PRESCHOOL PERIOD (3 to 6 years)	MIDDLE CHILDHOOD (6 to 12 years)
• Height and weight continue to increase rapidly. • The body becomes less rounded and more muscular. • The brain grows larger, neural interconnections continue to develop, and lateralization emerges. • Gross and fine motor skills advance quickly. Children can throw and catch balls, run, use forks and spoons, and tie shoelaces.	• Growth becomes slow and steady. Muscles develop, and "baby fat" is lost. • Gross motor skills (biking, swimming, skating, ball handling) and fine motor skills (writing, typing, fastening buttons) continue to improve. 
• Children show egocentric thinking (viewing world from their own perspective) and "centration," a focus on only one aspect of a stimulus. • Memory, attention span, and symbolic thinking improve, and intuitive thought begins. • Language (sentence length, vocabulary, syntax, and grammar) improves rapidly. 	• Children apply logical operations to problems. • Understanding of conservation (that changes in shape do not necessarily affect quantity) and transformation (that objects can go through many states without changing) emerge. • Children can "decenter"—take multiple perspectives into account. • Memory encoding, storage, and retrieval improve, and control strategies (meta-memory) develop. • Language pragmatics (social conventions) and metalinguistic awareness (self-monitoring) improve.
• Children develop self-concepts, which may be exaggerated. • A sense of gender and racial identity emerges. • Children begin to see peers as individuals and form friendships based on trust and shared interests. • Morality is rule based and focused on rewards and punishments. • Play becomes more constructive and co-operative, and social skills become important.	• Children refer to psychological traits to define themselves. Sense of self becomes differentiated. • Social comparison is used to understand one's standing and identity. • Self-esteem grows differentiated, and a sense of self-efficacy (an appraisal of what one can and cannot do) develops. • Children approach moral problems intent on maintaining social respect and accepting what society defines as right. • Friendship patterns of boys and girls differ. Boys mostly interact with boys in groups, and girls tend to interact singly or in pairs with other girls.
Preoperational stage	Concrete operational stage
Initiative-versus-guilt stage	Industry-versus-inferiority stage
Phallic stage	Latency period
Preconventional morality level	Conventional morality level

	ADOLESCENCE (12 to 20 years)	**YOUNG ADULTHOOD** (20 to 40 years)
PHYSICAL DEVELOPMENT	 • Girls begin the adolescent growth spurt around age 10, boys around age 12. • Girls reach puberty around age 11 or 12, boys around age 13 or 14. • Primary sexual characteristics develop (affecting the reproductive organs), as do secondary sexual characteristics (pubic and underarm hair in both sexes, breasts in girls, deep voices in boys).	• Physical capabilities peak in the twenties, including strength, senses, coordination, and reaction time. • Growth is mostly complete, although some organs, including the brain, continue to grow. • For many young adults, obesity becomes a threat for the first time, as body fat increases. • Stress can become a significant health threat. • In the mid-thirties, disease replaces accidents as the leading cause of death.
COGNITIVE DEVELOPMENT	• Abstract thought prevails. Adolescents use formal logic to consider problems in the abstract. • Relative, not absolute, thinking is typical. • Verbal, mathematical, and spatial skills improve. • Adolescents are able to think hypothetically, divide attention, and monitor thought through meta-cognition. • Egocentrism develops, with a sense that one is always being observed. Self-consciousness and introspection are typical. • A sense of invulnerability can lead adolescents to ignore danger.	• As world experience increases, thought becomes more flexible and subjective, geared to adept problem solving. • Intelligence is applied to long-term goals involving career, family, and society. • Significant life events of young adulthood may shape cognitive development.
SOCIAL/ PERSONALITY DEVELOPMENT	• Self-concept becomes organized and accurate and reflects others' perceptions. Self-esteem grows differentiated. • Defining identity is a key task. Peer relationships provide social comparison and help define acceptable roles. Popularity issues become acute; peer pressure can enforce conformity. • Adolescents' quest for autonomy can bring conflict with parents as family roles are renegotiated. • Sexuality assumes importance in identity formation. Dating begins.	• Forming intimate relationships becomes highly important. Commitment may be partly determined by the attachment style developed in infancy. • Marriage and children bring developmental changes, often stressful. Divorce may result, with new stresses. • Identity is largely defined in terms of work, as young adults consolidate their careers.

THEORIES & THEORISTS

Jean Piaget	Formal operations stage	
Erik Erikson	Identity-versus-confusion stage	Intimacy-versus-isolation stage
Sigmund Freud	Genital stage	
Lawrence Kohlberg	Postconventional morality level may be reached	

MIDDLE ADULTHOOD
(40 to 65 years)

LATE ADULTHOOD
(65 years to death)

- Physical changes become evident. Vision declines noticeably, as does hearing, but less obviously.
- Height reaches a peak and declines slowly. Osteoporosis speeds this process in women. Weight increases, and strength decreases.
- Reaction time slows, but performance of complex tasks is mostly unchanged due to lifelong practice.
- Women experience menopause, with unpredictable effects. The male climacteric brings gradual changes in men's reproductive systems.

- Wrinkles and grey or thinning hair are marks of late adulthood. Height declines as backbone disk cartilage thins. Women are especially susceptible to osteoporosis.
- The brain shrinks, and the heart pumps less blood through the body. Reactions slow, and the senses become less acute. Cataracts and glaucoma may affect the eyes, and hearing loss is common.
- Chronic diseases, especially heart disease, grow more common. Mental disorders, such as depression and Alzheimer's disease, may occur.

- Some loss of cognitive functioning may begin in middle adulthood, but overall cognitive competence holds steady because adults use life experience and effective strategies to compensate.
- Slight declines occur in the efficiency of retrieval from long-term memory.

- Cognitive declines are minimal until the eighties. Cognitive abilities can be maintained with training and practice, and learning remains possible throughout the lifespan.
- Short-term memory and memory of specific life episodes may decline, but other types of memory are largely unaffected.

- People in middle adulthood take stock, appraising accomplishments against a "social clock" and developing a consciousness of mortality.
- Middle adulthood, despite the supposed "midlife crisis," usually is tranquil and satisfying. Individuals' personality traits are generally stable over time.
- While marital satisfaction is usually high, family relationships can present challenges.
- The view of one's career shifts from outward ambition to inner satisfaction or, in some cases, dissatisfaction. Career changes are increasingly common.

- Basic personality traits remain stable, but changes are possible. "Life review," a feature of this period, can bring either fulfillment or dissatisfaction.
- Retirement is a major event of late adulthood, causing adjustments to self-concept and self-esteem.
- A healthy lifestyle and continuing activity in areas of interest can bring satisfaction in late adulthood.
- Typical circumstances of late adulthood (reduced income, the aging or death of a spouse, a change in living arrangements) cause stress.

Generativity-versus-stagnation stage

Ego-integrity-versus-despair stage

Discovering *the* Lifespan

Canadian Edition

Robert S. Feldman
University of Massachusetts Amherst

Oriane Landry
McMaster University

PEARSON

Toronto

Vice-President, Editorial Director: Gary Bennett
Editor-in-Chief: Michelle Sartor
Acquisitions Editor: Matthew Christian
Signing Representative: Duncan Mackinnon
Marketing Manager: Lisa Gillis
Senior Developmental Editor: Lise Dupont
Project Manager: Rachel Thompson
Production Editor: Sapna Rastogi (Cenveo® Publisher Services)
Copy Editor: Julie Fletcher
Proofreaders: Audrey Dorsch, Colleen Ste. Marie
Compositor: Cenveo® Publisher Services
Photo Researcher: Kerri Wilson (PreMediaGlobal)
Permissions Researcher: Marnie Lamb
Art Director: Julia Hall
Cover and Interior Designer: Miguel Acevedo
Cover Image: Katie Edwards / Getty Images

To Jon, Leigh, Josh, Julie, and Sarah.

—Robert S. Feldman

To all my friends and family whose trials and triumphs inspire me in my teaching. You are never alone.

—Oriane Landry

10 9 8   [WEB]

Library and Archives Canada Cataloguing in Publication

Feldman, Robert S. (Robert Stephen), 1947–
       Discovering the lifespan / Robert S. Feldman, Oriane
Landry.—1st Canadian ed.

Includes bibliographical references and index.
ISBN 978-0-13-274478-2

    1. Developmental psychology—Textbooks. 2. Life cycle,
Human—Textbooks. 3. Human growth—Textbooks. I. Landry,
Oriane, 1975– II. Title.

BF713.F44 2013   155   C2012-905501-8

ISBN 978-0-13-274478-2

Brief Contents

Contents

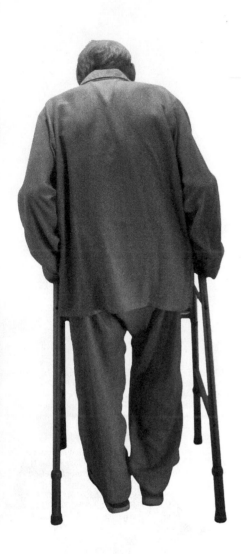

Text Credits

Chapter 1 Page 4, Moreton, C. (2007, January 13). World's first test-tube baby Louise Brown has a child of her own. The Independent, January 14, 2007 Copyright © 2007 Reprinted by permission of the Independent. www.independent.co.uk;. p. 7 Morelli, G.A., Rogoff, B., Oppenheim, D., & Goldsmith, D. (1992). Cultural variation in infants' sleeping arrangements: Questions of independence [Special section: Cross-cultural studies of development]. *Developmental Psychology*, 28, 604-613; p. 14 Watson, J.B. (1925). *Behaviorism*. New York: Norton; p. 22 Hunt, M. (1993). *The story of psychology*. New York: Doubleday.

Chapter 2 Page 52, Miller G. 2010. Epigenetics. The seductive allure of behavioral epigenetics. *Science*. 329(5987):24-7; p. 63 Brazelton, T. B. (1969). *Infants and mothers: Differences in development* (Rev. ed.). New York: Dell; p. 65 Knight, K. (1994, March). Back to basics. *Essence*, pp. 122–138; p. 38, figure 2-2, Rising Multiples. Statistics Canada. (2012). Table 102-4515. Live births and fetal deaths (stillbirths), by type (single or multiple), Canada, provinces and territories, annual (number). Accessed April 11, 2012; p. 41, figure 2-5, Based on data from International Human Genome Sequencing Consortium. (2001). Initial sequencing and analysis of the human genome. *Nature*, 409, 860-921; p. 48, figure 2-6, Bouchard, T.J., & McGue, M. (1981). Familial studies of intelligence: A review. *Science*, 212, 1055-1059. Used by permission of Dr. Thomas Bouchard; p. 49, figure 2-7, Tellegen, A., Lykken, D.T., Bouchard, T.J., Jr., Wilcox, K.J., Segal, N.L., & Rich, S. (1988). Personality similarity in twins reared apart and together. *Journal of Personality and Social Psychology*, 54, 1031-1039; p. 51, figure 2-8, From *Schizophrenia Genesis: The Origins of Madness* ©1991 by W.H. Freeman and Company. Used with permission; p. 53, figure 2-9, From *Before we were born* (6th ed.), K.L. Moore & T.V.N. Persaud, Copyright Elsevier (2003); p. 56, figure 2-11, Andersen, A. M. N., Wohlfahrt, J., Christens, P., Olsen, J., & Melbye, M. (2000). Maternal age and fetal loss: Population based register linkage study. *BMJ*, 320, 1708-1712; Adapted from Menken, J., Trussell, J., & Larsen, U. (1986). Age and infertility. *Science*, 233, 1389-1394; Adapted from Heffner, L. J. (2004). Advanced maternal age–how old is too old? *New England Journal of Medicine*, 351(19), 1927-1929; and Hook, E. B., Cross, P. K., & Schreinemachers, D. M. (1983). Chromosomal abnormality rates at amniocentesis and in live-born infants. *Journal of the American Medical Association*, 249(15), 2034-2038; p. 58, figure 2-12, From *Before we are born: Basic embryology and birth defects*, K.L. Moore, Copyright Elsevier (1974); p. 69, figure 2-14, The World Factbook, 2007; p. 72, figure 2-16, International Cesarean Awareness Network. (2004.) Available online at http://www.ican-online.org; p. 75, figure 2-17, The Canadian Maternity Experiences Survey (MES) 2006-2007. Public Health Agency of Canada, 2009. Reproduced with permission from the Minister of Health, 2012; p. 78, table 2-5, Republished with permission of ABC-CLIO, from Very-low-birthweight newborns and parents as early social partners. In S.L. Friedman & M.D. Sigman (Eds.), The psychological development of low-birthweight children. Eckerman, C.O., & Oehler, J.M., 1992; permission conveyed through Copyright Clearance Center, Inc.

Chapter 3 Page 128, Brazelton, T.B. (1983). Infants and mothers: Differences in development (Rev. ed.). New York: Dell; p. 85, figure 3-1, Height and Weight Growth (Adapted from Cratty, B. J. (1979). PERCEPTUAL AND MOTOR DEVELOPMENT IN INFANTS AND CHILDREN, 2e, pg. 222.); p. 87, figure 3-3, Van de Graaf, K. (1998). *Human anatomy* (5th ed., p. 339). Boston: McGraw-Hill; figure 3-4, Reprinted by permission of the publisher from THE POSTNATAL DEVELOPMENT OF THE HUMAN CEREBRAL CORTEX, VOLUMES I-VIII, by J. LeRoy Conel, Cambridge, Mass.: Harvard University Press, Copyright © 1939, 1941, 1947, 1951, 1955, 1959, 1963, 1967 by the President and Fellows of Harvard College. Copyright © renewed 1967, 1969, 1975, 1979, 1983, 1987, 1991; p. 90, figure 3-5, Used by permission of Howard Roffwarg, M.D. Roffwarg, H.P., Muzio, J.N., & Dement, W.C. (1966). Ontogenic development of the human sleep-dream cycle. *Science*, 152, 604-619; p. 94, figure 3-6, Data source: Pediatrics, Vol. 89, Pages 91–97, Copyright 1992 by the American Academy of Pediatrics; p. 100, figure 3-8, Fantz, R.L. (1961). The origin of form perception. *Scientific American*, 204, 66-72; p. 117, figure 3-12, Bornstein, M.H., & Lamb, M.E. (1992). Development in infancy: An introduction. New York: McGraw-Hill; p. 126, figure 3-15, Reprinted by permission of the publisher from INFANCY: ITS PLACE IN HUMAN DEVELOPMENT by Jerome Kagan, Richard B. Kearsley, and Philip R. Zelazo, p. 107, Cambridge, Mass.: Harvard University Press, Copyright © 1978 by the President and Fellows of Harvard College; p. 95, table 3-3, Data source: Pediatrics, Vol. 89, Pages 91–97, Copyright 1992 by the American Academy of Pediatrics; p. 113, table 3-6, *Bayley Scales of Infant Development*". Copyright © 1969 NCS Pearson, Inc. Reproduced with permission. All rights reserved. *Bayley Scales of Infant Development* is a trademark, in the US and/or other countries, of Pearson Education, Inc. or its affiliates(s); p. 119, table 3-7, Adapted from Brown, R., & Fraser, C. (1963). The acquisition of syntax: Problems and processes. In C. N. Cofer & B. S. Musgrave (Eds.), *Verbal behavior and learning*. New York: McGraw-Hill. 158–201.

Chapter 4 Page 155, Ceci, S.J., & Bruck, M. (1993). The suggestibility of the child witness: A historical review and synthesis. *Psychological Bulletin*, 113, 403-439; p. 156, Ceci, S.J., & Bruck, M. (1993). The suggestibility of the child witness: A historical review and synthesis. *Psychological Bulletin*, 113, 403-439. Bruck, M., & Ceci, S. (2004). Forensic developmental psychology: Unveiling four common misconceptions. *Current Directions in Psychological Science*, 13, 229-232; p. 156, Tharp, R.G., (1989). Psychocultural variables and constants: Effects on teaching and learning in schools. American Psychologist, 44 [Special issue: Children and their development: Knowledge base, research agenda, and social policy application], 349-359; p. 174, Reprinted with permission of Terry Carson, parenting coach; p. 178, Katz, L.G. (1989, December). Beginners' ethics. *Parents*, p. 213; p. 143, figure 4-1, © 2012. Dietitians of Canada. All rights reserved. This document is available from the Dietitians of Canada website at http://www.dietitians.ca; p. 146, figure 4-2, Society for Research in Child Development; p. 159, figure 4-6, By permission of Jean Berko Gleason; p. 161, figure 4-7, This information was reprinted with permission from the Henry J. Kaiser Family Foundation. The Kaiser Family Foundation, a leader in health policy analysis, health journalism and communication, is dedicated to filling the need for trusted, independent information on the major health issues facing our nation and its people. The Foundation is a non-profit private operating foundation, based in Menlo Park, California; p. 162, figure 4-8, Bushnik, T., (2006).

Child Care in Canada. Statistics Canada Catalogue no. 89-599-MIE. Ottawa. 99 p. Children and Youth Research Paper Series, no. 3, www.statcan.gc.ca/pub/89-599-m/89-599-m2006003-eng.pdf (accessed March 11, 2011); p. 174, figure 4-9, The Canadian Incidence Study of Reported Child Abuse and Neglect. Health Canada, 1998. Reproduced with permission from the Minister of Health, 2012; p,175, figure 4-10, The Canadian Incidence Study of Reported Child Abuse and Neglect. Health Canada, 1998. Reproduced with permission from the Minister of Health, 2012; p. 177, figure 4-11, Used by permission of Carol Donner Lescoulie; p. 183, figure 4-13, Center for Media & Public Affairs; p. 148, table 4-1, Corbin, A Textbook of Motor Development, 1e. Copyright © 1973 The McGraw-Hill Companies. Reprinted with permission.

Chapter 5 Page 193, Segal, J., & Segal, Z. (1992, September). No more couch potatoes. *Parents*, p. 235; p. 211, Mead, M. (1942). Environment and education, a symposium held in connection with the fiftieth anniversary celebration of the University of Chicago. Chicago: University of Chicago; p. 229, Damon, W. (1983). *Social and personality development*. New York: Norton; p. 233, Goodwin, M.H. (1990). Tactical uses of stories: Participation frameworks within girls' and boys' disputes. *Discourse Processes*, 13, 33-71; p. 192, figure 5-1, Adapted from Shields, M. (2004). Measured obesity: Overweight Canadian children and adolescents. Nutrition: Findings from the Canadian Community Health Survey. Issue 1. Component of Statistics Canada Catalogue no. 82-620-MWE2005001; p. 195, figure 5-2, Adapted from Cratty, B. J., PERCEPTUAL AND MOTOR DEVELOPMENT IN INFANTS AND CHILDREN, 3rd ed. Copyright © Pearson Education, Inc. Reprinted with permission from Pearson Education, Inc.; p. 203, figure 5-3, Dasen, P., Ngini, L., & Lavallee, M. (1979). Cross-cultural training studies of concrete operations. In L.H. Eckenberger, W.J. Lonner, & Y.H. Poortinga (Eds.), *Cross-cultural contributions to psychology*. Amsterdam: Swets & Zeitlinger; p. 207, figure 5-4, Primary Languages Spoken in the Home, 1971-2006 (Statistics Canada, 1971, 1981, 1991, 2001, 2006 Census of the Population. Statistics Canada. (2006). Population by mother tongue, by province and territory. 2006 Census of the Population (summary table). Retrieved on June 3, 2012 from http://www.statcan.gc.ca/tables-tableaux/sum-som/l01/cst01/demo11a-eng.htm; p. 216, figure 5-7, Walters, E., & Gardner, H. (1986). The theory of multiple intelligences: Some issues and answers. In R. J. Sternberg & R. K. Wagner (Eds.), *Practical intelligence*. Cambridge, England: Cambridge University Press; p. 231, figure 5-8, EDUCATIONAL PSYCHOLOGY BY K. A. Dodge. Copyright 1985 by Taylor & Francis Informa UK Ltd—Journals. Reproduced with permission of Taylor & Francis Informa UK Ltd—Journals in the format Textbook via Copyright Clearance Center; p. 226, table 5-1, Used by permission of David. A Goslin. Kohlberg, L. (1969.) Stage and sequence: The cognitive-developmental approach to socialization. In David A. Goslin (Ed.), *The handbook of socialization theory and research* (pp. 347–480). Chicago: Rand McNally.

Chapter 6 Page 252, Beckman, M. (2004, July 30). Neuroscience: Crime, culpability, and the adolescent brain. *Science*, 305, pp. 596-599; p. 253, The Anti Drug.website. Teens Today: Real Teen Stories: Amy's Story. Retrieved on May 29, 2012 from http://www.theantidrug.com/advice/teens-today/teens-and-technology/real-teen-stories.aspx; p. 258, CBC News; p. 267, Fields-Meyer, T. (1995, September 25). Having their say. *People*, 50-60; p. 268, *LAGRECA, THROUGH THE EYES OF THE CHILD: OBTAINING SELF REPORTS FROM CHILDREN AND ADOLESCENTS, 1st Ed., ©1990. Reprinted and Electronically reproduced by permission of Pearson Education, Inc., Upper Saddle River, New Jersey*; p. 274, Brant Castellano, M. (2008). Reflections on identity and empowerment: Recurring themes in the discourse on and with Aboriginal youth. *Horizons*, 10(1), 7-12; p., Public Health Service; p. 275, Public Health Service; p. 284, Gregory, S. (1856). Facts for young women. Boston: G. Gregory; p. 245, figure 6-1, Adapted from Cratty, B. (1986). *Perceptual and motor development in infants and children* (3rd ed.). Englewood Cliffs, NJ: Prentice-Hall; p. 247, figure 6-2, Tanner, J.M. (1978). Education and physical growth (2nd ed.). New York: International Universities Press; p. 251, figure 6-3, Sowell, E.R., Thompson, P.M., Holmes, C.J., Jernigan, T.L., & Toga, A.W. (1999). In vivo evidence for post-adolescent brain maturation in frontal and striatal regions. Nature Neuroscience, 10, 859-861; Reprinted by permission from Macmillan Publishers Ltd: Nature Neuroscience, 10. Sowell, E.R., Thompson, P.M., Holmes, C.J., Jernigan, T.L., & Toga, A.W. In vivo evidence for post-adolescent brain maturation in frontal and striatal regions. 859-861. Copyright 1999; p. 253, figure 6-4, Adapted from Health Canada, 2010 with the permission from the Minister of Health, 2012. Canadian Alcohol and Drug Use Monitoring Survey (CADUMS). Adapted from "Table 4: Changes between CAS 2004 and CADUMS 2008 and 2009 by age: Drugs" and from "Table 9: Changes between CAS 2004 and CADUMS 2008 and 2009 by age: Alcohol." Retrieved September 28, 2012 from http://www.hc-sc.gc.ca/hp-ps/drugs-drogues/stat/_2009/tablestableaux-eng.php; p. 254, figure 6-5, Based on raw data obtained from Adlaf, Demers, & Gliksman. (2005). *Canadian Campus Survey 2004*. Toronto, ON: Centre for Addiction and Mental Health; p. 256, figure 6-6, Canadian Guidelines on Sexually Transmitted Infections, 2010. Public Health Agency of Canada, 2010. Reproduced with permission from the Minister of Health, 2012; p. 265, figure 6-7, Statistics Canada. (2010). Table 358-0153 - Canadian Internet use survey, Internet use, by age group and Internet activity, occasional (percent). CANSIM (database); p. 277, figure 6-8, PRIMEDIA/Roper. (1999). Roper National Youth Survey. Storrs, CT: Roper Center for Public Opinion Research; p. 278, figure 6-9, Larson, R.W., Richards, M.H., Moneta, G., Holmbeck, G., & Duckett, E. (1996). Changes in adolescents' daily interactions with their families from ages 10 to 18: Disengagement and transformation. Developmental Psychology, 32, 744-754; p., figure 6-11, Roterman, M. (2008). Trends in teen sexual behaviour and condom use. Health Matters. Statistics Canada, Catalogue no. 82-003-XPE. Health Reports, Vol. 19, no. 3, September 2008. Retrieved May 2, 2012, from http://www.statcan.gc.ca/pub/82-003-x/2008003/article/10664-eng.pdf; p. 270, table 6-2, "Figure of Erikson's Stages of Personality Development," from CHILDHOOD AND SOCIETY by Erik H. Erikson. Copyright 1950, © 1963 by W. W. Norton & Company, Inc., renewed © 1978, 1991 by Erik H. Erikson. Used by permission of W. W. Norton & Company, Inc.; p. 281, table 6-3, Adapted from Suitor, J. J., Minyard, S. A., & Carter, R. S. (2001), "'Did you see what I saw?' Gender differences in perceptions of avenues to prestige among adolescents," Sociological Inquiry, 71, 437–454. Copyright © 2001 Blackwell Publishing. Reprinted with permission of John Wiley & Sons Ltd.

Chapter 7 Page 294, Murguia, A., Peterson, R.A., & Zea, M.C. (1997, August). Cultural health beliefs. Paper presented at the annual meeting of the American Psychological Association, Toronto, Canada; p. 305, Based on Wagner, R.K., & Sternberg, R.J. (1985). Alternate conceptions of intelligence and their implications for education. *Review of Educational Research*, 54, 179-223; p. 307, Stanovich, K.E. (2009, November/December). The thinking that IQ tests miss. *Scientific American*, pp. 34-39; p. 313, Sadker, M., & Sadker, D. (1994). *Failing at fairness: How America's schools cheat girls*. New York: Scribner's; p. 315, Steele, C.M., & Aronson, J. (1995). Stereotype threat and the intellectual test performance of African Americans. Journal of Personality and Social Psychology, 69, 797-811; p. 326, Cowan, C.P., & Cowan, P.A. (1992). *When partners become parents*. New York: Basic Books; p. 334, Unger, R., & Crawford, M. (1992). *Women and gender: A feminist psychology* (2nd ed.). New York: McGraw-Hill; p. 294, figure 7-1, Adapted from Blair, S. N., Kohl, H. W., III, Paffenbarger, R. S., Jr., Clark, D. G., Cooper, K. H., and Gibbons, L. W. (1989). Physical fitness and all-cause mortality: A prospective study of healthy men and women. *Journal of the American Medical Association*, 262, pp. 2395–2401; p. 296, figure 7-2, Statistics Canada. (2009, June 25). Canadian Community Health Survey. The Daily; p. 304, figure 7-3, Schaie, K.W. (1977-1978). Toward a stage theory of adult cognitive development. *Journal of Aging and Human Development*, 8(2), 129-138. © 1977-1978 Baywood Publishing, Amityville, NY; p. 306, figure 7-4, Robert J. Sternberg, Richard K. Wagner, Current Directions in Psychological Science (2, 1), pp. 1-4, copyright © 1993 by SAGE Publications. Reprinted by Permission of SAGE Publications; p. 308, figure 7-5, JOURNAL OF GERONTOLOGY by W. Dennis. Copyright 1966 by The Gerontological Society of America. Reproduced with permission of The Gerontological Society of America in the format Textbook via Copyright Clearance Center; p. 310, figure 7-6, Statistics Canada. Survey of Labour and Income Dynamics, 2006; p. 313, figure 7-7, Benton, S.A., Robertson, J.M., Tseng, W.-C., Newton, F.B., & Benton, S.L. (2003). Changes in counseling center client problems across 13 years. *Professional Psychology: Research and Practice*, 34, 66-72; p. 314, figure 7-8, ©1990 American Council on Education. Reprinted with permission; p. 327, figure 7-9, Milan, A., Vézina, M., & Wells, C. (2006). 2006 Census: Family portrait: Continuity and change in Canadian families and households in 2006: Findings. Statistics Canada Catalogue no. 97-553-XWE2006001; p. 328, figure 7-10, Statistics Canada (2011). Fig 6-13. For 1921-1975 : Statistics Canada. Marriage and Conjugal Life in Canada, Current Demographic Analysis. Cat. number 91-543E, Table I; for 1976 2002 : Statistics Canada. Demography Division; and for 2003: Statistics Canada. Mean age and median age of males and females, by type of marriage and marital status, Canada, provinces and territories, annual. CANSIM no. 101-1002; p. 330, figure 7-11, Marshall, A.K. (2006). In the StatsCan publication 'Perspectives on Labour and Income,' Vol. 7(7), 2006; p. 335, figure 7-12, Adapted from Statistics Canada, CANSIM table 202-0409. Income of individuals by sex, age group, and income source, 2009 constant dollars, annual. Available online at Statistics Canada http://www5.statcan.gc.ca/ cansim/a16?lang=eng&smonth=1&syear=1976&emonth=1&eyear=20 09&requestID=2011081510533820461&csid=Accessed August 15, 2011; p. 299, table 7-1, Sheldon Cohen, Tom Kamarck and Robin Mermelstein. "A Global Measure of Perceived Stress." *Journal of Health and Social Behavior, Vol. 24, No. 4 (Dec., 1983)*, Appendix A; p. 317, table 7-2, Colarusso & Nemiroff, 1981; p. 322, table 7-4, Buss, D.M., et al., Journal of Cross-Cultural Psychology, 21(1). pp. 5-47, © 1990 by SAGE. Reprinted by Permission of SAGE Publications.

Chapter 8 Page 352, Layton, J. (2011, August 21). [Letter to Canadians]; p. 353, Tara Flanagan is a single mom, a university professor, and a breast cancer survivor; p. 369, Enright, E. (2004, July & August). A house divided. *AARP Magazine*, pp. 54, 57; p. 379, *Success Stories: Remzi: From a refugee to a Rhodes Scholar, http://www.cic.gc.ca/english/department/media/stories/remzi.asp, Citizenship and Immigration Canada, 2011*. Reproduced with the permission of the Minister of Public Works and Government Services Canada, 2012; p 345, figure 8-1, From "The Benefits of Exercise," from A. G. DiGiovanna, Human Aging: Biological Perspectives. Copyright © 1994 The McGraw-Hill Companies, Inc. Reprinted with permission; p. 349, figure 8-2, Adapted from Skarborn, M., & Nicki, R. (2000). Table 3. Worry in pre- and post-retirement persons. *International Journal of Aging and Human Development*, 50(1), 61-71; p. 350, figure 8-3, Baum, A. (1994). Behavioral, biological, and environmental interactions in disease processes. In S. Blumenthal, K. Matthews, & S. Weiss (Eds.), *New research frontiers in behavioral medicine: Proceedings of the National Conference*. Washington, DC: NIH Publications; p. 353, figure 8-4, Canadian Cancer Society's Steering Committee on Cancer Statistics. *Canadian Cancer Statistics 2011*. Toronto, ON: Canadian Cancer Society; 2011; p. 357, figure 8-5, K. W. Schaie, "Longitudinal Studies of Adult Psychological Development," 1985. Copyright © Guilford Press. Reprinted with permission; p. 365, figure 8-6, Costa, P.T., Jr., & McCrae, R.R. (1989). Personality continuity and the changes of adult life. In M. Storandt & G.R. VandenBos (Eds.), *The adult years: Continuity and change*. Washington, DC: American Psychological Association; p. 368, figure 8-7, Rollins, B., & Cannon, K. (1974). Marital satisfaction over the family life cycle: A reevaluation. *Journal of Marriage and the Family*, 36(2), 271-282; p. 363, table 8-1, From *Transformations*, by R. L. Gould & M. D. Gould, 1978, New York: Simon & Schuster.

Chapter 9 Page 386, Winter, J.W. (2011). Easy rider. *Senior Living Magazine*. © 2011 Stratis Publishing Ltd.; p. 395, Bialystok, E., Craik, F.I.M., & Freedman, M. (2007). Bilingualism as a protection against the onset of symptoms of dementia. *Neuropsychologia*, 45, 459-464; p. 401, Dent, C. (1984). Development of discourse rules: Children's use of indexical reference and cohesion. Developmental Psychology, 20, 229-234; p. 401, Used by permission of Nick Rockel. November 30, 2010. Brenda Milner unlocks the mysteries of memory. The Globe and Mail; p. 403, McCartney, M. (2006, March 11). Mind gains: We are living longer but will we be able to keep our minds active enough to enjoy it? *Financial Times* (London, England), p. 1. Retrieved March 4, 2007 from LexisNexis Academic; p., Reprinted with the permission of Touchstone, a Division of Simon & Schuster, Inc., from THE NEW OURSELVES, GROWING OLDER, REVISED AND UPDATED by Paula Doress-Worters and Diana Laskin Siegal. Copyright © 1987, 1994 by Paula Doress-Worters and Diana Laskin Siegal. All rights reserved; p. 421, Reprinted with the permission of Touchstone, a Division of Simon & Schuster, Inc., from THE NEW OURSELVES, GROWING OLDER, REVISED AND UPDATED by Paula Doress-Worters and Diana Laskin Siegal. Copyright © 1987, 1994 by Paula Doress-Worters and Diana Laskin Siegal. All rights reserved; p. 425, *Excerpted from the Harvard Health Letter October, 1995 © 1995, Harvard University. For more information visit:**health.harvard.edu** NOTE: **Harvard Health Publications does not endorse any products or medical procedures**; p. 387, figure 9-1, HRSDC calculations based on Statistics Canada. Estimates of population, by age group and sex for July 1, Canada, provinces and territories, annual (CANSIM Table 051-0001); and Statistics Canada. Projected population, by projection scenario, sex and age group as of July 1, Canada, provinces and territories, annual (CANSIM table 052-0005). Ottawa: Statistics Canada, 2010; figure 9-2, United Nations Population Division. (2002). *World population ageing: 1950-2050*. New York: United Nations; p. 391, figure 9-3, National Highway Traffic Safety Administration. (1994). Age-related incidence of traffic accidents. Washington, DC: National Highway Traffic Safety Administration; p. 398, figure 9-6, Statistics Canada, 2009. Statistics Canada, Life Tables, Canada, Provinces and Territories, Catalogue no. 84-537-XPB; and Canadian Vital Statistics, Birth and Death Databases; and Demography Division (population estimates); p. 399, figure 9-7, Turcotte & Schellenberg. (2007). A portrait of seniors in Canada. Chart 6.2. Reprinted with permission; p. 402, figure 9-8, Schaie, K. W. (1994). "The course of adult intellectual development." p. 307 American Psychologist, 49, 304–313. Copyright © 1994 by the American Psychological Association. Reproduced with permission; p. 405, figure 9-9, Rubin, D.C. (1986). *Autobiographical memory*. Cambridge, England: Cambridge University Press; p. 216, figure 9-10, Turcotte & Schellenberg, 2007. A portrait of seniors in Canada. Chart 6.2. Reprinted with permission; p. 420, figure 9-11, Statistics Canada, 2006, Census of the Population; p. 423, figure 9-12, Federal Interagency Forum on Age-Related Statistics. (2000). Older Americans 2000: Key indicators of well-being. Hyattsville, MD: Federal Interagency Forum on Age-Related Statistics; p. 389, table 9-1, From "The Myths of Aging" from Palmore, E. B. (1982). THE FACTS ON AGING QUIZ. New York: Springer. Reprinted with permission from the author.

Chapter 10 Page 430, CBC News; p. 436, Excerpted from Yedidia, M.J., & MacGregor, B. (2001). Confronting the prospect of dying: Reports of terminally ill patients. Journal of Pain and Symptom Management, 22, 807-819; p. 442, Wilson, D., Truman, C. D., Thomas, R., Fainsinger, R., Kovacs-Burns, K., Froggatt, K., & Justice, C. (2009). The rapidly changing location of death in Canada, 1994-2004. Social Science and Medicine 68, 1752-1758; p. 443, Lewis, C.S. (1985). A grief observed. In E.S. Shneidman (Ed.), Death: Current perspectives (3rd ed.). Palo Alto, CA: Mayfield; p. 436, Kübler-Ross, E. (Ed.). (1975). Death: The final stage of growth. Englewood Cliffs, NJ: Prentice-Hall.

Preface

I've never met an instructor of a lifespan development course who didn't feel that he or she was fortunate to teach the course. The subject matter is inherently fascinating, and there is a wealth of information to convey that is at once fascinating and practical. Students come to the course with anticipation, motivated to learn about a topic that, at its core, is about their own lives and the lives of every other human being.

At the same time, the course presents unique challenges. For one thing, the breadth of lifespan development is so vast that it is difficult to cover the entire field within the confines of a traditional college or university term. In addition, many instructors find traditional lifespan development texts too long. Students are concerned about the length of the texts and have trouble reading the entire book within the timeframe of the course. As a result, instructors are often reluctant to assign the complete text and are forced to drop material, often arbitrarily.

Finally, instructors often wish to incorporate into their classes computer-based electronic media that promote understanding of key concepts and take advantage of students' capabilities with electronic media. Yet traditional lifespan development textbooks do little to integrate the electronic media with the book. Consequently, in most courses, the book and accompanying electronic media stand largely in isolation from one another. This lack of integration diminishes the potential impact of both traditional and electronic media and the advantages that an integration of the two could produce in terms of helping students engage with, and learn from, the subject matter.

Discovering the Lifespan, **Canadian Edition**, directly addresses these challenges. The book, which is based on the highly popular *Development Across the Life Span*, is some 25 percent shorter than traditional lifespan books. At the same time, it maintains the student friendliness that has been the hallmark of the original. It is rich in examples and illustrates the applications that can be derived from the research and theory of lifespan developmentalists.

The book uses a modular approach to optimize student learning. Each chapter is divided into three modules, and, in turn, each module is divided into several smaller sections. Consequently, rather than facing long, potentially daunting chapters, students encounter material that is divided into smaller, more manageable chunks. Of course, presenting material in small sections also happens to represent a structure that psychological researchers long ago identified as optimal to promote learning.

The modular approach has another advantage: It allows instructors to customize instruction by assigning only those modules that fit their course. Each of the book's chapters focuses on a particular period of the lifespan, and, within each chapter, separate modules address the three main conceptual approaches to the period: physical development, cognitive development, and social and personality development. Because of the flexibility of this structure, instructors who wish to highlight a particular theoretical or topical approach to lifespan development can do so easily.

Finally, *Discovering the Lifespan,* **Canadian Edition**, provides complete integration between the book and a huge array of electronic media in **MyDevelopmentLab**, including online assessments, development videos, and other engaging activities that extend the text and make concepts come alive. **MyVirtualLife** is included within MyDevelopmentLab. This interactive resource is two simulations in one. The first simulation allows you to raise a child from birth to age 18 and to monitor the effects of your parenting decisions over time. The second simulation encourages you to make first-person decisions and to see the impact of those decisions on your simulated future self over time. Both MyDevelopmentLab and MyVirtualLife are referenced throughout the book in an engaging way, enticing students to go online and to make use of the electronic materials that will help them understand the material in the book more deeply.

An Introduction to *Discovering the Lifespan,* Canadian Edition

Discovering the Lifespan, **Canadian Edition,** provides a broad overview of the field of human development, covering the entire range of the human life, from the moment of conception through death. The text furnishes students with a broad, comprehensive introduction to the

field, covering basic theories and research findings, as well as highlighting current applications outside the laboratory. It covers the lifespan chronologically, encompassing the prenatal period, infancy and toddlerhood, the preschool years, middle childhood, adolescence, early and middle adulthood, and late adulthood. Within these periods, it focuses on physical, cognitive, and social and personality development.

In a unique departure from traditional lifespan development texts, each chapter integrates the physical, cognitive, and social and personality domains within each chronological period. Chapters begin with a compelling story about an individual representing the age period covered by the chapter, and the chapter ends by refocusing on that individual and integrating the three domains. At the same time, chapters drive students to **MyDevelopmentLab** through marginal queries and reminders about the rich media content available to them.

The book also blends and integrates theory, research, and applications, focusing on the breadth of human development. Furthermore, rather than attempting to provide a detailed historical record of the field, it focuses on the here-and-now, drawing on the past where appropriate, with a view toward delineating the field as it now stands and the directions toward which it is evolving. Similarly, while providing descriptions of classic studies, the emphasis is more on current research findings and trends.

The book strives to be user-friendly. Written in a direct, conversational voice, it replicates as much as possible a dialogue between authors and student. The text is meant to be understood and mastered on its own by students of every level of interest and motivation. To that end, it includes a variety of pedagogical features that promote mastery of the material and encourage critical thinking.

Features

- **Chapter-Opening Prologues.** Each of the chapters starts with an attention-grabbing account of an individual who is at the developmental stage covered by the chapter. The material in the prologue sets the stage for the chapter, and the content is addressed again in the end of the chapter when the physical, cognitive, and social and personality aspects are integrated.

- **Module-Opening Vignette and Looking Ahead.** Modules (which are nestled within chapters) begin with short vignettes describing an individual or situation that is relevant to the basic developmental issues being addressed in the module.

- **Learning Objectives.** The learning objectives, which are posed as questions, permit students to clearly understand what they are expected to learn in a given section of the book. The learning objectives are tied to review summaries at the end of every section of the book, and they are also keyed to the test bank.

- **From Research to Practice.** Each chapter includes a box that describes current developmental research or research issues applied to everyday problems.

- **Cultural Dimensions.** Every chapter has several "Cultural Dimensions" sections incorporated into the text. These sections highlight issues relevant to today's multicultural society, for example discussions about how cultural practices influence development from baby's first steps through attitudes and rituals surrounding death; gay and lesbian relationships; and gender and ethnic differences in life expectancy.

- **Focus on Research.** Each chapter includes a box that describes an interesting area of research currently underway in Canada. These boxes are intended to highlight some of the groundbreaking, and just plain interesting, research taking place in your backyard. Much of this research challenges popular beliefs—a reminder to always question "conventional wisdom" and to ask yourself "How do I know this is true?"

- **Becoming an Informed Consumer of Development.** Every chapter includes information on specific uses that can be derived from research conducted by developmental investigators. For instance, the text provides concrete information on how to encourage children to become more physically active, help troubled adolescents who might be contemplating suicide, and plan and live a good retirement.

- **Review, Check, and Apply Sections.** Each module is divided into several subsections. At the end of each section is a short recap of the chapter's main points, a series of questions about the chapter content, and a question designed to help students to apply the chapter content to the real world. In addition, students are encouraged to use the online resources associated with the chapter.
- **"From the Perspective of . . ." Questions.** Students will encounter frequent questions throughout the text designed to show the applicability of the material to a variety of professions, including education, nursing, social work, and health care.
- **Running Glossary.** Key terms are defined in the margin of the page.
- **End-of-Chapter Integrative Material.** At the end of each chapter, the chapter-opening prologue is recapped and addressed from the three domains of physical, cognitive, and social and personality development. In addition, questions address the prologue from the perspective of people such as parents, professional caregivers, nurses, and educators.

A Final Note

We are very excited about this new edition of *Discovering the Lifespan*. We believe its length, structure, and media and text integration will help students learn the material in a highly effective way. Just as important, we hope it will spark and nurture students' interest in the field of lifespan development, drawing them into its way of looking at the world, building their understanding of developmental issues, and showing them how the field can have a significant impact on their own and others' lives.

Teaching and Learning Resources

Discovering the Lifespan is accompanied by a superb set of teaching and learning materials. See the list below for more details.

- **Instructor's Resource Manual (ISBN 978-0-13-313808-5).** Designed to make your lectures more effective and save you preparation time, this extensive resource gathers together the most effective activities and strategies for teaching your course. The Instructor's Resource Manual includes learning objectives, key terms and concepts, self-contained lecture suggestions and class activities for each chapter with handouts, supplemental reading suggestions, and an annotated list of additional multimedia resources. The Instructor's Resource Manual can be downloaded via the Instructor's Resource Centre at www.pearsonhighered.ca/IRC or the MyDevelopmentLab® platform.
- **PowerPoint Presentations (ISBN 978-0-13-313806-1).** The PowerPoints provide an active format for presenting concepts from each chapter and feature relevant figures and tables from the text. Available for download via the Instructor's Resource Centre at www.pearsonhighered.ca/ IRC or the MyDevelopmentLab® platform.
- **Test Item File (ISBN 978-0-13-315158-9).** The test bank contains multiple choice, true or false, and essay questions. Each question has been checked to ensure that the correct answer is identified and that the page reference is accurate. An additional feature of the test bank is the classification of each question as factual, conceptual, or applied. This allows professors to customize their tests and to ensure a balance of question types. The test item file is available for download via the Instructor's Resource Centre at www.pearsonhighered.ca/IRC or the MyDevelopmentLab® platform.
- **MyTest (ISBN 978-0-13-313810-8).** This powerful assessment-generation program helps instructors to easily create and print quizzes and exams. Questions and tests can be authored online, allowing instructors ultimate flexibility and the ability to efficiently manage assessments any time, anywhere! Instructors can easily access existing questions and edit, create, and store them using simple drag-and-drop techniques and Word-like controls. Data with each question provide information on difficulty level and the page number of the corresponding text discussion. In addition, each question maps to the text's major section and learning objective. For more information, go to www.PearsonMyTest.ca/IRC or the MyDevelopmentLab® platform.

- **MyDevelopmentLab.** The new MyDevelopmentLab combines proven learning applications with powerful assessment to engage students, assess their learning, and help them succeed. With assessment tied to every video, application, and chapter, students receive immediate feedback, and instructors can see what their students know with just a few clicks. Instructors can also personalize MyDevelopmentLab to meet the needs of their students.
  - **An individualized study plan for each student,** based on performance results from chapter pretests, helps students focus on the specific topics where they need the most support. The personalized study plan arranges content from less complex thinking (like remembering and understanding) to more complex critical thinking skills (like applying and analyzing) and is based on Bloom's taxonomy. Every level of the study plan provides a formative assessment quiz.
  - **Media assignments** for each chapter—including videos with assignable questions—feed directly into the gradebook, enabling instructors to track student progress automatically.
  - **The Pearson eText** lets students access their textbook anytime and anywhere, and any way they want, including listening online.

- **MyVirtualLife.** Included within MyDevelopmentLab or sold as a stand-alone product, MyVirtualLife is an interactive resource with two simulations in one. The first simulation allows students to raise a child from birth to age 18 and to monitor the effects of their parenting decisions over time. The second simulation encourages students to make first-person decisions and to see the impact of those decisions on their simulated future selves over time. At each age, students are given feedback about the various milestones their child has attained; key stages of the child's development will include personalized feedback. As in real life, certain "unplanned" events might occur randomly. Students take a personality test at the beginning of the program, the results of which will have an impact on the temperament of their child or simulated future selves. Observational videos are included throughout the program to help illustrate key concepts. Critical thinking questions within the program help students to apply to their own virtual person what they are learning in class and in their textbook. These questions can be assigned or used as the basis for in-class discussion.

- **MyDevelopmentLab Video Series.** The MyDevelopmentLab Video Series engages students in the study of human development. Hundreds of observational videos and interviews, from prenatal development through the end of the lifespan, bring to life a wide range of topics typically covered in child, adolescent, and lifespan development courses. New cross-cultural videos shot on location in several countries allow students to observe similarities and differences in human development across cultures throughout the lifespan. These videos can be accessed online via MyDevelopmentLab and are also available on DVD. Contact your Pearson sales rep for more information.

  - **CourseSmart Online Textbooks** are also available. CourseSmart goes beyond traditional expectations, providing instant, online access to the textbook and course materials at a lower cost than the print edition (average savings of 60 percent). With instant access from any computer and full electronic search functionality, CourseSmart allows students to find content quickly, no matter where they are. And with online tools like highlighting and note-taking, students can save time and study efficiently.

    Instructors can save time and avoid hassle with a digital eTextbook that allows them to search for the most relevant content at the very moment they need it. Whether for evaluating textbooks or creating lecture notes to help students with difficult concepts, CourseSmart can make life a little easier. See all the benefits at www.coursesmart.com/instructors or www.coursesmart.com/students.

Supplementary Texts

Contact your Pearson representative to package any of these supplementary texts with *Discovering the Lifespan*, **Canadian Edition**.

- *Current Directions in Developmental Psychology* **(ISBN 0205597505).** Readings from the American Psychological Society. This exciting reader includes more than 20 articles that have been carefully selected for the undergraduate audience and taken from the very accessible *Current Directions in Psychological Science* journal. These timely, cutting-edge articles allow instructors to bring their students real-world perspective about today's most current and pressing issues in psychology. Available in print or within MyDevelopmentLab.

- *Twenty Studies That Revolutionized Child Psychology* **(ISBN 0130415723).** This brief text by Wallace E. Dixon, Jr., presents the seminal research studies that have shaped modern developmental psychology, and provides an overview of the environment that gave rise to each study, its experimental design, its findings, and its impact on current thinking in the discipline.

- *Human Development in Multicultural Context: A Book of Readings* **(ISBN 0130195235).** Written by Michele A. Paludi, this compilation of readings highlights cultural influences in developmental psychology.

- *The Psychology Major: Careers and Strategies for Success,* **5th Edition (ISBN 0205829651).** Written by Eric Landrum (Idaho State University) and Stephen Davis (Emporia State University), this 160-page paperback provides valuable information on career options available to psychology majors, tips for improving academic performance, and a guide to the APA style of research reporting.

Acknowledgments from Oriane Landry

I would first like to thank the team at Pearson for giving me the opportunity to bring this book to classrooms across Canada: Duncan Mackinnon, who brought me into the Pearson family; Lise Dupont and Matthew Christian, who functioned as my right- and left-hand advisors and advocates through much of this process; and my production-editorial team: Rachel Thompson, Project Manager; Sapna Rastogi, Production Editor; Julie Fletcher, copy editor; and Audrey Dorsch, proofreader. I would also like to thank Sandra Hessels and my three research assistants: Meghan Tower, Chantelle McMullin, and Marissa Ley, who spent countless hours digging up Statistics Canada and other data. Adapting a US text involves more than just converting the apothecaries' Imperial system of measurement to metric and inserting Canadian spellings; looking at American and Canadian data side by side gave me a new appreciation of Canadian culture. On the subject of data, Statistics Canada is a national treasure, and this book would not have been possible without that resource.

I would also like to thank the reviewers of this Canadian edition, who provided excellent suggestions and comments, reflecting the diverse populations of students they teach. Ultimately this will be the textbook about which your students will ask the same questions mine always did, and I hope that, with your feedback, we've created a volume that reflects what you feel is essential to your students' learning. Set out below are the reviewers' names in alphabetical order:

Alice S. Barron, St. Clair College; Sue Davis-Mendelow, Humber College; Laura Hotham, Niagara College; Louise Jarrold, Dawson College; Jacqueline Kampman, Thompson Rivers University; Jason Morris, St. Clair College; Jennifer Potton-Roberts, Mohawk College; Ravi Ramkissoonsingh, Niagara College; Maria Roberts, Centennial College; Lina Rossi, Fanshawe College; Mary Ann Smith, Fanshawe College; Alwin Spence, John Abbott College; Joel St. Pierre, Mohawk College; Stephanie Yamin, University of Ottawa.

Although there are too many people at various institutions to thank in this small space—people who facilitated my career development to this point and who merit gracious acknowledgment—a few deserve special mention. Thank you to Jake Burack, Peter Mitchell,

Tomáš Paus, Bruce Morton, Rob Nicolson, Bruce Earhard, Ray Klein, and David Shore; each of you opened doors at critical points during my journey, and I would not be where I am today otherwise. A special thank you also to Susanne Lajoie for helping to close a door when it needed closing.

To my partner and progeny, thank you for all your support throughout the development of this Canadian Edition (and through the tough times over the past 10 years leading up to this point), and thank you for the experience of parenthood. It's one thing to work with children professionally; it's a whole new world when you become a "mom."

Finally, to my parents: thank you for the genes, and thank you for a healthy prenatal and postnatal environment; and to my grandparents, thank you for raising my parents to raise me to be the person I am today.

Oriane Landry
McMaster University

Acknowledgments from Robert S. Feldman

I am grateful to the reviewers of the US first and second editions who provided a wealth of comments, constructive criticism, and encouragement.

Many others deserve a great deal of thanks. I am indebted to the numerous people who provided me with a superb education, first at Wesleyan University and later at the University of Wisconsin. Specifically, Karl Scheibe played a pivotal role in my undergraduate education, and the late Vernon Allen acted as mentor and guide through my graduate years. It was in graduate school that I learned about development, being exposed to such experts as Ross Parke, John Balling, Joel Levin, Herb Klausmeier, and many others. My education continued when I became a professor. I am especially grateful to my colleagues at the University of Massachusetts, who make the university such a wonderful place in which to teach and do research.

Several people played important roles in the development of this book. Edward Murphy, Amy Henry, and Christopher Poirier provided significant research and editorial support. In addition, John Graiff was essential in juggling and coordinating the multiple aspects of writing a book. I am very grateful for his help.

I am also thankful to the superb Pearson team that was instrumental in the inception and development of this book. Jeff Marshall, Executive Editor, conceived of the format of this book, and he has brought creativity and a wealth of good ideas to the project. Apart from being a relentless taskmaster, Jeff is a fantastic editor, and I count myself lucky to work with him. I'm also extremely grateful to LeeAnn Doherty, Associate Editor, who stayed on top of every aspect of the project and brought inventiveness and imagination to the book. I can't thank her enough for her way-beyond-the-call-of duty efforts and patience with me.

Editorial Director Craig Campanella and Editor in Chief Jessica Mosher stood behind the project, and I'm very grateful for their support. On the production end of things, Marianne Peters-Riordan, the Production Supervisor, and Mary Siener, Designer, helped give the book its distinctive look. Finally, I'd like to thank (in advance) Marketing Manager Nicole Kunzmann, on whose skills I'm counting.

I also wish to acknowledge the members of my family who play such an essential role in my life. My brother, Michael, my sisters-in-law and brother-in-law, and my nieces and nephews all make up an important part of my life. In addition, I am always indebted to the older generation of my family who led the way in a manner I can only hope to emulate. I will always be obligated to Harry Brochstein, Mary Vorwerk, and Ethel Radler. Most of all, the list is headed by my father, the late Saul Feldman, and my mother, Leah Brochstein.

In the end, it is my immediate family who deserve the greatest thanks. My son Jon, his wife, Leigh, and my grandson, Alex; my son Josh, and his wife, Julie; and my daughter, Sarah, are not only nice, smart, and good-looking, but my pride and joy. And ultimately my wife, Katherine Vorwerk, provides the love and grounding that make everything worthwhile. I thank them, with all my love.

Robert S. Feldman
University of Massachusetts at Amherst

About the Authors

Robert S. Feldman is Professor of Psychology and Dean of the College of Social and Behavioral Sciences at the University of Massachusetts Amherst. A recipient of the College Distinguished Teacher Award, he teaches psychology classes ranging from 15 to nearly 500 students. During the course of more than two decades as a college instructor, he has taught both undergraduate and graduate courses at Mount Holyoke College, Wesleyan University, and Virginia Commonwealth University, in addition to the University of Massachusetts.

Feldman, who initiated the Minority Mentoring Program at the University of Massachusetts, also has served as a Hewlett Teaching Fellow and Senior Online Teaching Fellow. He initiated distance learning courses in psychology at the University of Massachusetts.

Feldman is actively involved in promoting the field of psychology. He is on the Board of Directors of the Federation of Associations in Behavioral and Brain Sciences (FABBS), and is on the board of the FABBS Foundation. A Fellow of both the American Psychological Association and the Association for Psychological Science, Professor Feldman received a B.A. with High Honors from Wesleyan University and an M.S. and Ph.D. from the University of Wisconsin–Madison.

He is a winner of a Fulbright Senior Research Scholar and Lecturer award, and he has written more than 150 books, book chapters, and scientific articles. He has edited _Development of Nonverbal Behavior in Children_ (Springer-Verlag), _Applications of Nonverbal Behavioral Theory and Research_ (Erlbaum), and co-edited _Fundamentals of Nonverbal Behavior_ (Cambridge University Press). He is also author of _Child Development_, _Understanding Psychology_, and _P.O.W.E.R. Learning: Strategies for Success in College and Life_. His books have been translated into a number of languages, including Spanish, French, Portuguese, Dutch, Chinese, and Japanese.

His research interests include honesty and deception in everyday life and the use of nonverbal behaviour in impression management. His research has been supported by grants from the National Institute of Mental Health and the National Institute on Disabilities and Rehabilitation Research.

Feldman loves music, is an enthusiastic—if not exactly expert—pianist, and he enjoys cooking and travelling. He has three children, and he and his wife, a psychologist, live in western Massachusetts, in a home overlooking the Holyoke mountain range.

Oriane Landry is Assistant Professor in the Psychology, Neuroscience, and Behaviour Department at McMaster University, where she teaches courses in infancy through adulthood as well as research methods. She has also taught courses in developmental psychology, child psychopathology, research methods, and statistics at Dalhousie University and the University of Western Ontario.

Dr. Landry received a B.A. from Dalhousie University and an M.A. and Ph.D from McGill University. She was also a Post Doctoral Fellow at the University of Nottingham, UK. Her main research interests are the early development of cognitive processes, especially attention, in typical children and in children with autism. _Discovering the Lifespan,_ Canadian Edition, is her first textbook.

Introduction

Most days Joanna still felt like she was 25, but every once in a while she caught a glimpse of a 37-year-old looking back at her in the mirror. She had a challenging career that she loved, a supportive partner, and two children who brought her joy—most of the time.

Her two children were like night and day. Her son, Tom, had been a calm and happy baby and was still a mellow, easygoing 10-year-old. Her 6-year-old daughter, Adele, on the other hand, drove Joanna crazy. As a baby Adele never seemed to sleep. Potty training took forever. She never listened and kept at it until she got what she wanted. She flew into tantrums at the drop of a hat. Both children were both popular, and Adele was enrolled in a program for gifted children at her school. Tom was capable, but less motivated. Joanna often wondered what, if anything, she had done when they were little to make them so different. At other times, she saw Tom and Adele as miniature versions of herself or their father. Adele was stubborn, like her father. Tom was easily distracted, like Joanna.

Joanna was also beginning to worry about her parents. Would their retirement savings be enough? How much longer would they be in good health? Would she

MODULE **1.1** Beginnings

Nature vs. nurture: Which has the greater influence? see page 4.

MODULE **1.2** Theoretical Perspectives on Lifespan Development

Is one right and one wrong? see page 11.

have to take care of them? What about her in-laws? When she caught the eye of that 37-year-old in the mirror, a million thoughts rushed through her mind and for a brief moment, she felt a lot older.

Lifespan development is a diverse and growing field with a broad focus and wide applicability. It covers the entire lifespan of the individual from birth to death, examining the ways in which people develop physically, intellectually, and socially. It asks and attempts to answer questions about the ways in which people change and remain the same over the years of their life.

Many of the questions that developmentalists ask are, in essence, the scientist's version of the questions that parents ask about their children and themselves: how the genetic legacy of parents plays out in their children; how children learn; why children make the choices they make; whether personality characteristics are inherited and whether they change or are stable over time; how a stimulating environment affects development; and many others. To find the answers, of course, developmentalists use the highly structured, formal scientific method, while parents frequently use a more informal strategy of waiting, observing, engaging, and loving their kids.

In this chapter, we will introduce the field of lifespan development. We first discuss the breadth of the field, both in the range of years it covers and in the topics it addresses, and we look at the major theoretical perspectives that have examined those topics. We also describe the key features of the scientific method—the main approach that scientists take to answering questions of interest.

MODULE 1.3 Research Methods

What kind of research could you conduct using Joanna's household?

see page 22.

MyVirtualLife

How much of your child's personality is inherited through genetics and how much comes from how he or she is raised? How will your decisions affect your child's development?

Log onto My Virtual Life through MyDevelopmentLab and start making those choices.

MODULE 1.1 Beginnings

New Conceptions

What if, for your entire life, the image that others held of you was coloured by the way in which you were conceived?

In some ways, that's what it has been like for Louise Brown, who was the world's first "test tube baby," born by in vitro fertilization (IVF), a procedure in which fertilization of a mother's egg by a father's sperm takes place outside the mother's body.

Louise was a preschooler when her parents told her how she was conceived, and throughout her childhood she was bombarded with questions. It became routine to explain to her classmates that she in fact was not born in a laboratory.

As a child, Louise sometimes felt completely alone. But as she grew older, her isolation declined as more and more children were born in the same manner.

In fact, today Louise is hardly isolated. More than 1.5 million babies have been born using the procedure, which has become almost routine. And at the age of 28, Louise became a mother herself, giving birth to a baby boy named Cameron—conceived, by the way, in the old-fashioned way. (Moreton, 2007)

Louise Brown's conception might have been novel, but her development since then has followed a predictable pattern. While the specifics of every person's development vary, the broad strokes set in motion in that test tube 35 years ago are remarkably similar to everyone else's. Justin Beiber or your little brother, the Queen of England or your grandmother—all are traversing the territory known as lifespan development.

Louise Brown's conception was and is just one of the brave new worlds of the day. Issues that affect human development range from cloning to poverty to the prevention of AIDS and cancer. Underlying these are even more fundamental issues: How do we develop physically? How does our understanding of the world change throughout our lives? And how do our personalities and social relationships develop as we move through the lifespan?

These questions and many others are central to lifespan development. The field encompasses a broad span of time and a wide range of areas. Consider the range of interests that different specialists might focus on when considering Louise Brown:

- Lifespan development researchers who investigate behaviour at the biological level might ask if Louise's functioning before birth was affected by her conception outside the womb.
- Specialists in lifespan development who study genetics might examine how the genetic endowment from Louise's parents affects her later behaviour.
- Lifespan development specialists who investigate thinking processes might examine how Louise's understanding of the circumstances of her conception changed as she grew older.
- Other researchers in lifespan development, who focus on physical growth, might consider whether her growth rate differed from children conceived more traditionally.
- Lifespan development experts who specialize in the social world and social relationships might look at the ways that Louise interacted with others and the kinds of friendships she developed.

Although their interests take many forms, these specialists share one concern: understanding the growth and change that occur during life. Taking many different approaches, developmentalists study how both our biological inheritance from our parents and the environment in which we live jointly affect our future behaviour, personality, and potential as human beings.

Whether they focus on heredity or environment, all developmental specialists acknowledge that neither alone can account for the full range of human development. Instead, we must look at the interaction of heredity and environment, and attempt to grasp how both underlie human behaviour.

In this module, we orient ourselves to the field of lifespan development. We begin with a discussion of the scope of the discipline, illustrating the wide array of topics it covers and the full range of ages it examines. We also survey the key issues and controversies of the field and consider the broad perspectives that developmentalists take. Finally, we discuss the ways developmentalists use research to ask and answer questions.

An Orientation to Lifespan Development

LO1 What is lifespan development?

LO2 What are the different sources of influence on human development?

LO3 What are the key issues in the field of development?

LEARNING OBJECTIVES

Have you ever wondered at the way an infant tightly grips your finger with tiny, perfectly formed hands? Or marvelled at how a preschooler methodically draws a picture? Or at the way an adolescent can make involved decisions about whom to invite to a party or the ethics of downloading music files? Or the way a middle-aged politician can deliver a long, flawless speech from memory? Or what makes a grandfather at 80 so similar to the father he was at 40?

If you've ever wondered about such things, you are asking the kinds of questions posed by scientists in the field of lifespan development. **Lifespan development** is the field of study that examines patterns of growth, change, and stability in behaviour that occur throughout the lifespan.

Like members of other scientific disciplines, researchers in lifespan development test their assumptions by applying *scientific* methods. They develop theories about development and use methodical, scientific techniques to systematically validate the accuracy of their assumptions.

Lifespan development focuses on *human* development. Although some developmentalists study nonhuman species, the vast majority study people. Some seek to understand universal principles of development, while others focus on how social and cultural differences affect development. Still others aim to understand the traits and characteristics that differentiate one person from another. Regardless of approach, however, all developmentalists view development as a continuing process throughout the lifespan.

As developmental specialists focus on change during the lifespan, they also consider stability. They ask in which areas and in what periods people show change and growth, and when and how behaviour reveals consistency and continuity with prior behaviour.

Finally, developmentalists assume that the process of development persists from the moment of conception to the moment of death, with people changing in some ways right up to the end of their lives and in other ways exhibiting remarkable stability. Developmentalists believe that no single period governs all development, but instead that people maintain the capacity for substantial growth and change throughout their lives.

Characterizing Lifespan Development: The Scope of the Field

Clearly, the definition of lifespan development is broad and the scope of the field extensive. Typically, lifespan development specialists cover several diverse areas, choosing to specialize in both a topical area and an age range.

Topical Areas in Lifespan Development. Some developmentalists focus on **physical development**, examining the ways in which the body's makeup—the brain, nervous system, muscles, and senses, and the need for food, drink, and sleep—helps determine behaviour. For example, one specialist in physical development might examine the effects of malnutrition on the pace of growth in children, while another might look at how athletes' physical performance declines during adulthood.

Other developmental specialists examine **cognitive development**, seeking to understand how growth and change in intellectual capabilities influence a person's behaviour. Cognitive developmentalists examine learning, memory, problem solving, and intelligence. For example, specialists in cognitive development might want to see how problem-solving skills change over the course of life, or whether cultural differences exist in the way people explain their academic successes and failures, or how traumatic events experienced early in life are remembered later in life.

lifespan development the field of study that examines patterns of growth, change, and stability in behaviour that occur throughout the entire lifespan

physical development development involving the body's physical makeup, including the brain, nervous system, muscles, and senses, and the need for food, drink, and sleep

cognitive development development involving the ways that growth and change in intellectual capabilities influence a person's behaviour

personality development development involving the ways that enduring characteristics that differentiate one person from another change over the lifespan

social development the way in which individuals' interactions with others and their social relationships grow, change, and remain stable over the course of life

Finally, some developmental specialists focus on personality and social development. **Personality development** is the study of stability and change in the characteristics that differentiate one person from another over the lifespan. **Social development** is the way in which individuals' interactions and relationships with others grow, change, and remain stable over the course of life. A developmentalist interested in personality development might ask whether there are stable, enduring personality traits throughout the lifespan, while a specialist in social development might examine the effects of racism or poverty or divorce on development. These three major topic areas—physical, cognitive, and social and personality development—are summarized in Table 1-1.

Age Ranges and Individual Differences. In addition to choosing a particular topical area, developmentalists also typically look at a particular age range. The lifespan is usually divided into broad age ranges: the prenatal period (from conception to birth); infancy (birth to 2); early childhood (2 to 6); middle childhood (6 to 12); adolescence (12 to 20); young adulthood (20 to 40); middle adulthood (40 to 65); and late adulthood (65 to death).

It's important to keep in mind that these periods are social constructions. A *social construction* is a shared notion of reality that is widely accepted but is a function of society and culture at a given time. Thus, the age ranges within a period—and even the periods themselves—are in many ways arbitrary and culturally derived. For example, we'll see how the concept of childhood as a special period did not even exist during the seventeenth

TABLE 1-1 APPROACHES TO LIFESPAN DEVELOPMENT

Orientation	Defining Characteristics	Examples of Question Asked*
Physical development	Emphasizes how brain, nervous system, muscles, sensory capabilities, and needs for food, drink, and sleep affect behaviour	• What determines the sex of a child? (2.1) • What are the long-term results of premature birth? (2.3) • What are the benefits of breast milk? (3.1) • What are the consequences of early or late sexual maturation? (6.1) • What leads to obesity in adulthood? (7.1) • How do adults cope with stress? (8.1) • What are the outward and internal signs of aging? (9.1) • How do we define death? (10.1)
Cognitive development	Emphasizes intellectual abilities, including learning, memory, problem solving, and intelligence	• What are the earliest memories that can be recalled from infancy? (3.2) • What are the intellectual consequences of watching television? (4.2) • Do spatial reasoning skills relate to music practice? (4.2) • Are there benefits to bilingualism? (5.2) • How does an adolescent's egocentrism affect his or her view of the world? (6.2) • Are there genetic influences on intelligence? (5.2) • How does creativity relate to intelligence? (7.2) • Does intelligence decline in late adulthood? (9.2)
Personality and social development	Emphasizes enduring characteristics that differentiate one person from another, and how interactions with others and social relationships grow and change over the lifetime	• Do newborns respond differently to their mothers than to others? (2.3) • What is the best procedure for disciplining children? (4.3) • When does a sense of gender identity develop? (4.3) • How can we promote multicultural friendships? (5.3) • What are the causes of adolescent suicide? (6.3) • How do we choose a romantic partner? (7.3) • Do the effects of parental divorce last into old age? (9.3) • Do people withdraw from others in late adulthood? (9.3) • What emotions are involved in confronting death? (10.1)

*Numbers in parentheses indicate in which chapter and module the question is addressed.

century—children were seen then simply as miniature adults. Furthermore, while some periods have a clear-cut boundary (infancy begins with birth, the preschool period ends with entry into public school, and adolescence starts with sexual maturity), others don't.

For instance, consider the period of young adulthood, which, at least in Western cultures, is typically assumed to begin at age 20. That age is notable only because it marks the end of the teenage period. In fact, for many people, such as those enrolled in higher education, the age change from 19 to 20 has little special significance. For them, more substantial changes are likely to occur when they graduate. Furthermore, in some cultures, adulthood starts much earlier—as soon as a child can begin full-time work.

In short, substantial *individual differences* exist in the timing of events in people's lives. In part, this is a biological fact of life: People mature at different rates and reach developmental milestones at different points. However, environmental factors also play a significant role; for example, the typical age of marriage varies from one culture to another, depending in part on the functions that marriage plays in the culture.

This wedding of two children in India is an example of how environmental factors can play a significant role in determining the age when a particular event is likely to occur.

The Links Between Topics and Ages. Each of the broad topical areas of lifespan development—physical, cognitive, and social and personality development—plays a role throughout the lifespan. Consequently, some developmental experts might focus on physical development during the prenatal period, and others on physical development during adolescence. Some might specialize in social development during the preschool years, while others look at social relationships in late adulthood. Still others might take a broader approach, looking at cognitive development through every period of life.

In this book, we'll take a comprehensive approach, proceeding chronologically from the prenatal period to late adulthood and death. Within each period, we'll look at physical, cognitive, and social and personality development.

Cultural Dimensions

How Culture, Ethnicity, and Race Influence Development

Mayan mothers in Central America are certain that almost constant contact between themselves and their infant children is necessary for good parenting, and they are physically upset if contact is not possible. They are shocked when they see a North American mother lay her infant down, and they attribute the baby's crying to the poor parenting of the North American. (Morelli et al., 1992)

What are we to make of the two views of parenting depicted in this passage? Is one right and the other wrong? Probably not, if we take cultural context into consideration. Different cultures and subcultures have their own views of appropriate and inappropriate childrearing, just as they have different developmental goals for children (Greenfield, 1997; Haight, 2002; Tolchinsky, 2003; Feldman and Masalha, 2007).

Clearly, to understand development, developmentalists must take into consideration broad cultural factors, such as an orientation toward individualism or collectivism, as well as finer ethnic, socio-economic, and gender differences. If they succeed in doing this, not only can they achieve a better understanding of human development, but they might also be able to derive more precise applications for improving the human social condition.

To complicate the study of diverse populations, the terms *race* and *ethnic group* are often used inappropriately. *Race* is a biological concept, which should refer to classifications based on physical and structural characteristics of species. In contrast, *ethnic group* and *ethnicity* are broader concepts, referring to cultural background, nationality, religion, and language.

The concept of race has proven particularly problematic. It has inappropriately taken on nonbiological meanings ranging from skin colour to religion to culture. Moreover, as a concept it is exceedingly imprecise; depending on how it is defined, there are between 3 and 300 races, and no race is genetically distinct. The fact that 99.9% of humans' genetic makeup is identical makes the question of race seem insignificant (Bamshad and Olson, 2003; Helms et al., 2005; Smedley and Smedley, 2005).

To fully understand development, then, we need to take the complex issues associated with human diversity into account. In fact, only by looking for similarities among and differences between various cultural groups can developmental researchers distinguish universal principles of development from culturally determined differences. Lifespan development will continue its transition from a focus on Western development to a global focus (Bamshad et al., 2003; Fowers and Davidov, 2006; Matsumoto and Yoo, 2006).

cohort a group of people born at around the same time in the same place

Cohort Influences on Development: Developing with Others in a Social World

Bob, born in 1949, is a baby boomer; he was born soon after the end of World War II, when returning soldiers created an enormous spike in the birth rate. He was a university student in Montreal during the October Crisis. His mother, Leah, was born in 1922; her generation passed its childhood and teenage years in the shadow of the Great Depression. Bob's son, Jon, was born in 1975. Now building a career and starting a family, Jon is a member of what has been called Generation X. Jon's younger sister, Sarah, who was born in 1982, is part of the next generation, which sociologists have called the Millennial Generation.

These people are, in part, products of the social times in which they live. Each belongs to a particular **cohort**—a group of people born at around the same time in the same place. Such major social events as wars, economic upturns and depressions, famines, and epidemics have similar influences on members of a particular cohort (Mitchell, 2002; Dittmann, 2005).

Cohort effects are an example of *history-graded influences*—biological and environmental influences associated with a particular historical moment. For instance, people who lived in areas affected by the 1998 ice storm experienced shared biological and environmental challenges due to the event (King and Laplante, 2005; Laplante et al., 2004). Whether the influence is a short-term natural disaster or a longer lasting change in the way we live our lives, cohort effects can have powerful influences on large groups of people (Bonanno et al., 2006; Laugharne et al., 2007).

> ⮞ **From an educator's perspective:** How would a student's cohort membership affect his or her readiness for school? For example, what would be the benefits and drawbacks of coming from a cohort in which Internet use was routine, compared to earlier cohorts before the appearance of the Internet?

In contrast, *age-graded influences* are biological and environmental influences that are similar for individuals in a particular age group, regardless of when or where they are raised. For example, biological events such as puberty and menopause are universal events that occur at about the same time in all societies. Similarly, a sociocultural event such as entry into formal education can be considered an age-graded influence because it occurs in many cultures around age six.

Development is also affected by *sociocultural-graded influences*, the social and cultural factors present at a particular time for a particular individual, and depending on such variables as ethnicity, social class, and subcultural membership. For example, sociocultural-graded influences will be considerably different for white and non-white children, especially if one lives in poverty and the other in affluence (Rose et al., 2003).

Key Issues and Questions: Determining the Nature—and Nurture—of Lifespan Development

LEARNING OBJECTIVES

LO4 How do nature and nurture interact?

Lifespan development is a decades-long journey through shared milestones, with many individual routes along the way. For developmentalists, the variations in lifespan development raise many questions. What are the best ways to think about the enormous changes that a person undergoes from before birth to death? How important is chronological age? Is there a clear timetable for development? How can one begin to find common threads and patterns?

These questions have been debated since lifespan development became established as a separate field in the late nineteenth and early twentieth centuries, though a fascination with the nature and course of humans' development can be traced back to the ancient Egyptians and Greeks.

Continuous Change versus Discontinuous Change

One of the primary issues challenging developmentalists is whether development proceeds in a continuous or discontinuous fashion. In **continuous change**, development is gradual, with achievements at one level building on those of previous levels. Continuous change is quantitative; the underlying developmental processes remain the same over the lifespan. In this view, changes are a matter of degree, not of kind—like changes in a person's height. Some theorists suggest that changes in people's thinking abilities are also continuous, building on gradual improvements rather than developing entirely new processing capabilities.

In contrast, others see development as primarily a matter of **discontinuous change**, occurring in distinct stages. Each stage brings about behaviour that is assumed to be qualitatively different from behaviour at earlier stages. Consider cognitive development again. Some cognitive developmentalists suggest that our thinking changes in fundamental ways as we develop, not just quantitatively but also qualitatively.

Most developmentalists agree that it makes little sense to take an either/or position on this issue. While many types of developmental change are continuous, others are clearly discontinuous (Flavell, 1994; Heimann, 2003).

Critical and Sensitive Periods: Gauging the Impact of Environmental Events

If a woman contracts rubella (German measles) in the eleventh week of pregnancy, the consequences for the child she is carrying—possible blindness, deafness, and heart defects—can be devastating. However, if she contracts the same strain of rubella in the thirtieth week of pregnancy, harm to the child is unlikely.

These different outcomes demonstrate the concept of critical periods. A **critical period** is a specific time during development when a particular event will have its greatest consequences. During critical periods, certain kinds of environmental stimuli must be present for development to proceed normally (Uylings, 2006).

Although early specialists in lifespan development placed great emphasis on critical periods, recent thinking suggests that individuals are more malleable, particularly in the domain of personality and social development.

Consequently, developmentalists are now more likely to speak of **sensitive periods** than critical periods. In a sensitive period, organisms are particularly susceptible to certain kinds of stimuli in their environments. In contrast to a critical period, however, the absence of those stimuli during a sensitive period does not always produce irreversible consequences (Barinaga, 2000; Thompson and Nelson, 2001; Beauchaine, 2003).

Lifespan Approaches versus a Focus on Particular Periods

Early developmentalists tended to focus their attention on infancy and adolescence, to the exclusion of other parts of the lifespan. Today, however, developmentalists believe the entire lifespan is important, largely because developmental growth and change continue during every part of life—as we'll discuss throughout this book.

Furthermore, to fully understand the social influences on a person of a given age, we need to understand the person's social environment—in other words, the people who in large measure provide those influences. For instance, to understand infant development, we need to unravel the effects of the parents' ages on the infants' social environments. A 15-year-old first-time mother and an experienced 37-year-old mother will provide parental influences

continuous change gradual development in which achievements at one level build on those of previous levels

discontinuous change development that occurs in distinct steps or stages, with each stage bringing about behaviour that is assumed to be qualitatively different from behaviour at earlier stages

critical period a specific time during development when a particular event has its greatest consequences and the presence of certain kinds of environmental stimuli are necessary for development to proceed normally

sensitive period a point in development when organisms are particularly susceptible to certain kinds of stimuli in their environments, but the absence of those stimuli does not always produce irreversible consequences of very different sorts. Consequently, infant development is in part an outgrowth of adult development.

Additionally, as lifespan developmentalist Paul Baltes points out, development across the lifespan involves both gains and losses. With age, certain capabilities become more refined and sophisticated, while others decline. For example, vocabulary tends to grow throughout childhood and continue through most of adulthood, but certain physical abilities, such as reaction time, improve until early and middle adulthood, and then begin to decline (Baltes et al., 1999; Baltes, 2003).

The Relative Influence of Nature and Nurture on Development

One of the enduring questions of development is how much of our behaviour is due to genetics (nature) and how much to our physical and social environment (nurture) (Wexler, 2006).

Nature refers to traits, abilities, and capacities that are inherited from one's parents and encompasses any factor that is produced by the predetermined unfolding of genetic information—a process known as **maturation.** These genetic, inherited influences are at work as we move from the one-cell organism created at conception to the billions of cells that make up a fully formed human. Nature influences whether our eyes are blue or brown, whether we have thick hair throughout life or eventually go bald, and how good we are at athletics. Nature allows our brains to develop in such a way that we can read the words on this page.

In contrast, *nurture* refers to the environmental influences that shape behaviour. Some influences might be biological, such as the impact of a pregnant mother's use of cocaine on her unborn child or the amount and kind of food available to children. Other influences are more social, such as the ways parents discipline their children and the effects of peer pressure on an adolescent. Finally, some influences are a result of societal factors such as the socioeconomic circumstances in which people find themselves.

Developmentalists reject the notion that behaviour is solely the result of either nature or nurture; nevertheless, the nature–nurture question can cause heated debate. Take, for instance, intelligence. If intelligence is primarily determined by heredity and is largely fixed at birth, then efforts to improve intellectual performance later in life may be doomed to failure. In contrast, if intelligence is primarily a result of environmental factors, such as the amount and quality of schooling and home stimulation, then an improvement in social conditions could cause intelligence to increase.

Clearly, neither nature nor nurture stands alone in most developmental matters. The interaction of genetic and environmental factors is complex, in part because certain genetically determined traits have not only a direct influence on children's behaviour, but also an indirect influence in shaping children's *environments*. For example, children who cry a great deal—a trait that could be produced by genetic factors—might influence their environment by making their parents rush to comfort them whenever the children cry. The parents' responsivity to their children's genetically determined behaviour becomes an environmental influence on the children's subsequent development.

Similarly, although our genetic background orients us toward particular behaviours, those behaviours will not necessarily occur without an appropriate environment. For example, though we humans might all be born with the genetic potential to learn language, we learn only the languages to which we are exposed. A daffodil, which lacks those genes, will never learn French no matter how much exposure it receives.

In sum, the nature–nurture question is challenging. Ultimately, we should consider the *interaction* between nature and nurture. Equally, continuous versus discontinuous development is not an either/or proposition: Some forms of development fall toward the continuous end of the continuum, others lie closer to the discontinuous end, while still others lie somewhere in between. In short, few statements about development involve either/or absolutes (Rutter, 2006; Deater-Deckard and Cahill, 2006).

maturation the predetermined unfolding of genetic information

REVIEW, CHECK, AND APPLY

REVIEW

- Lifespan development is a scientific approach to understanding human growth and change throughout life, and encompasses physical, cognitive, and social and personality development.

- Membership in a cohort, based on age and place of birth, subjects people to influences based on historical events (history-graded influences). People are also subject to age-graded influences and sociocultural-graded influences.

- Four important issues in lifespan development are continuity versus discontinuity in development, the importance of critical periods, whether to focus on certain periods or on the entire lifespan, and the nature–nurture controversy.

CHECK YOURSELF

1. Three assumptions made by lifespan developmentalists include 1) a focus on human development, 2) an understanding of stability in addition to growth and change, and 3) _____.

   a. the perception that development persists throughout our entire lives

   b. the perception that childhood development changes are the only changes worth studying

   c. the idea that some periods of the lifespan are more important than others

   d. the perception that development is a stagnant process

2. Stages of the lifespan such as adolescence and middle age are universal across cultures and stable across history.

   - True

   - False

3. Grady believes that human development occurs in small, measurable amounts. His sister Andrea disagrees and suggests that human development is more distinct and steplike. Their argument is most reflective of the _____ issue.

   a. critical and sensitive period

   b. nature and nurture

   c. continuous and discontinuous

   d. lifespan approach and particular period

4. A _____ is a specific time during development when a particular event has its greatest consequence.

5. Nurture refers to traits, abilities, and capacities that are inherited from one's parents.

   - True

   - False

APPLYING LIFESPAN DEVELOPMENT

- What are some examples of the ways culture (either broad culture or aspects of culture) affects human development?

Answers: 1) a; 2) False; 3) c; 4) critical period; 5) False

MODULE 1.2 Theoretical Perspectives on Lifespan Development

Theoretical Perspectives on Lifespan Development

Until the seventeenth century in Europe, no concept of "childhood" existed. Instead, children were simply thought of as miniature adults. They were assumed to be subject to the same needs and desires as adults, to have the same vices and virtues, and to warrant no more privileges. They were dressed the same as adults, and their work hours were the same. Children also received the same punishments for misdeeds. If they stole, they were hanged; if they did well, they could achieve prosperity—at least so far as their station in life or social class would allow.

Society's view of childhood—and of what is appropriate to ask of children—has changed through the ages. These children worked full-time in mines in the early 1900s.

This view of childhood seems wrong-headed now, but at the time it reflected society's understanding of lifespan development. From this perspective, there were no differences due to age; except for size, people were assumed to be virtually unchanging, at least on a psychological level, throughout most of the lifespan (Aries, 1962; Acocella, 2003; Hutton, 2004; Wines, 2006).

It is easy to reject this medieval view but less clear how to formulate a contemporary substitute. Should our view of development focus on the biological aspects of change, growth, and stability over the lifespan, on the cognitive or social aspects, or on some other factors?

In fact, people who study lifespan development approach the field from different perspectives. Each perspective encompasses one or more **theories**—broad, organized explanations and predictions concerning phenomena of interest. A theory provides a framework for understanding the relationships among a seemingly unorganized set of facts or principles.

We will consider five major theoretical perspectives used in lifespan development: the psychodynamic, behavioural, cognitive, contextual, and evolutionary perspectives. Each emphasizes somewhat different aspects of development and steers developmentalists in particular directions. Furthermore, each perspective continues to evolve, as befits a dynamic discipline.

Five Frameworks

LEARNING OBJECTIVES

LO5 Which theoretical perspectives have guided lifespan development?

LO6 What are the main characteristics of each of these perspectives?

LO7 Who are some of the key figures in each of these perspectives?

The Psychodynamic Perspective: Focusing on the Inner Person

When Marianne was six months old, she was involved in a bloody automobile accident—or so her parents tell her, since she has no recollection of it. Now at age 24, she is having difficulty maintaining relationships, and her therapist is seeking to determine whether her current problems are a result of the earlier accident.

Looking for such a link might seem a bit far-fetched—but not to proponents of the **psychodynamic perspective**. Advocates of this perspective believe that much behaviour is motivated by inner forces, memories, and conflicts of which a person has little awareness or control. The inner forces, which may stem from childhood, influence behaviour throughout life.

Freud's Psychoanalytic Theory. The psychodynamic perspective is most closely associated with Sigmund Freud. Freud, who lived from 1856 to 1939, was a Viennese physician whose revolutionary ideas had a profound effect not only on psychology and psychiatry, but on Western thought in general (Masling and Bornstein, 1996).

Freud's **psychoanalytic theory** suggests that unconscious forces act to determine personality and behaviour. To Freud, the *unconscious* is a part of the personality about which a person is unaware. It contains infantile wishes, desires, demands, and needs that are hidden, because of their disturbing nature, from conscious awareness. Freud suggested that the unconscious is responsible for a good part of our everyday behaviour.

According to Freud, everyone's personality has three aspects: id, ego, and superego. The *id* is the raw, unorganized, inborn part of personality that is present at birth. It represents primitive drives related to hunger, sex, aggression, and irrational impulses. The id operates according to the *pleasure principle*, in which the goal is to maximize satisfaction and reduce tension.

The *ego* is the part of personality that is rational and reasonable. The ego acts as a buffer between the external world and the primitive id. The ego operates on the *reality principle*, in which instinctual energy is restrained in order to maintain the safety of the individual and help integrate the person into society.

Finally, Freud proposed that the *superego* represents a person's conscience, incorporating distinctions between right and wrong. The superego begins to develop around age five or six and is learned from an individual's parents, teachers, and other significant figures.

Freud also addressed personality development during childhood. He argued that **psychosexual development** occurs as children pass through distinct stages in which pleasure, or gratification, is focused on a particular biological function and body part. As illustrated in Table 1-2, Freud suggested that pleasure shifts from the mouth (the *oral stage*) to the anus (the *anal stage*) and eventually to the genitals (the *phallic stage* and the *genital stage*).

According to Freud, if children are unable to gratify themselves sufficiently during a particular stage, or if they receive too much gratification, fixation may occur. *Fixation* is behaviour reflecting an earlier stage of development due to an unresolved conflict. For instance, fixation at the oral stage might produce an adult unusually absorbed in oral activities—eating,

Sigmund Freud

theories explanations and predictions concerning phenomena of interest, providing a framework for understanding the relationships among an organized set of facts or principles

psychodynamic perspective the approach that states behaviour is motivated by inner forces, memories, and conflicts that are generally beyond people's awareness and control

psychoanalytic theory the theory proposed by Freud that suggests that unconscious forces act to determine personality and behaviour

psychosexual development according to Freud, a series of stages that children pass through in which pleasure, or gratification, is focused on a particular biological function and body part

TABLE 1-2 FREUD'S AND ERIKSON'S THEORIES

Approximate Age	Freud's Stages of Psychosexual Development	Major Characteristics of Freud's Stages	Erikson's Stages of Psychosocial Development	Positive and Negative Outcomes of Erikson's Stages
Birth to 12–18 months	Oral	Interest in oral gratification from sucking, eating, mouthing, biting	Trust vs. mistrust	*Positive:* Feelings of trust from environmental support *Negative:* Fear and concern regarding others
12–18 months to 3 years	Anal	Gratification from expelling and withholding feces; coming to terms with society's controls relating to toilet training	Autonomy vs. shame and doubt	*Positive:* Self-sufficiency if exploration is encouraged *Negative:* Doubts about self, lack of independence
3 to 5–6 years	Phallic	Interest in the genitals; coming to terms with Oedipal conflict, leading to identification with same-sex parent	Initiative vs. guilt	*Positive:* Discovery of ways to initiate actions *Negative:* Guilt from actions and thoughts
5–6 years to adolescence	Latency	Sexual concerns largely unimportant	Industry vs. inferiority	*Positive:* Development of sense of competence *Negative:* Feelings of inferiority, no sense of mastery
Adolescence to adulthood (Freud) Adolescence (Erikson)	Genital	Re-emergence of sexual interests and establishment of mature sexual relationships	Identity vs. identity confusion	*Positive:* Awareness of uniqueness of self, knowledge of role to be followed *Negative:* Inability to identify appropriate roles in life
Early adulthood (Erikson)			Intimacy vs. isolation	*Positive:* Development of loving, sexual relationships and close friendships *Negative:* Fear of relationships with others
Middle adulthood (Erikson)			Generativity vs. stagnation	*Positive:* Sense of contribution to continuity of life *Negative:* Trivialization of one's activities
Late adulthood (Erikson)			Ego-integrity vs. despair	*Positive:* Sense of unity in life's accomplishments *Negative:* Regret over lost opportunities of life

talking, or chewing gum. Freud also argued that fixation is represented through symbolic oral activities, such as the use of "biting" sarcasm.

Erikson's Psychosocial Theory. German psychoanalyst Erik Erikson, who lived from 1902 to 1994, provided an alternative psychodynamic view, emphasizing our social interaction with other people. In Erikson's view, society and culture both challenge and shape us. **Psychosocial development** encompasses changes in our interactions with and understandings of one another as well as in our knowledge and understanding of ourselves as members of society (Erikson, 1963).

psychosocial development the approach that encompasses changes in our interactions with and understandings of one another, as well as in our knowledge and understanding of ourselves as members of society

Erik Erikson

Erikson's theory suggests that development proceeds throughout our lives in eight stages (see Table 1-2), which emerge in a fixed pattern and are similar for all people. Each stage presents a crisis or conflict that the individual must resolve. Although no crisis is ever fully resolved, the individual must at least address the crisis of each stage sufficiently to deal with demands made during the next stage of development. Unlike Freud, who regarded development as relatively complete by adolescence, Erikson suggested that growth and change continue throughout the lifespan (De St. Aubin et al., 2004).

Assessing the Psychodynamic Perspective. Freud's insight that unconscious influences affect behaviour was a monumental accomplishment, and the fact that it seems at all reasonable to us shows how extensively the idea of the unconscious has pervaded thinking in Western cultures. In fact, work by contemporary researchers studying memory and learning suggests that we unconsciously carry with us memories that have a significant impact on our behaviour.

Some of the most basic principles of Freud's psychoanalytic theory have been questioned, however, because they have not been validated by research. In particular, the notion that childhood stages determine adult personalities has little research support. In addition, because much of Freud's theory was based on a limited population of upper-middle-class Austrians living during a strict, puritanical era, its application to broad, multicultural populations is questionable. Finally, because Freud's theory focuses primarily on male development, it has been criticized as sexist and interpreted as devaluing women (Crews, 1993; Guterl, 2002; Messer and McWilliams, 2003).

Erikson's view that development continues throughout the lifespan is highly important—and has received considerable support. However, his theory also has its drawbacks. Like Freud's theory, it focuses more on men than on women. Furthermore, its vagueness makes rigorous testing difficult. And, as with psychodynamic theories in general, using Erikson's theory to make definitive predictions about a given individual's behaviour is difficult. (Whitbourne et al., 1992; Zauszniewski and Martin, 1999; De St. Aubin and McAdams, 2004).

The Behavioural Perspective: Focusing on Observable Behaviour

When Elissa Sheehan was three years old, a large brown dog bit her, and she needed dozens of stitches and several operations. From the time she was bitten, she broke into a sweat whenever she saw a dog, and in fact never enjoyed being around any pet.

To a lifespan development specialist using the behavioural perspective, the explanation for Elissa's behaviour is straightforward: She has a learned fear of dogs. Rather than looking inside the organism at unconscious processes, the **behavioural perspective** suggests that the keys to understanding development are observable behaviour and environmental stimuli. If we know the stimuli, we can predict the behaviour. In this respect, the behavioural perspective reflects the view that nurture is more important to development than nature.

Behavioural theories reject the notion that people universally pass through a series of stages. Instead, people are affected by the environmental stimuli to which they happen to be exposed. Developmental patterns, then, are personal, reflecting a particular set of environmental stimuli, and behaviour is the result of continuing exposure to specific factors in the environment. Furthermore, developmental change is viewed in quantitative, rather than qualitative, terms. For instance, behavioural theories hold that advances in problem-solving capabilities as children age are largely a result of cumulative experiences, such as practice and previous success, rather than the result of changes in the *kind* of thinking that children can bring to bear on a problem.

Classical Conditioning: Stimulus Substitution.

> *Give me a dozen healthy infants, well-formed, and my own specified world to bring them up in and I'll guarantee to take any one at random and train him to become any type of specialist I might select—doctor, lawyer, artist, merchant-chief, and yes, even beggar-man and thief, regardless of his talents, penchants, tendencies, abilities. . . . (Watson, 1925)*

With these words, the American psychologist John B. Watson summed up the behavioural perspective. Watson, who lived from 1878 to 1958, believed strongly that we could gain a full understanding of development by carefully studying the stimuli that composed the

behavioural perspective the approach suggesting that the keys to understanding development are observable behaviour and outside stimuli in the environment

environment. In fact, he argued that by effectively controlling—or conditioning—a person's environment, virtually any behaviour could be produced.

Classical conditioning occurs when an organism learns to respond in a particular way to a neutral stimulus. For instance, if the sound of a bell is paired with the arrival of meat, a dog will learn to react to the bell alone in the same way it reacts to the meat—by salivating and wagging its tail. The behaviour is a result of conditioning, a form of learning in which the response associated with one stimulus (food) comes to be connected to another—in this case, the bell.

The same process of classical conditioning explains how we learn emotional responses. In the case of dog-bite victim Elissa Sheehan, for instance, Watson would say that one stimulus has been substituted for another: Elissa's unpleasant experience with a particular dog (the initial stimulus) has been transferred to other dogs and to pets in general.

John B. Watson

Operant Conditioning.   In addition to classical conditioning, the behavioural perspective accounts for other types of learning, especially what behaviouralists call operant conditioning. **Operant conditioning** is a form of learning in which a voluntary response is strengthened or weakened by its association with positive or negative consequences. It differs from classical conditioning in that the response being conditioned is voluntary and purposeful rather than automatic (such as salivating). In operant conditioning, formulated and championed by American psychologist B. F. Skinner (1904–1990), individuals learn to *operate* on their environments in order to bring about desired consequences (Skinner, 1975).

Whether children and adults will seek to repeat a behaviour depends on whether the behaviour is followed by reinforcement. In *reinforcement*, a behaviour is followed by a stimulus that increases the probability that the behaviour will be repeated. Hence, a student is apt to work harder if he or she receives good grades; workers are likely to labour harder if their efforts are tied to pay increases; and people are more apt to buy lottery tickets if they occasionally win. In addition, *punishment*—the introduction of an unpleasant or painful stimulus or the removal of a desirable stimulus—decreases the probability that a preceding behaviour will occur in the future.

In the language of operant conditioning, then, behaviour that is reinforced is more likely to be repeated, while behaviour that is not reinforced or is punished is likely to be *extinguished*. Principles of operant conditioning are used in **behaviour modification**, a formal technique for promoting the frequency of desirable behaviours and decreasing the incidence of unwanted ones. Behaviour modification has been used in situations ranging from teaching toilet training in toddlers to helping people with self-control problems stick to diets (Katz, 2001; Christophersen and Mortweet, 2003; Hoek and Gendall, 2006).

Social-Cognitive Learning Theory: Learning through Imitation.   A 5-year-old boy seriously injured his 22-month-old cousin while imitating a violent wrestling move the boy saw on television. Although the baby sustained spinal cord injuries, he improved and was discharged five weeks after his hospital admission (Reuters Health eLine, 2002).

Did TV cause the boy to injure his cousin? We can't know for sure, but it certainly seems possible, especially to social-cognitive learning theorists. According to Canadian developmental psychologist Albert Bandura and colleagues, a significant amount of learning is explained by **social-cognitive learning theory**, an approach that emphasizes learning by observing the behaviour of another person, called a *model* (Bandura, 1977, 1994, 2002).

Watch on **mydevelopmentlab**

To watch a video on social cognition, log onto MyDevelopmentLab.

> **From a social worker's perspective:** How do the concepts of social learning and modelling relate to the mass media, and how might exposure to mass media influence a child's family life?

If operant conditioning makes learning a matter of trial and error, social-cognitive learning theory sees learning as a product of observation. Social-cognitive learning theory holds that when we see the behaviour of a model being rewarded, we are likely to imitate that behaviour. For instance, in one classic experiment, children who were afraid of dogs were exposed to a model, nicknamed the "Fearless Peer," who was seen playing happily with a dog (Bandura et al., 1967). After exposure, the children who previously had been afraid were more likely to approach a strange dog than children who had not seen the model.

classical conditioning a type of learning in which an organism responds in a particular way to a neutral stimulus that does not normally bring about that type of response

operant conditioning a form of learning in which a voluntary response is strengthened or weakened by its association with positive or negative consequences

behaviour modification a formal technique for promoting the frequency of desirable behaviours and decreasing the incidence of unwanted ones

social-cognitive learning theory theory stating that learning occurs by observing the behaviour of another person, called a model

On the reality show *Survivor*, contestants often must learn new survival skills in order to be successful. What form of learning is prevalent?

Assessing the Behavioural Perspective. Research using the behavioural perspective has made significant contributions, ranging from the education of children with intellectual disabilities to the development of procedures for curbing aggression. At the same time, the perspective has experienced internal disagreements. For example, although both are part of the same behavioural perspective, classical and operant conditioning and social learning theory disagree in some basic ways. Classical and operant conditioning consider learning in terms of external stimuli and responses, in which the only important factors are the observable features of the environment. People and other organisms are like inanimate "black boxes"; what occurs inside the box is neither understood nor cared about.

To social learning theorists, such an analysis is oversimplified. They argue that mental activity, in the form of thoughts and expectations, is what makes people different from rats and pigeons. We cannot derive a full understanding of people's development without moving beyond external stimuli and responses.

In many ways, social learning theory has won this argument in recent decades. In fact, another perspective that focuses explicitly on internal mental activity—the cognitive perspective—has become enormously influential.

The Cognitive Perspective: Examining the Roots of Understanding

When 3-year-old Jake is asked why it sometimes rains, he answers "so the flowers can grow." When his 11-year-old sister, Lila, is asked the same question, she responds "because of evaporation from the surface of the Earth." And when their cousin Ajima, who is studying meteorology in graduate school, considers the same question, her extended answer includes a discussion of cumulonimbus clouds, the Coriolis effect, and synoptic charts.

To a developmental theorist using the cognitive perspective, the difference in the sophistication of the answers is evidence of a different degree of knowledge and understanding—or cognition. The **cognitive perspective** focuses on the processes that allow people to know, understand, and think about the world.

The cognitive perspective emphasizes how people internally represent and think about the world. By using this perspective, developmental researchers hope to understand how children and adults process information and how their ways of thinking and understanding affect their behaviour. Researchers also seek to learn how cognitive abilities change as people develop, the degree to which cognitive development represents quantitative and qualitative growth in intellectual abilities, and how different cognitive abilities are related to one another.

Piaget's Theory of Cognitive Development. No one has had a greater impact on the study of cognitive development than Jean Piaget, a Swiss psychologist who lived from 1896 to 1980. Piaget proposed that all people pass through a fixed sequence of universal stages of cognitive development—and that not only does the *quantity* of information increase in each stage, but the *quality* of knowledge and understanding changes as well. His focus was on the change in cognition that occurs as children move from one stage to the next (Piaget, 1952, 1962, 1983).

Broadly speaking, Piaget suggested that human thinking is arranged into *schemes*, organized mental patterns that represent behaviours and actions. In infants, schemes represent concrete behaviour—a scheme for sucking, for reaching, and for each separate behaviour. In older children, the schemes become more sophisticated and abstract, such as the skills involved in riding a bike or playing an interactive video game. Schemes are like intellectual computer software that directs and determines how data from the world are looked at and dealt with.

Piaget suggested that the growth in children's understanding of the world can be explained by two basic principles: assimilation and accommodation. *Assimilation* is the process in which people understand a new experience in terms of their current stage of cognitive development and existing ways of thinking. In contrast, *accommodation* refers to changes in existing ways of thinking in response to encounters with new stimuli or events. Assimilation and accommodation work in tandem to bring about cognitive development.

Assessing Piaget's Theory. Piaget has profoundly influenced our understanding of cognitive development and is one of the towering figures in lifespan development. He provided masterly descriptions of intellectual growth during childhood—descriptions that have stood

cognitive perspective the approach that focuses on the processes that allow people to know, understand, and think about the world

the test of literally thousands of investigations. Broadly, then, Piaget's view of cognitive development is accurate.

However, the specifics of the theory have been questioned. For instance, some cognitive skills clearly emerge earlier than Piaget suggested. Growing evidence suggests that particular cognitive skills are highly dependent on factors such as formal schooling and familiarity (Rogoff and Chavajay, 1995). As well, in every culture, some people never seem to reach Piaget's highest level of cognitive sophistication: formal, logical thought (Genovese, 2003; McDonald and Stuart-Hamilton, 2003).

Ultimately, the greatest criticism of Piaget's stage theory is that cognitive development is not necessarily as discontinuous as suggested. Many developmental researchers argue that growth is considerably more continuous. These critics have suggested an alternative perspective, known as the information-processing approach, which focuses on the processes that underlie learning, memory, and thinking throughout the lifespan.

Information-Processing Approaches. Information-processing approaches have become an important alternative to Piagetian approaches. **Information-processing approaches** to cognitive development seek to identify the ways individuals take in, use, and store information.

Information-processing approaches grew out of developments in computers. These approaches assume that even complex behaviour such as learning, remembering, categorizing, and thinking can be broken down into a series of individual, specific steps. They contend that children, like computers, have limited capacity for processing information. As children develop, though, they increase in terms of capacity and speed, and employ increasingly sophisticated strategies that allow them to process information more efficiently.

In stark contrast to Piaget's view, information-processing approaches assume that development is marked more by quantitative advances than qualitative ones. Our capacity to handle information changes with age, as does our processing speed and efficiency. Furthermore, information-processing approaches suggest that, as we age, we are better able to control the nature of processing and the strategies we choose to process information.

An information-processing approach that builds on Piaget's research is known as neo-Piagetian theory. In contrast to Piaget's original work, which viewed cognition as a single system of increasingly sophisticated general cognitive abilities, *neo-Piagetian theory* considers cognition as being made up of different types of individual skills. Using the terminology of information-processing approaches, neo-Piagetian theory suggests that cognitive development proceeds quickly in certain areas and more slowly in others. For example, reading ability and the skills needed to recall stories might progress sooner than the abstract computational abilities used in algebra or trigonometry. Furthermore, neo-Piagetian theorists believe that experience plays an even greater role in advancing cognitive development than traditional Piagetian approaches (Case, 1999; Case et al., 2001; Yan and Fischer, 2002).

Assessing Information-Processing Approaches. Information-processing approaches have become a central part of our understanding of development, but they do not offer a complete explanation of behaviour. For example, while they explain why some children can learn faster than others, they cannot explain the onset of new skills such as language, a new conceptual understanding, or creativity where, to a parent, it can seem as though the child woke up one morning a whole new person. In addition, these approaches do not take into account the social context in which development takes place—and theories that do so have become increasingly popular.

Cognitive Neuroscience Approaches. Among the most recent additions to the array of approaches are **cognitive neuroscience approaches**, which look at cognitive development at the level of brain processes. Like other cognitive perspectives, cognitive neuroscience approaches consider internal, mental processes, but they focus specifically on the neurological activity that underlies thinking, problem solving, and other cognitive behaviour.

Cognitive neuroscientists seek to identify actual locations and functions within the brain that are related to different types of cognitive activity. For example, using sophisticated brain scanning techniques, cognitive neuroscientists have demonstrated that thinking about the meaning of a word activates different areas of the brain than does thinking about how the word sounds when spoken.

information-processing approach the model that seeks to identify the ways individuals take in, use, and store information

cognitive neuroscience approach the approach that examines cognitive development through the lens of brain processes

Cognitive neuroscience approaches are also on the forefront of cutting-edge research that has identified genes associated with disorders ranging from physical problems such as breast cancer to psychological disorders such as schizophrenia and autism (Courchesne et al., 2003; Herbert et al., 2005; Akshoomoff, 2006; DeLisi and Fleischhaker, 2007). Identifying the genes that make one vulnerable to such disorders is the first step in genetic engineering, in which gene therapy can reduce the incidence of or even prevent the disorder from occurring.

Assessing Cognitive Neuroscience Approaches. Cognitive neuroscience approaches continue to revolutionize our understanding of human behaviour by helping us understand how the brain works, but they are infrequently used to answer developmental questions in the early years. There are a few very good reasons for this, one of which is cost. Different techniques and the dizzying pace at which the technology continues to advance can mean costs of tens of thousands to millions of dollars. The second challenge to researchers who dream of peering into the brains of babies is that few neuroimaging tools are appropriate for use with small children. For example, functional magnetic resonance imaging (fMRI) is used to examine which parts of the brain are active during different tasks. Getting a clear picture, however, requires participants to remain perfectly still for an extended period of time, and young children do not have enough control over their movements to co-operate. Further, the machine is large and noisy, and many children would be scared by the process. Other techniques, such as electroencephalography (EEG), which measures electrical activity in the brain, are easier to use with young children but limited relative to MRI. Nevertheless, as the technology advances, our understanding of how the brain develops will be very important in understanding how we develop as humans.

The Contextual Perspective: Taking a Broad Approach to Development

Although lifespan developmentalists often consider development in terms of physical, cognitive, personality, and social factors separately, doing so has one serious drawback: In the real world, none of these broad influences occurs in isolation from any other. Instead, the different types of influence interact constantly.

The **contextual perspective** considers the relationship between individuals and their physical, cognitive, personality, and social worlds. It suggests that a person's unique development cannot properly be viewed without seeing how that person is enmeshed within a rich social and cultural context. We'll consider two major theories that fall under this perspective: Bronfenbrenner's bioecological approach and Vygotsky's sociocultural theory.

The Bioecological Approach to Development. In acknowledging the problem with traditional approaches to lifespan development, the Russian American psychologist Urie Bronfenbrenner (1989, 2000, 2002) has proposed an alternative perspective—the bioecological approach. The **bioecological approach** suggests that five levels of the environment simultaneously influence individuals. Bronfenbrenner suggests that we cannot fully understand development without considering how a person is influenced by each of these levels.

- The *microsystem* is the everyday, immediate environment of children's daily lives. Homes, caregivers, friends, and teachers all are influences, but the child is not just a passive recipient. Instead, children actively help construct the microsystem, shaping their immediate world.

- The *mesosystem* connects the various aspects of the microsystem. The mesosystem binds children to parents, students to teachers, employees to bosses, friends to friends. It acknowledges the direct and indirect influences that bind us to one another.

- The *exosystem* represents broader influences: societal institutions such as local government, the community, schools, places of worship, and the local media. Each of these institutions can have an immediate and major impact on personal development, and each affects how the microsystem and mesosystem operate.

- The *macrosystem* represents the larger cultural influences on an individual, including society in general, types of governments, religious and political value systems, and other broad, encompassing factors.

contextual perspective the theory that considers the relationship between individuals and their physical, cognitive, personality, and social worlds

bioecological approach the perspective suggesting that different levels of the environment simultaneously influence individuals

- Finally, the *chronosystem* underlies each of the previous systems. It involves the way in which the passage of time—including historical events (such as the terrorist attacks of September 2001) and more gradual historical changes (such as changes in the number of women who work outside the home)—affects children's development.

The bioecological approach emphasizes the *interconnectedness of the influences on development.* Because the various levels are related to one another, a change in one part of the system affects other parts. For instance, a parent's job loss (involving the mesosystem) has an impact upon a child's microsystem. Similarly, the influences among family members are multidirectional. Parents don't just influence their child's behaviour—the child also influences the parents' behaviour.

Finally, the bioecological approach stresses the importance of broad cultural factors that affect development. Researchers in lifespan development increasingly look at how membership in cultural groups influences behaviour.

Consider, for instance, whether you agree that children should be taught that their classmates' assistance is essential to getting good grades in school; or that they should plan to continue their fathers' businesses; or that they should take their parents' advice in choosing a career. If you have been raised in the most widespread Western culture, you would likely disagree with all three statements, since they violate the premises of *individualism,* the dominant Western philosophy that emphasizes personal identity, uniqueness, freedom, and the worth of the individual.

On the other hand, if you were raised in a traditional Asian culture, the likelihood that you agree with the three statements is considerably greater because the statements reflect the value orientation known as collectivism. *Collectivism* is the notion that the well-being of the group is more important than that of the individual. People raised in collectivistic cultures sometimes emphasize the welfare of the group at the expense of their own personal well-being (Choi, 2002; Sedikides et al. 2003; Leung, 2005).

sociocultural theory the approach that emphasizes how cognitive development proceeds as a result of social interactions between members of a culture

Assessing the Bioecological Approach. Although Bronfenbrenner regards biological influences as an important component of the bioecological approach, ecological influences are central to the theory. In fact, some critics argue that the perspective pays insufficient attention to biological factors. Still, the bioecological approach is important because it suggests the multiple levels at which the environment affects children's development.

Vygotsky's Sociocultural Theory. To the Russian developmentalist Lev Semenovich Vygotsky, a full understanding of development is impossible without taking into account the culture in which people develop. Vygotsky's **sociocultural theory** emphasizes how cognitive development proceeds as a result of social interactions between members of a culture (Vygotsky, 1979, 1926/1997; Beilin, 1996; Winsler, 2003; Edwards, 2005).

Vygotsky, who lived a brief life from 1896 to 1934, argued that children's understanding of the world is acquired through their problem-solving interactions with adults and other children. As children play and co-operate with others, they learn what is important in their society and, at the same time, advance cognitively. Consequently, to understand development, we must consider what is meaningful to members of a given culture.

More than most other theories, sociocultural theory emphasizes that development is a *reciprocal transaction* between the people in a child's environment and the child. Vygotsky believed that people and settings influence the child, who in turn influences the people and settings. This pattern continues in an endless loop, with children being both recipients of socialization influences and sources of influence.

Assessing Vygotsky's Theory. Though Vygotsky died almost eight decades ago, his sociocultural theory has become increasingly influential because of growing acknowledgment of the importance of cultural factors in development. Children do not develop in a cultural vacuum. Instead, their attention is directed by society to certain areas and, as a consequence, they develop particular kinds of skills. Vygotsky was one of the

According to Vygotsky, children can develop cognitively in their understanding of the world and learn what is important in society through play and co-operation with others.

evolutionary perspective the theory that seeks to identify behaviour that is a result of our genetic inheritance from our ancestors

first developmentalists to recognize and acknowledge the importance of the cultural environment, and—as today's society becomes increasingly multicultural—sociocultural theory helps us understand the rich and varied influences that shape development (Matusov and Hayes, 2000; Reis et al., 2000; Fowers and Davidov, 2006).

Sociocultural theory is not without its critics, however. Some suggest that Vygotsky's strong emphasis on the role of culture and social experience led him to ignore the effects of biological factors on development. In addition, his perspective seems to minimize the role that individuals play in shaping their environment.

Evolutionary Perspectives: Our Ancestors' Contributions to Behaviour

An increasingly influential approach is the evolutionary perspective, the fifth and final developmental perspective that we will consider. The **evolutionary perspective** seeks to identify behaviour that is the result of our genetic inheritance from our ancestors (Blasi and Bjorklund, 2003; Buss and Reeve, 2003; Bjorklund and Hernandez Blasi, 2005; Goetz and Shackelford, 2006).

Evolutionary approaches grow out of the groundbreaking work of English naturalist Charles Darwin. In 1859, Darwin argued in *On the Origin of Species* that a process of natural selection creates traits in a species that are adaptive to its environment. Using Darwin's arguments, evolutionary approaches contend that our genetic inheritance not only determines such physical traits as skin and eye colour, but certain personality traits and social behaviours as well. For instance, some evolutionary developmentalists suggest that behaviours such as shyness and jealousy are produced in part by genetic causes, presumably because they helped increase the survival rate of humans' ancient relatives (Plomin and McClearn, 1993; Buss, 2003).

The evolutionary perspective draws heavily on the field of *ethology*, which examines the ways in which our biological makeup influences our behaviour. Austrian Konrad Lorenz (1903–1989) was a primary proponent of ethology. Lorenz discovered that newborn geese are genetically preprogrammed to become attached to the first moving object they see after birth. His work, which demonstrated the importance of biological determinants in influencing behaviour patterns, led developmentalists to consider the ways in which human behaviour might reflect inborn genetic patterns.

The evolutionary perspective encompasses one of the fastest-growing areas in the field of lifespan development: behavioural genetics. *Behavioural genetics* studies the effects of heredity on behaviour. Behavioural geneticists seek to understand how we might inherit certain behavioural traits and how the environment influences whether we actually display those traits. It also considers how genetic factors might produce psychological disorders such as schizophrenia (Eley et al., 2003; Gottlieb, 2003; Li, 2003; Bjorklund, 2005).

Assessing the Evolutionary Perspective. There is little argument among lifespan developmentalists that Darwin's evolutionary theory provides an accurate description of basic genetic processes, and the evolutionary perspective is increasingly visible in the field of lifespan development. However, applications of the evolutionary perspective have been subjected to considerable criticism.

Some developmentalists are concerned that, because of its focus on genetic and biological aspects of behaviour, the evolutionary perspective pays insufficient attention to the environmental and social factors involved in producing children's and adults' behaviour. Other critics argue that there is no good way to experimentally test theories derived from this approach because humans evolved so long ago. For example, it is one thing to say that jealousy helped individuals to survive more effectively and another thing to prove it. Still, the evolutionary approach has stimulated research on how our biological inheritance at least partially influences our traits and behaviours (Buss and Reeve, 2003; Quartz, 2003; Scher and Rauscher, 2003).

Konrad Lorenz, seen here with geese who from their birth have followed him, considered the ways in which behaviour reflects inborn genetic patterns.

Why "Which Approach Is Right?" Is the Wrong Question

We have considered the five major perspectives on development—psychodynamic, behavioural, cognitive, contextual, and evolutionary—summarized in Table 1-3 and applied there to the case of a young adult who is overweight. It would be natural to wonder which of the six perspectives provides the most accurate account of human development.

For several reasons, Which approach is right? is not an appropriate question. For one thing, each perspective emphasizes different aspects of development. For instance, the psychodynamic approach emphasizes unconscious determinants of behaviour, while behavioural perspectives emphasize overt behaviour. The cognitive perspective looks more at what people *think* than at what they do. The contextual perspective examines social and cultural influences on development, and the evolutionary perspective focuses on how inherited biological factors underlie development.

Each perspective is based on its own premises and focuses on different aspects of development—the way different maps of the same geographical area focus on different aspects and features of that area. In the same way, a specific developmental phenomenon may be looked at from a number of perspectives. In fact, some lifespan developmentalists use an *eclectic* approach, drawing on several perspectives simultaneously.

The various theoretical perspectives provide different ways of looking at development. Considering them together paints a fuller portrait of the many ways humans change and grow over the lifespan. However, not all theories and claims derived from the various perspectives are accurate. How do we choose among competing explanations? The answer is *research,* which we consider in the final part of this module.

TABLE 1-3 MAJOR PERSPECTIVES ON LIFESPAN DEVELOPMENT

Perspective	Key Ideas about Human Behaviour and Development	Major Proponents	Example
Psychodynamic	Behaviour throughout life is motivated by inner, unconscious forces, stemming from childhood, over which we have little control.	Sigmund Freud, Erik Erikson	This view might suggest that a young adult who is overweight has a fixation in the oral stage of development.
Behavioural	Development can be understood through studying observable behaviour and environmental stimuli.	John B. Watson, B. F. Skinner, Albert Bandura	In this perspective, a young adult who is overweight might be viewed as not being rewarded for good nutritional and exercise habits; for example, a diet that did not result in immediately observed weight loss was abandoned.
Cognitive	Emphasizes how changes or growth in the ways people know, understand, and think about the world affect behaviour.	Jean Piaget	This view might suggest that a young adult who is overweight hasn't learned effective ways to stay at a healthy weight and doesn't value good nutrition.
Contextual	Views development in terms of the interrelationship of a person's physical, cognitive, personality, and social worlds.	Urie Bronfenbrenner, Lev Vygotsky	In this perspective, being overweight is caused by a number of interrelated factors in a person's physical, cognitive, personality, and social worlds—for example, family and culturally supported eating habits.
Evolutionary	Behaviour is the result of genetic inheritance from our ancestors; traits and behaviour that are adaptive for promoting the survival of our species have been inherited through natural selection.	Influenced by early work of Charles Darwin, Konrad Lorenz	This view might suggest that a young adult might have a genetic tendency toward obesity because extra fat helped his or her ancestors to survive in times of famine.

REVIEW, CHECK, AND APPLY

REVIEW

- The psychodynamic perspective looks primarily at the influence of internal, unconscious forces on development.

- The behavioural perspective focuses on external, observable behaviours as the key to development.

- The cognitive perspective focuses on mental activity.

- The contextual perspective focuses on the relationship between individuals and their social context.

- The evolutionary perspective seeks to identify behaviour that is a result of our genetic inheritance.

CHECK YOURSELF

1. _____ are organized explanations and predictions concerning phenomena of interest and provide frameworks for understanding the relationships across variables.

   a. Evaluations

   b. Constitutions

   c. Intuitions

   d. Theories

2. The _____ perspective suggests that the key to understanding one's actions involves observation of those actions and the outside stimuli in the environment.

3. Which of the following is *not* a concern with Piaget's cognitive perspective?

   a. Everyone reaches Piaget's highest level of thought, suggesting that doing so isn't much of an achievement.

   b. Some cognitive skills appear much earlier than Piaget originally thought.

   c. The timing of cognitive skills differs as a function of culture.

   d. Cognitive development does not appear to be as discontinuous as Piaget suggested.

APPLYING LIFESPAN DEVELOPMENT

- Can you think of examples of human behaviour that may have been inherited from our ancestors because they helped survival and adaptation? Explain why you think this.

Answers: 1) d; 2) behavioural; 3) a

MODULE 1.3 Research Methods

Research Methods

The Egyptians had long believed that they were the most ancient race on earth, and Psamtik [King of Egypt in the seventh century, B.C.], driven by intellectual curiosity, wanted to prove that flattering belief. Like a good researcher, he began with a hypothesis: If children had no opportunity to learn a language from older people around them, they would spontaneously speak the primal, inborn language of humankind—the natural language of its most ancient people—which, he expected to show, was Egyptian.

To test his hypothesis, Psamtik commandeered two infants of a lower-class mother and turned them over to a herdsman to bring up in a remote area. They were to be kept in a sequestered cottage, properly fed and cared for, but were never to hear anyone speak so much as a word. The Greek historian Herodotus, who tracked the story down and learned what he calls "the real facts" from priests of Hephaestus in Memphis, says that Psamtik's goal "was to know, after the indistinct babblings of infancy were over, what word they would first articulate."

The experiment, he tells us, worked. One day, when the children were two years old, they ran up to the herdsman as he opened the door of their cottage and cried out "Becos!" Since this meant nothing to him, he paid no attention, but when it happened repeatedly, he sent word to Psamtik, who at once ordered the children brought to him. When he too heard them say it, Psamtik made inquiries and learned that becos was the Phrygian word for bread. He concluded that, disappointingly, the Phrygians were an older race than the Egyptians. (Hunt, 1993, pp. 1–2)

With the perspective of several thousand years, we can easily see the shortcomings—both scientific and ethical—in Psamtik's approach. Yet his procedure represents an improvement over mere speculation, and, as such, is sometimes looked upon as the first developmental experiment in recorded history (Hunt, 1993).

Theories and Hypotheses: Posing Developmental Questions

LO8 What roles do theories and hypotheses play in the study of development?

LO9 What do correlational studies tell us about development? What can't they tell us?

LEARNING OBJECTIVES

Questions such as those raised by Psamtik drive the study of development. In fact, developmentalists are still studying how children learn language. Others are working on such questions as the following: What are the effects of malnutrition on intellectual performance? How do infants form relationships with their parents, and does daycare disrupt such relationships? Why are adolescents particularly susceptible to peer pressure? Can mentally challenging activities reduce declines in intellectual abilities related to aging? Do any mental faculties improve with age?

To answer such questions, developmentalists, like all psychologists and other scientists, rely on the scientific method. The **scientific method** is the process of posing and answering questions using careful, controlled techniques that include systematic, orderly observation and the collection of data. The scientific method involves three major steps: (1) identifying questions of interest, (2) formulating an explanation, and (3) carrying out research that either lends support to the explanation or refutes it.

The scientific method involves the formulation of **theories**, broad explanations and predictions about phenomena of interest. For instance, the idea that there is a crucial bonding period between parent and child immediately after birth is a theory.

Developmental researchers use theories to form hypotheses. An **hypothesis** states a prediction in a way that permits the prediction to be tested. For instance, someone who subscribes to the general theory that "bonding is crucial" might derive the hypothesis that "effective bonding occurs only if it lasts for a certain length of time."

Choosing a Research Strategy: Answering Questions

Once researchers have formed an hypothesis, they must develop a research strategy to test its validity. There are two major categories of research: correlational research and experimental research. Correlational research seeks to identify whether an association or relationship exists between two factors. As we'll see, **correlational research** cannot determine whether one factor *causes* changes in the other. For instance, correlational research could tell us if there is an association between the number of minutes a mother and her newborn child are together immediately after birth and the quality of the mother–child relationship when the child reaches age two. Such correlational research indicates whether the two factors are *associated* or *related* to one another, but not whether the initial contact caused the relationship to develop in a particular way (Schutt, 2001).

In contrast, **experimental research** is designed to discover *causal* relationships between various factors. In experimental research, researchers deliberately introduce a change in a carefully structured situation in order to see the consequences of that change. For instance, a researcher conducting an experiment might vary the number of minutes that mothers and children interact immediately following birth, in an attempt to see whether the bonding time affects the mother–child relationship.

Because experimental research is able to answer questions of causality, it is fundamental to finding answers to various developmental hypotheses. However, some research questions cannot be answered through experiments—for either technical or ethical reasons (for example, designing an experiment in which a group of infants was offered no chance to bond with a caregiver at all would be unethical). In fact, a great deal of pioneering developmental research employed correlational techniques. Consequently, correlational research remains an important tool for developmental researchers.

scientific method the process of posing and answering questions using careful, controlled techniques that include systematic, orderly observation and the collection of data

theories broad explanations and predictions about phenomena of interest

hypothesis a prediction stated in a way that permits testing

correlational research research that seeks to identify whether an association or relationship between two factors exists

experimental research research designed to discover causal relationships between various factors

Correlational Studies

As we've noted, correlational research examines the relationship between two variables to determine whether they are associated, or *correlated*. For instance, researchers interested in the relationship between televised aggression and subsequent behaviour have found that children who watch a good deal of aggression on television—murders, crime shows, shootings, and the like—tend to be more aggressive than those who watch only a little. In other words, viewing aggression and actual aggression are strongly associated, or correlated (Center for Communication and Social Policy, 1998; Singer and Singer, 2000).

But can we conclude that the viewing of televised aggression *causes* the more aggressive behaviour? Not at all. Consider some of the other possibilities: It might be that being aggressive in the first place makes children more likely to choose to watch violent programs. In this case, the aggressive tendency causes the viewing behaviour, not the other way around.

Or consider that there may be a *third* factor operating on both the viewing and the aggression. Suppose, for example, that children of lower socioeconomic status are more likely to behave aggressively *and* to watch higher levels of aggressive television than those raised in more affluent settings. In this case, the third variable—socioeconomic status—causes *both* the aggressive behaviour and the television viewing. (The various possibilities are illustrated in Figure 1-1.)

In short, finding that two variables are correlated proves nothing about causality. Although it is possible that the variables are linked causally, this is not necessarily the case. Still, we have learned a lot from correlational studies. For instance, we have learned that the closer the genetic link between two people, the more highly associated is their intelligence. We have

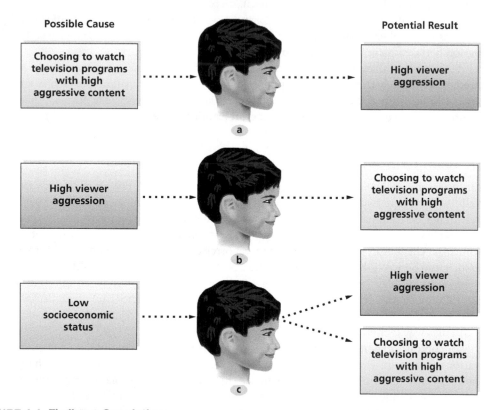

FIGURE 1-1 Finding a Correlation

Finding a correlation between two factors does not imply that one factor *causes* the other factor to vary. For instance, suppose a study found that viewing television shows with high levels of aggression is correlated with actual aggression in children. The correlation might reflect at least three possibilities: (a) watching television programs containing high levels of aggression causes aggression in viewers; (b) children who behave aggressively choose to watch TV programs with high levels of aggression; or (c) some third factor, such as a child's socioeconomic status, leads to both high viewer aggression and choosing to watch television programs with high levels of aggression. What other factors, besides socioeconomic status, might be plausible third factors?

learned that the more parents speak to their young children, the more extensive are the children's vocabularies. And we have learned that the better the nutrition infants receive, the fewer the cognitive and social problems they experience later (Plomin, 1994b; Hart, 2004; Colom et al., 2005).

Types of Correlational Studies. There are several types of correlational studies. **Naturalistic observation** is the observation of a naturally occurring behaviour without intervention. For instance, an investigator who wishes to learn how often preschool children share toys might observe a classroom over a three-week period, recording how often the preschoolers spontaneously share with one another. The key point is that the investigator observes without interfering (e.g., Beach, 2003; Prezbindowski and Lederberg, 2003).

While naturalistic observation has the advantage of seeing subjects in their "natural habitat," there is an important drawback: Researchers can exert no control over factors of interest. For instance, in some cases researchers might find so few naturally occurring instances of the behaviour of interest that they are unable to draw any conclusions at all. In addition, children who know they are being watched may modify their behaviour so that it is not representative of how they would behave if they were not being watched.

Ethnography. Increasingly, naturalistic observation employs *ethnography,* a method borrowed from anthropology and used to investigate cultural questions. In ethnography, the goal is to understand a culture's values and attitudes through careful, extended examination. Typically, researchers act as participant observers, living for a period of weeks, months, or even years in another culture. By carefully observing everyday life and conducting in-depth interviews, researchers can obtain a deep understanding of life within another culture (Fetterman, 1998; Dyson, 2003).

Case studies involve extensive, in-depth interviews with a particular individual or a small group of individuals. Often, they are used not just to learn about the individual being interviewed, but also to derive broader principles or draw tentative conclusions that might apply to others. For example, case studies have been conducted on children who display unusual genius and on children who have spent their early years in the wild, apparently without human contact. These case studies have provided important information to researchers, and have suggested hypotheses for future investigation (Lane, 1976; Goldsmith, 2000; Cohen and Cashon, 2003).

Using *diaries,* participants are asked to keep a record of their behaviour on a regular basis. For example, a group of adolescents might be asked to record each time they interact with friends for more than five minutes, thereby providing a way to track their social behaviour.

Surveys represent another sort of correlational research. In **survey research**, a group of people chosen to represent some larger population are asked questions about their attitudes, behaviour, or thinking on a given topic. For instance, surveys have been conducted about parents' use of punishment on their children and on attitudes toward breast-feeding. From the responses, inferences are drawn regarding the larger population that is represented by the individuals who have been surveyed.

Psychophysiological Methods. Some developmental researchers, particularly those using a cognitive neuroscience approach, make use of psychophysiological methods. **Psychophysiological methods** focus on the relationship between physiological processes and behaviour. For instance, a researcher might examine the relationship between blood flow in the brain and problem-solving ability. Similarly, some studies use infants' heart rate as a measure of their interest in stimuli to which they are exposed.

Among the most frequently used psychophysiological measures are the following:

- **Electroencephalogram (EEG).** The EEG uses electrodes placed on the skull to record electrical activity in the brain. The brain activity is transformed into a pictorial representation of brain-wave patterns, permitting the diagnosis of disorders such as epilepsy and learning disabilities.
- **Functional magnetic resonance imaging (fMRI) scan.** An fMRI provides a detailed, three-dimensional computer-generated image of brain activity by aiming a powerful magnetic field at the brain. It offers one of the best ways of learning about the operation of the brain, down to the level of individual nerves.

This fMRI shows activity in different regions of the brain.

naturalistic observation a type of correlational study in which some naturally occurring behaviour is observed without intervention in the situation

case studies studies that involve extensive, in-depth interviews with a particular individual or small group of individuals

survey research a type of study where a group of people chosen to represent some larger population are asked questions about their attitudes, behaviour, or thinking on a given topic

psychophysiological methods research that focuses on the relationship between physiological processes and behaviour

Experiments: Determining Cause and Effect

LO10 What are the characteristics of experimental research?

LO11 What are some of the ethical considerations?

In an **experiment**, an investigator or experimenter typically devises two different conditions (or *treatments*) and then compares how the behaviour of the participants exposed to each condition is affected. One group, the *treatment* or *experimental group*, is exposed to the treatment variable being studied; the other, the *control group*, is not.

For instance, suppose you want to see if exposure to movie violence makes viewers more aggressive. You might show a group of adolescents a series of movies with a great deal of violent imagery. You would then measure their subsequent aggression. This group would constitute the treatment group. For the control group you might show a second group of adolescents movies that contain no aggressive imagery, and measure their subsequent aggression. By comparing the amount of aggression displayed by members of the treatment and control groups, you would be able to determine if exposure to violent imagery produces aggression in viewers. In fact, this describes an experiment conducted at the University of Louvain in Belgium. Psychologist Jacques-Philippe Leyens and colleagues found that the level of aggression rose significantly for the adolescents who had seen the movies containing violence (Leyens et al., 1975).

The central feature of this experiment—and all experiments—is the comparison of the consequences of different treatments. The use of both treatment and control groups allows researchers to rule out the possibility that something other than the experimental manipulation produced the results found in the experiment. For instance, if a control group was not used, experimenters could not be certain that some other factor, such as the time of day the movies were shown or even the mere passage of time, produced the observed changes. By using a control group, experimenters can draw accurate conclusions about causes and effects.

Independent and Dependent Variables. The **independent variable** is the variable that researchers manipulate in the experiment (in our example, it is the type of movie participants saw—violent or nonviolent). In contrast, the **dependent variable** is the variable that researchers measure to see if it changes as a result of the experimental manipulation. In our example, the degree of aggressive behaviour shown by the participants after viewing violent or nonviolent films is the dependent variable. (One way to remember the difference: An hypothesis predicts how a dependent variable *depends* on the manipulation of the independent variable.) Every experiment has an independent and a dependent variable.

Experimenters must make sure their studies are not influenced by factors other than those they are manipulating. For this reason, they take great care to make sure that the participants in both the treatment and control groups are not aware of the purpose of the experiment (which could affect their responses or behaviour) and that the experimenters do not influence who is chosen for the control and treatment groups. The procedure that is used for this is known as random assignment. In *random assignment*, participants are assigned to different experimental groups or "conditions" purely on the basis of chance. This way the laws of statistics ensure that personal characteristics that might affect the outcome of the experiment are divided proportionally among the participants in the different groups, making the groups equivalent. Equivalent groups achieved by random assignment allow an experimenter to draw conclusions with confidence (Boruch, 1998).

Given these advantages, why aren't experiments always used? The answer is that there are some situations that a researcher, no matter how ingenious, simply cannot control. And there are some situations in which control would be unethical, even if it were possible. For instance, no researcher would be able to assign different groups of infants to parents of high and low socioeconomic status in order to learn the effects of such status on subsequent development. In situations in which experiments are logistically or ethically impossible, developmentalists employ correlational research.

Furthermore, keep in mind that a single experiment is insufficient to answer a research question definitively. Before complete confidence can be placed in a conclusion, research must be *replicated*, or repeated, sometimes using other procedures and techniques with other

experiment a process in which an investigator, called an experimenter, devises two different experiences for participants

independent variable the variable that researchers manipulate in an experiment

dependent variable the variable that researchers measure in an experiment and expect to change as a result of the experimental manipulation

participants. Sometimes developmentalists use a procedure called *meta-analysis*, which permits the results of many studies to be combined into one overall conclusion (Peterson and Brown, 2005).

Choosing a Research Setting. Deciding *where* to conduct a study can be as important as determining *what* to do. In the Belgian experiment on the influence of exposure to media aggression, the researchers used a real-world setting—a group home for boys who had been convicted of juvenile delinquency. They chose this **sample** (the group of participants selected for the experiment) because it was useful to have adolescents whose normal level of aggression was relatively high, and because they could incorporate the films into the everyday life of the home with minimal disruption.

Using a real-world setting (as in the aggression experiment) is the hallmark of a field study. A **field study** is a research investigation carried out in a naturally occurring setting. Field studies capture behaviour in real-life settings, where research participants might behave more naturally than in a laboratory.

Field studies may be used in both correlational studies and experiments. They typically employ naturalistic observation, the technique in which researchers observe a naturally occurring behaviour without intervening or changing the situation. A researcher might examine behaviour in a child-care centre, view the groupings of adolescents in high school corridors, or observe elderly adults in a senior centre.

In experimental research, developmentalists use controlled conditions to discover causal relationships between various factors.

Because it is often difficult to control the situation and environment enough to run an experiment in a real-world setting, field studies are more typical of correlational designs than experimental designs. Most developmental research experiments are conducted in laboratory settings. A **laboratory study** is a research investigation conducted in a controlled setting explicitly designed to hold events constant. The laboratory might be a room or building designed for research, such as a university psychology department. Researchers can exert enough control in a laboratory study to learn how their treatments affect participants.

Theoretical and Applied Research: Complementary Approaches

Developmental researchers typically focus on either theoretical research or applied research. **Theoretical research** is designed to test some developmental explanation and expand scientific knowledge, while **applied research** is meant to provide practical solutions to immediate problems. For instance, if we were interested in the processes of cognitive change during childhood, we might carry out a study of how many digits children of various ages can remember after one exposure to multidigit numbers—a theoretical approach. Alternatively, we might focus on the more practical question of how teachers can help children to remember information more easily. Such a study would represent applied research, because the findings are applied to a particular setting and problem.

As we discuss in the accompanying *From Research to Practice* box, research of both a theoretical and applied nature has played a significant role in shaping and resolving a variety of public policy questions.

Measuring Developmental Change

Growth and change are central to the work of all developmental researchers, and one of the thorniest research issues they face is the measurement of change and differences over age and time. To measure change, researchers have developed three major research strategies: longitudinal research, cross-sectional research, and sequential research.

Longitudinal Studies: Measuring Individual Change. If you were interested in learning how a child develops morally between ages three and five, the most direct approach would be to take a group of three-year-olds and follow them until they were five, testing them periodically.

This strategy illustrates longitudinal research. In **longitudinal research**, the behaviour of one or more study participants is measured as they age. Longitudinal research measures

sample the group of participants chosen for the experiment

field study a research investigation carried out in a naturally occurring setting

laboratory study a research investigation conducted in a controlled setting explicitly designed to hold events constant

theoretical research research designed specifically to test some developmental explanation and expand scientific knowledge

applied research research meant to provide practical solutions to immediate problems

longitudinal research research in which the behaviour of one or more participants in a study is measured as they age

From Research to Practice

Using Developmental Research to Improve Public Policy

Is the Universal Child Care Benefit improving access to childcare across Canada?

Does research support the legalization of marijuana?

What are the effects of same-sex marriage on the children of such unions?

Should preschoolers diagnosed with attention deficit hyperactivity disorder receive drugs to treat their condition?

Is D.A.R.E.—the national program designed to curb drug abuse in schoolchildren—effective?

Each of these questions represents a national policy issue that can be answered only by research. By conducting controlled studies, developmental researchers have made important contributions to education, family life, and health. The following examples demonstrate ways that public policy issues have been informed by research findings (Brooks-Gunn, 2003; Maton et al., 2004; Mervis, 2004; Aber et al., 2007):

- **Research findings can provide policy-makers a means of determining what questions to ask in the first place.** For example, studies of children's caregivers have led policymakers to question whether the benefits of infant daycare are outweighed by possible deterioration in parent–child bonds.

- **The findings and testimony of researchers are often part of the process by which laws are drafted.** Legislation is often based on findings from developmental researchers. For example, research revealed that children with developmental disabilities benefit from exposure to children without special needs. This finding ultimately led to passage of legislation

mandating that children with disabilities be placed in regular school classes as much as possible.

- **Policy-makers and other professionals use research findings to determine how best to implement programs.** Research has shaped programs designed to reduce the incidence of unsafe sex among teenagers, to increase the level of prenatal care for pregnant mothers, to raise class attendance rates in school-age children, and to promote flu shots.

- **Research techniques are used to evaluate the effectiveness of existing programs and policies.** It is often necessary to determine whether an existing program has been successful in accomplishing its goals. To do this, researchers employ formal evaluation techniques developed from basic research procedures. For instance, careful studies of D.A.R.E., a highly popular program meant to reduce children's use of drugs, began to find that the program was ineffective. Using the research findings of developmentalists, D.A.R.E. introduced new techniques—and preliminary findings suggest the revised program is more effective (Rhule, 2005; University of Akron, 2006).

By building upon research findings, developmentalists often work hand in hand with policy-makers, making a substantial impact on public policies.

- *What are some policy issues affecting children and adolescents that are currently being debated nationally?*

- *Despite the existence of research data that might inform policy about development, politicians rarely discuss such data in their speeches. Why do you think that is the case?*

---

change over time. By following many individuals over time, researchers can understand the general course of change across some period of life.

Longitudinal studies can provide a wealth of information about change over time, but they also have drawbacks. For one thing, they require a tremendous investment of time, because researchers must wait for participants to become older. Furthermore, participants often drop out over the course of the research because they lose interest, move away, become ill, or die.

In addition, participants might become "test-wise" and perform better each time they are assessed as they become more familiar with the procedure. Finally, they might be affected by the repeated presence of an experimenter or observer.

Consequently, despite the benefits of longitudinal research, particularly its ability to look at change within individuals, developmental researchers often turn to other methods. The alternative they choose most often is the cross-sectional study.

Cross-Sectional Studies. Suppose again that you want to consider how children's moral development—their sense of right and wrong—changes from age three to five. Instead of following the same children over several years, we might look simultaneously at three groups of children: three-year-olds, four-year-olds, and five-year-olds, perhaps presenting each group with the same problem and then seeing how they respond to it and explain their choices.

Such an approach typifies cross-sectional research. In **cross-sectional research**, people of different ages are compared at the same point in time. Cross-sectional studies provide information about differences in development between different age groups.

Cross-sectional research takes far less time than longitudinal research: Participants are tested at just one point in time. However, cross-sectional research has its own difficulties. Recall that every person belongs to a particular *cohort* of individuals born at around the same time in the same place. If we find that people of different ages vary along some dimension, the differences might be due to differences in cohort membership, not age *per se*.

cross-sectional research research in which people of different ages are compared at the same point in time

Consider a concrete example: If we find in a correlational study showing that people who are 25 perform better on a test of intelligence than those who are 75, several possibilities might explain why—other than that intelligence declines in old age. Instead, the finding might be attributable to cohort differences. The 75-year-olds might have had less formal education than the 25-year-olds because members of the older cohort were less likely to finish high school and attend college than members of the younger one. Or perhaps the older group received less adequate nutrition as infants than the younger group. In short, we cannot rule out the possibility that age-related differences in cross-sectional studies are actually cohort differences.

Cross-sectional studies have an additional and more basic disadvantage: They are unable to inform us about changes in individuals or groups. If longitudinal studies are like videos taken of a person at various ages, cross-sectional studies are like snapshots of entirely different groups. Although we can establish differences related to age, we cannot fully determine if such differences are related to change over time.

Sequential Studies. Because both longitudinal and cross-sectional studies have drawbacks, researchers have turned to some compromise techniques. Among the most frequently employed are sequential studies, which are essentially a combination of longitudinal and cross-sectional studies.

In **sequential studies**, researchers examine a number of different age groups at several points in time. For instance, an investigator interested in children's moral behaviour might begin a sequential study by examining the behaviour of three groups of children who are either three, four, or five years old when the study begins.

The study continues for the next several years, with each participant tested annually. Thus, the three-year-olds would be tested at ages three, four, and five; the four-year-olds at ages four, five, and six; and the five-year-olds at ages five, six, and seven. By combining the advantages of longitudinal and cross-sectional research, this approach permits developmental researchers to tease out the consequences of age *change* versus age *difference*. The major research techniques for studying development are summarized in Figure 1-2.

Ethics and Research

In the "study" conducted by Egyptian King Psamtik, two children were removed from their mothers and held in isolation in an effort to learn about the roots of language. If you found yourself thinking this was extraordinarily cruel, you are in good company. Clearly, such an experiment raises blatant ethical concerns, and nothing like it would ever be done today.

But sometimes ethical issues are more subtle. In order to deal with ethical problems, researchers use several ethical guidelines. Among these are principles involving freedom from harm, informed consent, the use of deception, and maintenance of participants' privacy (Canadian Institutes of Health Research, Natural Sciences and Engineering Research Council of Canada, and Social Sciences and Humanities Research Council of Canada, 2010):

- **Researchers must protect participants from physical and psychological harm.** The welfare, interests, and rights of participants come before those of researchers.

- **Researchers must obtain informed consent from participants before participants' involvement in a study.** To the best of their ability, participants must voluntarily agree to be in a study. If participants are under 18, parents or guardians must also provide consent.

- **The use of deception in research must be justified and cause no harm.** Although deception to disguise the true purpose of an experiment is permissible, any experiment that uses deception must undergo careful scrutiny by an independent panel before the experiment is conducted.

- **Participants' privacy must be maintained.** If participants are videotaped during a study, for example, they must give their permission for the videotapes to be viewed. Furthermore, access to the tapes must be carefully restricted.

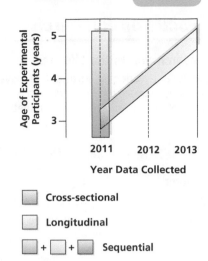

Cross-sectional

Longitudinal

+ + **Sequential**

FIGURE 1-2 Research Techniques for Studying Development

In a *cross-sectional study*, three-, four-, and five-year-olds are compared at a similar point in time (in 2011). In *longitudinal research*, a set of participants who are three years old in 2011 are studied when they are four years old (in 2012) and when they are five years old (in 2013). Finally, a *sequential study* combines cross-sectional and longitudinal techniques; here, a group of three-year-olds would be compared initially in 2011 with four- and five-year-olds, but would also be studied one and two years later, when they themselves were four and five years old. Although the graph does not illustrate this, researchers carrying out this sequential study might also choose to retest the children who were four and five in 2011 for the next two years. What advantages do the three kinds of studies offer?

sequential studies research in which a number of different age groups are examined over several points in time

Focus on Research

Research across the Lifespan

A wide and varied assortment of developmental research is taking place across the country. Table 1-4 gives a small sample of some of the diverse research questions and techniques used to study development across the lifespan. Each of these is described in greater detail in later chapters.

Table 1-4 EXAMPLES OF DEVELOPMENTAL RESEARCH TAKING PLACE ACROSS CANADA

Chapter	Topic	Place where research conducted
Chapter 2	How does maternal behaviour affect offspring?	McGill University, Montreal, Quebec
Chapter 3	What are the earliest signs of autism?	Canada-wide network
Chapter 4	Why are some children more aggressive than others?	Université de Montréal, Montreal, Quebec
Chapter 5	How do we curb bullying in our schools?	Queen's University, Kingston, Ontario
Chapter 6	Why is the rate of suicide in some Aboriginal communities so high?	University of British Columbia, Vancouver, and University of Victoria, British Columbia
Chapter 7	Why do we do *stupid* things?	Ontario Institute for Studies in Education, Toronto, Ontario
Chapter 8	Is perfectionism a good thing?	Dalhousie University, Halifax, Nova Scotia
Chapter 9	Is bilingualism good for your brain?	York University, Toronto, Ontario
Chapter 10	How do we make the best choices for our end-of-life care?	University of Alberta, Edmonton, Alberta

Thinking Critically about "Expert" Advice

Becoming an Informed Consumer of Development

If you immediately comfort crying babies, you'll spoil them.

If you let babies cry without comforting them, they'll be untrusting and clingy as adults.

* * *

Spanking is one of the best ways to discipline your child.

Never hit your child.

* * *

If a marriage is unhappy, children are better off if their parents divorce than if they stay together.

No matter how difficult a marriage is, parents should avoid divorce for the sake of their children.

There is no lack of advice on the best way to raise a child or, more generally, to lead one's life. From bestsellers such as *Men Are from Mars, Women Are from Venus* to magazine and newspaper columns that provide advice on every imaginable topic, to a myriad of websites and blogs, each of us is exposed to tremendous amounts of information.

Yet not all advice is equally valid. The mere fact that something is in print, on television, or on the Web does not make it legitimate or accurate. Fortunately, some guidelines can help distinguish when recommendations and suggestions are reasonable and when they are not:

- Consider the source of the advice. Information from established, respected organizations such as the Canadian Paediatric Society, the Canadian Psychological Association, or university or hospital websites reflects years of study and is usually accurate. If you don't know the organization, investigate it.

- Evaluate the credentials of the person providing advice. Trustworthy information tends to come from established, acknowledged researchers and experts, not from persons with obscure credentials or celebrities with no credentials. Consider where the author is employed and whether he or she has a particular political or personal agenda.

- Understand the difference between anecdotal evidence and scientific evidence. Anecdotal evidence is based on one or two instances of a phenomenon, haphazardly discovered or encountered; scientific evidence is based on careful, systematic procedures. If an aunt tells you that all her children slept through the night by two months of age and therefore your child will too, that is quite different from reading in a scientific report that 75 percent of children sleep through the night by nine months.

- If advice is based on research findings, a clear, transparent description of the studies on which the advice is based should be provided. Who were the participants? What methods were used? What do the results show? Think critically about the way the findings were obtained before accepting them.

- Don't overlook the cultural context of the information. An assertion may be valid in some contexts, but not in all. For example, it is typically assumed that providing infants the freedom to move about and exercise their limbs facilitates their muscular development and mobility. Yet in some cultures, infants spend most of their time closely bound to their mothers—with no apparent long-term damage (Kaplan and Dove, 1987; Tronick, 1995).

REVIEW, CHECK, AND APPLY

REVIEW

- Theories are systematically derived explanations of facts or phenomena. Theories suggest hypotheses, which are predictions that can be tested.

- Correlational studies examine relationships between factors without demonstrating causality, while experimental research seeks to discover cause-and-effect relationships.

- Researchers measure age-related change by longitudinal studies, cross-sectional studies, and sequential studies.

CHECK YOURSELF

1. Consider the following steps of the scientific method and rank them from first to last.

   _____ Formulating an explanation.

   _____ Carrying out research that either lends support to the explanation or refutes it.

   _____ Identifying questions of interest.

2. In order to make a prediction in such a way that permits it to be tested, one must make a(n)

   _____.

   a. theory

   b. hypothesis

   c. analysis

   d. judgment

3. If a control group is not used in an experiment, the researcher cannot rule out the possibility that something other than the treatment produced the observed outcome.

   - True

   - False

4. In a(n) _____, an investigator devises two conditions (treatment or control) and compares the outcomes of the participants exposed to those two different conditions in order to see how behaviour is affected.

   a. experiment

   b. correlational study

   c. interview

   d. naturalistic observation

APPLYING LIFESPAN DEVELOPMENT

- Formulate a theory about one aspect of human development and an hypothesis that relates to it.

Answers: 1) 2, 3, 1; 2) b; 3) True; 4) a

Putting It All Together
Introduction

JOANNA, the mother we met in the chapter opener, was reflecting upon her parenting skills, her children's personalities, and aging. She speculated—just as developmentalists do—about the role of genetics and environment in her children's development, considering issues like intelligence, resemblance, personality, schooling, and neighbourhood.

MODULE **1.1** Beginnings

- Many of Tom and Adele's characteristics will have a strong genetic component, but virtually all will represent some combination of genetics and environment. **(p. 10)**

MODULE **1.2** Theoretical Perspectives on Lifespan Development

- Tom and Adele will be influenced by the parenting they receive, the experiences they have, and the larger culture in which they live. **(pp. 12–21)**

- Joanna's experience of aging will progress through a number of stages. **(p. 13)**

- Correlational studies would help Joanna understand how her parenting might have influenced her children. **(pp. 24–25)**

- Experimental studies would help Joanna understand the best educational approaches for her children. **(pp. 26–27)**

What would a PARENT do?

- What strategies would you use to deal with a challenging child?

- How would you evaluate the different academic options for children?

- How would you prepare yourself for becoming the parent of a teenager?

  HINT Review pages 8–10.

  What's your response?

What would a HEALTH-CARE provider do?

- How would you prepare Joanna for her own aging process?

- How would you respond to her concerns and anxieties?

- What would tell her about the different options she will have for her aging parents?

  HINT Review pages 12–21.

  What's your response?

What would an EDUCATOR do?

- What strategies might you use to teach Tom and Adele?

- What might you tell Joanna about helping her children with homework?

  HINT Review page 30.

  What's your response?

What would YOU do?

- What would you say to Joanna about the differences between her children?

- What advice would you give to Joanna about aging?

  HINT Review pages 5–8.

  What's your response?

The Start of Life

CHAPTER 2

As Rachel's delivery date approached, she and her husband, Jack, thought the usual thoughts that occupy parents-to-be. They wondered whether they would have a daughter or a second son. They discussed what another son might look like, and which of them a daughter would resemble. They speculated about their baby's disposition, intelligence, and even potential career, and they congratulated themselves for having moved to a pleasant community with good public schools, a wealth of stimulating activities, and lots of places for kids to play safely.

A few months later, when Rachel's contractions began at four in the morning, she woke Jack and they drove to the hospital. She was pleased with her decision to use a midwife instead of an obstetrician, as she had done for her first birth. That time, her labour had lasted 31 hours and had been indescribably painful. With a midwife in attendance, Rachel was sure that the labour and birth would proceed more smoothly.

Rachel was also happy that she had had relatively few complications during her pregnancy. Her friend Janet, who was also pregnant, was having a tough time: her blood pressure was high, and she had to remain in bed for the last two months of her pregnancy.

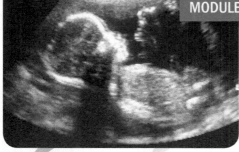

MODULE 2.1 Prenatal Development

What role is genetics playing in the prenatal development of Rachel and Jack's baby? see page 36.

MODULE 2.2 Prenatal Growth and Change

What is happening inside Rachel's expanding belly?

see page 53.

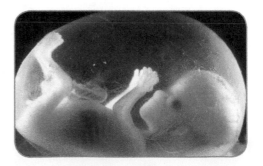

At the hospital, Rachel walked through her contractions, stopping to lean against the wall as each one peaked, until the midwife arrived. Four hours after labour began, the midwife told her that the birth was imminent. Rather than lie flat, a position that had necessitated the use of oxygen for her first birth, Rachel chose to kneel and pushed her baby—a daughter, Eva—into the world. As the baby was cleaned up and placed in Jack's arms, Rachel asked a nurse for some water. At that moment, Eva turned her head toward her mother. Jack said, "Look, Rachel, she recognizes the sound of your voice."

In this chapter, we start our voyage through the lifespan at its logical beginning: conception. We discuss genetics and the ways in which genetic information is transmitted from parents to child. We introduce a topic that receives a great deal of attention from developmentalists: the comparative roles of heredity and environment (or nature versus nurture) in forming the individual.

We finish the chapter with a discussion of the process of birth, including the ways women experience labour and the choices for care that parents have available before and during childbirth. We touch on some of the complications that can attend birth, including infants born significantly before or after their due date. We end with a discussion of the considerable abilities that a newborn possesses from the moment he enters the world—including the ability to recognize the voice of her mother as she asks for a glass of water.

What can Rachel and Jack expect during each stage of labour? see page 62.

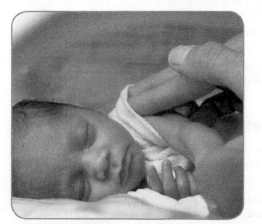

MyVirtualLife

What decisions would you make about birthing options and raising a newborn?

Log onto My Virtual Life through MyDevelopmentLab and start making those choices.

MODULE 2.1 Prenatal Development

The Future Is Now

Approaching the end of an uneventful pregnancy, Jana suddenly found herself admitted to hospital in preterm labour. It came out of the blue one Saturday night; Jana and Tim were having a dinner party. Later that night Jana began cramping. She had no risk factors and thought she would bring it up with her doctor on Monday. Then on Sunday, the cramping became worse—and strangely regular. The next thing Jana knew she was in the hospital on strict bed rest. She had no warning whatsoever.

When Jana got pregnant again, she and her doctor kept a close eye on her pregnancy. She was careful about activity and stress, and as her third trimester approached, she went on bed rest again. Her first son Stephen was born eight weeks prematurely. Her daughter, Caroline, was born only three weeks prematurely. Today Stephen, seven, has brain damage: His lungs were immature and his brain was deprived of oxygen during birth. Caroline, on the other hand, is an active, healthy two-year-old.

Unexpected pregnancy complications are just one of the many risks parents face in having the happy healthy children they dream of.

In this module, we'll examine what developmental researchers and other scientists have learned about ways that heredity and the environment work in tandem to affect people's lives. We begin with the basics of heredity, examining how we receive our genetic endowment. We'll consider an area of study—behavioural genetics—that specializes in the consequences of heredity on behaviour. We'll also discuss what happens when genetic factors cause development to go off track and how such problems are dealt with through genetic counselling and gene therapy.

But genes are only one part of the story of prenatal development. We'll also consider the child's environment—how family, socioeconomic status, and life events can affect a variety of characteristics including physical traits, intelligence, and even personality.

Finally, we'll focus on the first stage of development, tracing prenatal growth and change. We'll review some of the alternatives available to couples who find it difficult to conceive. We'll also talk about the stages of the prenatal period and how the prenatal environment offers both threats to and the promise of future growth.

Earliest Development

LEARNING OBJECTIVES

LO1 What is our basic genetic endowment?

LO2 How can human development go off track?

Watch on mydevelopmentlab

To watch the process you're reading about happening, check MyDevelopmentLab for an Observations Video on zygote development.

We humans begin the course of our lives simply.

Like individuals from tens of thousands of other species, we start as a single tiny cell weighing no more than one 20-millionth of an ounce. But from this humble beginning, in a matter of a few months, a living, breathing individual infant is born. That first cell is created when a male reproductive cell, a *sperm*, pushes through the membrane of the *ovum*, the female reproductive cell. These *gametes,* as the male and female reproductive cells are also called, contain huge amounts of genetic information. About an hour or so after the sperm enters the ovum, the two gametes suddenly fuse, becoming one cell, a **zygote**. The resulting combination of their genetic instructions—over two billion chemically coded messages—is sufficient to begin creating a whole person.

Genes and Chromosomes: The Code of Life

The blueprints for creating a person are stored and communicated in our **genes**, the basic units of genetic information. The roughly 25 000 human genes are the biological equivalent of "software" that programs the future development of all parts of the body's "hardware."

All genes are composed of specific sequences of **DNA (deoxyribonucleic acid) molecules**. The genes are arranged in specific locations and in a specific order along 46 **chromosomes**,

zygote the new cell formed by the process of fertilization

genes the basic unit of genetic information

rod-shaped portions of DNA that are organized in 23 pairs. Each of the sex cells—ovum and sperm—contains half this number, so that a child's mother and father each provide one of the two chromosomes in each of the 23 pairs. The 46 chromosomes (in 23 pairs) in the new zygote contain the genetic blueprint that will guide cell activity for the rest of the individual's life (Pennisi, 2000; International Human Genome Sequencing Consortium, 2001; see Figure 2-1). Through a process called *mitosis*, which accounts for the replication of most types of cells, nearly all the cells of the body will contain the same 46 chromosomes as the zygote.

Genes determine the nature and function of every cell in the body. For instance, they determine which cells will become part of the heart and which will become part of the muscles of the leg. Genes also establish how different parts of the body will function: how rapidly the heart will beat, or how much strength a muscle will have.

Moment of conception.

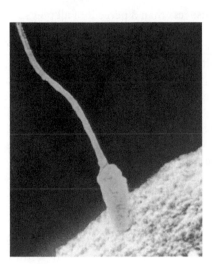

(a)

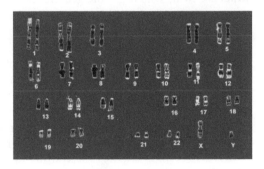

(b)

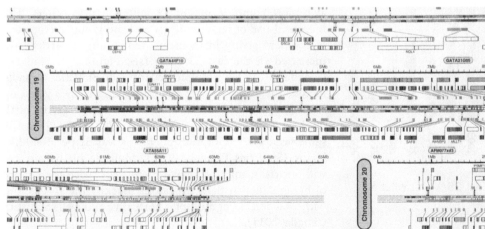

(c)

At the moment of conception (a), humans receive 23 pairs of chromosomes (b), half from the mother and half from the father. These chromosomes contain thousands of genes, shown in the computer-generated map (c).

DNA (deoxyribonucleic acid) molecules the substance that genes are composed of that determines the nature of every cell in the body and how each will function

chromosomes rod-shaped portions of DNA that are organized in 23 pairs

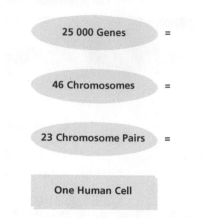

FIGURE 2-1 The Contents of a Single Human Cell
At the moment of conception, humans receive about 25 000 genes, contained on 46 chromosomes on 23 pairs.

If each parent provides just 23 chromosomes, what explains the vast diversity of human beings? The answer resides primarily in the processes that underlie the cell division of the gametes. When gametes—the sex cells, sperm and ova—are formed in the adult body in a process called *meiosis*, each gamete receives one of the two chromosomes that make up each of the 23 pairs. Because for each pair the chromosome that is chosen is largely a matter of chance, there are 2^{23}—or some eight million—different combinations possible. Furthermore, other processes, such as random transformations of particular genes and epigenetic modification, add to the variability of the genetic brew. The ultimate outcome: tens of *trillions* of possible genetic combinations.

With so many possible genetic mixtures, there is no likelihood that someday you'll bump into a genetic duplicate—unless you have an identical twin.

Multiple Births: Two—or More—for the Genetic Price of One

In humans, multiple births are cause for comment because less than 3 percent of all pregnancies produce twins, and the odds are even slimmer for producing triplets or more.

Why do multiple births occur? Some occur when a cluster of cells in the ovum splits off within the first two weeks after fertilization. The result is two genetically identical zygotes, which, because they come from the same original zygote, are called monozygotic. **Monozygotic twins** are twins who begin life genetically identical. Any differences in their future development can be attributed only to environmental factors.

However, multiple births are more commonly the result of two separate sperm fertilizing two separate ova at roughly the same time. Twins produced in this fashion are known as **dizygotic twins**. Because they are the result of two separate ovum–sperm combinations, they are no more genetically similar than two siblings born at different times. Triplets, quadruplets, and even more births are produced by either (or both) of the mechanisms that yield twins.

Thus, triplets may be some combination of monozygotic, dizygotic, or trizygotic.

Although the chances of having a multiple birth are typically slim, the odds rise considerably when fertility drugs are used before conception. Older women, too, are more likely to have multiple births, and multiple births are also more common in some families than in others. The increased use of fertility drugs and the rising average age of mothers giving birth means that multiple births have increased in the last 25 years (see Figure 2-2; Statistics Canada, 2012). For example, according to Statistics Canada, in 2008 the average age of birth mothers was 29.3 years, up from 27.7 in 1991, and the number of women giving birth in their early forties doubled from 1998 to 2008. In the same year, the rate of multiple births was 31 per 1000 live births (Statistics Canada, 2011). Multiple births are not without risks; multiples have more than twice the chance of being stillborn than singletons. Luckily the risk is low, with 98.4 percent of multiples born alive and well (Statistics Canada, 2011).

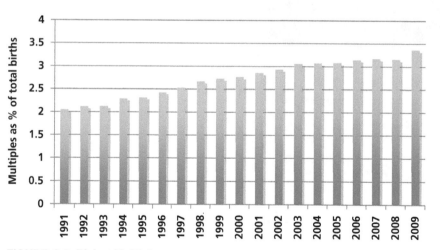

FIGURE 2-2 Rising Multiples
Multiple births have increased significantly over the last 25 years. What are some of the reasons for this phenomenon?
Source: Statistics Canada, 2012.

Boy or Girl? Establishing the Sex of the Child. In 22 of the 23 matched chromosome pairs, each chromosome is similar to the other member of its pair. The one exception is the twenty-third pair—the one that determines the sex of the child. In females, the twenty-third pair consists of two matching, relatively large X-shaped chromosomes, identified as XX. In males, on the other hand, one member of the pair is an X-shaped chromosome, but the other is a shorter, smaller Y-shaped chromosome. This pair is identified as XY.

Since a female's twenty-third pair of chromosomes are both Xs, an ovum will always carry an X chromosome. A male's twenty-third pair is XY, so each sperm could carry either an X or a Y chromosome. If the sperm contributes an X chromosome when it meets an

monozygotic twins twins produced by a single fertilized ovum

dizygotic twins twins who are produced when two separate ova are fertilized by two separate sperm at roughly the same time

ovum, the child will have an XX pairing on the twenty-third chromosome—and will be a female. If the sperm contributes a Y chromosome, the result will be an XY pairing—a male (see Figure 2-3).

The Basics of Genetics: The Mixing and Matching of Traits

What determined the colour of your hair? Why are you tall or short? What made you susceptible to hay fever? And why do you have so many freckles? To answer these questions, we need to consider the basic mechanisms through which the genes we inherit from our parents transmit information.

We can start by examining the discoveries of an Austrian monk, Gregor Mendel, in the mid-1800s. In a series of simple yet convincing experiments, Mendel cross-pollinated pea plants that always produced yellow seeds with pea plants that always produced green seeds. The result was not, as one might guess, a plant with a combination of yellow and green seeds. Instead, all of the resulting plants had yellow seeds. At first it appeared that the green-seeded plants had had no influence.

However, additional research on Mendel's part proved this was not true. He bred together plants from the new, yellow-seeded generation that had resulted from his original crossbreeding of the green-seeded and yellow-seeded plants. The consistent result was a ratio of three-quarters yellow seeds to one-quarter green seeds.

It was Mendel's genius to figure out why this ratio appeared so consistently. Based on his experiments with pea plants, he argued that when two competing traits, such as green or yellow colouring, were both present, only one could be expressed. The one that was expressed was called a **dominant trait**. Meanwhile, the other trait remained present in the organism, although unexpressed (displayed). This was called a **recessive trait**. In the case of the pea plants, the offspring plants received genetic information from both the green-seeded and yellow-seeded parents. However, the yellow trait was dominant, and consequently the recessive green trait did not assert itself.

Keep in mind, though, that genetic material from both parent plants is present in the offspring, even if unexpressed. The genetic information is known as the organism's genotype. A **genotype** is the underlying combination of genetic material present (but outwardly invisible) in an organism. In contrast, a **phenotype** is the observable trait, the trait that actually is seen. Although the offspring of the yellow-seeded and green-seeded pea plants all have yellow seeds (i.e., they have a yellow-seeded phenotype), the genotype consists of genetic information relating to both parents.

These principles apply to humans as well as plants—and to the majority of species. In humans, parents transmit genetic information to their offspring via the chromosomes they contribute through the gamete they provide during fertilization. Some of the genes form pairs called *alleles*, genes governing traits that may take alternate forms, such as hair or eye colour. For example, brown eye colour is a dominant trait (B); blue eyes are recessive (b). A child's allele may contain similar or dissimilar genes from each parent. If the child receives similar genes, he or she is said to be **homozygous** for the trait. On the other hand, if the child receives different forms of the gene from the parents, he or she is said to be **heterozygous**. In the case of heterozygous alleles (Bb), the dominant characteristic (brown eyes) is expressed. However, if the child happens to receive a recessive allele from each of the parents, and therefore lacks a dominant characteristic (bb), the child will display the recessive characteristic (in this case, blue eyes).

Transmission of Genetic Information

One example of this process at work is the transmission of *phenylketonuria (PKU)*, an inherited disorder in which a child is unable to make use of phenylalanine, an essential amino acid present in proteins found in milk and other foods. If untreated, PKU allows phenylalanine to build to toxic levels, causing brain damage and intellectual disability.

PKU is produced by a single allele, or pair of genes. As shown in Figure 2-4, we can label each gene of the pair with a *P* if it carries a dominant gene, which causes the normal production of phenylalanine, or with a *p* if it carries the recessive gene that produces PKU. In cases in which neither parent is a PKU carrier, both the mother's and the father's pairs of genes are the

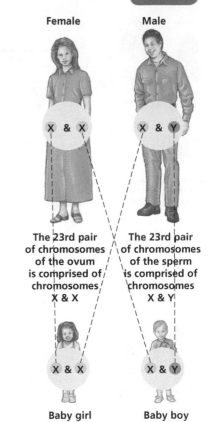

FIGURE 2-3 Determining Sex
When an ovum and sperm meet at the moment of fertilization, the ovum is certain to provide an X chromosome, while the sperm will provide either an X or a Y chromosome. If the sperm contributes its X chromosome, the child will have an XX pairing on the twenty-third chromosome and will be a girl. If the sperm contributes a Y chromosome, the result will be an XY pairing—a boy. Does this mean that girls are more likely to be conceived than boys?

dominant trait the one trait that is expressed when two competing traits are present

recessive trait a trait within an organism that is present, but is not expressed

genotype the underlying combination of genetic material present (but not outwardly visible) in an organism

phenotype an observable trait; the trait that actually is seen

homozygous inheriting from parents similar genes for a given trait

heterozygous inheriting from parents different forms of a gene for a given trait

FIGURE 2-4 PKU Probabilities
PKU, a disease that causes brain damage and intellectual disability, is produced by a single pair of genes inherited from mother and father. If neither parent carries a gene for the disease (a), a child cannot develop PKU. Even if one parent carries the recessive gene, but the other doesn't (b), the child cannot inherit the disease. However, if both parents carry the recessive gene (c), there is a one in four chance that the child will have PKU.

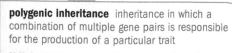

polygenic inheritance inheritance in which a combination of multiple gene pairs is responsible for the production of a particular trait

X-linked genes genes that are considered recessive and located only on the X chromosome

dominant form, symbolized as *PP*, in which case the child's genes will be *PP*, and the child will not have PKU.

Imagine what happens if one parent has the recessive *p* gene. In this case, symbolized as *Pp*, the parent will not have PKU, since the normal *P* gene is dominant. But the recessive gene can be passed down to the child. This is not so bad: If the child has only one recessive gene, it will not suffer from PKU. But what if both parents carry a recessive *p* gene? In this case, although neither parent has the disorder, it is possible for the child to receive a recessive gene from both parents. The child will have the *pp* genotype for PKU and will have the disorder.

Remember, though, that even children whose parents both have the recessive gene for PKU have only a 25 percent chance of inheriting the disorder. Due to the laws of probability, 25 percent of children with *Pp* parents will receive the dominant gene from each parent (these children's genotype would be *PP*), and 50 percent will receive the dominant gene from one parent and the recessive gene from the other (their genotypes would be either *Pp* or *pP*). Only the unlucky 25 percent who receive the recessive gene from each parent and end up with the genotype *pp* will suffer from PKU. Because phenylalanine is present in breast milk, testing infants at birth is an important and now routine procedure. Simply changing the infant's diet can prevent brain damage from this known genetic disorder.

Polygenic Traits. PKU illustrates the basic principles of genetic transmission, although PKU transmission is simpler than most cases. Relatively few traits are governed by a single pair of genes. Instead, most traits are the result of polygenic inheritance. In **polygenic inheritance**, a combination of multiple gene pairs is responsible for the production of a particular trait.

Furthermore, some genes come in several alternate forms, and still others act to modify the way that particular genetic traits (produced by other alleles) are displayed. Genes also vary in terms of their *reaction range*, the potential degree of variability in the expression of a trait due to environmental conditions. And some traits, such as blood type, are produced by genes in which neither member of a pair of genes can be classified as purely dominant or recessive. Instead, the trait is expressed in terms of a combination of the two genes—such as type AB blood.

A number of recessive genes, called **X-linked genes**, are located only on the X chromosome. Recall that in females, the twenty-third pair of chromosomes is an XX pair, while in males it is an XY pair. One result is that males have a higher risk for a variety of X-linked disorders, since males lack a second X chromosome that can counteract the genetic information that produces the disorder. For example, males are significantly more apt to have red-green colour blindness, a disorder produced by a set of genes on the X chromosome. Another example of a disorder produced by X-linked genes is *hemophilia*.

The Human Genome and Behavioural Genetics: Cracking the Genetic Code. Mendel's trailblazing achievements mark only the beginning of our understanding of genetics. The most recent milestone was reached early in 2001, when molecular geneticists succeeded in mapping the sequence of genes on each chromosome in humans. This is one of the most important accomplishments in the history of genetics (International Human Genome Sequencing Consortium, 2001).

Already, the mapping of the gene sequence has significantly advanced our understanding of genetics. For instance, the number of human genes, long thought to be 100 000, has been revised downward to 25 000—not many more than organisms that are far less complex (see Figure 2-5). Furthermore, scientists have discovered that 99.9 percent of the gene sequence is shared by all humans—meaning that many of the differences that seemingly separate people—such as race—are, literally, only skin-deep. Genome mapping will also help in the identification of disorders to which a given individual is susceptible (International Human Genome Sequencing Consortium, 2001; Human Genome Program, 2003; Gee, 2004; DeLisi and Fleischhaker, 2007; Gupta and State, 2007).

The field of behavioural genetics depends on the mapping of the human gene sequence. **Behavioural genetics** studies the effects of heredity on psychological characteristics. Rather than simply examining stable, unchanging characteristics such as hair or eye colour, behavioural genetics considers personality and behavioural characteristics. For example, behaviour geneticists study the genetic aspects of personality traits such as shyness, sociability, moodiness, and assertiveness, as well as psychological disorders, such as depression, attention deficit hyperactivity disorder, and schizophrenia (Conklin and Iacono, 2002; see Table 2-1). Researchers are even seeking to identify how genetic defects may be remedied (Peltonen and McKusick, 2001; Eley et al., 2003; Li, 2003).

Inherited and Genetic Disorders: When Development Deviates from the Norm

As we saw with PKU, a recessive gene responsible for a disorder may be passed on unknowingly from one generation to the next, revealing itself only when, by chance, it is paired with another recessive gene. When this happens, the gene will express itself, and the unsuspected genetic disorder will be inherited.

Another way that genes are a source of concern is that they might become physically damaged. Genes may break down due to wear and tear or chance events occurring during the cell-division processes of meiosis and mitosis. Sometimes, for no known reason, genes spontaneously change their form, a process called *spontaneous mutation*. Also, certain environmental factors, such as X-rays or even highly polluted air, might produce a malformation of genetic material. When damaged genes are passed on to a child, the results can be disastrous for physical and cognitive development (Samet et al., 2004).

In addition to PKU, which occurs once in 10 to 20 thousand births, other inherited and genetic disorders include the following:

- **Down's syndrome.** Instead of 46 chromosomes in 23 pairs, individuals with **Down's syndrome** have an extra chromosome on the twenty-first pair. Once referred to as mongolism, Down's syndrome is the most frequent cause of intellectual impairment. It occurs in about 1 out of 500 births, although the risk is much greater in mothers who are unusually young or old (Crane and Morris, 2006).

- **Fragile X syndrome. Fragile X syndrome** occurs when a particular gene is injured on the X chromosome. The result is mild to moderate intellectual impairment.

- **Sickle-cell anemia**. Around one-tenth of people of African descent carry genes that produce sickle-cell anemia, and 1 individual in 400 actually has the disease. **Sickle-cell anemia** is a

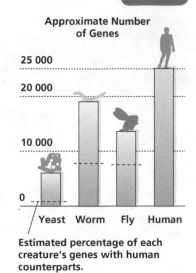

Approximate Number of Genes

25 000

20 000

10 000

0

Yeast   Worm   Fly   Human

Estimated percentage of each creature's genes with human counterparts.

FIGURE 2-5 Uniquely Human? Humans have about 25 000 genes, making them not much more genetically complex than some primitive species.
Source: Celera Genomics: International Human Genome Sequencing Consortium, 2001.

Mendelian inheritance	Chromosomal Abnormality	Multiple Interacting Genes (Heritable and Genetic Errors)
Huntington's disease	Down's syndrome	Schizophrenia
Fragile X	William's syndrome	Autism
PKU	Turner syndrome	Asthma
Cystic fibrosis	Klinefelter syndrome	Cancer

TABLE 2-1 GENETICALLY-BASED DISORDERS CAN BE INHERITED, CELL DIVISION ERRORS, AND MAY INVOLVE SINGLE OR MULTIPLE INTERACTING GENES

behavioural genetics the study of the effects of heredity on behaviour

Down's syndrome a disorder produced by the presence of an extra chromosome on the twenty-first pair; once referred to as mongolism

fragile X syndrome a disorder produced by injury to a gene on the X chromosome, producing mild to moderate mental retardation

sickle-cell anemia a blood disorder that gets its name from the shape of the red blood cells in those who have it

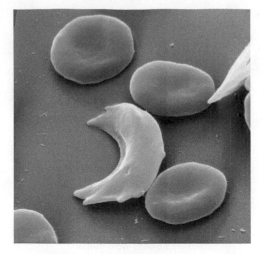

Sickle-cell anemia, named for the presence of misshapen red blood cells, is carried in the genes of 1 in 10 individuals of African descent.

blood disorder named for the shape of the red blood cells in those who have it. Symptoms include poor appetite, stunted growth, swollen stomach, and yellowish eyes. People afflicted with the most severe form rarely live beyond childhood. However, for those with less severe cases, medical advances have produced significant increases in life expectancy.

- **Tay-Sachs disease.** Occurring mainly in Jews of Eastern European ancestry and in French Canadians, **Tay-Sachs disease** usually causes death before its victims reach school age. There is no treatment for the disorder, which produces blindness and muscle degeneration prior to death.

- **Klinefelter's syndrome.** One male out of every 400 is born with **Klinefelter's syndrome**, which is the presence of an extra X chromosome. The resulting XXY complement produces underdeveloped genitals, extreme height, and enlarged breasts. Klinefelter's syndrome is one of a number of genetic abnormalities that result from receiving the improper number of sex chromosomes. For instance, there are disorders produced by having an extra Y chromosome (XYY), a missing second chromosome (called *Turner syndrome*) (X0), and three X chromosomes (XXX).

It is important to keep in mind that the mere fact a disorder has genetic roots does not mean that environmental factors do not also play a role. Consider sickle-cell anemia: Because the disease can be fatal in childhood, we'd expect that those who suffer from it would be unlikely to live long enough to pass it on. And this does seem to be true in North America. Compared with parts of West Africa, the incidence in North America is much lower.

Why the difference between North America and West Africa? Ultimately, scientists determined that carrying the sickle-cell gene raises immunity to malaria, a common disease in West Africa. This heightened immunity meant that people with the sickle-cell gene had a genetic advantage (in terms of resistance to malaria) that offset, to some degree, the disadvantage of being a carrier of the gene.

As we focus on genetic disorders, it is important to understand that in the vast majority of cases, the genetic mechanisms with which we are endowed work quite well. Overall, the vast majority of children born in Canada are healthy and normal. Moreover, due to advances in behavioural genetics, genetic difficulties can increasingly be forecast, anticipated, and planned for before birth, and parents can take steps before the child is born to reduce the severity of certain genetic conditions. In fact, as scientists' knowledge regarding the specific location of particular genes expands, predicting the genetic future is becoming an increasingly exact science.

Genetic Counselling: Predicting the Future from the Genes of the Present

If you knew that your mother and grandmother had died of Huntington's disease—a devastating, always fatal, inherited disorder marked by tremors and intellectual deterioration—how could you learn what your own chances of getting the disease are? The best way is through genetic counselling, a field that was nonexistent just a few decades ago. **Genetic counselling** focuses on helping people deal with issues relating to inherited disorders.

Genetic counsellors use a variety of data in their work. For instance, couples thinking about having a child might want to know the risks involved in a pregnancy. The counsellor will take a thorough family history, looking for a familial incidence of birth defects that might indicate a pattern of recessive or X-linked genes. In addition, the counsellor will take into account factors such as the age of the mother and father and any previous abnormalities in other children they might have already had (Fransen et al., 2006; Resta et al., 2006).

Typically, genetic counsellors suggest a thorough physical examination to identify physical abnormalities that the potential parents may be unaware of. In addition, samples of blood, skin, and urine might be used to isolate and examine specific chromosomes. Possible genetic defects, such as the presence of an extra sex chromosome, can be identified by assembling a *karyotype*, a chart containing enlarged photos of each of the chromosomes.

Prenatal Testing. If a woman is already pregnant, a variety of techniques can assess the health of her unborn child (see Table 2-2 for a list of currently available tests). The earliest is a *first-trimester screen,* which combines a blood test and ultrasound sonography in the eleventh to thirteenth week of pregnancy and which can identify chromosomal abnormalities and

Tay-Sachs disease a disorder that produces blindness and muscle degeneration prior to death; there is no treatment

Klinefelter's syndrome a disorder resulting from the presence of an extra X chromosome; the syndrome produces underdeveloped genitals, extreme height, and enlarged breasts.

genetic counselling the discipline that focuses on helping people deal with issues relating to inherited disorders

ultrasound sonography a process in which high-frequency sound waves scan the mother's womb to produce an image of the unborn baby, whose size and shape can then be assessed

other disorders such as heart problems. In **ultrasound sonography,** high-frequency sound waves bombard the mother's womb, producing an image of the unborn baby, whose size and shape can then be assessed. Most pregnant women in Canada today will undergo one to three ultrasounds, with no reason to suspect harm to the child. Whether repeated use of ultrasound sonography is risky is unclear—in most cases where mothers have undergone more than three ultrasounds, there were already reasons for concern. However, the advent of vanity ultrasounds—privately available for non-medicinal purposes such as keepsake videos—has led the U.S. Food and Drug Administration, the Society of Obstetricians and Gynaecologists of Canada, and Health Canada to issue an advisory against the use of ultrasound sonography for non-medicinal purposes (Society of Obstetricians and Gynaecologists of Canada, 2007). Despite this advisory, vanity ultrasounds have become increasingly available in most major cities across Canada.

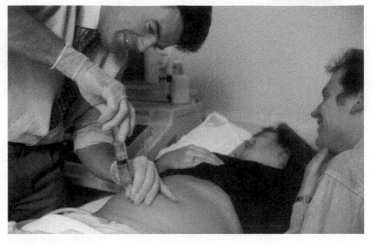

In amniocentesis, a sample of fetal cells is withdrawn from the amniotic sac and used to identify a number of genetic defects.

A more invasive test, **chorionic villus sampling (CVS)**, can be used if blood tests and ultrasound have identified a potential problem or if there is a family history of inherited disorders. CVS involves inserting a thin needle into the fetus and taking small samples of hair-like material that surrounds the embryo. The test carries a risk of causing miscarriage in between 1 in 100 to 1 in 200; because of the risk, CVS is rarely used unless there is an important reason to test the fetus early.

In **amniocentesis**, a small sample of fetal cells is drawn by a tiny needle inserted into the amniotic fluid surrounding the unborn fetus. Carried out 15 to 20 weeks into the pregnancy, amniocentesis can identify a variety of genetic defects with nearly 100 percent accuracy. In addition, it can determine the sex of the child. Amniocentesis carries a risk of infection and miscarriage similar to that of CVS, but is still less invasive and might be recommended in high-risk pregnancies.

After the various tests are complete, the couple will meet with the genetic counsellor again. Typically, counsellors avoid giving recommendations. Instead, they lay out the facts and present options for the parents, which typically range from doing nothing to taking more drastic steps, such as abortion.

chorionic villus sampling (CVS) a test that involves taking samples of hair-like material that surrounds the embryo; used to find genetic defects

amniocentesis the process of identifying genetic defects by examining a small sample of fetal cells drawn by a needle inserted into the amniotic fluid surrounding the unborn fetus

TABLE 2-2 FETAL DEVELOPMENT MONITORING TECHNIQUES

Technique	Description
Amniocentesis	Done between the fifteenth and twentieth week of pregnancy, this procedure examines a sample of the amniotic fluid, which contains fetal cells. Recommended if either parent carries Tay-Sachs, spina bifida, sickle-cell, Down's syndrome, muscular dystrophy, or Rh disease.
Chorionic villus sampling (CVS)	Done at 8 to 11 weeks, either transabdominally or transcervically, depending on where the placenta is located. Involves inserting a needle (abdominally) or a catheter (cervically) into the substance of the placenta but staying outside the amniotic sac and removing 10 to 15 milligrams of tissue. This tissue is manually cleaned of maternal uterine tissue and then grown in culture, and a karyotype is made, as with amniocentesis.
Embryoscopy	Examines the embryo or fetus during the first 12 weeks of pregnancy by means of a fibre optic endoscope inserted through the cervix. Can be performed as early as week five. Access to fetal circulation can be obtained through the instrument, and direct visualization of the embryo permits the diagnosis of malformations.
Fetal blood sampling (FBS)	Performed after 18 weeks of pregnancy by collecting a small amount of blood from the umbilical cord for testing. Used to detect Down's syndrome and most other chromosomal abnormalities in the fetuses of couples who are at increased risk of having an affected child. Many other diseases can be diagnosed using this technique.
Sonoembryology	Used to detect abnormalities in the first trimester of pregnancy. Involves high-frequency transvaginal probes and digital image processing. In combination with ultrasound, can detect more than 80% of all malformations.
Sonogram	Uses ultrasound to produce a visual image of the uterus, fetus, and placenta.
Ultrasound sonography	Uses very high frequency sound waves to detect structural abnormalities or multiple pregnancies, measure fetal growth, judge gestational age, and evaluate uterine abnormalities. Also used as an adjunct to other procedures such as amniocentesis.

Screening for Future Problems. The newest role of genetic counsellors is to test people, rather than their children, for susceptibility to disorders due to genetic abnormalities. For instance, Huntington's disease typically does not appear until people reach their forties. However, genetic testing can identify much earlier the flawed gene that produces Huntington's. Presumably, knowing that they carry the gene can help people prepare for the future (van't Spijker and ten Kroode, 1997; Ensenauer et al., 2005).

In addition to Huntington's disease, more than a thousand disorders, ranging from cystic fibrosis to ovarian cancer, can be predicted on the basis of genetic testing. Negative results can bring welcome relief, but positive results may produce just the opposite effect. In fact, genetic testing raises difficult practical and ethical questions (Johannes, 2003; Human Genome Project, 2006; Twomey, 2006).

Suppose, for instance, a woman is tested in her twenties for Huntington's and finds that she does not carry the defective gene. Obviously, she would be relieved. But suppose she finds that she does carry the flawed gene and will therefore get the disease. In this case, she might well experience depression and remorse. In fact, some studies show that 10 percent of people who find they have the flawed gene that leads to Huntington's disease never recover fully on an emotional level (Groopman, 1998; Hamilton, 1998; Myers, 2004; Wahlin, 2007).

Genetic testing is a complicated issue. It rarely provides a simple yes or no answer, instead typically presenting a range of probabilities. In some cases, the likelihood of becoming ill depends on the stressors in a person's environment. Personal differences also affect susceptibility to a disorder (Holtzman et al., 1997; Patenaude et al., 2002; Bonke et al., 2005).

> **From the perspective of a health-care provider:** What are some ethical and philosophical questions surrounding the issue of genetic counselling? Might it sometimes be unwise to know ahead of time about possible disorders that might affect your child or yourself?

Today many researchers and medical practitioners have moved beyond testing and counselling into actually modifying flawed genes. For example, in *germ line therapy*, cells with defective genes are taken from an embryo, repaired, and replaced.

REVIEW, CHECK, AND APPLY

REVIEW

- In humans, the male sex cell (the sperm) and the female sex cell (the ovum) provide the developing baby with 23 chromosomes each.

- A genotype is the underlying but invisible combination of genetic material present in an organism; a phenotype is the visible trait, the expression of the genotype.

- The field of behavioural genetics, a combination of psychology and genetics, studies the effects of genetics on behaviour.

CHECK YOURSELF

1. Sex cells (the ova and the sperm) are different from other cells because they

a. have twice the 46 chromosomes necessary so that when the cells combine and material is "spilled," the appropriate number of chromosomes will still be there.

b. each have half of the 46 chromosomes so that when they combine, the new zygote will have all the genetic information necessary.

c. are younger than all other cells in the developing human body.

d. are the only cells with chromosomal information.

2. According to Mendel, when competing traits are both present, only one trait, also known as the _____ trait, can be expressed.

3. Just because a disorder has genetic roots does not mean that environmental factors do not also play a role.

- True
- False

APPLYING LIFESPAN DEVELOPMENT

- How can the study of identical twins who were separated at birth help researchers determine the effects of genetic and environmental factors on human development?

Answers: 1) b; 2) dominant; 3) True

The Interaction of Heredity and Environment

LO3 How do the environment and genetics work together to determine human characteristics?

LO4 Which human characteristics are significantly influenced by heredity?

Like many other parents, Jared's mother, Leesha, and his father, Jamal, tried to figure out which of them their new baby resembled more. He seemed to have Leesha's big, wide eyes, and Jamal's generous smile. As he grew, they noticed that Jared's hairline was just like Leesha's, and his teeth made his smile resemble Jamal's. He also seemed to act like his parents. For example, he was a charming little baby, always ready to smile at people who visited the house—just like his friendly, jovial dad. He seemed to sleep like his mom, which was lucky since Jamal was an extremely light sleeper who could do with as little as four hours a night, while Leesha liked a regular seven or eight hours.

Were Jared's ready smile and regular sleeping habits something he just luckily inherited from his parents? Or did Jamal and Leesha provide a happy and stable home that encouraged these welcome traits? What causes our behaviour? Nature or nurture? Is behaviour produced by genetic influences or factors in the environment?

The simple answer is: There *is* no simple answer.

The Role of the Environment in Determining the Expression of Genes: From Genotypes to Phenotypes

As developmental research accumulates, it is becoming increasingly clear that to view behaviour as due to *either* genetic *or* environmental factors is inappropriate, since behaviour is the product of some combination of the two.

For instance, consider **temperament**, patterns of arousal and emotionality that represent consistent and enduring characteristics in an individual. Suppose we found—as increasing evidence suggests—that a small percentage of children are born with an unusual degree of physiological reactivity—a tendency to shrink from anything unusual. Such infants react to novel stimuli with a rapid increase in heartbeat and unusual excitability of the limbic system of the brain. By age four or five, children with heightened reactivity to stimuli are often considered shy by their parents and teachers. But not always: some of them behave indistinguishably from their peers at the same age (Kagan and Snidman, 1991; McCrae et al., 2000).

What makes the difference? The answer seems to be the children's environment. Children whose parents encourage them to be outgoing by arranging new opportunities for them may overcome their shyness. In contrast, children raised in a stressful environment marked by marital discord or a prolonged illness might be more likely to retain their shyness later in life (Kagan et al., 1993; Joseph, 1999; Propper and Moore, 2006). Jared, who was described earlier, might have been born with an easy temperament, which was easily reinforced by his caring parents.

Interaction of Factors. Such findings illustrate that many traits reflect **multifactorial transmission**, meaning that they are determined by a combination of both genetic and environmental factors. In multifactorial transmission, a genotype provides a range within which a phenotype can be expressed. For instance, people with a genotype that permits them to gain weight easily might vary in their actual body weight. They might be *relatively* slim, given their genetic heritage, but never able to get beyond a certain degree of thinness (Faith et al., 1997). In many cases, then, the environment determines how a particular genotype will be expressed as a phenotype (Wachs, 1992, 1993, 1996; Plomin, 1994a).

On the other hand, certain genotypes are relatively unaffected by environmental factors. For instance, pregnant women who were severely malnourished during famines caused by World War II had children who were, on average, unaffected physically or intellectually as

temperament patterns of arousal and emotionality that represent consistent and enduring characteristics in an individual

multifactorial transmission the determination of traits by a combination of both genetic and environmental factors in which a genotype provides a range within which a phenotype can be expressed

adults (Stein et al., 1975). Similarly, people will never grow beyond certain genetically imposed limitations in height, no matter how well or how much they eat—and the environment had little to do with Jared's hairline.

Although we can't attribute specific behaviours exclusively to nature or nurture, we can ask how much of a behaviour is caused by genetic factors and how much by environmental factors. We'll turn to this question next.

Studying Development: How Much Is Nature? How Much Is Nurture?

Developmental researchers use several strategies to study the relative influence of genetic and environmental factors on traits, characteristics, and behaviour. Their studies involve both nonhuman species and humans.

Nonhuman Animal Studies: Controlling Both Genetics and Environment. It is relatively simple to develop breeds of animals with genetically similar traits. The Butterball people do it all the time, producing Thanksgiving turkeys that grow especially rapidly so that they can be brought to market inexpensively. Similarly, strains of laboratory animals can be bred to share similar genetic backgrounds.

By observing genetically similar animals in different environments, scientists can determine, with reasonable precision, the effects of specific kinds of environmental stimulation. For example, to examine the effects of different environmental settings, researchers can raise some of the genetically similar animals in unusually stimulating environments, with lots of objects to climb over or through, and others in relatively barren environments. Conversely, by exposing groups of genetically *dissimilar* animals to *identical* environments, researchers can examine in a different way the role that genetic background plays.

Animal research offers substantial opportunities, but the drawback is that we can't be sure how well our findings can be generalized to people. We are also limited in what we can test. For example, we make extensive use of rats and mice for learning and memory, and cats for vision, but songbirds might provide the closest model for language. Many animal models for human behaviours exist, but no single animal models all human behaviours quite like a human.

Contrasting Relatedness and Behaviour: Adoption, Twin, and Family Studies. Obviously, researchers can't control either the genetic backgrounds or the environments of humans as they can with nonhumans. However, nature conveniently has provided ideal subjects for carrying out various kinds of "natural experiments": twins.

Recall that identical, monozygotic twins begin as *genetically* identical. Because their inherited backgrounds are precisely the same, any variations in their behaviour must be due entirely to environmental factors.

Identical twins would make great subjects for experiments about the roles of nature and nurture. For instance, by separating them at birth and placing them in totally different environments, researchers could clearly assess the impact of environment. Of course, ethical considerations make this impossible. What researchers can—and do—study, however, are identical twins who were adopted at birth and raised in substantially different environments (Bouchard and Pederson, 1999; Bailey et al., 2000; Richardson and Norgate, 2007). The difficulty is that this scenario does not present itself very often.

A few factors lead to similarities even when twins are separated at birth. Adoption agencies typically try to "match" the characteristics of birth mothers with those of adopting families (e.g., children tend to be placed with families of the same ethnicity and religion). Consequently, the home environments of the adopted twins often display similarities, and researchers can't always be entirely certain that differences in behaviour are due to differences in the environment.

Studies of nonidentical, dizygotic twins also present opportunities to learn about nature and nurture. Recall that dizygotic twins are genetically no more similar than siblings in a family born at different times. By comparing the behaviour of dizygotic twins with that of monozygotic twins (who were genetically identical), researchers can determine if monozygotic twins tend to be more similar on a particular trait than dizygotic twins. If so, researchers can assume that genetics play an important role in determining the expression of that trait.

Still another approach is to study people who are totally unrelated and therefore have dissimilar genetic backgrounds, but who share an environmental background. For instance, a family that adopts, at the same time, two very young unrelated children probably will provide them with similar environments. In this case, similarities in the children's characteristics and behaviour can be attributed with some confidence to environmental influences (Segal, 1993, 2000).

Finally, developmental researchers have examined groups of people in light of their degree of genetic similarity. For instance, if we find a high association on a particular trait between biological parents and their children, but a weaker association between adoptive parents and their children, we have evidence for the importance of genetics in determining the expression of that trait. On the other hand, if there is a stronger association on a trait between adoptive parents and their children than with the biological parents, or similar relationships between parents and their children regardless of relatedness, we have evidence for the importance of the environment in determining that trait. If a particular trait tends to occur at similar levels among genetically similar individuals, but at different levels among genetically distant individuals, genetics probably play a major role in the development of that trait (Rowe, 1994).

Developmental researchers using all these approaches, and more, for decades have come to the general conclusion that virtually all traits, characteristics, and behaviours result from the combination and interaction of nature and nurture (Robinson, 2004; Waterland and Jirtle, 2004).

Physical Traits: Family Resemblances

When patients entered the examining room of Dr. Cyril Marcus, they didn't realize that sometimes they were actually being treated by his identical twin brother, Dr. Stewart Marcus. So similar in appearance and manner were the twins that even long-time patients were fooled by this admittedly unethical behaviour, which occurred in a bizarre case made famous in the film *Dead Ringers*.

Monozygotic twins are merely the most extreme example of the fact that the more genetically similar two people are, the more likely they are to share physical characteristics. Tall parents tend to have tall children; and short parents, short children. Obesity also has a strong genetic component. For example, in one study, pairs of identical twins were put on diets that contained an extra 1000 calories a day—and ordered not to exercise. Over a three-month period, the twins gained almost identical amounts of weight. Moreover, different pairs of twins varied substantially in how much weight they gained, with some pairs gaining almost three times as much weight as other pairs (Bouchard et al., 1990).

Other, less obvious physical characteristics also show strong genetic influences. For instance, blood pressure, respiration rates, and even the age at which life ends are more similar in closely related individuals than in those who are less genetically alike (Jost and Sontag, 1944; Sorensen et al., 1988; Price and Gottesman, 1991).

Intelligence: More Research, More Controversy

No other nature–nurture issue has generated more research than intelligence. The reason is that intelligence, generally measured as an IQ score, is a highly valued human characteristic. In addition, intelligence is strongly related to scholastic success and, somewhat less strongly, to other types of achievement.

Genetics play a significant role in intelligence. As Figure 2-6 shows, in studies of both overall or general intelligence, and of specific subcomponents of intelligence (such as spatial skills, verbal skills, and memory), the closer the genetic link between two individuals, the greater the correspondence of their overall IQ scores.

Not only are genetics an important influence on intelligence, but the impact increases with age. For instance, as fraternal (that is, dizygotic) twins move from infancy to adolescence, their IQ scores become less similar. Not so with identical (monozygotic) twins, who become increasingly similar as they age (Brody, 1993; McGue et al., 1993).

Clearly, heredity plays an important role in intelligence, but to what degree is it inherited? Perhaps the most extreme view is held by psychologist Arthur Jensen (2003), who argues that as much as 80 percent of intelligence is a result of heredity. Others suggest more modest figures, ranging from 50 to 70 percent. It is critical to recall that these figures are averages across many people and say nothing about any individual's degree of inheritance (for example, Herrnstein and Murray, 1994; Devlin et al., 1997).

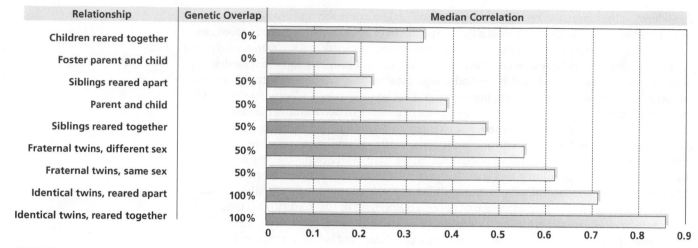

Relationship	Genetic Overlap	Median Correlation
Children reared together	0%	
Foster parent and child	0%	
Siblings reared apart	50%	
Parent and child	50%	
Siblings reared together	50%	
Fraternal twins, different sex	50%	
Fraternal twins, same sex	50%	
Identical twins, reared apart	100%	
Identical twins, reared together	100%	

FIGURE 2-6 Genetics and IQ

The closer the genetic link between two individuals, the greater the correspondence between their IQ scores. Why do you think there is a sex difference in the fraternal twins' figures? Might there be other sex differences, not shown on this chart, in other sets of twins or siblings?
Source: Bouchard & McGue, 1981.

It is also important to understand that, whatever role heredity plays, environmental factors such as exposure to books, good educational experiences, and intelligent peers are profoundly influential. In fact, in terms of public policy, environmental influences are the focus of efforts geared toward maximizing people's intellectual success. As developmental psychologist Sandra Scarr suggests, we should be asking what can be done to maximize the intellectual development of each individual (Scarr and Carter-Saltzman, 1982; Storfer, 1990; Bouchard, 1997).

> **From an educator's perspective:** Some people have used the proven genetic basis of intelligence to argue against strenuous educational efforts on behalf of individuals with below-average IQs. Does this viewpoint make sense based on what you have learned about heredity and environment? Why or why not?

Genetic and Environmental Influences on Personality: Born to Be Outgoing?

Do we inherit our personality?

We do, at least in part. Evidence suggests that some of our most basic personality traits have genetic roots. For example, two of the "big five" personality traits—neuroticism and extroversion—have been linked to genetic factors. *Neuroticism*, as the term is used by personality researchers, is the degree of emotional stability an individual characteristically displays. *Extroversion* is the degree to which a person seeks to be with others, to behave in an outgoing manner, and generally to be sociable. For instance, Jared, the baby described earlier, might have inherited an outgoing personality from his father, Jamal (Plomin and Caspi, 1998; Benjamin et al., 2002; Zuckerman, 2003).

How do we know which personality traits reflect genetics? Some evidence comes from direct examination of genes themselves. For instance, it appears that a specific gene is very influential in determining risk-taking behaviour and extravagance. This novelty-seeking gene affects the production of the brain chemical serotonin, making some people more prone than others to seek out novel situations and to take risks (Ebstein et al., 1996; Gillespie et al., 2003; Heck et al., 2009).

Are some children born to be outgoing and extroverted? The answer seems to be "yes."

Other evidence comes from studies of twins. In one major study, researchers looked at the personality traits of hundreds of pairs of twins. Because a good number of the twins were genetically identical but had been raised apart, it was possible to determine with some confidence the influence of genetic factors (Tellegen et al., 1988). The researchers found that certain traits reflected the contribution of genetics considerably more than others. As you can see in Figure 2-7, social potency (the tendency to be a masterful, forceful leader who enjoys being the centre of attention) and traditionalism (strict endorsement of rules and authority) are strongly associated with genetic factors (Harris et al., 2007).

Even less basic personality traits are linked to genetics, including political attitudes, religious interests and values, and attitudes toward human sexuality (Eley et al., 2003; Bouchard, 2004; Koenig et al., 2005).

Clearly, genetic factors play a role in determining personality—but so does the environment in which a child is raised. For example, some parents encourage high activity levels as a manifestation of independence and intelligence. Other parents might encourage lower levels of activity, feeling that more passive children will get along better in society. In part, these parental attitudes are culturally determined; Western parents might encourage higher activity levels, while parents in Asian cultures might encourage greater passivity. In both cases, children's personalities will be shaped in part by their parents' attitudes.

Because both genetic and environmental factors have consequences for a child's personality, personality development is a perfect example of the interplay between nature and nurture. Furthermore, it is not only individuals who reflect the interaction of nature and nurture—even entire cultures do, as we see next.

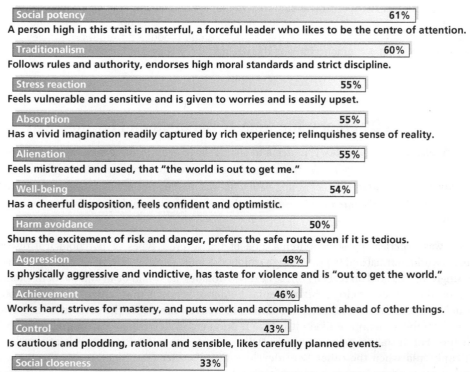

Social potency   **61%**
A person high in this trait is masterful, a forceful leader who likes to be the centre of attention.

Traditionalism   **60%**
Follows rules and authority, endorses high moral standards and strict discipline.

Stress reaction   **55%**
Feels vulnerable and sensitive and is given to worries and is easily upset.

Absorption   **55%**
Has a vivid imagination readily captured by rich experience; relinquishes sense of reality.

Alienation   **55%**
Feels mistreated and used, that "the world is out to get me."

Well-being   **54%**
Has a cheerful disposition, feels confident and optimistic.

Harm avoidance   **50%**
Shuns the excitement of risk and danger, prefers the safe route even if it is tedious.

Aggression   **48%**
Is physically aggressive and vindictive, has taste for violence and is "out to get the world."

Achievement   **46%**
Works hard, strives for mastery, and puts work and accomplishment ahead of other things.

Control   **43%**
Is cautious and plodding, rational and sensible, likes carefully planned events.

Social closeness   **33%**
Prefers emotional intimacy and close ties, turns to others for comfort and help.

FIGURE 2-7 **Inheriting Traits**
These traits are among the personality factors that are related most closely to genetic factors. The higher the percentage, the greater the degree to which the trait reflects the influence of heredity. Do these figures mean that "leaders are born, not made"? Why or why not?
Source: Adapted from Tellegen et al., 1988.

Cultural Dimensions

Cultural Differences in Physical Arousal: Might a Culture's Philosophical Outlook Be Determined by Genetics?

The Buddhist philosophy of many Asian cultures emphasizes harmony and peace. In contrast, many Western philosophies accentuate control over anxiety, fear, and guilt, which are assumed to be basic parts of the human condition.

Could such philosophical approaches reflect, in part, genetic factors? That is the controversial suggestion made by developmental psychologist Jerome Kagan and his colleagues. They speculate that the underlying temperament of a given society, determined genetically, might predispose people in that society toward a particular philosophy (Kagan et al., 1993; Kagan, 2010).

Kagan bases his admittedly speculative suggestion on well-confirmed findings that show clear differences in temperament between Caucasian and Asian children. For instance, one study that compared four-month-old infants in China, Ireland, and the United States found several relevant differences. In comparison to the Caucasian American babies and the Irish babies, the Chinese babies had significantly lower motor activity, irritability, and vocalization.

Kagan suggests that the Chinese, who enter the world temperamentally calmer, may find Buddhist notions of serenity more in tune with their nature. In contrast, Westerners, who are emotionally more volatile, tense, and prone to guilt, might be attracted to philosophies that focus on the control of unpleasant feelings, which are usual features of everyday experience (Kagan et al., 1994; Kagan, 2003).

Of course, neither philosophical approach is necessarily better or worse than the other, and neither temperament is superior or inferior. Any individual within a culture can be more or less temperamentally volatile, and the range of temperaments even within a single culture is vast. Finally, environmental conditions can have a significant effect on the portion of a person's temperament that is not genetically determined. What this speculation does reflect is the complex inter-

The Buddhist philosophy emphasizes harmony and peacefulness. Could this decidedly non-Western philosophy be a reflection, in part, of genetic causes?

action between culture and temperament. Religion might help mould temperament; temperament might make certain religious ideals more attractive.

To validate this intriguing notion would require additional research to determine just how the unique interaction of heredity and environment within a given culture can produce a framework for viewing and understanding the world.

Psychological Disorders: The Role of Genetics and Environment

Lewis Shiner was a young bodybuilder and should have been in his prime. Instead, he heard voices taunting him, telling him he wasn't good enough, and constantly questioning his sexuality. One day he lashed out at another young man who was making fun of him at the gym...the bully was his reflection in the mirror. The cuts from the mirror glass were deep, and Lewis was admitted to the hospital for the first time at age 19.

Shiner was experiencing schizophrenia, one of the severest types of psychological disorder. Shiner's world, normal and happy through childhood, took a tumble during adolescence as he increasingly lost his hold on reality. For the next two decades, he would be in and out of institutions.

How did Shiner develop schizophrenia? Evidence suggests that schizophrenia is brought about by genetic factors and runs in families. Moreover, the closer the genetic links between family members, the more likely it is that if one person develops schizophrenia, the other will too. For instance, a monozygotic twin has close to a 50 percent risk of developing schizophrenia when the other twin develops the disorder (see Figure 2-8). On the other hand, a niece or nephew of a person with schizophrenia has less than a 5 percent chance of developing the disorder (Prescott and Gottesman, 1993; Hanson and Gottesman, 2005).

However, these data also illustrate that genetics alone do not influence the development of the disorder. If genetics were the sole cause, the risk for an identical twin would be 100 percent. Consequently, other factors account for the disorder, ranging from structural abnormalities in the brain to a biochemical imbalance (for example, Lyons et al., 2002; Hietala et al., 2003).

It also seems that even if individuals harbour a genetic predisposition toward schizophrenia, they are not destined to develop the disorder. Instead, they might inherit an unusual sensitivity to stress in the environment. If stress is low, schizophrenia will not occur; if stress is sufficiently strong, schizophrenia will result. Still, for someone with a strong genetic predisposition, even relatively weak environmental stressors can lead to schizophrenia (Paris, 1999; Norman and Malla, 2001).

Schizophrenia is not the only psychological disorder to have a genetic association. Major depression, alcoholism, autism, and attention deficit hyperactivity disorder also have significant inherited components (Gallagher et al., 2003; Prescott et al., 2005; Dick et al., 2006).

These disorders, which are genetic but far from preordained, illustrate a fundamental principle regarding the relationship between heredity and environment. Genetics often produces a tendency toward a future course of development, but when and whether the characteristic will be displayed depends on the environment. Although a predisposition for schizophrenia might be present at birth, typically people do not show the disorder until adolescence—if at all.

Similarly, other traits are more likely to be displayed as the influence of parents and other socializing factors declines. For example, young adopted children may display traits that are relatively similar to those of their adoptive parents. As they get older and their parents' day-to-day influence declines, genetically influenced traits may begin to manifest themselves (Caspi and Moffitt, 1993; Arsenault et al., 2003; Poulton and Caspi, 2005).

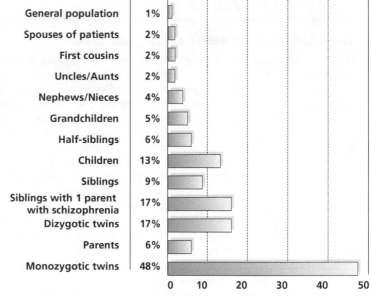

FIGURE 2-8 The Genetics of Schizophrenia
The psychological disorder of schizophrenia has clear genetic components. The closer the genetic links between someone with schizophrenia and another family member, the more likely it is that the other person will also develop schizophrenia.
Source: From *Schizophrenia Genesis: The Origins of Madness* ©1991 by W.H. Freeman and Company. Used with permission.

Can Genes Influence the Environment?

According to the developmental psychologist Sandra Scarr (1993, 1998), the genetic endowment provided to children by their parents not only determines their genetic characteristics, but also actively influences their environment. Scarr suggests three ways a child's genetic predisposition might influence his or her environment.

First, children tend to focus on aspects of their environment that are most in tune with their genetic abilities. For example, an active, aggressive child might gravitate toward sports, while a reserved child might be more engaged by academics or solitary pursuits like computer games or drawing. Or, one girl reading the school bulletin board might notice the upcoming tryouts for Little League baseball, while her less coordinated but more musically endowed friend might spot a poster recruiting students for an after-school chorus. In these examples the children are attending to those aspects of the environment in which their genetically determined abilities can flourish.

Second, the gene–environment influence might be more passive and less direct. For example, a particularly sports-oriented parent, who has genes that promote good physical coordination, might provide many opportunities for a child to play sports.

Finally, the genetically driven temperament of a child might *evoke* certain environmental influences. For instance, an infant's demanding behaviour might cause parents to be more attentive to the infant's needs than they would be otherwise. Or, a child who is genetically well coordinated might play ball with anything in the house so often that her parents notice and decide to give her some sports equipment.

In sum, determining whether behaviour is primarily attributable to nature or nurture is like shooting at a moving target. Not only are behaviours and traits a joint outcome of genetic and environmental factors, but the relative influence of genes and environment on specific characteristics shifts over the lifespan. Although the genes we inherit at birth set the stage for our future development, the constantly shifting scenery and the other characters in our lives determine just how our development eventually plays out. The environment both influences our experiences and is moulded by the choices we are temperamentally inclined to make.

Focus on Research

The Relationship between Parenting and Cancer

Using an animal model, Michael Meaney has spent years at McGill University studying the effects of maternal behaviour on offspring—rats, to be specific. Behaviour we might think of as demonstrating good mothering is shown by the mothers who spend a lot of time licking and grooming their pups. These mothers also take on a special position, called "arch-back," when nursing that makes it easier for pups to feed. Meaney's research group have demonstrated numerous benefits to pups of this high-licking–grooming type of mother, including regulating hormones that prepare the pup to better respond to stressful situations. The daughters of these high-licking–grooming mothers also go on to become high-licking–grooming mothers themselves. Is good mothering therefore genetically passed from mother to child? No. Animal models offer the unique opportunity to experimentally test this question by allowing researchers to deliberately switch the pups of high- and low-licking–grooming mothers, a technique called "cross-fostering." The switch in this case produced daughters that grew up to be like their foster mothers—not like their biological mothers. Nurture overcame nature.

So what does this all have to do with cancer? The story gets interesting here. Across campus, Moshe Szyf was studying the epigenetics of cancer—how our environment (for example the food we eat, toxin exposure, etc.) causes changes to our DNA, allowing cancer cells to grow. (If you thought your DNA was permanently fixed, guess again!) One day Meaney and Szyf started talking, then collaborating to examine the genes of the rat pups raised by high- and low-licking–grooming mothers. Not only was the high-licking–grooming mother changing hormones and brain structure in her offspring, but the changes could be detected at a genetic level; genetic changes that were passed on to the next generation. Nurture *changed* nature!

Meaney and Szyf's partnership is credited for creating the field of *behavioural epigenetics*, the study of how molecular changes to genes brought about by the environment affect behaviour—from behavioural problems to psychiatric difficulties to the onset of neurological disease. The field of behavioural epigenetics is still in its infancy, and the greatest challenge is testing whether the findings apply equally to humans. But the simple finding that maternal behaviour altered the activity of genes in ways that could be passed to future generations truly turns the nature versus nurture debate on its head! (Miller, 2010)

The environment in which we are raised affects not only our behaviour but also our biology.

REVIEW, CHECK, AND APPLY

REVIEW

- Human characteristics and behaviour are a joint outcome of genetic and environmental factors.

- Genetic influences have been identified in physical characteristics, intelligence, personality traits and behaviours, and psychological disorders.

- There is some speculation that entire cultures might be predisposed genetically toward certain types of philosophical viewpoints and attitudes.

CHECK YOURSELF

1. Most behavioural traits are a product of genetic influence and environmental factors. This is also known as _____.

   a. systematic desensitization

   b. creative orientation

   c. genetic predetermination

   d. multifactorial transmission

2. Instead of asking whether behaviour is caused by genetic *or* environmental influence, we should be asking *how much* of behaviour is caused by genetic factors and *how much* is caused by environmental factors.

   - True

   - False

3. According to psychologist Jerome Kagan, differences in temperament between Chinese and American children suggest a culture's philosophical outlook may be related to _____ factors.

APPLYING LIFESPAN DEVELOPMENT

- How might an environment different from the one you experienced have affected the development of personality characteristics that you believe you inherited from one or both of your parents?

MODULE 2.2 Prenatal Growth and Change

At her first appointment with Robert and Lisa, the midwife checked the results of tests to confirm the couple's home pregnancy test. "Yep, you're going to have a baby," she said to Lisa. "You'll need to set up monthly visits for the next six months, then more frequently as your due date approaches. Pick up some prenatal vitamins at a pharmacy and read these guidelines about diet and exercise. You don't smoke, do you? Good." Then she turned to Robert. "How about you? Do you smoke?" After many more minutes of instructions and advice, she left the couple feeling slightly dazed, but ready to do whatever they could to have a healthy baby.

From the moment of conception, development proceeds relentlessly. Much of it is guided by the complex set of genetic guidelines inherited from the parents, but much is also influenced from the start by environmental factors (Leavitt and Goldson, 1996). And both parents, like the bewildered Lisa and Robert, will have the chance to provide a good prenatal environment.

The Prenatal Period

L05 What happens during the prenatal stages of development?

LEARNING OBJECTIVES

Fertilization: The Moment of Conception

When most of us think about the facts of life, we tend to focus on the events that cause a male's sperm cells to begin their journey toward a female's ovum. Yet the sex act that creates the potential for conception is both the consequence and the start of a long string of events that precede and follow **fertilization**, or conception: the joining of sperm and ovum to create the single-celled zygote from which all of us began our lives.

Both the male's sperm and the female's ovum come with a history of their own. Females are born with around 400 000 ova located in the two ovaries (see Figure 2-9 for the basic anatomy of the female reproductive organs). However, the ova do not mature until the female reaches puberty. From that point until she reaches menopause, the female will ovulate about every 28 days. During ovulation, an egg is released from one of the ovaries and pushed by minute hair cells through the fallopian tube toward the uterus. If the ovum meets a sperm in the fallopian tube, fertilization takes place (Aitken, 1995).

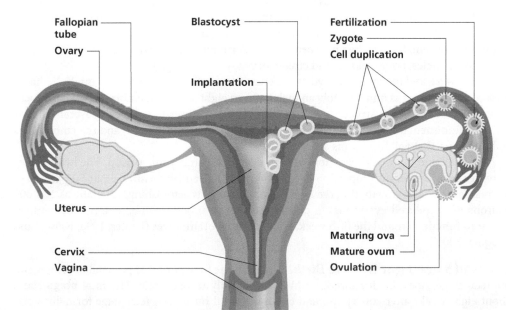

FIGURE 2-9 Anatomy of the Female Reproductive Organs
The basic anatomy of the female reproductive organs is illustrated in this cutaway view.
Source: Moore & Persaud, 2003.

fertilization the process by which a sperm and an ovum—the male and female gametes, respectively—join to form a single new cell

Sperm, which look a little like microscopic tadpoles, have a shorter lifespan. They are created by the testicles at a rapid rate: An adult male typically produces several hundred million sperm a day. Consequently, the sperm ejaculated during sexual intercourse are of considerably more recent origin than the ovum to which they are heading.

When sperm enter the vagina, they begin a winding journey through the cervix—the opening into the uterus—and into the fallopian tube, where fertilization can take place. However, only a tiny fraction of the 300 million cells that are typically ejaculated during sexual intercourse will ultimately survive the arduous journey. That's usually okay, though: It takes only one sperm to fertilize an ovum, and each sperm and ovum contains all the genetic data necessary to produce a new human.

The Stages of the Prenatal Period: The Onset of Development

The prenatal period consists of three phases: the germinal, embryonic, and fetal stages.

The Germinal Stage: Fertilization to Two Weeks. During the **germinal stage**, the first—and shortest—stage of the prenatal period, the zygote begins to divide and grow in complexity. The fertilized egg (now called a *blastocyst*) travels toward the *uterus*, where it becomes implanted in the uterus's wall, which is rich in nutrients. The germinal stage is characterized by methodical cell division, which gets off to a quick start: Three days after fertilization, the organism consists of some 32 cells, and by the next day the number doubles. Within a week, it comprises 100 to 150 cells, and the number rises with increasing rapidity.

The cells of the organism become not only more numerous, but also more specialized. For instance, some cells form a protective layer around the mass of cells, while others begin to establish the rudiments of a placenta and umbilical cord. When fully developed, the **placenta** serves as a conduit between the mother and fetus, providing nourishment and oxygen via the *umbilical cord*. In addition, waste materials from the developing child are removed through the umbilical cord.

The Embryonic Stage: Two Weeks to Eight Weeks. By the end of the germinal period—just two weeks after conception—the organism is firmly secured to the wall of the mother's uterus. At this point, the child is called an *embryo*. The **embryonic stage** is the period from two to eight weeks following fertilization. During this stage the major organs and basic anatomy develop.

At the beginning of this stage, the developing child has three distinct layers, each of which will form a different set of structures that eventually make up every part of the body. The outer layer of the embryo, the *ectoderm*, will form skin, hair, teeth, sense organs, and the brain and spinal cord. The *endoderm*, the inner layer, produces the digestive system, liver, pancreas, and respiratory system. Sandwiched between the ectoderm and endoderm is the *mesoderm*, from which the muscles, bones, blood, and circulatory system are forged.

If you were looking at an embryo at the end of the embryonic stage, you might be hard-pressed to identify it as human. Only an inch long, an eight-week-old embryo has what appear to be gills and a tail-like structure. On the other hand, a closer look reveals several familiar features. Rudimentary eyes, nose, lips, and even teeth can be recognized, and the embryo has stubby bulges that will form arms and legs.

The head and brain undergo rapid growth during the embryonic period. The head begins to represent a significant proportion of the embryo's size, encompassing about 50 percent of its total length. The growth of nerve cells, called *neurons*, is astonishing: As many as 100 000 neurons are produced every minute during the second month of life! The nervous system begins to function around the fifth week, emitting weak brain waves (Lauter, 1998; Nelson and Bosquet, 2000).

The Fetal Stage: Eight Weeks to Birth. Not until the final period of prenatal development, the fetal stage, does the developing child become easily recognizable. The **fetal stage** starts about eight weeks after conception and continues until birth. The fetal stage formally starts when the major organs have differentiated.

Now called a **fetus**, the developing child undergoes astoundingly rapid change. He increases in length some 20 times, and his proportions change dramatically. At two months,

germinal stage the first—and shortest—stage of the prenatal period, which takes place during the first two weeks following conception

placenta a conduit between the mother and fetus, providing nourishment and oxygen via the umbilical cord

embryonic stage the period from two to eight weeks following fertilization during which significant growth occurs in the major organs and body systems

fetal stage the stage that begins at about eight weeks after conception and continues until birth

fetus a developing child, from eight weeks after conception until birth.

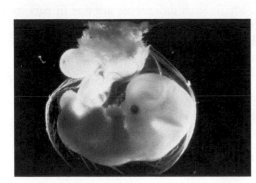

(a) Fetus at 5–6 weeks

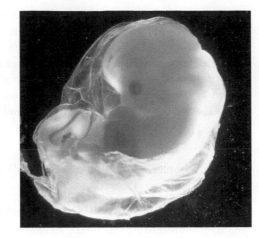

(b) Fetus at 8 weeks

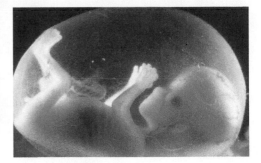

(c) Fetus at 14 weeks

around half the fetus will ultimately be her head; by five months, the head accounts for just over a quarter of her total size (see Figure 2-10). The fetus also substantially increases in weight. At four months, the fetus weighs an average of about 113 grams (4 ounces); at seven months, he weighs about 1800 grams (3 pounds); and at the time of birth the average child weighs just over 3100 grams (7 pounds).

At the same time, the developing child is rapidly becoming more complex. Organs become more differentiated and start to work. By three months, for example, the fetus swallows and urinates. In addition, the interconnections between the different parts of the body become more complex and integrated. Arms develop hands; hands develop fingers; fingers develop nails.

As this is happening, the fetus makes herself known to the outside world. In the earliest stages of pregnancy, mothers may be unaware that they are, in fact, pregnant. As the fetus becomes increasingly active, however, most mothers take notice. By four months, a mother can feel the movement of her child, and several months later, others can feel the baby's kicks through the mother's skin. In addition, the fetus can turn, do somersaults, cry, hiccup, clench his fists, open and close his eyes, and suck his thumb.

The brain, too, becomes increasingly sophisticated. The left and right halves of the brain, known as *hemispheres*, grow rapidly, and the interconnections between neurons become more complex. The neurons become coated with an insulating material called *myelin* that helps speed the transmission of messages from the brain to the rest of the body.

In weeks 8 to 24 following conception, hormones are released that lead to the increasing differentiation of male and female fetuses. For example, high levels of androgen are produced in males; androgen affects the size of brain cells and the growth of neural connections, and some scientists speculate that this may ultimately lead to differences in male and female brain structure and even to later variations in gender-related behaviour (Berenbaum and Bailey, 2003; Reiner and Gearhart, 2004; Knickmeyer and Baron-Cohen, 2006).

From week 24 onward, the senses (except for vision—it's pretty dark in there) are hard at work and the fetus demonstrates learning. Across a number of studies, newborns differentiated between things to which they were exposed in utero and things that were new, including their mother's voice, the rhythm of their mother's language, flavours and scents from their mother's diet, and music (Fifer and Moon, 2003; Oostindjer et al., 2009). For example, researchers Anthony DeCasper and Melanie Spence (1986) asked a group of pregnant mothers to read aloud the Dr. Seuss story *The Cat in the Hat* two times a day during the latter months of pregnancy. Three days after the babies were born, they appeared to recognize the story, responding more to it than to another story with a different rhythm.

By the last 10 weeks of the fetal period, brain waves indicate that the fetus passes through different stages of sleep and wakefulness, including REM sleep, the stage associated with dreaming. REM sleep is believed to be important for brain development (Mirmiran et al., 2003).

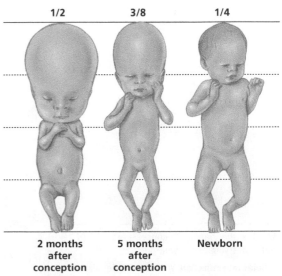

FIGURE 2-10 **Body Proportions**
During the fetal period, the proportions of the body change dramatically. At two months, the head represents about half the fetus, but by the time of birth, it is one-quarter of the fetus's total size.

Just as no two adults are alike, no two fetuses are the same. Some fetuses are exceedingly active (a trait that will probably remain with them after birth), while others are more sedentary. Some have relatively quick heart rates, while others have slower rates (DiPietro et al., 2002; Niederhofer, 2004; Tongsong et al., 2005). Such differences are due in part to genetic characteristics inherited at the moment of fertilization. Other differences, though, are caused by the nature of the environment in which the child spends her first nine months. The prenatal environment can affect infants' development in many ways—for good or ill.

Pregnancy Problems

For some couples, conception presents challenges—both physical and ethical—that relate to pregnancy.

Infertility. Some 15 percent of couples suffer from **infertility**, the inability to conceive after 12 to 18 months of trying. Infertility is correlated with age. The older the parents, the more likely infertility will occur; see Figure 2-11.

In men, infertility typically results from producing too few sperm. Use of illicit drugs or cigarettes and previous bouts of sexually transmitted diseases also increase infertility. For women, the most common cause is failure to release an egg through ovulation. This may occur because of a hormone imbalance, a damaged fallopian tube or uterus, stress, or abuse of alcohol or drugs (Gibbs, 2002; Pasqualotto et al., 2005; Lewis et al., 2006).

Several treatments for infertility exist. Some difficulties can be corrected through the use of drugs or surgery. Another option might be **artificial insemination**, a procedure in which a man's sperm is placed directly into a woman's reproductive tract by a physician. In some situations, the woman's husband provides the sperm, while in others sperm is provided by an anonymous donor from a sperm bank.

In other cases, fertilization takes place outside the mother's body. **In vitro fertilization (IVF)** is a procedure in which a woman's ova are removed from her ovaries, and fertilized with a man's sperm in a laboratory. The fertilized egg is then implanted in a woman's uterus. Similarly, *gamete intrafallopian transfer (GIFT)* and *zygote intrafallopian transfer (ZIFT)* are procedures in which an egg and sperm, or a fertilized egg, are implanted in a woman's fallopian tubes. In IVF, GIFT, and ZIFT, implantation is usually done in the woman who provided

infertility the inability to conceive after 12 to 18 months of trying to become pregnant

artificial insemination a process of fertilization in which a man's sperm is placed directly into a woman's reproductive tract by a physician

in vitro fertilization (IVF) a procedure in which a woman's ova are removed from her ovaries and fertilized with a man's sperm in a laboratory

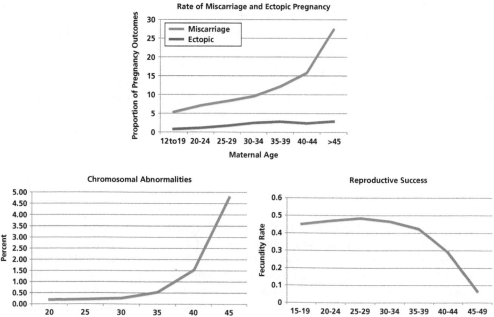

FIGURE 2-11 **Older Women and Risks of Pregnancy**
Not only does the rate of infertility increase as women get older, but the risk of chromosomal abnormality increases as well.
Source: Adapted from Andersen et al., 2000; Hefner, 2004; Hook, 1983; Menken et al., 1986.

the donor eggs. More rarely, a *surrogate mother* is used. The surrogate mother is artificially inseminated by the biological father or implanted with a fertilized egg and brings the baby to term (Frazier et al., 2004; Kolata, 2004).

In vitro fertilization has achieved success rates as high as 33 percent for younger women, but the success rate is lower for older women. Furthermore, reproductive technologies are becoming increasingly sophisticated, permitting parents to choose the sex of their baby. One technique is to separate sperm carrying the X and Y chromosome and implant the desired type into a woman's uterus. In another technique, eggs are removed from a woman and fertilized with sperm through in vitro fertilization. Three days after fertilization, the embryos are tested to determine their sex. If they are the desired gender, they are then implanted into the mother (Duenwald, 2003, 2004; Kalb, 2004).

Ethical Issues. The use of surrogate mothers, in vitro fertilization, and sex selection techniques presents a web of ethical and legal issues, as well as many emotional concerns. In some cases, surrogate mothers have refused to give up the child after birth, while in others the surrogate mother has sought to have a role in the child's life. In such cases, the rights of the mother, the father, the surrogate mother, and ultimately the baby are in conflict. Even more troubling are concerns raised by sex selection techniques, which are largely illegal in Canada.

Is it ethical to terminate the life of an embryo because of its sex? Do cultural pressures that might favour boys over girls make permissible medical intervention to produce male offspring? And—even more disturbing—will it be permissible in the future to preselect babies for other genetic characteristics, such as blue eyes, high intelligence, or a cheerful personality? While not feasible now, such selection might someday be possible.

Miscarriage and Abortion. A *miscarriage*—known as a spontaneous abortion—occurs when the embryo detaches from the wall of the uterus and is expelled before the child can survive outside the womb. Some 15 to 20 percent of pregnancies end in miscarriage, usually in the first several months. Many occur so early that the mother doesn't know that she had a miscarriage or that she was pregnant. Some sort of genetic abnormality accounts for most miscarriages.

In *abortion*, a mother chooses to terminate pregnancy. Abortion is a difficult choice for any woman in that it involves complex physical, psychological, legal, and ethical issues. While the decision to have an abortion is always difficult to make, research suggests that the impact on a woman's psychological well-being is no different than that of bringing an unwanted pregnancy to term (Fergusson et al., 2006; Major et al., 2009).

The Prenatal Environment: Threats to Development

LO6　What are the threats to the fetal environment and what can be done about them?

LEARNING OBJECTIVES

According to the Siriono people of South America, a pregnant woman who eats the meat of certain animals risks having a child who acts and looks like those animals. According to opinions on some TV talk shows, a pregnant mother should never lose her temper or else her child may enter the world angry (Cole, 1992).

While these views are folkloric, certain aspects of a mother's and father's behaviour, both before and after conception, can produce lifelong consequences for the child. Some problems show up immediately, but others don't appear until years later (Groome et al., 1995; Couzin, 2002). Some of the most profound problems are caused by teratogenic agents. A **teratogen** is an environmental agent such as a drug, chemical, virus, or other factor that affects and potentially harms the fetus. Although the placenta is responsible for keeping teratogens from the fetus, it is not 100 percent successful, and probably every fetus is exposed to some teratogens.

The timing and quantity of exposure to a teratogen are crucial. At some phases of prenatal development, a certain teratogen may have only a minimal impact, while at other stages the consequences can be profound. Generally, teratogens have their severest effects during periods of especially rapid prenatal development.

teratogen a factor that produces a birth defect

In the first two weeks, damage would most likely lead to death. In the early formation of organs, exposure to teratogens can lead to structural damage, whereas later exposure to a fully formed organ can lead to functional damage. The different maturational timetables of the organs then make each organ system vulnerable at different times. For example, the brain is most susceptible to structural damage 15 to 25 days after conception, while the heart is most vulnerable 20 to 40 days after conception (see Figure 2-12; Needleman and Bellinger, 1994; Bookstein et al., 1996; Pajkrt et al., 2004).

Mothers' Diet. A mother's diet clearly plays an important role in fetal development. A mother who eats a varied diet high in nutrients is apt to have fewer complications during pregnancy, an easier labour, and a generally healthier baby than a mother whose diet is restricted in nutrients (Kaiser and Allen, 2002; Guerrini et al., 2007).

The problem of diet is of immense global concern, since there are 800 million hungry people in the world and close to one *billion* people vulnerable to hunger. Clearly, hunger on such a massive scale affects millions of children (United Nations, 2004).

Fortunately, there are ways to counteract maternal malnutrition. Dietary supplements for mothers can reverse some of the problems produced by a poor diet. Furthermore, research shows that babies who were malnourished as fetuses, but who are subsequently raised in enriched environments, can overcome some of the effects of early malnutrition. However, the reality is that most of the world's children whose mothers were malnourished *before* their birth will continue to be malnourished after birth (Grantham-McGregor et al., 1994; Olness, 2003). There is also emerging evidence that timing of malnutrition and later (over)compensation may contribute to tendencies towards obesity.

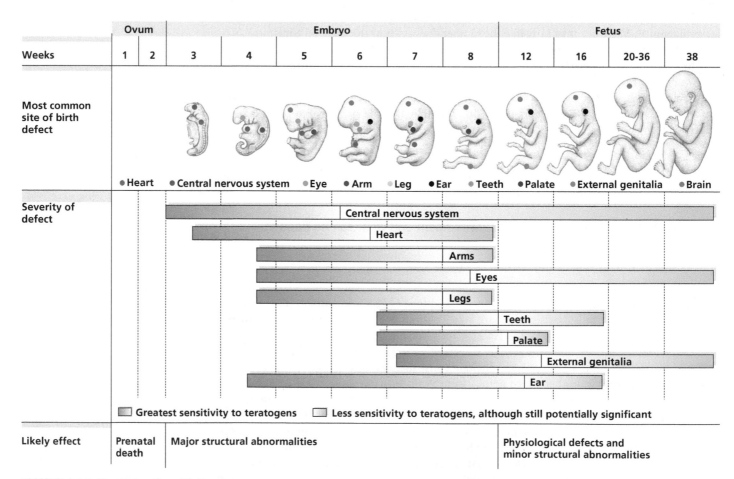

FIGURE 2-12 Teratogen Sensitivity
Depending on their state of development, some parts of the body vary in their sensitivity to teratogens.
Source: Reprinted from Moore, K.L. *Before we are born: Basic embryology and birth defects* (Philadelphia: Saunders, 1974), p. 96, with permission from Elsevier.

Mothers' Age.   More women are giving birth later in life than just two or three decades ago. This change is largely due to transformations in society, as more women choose to continue their education with advanced degrees and to start careers before having their first child (Gibbs, 2002; Wildberger, 2003; Bornstein et al., 2006).

The number of women who give birth in their thirties and forties has grown considerably since the 1970s—a situation that could have consequences for both mothers' and children's health. Women over 35 who give birth are at greater risk for a variety of pregnancy and birth complications than younger women. They are more apt to give birth prematurely and to have children with low birth weights, in part because of a decline in the condition of their eggs. By the time women reach age 42, 90 percent of their eggs are no longer normal (Cnattingius et al., 1993; Gibbs, 2002). Older mothers are also considerably more likely to give birth to children with Down's syndrome. About 1 in 100 babies born to mothers over 40 has Down's syndrome; for mothers over 50, the incidence increases to one in four (Gaulden, 1992). On the other hand, some research shows that older mothers are not automatically at risk. For instance, one study found that when women in their forties who have not experienced health difficulties are considered, they are no more likely to have prenatal problems than women in their twenties (Ales et al., 1990; Dildy et al., 1996).

Women who become pregnant during adolescence also face elevated levels of risk. They are more likely to have premature deliveries, and the mortality rate of infants born to adolescent mothers is twice that for mothers in their twenties (Kirchengast and Hartmann, 2003).

Mothers' Prenatal Support.   The higher mortality rate for such babies reflects more than just physiological problems related to the mother's age. Many teenage mothers do not have enough money or social support, which prevents them from getting good prenatal care and parenting support after the baby is born. The social circumstances that might have set the stage for the pregnancy in the first place, such as poverty or a lack of parental involvement and supervision, usually persist after the birth takes place (DePietro, 2004; Huizink et al., 2004).

Mothers' Health.   Depending on when it strikes, an illness in a pregnant woman can have devastating consequences. For instance, the onset of *rubella* (German measles) before the eleventh week of pregnancy can cause blindness, deafness, heart defects, or brain damage in the baby. In later stages of a pregnancy, however, rubella has less serious effects.

Several other diseases can affect a developing fetus, depending on when they are contracted. For instance, *chicken pox* can produce birth defects, while *mumps* can increase the risk of miscarriage.

Some sexually transmitted diseases (STDs), such as *syphilis*, can be transmitted directly to the fetus, who will be born with the disease. Some STDs, such as *gonorrhea*, are communicated to the child as it passes through the birth canal to be born.

Mothers who have *AIDS (acquired immune deficiency syndrome)* or who are carriers of the virus can pass it on to their fetuses through the blood that reaches the placenta. However, if mothers with AIDS are treated with antiviral drugs such as AZT during pregnancy, fewer than 5 percent of infants are born with the disease. Those infants who are born with AIDS must remain on antiviral drugs their entire lives (Nesheim et al., 2004).

Mothers' Drug Use.   The use of many kinds of drugs—both legal and illegal—poses serious risks to the unborn child. Even over-the-counter remedies for common ailments can have surprisingly injurious consequences. For instance, aspirin taken for a headache can lead to fetal bleeding and growth impairments (Griffith et al., 1994).

Some drugs taken by mothers cause problems for their children decades later. As recently as the 1970s, the artificial hormone *DES (diethylstilbestrol)* was frequently prescribed to prevent miscarriage. Only later was it found that the daughters of mothers who took DES stood a much higher than normal chance of developing a rare form of vaginal or cervical cancer and had more difficulties during their own pregnancies. Sons of the mothers who had taken DES also had problems, including a higher-than-average rate of reproductive difficulties (Adams Hillard, 2001; Schecter et al., 2005).

fetal alcohol syndrome (FAS) a disorder caused by the pregnant mother's consuming substantial quantities of alcohol during pregnancy, potentially resulting in mental retardation and delayed growth in the child

fetal alcohol effects (FAE) a condition in which children display some, although not all, of the problems of fetal alcohol syndrome due to the mother's consumption of alcohol during pregnancy

Birth control or fertility pills taken by pregnant women before they are aware of their pregnancy can also cause fetal damage. Such medicines contain sex hormones that, when produced naturally, relate to sexual differentiation in the fetus and gender differences after birth; these drugs can cause significant damage to developing brain structures (Miller, 1998; Brown et al., 2002).

Illicit drugs can also pose a risk to prenatal children. Consider *marijuana,* a commonly used drug that, if used during pregnancy, can restrict the oxygen that reaches the fetus. After birth, these infants might be irritable, nervous, and easily disturbed. At age 10, children who were exposed to marijuana prenatally show learning and memory deficits (Porath and Fried, 2005; Huizink and Mulder, 2006; Jones, 2006).

During the early 1990s, *cocaine* use by pregnant women led to the birth of thousands of so-called "crack babies." Cocaine restricts the arteries that lead to the fetus, significantly reducing the flow of blood and oxygen and increasing the risk of birth defects, disabilities, and fetal death.

Children whose mothers were addicted to cocaine might themselves be born addicted and have to undergo painful withdrawal. Even if not addicted, they are often shorter and weigh less than average, and they might have serious respiratory problems, visible birth defects, or seizures. They behave quite differently from other infants: Their reactions to stimulation are muted, but once they start to cry, they can be hard to soothe (Singer et al., 2000; Eiden et al., 2007).

It is difficult to determine the long-term effects of mothers' cocaine use in isolation, because such drug use is often accompanied by poor prenatal care and impaired nurturing after birth. In many cases, neglectful caregiving by mothers who use cocaine, not exposure to the drug, causes the children's problems. Treatment of these children requires not only that the mother stop using the drug, but also that she or other caregivers provide improved care to the infant (Brown et al., 2004; Jones, 2006). In one large-scale follow-up study, children exposed to cocaine prenatally were found to be at risk for cognitive problems, but also that better home environments could offset that risk (Singer et al., 2004).

Mothers' Use of Alcohol and Tobacco. Evidence strongly suggests that even small amounts of alcohol or nicotine take by pregnant women can disrupt the development of the fetus. The children of alcoholics who consume substantial quantities of alcohol during pregnancy are at the greatest risk. Approximately 1 out of every 750 infants is born with **fetal alcohol syndrome (FAS)**, a disorder that can includes cognitive impairments, delayed growth, and facial deformities. FAS is now the primary preventable cause of intellectual disability (Steinhausen and Spohr, 1998; Burd et al., 2003; Calhoun and Warren, 2007).

Even mothers who use smaller amounts of alcohol during pregnancy place their child at risk. **Fetal alcohol effects (FAE)** is a condition in which children display some, but not all, of the problems of FAS due to their mother's consumption of alcohol during pregnancy (Streissguth, 1997; Baer et al., 2003).

Children who do not have FAE can still be affected. Studies find that maternal consumption of just two alcoholic drinks a day during pregnancy is associated with lower intelligence in their offspring at age seven, and that relatively small quantities of alcohol taken during pregnancy can have adverse effects on children's future behaviour and psychological functioning (Johnson et al., 2001; Lynch et al., 2003; Mattson et al., 2006).

Because of these risks, physicians today counsel pregnant women and women who are trying to become pregnant to stop drinking alcohol entirely. They also caution against smoking, another practice proven to have an adverse effect on an unborn child.

Smoking has many consequences, none good. First, it reduces the oxygen content and increases the carbon monoxide content of the mother's blood, which quickly restricts the oxygen available to the fetus. In addition, the nicotine and other toxins in cigarettes slow the respiration rate of the fetus and speed up its heart.

The end result is an increased possibility of miscarriage and a higher likelihood of death during infancy. Furthermore, smokers are twice as likely as non-smokers to have babies with

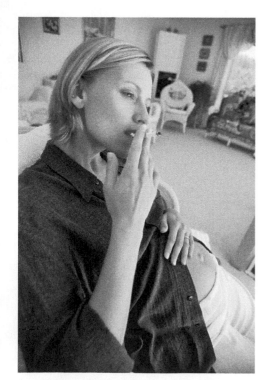

Pregnant women who use tobacco place their unborn children at significant risk.

an abnormally low birth weight, and smokers' babies are shorter, on average, than those of non-smokers (Dejin-Karlsson et al., 1998; Wakschalg et al., 2006). Emerging evidence also indicates that smoking during pregnancy might cause subtle brain damage contributing to later behavioural and cognitive problems.

Do Fathers Affect the Prenatal Environment? It would be easy to believe that fathers, having done their part to cause conception, have no further effect on the *prenatal* environment of the fetus, but it turns out that a father's behaviour may well have an influence. In fact, health practitioners are applying new research to suggest ways fathers can support healthy prenatal development.

For instance, fathers-to-be should avoid smoking. Second-hand smoke might affect the health of the mother and her unborn child. The more the father smokes, the lower the birth weight of his children (Hyssaelae et al., 1995; Tomblin et al., 1998).

Similarly, alcohol and drug use by a father can have significant effects on the fetus. Alcohol and drugs impair sperm and can lead to chromosomal damage, which can affect the fetus at conception. In addition, alcohol and drug use can create stress in the mother by producing an unhealthy environment. And workplace toxins such as lead or mercury can bind to sperm and cause birth defects (Wakefield et al., 1998; Choy et al., 2002; Dare et al., 2002).

Finally, fathers who are physically or emotionally abusive to their pregnant wives can harm their unborn children by increasing maternal stress or causing actual physical damage. An estimated 4 to 8 percent of women face physical abuse during pregnancy (Gilliland and Verny, 1999; Gazmararian et al., 2000; Bacchus et al., 2006; Martin et al., 2006).

From the perspective of a health-care provider: In addition to avoiding smoking, what other sorts of things might fathers-to-be do to help their unborn children develop normally in the womb?

From Research to Practice

Optimizing the Prenatal Environment

For a mother-to-be, pregnancy advice can be very overwhelming: Eat this, don't eat that; exercise, but not too much. Avoid stress—if you weren't stressed before, you are now! In the vast majority of cases, pregnancy and birth proceed without mishap. Being able to determine whether advice is research-based or an old wives tale is important. One way to tell the difference is to evaluate the source. Reputable sources include your health-care providers and federal, provincial, or regional health authorities. Many hospitals offer online resources: Motherisk, based out of Sick Kids Hospital in Toronto offers information and telephone counselling on topics ranging from morning sickness, nutrition, and herbal products, to cancer and HIV during pregnancy.

Another way to evaluate advice is by remembering that research-based advice should offer a well-reasoned explanation of why or how something works. Examples include the following:

- As an estimated 50 percent of pregnancies are unplanned, a healthy lifestyle (including sufficient folic acid) is always a good idea. The first few weeks of pregnancy are the most critical, and you might not even know you're pregnant.

- Don't use alcohol or other drugs. If you take medication for a chronic health condition, discuss your options with your doctor, who will weigh the risks to the fetus versus the risks to you. This includes all over-the-counter and herbal supplements, which can act like drugs in your body. (That's why you take them, right?) For example, many women experience constipation during pregnancy and turn to a laxative herbal tea of fennel and anise—don't! Some herbs disrupt hormones, and these particular herbs are known to mimic estrogen. A better choice is prune juice.

- Monitor caffeine intake. Although it is not clear that caffeine produces birth defects, it is known that the caffeine in coffee, tea, and chocolate can pass to the fetus, acting as a stimulant. There isn't much evidence that it will cause problems for your child after birth, but heavy consumption (defined as 300 mg/day) increases the risk of miscarriage. If you regularly drink more than the equivalent of two medium double-doubles per day, you might want to cut back before pregnancy.

- Avoid foods at high risk of food-borne illness. The "what to eat and what not to eat" advice can be overwhelming, but essentially boils down to the following: Try to get balanced nutrition and avoid food poisoning. Soft cheeses, raw fish (sushi), eggs or meat, alfalfa sprouts—harmful bacteria are everywhere and, at best, are a nuisance to a healthy adult, but at worst, are potentially life-threatening to a fetus.

REVIEW, CHECK, AND APPLY

REVIEW

- Fertilization joins the sperm and ovum to start prenatal development. The prenatal period consists of three stages: germinal, embryonic, and fetal.

- The prenatal environment significantly influences the development of the baby. The diet, age, prenatal support, and illnesses of mothers can affect their babies' health and growth.

- Mothers' use of drugs, alcohol, tobacco, and caffeine can adversely affect the health and development of the unborn child. The behaviour of fathers and others can also affect the child.

CHECK YOURSELF

1. Match the following descriptions of prenatal development to their appropriate labels: germinal, embryonic, and fetal.

   a. This stage lasts from eight weeks until birth and involves the differentiation of major organs.

   _____

   b. This stage lasts from the second to eighth week following fertilization, when the major organs and basic anatomy begin developing.

   _____

   c. The first and shortest stage, during which the zygote begins to divide and grow in complexity; the first two weeks following conception.

   _____

2. A _____ is an environmental agent such as a drug, chemical, virus, or other factor that produces a birth defect.

APPLYING LIFESPAN DEVELOPMENT

- Studies show that "crack babies" who are now entering school have significant difficulty dealing with multiple stimuli and forming close attachments. How might both genetic and environmental influences have combined to produce these results?

Answers: 1) a—fetal, b—embryonic, c—germinal; 2) teratogen

MODULE 2.3 Birth and the Newborn Infant

Welcome to the NICU

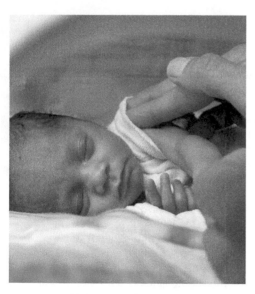

When Anne began to have contractions shortly after midnight, she thought it was just constipation pains. The following day, Sunday, she continued to have pains, but they were bearable and she had a prenatal check-up scheduled the next morning. At 6:00 p.m. the pains began to get worse, and strangely regular.

"I was only thirty-one weeks. It didn't occur to me that something might be wrong, that I might be in labour. When the cramps began to occur at regular seven-minute intervals, I thought, this is very strange, this has never happened before."

She went to the hospital, still believing they would give her a laxative and send her home. "But I really wanted that laxative . . . when the doctor told me I was in labour, I was completely shocked."

Despite the medical team's best efforts to stop labour, three days later, Amelia was born. "She was so tiny, she only weighed 1690 grams, she was in an incubator hooked up to so many tubes. I was torn between my desire to hold her and my fear of breaking her. She looked so fragile."

After six weeks in the Neonatal Intensive Care Unit (NICU), Amelia was ready to go home. "I saw so many babies, smaller babies, sicker babies. . . . I knew Amelia was ready, but I wasn't. After so much support from the nurses, I was scared to go home."

Infants are not meant to be born as early as Amelia. Yet 8 percent of babies in Canada are born early, and the outlook for them is improving dramatically.

All births, even full-term births, entail a mixture of excitement and anxiety. Usually delivery goes smoothly and, in an amazing and joyous moment, a new being enters the world. The excitement soon yields to wonder at this extraordinary new person. Babies enter the world with surprising capabilities, ready to respond to the world and the people in it.

In this module we'll examine the delivery and birth of a child, and take an initial look at the newborn. We'll first consider labour and delivery, exploring how the process usually proceeds—as well as some alternative approaches.

We'll next examine some possible birth complications, from premature birth to infant mortality. Finally, we'll consider the remarkable capabilities of newborns. We'll look at their physical and perceptual abilities, their immediate ability to learn, and at skills that help form the foundations of their relationships with others.

Birth

L07 What is the normal process of labour?

Her head was cone-shaped. Although I knew this was due to the normal movement of the head bones as she came through the birth canal and would change in a few days, I was still startled. She also had some blood on the top of her head and was damp, a result of the amniotic fluid in which she had spent the last nine months. There was some white, cheesy substance over her body, which the nurse wiped off just before she placed her in my arms. I could see a bit of downy hair on her ears, but I knew this, too, would disappear before long. Her nose looked a little as if she had been on the losing end of a fistfight: It was squashed into her face, flattened by its trip through the birth canal. But as she seemed to fix her eyes on me and grasped my finger, it was clear that she was nothing short of perfect. (Adapted from Brazelton, 1969)

For those of us accustomed to thinking of newborns in the images of baby food commercials, this portrait of a typical newborn may be surprising. Yet most **neonates**—the term used for newborns—resemble this one. Make no mistake, however: Babies are a welcome sight to their parents from the moment of birth.

The neonate's odd appearance is a result of its journey from the uterus, down the birth canal, and into the world. We can trace this journey, beginning with the release of the chemicals that initiate labour.

Labour: The Process of Birth Begins

About 266 days after conception, a protein called *corticotropin-releasing hormone* (CRH) triggers the release of various hormones, and the process that leads to birth begins. One critical hormone is *oxytocin*, from the mother's pituitary gland. When the concentration of oxytocin becomes high enough, the uterus begins periodic contractions (Smith, 1999; Hertelendy and Zakar, 2004).

During the prenatal period, the uterus, which is composed of muscle tissue, slowly expands as the fetus grows. For most of the pregnancy the uterus is inactive, but after the fourth month it occasionally contracts to ready itself for the delivery. These *Braxton-Hicks contractions* are sometimes called "false labour" because they can fool eager and anxious parents.

When birth is imminent, the uterus begins to contract intermittently. The increasingly intense contractions force the head of the fetus against the *cervix*, which is the neck of the uterus that separates it from the vagina. Eventually, the contractions become strong enough to propel the fetus slowly down the birth canal until it enters the world (Mittendorf et al., 1990). This exertion and the narrow birth passageway often give newborns a battered, cone-head appearance.

Labour proceeds in three stages (see Figure 2-13). In the *first stage of labour,* the uterine contractions initially occur around every 8 to 10 minutes and last about 30 seconds. As labour proceeds, the contractions occur more frequently and last longer. Toward the end of labour, the contractions may occur every two minutes and last almost two minutes. As the first stage of labour ends, the contractions reach their greatest intensity in a period known as *transition.* The mother's cervix fully opens, eventually expanding enough (usually to around 10 cm) to allow the baby's head to pass through.

The first stage of labour is the longest. Its duration varies, depending on the mother's age, ethnicity, number of prior pregnancies, and other factors. Typically, labour takes 16 to 24 hours for first-born children, but there are wide variations. Labour becomes shorter for subsequent children.

During the *second stage of labour,* which typically lasts around 90 minutes, the baby's head proceeds further with each contraction, increasing the size of the vaginal opening. Because the area between the vagina and rectum must stretch, an incision called an **episiotomy** is sometimes made to increase the size of the opening of the vagina. However, this practice is now seen as potentially harmful, and the number of episiotomies has fallen drastically in the last decade (Goldberg et al., 2002; Graham et al., 2005).

The second stage of labour ends when the baby has completely left the mother's body. Finally, in the *third stage of labour* the child's umbilical cord (still attached to the neonate) and the placenta are expelled from the mother. This stage is the quickest and easiest, taking just a few minutes.

neonates newborns

episiotomy an incision sometimes made to increase the size of the opening of the vagina to allow the baby to pass

Stage 1

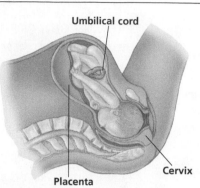

Uterine contractions initially occur every 8 to 10 minutes and last 30 seconds. Toward the end of labour, contractions may occur every 2 minutes and last as long as 2 minutes. As the contractions increase, the cervix, which separates the uterus from the vagina, becomes wider, eventually expanding to allow the baby's head to pass through.

Stage 2

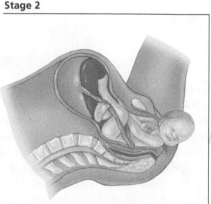

The baby's head starts to move through the cervix and birth canal. Typically lasting around 90 minutes, the second stage ends when the baby has completely left the mother's body.

Stage 3

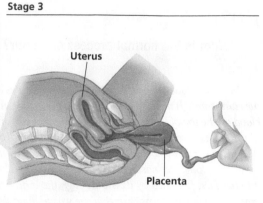

The child's umbilical cord (still attached to the neonate) and the placenta are expelled from the mother. This stage is the quickest and easiest, taking just a few minutes.

FIGURE 2-13 **The Three Stages of Labour**

How women react to labour reflects cultural factors. Although the physiological aspects of labour appear to be the same everywhere, expectations and interpretations vary significantly across cultures (Scopesi et al., 1997; Callister et al., 2003).

For instance, there is a kernel of truth to popular stories about women in some societies putting down their tools, giving birth, and immediately returning to work with their neonates on their backs. Accounts of the !Kung people in Africa describe women giving birth without much ado—or assistance—and quickly recovering. On the other hand, many societies regard childbirth as dangerous or even as an illness.

Birth: From Fetus to Neonate

Birth occurs when the fetus emerges fully from its mother's body. In most cases, babies automatically make the transition from the placenta to their lungs for oxygen. Consequently, most newborns spontaneously cry, which helps them clear their lungs and breathe on their own. What happens next varies widely. In Western cultures, health-care workers are almost always on hand for the birth. In 2008, 98.7 percent of births in Canada took place in a hospital (Statistics Canada, 2011), but worldwide, health-care workers are present for only about 50 percent of births (United Nations, 1990).

The Apgar Scale. In most cases, the newborn undergoes a quick visual inspection. While parents lovingly count fingers and toes, health-care workers use the **Apgar scale**, a standard measurement system that looks for a variety of indicators of good health. Developed by physician Virginia Apgar, the scale directs attention to five basic qualities, recalled most easily by using Apgar's name as a guide: *a*ppearance (colour), *p*ulse (heart rate), *g*rimace (reflex irritability), *a*ctivity (muscle tone), and *r*espiration (respiratory effort).

The newborn receives a score ranging from 0 to 2 on each of the five qualities, for an overall score between 0 and 10. Most score 7 or above; the 10 percent who score under 7 require help to start breathing. Newborns who score under 4 need immediate, life-saving intervention. A newborn with a score of 4, for example, might have pale or blue-grey skin colouring, indicating poor circulation; a pulse below 100 beats per minute; show little to no activity; or may show slow, irregular, or no breathing. The quick evaluation allows quick intervention, and many infants will show improvements in circulation, heart rate, response and activity, and breathing within five minutes (Apgar, 1953).

Apgar scale a standard measurement system that looks for a variety of indications of good health in newborns

In addition to problems or defects already present in the fetus, the process of birth itself can sometimes cause difficulties. Oxygen deprivation is one of the most profound. At times during labour, the umbilical cord may get wrapped around the baby's neck or pinched during a prolonged contraction, thereby cutting off the supply of oxygen. Lack of oxygen for a few seconds is not harmful, but any longer can cause serious harm. A restriction of oxygen, or **anoxia**, lasting a few minutes can produce cognitive deficits such as language delays and even intellectual impairment due to brain cell death (Hopkins-Golightly et al., 2003).

Physical Appearance and Initial Encounters. After assessing the newborn's health, health-care workers deal with the remnants of the child's passage through the birth canal. They typically clean away the *vernix*, the thick, greasy substance (like cottage cheese) that covers the newborn and smoothes the passage through the birth canal. A fine, dark fuzz known as *lanugo* covers the newborn's body (and will disappear later). The newborn's eyelids might be puffy from fluids that accumulated during labour, and blood or other fluids might remain on parts of her body.

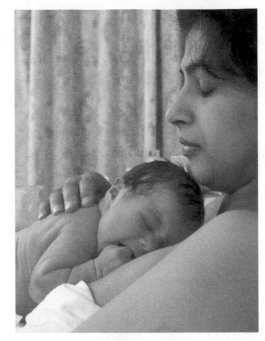

The newborn is then handed to the parent or parents for their first, miraculous encounter with their child. The importance of this initial encounter has become a matter of controversy. Some psychologists and physicians argued in the 1970s and early 1980s that **bonding**, the close physical and emotional contact between parent and child during the period immediately following birth, was crucial for lasting parent–child relationships. Their arguments were based in part on research on ducklings, which revealed a critical period just after birth when organisms had a unique readiness to learn, or *imprint*, from members of their species who happened to be present (Lorenz, 1957).

As applied to humans, this critical period would begin at birth and last only a few hours. During this period, skin-to-skin contact between mother and child supposedly leads to deep, emotional bonding—and if something prevents that contact, the mother–child bond will forever be lacking. The use of incubators or the hospital nursery—common at the time—was called into question (deChateau, 1980; Eyer, 1992).

Although observation of nonhuman animals highlights the importance of contact between mother and offspring following birth, research on humans suggests that immediate physical contact is less critical.

There was just one problem: Evidence for the critical period was lacking. Developmental researchers who carefully reviewed the research literature found little support for the idea. Although mothers who have early physical contact with their babies are more responsive to them, the difference lasts only a few days. Furthermore, there are no lingering reactions to separations following birth, even those that last several days (Redshaw, 1997; Else-Quest et al., 2003; Weinberg, 2004; Miles et al., 2006).

Although bonding immediately following birth does not seem critical, newborns do need touch and gentle massage soon after birth to stimulate the production of chemicals in the brain that initiate growth (Field, 2001). Skin-to-skin contact has numerous benefits, including promoting lactation in the mother, promoting growth in premature infants, improving sleep, and promoting social development in the first three months (Bigelow and Power, 2012). The critical period, however, might be months, not hours.

Approaches to Childbirth: Where Medicine and Attitudes Meet

Ester Iverem knew herself well enough to know that she didn't like the interaction she had with medical doctors. So she opted for a nurse-midwife who allowed her to use a birthing stool and to have her husband, Nick Chiles, by her side. When contractions began, Iverem and Chiles went for a walk, stopping periodically to rock—a motion, she says, "similar to the way children dance when they first learn how, shifting from foot to foot." That helped her work through the really powerful contractions.

> *I sat on the birthing chair [a Western version of the traditional African stool, which lies low to the ground and has an opening in the middle for the baby to come through] and Nick was sitting right behind me. When the midwife said "Push!" the baby's head just went "pop!," and out he came." Their son, Mazi (which means "Sir" in Ibo) Iverem Chiles, was placed on Ester's breast while the midwives went to prepare for his routine examination. (Knight, 1994, p. 122)*

anoxia a restriction of oxygen to the baby, lasting a few minutes during the birth process, that can produce brain damage

bonding close physical and emotional contact between parent and child during the period immediately following birth, argued by some to affect later relationship strength

Parents have developed strategies to help them deal with giving birth—a process that animals manage without much apparent thought. Parents find themselves deciding if the birth should take place in a hospital or in the home; if a physician, nurse, or midwife should assist; if the father's presence is desirable; if siblings and other family members should be on hand.

Most of these questions, of course, are matters not of fact but of values and opinions. No single approach will be effective for everyone, and no conclusive research indicates that one procedure is significantly more effective than another. And not only are personal preferences involved, culture also plays a role in the choice of birthing procedures.

Childbirth Attendants: Who Delivers? Traditionally, *obstetricians,* physicians who specialize in delivering babies, have been the childbirth attendants of choice. Recently, more mothers have chosen to use a *midwife,* who stays with the mother through labour and delivery. Midwives—most often nurses specializing in childbirth—are used primarily for pregnancies with no expected complications. Midwifery is regulated by most provinces in Canada, and some provinces have special Aboriginal midwifery clauses. Nevertheless, in 2002 only 3 percent of Canadian women chose a midwife for prenatal care. In contrast, 70 percent of women in the UK and New Zealand are seen by midwives, and 90 percent in Holland. Home birth is common in countries at all levels of economic development. For instance, a third of all births in the Netherlands occur at home (Ayoub, 2005). In contrast, only 1.3 percent of Canadian women give birth outside of a hospital—including birthing centres and home births.

The newest trend is also one of the oldest: the use of a *doula* (pronounced doo-lah). A doula provides emotional, psychological, and educational support during birth. A doula does not replace an obstetrician or midwife and does not do medical exams. Instead, doulas provide the mother with support and suggest consideration of birthing alternatives. This represents a return to a centuries-old tradition in which supportive, experienced older women serve as birthing assistants and guides.

Research suggests that doulas are beneficial, speeding deliveries and reducing reliance on drugs. Yet concerns remain. Unlike certified midwives, doulas do not have to be certified or specially trained (Stein et al., 2003; Carmichael, 2004; Breedlove, 2005; Ballen and Fulcher, 2006).

From the perspective of a health-care provider: While nearly 99 percent of Canadian births take place in hospital, circumstances are much different worldwide. What do you think are some reasons for this, and what are the implications of this statistic?

Use of Anesthesia and Pain-Reducing Drugs. Certainly the ongoing discovery of pain-reducing drugs is one of the greatest advances of modern medicine, but the use of medication during childbirth has both benefits and pitfalls. Slightly more than half of Canadian women choose *epidural anesthesia,* which produces numbness from the waist down. Traditional epidurals immobilize women and can prevent them from helping to push the baby. A newer form—a *walking epidural* or *dual spinal-epidural*—uses smaller needles and administers doses continuously. This permits women to move more freely and has fewer side effects. Use of epidurals varies widely across the country, from less than 10 percent in Nunavut to nearly 70 percent in Quebec. Part of the variability is due to access; limited access to anesthesiologists in rural areas decreases availability of the service. To quote one expectant parent, "If we want an epidural, we can't go into labour between 7pm and 7am."

It is important to remember that pain reduction comes at a cost. Drugs reach not just the mother but the fetus as well, and the stronger the drug, the greater its effects on the fetus and neonate. For example, anesthetics may temporarily depress the flow of oxygen to the fetus and slow labour. In addition, newborns whose mothers have been anesthetized are less physiologically responsive, show poorer motor control during the first days after birth, cry more, and may have more difficulty breastfeeding. Further, because of the size difference, doses that might have a minimal effect on the mother can have a magnified effect on the fetus (Ransjö-Arvidson et al., 2001; Torvaldsen et al., 2006).

In Lamaze classes, parents are taught relaxation techniques to prepare for childbirth and to reduce the need for anesthetics.

However, most research suggests that drugs, as currently used, produce only minimal risks and have no significant effect on a child's later well-being (Shute, 1997; ACOG, 2002; Albers et al., 2007). In a joint policy statement, the Society of Obstetricians and Gynaecologists (2008) include pharmacological and non-pharmacological pain relief equally in their definition of "normal childbirth."

Postdelivery Hospital Stay: Deliver, Then Depart? A generation or two ago, even a healthy uncomplicated delivery usually involved a five-day stay in hospital. Today, the average stay is two days. A few studies support the claim that early discharge increases the number of newborns readmitted to hospital, most often for jaundice and or dehydration. Thus, it is recommended that all newborns be seen by a family physician or pediatrician within two days of discharge. Women in many parts of Canada are also offered home visits by public health nurses, who provide support for everything from breast-feeding to accessing local services to screening for postpartum depression (Johnson et al., 2002; Lee et al., 1995; Lui et al., 2000; Wen et al., 1998).

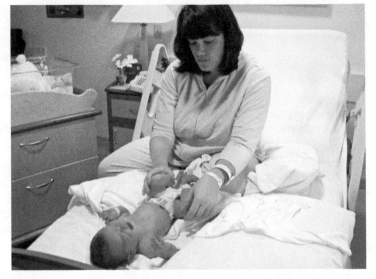
Some mothers are eager to get home after the birth of their child. Others express concern about going home too soon.

Newborn Medical Screening. Just after birth, newborns typically are tested for a variety of diseases and genetic conditions. The exact number of tests that a newborn experiences varies drastically. In some provinces, only three tests are mandated, while others provide 29. In some parts of the US and Europe, more than 40 disorders are screened for. Surprisingly, in 2005, Ontario was the province with the worst screening program, testing infants for only three disorders: PKU, congential hypothyroidism, and hearing. Further, Ontario was the only province that did not have a central computerized system for recording and follow-up of infants with positive screening test results (Hanley, 2005). The following year, Newborn Screening Ontario opened in Ottawa—a centralized laboratory where screening takes place today for 28 disorders, all from a tiny drop of blood taken from the newborn's heel. Sometimes research affects immediate public policy change!

Dealing with Labour

Becoming an Informed Consumer of Development

Every woman who is soon to give birth has some fear of labour. Most have heard gripping tales of extended, 48-hour labours. Still, few mothers would deny that the rewards of giving birth are worth the effort.

There is no right or wrong way to deal with labour. However, several strategies can help make the process as positive as possible:

- **Be flexible.** Although you might have carefully devised your birth plan, don't feel obliged to follow through exactly. If one strategy is ineffective, try another.

- **Communicate with your health-care providers.** Let them know what you are experiencing and ask for help and information. They should be able to give you an indication of how much longer you will be in labour, which can help you feel you can handle it.

- **Remember that labour is . . . laborious.** Expect to become fatigued, but realize that toward the end you might well get a second wind.

- **Accept your partner's support.** If a spouse or other partner is present, allow that person to make you comfortable and provide support. Research has shown that women who are supported by a spouse or partner have a more comfortable birth experience (Bader, 1995; Kennell, 2002).

- **Be realistic and honest about your reactions to pain.** Even if you had planned an unmedicated delivery, realize that you might find the pain hard to bear. At that point, consider drugs. Asking for pain medication is not a sign of failure.

- **Focus on the big picture.** Keep in mind that labour is part of a process that leads to an event unmatched in the joy it can bring.

REVIEW

- Labour proceeds through three stages.
- Immediately after birth, birthing attendants usually examine the neonate, using a measurement system such as the Apgar scale.
- Birthing options include the use of anesthetics during birth and alternatives to traditional hospital birthing, such as the use of a birthing centre, as well as the use of a midwife.

CHECK YOURSELF

1. Labour proceeds in three stages. The longest stage of labour is _____.

   a. the first stage

   b. the second stage

   c. the third stage

   d. hard to determine

2. Women appear to respond differently to labour as a function of culture.

   - True
   - False

3. The _____ scale measures infant health by assessing appearance (colour), pulse (heart rate), grimace (reflex irritability), activity (muscle tone), and respiration (respiratory effort).

   a. Bronfenbrenner

   b. Brazelton

   c. Anoxia

   d. Apgar

4. Which of the following factors influence a woman's delivery? (Check all that apply.)

   a. her preparation for childbirth

   b. the support she has before and during delivery

   c. her culture's view of pregnancy and delivery

   d. the specific nature of the delivery itself

   e. the weather on the day of delivery

APPLYING LIFESPAN DEVELOPMENT

- Why might cultural differences exist in expectations and interpretations of labour?

Answers: 1) a; 2) True; 3) d; 4) a–d

Birth Complications

L08 **What complications can occur at birth, and what are their causes, effects, and treatments?**

The infant mortality rate in Canada varies widely, from 3.3 deaths per 1000 births in Nova Scotia to 15.1 deaths per 1000 births in Nunavut. Overall, Canada ranks fourteenth among industrialized countries, with 5.1 deaths for every 1000 live births (Statistics Canada, 2010; *The World Factbook*, 2007; see Figure 2-14).

Why do infants have a greater chance of survival in some regions than in others? To answer this question, we need to consider the problems that can occur during labour and delivery.

Preterm Infants: Too Soon, Too Small

Like Amelia, whose birth was described in the module prologue, 8 percent of infants are born early. **Preterm infants**, or premature infants, are born prior to 37 weeks gestation. Because they have not had time to develop fully, preterm infants are at high risk for illness and death (Jeng et al., 1998).

The danger largely depends on the child's weight at birth. Although the average newborn weighs around 3400 grams, **low-birth-weight infants** weigh less than 2500 grams. Fewer than 7 percent of newborns are in the low-birth-weight category, but these account for most newborn deaths (Gross et al., 1997).

Not all low-birth-weight infants are preterm. **Small-for-gestational-age infants** are infants who, because of delayed fetal growth, weigh 90 percent (or less) of the average weight of infants of the same gestational age. Small-for-gestational-age infants are sometimes also preterm, but might not be (Meisels and Plunket, 1988; Shiono and Behrman, 1995).

If the baby is not very premature and the weight at birth is not extremely low, the threat is relatively minor. In such cases, the best treatment might be to keep the baby in the hospital to gain weight. Additional weight is critical because fat layers help prevent chilling in neonates, who are not very efficient at regulating body temperature.

Newborns who are born more prematurely and who have birth weights significantly below average face a tougher road. They are highly vulnerable to infection and, because their

preterm infants infants who are born prior to 37 weeks gestation (also known as premature infants)

low-birth-weight infants infants who weigh less than 2500 grams (around 5 1/2 pounds) at birth

small-for-gestational-age infants infants who, because of delayed fetal growth, weigh 90 percent (or less) of the average weight of infants of the same gestational age

very-low-birth-weight infants infants who weigh less than 1250 grams or who, regardless of weight, have been in the womb less than 30 weeks

lungs are not fully developed, they have problems taking in oxygen. As a consequence, they can experience *respiratory distress syndrome (RDS)*, with potentially fatal consequences.

To deal with respiratory distress syndrome, low-birth-weight infants are often placed in incubators, enclosures in which temperature and oxygen content are carefully monitored. Too low a concentration of oxygen will not provide relief, and too high a concentration can damage the delicate retinas of the eyes, leading to permanent blindness.

Preterm neonates are unusually sensitive to the sights, sounds, and sensations they experience, and their breathing might be interrupted or their heart rates can slow. They are often unable to move smoothly, instead moving with uncoordinated arm and leg movements that can be disconcerting to parents (Miles et al., 2006).

Despite the difficulties they experience at birth, the majority of preterm infants eventually develop normally. However, they develop more slowly and can be susceptible to subtle problems later. Significantly more children born preterm require special education services in school. For instance, some show learning disabilities, behaviour disorders, or lower-than-average IQ scores. Others have difficulties with physical coordination. Still, around 60 percent of preterm infants are free of even minor problems (Nadeau et al., 2001; Arseneault et al., 2003; Dombrowski et al., 2007; Chyi et al., 2008). The earlier the preterm birth, the greater the risk of long-term problems.

Very-Low-Birth-Weight Infants: The Smallest of the Small.
The story is less positive for the most extreme cases of prematurity. **Very-low-birth-weight infants** weigh less than 1250 grams or, regardless of weight, have been in the womb less than 30 weeks.

Very-low-birth-weight infants are not only tiny, they hardly seem to belong to the same species as full-term newborns. Their eyes might be fused shut and their earlobes can look like flaps of skin on the sides of their heads. Their skin is a darkened red colour, whatever their race.

Very-low-birth-weight babies are in grave danger from the moment they are born because their organ systems are immature. Before the mid-1980s, these babies would not have survived; recent medical advances have pushed the *age of viability*, the point at which an infant can survive prematurely, to about 22 weeks—some 4 months earlier than the normal term. Of course, the longer the baby stays in the womb after conception, the better the outcome (see Figure 2-15).

If a very-low-birth-weight preterm infant survives, the medical costs can be astonishing—between 3 and 50 times higher than the medical costs for a full-term child during the first three years of life. This fact has engendered ethical debates about the expenditure of substantial financial and human resources in cases in which a positive outcome may be unlikely (Prince, 2000; Petrou, 2006). Still, emerging evidence suggests that high-quality care can provide protection from some of the risks of prematurity, and that by the time they reach adulthood, premature babies may be little different from other adults (Hack, 2009).

Research also shows that care matters. For example, "Kangaroo Care," in which infants are held skin-to-skin against their parents' chests,

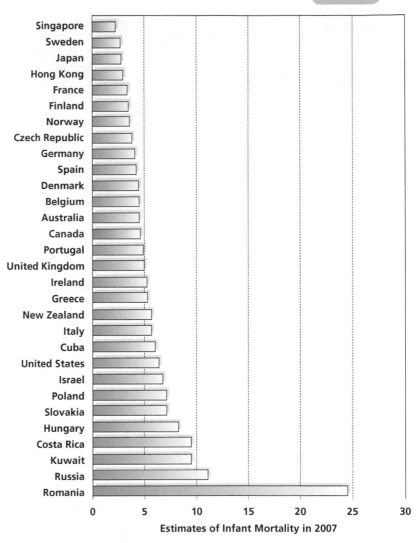

FIGURE 2-14 International Infant Mortality
Infant mortality rates in selected countries. Note Canada's position. What are some of the reasons for such a wide range between industrialized countries?
Source: *The World Factbook*, 2007.

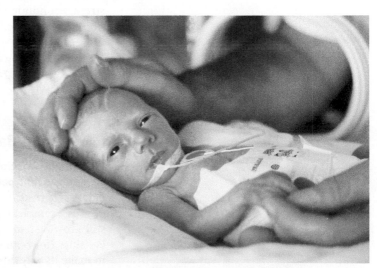

Preterm infants stand a much greater chance of survival today than they did even a decade ago.

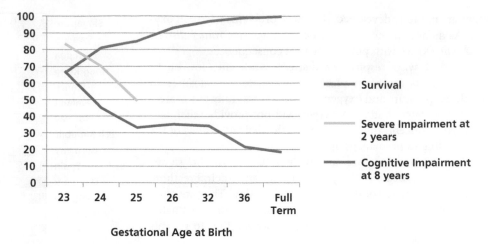

Gestational Age at Birth

FIGURE 2-15 **Outcomes and Gestational Age**
Survival for preterm infants has improved substantially in recent decades. Very young survivors, however, face significant risk of severe neurological impairment.
Source: Whyte et al., 1993; Wood et al., 2000; Effer et al., 2002; Hoekstra et al., 2004; Chyi et al., 2008.

appears to help preterm infants develop. Massaging preterm infants several times a day triggers the release of hormones that promote weight gain, muscle development, and the ability to cope with stress (Field, 2001; Feldman and Eidelman, 2003; Tallandini and Scalembra, 2006).

What Causes Preterm and Low-Birth-Weight Deliveries? About half of preterm and low-birth-weight births are unexplained, but several known causes account for the remainder. In some cases, the cause arises from difficulties in the mother's reproductive system. For instance, twins place unusual stress on their mothers, which can lead to early labour. In fact, most multiple births are preterm to some degree (Paneth, 1995; Cooperstock et al., 1998; Tan et al., 2004).

In other cases, preterm and low-birth-weight babies are a result of the maturity of the mother's reproductive system. Young mothers—under age 15—are more prone to deliver prematurely, as are mothers over age 40. In addition, a woman who becomes pregnant within six months of her previous delivery is more likely to have a preterm or low-birth-weight infant than a woman whose reproductive system has had a chance to recover. The father's age matters, too: wives of older fathers are more likely to have preterm deliveries (Smith et al., 2003; Branum, 2006).

Finally, factors that affect the general health of the mother—nutrition, medical care, stress, economic support—all are related to prematurity and low birth weight. In addition, the increased rate of preterm births from a generation ago is directly related to the decreased infant mortality rate—sometimes a preterm delivery is medically necessary for the well-being of the mother or the child (Canadian Institute for Health Information, 2009). See Table 2-3 for a summary of factors associated with increased risk of low birth weight (Carlson and Hoem, 1999; Stein et al., 2000; Field et al., 2008; Murray and Zentner, 2009).

Postmature Babies: Too Late, Too Large

One might imagine that a baby who spends extra time in the womb might have some advantages, but **postmature infants**—those still unborn two weeks after the mother's due date—face risks.

For example, the blood supply from the placenta can become insufficient to nourish the still-growing fetus. A decrease in blood to the brain can lead to brain damage. Similarly, labour is riskier (for both mother and child) if a fetus nearly the size of a one-month-old infant has to make its way through the birth canal (Shea et al., 1998; Fok, 2006).

Postmature infants are less of a problem than preterm babies because medical practitioners can induce labour artificially through drugs or perform a Caesarean delivery.

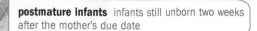

postmature infants infants still unborn two weeks after the mother's due date

TABLE 2-3 FACTORS ASSOCIATED WITH INCREASED RISK OF LOW BIRTH WEIGHT

I. Demographic Risks

  A. Age (less than 17; over 49)

  B. Low socioeconomic status

II. Medical Risks Predating Pregnancy

  A. Number of previous pregnancies (0 or more than 4)

  B. Low weight for height

  C. Genitourinary anomalies/surgery

  D. Selected diseases such as diabetes, chronic hypertension

  E. Nonimmune status for selected infections such as rubella

  F. Poor obstetric history, including previous low-birth-weight infant, multiple spontaneous abortions

  G. Maternal genetic factors (such as low maternal weight at own birth)

III. Medical Risks in Current Pregnancy

  A. Multiple pregnancy

  B. Poor weight gain

  C. Short interpregnancy interval

  D. Low blood pressure

  E. Hypertension/pre-eclampsia/toxemia

  F. Selected infections such as asymptomatic bacteriuria, rubella, and cytomegalovirus

  G. First- or second-trimester bleeding

  H. Placental problems such as placenta previa, abruptio placentae

  I. Severe morning sickness

  J. Anemia/abnormal hemoglobin

  K. Severe anemia in a developing baby

  L. Fetal anomalies

  M. Incompetent cervix

  N. Spontaneous premature rupture of membrane

IV. Behavioural and Environmental Risks

  A. Smoking

  B. Poor nutritional status

  C. Alcohol and other substance abuse

  D. DES exposure and other toxic exposure, including occupational hazards

  E. High altitude

V. Health-Care Risks

  A. Absent or inadequate prenatal care

  B. Iatrogenic prematurity

VI. Evolving Concepts of Risks

  A. Stress—physical and psychosocial

  B. Uterine irritability

  C. Events triggering uterine contractions

  D. Cervical changes detected before onset of labour

  E. Selected infections such as mycoplasma and chlamydia trachomatis

  F. Inadequate plasma volume expansion

  G. Progesterone deficiency

Caesarean Delivery: Intervening in the Process of Birth

> **Caesarean delivery** a birth in which the baby is surgically removed from the uterus, rather than travelling through the birth canal
>
> **fetal monitor** a device that measures the baby's heartbeat during labour

As Elena entered her eighteenth hour of labour, her obstetrician began to look concerned. She told Elena and her partner, Paula, that the fetus's heart rate had begun to repeatedly fall after each contraction. After trying some simple remedies, such as repositioning Elena on her side, the obstetrician came to the conclusion that the fetus was in distress. She told them that the baby should be delivered immediately by Caesarean delivery.

Elena became one of the nearly 25 percent of mothers in Canada who have a Caesarean delivery each year. In a **Caesarean delivery** (sometimes known as a *C-section*), the baby is surgically removed from the uterus, rather than travelling through the birth canal.

Caesarean deliveries are most often called for when the fetus shows distress of some sort (for example, a sudden rise in heart rate), or if blood flows from the mother's vagina during labour. In addition, mothers over age 40 are more likely to have Caesarean deliveries than younger ones (Dulitzki et al., 1998; Gilbert et al., 1999; Tang et al., 2006).

Caesarean deliveries are sometimes performed when the baby is in *breech position*—feet first in the birth canal. Breech position births, which occur in about 1 of 25 births, place the baby at risk because the umbilical cord is more likely to be compressed, depriving the baby of oxygen. Caesarean deliveries are also more likely in *transverse position* births, in which the baby lies crosswise in the uterus, or when the baby's head is so large it has trouble moving through the birth canal. Caesarean deliveries are also used in cases of placenta previa—when the placenta has grown partially or completely over the cervical opening.

The routine use of **fetal monitors**, which measure the baby's heartbeat during labour, has contributed to a soaring rate of Caesarean deliveries—

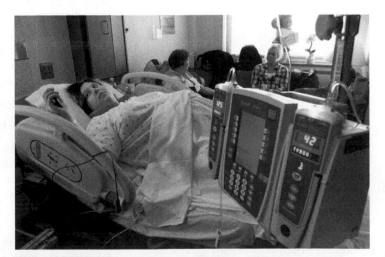

The use of fetal monitoring has contributed to a sharp increase in Caesarean deliveries in spite of evidence showing few benefits from the procedure.

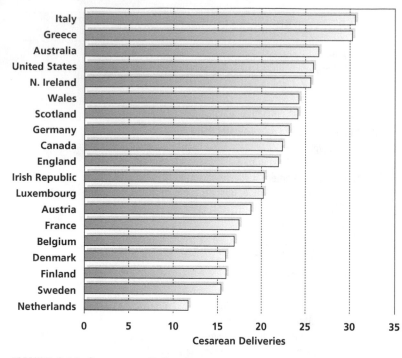

FIGURE 2-16 Caesarean Deliveries
The rate at which Caesarean deliveries are performed varies substantially from one country to another. Canada is near the middle of the pack. Why do you think such international differences occur?
Source: International Cesarean Awareness Network, 2004.

arguably by causing doctors to perceive greater risks than are present. In contrast, many other countries have substantially lower rates of Caesarean deliveries (see Figure 2-16), and there is no association between successful birth consequences and the rate of Caesarean deliveries.

Concerns have been raised in recent years about increasing rates of Caesarean—fewer than one in five women will have a Caesarean delivery for the first time this year, but among women who previously had a Caesarean, the rate is more than four in five. This is in part because the factors that led to the first Caesarean might be present a second time, but also because factors related to the previous surgery might make vaginal delivery risky. After two Caesareans, all subsequent pregnancies will be delivered that way, and each carries greater risk. Caesareans are major surgeries that carry dangers. The mother's recovery can be lengthy, and the risk of maternal infection is higher. In addition, a Caesarean delivery presents some risks for the baby. The relatively easy passage of Caesarean babies through the birth canal may deter the normal release of certain stress-related hormones, such as catecholamines, that help prepare the neonate to deal with the stress of the outside world. In fact, babies born without labour are more likely to experience breathing problems upon birth than those who experience at least some labour (Hales et al., 1993; Durik et al., 2000).

Medical authorities now recommend that fetal monitors not be used routinely. Evidence shows that outcomes are no better for newborns who have been monitored. In addition, monitors indicate fetal distress when there is none—false alarms—with disquieting regularity. Monitors should be used primarily in high-risk pregnancies and in cases of preterm and postmature babies (Farine et al., 2006).

Mortality and Stillbirth: The Tragedy of Premature Death

Sometimes a child does not live to pass through the birth canal. **Stillbirth**, the delivery of a child who is not alive, occurs in fewer than 1 out of 100 deliveries. If the death is detected before labour begins, labour is typically induced, or physicians might perform a Caesarean to remove the body as soon as possible. In other cases of stillbirth, the baby dies during its travels through the birth canal.

The overall rate of **infant mortality** (defined as death within the first year of life) is 7 deaths per 1000 live births. Infant mortality generally has been declining since the 1960s (MacDorman et al., 2005).

The loss of a baby is tragic and the impact on parents enormous. The juxtaposition of the dawning of life and an early death may make the death particularly difficult to deal with. Depression is common (Finkbeiner, 1996; McGreal et al., 1997; Murray et al., 2000).

Postpartum Depression: Moving from the Heights of Joy to the Depths of Despair

Renata had been overjoyed when she found out that she was pregnant and had spent the months of her pregnancy happily preparing for her baby's arrival. The birth was routine, the baby a healthy, pink-cheeked boy. But a few days after her son's birth, she sank into the depths of depression. Constantly crying, confused, feeling incapable of caring for her child, she was experiencing unshakable despair.

The diagnosis: postpartum depression. *Postpartum depression*, a period of deep depression following the birth of a child, affects some 10 percent of new mothers. The deep sadness that is its main symptom may last for months or even years. In about 1 in 500 cases, the symptoms evolve into a total break with reality. In extremely rare instances, postpartum depression

stillbirth the delivery of a child who is not alive, occurring in fewer than 1 in 100 deliveries

infant mortality death within the first year of life

can turn deadly. In 2011 the Ontario Court of Appeals upheld the legal distinction between infanticide, which is legally defined as a mother wilfully killing her newborn while suffering mental disturbance related to childbirth, and homicide.

The onset of depression usually comes as a complete surprise. Certain mothers seem more likely to become depressed, such as those who have been clinically depressed at some point in the past or who have depressed family members. Furthermore, women who are unprepared for the range of emotions that follow birth—some positive, some negative—may be more prone to depression.

Finally, postpartum depression may be triggered by the pronounced swings in hormone production that occur after birth. During pregnancy, the production of estrogen and progesterone increases significantly. However, 24 hours after birth they plunge to normal levels. This rapid change may result in depression (Honey et al., 2003; Verkerk et al., 2003; Klier et al., 2007).

Whatever the cause, maternal depression leaves its marks on the infant. As we'll soon see, babies are born with impressive social capacities, and they are highly attuned to their mothers' moods. When depressed mothers interact with their infants, they are likely to display little emotion and to act detached and withdrawn. This leads infants to display fewer positive emotions and to withdraw from contact not only with their mothers but with other adults as well (Hay et al., 2003; Nylen et al., 2006).

REVIEW, CHECK, AND APPLY

REVIEW

- Preterm infants can have substantial difficulties after birth and later in life.
- Preterm and low-birth-weight deliveries can be caused by health, age, and pregnancy-related factors in the mother. Income is also an important factor.
- Infant mortality rates can be lowered by the availability of inexpensive health care and good education programs for mothers-to-be.

CHECK YOURSELF

1. The amount of danger facing preterm infants largely depends on the child's _____ at birth.

2. The point at which an infant can survive prematurely is also known as the age of survivability.
   - True
   - False

3. _____, defined as death within the first year of life, has been declining since the 1960s.
   a. Infant decline
   b. Infant mortality
   c. Life expectancy
   d. Age of viability

APPLYING LIFESPAN DEVELOPMENT

- What are some ethical considerations arising from providing intensive medical care to very-low-birth-weight babies? Do you think such interventions should be routine practice? Why or why not?

Answers: 1) weight; 2) False; 3) d

The Competent Newborn

L09 What capabilities does the newborn have?

LEARNING OBJECTIVES

Relatives gathered around the infant car seat and its occupant, Kaita Castro, born just two days before. This was Kaita's first day home from the hospital. Kaita's nearest cousin, four-year-old Tabor, seemed uninterested in the new arrival. "Babies can't do anything fun. They can't even do anything at all," he said.

Kaita's cousin Tabor is partly right. There are many things babies cannot do, such as walk and care for themselves. Why are human infants born so dependent, while members of other species seem to arrive much better equipped?

One reason is that, in a sense, humans are born too soon. The brain of the average newborn is just one-quarter of what it will be at adulthood. In comparison, the brain of the macaque monkey, which is born after just 24 weeks of gestation, is 65 percent of its adult size. Because of the relative puniness of the infant human brain, some have suggested that we emerge from the womb 6 to 12 months too early. In reality, evolution knew what it was doing: If we stayed inside our mothers' bodies an additional half year to a year, our heads would be so large that we'd never manage to get through the birth canal (Schultz, 1969; Gould, 1977; Kotre and Hall, 1990).

The relatively underdeveloped brain of the human newborn helps explain the infant's apparent helplessness. But developmental researchers are coming to realize that infants enter this world with an astounding array of capabilities in all domains of development: physical, cognitive, and social.

Physical Competence: Meeting the Demands of a New Environment

The world the neonate faces is markedly different from the "womb world." Consider, for instance, the significant changes that Kaita Castro encountered as she began the first moments of life in her new environment.

Kaita's first task was to bring air into her body. Inside her mother, the umbilical cord delivered air and removed carbon dioxide. The outside world was different: Once the umbilical cord was cut, Kaita's respiratory system had to start its lifetime's work.

For Kaita, the task was automatic. Most newborn babies begin to breathe on their own as soon as they are exposed to air. The ability to breathe immediately indicates that the respiratory system is reasonably well developed, despite its lack of rehearsal in the womb.

Neonates emerge from the uterus more practised in other types of physical activities. For example, newborns such as Kaita have **reflexes**—unlearned, organized, involuntary responses that occur automatically in the presence of certain stimuli. Some reflexes have been rehearsed for several months before birth. The *sucking reflex* and the *swallowing reflex* permit Kaita to ingest food right away. The *rooting reflex,* which involves turning in the direction of a stimulus (such as a light touch) near the mouth, is also related to eating. It guides Kaita toward nearby sources of food, such as a nipple.

Other reflexes that present themselves at birth—coughing, sneezing, and blinking—help the infant avoid stimuli that are potentially bothersome or hazardous. Kaita's sucking and swallowing reflexes, which help her to consume her mother's milk, are coupled with the newfound ability to digest nutrients. The newborn's digestive system initially produces feces in the form of *meconium,* a greenish-black substance that is a remnant of the neonate's days as a fetus.

Because the liver, a critical component of the digestive system, does not always work effectively at first, almost half of newborns develop a yellowish tinge to their bodies and eyes. This *neonatal jaundice* is most prevalent in preterm and low-weight neonates and is typically not dangerous. Treatment involves placing the baby under fluorescent lights or administering medicine.

◉ Watch on **mydevelopmentlab**

To watch infants demonstrate the reflexes you have been reading about, log onto MyDevelopmentLab.

Sensory Capabilities: Experiencing the World

Just after Kaita was born, her father was certain that she looked directly at him. Did she, in fact, see him?

This is a hard question to answer. When sensory experts talk of "seeing," they mean both a sensory reaction to stimulation and an interpretation of that stimulation (the distinction between sensation and perception). Furthermore, it is tricky to pinpoint the specific sensory skills of newborns who can't explain what they are experiencing.

Still, it is clear that neonates such as Kaita can see to some extent. Although their visual acuity is not fully developed, newborns actively pay attention to certain types of information in their environment.

For instance, they attend to high-information elements in their field of vision, such as objects that sharply contrast with the rest of the environment. Furthermore, they can discriminate levels of brightness. There is even evidence that they may have a rudimentary sense of size constancy—the awareness that objects stay the same size even though the size of the image on the retina varies with distance (Slater et al., 1990; Slater and Johnson, 1998; Chien et al., 2006).

Starting at birth, infants are able to distinguish colours and even show preferences for particular ones.

In addition, not only can newborn babies distinguish different colours, they seem to prefer particular ones. For example, they can distinguish between red, green, yellow, and blue, and they take more time staring at blue and green objects (Adams et al., 1986; Alexander and Hines, 2002).

Newborns also clearly can hear. They react to certain sounds, showing startle reactions to loud, sudden noises, for instance. They also recognize sounds. For example, a crying newborn, hearing other newborns crying, will continue to cry. But on hearing a recording of its own crying, the newborn is more likely to stop crying, as if recognizing a familiar sound (Dondi et al., 1999; Fernald, 2001).

The auditory system is not completely developed, however, and auditory acuity is not as great as it will be. Moreover, amniotic fluid, which is initially trapped in the middle ear, must drain before the newborn can fully hear.

In addition to sight and hearing, the senses of smell and taste are also well developed. Place peppermint near the nose, and newborns suck and increase their physical activity; put something sour on their lips and they pucker. Other tastes evoke other facial expressions. Such findings clearly suggest that the senses of touch, smell, and taste are reasonably sophisticated at birth (Marlier et al., 1998; Cohen and Cashon, 2003).

Furthermore, newborns are clearly sensitive to touch. For instance, they respond to stimuli such as the hairs of a brush, and they are aware of puffs of air so weak that adults cannot notice them. In fact, the newborn's sensitivity to touch—and to pain—is part of the controversy surrounding circumcision of male infants, as discussed next.

Circumcision of Newborn Male Infants: The Unkindest Cut?

Circumcision is the surgical removal of part or all of the foreskin from the penis, and it is most commonly performed shortly after birth. Parents usually choose circumcision for a combination of health, religious, cultural, and traditional reasons. Around the world, rates of circumcision vary, from very rare in Central America, the Caribbean, and parts of Europe, to very common in the Middle East and parts of Africa. Rates in Canada are near the middle, with slightly less than half of male infants undergoing the procedure. There is also great variability across Canada, ranging from 6.8 percent in Nova Scotia to 44.3 percent in Alberta (see Figure 2-17; Public Health Agency of Canada, 2009). Physicians within Canada have long held that the practice is unnecessary.

But new research has added a twist: Circumcision provides protection against sexually transmitted diseases. A number of studies in Africa have found that circumcised men are less likely to become infected with HIV, even when other factors such as hygiene are controlled. In fact, when large experimental studies in Kenya and Uganda found compelling evidence that circumcision cut the risk of HIV infection nearly in half, researchers stopped the studies early to allow the uncircumcised men in the control groups to be circumcised and gain the same

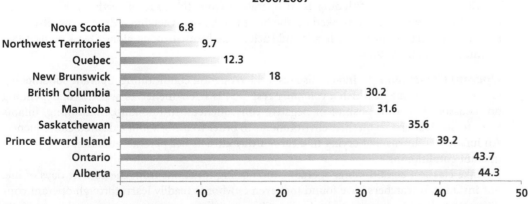

Proportion (%) of Males Circumcised, by Province/Territory, Canada, 2006/2007

FIGURE 2-17 **Circumcision Rates across Canada**
Source: Public Health Agency of Canada, 2009.

classical conditioning a type of learning in which an organism responds in a particular way to a neutral stimulus that would not normally cause that type of response

operant conditioning a form of learning in which a voluntary response is strengthened or weakened, depending on its association with positive or negative consequences

habituation the decrease in the response to a stimulus that occurs after repeated presentations of the same stimulus

protective benefits (American Academy of Family Physicians, 2002; Meier et al., 2006; Mills and Seigfried, 2006; National Institutes of Health, 2006).

Circumcision can produce other medical benefits. The risk of urinary tract infections is reduced in circumcised males, especially during the first year of life, and the risk of penile cancer is about three times higher in uncircumcised men than in men who were circumcised at birth (Frisch et al., 1995; American Academy of Pediatrics, 1999).

On the other hand, circumcision is not without complications. The most common are bleeding and infection, both of which are easily treated. The procedure is also painful and stressful to the infant, as it is typically done without general anesthesia. Further, some experts believe that circumcision reduces sensation and sexual pleasure later in life, while others argue that it is unethical to remove a healthy body part without a person's consent when there is no medical need to do so.

One thing is clear: circumcision is highly controversial and evokes strong emotions. The decision ultimately comes down to personal preferences and values (Goldman, 2004).

Early Learning Capabilities

One-month-old Michael Samedi was on a car ride with his family when a violent thunderstorm suddenly began. Flashes of lightning were quickly followed by loud thunderclaps. Michael, clearly disturbed, began to sob. With each new thunderclap, the pitch and fervour of his crying increased. Unfortunately, before very long it wasn't just the thunder that would raise Michael's anxiety; the lightning alone was enough to make him cry out. In fact, even as an adult, Michael feels his chest tighten and his stomach churn at the mere sight of lightning.

Classical Conditioning. The source of Michael's fear is classical conditioning, a type of learning first identified by Ivan Pavlov (and discussed in Module 1.2). In **classical conditioning** an organism learns to respond in a particular way to a neutral stimulus that normally does not bring about that type of response.

Pavlov discovered that by repeatedly pairing two stimuli, such as the sound of a bell and the arrival of meat, he could make hungry dogs learn to respond (in this case by salivating) not only when the meat was presented, but even when the bell was sounded without the meat (Pavlov, 1927).

The key feature of classical conditioning is stimulus substitution, in which a stimulus that doesn't naturally bring about a particular response is paired with a stimulus that does evoke that response. Repeatedly presenting the two stimuli together results in the second stimulus taking on the properties of the first. In effect, the second stimulus is substituted for the first.

One of the earliest examples of classical conditioning shaping human emotions was the case of 11-month-old "Little Albert" (Watson and Rayner, 1920). Although he initially adored furry animals and showed no fear of rats, Little Albert learned to fear them when, during a laboratory demonstration, a loud noise was sounded every time he played with a cute and harmless white rat. In fact, the fear generalized to other furry objects, including rabbits and even a Santa Claus mask. (By the way, this demonstration would be considered unethical today and would never be conducted.)

Clearly, classical conditioning is in operation from the time of birth. One- and two-day-old newborns who are stroked on the head just before receiving a drop of sweet-tasting liquid soon learn to turn their heads and suck at the head-stroking alone (Blass et al., 1984; Dominguez et al., 1999).

Operant Conditioning. Infants also respond to operant conditioning. **Operant conditioning** is a form of learning in which a *voluntary* response is strengthened or weakened, depending on its association with positive or negative consequences. In operant conditioning, infants learn to act deliberately on their environments in order to bring about a desired consequence. An infant who learns that crying in a certain way attracts her parents' attention is displaying operant conditioning.

Like classical conditioning, operant conditioning functions from the earliest days of life. For instance, researchers have found that even newborns readily learn through operant conditioning to keep sucking on a nipple when it permits them to continue hearing their mothers read a story or to listen to music (DeCasper and Fifer, 1980; Lipsitt, 1986).

TABLE 2-4   THREE BASIC PROCESSES OF LEARNING

Type	Description	Example
Classical conditioning	A situation in which an organism learns to respond in a particular way to a neutral stimulus that normally does not bring about that type of response.	A hungry baby stops crying when her mother picks her up because she has learned to associate being picked up with subsequent feeding.
Operant conditioning	A form of learning in which a voluntary response is strengthened or weakened, depending on its positive or negative consequences.	An infant who learns that smiling at his or her parents brings positive attention might smile more often.
Habituation	The decrease in the response to a stimulus that occurs after repeated presentations of the same stimulus.	A baby who showed interest and surprise at first seeing a novel toy might show no interest after seeing the same toy several times.

Habituation.   Probably the most primitive form of learning is habituation. **Habituation** is the decrease in the response to a stimulus that occurs after repeated presentations of the same stimulus.

Habituation in infants relies on the fact that when newborns are presented with a new stimulus, they produce an *orienting response* in which they become quiet and attentive and experience a slowed heart rate as they take in the novel stimulus. When the novelty wears off, the infant no longer reacts. If a new and different stimulus is presented, the infant once again reacts with an orienting response. When this happens, we can say that the infant recognizes the original stimulus and can distinguish it from others.

Researchers have several ways of studying habituation. They examine changes in sucking, which stops temporarily when a new stimulus is presented. Other measures of habituation include changes in heart rate, respiration rate, and the length of time spent looking at a stimulus.

The development of habituation is linked to physical and cognitive maturation. It is present at birth and becomes more pronounced during the first 12 weeks. Difficulties with habituation are a sign of developmental problems (see Table 2-4; Moon, 2002).

Social Competence: Responding to Others

Soon after Kaita was born, her older brother looked into her crib and opened his mouth wide, pretending to be surprised. Kaita's mother was amazed when Kaita imitated his expression, opening her mouth as if *she* were surprised.

Researchers registered surprise of their own when they found that newborns could apparently imitate others' behaviour. Although infants have all the facial muscles needed to express basic emotions, the appearance of such expressions was assumed to be random. But beginning in the late 1970s, developmental researchers found that when a newborn was exposed to an adult modelling a behaviour that the infant had already performed spontaneously, such as opening the mouth or sticking out the tongue, the newborn appeared to imitate the behaviour (Meltzoff and Moore, 1977; Meltzoff and Moore, 2002; Nagy, 2006).

Even more exciting were findings from studies conducted by developmental psychologist Tiffany Field and her colleagues (Field, 1982; Field and Walden, 1982; Field et al., 1984). They first showed that infants could discriminate between such basic facial expressions as happiness, sadness, and surprise. The researchers then exposed newborns to an adult model with a happy, sad, or surprised facial expression. The results suggested that newborns produced a reasonably accurate imitation of the adult's expression.

This result was questioned, however, when subsequent research found consistent evidence for only one movement: sticking out the tongue. And even that seemed to disappear around the age of two months. Since it seems unlikely that imitation would be limited to a single gesture of only a few months' duration, researchers began to question the earlier findings. In fact, some researchers suggested that sticking out the tongue was not imitation, but merely an exploratory behaviour (Anisfeld, 1996; Bjorklund, 1997; Jones, 2006).

👁 Watch on **mydevelopmentlab**

Do you understand habituation?
To learn more about it, check MyDevelopmentLab for an Observations Video.

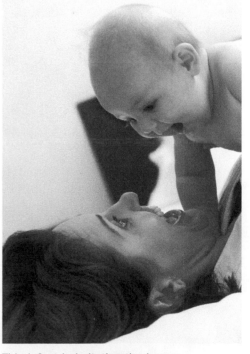

This infant is imitating the happy expressions of the adult. Why is this important?

states of arousal different degrees of sleep and wakefulness through which newborns cycle, ranging from deep sleep to great agitation

TABLE 2-5 FACTORS THAT ENCOURAGE SOCIAL INTERACTION BETWEEN FULL-TERM NEWBORNS AND THEIR PARENTS

Full-Term Newborn	Parent
Has organized states	Helps regulate infant's states
Attends selectively to certain stimuli	Provides these stimuli
Behaves in ways interpretable as specific communicative intent	Searches for communicative intent
Responds systematically to parent's acts	Wants to influence newborn, feel effective
Acts in temporally predictable ways	Adjusts actions to newborn's temporal rhythms
Learns from, adapts to parent's behaviour	Acts repetitively and predictably

Source: Eckerman and Oehler, 1992.

The jury is still out on exactly when true imitation begins, although it seems clear that some forms of imitation begin early. Imitative skills are important because effective social interactions rely in part on the ability to react to other people in an appropriate way and to understand the meaning of others' emotional states (Heimann, 2001; Meltzoff, 2002; Rogers and Williams, 2006; Zeedyk and Heimann, 2006).

Several other aspects of newborns' behaviour also act as forerunners for more formal types of social interaction that develop later. As shown in Table 2-5, certain characteristics of neonates mesh with parental behaviour to help produce a social relationship between child and parent, as well as relationships with others (Eckerman and Oehler, 1992).

For example, newborns cycle through various **states of arousal**—different degrees of sleep and wakefulness, that range from deep sleep to great agitation. Caregivers become involved in easing the baby through transitions from one state to another. For instance, a father who rhythmically rocks his crying daughter to calm her is engaged with her in a joint activity that is a prelude to future social interactions of different sorts. Similarly, newborns pay particular attention to their mother's voice, in part because they have become familiar with it after months in the womb. In turn, parents and others modify their speech when talking to infants to gain their attention and encourage interaction, using a different pitch and tempo than they use with older children and adults (DeCasper and Fifer, 1980; Trainor et al., 2000; Kisilevsky et al., 2003; Newman and Hussain, 2006).

The outcome of the social interactive capabilities of the newborn infant, and the responses from parents, is a paved path for future social interactions. In sum, then, neonates display remarkable physical, perceptual, *and* social capabilities.

From a child-care worker's perspective: Developmental researchers no longer view the neonate as a helpless, incompetent creature, but rather as a remarkably competent, developing human being. What do you think are some implications of this change in viewpoint for methods of childrearing and childcare?

REVIEW, CHECK, AND APPLY

REVIEW

- Newborns' respiratory and digestive systems begin to function at birth. They have an array of reflexes to help them eat, swallow, find food, and avoid unpleasant stimuli.
- Newborns' sensory competence includes the ability to distinguish objects in the visual field and to see colour differences, the ability to hear and to discern familiar sounds, and sensitivity to touch, odours, and tastes.
- The processes of classical conditioning, operant conditioning, and habituation demonstrate infants' learning capabilities.

CHECK YOURSELF

1. In order to survive the first few minutes or even days, infants are born with _____, or unlearned, organized, involuntary responses that occur automatically in the presence of certain stimuli.

2. Evidence suggests that infants have size constancy, meaning they are aware that objects stay the same size even though the size of the image on the retina varies with distance.

   - True
   - False

3. An infant learning through _____ learns to respond in a particular way to a neutral stimulus that would not normally bring about that type of response.

   a. reward
   b. classical conditioning
   c. operant conditioning
   d. social learning

APPLYING LIFESPAN DEVELOPMENT

- Can you think of examples of the use of classical conditioning on adults in everyday life, in such areas as entertainment, advertising, or politics?

Answers: 1) reflexes; 2) True; 3) b

Putting It All Together
Beginnings

Rachel and Jack, the parents we met in the chapter opener, looked forward to the birth of their second child. They speculated—as developmentalists do—about the role of genetics and environment in their children's development, considering issues like intelligence, resemblance, personality, schooling, and neighbourhood. For the birth itself, they had many options available. Rachel and Jack chose to use a midwife rather than an obstetrician and to give birth at a traditional hospital, but in a non-traditional way. And when their baby was born, both felt pride and happiness as baby Eva reacted to the sound of her mother's voice, which she had heard from her intimate perch inside Rachel's body.

MODULE **2.1** Prenatal Development

- Rachel and Jack considered the role of genetics (nature) versus environment (nurture) in thinking about what their child would be like **(pp. 36–37).**

- Like all parents, Rachel and Jack contributed 23 chromosomes each at conception. Their baby's sex was determined from the particular mix of one pair of chromosomes **(p. 38).**

- They also considered how their new child would develop physically, intellectually (or cognitively), and socially **(pp. 45–49).**

MODULE **2.2** Prenatal Growth and Change

- Many of Eva's characteristics will have a strong genetic component, but virtually all will represent some combination of genetics and environment **(pp. 45–49).**

- Eva's prenatal development started as a fetus and progressed through a number of stages **(p. 54).**

- Rachel's labour was intense and painful, although others experience labour in different ways due to individual and cultural differences **(pp. 63–67)**.

- Rachel chose to use a midwife, one of several new birthing methods **(p. 66)**.

- Like the vast majority of births, Eva's was completely normal and successful **(p. 68)**.

- Although Baby Eva seemed helpless and dependent, she actually possessed from birth an array of useful capabilities and skills **(pp. 73–78)**.

What would a PARENT do?

- What strategies would you use to prepare yourself for the upcoming birth of your child?

- How would you evaluate the different options for prenatal care and delivery?

- How would you prepare your older child for the birth of a new baby?

    HINT Review pages 57–67.

    What's your response?

What would a HEALTH-CARE PROVIDER do?

- How would you prepare Rachel and Jack for the upcoming birth of their baby?

- How would you respond to their concerns and anxieties?

- What would tell them about the different options they have for giving birth?

    HINT Review pages 57–67, 71–73.

    What's your response?

What would an EDUCATOR do?

- What strategies might you use to teach Rachel and Jack about the stages of pregnancy and the process of birth?

- What might you tell them about infancy to prepare them for caring for their child?

    HINT Review pages 65–66, 73–78.

    What's your response?

What would YOU do?

- What would you say to Rachel and Jack about the impending birth of their child?

- What advice would you give to Rachel and Jack about prenatal care and their decision about the use of a midwife?

    HINT Review pages 65–66.

    What's your response?

3 Infancy

T he first few months of Alex's infancy went by in a blur. Although everyone had warned his parents that their lives would change with his birth, they weren't prepared for the sheer amount of work that infancy would require. Not only were they physically exhausted from a lack of sleep, but the many decisions they had to make were daunting.

How should they respond when Alex began to cry in the middle of the night? Should Leigh only breast-feed Alex or supplement breast-feeding with a bottle? Should they use cloth or disposable diapers? Should they call their physician when Alex, who was occasionally fussy after meals, got diarrhea? What kind of mobile should hang over Alex's crib? How should they try to encourage Alex's physical and intellectual development?

Yet there was not a moment when they questioned their decision to have a child. Alex was good-looking, strong, and growing rapidly. He generally had a wonderful disposition. The best time of day was the morning, right after he woke up, when he showered his parents with huge, toothless smiles. His smiles could melt anyone's heart, and his parents were entranced. Alex was the best!

MODULE 3.1 Physical Development in Infancy

What basic reflexes are we born with? see page 84.

MODULE 3.2 Cognitive Development in Infancy

Do infants have a memory?

see page 103.

All infants, whether they have good dispositions like Alex or are fussy and demanding, are engaging, energetic, and challenging. They change constantly as they develop physically, cognitively, socially—and find their own unique personality.

In this chapter, we examine infancy, the period of the lifespan that starts at birth and continues through the first two years of life. We'll first discuss the ways in which infants grow physically and examine their remarkably rapid progress from largely instinctual beings to individuals with a range of complex physical abilities.

Turning to infants' cognitive development, we'll discuss the notion of stages of development, as well as some alternative views. We'll consider the amazing growth in learning, memory, and language that infants experience—and adults witness with awe.

Finally we will examine social and personality development. We will look at personality and temperament and observe how gender differences are a matter of both genes and environment. We'll see how infants begin to develop as social beings, moving from interactions with their parents to relations with other adults and children.

Above all, we'll marvel at the rate of infants' progress, and we will get a preview of the ways in which characteristics that emerge from infancy continue to influence the individual into adulthood. As we proceed, keep in mind how the seeds of our futures appear in our earliest beginnings.

MODULE **3.3** Social and Personality Development in Infancy

Do infants know who they are?

see page 123.

MyVirtualLife

What decisions would you make while raising an infant? What would the consequences of those decisions be?

Find out by logging onto My Virtual Life and raising your child from birth to 18 years.

MODULE 3.1 Physical Development in Infancy

First Steps

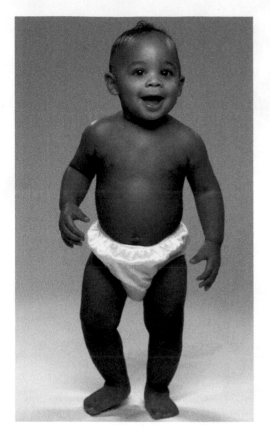

We had intimations that his first steps would not be too far in the future. Josh had previously dragged himself up, and, clutching the side of chairs and tables, managed to progress slowly around our living room. For the last few weeks, he'd even been able to stand, unmoving, for several moments without holding on.

But walking? It seemed too early: Josh was only 10 months old, and the books we read told us that most children would not take their first steps on their own until they were a year old. Our older son, Jon, hadn't walked until he was 14 months of age.

So when Josh suddenly lurched forward, taking one awkward step after another, away from the safety of the furniture, and moved toward the centre of the room, we were astounded. Despite the appearance that he was about to keel over at any second, he moved one, then two, then three steps forward, until our awe at his accomplishment overtook our ability to count each step.

Josh tottered all the way across the room, until he reached the other side. Not quite knowing how to stop, he toppled over, landing in a happy heap. It was a moment of pure glory.

Josh's first steps at 10 months were just one in the succession of milestones that characterize the dramatic physical attainments of infancy. In this module we consider the nature of physical development during infancy, a period that starts at birth and continues until the second birthday. We begin by discussing the pace of growth during infancy, noting obvious changes in height and weight as well as less apparent changes in the nervous system. We also consider how infants quickly develop increasingly stable patterns in such basic activities as sleeping, eating, and attending to the world.

Our discussion then turns to infants' thrilling gains in motor development as skills emerge that eventually will allow an infant to roll over, take the first step, and pick up a cookie crumb from the floor—skills that ultimately form the basis of later, even more complex behaviours. We start with basic, genetically determined reflexes and consider how even these can be modified through experience. We also discuss the nature and timing of the development of particular physical skills, look at whether their emergence can be speeded up, and consider the importance of early nutrition to infants' development.

Finally, we explore how infants' senses develop. We investigate how sensory systems like hearing and vision operate, and how infants sort through the raw data from their sense organs and transform it into meaningful information.

Growth and Stability

LEARNING OBJECTIVES

LO1 How do the human body and nervous system develop?

LO2 Does the environment affect the pattern of development?

LO3 What developmental tasks must infants accomplish in this period?

The average newborn weighs just over 3 kg, which is less than the weight of the average Thanksgiving turkey. His length is about 50 cm, shorter than a loaf of French bread. She is helpless; if left to fend for herself, she could not survive.

Yet after just a few years, the story is very different. Babies become much larger, they are mobile, and they become increasingly independent. How does this growth happen? We can answer this question first by describing the changes in weight and height that occur over the first two years of life, and then by examining some of the principles that underlie and direct that growth.

Physical Growth: The Rapid Advances of Infancy

Infants grow at a rapid pace over the first two years of their lives (see Figure 3-1). By the age of five months, the average infant's birth weight has doubled to around 7 kg. By the first birthday, the baby's weight has tripled to about 10 kg. Although the pace of weight gain slows during the second year, it continues to increase. By the end of her second year, the average child weighs around four times as much as she did at birth. Of course, there is a good deal of variation among infants. Height and weight measurements, which are taken regularly during physician's visits in a baby's first year, provide a way to spot problems in development.

The weight gains of infancy are matched by increased length. By the end of the first year, the typical baby grows almost 50 percent taller, to 77 cm. By their second birthdays, children average a height of 91 cms.

Not all parts of an infant's body grow at the same rate. For instance, at birth the head accounts for one-quarter of the newborn's entire body size. During the first two years of life, the rest of the body begins to catch up. By the age of two the baby's head is only one-fifth of body length, and by adulthood it is only one-eighth (see Figure 3-2).

There are also gender differences in weight and length. Girls generally are slightly shorter and weigh slightly less than boys, and these differences remain throughout childhood (and, as we will see later in the book, the disparities become considerably greater during adolescence).

Four Principles of Growth. The disproportionately large size of infants' heads at birth is an example of one of four major principles that govern growth. The **cephalocaudal principle** states that growth follows a direction and pattern that begins with the head and upper body parts and then proceeds to the rest of the body. The word *cephalocaudal* is derived from Greek and Latin roots meaning "head-to-tail." The cephalocaudal growth principle means that we develop visual abilities (located in the head) well before we master the ability to walk (closer to the end of the body). The cephalocaudal principle operates both prenatally and after birth.

Three other principles (summarized in Table 3-1) help explain the patterns by which growth occurs. The **proximodistal principle** states that development proceeds from the centre of the body outward—that the trunk of the body grows before the extremities of the arms and legs. Similarly, only after growth has occurred in the arms and legs can the fingers and toes grow. Related to this is the way complex skills build upon simpler ones. The **principle of hierarchical integration** states that simple skills typically develop separately and independently. Later, however, these simple skills are integrated into more complex ones. Thus, the relatively complex skill of grasping something in the hand cannot be mastered until the developing infant learns how to control—and integrate—the movements of the individual fingers. Finally, the fourth and last major principle of growth is the **principle of the independence of systems**,

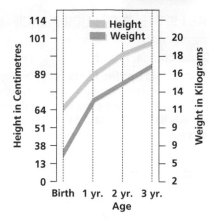

FIGURE 3-1 Height and Weight Growth
Although the greatest increase in height and weight occurs during the first year of life, children continue to grow throughout infancy and toddlerhood.
Source: Adapted from Cratty, B. J. (1979). *Perceptual and Motor Development in Infants and Children*, 2e, pg. 222. © Copyright © 1979 Pearson Education, Inc. Reprinted with permission of Pearson Education, Inc.

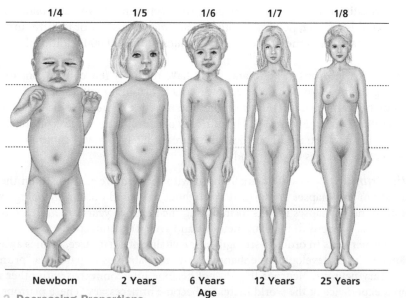

FIGURE 3-2 Decreasing Proportions
At birth, the head represents one-quarter of the neonate's body. By adulthood, the head is only one-eighth the size of the body. Why is the neonate's head so large?

cephalocaudal principle the principle that growth follows a pattern that begins with the head and upper body parts and then proceeds down to the rest of the body

proximodistal principle the principle that development proceeds from the centre of the body outward

principle of hierarchical integration the principle that simple skills typically develop separately and independently but are later integrated into more complex skills

principle of the independence of systems the principle that different body systems grow at different rates

TABLE 3-1 THE MAJOR PRINCIPLES GOVERNING GROWTH

Cephalocaudal Principle	Proximodistal Principle	Principle of Hierarchical Integration	Principle of the Independence of Systems
Growth follows a pattern that begins with the head and upper body parts and then proceeds to the rest of the body. Based on Greek and Latin roots meaning "head-to-tail."	Development proceeds from the centre of the body outward. Based on the Latin words for "near" and "far."	Simple skills typically develop separately and independently. Later they are integrated into more complex skills.	Different body systems grow at different rates.

which suggests that different body systems grow at different rates. This principle means that growth in one system does not necessarily imply that growth is occurring in others. For instance, the patterns of growth for body size, the nervous system, and sexual characteristics are independent.

The Nervous System and Brain: The Foundations of Development

When Rina was born, she was the first baby among her parents' circle of friends. These young adults marvelled at the infant, oohing and aahing at every sneeze and smile and whimper, trying to guess their meaning. Whatever feelings, movements, and thoughts Rina was experiencing, they were all brought about by the same complex network: the infant's nervous system. The *nervous system* comprises the brain and the nerves that extend throughout the body.

Neurons are the basic cells of the nervous system. Figure 3-3 shows the structure of an adult neuron. Like all cells in the body, neurons have a cell body containing a nucleus. But unlike other cells, neurons have a distinct ability: They can communicate with other cells, using a cluster of fibres called *dendrites* at one end. Dendrites receive messages from other cells. At their opposite end, neurons have a long extension called an *axon*, the part of the neuron that carries messages destined for other neurons. Neurons do not actually touch one another. Rather, they communicate with other neurons by means of chemical messengers, or *neurotransmitters*, that travel across the small gaps known as **synapses**, between neurons.

Although estimates vary, infants are born with between 100 and 200 billion neurons. In order to reach this number, neurons multiply at an amazing rate prior to birth. In fact, at some points in prenatal development, cell division creates some 250 000 additional neurons every minute.

At birth, most neurons in an infant's brain have relatively few connections to other neurons. During the first two years of life, however, a baby's brain will establish billions of new connections between neurons. Furthermore, the network of neurons becomes increasingly complex, as illustrated in Figure 3-4. The intricacy of neural connections continues to increase throughout life. In fact, in adulthood a single neuron is likely to have a minimum of 5000 connections to other neurons or other body parts.

Synaptic Pruning. Babies are actually born with many more neurons than they need. In addition, although synapses are formed throughout life based on our changing experiences, the billions of new synapses infants form during the first two years are more numerous than necessary. What happens to the extra neurons and synaptic connections?

Like a farmer who, in order to strengthen the vitality of a fruit tree, prunes away unnecessary branches, brain development enhances certain capabilities in part by a "pruning down" of unnecessary neurons. Neurons that do not become interconnected with other neurons as the infant's experience of the world increases become unnecessary. These neurons eventually die out, increasing the efficiency of the nervous system.

Watch on **mydevelopmentlab**

To watch an animation of the synaptic development process you just read about, log onto MyDevelopmentLab.

neuron the basic nerve cell of the nervous system

synapse the gap at the connection between neurons, through which neurons chemically communicate with one another

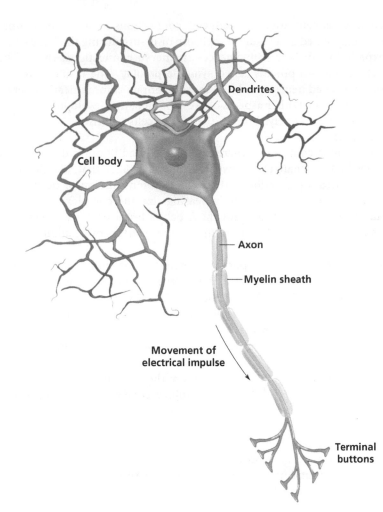

FIGURE 3-3 The Neuron
The basic element of the nervous system, the neuron comprises a number of components.
Source: From Kent Van De Graff, *Human Anatomy*, 5e. Copyright © 2000 The McGraw-Hill Companies. Reprinted with permission.

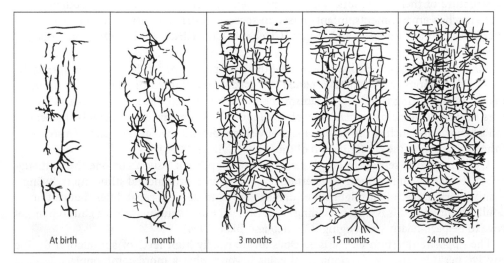

FIGURE 3-4 Neuron Networks
Over the first two years of life, networks of neurons become increasingly complex and interconnected. Why are these connections important?
Source: From THE POSTNATAL DEVELOPMENT OF THE HUMAN CEREBRAL CORTEX, Vol I–VIII by Jesse LeRoy Conel, Cambridge, Mass.: Harvard University Press, Copyright © 1939, 1975 by the President and Fellows of Harvard College.

As unnecessary neurons are being reduced, connections between remaining neurons are expanded or eliminated as a result of their use or disuse during the baby's experiences. If a baby's experiences do not stimulate certain nerve connections, these, like unused neurons, are eliminated—a process called **synaptic pruning**. The result of synaptic pruning is to allow established neurons to build more elaborate communication networks with other neurons. Unlike most other aspects of growth, then, the development of the nervous system proceeds most effectively through the loss of cells (Johnson, 1998; Mimura et al., 2003; Iglesias et al., 2005).

After birth, neurons continue to increase in size. In addition to dendrite growth, the axons of neurons become coated with **myelin**, a fatty substance that, like the insulation on an electric wire, provides protection and speeds the transmission of nerve impulses. So even though many neurons are lost, the increasing size and complexity of the remaining ones contribute to impressive brain growth. A baby's brain triples in weight during the first two years of life, and it reaches more than three-quarters of its adult weight and size by age two.

As they grow, the neurons also reposition themselves, becoming arranged by function. Some move into the **cerebral cortex**, the upper layer of the brain, while others move to *subcortical levels*, which are below the cerebral cortex. The subcortical levels, which regulate such fundamental activities as breathing and heart rate, are the most fully developed at birth. As time passes, however, the cells in the cerebral cortex, which are responsible for higher-order processes such as thinking and reasoning, become more developed and interconnected.

Although the brain is protected by the bones of the skull, it is highly sensitive to some forms of injury. One particularly devastating injury comes from a form of child abuse called *shaken baby syndrome,* in which an infant is shaken by a caretaker, usually out of frustration or anger due to a baby's crying. Shaking can lead the brain to rotate within the skull, causing blood vessels to tear and destroying the intricate connections between neurons. Shaken baby syndrome produces severe medical problems, long-term physical and learning disabilities, and often death (Gerber and Coffman, 2007; Jayawant and Parr, 2007).

Environmental Influences on Brain Development. Brain development, much of which unfolds automatically because of genetically predetermined patterns, is also strongly susceptible to environmental influences. In fact, the brain's **plasticity**, the degree to which a developing structure or behaviour is modifiable due to experience, is relatively great. For instance, as we've seen, an infant's sensory experience affects both the size of individual neurons and the structure of their interconnections. Consequently, compared with those brought up in more enriched environments, infants raised in severely restricted settings are likely to show differences in brain structure and weight (Cicchetti, 2003; Cirulli et al., 2003; Couperus and Nelson, 2006).

Furthermore, researchers have found that there are particular sensitive periods during the course of development. A **sensitive period** is a specific but limited time, usually early in an organism's life, during which the organism is particularly susceptible to environmental influences relating to some particular facet of development. A sensitive period can be associated with a behaviour—such as the development of vision—or with the development of a structure of the body, such as the configuration of the brain (Uylings, 2006).

The existence of sensitive periods raises several important issues. For one thing, it suggests that unless an infant receives a certain level of early environmental stimulation during a sensitive period, the infant might suffer damage or fail to develop capabilities that can never be fully regained. If this is true, providing successful later intervention for such children might prove to be particularly challenging (Gottlieb and Blair, 2004).

The opposite question also arises: Does an unusually high level of stimulation during sensitive periods produce developmental gains beyond what a more commonplace level of stimulation would provide?

Such questions have no simple answers. Determining how unusually impoverished or enriched environments affect later development is one of the major questions addressed by developmental researchers as they try to find ways to maximize opportunities for developing

synaptic pruning the elimination of neurons as the result of disuse or lack of stimulation

myelin a fatty substance that helps insulate neurons and speeds the transmission of nerve impulses

cerebral cortex the upper layer of the brain

plasticity the degree to which a developing structure or behaviour is modifiable due to experience

sensitive period a specific, but limited, time, usually early in an organism's life, during which the organism is particularly susceptible to environmental influences relating to some particular facet of development

children. In the meantime, many developmentalists suggest that there are many simple ways parents and caregivers can provide a stimulating environment that will encourage healthy brain growth. Cuddling with, talking and singing to, and playing with babies—all help enrich their environment (Lafuente et al., 1997; Garlick, 2003).

> ⊙ **From a social worker's perspective:** What are some cultural or subcultural influences that might affect parents' childrearing practices?

rhythms repetitive, cyclical patterns of behaviour

state the degree of awareness an infant displays to both internal and external stimulation

Integrating the Bodily Systems: The Life Cycles of Infancy

If you happen to overhear new parents discuss their newborns, chances are that one or several bodily functions will come up. In the first days of life, infants' body rhythms—waking, eating, sleeping, and eliminating waste—govern the infant's behaviour, often at seemingly random times.

These most basic activities are controlled by a variety of bodily systems. Although each of these individual behavioural patterns probably is functioning quite effectively, it takes some time and effort for infants to integrate the separate behaviours. In fact, one of the neonate's major missions is to make its individual behaviours work in harmony, helping it, for example, to sleep through the night (Ingersoll and Thoman, 1999; Waterhouse and DeCoursey, 2004).

Rhythms and States. One of the most important ways that behaviour becomes integrated is through the development of various **rhythms**, which are repetitive, cyclical patterns of behaviour. Some rhythms are immediately obvious, such as the change from wakefulness to sleep. Others are more subtle but still easily noticeable, such as breathing and sucking. Still other rhythms require careful observation to be noticed. For instance, newborns may go through periods in which they jerk their legs in a regular pattern every minute or so. Although some of these rhythms are apparent just after birth, others emerge slowly over the first year as the neurons of the nervous system become increasingly integrated (Thelen and Bates, 2003).

One major body rhythm is an infant's **state**—the degree of awareness he or she displays to both internal and external stimulation. States include various levels of wakeful behaviours, such as alertness, fussing, and crying, and different levels of sleep as well. Each change in state brings about a change in the amount of stimulation required to get the infant's attention (Diambra and Menna-Barreto, 2004).

Sleep: Perchance to Dream? At the beginning of infancy, sleep is the major state that occupies a baby's time—much to the relief of exhausted parents who often regard sleep as a welcome respite from caregiving responsibilities. On average, newborn infants sleep some 16 to 17 hours a day. However, there are wide variations. Some sleep more than 20 hours, while others sleep as little as 10 hours a day (Peirano et al., 2003; Buysse, 2005).

Infants sleep a lot, but you shouldn't wish to "sleep like a baby." The sleep of infants comes in fits and starts. Rather than covering one long stretch, sleep initially comes in spurts of around two hours, followed by periods of wakefulness. Because of this, infants—and their sleep-deprived parents—are "out of sync" with the rest of the world, for whom sleep comes at night and wakefulness during the day (Groome et al., 1997; Burnham et al., 2002). Most babies do not sleep through the night for several months. Parents' sleep is interrupted, sometimes several times a night, by the infant's cries for food and physical contact.

Luckily for their parents, infants gradually settle into a more adult-like pattern. After a week, babies sleep a bit more at night and are awake for slightly longer periods during the day. Typically, by 16 weeks infants begin to sleep as much as 6 continuous hours at night, and daytime sleep falls into regular nap-like patterns. Most infants sleep through the night by the end of the first year, and the total amount of sleep they need each day is reduced to about 15 hours (Mao, 2004).

Hidden beneath the supposedly tranquil sleep of infants is another cyclic pattern. During periods of sleep, an infant's heart rate increases and becomes irregular, their blood pressure

Infants sleep in spurts, often making them out of sync with the rest of the world.

rises, and they begin to breathe more rapidly (Montgomery-Downs and Thomas, 1998). Sometimes, although not always, their closed eyes begin to move in a back-and-forth pattern, as if they were viewing an action-packed scene. This period of active sleep is similar, although not identical, to the **rapid eye movement (REM) sleep** of older children and adults, and it is associated with dreaming.

At first, this active, REM-like sleep takes up around one-half of an infant's sleep, compared with just 20 percent of an adult's sleep (see Figure 3-5). However, the quantity of active sleep quickly declines, and by the age of six months, it amounts to just one-third of total sleep time (Burnham et al., 2002; Staunton, 2005).

The appearance of active sleep periods that are similar to REM sleep in adults raises the intriguing question of whether infants dream during those periods. No one knows the answer, although it seems unlikely. First of all, young infants do not have much to dream about, given their relatively limited experiences. Furthermore, the brain waves of sleeping infants appear to be qualitatively different from those of adults who are dreaming. It is not until the baby reaches three or four months of age that the wave patterns become similar to those of dreaming adults, suggesting that young infants are not dreaming during active sleep—or at least are not doing so in the same way adults do (McCall, 1979; Parmelee and Sigman, 1983; Zampi et al., 2002).

What is the function then of REM sleep in infants? Although we don't know for certain, some researchers think it provides a means for the brain to stimulate itself—a process called *autostimulation* (Roffwarg et al., 1966). Stimulation of the nervous system is particularly important in infants who spend so much time sleeping and relatively little in alert states.

Infants' sleep cycles seem largely preprogrammed by genetic factors, but environmental influences also play a part. For instance, cultural practices affect infants' sleep patterns. Among the Kipsigis of Africa, infants sleep with their mothers at night and are allowed to nurse whenever they wake. In the daytime, they accompany their mothers during daily

rapid eye movement (REM) sleep a period of sleep in older children and adults; associated with dreaming

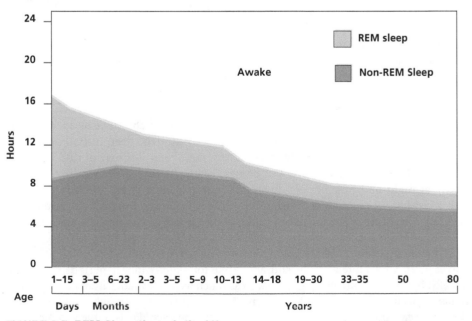

FIGURE 3-5 REM Sleep through the Lifespan
As we age, the proportion of REM sleep increases as the proportion of non-REM sleep declines. In addition, the total amount of sleep declines as we get older.
Source: Adapted from Roffwarg, Muzio, and Dement, 1966.

chores, often napping while strapped to their mothers' backs. Because they are often out and on the go, Kipsigis infants do not sleep through the night until much later than babies in Western societies, and for the first eight months of life, they seldom sleep longer than three hours at a stretch. In comparison, eight-month-old infants in Western societies might sleep as long as eight hours at a time (Super and Harkness, 1982; Anders and Taylor, 1994; Gerard et al., 2002).

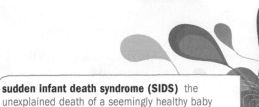

sudden infant death syndrome (SIDS) the unexplained death of a seemingly healthy baby

SIDS: The Unanticipated Killer

For a tiny percentage of infants, the rhythm of sleep is interrupted by a deadly affliction: sudden infant death syndrome, or SIDS. **Sudden infant death syndrome (SIDS)** is a disorder in which seemingly healthy infants die in their sleep. Put to bed for a nap or for the night, an infant simply never wakes up.

SIDS strikes about 1 in 2000 infants in Canada each year. Although it seems to occur when the normal patterns of breathing during sleep are interrupted, scientists have been unable to discover why that might happen. It is clear that infants don't smother or choke; they die a peaceful death, simply ceasing to breathe (Rusen et al., 2004). Some research suggests impaired brain function caused by maternal alcohol use and smoking; autopsy reveals dysfunction in the medulla, a part of the brain involved in regulating autonomic functions like breathing, heart rate, and temperature control (Kinney et al., 2003).

While no reliable means for preventing the syndrome has been found, the Canadian Paediatric Society recommends that babies sleep on their backs rather than on their sides or stomachs—called the *back-to-sleep* guideline. Interestingly, pacifier use at nap and bedtime is associated with decreased risk of SIDS. Risk is increased when infants are exposed to second-hand smoke or when put to sleep in unsafe locations such as with soft bedding or pillows on a couch. Certain conditions of bedsharing also increase risk: if the adult is a smoker, is exhausted or impaired by drugs or alcohol, or is not used to bedsharing with the infant (Canadian Paediatric Society, 2004).

The number of deaths from SIDS has decreased significantly since these guidelines were developed. Still, SIDS is the leading cause of death in the first year (Eastman, 2003; Daley, 2004).

REVIEW, CHECK, AND APPLY

REVIEW

- The major principles of growth are the cephalocaudal principle, the proximodistal principle, the principle of hierarchical integration, and the principle of the independence of systems.

- The development of the nervous system first entails the development of billions of neurons and interconnections among them. Later, the numbers of both neurons and connections decrease as a result of the infant's experiences.

- Babies integrate their individual behaviours by developing rhythms—repetitive, cyclical patterns of behaviour.

CHECK YOURSELF

1. The _____ principle states that growth begins with the head and proceeds down to the rest of the body; the _____ principle states that development proceeds from the centre of the body outward.

 a. cephalocaudal; proximodistal

 b. proximodistal; cephalocaudal

 c. hierarchical integration; independence of systems

 d. independence of systems; hierarchical integration

2. The process of synaptic pruning allows established neurons to build stronger networks and reduces unnecessary neurons during the first two years of life.

 - True

 - False

3. Although brain development is largely genetically predetermined, it is also susceptible to environmental experiences; the ability of the brain to be modifiable by the environment is called (a) _____.

 a. plasticity

 b. synaptic pruning

 c. sensitive period

 d. critical period

APPLYING LIFESPAN DEVELOPMENT

- What evolutionary advantage could there be for infants to be born with more nerve cells than they actually need or use? How might our understanding of synaptic pruning affect the way we treat infants?

Answers: 1) a; 2) True; 3) a

Motor Development

LEARNING OBJECTIVES

LO4 What are reflexes and what purpose do they serve?

LO5 What is the role of nutrition in physical development?

Suppose you were hired by a genetic engineering firm to redesign newborns and were charged with replacing the current version with a new, more mobile one. The first change you'd probably consider in carrying out this (luckily fictitious) job would be in the conformation and composition of the baby's body.

The shape and proportions of newborn babies simply are not conducive to easy mobility. Their heads are so large and heavy that young infants lack the strength to raise them. Because their limbs are short in relation to the rest of their body, movements are further impeded. Furthermore, their bodies are mainly fat, with a limited amount of muscle; the result is that newborns lack strength.

Fortunately, infants soon begin to develop a remarkable amount of mobility. In fact, even at birth they have an extensive repertoire of behavioural possibilities brought about by innate reflexes, and their range of motor skills grows rapidly during the first two years of life.

Reflexes: Our Inborn Physical Skills

When her father pressed three-day-old Christina's palm with his finger, she responded by tightly winding her small fist around his finger and grasping it. When he moved his finger upward, she held on so tightly that it seemed he might be able to lift her completely off her crib floor.

The Basic Reflexes. In fact, her father was right: Christina probably could have been lifted in this way. The reason for her resolute grip was activation of one of the dozens of reflexes with which infants are born. **Reflexes** are unlearned, organized, involuntary responses that occur automatically in the presence of certain stimuli. Newborns enter the world with a repertoire of reflexive behavioural patterns that help them adapt to their new surroundings and serve to protect them.

reflexes unlearned, organized, involuntary responses that occur automatically in the presence of certain stimuli

TABLE 3-2 SOME BASIC REFLEXES IN INFANTS

Reflex	Approximate Age of Disappearance	Description	Possible Function
Rooting reflex	3 weeks	Neonate's tendency to turn its head toward things that touch its cheek.	Food intake
Stepping reflex	2 months	Movement of legs when held upright with feet touching the floor.	Prepares infants for independent locomotion
Swimming reflex	4–6 months	Infant's tendency to paddle and kick in a sort of swimming motion when lying face down in a body of water.	Avoidance of danger
Moro reflex	6 months	Activated when support for the neck and head is suddenly removed. The arms of the infant are thrust outward and then appear to grasp onto something.	Similar to primate's protection from falling
Babinski reflex	8–12 months	An infant fans out its toes in response to a stroke on the outside of its foot.	Unknown
Startle reflex	Remains in different form	An infant, in response to a sudden noise, flings out arms, arches its back, and spreads its fingers.	Protection
Eye-blink reflex	Remains	Rapid shutting and opening of eye on exposure to direct light.	Protection of eye from direct light
Sucking reflex	Remains	Infant's tendency to suck at things that touch its lips.	Food intake
Gag reflex	Remains	An infant's reflex to clear its throat.	Prevents choking

As we can see from the list of reflexes in Table 3-2, many reflexes clearly represent behaviour that has survival value, helping to ensure the well-being of the infant. For instance, the *swimming reflex* makes a baby who is lying face down in a body of water paddle and kick in a sort of swimming motion. The obvious consequence of such behaviour is to help the baby move from danger and survive until a caregiver can come to its rescue. Similarly, the *eye-blink reflex* seems designed to protect the eye from too much direct light, which might damage the retina.

Given the protective value of many reflexes, it might seem beneficial for them to remain with us for our entire lives. In fact, some do: The eye-blink reflex remains functional throughout the full lifespan. On the other hand, quite a few reflexes, such as the swimming reflex, disappear after a few months. Why should this be the case?

Researchers who focus on evolutionary explanations of development attribute the gradual disappearance of reflexes to the increase in voluntary control over behaviour that occurs as infants become more able to control their muscles. In addition, it might be that reflexes form the foundation for future, more complex behaviours. As these more intricate behaviours become well learned, they encompass the earlier reflexes. Finally, it is possible that reflexes stimulate parts of the brain responsible for more complex behaviours, helping them develop (Myklebust and Gottlieb, 1993; Zelazo, 1998; Lipsitt, 2003).

Ethnic and Cultural Differences and Similarities in Reflexes. Although reflexes are, by definition, genetically determined and universal throughout all infants, there are actually some cultural variations in the ways they are displayed. For instance, consider the *Moro reflex* (often called the *startle response*, but not to be confused with the startle reflex), which is activated when support for the neck and head is suddenly removed. The Moro reflex consists of the infant's arms thrusting outward and then appearing to seek to grasp onto something. Most scientists feel that the Moro reflex represents a leftover response that we humans have inherited from our nonhuman ancestors. The Moro reflex is an extremely useful behaviour for monkey babies, who travel about by clinging to their mothers' backs. If they lose their grip, they fall down unless they are able to grasp quickly onto their mother's fur—using a Moro-like reflex (Prechtl, 1982; Zafeiriou, 2004).

The Moro reflex is found in all humans, but it appears with significantly different vigour in different children. Some differences reflect cultural and ethnic variations (Freedman and

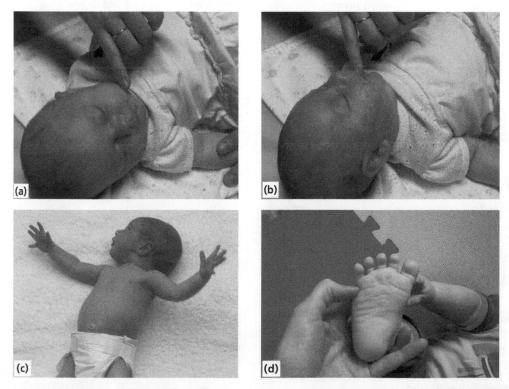

Infants showing (a, b) the rooting reflex, (c) the startle reflex, and (d) the Babinski reflex.

DeBoer 1979). For example, differences in the Moro reflex have been observed between Caucasian and Aboriginal infants (and between Aboriginal groups). These differences are believed to reflect genetic variability related to temperament (which will be discussed in Module 3.3).

Motor Development in Infancy: Landmarks of Physical Achievement

Probably no physical changes are more obvious—and more eagerly anticipated—than the increasing array of motor skills that babies acquire during infancy. Most parents can remember their child's first steps with a sense of pride and awe at how quickly she or he changed from a helpless infant, unable even to roll over, into a person who could navigate quite effectively in the world.

Gross Motor Skills. Even though the motor skills of newborn infants are not terribly sophisticated, at least compared with attainments that will soon appear, young infants still are able to accomplish some kinds of movement. For instance, when placed on their stomachs they wiggle their arms and legs and may try to lift their heavy heads. As their strength increases, they are able to push hard enough against the surface on which they are resting to propel their bodies in different directions. They often end up moving backwards rather than forwards, but by the age of six months they become rather accomplished at moving themselves in particular directions. These initial efforts are the forerunners of crawling, in which babies coordinate the motions of their arms and legs and propel themselves forward. Crawling appears typically between 8 and 10 months. (Figure 3-6 provides a summary of some of the milestones of normal motor development.)

Walking comes later. At around nine months, most infants are able to walk by supporting themselves on furniture, and half of all infants can walk well by the end of their first year of life.

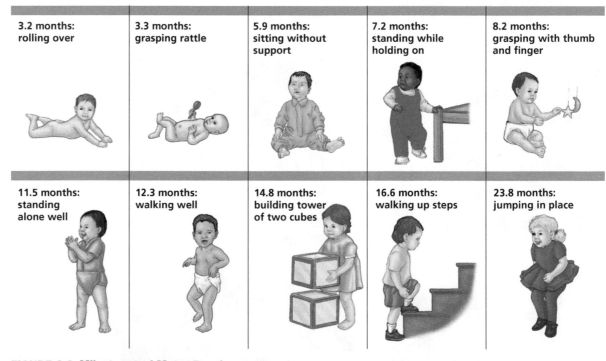

FIGURE 3-6 Milestones of Motor Development
Fifty percent of children are able to perform each skill at the month indicated in the figure. However, the specific timing at which each skill appears varies widely. For example, one-quarter of children are able to walk well at 11 months; by 15 months, 90% of children are walking well. Is knowledge of such average benchmarks helpful or harmful to parents?
Source: Adapted from Frankenburg et al., 1992.

At the same time infants are learning to move around, they are perfecting the ability to remain in a stationary sitting position. At first, babies cannot remain seated upright without support. But they quickly master this ability, and most are able to sit without support by the age of six months.

Fine Motor Skills. At the same time infants are perfecting their gross motor skills, such as sitting upright and walking, they are also making advances in their fine motor skills (see Table 3-3). For instance, by the age of three months, infants show some ability to coordinate the movements of their limbs.

Furthermore, although infants are born with a rudimentary ability to reach toward an object, this ability is neither very sophisticated nor very accurate, and it disappears around the age of four weeks. A different, more precise, form of reaching reappears at four months. It takes some time for infants to coordinate successful grasping after they reach out, but in fairly short order they are able to reach out and hold onto an object of interest (Claxton et al., 2003).

The sophistication of an infant's fine motor skills continues to grow. By the age of 11 months, infants are able to pick up off the ground objects as small as marbles—something caregivers need to be concerned about, since the next place such objects often go is the mouth. By the time they are two years old, children can carefully hold a cup, bring it to their lips, and take a drink without spilling a drop.

Grasping, like other motor advances, follows a sequential developmental pattern in which simple skills are combined into more sophisticated ones. For example, infants first begin picking things up with their whole hand. As they get older, they use a *pincer grasp,* where thumb and index finger meet to form a circle. The pincer grasp allows for considerably more precise motor control.

Developmental Norms: Comparing the Individual to the Group. Keep in mind that the timing of the milestones in motor development that we have been discussing is based on norms. **Norms** represent the average performance of a large sample of children of a given age. They permit comparisons between a particular child's performance on a particular behaviour, and the average performance of the children in the norm sample.

For instance, one of the most widely used techniques to determine infants' normative standing is the **Brazelton Neonatal Behavioral Assessment Scale (NBAS)**, a measure designed to determine infants' neurological and behavioural responses to their environment.

The NBAS takes about 30 minutes to administer and includes 27 separate categories of responses that constitute four general aspects of infants' behaviour: interactions with others (such as alertness and cuddliness); motor behaviour; physiological control (such as the ability to be soothed after being upset); and responses to stress (Brazelton, 1973, 1990; Davis and Emory, 1995; Canals et al., 2003).

Although the norms provided by scales such as the NBAS are useful in making broad generalizations about the timing of various behaviours and skills, they must be interpreted with caution. Because norms are averages, they mask substantial individual differences in the times when children attain various achievements.

Norms are useful only to the extent that they are based on data from a large, heterogeneous, culturally diverse sample of children. Unfortunately, many of the norms on which developmental researchers have traditionally relied have been based on groups of infants who are predominantly Caucasian and from the middle and upper socioeconomic strata (for example, Gesell, 1946). The reason: much of the research was conducted on college campuses, using the children of graduate students and faculty.

This limitation would not be critical if no differences existed in the timing of development in children from different groups. But they do. For example, as a group, babies of African descent (in Africa, the Caribbean, the US, and England) and Australian Aboriginals showed more rapid motor development than babies of European descent in early infancy. The pattern was more pronounced in rural than in urbanized Blacks. These patterns led to speculation that among traditionally nomadic groups, "readiness to travel" might have been genetically selected (Freedman and DeBoer, 1979). Around the world there are various means of transporting infants—slings, swaddling, cradleboards.

TABLE 3-3 MILESTONES OF FINE MOTOR DEVELOPMENT

Age (months)	Skill
3	Opens hand prominently
3	Grasps rattle
8	Grasps with thumb and finger
11	Holds crayon adaptively
14	Builds tower of two cubes
16	Places pegs in board
24	Imitates strokes on paper
33	Copies circle

Source: From Frankenburg, W. K., Dodds, J., Archer, P., Shapiro, H., and Brunsneck, B., The Denver II: A Major Revision and Restandardization of the Denver Developmental Screening Test, *Pediatrics*, 89, pp. 91–97, 1992. Reprinted with permission from Dr. William K. Frankenburg.

norms the average performance of a large sample of children of a given age

Brazelton Neonatal Behavioral Assessment Scale (NBAS) a measure designed to determine infants' neurological and behavioural responses to their environment

Nomadic lifestyles require infants to be portable soon after birth. Other cultures practise a "lying-in" period with newborns. Concerns have also been expressed about neurotoxicity in populations whose environment is becoming increasingly contaminated. For example, mercury levels in the Arctic might be responsible for different patterns of reflex and motor development observed in Northern Quebec Cree and Inuit populations. These and other cultural factors might also have a significant effect on the rate of motor development (Werner, 1972; Keefer et al., 1991; Gartstein et al., 2003; deOnis et al., 2007; El-Hayek, 2007).

Cultural Dimensions

Motor Development Across Cultures

Among the Ache people, who live in the rain forest of South America, infants face an early life of physical restriction. Because the Ache lead a nomadic existence, living in a series of tiny camps in the rain forest, open space is at a premium. Consequently, for the first few years of life, infants spend nearly all their time in direct physical contact with their mothers. Even when they are not physically touching their mothers, they are permitted to venture no more than a few feet away.

Infants among the Kipsigis people, who live in a more open environment in rural Kenya, Africa, lead quite a different existence. Their lives are filled with activity and exercise. Parents seek to teach their children to sit up, stand, and walk from the earliest days of infancy. For example, very young infants are placed in shallow holes in the ground designed to keep them in an upright position. Parents begin to teach their children to walk starting at the eighth week of life. The infants are held with their feet touching the ground, and they are pushed forward.

Clearly, the infants in these two societies lead very different lives (Super, 1976; Kaplan and Dove, 1987). But do the relative lack of early motor stimulation for Ache infants and the efforts of the Kipsigis to encourage motor development really make a difference?

The answer is both yes and no. It's "yes" in that Ache infants tend to show delayed motor development, relative both to Kipsigis infants and to children raised in Western societies. Although their social abilities are no different, Ache children tend to begin walking at around 23 months, about a year later than the typical child in Canada. In contrast, Kipsigis children, who are encouraged in their motor development, learn to sit up and walk several weeks earlier, on average, than Canadian children.

In the long run, however, the differences between Ache, Kipsigis, and Western children disappear. By late childhood, about age six, there is no evidence of differences in general, overall motor skills among Ache, Kipsigis, and Western children.

As we see with the Ache and Kipsgis babies, variations in the timing of motor skills seem to depend in part on parental expectations of what is the "appropriate" schedule for the emergence of specific skills. For instance, one study examined the motor skills of infants who lived in a single city in England, but whose mothers varied in ethnic origin. In the research, English, Jamaican, and Indian mothers' expectations were first assessed regarding several markers of their infants' motor skills. The Jamaican mothers expected their infants to sit and walk significantly earlier than the English and Indian mothers, and the actual emergence of these activities was in line with their expectations. The source of the Jamaican infants' earlier mastery seemed to lie in the treatment of the children by their

Cultural influences affect the rate of the development of motor skills.

parents. For instance, Jamaican mothers gave their children practice in stepping quite early in infancy (Hopkins and Westra, 1989, 1990).

In sum, cultural factors help determine the time at which specific motor skills appear. Activities that are an intrinsic part of a culture are more apt to be purposely taught to infants in that culture, leading to the potential of their earlier emergence (Nugent et al., 1989).

Nutrition in Infancy: Fuelling Motor Development

Rosa sighed as she sat down to nurse the baby—again. She had fed four-week-old Juan about every hour today, and he still seemed hungry. Some days, it seemed like all she did was breast-feed her baby. "Well, he must be going through a growth spurt," she decided, as she settled into her favourite rocking chair and put the baby to her nipple.

The rapid physical growth that occurs during infancy is fuelled by the nutrients that infants receive. Without proper nutrition, infants cannot reach their physical potential, and they might suffer cognitive and social consequences as well (Tanner and Finn-Stevenson, 2002; Costello et al., 2003; Gregory, 2005).

Although vast individual differences exist in what constitutes appropriate nutrition—infants differ in terms of growth rates, body composition, metabolism, and activity levels—some broad guidelines do hold. In general, infants should consume more than 100 calories per day for each kilogram they weigh—an allotment that is twice the suggested caloric intake for adults (Dietz and Stern, 1999; Skinner et al., 2004).

Typically, though, it's not necessary to count calories for infants. Most infants regulate their caloric intake quite effectively on their own. If they are allowed to consume as much they seem to want, and are not pressured to eat more, they will do fine.

Malnutrition. *Malnutrition,* the condition of having an improper amount and balance of nutrients, produces several results, none good. For instance, malnutrition is more common among children living in many developing countries than among children who live in more industrialized, affluent countries. Malnourished children in these countries begin to show a slower growth rate by the age of six months. By the time they reach the age of two, their height and weight are only 95 percent the height and weight of children in more industrialized countries.

Children who have been chronically malnourished during infancy later score lower on IQ tests and tend to do less well in school. These effects may linger even after the children's diet has improved substantially (Grantham-McGregor et al., 2001; Ratanachu-Ek, 2003).

Severe malnutrition during infancy may lead to several disorders. Malnutrition during the first year can produce *marasmus*, a disease in which infants stop growing. Marasmus, attributable to a severe deficiency in proteins and calories, causes the body to waste away and ultimately results in death. Older children are susceptible to *kwashiorkor*, a disease in which a child's stomach, limbs, and face swell with water. To a casual observer, it appears that a child with kwashiorkor is actually chubby. However, this is an illusion: The child's body is in fact struggling to make use of the few nutrients that are available.

> **From an educator's perspective:** Why might malnourishment, which slows physical growth, affect IQ scores and school performance? How might malnourishment affect education in Third World countries?

In some cases, infants who receive sufficient nutrition act as though they have been deprived of food. Looking as though they suffer from marasmus, they are underdeveloped, listless, and apathetic. The real cause, though, is emotional: They lack sufficient love and emotional support. In such cases, known as **nonorganic failure to thrive**, children stop growing not for biological reasons but due to a lack of stimulation and attention from their parents. Usually occurring by the age of 18 months, nonorganic failure to thrive can be reversed through intensive parent training or by placing children in a foster home where they can receive emotional support.

Obesity. It is clear that malnourishment during infancy has potentially disastrous consequences for an infant. Less clear, however, are the effects of *obesity,* defined as weight greater than 20 percent above the average for a given height. While there is no clear correlation between obesity during infancy and obesity at the age of 16, some research suggests that overfeeding during infancy can lead to the creation of an excess of fat cells, which remain in the body throughout life and may predispose a person to be overweight. In fact, weight

nonorganic failure to thrive a disorder in which infants stop growing due to a lack of stimulation and attention as the result of inadequate parenting

gains during infancy are associated with weight at age six. Other research shows an association between obesity after the age of six and adult obesity, suggesting that obesity in babies ultimately may be found to be associated with adult weight problems. A clear link between overweight babies and overweight adults, however, has not yet been found (Gunnarsdottir and Thorsdottir, 2003; Toschke et al., 2004; Dennison et al., 2006).

Although the evidence linking infant obesity to adult obesity is inconclusive, it's plain that the societal view that "a fat baby is a healthy baby" is not necessarily correct. Parents should concentrate less on their baby's weight and more on providing appropriate nutrition. But just what constitutes proper nutrition? Probably the biggest question revolves around whether infants should be breast-fed or given a formula of commercially processed cow's milk with vitamin additives, as we consider next.

Breast or Bottle?

In ancient times, infants were typically breast-fed for the first 12–18 months, sometimes longer. Industrialization brought in new attitudes and trends towards artificial feedings earlier and earlier—and increasing infant mortality! In the 1920s, a US government-issued childcare manual recommended feeding infants cod liver oil, orange juice, and formula. In the 1940s, the Canadian government issued a childcare manual recommending that breast-feeding was best (Canadian Paediatric Society, 2004b). Whether and for how long mothers today breast-feed depends on numerous factors.

The Canadian Paediatric Society and World Health Organization agree: For the first six months of life, there is no better food for an infant than breast milk. Breast milk not only contains all the nutrients necessary for growth, but it also seems to offer some degree of immunity to a variety of childhood diseases, such as respiratory illnesses, ear infections, diarrhea, and allergies. Breast milk is more easily digested than cow's milk or formula, and it is sterile, warm, and convenient for the mother to dispense. Breast milk also changes in composition as the child matures. Some researchers even argue that breast milk enhances cognitive growth, leading to high adult intelligence (Feldman and Eidelman, 2003; Canadian Paediatric Society, 2005; Der et al., 2006).

Breast-feeding is not a cure-all for infant nutrition and health, and the millions of mothers who must use formula (for example, those physically unable to produce milk or who are prevented from breast-feeding by social factors such as work schedules) should not be concerned that their children are suffering significant harm. While some research might show cognitive advantages for breast-fed children, recent research suggests that infants fed formula show equivalent cognitive performance in preschool (Birch et al., 2000; Auestad et al., 2003; Rabin, 2006).

Introducing Solid Foods: When and What?

Although pediatricians agree that breast milk is the ideal initial food, at some point infants require more nutriments than breast milk alone can provide. The Canadian Paediatric Society suggests that babies should start iron-enriched solids at around six months, while continuing to breast-feed for as long as desired by mother and infant (Canadian Paediatric Society, 2004; 2005).

Solid foods are introduced into an infant's diet gradually, one at a time, so that parents can be aware of the infant's preferences and allergies. Most often cereal comes first, followed by strained fruits. Vegetables and other foods typically are introduced next, although the order varies significantly from one infant to another.

The timing of *weaning*, the gradual cessation of breast- or bottle-feeding, varies greatly. Weaning is considered to begin when formula or solid food is introduced, and is complete when breast-feeding is completely eliminated. In developed countries, weaning is often tied to the mother's return to work. In countries where women return to work earlier, weaning typically occurs earlier. In Canada, where many women take advantage of 12 months of maternity leave, breast-feeding rates are higher, and 63 percent report breast-feeding beyond 3 months. The most common reason for a mother's decision to wean is perceived inadequate milk supply (Canadian Paediatric Society, 2004). On the other hand, some mothers continue breast-feeding for two or three years or beyond.

sensation the physical stimulation of the sense organs

perception the sorting out, interpretation, analysis, and integration of stimuli involving the sense organs and brain

REVIEW, CHECK, AND APPLY

REVIEW

- Reflexes are universal, genetically determined physical behaviours.

- During infancy, children reach a series of milestones in their physical development on a fairly consistent schedule, with some individual and cultural variations.

- Nutrition strongly affects physical development.

- The advantages of breast-feeding are numerous.

CHECK YOURSELF

1. _____ are unlearned, organized, involuntary responses that occur automatically in the presence of certain stimuli.

2. Which of the following is *not* one of the consequences of malnutrition during infancy?

    a. Malnourished children sleep, on average, six to eight hours less than non-malnourished children of the same age.

    b. Malnourished children show a slower growth rate by the age of six months.

    c. Malnourished children score lower on IQ tests later in life.

    d. Malnourished children have a lower height and weight by age two than non-malnourished children.

3. Breast-feeding has been associated with enhanced health.

- True
- False

APPLYING LIFESPAN DEVELOPMENT

- What advice might you give a friend who is concerned that her infant is still not walking at 14 months, when every other baby she knows started walking by the first birthday?

Answers: 1) Reflexes; 2) a; 3) True

The Development of the Senses

LO6 What sensory capabilities do infants possess?

LEARNING OBJECTIVES

William James, one of the founding fathers of psychology, believed the world of the infant is a "blooming, buzzing confusion" (James, 1890/1950). Was he right?

In this case, James's wisdom failed him. The newborn's sensory world does lack the clarity and stability that we can distinguish as adults, but day by day the world grows increasingly comprehensible as the infant's ability to sense and perceive the environment develops. In fact, babies appear to thrive in an environment enriched by pleasing sensations.

The processes that underlie infants' understanding of the world around them are sensation and perception. **Sensation** is the physical stimulation of the sense organs, and **perception** is the mental process of sorting out, interpreting, analyzing, and integrating stimuli from the sense organs and brain.

The study of infants' capabilities in the realm of sensation and perception challenges the ingenuity of investigators. As we'll see, researchers have developed a number of procedures for understanding sensation and perception in different realms.

Visual Perception: Seeing the World

From the time of Lee Eng's birth, everyone who met him felt that he gazed at them intently. His eyes seemed to meet those of visitors. They seemed to bore deeply and knowingly into the faces of people who looked at him.

How good, in fact, was Lee's vision, and what, precisely, could he make out in his environment? Quite a bit, at least up close. According to some estimates, a newborn's distance vision ranges from 20/200 to 20/600, which means that an infant can see with accuracy up to 20 feet, where an adult with normal vision is able to see with similar accuracy from a distance of between 200 and 600 feet (Haith, 1991).

These figures indicate that infants' distance vision is one-tenth to one-third that of the average adult's. This isn't so bad, actually:

While an infant's distant vision is 10 to 30 times poorer than the average adult's, the vision of newborns provides the same degree of distance acuity as the uncorrected vision of many adults who wear eyeglasses or contact lenses.

FIGURE 3-7 Visual Cliff
The "visual cliff" experiment examines the depth perception of infants. Most infants in the age range of 6 to 14 months cannot be coaxed to cross the cliff, apparently responding to the fact that the patterned area drops several feet.

The vision of newborns provides the same degree of distance acuity as the uncorrected vision of many adults who wear eyeglasses or contact lenses. (If you wear glasses or contact lenses, remove them to get a sense of what an infant can see of the world.) Furthermore, infants' distance vision grows increasingly acute. By six to eight months of age, the average infant's vision is nearly identical to that of adults', and most infants achieve 20/20 vision by two to three years (Aslin, 1987; Cavallini et al., 2002; Slater et al., 2007).

Depth perception is a particularly useful ability, helping babies acknowledge heights and avoid falls. In a classic study, developmental psychologists Eleanor Gibson and Richard Walk (1960) placed infants on a sheet of heavy glass. A checkered pattern appeared under one-half of the glass sheet, creating the appearance that the infant was on a stable floor. However, in the middle of the glass sheet, the pattern dropped down several feet, forming an apparent "visual cliff." Gibson and Walk asked whether infants would willingly crawl across the cliff when called by their mothers (see Figure 3-7).

The results were clear: Most of the infants in the study, who ranged in age from 6 to 14 months, could not be coaxed over the apparent cliff. Clearly most of them had already developed the ability to perceive depth by that age (Campos et al., 1970).

Infants also show clear visual preferences, which are present from birth. Given a choice, infants reliably prefer to look at patterned stimuli than to look at simpler stimuli (see Figure 3-8). How do we know? Developmental psychologist Robert Fantz (1963) created a classic test. He built a chamber in which babies could lie on their backs and see pairs of visual stimuli above them. Fantz could determine which of the stimuli the infants were looking at by observing the reflections of the stimuli in their eyes.

Fantz's work was the impetus for a great deal of research on the preferences of infants, most of which points to a critical conclusion: Infants are genetically preprogrammed to prefer particular kinds of stimuli. For instance, just minutes after birth, they show preferences for certain colours, shapes, and configurations of various stimuli. They prefer curved over straight lines, three-dimensional figures to two-dimensional ones, and human faces to non-faces. Such capabilities might be a reflection of the existence of highly specialized cells in the brain that react to stimuli of a particular pattern, orientation, shape, and direction of movement (Rubenstein et al., 1999; Hubel and Wiesel, 1979, 2004; Kellman and Arterberry, 2006).

However, genetics are not the sole determinant of infant visual preferences. Just a few hours after birth, infants have already learned to prefer their own mother's face to other faces. Similarly, between the ages of six and nine months, infants become more adept at distinguishing between the faces of humans, while they become less able to distinguish faces of members of other species. They also distinguish between male and female faces. Such findings provide more clear evidence of how heredity and environmental experiences are woven together to determine an infant's capabilities (Pascalis et al., 2002; Ramsey-Rennels and Langlois, 2006; Turati et al., 2006).

Auditory Perception: The World of Sound

What is it about a mother's lullaby that helps soothe crying babies like Alex, whose case we discussed at the beginning of this chapter? Some clues emerge when we look infants' capabilities in the realm of auditory sensation and perception.

Infants hear from the time of birth—and even before, as the ability to hear begins prenatally. Even in the womb, the fetus responds to sounds outside of its mother. Furthermore, infants are born with preferences for particular sound combinations (Schellenberg and Trehub, 1996; Trehub, 2003).

Because they have had some practice hearing before birth, it is not surprising that infants have reasonably good auditory perception after they are born. In fact, infants actually are more sensitive to certain very high and very low frequencies than adults—a sensitivity that seems to increase during the first two years of life. On the other hand, infants are initially less sensitive than adults to middle-range frequencies. Eventually, however, their capabilities within the middle range improve (Fenwick and Morongiello, 1991; Werner and Marean, 1996; Frenald, 2001).

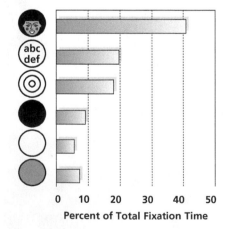

Percent of Total Fixation Time

FIGURE 3-8 Preferring Complexity
In a classic experiment, researcher Robert Fantz found that two- and three-month-old infants preferred to look at more complex stimuli than to look at simple ones.
Source: Adapted from Fantz, 1961.

In addition to the ability to detect sound, infants need several other abilities in order to hear effectively. For instance, *sound localization* permits us to pinpoint the direction from which a sound is emanating. Compared to adults, infants have a slight handicap in this task because effective sound localization requires the use of the slight difference in the times at which a sound reaches our two ears. Sound that we hear first in the right ear tells us that the source of the sound is to our right. Because infants' heads are smaller than those of adults, the ability to time the arrival of sound at the two ears is less than it is in adults; therefore, they have difficulty determining from which direction sound is coming.

However, despite the potential limitation brought about by their smaller heads, infants' sound localization abilities are actually fairly good even at birth, and they reach adult levels of success by 18 months. Furthermore, young infants are capable of making the fine discriminations that their future understanding of language will require (Bijeljac-Babic et al., 1993; Fenwick et al., 1998).

Smell and Taste

What do infants do when they smell a rotten egg? Pretty much what adults do—crinkle their noses and generally look unhappy. On the other hand, the scents of bananas and butter produce a pleasant reaction on the part of infants (Steiner, 1979; Pomares et al., 2002).

The sense of smell is so well developed, even among very young infants, that at least some 12- to 18-day-old babies can distinguish their mothers on the basis of smell alone. For instance, in one experiment infants were exposed to the smell of gauze pads worn under the arms of adults the previous evening. Infants who were being breast-fed were able to distinguish their mothers' scent from those of other adults. However, not all infants could do this: Those who were being bottle-fed were unable to make the distinction. Moreover, both breast-fed and bottle-fed infants were unable to distinguish their fathers on the basis of odour (Porter et al., 1988; Mizuno and Ueda, 2004).

Infants seem to have an innate sweet tooth (even before they have teeth!), and they show facial expressions of disgust when they taste something bitter. Very young infants smile when a sweet-tasting liquid is placed on their tongues. They also suck harder at a bottle if it is sweetened. Since breast milk has a sweet taste, it is possible that this preference is part of our evolutionary heritage, retained because it offered a survival advantage (Porges et al., 1993; Liem and Mennella, 2002; Silveira et al., 2007).

Sensitivity to Pain and Touch

Infants are born with the capacity to experience pain. Obviously, no one can be sure if the experience of pain in children is identical to that in adults, any more than we can tell if an adult friend who complains of a headache is experiencing pain that is more or less severe than our own pain when we have a headache.

What we do know is that pain produces distress in infants. Their heartbeat increases, they sweat, show facial expressions of discomfort, and change the intensity and tone of crying when they are hurt (Simons et al., 2003; Warnock and Sandrin, 2004).

There appears to be a developmental progression in reactions to pain. For example, a newborn infant who has her heel pricked for a blood test responds with distress, but it takes her several seconds to show the response. In contrast, only a few months later, the same procedure brings a much more immediate response. It is possible that the delayed reaction in infants is produced by the relatively slower transmission of information within the newborn's less-developed nervous system (Anand and Hickey, 1992; Axia et al., 1995; Puchalsi and Hummel, 2002).

Responding to Touch. Touch is one of the most highly developed sensory systems in a newborn. It is also one of the first to develop: Evidence shows that by 32 weeks after conception, the entire body is sensitive to touch. Furthermore, several of the basic reflexes present at birth, such as the rooting reflex, require touch sensitivity to operate. An infant must sense a touch near the mouth in order to seek automatically a nipple to suck (Haith, 1986).

Infants' abilities in the realm of touch are particularly helpful in their efforts to explore the world. Several theorists have suggested that one of the ways children gain information about the world is through touching. As mentioned earlier, at the age of six months, infants are apt to place almost any object in their mouths, apparently taking in data about its configuration from their sensory responses to the feel of it in their mouths (Ruff, 1989).

By the age of four months infants are able to discriminate their own names from other, similar sounding, words. What are some ways an infant is able to discriminate his or her name from other words?

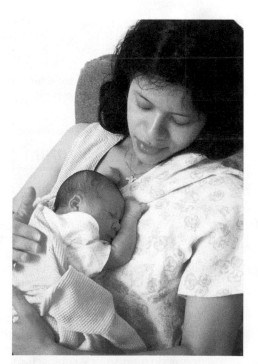

Infants' sense of smell is so well developed they can distinguish their mothers on the basis of smell alone.

multimodal approach to perception the approach that considers how information that is collected by various individual sensory systems is integrated and coordinated

affordances the action possibilities that a given situation or stimulus provides

Multimodal Perception: Combining Individual Sensory Inputs

When Eric Pettigrew was seven months old, his grandparents presented him with a squeaky rubber doll. As soon as he saw it, he reached out for it, grasped it in his hand, and listened as it squeaked. He seemed delighted with the gift.

One way of considering Eric's sensory reaction to the doll is to focus on each of the senses individually: what the doll looked like to Eric, how it felt in his hand, and what it sounded like. In fact, this approach has dominated the study of sensation and perception in infancy.

However, let's consider another approach: We might examine how the various sensory responses are integrated with one another. Instead of looking at each individual sensory response, we could consider how the responses work together and are combined to produce Eric's ultimate reaction. The **multimodal approach to perception** considers how information that is collected by various individual sensory systems is integrated and coordinated.

> **From a health-care worker's perspective:** People who are born without the use of one sense often develop unusual abilities in one or more other senses. What can health-care professionals do to help infants who are lacking in a particular sense?

Although the multimodal approach is a relatively recent innovation in the study of how infants understand their sensory world, it raises some fundamental issues about the development of sensation and perception. For instance, some researchers argue that sensations are initially integrated with one another in the infant, while others maintain that the infant's sensory systems are initially separate and that brain development leads to increasing integration (De Gelder, 2000; Lickliter and Bahrick, 2000; Lewkowicz, 2002).

We do not know yet which view is correct. However, it does appear that by an early age infants are able to relate what they have learned about an object through one sensory channel to what they have learned about it through another. For instance, even one-month-old infants are able to recognize by sight objects that they have previously held in their mouths but never seen (Meltzoff, 1981; Steri and Spelke, 1988). Clearly, some cross-talk between various sensory channels is already possible a month after birth.

Their abilities in multimodal perception showcase the sophisticated perceptual abilities of infants, abilities which continue to grow throughout the period of infancy. Such perceptual growth is aided by infants' discovery of **affordances**, the options that a given situation or stimulus provides. For example, infants learn that they might potentially fall when walking down a steep ramp—that is, the ramp *affords* the possibility of falling. Such knowledge is crucial as infants make the transition from crawling to walking. Similarly, infants learn that an object shaped in a certain way can slip out of their hands if not grasped correctly. For example, Eric is learning that his toy has several affordances: He can grab it and squeeze it, listen to it squeak, and even chew comfortably on it if he is teething (Adolph, 1997; McCarty and Ashmead, 1999; Flom and Bahrick, 2007; Wilcox et al., 2007).

The senses of sight and touch are integrated by infants through multimodal perception.

Exercising Your Infant's Body and Senses

Becoming an Informed Consumer of Development

Recall how cultural expectations and environments affect the age at which various physical milestones, such as the first step, occur. While most experts feel attempts to accelerate physical and sensory-perceptual development yield little advantage, parents should ensure that their infants receive sufficient physical and sensory stimulation. There are several specific ways to accomplish this goal:

- Carry the baby in different positions—in a backpack, in a front-pack, or in a football hold with the infant's head in the palm of your hand and its feet lying on your arm. This lets the infant view the world from several perspectives.

- Let infants explore their environment. Don't contain them too long in a barren environment. Let them crawl or wander around—after

first making the environment "childproof" by removing dangerous objects.

- Engage in "rough-and-tumble" play. Wrestling, dancing, and rolling around on the floor—if not violent—are activities that are fun and that stimulate older infants' motor and sensory systems.

- Let babies touch their food and even play with it. Infancy is too early to start teaching table manners. It's also a good way for them to gauge temperature and avoid putting food in their mouths that is too hot.

- Provide toys that stimulate the senses, particularly toys that can stimulate more than one sense at a time. For example, brightly coloured, textured toys with movable parts are enjoyable and help sharpen infants' senses.

REVIEW, CHECK, AND APPLY

REVIEW

- Infants' sensory abilities are surprisingly well developed at or shortly after birth. Their perceptions help them explore and begin to make sense of the world.

- Very early, infants can see depth and motion, distinguish colours and patterns, localize and discriminate sounds, and recognize the sound and smell of their mothers.

- Infants are sensitive to pain and touch, and most medical authorities now advocate for procedures, including anesthesia, that minimize infants' pain.

CHECK YOURSELF

1. _____ is the physical stimulation of the sense organs, and _____ is the mental process of interpreting and integrating stimuli from the brain.

2. We know that infants experience pain because their heartbeat increases, they sweat, they show discomfort, and their crying changes tone.

   - True
   - False

3. The _____ considers how information that is collected by various individual sensory systems is integrated and coordinated.

   a. multimodal approach to perception

   b. affordance theory

   c. multidisciplinary motor development cycle

   d. macrosystem

Answers: 1) Sensation/perception; 2) True; 3) a

MODULE 3.2 Cognitive Development in Infancy

The Electric Nanny

Tim, 2, and his sister Jane, 10 months, are typical Canadian babies. When their mother Anna needs to keep them occupied, she turns on Treehouse TV or pops in a Baby Einstein DVD. "Jane loves the Baby Einstein DVDs. Maybe she just likes the music and colours, but I like to think she's learning too. Tim is getting too old for them though—he prefers Caillou and Curious George. I like that I can prepare supper or do the laundry and know they won't get into any mischief, and if they are learning something, all the better!"

Can infants really become miniature Einsteins by watching educational media? What concepts are babies as young as 10-month-old Jane actually grasping, and what intellectual abilities remain undeveloped at that age? Can an infant's cognitive development really be accelerated through intellectual stimulation, or does the process unfold on its own timetable despite the best efforts of parents to hasten it?

We address these questions in this module as we consider cognitive development during the first years of life, focusing on how infants develop their knowledge and understanding of the world. We first discuss the work of Swiss psychologist Jean Piaget, whose theory of developmental stages served as a highly influential impetus for a considerable amount of work on cognitive development.

We then cover more contemporary views of cognitive development, examining information-processing approaches that seek to explain how cognitive growth occurs. We also examine memory in infants and address individual differences in intelligence.

Finally, we consider language, the cognitive skill that permits infants to communicate with others. We look at the roots of language in prelinguistic speech and trace the milestones indicating the development of language skills in the progression from the baby's first words to phrases and sentences.

Piaget's Approach to Cognitive Development

L07 What are the fundamental features of Piaget's theories of cognitive development?

L08 How has Piaget's theory been supported and challenged?

Swiss psychologist Jean Piaget.

Olivia's dad is wiping up the mess around the base of her high chair—for the third time today! It seems to him that 14-month-old Olivia takes great delight in dropping food from the high chair. She also drops toys, spoons, anything it seems, just to watch how it hits the floor. She almost appears to be experimenting to see what kind of noise or what size of splatter is created by each different thing she drops.

Swiss psychologist Jean Piaget (1896–1980) probably would have said that Olivia's dad is right in theorizing that Olivia is conducting her own series of experiments to learn more about the workings of her world. Piaget's views of the ways infants learn could be summed in a simple equation: *Action = Knowledge.*

Piaget argued that infants do not acquire knowledge from facts communicated by others, nor through sensation and perception. Instead, Piaget suggested that knowledge is the product of direct motor behaviour. Although many of his basic explanations and propositions have been challenged by subsequent research, as we'll discuss later, the view that in significant ways infants learn by doing remains unquestioned (Piaget, 1952, 1962, 1983; Bullinger, 1997).

Key Elements of Piaget's Theory

As we first noted in Module 1.2, Piaget's theory is based on a stage approach to development. He assumed that all children pass through a series of four universal stages in a fixed order from birth through adolescence: sensorimotor, preoperational, concrete operational, and formal operational. He also suggested that movement from one stage to the next occurs when a child reaches an appropriate level of physical maturation *and* is exposed to relevant experiences. Without such experience, children are assumed to be incapable of reaching their cognitive potential. Some approaches to cognition focus on changes in the *content* of children's knowledge about the world, but Piaget argued that it was critical to also consider the changes in the *quality* of children's knowledge and understanding as they move from one stage to another.

For instance, as they develop cognitively, infants experience changes in their understanding about what can and cannot occur in the world. Consider a baby who participates in an experiment during which she is exposed to three identical versions of her mother all at the same time, thanks to some well-placed mirrors. A three-month-old infant will interact happily with each of these images of mother. However, by five months of age, the child becomes quite agitated at the sight of multiple mothers. Apparently by this time the child has figured out that she has but one mother, and viewing three at a time is thoroughly alarming (Bower, 1977). To Piaget, such reactions indicate that a baby is beginning to master principles regarding the way the world operates, indicating that she has begun to construct a mental sense of the world that she didn't have two months earlier.

Piaget believed that the basic building blocks of the way we understand the world are mental structures called **schemes**—organized patterns of functioning—that adapt and change with mental development. At first, schemes are related to physical, or sensorimotor, activity, such as picking up or reaching for toys. As children develop, their schemes move to a mental level, reflecting thought. Schemes are similar to computer software: They direct and determine how data from the world, such as new events or objects, are considered and dealt with (Achenbach, 1992; Rakison and Oakes, 2003).

If you give a baby a new cloth book, for example, she will touch it, mouth it, perhaps try to tear it or bang it on the floor. To Piaget, each of these actions represents a scheme, and they are the infant's way of gaining knowledge and understanding of this new object.

Piaget suggested that two principles underlie the growth in children's schemes: assimilation and accommodation. **Assimilation** is the process by which people understand an experience in terms of their current stage of cognitive development and way of thinking. Assimilation occurs, then, when a stimulus or event is acted upon, perceived, and understood in accordance with existing patterns of thought. For example, an infant who tries to suck on any toy in the same way is assimilating the objects to her existing sucking scheme. Similarly, a child who encounters a flying squirrel at a zoo and calls it a "bird" is assimilating the squirrel to his existing scheme of bird.

In contrast, when we change our existing ways of thinking, understanding, or behaving in response to encounters with new stimuli or events, **accommodation** takes place. For instance, when a child sees a flying squirrel and calls it "a bird with a tail," he is beginning to *accommodate* new knowledge, modifying his scheme of bird.

scheme an organized pattern of sensorimotor functioning

assimilation the process in which people understand an experience in terms of their current stage of cognitive development and way of thinking

accommodation changes in existing ways of thinking that occur in response to encounters with new stimuli or events

sensorimotor stage (of cognitive development) Piaget's initial major stage of cognitive development, which can be broken down into six substages

Piaget believed that the earliest schemes are primarily limited to the reflexes with which we are all born, such as sucking and rooting. Infants start to modify these simple early schemes almost immediately, through the processes of assimilation and accommodation, in response to their exploration of the environment. Schemes quickly become more sophisticated as infants become more advanced in their motor capabilities—to Piaget, a signal of the potential for more advanced cognitive development. Because Piaget's sensorimotor stage of development begins at birth and continues until the child is about two years old, we consider it here in detail.

The Sensorimotor Period: The Earliest Stage of Cognitive Growth

Piaget suggests that the **sensorimotor stage**, the initial major stage of cognitive development, can be broken down into six substages. These are summarized in Table 3-4. It is important to keep in mind that although the specific substages of the sensorimotor period may at first appear to unfold with great regularity, as though infants reach a particular age and smoothly proceed into the next substage, the reality of cognitive development is somewhat different. First, the ages at which infants actually reach a particular stage vary a good deal among different children. The exact timing of a stage reflects an interaction between the infant's level of physical maturation and the nature of the social environment in which the child is being raised.

Piaget viewed development as a more gradual process than the notion of different stages might seem to imply. Infants do not go to sleep one night in one substage and wake up the next morning in the next one. Instead, there is a rather steady shifting of behaviour as a child moves toward the next stage of cognitive development. Infants also pass through periods of transition in which some aspects of their behaviour reflect the next higher stage, while other aspects indicate their current stage (see Figure 3-9).

TABLE 3-4   PIAGET'S SIX SUBSTAGES OF THE SENSORIMOTOR STAGE

Substage	Age	Description	Example
Substage 1: Simple reflexes	First month of life	During this period, the various reflexes that determine the infant's interactions with the world are at the centre of its cognitive life.	The sucking reflex causes the infant to suck at anything placed in its lips.
Substage 2: First habits and primary circular reactions	From 1 to 4 months	At this age infants begin to coordinate what were separate actions into single, integrated activities.	An infant might combine grasping an object with sucking on it, or staring at something with touching it.
Substage 3: Secondary circular reactions	From 4 to 8 months	During this period, infants take major strides in shifting their cognitive horizons beyond themselves and begin to act on the outside world.	A child who repeatedly picks up a rattle in her crib and shakes it in different ways to see how the sound changes is demonstrating her ability to modify her cognitive scheme about shaking rattles.
Substage 4: Coordination of secondary circular reactions	From 8 to 12 months	In this stage infants begin to use more calculated approaches to producing events, coordinating several schemes to generate a single act. They achieve object performance during this stage.	An infant will push one toy out of the way to reach another toy that is lying, partially exposed, under it.
Substage 5: Tertiary circular reactions	From 12 to 18 months	At this age infants develop what Piaget regards as the deliberate variation of actions that bring desirable consequences. Rather than just repeating enjoyable activities, Infants appear to carry out miniature experiments to observe the consequences.	A child will drop a toy repeatedly, varying the position from which he drops it, carefully observing each time to see where it falls.
Substage 6: Beginnings of thought	From 18 months to 2 years	The major achievement of Substage 6 is the capacity for mental representation or symbolic thought. Piaget argued that only at this stage can infants imagine where objects that they cannot see might be.	Children can even plot in their heads unseen trajectories of objects, so that if a ball rolls under a piece of furniture, they can figure out where it is likely to emerge on the other side.

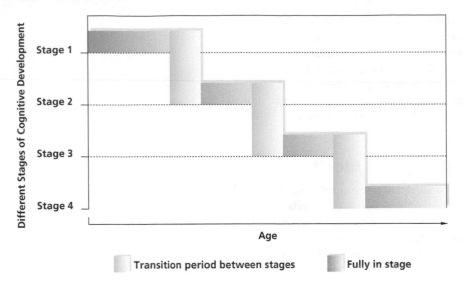

FIGURE 3-9 **Transitions**

Infants do not suddenly shift from one stage of cognitive development to the next. Instead, Piaget argues that there is a period of transition in which some behaviour reflects one stage, while other behaviour reflects the more advanced stage. Does this gradualism argue against Piaget's interpretation of stages?

Substage 1: Simple Reflexes. The first substage of the sensorimotor period is *Substage 1: Simple reflexes,* encompassing the first month of life. During this time, the various inborn reflexes, described in Module 3.1, are at the centre of a baby's physical and cognitive life, determining the nature of his or her interactions with the world. At the same time, some of the reflexes begin to accommodate the infant's experience with the nature of the world. For instance, an infant who is being breast-fed, but who also receives supplemental bottles, may start to change the way he or she sucks, depending on whether a nipple is on a breast or a bottle.

Substage 2: First Habits and Primary Circular Reactions. *Substage 2: First habits and primary circular reactions,* the second substage of the sensorimotor period, occurs from one to four months of age. In this period, infants begin to coordinate what were separate actions into single, integrated activities. For instance, an infant might combine grasping an object with sucking on it, or staring at something while touching it.

If an activity engages a baby's interests, he or she may repeat it over and over, simply for the sake of continuing to experience it. This repetition of a chance motor event helps the baby start building cognitive schemes through a process known as a *circular reaction. Primary circular reactions* are schemes reflecting an infant's repetition of interesting or enjoyable actions which focus on the infant's own body, just for the enjoyment of doing them.

Substage 3: Secondary Circular Reactions. *Substage 3: Secondary circular reactions* are more purposeful. According to Piaget, this third stage of cognitive development in infancy occurs from four to eight months of age. During this period, a child begins to act upon the outside world. For instance, infants now seek to repeat enjoyable events in their environments if they happen to produce them through chance activities. A child who repeatedly picks up a rattle in her crib and shakes it in different ways to see how the sound changes is demonstrating her ability to modify her cognitive scheme about shaking rattles. She is engaging in what Piaget calls *secondary circular reactions,* which are schemes regarding repeated actions that bring about a desirable consequence.

Substage 4: Coordination of Secondary Circular Reactions. Some major leaps forward occur in *Substage 4: Coordination of secondary circular reactions,* which lasts from around 8 months to 12 months. In Substage 4, infants begin to employ *goal-directed behaviour* in which several schemes are combined and coordinated to generate a single act to solve a problem. For instance, they will push one toy out of the way to reach another toy that is lying, partially exposed, under it.

Infants' newfound purposefulness, their ability to use means to attain particular ends, and their skill in anticipating future circumstances owe their appearance in part to the developmental achievement of object permanence that emerges in Substage 4. **Object permanence,** according to Piaget, is the realization that people and objects exist even when they cannot be seen. It is a simple principle, but its mastery has profound consequences.

Consider, for instance, seven-month-old Chu, who has yet to learn the idea of object permanence. Chu's mother shakes a rattle in front of him, then takes the rattle and places it under a blanket. To Chu, who has not mastered the concept of object permanence, the rattle no longer exists. He will make no effort to look for it.

Several months later, when he reaches Substage 4, the story is quite different (see Figure 3-10). This time, as soon as his mother places the rattle under the blanket, Chu tries to toss the cover aside, eagerly searching for the rattle. Chu clearly has learned that the object continues to exist even when it cannot be seen. For the infant who achieves an understanding of object permanence, then, out of sight is decidedly not out of mind.

◉ Watch on **mydevelopmentlab**

To see a video of an infant demonstrating the principle of object permanence that you've been reading about, log onto MyDevelopmentLab.

object permanence the realization that people and objects exist even when they cannot be seen

Before Object Permanence

After Object Permanence

FIGURE 3-10 **Object Permanence**

Before an infant has understood the idea of object permanence, he will not search for an object that has been hidden right before his eyes. But several months later, he will search for it, illustrating that he has attained object permanence. Why is the concept of object permanence important?

The attainment of object permanence extends not only to inanimate objects, but to people, too. It gives Chu the security that his father and mother still exist even when they have left the room.

Substage 5: Tertiary Circular Reactions. *Substage 5: Tertiary circular reactions* is reached at around the age of 12 months and extends to 18 months. As the name of the stage indicates, during this period infants develop these reactions, which are schemes regarding the deliberate variation of actions that bring desirable consequences. Rather than just repeating enjoyable activities, as they do with secondary circular reactions, infants appear to carry out miniature experiments to observe the consequences.

For example, Piaget observed his son Laurent dropping a toy swan repeatedly, varying the position from which he dropped it, carefully observing each time to see where it fell. Instead of just repeating the action each time, Laurent made modifications in the situation to learn about their consequences. As you may recall from our discussion of research methods in Module 1.3, this behaviour represents the essence of the scientific method: An experimenter varies a situation in a laboratory to learn the effects of the variation. To infants in Substage 5, the world is their laboratory, and they spend their days leisurely carrying out one miniature experiment after another.

Substage 6: Beginnings of Thought. The final stage of the sensorimotor period is *Substage 6: Beginnings of thought*, which lasts from around 18 months to 2 years. The major achievement of Substage 6 is the capacity for mental representation, or symbolic thought. A *mental representation* is an internal image of a past event or object. Piaget argued that by this stage infants can imagine where objects might be that they cannot see. They can even plot in their heads unseen trajectories of objects, so if a ball rolls under a piece of furniture, they can figure out where it is likely to emerge on the other side.

 From a caregiver's perspective: What are some implications for childrearing practices of Piaget's observations about the ways children gain an understanding of the world? Would you use the same approaches in childrearing for a child growing up in a non-Western culture?

With the attainment of the cognitive skill of deferred imitation, children are able to imitate people and scenes they have witnessed in the past.

Appraising Piaget: Support and Challenges

Most developmental researchers would probably agree that in many significant ways, Piaget's descriptions of how cognitive development proceeds during infancy are quite accurate (Harris, 1983, 1987; Marcovitch et al., 2003). Yet there is substantial disagreement over the validity of the theory and many of its specific predictions.

Let's start with what is clearly accurate about the Piagetian approach. Piaget was a masterful reporter of children's behaviour, and his descriptions of growth during infancy remain a monument to his powers of observation. Furthermore, literally thousands of studies have supported Piaget's view that children learn much about the world by acting on objects in their environment. Finally, the broad outlines sketched out by Piaget of the sequence of cognitive development and the increasing cognitive accomplishments that occur during infancy are generally accurate (Gratch and Schatz, 1987; Kail, 2004). On the other hand, specific aspects of the theory have come under increasing scrutiny—and criticism—in the decades since Piaget carried out his pioneering work. For example, some researchers question the stage conception that forms the basis of Piaget's theory. Although, as we noted earlier, even Piaget acknowledged that children's transitions between stages are gradual, critics contend that development proceeds in a much more continuous fashion. Rather than showing major leaps of competence at the end of one stage and the beginning of the next, improvement comes in more gradual increments, growing step by step in a skill by skill manner (Siegler, 2003; Lavelli and Fogel, 2005).

Other critics dispute Piaget's notion that cognitive development is grounded in motor activities. They charge that Piaget overlooked the importance of the sensory and perceptual systems that are present from a very early age in infancy—systems about which Piaget knew little, since so much of the research illustrating how sophisticated they are even in infancy was done relatively recently (Decarrie, 1969; Butterworth, 1994).

To bolster their views, Piaget's critics also point to more recent studies that cast doubt on Piaget's view that infants are incapable of mastering the concept of object permanence until they are close to a year old. For instance, some work suggests that younger infants did not appear to understand object permanence because the techniques used to test their abilities were not sensitive enough to their true capabilities (Aguiar and Baillargeon, 2002; Baillargeon, 2004; Krojgaard, 2005).

It might be that a four-month-old doesn't search for a rattle hidden under a blanket because she hasn't learned the motor skills necessary to do the searching—not because she doesn't understand that the rattle still exists. Similarly, the apparent inability of young infants to comprehend object permanence may reflect more about their memory deficits than their lack of understanding of the concept: The memories of young infants may be poor enough that they simply do not recall the earlier concealment of the toy. In fact, when more age-appropriate tasks are employed, some researchers have found indications of object permanence in children as young as 3 1/2 months (Aguiar and Baillargeon, 2002; Wang et al., 2005; Ruffman et al., 2006).

Piaget's work also seems to describe children from developed Western countries better than those in non-Western cultures. For instance, some evidence suggests that some cognitive skills emerge on a slightly different timetable for children in non-Western cultures than for children in Western cultures. Infants raised in the Ivory Coast of Africa, for example, reach the various substages of the sensorimotor period at an earlier age than infants reared in France (Dasen et al., 1978; Rogoff and Chavajay, 1995; Mistry and Saraswathi, 2003). Cultural differences would be unlikely to dissuade Piaget. He always believed that children's unique experiences, which would include culturally specific childrearing practices, could affect the rate of development. What he would emphasize as universal is the order of stages.

Even Piaget's most passionate critics concede that he has provided us with a masterful description of the broad outlines of cognitive development during infancy. His shortcomings seem to be in underestimating the capabilities of younger infants and in his claims that sensorimotor skills develop in a consistent, fixed pattern. Still, his influence has been enormous, and although the focus of many contemporary developmental researchers has shifted to newer information-processing approaches, which we discuss next, Piaget remains a towering and pioneering figure in the field of development (Roth et al., 2000; Kail, 2004).

Appraising Piaget: Research on babies in non-Western cultures suggests that Piaget's stages are not universal, but are to some degree culturally derived.

REVIEW, CHECK, AND APPLY

REVIEW

- Piaget's theory of human cognitive development involves a succession of stages through which children progress from birth to adolescence.

- As infants move from one stage to another, the way they understand the world changes.

- The sensorimotor stage, from birth to about two years, involves a gradual progression through simple reflexes, single coordinated activities, interest in the outside world, purposeful combinations of activities, manipulation of actions to produce desired outcomes, and symbolic thought. The sensorimotor stage has six substages.

CHECK YOURSELF

1. According to Piaget, a child can only move from one cognitive stage to another when he or she _____ and is exposed to relative experiences.

   a. is adequately nourished

   b. is born with an adequate genetic predisposition for learning

   c. has remembered his or her goal of learning

   d. reaches an appropriate level of physical maturation

2. Infants' schemes for understanding the world usually involve their physical or sensorimotor activities.

   - True

   - False

3. In general, when it comes to infant cognitive development, it appears that Piaget

   a. overestimated infants and what they could do.

   b. underestimated infants and what they could do.

   c. was more accurate about adolescent cognitive development.

   d. overestimated the role of culture.

APPLYING LIFESPAN DEVELOPMENT

- Think of a common young children's toy with which you are familiar. How might its use be affected by the principles of assimilation and accommodation?

Answers: 1) d; 2) True; 3) b

Information-Processing Approaches to Cognitive Development

LO9   How do infants process information?

LO10   How is infant intelligence measured?

Amber, three months old, breaks into a smile as her brother Marcus stands over her crib, picks up a doll, and makes a whistling noise through his teeth. In fact, Amber never seems to tire of Marcus's efforts at making her smile, and soon whenever Marcus appears and simply picks up the doll, her lips begin to curl into a smile.

Clearly, Amber remembers Marcus and his humorous ways. But *how* does she remember him? And how much else can Amber remember?

To answer questions such as these, we need to diverge from the road that Piaget laid out for us. Rather than seeking to identify the universal, broad milestones in cognitive development through which all infants pass, as Piaget tried to do, we must consider the specific processes by which individual babies acquire and use the information to which they are exposed. We need, then, to focus less on the qualitative changes in infants' mental lives and consider more closely their quantitative capabilities.

Information-processing approaches to cognitive development seek to identify the way that individuals take in, use, and store information. According to this approach, the quantitative changes in infants' abilities to organize and manipulate information represent the hallmarks of cognitive development.

Taking this perspective, cognitive growth is characterized by increasing sophistication, speed, and capacity in information-processing. Earlier, we compared Piaget's idea of schemes to computer software, which directs the computer in how to deal with data from the world. We might compare the information-processing perspective on cognitive growth to the improvements that come from both hardware upgrades (brain maturation) and the use of

Information-processing approaches the model that seeks to identify the way that individuals take in, use, and store information

more efficient programs that lead to increased speed and sophistication in the processing of information. Information-processing approaches, then, focus on the types of "mental programs" that people use when they seek to solve problems (Reyna, 1997; Siegler, 1998; Cohen and Cashon, 2003).

Encoding, Storage, and Retrieval: The Foundations of Information-Processing

Information-processing has three basic aspects: encoding, storage, and retrieval (see Figure 3-11). *Encoding* is the process by which information is initially recorded in a form usable to memory. Infants and children—indeed, all people—are exposed to a massive amount of information; if they tried to process it all, they would be overwhelmed. Consequently, they encode selectively, picking and choosing the information to which they will pay attention.

Even if someone has been exposed to the information initially and has encoded it in an appropriate way, there is still no guarantee that he or she will be able to use it in the future. Information must also have been stored in memory adequately. *Storage* refers to the placement of material into memory. Finally, success in using the material in the future depends on retrieval processes. *Retrieval* is the process by which material in memory storage is located, brought into awareness, and used.

We can use our comparison to computers again here. Information-processing approaches suggest that the processes of encoding, storage, and retrieval are analogous to different parts of a computer. Encoding can be thought of as a computer's keyboard, through which one inputs information; storage is the computer's hard drive, where information is stored; and retrieval is analogous to software that accesses the information for display on the screen. Only when all three processes are operating—encoding, storage, and retrieval—can information be processed.

Automatization. In some cases, encoding, storage, and retrieval are relatively automatic, while in other cases they are deliberate. *Automatization* is the degree to which an activity requires attention. Processes that require relatively little attention are automatic; processes that require relatively large amounts of attention are controlled. For example, some activities such as walking, eating with a fork, or reading may be automatic for you, but at first they required your full attention.

Automatic mental processes help children in their initial encounters with the world by enabling them to easily and "automatically" process information in particular ways. For instance, by the age of five, children automatically encode information in terms of frequency. Without a lot of attention to counting or tallying, they become aware, for example, of how often they have encountered various people, permitting them to differentiate familiar from unfamiliar people (Hasher and Zacks, 1984).

Some of the things we learn automatically are unexpectedly complex. For example, infants have the ability to learn subtle statistical patterns and relationships; these results are consistent with a growing body of research showing that the mathematical skills of infants are surprisingly good. For example, infants have an innate grasp of certain basic mathematical functions and statistical patterns. This inborn proficiency is likely to form the basis for learning more complex mathematics and statistical relationships later in life, and even language (Saffran, 2003; Gelman and Gallistel, 2004; McCrink and Wynn, 2004; vanMarle and Wynn, 2006).

FIGURE 3-11 Information-Processing
The process by which information is encoded, stored, and retrieved.

Memory During Infancy: They Must Remember This . . .

Simona's father tells stories of Simona's infancy, some so often she sometimes feels like she's remembering them, but the only memory she truly knows is her own memory is of a tricycle accident when she was four. How does she know the difference? The stories her father tells play like movies in her mind, and sometimes not from her own perspective. Her tricycle accident, on the other hand, she sees from her perspective, including what happened before the adults arrived on the scene.

How likely is it that Simona truly remembers nothing of her infancy? And if she ever does recall her first two years of life, how accurate will her memories be? To answer these questions, we need to consider the qualities of memory that exist during infancy.

Memory Capabilities in Infancy. Certainly, infants have **memory** capabilities, defined as the process by which information is initially recorded, stored, and retrieved. As we've seen, infants can distinguish new stimuli from old, and this implies that some memory of the old must be present. Unless the infants had some memory of an original stimulus, it would be impossible for them to recognize that a new stimulus differed from the earlier one (Newcombe et al., 1995).

However, infants' capability to distinguish new stimuli from old tells us little about how age brings changes in the capacities of memory and in its fundamental nature. Do infants' memory capabilities increase as they get older? The answer is clearly affirmative. In one study, infants were taught that they could move a mobile hanging over the crib by kicking their legs (see photo). It took only a few days for two-month-old infants to forget their training, but six-month-old infants still remembered for as long as three weeks (Rovee-Collier, 1993, 1999).

Furthermore, infants who were later prompted to recall the association between kicking and moving the mobile showed evidence that the memory continued to exist even longer. Infants who had received just two training sessions lasting nine minutes each still recalled about a week later, as illustrated by the fact that they began to kick when placed in the crib with the mobile. Two weeks later, however, they made no effort to kick, suggesting that they had forgotten entirely.

But they hadn't: When the babies saw a reminder—a moving mobile—their memories were apparently reactivated. In fact, the infants could remember the association, following prompting, for as long as an additional month. Other evidence confirms these results, suggesting that hints can reactivate memories that at first seem lost, and that the older the infant, the more effective such prompting is (Hildreth et al., 2003; Bearce and Rovee-Collier, 2006).

The Duration of Memories. Although the processes that underlie memory retention and recall seem similar throughout the lifespan, the quantity of information stored and recalled does differ markedly as infants develop. Older infants can retrieve information more rapidly and they can remember it longer. But just how long? Can memories from infancy be recalled, for example, after babies grow up?

Researchers disagree on the age from which memories can be retrieved. Although early research supported the notion of **infantile amnesia**—the lack of memory for experiences occurring prior to three years of age—more recent research shows that infants do retain memories. For example, six-month-old children exposed to an unusual series of events, such as intermittent periods of light and dark and unusual sounds, have some memories of their participation in the earlier experience two years later (Howe et al., 2004; Neisser, 2004).

Still, although it is at least theoretically possible for memories to remain intact from a very young age—if subsequent experiences do not interfere with their recollection—in most cases, memories of personal experiences in infancy do not last into adulthood. Memories of personal experience seem not to become accurate before age 18 to 24 months (Howe, 2003; Howe et al., 2004).

The Cognitive Neuroscience of Memory. Some of the most exciting research on the development of memory is coming from studies of the neurological basis of memory. Advances in brain scan technology, as well as studies of adults with brain damage, suggest that there are two separate systems involved with long-term memory. These two systems, called explicit memory and implicit memory, retain different sorts of information.

Explicit memory is memory that is conscious and that can be recalled intentionally. When we try to recall a name or phone number, we're using explicit memory. In comparison, *implicit memory* consists of memories of which we are not consciously aware, but that affect performance and behaviour. Implicit memory consists of motor skills, habits, and activities

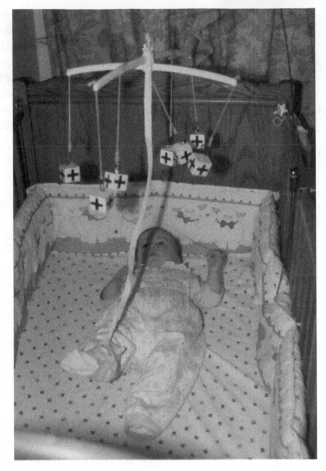

Infants who learned they can control this mobile by kicking their feet demonstrate memory when they spontaneously kick for the same mobile on a later occasion.

memory the process by which information is initially recorded, stored, and retrieved

infantile amnesia the lack of memory for experiences that occurred prior to three years of age

that can be remembered without conscious cognitive effort, such as how to ride a bike or climb stairs.

Explicit and implicit memories emerge at different rates and involve different parts of the brain. The earliest memories seem to be implicit, and they involve the cerebellum and brain stem. The forerunner of explicit memory involves the hippocampus, but true explicit memory doesn't emerge until the second half of the first year. When explicit memory does emerge, it involves an increasing number of areas of the cortex of the brain (Bauer et al., 2003; Bauer, 2004; Squire and Knowlton, 2005).

Individual Differences in Intelligence: Is One Infant Smarter than Another?

Maddy is a bundle of curiosity and energy. At six months of age, she cries heartily if she can't reach a toy, and when she sees a reflection of herself in a mirror, she gurgles and seems, in general, to find the situation quite amusing.

***

Bailey, at six months, is a good deal more inhibited than Maddy. He doesn't seem to care much when a ball rolls out of his reach, losing interest in it rapidly. And, unlike Maddy, when he sees himself in a mirror, he pretty much ignores the reflection.

As anyone who has spent any time at all observing more than one baby can tell you, not all infants are alike. Some are full of energy and life, apparently displaying a natural-born curiosity, while others seem, by comparison, somewhat less interested in the world around them. Does this mean that such infants differ in intelligence?

Answering questions about how and to what degree infants vary in their underlying intelligence is not easy. Although it is clear that different infants show significant variations in their behaviour, the issue of just what types of behaviour might be related to cognitive ability is complicated. Interestingly, the examination of individual differences between infants was the initial approach taken by developmental specialists to understand cognitive development, and such issues still represent an important focus within the field.

What Is Infant Intelligence? Developmental specialists have devised several approaches (summarized in Table 3-5) to illuminate the nature of individual differences in intelligence during infancy.

Developmental Scales. Developmental psychologist Arnold Gesell formulated the earliest measure of infant development, which was designed to distinguish between typically developing and atypically developing babies (Gesell, 1946). Gesell based his scale on examinations of hundreds of babies. He compared their performance at different ages to learn what behaviours were most common at a particular age. If an infant varied significantly from the norms of a given age, he was considered to be developmentally delayed or advanced.

TABLE 3-5 APPROACHES USED TO DETECT DIFFERENCES IN INTELLIGENCE DURING INFANCY

Developmental quotient	Formulated by Arnold Gesell, the developmental quotient is an overall development score that relates to performance in four domains: motor skills (balance and sitting), language use, adaptive behaviour (alertness and exploration), and personal-social behaviour.
Bayley Scales of Infant Development	Developed by Nancy Bayley, the Bayley Scales of Infant Development evaluate an infant's development from 2 to 42 months. The Bayley Scales focus on two areas: mental (senses, perception, memory, learning, problem solving, and language) and motor abilities (fine and gross motor skills).
Visual-recognition memory measurement	Measures of visual-recognition memory, the memory of and recognition of a stimulus that has been previously seen, also relate to intelligence. The more quickly an infant can retrieve a representation of a stimulus from memory, the more efficient, presumably, is that infant's information-processing.

TABLE 3-6 SAMPLE ITEMS FROM THE BAYLEY SCALES OF INFANT DEVELOPMENT

Age	Mental Scale	Motor Scale
2 months	Turns head to sound	Holds head erect/steady for 15 seconds
	Reacts to disappearance of face	Sits with support
6 months	Lifts cup by handle	Sits alone for 30 seconds
	Looks at pictures in book	Grasps foot with hands
12 months	Builds tower of two cubes	Walks with help
	Turns pages of book	Grasps pencil in middle
17–19 months	Imitates crayon stroke	Stands alone on right foot
	Identifies objects in photo	Walks up stairs with help
23–25 months	Matches pictures	Laces three beads
	Imitates a two-word sentence	Jumps distance of four inches
38–42 months	Names four colours	Copies circle
	Uses past tense	Hops twice on one foot
	Identifies gender	Walks down stairs, alternating feet

Following the lead of researchers who sought to quantify intelligence through a specific score (known as an intelligence quotient, or IQ, score), Gesell developed a developmental quotient, or DQ. The **developmental quotient** is an overall developmental score that relates to performance in four domains: motor skills (for example, balance and sitting), language use, adaptive behaviour (such as alertness and exploration), and personal-social (for example, adequately feeding and dressing oneself).

Later researchers have created other developmental scales. For instance, Nancy Bayley developed one of the most widely used measures for infants. The **Bayley Scales of Infant Development** evaluate an infant's development from 2 to 42 months. The Bayley Scales focus on two areas: mental and motor abilities. The mental scale focuses on the senses, perception, memory, learning, problem solving, and language, while the motor scale evaluates fine and gross motor skills (see Table 3-6). Like Gesell's approach, the Bayley yields a developmental quotient (DQ). A child who scores at an average level—meaning average performance for other children at the same age—receives a score of 100 (Bayley, 1969; Black and Matula, 1999; Gagnon and Nagle, 2000).

The virtue of approaches such as those taken by Gesell and Bayley is that they provide a good snapshot of an infant's current developmental level. Using these scales, we can tell in an objective manner whether a particular infant falls behind or is ahead of his or her same-age peers. The scales are particularly useful in identifying infants who are substantially behind their peers and who therefore need immediate special attention (Culbertson and Gyurke, 1990; Aylward and Verhulst, 2000).

What such scales are *not* useful for is predicting a child's future course of development. A child whose development is identified by these measures as relatively slow at the age of 1 year will not necessarily display slow development at age 5, or 12, or 25. The association between most measures of behaviour during infancy and adult intelligence, then, is minimal (Siegel, 1989; DiLalla et al., 1990; Molffese and Acheson, 1997).

>  **From a nurse's perspective:** In what ways is the use of such developmental scales as Gesell's or Bayley's helpful? In what ways is it dangerous? How would you maximize the helpfulness and minimize the danger if you were advising a parent?

developmental quotient an overall developmental score that relates to performance in four domains: motor skills, language use, adaptive behaviour, and personal-social

Bayley Scales of Infant Development a measure that evaluates an infant's development from 2 to 42 months

Information-Processing Approaches to Individual Differences in Intelligence.
Contemporary approaches to infant intelligence suggest that the speed with which infants
process information may correlate most strongly with later intelligence, as measured by IQ
tests administered during adulthood.

How can we tell if a baby is processing information quickly? Most researchers use habituation tests. Infants who process information efficiently ought to be able to learn about stimuli
more quickly. Consequently, we would expect that they would turn their attention away from
a given stimulus more rapidly than those who are less efficient at information-processing,
leading to the phenomenon of habituation. Similarly, measures of *visual-recognition memory*,
the memory and recognition of a stimulus that has been previously seen, also relate to IQ. The
more quickly an infant can retrieve a representation of a stimulus from memory, the more
efficient, presumably, is that infant's information-processing (Rose et al., 2002; Robinson and
Pascalis, 2005).

Research using an information-processing framework clearly suggests a relationship
between information-processing efficiency and cognitive abilities: Measures of how quickly
infants lose interest in stimuli that they have previously seen, as well as their responsiveness
to new stimuli, correlate moderately well with later measures of intelligence. Infants who
are more efficient information processors during the 6 months following birth tend to have
higher intelligence scores between 2 and 12 years of age, as well as higher scores on other
measures of cognitive competence such as language and reading (Sigman et al., 2000; Rose
et al., 2004).

Although information-processing efficiency during infancy relates moderately well to
later IQ scores, we need to keep in mind two qualifications. Even though there is an association between early information-processing capabilities and later measures of IQ, the correlation is only moderate in strength. Consequently, we should not assume that intelligence is
somehow permanently fixed in infancy.

Assessing Information-Processing Approaches.   The information-processing perspective
on cognitive development during infancy is very different from Piaget's. Rather than focusing
on broad explanations of the *qualitative* changes that occur in infants' capabilities, as Piaget
does, information-processing looks at *quantitative* change. Piaget sees cognitive growth occurring in fairly sudden spurts; information-processing sees more gradual, step-by-step
growth. (Think of the difference between a track-and-field runner leaping hurdles versus a
slow-but-steady marathon racer.)

Because information-processing researchers consider cognitive development in terms
of a collection of individual skills, they are often able to use more precise measures of
cognitive ability, such as processing speed and memory recall, than proponents of Piaget's
approach. Still, the very precision of these individual measures makes it harder to get an
overall sense of the nature of cognitive development, something at which Piaget was a
master. It's as if information-processing approaches focus more on the individual pieces of
the puzzle of cognitive development, while Piagetian approaches focus more on the whole
puzzle.

Ultimately, both Piagetian and information-processing approaches provide an account of
cognitive development in infancy. Coupled with advances in understanding the biochemistry
of the brain and theories that consider the effects of social factors on learning and cognition,
the two help us paint a full picture of cognitive development. (Also see the *From Research to
Practice* box.)

From Research to Practice

Do Educational Media for Infants Enhance Their Cognitive Development? Taking the Einstein Out of Baby Einstein

Gemma is 11 months old, and already her toybox is full.

"We have a routine. We dance in the morning, we do a half-hour of Baby Einstein after lunch, and we get out the Leapster after nap. My sister tells me I'm wasting my money, but I want the best for Gemma. Money is no object," says Gemma's mother, Mabel.

Mabel's philosophy captures the sentiments of many parents, who believe that exposing infants to educational media like the Baby Einstein series of videos may be beneficial to their cognitive growth. For instance, one survey found that about half the parents agreed that educational media are "very important" contributors to their children's intellectual development. And there is certainly a wide variety of products to try, ranging from DVDs to computer games and electronic devices, that are marketed with claims of having educational value. But one important question for parents is whether their infant children are really deriving any benefit from these products—and if they are not, is it truly a safe assumption that such products are completely harmless (Wartella et al., 2004)?

A report from the Kaiser Family Foundation reveals that the marketing of educational media for infants is far outpacing the research on its effectiveness. In fact, practically no such research evidence exists. One part of the reason is the difficulty in conducting such research experimentally; much of the limited evidence is based on correlational studies that cannot rule out such factors as natural intelligence or parental education—or even discern true benefits of the media exposure from normal cognitive development over time (Garrison and Christakis, 2005).

Another part of the reason for the lack of research on the effectiveness of electronic media is that companies producing such products are reluctant to test the claims that their products are of value. Although they do conduct research on whether children can understand the media well enough to use it, their research on actual beneficial outcomes is very limited (Rideout et al., 2003).

However, an overreliance on educational media products can actually be harmful. Consider the research of language expert Patricia Kuhl, who has found that infants don't learn language from media such as an audio or a videotape. Nine-month-old anglophone infants who interacted with a Mandarin-speaking adult acquired a sensitivity to the sounds of the Mandarin language—but infants who were exposed to the language through audio and video media did not. Social interaction seems to be a critical part of language learning. Without social context, the language lessons were little more than meaningless noise to the infants. Other research also shows that very young children learn better from live demonstrations than they do from videotapes, failing to imitate actions on a video that they *can* imitate from a live model and failing to use information on a TV screen when they *could* use the same information if they thought the TV was a window into another room. Thus, the research suggests that parents should hold off on the electronic media until age two or three, and even then it's no substitute (Troseth and DeLoache, 1998; Kuhl et al., 2003; Anderson and Pempek, 2005; Arnold and Colburn, 2007).

- Do you think that educational media for infants is worth a try, despite the lack of scientific research supporting its use? Why? Under what conditions might its use actually have undesirable consequences?

- Why do you think parents generally do not seem to be concerned about the lack of scientific evidence for the effectiveness of educational media for infants?

REVIEW, CHECK, AND APPLY

REVIEW

- Information-processing approaches consider quantitative changes in children's abilities to organize and use information. Cognitive growth is regarded as the increasing sophistication of encoding, storage, and retrieval.

- Infants clearly have memory capabilities from a very early age, although the duration and accuracy of such memories are unresolved questions.

- Traditional measures of infant intelligence focus on behavioural attainments, which can help identify developmental delays or advances.

CHECK YOURSELF

1. The information-processing approach to cognitive development emphasizes the increased sophisti-

cation, speed, and _____ associated with cognitive growth.

   a. capacity

   b. circular reactions

   c. categorization

   d. analysis

2. Infants have memory capabilities from a very early age, although the duration and accuracy of such memories are unresolved questions.

   • True

   • False

3. When Justin first learned to walk he had a difficult time coordinating the movements to lift or carry an object. After much practice the motions became more fluid and each component of the process required less attention. According to the

information-processing model, this would be an example of _____.

APPLYING LIFESPAN DEVELOPMENT

- What information from this module could you use to refute the claims of books or educational programs that promise to help parents increase their babies' intelligence or instill advanced intellectual skills in infants? Based on valid research, what approaches would you use for intellectual development of infants?

Answers: 1) a; 2) True; 3) automatization

The Roots of Language

LO11 By what process do children learn to use language?

LO12 How do children influence adults' language?

> **language** the systematic, meaningful arrangement of symbols, which provides the basis for communication

Vicki and Dominic were engaged in a friendly competition over whose name would be the first word their baby, Maura, said. "Say 'mama,'" Vicki would coo, before handing Maura over to Dominic for a diaper change. Grinning, he would take her and coax, "No, say 'daddy.'" Both parents ended up losing—and winning—when Maura's first word sounded more like "baba," and seemed to refer to her bottle.

Mama. No. Cookie. Dada. Kitty. Most parents can remember their baby's first word, and no wonder. It's an exciting moment, this emergence of a skill that is, arguably, unique to human beings.

But those initial words are just the first and most obvious manifestations of language. Many months earlier, infants begin to understand the language used by others to make sense of the world around them. How does this linguistic ability develop? What is the pattern and sequence of language development? And how does the use of language transform the cognitive world of infants and their parents? We consider these questions, and others, as we address the development of language during the first years of life.

The Fundamentals of Language: From Sounds to Symbols

Language, the systematic, meaningful arrangement of symbols, provides the basis for communication. But it does more than this: It is closely tied to the way we think and understand the world. It enables us to reflect on people and objects and to convey our thoughts to others.

Language has several formal characteristics that must be mastered as linguistic competence is developed. They include the following:

- **Phonology.** Phonology refers to the basic sounds of language, called *phonemes,* that can be combined to produce words and sentences. For instance, the "a" in "mat" and the "a" in "mate" represent two different phonemes in English. Although English employs just 40 phonemes to create every word in the language, other languages have as many as 85 phonemes—and some as few as 15 (Akmajian et al., 1984).

- **Morphemes.** A morpheme is the smallest language unit that has meaning. Some morphemes are complete words, while others add information necessary for interpreting a word, such as the endings "-s" for plural and "-ed" for past tense.

- **Semantics.** Semantics are the rules that govern the meaning of words and sentences. As their knowledge of semantics develops, children are able to understand the subtle distinction between "Ellie was hit by a ball" (an answer to the question of why Ellie doesn't want to play catch) and "A ball hit Ellie" (used to announce the current situation).

In considering the development of language, we need to distinguish between linguistic *comprehension,* the understanding of speech, and linguistic *production,* the use of language to communicate. One principle underlies the relationship between the two: Comprehension precedes production. An 18-month-old might be able to understand a complex series of directions ("pick up your coat from the floor and put it on the chair by the fireplace") but might not yet have strung more than two words together when speaking for herself. Throughout infancy comprehension also outpaces production. For example, during infancy, comprehension of words expands at a rate of 22 new words a month, while production of words increases at a rate of about 9 new words a month, once talking begins (Benedict, 1979; Tincoff and Jusczyk, 1999; Rescorla et al., 2001; see Figure 3-12).

Early Sounds and Communication. Spend 24 hours with even a very young infant and you will hear a variety of sounds: cooing, crying, gurgling, murmuring, and assorted types of other noises. These sounds, although not meaningful in themselves, play an important role in linguistic development, paving the way for true language (Bloom, 1993; O'Grady and Aitchison, 2005).

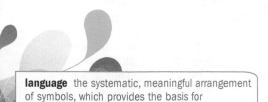

Although we tend to think of language in terms of the production of words and then groups of words, infants can begin to communicate linguistically well before they say their first word.

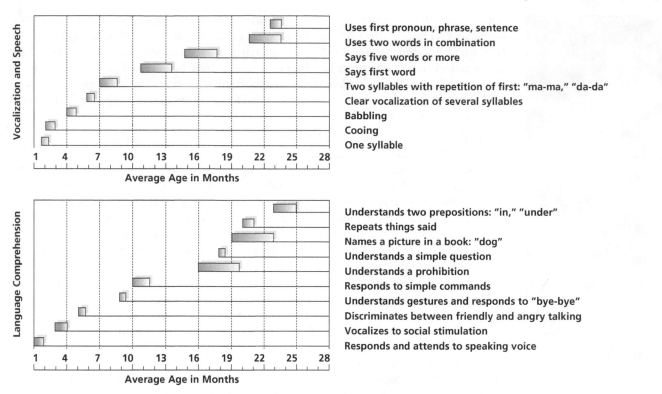

Uses first pronoun, phrase, sentence
Uses two words in combination
Says five words or more
Says first word
Two syllables with repetition of first: "ma-ma," "da-da"
Clear vocalization of several syllables
Babbling
Cooing
One syllable

Understands two prepositions: "in," "under"
Repeats things said
Names a picture in a book: "dog"
Understands a simple question
Understands a prohibition
Responds to simple commands
Understands gestures and responds to "bye-bye"
Discriminates between friendly and angry talking
Vocalizes to social stimulation
Responds and attends to speaking voice

FIGURE 3-12 Comprehension Precedes Production
Throughout infancy, the comprehension of speech precedes the production of speech.
Source: Adapted from Bornstein and Lamb, 1992.

Prelinguistic communication is communication through sounds, facial expressions, gestures, imitation, and other nonlinguistic means. When a father responds to his daughter's "ah" with an "ah" of his own, and then the daughter repeats the sound, and the father responds once again, they are engaged in prelinguistic communication. Clearly, the "ah" sound has no particular meaning. However, its repetition, which mimics the give-and-take of conversation, teaches the infant something about turn-taking and the back-and-forth of communication (Reddy, 1999).

babbling making speechlike but meaningless sounds

The most obvious manifestation of prelinguistic communication is babbling. **Babbling**—making speechlike but meaningless sounds—starts at the age of two or three months and continues until around the age of one year. When they babble, infants repeat the same vowel sound over and over, changing the pitch from high to low (as in "ee-ee-ee," repeated at different pitches). After the age of five months, the sounds of babbling begin to expand, reflecting the addition of consonants (such as "bee-bee-bee-bee").

Babbling is a universal phenomenon, accomplished in the same way throughout all cultures. While they are babbling, infants spontaneously produce all the sounds found in every language, not just the language they hear people around them speaking.

Babbling typically follows a progression from simple to more complex sounds. Although exposure to the sounds of a particular language does

Deaf infants who are exposed to sign language do their own type of babbling, related to the use of signs.

By the age of two, most children use two-word phrases, such as "ball play."

not seem to influence babbling initially, eventually experience does make a difference. By the age of six months, babbling reflects the sounds of the language to which infants are exposed (Blake and Boysson-Bardies, 1992). The difference is so noticeable that even untrained listeners can distinguish between babbling infants who have been raised in cultures in which French, Arabic, or Cantonese languages are spoken. Furthermore, the speed at which infants begin honing in on their own language is related to the speed of later language development (Oller et al., 1997; Tsao et al., 2004).

First Words. When a mother and father first hear their child say "Mama" or "Dada," or even "baba," as Maura, the baby described earlier in this section did, it is hard to be anything but delighted. Their initial enthusiasm might be dampened a bit, however, when they find that the same sound is used to ask for a cookie, a doll, and a ratty old blanket.

First words generally are spoken somewhere around the age of 10 to 14 months, but may occur as early as 9 months. Once an infant starts to produce words, vocabulary increases at a rapid rate. By the age of 15 months, the average child has a vocabulary of 10 words and methodically expands until the one-word stage of language development ends at around 18 months. Once that happens, a sudden spurt in vocabulary occurs. In just a short period—a few weeks somewhere between 16 and 24 months of age—an explosion of language occurs in which a child's vocabulary typically increases from 50 to 400 words (Gleitman and Landau, 1994; Fernald et al., 1998; Nazzi and Bertoncini, 2003).

The first words in children's early vocabularies typically regard objects and things, both animate and inanimate. Most often they refer to people or objects who constantly appear and disappear ("Mama"), to animals ("kitty"), or to temporary states ("wet"). These first words are often **holophrases**, one-word utterances that stand for a whole phrase, whose meaning depends on the particular context in which they are used. For instance, a youngster may use the phrase "ma" to mean, depending on the context, "I want to be picked up by Mom" or "I want something to eat, Mom" or "Where's Mom?" (Dromi, 1987; O'Grady and Aitchison, 2005).

The unique properties of specific languages have an effect on the type of first words spoken. For example, unlike English-speaking infants, who are more apt to use nouns initially, Chinese Mandarin-speaking infants use more verbs than nouns. This is attributed to differences in the structures of the languages; Mandarin and Japanese are more "verb-friendly" languages and thus verbs are more prominent in children's early vocabularies (Fernald and Marchman, 2006). On the other hand, by the age of 20 months, remarkable cross-cultural similarities occur in the types of words spoken. For example, a comparison of 20-month-olds in Argentina, Belgium, France, Israel, Italy, and the Republic of Korea found that children's vocabularies in every culture contained greater proportions of nouns than other classes of words (Tardif, 1996; Bornstein et al., 2004).

First Sentences. When Aaron was 19 months old, he heard his mother coming up the back steps, as she did every day just before dinner. Aaron turned to his father and distinctly said, "Ma come." In stringing those two words together, Aaron took a giant step in his language development.

The increase in vocabulary that comes at around 18 months is accompanied by another accomplishment: the linking together of individual words into sentences that convey a single thought. Although there is a good deal of variability in the time at which children first create two-word phrases, it is generally around 8 to 12 months after they say their first word.

The linguistic advance represented by two-word combinations is important because the linkage not only provides labels for things in the world but also indicates the relations between them. For instance, the combination may declare something about possession ("Mama key") or recurrent events ("dog bark"). Interestingly, most early sentences don't represent demands or even necessarily require a response. Instead, they are often merely comments and observations about events occurring in the child's world (Halliday, 1975; O'Grady and Aitchison, 2005).

Two-year-olds using two-word combinations tend to employ particular sequences that are similar to the ways in which adult sentences are constructed. For instance, sentences in English typically follow a pattern in which the subject of the sentence comes first, followed by the verb, and then the object ("Josh threw the ball"). Children's speech most often uses a similar order, although not all the words are initially included. Consequently, a child might say

holophrases one-word utterances that stand for a whole phrase, the meaning of which depends on the particular context in which they are used

"Josh threw" or "Josh ball" to indicate the same thought. What is significant is that the order is typically not "threw Josh" or "ball Josh," but rather the usual order of English, which makes the utterance much easier for an English speaker to comprehend (Brown, 1973; Hirsh-Pasek and Michnick-Golinkoff, 1995; Masataka, 2003).

Although the creation of two-word sentences represents an advance, the language used by children still is by no means adultlike. As we've just seen, two-year-olds tend to leave out words that aren't critical to the message, similar to the way we might write a telegram for which we were paying by the word (note the similarity to text messaging today). For that reason, their talk is often called **telegraphic speech**. Rather than saying, "I showed you the book," a child using telegraphic speech might say, "I show book." "I am drawing a dog" might become "drawing dog" (see Table 3-7).

Early language has other characteristics that differentiate it from the language used by adults. For instance, consider Sarah, who refers to the blanket she sleeps with as "blankie." When her Aunt Ethel gives her a new blanket, Sarah refuses to call the new one a "blankie," restricting the word to her original blanket.

Sarah's inability to generalize the label of "blankie" to blankets in general is an example of **underextension**, using words too restrictively, which is common among children just mastering spoken language. Underextension occurs when language novices think that a word refers to a specific instance of a concept, instead of to all examples of the concept (Caplan and Barr, 1989; Masataka, 2003). This suggests that children's first bias is to assume labels are the names of things. Thus, "mama" refers to Sarah's mother, not just anyone's mother and "kitty" refers to Sarah's cat, not other cats.

As infants like Sarah grow more adept with language, the opposite phenomenon occurs. In **overextension**, words are used too broadly, overgeneralizing their meaning. For example, when Sarah refers to buses, trucks, and tractors as "cars," she is guilty of overextension, making the assumption that any object with wheels must be a car. Although overextension reflects speech errors, it also shows that advances are occurring in the child's thought processes: The child is beginning to develop general mental categories and concepts (Johnson and Eilers, 1998; McDonough, 2002). Sarah now understands that "mama" isn't just her mother but is a class of people and "kitty" is a class of animals. This understanding of categories begins with excessively broad categories that are gradually refined as children learn more about the world.

Infants also show individual differences in the style of language they use. For example, some use a **referential style** in which language is used primarily to label objects. Others tend to use an **expressive style** in which language is used primarily to express feelings and needs about oneself and others (Bates et al., 1994; Nelson, 1996). Language styles reflect, in part, cultural factors. For example, anglophone mothers label objects more frequently than do Japanese mothers, encouraging a more referential style of speech. In contrast, mothers in Japan are more apt to speak about social interactions, encouraging a more expressive style of speech (Fernald and Marchman, 2006).

telegraphic speech speech in which words not critical to the message are left out

underextension the overly restrictive use of words, common among children just mastering spoken language

overextension the overly broad use of words, overgeneralizing their meaning to label objects

referential style a style of language use in which language is used primarily to label objects

expressive style a style of language use in which language is used primarily to express feelings and needs about oneself and others

TABLE 3-7   CHILDREN'S IMITATION OF SENTENCES SHOWING DECLINE OF TELEGRAPHIC SPEECH

	Eve, 25.5 Months	Adam, 28.5 Months	Helen, 30 Months	Ian, 31.5 Months	Jimmy, 32 Months	June, 35.5 Months
I showed you the book.	I show book.	(I show) book.	C	I show you the book.	C	Show you the book.
I am very tall.	(My) tall.	I (very) tall.	I very tall.	I'm very tall.	Very tall.	I very tall.
It goes in a big box.	Big box.	Big box.	In big box.	It goes in the box.	C	C
I am drawing a dog.	Drawing dog.	I draw dog.	I drawing dog.	Dog.	C	C
I will read the book.	Read book.	I will read book.	I read the book.	I read the book.	C	C
I can see a cow.	See cow.	I want see cow.	C	Cow.	C	C
I will do that again.	Do again.	I will that again.	I do that.	I again.	C	C

C=correct imitation.

Source: Adapted from R. Brown and C. Fraser, 1963.

learning theory approach the theory that language acquisition follows the basic laws of reinforcement and conditioning

nativist approach the theory that a genetically determined, innate mechanism directs language development

universal grammar Noam Chomsky's theory that all the world's languages share a similar underlying structure

language-acquisition device (LAD) a neural system of the brain hypothesized to permit understanding of language

The Origins of Language Development

The immense strides in language development during the preschool years raise a fundamental question: How does proficiency in language come about? Linguists are deeply divided on how to answer this question.

Learning Theory Approaches: Language as a Learned Skill. One view of language development emphasizes the basic principles of learning. According to the **learning theory approach**, language acquisition follows the basic laws of reinforcement and conditioning discussed in Module 1.2 (Skinner, 1957). For instance, a child who articulates the word "da" might be hugged and praised by her father, who jumps to the conclusion that she is referring to him. This reaction reinforces the child, who is more likely to repeat the word. In sum, the learning theory perspective on language acquisition suggests that children learn to speak by being rewarded for making sounds that approximate speech. Through the process of *shaping*, language becomes more and more similar to adult speech.

There's a problem, though, with the learning theory approach. It doesn't seem to adequately explain how children acquire the rules of language as readily as they do. For instance, young children are reinforced when they make errors. Parents are apt to be just as responsive if their child says, "Why the dog won't eat?" as they are if the child phrases the question more correctly ("Why won't the dog eat?"). Both forms of the question are understood correctly, and both elicit the same response; reinforcement is provided for both correct and incorrect language usage. Under such circumstances, learning theory is hard put to explain how children learn to speak properly.

Children are also able to move beyond specific utterances they have heard, and produce novel phrases, sentences, and constructions, an ability that also cannot be explained by learning theory. Furthermore, children can apply linguistic rules to nonsense words. In one study, four-year-old children heard the nonsense verb "to pilk" in the sentence "the bear is pilking the horse." Later, when asked what was happening to the horse, they responded by placing the nonsense verb in the correct tense and voice: "He's getting pilked by the bear."

Nativist Approaches: Language as an Innate Skill. Such conceptual difficulties with the learning theory approach have led to the development of an alternative, championed by the linguist Noam Chomsky and known as the nativist approach (1968, 1978, 1991, 1999, 2005). The **nativist approach** argues that there is a genetically determined, innate mechanism that directs the development of language. According to Chomsky, people are born with an innate capacity to use language, which emerges, more or less automatically, due to maturation.

Chomsky's analysis of different languages suggests that all the world's languages share a similar underlying structure, which he calls **universal grammar**. In this view, the human brain is wired with a neural system called the **language-acquisition device (LAD)** that both permits the understanding of language structure and provides a set of strategies and techniques for learning the particular characteristics of the language to which a child is exposed. In this view, language is uniquely human, made possible by a genetic predisposition to both comprehend and produce words and sentences (Nowak et al., 2001, 2002; Hauser et al., 2002; Lidz and Gleitman, 2004).

Support for Chomsky's nativist approach comes from recent findings identifying a specific gene related to speech production. Further support comes from research showing that language processing in infants involves brain structures similar to those in adult speech processing, suggesting an evolutionary basis to language (see Figure 3-13; Wade, 2001; Monaco, 2005; Dehaene-Lambertz et al., 2006).

On the other hand, the view that language is an innate ability unique to humans also has its critics. For instance, some researchers argue that certain primates are able to learn at least the basics of language, an ability that calls into question the uniqueness of the human linguistic capacity. Others point out that although humans may be genetically primed to use language, its use still requires significant social experience in order for it to be used effectively (MacWhinney, 1991; Savage-Rumbaugh et al., 1993; Goldberg, 2004).

The Computational Approaches. Neither the learning theory nor the nativist perspective fully explains language acquisition. Instead there appear to be sophisticated computational strategies at work in the brains of infants, taking in the language they hear, processing it like

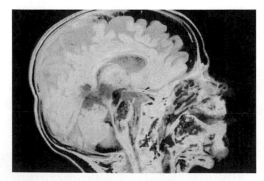

FIGURE 3-13 Infant's Speech Processing
This fMRI scan of a three-month-old infant shows speech processing activity similar to that of an adult, suggesting there might be an evolutionary basis to language.

raw data, and honing in on the rules of their native language. Beginning in utero, infants hear the rhythm of their mother's speech. Following birth, infants show a preference to hear a language that matches that rhythm over a language with a very different rhythm. Infants are also born with the ability to perceptually distinguish between all phonemes of all languages, but by 10–12 months they become "culture-bound listeners"—only able to distinguish the phonemes present in the language they hear on a day-to-day basis. Infants also appear to use statistical learning to identify word patterns, distinguishing between phoneme strings that are highly probable in a given language versus phoneme strings that are highly unlikely. This perspective suggests that language development is produced through a combination of genetically determined predispositions and environmental circumstances that help teach language (Saffran, 2003; Werker and Yeung, 2005; Kuhl, 2007).

infant-directed speech a type of speech directed toward infants, characterized by short, simple sentences

Speaking to Children: The Language of Infant-Directed Speech

Say the following sentence aloud: Do you like the applesauce?

Now pretend that you are going to ask the same question of an infant, and speak it as you would for a young child's ears.

Chances are several things happened when you translated the phrase for the infant. First of all, the wording probably changed, and you may have said something like, "Does baby like the apple sauce?" At the same time, the pitch of your voice probably rose, your general intonation most likely had a singsong quality, and you probably separated your words carefully.

Infant-Directed Speech.   The shift in your language was due to your use of **infant-directed speech**, also known as *motherese,* a style of speech that characterizes much of the verbal communication directed toward infants by mothers, fathers, grandparents, and even older siblings.

Infant-directed speech is characterized by short, simple sentences. Pitch becomes higher, the range of frequencies increases, and intonation is more varied. There is also repetition of words, and topics are restricted to items that are assumed to be comprehensible to infants, such as concrete objects in the baby's environment.

Sometimes infant-directed speech includes amusing sounds that are not even words, imitating the prelinguistic speech of infants. In other cases, it has little formal structure, but is similar to the kind of telegraphic speech that infants use as they develop their own language skills.

Infant-directed speech changes as children become older. Around the end of the first year, infant-directed speech takes on more adultlike qualities. Sentences become longer and more

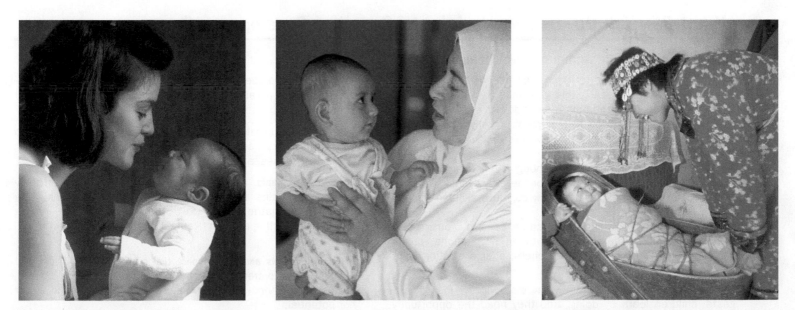

Infant-directed speech includes the use of short, simple sentences and is said in a pitch that is higher than that used with older children and adults.

complex, although individual words are still spoken slowly and deliberately. Pitch is also used to focus attention on particularly important words.

Some adults are under the mistaken belief that infant-directed speech is silly and harmful. Infant-directed speech actually plays an important role in infants' acquisition of language. As discussed next, infant-directed speech occurs all over the world, though there are cultural variations. Newborns prefer to listen to infant-directed speech over regular adult language, a fact that suggests that they may be particularly receptive to it. Furthermore, some research suggests that babies who are exposed to a great deal of infant-directed speech early in life seem to begin to use words and exhibit other forms of linguistic competence earlier (Liu et al., 2003; Thiessen et al., 2005; Englund and Behne, 2006; Werker et al., 2007).

Cultural Dimensions

Is Infant-Directed Speech Similar across All Cultures?

Do mothers in Canada, Japan, and Russia speak the same way to their infants?

In some respects, they clearly do. Although the words themselves differ across languages, the way the words are spoken to infants is quite similar. According to a growing body of research, there are basic similarities across cultures in the nature of infant-directed speech (Papousek and Papousek, 1991; Rabain-Jamin and Sabeau-Jouannet, 1997; Werker et al., 2007).

For example, 6 of the 10 most frequent major characteristics of speech directed at infants used by native speakers of English and Spanish are common to both languages: exaggerated intonation, high pitch, lengthened vowels, repetition, lower volume, and heavy stress on certain key words (such as emphasizing the word "ball" in the sentence, "No, that's a ball") (Blount, 1982). Similarly, mothers speaking English, Swedish, and Russian all exaggerate and elongate the pronunciation of the three vowel sounds of "ee," "ah," and "oh" when speaking to infants in similar ways, despite differences in the languages in which the sounds are used (Kuhl et al., 1997).

Even deaf mothers use a form of infant-directed speech: When communicating with their infants, deaf mothers use sign language at a significantly slower tempo than when communicating with adults, and they frequently repeat the signs, and use simpler and exaggerated gestures (Swanson et al., 1992; Masataka, 1996, 1998, 2000; Brand et al., 2002).

What Can You Do to Promote Infants' Cognitive Development?

Becoming an Informed Consumer of Development

All parents want their children to reach their full cognitive potential, but sometimes efforts to reach this goal take a bizarre path. For instance, some parents spend hundreds of dollars enrolling in workshops with titles such as "How to Multiply Your Baby's Intelligence" and buying books with titles such as *How to Teach Your Baby to Read* (Doman and Doman, 2002).

Do such efforts ever succeed? Although some parents swear they do, there is no scientific support for the effectiveness of such programs. For example, despite the many cognitive skills of infants, no infant can actually read.

On the other hand, certain things can be done to promote cognitive development in infants. The following suggestions, based upon findings of developmental researchers, offer a starting point (Schulman, 1991; Gopnik et al., 2000):

- **Provide infants the opportunity to explore the world.** As Piaget suggests, children learn by doing, and they need the opportunity to explore and probe their environment. Make sure the environment contains a variety of toys, books, and other sources of stimulation.

- **Be responsive to infants on both a verbal and a nonverbal level.** Try to speak *with* babies, as opposed to *at* them. Ask questions, listen to their responses, and provide further communication.

- **Read to your infants.** Reading is associated with later literacy skills and begins to create a lifelong reading habit. The Canadian Paediatric Society (2006) recommends daily reading to children starting at birth (Reutzel et al., 2006; Weigel et al., 2006).

- **Don't push infants and don't expect too much too soon.** Your goal should not be to create a genius, but rather to provide a warm, nurturing environment that will allow an infant to reach his or her potential.

REVIEW, CHECK, AND APPLY

REVIEW

- Before they speak, infants understand many adult utterances and engage in several forms of prelinguistic communication.

- Children typically produce their first words between 10 and 14 months, and rapidly increase their vocabularies from that point on, especially during a spurt at about 18 months.

- Learning theorists believe that basic learning processes account for language development, whereas nativists like Noam Chomsky and his followers argue that humans have an innate language capacity. The interactionists suggest that language is a consequence of both environmental and innate factors.

CHECK YOURSELF

1. Like other two-year-olds, Mason can say "doggie bye bye" and "milk gone." These two-word phrases are examples of _____ speech.

   a. holophrastic

   b. telegraphic

   c. interpretive

   d. active

2. One theory, the _____ approach, suggests that a genetically determined, innate mechanism directs language development.

3. Whenever nine-month-old Ana's mother talks to her, she uses short, simple sentences, repetitive words, and higher pitches. This shift in language is consistent with the use of _____ speech.

   a. infant-directed

   b. telegraphic

   c. nativist

   d. interactionist

APPLYING LIFESPAN DEVELOPMENT

- What are some ways in which children's linguistic development reflects their acquisition of new ways of interpreting and dealing with their world?

Answers: 1) b; 2) nativist; 3) a

MODULE 3.3 Social and Personality Development in Infancy

The Velcro Chronicles

The child-care centre had a rule: socks or slippers at all times. Generally speaking, rules are not challenged in the baby room. But suddenly, one day in April, it was all the teachers could do to keep socks on the children's feet. The teachers thought they would be safe taking the children outside to play, bundled into shoes, coats, and hats for a sunny but crisp morning. But no. It started with 14-month-old Caleb—he mastered the Velcro closure on his shoes and suddenly was barefoot in the grass. No sooner did the teachers get his shoes back on, than 13-month-old Brooke did the same thing. Then Gabby. Then Isaac. Then, with a squeal, Brooke applied the same principle and flung her hat in the air with glee!

As babies like these show us, children are sociable from a very early age. This anecdote also demonstrates one of the side benefits of infants' participation in childcare, and something research has begun to suggest: Through their social interactions, babies acquire new skills and abilities from more "expert" peers. Infants, as we will see, have an amazing capacity to learn from other children, and their interactions with others can play a central role in their developing social and emotional worlds.

In this module we consider social and personality development in infancy. We begin by examining the emotional lives of infants, considering which emotions they feel and how well they can read others' emotions, and how babies view their own and others' mental lives.

We then turn to infants' social relationships. We look at how they forge bonds of attachment and the ways they interact with family members and peers. Finally, we cover the characteristics that differentiate one infant from another and discuss differences in the way children are treated, depending on their gender.

Developing the Roots of Sociability

LO13 Do infants experience emotions?

LO14 What sort of mental lives do infants have?

Germaine smiles when he catches a glimpse of his mother. Tawanda looks angry when her mother takes away the spoon that she is playing with. Sydney scowls when a loud plane flies overhead.

A smile. A look of anger. A scowl. The emotions of infancy are written all over a baby's face. Yet do infants experience emotions in the same way that adults do? When do they become capable of understanding what others are experiencing emotionally? And how do they use others' emotional states to make sense of their environment? We consider some of these questions as we seek to understand how infants develop emotionally and socially.

Emotions in Infancy: Do Infants Experience Emotional Highs and Lows?

Anyone who spends any time at all around infants knows they display facial expressions that seem indicative of their emotional states. In situations in which we expect them to be happy, they seem to smile; when we might assume they are frustrated, they show anger; and when we might expect them to be unhappy, they look sad.

In fact, these basic facial expressions are remarkably similar across the most diverse cultures. Whether we look at babies in India, Canada, or the jungles of New Guinea, the expression of basic emotions is the same (see Figure 3-14). Furthermore, the nonverbal expression of emotion, called *nonverbal encoding*, is fairly consistent among people of all ages. These consistencies have led researchers to conclude that we are born with the capacity to display basic emotions (Scharfe, 2000; Sullivan and Lewis, 2003; Ackerman and Izard, 2004).

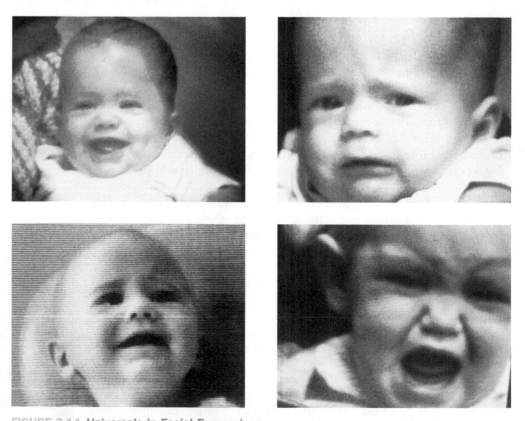

FIGURE 3-14 Universals in Facial Expressions
Across every culture, infants show similar facial expressions relating to basic emotions. Do you think such expressions are similar in nonhuman animals?

Infants display a fairly wide range of emotional expressions. Almost all mothers report that by the age of one month their babies have non-verbally expressed interest and joy. Careful coding of infants' nonverbal expressions shows that interest, distress, and disgust are present at birth, and that other emotions emerge over the next few months. Such findings are consistent with the work of the famous naturalist Charles Darwin, whose 1872 book *The Expression of the Emotions in Man and Animals* argued that humans and primates have an inborn, universal set of emotional expressions—a view consistent with today's evolutionary approach to development (Izard, 1982; Sroufe, 1996; Benson, 2003).

Although infants display similar *kinds* of emotions, the *degree* of emotional expressivity varies among infants. Children in different cultures show reliable differences in emotional expressiveness, even during infancy. For example, by the age of 11 months, Chinese infants are generally less expressive than European, American, and Japanese infants (Camras et al., 2002; Izard et al., 2003; Buss and Kiel, 2004).

When infants smile at a person, rather than a nonhuman stimulus, they are displaying a social smile.

Stranger Anxiety and Separation Anxiety. "She used to be such a friendly baby," thought Erika's mother. "No matter whom she encountered, she had a big smile. But almost the day she turned seven months old, she began to react to strangers as if she were seeing a ghost. Her face crinkles up with a frown, and she either turns away or stares at them with suspicion. It's as if she has undergone a personality transplant."

What happened to Erika is, in fact, quite typical. By the end of the first year, infants often develop both stranger anxiety and separation anxiety. **Stranger anxiety** is the caution and wariness displayed by infants when encountering an unfamiliar person. Such anxiety typically appears in the second half of the first year.

What brings on stranger anxiety? Brain development and the increased cognitive abilities of infants play a role. As infants' memory develops, they are able to separate the people they know from the people they don't. The same cognitive advances that allow them to respond so positively to those people with whom they are familiar also give them the ability to distinguish people who are unfamiliar. Furthermore, between six and nine months, infants begin trying to make sense of their world, trying to anticipate and predict events. When something happens that they don't expect—such as the appearance of an unknown person—they experience fear (Ainsworth, 1973; Kagan et al., 1978).

Separation anxiety is the distress displayed by infants when a customary care provider departs. Separation anxiety, which is also universal across cultures, usually begins at about seven or eight months (see Figure 3-15). It peaks at around 14 months, and then decreases. Separation anxiety is largely attributable to the same triggers as stranger anxiety. Infants' growing cognitive skills allow them to ask reasonable questions—questions for which they are too young to understand the answer: "Why is my mother leaving?" "Where is she going?" and "Will she come back?"

Stranger anxiety and separation anxiety represent important social progress. They reflect both cognitive advances and the growing emotional and social bonds between infants and their caregivers—bonds that we'll consider later in the module when we discuss infants' social relationships.

Smiling. As Luz lay sleeping in her crib, her mother and father caught a glimpse of the most beautiful smile crossing her face. Her parents were sure that Luz was having a pleasant dream. Were they right?

Probably not. The earliest smiles expressed during sleep probably have little meaning, although no one can be absolutely sure. They could be in response to pleasurable bodily sensations. By six to nine weeks babies begin to smile reliably at the sight of stimuli that please them, including toys, mobiles, and—to the delight of parents—people. The first smiles tend to be relatively indiscriminate, as infants first begin to smile at the sight of almost anything they find amusing. However, as they get older, they become more selective in their smiles.

⊙—Watch on **mydevelopmentlab**

Has your virtual child shown any stranger anxiety? How are you addressing it?
To see a child display stranger anxiety, watch the video in MyDevelopmentLab.

⊙—Watch on **mydevelopmentlab**

Has your virtual child experienced separation anxiety? How will you handle outside childcare?
Watch a child display separation anxiety in the video in MyDevelopmentLab.

stranger anxiety the caution and wariness displayed by infants when encountering an unfamiliar person

separation anxiety the distress displayed by infants when a customary care provider departs

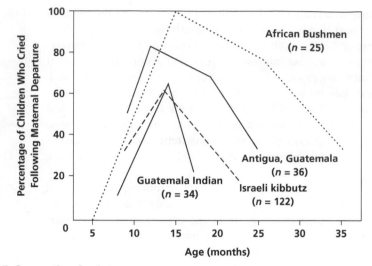

FIGURE 3-15 Separation Anxiety
Separation anxiety, the distress displayed by infants when their usual care provider leaves their presence, is a universal phenomenon beginning at around the age of seven or eight months. It peaks at around the age of 14 months and then begins to decline. Does separation anxiety have survival value for humans?
Source: From INFANCY: ITS PLACE IN HUMAN DEVELOPMENT by Jerome Kagan, Richard P. Kearsley, and Phillip R. Zelazo., p. 107 , Cambridge, Mass.: Harvard University Press, Copyright © 1978 by the President and Fellows of Harvard University College.

A baby's smile in response to another person, rather than to nonhuman stimuli, is considered a *social smile*. As babies get older, their social smiles become directed toward particular individuals, not just anyone. By the age of 18 months, social smiling, directed more toward mothers and other caregivers, becomes more frequent than smiling directed toward nonhuman objects. Moreover, if an adult is unresponsive to a child, the amount of smiling decreases. In short, by the end of the second year children are quite purposefully using smiling to communicate their positive emotions, and they are sensitive to the emotional expressions of others. They can even match happy and sad facial expressions to happy and sad voices (Muir et al., 2005; Bigelow and Rochat, 2006; Fogel et al., 2006).

Decoding Others' Facial Expressions. In Module 2.3, we discussed the possibility that neonates can imitate adults' facial expressions even minutes after birth. Although their imitative abilities certainly do not imply that they can understand the meaning of others' facial expressions, such imitation does pave the way for *nonverbal decoding* abilities, which begin to emerge fairly soon. Using these abilities, infants can interpret others' facial and vocal expressions that carry emotional meaning. For example, they can tell when a caregiver is happy to see them and pick up on worry or fear in the faces of others (Bornstein and Arterberry, 2003; Hernandez-Reif et al., 2006; Striano and Vaish, 2006).

In the first six to eight weeks, infants' visual precision is sufficiently limited that they cannot pay much attention to others' facial expressions. But they soon begin to discriminate among different facial expressions of emotion and even seem to be able to respond to differences in emotional intensity conveyed by facial expressions. By the time they reach the age of four months, infants already have begun to understand the emotions that lie behind the facial and vocal expressions of others (Nelson, 1987; Adamson and Frick, 2003; Bertin and Striano, 2006).

Social Referencing: Feeling What Others Feel

Twenty-three-month-old Stephania watches as her older brother Eric and his friend Chen argue loudly with each other and begin to wrestle. Uncertain of what is happening, Stephania glances at her mother. Her mother, though, wears a smile, knowing that Eric and Chen are just playing. On seeing her mother's reaction, Stephania smiles too, mimicking her mother's facial expression.

Watch on mydevelopmentlab

After reading about social referencing, watch how it operates in the video on MyDevelopmentLab.

Like Stephania, most of us have been in situations in which we feel uncertain. In such cases, we sometimes turn to others to see how they are reacting. This reliance on others, known as social referencing, helps us decide what an appropriate response ought to be.

Social referencing is the intentional search for information about others' feelings to help explain the meaning of uncertain circumstances and events. Like Stephania, we use social referencing to clarify the meaning of a situation and so to reduce our uncertainty about what is occurring.

Social referencing first occurs around the age of eight or nine months. It is a fairly sophisticated social ability: Infants need it not only to understand the significance of others' behaviour by using such cues as their facial expressions, but also to understand the meaning of those behaviours within the context of a specific situation (Mumme and Fernald, 2003; de Rosnay et al., 2006; Carver and Vaccaro, 2007).

> **From a social worker's perspective:** In what situations do adults rely on social referencing to work out appropriate responses? How might social referencing be used to influence parents' behaviour toward their children?

Research suggests that this 18-month-old is exhibiting a clearly developing sense of self.

The Development of Self: Do Infants Know Who They Are?

Elysa, eight months old, crawls past the full-length mirror that hangs on a door in her parents' bedroom. She barely pays any attention to her reflection as she moves by. On the other hand, her cousin Brianna, who is almost two years old, stares at herself in the mirror as she passes—and laughs as she notices, then rubs off, a smear of jelly on her forehead.

Perhaps you have had the experience of catching a glimpse of yourself in a mirror and noticing a hair out of place. You probably reacted by attempting to push the unruly hair back into place. Your reaction shows more than that you care about how you look. It implies that you have a sense of yourself, the awareness and knowledge that you are an independent social entity to which others react, and which you attempt to present to the world in ways that reflect favourably upon you.

However, we are not born with the knowledge that we exist independently from others and the larger world. Very young infants do not have a sense of themselves as individuals; they do not recognize themselves in photos or mirrors. However, the roots of **self-awareness**—knowledge of oneself—begin to grow after the age of 12 months.

We know this from a simple but ingenious experimental technique in which an infant's nose or forehead is secretly coloured with a big red spot (also called the "rouge test" because of the type of make-up originally used). Then the infant is seated in front of a mirror. If infants touch their noses or attempt to wipe off the spot, we have evidence that they have at least some knowledge of their physical characteristics. Although some infants as young as 12 months seem startled on seeing the red spot, for most a reaction does not occur until between 17 and 24 months of age. The same results occur when infants are shown photographs of themselves; even though the photo was taken moments before, younger infants show no sign that they understand they are seeing a picture of themselves. This awareness is one step in infants' understanding of themselves as independent objects (Gallup, 1977; Asendorpf et al., 1996; Rochat, 2004).

Theory of Mind: Infants' Perspectives on the Mental Lives of Others—and Themselves

What are infants' thoughts about thinking? Infants begin to understand certain things about their own and others' mental processes at quite an early age, developing a **theory of mind**, their knowledge and beliefs about how the mind works and how it influences behaviour. Theories of mind are the explanations that children use to explain how others think.

For instance, cognitive advances during infancy (discussed in Module 3.2) permit older infants to see people in a very different way from other objects. They learn to see other people as *compliant agents*, beings similar to themselves who behave under their own power and who have the capacity to respond to infants' requests (Poulin-Dubois, 1999; Rochat, 1999, 2004).

Watch on **mydevelopmentlab**

By the time your virtual child turns one, he or she will begin to exhibit self-awareness. To observe a child demonstrating self-awareness, watch the video in MyDevelopmentLab.

social referencing the intentional search for information about others' feelings to help explain the meaning of uncertain circumstances and events

self-awareness knowledge of oneself

theory of mind knowledge and beliefs about how the mind works and how it affects behaviour

empathy an emotional response that corresponds to the feelings of another person

In addition, children's capacity to understand intentionality and causality grows during infancy. They begin to understand that others' behaviours have some meaning and that the behaviours they see people enacting are designed to accomplish particular goals, in contrast to the "behaviours" of inanimate objects. For example, a child comes to understand that his father has a specific goal when he is in the kitchen making sandwiches. In contrast, his father's car is simply parked in the driveway, having no mental life or goal (Golinkoff, 1993; Ahn et al., 2000).

Another piece of evidence for infants' growing sense of mental activity is that by the age of two, infants begin to show very clear signs of empathy. **Empathy** is an emotional response that corresponds to the feelings of another person. The earliest signs of empathy are thought to occur when infants demonstrate contagious crying, a phenomenon observed in preterm neonates as young as 34 weeks gestation. Hoffman referred to this as global empathy because it was non-specific but is a clear indication that the infant is mirroring another's emotional response—the hallmark of empathy. As infants get older, they are capable of more deliberate responses to others' emotional responses. For example, 18-month-olds will go to considerable effort to help an adult, and can sometimes attempt to comfort others or show concern for them. In order to do this, they need to be aware of the emotional states of others (Hoffman, 1987; Gauthier, 2003; Mumme and Fernald, 2003; Warneken and Tomasello, 2006).

◉─ **Watch** on **mydevelopmentlab**

To see the theory of mind at work, watch the video in MyDevelopmentLab.

REVIEW, CHECK, AND APPLY

REVIEW

- Infants appear to express and experience emotions, and their emotions broaden in range to reflect increasingly complex emotional states.
- The ability to decode the non-verbal facial and vocal expressions of others develops early in infants.
- Infants develop self-awareness, the knowledge that they exist separately from the rest of the world, after about 12 months of age, and by the age of 2, children have developed the rudiments of a theory of mind.

CHECK YOURSELF

1. _____ is the caution and wariness expressed by infants when encountering an unfamiliar person.

2. Marcel has been attending daycare without incident since he was 4 months old. Now at around 14 months he starts to express difficulty when his mother leaves. He cries, shouts "No!", and then grabs her leg as she attempts to leave for work. Which of the following concepts best explains Marcel's change in behaviour?

   a. stranger anxiety

   b. intuition

   c. egocentrism

   d. separation anxiety

3. When Darius bumped his knee on the table, he gazed at his mother to look at her reaction. When he saw that she was alarmed, he began crying. This is an example of _____.

APPLYING LIFESPAN DEVELOPMENT

- Why would the sad or flat emotional expressiveness of a depressed parent be hard on an infant? How might it be counteracted?

Answers: 1) Stranger anxiety; 2) d; 3) social referencing

Forming Relationships

LEARNING OBJECTIVES

LO15 What is attachment in infancy and how does it affect a person's future social competence?

LO16 What roles do other people play in infants' social development?

Louis Moore became the centre of attention on the way home [from the hospital]. His father brought Martha, aged 5, and Tom, aged 3, to the hospital with him when Louis and his mother were discharged. Martha rushed to see "her" new baby and ignored her mother. Tom clung to his mother's knees in the reception hall of the hospital.

A hospital nurse carried Louis to the car. . . . The two older children immediately climbed over the seat and swamped mother and baby with their attention. Both children stuck their faces into his, smacked at him, and talked to him. They soon began to fight over him with loud voices. The loud argument and the jostling of his mother upset Louis, and he started to cry. He let out a wail that came like a shotgun blast into the noisy car. The children quieted immediately and looked with awe at this new infant. His insistent wails drowned out their bickering. He had already asserted himself in their eyes. (Brazelton, 1983, p. 48)

The arrival of a newborn brings a dramatic change to a family's dynamics. No matter how welcome a baby's birth, it causes a fundamental shift in the roles that people play within the family. Mothers and fathers must start to build a relationship with their infant, and older children must adjust to the presence of a new member of the family and build their own alliance with their infant brother or sister.

Although the process of social development during infancy is neither simple nor automatic, it is crucial: The bonds that grow between infants and their parents, siblings, family, and others provide the foundation for a lifetime's worth of social relationships.

Attachment: Forming Social Bonds

The most important aspect of social development that takes place during infancy is the formation of attachment. **Attachment** is the positive emotional bond that develops between a child and a particular, special individual. When children experience attachment to a given person, they feel pleasure when they are with them and feel comforted by their presence at times of distress—like the infant, Alex, described in the chapter opener, who cried in his crib until his mother or father came to comfort him. The nature of our attachment during infancy affects how we relate to others throughout the rest of our lives (Fraley, 2002; Grossmann and Waters, 2005; Hofer, 2006).

To understand attachment, the earliest researchers turned to the bonds that form between parents and children in the nonhuman animal kingdom. For instance, ethologist Konrad Lorenz (1965) observed that newborn goslings have an innate tendency to follow their mother, the first moving object to which they typically are exposed after birth. Lorenz found that goslings whose eggs were raised in an incubator and who viewed him just after hatching would follow his every movement, as if he were their mother. As we discussed in Module 1.2, he labelled this process *imprinting*: behaviour that takes place during a critical period and involves attachment to the first moving object that is observed.

Lorenz's findings suggested that attachment was based on biologically determined factors, and other theorists agreed. For instance, Freud suggested that attachment grew out of a mother's ability to satisfy a child's oral needs. Similarly, John Bowlby (1951) argued that attachment is based primarily on infants' needs for safety and security. As they develop, infants come to learn that their safety is best provided by a particular individual, typically the mother, and they develop a relationship with the primary caregiver that is qualitatively different from the bonds formed with others. In his view, attachment provides a type of home base. As children become more independent, they can progressively roam further away from their secure base.

The Ainsworth Strange Situation and Patterns of Attachment. Developmental psychologist Mary Ainsworth built on Bowlby's theorizing to develop a widely used experimental technique to measure attachment (Ainsworth et al., 1978). The **Ainsworth Strange Situation** consists of a sequence of staged episodes that illustrate the strength of attachment between a child and (typically) his or her mother. The "strange situation" follows this general eight-step pattern: (1) The mother and baby enter an unfamiliar room; (2) the mother sits down, leaving the baby free to explore; (3) an adult stranger enters the room and converses first with the mother and then with the baby; (4) the mother exits the room, leaving the baby alone with the stranger; (5) the mother returns, greeting and comforting the baby, and the stranger leaves; (6) the mother departs again, leaving the baby alone; (7) the stranger returns; and (8) the mother returns and the stranger leaves (Ainsworth et al., 1978).

Infants' reactions to the various aspects of the Strange Situation vary considerably, depending on the nature of their attachment to their mothers. One-year-olds typically show one of four major patterns—secure, avoidant, ambivalent, and disorganized-disoriented (summarized in Table 3-8). Children who have a **secure attachment pattern** use the mother as the type of home base that Bowlby described. These children seem at ease in the Strange

attachment the positive emotional bond that develops between a child and a particular individual

Ainsworth Strange Situation a sequence of staged episodes that illustrate the strength of attachment between a child and (typically) his or her mother

secure attachment pattern a style of attachment in which children use the mother as a kind of home base and are at ease when she is present; when she leaves, they become upset and go to her as soon as she returns

TABLE 3-8 CLASSIFICATIONS OF INFANT ATTACHMENT

Classification Criteria

Label	Seeking Proximity with Caregiver	Maintaining Contact with Caregiver	Avoiding Proximity with Caregiver	Resisting Contact with Caregiver
Secure	High	High (if distressed)	Low	Low
Avoidant	Low	Low	High	Low
Ambivalent	High	High (often pre-separation)	Low	High
Disorganized-disoriented	Inconsistent	Inconsistent	Inconsistent	Inconsistent

Situation as long as their mothers are present. They explore independently, returning to her occasionally. Although they may or may not appear upset when she leaves, securely attached children immediately go to her when she returns and seek contact. Most children—about two-thirds—fall into the securely attached category.

In contrast, children with an **avoidant attachment pattern** do not seek proximity to the mother, and after she has left, they typically do not seem distressed. Furthermore, they seem to avoid her when she returns. It is as if they are indifferent to her behaviour. Some 20 percent of 1-year-old children are in the avoidant category.

Children with an **ambivalent attachment pattern** display a combination of positive and negative reactions to their mothers. Initially, ambivalent children are in such close contact with the mother that they hardly explore their environment. They appear anxious even before the mother leaves, and when she does leave, they show great distress. But upon her return, they show ambivalent reactions, seeking to be close to her but also hitting and kicking, apparently in anger. About 10 to 15 percent of 1-year-olds fall into the ambivalent classification (Cassidy and Berlin, 1994).

Although Ainsworth identified only three categories, a more recent expansion of her work finds that there is a fourth category: disorganized-disoriented. Children who have a **disorganized-disoriented attachment pattern** show inconsistent, contradictory, and confused behaviour. They may run to the mother when she returns but not look at her, or seem initially calm and then suddenly break into angry weeping. Their confusion suggests that they may be the least securely attached children of all. About 5 to 10 percent of all children fall into this category (Mayseless, 1996; Cole, 2005).

The quality of attachment between infants and their mothers has significant consequences for relationships at later stages of life. For example, boys who are securely attached at the age of one year show fewer psychological difficulties at older ages than do avoidant or ambivalent children. Similarly, children who are securely attached as infants tend to be more socially and emotionally competent later, and others view them more positively (Aviezer et al., 2002; Mikulincer and Shaver, 2005; Simpson et al., 2007).

Producing Attachment: The Roles of the Mother and Father

As five-month-old Annie cries passionately, her mother comes into the room and gently lifts her from her crib. After just a few moments, as her mother rocks Annie and speaks softly, Annie's cries cease, and she cuddles in her mother's arms. But the moment her mother places her back in the crib, Annie begins to wail again, leading her mother to pick her up once again.

The pattern is familiar to most parents. The infant cries, the parent reacts, and the child responds in turn. Such seemingly insignificant sequences as these, repeatedly occurring in the lives of infants and parents, help pave the way for the development of relationships between children, their parents, and the rest of the social world. We'll consider how each of the major caregivers and the infant play a role in the development of attachment.

> **From a social worker's perspective:** What might a social worker seeking to find a good home for a foster child look for when evaluating potential foster parents?

avoidant attachment pattern a style of attachment in which children do not seek proximity to the mother; after the mother has left, they seem to avoid her when she returns as if they are angered by her behaviour

ambivalent attachment pattern a style of attachment in which children display a combination of positive and negative reactions to their mothers; they show great distress when the mother leaves, but upon her return they may simultaneously seek close contact but also hit and kick her

disorganized-disoriented attachment pattern a style of attachment in which children show inconsistent, often contradictory behaviour, such as approaching the mother when she returns but not looking at her; they may be the least securely attached children of all

Mothers and Attachment. Sensitivity to their infants' needs and desires is the hallmark of mothers of securely attached infants. Such a mother tends to be aware of her child's moods, and she takes into account her child's feelings as they interact. She is also responsive during face-to-face interactions, provides feeding "on demand," and is warm and affectionate to her infant (Ainsworth, 1993; Thompson et al., 2003; McElwain and Booth-LaForce, 2006).

It is not only a matter of responding in *any* fashion to their infants' signals that separates mothers of securely attached and insecurely attached children. Mothers of secure infants tend to provide the appropriate level of response. In fact, overly responsive mothers are just as likely to have insecurely attached children as under-responsive mothers. In contrast, mothers whose communication involves *interactional synchrony*, in which caregivers respond to infants appropriately and both caregiver and child match emotional states, are more likely to produce secure attachment (Belsky et al., 1984; Kochanskya, 1998; Hane et al., 2003).

Fathers and Attachment. Up to now, we've barely touched upon one of the key players involved in the upbringing of a child: the father. In fact, if you look at the early theorizing and research on attachment, you'll find little mention of the father and his potential contributions to the life of the infant (Tamis-LeMonda and Cabrera, 1999).

However, it is increasingly clear that infants can form their primary initial relationship with their fathers—or whoever takes on the primary caregiver role—and much of what we have said about mothers' attachment expands to any primary caregiver. That the primary caregiver is the primary attachment figure is very important. Secondary caregivers spend time with infants, often in play activities, whereas the primary caregiver tends to spend time with infants in routine activities such as changing diapers and feeding. This person who cares for your day-to-day needs is therefore a very good candidate to use as a secure base. Further, fathers' expressions of nurturance, warmth, affection, support, and concern are extremely important to their children's emotional and social well-being. Some psychological disorders, such as substance abuse and depression, have been found to be related more to fathers' than mothers' behaviour (Veneziano, 2003; Parke, 2004; Roelofs et al., 2006).

A growing body of research highlights the importance of a father's demonstration of love for his children. In fact, certain disorders such as depression and substance abuse have been found to be more related to fathers' than to mothers' behaviour.

Infants' Sociability with Their Peers: Infant–Infant Interaction

How sociable are infants with other children? Although it is clear that they do not form "friendships" in the traditional sense, babies do react positively to the presence of peers from early in life, and they engage in rudimentary forms of social interaction.

Infants' sociability is expressed in several ways. From the earliest months of life, they smile, laugh, and vocalize while looking at their peers. They show more interest in peers than in inanimate objects and pay greater attention to other infants than they do to a mirror image of themselves. They also begin to show preferences for peers with whom they are familiar compared with those they do not know. For example, studies of identical twins show that twins exhibit a higher level of social behaviour toward each other than toward an unfamiliar infant (Field, 1990; Legerstee et al., 1998).

Infants' level of sociability rises with age. Nine- to twelve-month-olds mutually present and accept toys, particularly if they know each other. They also play social games, such as peek-a-boo or crawl-and-chase. Such behaviour is important, as it serves as a foundation for future social exchanges in which children will try to elicit responses from others and then offer reactions to those responses. These kinds of exchanges are important to learn, since they continue even into adulthood. For example, someone who says, "Hi, what's up?" might be trying to elicit a response to which he or she can then reply (Endo, 1992; Eckerman and Peterman, 2001).

Japanese parents seek to avoid separation and stress during infancy and do not foster independence. As a result, Japanese children often have the appearance of being less securely attached according to the Strange Situation, but using other measurement techniques they might well score higher in attachment.

Cultural Dimensions

Does Attachment Differ Across Cultures?

John Bowlby's observations of the biologically motivated efforts of the young of other species to seek safety and security were the basis for his views on attachment and his reason for suggesting that seeking attachment was biologically universal, an effort that we should find not only in other species, but among humans of all cultures as well.

However, research has shown that human attachment is not as culturally universal as Bowlby predicted. Around the world, most researchers have found secure attachment to be most common, ranging from 50 to 70 percent of infants. But some cultural practices have also been found to influence attachment, especially insecure attachment styles. For example, one study of Northern German infants showed high rates of insecure classification, and most fell into the avoidant category. Southern German infants did not show this pattern. The high rate of avoidant classification was attributed to a culture of parenting that encouraged independence at a young age. Another study conducted in Israel found that the cultural practice of communal sleeping rather than sleeping with parents was associated with insecure attachment. Finally, comparisons of Chinese and Canadian children show that Chinese children are more inhibited than Canadians in the Strange Situation (Grossmann et al., 1982; Takahashi, 1986; Chen et al., 1998; Rothbaum et al., 2000).

Do such findings suggest that we should abandon the notion that attachment is a universal biological tendency? Not necessarily. Most of the data on attachment have been obtained by using the Ainsworth Strange Situation, which might not be the most appropriate measure in non-Western cultures. For example, Japanese parents seek to avoid separation and stress during infancy, and they don't strive to foster independence to the same degree as parents in many Western societies. Because of their relative lack of prior experience in separation, then, infants placed in the Strange Situation may experience unusual stress—producing the appearance of less secure attachment in Japanese children. If a different measure of attachment were used, one that could be administered later in infancy, more Japanese infants could likely be classified as secure. In short, our perception of attachment is affected by cultural norms and expectations (Nakagawa et al., 1992; Vereijken et al., 1997; Dennis et al., 2002).

Focus on Research

In Search of the Cause of Autism

Approximately 10 years ago, a very ambitious project began to document the onset of autism. Autism is a developmental disorder that causes severe impairment to children's language, communication, and social skills, and affects nearly 1 in 150 children in Canada. Approximately half of children with autism also have intellectual disabilities, sometimes quite severe, but it's also not unusual to find extreme giftedness, sometimes referred to as *savant skills*. The challenge with autism is that it is difficult to diagnose before the age of three. Why? Because a key diagnostic criteria is delayed language development. The age of diagnosis sometimes leads to falsely coincident ideas about the cause of autism, the most dangerous being the claims that chemical preservatives in vaccines cause autism (fears which have led to unnecessary outbreaks of diseases such as the measles and to wasted resources repeatedly disproving the link).

But autism takes hold long before a doctor makes the official diagnosis. Short of documenting every detail of the development of 1500 children and waiting for 10 to develop a confirmable case, a nationwide research team led by Susan Bryson at Dalhousie University and Lonnie Zwaigenbaum at the University of Alberta developed a plan: focus on children at the highest risk. While geneticists have been unable to identify the genetics underlying autism, we know that it does run in families. A newborn with one sibling with autism is 3 to 12 times more likely to be diagnosed than a newborn with no diagnosed siblings. A newborn with two diagnosed siblings is 12 to 37 times more likely to eventually be diagnosed. The research solution is to keep a close eye on the new baby siblings of children already diagnosed. The *baby sibs* model, as it's known, has been taken up by research groups around the world. When families of children with autism find themselves pregnant, they are invited to join the research. Some research groups even document the pregnancy. The new baby sibling is then engaged in a large battery of tests at regular intervals. A multitude of findings have emerged from this research, but the key is that subtle signs of autism are present by 12 months. Consistent with neurological theory, no signs have yet been detected at six months. Between 6 and 12 months, neurodevelopment is supposed to begin pruning unnecessary pathways, allowing strengthening of the ones we use and making us specialists, whether in our native language or in recognizing human faces but not monkey faces. The current thinking in autism research is that this pruning does not occur properly, leading to unusually large heads among children with autism. When it comes to brains, bigger isn't always better, and it is thought that lack of pruning leaves the brain very inefficiently wired. This in turn could explain some of the unusual skills—as well as the impairments—often found in autism.

The single most effective treatment of autism is early behavioural intervention, and the earlier the better. Techniques such as Pivotal Response Treatment are intensive and targeted training sessions that focus on teaching the fundamental skills that underlie language and social communication. What causes autism remains a mystery. As the baby sibs projects continue, we are slowly getting closer to the answer (Zwaigenbaum et al., 2005; DiCicco-Bloom et al., 2006; Bryson et al., 2007; Gamliel et al., 2009; Rogers, 2009; Smith et al., 2010).

Finally, as infants age, they begin to imitate each other (Russon and Waite, 1991). For instance, 14-month-old infants who are familiar with one another sometimes reproduce each other's behaviour (Mueller and Vandell, 1979). Such imitation serves a social function and can also be a powerful teaching tool.

To some developmentalists, the capacity of young children to engage in imitation suggests that imitation might be inborn. In support of this view, research has identified a class of neurons in the brains of monkeys that could be related to an innate ability to imitate. *Mirror neurons* are neurons that fire not only when an individual enacts a particular behaviour, but also when the individual simply observes *another* carrying out the same behaviour (Falck-Ytter, 2006).

REVIEW, CHECK, AND APPLY

REVIEW

- Attachment, the positive emotional bond between an infant and a significant individual, affects a person's later social competence as an adult.

- Infants and the people with whom they interact engage in reciprocal socialization as they mutually adjust to one another's interactions.

- Infants react differently to other children than to inanimate objects, and gradually they engage in increasing amounts of peer social interaction.

CHECK YOURSELF

1. _____ is the positive emotional bond that develops between a child and a particular individual.

2. Children who are attached to their primary caregivers feel _____ when they are with them and feel _____ during times of distress.

   a. concern; sad

   b. pleasure; comforted

   c. overwhelmed; distraught

   d. confused; comfort

3. One way mothers can improve the likelihood of secure attachment in their children is to respond to their needs appropriately. Another name for this communication in which mothers and children match emotional states is

   a. emotion matching.

   b. goodness of fit.

   c. interactional synchrony.

   d. environmental assessment.

APPLYING LIFESPAN DEVELOPMENT

- In what sort of society might an avoidant attachment style be encouraged by cultural attitudes toward childrearing? In such a society, would characterizing the infant's consistent avoidance of its mother as anger be an accurate interpretation?

Answers: 1) Attachment; 2) b; 3) c

Differences Among Infants

L017   What individual differences distinguish one infant from another?

LEARNING OBJECTIVES

Lincoln was a difficult baby, his parents both agreed. For one thing, it seemed like they could never get him to sleep at night. He cried at the slightest noise—a problem since his crib was near the windows facing a busy street. Worse yet, once he started crying, it seemed to take forever to calm him down again. One day his mother, Aisha, was telling her mother-in-law, Mary, about the challenges of being Lincoln's mom. Mary recalled that her own son, Lincoln's father Malcom, had been much the same way. "He was my first child, and I thought this was how all babies acted. So, we just kept trying different ways until we found out how he worked. I remember, we put his crib all over the apartment until we finally found out where he could sleep, and it ended up being in the hallway for a long time. Then his sister, Maleah, came along, and she was so quiet and easy, I didn't know what to do with my extra time!"

As the story of Lincoln's family shows, babies are not all alike, and neither are their families. In fact, as we'll see, some of the differences among people seem to be present from the moment we are born. The differences among infants include overall personality and temperament, and differences in the lives they lead—differences based on their gender, the nature of their families, and the ways in which they are cared for.

personality the sum total of the enduring characteristics that differentiate one individual from another

Erikson's theory of psychosocial development the theory that considers how individuals come to understand themselves and the meaning of their own and others' behaviour

trust-versus-mistrust stage according to Erikson, the period during which infants develop a sense of trust or mistrust, largely depending on how well their needs are met by their caregivers

autonomy-versus-shame-and-doubt stage the period during which, according to Erikson, toddlers (aged 18 months to 3 years) develop independence and autonomy if they are allowed the freedom to explore, or shame and self-doubt if they are restricted and overprotected

temperament patterns of arousal and emotionality that are consistent and enduring characteristics of an individual

Personality Development: The Characteristics That Make Infants Unique

The origins of **personality**, the sum total of the enduring characteristics that differentiate one individual from another, stem from infancy. From birth onward, infants begin to show unique, stable traits and behaviours that ultimately lead to their development as distinct, special individuals (Caspi, 2000; Kagan, 2000; Shiner et al., 2003).

According to psychologist Erik Erikson, whose approach to personality development we first discussed in Module 1.2, infants' early experiences are responsible for shaping one of the key aspects of their personalities: whether they will be basically trusting or mistrustful.

Erikson's theory of psychosocial development considers how individuals come to understand themselves and the meaning of others'—and their own—behaviour (Erikson, 1963). The theory suggests that developmental change occurs throughout people's lives in eight distinct stages, the first of which occurs in infancy.

According to Erikson, during the first 18 months of life, we pass through the **trust-versus-mistrust stage**. During this period, infants develop a sense of trust or mistrust, largely depending on how well their needs are met by their caregivers. Mary's attention to Malcom's needs, in the previous example, probably helped him develop a basic sense of trust in the world. Erikson suggests that if infants are able to develop trust, they experience a sense of hope, which permits them to feel as if they can fulfill their needs successfully. On the other hand, feelings of mistrust lead infants to see the world as harsh and unfriendly, and they may have later difficulties in forming close bonds with others.

During the end of infancy, children enter the **autonomy-versus-shame-and-doubt stage**, which lasts from around 18 months to 3 years. During this period, children develop independence and autonomy if parents encourage exploration and freedom within safe boundaries. However, if children are restricted and overly protected, they feel shame, self-doubt, and unhappiness.

Erikson argues that personality is primarily shaped by infants' experiences. However, as we discuss next, other developmentalists concentrate on consistencies of behaviour that are present at birth, even before the experiences of infancy. These consistencies are viewed as largely genetically determined and as providing the raw material of personality.

Temperament: Stabilities in Infant Behaviour

Sarah's parents thought there must be something wrong. Unlike her older brother Josh, who had been so active as an infant that he seemed never to be still, Sarah was much more placid. She took long naps and was easily soothed on those relatively rare occasions when she became agitated. What could be producing her extreme calmness?

The most likely answer: The difference between Sarah and Josh reflected differences in temperament. As we first discussed in Module 3.1, **temperament** encompasses patterns of arousal and emotionality that are consistent and enduring characteristics of an individual (Rothbart et al., 2000; Kochanska, 2004).

Temperament refers to *how* children behave, as opposed to *what* they do or *why* they do it. Infants show temperamental differences in general disposition from the time of birth, largely due initially to genetic factors, and temperament tends to be fairly stable well into adolescence. On the other hand, temperament is not fixed and unchangeable: Childrearing practices can modify temperament significantly. In fact, some children show little consistency in temperament from one age to another (McCrae et al., 2000; Rothbart et al., 2000; Rothbart and Derryberry, 2002).

Temperament is reflected in several dimensions of behaviour. One central dimension is *activity level,* which reflects the degree of overall movement. Some babies (like Sarah and Maleah, in the earlier examples) are relatively placid, and their movements are slow and almost leisurely. In contrast, the activity level of other infants (like Josh) is quite high, with strong, restless movements of the arms and legs.

Another important dimension of temperament is the nature and quality of an infant's mood, and, in particular, a child's *irritability*. Some infants are easily disturbed and cry easily, while others are relatively easygoing. Irritable infants fuss a great deal, and they are easily

TABLE 3-9 DIMENSIONS OF TEMPERAMENT

Dimension	Definition
Activity level	Proportion of active time periods to inactive time periods
Approaches withdrawal	The response to a new person or object, based on whether the child accepts the new situation or withdraws from it
Adaptability	How easily the child is able to adapt to changes in his or her environment
Quality of mood	The contrast of the amount of friendly, joyful, and pleasant behaviour with unpleasant, unfriendly behaviour
Attention span and persistence	The amount of time the child devotes to an activity and the effect of distraction on that activity
Distractibility	The degree to which stimuli in the environment alter behaviour
Rhythmicity (regularity)	The regularity of basic functions such as hunger, excretion, sleep, and wakefulness
Intensity of reaction	The energy level or reaction of the child's response
Threshold of responsiveness	The intensity of stimulation needed to elicit a response

upset. They are also difficult to soothe when they do begin to cry. (Other aspects of temperament are listed in Table 3-9.)

Categorizing Temperament: Easy, Difficult, and Slow-to-Warm Babies. Because temperament can be viewed along so many dimensions, some researchers have asked whether there are broader categories that can be used to describe children's overall behaviour. According to Alexander Thomas and Stella Chess, who carried out a large-scale study of a group of infants (Thomas and Chess, 1980), babies can be described according to one of several profiles:

- **Easy babies.** Easy babies have a positive disposition. Their body functions operate regularly, and they are adaptable. They are generally positive, showing curiosity about new situations, and their emotions are moderate or low in intensity. This category applies to about 40 percent (the largest number) of infants.
- **Difficult babies.** Difficult babies have more negative moods and are slow to adapt to new situations. When confronted with a new situation, they tend to withdraw. About 10 percent of infants belong in this category.
- **Slow-to-warm babies.** Slow-to-warm babies are inactive, showing relatively calm reactions to their environment. Their moods are generally negative, and they withdraw from new situations, adapting slowly. Approximately 15 percent of infants are slow-to-warm.

As for the remaining 35 percent, they cannot be consistently categorized. These children show various combinations of characteristics. For instance, one infant might have relatively sunny moods, but react negatively to new situations, or another may show little stability of any sort in terms of general temperament. More elaborate descriptions of temperament, such as the dimensions listed in Table 3-9, can provide a greater understanding of those children who could not be classified using Thomas and Chess's system.

The Consequences of Temperament: Does Temperament Matter? One obvious question to emerge from the findings of the relative stability of temperament is whether a particular kind of temperament is beneficial. The answer seems to be that no single type of temperament is invariably good or bad. Instead, children's long-term adjustment depends on the **goodness-of-fit** of their particular temperament and the nature and demands of the environment in which they find themselves. For instance, children with a low activity level and low irritability may do particularly well in an environment in which they are left to explore on their own and are allowed largely to direct their own behaviour. In contrast, high-activity-level, highly irritable children may do best with greater direction, which permits them to channel their energy in particular directions (Thomas and Chess, 1977, 1980; Strelau, 1998; Schoppe-Sullivan et al., 2007). Mary, the grandmother in the earlier example, found ways to adjust the environment for her son, Malcom. Malcom and Aisha may need to do the same for their own son, Lincoln.

easy babies babies who have a positive disposition; their body functions operate regularly, and they are adaptable

difficult babies babies who have negative moods and are slow to adapt to new situations; when confronted with a new situation, they tend to withdraw

slow-to-warm babies babies who are inactive, showing relatively calm reactions to their environment; their moods are generally negative, and they withdraw from new situations, adapting slowly

goodness-of-fit the notion that development is dependent on the degree of match between children's temperament and the nature and demands of the environment in which they are being raised

Some research suggests that certain temperaments are, in general, more adaptive than others. For instance, difficult children, in general, are more likely to show behaviour problems by school age than those classified in infancy as easy children. But not all difficult children experience problems. The key determinant seems to be the way parents react to their infants' difficult behaviour. If they react by showing anger and inconsistency—responses that their child's difficult, demanding behaviour readily evokes—then the child is ultimately more likely to experience behaviour problems. On the other hand, parents who display more warmth and consistency in their responses are more likely to have children who avoid later problems (Thomas et al., 1968; Teerikangas et al., 1998; Pauli-Pott et al., 2003).

Gender: Boys in Blue, Girls in Pink

"It's a boy." "It's a girl." One of these two statements, or some variant, is probably the first announcement made after the birth of a child. From the moment of birth, girls and boys are treated differently. Their parents send out different kinds of birth announcements. They are dressed in different clothes and wrapped in different-coloured blankets. They are given different toys, and their rooms decorated with different themes (Bridges, 1993; Coltrane and Adams, 1997; Serbin et al., 2001).

Parents play with boy and girl babies differently: From birth on, fathers tend to interact more with sons than daughters, while mothers interact more with daughters. Because, as we noted earlier in the module, mothers and fathers play in different ways (with fathers typically engaging in more physical, rough-and-tumble activities and mothers in traditional games such as peek-a-boo), male and female infants are clearly exposed to different styles of activity and interaction from their parents (Parke, 1996; Laflamme et al., 2002; Clearfield and Nelson, 2006).

The behaviour exhibited by girls and boys is interpreted in very different ways by adults. For instance, when researchers showed adults a video of an infant whose name was given as either "John" or "Mary," adults perceived "John" as adventurous and inquisitive, while "Mary" was fearful and anxious, although it was the same baby performing a single set of behaviours (Condry and Condry, 1976). In another study, adults interacted with a baby and were told it was a girl or a boy—or they were not told the gender. The adults chose toys, played with and made attributions about the baby's behaviour reflecting the perceived gender of the baby, but in all cases it was the same baby (Seavey et al., 1975; Sidorowicz and Lunney, 1980). Clearly, adults view the behaviour of children through the lens of gender. **Gender** refers to the sense of being male or female. The term "gender" is often used to mean the same thing as "sex," but they are not actually the same. *Sex* typically refers to sexual anatomy and sexual behaviour, while gender refers to the social perceptions of maleness or femaleness.

Gender Differences. There is a considerable amount of disagreement over both the extent and causes of such gender differences, even though most agree that boys and girls do experience at least partially different worlds based on gender. Some gender differences are fairly clear from the time of birth. For example, male infants tend to be more active and fussier than female infants. Boys' sleep tends to be more disturbed than that of girls. Boys grimace more, although no gender difference exists in the overall amount of crying. There is also some evidence that male newborns are more irritable than female newborns, although the findings are inconsistent. Differences between male and female infants, however, are generally minor (Eaton and Enns, 1986; Crawford and Unger, 2004).

Gender differences emerge more clearly as children age, and become increasingly influenced by the gender roles that society sets out for them. For instance, by the age of one year, infants are able to distinguish between males and females. Girls at this age prefer to play with dolls or stuffed animals, while boys seek out blocks and trucks. Often, of course, these are the only options available to them, due to the choices their parents and other adults have made in the toys they provide (Serbin et al., 2001; Cherney et al., 2003).

By the time they reach the age of two, boys behave more independently and less compliantly than girls. Much of this behaviour can be traced to parental reactions to earlier behaviour. For instance, when a child takes his or her first steps, parents tend to react differently, depending on the child's gender: Boys are encouraged more to go off and explore the world,

gender the sense of being male or female

while girls are hugged and kept close. It is hardly surprising, then, that by the age of two, girls tend to show less independence and greater compliance (Kuczynski and Kochanska, 1990; Poulin-Dubois et al., 2002).

Societal encouragement and reinforcement do not, however, completely explain differences in behaviour between boys and girls. For example, one study examined girls who were exposed before birth to abnormally high levels of *androgen*, a masculinizing hormone, because their mothers unwittingly took a drug containing the hormone while pregnant. Later, these girls were more likely to play with toys stereotypically preferred by boys (such as cars) and less likely to play with toys stereotypically associated with girls (such as dolls). Although there are many alternative explanations for these results—you can probably think of several yourself—one possibility is that increased exposure to masculinizing hormones affected the brain development of the girls, leading them to favour toys that involve certain kinds of preferred skills (Levine et al., 1999; Mealey, 2000; Servin et al., 2003).

In sum, differences in behaviour between boys and girls begin in infancy, and—as we will see in future modules—continue throughout childhood (and beyond). Although gender differences have complex causes, representing some combination of innate, biologically related factors and environmental factors, they play a profound role in the social and emotional development of infants.

REVIEW, CHECK, AND APPLY

REVIEW

- According to Erikson, during infancy individuals move from the trust-versus-mistrust stage of psychosocial development to the autonomy-versus-shame-and-guilt stage.

- Temperament encompasses enduring levels of arousal and emotionality that are characteristic of an individual.

- Gender differences become more pronounced as infants age.

CHECK YOURSELF

1. Patterns of arousal and emotionality that are consistent and enduring in an individual are known as an individual's _____.

2. _____ are prescribed by societies as activities or positions appropriate for males and females.
   a. Gender expectations
   b. Sex roles
   c. Gender roles
   d. Sex expectations

3. Autism is caused by vaccines.
   - True
   - False

APPLYING LIFESPAN DEVELOPMENT

- If you were designing a prenatal class for first-time parents about what to expect from their baby, what would you emphasize?

Answers: 1) temperament; 2) c; 3) False

Putting It All Together
Infancy

FOUR-MONTH-OLD ALEX (whom we met in the Chapter 3 opener) was a model infant in almost every respect. However, one aspect of his behaviour posed a dilemma: how to respond when he woke up in the middle of the night and cried despondently. It usually was not a matter of being hungry, because typically he had been fed recently. And it was not caused by his diaper being soiled, because usually that had been changed recently. Instead, it seemed that Alex just wanted to be held and entertained, and when he wasn't, he cried and shrieked dramatically until someone came to him.

MODULE **3.1** Physical Development

- Alex's body is developing various rhythms (repetitive, cyclical patterns of behaviour) that are responsible for the change from sleep to wakefulness **(p. 89)**.

- Alex will sleep in spurts of around two hours, followed by periods of wakefulness, until about 16 weeks, when he will begin to sleep as much as six continuous hours **(pp. 89–90)**.

- Since Alex's sense of touch is one of his most highly developed senses (and one of the earliest developed), Alex will respond to gentle touches, such as a soothing caress, which can calm a crying, fussy infant **(p. 101)**.

MODULE **3.2** Cognitive Development

- Alex has learned that his behaviour (crying) can produce a desired effect (someone holding and entertaining him) **(p. 104)**.

- As Alex's brain develops, he is able to separate people he knows from people he doesn't; this is why he responds so positively when someone he knows comes to comfort him during the night **(p. 111)**.

- Alex has developed attachment (the positive emotional bond between him and particular individuals) to those who care for him **(p. 129)**.

- In order to feel secure, Alex needs to know that his caregivers will provide an appropriate response to the signals he is sending **(p. 131)**.

- Part of Alex's temperament is that he is irritable. Irritable infants can be fussy and are difficult to soothe when they do begin to cry **(p. 134)**.

- Since irritability is relatively stable, Alex will continue to display this temperament at age one and even age two **(p. 135)**.

What would a PARENT do?

- What strategies would you use in dealing with Alex? Would you go to him every time he cried? Or would you try to wait him out, perhaps setting a time limit before going to him?

  HINT Review pages 130–131.

  What's your response?

What would a HEALTH CARE PROVIDER do?

- How would you recommend that Alex's caregivers deal with the situation? Are there any dangers that the caregivers should be aware of?

  HINT Review pages 134–135.

  What's your response?

What would a SOCIAL WORKER do?

- Neighbours contacted child services because they were concerned that Alex was crying too much. If you were a social worker, what might you look for when you conduct a home visit?

  HINT Review pages 89, 97, 130, 134.

  What's your response?

What would YOU do?

- How would you deal with Alex? What factors would affect your decision? Based on your reading, how do you think Alex will respond?

  HINT Review pages 130–135.

  What's your response?

CHAPTER 4

The Early Childhood and Preschool Years

Maureen Cronin, Julie Murphy's first preschool teacher, made a point of observing Julie's first weeks closely. At three years, four months, Julie was in the younger group, and she was physically small. She was also shy and quiet.

On her second day, Julie settled into a corner and eventually took a wooden jigsaw puzzle from the toy box. James, an older and bigger boy, approached Julie and, telling her she had his favourite puzzle, took it from her. Maureen watched as Julie's look of surprise turned to resignation. Maureen recalled that Julie had an older brother at home, and guessed that she must be used to this sort of thing.

Over the course of the year, Maureen intervened when bigger kids imposed their will on smaller ones. She would help the shyer children assert themselves and develop strategies for communicating effectively, and she would talk about the virtues of sharing. There were other issues, as well, that she (and the preschoolers' parents) dealt with: how to encourage the development of Julie's language skills, how to support her to behave independently, how to best provide discipline, how to determine the amount and kind of television she can

MODULE 4.1 Physical Development in the Preschool Years

When—and how—should children be toilet trained? see page 142.

MODULE 4.2 Cognitive Development in the Preschool Years

How accurate is a preschooler's memory? see page 150.

watch, how to encourage the development of her motor skills, and a host of other tough issues.

Toward the end of the school year, Maureen saw a familiar scene developing. While Julie was looking at a favourite picture book, James, who still was something of a bully, tried to take it away. This time, though—in contrast to her behaviour at the start of the school year—Julie held on to it, saying in a loud voice, "Go get your own. I have this one." As James retreated in surprise, Maureen smiled, silently congratulating the now older, wiser, more assertive, and more verbal Julie.

The preschool period is an exciting time in children's lives. In one sense, the preschool years mark a time of preparation: a period spent anticipating and getting ready for the start of a child's formal education. But it is a mistake to take the label "preschool" too literally. The years between two and six are hardly a mere way station in life, an interval spent waiting for the next, more important period to start. Instead, the preschool years are a time of tremendous change and growth.

In this chapter, we focus on the physical, cognitive, and social growth typical of the preschool years. We begin by considering the physical changes children undergo. We discuss weight and height, nutrition, and health and wellness. The brain and its neural pathways change too, and we will look at how both gross and fine motor skills change over the preschool years.

MODULE **4.3** Social and Personality Development in the Preschool Years

Viewing violence on TV:
Does it matter? see page 164.

MyVirtualLife

Experience the challenges and delights of the preschool years by helping your own virtual child through these years.

Log onto MyDevelopmentLab to get started.

Intellectual development is the focus of the next section of the chapter. We examine the major approaches to cognitive development, including Piaget's stage theory, information-processing approaches, and an emerging view of cognitive development that gives great weight to the influence of culture. We also consider the important advances in language development that occur during the preschool years, and we discuss several factors that influence cognitive development, including exposure to television and participation in child-care and preschool programs.

Finally, we look at social and personality development in these years, focusing first on how children figure out who they are and develop a sense of racial and gender identity. We discuss the nature of their friendships and the significance of the ways that they play together. We next look at parents, considering the different styles of parenting that are common today, as well as the implications for their children's future development and personalities. We conclude with a look at the ways in which preschool-age children begin to develop a moral sense and learn how to control aggression.

MODULE 4.1 Physical Development in the Preschool Years

Aaron

Aaron, a wildly energetic preschooler who has just turned three, was trying to stretch far enough to reach the bowl of cookies that he spied sitting on the kitchen counter. Because the bowl was just beyond his grasp, he pushed a chair from the kitchen table over to the counter and climbed up.

He still couldn't reach the cookies from the chair, so Aaron climbed onto the kitchen counter and crawled over to the cookie bowl. He pried the lid off the jar, thrust his hand in, pulled out a cookie, and began to munch on it.

But not for long. His curiosity getting the better of him, he grabbed another cookie and began to work his body along the counter towards the sink. He climbed in, twisted the cold water faucet to the "on" position, and happily splashed in the cold water.

Aaron's father, who had left the room for only a moment, returned to find Aaron sitting in the sink, soaked, with a contented smile on his face.

Three years ago, Aaron could not even lift his head. Now he can move with confidence—pushing furniture, opening jars, turning knobs, and climbing on chairs. These advances in mobility are challenging to parents, who must rise to a whole new level of vigilance in order to prevent injuries, the greatest threat to preschoolers' physical well-being. (Think what would have happened if Aaron had turned on the hot water, rather than the cold, when he reached the sink.)

Parents and caregivers also must worry about colds and other illnesses, and especially in recent years, about making sure their child gets enough of the right kinds of food to eat. As they watch their child grow active, they must insist on quiet time and a bedtime that will afford their child adequate sleep. If this seems like a long list of worries, remember that the list of delights that the preschool years bring is far longer.

The Growing Body

LEARNING OBJECTIVES

LO1 What is the state of children's bodies and overall health during the preschool years?

During the preschool years, children experience rapid advances in their physical abilities that are nothing short of astounding. Just how far they develop is apparent when we look at the changes they undergo in their size, shape, and physical abilities.

By age two, the average child in Canada weighs around 10 to 14 kilograms and is close to 90 centimetres tall. By the time the child is six years old, he or she weighs about 20 kilograms and stands 120 centimetres tall (Dieticians of Canada, 2010; see Figure 4-1).

These averages mask significant individual differences. For instance, 15 percent of six-year-olds weigh 24 kilograms or more, and 15 percent weigh 16 kilograms or less. Furthermore, average differences between boys and girls increase during the preschool years. Although at age two the differences are relatively small, during the preschool years boys start becoming taller and heavier, on average, than girls.

Economics also affects these averages. The better nutrition and health care typically received by children in developed countries translates into differences in growth. For instance, the average Swedish four-year-old is as tall as the average six-year-old in Bangladesh (United Nations, 1991; Leathers and Foster, 2004). Even within a culture, children in families with incomes below the poverty level are more likely to be short than children raised in more affluent homes (Barrett and Frank, 1987; Ogden et al., 2002).

Changes in Body Shape and Structure

The bodies of a two-year-old and a six-year-old vary not only in height and weight, but also in shape. During the preschool years, boys and girls become less round and more slender. Moreover, their arms and legs lengthen, and the size relationship between the head and the rest of the body becomes proportionally more adult-like, as was illustrated in Module 3.1. In fact, by the time children reach age six, their proportions are similar to those of adults.

Other physical changes occur internally. Muscle size increases, and children grow stronger. Bones become sturdier, and the sense organs continue to develop. For instance, the *Eustachian tube* in the ear changes its orientation so radically that it may cause the earaches that are so common with preschoolers.

Nutrition: Eating the Right Foods

Because the rate of growth is slower than during infancy, preschoolers need less food, which may cause parents to worry. However, children tend to be adept at eating enough if they are provided with nutritious meals. In fact, anxiously encouraging children to eat more than they want may lead to **obesity**, which is defined as a body weight more than 20 percent higher than the average weight for a person of a given age and height. The prevalence of obesity among older preschoolers has increased significantly over the last 20 years.

The best strategy for parents is to make sure that they make a variety of low-fat, high-nutrition foods available to preschoolers. Foods that have a relatively high iron content are particularly important: Iron-deficiency anemia, which causes constant fatigue, is one of the prevalent nutritional problems facing children raised in developed countries (Ranade, 1993).

Within these bounds, children should be given the opportunity to develop their own preferences. Exposing children to new foods by encouraging them to take just one bite is a relatively low-stress way of expanding children's diets (Shapiro, 1997).

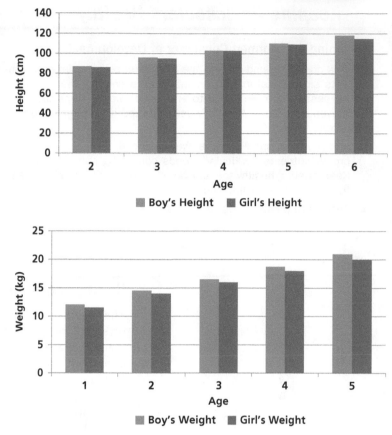

Boy's Height   **Girl's Height**

Boy's Weight   **Girl's Weight**

FIGURE 4-1 **Gaining Height and Weight**
The preschool years are marked by steady increases in height and weight. The figures show the median point for boys and girls at each age, in which 50% of children in each category are above this height or weight level and 50% are below.
Source: Based on the World Health Organization (WHO) Child Growth Standards (2006) and WHO Reference (2007) adapted for Canada by Dietitians of Canada, Canadian Paediatric Society, the College of Family Physicians of Canada, and Community Health Nurses of Canada. © Dieticians of Canada, 2010. Reproduced with permission.

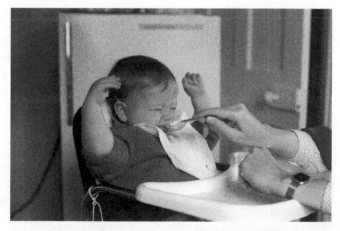

Encouraging children to eat more than they seem to want naturally may lead them to increase their food intake beyond an appropriate level.

From a health-care worker's perspective: How might biology and environment combine to affect the physical growth of a child adopted as an infant from a developing country and reared in a more industrialized one?

obesity body weight more than 20 percent higher than the average weight for a person of a given age and height

Keeping Preschoolers Healthy

Becoming an Informed Consumer of Development

There is no way around it: Even the healthiest preschooler occasionally gets sick. Social interaction with others ensures that illnesses will be passed from one child to another. However, some diseases are preventable, and others can be minimized if simple precautions are taken:

- Preschoolers should eat a well-balanced diet containing the proper nutrients, particularly foods containing sufficient protein. Keep offering healthy foods; even if children initially reject them, they might grow to like them.

- Encourage preschoolers to exercise.

- Children should get as much sleep as they wish. Being fatigued makes children more susceptible to illness.

- Children should avoid contact with others who are ill. If they play with kids who are sick, parents should make sure they and their children wash their hands thoroughly.

- Finally, be sure that children follow an appropriate schedule of immunizations.

The danger of injuries during the preschool years is in part a result of children's high levels of physical activity. It is important to take protective measures to reduce the hazards.

Health and Illness

The majority of children in Canada are reasonably healthy during this period, with the average preschooler experiencing 7 to 10 colds and other minor respiratory illnesses in each of the years from age three to five (Denny and Clyde, 1983; Kalb, 1997). Although distressing and unpleasant, minor illnesses can offer unexpected benefits, including the physical advantage of building up immunity to more severe illnesses.

The greatest risk that preschoolers face comes from neither illness nor nutritional problems but from accidents: injury is the leading cause of death among Canadian children. Among children visiting an emergency room, fractures, open wounds, and superficial wounds account for 60 percent of all injuries, with head/neck (35 percent) and arm (34 percent) injuries being most common. For one- to four-year-olds, 55 percent of injuries tend to occur during sports or leisure activities and 73 percent are likely to occur at home (Health Canada, 1998).

When we combine the high levels of physical activity, curiosity, and lack of judgment that characterize preschoolers, it is no wonder that preschoolers are accident-prone. Furthermore, some children are more apt than others to take risks and consequently to be injured. Boys, who typically are more active than girls and tend to take more risks, have a higher rate of injuries. Economic factors also play a role. Children raised under conditions of poverty in urban areas, whose inner-city neighbourhoods might contain more hazards than more affluent areas, are two times more likely to die of injuries than children living in affluence (Morrongiello et al., 2000; Morrongiello and Hogg, 2004).

Parents and caregivers can take precautions to prevent injuries, starting by childproofing homes and classrooms with electrical outlet covers and childproof locks on cabinets, but most importantly through supervision. Car seats and bike helmets can help prevent injuries from accidents.

Parents and teachers also need to be aware of the dangers from long-term hazards. For example, lead poisoning is a significant danger for many children due to their smaller body weight, developing brains, and tendency to put objects in their mouths. Despite stringent legal restrictions on the amount of lead in paint and gasoline, lead is still found on painted walls and window frames—particularly in older homes—and in gasoline, ceramics, lead-soldered pipes, automobile and truck exhaust, and even dust and water. In recent years, concerns have grown about the use of lead-based paints on children's toys.

Lead can permanently harm children. Exposure to lead has been linked to lower intelligence, problems in verbal and auditory processing, and hyperactivity and distractibility. High lead levels have also been linked to higher levels of antisocial behaviour, including aggression and delinquency in school-age children. At yet higher levels of exposure, lead poisoning results in illness and death (Morgan et al., 2001; Canfield et al., 2003; Coscia et al., 2003; Jusko et al., 2008; Wasserman et al., 2003).

REVIEW, CHECK, AND APPLY

REVIEW

- The preschool period is marked by steady physical growth and rapid advances in physical ability.
- Preschoolers tend to eat less than they did as babies, but generally regulate their food intake appropriately, if they are given nutritious options and the freedom to develop their own choices and controls.
- The preschool period is generally the healthiest time of life, with only minor illnesses threatening children. Accidents and environmental hazards are the greatest threats.

CHECK YOURSELF

1. During the preschool years, boys on the average start becoming taller and heavier than girls.
   - True
   - False

2. Which of the following suggestions is *not* recommended for preventing obesity in children?
   a. Provide food that is high in nutritional value.
   b. Make sure meals are low in fat.
   c. Ensure a consistent diet with little variety.
   d. Allow children to develop their own food preferences.

3. Which of the following benefits was included in the discussion of minor illnesses in preschoolers?
   a. Prevents the development of empathy
   b. Builds up immunities
   c. Permits children to understand their bodies
   d. Helps children develop coping skills

APPLYING LIFESPAN DEVELOPMENT

- What are some ways that increased understanding of issues relating to the physical development of preschoolers might help parents and caregivers in their care of children?
- Do you think the fact that preschool boys are more risk-prone than girls is genetic, environmental, or both? Why?

Answers: 1) True; 2) c; 3) b

The Growing Brain

L02   How do preschool children's brains and physical skills develop?

LEARNING OBJECTIVES

The brain grows at a faster rate than any other part of the body. Two-year-olds have brains that are about three-quarters the size and weight of an adult brain. By age five, children's brains are 90 percent the weight of an average adult's brain weight. By comparison, the average five-year-old's total body weight is just 30 percent the weight of average adult's body weight (Lowrey, 1986; Schuster and Ashburn, 1986; Nihart, 1993).

Why does the brain grow so rapidly? One reason is an increase in the number of interconnections among cells, which supports more complex communication between neurons and permits the rapid growth of cognitive skills. In addition, the amount of **myelin**—protective insulation that surrounds parts of neurons—increases, which speeds the transmission of electrical impulses along brain cells.

The Links Between Brain Growth and Cognitive Development

Neuroscientists are beginning to understand the ways in which brain growth is related to cognitive development. While we do not yet know the direction of causality (does brain development produce cognitive advances, or vice versa?), we can clearly see the relationship.

For example, there are periods during childhood when the brain shows unusual growth spurts, and these periods are linked to advances in cognitive abilities. One study that measured electrical activity in the brain found unusual spurts at between one and a half and two years, a time when language abilities increase rapidly. Other spurts occurred around other ages when cognitive advances are particularly intense (see Figure 4-2; Fischer and Rose, 1995; Mabbott et al., 2006; Westermann et al., 2007).

Other research has suggested that the increases in myelin in the brain (discussed earlier) might be related to preschoolers' growing cognitive capabilities. For example, myelination of the *reticular formation*, an area of the brain associated with attention and concentration, is completed by the time children are about five. This might be associated with children's

myelin protective insulation that surrounds parts of neurons—which speeds the transmission of electrical impulses along brain cells but also adds to brain weight

lateralization the process in which certain cognitive functions are located more in one hemisphere of the brain than in the other

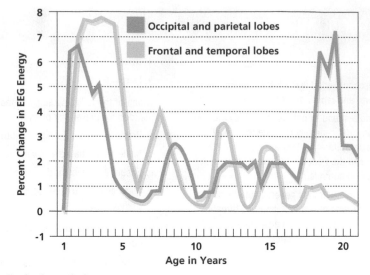

FIGURE 4-2 Brain Growth Spurt

According to one study, electrical activity in the brain has been linked to advances in cognitive abilities at various stages across the lifespan. In this graph, activity increases dramatically between one-and-a-half and two years, a period during which language rapidly develops.

Source: Fischer and Rose, 1995.

growing attention spans as they approach school age. The improvement in memory that occurs during the preschool years might also be associated with myelination: During the preschool years, myelination is completed in the hippocampus, an area associated with memory (Rolls, 2000).

In addition, there is significant growth in the nerves connecting the *cerebellum*, a part of the brain that controls balance and movement, to the *cerebral cortex*, the structure responsible for sophisticated information-processing. The growth in these nerve fibres is related to the significant advances in motor skills and cognitive processing during the preschool years (Carson, 2006; Gordon, 2007).

Brain Lateralization

By the end of the preschool period, the *corpus callosum*, a bundle of nerve fibres that connects the two hemispheres of the brain, becomes considerably thicker, developing as many as 800 million individual fibres that help coordinate brain functioning between the two hemispheres. At the same time, the two halves of the brain become increasingly differentiated and specialized. **Lateralization**, the process in which certain functions are located more in one hemisphere than the other, becomes more pronounced during the preschool years.

For most people, the left hemisphere is primarily involved with tasks that necessitate verbal competence, such as speaking, reading, thinking, and reasoning. The right hemisphere develops its own strengths, especially in nonverbal areas such as comprehension of spatial relationships, recognition of patterns and drawings, music, and emotional expression (McAuliffe and Knowlton, 2001; Koivisto and Revonsuo, 2003; Pollak et al., 2004; see Figure 4-3).

Each hemisphere also begins to process information in a slightly different manner. The left hemisphere processes data sequentially, one piece at a time. The right hemisphere processes information in a more global manner, reflecting on it as a whole (Gazzaniga, 1983; Springer and Deutsch, 1989; Leonard et al., 1996).

While there is some specialization, in most respects the two hemispheres act in tandem and are interdependent. In fact, each hemisphere can perform most of the tasks of the other. For example, the right hemisphere does some language processing and plays an important role in language comprehension (Knecht et al., 2000; Corballis, 2003; Hutchinson et al., 2003).

There are also individual and cultural differences in lateralization. For example, many of the 10 percent of people who are left-handed or ambidextrous (able to use both hands interchangeably) have language centred in the right hemisphere or have no specific language

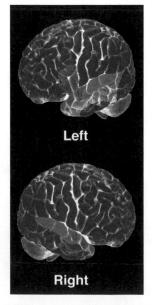

FIGURE 4-3 Looking into the Brain

This series of PET brain scans illustrates that activity in the right or left hemisphere of the brain differs according to the task in which a person is engaged. How might educators use this finding in their approach to teaching?

centre (Banich and Nicholas, 1998; Compton and Weissman, 2002). Literacy also influences lateralization (Petersson et al., 2007).

Even more intriguing are differences in lateralization related to gender and culture. For instance, starting during the first year and continuing in the preschool years, boys and girls show some hemispheric differences associated with lower-body reflexes and the processing of auditory information. Boys also clearly tend to show greater lateralization of language in the left hemisphere; among females, language is more evenly divided between the hemispheres. Such differences may help explain why girls' language development proceeds more rapidly during the preschool years than boys' (Gur et al., 1982; Grattan et al., 1992; Bourne and Todd, 2004).

REVIEW, CHECK, AND APPLY

REVIEW

- In addition to physical growth, the preschool period is marked by rapid brain growth. The increase in myelin in the brain is particularly important for intellectual development.

- Among other changes, the brain develops lateralization, a tendency of the two hemispheres to adopt specialized tasks.

CHECK YOURSELF

1. During the preschool years, the two halves of the brain become more specialized in a process called _____.

2. Language differences between the male and female brains might not be just the product of genetics; the environment might play a role as well. For example, females might have better language skills because

    a. their brains are different in size.

    b. males are not equipped to learn language at the same pace as are females.

    c. they listen to language more intently when in the womb.

    d. they receive more encouragement for verbal skills than do boys.

APPLYING LIFESPAN DEVELOPMENT

- Does brain growth cause cognitive development, or does cognitive development cause the brain to grow? Pick a side in this endless argument and defend it.

- What do you imagine thinking, planning, and reflection might be like if the two hemispheres of the brain could not communicate with each other (as is the case in some individuals with severe head injuries)?

Answers: 1) lateralization; 2) d

Motor Development

LO3 How does motor development evolve in preschool children?

LEARNING OBJECTIVES

Anya sat in the sandbox at the park, chatting with the other parents and playing with her two children, 5-year-old Nicholai and 13-month old Smetna. While she chatted, she kept a close eye on Smetna, who would still put sand in her mouth sometimes if she wasn't stopped. Today, however, Smetna seemed content to run the sand through her hands and try to put it into a bucket. Nicholai, meanwhile, was busy with two other boys, rapidly filling and emptying the other sand buckets to build an elaborate sand city, which they would then destroy with toy trucks.

When children of different ages gather at a playground, it's easy to see that preschool children have come a long way in their motor development. Both their gross and fine motor skills have become increasingly fine-tuned. Smetna, for example, is still mastering putting sand into a bucket, while her older brother Nicholai uses that skill easily as part of his larger goal of building a sand city.

Gross Motor Skills

By the time they are three, children have mastered a variety of skills: jumping, hopping on one foot, skipping, and running. By four and five, their skills have become more refined as

TABLE 4-1 MAJOR GROSS MOTOR SKILLS IN EARLY CHILDHOOD

2-Year-Olds	3-Year-Olds	4-Year-Olds	5-Year-Olds
Walk well; running improves with practice	Cannot turn or stop suddenly or quickly	Have more effective control of stopping, starting, and turning	Start, turn, and stop effectively in games
Jump off floor with both feet or from a height of 30 cm	Jump a distance of 36 to 60 centimetres	Jump a distance of 60 to 83 centimetres	Can make a running jump of 71 to 91 centimetres
Ascend and descend a stairway, one step at a time, leading with the same foot	Ascend a stairway unaided, alternating the feet	Descend a long stairway alternating the feet, if supported	Descend a long stairway alternating the feet
Can balance on one foot, left or right	Can hop, using largely an irregular series of jumps with some variations added	Hop 4 to 6 steps on one foot	Easily hop a distance of 4.88 metres

Source: From Corbin, *A Textbook of Motor Development,* 1e. Copyright © 1973 The McGraw-Hill Companies. Reprinted with permission.

During the preschool years, children grow in both fine and gross motor skills.

they have gained increasing control over their muscles. For instance, at four they can throw a ball with enough accuracy that a friend can catch it, and by age five they can toss a ring and have it land on a peg 1.5 metres away. Five-year-olds can learn to ride bikes, climb ladders, and ski downhill—activities that all require considerable coordination (Clark and Humphrey, 1985). (Table 4-1 summarizes major gross motor skills that emerge during the preschool years.)

These achievements may be related to brain development and myelination of neurons in areas of the brain related to balance and coordination. Another likely reason is that children spend a great deal of time practising these skills. During this period, the general level of activity is extraordinarily high. In fact, the activity level is higher at age three than at any other point in the entire lifespan (Eaton and Yu, 1989; Poest et al., 1990).

Girls and boys differ in certain aspects of gross motor coordination in part because of differences in muscle strength, which is usually somewhat greater in boys than in girls. For instance, boys can typically throw a ball better and jump higher, and a boy's overall activity level tends to be greater than a girl's (Eaton and Yu, 1989). On the other hand, girls generally surpass boys in tasks that involve limb coordination. For instance, at age five, girls are better than boys at jumping jacks and balancing on one foot (Cratty, 1979).

Another aspect of muscular skills—one that parents often find most problematic—is bowel and bladder control.

The Potty Question: When—and How—Should Children Be Toilet Trained?

Few questions engage as much discussion among preschoolers' caretakers than when toilet training should begin and what methods should be used. Current guidelines of the Canadian Paediatric Society support the position of pediatrician T. Berry Brazelton, who suggests that there is no single time to begin toilet training and that training should begin only when children are ready (Brazelton, 1997; Brazelton et al., 1999).

When are children "ready"? The signs of readiness include staying dry at least two hours at a time during the day or waking up dry after naps; regular and predictable bowel movements; an indication, through facial expressions or words, that urination or a bowel movement is about to occur; the ability to follow simple directions; the ability to get to the bathroom and undress alone; discomfort with soiled diapers; asking to use the toilet or potty chair; and the desire to wear underwear.

Furthermore, children must be ready not only physically, but emotionally, and if they show strong signs of resistance to toilet training, toilet training should be put off. Although some children show signs of readiness for toilet training between 18 and 24 months, some are not ready until 30 months or older (Stadtler et al., 1999; Fritz and Rockney, 2004).

handedness the preference of using one hand over another

Partially in response to changing guidelines, toilet training has begun later over the last few decades. In the 1920s and '30s, a parent-centred approach replaced the earlier child-centred approach, only to return to the child-centred approach a generation or two later. For example, in 1957, 92 percent of children were toilet trained by 18 months. In 1999, only 25 percent were toilet trained at that age, and just 60 percent of 36-month-olds were toilet trained. Some 2 percent were still not toilet trained at the age of 4 (Goode, 1999).

Fine Motor Skills

At the same time, children are progressing in their ability to use fine motor skills, which involve more delicate, smaller body movements such as using a fork and spoon, cutting with scissors, tying shoelaces, and playing the piano.

The skills involved in fine motor movements require practice. The emergence of fine motor skills shows clear developmental patterns. At age three, children can draw a circle and square with a crayon, and they can undo their clothes when they go to the bathroom. They can put a simple jigsaw puzzle together, and they can fit blocks of different shapes into matching holes. However, they do not show much precision and polish in these tasks—often, for example, forcing puzzle pieces into place.

By age four, their fine motor skills are better. They can draw a person that looks like a person, and they can fold paper into triangular designs. And by the time they are five, they can hold and manipulate a thin pencil properly.

Handedness. How do preschoolers decide which hand to hold the pencil in as they work on their fine motor skills? For most, their choice was made soon after conception.

Beginning in early infancy, many children show signs of a preference for the use of one hand over the other—the development of **handedness**. Some 90 percent are right-handed and 10 percent are left-handed, and more boys than girls are left-handed. Advances in ultrasound technology have allowed researchers to see that similar proportions of children prefer to suck their right thumb than their left thumb as early as at eight weeks gestation. In one study, researchers were able to follow up with children whose fetal thumb-sucking was recorded at 10–11 weeks gestation. At 10–12 years old, all those who preferred their right thumb were right-handed, and most of those who preferred their left thumb were left-handed (Hepper et al., 2005). As children in the preschool period practise their fine motor skills they try out both hands, but for most children handedness was already decided long before birth.

REVIEW, CHECK, AND APPLY

REVIEW

- Gross and fine motor development advances rapidly during the preschool years.
- Boys' and girls' gross motor skills begin to diverge, with boys typically doing better at tasks requiring strength and girls doing better at tasks requiring coordination.

CHECK YOURSELF

1. During the preschool years, there is significant pruning in the nerves connecting the cerebellum (the part of the brain that controls balance and movement) to the cerebral cortex (the structure responsible for sophisticated information-processing).
   - True
   - False

2. In addition to changes in myelination, another reason that motor skills develop so rapidly during the preschool years is that children spend a great deal of time
   a. using mental imagery.
   b. practising them.
   c. observing adults performing the same behaviours.
   d. sleeping.

APPLYING LIFESPAN DEVELOPMENT

- To what extent do you think that gender differences in the development of gross motor skills are genetic versus environmental?

- If it could be shown that left-handers had a greater likelihood to be gifted than right-handers, would it make sense to train children to use their left hands for everyday tasks? Why?

Answers: 1) False; 2) b

MODULE 4.2 Cognitive Development in the Preschool Years

Sam and Gill

Three-year-old Sam was talking to himself in two very different voices. "Find your shoes," he said in a low voice. "Not today. I'm not going. I hate the shoes," he said in a higher-pitched voice. The lower voice answered, "You are a bad boy. Find the shoes, bad boy." The higher-voiced response was "No, no, no." Sam's parents realized that he was playing a game with his imaginary friend, Gill—a bad boy who often disobeyed his mother. In fact, according to Sam's musings, Gill often was guilty of the very same misdeeds for which his parents blamed Sam.

In some ways, the intellectual sophistication of three-year-olds is astounding. Their creativity and imagination leap to new heights, their language is increasingly sophisticated, and they reason and think about the world in ways that would have been impossible even a few months earlier. But what underlies the dramatic advances in intellectual development of the preschool years? In this module we will consider a number of approaches to understanding children's thinking and the development of cognitive abilities in the preschool years.

Piaget's Approach

LEARNING OBJECTIVES

LO4 How does Piaget interpret cognitive development during the preschool years?

LO5 What are some challenges to Piaget's view?

Piaget's Stage of Preoperational Thinking

Jean Piaget, whose stage approach to cognitive development we discussed in Chapter 3, saw the preschool years as a time of both stability and change. He placed the preschool years into a single stage of cognitive development—the preoperational stage—which lasts from age two until around age seven.

During the **preoperational stage**, children's use of symbolic thinking grows, mental reasoning emerges, and the use of concepts increases. Seeing Mom's car keys might prompt the question, "Go to store?" as the child learns that the keys are a symbol of a car ride. In this way, children become better at representing events internally and less dependent on sensorimotor activity to understand the world around them. Yet they are still not capable of **operations**: organized, formal, logical mental processes.

According to Piaget, a key aspect of preoperational thought is *symbolic function*, the ability to use a mental symbol, a word, or an object to stand for or represent something that is not physically present. For example, preschoolers can use a mental symbol for a car (the word "car"), and they understand that a small toy car is representative of the real thing. They have no need to get behind the wheel of an actual car to understand its basic purpose and use.

The Relation between Language and Thought. Symbolic function is at the heart of one of the major advances of the preoperational period: the increasingly sophisticated use of language. Piaget suggested that the advances in language during the preschool years reflect improvements over the type of thinking that is possible during the earlier sensorimotor period. Instead of slow, sensorimotor-based thinking, symbolic thought, which relies on improved linguistic ability, allows preschoolers to represent actions virtually, at much greater speed.

Even more important, language allows children to think beyond the present to the future. Rather than being grounded in the here and now, preschoolers can imagine future possibilities through language in the form of fantasies and daydreams.

Centration: What You See Is What You Think. Place a dog mask on a cat and what do you get? According to three- and four-year-old preschoolers, a dog. To them, a cat with a dog mask ought to bark like a dog, wag its tail like a dog, and eat dog food. In every respect, the cat has been transformed into a dog (deVries, 1969).

preoperational stage according to Piaget, the stage from approximately age two to age seven in which children's use of symbolic thinking grows, mental reasoning emerges, and the use of concepts increases

operations organized, formal, logical mental processes

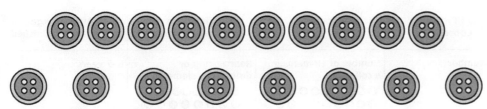

FIGURE 4-4 Which Row Contains More Buttons?
When preschoolers are shown these two rows and asked which row has more buttons, they usually respond that the lower row of buttons contains more, because it looks longer. They answer in this way even though they know quite well that 10 is greater than 8. Do you think preschoolers can be *taught* to answer correctly?

To Piaget, the root of this belief is centration, a key element, and limitation, of thinking in the preoperational period. **Centration** is the process of concentrating on one limited aspect of a stimulus—typically its superficial elements—and ignoring others. These elements come to dominate preschoolers' thinking, leading to inaccuracy.

Centration is the cause of the error illustrated in Figure 4-4. Asked which row contains more buttons, children who are four or five usually choose the row that looks longer, rather than the one that actually contains more buttons. This occurs even though children this age know quite well that 10 is more than 8. Rather than taking into account their understanding of quantity, they focus on appearance.

Preschoolers' focus on appearances might be related to another aspect of preoperational thought, the lack of conservation.

Conservation: Learning That Appearances are Deceiving. Consider the following scenario:

Four-year-old Jaime is shown two drinking glasses. One is short and broad; the other, tall and thin. A teacher half-fills the short, broad glass with apple juice. The teacher then pours the juice into the tall, thin glass. The juice fills the tall glass almost to the brim. The teacher asks Jaime a question: Is there more juice in the second glass than there was in the first?

If you view this as an easy task, so do children like Jaime. The problem is that they almost always get it wrong.

Most four-year-olds say that there is more apple juice in the tall, thin glass than there was in the short, broad one. In fact, if the juice is poured back into the shorter glass, they are quick to say that there is now less juice than there was in the taller.

The reason is that children of this age have not mastered conservation. **Conservation** is the knowledge that quantity is unrelated to the arrangement and physical appearance of objects. Some other conservation tasks are shown in Figure 4-5.

Why do children in the preoperational stage make conservation errors? Piaget suggests that the main reason is that their tendency toward centration prevents them from focusing on the relevant features of the situation. Furthermore, they cannot follow the sequence of transformations that accompanies changes in the appearance of a situation.

Incomplete Understanding of Transformation. A preoperational, preschool child who sees several worms during a walk in the woods may believe that they are all the same worm. The reason: She views each sighting in isolation, unable to understand that a transformation would be necessary for a worm to move quickly from one location to the next.

As Piaget used the term, **transformation** is the process in which one state is changed into another. For instance, adults know that if a pencil that is held upright is allowed to fall down, it passes through a series of successive stages until it reaches its final, horizontal resting spot. In contrast, children in the preoperational period are unable to envision or recall the successive transformations that the pencil followed in moving from the upright to the horizontal position. To overcome the error committed in Figure 4-4, children need to understand that to have *more* buttons, you would have to *add* buttons; that transformation requires you to add or remove something.

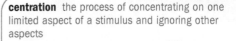

Watch on **mydevelopmentlab**

To see a re-enactment of the scenario you've just read about, log onto MyDevelopmentLab and check out the video clip "Conservation."

centration the process of concentrating on one limited aspect of a stimulus and ignoring other aspects

conservation the knowledge that quantity is unrelated to the arrangement and physical appearance of objects

transformation the process in which one state is changed into another

Type of Conservation	Modality	Change in Physical Appearance	Average Age Invariance Is Grasped
Number	Number of elements in a collection 	Rearranging or dislocating elements 	6–7 years
Substance (mass)	Amount of a malleable substance (e.g., clay or liquid) 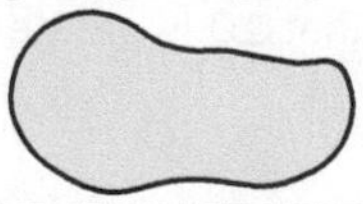	Altering shape 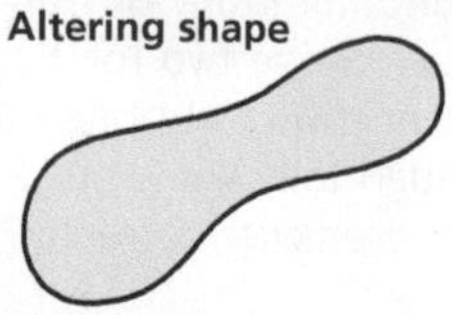	7–8 years
Length	Length of a line or object 	Altering shape or configuration 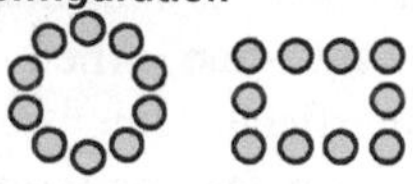	7–8 years
Area	Amount of surface covered by a set of plane figures 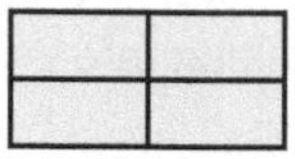	Rearranging the figures 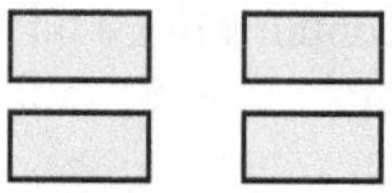	8–9 years
Weight	Weight of an object 	Altering shape 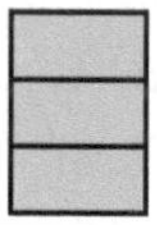	9–10 years
Volume	Volume of an object (in terms of water displacement) 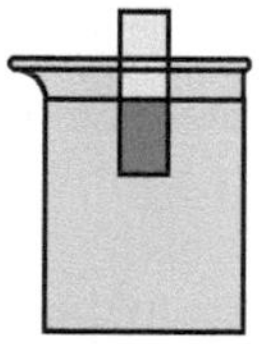	Altering shape 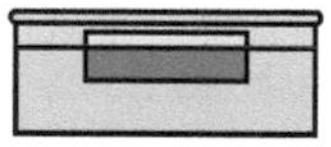	14–15 years

FIGURE 4-5 Common Tests of Children's Understanding of the Principle of Conservation
Why is it important for preschoolers to develop a sense of conservation?

Watch on **mydevelopmentlab**

To watch an experiment that demonstrates egocentrism in preschoolers, check out the video clip "Egocentrism" on MyDevelopmentLab.

egocentric thought thinking that does not take into account the viewpoints of others

Egocentrism: The Inability to Take Others' Perspectives. Another hallmark of the preoperational period is egocentric thinking. **Egocentric thought** is thinking that does not take into account the viewpoints of others. Preschoolers do not understand that others have different perspectives. Egocentric thought takes two forms: lack of awareness that others see things from a different physical perspective, and failure to realize that others may hold thoughts, feelings, and points of view that differ from theirs. (Note that egocentric thought does *not* imply intentional selfishness or a lack of consideration.)

Egocentric thinking lies behind children's lack of concern over their nonverbal behaviour and the impact it has on others. For instance, a four-year-old who receives a gift of socks may frown as he opens the package, unaware that his face can be seen by others and reveals his true feelings (Feldman, 1992).

Egocentrism largely explains why many preschoolers talk to themselves, even in the presence of others, and often ignore what others are telling them. This behaviour illustrates the egocentric nature of preoperational children's thinking: the lack of awareness that their behaviour acts as a trigger to others' reactions and responses. Consequently, much of preschoolers' verbal behaviour has no social motivation but is meant purely for their own consumption.

Egocentrism can also be seen in hiding games. In hide-and-seek, three-year-olds might "hide" by covering their faces with a pillow—even though they remain in plain view. Their reasoning: If they cannot see others, others cannot see them. They assume that everyone else shares their view.

The Emergence of Intuitive Thought. Because Piaget labelled this the "*pre*operational period" and focused on cognitive deficiencies, it is easy to assume that preschoolers are marking time, but the period is far from idle. Cognitive development proceeds steadily, and new abilities emerge, including intuitive thought.

Intuitive thought refers to preschoolers' use of primitive reasoning and their avid acquisition of world knowledge. From about ages four through seven, curiosity blossoms. Children ask "Why?" questions about nearly everything. At the same time, they might act as if they are authorities on particular topics, certain that they have the final word on an issue. Their intuitive thought leads them to believe that they know answers to all kinds of questions, with little or no logical basis for this confidence.

In the late stages of the preoperational period, children's intuitive thinking prepares them for more sophisticated reasoning. For instance, preschoolers come to understand that pushing harder on the pedals makes a bicycle move faster, or that pressing a button on a remote control makes the television change channels. By the end of the preoperational stage, preschoolers begin to grasp *functionality*, the idea that actions, events, and outcomes are related to one another in fixed patterns. They also become aware of *identity*, the understanding that certain things stay the same, regardless of changes in shape, size, and appearance—for instance, that a lump of clay contains the same amount of clay whether it is clumped into a ball or stretched out like a snake. Comprehension of identity is necessary for children to develop an understanding of conservation (the understanding, as we discussed earlier, that quantity is not related to physical appearances). Piaget regarded the development of conservation as the transition from the preoperational period to the next stage, *concrete operations*, which we will discuss in the next chapter.

Evaluating Piaget's Approach to Cognitive Development. Piaget, a masterly observer of children's behaviour, provided a detailed portrait of preschoolers' cognitive abilities. The broad outlines of his approach have given us a useful way of thinking about the progressive advances in cognitive ability during the preschool years (Siegal, 1997).

However, as we discussed earlier, Piaget's theory is based on extensive observations of relatively few children. Recent experimental investigations suggest that, in certain regards, Piaget underestimated children's capabilities.

Take, for instance, Piaget's assertion that preschoolers have little understanding of numbers, as shown by their inability to grasp conservation and reversibility (the understanding that a transformation can be reversed to return something to its original state). Recent experimental work calls that assertion into question. For instance, developmental psychologist Rochel Gelman has found that children as young as three can easily tell the difference between rows of two and three toy animals, regardless of the animals' spacing. Older children are able to identify which of two numbers is larger and even infants show a rudimentary understanding of addition and subtraction (Gelman, 1982, 2006; Wynn, 1992; Sophian et al., 1997; Vilette, 2002).

Gelman concluded that children have an innate ability to count, akin to the ability to use language that some theorists see as universal and genetically determined. This is clearly at odds with Piagetian notions, which suggest that children's numerical abilities do not blossom until after the preoperational period.

Some developmentalists (particularly those who favour the information-processing approach) also believe that cognitive skills develop in a more continuous manner than Piaget's theory implies. They believe that rather than thought changing in quality, as Piaget argues, the changes in thinking ability are more quantitative, improving gradually (Gelman and Baillargeon, 1983; Case, 1991).

There are further difficulties with Piaget's view. His contention that conservation does not emerge until the end of the preoperational period has not stood up to experimental scrutiny. Children can learn to answer correctly on conservation tasks if they are given certain training and experiences. The fact that one can improve children's performance argues against the

intuitive thought thinking that reflects preschoolers' use of primitive reasoning and their avid acquisition of knowledge about the world.

Piagetian view that children in the preoperational period have not reached a level of cognitive maturity to understand conservation (Siegler, 1995).

In sum, Piaget tended to concentrate on preschoolers' *deficiencies* in logical thought. By focusing more on children's competence, recent theorists have found evidence for a surprising degree of capability in preschoolers.

REVIEW, CHECK, AND APPLY

REVIEW

- According to Piaget, children in the preoperational stage develop symbolic function, a change in their thinking that is the foundation of further cognitive advances.

- Preoperational children are hampered by a tendency toward egocentric thought.

- Recent developmentalists, while acknowledging Piaget's gifts and contributions, take issue with his underestimation of preschoolers' capabilities.

CHECK YOURSELF

1. Children in Piaget's _____ stage begin using symbolic thinking; however, they are not capable

of _____, or organized, logical mental processes that characterize schoolchildren.

2. Egocentric thought can involve the lack of awareness that others see things from a different physical perspective and _____ .

   a. the inability to present their own perspectives to others

   b. their unwillingness to consider how their perspectives have been consistent over time

   c. failure to realize that others might hold thoughts, feelings, and points of view that differ from theirs

   d. that preoperational children are intentionally selfish and inconsiderate

3. Piaget's perspective has been criticized by others because he overestimated children's abilities.

- True
- False

APPLYING LIFESPAN DEVELOPMENT

- Do you think it is possible to break a preschooler's habit of egocentric thought by directly teaching him to take another person's point of view? Would showing him a picture of himself "hidden" behind a chair change his thinking? Why?

Answers: 1) preoperational/operations; 2) c; 3) False

Information-Processing and Vygotsky's Approach to Cognitive Development

LEARNING OBJECTIVES

LO6 How do other views of cognitive development differ from Piaget's?

Information-Processing Approaches: Cognitive Development through Skill Growth

Even as an adult, Ethan has clear recollections of his first trip to a farm, which he took when he was three years old. He was visiting his godfather and the two of them went to a nearby farm. Ethan recounts seeing what seemed like hundreds of chickens, and he clearly recalls his fear of the pigs, who seemed huge, smelly, and frightening. Most of all, he recalls the thrill of riding on a horse with his godfather.

The fact that Ethan has a clear memory of his farm trip is not surprising: Most people have unambiguous, and seemingly accurate, memories dating as far back as age three. But are the processes used to form memories at that age similar to those that operate later in life? More broadly, what general changes in the processing of information occur during the preschool years?

Information-processing approaches focus on changes in the kinds of "mental programs" that children use when approaching problems. They compare the changes in children's cognitive abilities during the preschool years to the way a computer program becomes more sophisticated as a programmer modifies it based on experience. For many child developmentalists, information-processing approaches represent the dominant, most comprehensive, and most accurate explanation of how children develop cognitively (Siegler, 1994; Lacerda et al., 2001).

We'll focus on two areas that highlight the approach taken by information-processing theorists: understanding numbers and memory development.

Preschoolers' Understanding of Numbers. As we saw earlier, preschoolers have a greater understanding of numbers than Piaget thought. Researchers using information-processing approaches have found increasing evidence for the sophistication of preschoolers' numerical understanding. The average preschooler is not only able to count, but to do so in a fairly systematic, consistent manner (Siegler, 1998).

For instance, developmental psychologist Rochel Gelman suggests that preschoolers follow set principles in their counting. Shown a group of items, they know they should assign just one number to each item and count each item only once. Moreover, even when they get the *names* of numbers wrong, they are consistent in their usage. For instance, a four-year-old who counts three items as "one, three, seven" will say "one, three, seven" when counting another group of different items. And if asked, she will probably say that there are seven items in the group (Gelman and Gallistel, 2001; Gelman, 2006).

This preschooler may recall this ride in six months, but by the time he is 12, it will probably be forgotten. Can you explain why?

Memory: Recalling the Past. Think back to your own earliest memory. If you are like Ethan, described earlier, and most other people too, your earliest memory is probably of an event that occurred after age three. **Autobiographical memory**, memory of particular events from one's own life, achieves little accuracy until then and increases gradually throughout the preschool years (Sutton, 2002; Ross and Wilson, 2003; De Roten et al., 2004; Nelson and Fivush, 2004). The accuracy of preschoolers' memories is partly determined by when the memories are assessed. Not all autobiographical memories last into later life. For instance, a child may remember the first day of kindergarten six months or a year later, but later in life might not remember it at all. Further, unless an event is particularly vivid or meaningful, it is not likely to be remembered at all.

Preschoolers' autobiographical memories not only fade, but may not be wholly accurate. For example, if an event happens often, it can be hard to remember one specific time it happened. Preschoolers' memories of familiar events are often organized into **scripts**, broad representations in memory of events and the order in which they occur. For example, a young preschooler might represent eating in a restaurant in terms of a few steps: talking to a server, getting the food, and eating. With age, the scripts become more elaborate: getting in the car, being seated at the restaurant, choosing food, ordering, waiting for the meal to come, eating, ordering dessert, and paying for the food. Particular instances of such scripted events are recalled with less accuracy than events that are unscripted (Fivush et al., 1992; Sutherland et al., 2003).

Preschoolers' memories are also susceptible to suggestion. This is a special concern when children testify in legal situations, such as when abuse is suspected.

Children's Eyewitness Testimony: Memory on Trial

I was looking and then I didn't see what I was doing and it got in there somehow. . . . The mousetrap was in our house because there's a mouse in our house. . . . The mousetrap is down in the basement, next to the firewood. . . . I was playing a game called "Operation" and then I went downstairs and said to Dad, "I want to eat lunch," and then it got stuck in the mousetrap. . . . My daddy was down in the basement collecting firewood. . . . [My brother] pushed me [into the mousetrap]. . . . It happened yesterday. The mouse was in my house yesterday. I caught my finger in it yesterday. I went to the hospital yesterday. (Ceci and Bruck, 1993, p. A23)

Despite the detailed account by this four-year-old boy of his encounter with a mousetrap and subsequent trip to the hospital, there's a problem: The incident never happened, and the memory is entirely false.

The four-year-old's explicit memory of an imaginary incident was the product of a study on children's memory. Each week for 11 weeks, the boy was told, "You went to the hospital because your finger got caught in a mousetrap. Did this ever happen to you?"

autobiographical memory memory of particular events from one's own life

scripts broad representations in memory of events and the order in which they occur

The first week, the child accurately said, "No. I've never been to the hospital." But by the second week, the answer changed to, "Yes, I cried." In the third week, the boy said, "Yes. My mom went to the hospital with me." By the eleventh week, the answer had expanded to the quote above (Ceci and Bruck, 1993; Bruck and Ceci, 2004).

The research study that elicited the child's false memories is part of a new and rapidly growing field: forensic developmental psychology. *Forensic developmental psychology* focuses on the reliability of children's autobiographical memories in the context of the legal system, when they might be witnesses or victims (Bruck and Ceci, 2004; Goodman, 2006).

Children's memories are susceptible to the suggestions of adults asking them questions. This is particularly true of preschoolers, who are considerably more vulnerable to suggestion than either adults or school-age children. The error rate is heightened when the same question is asked repeatedly. False memories of the "mousetrap" variety just reported, in fact, can be more persistent than actual memories. In addition, when questions are highly suggestive (that is, when questioners attempt to lead a person to particular conclusions), children are more apt to make mistakes (Powell et al., 2003; Bruck and Ceci, 2004; Loftus and Bernstein, 2005).

Information-Processing in Perspective. According to information-processing approaches, cognitive development consists of gradual improvements in the ways people perceive, understand, and remember information. With age and practice, preschoolers process information more efficiently and with greater sophistication, and they are able to handle increasingly complex problems. In this view, it is these quantitative advances in information-processing—and not the qualitative changes suggested by Piaget—that constitute cognitive development (Case and Okamoto, 1996; Goswami, 1998; Zhe and Siegler, 2000).

For information-processing proponents, the reliance on well-defined processes that can be tested by research is one of the perspective's most important features. Rather than relying on somewhat vague concepts, such as Piaget's notions of assimilation and accommodation, information-processing approaches provide a comprehensive, logical set of concepts.

For instance, as preschoolers grow older, they have longer attention spans, can monitor and plan what they are attending to more effectively, and become increasingly aware of their cognitive limitations. This places some of Piaget's findings in a different light. For instance, increased attention allows older children—as distinct from preschoolers—to attend to both the height *and* width of tall and short glasses and to understand that the amount of liquid in the glasses stays the same when it is poured back and forth—that is, to grasp conservation (Miller and Seier, 1994; Hudson et al., 1997).

Yet information-processing approaches have their detractors. One important criticism is that information-processing approaches "lose the forest for the trees" by paying so much attention to the detailed, individual sequence of mental processes that they never adequately paint a comprehensive picture of cognitive development—which Piaget clearly did quite well.

Information-processing approaches have been highly influential over the past several decades. They have inspired a tremendous amount of research that has helped us gain some insights into how children develop cognitively.

Vygotsky's View of Cognitive Development: Taking Culture into Account

As her daughter watches, a member of the Chilcotin Indian tribe prepares a salmon for dinner. When the daughter asks a question about a small detail of the process, the mother takes out another salmon and repeats the entire process. According to the tribal view of learning, understanding and comprehension can come only from grasping the total procedure, and not from learning about the individual subcomponents of the task. (Tharp, 1989)

Russian developmental psychologist Lev Vygotsky proposed that the focus of cognitive development should be on a child's social and cultural world, as opposed to the Piagetian approach concentrating on individual performance.

The Chilcotin view of how children learn about the world contrasts with the prevalent view of Western society, which assumes that only by mastering the separate parts of a problem can one fully comprehend it. Do differences in the ways particular cultures and societies approach problems influence cognitive development? According to Russian developmental psychologist Lev Vygotsky, who lived from 1896 to 1934, the answer is a clear "yes."

Vygotsky viewed cognitive development as the product of social interactions. Instead of concentrating on individual performance, Vygotsky's increasingly influential view focuses on the social aspects of development and learning.

Vygotsky saw children as apprentices, learning cognitive strategies and other skills from adult and peer mentors who not only present new ways of doing things, but also provide assistance, instruction, and motivation. Consequently, he focused on the child's social and cultural world as the source of cognitive development. According to Vygotsky, children gradually grow intellectually and begin to function on their own because of the assistance that adult and peer partners provide (Vygotsky, 1979; 1926/1997; Tudge and Scrimsher, 2003).

Vygotsky contended that culture and society establish the institutions, such as preschools and play groups, that promote development by providing opportunities for cognitive growth. Furthermore, by emphasizing particular tasks, culture and society shape the nature of specific cognitive advances. Unless we look at what is important and meaningful to members of a given society, we can seriously underestimate the nature and level of cognitive abilities that ultimately will be attained (Tappan, 1997; Schaller and Crandall, 2004). For example, children's toys reflect what is important and meaningful in a particular society. In Western societies, preschoolers commonly play with toy wagons, automobiles, and other vehicles, in part reflecting the mobile nature of the culture.

Vygotsky's approach is therefore quite different from Piaget's. Where Piaget looked at children and saw junior scientists working by themselves to develop an independent understanding of the world, Vygotsky saw cognitive apprentices learning from master teachers the skills valued in the child's culture (Kitchener, 1996; Fernyhough, 1997).

The Zone of Proximal Development and Scaffolding: Foundations of Cognitive Development.

Vygotsky proposed that children's cognitive abilities increase through exposure to information that is new enough to be intriguing, but not too difficult to contend with. He called this the **zone of proximal development (ZPD)**, the level at which a child can *almost,* but not fully, perform a task independently, but can do so with the assistance of someone more competent. For cognitive development to occur, new information must be presented—by parents, teachers, or more skilled peers—within the zone of proximal development. For example, a preschooler might not be able to figure out by herself how to stick a handle on the clay pot she's making, but she can do it with advice from her teacher (Blank and White, 1999; Chaiklin, 2003; Kozulin, 2004).

The concept of the zone of proximal development suggests that even though two children might be able to achieve the same amount without help, if one child receives aid, he or she might improve substantially more than the other. The greater the improvement that comes with help, the larger the zone of proximal development.

The assistance or structuring provided by others has been termed *scaffolding* after the temporary scaffolds that aid in building construction. **Scaffolding** is the support for learning and problem solving that encourages independence and growth (Puntambekar and Hübscher, 2005). As in construction, the scaffolding that older people provide, which facilitates the completion of identified tasks, is removed once children can solve a problem on their own (Rogoff, 1995; Warwick and Maloch, 2003).

To Vygotsky, scaffolding not only helps children solve specific problems, it also aids in the development of their overall cognitive abilities. In education, scaffolding involves, first of all, helping children think about and frame a task appropriately. In addition, a parent or teacher is likely to provide clues to help with task completion that fit the child's level of development and to model behaviour that can lead to task completion.

> **From an educator's perspective:** If children's cognitive development is dependent on interactions with others, what obligations does society have regarding such social settings as preschools and neighbourhoods?

One key aspect of the aid that more accomplished individuals provide to learners comes in the form of cultural tools. *Cultural tools* are actual, physical items (e.g., pencils, paper, calculators, computers, and so forth), as well as an intellectual and conceptual framework for solving problems. The framework includes the language that is used within a culture, its

Watch on **mydevelopmentlab**

Log onto MyDevelopmentLab and watch several videos of the zone of proximal development principle displayed in preschoolers.

Watch on **mydevelopmentlab**

To watch a teacher using the scaffolding technique with preschoolers, log onto MyDevelopmentLab and watch the video clip "Scaffolding."

zone of proximal development (ZPD) according to Vygotsky, the level at which a child can *almost,* but not fully, perform a task independently, but can do so with the assistance of someone more competent

scaffolding the support for learning and problem solving that encourages independence and growth

alphabetical and numbering schemes, its mathematical and scientific systems, and even its religious systems. These cultural tools provide a structure that can be used to help children define and solve specific problems, as well as an intellectual point of view that encourages cognitive development.

For example, consider the cultural differences in how people talk about distance. In cities, distance is usually measured in blocks ("the store is about 15 blocks away"). To a child from a rural background, more culturally meaningful terms are needed, such as metres or kilometres, or such practical measurements as "a stone's throw," or references to known distances and landmarks ("about half the distance to town" or "five houses down the road"). To make matters more complicated, "how far" questions are sometimes answered in terms not of distance, but of time ("it's about 15 minutes to the store"), which will be understood variously to refer to walking or riding time, depending on context—and, if riding time, to different forms of riding (by ox cart, bicycle, bus, canoe, or automobile), again depending on cultural context. The nature of the tools available to children to solve problems and perform tasks is highly dependent on the culture in which they live.

Evaluating Vygotsky's Contributions. Vygotsky's view has become increasingly influential, which is remarkable given that he died in 1934 at the age of 37 (Van Der Veer and Valsiner, 1993, 1994; Winsler, 2003). His work was not translated into English until nearly 30 years after his death. Compare that to Piaget, born the same year, who died in 1980 after a long research career. Vygotsky's influence has grown because his ideas help explain a growing body of research on the importance of social interaction in promoting cognitive development. The idea that children's comprehension of the world flows from their interactions with their parents, peers, and other members of society is increasingly well supported. It is also consistent with a growing body of multicultural and cross-cultural research, which finds evidence that cognitive development is shaped, in part, by cultural factors (Daniels, 1996; Scrimsher and Tudge, 2003).

Vygotsky's melding of the cognitive and social worlds of children has been an important advance in our understanding of cognitive development.

REVIEW, CHECK, AND APPLY

REVIEW

- Proponents of information-processing approaches argue that quantitative changes in children's processing skills largely account for their cognitive development.

- Instead of focusing on children's cognitive limitations, developmentalists using an information-processing approach focus on the cognitive advances that enable children to develop considerable abilities.

- Vygotsky believed that children develop cognitively within a context of culture and society. His theory includes the concepts of the zone of proximal development and scaffolding.

CHECK YOURSELF

1. According to the information-processing approach of cognitive development, memories of particular events occurring in one's own life are also known as

   a. autobiographical memory.

   b. explicit memory.

   c. personal memory.

   d. cultural memory.

2. _____ believed that children learn about their world through their interactions with others.

   a. Vygotsky

   b. Piaget

   c. Siegler

   d. Gelman

3. One reason Vygotsky has only begun to have an influence in psychology is because he was largely unknown to developmentalists.

   - True

   - False

APPLYING LIFESPAN DEVELOPMENT

- Do you agree with the view that information-processing approaches see too many trees and lose sight of the forest? Or do you think that Piaget saw too much forest without accounting for enough trees? Explain.

- In what ways have educators and others begun to apply Vygotsky's ideas in schools and communities? Should governments take an active role in this?

Answers: 1) a; 2) a; 3) True

The Growth of Language and Learning

LO7   How does language develop in the preschool years?

LO8   What effect does television have on preschoolers?

LO9   What kinds of preschool educational programs are available?

"I better save kids, save kids. This is four year olds. Some four year olds like earrings and they wear earrings. I'm not letting myself get earrings. Oh they're so [unintelligible]. I'm joking. No you're not. Oh look it's a car with a remote control. I think if you download exit you can buy. But that cost hundreds of dollars. Why are you buying this, why? It hurts my feelings. I never get what I want. [starts singing a song]"

Listen to Julie, at age four. In addition to recognizing most letters of the alphabet, printing the first letter of her name, and writing the word "HI," she is capable of producing these complex sentences.

During the preschool years, children's language skills reach new heights of sophistication. They begin the period with reasonable linguistic capabilities, but with significant gaps in both comprehension and production. In fact, no one would mistake a four-year-old's language for an adult's. However, by the end of the preschool years, children can hold their own with adults, comprehending and producing language with many of the qualities of adults' language. How does this transformation occur?

Language Development

Language blooms so rapidly between the late twos and the mid-threes that researchers have yet to understand the exact pattern. What is clear is that sentence length increases steadily, and the number of ways children combine words and phrases to form sentences—known as **syntax**—doubles each month. By the time a preschooler is three, the various combinations reach into the thousands (Wheeldon, 1999, Pinker, 2005).

There are also enormous leaps in the number of words children use. By age six, the average child has a vocabulary of around 14 000 words—acquired at a rate of nearly one new word every 2 hours, 24 hours a day. They manage this feat through a process known as **fast mapping**, in which new words are associated with their meaning after only a brief encounter (Clark, 1983; Fenson et al., 1994; Ganger and Brent, 2004).

By the age of three, preschoolers routinely use plural and possessive forms of nouns (such as "boys" and "boy's"), the past tense (adding "-ed" at the end of words), and articles ("the" and "a"). They can ask, and answer, complex questions ("Where did you say my book is?" and "Those are trucks, aren't they?").

Preschoolers' skills extend to the appropriate formation of words that they have never before encountered. For example, in one classic experiment (Berko, 1958), the experimenter told the children that a figure was a "wug," and then showed them a card with two of the cartoon figures. "Now there are two of them," the children were told, and they were then asked to supply the missing word in the sentence, "There are two _____" (the answer to which, of course, is "wugs"). See Figure 4-6.

Not only did children show that they knew rules about the plural forms of nouns, but they also understood possessive forms of nouns and the third-person singular and past-tense forms of verbs—all for words that they had never encountered, since they were nonsense words with no real meaning (O'Grady and Aitchison, 2005).

Preschoolers also learn what *cannot* be said as they acquire the principles of grammar. **Grammar** is the system of rules that determine how our thoughts can be expressed. For instance, preschoolers come to learn that "I am sitting" is correct, while the similarly structured "I am knowing [that]" is incorrect. Although they still make frequent mistakes of one sort or another, three-year-olds follow the principles of grammar most of the time. Some errors are very noticeable—such as the use of "mens" and "catched"—and quite

This is a wug.

Now there is another one. There are two of them. There are two _____.

FIGURE 4-6 Appropriate Formation of Words

Even though no preschooler—like the rest of us—is likely to have ever before encountered a wug, they are able to produce the appropriate word to fill in the blank (which, for the record, is *wugs*).

Source: Reprinted by permission of Jean Berko Gleason.

---

syntax the way in which an individual combines words and phrases to form sentences

fast mapping instances in which new words are associated with their meaning after only a brief encounter

grammar the system of rules that determine how our thoughts can be expressed

regular. When a three-year-old says "I runned to the park," she is actually demonstrating that she understands the rules for conjugating regular verbs, referred to as *overregularization*. Gradually she will also learn all the irregular verbs (deVilliers and deVilliers, 1992; Pinker, 1994; Guasti, 2002).

Private Speech and Social Speech. In even a short visit to a preschool, you're likely to notice some children talking to themselves during play periods. A child might be reminding a doll about a trip to the grocery store later, or, while playing with a toy racing car, might speak of an upcoming race. In some cases, the talk is sustained, as when a child, working on a puzzle, says things like, "This piece goes here. . . . Uh-oh, this one doesn't fit. . . . Where can I put this piece? . . . . This can't be right."

Some developmentalists suggest that **private speech**, speech by children that is spoken and directed to themselves, performs an important function. For instance, Vygotsky suggested that it is used as a guide to behaviour and thought. By communicating with themselves through private speech, children are able to try out ideas, acting as their own sounding boards. In this way, private speech facilitates children's thinking and helps them control their behaviour—much as you might say "Take it easy" or "Calm down" when trying to control your anger over some situation. In Vygotsky's view, then, private speech serves an important social function and is also a forerunner to the internal dialogues that we use when we reason with ourselves during thinking (Winsler et al., 1997; Winsler et al., 2003).

In addition, private speech might be a way for children to practise the practical skills required in conversation, known as *pragmatics*. **Pragmatics** is the aspect of language relating to communicating effectively and appropriately with others. The development of pragmatic abilities permits children to understand the basics of conversations—turn-taking, sticking to a topic, and what should and should not be said, according to the conventions of society. When children are taught that the appropriate response to receiving a gift is "thank you," or that they should use different language in various settings (on the playground versus in the classroom), they are learning the pragmatics of language.

The preschool years also mark the growth of social speech. **Social speech** is speech directed toward another person and meant to be understood by that person. Before age three, children seem to speak sometimes for their own entertainment, apparently uncaring whether anyone else can understand. However, during the preschool years, children begin to direct their speech to others, wanting others to listen and becoming frustrated when they cannot make themselves understood. As a result, they begin to adapt their speech to others through pragmatics, as discussed earlier.

Learning from the Media: Television and the Internet

Ask almost any preschooler, and she or he will be able to identify Elmo, as well as Big Bird, Bert, Ernie, and a host of other characters: the members of the cast of *Sesame Street*. *Sesame Street* is the most successful television show in history targeted at preschoolers; its audience is in the millions.

But *Sesame Street* is not all that preschoolers are watching on television, and more recently the Internet and computers play a central role in many Canadian households. Television is a particularly potent stimulus, with the average preschooler watching more than 21 hours of TV a week. In more than a third of households with children two to seven years of age, the television is on "most of the time." In comparison, preschoolers spend three-quarters of an hour reading on the average day (see Figure 4-7; Robinson and Bianchi, 1997; Roberts et al., 1999; Bryant and Bryant, 2001, 2003).

Computers are also becoming influential in the lives of preschoolers. Seventy percent of preschoolers between the ages of four and six have used a computer, and a quarter of them use one every day. Those who use a computer use it an average of an hour a day, and the majority use it by themselves. With help from their parents, almost one-fifth have sent an email (Rideout et al., 2003).

It's too early to know the effects of computer usage—and of other new media such as video games and hand-held devices—on preschoolers' language and cognitive development.

private speech speech by children that is spoken and directed to themselves

pragmatics the aspect of language that relates to communicating effectively and appropriately with others

social speech speech directed toward another person and meant to be understood by that person

However, there is a wealth of research on the consequences of viewing television, and we consider it next.

Television: Controlling Exposure. Despite the introduction of a number of high-quality educational programs in recent decades, many children's programs are not of high quality or are not appropriate for a preschool audience. Furthermore, while parents may turn on high-quality programs like *Sesame Street* for an hour each day, children are often exposed to far more background television being viewed by older siblings and adults. In one study, 50 percent of households reported that the TV is on all day (Rideout et al., 2003). Some researchers argue that exposure to the medium itself, regardless of the program, contributes to attention problems (Christakis et al., 2004) and obesity (Canadian Paediatric Society, 2003), and most agree that television viewing takes time away from more beneficial physical, social, and educational activities, and sleep. The Canadian Paediatric Society recommends that children watch no more than one hour of television per day and that televisions and video game equipment never be located in children's bedrooms (Canadian Paediatric Society, 2003).

Preschoolers are not particularly "television literate." They often do not fully understand the plots of the stories they are viewing, are unable to recall significant story details after viewing a program, and make limited and often erroneous inferences about the motivations of characters. Moreover, preschool children may have difficulty separating fantasy from reality, with some believing, for example, that there is a real Big Bird living on *Sesame Street* (Wright et al., 1994; Kimura and Kato, 2006).

Similarly, preschoolers exposed to TV advertising are not able to critically understand and evaluate the messages they see. Consequently, they are likely to fully accept advertisers' claims about their product. The likelihood of children believing advertising messages is so high that the American Psychological Association has recommended placing restrictions on advertising targeting children under age eight (Kunkel et al., 2004). Similar restrictions are in place in Canada for television, but not the Internet. This is of particular concern when families with preschoolers replace a traditional cable television with Internet-based "free" streaming video.

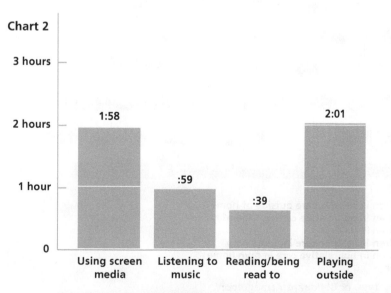

Note: Average is among all children, across all days of the week, including those who don't do certain activities yet at all.

FIGURE 4-7

Amount of Time Children 0–6 Spend Each Day, on Average

As they get older and their information-processing capabilities improve, preschoolers' understanding of the material they see on television improves. They remember things more accurately, and they are better able to focus on the central message of a show. This improvement suggests that the powers of the medium of television may be harnessed to bring about cognitive gains—exactly what the producers of *Sesame Street* have done for 40 years (Singer and Singer, 2000; Crawley et al., 2002; Berry, 2003; Fisch, 2004).

Early Childhood Education: Taking the "Pre" Out of the Preschool Period

The term "preschool period" is something of a misnomer: More than half of children in Canada between one and five years old are in some form of care outside the home, much of it designed either explicitly or implicitly to teach skills that will enhance intellectual and social abilities (Bushnik, 2006; see Figure 4-8). There are several reasons for this, but one major factor is the rise in the number of families in which both parents work outside the home. For instance, a high proportion of fathers work outside the home, and close to 75 percent of women with children under six are employed, most of them full-time. Despite increasing social acceptance of the "stay-at-home-dad", 4.4 times as many women as men stopped working for "personal or family reasons" in 2006 (Bushnik, 2006).

However, there is another reason that preschools are popular: Developmental psychologists have found evidence that children can benefit substantially from involvement in some form of educational activity before they enrol in formal schooling, which typically takes place at age five. When compared to children who stay at home and have no formal educational involvement, most children enrolled in high-quality preschools experience clear cognitive and social benefits (National Institute of Child Health and Human Development, 1999, 2000; Campbell et al., 2002).

The Varieties of Early Education. The variety of early education alternatives is vast. Some outside-the-home care for children is little more than babysitting, while other options are designed to promote intellectual and social advances. Among the major choices are the following:

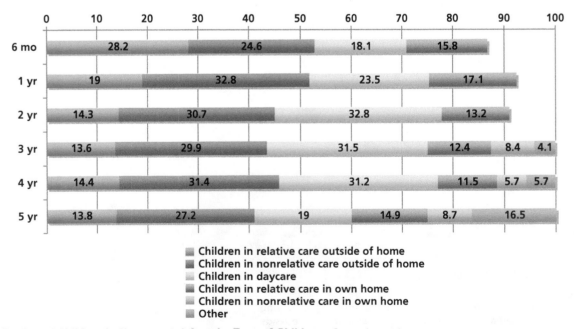

FIGURE 4-8 Distribution of Children in Nonparental Care by Type of Childcare Arrangement
Approximately half of children in Canada are enrolled in some form of care outside the home—part of a trend that is the result of more parents being employed full-time. Evidence suggests that children can benefit from early childhood education.
Note: Data for children two and younger in "nonrelative care in own home" and "other" categories was unavailable.
Source: Bushnik, 2006, Child Care in Canada. Statistics Canada, National Longitudinal Study of Children and Youth Statistics Canada, 2006.

- *Child-care centres* typically provide care for children outside the home, while their parents are at work. Although many child-care centres aim to provide some form of intellectual stimulation or explicit school-readiness programs, their primary purpose tends to be more social and emotional than cognitive.

- Some childcare is provided in *family-run child-care centres*, small operations run in private homes. Because centres in some areas are unlicensed, the quality of care can be uneven. Because teachers in licensed child-care programs are more often trained professionals than those who provide this unlicensed childcare, the quality of care is often higher in licensed programs.

- *Preschools* are explicitly designed to provide intellectual and social experiences for children. They tend to be more limited in their schedules than family-run care centres, typically providing care for only three to five hours per day. Because of this limitation, preschools mainly serve children from middle and higher socioeconomic levels, in cases where parents don't need to work full-time.

Like child-care centres, preschools vary enormously in the activities they provide. Some emphasize social skills while others focus on intellectual development. Some do both.

The Effectiveness of Childcare.

How effective are such programs? Most research suggests that preschoolers enrolled in child-care centres show intellectual development that at least matches that of children cared for at home, and often is better. For instance, some studies find that preschoolers in childcare are more verbally fluent, show memory and comprehension advantages, and even achieve higher IQ scores than at-home children. Other studies find that early and long-term participation in childcare is particularly helpful for children from lower-income homes or who are at risk for negative developmental outcomes (Campbell et al., 2002; Clarke-Stewart and Allhusen, 2002; Vandell, 2004).

Similar advantages are found for preschoolers' social development. Children in high-quality programs tend to be more self-confident, independent, and knowledgeable about the social world in which they live than those who do not participate. On the other hand, not all the outcomes of outside-the-home care are positive: Some studies report that children in childcare are less polite, less compliant, less respectful of adults, and sometimes more competitive and aggressive than their peers. Furthermore, children who spend more than 10 hours a week in preschools have a slightly higher likelihood of being disruptive in class (Clarke-Stewart and Allhusen, 2002; NICHD Early Child Care Research Network, 2003; Belsky et al., 2007). That said, associations between increased hours in childcare and developmental problems may be masking other issues—for example, single parents are more likely to live in low-income, high-risk areas, have access to poorer-quality childcare, and have greater need for longer hours of care. When we look at the association between number of hours in childcare and developmental outcome, we need to consider why children differ in the number of hours they are enrolled in childcare.

It is also important to keep in mind that not all early childhood care programs are equally effective. High-quality care provides intellectual and social benefits, while low-quality care not only is unlikely to furnish benefits, but actually may harm children (Maccoby and Lewis, 2003; Votruba-Drzal et al., 2004; NICHD Early Child Care Research Network, 2006).

The Quality of Childcare.

How can we define "high quality"? The major characteristics of high-quality care include the following (Love et al., 2003; Vandell et al., 2005; Layzer and Goodson, 2006):

- The care providers are well trained.
- The child-care centre has an appropriate overall size and ratio of care providers to children. Recommended teacher-to-child ratios are 1:3 for infants and 1:4 for toddlers. Provincial regulations allow much higher ratios for three- to five-year–olds; however, children thrive when ratios are smaller (Friendly et al., 2009).
- The curriculum of a child-care facility is not left to chance, but is carefully planned out and coordinated among the teachers.
- The language environment is rich, with a great deal of conversation.

- The caregivers are sensitive to children's emotional and social needs, and they know when and when not to intervene.
- Materials and activities are age appropriate.
- Basic health and safety standards are followed.

> **From an educator's perspective:** What do you think might be some implications for a preschool teacher who has children from diverse backgrounds in the classroom?

REVIEW, CHECK, AND APPLY

REVIEW

- In the preschool years, children rapidly increase in linguistic ability, developing an improved sense of grammar and shifting gradually from private to social speech.

- Preschoolers watch television at high levels, with mixed consequences.

- Preschool educational programs are beneficial if they are of high quality, with trained staff, a developmentally appropriate educational curriculum, proper group sizes, and small staff–student ratios.

CHECK YOURSELF

1. Being able to combine words and phrases in order to form sentences is also known as _____.

2. Preschoolers are able to learn the meaning of words after only a brief encounter. This is also known as _____.
   a. synaptic explosion
   b. word unification
   c. social speech
   d. fast mapping

3. When it comes to childcare, the key factor to effectiveness is _____.
   a. size
   b. program type
   c. age of the child
   d. quality

APPLYING LIFESPAN DEVELOPMENT

- Is private speech egocentric or useful? Do adults ever use private speech? What functions does it serve?

- In your view, how do thought and language interact in preschoolers' development? Is it possible to think without language? How do children who have been deaf from birth think?

Answers: 1) syntax; 2) d; 3) d

MODULE 4.3 Social and Personality Development in the Preschool Years

Feeling His Mother's Pain

When Cathy opened the mail, she sat down on the couch and cried. It was just too much: her boss had yelled at her at work, her babysitter cancelled for Friday night (so much for date night), and now in the mail was a reassessment letter from the Canada Revenue Agency—she owed $2148. Christmas was just around the corner, and she didn't know where she would get the money. With the letter, and her head, in her hands, she just cried. Her two-year-old son, hearing her sobs, came to the rescue. He offered his sookie and said, "Boo-boo kiss?"

Like most two-year-olds, Cathy's son could not only share his mother's pain but was able to find a way to try to soothe it. During the preschool years, children's ability to understand others' emotions begins to grow, and it colours their relationships with others.

In this module, we address social and personality development during the preschool period. We begin by examining how children continue to form a sense of self, focusing on how they develop their self-concepts, including their concept of gender. Next we focus on preschoolers' social lives, especially how they play with one another, and we consider how parents and other authority figures use discipline to shape children's behaviour.

Finally, we examine two key aspects of social behaviour: moral development and aggression. We consider how children develop a notion of right and wrong and we look at factors that lead preschool-age children to behave aggressively.

Forming a Sense of Self

L010 How do preschool-age children develop a concept of themselves?

L011 Ho do children develop their sense of racial identity and gender?

Psychosocial development relates to changes in an understanding of oneself and others' behaviour.

Although the question "Who am I?" is not explicitly posed by most preschool-age children, it underlies much of their development during the preschool years, and the answer may affect them for the rest of their lives.

Psychosocial Development: Resolving the Conflicts

Mary-Alice's preschool teacher raised her eyebrows slightly when the four-year-old took off her coat. Mary-Alice, usually dressed in well-matched play suits, was a medley of prints. She had on a pair of flowered pants, along with a completely clashing plaid top. The outfit was accessorized with a striped headband, socks in an animal print, and Mary-Alice's polka-dotted rain boots. Mary-Alice's mom gave a slightly embarrassed shrug. "Mary-Alice got dressed all by herself this morning," she explained as she handed over a bag containing spare shoes, just in case the rain boots became uncomfortable during the day.

Psychoanalyst Erik Erikson might well have praised Mary-Alice's mother for helping Mary-Alice develop a sense of initiative (if not of fashion), and thereby promoting her psychosocial development. **Psychosocial development** encompasses changes in individuals' understanding of themselves and of others' behaviour. According to Erikson, society and culture present a series of challenges that shift as people age. Erikson believed that people pass through eight distinct stages, each characterized by a crisis or conflict that the person must resolve. Our experiences as we try to resolve these conflicts lead us to develop ideas about ourselves that can last for the rest of our lives.

According to Erikson, in the early part of the preschool period, children are said to be completing the autonomy-versus-shame-and-doubt stage and entering what Erikson called the **initiative-versus-guilt stage**, which lasts from around age three to age six. During this period, children face conflicts between the desire to act independently of their parents and the guilt that comes if they don't succeed. They come to see themselves as persons in their own right, and they begin to make decisions on their own.

Parents (like Mary-Alice's mother) who react positively can help their children resolve these opposing feelings. By providing their children with opportunities to act self-reliantly, while still giving them direction and guidance, parents can support their children's initiative. On the other hand, parents who discourage their children's independence may contribute to a sense of guilt that persists throughout their lives and affects their self-concept, which begins to develop during this period.

Self-Concept in the Preschool Years: Thinking About the Self

If you ask preschool-age children to specify what makes them different from other kids, they readily respond with answers like, "I'm a good runner" or "I'm a big girl." Such answers relate to **self-concept**—their identity, or their set of beliefs about what they are like as individuals (Brown, 1998; Tessor et al., 2000; Marsh et al., 2002).

psychosocial development according to Erikson, development that encompasses changes both in the understandings individuals have of themselves as members of society and in their comprehension of the meaning of others' behaviour

initiative-versus-guilt stage according to Erikson, the period during which children aged three to six years experience conflict between independence of action and the sometimes negative results of that action

self-concept one's identity or set of beliefs about what one is like as an individual

Cultural Dimensions

Developing Ethnic Awareness

The preschool years mark an important turning point for children. Their answer to the question of who they are begins to take into account their ethnic identity.

For most preschool-age children, ethnic awareness comes relatively early. Certainly, even infants are able to distinguish different skin colours, but it is only later that children begin to attribute meaning to different ethnic characteristics.

By the time they are three or four years of age, preschool-age children notice differences among people based on skin colour, and they begin to identify themselves as a member of a particular group, such as "Mohawk" or "Black." Although at first they do not realize that ethnicity is an enduring feature of who they are, later they begin to understand the significance that society places on ethnic membership (Bernal and Knight, 1993; Sheets and Hollins, 1999; Hall and Rowan, 2003).

Some preschoolers have mixed feelings about their ethnic identity. Some experience **race dissonance**, the phenomenon in which minority children indicate preferences for majority values or people. For instance, some studies find that as many as 90 percent of African American children, when asked about their reactions to drawings of Black and white children, react more negatively to those depicting Black children. However, this reaction does not translate into lower self-esteem; rather, the white preference appears to be a result of the powerful influence of the dominant culture, rather than a disparagement of their own race (Holland, 1994). These results have been replicated in numerous minority groups, including remote Northern Canadian Aboriginal groups, with experimenters of the same ethnicity and speaking the local Native language (Cornblum, 1996). This suggests that children are aware of which group has status and power from a very early age.

Children's self-concepts are not necessarily accurate. In fact, preschool children typically overestimate their skills and knowledge across all domains of expertise. Consequently, their view of the future is quite rosy: They expect to win the next game they play, to beat all opponents in an upcoming race, to write great stories when they grow up. Even when they have just experienced failure at a task, they are likely to expect to do well in the future. This optimistic view arises because they do not yet compare themselves and their performance against others, thereby gaining the freedom to take chances and try new activities (Dweck, 2002; Wang, 2004).

Preschool-age children's view of themselves reflects their culture. For example, many Asian societies tend to have a **collectivistic orientation**, in which individuals tend to regard themselves as parts of a larger social network in which they are interconnected with and responsible to others. In contrast, children in Western cultures are more likely to develop an **individualistic orientation** that emphasizes personal identity and the uniqueness of the individual, seeing themselves as self-contained and autonomous, in competition with others for scarce resources (Markus and Kitayama, 1991; Dennis et al., 2002; Lehman et al., 2004; Wang, 2004, 2006).

Preschoolers' developing self-concepts can also be affected by their culture's attitudes toward various racial and ethnic groups. Preschoolers' awareness of their ethnic or racial identity is subtly influenced by the attitudes of the people, schools, and other cultural institutions with which they come into contact.

Gender Identity: Developing Femaleness and Maleness

Boys' awards: Very Best Thinker, Most Eager Learner, Most Imaginative, Most Enthusiastic, Most Scientific, Best Friend, Mr. Personality, Hardest Worker, Best Sense of Humour.

Girls' awards: All-Around Sweetheart, Sweetest Personality, Cutest Personality, Best Sharer, Best Artist, Biggest Heart, Best Manners, Best Helper, Most Creative.

What's wrong with this picture? To one parent, whose daughter received one of the girls' awards during a kindergarten graduation ceremony, quite a bit. While the girls were getting pats on the back for their pleasing personalities, the boys were receiving awards for their intellectual and analytic skills (Deveny, 1994).

This situation is not rare: Girls and boys often live in very different worlds beginning at birth and continuing into the preschool years and beyond (Coltrane and Adams, 1997; Maccoby, 1999; Martin and Ruble, 2004).

race dissonance the phenomenon in which minority children indicate preferences for majority values or people

collectivistic orientation a philosophy that promotes the notion of interdependence

individualistic orientation a philosophy that emphasizes personal identity and the uniqueness of the individual

Gender—the sense of being male or female—is well established by the time children reach the preschool years. By age two, children consistently label people as male or female (Poulin-Dubois et al., 1994; Raag, 2003; Campbell et al., 2004).

Gender shows up in play. Preschool boys spend more time than girls in rough-and-tumble play, while preschool girls spend more time in organized games and role-playing. During this time, boys begin to play more with boys, and girls with girls, a trend that increases during middle childhood. Girls begin to prefer same-sex playmates a little earlier than boys. They first have a clear preference for interacting with other girls at age two, while boys don't show much preference for same-sex playmates until age three (Boyatzis et al., 1999; Martin and Fabes, 2001; Raag, 2003).

Preschool-age children often have very strict ideas about how boys and girls are supposed to act. In fact, their expectations about gender-appropriate behaviour are even more gender-stereotyped than those of adults. Beliefs in gender stereotypes become increasingly pronounced up to age five, and although they become somewhat less rigid by age seven, they do not disappear. In fact, the gender stereotypes held by preschoolers resemble those held by traditional adults in society (Eichstedt et al., 2002; Serbin et al., 2002; Lam and Leman, 2003).

Like adults, preschoolers expect that males are more apt to have traits involving competence, independence, forcefulness, and competitiveness. In contrast, females are viewed as more likely to have traits such as warmth, expressiveness, nurturance, and submissiveness. Although these are *expectations*, and say nothing about the way that men and women actually behave, such expectations provide the lens through which preschool-age children view the world and affect their behaviour as well as the way they interact with peers and adults (Durkin and Nugent, 1998; Blakemore, 2003; Gelman et al., 2004).

During the preschool period, differences in play according to gender become more pronounced. In addition, boys tend to play with boys, and girls with girls.

> **From a child-care provider's perspective:** If a girl in a preschool child-care setting loudly tells a boy that he can't play with the dolls in the play area because he's a boy, what is the best way to handle the situation?

Why should gender play such a powerful role during the preschool years (as well as during the rest of the lifespan)? Developmentalists have proposed several explanations.

Biological Perspectives. It is hardly surprising that the biological characteristics associated with sex lead to gender differences. Hormones, for example, have been found to affect gender-based behaviours. Girls exposed to unusually high levels of *androgens* (masculinizing hormones) prenatally are more likely to display "typically male" behaviours than their sisters who were not exposed to androgens (Money and Ehrhardt, 1972; Hines et al., 2002; Servin et al., 2003).

Androgen-exposed girls preferred boys as playmates and spent more time than other girls playing with toys associated with the male role, such as cars and trucks. Similarly, boys exposed prenatally to atypically high levels of female hormones are apt to display more behaviours that are stereotypically female than is usual (Berenbaum and Hines, 1992; Hines and Kaufman, 1994; Servin et al., 2003; Knickmeyer and Baron-Cohen, 2006).

Some developmentalists see gender differences as serving the biological goal of survival of the species. Using an evolutionary approach, these theorists suggest that males with stereotypically masculine qualities, such as forcefulness and competitiveness, might have been able to attract females who could give them hardy offspring. Females who excelled at stereotypically feminine tasks, such as nurturing, may have been valued because they could help their children survive the dangers of childhood (Geary, 1998; Browne, 2006; Ellis, 2006).

Of course, it is difficult to attribute behavioural characteristics unambiguously to biological factors. Because of this, we must consider other explanations for gender differences.

gender identity the perception of oneself as male or female

gender schema a cognitive framework that organizes information relevant to gender

gender constancy the belief that people are permanently males or females, depending on fixed, unchangeable biological factors

androgynous a state in which gender roles encompass characteristics thought typical of both sexes

Social Learning Approaches. According to social learning approaches, children learn gender-related behaviour and expectations by observing others, including parents, teachers, siblings, and even peers. A boy might admire a major league baseball player and become interested in sports. A girl might watch her babysitter practising cheerleading moves and begin to try them herself. Observing the praise and honour that gender-appropriate behaviour earns leads the child to emulate that behaviour (Rust et al., 2000).

Books and the media, and in particular television and video games, also play a role in perpetuating traditional views of gender-related behaviour. Analyses of the most popular television shows find that male characters outnumber female characters by two to one. Furthermore, females are more apt to appear with males, whereas female–female relationships are relatively uncommon (Calvert et al., 2003).

Television also presents men and women in traditional gender roles. Television shows typically define female characters in terms of their relationships with males. Females are more likely to appear as victims than males (Wright et al., 1995; Turner-Bowker, 1996). They are less likely to be presented as productive or as decision makers, and more likely to be portrayed as characters interested in romance, their homes, and their families. Such models, according to social learning theory, have a powerful influence on preschoolers' definitions of appropriate behaviour (Browne, 1998; Nathanson et al., 2002; Scharrer et al., 2006).

In some cases, preschoolers learn social roles directly, not through models. For example, preschool-age children might be told by their parents to act like a "little girl" or "little man." What this generally means is that girls should behave politely and boys should be tough. Such direct training sends a clear message about expected behaviour for the different genders (Witt, 1997; Leaper, 2002).

Cognitive Approaches. In the view of some theorists, one aspect of forming a clear sense of identity is the desire to establish a **gender identity**, a perception of oneself as male or female. To do this, children develop a **gender schema**, a cognitive framework that organizes information relevant to gender (Martin, 2000; Barberá, 2003; Martin and Ruble, 2004).

Gender schemas serve as a lens through which preschoolers view the world, encompassing "rules" about what is appropriate and inappropriate for males and females. Some girls may decide that wearing pants is what boys do and apply the rule so rigidly that they refuse to wear anything but dresses. Or a preschool boy may reason that it is inappropriate for him to wear makeup for a school play because makeup is worn by girls—even though all the other boys and girls are wearing it.

According to *cognitive-developmental theory*, proposed by Lawrence Kohlberg, this rigidity is in part a reflection of preschoolers' understanding of gender (Kohlberg, 1966). Specifically, young preschoolers erroneously believe that sex differences are based not on biological factors but on differences in appearance or behaviour. Employing this view of the world, a boy may think he could turn into a girl if he put on a dress and tied his hair in a ponytail (remember the example of the cat with the dog mask from Module 4.2?). However, by age four or five, children develop an understanding of **gender constancy**—the awareness that people are permanently males or females, depending on fixed, unchangeable biological factors.

Interestingly, gender schemas appear well before children understand gender constancy. Even young preschool-age children assume that certain behaviours are appropriate—and others are not—on the basis of stereotypic views of gender (Warin, 2000; Martin et al., 2002; Martin and Ruble, 2004).

Is it possible to avoid viewing the world in terms of gender schemas? According to Sandra Bem (1987), one way is to encourage children to be **androgynous**, a state in which gender roles encompass characteristics thought typical of both sexes. For instance, parents and caregivers can encourage preschool children to see males as assertive but at the same time warm and tender. Similarly, girls might be encouraged to see the female role as both empathetic and tender, as well as competitive, assertive, and independent.

Like the other approaches to gender development, the cognitive perspective does not imply that differences between the two sexes are in any way improper or inappropriate. Instead, it suggests that preschoolers should be taught to treat others as individuals. Furthermore, preschoolers need to learn the importance of fulfilling their own talents and of acting as individuals and not as representatives of a gender.

REVIEW

- According to Erikson's psychosocial development theory, preschool-age children move from the autonomy-versus-shame-and-doubt stage to the initiative-versus-guilt stage.

- During the preschool years, children develop their self-concepts—beliefs about themselves that they derive from their own perceptions, their parents' behaviours, and society.

- Racial, ethnic, and gender awareness begin to form in the preschool years.

CHECK YOURSELF

1. According to Erikson (1963), during the preschool years, children face a key conflict relating to psy-

chosocial development that involves the development of _____.
   a. repression
   b. identity
   c. initiative
   d. trust

2. Five-year-old Kayla has been practising her rope-skipping skills for the past six weeks so she can enter a contest at her school. After one afternoon of practice she tells her mother, "I am a terrific skipper." This statement is an example of Kayla's increasing understanding of her identity, or _____.

3. Biological characteristics associated with a person's sex do not appear to be related to gender differences.

- True
- False

- What sorts of activities might you encourage a preschool boy to undertake to help him adopt a less stereotypical gender schema?

Answers: 1) c; 2) self-concept; 3) False

Friends and Family: Preschoolers' Social Lives

LO12 In what sorts of social relationships and play do preschool-age children engage?

LO13 What sorts of disciplinary styles do parents employ, and what effects do they have?

LO14 What factors contribute to child abuse and neglect?

When Logan was three, he met his first best friend, Noah. Logan and Noah, who lived in the same apartment building in Saskatoon, were inseparable. They played incessantly with toy cars, racing them up and down the apartment hallways until some of the neighbours began to complain about the noise. They pretended to read to one another, and sometimes they slept over at each other's home—a big step for a three-year-old. Neither boy seemed more joyful than when he was with his "best friend"—the term each used for the other.

An infant's family can provide nearly all the social contact he or she needs. As preschoolers, however, many children, like Logan and Noah, begin to discover the joys of peer friendships. Let's take a look at both sides of preschoolers' social development—friends and family.

The Development of Friendships

Before age three, most social activity involves simply being in the same place at the same time, without real social interaction. However, at around age three, children begin to develop real friendships as peers are seen as individuals who hold special qualities and rewards. While preschoolers' relations with adults reflect children's needs for care, protection, and

As preschoolers get older, their conception of friendship evolves and the quality of their interactions changes.

According to developmentalist Lev Vygotsky, children are able, through make-believe play, to practise activities that are part of their particular culture and to broaden their understanding of the way the world functions.

👁 **Watch on mydevelopmentlab**

> To see all the types of play you've been reading about displayed in preschoolers, watch the clip "Parten's Play Categories" on MyDevelopmentLab.

functional play play that involves simple, repetitive activities typical of three-year-olds

constructive play play in which children manipulate objects to produce or build something

parallel play action in which children play with similar toys in a similar manner, but do not interact with each other

onlooker play action in which children simply watch others at play, but do not actually participate themselves

associative play play in which two or more children actually interact with one another by sharing or borrowing toys or materials, although they do not do the same thing

co-operative play play in which children genuinely interact with one another, taking turns, playing games, or devising contests

direction, their relations with peers are based more on the desire for companionship, play, and fun. Gradually they come to view friendship as a continuing state that offers not just immediate pleasure, but the promise of future activity (Harris, 1998, 2000; Hay et al., 2004).

Interactions with friends change during the preschool period. For three-year-olds, the focus of friendship is the enjoyment of doing things together and playing jointly. Older preschoolers pay more attention to trust, support, and shared interests (Park et al., 1993). Throughout the entire period, however, play remains an important part of friendship.

Playing by the Rules: The Work of Play. In Rosie Graiff's class of three-year-olds, Minnie bounces her doll's feet on the table as she sings softly to herself. Ben pushes his toy car across the floor, making motor noises. Sarah chases Abdul around and around the perimeter of the room.

Play is more than what children of preschool age do to pass the time. Instead, play helps preschoolers develop socially, cognitively, and physically (Roopnarine, 2002; Lindsey and Colwell, 2003; Blundon and Schaefer, 2006; Samuelsson and Johansson, 2006).

Categorizing Play. At the beginning of the preschool years, children engage in **functional play**—simple, repetitive activities typical of three-year-olds, such as pushing cars on the floor, skipping, and jumping. Functional play involves doing something to be active rather than to create something (Rubin et al., 1983; Bober et al., 2001; Kantrowitz and Evans, 2004).

By age four, children become involved in a more sophisticated form of play. In **constructive play** children manipulate objects to produce or build something. A child who builds a house out of Legos or puts a puzzle together is involved in constructive play: He or she has an ultimate goal—to produce something. The creation need not be novel, since children may repeatedly build a house of blocks, let it fall, and then rebuild it.

Constructive play gives children a chance to practise their physical and cognitive skills and fine muscle movements. They gain experience in solving problems about the ways and the sequences in which things fit together. They also learn to co-operate with others as the social nature of play becomes more important to them (Power, 1999; Edwards, 2000; Shi, 2003).

The Social Aspects of Play. If two preschoolers sit side by side at a table, each assembling a different puzzle, are they engaged jointly in play?

According to pioneering work done by Mildred Parten (1932), the answer is yes. She suggests that these preschoolers are engaged in **parallel play**, in which children play with similar toys, in a similar manner, but do not interact with each other. Preschoolers also engage in another form of play, a highly passive one: onlooker play. In **onlooker play**, children simply watch others at play, but do not actually participate themselves.

As they get older, however, preschool-age children engage in more sophisticated forms of social play that involve greater interaction. In **associative play**, two or more children interact with one another by sharing or borrowing toys or materials, although they do not do the same thing. In **co-operative play**, children genuinely play with one another, taking turns, playing games, or devising contests.

Solitary and onlooker play continue in the later stages of the preschool period. There are simply times when children prefer to play by themselves. And when newcomers join a group, one strategy for becoming part of the group—often successful—is to engage in onlooker play, waiting for an opportunity to join the play more actively (Howes et al., 1989; Hughes, 1995; Lindsey and Colwell, 2003).

The nature of pretend or make-believe play also changes during this period, becoming in some ways more *un*realistic—and imaginative—as preschoolers shift from using only realistic objects to using less concrete ones. Thus, at the start of the preschool period, children may pretend to listen to a radio only if they have a plastic radio on hand. Later, they may use an entirely different object, such as a large cardboard box, as a pretend radio (Bornstein et al., 1996).

Vygotsky (1930/1978) argued that pretend play, particularly if it involves social play, is an important means for expanding preschool-age children's cognitive skills. Through make-believe play, children are able to "practise" activities (such as pretending to use a computer or read a book) that are a part of their particular culture, and to broaden their understanding of the way the world functions.

> **From an educator's perspective:** How might a nursery school teacher encourage a shy child to join a group of preschoolers who are playing?

Watch on **mydevelopmentlab**

Log onto MyDevelopmentLab and watch the video clip "Sociodramatic Play" to see preschoolers engaging in different types of social play.

Preschoolers' Theory of Mind: Understanding What Others Are Thinking

Alongside changes in children's play is the continuing development of preschoolers' theory of mind—their knowledge and beliefs about how the mind operates. Using their theory of mind, preschool children increasingly see the world from others' perspectives. Children as young as two are able to understand that others have emotions. By age three or four, preschoolers know that they can imagine something that is not physically present, such as a zebra, and that others can do the same. They can also pretend that something has happened and react as if it really had occurred, a skill that becomes part of their imaginative play (Čadinu and Kiesner, 2000; Mauritzson and Saeljoe, 2001; Andrews et al., 2003).

Preschool-age children also become more insightful regarding the motives and reasons behind people's behaviour. They begin to understand that their mother is angry because she was late for an appointment, even if they themselves haven't seen her be late. Furthermore, by age four, children's understanding that people can be fooled by physical reality (such as magic tricks involving sleight-of-hand) becomes surprisingly sophisticated. This increase in understanding helps children become more socially skilled as they gain insight into what others are thinking (Nguyen and Frye, 1999; Fitzgerald and White, 2002; Eisbach, 2004).

There are limits, however, to three-year-olds' theory of mind. For instance, their understanding of "belief" is incomplete, as illustrated by their performance on the *false belief* task. In the false belief task, preschoolers are shown a doll named Maxi who places chocolate in a cabinet and then leaves. After Maxi is gone, his mother moves the chocolate somewhere else.

Preschoolers are then asked where Maxi will look for the chocolate when he returns. Three-year-olds answer (erroneously) that Maxi will look for it in the new location. In contrast, four-year-olds correctly realize that Maxi has the false belief that the chocolate is still in the cabinet, and that's where he will look for it (Wimmer, 2000; Ziv and Frye, 2003; Flynn et al., 2004; Amsterlaw and Wellman, 2006).

Preschoolers' Family Lives

Four-year old Benjamin was watching TV while his mom cleaned up after dinner. After a while, he wandered in and grabbed a towel, saying, "Mommy, let me help you do the dishes." Surprised by this unprecedented behaviour, she asked him, "Where did you learn to do dishes?"

"I saw it on TV," he replied, "only it was the dad helping. Since we don't have a dad, I figured I'd do it."

For many preschool-age children, life does not mirror idyllic TV programs. Many face the realities of an increasingly complicated world. For instance, in 1961, 11 percent of families were headed by a single parent. In 2004, a single parent headed 25 percent of Canadian families (Bushnik, 2006).

Still, for most children the preschool years are not a time of turmoil. Instead, the period is characterized by growing interactions with the world at large. Preschoolers form genuine friendships and develop close ties with other children—a circumstance facilitated by a warm, supportive home environment. Research finds that strong, positive relationships between parents and children encourage children's relationships with others (Sroufé, 1994; Howes et al., 1998).

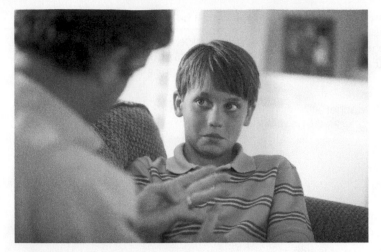

Children with authoritative parents tend to be well adjusted, in part because the parents are supportive and take the time to explain things. What are the consequences of parents who are too permissive? Too authoritarian? Too uninvolved?

Effective Parenting: Teaching Desired Behaviour

While she thinks no one is looking, Marie-Eve goes into her brother Alexandre's bedroom, where he has been saving the last of his Halloween candy. Just as she takes his last Reese's Peanut Butter Cup, the children's mother walks into the room and immediately takes in the situation.

If you were Marie-Eve's mother, which of the following reactions seems most reasonable?

1. Tell Marie-Eve to go to her room and stay there for the rest of the day, and take away access to her favourite blanket, the one she sleeps with every night and during naps.
2. Mildly tell Marie-Eve that what she did was not such a good idea, and she shouldn't do it in the future.
3. Explain to Marie-Eve why her action would upset her brother, and tell her to go to her room for an hour as punishment.
4. Forget about it, and let the children sort it out themselves.

Each of these responses represents one of the major parenting styles identified by Diana Baumrind (1971, 1980) and updated by Eleanor Maccoby and colleagues (Baumrind, 1971, 1980; Maccoby and Martin, 1983).

1. **Authoritarian parents** are controlling, punitive, rigid, and cold. Their word is law, and they value strict, unquestioning obedience. They do not tolerate expressions of disagreement.

2. **Permissive parents** provide lax and inconsistent feedback. They provide a loving and supportive environment, but have low maturity demands. They place little or no limits or control on their children's behaviour.

3. **Authoritative parents** are firm, setting clear and consistent limits. Although they tend to be relatively strict, like authoritarian parents, they are loving and emotionally support-ive. They also try to reason with their children, explaining why they should behave in a particular way ("Alexandre is going to be upset") and communicating the rationale for any punishment they might impose. Authoritative parents encourage their children to be independent.

4. **Uninvolved parents** show virtually no interest in their children, displaying indifferent, rejecting behaviour. They are detached emotionally and see their role as no more than feeding, clothing, and providing shelter. In its most extreme form, uninvolved parenting results in *neglect,* a form of child abuse. (The four patterns are summarized in Table 4-2.)

Parents' disciplinary styles usually produce differences in children's behaviour—although there are many exceptions (Collett et al., 2001; Snyder et al., 2005; Arredondo et al., 2006; Simons and Conger, 2007):

- Children of authoritarian parents tend to be withdrawn, show little sociability, are not very friendly, and often behave uneasily around their peers. Girls are especially dependent on their parents, whereas boys are unusually hostile.
- Children of permissive parents tend to be dependent and moody, and are low in social skills and self-control.
- Children of authoritative parents fare best. They generally are independent, friendly, self-assertive, and co-operative. They have strong motivation to achieve, and are typically suc-cessful and likable. They regulate their own behaviour effectively, including their emotions and their relationships.
- Children of uninvolved parents are the worst off, showing disrupted emotional devel-opment. They feel unloved and emotionally detached, and their physical and cognitive development may be impeded as well.

authoritarian parents parents who are controlling, punitive, rigid, and cold, and whose word is law. They value strict, unquestioning obedience from their children and do not tolerate expressions of disagreement

permissive parents parents who provide lax and inconsistent feedback and require little of their children

authoritative parents parents who are firm, setting clear and consistent limits, but who try to reason with their children, giving explanations for why they should behave in a particular way

uninvolved parents parents who show almost no interest in their children and engage in indifferent, rejecting behaviour

TABLE 4-2   PARENTING STYLES

How Demanding Parents Are of Children	Demanding	Undemanding
How Responsive Parents Are to a Child	**Authoritative**	**Permissive**
Highly Responsive	**Characteristics:** firm, setting clear and consistent limits	**Characteristics:** lax and inconsistent feedback
	Relationship with Children: Although they tend to be relatively strict, like authoritarian parents they are loving and emotionally supportive and encourage their children to be independent. They also try to reason with their children, giving explanations for why they should behave in a particular way, and communicating the rationale for any punishment they might impose.	**Relationship with Children:** Like authoritarian parents, they are loving and supportive, but fall short in encouraging independence and discipline. They may be very well-intentioned but misguided in trying to keep children happy.
	Authoritarian	**Uninvolved**
Low Responsive	**Characteristics:** controlling, punitive, rigid, cold	**Characteristics:** displaying indifferent, rejecting behaviour
	Relationship with Children: Their word is law, and they value strict, unquestioning obedience from their children. They also do not tolerate expressions of disagreement.	**Relationship with Children:** They are detached emotionally and see their role as only providing food, clothing, and shelter. In its extreme form, this parenting style results in neglect, a form of child abuse.

Of course, no classification system is an infallible predictor of how children will fare. In a significant number of cases the children of authoritarian and permissive parents develop successfully, and other factors need to be taken into account.

Furthermore, most parents are inconsistent, switching from their dominant mode to one of the others. For instance, when a child darts into the street, an authoritarian style is generally the most effective. Two parents might have different styles, and major life events such as divorce can lead to a change in parenting style (Janssens and Dekovic, 1997; Holden and Miller, 1999; Eisenberg and Valiente, 2002; Gershoff, 2002).

Cultural Differences in Childrearing Practices. It's important to keep in mind that the findings regarding childrearing styles we have been discussing are chiefly applicable to Western societies. The style of parenting that is most successful can depend quite heavily on the norms of a particular culture—and what parents in a particular culture are taught regarding appropriate childrearing practices (Claes et al., 2003; Giles-Sims and Lockhart, 2005; Dwairy et al., 2006; Hulei et al., 2006).

For example, the Chinese concept of *chiao shun* suggests that parents should learn to be strict, firm, and in tight control of their children's behaviour. They accept that they have a duty to train their children to adhere to socially and culturally desirable standards of behaviour, particularly in their school performance. Children's acceptance of this style is seen as a sign of parental respect (Chao, 1994; Wu et al., 2002).

In short, childrearing practices reflect cultural perspectives on the nature of children as well as on the appropriate role of parents. No one parenting pattern or style is universally appropriate (Harwood et al., 1996; Hart et al., 1998; Wang and Tamis-LeMonda, 2003.) Similarly, it is important to keep in mind that parents are not the sole influence on children's development. Sibling and peer influences play a significant role, as does the child's unique genetic endowment (Reiss et al., 2000; Boivin et al., 2005; Loehlin et al., 2005).

From Research to Practice

Parenting Coaches: Teaching Parents to Parent

Samantha, a single mom, was getting very frustrated with the constant fighting and roughhousing between her two boys (aged three and five). Ultimately, her older boy would cause the younger one to start crying, at which point Samantha was forced to intervene. The situation recurred almost daily, as soon as Samantha returned home from work. Wanting only to come home and relax, Samantha was becoming frustrated instead. Moreover, she was becoming stressed out. Her scolding of the boys wasn't working. In fact, the situation was getting worse. (Carson, 2009)

She called her personal parent coach to find out how to deal with the situation.

Personal parent coach? Parents are increasingly turning to a profession that didn't exist only few years ago—*parent coaching*—to help them navigate the trials of parenthood.

Less expensive than formal therapy, but more systematic than a next-door neighbour, parent coaching combines advice and support. Some parent coaches offer specific strategies, while others teach the basics of child development to help parents put their child's behaviour in perspective (Marchant et al., 2004). For some parents,

coaching is a lifeline, providing access to a more experienced parent and setting up a relationship with another adult who can offer social support (Smith, 2005).

Although many parents swear by parent coaches, their effectiveness has not been established by research, which in part reflects the newness of the field. In addition, the qualifications of parent coaches vary widely. While some have had formal training in child development, the only qualifications of others is having raised a child themselves (Leonard, 2005).

Because parent coaches are not licensed, parents should adopt a buyer-beware attitude and examine credentials carefully. Until the field becomes more regulated—and the value of parent coaches has been formally established—parents should be cautious.

- *If you were conducting an interview with a potential parent coach, what questions would you ask?*
- *Do you think parent coaches should be licensed and/or paid for by the government? Why or why not?*

Child Abuse and Psychological Maltreatment: The Grim Side of Family Life

While the number of child homicides is quite small in Canada (four per million children and youth), the majority were committed by a family member. An estimated 1 to 2 percent of children are victims of abuse. Abuse takes several forms, ranging from physical abuse to psychological mistreatment (see Figure 4-9). More than 50 percent of children in substantiated abuse investigations showed considerable problems in functioning (Trainor and Mihorean, 2001).

Physical Abuse. Physical abuse can occur in any household, regardless of economic well-being or social status. It is most prevalent in families living in stressful environments. Poverty,

This nine-day-old infant, named Baby Vinnie, was found after being abandoned on the steps behind a church. He later was adopted by a foster family.

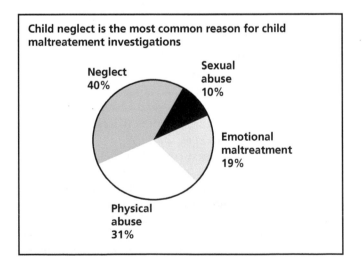

Child neglect is the most common reason for child maltreatement investigations

Neglect 40%

Sexual abuse 10%

Emotional maltreatment 19%

Physical abuse 31%

FIGURE 4-9 Types of Child Abuse
Neglect is the most frequent form of abuse. How can educators and health-care providers help identify cases of child abuse?
Source: Health Canada, The Canadian Incidence Study of Reported Child Abuse and Neglect, 1998.

TABLE 4-3   WHAT ARE THE WARNING SIGNS OF CHILD ABUSE?

Because child abuse is typically a secret crime, identifying the victims of abuse is particularly difficult. Still, several signs indicate that a child is the victim of violence (Robbins, 1990):

- visible, serious injuries that have no reasonable explanation
- bite or choke marks
- burns from cigarettes or immersion in hot water
- feelings of pain for no apparent reason
- fear of adults or care providers
- inappropriate attire in warm weather (long sleeves, long pants, high-necked garments)—possibly to conceal injuries to the neck, arms, and legs
- extreme behaviour—highly aggressive, extremely passive, extremely withdrawn
- fear of physical contact

If you suspect a child is a victim of aggression, it is your responsibility to act. Call your local police or the department of community/family services in your region. Talk to a teacher or a member of the clergy. Remember, by acting decisively you can literally save someone's life.

single-parenthood, and higher-than-average levels of marital conflict help create such environments. Biological parents are much more often the perpetrators, with fathers and mothers almost equally accounting for 46 percent and 43 percent of cases, respectively (see Figure 4-10). Forty-six percent were isolated incidents, and 69 percent were inappropriate forms of punishment (Health Canada, The Canadian Incidence Study of Reported Child Abuse and Neglect, 1998).

Notably, while maltreatment overall occurs more in single- than in dual-parent households, this is not the case for physical abuse. In half of cases of physical abuse, caregivers suffered from substance abuse or mental health issues, 35 percent experienced abuse themselves in childhood and, as adults, 28 percent experienced a lack of supports, and 21 percent experienced spousal violence (Trainor and Mihorean, 2001). (Table 4-3 lists some of the warning signs of abuse.)

Abused children are more likely to be fussy, resistant to control, and not readily adaptable to new situations. They have more headaches and stomach aches, experience more bedwetting, are generally more anxious, and may show developmental delays. Children in certain age groups are also more likely to be the targets of abuse: Risk of physical abuse increases with age for both boys and girls; however, the risk of sexual abuse is highest for 4- to 7-year-olds (boys and girls) and 12- to 15-year-old girls (Trainor and Mihorean, 2001).

Reasons for Physical Abuse.   Why does physical abuse occur? Most parents do not intend to hurt their children. In fact, most parents who abuse their children later express bewilderment and regret about their behaviour.

One reason for child abuse is the vague demarcation between permissible and impermissible forms of physical violence. A 1998 study of investigated child maltreatment cases found that in 69 percent of substantiated cases of physical abuse, the abuse was categorized as inappropriate punishment (Trainor and Mihorean, 2001). According to the study authors, many cases of physical abuse were linked to punishment or confused with discipline, including spanking that led to physical harm. Despite efforts to discourage spanking, it remains legal for parents and teachers to use corporal punishment in Canada and spanking remains widely endorsed by the general public. Surveys conducted in Quebec and Manitoba found approximately two-thirds of adults believe spanking to be

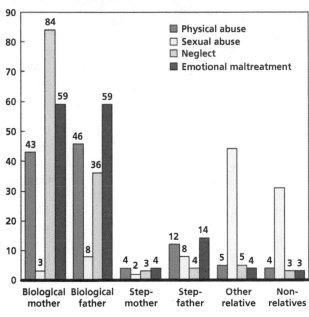

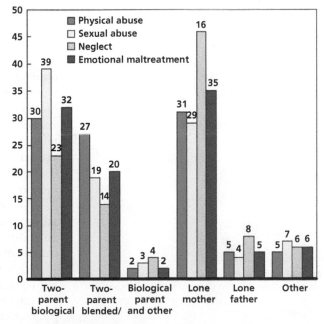

FIGURE 4-10 Perpetrators of Abuse

Most abuse happens at the hands of biological parents. Children of single mothers are at highest risk for neglect.
Source: Health Canada, The Canadian Incidence Study of Reported Child Abuse and Neglect, 1998.

Two of the children in this large family allegedly were singled out for abuse by their parents and were severely malnourished, while the other children were seemingly well cared for. What might account for this unusual situation?

a necessary parenting tool, in large part because equal numbers were themselves spanked as children and see no negative consequences. A survey conducted in the United States reported that almost half of mothers with children under four have spanked their child in the previous week, and close to 20 percent believe it is appropriate to spank a child less than one year of age. In some other cultures, physical discipline is even more common (Durrant, 1994; Straus et al., 2003; Lansford et al., 2005; Deb and Adak, 2006; Shor, 2006; Gagné et al., 2007).

Unfortunately, the line between "spanking" and "beating" is fuzzy, and spankings begun in anger can escalate into abuse. In fact, increasing scientific evidence suggests that spanking should be avoided entirely. Although physical punishment might produce immediate compliance, there are serious long-term side effects. For example, spanking is associated with inferior parent–child relationships, poorer mental health for both child and parent, higher levels of delinquency, and more antisocial behaviour. Spanking also teaches children that violence is an acceptable solution to problems. Consequently, the American Academy of Pediatrics and the Canadian Paediatric Society strongly recommend *against* the use of physical punishment of any sort (American Academy of Pediatrics, 1998; Canadian Paediatric Society, 2004; Gershoff, 2002; Kazdin and Benjet, 2003; Afifi et al., 2006).

Privacy is another factor that leads to high rates of abuse in Western countries. In most Western cultures, children are raised in private, isolated households. In many other cultures, childrearing is the joint responsibility of several people and even society as a whole, and other people are available to help out when a parent's patience is tested (Chaffin, 2006; Elliott and Urquiza, 2006).

The Cycle of Violence Hypothesis. Many people who abuse children were themselves abused as children. According to the **cycle of violence hypothesis**, the abuse and neglect that children suffer predisposes them as adults to abuse and neglect their own children (Miller-Perrin and Perrin, 1999; Widom, 2000; Heyman and Slep, 2002).

According to this hypothesis, victims of abuse have learned from their childhood experiences that violence is an appropriate and acceptable form of discipline, and they have failed to learn the skills needed to solve problems and instill discipline without violence (Straus et al., 1997; Blumenthal, 2000; Ethier et al., 2004).

Of course, being abused as a child does not inevitably lead to abuse of one's own children. In fact, statistics show that only about one-third of people who were abused or neglected as children abuse their own children (Cicchetti, 1996; Straus and McCord, 1998).

Psychological Maltreatment. Children might also be the victims of more subtle forms of mistreatment. **Psychological maltreatment** occurs when parents or other caregivers harm children's behavioural, cognitive, emotional, or physical functioning. This maltreatment might take the form of overt behaviour or neglect (Hart et al., 1996; Higgins and McCabe, 2003).

For example, abusive parents might frighten, belittle, or humiliate their children, who might be made to feel like disappointments or failures. Parents might say that they wish that their children had never been born. Children might be threatened with abandonment or even death. In other instances, older children might be exploited or forced to seek employment and then to give their earnings to their parents.

In other cases of psychological maltreatment, the abuse takes the form of neglect. Parents might ignore their children or act emotionally unresponsive. The children might be given unrealistic responsibilities or left to fend for themselves. Neglect accounts for 40 percent of child maltreatment investigations in Canada (Trainor and Mihorean, 2001).

While some children are sufficiently resilient to survive psychological maltreatment, lasting damage often results. Psychological maltreatment has been associated with low self-esteem, lying, misbehaviour, and underachievement in school. In extreme cases, it can produce criminal behaviour, aggression, and murder. In other instances, children who have been psychologically maltreated become depressed and even commit suicide (Shonk and Cicchetti, 2001; Eigsti and Cicchetti, 2004; Koenig et al., 2004).

One reason that psychological maltreatment—as well as physical abuse—produces so many negative consequences is that the brains of victims undergo permanent changes due

cycle of violence hypothesis the theory that the abuse and neglect that children suffer predisposes them as adults to abuse and neglect their own children

psychological maltreatment abuse that occurs when parents or other caregivers harm children's behavioural, cognitive, emotional, or physical functioning

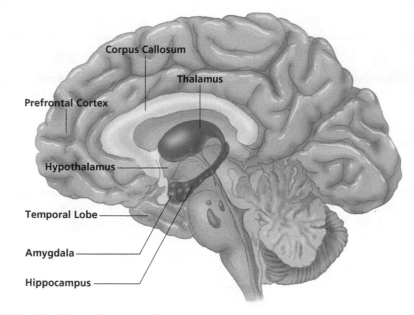

FIGURE 4-11 **Abuse Alters the Brain**
The limbic system, comprising the hippocampus and amygdala, can be permanently altered as a result of childhood abuse.
Source: *Scientific American*, 2002.

to the abuse (see Figure 4-11). For example, childhood maltreatment can lead to reductions in the size of the amygdala and hippocampus in adulthood. The stress, fear, and terror that accompany abuse can also produce permanent changes in the brain due to overstimulation of the limbic system. Because the limbic system is involved in the regulation of memory and emotion, the result can be antisocial behaviour during adulthood (Teicher et al., 2002; Bremner, 2003; Teicher et al., 2003; Watts-English et al., 2006).

Resilience: Overcoming the Odds

Given the seriousness of child abuse and the damage it can cause, it's remarkable that not all children who have been abused are permanently scarred. In fact, some do surprisingly well. What enables some children to overcome stress and trauma that in most cases haunts others for life?

The answer appears to be resilience. **Resilience** is the ability to overcome high-risk circumstances such as extremes of poverty, prenatal stress, or violence in the home. Several factors seem to reduce and, in certain cases, eliminate some children's reactions to difficult circumstances (Luthar et al., 2000; Trickett et al., 2004).

According to developmental psychologist Emmy Werner, resilient children tend to have temperaments that evoke positive responses. They tend to be affectionate, easy-going, and good-natured. They are easily soothed as infants, and elicit care from the most nurturant people in any given environment. In a sense, resilient children make their own environments by drawing out behaviour in others that they need for their own development (Werner, 1995; Werner and Smith, 2002). As they grow to school age, they are socially pleasant, outgoing, and have good communication skills. They tend to be intelligent and independent, feeling that they can shape their own fate without depending on others or luck (Curtis and Cicchetti, 2003; Kim and Cicchetti, 2003; Haskett et al., 2006).

These characteristics suggest ways to help children who are at risk. Programs that have been successful in helping especially vulnerable children provide competent and caring adult models who teach the children problem-solving skills and help them to communicate their needs to those who are in a position to help (Davey et al., 2003; Maton et al., 2004; Condly, 2006).

Watch on **mydevelopmentlab**

What type of temperament does your virtual child seem to have? To watch children displaying all the different temperaments, log onto MyDevelopmentLab and watch the video clip "Temperament."

resilience the ability to overcome circumstances that place a child at high risk for psychological or physical damage.

Disciplining Children

Becoming an Informed Consumer of Development

The question of how to discipline children has been raised for generations. Answers from developmentalists today include the following (O'Leary, 1995; Brazelton and Sparrow, 2003; Flouri, 2005):

- **For most children in Western cultures, authoritative parenting works best.** Parents should be firm and consistent, providing clear direction and rules, but explaining why the rules make sense, using language that children can understand.

- **Spanking is never an appropriate discipline technique** according to the experts. Not only is spanking ineffective, but it leads to additional unwanted outcomes, such as the potential for more aggressive behaviour (Canadian Paediatric Society, 2004).

- **Use *time-out* for punishment.** It is best to remove children from a situation in which they have misbehaved and take away enjoyable activities for a set period.

- **Tailor parental discipline to the characteristics of the child and the situation.** Try to keep the child's personality in mind, and adapt discipline to it. Modify expectations as developmentally appropriate.

- **Use routines (such as a bath routine or a bedtime routine) to avoid conflict.** To avoid a nightly struggle, make the potential conflict situation predictably enjoyable. For instance, routinely reading a bedtime story or engaging in a nightly "wrestling" match with the child can defuse potential battles.

REVIEW, CHECK, AND APPLY

REVIEW

- In the preschool years, children develop friendships on the basis of personal characteristics, trust, and shared interests.

- The character of preschoolers' play changes over time, growing more sophisticated, interactive, and co-operative, and relying increasingly on social skills.

- There are several distinct childrearing styles, including authoritarian, permissive, authoritative, and uninvolved.

CHECK YOURSELF

1. When it comes to play, younger preschoolers focus on _____ and older preschoolers focus on _____ .

   a. sharing activities; trust and shared interests

   b. trust and shared interests; sharing activities

   c. parallel play; solitary play

   d. communicative play; nonverbal play

2. As preschoolers get older, their play shifts from more social to more functional.

   - True
   - False

3. Which of the following characteristics is *not* typical of a child who has authoritative parents?

   a. independent

   b. achievement-oriented

   c. dependent

   d. likeable

APPLYING LIFESPAN DEVELOPMENT

- What role do reality television shows about parenting have in educating parents? Do you think they are well-informed? Do you think they are effective?

Answers: 1) a; 2) False; 3) c

Moral Development and Aggression

LEARNING OBJECTIVES

LO15 How do children develop a sense of right and wrong?

LO16 How does aggression develop in preschool-age children?

During snack time at preschool, playmates Jan and Meg inspected the goodies in their lunch boxes. Jan found two appetizing cream-filled cookies. Meg's snack offered less tempting carrot and celery sticks. As Jan began to munch on one of her cookies, Meg looked at the cut-up vegetables and burst into tears. Jan responded to Meg's distress by offering her companion one of her cookies, which Meg gladly accepted. Jan was able to put herself in Meg's place, understand Meg's thoughts and feelings, and act compassionately. (Katz, 1989, p. 213)

In this short scenario we see many of the key elements of morality, preschool style. Changes in children's views of the right way to behave are an important element of growth during the preschool years.

At the same time, the kind of aggression displayed by preschoolers also changes. We can consider the development of morality and aggression as two sides of the coin of human conduct, and both involve a growing awareness of others.

Developing Morality: Following Society's Rights and Wrongs

Moral development refers to changes in people's sense of justice and of what is right and wrong, and in their behaviour related to moral issues. Developmentalists have considered moral development in terms of children's reasoning about morality, attitudes toward moral lapses, and behaviour when faced with moral issues. In the process of studying moral development, several approaches have evolved (Langford, 1995; Grusec and Kuczynski, 1997).

Preschoolers believe in immanent justice. This child may worry that she will be punished even if no one sees her carrying out the misdeed.

Piaget's View of Moral Development. Child psychologist Jean Piaget was one of the first to study moral development. He suggested that moral development, like cognitive development, proceeds in stages (Piaget, 1932). He called the earliest stage *heteronomous morality*, in which rules are seen as invariant and unchangeable. During this stage, which lasts from about age four through age seven, children play games rigidly, assuming that there is one and only one way to play. At the same time, though, they might not even fully grasp game rules. Consequently, a group of children could be playing together, with each child playing according to a slightly different set of rules. Nevertheless, they enjoy playing with each other. Piaget suggests that every child may "win" such a game, because winning means having a good time, as opposed to competing.

Heteronomous morality is ultimately replaced by two later stages of morality: incipient co-operation and autonomous co-operation. In the *incipient co-operation stage*, which lasts from around age 7 to age 10, children's games become more clearly social. Children learn the actual rules and play according to this shared knowledge. Rules are still seen as largely unchangeable, and children believe that there is a "right" way to play the game.

Not until the autonomous co-operation stage, which begins at about age 10, do children become fully aware that formal game rules can be modified if the players agree. This is the beginning of the understanding that rules of law are created by people and are subject to change according to the will of people.

Social Learning Approaches to Morality. Whereas Piaget emphasizes how limitations in preschoolers' cognitive development lead to particular forms of moral *reasoning*, social learning approaches focus more on how the environment in which preschoolers operate produces **prosocial behaviour**—helping behaviour that benefits others (Eisenberg et al., 1999; Eisenberg, 2004).

Social learning approaches acknowledge that some instances of children's prosocial behaviour stem from situations in which they have received positive reinforcement for acting in a moral way. For instance, when Claire's mother tells her she has been a "good girl" for sharing a box of candy with her brother, Claire's behaviour has been reinforced. As a consequence, she is more likely to engage in sharing behaviour in the future.

However, not all prosocial behaviour has to be directly reinforced. According to social learning theorists, children also learn moral behaviour indirectly by observing the behaviour of others, called *models* (Bandura, 1977). Children imitate models who receive reinforcement for their behaviour and they ultimately learn to perform the behaviour themselves. For example, when Claire's friend Jake watches Claire share her candy with her brother, and Claire is praised for her behaviour, Jake is more likely to engage in sharing behaviour himself at some later point. Unfortunately, the opposite also holds true: If a model behaves selfishly, children who observe such behaviour tend to behave more selfishly themselves (Staub, 1971; Grusec, 1982, 1991).

Children do more than simply mimic behaviour that they see rewarded in others. When they observe moral conduct, they are reminded of society's norms about the importance of moral behaviour as conveyed by parents, teachers, and other authority figures. They notice the connections between particular situations and certain kinds of behaviour. This increases the likelihood that similar situations will elicit similar behaviour later.

moral development the changes in people's sense of justice and of what is right and wrong, and in their behaviour related to moral issues

prosocial behaviour helping behaviour that benefits others

Aggression, both physical and verbal, is present throughout the preschool period.

Consequently, modelling paves the way for the development of more general rules and principles in a process called **abstract modelling**. Rather than always modelling the particular behaviour of others, older preschoolers begin to develop generalized principles that underlie the behaviour they observe. After observing repeated instances in which a model is rewarded for acting in a morally desirable way, children begin the process of inferring and learning the general principles of moral conduct (Bandura, 1991).

Empathy and Moral Behaviour. According to some developmentalists, **empathy**—the understanding of what another individual feels—lies at the heart of some kinds of moral behaviour. Think back to Cathy's son, who used his "sookie" to try to heal what was making his mother cry. For her son to understand that Cathy needed comforting, it was necessary for him to feel empathy with her unhappiness. Although he might have been confused about the source of her pain, Cathy's son realized that she seemed hurt and warranted sympathy.

The roots of empathy grow early. Newborn infants cry when they hear other infants crying (Buhler and Hetzer, 1928, c.f. Geangu et al., 2010). By ages two and three, toddlers will often offer gifts and spontaneously share toys with other children and adults, even with strangers (Stanjek, 1978; Radke-Yarrow et al., 1983; Zahn-Wexler and Radke-Yarrow, 1990).

During the preschool years, empathy continues to grow as children's ability to monitor and regulate their emotional and cognitive responses increases. Some theorists believe that increasing empathy (along with other positive emotions, such as sympathy and admiration) leads children to behave morally. In addition, some negative emotions—such as anger at an unfair situation or shame over previous transgressions—also can promote moral behaviour (Miller and Jansen op de Haar, 1997; Valiente et al., 2004; Decety and Jackson, 2006).

Aggression and Violence in Preschoolers: Sources and Consequences

Four-year-old Duane could not contain his anger and frustration any more. Although he usually was mild-mannered, Duane finally snapped when Eshu began to tease him about the split in his pants and kept it up for several minutes. Rushing over to Eshu, Duane pushed him to the ground and began to hit him with his small, closed fists. Because he was so distraught, Duane's punches were not terribly effective, but they were severe enough to hurt Eshu and bring him to tears before the preschool teachers could intervene.

Aggression among preschoolers is common, though attacks such as this are not. Verbal hostility, shoving matches, kicking, and other forms of aggression can occur throughout the preschool period, although the degree to which aggression is acted out changes with age.

Eshu's taunting is also a form of aggression. **Hostile aggression** is intentional injury or harm to another person. Aggression can be direct, such as one child running up to and hitting another, or it can be indirect, occurring behind the victim's back. Toddlers and younger preschoolers are most likely to engage in direct physical and verbal aggression; indirect aggression requires more sophisticated social and cognitive skills. A certain degree of aggressive behaviour is normal in young children as they have limited skills to deal with anger and frustration.

In most children, the amount of aggression declines as they move through the preschool years, as does the frequency and average length of episodes of aggressive behaviour (Cummings et al., 1989; Persson, 2005).

The child's personality and social development contribute to this decline in aggression. Throughout the preschool years, children become better at controlling the emotions that they are experiencing. **Emotional self-regulation** is the capability to adjust emotions to a desired state and level of intensity. Starting at age two, children are able to talk about their feelings, and they engage in strategies to regulate them. As they get older, they develop more effective

⊙ Watch on mydevelopmentlab

Log onto MyDevelopment Lab and watch the video clips "Relational Aggression" and "Reactive Aggression" to get a better understanding of the types of aggression and what they look like in children.

abstract modelling the process in which modelling paves the way for the development of more general rules and principles

empathy the understanding of what another individual feels

hostile aggression intentional injury or harm to another person

emotional self-regulation the capability to adjust emotions to a desired state and level of intensity

strategies, learning to better cope with negative emotions. In addition to increasing their self-control, children also develop sophisticated social skills. Most learn to use language to express their wishes and to negotiate with others (Eisenberg and Zhou, 2000; Philippot and Feldman, 2005; Zeman et al., 2006).

Despite these typical declines in aggression, some children remain aggressive throughout the preschool period. Furthermore, aggression is a relatively stable characteristic: The most aggressive preschoolers tend to be the most aggressive children during the school-age years (Rosen, 1998; Tremblay, 2001; Schaeffer et al., 2003).

Boys typically show higher levels of physical, instrumental aggression than girls. **Instrumental aggression** is aggression motivated by the desire to obtain a concrete goal, such as playing with a desirable toy that another child is playing with. Most aggression displayed by toddlers and younger preschoolers is instrumental—if you come between me and my goal, you might get hurt! Luckily they aren't very strong and are easily disciplined at this age.

On the other hand, although girls show lower levels of instrumental aggression, they are more likely to practise **relational aggression**, which is nonphysical aggression that is intended to hurt another person's feelings. Such aggression may manifest as name-calling, withholding friendship, or simply saying mean, hurtful things that make the recipient feel bad. This form of aggression requires the more sophisticated language and social skills that develop later in the preschool years (Underwood, 2003; Werner and Crick, 2004; Murray-Close et al., 2006).

> **instrumental aggression** aggression motivated by the desire to obtain a concrete goal
>
> **relational aggression** nonphysical aggression that is intended to hurt another person's psychological well-being

The Roots of Aggression in Instinct.   How can we explain the aggression of preschoolers? Some theoreticians suggest that aggression is an instinct, part and parcel of the human condition. For instance, Freud's psychoanalytic theory suggests that we all are motivated by sexual and aggressive instincts (Freud, 1920). And ethologist Konrad Lorenz, an expert in animal behaviour, argues that animals—including humans—share a fighting instinct that stems from primitive urges to preserve territory, maintain a steady supply of food, and weed out weaker animals (Lorenz, 1966, 1974).

Social Learning Approaches to Aggression.   The day after Duane lashed out at Eshu, Lynn, who had watched the entire scene, got into an argument with Ilya. They verbally bickered for a while, and suddenly Lynn balled her hand into a fist and tried to punch Ilya. The preschool teachers were stunned: It was rare for Lynn to get upset, and she had never displayed aggression before.

Focus on Research

The Truth behind the Terrible Twos

Who has not heard parents talk about the *terrible twos*? Two-year-olds are notorious for tantrums and screams of "NO!" Researchers in Montreal have also found that this is the age at which aggression in humans is at its peak. The research team, led by Richard Tremblay at the Université de Montréal, have been studying a large group of children from birth in order to understand the origins of aggression. As they explain in the National Film Board documentary *The Origins of Human Aggression* (Gervais and Tremblay, 2005), aggressive acts committed by two-year-olds are measured as number of assaults committed per hour. In contrast, adolescent aggression is measured as the number of assaults committed per week or month. As many as one in four social interactions initiated by two-year-olds is aggressive; fortunately, these children are small and not very strong. Tremblay's research supports evolutionary theories arguing that, as with other animals, a certain degree of aggression is adaptive in humans. Also, like other social animals, children must learn how much is too much because those who do not learn to control their aggression will be excluded from the social group. By four years old, most children have

dramatically reduced their aggression. Three cognitive changes are believed to help children control their aggression.

1) General improvements in cognitive control allow children to stop and think before reacting emotionally.

2) Improvements in "theory of mind" (described earlier in this chapter) allow children to better consider conflicts from the other person's perspective.

3) Improvements in language provide children with a new tool to resolve conflicts, express frustration, and ask for help.

Social learning theorists have long argued that children learn to be aggressive by watching aggressive models, especially if the model was rewarded, but believed that children would otherwise be very peaceful. Tremblay's research demonstrates that the social learning theorists are only partially correct; that rather than simply learning aggression from models, children need to learn to curb their aggression as well.

FIGURE 4-12 Modelling Aggression
This series of photos is from Albert Bandura's classic Bobo doll experiment, designed to illustrate social learning of aggression. The photos clearly show how the adult model's aggressive behaviour (in the first row) is imitated by children who had viewed the aggressive behaviour (second and third rows).

Is there a connection between the two events? Social learning theorists would answer yes, because to them aggression is largely a learned behaviour based on children's observation and prior learning. To understand the causes of aggressive behaviour, then, we should look at the system of rewards and punishments in a child's environment.

Social learning approaches emphasize how social and environmental conditions teach individuals to be aggressive. Using a behavioural perspective, they argue that aggressive behaviour is learned through direct reinforcement. For instance, preschool-age children might learn that they can continue to play with the most desirable toys by aggressively refusing their classmates' requests for sharing. In the parlance of traditional learning theory, they have been reinforced for acting aggressively, and they are more likely to behave aggressively in the future.

But as we saw when discussing morality, social learning approaches suggest that reinforcement also comes indirectly. Research suggests that exposure to aggressive models leads to increased aggression, particularly if the observers are themselves angered, insulted, or frustrated. For example, Albert Bandura and his colleagues illustrated the power of models in a classic study of preschool-age children (Bandura et al., 1963). One group of children watched a film of an adult playing aggressively and violently with a Bobo doll (a large, inflated plastic clown designed as a punching bag that always returns to an upright position after being knocked over)(see Figure 4-12). In comparison, children in another condition watched a film of an adult playing sedately with a set of Tinkertoys. Later, the preschool-age children were allowed to play with a number of toys, which included both the Bobo doll and the Tinkertoys. But first, the children were led to feel frustrated by being refused the opportunity to play with a favourite toy.

As predicted by social learning approaches, the preschool-age children modelled the behaviour of the adult. Those who had seen the aggressive model playing with the Bobo

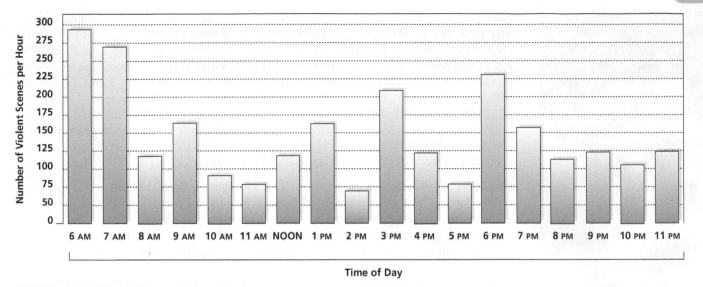

FIGURE 4-13 Acts of Violence
A survey of the violence shown on the major TV networks and several cable channels on one particular weekday found acts of violence during every time period. Do you think depictions of violence on TV should be regulated?
Source: Center for Media and Public Affairs, 1995.

doll were considerably more aggressive than those who had watched the calm, unaggressive model playing with the Tinkertoys. The children were also more aggressive if they saw the adult rewarded for aggressive behaviour than if they saw the adult reprimanded for aggressive behaviour. Thus, preschoolers don't have to experience rewards and punishments themselves, they also learn from watching how others are rewarded or punished.

Viewing Violence on TV: Does It Matter? The majority of preschool-age children are exposed to aggression via television. Children's television programs contain higher levels of violence (69 percent) than other types of programs (57 percent). In an average hour, children's programs contain more than twice as many violent incidents as other types of programs (see Figure 4-13; Wilson, 2002).

This high level of televised violence, viewed in light of research findings on modelling aggression, raises a significant question: Does viewing aggression increase the likelihood that children (and later adults) will perform aggressive acts?

Longitudinal studies have found that children's preferences for violent television shows at age 8 are correlated with the seriousness of criminal convictions by age 30 (Eron, 1982). Other evidence supports the notion that observation of media violence can lead to a greater readiness to act aggressively, bullying, and insensitivity to the suffering of victims of violence (Anderson et al., 2003; Huesmann et al., 2003; Slater et al., 2003; Ostrov et al., 2006). The vast majority of research linking television violence and aggression is correlational. In other words, in most of the studies conducted to date, children are not randomly assigned to watch violent or non-violent programming, but children who already watch more violent programming and have different attitudes toward what they are watching are also more aggressive. Therefore, we are stuck with the problem that children who will be more aggressive also prefer to watch violent programs, and continued viewing may compound problems over time.

> **From an educator's perspective:** How might a preschool teacher or parent help children notice the violence in the programs they watch and protect them from its effects?

Television is not the only source of media violence. Many video games contain highly aggressive behaviour, and many children play such games. For example, 14 percent of children age three and younger and around 50 percent of those four to six play video games. Because research conducted with adults shows that playing violent video games is

Social learning explanations of aggression suggest that children's observation of aggression on television can result in actual aggression.

associated with behaving aggressively, children who play video games containing violence may be at risk for behaving aggressively. In many of these experiments, adult participants are randomly assigned to play a violent or a non-violent video game and then tested in an aggression-provoking situation up to 24 hours later. While there are ethical concerns about conducting similar experiments with children, the assumption is that if a causal link exists with adults, one would very likely appear in children as well (Bushman and Anderson, 2001, 2002; Funk et al., 2003; Rideout, et al., 2003; Anderson et al., 2004).

Furthermore, just as exposure to aggressive models leads to aggression, observation of *non*aggressive models can *reduce* aggression. Preschoolers can actually learn how to avoid confrontation and to control their aggression, as we'll discuss later.

Cognitive Approaches to Aggression: The Thoughts behind Violence. Two children, waiting for their turn in a game of kickball, inadvertently knock into one another. One child's reaction is to apologize; the other's is to shove, saying angrily, "Cut it out."

Despite the fact that each child bears the same responsibility for the minor event, they have different reactions. What the first child sees as an accident, the second child sees as a provocation.

The cognitive approach to aggression suggests that to understand preschoolers' moral development it is necessary to examine their interpretations of others' behaviour and of the environmental context of the behaviour. According to developmental psychologist Kenneth Dodge and his colleagues, some children are more prone than others to assume that actions are aggressively motivated. They are unable to pay attention to the appropriate cues in a situation and therefore interpret the behaviours in the situation erroneously, assuming that what is happening is hostile. Subsequently, in deciding how to respond, they base their behaviour on their inaccurate interpretation, behaving aggressively in response to a situation that never in fact existed (Dodge and Coie, 1987; Dodge and Crick, 1990; Petit and Dodge, 2003).

Although the cognitive approach describes the process that leads some children to behave aggressively, it fails to explain why they perceive situations inaccurately and why they so readily respond with aggression. On the other hand, the cognitive approach is useful in pointing out a means to reduce aggression: By teaching preschool-age children to interpret situations more accurately, we can induce them to be less prone to view others' behaviour as motivated by hostility and less likely to respond with aggression themselves.

Increasing Moral Behaviour and Reducing Aggression in Preschool-age Children

Becoming an Informed Consumer of Development

Here are some practical and readily accomplished strategies for encouraging moral conduct and reducing aggression, based on ideas from the many approaches we have discussed (Goldstein, 1999; Bor and Bor, 2004):

- **Provide opportunities for preschool-age children to observe others acting in a co-operative, helpful, prosocial manner.** Encourage them to interact with peers in joint activities in which they share a common goal. Such co-operative activities can teach the importance and desirability of working with—and helping—others.

- **Do not ignore aggressive behaviour.** Parents and teachers should intervene when they see aggression in preschoolers, sending a clear message that aggression is an unacceptable way to resolve conflicts.

- **Help preschoolers devise alternative explanations for others' behaviour.** With children who are prone to aggression and apt to view others' conduct as more hostile than it actually is, parents and teachers should help them see that the behaviour of their peers has several possible interpretations.

- **Monitor preschoolers' television viewing, particularly the violence that they view.** Discourage preschoolers from watching shows depicting aggression and encourage them instead to watch shows that are designed, in part, to foster moral conduct, such as *Sesame Street*, *My Big Big Friend*, and *Caillou*.

- **Help preschoolers understand their feelings.** When children become angry—and all children do—they must learn to deal with their feelings constructively. Tell them *specific* things they can do to improve the situation. ("I see you're really angry with Jake for not giving you a turn. Don't hit him, but tell him you want a chance to play with the game.")

- **Explicitly teach reasoning and self-control.** Preschoolers can understand the rudiments of moral reasoning, and they should be reminded why certain behaviours are desirable. For instance, explicitly saying "If you take all the cookies, others will have no dessert" is preferable to saying, "Good children don't eat all the cookies."

REVIEW, CHECK, AND APPLY

REVIEW

- Piaget believed that preschoolers are in the heteronomous morality stage of moral development, in which rules are seen as invariant and unchangeable.

- Social learning approaches to moral development emphasize the importance of reinforcement for moral actions and the observation of models of moral conduct. Psychoanalytic and other theories focus on children's empathy with others and their wish to help others so they can avoid unpleasant feelings of guilt themselves.

- Aggression typically declines in frequency and duration as children become more able to regulate their emotions and use language to negotiate disputes.

CHECK YOURSELF

1. Changes in our sense of justice or an understanding of behaviours related to what is right and wrong is also known as _____.

   a. behavioural concern

   b. moral development

   c. perspective taking

   d. self-reflection

2. According to the _____ theory, the factor that increases the likelihood that a preschooler will engage in prosocial behaviour is his or her environment.

   a. cognitive-behavioural

   b. social-learning

   c. psychoanalytic

   d. humanistic

3. Aggression is an unstable characteristic in that aggressive preschoolers rarely grow up to be aggressive adults.

   - True

   - False

APPLYING LIFESPAN DEVELOPMENT

- If high-prestige models of behaviour are particularly effective in influencing moral attitudes and actions, are there implications for individuals in such industries as sports, advertising, and entertainment?

Answers: 1) a; 2) b; 3) False

Putting It All Together
The Early Childhood and Preschool Years

JULIE, whom we met in the chapter opener as a three-year-old in her first days of preschool, was initially shy and passive. She appeared to accept that older and larger children, particularly boys, had a right to tell her what to do and to take things from her that they wanted. She saw little choice but to let these things happen, since she was powerless to stop them. However in the span of one short year, Julie decided that she had had enough. Instead of accepting the "rule" that bigger kids could do whatever they wanted, she would protest against its unfairness. Instead of silently allowing other kids to dominate her, she would use her newfound moral sense, together with her evolving language skills, to warn them off. Julie had put together all the developmental tools that she now had to make her world a fairer and better place.

MODULE 4.1 Physical Development

- Julie grew bigger, heavier, and stronger during these years. **(p. 143)**

- Her brain grew and, with it, her cognitive abilities, including the ability to plan and to use language as a tool. **(pp. 145–146)**

- She learned to use and control her gross and fine motor skills. **(p. 148)**

MODULE 4.2 Cognitive Development

- During the preschool years, Julie's memory capabilities increased. **(p. 155)**

- She watched others and learned from her peers and from adults how to handle different situations. **(p. 157)**

- She also used her growing language skills to function more effectively. **(p. 160)**

- As with other preschool-age children, Julie's play was a way to grow socially, cognitively, and physically. **(p. 170)**

- Julie learned the rules of play, such as turn taking and playing fairly. **(p. 170)**

- She also developed theories of mind that help her to understand what others are thinking. **(p. 171)**

- She developed the beginnings of a sense of justice and moral behaviour. **(p. 179)**

- Julie was able to adjust her emotions to a desired intensity level and use language to express her wishes and deal with others. **(p. 184)**

What would a PARENT do?

- How would you help Julie become more assertive, both at home and at school? How would you help her prepare to deal with bullies in preschool and her big brother at home?

  HINT Review page 168.

  What's your response?

What would a HEALTH-CARE PROVIDER do?

- How would you help Julie's parents provide appropriate kinds of discipline for Julie and her older brother? How would you help her parents optimize their home environment to promote physical, cognitive, and social development for their children?

  HINT Review pages 172–173.

  What's your response?

What would an EDUCATOR do?

- What strategies would you use to promote cognitive and social development? How would you deal with instances of bullying in your preschool classroom, both children who were victimized as well as bullies?

  HINT Review pages 180–184.

  What's your response?

What would You do?

- What would you do to promote Julie's development? What specific advice would you give to Julie's parents and teacher on how to help Julie overcome her shyness and to interact more effectively with other children?

  HINT Review pages 169–171.

  What's your response?

Middle Childhood

Ryan was thrilled to *finally* reach grade 1. On the "Wishing Star" he made for Parents' Night, he had his teacher write his wish for the year: "My #1 wish: I want to read and write."

But reading and writing were proving difficult for Ryan. It was hard for him to decode even simple words, and hand–eye coordination made writing a chore, often resulting in a heavily smudged page.

In most ways, Ryan's physical and cognitive development was right on target for his seven years. He was an enthusiastic hiker, and he was able to memorize complex stories. Testing showed that Ryan's intelligence was above average, but vision and motor problems were frustrating his attempts to achieve normal developmental goals.

These frustrations affected Ryan's social development, too. He spent several hours each day in the special needs room, and could neither track the path of a soccer ball during a game nor ride a two-wheel bike. His social status was low. Several peers made fun of him, and he responded by withdrawing further into himself.

MODULE 5.1 Physical Development in Middle Childhood

How do visual, auditory, and speech impairments affect a child's social and personality development? see page 190.

MODULE 5.2 Cognitive Development in Middle Childhood

Schooling around the world and across genders: Who gets educated?

see page 201.

Ryan's parents and teachers kept in constant contact to discuss how best to support him both academically and socially. He worked with a reading specialist, and the school provided physical therapy services to help Ryan develop his motor skills.

The early intervention worked. It boosted Ryan's grades and his self-esteem. By the end of grade 2, he was riding his bike all over the neighborhood, reading at a grade 6 level, and writing rather than dictating stories about his favourite subject—pirates. In the regular classroom all day now, he made three close friends with whom he played *Star Wars* at recess, a happy, laughing, confident child.

In middle childhood, children enter school eager to learn all they can about the world. Often the regular classroom setting serves them well and contributes to their physical, intellectual, and social development; sometimes, however, children display needs or deficits that require special interventions—such as the reading specialist and physical therapist provided for Ryan—to make the most of their abilities and keep their self-esteem intact.

In this chapter, we follow children taking the crucial step into formal schooling. We look at the physical changes that prepare them for new challenges. We discuss the patterns of growth—and excess—that are typical of this period and the new levels of motor skills that enable them to perform actions as diverse as throwing a ball and playing

How does divorce affect a child's development? see page 221.

MyVirtualLife

How would you approach raising a child during middle childhood? What decisions would you make, and what would the consequences of those decisions be?

Find out by logging onto *My Virtual Life* through MyDevelopmentLab.

the violin. We also discuss threats to their well-being and consider the special needs that can impinge on children's school lives.

Next we consider the growing intellectual and conceptual skills and the increasingly sophisticated use of language that are hallmarks of this period. We visit the place where they spend most of their time: school. We consider reading and the policy dispute over the best way to teach it. We also address the surprisingly controversial topic of intelligence.

Finally, we consider school-age children as members of society, including their membership in school and family. We look at the ways school-age children understand themselves and develop self-esteem. We consider how they relate to one another, including members of the opposite sex. We then examine the many shapes and configurations that families take.

MODULE 5.1 Physical Development in Middle Childhood

Batter up!

It is a hot summer day in Southwestern Ontario. Adults move slowly through the humid air, but not eight-year-old Suzanne McGuire. A look of triumph crosses her face as she rounds the corner from third base to home plate.

Moments before, she was waiting for the pitcher to throw the ball. Her first two turns at bat, Suzanne had struck out, leaving her unhappy and a bit humiliated.

On her third turn at bat, though, the pitch looked perfect. She swung at it with confidence and high hope. When the bat connected with the ball, lobbing it well beyond the left fielder for a home run, a moment she would never forget was created.

Suzanne McGuire has come a long way since the preschool years, when quick, coordinated running and batting to the mark were not possible.

Such moments characterize middle childhood, when children's physical, cognitive, and social skills reach new heights. Beginning at age 6 and continuing to about age 12, this period is often called the school years. Physical growth is remarkable. Motor skills soar.

We begin by examining physical and motor development in middle childhood. We discuss how children's bodies change, and the twin problems of malnutrition and obesity. We examine the development of gross motor skills, like swinging a bat, and fine motor skills, like playing scales on a piano. We discuss the health of children during this period, including their psychological health.

We finish the module by considering the sensory and learning difficulties of children with special needs. We also discuss a disorder, the incidence of which has grown in importance in recent decades: attention deficit hyperactivity disorder (ADHD).

The Growing Body

LEARNING OBJECTIVES

LO1 In what ways do children grow during the school years, and what factors influence their growth?

Cinderella, dressed in yella,
Went upstairs to kiss her fellah.
But she made a mistake and she kissed a snake.
How many doctors did it take?
One, two...

While the other girls chanted this skipping rhyme, Kat proudly displayed her new ability to jump backwards. Now in grade 2, Kat was becoming quite good at skipping rope. In grade 1, she simply had not been able to master it, but over the summer, she had spent many hours practising, and now that practice was paying off.

As Kat is gleefully experiencing, children make great physical strides in middle childhood, mastering many new skills. How does this progress occur? We'll first consider typical physical growth during this period, then turn our attention to exceptional children.

Slow but steady: These words characterize the nature of growth during middle childhood. In contrast to the swift growth from birth to age five and the remarkable growth spurt of adolescence, middle childhood is relatively tranquil. The body has not shifted into neutral; physical growth continues, but at a more steady pace than in the pre-school years.

Variations of 15 cm in height between children of the same age are not unusual and are well within normal ranges.

Height and Weight Changes

In elementary school, children grow, on average, 7 cm a year. By age 11, the average height for girls is 144 cm, while boys average 143 cm. This is the only period in life when girls tend to be taller than boys. This reflects the slightly more rapid physical development of girls, who start their adolescent growth spurt around age 10.

Weight gain in middle childhood follows a similar pattern; boys and girls both gain around 3 kg a year. Weight is also redistributed. As "baby fat" disappears, children's bodies become more muscular and their strength increases.

These average height and weight increases disguise significant individual differences. Children of the same age can be 15 to 17 cm apart in height.

Cultural Patterns of Growth

Most children in Canada receive sufficient nutrients to grow to their full potential. In other parts of the world, however, inadequate nutrition and disease take their toll, producing children who are shorter and weigh less. The discrepancies can be dramatic: Poor children in cities such as Calcutta, Hong Kong, and Rio de Janeiro are smaller than affluent children in the same cities.

In affluent industrialized nations, most variations in height and weight are the result of people's unique genetic inheritance, including genetic factors relating to ethnic background. Children with Asian heritage tend to be shorter than those of northern and central European ancestry. In addition, the rate of growth is generally more rapid for children of African heritage (Deurenberg et al., 2002; Deurenberg et al., 2003).

Even within ethnic groups, individuals vary significantly. We cannot attribute ethnic differences solely to genetic factors because dietary customs as well as variations in levels of affluence also may contribute to differences. In addition, severe stress—brought on by factors such as exposure to conflict or parental alcoholism—can affect the pituitary gland, thereby affecting growth (Powell et al., 1967; Koska et al., 2002).

Nutrition

There is a relationship between size and nutrition, but size isn't the only thing affected by diet. For instance, nutrition is related to social and emotional functioning at school age. Children who receive more nutrients are more involved with their peers, show more positive emotion, and have less anxiety than children with less adequate nutrition. Nutrition is also linked to cognitive performance. For example, in one study, children in Kenya who were well-nourished performed better on a test of verbal abilities and on other cognitive measures than those who had mild to moderate undernutrition. Malnutrition may influence cognitive development by dampening children's curiosity, responsiveness, and motivation to learn (McDonald et al., 1994; Brown and Pollitt, 1996; Wachs, 2002; Grigorenko, 2003).

Although undernutrition and malnutrition clearly lead to physical, social, and cognitive difficulties, in some cases *over*nutrition—the intake of too many calories—leads to problems of its own, in particular childhood obesity.

Inadequate nutrition and disease affect growth significantly. Children in poorer areas of cities such as Calcutta, Hong Kong, and Rio de Janeiro are smaller than their counterparts in affluent areas of the same cities.

Childhood Obesity

When her mother asks if she would like bread with her meal, Ruthellen replies that she'd better not—she thinks she might be getting fat. Ruthellen, who is of normal weight and height, is six years old.

Although height can be of concern to both children and parents, weight is an even greater worry for some. Weight concerns can border on obsession, particularly in girls. Many 6-year-old girls worry about becoming "fat," and some 40 percent of girls aged 9 to 10 are trying to lose weight. Their concern with weight often reflects a cultural preoccupation with slimness, which permeates a great deal of Western society (Schreiber et al., 1996; Greenwood and Pietromonaco, 2004).

Despite the prevalent view that thinness is a virtue, childhood obesity is rising. *Obesity* is defined as having excess body fat and is calculated using body mass index (BMI), which is based on height, weight and, for children, age. Unlike adults, the cut-off BMI for children varies as a function of age and gender. A BMI of 20 would be considered obese for a 6-year-old, overweight but not obese for a 9-year-old, and perfectly healthy for a 12-year-old or adult. The rate of childhood obesity has risen dramatically in recent decades. Among school-aged children, 18 percent are overweight and 8 percent are obese. In 1978, 13 percent were overweight and obesity was rare (see Figure 5-1; Sheilds, 2004).

The costs of childhood obesity last a lifetime. Obese children are more likely to be overweight as adults and have a greater risk of heart disease, diabetes, and other diseases. Some scientists believe an epidemic of obesity could be leading

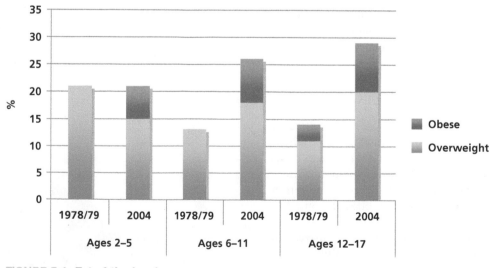

FIGURE 5-1   Fat of the Land
The percentage of children and adolescents who are overweight has increased dramatically in recent decades.
Source: Adapted from Sheilds, 2004.

to a decline in lifespan (Freedman et al., 2004; Olshansky et al., 2005; Krishnamoorthy et al., 2006).

Genetic and social characteristics as well as diet influence obesity. Particular inherited genes predispose certain children to be overweight. For example, adopted children's weight tends to reflect that of their birth parents rather than the weight of their adoptive parents (Zhang et al., 1994; Whitaker et al., 1997). Children with African heritage are more prone to obesity than children from Asian heritage. Children of Aboriginal heritage are at highest risk. Obesity also varies regionally, with the highest rates in the Atlantic and Prairie provinces, and the lowest rates in BC, Quebec, and Alberta. However, only 25 to 40 percent of obesity seems to be explained by genetic heritage (Sheilds, 2004; Canadian Paediatric Society, 2002).

Social factors also affect children's weight problems. Parents need to model healthy eating and lifestyle options as well as provide healthy options. For example, children who eat fewer than five servings of fruits and vegetables per day are more likely to be overweight or obese. Parents who stock their kitchen with fruits and vegetables as available snacks and who model healthy snacking behaviour are more likely to have children who choose an apple or banana as an after-school snack. Children also need to control their own eating. Parents who are controlling and directive about their children's eating may produce children who lack internal controls to regulate their own food intake (Johnson and Birch, 1994; Faith et al., 1997; Wardle et al., 2001).

Given how energetic children this age can be, it is surprising that a major factor in childhood obesity is a lack of exercise. School-age children tend to engage in relatively little exercise and are not particularly fit. Around 40 percent of boys aged 6 to 12 are unable to do more than one pull-up, and a quarter can't do any. Furthermore, children have shown little or no improvement in the amount of exercise they get, despite national efforts to increase the fitness of school-age children, in part because many schools have reduced the time available for recess and gym classes. Among children aged 5 to 12, 30 percent of girls and 50 percent of boys are physically active. These rates of physical activity drop in adolescence to 25 percent of girls and 40 percent of boys (Canadian Paediatric Society, 2002; Moore et al., 2003; Sallis and Glanz, 2006; Weiss and Raz, 2006).

Why is this level of exercise relatively low? One answer is that many kids watch television and play computer or video games instead of engaging in physical activity. Not only do such sedentary activities prevent exercise, but children often snack while viewing TV or surfing the

Keeping Children Fit

Becoming an Informed Consumer of Development

Here is a brief portrait of a contemporary child: Sam works all week at a school desk and gets no regular physical exercise. On weekends he spends many hours sitting in front of the TV, often snacking on sodas and sweets. Both at home and at restaurants, his meals feature high-calorie, fat-saturated foods (Segal and Segal, 1992, p. 235).

Although this scenario fits many adults, Sam is just six. Many school-age children like Sam get little or no regular exercise and consequently are physically unfit and at risk for obesity and other health problems.

To encourage children to be more physically active (Tyre and Scelfo, 2003; Okie, 2005) here are some tips:

- **Make exercise fun.** Children repeat what they enjoy. Overly competitive activities or those that sideline children with inferior skills can create a lifelong distaste for exercise.

- **Be an exercise role model.** Children who see their parents, teachers, or adult friends exercising regularly may view fitness as a regular part of their lives, too.

- **Gear activities to the child's physical level and motor skills.** Use child-size equipment to help children feel successful.

- **Encourage the child to find a partner.** Roller skating, hiking, and many other activities are more fun when shared with a friend, sibling, or parent.

- **Start slowly.** Ease sedentary children into regular physical activity. Try 5 minutes of exercise daily. Over 10 weeks, aim for 30 minutes three to five times a week.

- **Urge participation in organized sports activities, but do not push too hard.** Not every child is athletically inclined. Make participation and enjoyment—not winning—the goal.

- **Don't use physical activity as a punishment.** Encourage children to join organized activities they enjoy.

- **Provide a healthy diet.** Children don't buy the groceries. Parents need to ensure healthy options are available. Good nutrition gives children energy; pop, sweetened drinks, and sugary, fatty snack foods do not.

Web. Children who spend more than two hours per day in "screen time" are more likely to be overweight or obese than children who spend one hour or less per day in front of a screen. Another factor in childhood obesity, according to a recent survey conducted by the YMCA, is that parents today are reluctant to allow children in this age group to be unsupervised outdoors, which in turn means children are less likely to walk to and from school or play outdoors after school (Sheilds, 2004; Tartamella et al., 2005; Anderson and Butcher, 2006; Taveras et al., 2006; Kim, 2011).

REVIEW, CHECK, AND APPLY

REVIEW

- In middle childhood, height and weight increase gradually.
- Differences in height and weight are influenced by both genetic and social factors.
- Adequate nutrition promotes physical, social, and cognitive development, while poor nutrition and a sendentary lifestyle can lead to obesity.

CHECK YOURSELF

1. Due to the sudden changes taking place during this stage, the sight of children of the same age who are 15 cm apart in height is not uncommon in middle school.
   - True
   - False

2. Which of the following is *not* a long-term outcome associated with childhood obesity?
   a. cognitive deficits
   b. being overweight as adults
   c. greater risk of heart disease
   d. higher prevalence of diabetes

APPLYING LIFESPAN DEVELOPMENT

- What are some aspects of Western culture that might contribute to obesity among school-age children?

LEARNING OBJECTIVES

Motor Development and Safety

LO2 What are the main health concerns at this age?

Although the fitness level of children is lower than we might wish, this does not mean children are physically incapable. In fact, even without regular exercise, children's gross and fine motor skills develop substantially over the course of the school years.

Gross Motor Skills

One important improvement in gross motor skills is in muscle coordination. Watching a softball player pitch a ball past a batter to her catcher—or watching Kat, the girl skipping rope described earlier in the module—we are struck by the many skills children have mastered since their awkward preschool days. Most can readily learn to ride a bike, skate, swim, and skip rope (Cratty, 1986; see Figure 5-2).

Years ago developmentalists concluded that gender differences in gross motor skills became increasingly pronounced during these years, with boys outperforming girls (Espenschade, 1960). However, when comparing boys and girls who regularly take part in similar activities—such as softball   gender variations are minimal (Hall and Lee, 1984; Jurimae and Saar, 2003).

Why the change? Expectations probably played a role. Society did not expect girls to be highly active and told girls they would do worse than boys in sports. The girls' performance reflected that message.

During middle childhood, children master many types of skills that earlier they could not perform well, such as riding a bike, skating, swimming, and skipping rope. Is the same true for children of other cultures?

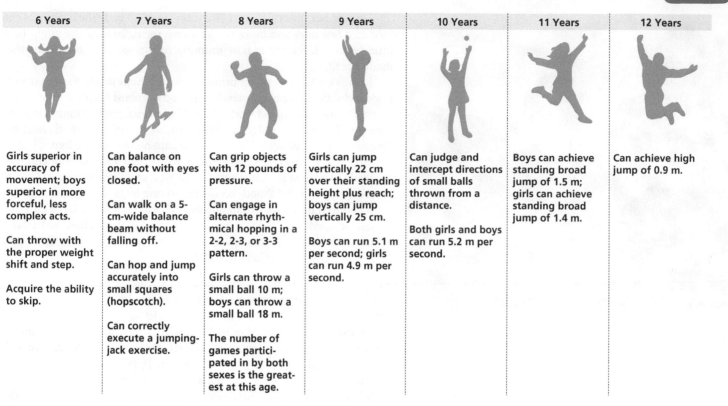

6 Years	7 Years	8 Years	9 Years	10 Years	11 Years	12 Years
Girls superior in accuracy of movement; boys superior in more forceful, less complex acts. Can throw with the proper weight shift and step. Acquire the ability to skip.	Can balance on one foot with eyes closed. Can walk on a 5-cm-wide balance beam without falling off. Can hop and jump accurately into small squares (hopscotch). Can correctly execute a jumping-jack exercise.	Can grip objects with 12 pounds of pressure. Can engage in alternate rhythmical hopping in a 2-2, 2-3, or 3-3 pattern. Girls can throw a small ball 10 m; boys can throw a small ball 18 m. The number of games participated in by both sexes is the greatest at this age.	Girls can jump vertically 22 cm over their standing height plus reach; boys can jump vertically 25 cm. Boys can run 5.1 m per second; girls can run 4.9 m per second.	Can judge and intercept directions of small balls thrown from a distance. Both girls and boys can run 5.2 m per second.	Boys can achieve standing broad jump of 1.5 m; girls can achieve standing broad jump of 1.4 m.	Can achieve high jump of 0.9 m.

FIGURE 5-2 Gross Motor Skills Developed Between 6 and 12 Years
Source: Adapted from Cratty, B. J., *Perceptual and motor development in infants and children*, 3rd ed. Copyright © Pearson Education, Inc. Reprinted with permission from Pearson Education, Inc.

Today, society's message has changed, at least officially. For instance, the Canadian Paediatric Society encourages that boys and girls have access to the same sports opportunities, and the American Academy of Pediatrics suggests that boys and girls should engage in the same sports and games and that they can do so in mixed-gender groups. There is no reason to separate the sexes in physical exercise and sports until puberty, when the smaller size of females makes them more susceptible to injury in contact sports (Raudsepp and Liblik, 2002; Vilhjalmsson and Kristjansdottir, 2003; American Academy of Pediatrics, 1989, 2004).

Fine Motor Skills

Typing at a computer keyboard, writing in cursive with pen or pencil, drawing detailed pictures—these are some of the accomplishments that depend on the improved fine motor coordination of early and middle childhood. Six- and seven-year-olds are able to tie their shoes and fasten buttons; by age eight, they can use each hand independently. By 11 and 12, they can manipulate objects almost as capably as adults.

One reason fine motor skills improve is that the amount of myelin in the brain increases significantly between the ages of six and eight (Lecours, 1982), raising the speed at which electrical impulses travel between neurons. Messages reach muscles more rapidly and control them better. Myelin also provides protective insulation that surrounds parts of nerve cells.

Health During Middle Childhood

Imani was miserable. Her nose was running, her lips were chapped, and her throat was sore. Although she had stayed home from school and watched old reruns on TV, she still felt that she was suffering mightily.

Children's access to computers and the Internet needs to be monitored.

Despite her misery, Imani's situation is not so bad. She'll get over the cold in a few days and be none the worse for it. In fact, she might be a little *better* off, for she is now immune to the specific cold germs that made her ill.

Imani's cold could end up being the most serious illness she gets during middle childhood. This is generally a period of robust health, and most ailments children do contract tend to be mild and brief. Routine immunizations have produced a considerably lower incidence of the life-threatening illnesses that 50 years ago claimed a significant number of children.

However, illness is not uncommon. More than 90 percent of children are likely to have at least one serious medical condition over the six-year period of middle childhood, according to one large survey. And though most children have short-term illnesses, about one in nine has a chronic, persistent condition, such as repeated migraine headaches, and nearly one in four deaths in this age group is the result of cancer (Dey and Bloom, 2005; Statistics Canada, 2009).

Accidents. Accidental injury is also a leading cause of death for children, accounting for more than one in five deaths among children between the ages of five and nine (Statistics Canada, 2009). The rate of injury for children rises due to increased independence and mobility. Boys are more apt to be injured than girls, probably because their overall level of physical activity is greater (Noonan, 2003a).

The increased mobility of this age can lead to several kinds of accidents. Children who regularly walk to school, many doing so alone for the first time, face the perils posed by cars and trucks. Their lack of experience can lead them to misjudge how far they are from an oncoming vehicle. Bicycle accidents pose an increasing risk, particularly as children venture out onto busier roads (Thomson et al., 1998).

The most frequent injuries to children result from motor vehicle accidents, and most often as passenger. Motor vehicle crashes annually kill 2 out of every 100 000 children between the ages of five and nine, accounting for half of accidental deaths. Drowning, which makes headlines every summer, is a distant second, accounting for approximately one quarter of accidental deaths in this age group. Other leading causes of accidental death include fire and suffocation (PHAC, 2009).

In cars, using seat belts consistently and booster seats for children under 145 cm reduces injuries. Bicycle helmets have significantly reduced head injuries resulting from bike accidents; in many cities, helmet use is mandatory. Knee and elbow pads have proven to reduce injuries in roller-blading and skateboarding accidents (Lee et al., 2005).

Safety in Cyberspace. The newest threat to children's safety comes from a source that was unheard of a generation ago: the Internet and the World Wide Web. Although claims that cyberspace is overrun with pornography and child molesters are exaggerated—and the benefits of the Internet are many—it is true that cyberspace makes material available that many parents find objectionable (Brant, 2003).

Computer software developers have devised programs that will block particular computer sites, but most experts feel the most reliable safeguard is parental supervision. One challenge parents face is that they might not be fully literate in the new media. Parents should warn their children never to provide personal information, such as home addresses or telephone numbers, to people on public computer "bulletin boards" or in chat rooms. In addition, children should not hold face-to-face meetings with people they meet via computer, at least not without a parent present.

> **From an educator's perspective:** Do you think using blocking software or computer chips to screen offensive Internet content is a practical idea? Are such controls the best way to keep children safe in cyberspace?

The Canadian Paediatric Association recommends that children should not have televisions, computers, or video game equipment in their bedrooms; such media should be in shared areas of the home where parents can more readily monitor usage—both quantity and quality (Canadian Paediatric Society, 2003).

Psychological Disorders

Tevin is planning his seventh birthday party. "Right now he's excited," says his mom, Candice. "He's a party-planning machine, although his vision for the party is quickly getting out of control. It's a delicate balance. I like to encourage him when he's in these up moods, but at the same time we have to keep him under control. He gets very hyper. If I set too many limits I'm afraid I'll set off a spectacular tantrum."

And a tantrum he has, later that day. During supper, Tevin refuses to eat and says he has a stomach ache. An hour later he wants to cancel the party, and he collapses in tears and screams to "Go away!"

Bipolar disorder such as Tevin's is diagnosed when a person cycles back and forth between two extreme emotional states: unrealistically high spirits and energy, and depression. For years, most people neglected the symptoms of such psychological disorders in children, and even today the symptoms might be overlooked. Yet such disorders are a common problem: an estimated 14 percent of children and adolescents in Canada have a psychological disorder that produces at least some impairment. For example, about 5 percent of preteens suffer from childhood depression, and 13 percent of children between 9 and 17 experience an anxiety disorder (Kalb, 2003; Beardslee and Goldman, 2003; Tolan and Dodge, 2005; Cicchetti and Cohen, 2006; CIHI, 2009).

Psychological disorders might be neglected because children and adults express symptoms differently. For example, depression in children is expressed with a lot of physical complaints (headache, stomach ache) and crankiness, rather than sadness. Bipolar disorder may be frequently mistaken for ADHD. Even when such disorders are diagnosed accurately, the correct treatment can be elusive. Approximately 0.4 percent of children 5 to 11 years old and 2 percent of adolescents receive prescriptions for antidepressant drugs each year, even though such drugs have never been approved for use in children under 18 years old. But because the drugs have been approved for adults, physicians who prescribe them for children are acting legally, a discretionary practice called "off-label use" (Katz et al., 2008; Goode, 2004; Health Canada, 2004).

Advocates for the use of antidepressants such as Prozac, Zoloft, Paxil, and Wellbutrin for children suggest that drug therapies can successfully treat their depression and other psychological disorders. Drugs may provide the only relief in cases where traditional therapies that use verbal methods are ineffective. At least one clinical test shows that the drugs are effective with children (Emslie et al., 1997; Garland, 2004).

Critics, however, question the long-term effectiveness of antidepressants for children. No one knows the consequences of their use on the developing brain, nor the overall long-term effects. Little is known about the correct dosage for age or size, and some observers suggest that children's versions of the drugs, in orange- or mint-flavored syrups, might lead to overdoses or eventually encourage the use of illegal drugs (Strauch, 1997; Goode, 2004).

Finally, some evidence links antidepressants with an increased risk of suicide. The possible link prompted Health Canada to issue a warning about a class of antidepressants known as SSRIs in 2003. Some experts have urged that use with children and adolescents be banned completely (Satel, 2004; Vedantam, 2004). The Health Canada warning did lead to a significant reduction in prescriptions, but the rate remains high (Katz et al., 2008). However, while the antidepressants were associated with increased risk of suicide, the risk of suicide from untreated depression is also high.

Although the use of antidepressants to treat children is controversial, clearly childhood depression and other psychological disorders remain a significant problem. These disorders must not be ignored. Not only are they disruptive during childhood, they also put children at risk for future disorders (Marmar et al., 2002; Mash and Barkley, 2003; Wals and Verhulst, 2005).

As we'll see next, adults also need to pay attention to other special needs that affect many school-age children.

REVIEW, CHECK, AND APPLY

REVIEW

- Gross motor skills continue to improve during the school years.

- Muscular coordination and manipulative skills advance to near adult levels.

- Threats to safety include accidents, a result of increased independence and mobility, and unsupervised access to cyberspace.

CHECK YOURSELF

1. One explanation for the advances in fine motor skills during middle school involves the increase in the amount of _____ in the brain.

2. When it comes to school-age children and injuries associated with accidents, which of the following statements is true?

   a. The number of accidents occurring in the school-age years is significantly fewer than in earlier years.

   b. Girls are significantly more likely to be injured in accidents than are boys.

   c. There is no relationship between gender and the prevalence of injuries associated with accidents.

   d. Boys are significantly more likely than girls to be injured.

APPLYING LIFESPAN DEVELOPMENT

- How would you design an experiment to examine the roots of gender differences in gross motor skills? What impediments would you encounter in doing so?

Answers: 1) myelin; 2) d

Children with Special Needs

LEARNING OBJECTIVES

LO3 What special needs might become apparent during these years and how can they be met?

An estimated 5 to 10 percent of children have a learning disability, and another 5 to 10 percent have other disabilities. Although every child has different capabilities, children with *special needs* differ significantly in physical attributes or learning abilities. Their needs present major challenges for care providers and teachers.

We turn now to the most prevalent disorders affecting children of normal intelligence: sensory difficulties, learning disabilities, and attention deficit disorders. (We will consider the special needs of children who are significantly below and above average in intelligence later in the module.)

Sensory Difficulties: Visual, Auditory, and Speech Problems

Anyone who has lost his or her eyeglasses or a contact lens knows how difficult even basic, everyday tasks must be for the sensory impaired. To function without adequate vision, hearing, or speech poses a tremendous challenge.

Visual impairment has both a legal and an educational meaning. Legal impairment is defined precisely: *Blindness* is visual acuity below 20/200 after correction (meaning the inability to see at 20 feet what is typically seen at 200 feet), while *partial sightedness* is visual acuity of less than 20/70 after correction.

Even if a child is not legally blind, visual problems may seriously affect school work. For one thing, the legal criterion pertains solely to distance vision, while most school tasks require close-up vision. The legal definition does not consider abilities in the perception of colour, depth, and light, either—all of which might influence a student's success. About one student in a thousand requires special education services due to visual impairment.

Most severe visual problems are identified fairly early, but impairment can go undetected. Visual problems can also emerge gradually as development brings changes in the apparatus of the eye. Parents and teachers need to look out for frequent eye irritation (redness, sties, or infection); continual blinking and facial contortions when reading; holding reading material unusually close to the face; difficulty writing; and frequent headaches, dizziness, or burning eyes. All are signs of visual problems.

Auditory impairments can cause social as well as academic problems since much peer interaction involves informal conversation. Hearing loss, affecting 1 to 2 percent of the school-

Auditory impairments can produce both academic and social difficulties, and they may lead to speech difficulties.

age population, goes beyond just not hearing enough and varies on a number of dimensions (Yoshinaga-Itano, 2003; Smith et al., 2005).

In some cases, hearing is impaired at only certain frequencies or pitches. For example, the loss may be great at pitches in the normal speech range yet minimal in other frequencies, such as those of very high or low sounds. Different levels of amplification at different frequencies might be required; a hearing aid that amplifies all frequencies equally may be ineffective, amplifying sounds the child can hear to an uncomfortable degree.

How a child adapts depends on when the hearing loss begins. The effects will likely be more severe in a child with little or no exposure to the sound of language, producing an inability to understand or produce speech. For a child who has learned language, hearing loss will not seriously affect subsequent linguistic development.

Severe and early loss of hearing can impair abstract thinking. Concrete concepts can be visually illustrated but abstract concepts depend on language for meaning. For example, it is difficult to explain the concept of "freedom" or "soul" without use of language (Butler and Silliman, 2002; Marschark and Spencer, 2003).

Auditory difficulties can be accompanied by **speech impairments**, one of the most public types of exceptionality: Speech that deviates from the norm is obvious whenever the child speaks. It also interferes with communication and can produce maladjustment in the speaker. Speech impairments occur in around 3 to 5 percent of the school-age population (Bishop and Leonard, 2001).

Stuttering, the most common speech impairment, produces substantial disruption in the rhythm and fluency of speech. Despite much research, no specific cause has been identified. Occasional stuttering is not unusual in young children—or even normal adults—but chronic stuttering can be a severe problem. Stuttering hinders communication and can be embarrassing or stressful for children, who may come to fear conversation and speaking aloud in class (Whaley and Parker, 2000; Altholz and Golensky, 2004).

Parents and teachers can help children who stutter by not drawing attention to the issue and by giving children sufficient time to finish what they are saying, no matter how protracted the statement becomes. Finishing a sentence for a stutterer or otherwise correcting their speech does not help stutterers (Ryan, 2001).

Learning Disabilities: Discrepancies between Achievement and Capacity to Learn

As many as 1 in 10 children are labelled as having learning disabilities. **Learning disabilities** interfere with a child's ability to listen, speak, read, write, reason, or do math. As an ill-defined category, learning disabilities are diagnosed when children's academic performance falls substantially below their potential and opportunity to learn (Lerner, 2002; Bos and Vaughn, 2005).

Such a broad definition includes a wide and varied range of difficulties. For instance, *dyslexia* is a disability involving written language. Dyslexia is the most frequently diagnosed learning disability and interferes with children's ability to learn how to read and write. Dyslexia is not fully understood, but the problem might lie in the part of the brain that breaks words into the sound elements that make up language. The majority of children with dyslexia have difficulty with phonological processing and awareness, mapping spoken sounds to letters, starting in the preschool years (Paulesu et al., 2001; McGough, 2003; Lachmann et al., 2005; van Bergen et al., 2011).

Although learning disabilities are generally attributed to some form of brain dysfunction, probably due in part to genetic factors, their causes are not well understood. Some experts suggest that environmental causes such as poor early nutrition or allergies could contribute (Shaywitz, 2004).

Attention Deficit Hyperactivity Disorder

David is a loving seven-year-old boy. "Teachers hate me. They're always telling me to pay attention and stop fidgeting."

"We don't hate him," says his teacher, Alice Nash, "but I know he can do better. When he applies himself, if it's a project he likes, he does really well. But it's hard to get him to focus on

visual impairment difficulty in seeing that can include blindness or partial sightedness

auditory impairment a special need that involves the loss of hearing or some aspect of hearing

speech impairment speech that deviates so much from the speech of others that it calls attention to itself, interferes with communication, or produces maladjustment in the speaker

stuttering substantial disruption in the rhythm and fluency of speech; the most common speech impairment

learning disabilities difficulties in the acquisition and use of listening, speaking, reading, writing, reasoning, or mathematical abilities

the more boring tasks. Plus, he's disruptive and destructive. He keeps digging at his desk with his pencil. There are marks and gouges all over."

Attention deficit hyperactivity disorder (ADHD)
a learning disability marked by inattention, impulsiveness, a low tolerance for frustration, and generally a great deal of inappropriate activity

David suffers from a disorder unheard of just a few decades ago—**attention deficit hyperactivity disorder (ADHD)**. This disorder is marked by inattention, impulsiveness, low tolerance for frustration, and a great deal of inappropriate activity. All children show such traits at times, but for children with ADHD such behaviour is common, interfering with their home and school functioning (Goldman, 2010; Nigg, 2001; Whalen et al., 2002).

It is often difficult to distinguish between children who are highly active and those with ADHD, especially at younger ages. Common symptoms include the following:

- persistent difficulty in finishing tasks, following instructions, and organizing work
- fidgeting, squirming, inability to watch an entire television program
- frequent interruption of others or excessive talking
- a tendency to jump into a task before hearing all the instructions
- difficulty in waiting or remaining seated

Lacking a simple test to identify ADHD, it is hard to know for sure how many children have the disorder. Most estimates suggest that ADHD affects 3 to 7 percent of those under the age of 18, and affects two to four times more boys than girls. Accurate diagnosis requires an extensive evaluation by a trained clinician and interviews with parents and teachers (Goldman, 2010; Sax and Kautz, 2003).

Considerable controversy surrounds the treatment of ADHD. Many physicians routinely prescribe drugs such as Ritalin or Dexadrine (which, paradoxically, are stimulants) because they reduce activity in hyperactive children (Volkow et al., 2001; Kaplan et al., 2004; HMHL, 2005). Giving stimulants to hyperactive children seems counterintuitive to most people, but the hyperactive impulsive behaviour is thought to be caused by inefficient brain signals. Speeding up the brain makes it work better in the same way that many adults get improved focus from caffeine.

Although such drugs can effectively increase attention span and compliance, the side effects (such as irritability, reduced appetite, depression, and sleep problems) can be considerable, and the long-term health consequences are unclear. Although the drugs can boost school performance in the short run, the evidence for continued improvement is mixed. Some studies suggest that after a few years, children treated with drugs perform no better than untreated ADHD children. The number of children being given drugs, however, has increased significantly in the last decade. The Canadian Paediatric Society recommends that if children need drug treatment for ADHD, newer extended-release drugs are preferred over the older immediate-acting drugs (Hallahan et al., 2000; Marshall, 2000; Zernike and Petersen, 2001; Feldman and Bélanger, 2009).

In addition to drugs, behaviour therapy is also recommended to treat ADHD. Parents and teachers learn techniques that primarily use rewards (such as verbal praise) to improve behaviour. Parents and teachers also need to impose more structure on children with ADHD as children with ADHD have difficulty with self-control and self-regulation. Teachers can increase the structure of classroom activities, among other management techniques, as ADHD children find unstructured tasks difficult. Parents can help children have sparse, uncluttered bedrooms, teach scheduling and have posted schedules, and assist with well-labelled organizational systems (Chronis et al., 2006; DuPaul and Weyandt, 2006).

Research showing links between ADHD and children's diet, particularly in terms of fatty acids or food additives, have prompted dietary treatments. While it seems that artificial food colourings, preservatives, and refined sugar contribute to increased hyperactivity for children whether or not they have ADHD, dietary treatments targeting these culprits are usually insufficient by themselves. In recent years an elimination diet in which children eat rice, turkey, lamb, vegetables, fruits, margarine, vegetable oil, tea, pear juice, and water showed significant reduction in symptoms. While this was a single, and somewhat controversial study, it is clear that more research on diet and ADHD is needed (Adesman, 2011; Cruz and Bahna, 2006; Stevenson, 2003; Pelsser et al., 2009; Stevens et al., 2011).

REVIEW, CHECK, AND APPLY

REVIEW

- Many children have special needs relating to vision, hearing, and speech disabilities that can impact their social relationships and school performance.

- Learning disabilities include difficulties in acquiring and using listening, speaking, reading, writing, reasoning, or mathematical abilities.

- Attention deficit hyperactivity disorder poses attention, organization, and activity problems for 3 to 7 percent of school-age children.

CHECK YOURSELF

1. _____, the most common speech impairment, involves a substantial disruption in the rhythm and fluency of speech.

2. Although most children may, at one time or another, display symptoms of attention deficit hyperactivity disorder (ADHD), a diagnosis of ADHD requires all of the following elements, *except*

    _____.

    a. common ADHD behaviours

    b. ADHD behaviours for more than three weeks

    c. ADHD behaviours interfering with home functioning

    d. ADHD behaviours interfering with school functioning

APPLYING LIFESPAN DEVELOPMENT

- If hearing is associated with abstract thinking, how do people who were born deaf think?

Answers: 1) Stuttering; 2) a

MODULE 5.2 Cognitive Development in Middle Childhood

Lucy and *The Giant Peach*

Lucy is well-known in her local library. The eight-year-old goes to the library every day after school until suppertime. "Except on Mondays when the library is closed. Mondays I hang out in the park or go to a friend's house." Lucy lives with her mother, a single parent who can't afford a lot of afterschool programs, "…or to feed that appetite for reading she's got," laughs her mother. "The library is a godsend. It's free, and I know she won't get into any trouble there while I'm at work."

    Her favourite book is James and The Giant Peach *by Roald Dahl. "I've read all his books, but* The Giant Peach *I read four times."*

Middle childhood is often referred to as the "school years" because it marks the beginning of formal education for most children. Sometimes the physical and cognitive growth that occurs during middle childhood is gradual, other times it is sudden—but always it is remarkable.

During middle childhood, children blossom with ideas and plans—and the language to express them orally and in writing. It is during this period that much of their future development is charted.

We begin our discussion by examining several approaches to describe and explain cognitive development, including Piagetian and information-processing theories and the important ideas of Vygotsky. We look at language development and the questions surrounding bilingualism.

Next we consider several issues involving schooling. After discussing the scope of education throughout the world, we examine the critical skill of reading and the nature of multicultural education. The chapter ends with a discussion of intelligence, a characteristic closely tied to school success. We look at the nature of IQ tests and at the education of children who are either significantly below or above the intellectual norm.

Intellectual and Language Development

LO4 In what ways do children develop cognitively during these years, according to major theoretical approaches?

LO5 How does language develop during the middle childhood period?

LEARNING OBJECTIVES

Jared's parents were delighted when he came home from kindergarten one day and announced he had learned why the sky was blue. He talked about the Earth's atmosphere—although he mispronounced the word—and how tiny bits of moisture in the air reflected the sunlight. His explanation had rough edges (he couldn't quite grasp what "atmosphere" was), but he had the general idea. His parents felt it was quite an achievement for their five-year-old.

Fast-forward six years. Jared, now 11, has already invested an hour in his homework. Having completed a two-page worksheet on multiplying and dividing fractions, he is working on his social studies project. He is taking notes for his report, which will explain the factors leading up to and the aftermath of the Acadian Deportation.

Cognitive development makes substantial advances in middle childhood.

Jared's vast intellectual advances are not uncommon. During middle childhood, cognitive abilities broaden, and children increasingly understand and master complex skills. But their thinking is not yet fully mature.

Several perspectives explain the cognitive advances and limitations of middle childhood.

Piagetian Approaches to Cognitive Development

Let's return to Jean Piaget's view of the preschooler considered in Chapter 4. From Piaget's perspective, preschoolers think *preoperationally*. They are largely egocentric and lack the ability to use *operations*—organized, formal, logical mental processes.

The Rise of Concrete Operational Thought. All this changes during the school years in what Piaget calls the **concrete operational stage**. Occurring between ages 7 and 12, this stage is characterized by the active, and appropriate, use of logic. Concrete operational thought applies *logical operations* to concrete problems. For instance, when children in this stage confront a conservation problem (such as determining whether the amount of liquid poured from one container to another of a different shape stays the same), they use cognitive and logical processes to answer, no longer judging solely by appearance. They are able to reason correctly that, since none of the liquid has been lost, the amount stays the same. Being less egocentric, they can consider multiple aspects of a situation, an ability known as **decentring**. Jared, the grade 6 student described earlier, used decentring to consider the views of the various factions behind the Acadian Deportation.

The shift from preoperational to concrete operational thought takes time. Children shift between these modes of thought before concrete operations take a firm hold—they are able to answer conservation problems but unable to explain why. When asked for their reasoning, they might simply respond, "Because."

However, once concrete operations take hold, children make several cognitive leaps, such as the concept of *reversibility*—the notion that transformations to a stimulus can be reversed. Grasping this, children realize that a ball of clay squeezed into a long, thin rope can become a ball again. More abstractly, this concept allows children to understand that if 3 + 5 equals 8, then 5 + 3 also equals 8—and, later, that 8 − 3 equals 5.

Concrete operational thinking also permits children to grasp such concepts as the relationship between time and speed. For instance, consider the problem in which two cars travelling routes of a different length start and finish at the same points in the same amount of time. Children entering the concrete operational period reason that the cars' speeds are the same. However, between ages 8 and 10, children begin to understand that for both cars to arrive simultaneously at the finish point, the car travelling the longer route must be moving faster.

Despite these advances, children's thinking still has one critical limitation. They remain tied to concrete, physical reality. Furthermore, they cannot understand truly abstract or hypothetical questions, or ones involving formal logic, such as concepts like free will or determinism.

Piaget in Perspective: Right and Wrong. As we learned earlier, researchers who followed Piaget have found much to applaud—and much to criticize.

👁 Watch on **mydevelopmentlab**

To watch a video clip on concrete operational thinking, log onto MyDevelopmentLab.

concrete operational stage the period of cognitive development between 7 and 12 years of age, which is characterized by the active, and appropriate, use of logic

decentring the ability to take multiple aspects of a situation into account

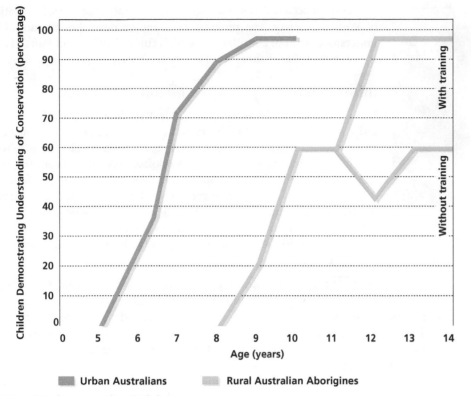

FIGURE 5-3 Conservation Training

Rural Australian Aborigine children trail their urban counterparts in the development of their understanding of conservation; with training, they later catch up. Without training, around half of 14-year-old Aborigines do not have an understanding of conservation. What can be concluded from the fact that training influences the understanding of conservation?
Source: Adapted from Dasen et al., 1979.

Piaget was a virtuoso observer of children. His many books contain brilliant, careful observations of children at work and play. His theories have had powerful educational implications, and many schools use his principles to guide instruction (Flavell, 1996; Siegler and Ellis, 1996; Brainerd, 2003).

In some ways, Piaget's approach succeeded in describing cognitive development (Lourenco and Machado, 1996). At the same time, critics have raised compelling and reasonable grievances about the interpretations. As noted earlier, many researchers argue that Piaget underestimated children's capabilities, in part due to the limitations of the mini-experiments he conducted. When a broader array of experimental tasks is used, children show less consistency within stages than Piaget predicted (Siegler, 1994; Bjorklund, 1997). Increasing evidence suggests that children's cognitive abilities emerge earlier than Piaget envisioned. Some children demonstrate concrete operational thinking before age seven, when Piaget suggested these abilities first appear.

Still, we cannot dismiss Piaget. Although some early cross-cultural research implied that children in certain cultures remain preoperational, failing to master conservation and develop concrete operations, more recent research suggests otherwise. For instance, with proper training in conservation, children in non-Western cultures who do not conserve learn to do so. In one study, urban Australian children—who develop concrete operations on Piaget's timetable—were compared to rural Aborigine children, who typically do not conserve at the age of 14 (Dasen et al., 1979). With training, the rural Aborigine children showed conservation skills similar to those of their urban counterparts, although about three years later (see Figure 5-3).

When children are interviewed by researchers from their own culture, who share their language and customs, and whose reasoning tasks relate to important cultural domains, the children are much more likely to display concrete operational thinking (Nyiti, 1982; Jahoda, 1983). Such research suggests that Piaget was right in arguing that concrete operations are universally achieved during middle childhood. Performance differences between Western and some non-Western children on Piagetian measures of conservation and concrete operations

Students working in co-operative groups benefit from the insights of others.

probably reflect a difference in experiences, notably the formal education of Western society. The progress of cognitive development cannot be understood without considering a child's culture (Beilin and Pufall, 1992; Berry et al., 1992; Mishra, 1997; Lau et al., 2004).

Information-Processing in Middle Childhood

It is a significant achievement for grade 1 students to learn basic math tasks, such as single-digit addition and subtraction, as well as the spelling of simple words like "dog." But by grade 6, children are able to work with fractions and decimals, completing a worksheet like the one done by Jared, the boy cited earlier. They can spell words like "exhibit" and "residence."

According to *information-processing approaches*, children handle information with increasing sophistication. Like computers, they process more data as the size of their memories increases and the "programs" they use to do this become more complex (Kuhn et al., 1995; Kail, 2003; Zelazo et al., 2003).

Memory. As noted, **memory** in the information-processing model is the ability to encode, store, and retrieve information. For a child to remember a piece of information, the three processes must all function properly. Through *encoding*, the child records the information in a form usable to memory. Children who never learned that $5 + 6 = 11$, or who didn't heed this fact when it was taught, will never be able to recall it. They never encoded the information in the first place.

But exposure to a fact is not enough; the information also has to be *stored*. In our example, the information that $5 + 6 = 11$ must be placed and maintained in the memory system. Finally, proper memory functioning requires that stored material must be *retrieved*. Through retrieval, material in storage is located, made conscious, and used.

During middle childhood, short-term memory (also referred to as *working memory*) capacity greatly improves. Children are increasingly able to hear a string of digits ("1-5-6-3-4") and then repeat them in reverse order ("4-3-6-5-1"). In the early preschool period, they can remember and reverse only about two digits; by early adolescence, they can perform the task with as many as six digits. They also use more sophisticated strategies for recalling information, which training can improve (Bjorklund et al., 1994; Halford et al., 1994; Cowan et al., 2002).

Memory capacity may shed light on another issue in cognitive development. Some developmental psychologists suggest that preschool children might have difficulty solving conservation problems due to memory limitations (Siegler and Richards, 1982). They argue that young children simply might not be able to recall all the necessary information to solve such problems.

Metamemory, a grasp of the processes that underlie memory, also emerges and improves during middle childhood. By the start of grade 1, when their theory of mind becomes more sophisticated, children have a general notion of what memory is. They understand that some people have better memories than others (Schneider and Pressley, 1989; Lewis and Mitchell, 1994; Cherney, 2003).

School-age children understand memory in more sophisticated ways as they increasingly engage in *control strategies*—intentionally used tactics to improve cognitive processing. For instance, school-age children know that rehearsal, the repetition of information, improves memory, and they increasingly make use of this strategy. They also progress in organizing material into coherent patterns, a strategy that improves recall. For instance, faced with memorizing a list including cups, knives, forks, and plates, older school-age children are more likely than younger ones to group the items into coherent patterns—cups and plates, and forks and knives (Pressley and Van Meter, 1993; Weed et al., 1990; Sang et al., 2002).

Improving Memory. School-age children can learn to use control strategies more effectively, although teaching these strategies is not simple. For instance, children need to know not only how to use a memory strategy, but also when and where to use it.

An innovative technique called the *keyword strategy*, for example, can help students learn a foreign language, the provincial and territorial capitals, or any information that pairs two sets of words or labels that sound alike (Pressley and Levin, 1983; Pressley, 1987). For instance, in learning foreign language vocabulary, a foreign word such as the Spanish word for duck (*pato,*

memory the process by which information is initially recorded, stored, and retrieved

metamemory an understanding about the processes that underlie memory, which emerges and improves during middle childhood

pronounced *pot-o*) is paired with a common English word—in this case it might be "pot." The English word is the keyword. Once the keyword is chosen, children then form a mental image of the two words interacting with one another. For instance, a student might use an image of a duck taking a bath in a pot to remember the word *pato*.

Vygotsky's Approach to Cognitive Development and Classroom Instruction

Learning environments can encourage children to adopt these strategies as well. Recall that Russian developmentalist Lev Vygotsky proposed that cognitive advances occur through teaching within a child's *zone of proximal development*, or ZPD. In the ZPD, a child can almost, but not quite, understand or perform a task.

Vygotsky's approach has particularly encouraged the development of classroom practices that promote children's active participation in their learning (for example, Holzman, 1997). Consequently, classrooms are seen as places where children should experiment and try out new activities (Vygotsky, 1926/1997).

According to Vygotsky, education should focus on activities that involve interaction with others. Both child–adult and child–child interactions can promote cognitive growth. The interactions must be carefully structured to fall within each child's zone of proximal development.

Vygotsky's work has influenced several current and noteworthy innovations. For example, *co-operative learning*, where children work in groups to achieve a common goal, uses several aspects of Vygotsky's theory. Students working in co-operative groups benefit from the insights of others. A wrong turn by one child can be corrected by others in the group. On the other hand, not every group member is equally helpful: As Vygotsky's approach would imply, individual children benefit most when some of the group members are more competent at the task and can act as experts (Slavin, 1995; Karpov and Haywood, 1998; Gillies and Boyle, 2006).

> **From an educator's perspective:** Suggest how a teacher might use Vygotsky's approach to teach 10-year-olds about Canadian history.

Reciprocal teaching, a technique to teach reading comprehension strategies, is another practice that reflects Vygotsky's approach to cognitive development. Students learn to skim the content of a passage, ask questions about its meaning, summarize, and predict what will happen next. The reciprocal nature of this technique gives students a chance to adopt the role of teacher. Teachers initially lead students through the comprehension strategies. Gradually, students progress through their zones of proximal development, taking increasing control of the strategies until they assume the teaching role. The method has impressively raised comprehension levels, particularly for students with reading difficulties (Palincsar et al., 1993; Greenway, 2002; Takala, 2006).

Language Development: What Words Mean

If you listen to school-age children, their speech sounds similar to that of adults. However, the apparent similarity is deceiving. The linguistic sophistication of children—particularly early in the school-age period—still needs refining to reach adult levels.

Mastering the Mechanics of Language.   Vocabulary continues to increase rapidly during the school years. The average 6-year-old has a vocabulary of from 8000 to 14 000 words, and another 5000 words appear from ages 9 to 11.

Children's mastery of grammar also improves. For instance, the passive voice is seldom used during the early school-age years (as in "The dog was walked by Jon," compared with the active-voice "Jon walked the dog"). Six- and seven-year-olds rarely use conditional sentences, such as "If Sarah will set the table, I will wash the dishes." During middle childhood, however, the use of passive voice and conditional sentences increases. In addition, children's understanding of *syntax*, the rules governing how words and phrases can be combined to form sentences, grows.

By grade 1, most children pronounce words quite accurately. However, certain *phonemes*, units of sound, remain troublesome. For instance, the ability to pronounce *j*, *v*, *th*, and *zh* sounds develops later.

School-age children also may have trouble decoding sentences when the meaning depends on *intonation*, or tone of voice. Consider the sentence, "George gave a book to David and he gave one to Bill." If the word "he" is emphasized, the meaning is "George gave a book to David and David gave a different book to Bill." But if the word "and" is emphasized then the meaning becomes "George gave a book to David and George also gave a book to Bill." School-age children cannot easily sort out such subtleties (Moshman et al., 1987; Woolfolk, 1993).

Conversational skills also develop as children become more competent in using *pragmatics*, the rules governing the use of language to communicate in social settings.

For example, although children in early childhood are aware of the rules of conversational turn-taking, their use is sometimes primitive. Consider the following conversation between six-year-olds Yonnie and Max:

Yonnie: My dad drives a FedEx truck.

Max: My sister's name is Molly.

Yonnie: He gets up really early in the morning.

Max: She wet her bed last night.

Later, however, conversations show more give and take, with children responding to each other's comments. For instance, this conversation between 11-year-olds Mia and Josh reflects a greater mastery of pragmatics:

Mia: I don't know what to get Claire for her birthday.

Josh: I'm getting her earrings.

Mia: She already has a lot of jewellery   .

Josh: I don't think she has that much.

Metalinguistic Awareness.   A significant development in middle childhood is children's increasing understanding of their own use of language, or **metalinguistic awareness**. By age five or six, they understand that a set of rules governs language. In the early years they learn and comprehend these rules implicitly, but during middle childhood they understand them more explicitly (Kemper and Vernooy, 1994; Benelli et al., 2006).

Metalinguistic awareness helps children's comprehension when information is fuzzy or incomplete. For instance, when preschoolers receive ambiguous or unclear information, such as directions for a complicated game, they rarely ask for clarification, and tend to blame themselves for any confusion. By age seven or eight, children realize that miscommunication may be due to the person communicating with them as well. Consequently, school-age children are more likely to ask for clarifications (Beal and Belgrad, 1990; Kemper and Vernooy, 1994; Apperly and Robinson, 2002).

How Language Promotes Self-Control.   Their growing sophistication with language helps children control and regulate their behaviour. In one experiment, children were told they could have one marshmallow treat if they chose to eat it immediately, but two treats if they waited. Most of the children, who ranged in age from four to eight, chose to wait, but the strategies they used differed significantly.

The four-year-olds often chose to look at the marshmallows while waiting, a strategy that was not terribly effective. In contrast, six- and eight-year-olds used language to help overcome temptation, although in different ways. The six-year-olds spoke and sang to themselves, reminding themselves they would get more treats if they waited. The eight-year-olds focused on aspects of the marshmallows unrelated to taste, such as appearance, which helped them to wait.

In short, children used "self-talk" to regulate their behaviour. Their self-control grew as their linguistic capabilities increased.

Bilingualism and Multilingualism: Speaking in Many Tongues

Rosa grew up the youngest of nine children of Italian immigrants. Growing up in suburban Montreal, she learned both French in school and English in the community. Her mother never learned English, and her older siblings identified Italian as their mother tongue, but were fully

metalinguistic awareness an understanding of one's own use of language

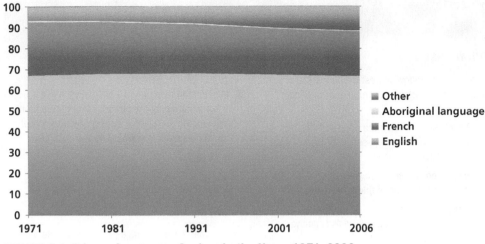

FIGURE 5-4 **Primary Languages Spoken in the Home 1971–2006**
Source: Statistics Canada, 2006 Census of the Population.

fluent in both English and French. Rosa, as the youngest surrounded by English-speaking siblings, never really learned Italian. Yet she never had a problem communicating with her mother—they always communicated through her siblings.

Across Canada, the voices with which children speak are changing. While **bilingualism**—the use of more than one language—is not unusual in Canada, an increasing number of families are also considered multilingual (Statistics Canada, 2006, Census of the Population; see Figure 5-4), speaking a language other than English or French at home, and potentially using both English and French outside the home. On the 2006 Census, 15 percent of Canadian households reported speaking more than one language regularly *within* the home. The combination of English and French represents only 25 percent of these households; 65 percent speak English and another language, and 7 percent speak French and another language. Only 3 percent of Anglophones speak another language at home, compared to 11 percent of Francophones and 47 percent of those who report another "mother tongue."

There are many levels on which to understand the issue of bilingualism and multilingualism. For an increasing number of families, bilingualism begins at birth for children when parents speak different languages. For other children, immigration to Canada puts children in a position of having to learn English or French quickly. For a third group of children, learning and becoming proficient in two or more languages is considered by their parents to be a future advantage. A generation ago, bilingualism for most Canadians meant French and English. Today, there are increasing options and increasing numbers of children learning three languages.

Being bilingual, regardless of the languages, may also offer cognitive advantages. With a wider range of linguistic possibilities to choose from in assessing a situation, speakers of two languages show greater cognitive flexibility. They solve problems with greater creativity and versatility, although this particular finding is controversial. Learning two languages, especially from an early age, might facilitate cognitive flexibility. On the other hand, children who are more cognitively flexible may have an easier time learning a second language. Learning in one's native tongue is also associated with higher self-esteem in minority students (Romaine, 1994; Wright and Taylor, 1995; Barker et al., 2001).

Bilingual students often have greater metalinguistic awareness, understanding the rules of language more explicitly. Some research shows they may score higher on intelligence tests. One survey of French- and English-speaking schoolchildren found that bilingual students scored significantly higher on both verbal and nonverbal tests of intelligence (Lambert and Peal, 1972; Bochner, 1996; Crutchley, 2003; Swanson et al., 2004). Because many linguists believe universal processes underlie language acquisition, native language instruction may enhance instruction in a second language (Perozzi and Sanchez, 1992; Yelland et al., 1993; Kecskes and Papp, 2000).

bilingualism the use of more than one language

REVIEW, CHECK, AND APPLY

REVIEW

- Piaget believed school-age children are in the concrete operational stage, while information-processing approaches focus on quantitative improvements in memory and in the sophistication of the mental programs children use.

- Vygotsky suggests schoolchildren should have the opportunity to experiment and participate actively with their peers in their learning.

- Children gain increasing control over the memory processes—encoding, storage, and retrieval—and the development of metamemory improves cognitive processing and memorization.

- As language develops, vocabulary, syntax, and pragmatics improve, metalinguistic awareness grows, and language is used as a self-control device.

CHECK YOURSELF

1. Which of the following best describes Piaget's approach to cognitive development in middle childhood?

   a. Piaget overestimated the degree to which young children could problem-solve because of the types of tasks he used.

   b. Piaget considered the degree to which culture influences the kind of things we learn.

   c. Piaget's approach provided totally accurate descriptions of young children's cognitive development.

   d. Piaget's theory has had powerful implications for schools and educational materials.

2. Children who have the ability to focus on more than one aspect of a problem at a time are capable of _____.

   a. centring

   b. decentring

   c. irreversibility

   d. mental repression

3. As children reach middle childhood they get better at understanding the processes that underlie their own memory, including strategies for doing better on tasks requiring memory.

   - True

   - False

APPLYING LIFESPAN DEVELOPMENT

- Do adults use language (and self-talk) as a self-control device? How?

Answers: 1) d; 2) b; 3) True

Schooling: The Three Rs (and More) of Middle Childhood

LEARNING OBJECTIVES

LO6   What are some trends in schooling today?

As the six other children in his reading group turned to him, Glenn shifted uneasily in his chair. Reading was hard for him, and he always felt anxious when asked to read aloud. But with his teacher's encouraging nod, he plunged in, hesitant at first, then gaining momentum as he read the story of a mother's first day on a new job. He was happy and proud to find that he could read the passage quite nicely. He broke into a broad smile when his teacher said, "Well done, Glenn."

Such moments, repeated over and over, make—or break—a child's educational experience. School is society's formal attempt to transfer its accumulated knowledge, beliefs, values, and wisdom to new generations. The success of this transfer determines, in a very real sense, the future fortunes of the world, as well as the success of each student.

Schooling Around the World and across Genders: Who Gets Educated?

In most developed countries, a primary school education is both a universal right and a legal requirement. Virtually all children in developed countries enjoy a free education through grade 12.

Elsewhere, children are not always so fortunate. More than 160 million of the world's children do not even receive a primary education. An additional 100 million children are educated only to a level comparable to our elementary school, and close to a billion individuals (two-thirds of them women) are illiterate throughout their lives.

In almost all developing countries, fewer females than males receive formal education, a discrepancy found at every level of schooling. Even in developed countries, women lag behind men in their exposure to science and technological topics. These differences reflect widespread, deeply held cultural and parental biases that favour males over females. Boys and girls in Canada share equal access to educational opportunities, especially in the early years.

Reading: Learning to Decipher the Meaning Behind Words

The efforts of Lucy (described in the prologue) to improve her reading are significant, for there is no task more fundamental to learning than reading. Reading involves a significant number of skills, from low-level cognitive skills (the identification of single letters and letter–sound association) to higher-level skills (matching written words with meanings stored in memory, and using context and prior knowledge to determine a sentence's meaning).

In almost all developing countries, more males than females receive formal education.

Reading Stages. Learning to read usually occurs in several broad and frequently overlapping stages (Chall, 1979, 1992). In *Stage 0*, from birth to grade 1, children learn the prerequisites for reading, including letter identification, recognition of familiar words (such as their name or "stop" on a stop sign), and perhaps writing their name.

Stage 1, in grades 1 and 2, introduces real reading, but it largely involves *phonological recoding* skills. At this stage, children sound out words by blending the letters together. They also finish learning their letters and the corresponding sounds.

In *Stage 2*, typically in grades 2 and 3, children learn to read aloud with fluency. However, the effort involved in sounding out words leaves little energy to process their meaning. Lucy's flawless reading of *James and the Giant Peach* shows that she has attained this stage.

In *Stage 3*, grades 4 to 8, reading becomes a means to an end. Whereas earlier reading was its own accomplishment, by this point children read to learn about the world. However, even at this age, comprehension is not complete. For instance, comprehension depends on the information being presented from a single perspective.

In the final period, *Stage 4*, children can read and process information that reflects multiple viewpoints. This ability, starting with the transition to high school, permits children a far more sophisticated understanding of material. Great works of literature are not read at earlier stages, partly because younger children lack the necessary vocabulary, but mostly because they lack the ability to understand the multiple viewpoints presented in sophisticated literature.

How Should We Teach Reading? Educators have long been engaged in a debate over the most effective means of teaching reading. This debate centres on a disagreement about how information is processed during reading. According to proponents of *code-based approaches to reading*, teachers should focus on the basic skills that underlie reading. Code-based approaches emphasize the components of reading, such as letter sounds and combinations—phonics—and how letters and sounds combine to make words. They suggest that reading consists of processing the components of words, combining them into words, and using these to derive the meaning of sentences and passages (Vellutino, 1991; Jimenez and Guzman, 2003; Gray et al., 2007).

In contrast, some educators argue that the most successful approach is *whole language*, which regards reading as a natural process, similar to the acquisition of oral language. According to this view, children learn to read through authentic writing, such as sentences, stories, poems, lists, and charts. Rather than sounding out words, children make guesses about the meaning of words based on the context. Children become proficient readers, learning whole words and phrases through such a trial-and-error approach (Shaw, 2003; Sousa, 2005; Donat, 2006).

In Canada, decisions about how to best teach children to read are often made by individual school boards, and many of these curriculum decisions reflect the unique needs of the students

cultural assimilation model the model that fostered the view of American society as the proverbial melting pot

pluralistic society model the concept that Canadian society is made up of diverse, coequal cultural groups that should preserve their individual cultural features

bicultural identity maintaining one's original cultural identity while integrating oneself into the dominant culture

multicultural education a form of education in which the goal is to help minority students develop confidence in the culture of the majority group while maintaining positive group identities that build on their original cultures

they serve; approximately half of children pick up reading using a whole languge approach, and half learn better with a code-based approach. The Canadian Language and Literacy Research Network (2009) does not endorse a single method as superior, but rather emphasizes that literacy begins at birth and at home. According to the Canadian Language and Literacy Research Network, 1 in 5 children enter school without the necessary early language and literacy skills, and 42 percent of adults lack the literacy skills to fully participate in society.

Educational Trends: Beyond the Three *R*s

As the Canadian population becomes more diverse, elementary schools are paying increased attention to student diversity issues and multiculturalism. And with good reason: Cultural as well as language differences affect students socially and educationally.

Cultural Assimilation or Pluralistic Society? Traditionally, public school was the great melting pot where children from minority cultures came together to be taught the dominant culture in the dominant language. The **cultural assimilation model** has the goal of assimilating individual cultural identities into a unique, unified culture. In practice in the public school system this meant that non-English speakers were discouraged from using their native language and were totally immersed in English (or, in Quebec, non-French speakers were immersed in French).

> **From an educator's perspective:** Should one goal of society be to foster the cultural assimilation of children from other cultures? Why or why not? What was your experience as a child? To what extent was diversity emphasized in your school versus our common Canadian culture?

But isn't Canada's official multiculturalism model that of a **pluralistic society model**, in which society is made up of diverse, coequal cultural groups that preserve their unique cultural features? Welcome to the paradox of multicultural education in Canada.

There are signs that the pluralistic model is infiltrating schools. The pluralistic model grew in part from the belief that teachers who emphasized the dominant culture and discouraged nonnative English speakers from using their native tongues in effect devalued subcultural heritages and lowered the self-esteem of those students. Instructional materials inevitably feature culture-specific events and understandings. Thus, minority children might never be exposed to important aspects of their culture. This practice has been particularly devastating for Aboriginal children who risked missing important components of their heritage.

In recent years, educators have argued that students from diverse cultures enrich and broaden the education of all students. Pupils and teachers exposed to other cultures better understand the world and become sensitive to the values and practices of others.

Fostering a Bicultural Identity. Most educators now agree that minority children should develop a **bicultural identity**, where schools support children's original cultural identities while also integrating them into the dominant culture. In this view, an individual lives as a member of two cultures, with two cultural identities, without having to choose one over the other (Lu, 2001; Oyserman et al., 2003; Vyas, 2004).

The best way to achieve this goal is not clear. Consider children who enter school speaking only Hindi. A "melting-pot" technique would immerse them in classes taught in English while providing a crash course in English language (and little else) until the children gain a reasonable proficiency. Unfortunately, this approach has a major drawback: Until they are proficient, students fall farther and farther behind their peers (First and Cardenas, 1986).

More contemporary bicultural approaches encourage children to maintain membership in more than one culture. For a Hindi-speaking child, instruction would begin in Hindi and shift rapidly to include English. The school would also conduct a multicultural program for all children, where material on the cultures of all students is presented. Such instruction is meant to enhance the self-image of every student (Wright and Taylor, 1995; Bracey et al., 2004; Fowers and Davidov, 2006).

Although most experts favour bicultural approaches, the general public does not always agree. Having two official languages, and recognizing the status of Aboriginal languages complicates matters further. Across Canada, children may be educated in a multitude of languages.

Cultural Dimensions

Multicultural Education

Classrooms in Canada have always been populated by students with diverse backgrounds and experiences. Only recently, though, have variations in student backgrounds been viewed as a major challenge—and opportunity—that educators face.

In fact, this diversity in the classroom relates to a fundamental objective of education, which is to transmit the information a society deems important. As the famous anthropologist Margaret Mead (1942) once said, "In its broadest sense, education is the cultural process, the way in which each newborn human infant, born with a potentiality for learning greater than that of any other mammal, is transformed into a full member of a specific human society, sharing with the other members of a specific human culture" (p. 633).

Culture, then, can be seen as a set of behaviours, beliefs, values, and expectations shared by the members of a society. But culture is not simply "Western culture" or "Asian culture." It is also made up of *subcultural* groups. Membership in a cultural or subcultural group might be of minor concern to educators if it didn't substantially impact the way students experience school. In recent years, considerable thought has gone into providing **multicultural education**, with the goal of helping students develop competence in the majority culture while maintaining positive group identities built on their original cultures (Nieto, 2005).

Pupils and teachers exposed to a diverse group could better understand the world and gain a greater sensitivity to the values and needs of others. What are some ways of developing greater sensitivity in the classroom?

REVIEW, CHECK, AND APPLY

REVIEW

- Schooling is considered a legal right in many countries, but millions of the world's children do not receive even a primary education.

- Reading skills generally develop in several stages.

- When children are educated in a second language, learning the new language may overshadow learning material and the students risk falling behind.

CHECK YOURSELF

1. According to the _____ approach to reading, reading should be taught by presenting the basic skills underlying reading. Examples include phonics and how letters and words are combined to make words.

   a. whole-language

   b. linguistic

   c. code-based

   d. dynamic

2. The goal of multicultural education is to help minority students develop competence in the culture of the majority group while maintaining positive group identities that build on their original cultures.

   - True
   - False

APPLYING LIFESPAN DEVELOPMENT

- Do you think that the emphasis on the traditional three *R*s in middle school is appropriate? Do less "academic" subjects have a place in the regular curriculum, or should they be dealt with as "add-ons" and after-school activities. Why?

Answers: 1) c; 2) True

Intelligence: Determining Individual Strengths

L07 How can intelligence be measured, and how are exceptional children educated?

LEARNING OBJECTIVES

"Why should you tell the truth?" "How far is Vancouver from Yellowknife?" "A table is made of wood; a window of _____."

The Wechsler Intelligence Scale for Children–Fourth Edition (WISC-IV) is widely used as an intelligence test that measures verbal and performance (non-verbal) skills.

As 10-year-old Petra sat hunched over her desk, faced with a series of questions like these, she tried to guess the point of the test she was taking. Clearly, the test covered material not discussed by her grade 5 teacher, Ms. Forsythe.

"What number comes next in this series: 1, 3, 7, 15, 31, _____?"

As she worked through the test, she gave up trying to guess its rationale. She'd leave that to her teacher and simply try to figure out the correct answers.

Petra was taking an intelligence test. It might surprise her to learn that others also questioned the meaning and importance of the test. Intelligence test items are painstakingly prepared, and the tests are designed to predict academic success (for reasons we'll soon discuss).

Understanding just what intelligence means has proven a major challenge for researchers in defining what separates intelligent from unintelligent behaviour. Although nonexperts have their own definitions (one survey found that laypersons view intelligence as three components: problem-solving ability, verbal ability, and social competence), it has been more difficult for experts to concur (Sternberg et al., 1981; Howe, 1997). Still, a general definition of intelligence is possible: **Intelligence** is the capacity to understand the world, think with rationality, and use resources effectively when faced with challenges (Wechsler, 1975).

To understand how researchers have variously approached the task of defining intelligence and devising *intelligence tests*, we need to consider some of the historical milestones in this area.

Intelligence Benchmarks: Differentiating the Intelligent from the Unintelligent

Paris schools faced a problem as the twentieth century began: Regular instruction was failing many students. The French Minister of Instruction asked psychologist Alfred Binet to devise a method for identifying students who might benefit from special instruction.

Binet's Test. Binet took a practical approach. Years of observation suggested that prior tests for intelligence—some based on reaction time or eyesight—were ineffectual. Binet, using a trial-and-error approach, administered items and tasks to students identified as either "bright" or "dull." He retained the tasks that the bright students completed correctly and the dull students failed. Tasks that did not discriminate were discarded. The end result was a test that reliably distinguished fast and slow learners.

Binet's pioneering efforts left three important legacies. The first was his pragmatic approach to constructing intelligence tests. Binet did not have theoretical preconceptions about what intelligence was. Instead, he used a trial-and-error approach to psychological measurement that continues to be the predominant approach to test construction. His definition of intelligence as *that which his test measured* has been adopted by many modern researchers, and it is particularly popular among test developers who wish to avoid arguments about the underlying nature of intelligence.

Binet's legacy links intelligence and school success. His approach to constructing a test ensured that intelligence—defined as performance on the test—and school success would be virtually identical. Thus, Binet's intelligence test, and today's tests that use his methods, are reasonable predictors of school performance. They do not, however, provide useful information for other attributes, such as social skills or personality traits, which are largely unrelated to academic proficiency.

Finally, Binet developed a method to link each intelligence test score with a **mental age**—the age of the children who, on average, achieved that score. If a 6-year-old girl scored 30 on the test, and this was the average score for 10-year-olds, her mental age would be 10. Similarly, a 15-year-old boy who scored a 90—matching the mean score for 15-year-olds—would have a mental age of 15.

The mental age (MA) and **chronological age (CA)** in combination provide a measure of *relative* intelligence—the **intelligence quotient**, or **IQ score**. The traditional method of calculating an IQ score uses the following formula, in which MA equals mental age and CA equals chronological age:

intelligence the capacity to understand the world, think with rationality, and use resources effectively when faced with challenges

mental age the typical intelligence level found for people at a given chronological age

chronological age the actual age of the child taking the intelligence test

intelligence quotient (or IQ score) a score that accounts for a student's mental and chronological age

$$IQ\ score = \frac{MA}{CA} \times 100$$

Stanford-Binet Intelligence Scales, Fifth Edition (SB5) a test consisting of a series of items that vary according to the age of the person being tested

Wechsler Intelligence Scale for Children, Fourth Edition (WISC-IV) a test for children that provides separate measures of verbal and performance (or nonverbal) skills, as well as a total score

As this formula demonstrates, people whose mental age is equal to their chronological age will always have an IQ of 100. If the chronological age exceeds the mental age (implying below-average intelligence), the score will be below 100; and if the chronological age is lower than the mental age (suggesting above-average intelligence), the score will be above 100.

Using this formula, known as the ratio IQ, consider our example of a 14-year-old who scores a mental age of 16. This student's IQ is 16/14 × 100, or 114. In comparison, the IQ of a 6-year-old scoring a mental age of 8 is 8/6 × 100, or 133—a higher IQ score.

IQ scores today are calculated in a more complex and sophisticated manner (in part because the tests are more complex). Rather than identify at which age a given performance would be average, the performance of all children in an age group is ranked and standardized. The average IQ score is set at 100; exactly half of the population should score above, and half should score below this point. Two-thirds of all people fall within 15 points of 100, scoring between 85 and 115 (see Figure 5-5). Beyond this range, the percentage of people in the same score category drops significantly. The old ratio IQ formula continues to be used today to estimate mental age for children who are particularly high or low functioning.

Measuring IQ: Present-Day Approaches to Intelligence. Since Binet, intelligence tests have become increasingly accurate measures of IQ, though most remain rooted in his original work. For example, one of the most widely used tests—the **Stanford-Binet Intelligence Scales, Fifth Edition (SB5)**—began as an American revision of Binet's original test. The test consists of age-appropriate items—for example, young children are asked about everyday activities or given complex figures to copy. Older people are asked to explain proverbs, solve analogies, and describe similarities between word groups. Test takers are given progressively more difficult problems to determine the most difficult item that can be completed.

The **Wechsler Intelligence Scale for Children, Fourth Edition (WISC-IV)** is another widely used test. The test (an offshoot of the *Wechsler Adult Intelligence Scale*) breaks the total score into measures of verbal and performance (or non-verbal) skills. As you can see from

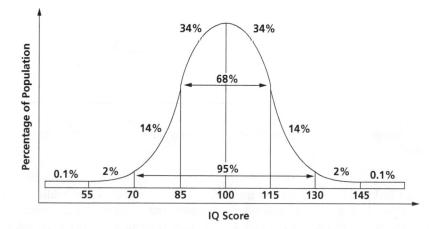

FIGURE 5-5 IQ Score Distribution
IQ test scores today are *standardized* so that in any given age group the average performance will be 100. Two-thirds of test takers will score between 85 and 115, which is considered average performance. Only 5 percent of test-takers will score below 70 or above 130.

Name	Goal of Item	Example
Verbal Scale		
Information	Assess general information	How many nickels make a dime?
Comprehension	Assess understanding and evaluation of social norms and past experience	What is the advantage of keeping money in the bank?
Arithmetic	Assess math reasoning through verbal problems	If two buttons cost 15 cents, what will be the cost of a dozen buttons?
Similarities	Test understanding of how objects or concepts are alike, tapping abstract reasoning	In what way are an hour and a week alike?
Performance Scale		
Digit symbol	Assess speed of learning	Match symbols to numbers using key. 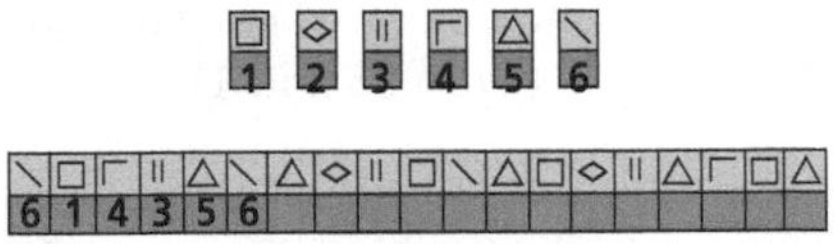
Picture completion	Visual memory and attention	Identify what is missing. 
Object assembly	Test understanding of relationship of parts to wholes	Put pieces together to form a whole. 

FIGURE 5-6 Measuring Intelligence
The Wechsler Intelligence Scales for Children (WISC-IV) includes items such as these. What do such items cover? What do they miss?

Kaufman Assessment Battery for Children, Second Edition (KABC-II) an intelligence test that measures children's ability to integrate different stimuli simultaneously and to use step-by-step thinking

Figure 5-6, word problems are used to test skills such as comprehension, while typical nonverbal tasks include copying a complex design, sequencing pictures, and assembling objects. The test's separate portions make it easier to identify specific problems a test taker might have. For example, significantly higher scores on the performance part than on the verbal part may indicate linguistic development difficulties (Zhu and Weiss, 2005).

The **Kaufman Assessment Battery for Children, Second Edition (KABC-II)** takes a different approach. It tests children's ability to integrate different kinds of stimuli simultaneously and to use sequential thinking. The KABC-II's special virtue is its flexibility. It allows the test giver to use alternative wording or gestures, or even to pose questions in a different language, in order to maximize performance. This makes testing more valid and equitable for children to whom English is a second language (Kaufman et al., 2005).

What do the IQ scores mean? For most children, they are reasonable predictors of school performance. That's not surprising, given that intelligence tests were developed to identify students who were having difficulties (Sternberg and Grigorenko, 2002).

But the story differs for performance outside of school; for example, although people with higher scores tend to finish more years of schooling, once this is statistically controlled for, IQ scores do not closely relate to income and later success in life. Two people with different scores might both earn a bachelor's degree at the same college, but the person with a lower IQ might have a higher income and a more successful career. These difficulties with traditional IQ scores have led researchers to consider alternative approaches (McClelland, 1993).

What IQ Tests Don't Tell: Alternative Conceptions of Intelligence. The intelligence tests used most today regard intelligence as a single factor, a unitary mental ability. This attribute is commonly called *g* (Spearman, 1927; Lubinski, 2004). Assumed to underlie performance on every aspect of intelligence, the *g* factor is what IQ tests presumably measure.

However, many theorists disagree that intelligence is unidimensional. Some developmentalists suggest that two kinds of intelligence exist: fluid and crystallized (Catell, 1967, 1987). **Fluid intelligence** reflects information-processing capabilities, reasoning, and memory; for example, a student asked to group a series of letters according to some criterion or to remember a set of numbers would be using fluid intelligence. In contrast, **crystallized intelligence** is the cumulative information, skills, and strategies people have learned and can apply in solving problems. A student would likely use crystallized intelligence to solve a puzzle or find the solution to a mystery (McGrew, 2005; Alfonso et al., 2005). Fluid intelligence could be tuned with practice, but crystallized intelligence is very much a product of education and environment.

Other theorists divide intelligence into even more parts. Psychologist Howard Gardner suggests that we have at least eight distinct intelligences, each relatively independent (see Figure 5-7). Gardner suggests that these intelligences operate together, depending on the activity we engage in (Gardner, 2000, 2003; Chen and Gardner, 2005; Gardner and Moran, 2006).

From an educator's perspective: Does Howard Gardner's theory of multiple intelligences suggest that classroom instruction should be modified from an emphasis on the traditional 3Rs of reading, writing, and arithmetic?

Russian psychologist Lev Vygotsky, whose cognitive development approach we discussed earlier, took a very different approach to intelligence. He suggested we assess intelligence by looking not only at fully developed cognitive processes, but those in current development as well. To do this, he contended that assessment tasks should involve co-operative interaction between the assessed individual and the assessor—a process called *dynamic assessment*. In short, intelligence is reflected both in how children perform on their own and how they perform when helped by adults (Vygotsky, 1926/1976; Daniels, 1996; Brown and Ferrara, 1999).

Psychologist Robert Sternberg (1987, 1990, 2003a), taking another approach, suggests intelligence is best viewed as information-processing. In this view, how people store material in memory and later use it to solve intellectual tasks provides the most precise concept of intelligence. Rather than focusing on the subcomponents that make up the *structure* of intelligence, information-processing approaches examine the *processes* underlying intelligent behaviour.

Studies of the nature and speed of problem-solving processes show that people with higher intelligence levels differ from others in the number of problems they solve and the methods they use. People with high IQ scores spend more time on the initial stages of problem solving, retrieving relevant information from memory. In contrast, those who score lower tend to skip ahead and make less-informed guesses. The processes used in solving problems might reflect important differences in intelligence (Sternberg, 1982, 1990).

Sternberg's work on information-processing approaches led him to develop the **triarchic theory of intelligence**. In this model, three aspects of information-processing denote intelligence: the componential/analytic, the experiential/creative, and the contextual/practical. The *componential* aspect reflects how efficiently people process and analyze information.

fluid intelligence intelligence that reflects information-processing capabilities, reasoning, and memory

crystallized intelligence the accumulation of information, skills, and strategies that people have learned through experience and that they can apply to problem-solving

triarchic theory of intelligence a model that states that intelligence consists of three aspects of information-processing: the componential element, the experiential element, and the contextual element

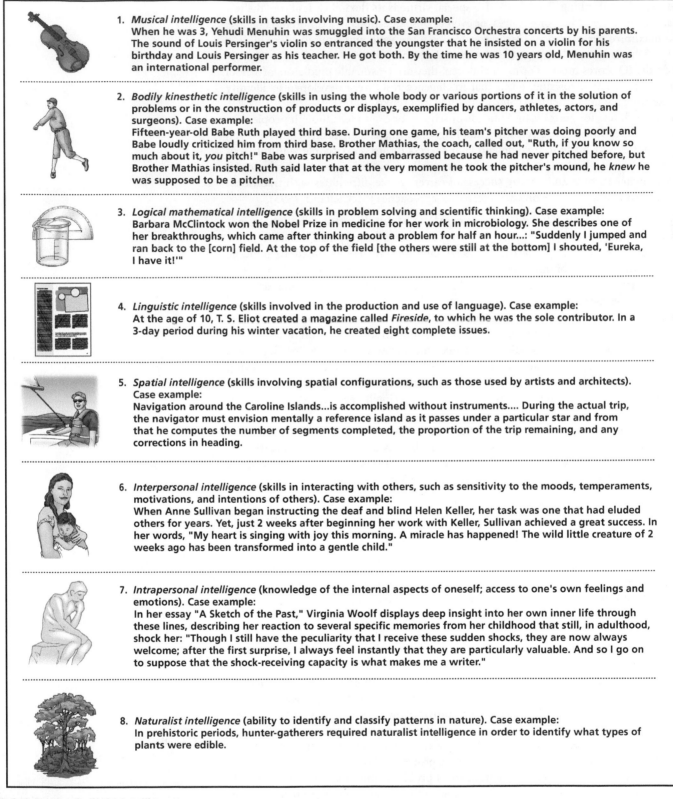

1. *Musical intelligence* (skills in tasks involving music). Case example:
   When he was 3, Yehudi Menuhin was smuggled into the San Francisco Orchestra concerts by his parents. The sound of Louis Persinger's violin so entranced the youngster that he insisted on a violin for his birthday and Louis Persinger as his teacher. He got both. By the time he was 10 years old, Menuhin was an international performer.

2. *Bodily kinesthetic intelligence* (skills in using the whole body or various portions of it in the solution of problems or in the construction of products or displays, exemplified by dancers, athletes, actors, and surgeons). Case example:
   Fifteen-year-old Babe Ruth played third base. During one game, his team's pitcher was doing poorly and Babe loudly criticized him from third base. Brother Mathias, the coach, called out, "Ruth, if you know so much about it, *you* pitch!" Babe was surprised and embarrassed because he had never pitched before, but Brother Mathias insisted. Ruth said later that at the very moment he took the pitcher's mound, he *knew* he was supposed to be a pitcher.

3. *Logical mathematical intelligence* (skills in problem solving and scientific thinking). Case example:
   Barbara McClintock won the Nobel Prize in medicine for her work in microbiology. She describes one of her breakthroughs, which came after thinking about a problem for half an hour...: "Suddenly I jumped and ran back to the [corn] field. At the top of the field [the others were still at the bottom] I shouted, 'Eureka, I have it!'"

4. *Linguistic intelligence* (skills involved in the production and use of language). Case example:
   At the age of 10, T. S. Eliot created a magazine called *Fireside*, to which he was the sole contributor. In a 3-day period during his winter vacation, he created eight complete issues.

5. *Spatial intelligence* (skills involving spatial configurations, such as those used by artists and architects). Case example:
   Navigation around the Caroline Islands...is accomplished without instruments.... During the actual trip, the navigator must envision mentally a reference island as it passes under a particular star and from that he computes the number of segments completed, the proportion of the trip remaining, and any corrections in heading.

6. *Interpersonal intelligence* (skills in interacting with others, such as sensitivity to the moods, temperaments, motivations, and intentions of others). Case example:
   When Anne Sullivan began instructing the deaf and blind Helen Keller, her task was one that had eluded others for years. Yet, just 2 weeks after beginning her work with Keller, Sullivan achieved a great success. In her words, "My heart is singing with joy this morning. A miracle has happened! The wild little creature of 2 weeks ago has been transformed into a gentle child."

7. *Intrapersonal intelligence* (knowledge of the internal aspects of oneself; access to one's own feelings and emotions). Case example:
   In her essay "A Sketch of the Past," Virginia Woolf displays deep insight into her own inner life through these lines, describing her reaction to several specific memories from her childhood that still, in adulthood, shock her: "Though I still have the peculiarity that I receive these sudden shocks, they are now always welcome; after the first surprise, I always feel instantly that they are particularly valuable. And so I go on to suppose that the shock-receiving capacity is what makes me a writer."

8. *Naturalist intelligence* (ability to identify and classify patterns in nature). Case example:
   In prehistoric periods, hunter-gatherers required naturalist intelligence in order to identify what types of plants were edible.

FIGURE 5-7 Gardner's Eight Intelligences
Howard Gardner has theorized that there are eight distinct intelligences, each relatively independent.
Source: From "Gardner's Eight Intelligences" from Walters, E., and Gardner, H. (1986). The theory of multiple intelligences: Some issues and answers. In R. J. Sternberg and R. K. Wagner (Eds.) *Practical Intelligence*. Cambridge, England: Cambridge University Press.

Efficiency here allows people to infer relationships among different parts of a problem, solve the problem, and then evaluate their solution. People with a strong componential element score highest on traditional tests of intelligence (Sternberg, 2005).

The *experiential* element is the insightful component of intelligence. People with a strong experiential element can easily compare new material with what they know, and can combine and relate known facts in novel and creative ways. Finally, the *contextual* element concerns practical intelligence, or ways of dealing with everyday demands. The contextual element includes skills such as social skills and "street smarts"—elements clearly missing from traditional IQ tests.

In Sternberg's view, people vary in the degree to which they possess each of these elements. Our level of success at any task reflects the match between the task and our own pattern of strength on these three components (Sternberg, 1991, 2003b, 2007).

Group Differences in IQ

A "jontry" is an example of a

   (a) rulpow

   (b) flink

   (c) spudge

   (d) bakwoe

If you found an item composed of nonsense words such as this on an intelligence test, you would likely complain. What sort of intelligence test uses items that incorporate meaningless terms?

Yet for some people, the items used on traditional intelligence tests might appear nonsensical. As a hypothetical example, suppose rural children were asked details about subways, while urban students were asked about the mating practices of sheep. In both cases, we would expect the test takers' prior experiences to substantially affect their ability to answer the questions. On an IQ test, such questions could rightly be seen as a measure of prior experience rather than of intelligence.

⊙ **Watch** on **mydevelopmentlab**

How is your virtual child doing in school? Do you think that standardized testing should be used to assess his or her performance in school? Watch Robert Guthrie discuss the validity of intelligence tests on MyDevelopmentLab.

Performance on traditional IQ tests is dependent in part on test-takers' prior experiences and cultural background. How might formal schooling or farming influence a child's performance on a traditional IQ test?

Although traditional IQ tests are not so obviously dependent upon test takers' prior experiences, cultural background and experience can affect test scores. In fact, many feel that traditional measures of intelligence are culturally biased (Ortiz and Dynda, 2005). Subtle differences, for example in language usage, require that even different countries that appear to share a common language like English have to have unique sets of norms for comparing performance. We cannot directly compare children from Alberta, Texas, and Australia.

Explaining Group Differences in IQ. How cultural background and experience affect IQ test scores has led to much debate among researchers, fuelled by the finding that certain ethnic groups' IQ scores are consistently higher or lower, on average, than those of other groups. For example, the mean score of Blacks tends to be lower than the mean score of whites, which tends to be lower than the mean score of Asians—although the measured difference varies a great deal depending on the IQ test employed (Fish, 2001; Maller, 2003).

The question that emerges from such differences is whether they reflect differences in intelligence or biases in intelligence tests. For example, if one group outperforms another on an IQ test, is it because they are more familiar with the language of the test items? Is it because one group is more familiar with the process of test taking? Is it because one group has more experience with the types of questions or problems presented on the test? Some researchers have used racial and gender differences in IQ as arguments for genetically based differences, implying that from birth one group has greater potential than another (for example, Herrnstein and Murray, 1994). Other researchers argue that race does not really exist on a genetic level, but that culture, which is often intertwined with social constructions of race, exerts a very powerful influence on what children do with their potential.

Take the stereotype of the Asian mathematics advantage. Is the difference due to genetic differences in mathematical abilities? Or is it more likely the result of cultural differences in both educational practice and attitude. For example, researchers compared students in Japan and the United States, two countries in which students show very different mathematics abilities. They found that Japanese schools spend more time and place greater emphasis on mathematics instruction and mastery than do American schools. But they also found that Japanese parents and teachers believe more strongly in effort than inborn competence. When the culture as a whole communicates to children that a skill is important and that everyone can master it if they just keep trying, it's not surprising that children achieve more. In contrast, a cultural message that abilities are inborn communicates to children that if at first they don't succeed, they should give up and do something else (Stigler and Stevenson, 1991; Serpell and Hatano, 1997).

> ◯➔ **From an educator's perspective:** Canadian students' mathematics performance is much more similar to that of Japanese students than American students. Is this performance better explained by genetic or cultural differences?

This boy with Down's syndrome is participating fully in his grade 5 class.

Similarly, Jelani Mandara argues that, over generations, minority groups such as African Americans internalized the racism they experienced, creating a culture that de-emphasized academic achievement. This cultural attitude toward education then led children to underachieve and expect little. When socioeconomic status and related factors (such as parental education levels and attitudes toward education) are matched between Black students and white students, the academic disparity disappears (Mandara, 2011).

Most experts agree that intelligence is equally influenced by genetics and environment. Genes are seen to affect experiences, and experiences are viewed as influencing the expression of genes. Psychologist Eric Turkheimer found evidence that while environmental factors play a larger role in the IQ of poor children, genes are more influential for affluent children. If we focus on the large portion that is environmentally determined, modifying social and educational conditions is a more promising strategy to increase cognitive functioning (Turkheimer et al., 2003; Weiss, 2003).

Ultimately, determining the absolute degree to which intelligence is influenced by genetic and environmental factors may be less important than improving children's living conditions and educational experiences.

Enriching the quality of children's environments will better permit all children to reach their full potential and to maximize their contributions to society (Wachs, 1996; Wickelgren, 1999; Posthuma and de Geus, 2006).

Below and Above Intelligence Norms: Intellectual Disabilities and Intellectual Giftedness

Although Connie kept pace with her peers in kindergarten, by grade 1, she was academically the slowest in almost every subject. She tried hard, but it took her longer than the others to absorb new material, and she regularly required special attention to keep up with the class.

In some areas, though, she excelled: When asked to draw or produce something with her hands, her performance exceeded her classmates'. She produced beautiful work that was much admired. The other students in the class felt that there was something different about Connie, but they couldn't identify the source of the difference and spent little time pondering the issue.

Connie's parents and teacher, though, knew what made her special. Extensive testing in kindergarten had shown that Connie's intelligence was well below normal, and she was officially classified as a student with special needs.

If Connie had been attending school a generation ago, she would most likely have been placed in a special needs classroom as soon as her low IQ was identified. Such students—with a range of afflictions including emotional difficulties, severe reading problems, and physical disabilities such as multiple sclerosis, as well those with lower IQs—were usually kept separate from the regular educational process, either in special schools, or **mainstreamed**, a term for a special education classroom within a regular school allowing for social interaction but separating children for academic instruction.

Today, the most prevalent philosophy is termed **inclusive education**. Inclusive education is the integration of all students, even the most severely disabled, into regular classes, thereby eliminating separate special education programs. In theory, it is the model that best serves the child with a disability by providing a fully integrated life, promoting social skills, daily living skills, and academic skills to the best of the individual's ability. Inclusion is also beneficial to the students without special needs in the classroom, as it promotes acceptance and accommodation of those who are differently abled from an early age.

Inclusion is not a cheaper alternative to special education classes or special schools, and when the necessary supports are not made available, children are set up to fail. Because this sometimes happens, inclusion is a controversial philosophy. Parents and teachers sometimes perceive that the child with special needs is monopolizing the teacher's time, and parents of children with special needs sometimes prefer the increased support provided in special education classrooms or separate specialized schools (Kavale and Forness, 2000; Kavale, 2002; Brehm, 2003; Gersten and Dimino, 2006).

Regardless of how they are educated, children whose intelligence is significantly beyond the typical range represent a challenge for educators. We will consider both those who are below and those above the norms.

Below the Norm: Intellectual Disability (Mental Retardation). Approximately 2 percent of the population is considered to have an intellectual disability. **Intellectual disability**—also known as **mental retardation**—is characterized by significant limitations in intellectual functioning and in adaptive behaviour involving conceptual, social, and practical skills (AAMR, 2002). Although educators increasingly use the terms *intellectual disabilities*, *developmental delay*, and *cognitive impairment*, "mental retardation" continues to be a widely used medical term (although people who consider the term offensive will be pleased that its use is fading). Because intelligence is so highly valued in our society, labelling is particularly difficult with this population because they continue to be marginalized, regardless of the term used to describe them.

 From an educator's perspective: What is the difference between saying a child is impaired versus saying a child has an impairment? What is the difference between calling a child "retarded" and calling a child "gifted"? How do labelling and the language of labels affect children?

mainstreamed an approach in which children with special needs attend the same school as children without special needs, sharing social activities but learning in a separate class

inclusive education an educational approach in which children with special needs are integrated into the traditional classroom and are provided with a broad range of in-class supports

intellectual disability (mental retardation) a significantly below-average level of intellectual functioning that occurs with related limitations in two or more skill areas

Most cases of intellectual disability are classified as *familial*, meaning that no cause is apparent beyond a history of lower IQ in the family. These individuals tend to have IQs between 60 and 70 and, in many respects, reflect the simple fact that, by definition, 2.5 percent of individuals have to be in the left-most end of the IQ distribution. For a 10-year-old, this means functioning three to four years behind peers; however, education, future employment, and adult independent living are very reasonable aspirations. Among most individuals with very low IQs there is a clear biological—or *organic*—cause. The most common such causes are genetic errors such as *Down's syndrome*, caused by the presence of an extra chromosome. Birth complications, such as a temporary lack of oxygen or exposure to toxins in utero, can also lead to intellectual disability. *Fetal alcohol syndrome*, resulting from the mother's use of alcohol while pregnant, is the most common preventable developmental disorder (Burd, 2003; Plomin, 2005; West and Blake, 2005; Manning and Hoyme, 2007).

Intellectual disability is diagnosed not only on the basis of low IQ but also on delays in adaptive functioning, also known as daily living skills. Examples include dressing independently, preparing a cold snack or meal, or walking to and from school independently. Significant variation exists in the abilities of people with delays, ranging from those who can be taught to work and function with little special attention to those who are virtually untrainable and who never develop speech or such basic motor skills as crawling or walking. Even two individuals with the same scores on an IQ test may have very different levels of adaptive functioning. Each child is unique, and special needs must be assessed on an individual basis. Many could grow up to lead independent or semi-independent lives; others require permanent care.

Above the Norm: Gifted.

Her first words were a two-word sentence when she was barely eight months old. By 18 months she recognized signs for Sobeys and Sears, as well as her own name. By age three, her preschool teacher commented that her vocabulary was bigger than the teacher's, and she could read a few words.

It sometimes surprises people that the gifted and talented are considered to have a form of exceptionality, with needs as special as those with very low IQs. Yet the 2.5 percent of children at the right-most end of the IQ distribution present special challenges of their own.

There is no formal agreed upon definition of **gifted** students, but many researchers accept the measure of IQ greater than 130. In addition to intellectual exceptionality, unusual potential in nonacademic areas is also included in the concept. Gifted and talented children, no less than students with low IQs, warrant special concern—although programs for them are often the first to be dropped when schools face budgetary problems (Robinson et al., 2000; Schemo, 2004; Mendoza, 2006).

Despite the stereotype that labels the gifted "unsociable," "poorly adjusted," and "neurotic," research suggests that highly intelligent people tend to be outgoing, well adjusted, and popular (Howe, 2004; Bracken and Brown, 2006; Shaunessy et al., 2006).

For instance, one landmark, long-term study of 1500 gifted students, which began in the 1920s, found that the gifted were healthier, better coordinated, and psychologically better adjusted than their less intelligent classmates. Furthermore, they received more awards and distinctions, earned more money, and made many more contributions in art and literature than the average person. By the time they had reached age 40, they had collectively produced more than 90 books, 375 plays and short stories, and 2000 articles, and they had registered more than 200 patents. Perhaps not surprisingly, they reported greater satisfaction with their lives than the nongifted (Terman and Oden, 1959; Sears, 1977; Shurkin, 1992; Reis and Renzulli, 2004).

Yet being gifted and talented is no guarantee of school success. The verbal abilities that allow the expression of ideas and feelings can just as easily voice glib and persuasive statements that happen to be inaccurate. Furthermore, teachers sometimes misinterpret the humour, novelty, and creativity of unusually gifted children and regard their intellectual fervour as disruptive or inappropriate. And peers may be unsympathetic: Some very bright children try to hide their intelligence in an effort to fit in (Swiatek, 2002).

Educating the Gifted and Talented.

Educators have devised two approaches to teaching children with exceptionally high ability: acceleration and enrichment. **Acceleration** allows gifted students to move ahead at their own pace, even if this means skipping grade levels. The

gifted a term for children who show evidence of high-performance capability in areas such as intellect, creativity, artistic ability, leadership capacity, or specific academic fields

acceleration special programs that allow gifted students to move ahead at their own pace, even if this means skipping to higher grade levels

materials in acceleration programs are not always different; they may simply be provided at a faster pace than for the average student.

An alternative approach is **enrichment**, through which students are kept at grade level but are enrolled in special programs and given individual activities to allow greater depth of study. In enrichment, the material differs not only in the timing of its presentation, but in its sophistication as well. Thus, enrichment materials are designed to provide an intellectual challenge to the gifted student, encouraging higher-order thinking, while keeping the child with his or her peer group (Worrell et al., 2001).

> **enrichment** an approach through which students are kept at grade level but are enrolled in special programs and given individual activities to allow greater depth of study on a given topic

REVIEW, CHECK, AND APPLY

REVIEW

- Measuring intelligence has traditionally been a matter of testing skills that promote academic success.

- Recent theories of intelligence suggest there could be several distinct intelligences or several components of intelligence that reflect different ways of processing information.

- Educators attempt to deal with large numbers of exceptional students whose intellectual and other skills are significantly lower or higher than normal.

CHECK YOURSELF

1. Intelligence is the capacity to understand the world, think with rationality, and use resources effectively when faced with challenges.
   - True
   - False

2. According to Howard Gardner, we have at least eight distinct intelligences, each relatively independent.
   - True
   - False

3. For children whose intelligence falls below the normal range, the prevalent philosophy is that they be educated in the _____ environment.
   - **a.** inclusive
   - **b.** average educational
   - **c.** least restrictive
   - **d.** most restrictive

APPLYING LIFESPAN DEVELOPMENT

- How do fluid and crystallized intelligence interact? Which of the two is likely to be more influenced by genetics and which by environment? Why?

Answers: 1) True; 2) True; 3) a

MODULE 5.3 Social and Personality Development in Middle Childhood

Play Time

It's a Wednesday afternoon in April, and six boys are playing in Amy Moore's backyard—her two sons and four neighbourhood children. The boys have built something elaborate out of an enormous cardboard box from Amy's new refridgerator. "I don't know what they built, but they seem to be having fun!"

Andy, seven, and Brian, nine, are transforming the box into a spaceship. They have markers and scissors. Trevor and Evan, eight-year-old twins from next door, are working on the rockets. Michel, Brian's best friend, is designing an instrument panel out of bottle caps and other items retrieved from the recycling bin. Gareth, Andy's classmate, is describing the aliens and planets they will encounter on their adventure.

For Andy and Brian, afternoons like these are more than a way to pass time. They also allow for the formation of social relationships, a key developmental task during middle childhood.

In this module, we focus on social and personality development during this period. It is a time when children's views of themselves undergo significant changes: they form new bonds with friends and family, and they become increasingly attached to social institutions outside the home.

We start our consideration of personality and social development for this age group by examining the changes in how children see themselves. We discuss how they view their personal characteristics, and examine the complex issue of self-esteem.

Next, we turn to relationships. We discuss the stages of friendship and the ways gender and ethnicity affect how and with whom children interact. We also examine how to improve children's social competence.

The last part of the module explores the central societal institution in children's lives: the family. We consider the consequences of divorce, self-care children, and the phenomenon of group care.

The Developing Self

LEARNING OBJECTIVES

LO8 In what ways do children's views of themselves change during middle childhood?

LO9 Why is self-esteem important during these years?

LO10 How does a child's sense of right and wrong change as he or she ages?

Ten-year-old Layne surveys the backyard from his treehouse. "My father and I built it together," he says proudly. "Next, we're going to build a go-kart. There is a race on the big hill every year, and this year we're going to win! We'll get a big trophy. I'll put it in my treehouse. Maybe we need to build a trophy case in here," he says, turning to survey the inside of the treehouse.

Layne's growing sense of competence is reflected in his description of how he and his father built his treehouse. Conveying what psychologist Erik Erikson calls "industriousness," Layne's quiet pride in his accomplishment illustrates one way children's views of themselves evolve.

Psychosocial Development in Middle Childhood: Industry versus Inferiority

According to Erik Erikson, middle childhood is largely about competence. Lasting from roughly age 6 to 12, the **industry-versus-inferiority stage** is characterized by efforts to meet the challenges presented by parents, peers, school, and the complex modern world.

During this period, children direct their energies to mastering the enormous body of information presented in school and to making a place for themselves in their social worlds. Success in this stage brings feelings of mastery and a growing sense of competence, like those expressed by Layne regarding his building experience. On the other hand, difficulties in this stage lead to feelings of failure and inadequacy. As a result, children may withdraw from academic pursuits, showing less interest and motivation to excel, and from interactions with peers.

The sense of industry that children such as Layne attain at this stage has lasting effects. One study examined how childhood industriousness and hard work were related to adult behaviour by following a group of 450 men over a 35-year period, starting in early childhood (Vaillant and Vaillant, 1981). The men who were most industrious and hardworking as children were most successful as adults, both professionally and personally. In fact, childhood industriousness was more closely associated with adult success than was intelligence or family background.

Understanding One's Self: A New Response to "Who Am I?"

During middle childhood, children seek to answer the question "Who am I?" Although the question will assume greater urgency in adolescence, elementary-age children still try to find their place in the world.

The Shift in Self-Understanding from the Physical to the Psychological. The cognitive advances discussed in the previous chapter

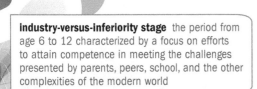

industry-versus-inferiority stage the period from age 6 to 12 characterized by a focus on efforts to attain competence in meeting the challenges presented by parents, peers, school, and the other complexities of the modern world

As children become older, they begin to characterize themselves in terms of their psychological attributes as well as their physical achievements.

aid children in their quest for self-understanding. They begin to view themselves less in terms of external, physical attributes and more in terms of psychological traits (Marsh and Ayotte, 2003; Sotiriou and Zafiropoulou, 2003; Lerner et al., 2005).

For instance, 6-year-old Carey describes herself as "a fast runner and good at drawing"—characteristics dependent on motor skills in external activities. In contrast, 11-year-old Meiping characterizes herself as "pretty smart, friendly, and helpful to my friends." Because of her increasing cognitive skills, Meiping's view of herself is based on psychological characteristics, inner traits that are more abstract.

Children's views of who they are also become more complex. In Erikson's view, children are seeking endeavours where they can be successfully industrious. As they get older, children discover their strengths and weaknesses. Ten-year-old Ginny, for instance, comes to understand she is good at arithmetic but not very good at spelling; 11-year-old Alberto decides he is good at softball but lacks the stamina to play soccer well.

Children's self-concepts become divided into personal and academic spheres. They evaluate themselves in four major areas, each of which can be broken down further. For example, the nonacademic self-concept includes physical appearance, peer relations, and physical ability, while the academic self-concept is similarly divided. Research on students' self-concepts in English, mathematics, and non-academic realms shows that the separate realms do not always correlate, although overlap exists. For example, a child who sees herself as a star math student will not necessarily feel she is great at English (Burnett and Proctor, 2002; Marsh and Ayotte, 2003; Marsh and Hau, 2004).

Self-Esteem: Developing a Positive—or Negative—View of Oneself

Children don't dispassionately view themselves as just a list of physical and psychological traits. Instead, they judge themselves as being good or bad in particular ways. **Self-esteem** is an individual's overall and specific self-evaluation. Whereas self-concept reflects beliefs and cognitions about the self (*I am good at trumpet; I am not so good at social studies*), self-esteem is more emotionally oriented (*everybody thinks I'm a nerd*). (Davis-Kean and Sandler, 2001; Bracken and Lamprecht, 2003).

Self-esteem develops in important ways during middle childhood. As noted, children increasingly compare themselves to others, assessing how they measure up to society's standards. They also increasingly develop their own internal standards of success and measure how well they compare to those. One advance that occurs in this period is that, as with self-concept, self-esteem becomes increasingly differentiated. At age seven, most children have self-esteem that reflects a global, fairly simple view of themselves. Overall positive self-esteem makes them believe they are relatively good at all things. If their overall self-esteem is negative, they feel inadequate at most things (Harter, 1990b; Lerner et al., 2005).

As children move into middle childhood, however, their self-esteem is higher for some areas and lower in others; for example, a boy's overall self-esteem may be positive in some areas (such as artistic ability) and negative in others (such as athletic skills).

Change and Stability in Self-Esteem. Overall self-esteem is generally high during middle childhood, but begins to decline around age 12, affected mainly by the change of schools: Students leaving elementary school and entering junior high school show a decline in self-esteem, which then gradually rises again. This environmental change also coincides with children's shift from making comparisons between themselves and an objective standard, to comparing themselves to peers (Twenge and Campbell, 2001; Robins and Trzesniewski, 2005).

Some children, though, have chronically low self-esteem. These children face a tough road, in part because low self-esteem ensnares them in a cycle of failure that becomes difficult to break. For instance, Harry, a student with chronically low self-esteem, is facing an important test. Because of his low self-esteem, he expects to do poorly. Thus, he is so anxious that he cannot concentrate or study effectively. He also might not study much, figuring that if he's going to do badly anyway, why bother?

Of course, Harry's anxiety and lack of effort bring the result he expected: He does poorly on the test. This failure confirms Harry's expectation, reinforces his low self-esteem, and the cycle of failure continues.

self-esteem an individual's overall and specific positive and negative self-evaluation

Students with high self-esteem fall into a cycle of success. Higher expectations lead to more effort and less anxiety, increasing the odds of success. In turn, success affirms the high self-esteem that began the cycle.

> ⭕ **From an educator's perspective:** What can teachers do to help children whose low self-esteem is causing them to fail? How can this cycle of failure be broken?

Parents can help break the failure cycle by promoting their child's self-esteem. The best way to do this is to use the *authoritative* childrearing style discussed previously. Authoritative parents are warm and emotionally supportive, but set clear limits for behaviour. Other parenting styles have negative effects on self-esteem. Highly punitive and controlling parents send a message to their children that the children are untrustworthy and unable to make good decisions—which can undermine children's sense of adequacy. Highly permissive parents, who indiscriminately praise and reinforce their children regardless of actual performance, can create a false sense of self-esteem, which can be just as damaging (DeHart et al., 2006; Rudy and Grusec, 2006; Bender et al., 2007).

Ethnicity and Self-Esteem. If you were a member of a group that routinely experienced prejudice and discrimination, your self-esteem would likely be affected. Early research confirmed that hypothesis. A set of pioneering studies more than a generation ago found that African American children shown Black and white dolls preferred the white dolls over the Black ones (Clark and Clark, 1947). The interpretation drawn from the study: The self-esteem of the African American children was low.

However, more recent research has shown these assumptions to be overstated. The picture is more complex. For example, although white children initially show higher self-esteem, Black children begin to show slightly higher self-esteem than white children around age 11. This shift occurs as Black children become more identified with their racial group, develop more complex views of racial identity, and increasingly view the positive aspects of their group membership (Gray-Little and Hafdahl, 2000; Oyserman et al., 2003; Tatum, 2007).

Aboriginal children show similar patterns. The pioneering study conducted with African American children was repeated with Aboriginal children in Canada. Even children in a remote northern community tested by a researcher of their own group speaking their own language preferred the white doll. The interpretation: From a young age, children are sensitive to the status of different groups and identify desire to be part of the higher status group (Corenblum, 1996).

One explanation for the complex relationship between self-esteem and minority group status comes from *social identity theory*. According to the theory, minority group members are likely to accept the majority group's negative views only if they perceive that there is little possibility of changing the power and status differences between the groups. If minority group members feel that prejudice and discrimination can be reduced, and they blame society for the prejudice and not themselves, self-esteem should not differ between majority and minority groups (Tajfel, 1982; Turner and Onorato, 1999).

In fact, as group pride and ethnic awareness on the part of minority group members has grown, differences in self-esteem between members of different ethnic groups have narrowed. This trend has been supported by increased sensitivity to the importance of multiculturalism (Goodstein and Ponerotto, 1997; Negy et al., 2003; Lee, 2005; Tatum, 2007).

In pioneering research conducted several decades ago, non-white girls' preference for white dolls was viewed as an indication of low self-esteem. More recent evidence, however, suggests that this doll preference is not an indicator of self-esteem.

Moral Development

Your wife is near death from an unusual kind of cancer. One drug exists that the physicians think might save her—a form of radium that a scientist in a nearby city has recently developed. The drug, though, is expensive to manufacture, and the scientist is charging 10 times what the drug costs him

Cultural Dimensions

Are Children of Immigrant Families Well Adjusted?

Canada continues to welcome a large number of immigrants each year: 8 newcomers per 1000 people, a rate that has remained relatively stable for years (Statistics Canada, 2009).

Among these immigrants, the children are faring quite well. In some ways they are better off than their nonimmigrant peers. They tend to have equal or better grades in school than children whose parents were born in Canada. Psychologically, they also do quite well, showing similar levels of self-esteem to nonimmigrant children, although they do report feeling less popular and less in control of their lives (Kao and Tienda, 1995; Kao, 2000; Harris, 1999).

Why is the adjustment of these children generally so positive? One answer is that often their socioeconomic status is higher. In spite of stereotypes that immigrant families come from lower social classes, many are well educated and seek greater opportunities.

But socioeconomic status is only part of the story. Even the immigrant children who are not financially well off are often more highly motivated to succeed and place greater value on education than do nonimmigrant children. In addition, many immigrant children come from societies that emphasize collectivism and may feel more obligation and duty toward their family to succeed. Finally, their native country can give some immigrant children a strong enough cultural identity to prevent them from adopting undesirable "Western" behaviours—such as materialism or selfishness (Fuligini et al., 1999; Fuligni and Yoshikawa, 2003).

During middle childhood, then, it appears that immigrant children typically do well. The story is less clear, however, during adolescence

and adulthood. Research is just beginning to clarify how immigrants cope over their lifespan (Fuligini, 1998; Portes and Rumbaut, 2001).

Immigrant children tend to fare quite well, partly because many come from societies that emphasize collectivism, and consequently they may feel more obligation and duty to their family to succeed. What are some other cultural differences that can lead to the success of immigrant children?

to make. He pays $1000 for the radium and charges $10 000 for a small dose. You have gone to everyone you know to borrow money, but you can only get $2500—one-quarter of what you need. You've told the scientist that your wife is dying and have asked him to sell it more cheaply or let you pay later. But the scientist has said, "No, I discovered the drug and I'm going to make money from it." In desperation, you consider breaking into the scientist's laboratory to steal the drug for your wife. Should you do it?

According to developmental psychologist Lawrence Kohlberg and his colleagues, the justification that children give when answering this question reveals central aspects of their sense of morality and justice. He suggests that people's responses to moral dilemmas such as this one reveal their stage of moral development—as well as information about their level of cognitive development (Kohlberg, 1984; Colby and Kohlberg, 1987).

Kohlberg contends that people pass through stages as their sense of right and wrong evolves and the reasoning they use to make moral judgments changes. Younger school-age children tend to think in terms of either concrete, unvarying rules ("It is always wrong to steal" or "I'll be punished if I steal") or the rules of society ("Good people don't steal" or "What if everyone stole?").

By adolescence, however, individuals can reason on a higher plane if they have reached Piaget's stage of formal operations. They are capable of comprehending abstract, formal principles of morality, and they consider broader issues of morality and of right and wrong in cases like the one just presented ("Stealing might be acceptable if you are following your own conscience and doing the right thing").

Kohlberg suggests that moral development emerges in a three-level sequence, further subdivided into six stages (see Table 5-1). At the lowest level, *preconventional morality* (Stages 1 and 2), people follow rigid rules based on punishments or rewards (for example, a student might evaluate the moral dilemma in the story by saying it was not worth stealing the drug because you could go to jail). Like the egocentric preoperational child, right and wrong are based largely on self-interest.

◉ Watch on mydevelopmentlab

Log onto MyDevelopmentLab and watch the video on moral development. In the interviews, children display Kohlberg's theories, which you've just been reading about.

TABLE 5-1 KOHLBERG'S SEQUENCE OF MORAL REASONING

Level	Stage	Sample Moral Reasoning	
		In Favour of Stealing	Against Stealing
LEVEL 1 **Preconventional morality:** At this level, the concrete interests of the individual are considered in terms of rewards and punishments.	**STAGE 1** Obedience and punishment orientation: At this stage, people stick to rules in order to avoid punishment, and obedience occurs for its own sake.	"If you let your wife die, you will get in trouble. You'll be blamed for not spending the money to save her, and there'll be an investigation of you and the druggist for your wife's death."	"You shouldn't steal the drug because you'll get caught and sent to jail if you do. If you do get away, your conscience will bother you thinking how the police will catch up with you at any minute."
	STAGE 2 Reward orientation: At this stage, rules are followed only for a person's own benefit. Obedience occurs because of rewards that are received.	"If you do happen to get caught, you could give the drug back and you wouldn't get much of a sentence. It wouldn't bother you much to serve a little jail term, if you have your wife when you get out."	"You may not get much of a jail term if you steal the drug, but your wife will probably die before you get out, so it won't do much good. If your wife dies, you shouldn't blame yourself; it isn't your fault she has cancer."
LEVEL 2 **Conventional morality:** At this level, people approach moral problems as members of society. They are interested in pleasing others by acting as good members of society.	**STAGE 3** "Good boy" morality: Individuals at this stage show an interest in maintaining the respect of others and doing what is expected of them.	"No one will think you're bad if you steal the drug, but your family will think you're an inhuman husband if you don't. If you let your wife die, you'll never be able to look anybody in the face again."	"It isn't just the druggist who will think you're a criminal; everyone else will, too. After you steal the drug, you'll feel bad thinking how you've brought dishonour on your family and yourself; you won't be able to face anyone again."
	STAGE 4 Authority and social-order-maintaining morality: People at this stage conform to society's rules and consider that "right" is what society defines as right.	"If you have any sense of honour, you won't let your wife die just because you're afraid to do the only thing that will save her. You'll always feel guilty that you caused her death if you don't do your duty to her."	"You're desperate and you may not know you're doing wrong when you steal the drug. But you'll know you did wrong after you're sent to jail. You'll always feel guilty for your dishonesty and law-breaking."
LEVEL 3 **Postconventional morality:** At this level, people use moral principles, which are seen as broader than those of any particular society.	**STAGE 5** Morality of contract, individual rights, and democratically accepted law: People at this stage do what is right because of a sense of obligation to laws that are agreed upon within society. They perceive that laws can be modified as part of changes in an implicit social contract.	"You'll lose other people's respect, not gain it, if you don't steal. If you let your wife die, it will be out of fear, not out of reasoning. So you'll just lose self-respect and probably the respect of others, too."	"You'll lose your standing and respect in the community and violate the law. You'll lose respect for yourself if you're carried away by emotion and forget the long-range point of view."
	STAGE 6 Morality of individual principles and conscience: At this final stage, a person follows laws because they are based on universal ethical principles. Laws that violate the principles are disobeyed.	"If you don't steal the drug, and if you let your wife die, you'll always condemn yourself for it afterward. You won't be blamed and you'll have lived up to the outside rule of the law, but you won't have lived up to your own standards of conscience."	"If you steal the drug, you won't be blamed by other people, but you'll condemn yourself because you won't have lived up to your own conscience and standards of honesty."

Source: Adapted from Kohlberg, 1969.

In the next level, *conventional morality* (Stages 3 and 4), people approach moral problems as good, responsible members of society. Some would decide *against* stealing the drug because they would feel guilty or dishonest for violating social norms. Others would decide *in favour* of stealing the drug because they would be unable to face others if they did nothing. All of these people would be reasoning at the conventional level of morality. Right and wrong are defined by family or society.

Finally, individuals using *postconventional morality* (Stages 5 and 6) invoke universal moral principles that are considered broader than the rules of their particular society. People who would condemn themselves if they did not steal the drug because they would be violating their own moral principles are reasoning at the postconventional level. Right and wrong are now defined by principles such as "the greater good" and "the betterment of society" and may be in direct conflict with both the individual's self-interest and local laws.

Kohlberg's theory proposes that people move through the stages in a fixed order and are unable to reach the highest stage until adolescence, due to constraints in cognitive development before then (Kurtines and Gewirtz, 1987). However, not everyone is presumed to reach the highest stages: Kohlberg found that postconventional reasoning is in fact relatively rare.

Although Kohlberg's theory provides a good account of the development of moral *judgments*, the links with moral *behaviour* are less strong. For example, students at higher stages of moral reasoning are less likely to engage in antisocial behaviour at school and in the community. One experiment found that 15 percent of students who reasoned at the postconventional level cheated when given the opportunity, compared to 55 percent of students at the conventional level and 70 percent of students at the preconventional level. Though those at higher levels cheated less, a few postconventional students still cheated. Clearly, high moral reasoning doesn't guarantee the most moral behaviour all the time (Snarey, 1995; Killen and Hart, 1995; Hart et al., 2003; Semerci, 2006).

Kohlberg's theory has also been criticized because it is based solely on observations of Western cultures. In fact, cross-cultural research finds that those in more industrialized, technologically advanced cultures move through the stages more rapidly than members of nonindustrialized countries. One explanation is that Kohlberg's higher stages are based on moral reasoning involving governmental and societal institutions such as the police and court system. In less industrialized areas, morality may be based more on relationships between people. In short, the nature of morality may differ in diverse cultures, and Kohlberg's theory is more suited for Western cultures (Fu et al., 2007).

Another problematic aspect of Kohlberg's theory is the difficulty it has explaining *girls'* moral judgments. Because the initial theory was based largely on data from males, some researchers have argued that it better describes boys' moral development than girls'. This would explain the surprising finding that women typically score at a lower level than men on tests of moral judgments using Kohlberg's stages. This result has led to an alternative account of moral development for girls.

Moral Development in Girls. Psychologist Carol Gilligan (1982, 1987) has suggested that differences in the ways boys and girls are raised in our society lead to basic distinctions in how men and women view moral behaviour. According to Gilligan, boys view morality primarily in terms of broad principles such as justice or fairness, while girls see it in terms of responsibility toward individuals and willingness to sacrifice themselves to help specific individuals within the context of particular relationships. Compassion for individuals, then, is a greater factor in moral behaviour for women than it is for men (Gilligan et al., 1988; Gilligan et al., 1990; Gump et al., 2000).

Gilligan views morality as developing among females in a three-stage process (summarized in Table 5-2). In the first stage, called "orientation toward individual survival," females first concentrate on what is practical and best for them, gradually making a transition from selfishness to responsibility—that is, thinking about what would be best for others. In the second stage, termed "goodness as self-sacrifice," females begin to think they must sacrifice their own wishes to those of others.

Ideally, women make a transition from "goodness" to "truth," in which they take into account their own needs, too. This transition leads to the third stage, "morality of nonviolence," in which women decide that hurting anyone is immoral—including themselves. This realization

TABLE 5-2 GILLIGAN'S THREE STAGES OF MORAL DEVELOPMENT IN WOMEN

Stage	Characteristics	Example
STAGE 1 Orientation toward individual survival	Initial concentration is on what is practical and best for self. Gradual transition from selfishness to responsibility, which includes thinking about what would be best for others.	A grade 1 student might insist on playing only games of her own choosing when playing with a friend.
STAGE 2 Goodness as self-sacrifice	Initial view is that a woman must sacrifice her own wishes to what other people want. Gradual transition from "goodness" to "truth," which takes into account needs of both self and others.	Now older, the same girl might believe that to be a good friend, she must play the games her friend chooses, even if she herself doesn't like them.
STAGE 3 Morality of nonviolence	A moral equivalence is established between self and others. Hurting anyone—including one's self—is seen as immoral. Most sophisticated form of reasoning, according to Gilligan.	The same girl might realize that both friends must enjoy their time together and look for activities that both she and her friend can enjoy.

establishes a moral equivalence between themselves and others and represents, according to Gilligan, the most sophisticated level of moral reasoning.

Gilligan's sequence of stages is quite different from Kohlberg's, and some developmentalists have suggested that her rejection of Kohlberg's work is too sweeping—that gender differences are less pronounced than first thought (Colby and Damon, 1987). For instance, some researchers argue that both males and females use similar "justice" and "caring" orientations in making moral judgments, depending on the situation and wording of the question. Other critics point out that these gender differences are not found in children, that the gender differences are seen only in adults, suggesting that the difference is a product of socialization. Clearly, the question is far from settled (Walker et al., 1987; Tangney and Dearing, 2002; Weisz and Black, 2002; Jorgensen, 2006; Tappan, 2006).

REVIEW, CHECK, AND APPLY

REVIEW

- According to Erikson, children at this time are in the industry-versus-inferiority stage.

- In middle childhood, children begin to use social comparison and self-concepts based on psychological rather than physical characteristics.

- According to Kohlberg, moral development proceeds from a concern with rewards and punishments, through a focus on social conventions and rules, toward a sense of universal moral principles. Gilligan has suggested, however, that girls may follow a different progression of moral development.

CHECK YOURSELF

1. According to Erikson, children ages 6 to 12 focus on efforts to meet the challenges presented by parents, peers, and school. This stage is _____.

   a. autonomy versus shame and doubt

   b. trust versus mistrust

   c. self versus others

   d. industry versus inferiority

2. As children develop a better self-understanding in middle childhood, they begin to view themselves less in terms of physical attributes and more in terms of their _____.

   a. familial relationships

   b. psychological traits

   c. environmental characteristics

   d. motor skills

3. According to _____, people pass through a series of six stages as their sense of justice and their level of reasoning evolves with age and cognitive development.

APPLYING LIFESPAN DEVELOPMENT

- Kohlberg and Gilligan each suggest there are three major levels of moral development. Are any of their levels comparable? In which level of either theory do you think that the largest discrepancy between males and females would be observed?

Relationships: Building Friendship in Middle Childhood

LO11   What sorts of relationships and friendships are typical of middle childhood?

LO12   How do gender and ethnicity affect friendship?

Friends influence development in several ways. Friendships provide children with information about the world as well as themselves. Friends provide emotional support that allows children to respond more effectively to stress. Having friends makes a child a less likely target of aggression. Friendship can teach children how to manage their emotions and help them interpret their own emotional experiences (Berndt, 2002). Friendships teach children how to communicate and interact with others. They also foster intellectual growth by increasing children's range of experiences (Harris, 1998; Nangle and Erdley, 2001; Gifford-Smith and Brownell, 2003).

Friends and other peers become increasingly influential at this stage, but parents and other family members remain significant. Most developmentalists believe that children's psychological functioning and their general development is the product of multiple factors, including peers and parents (Vandell, 2000; Parke et al., 2002). (We'll talk more about the family's influence later in this module.)

Stages of Friendship: Changing Views of Friends

At this stage, a child's concept of friendship passes through three distinct stages, according to developmental psychologist William Damon (Damon and Hart, 1988).

Stage 1: Basing Friendship on Others' Behaviour.   In this stage, from around age four to seven, children see friends as others who like them and with whom they share toys and other activities. They view the children they spend the most time with as their friends. A kindergartner who was asked, "How do you know that someone is your best friend?" responded:

> I sleep over at his house sometimes. When he's playing ball with his friends he'll let me play. When I slept over, he let me get in front of him in 4-squares. He likes me. (Damon, 1983, p. 140)

What children in this stage seldom do, however, is consider others' personal qualities as the basis of friendships. Instead, they use a concrete approach, primarily choosing friends for their behaviour. They like those who share, shun those who don't share, who hit, or who don't play with them. In the first stage, friends are viewed largely as presenting opportunities for pleasant interactions.

Stage 2: Basing Friendship on Trust.   In the next stage, children's view of friendship becomes complicated. Lasting from around age 8 to 10, this stage involves taking others' personal qualities and traits as well as the rewards they provide into consideration. But the centrepiece of friendship in this second stage is mutual trust. Friends are seen as those one can count on to help out when needed. Violations of trust are taken very seriously, and friends cannot make amends just by engaging in positive play, as they might at earlier ages. Instead, the expectation is that formal explanations and apologies must occur before friendship can resume.

Stage 3: Basing Friendship on Psychological Closeness.   The third stage of friendship begins toward the end of middle childhood, from age 11 to 15, when children develop the view of friendship they will hold in adolescence. Although we'll discuss this perspective in detail later, the main criteria for friendship shift toward intimacy and loyalty. Friendship becomes characterized by feelings of closeness, usually brought on by

Mutual trust is considered to be the centrepiece of friendship during middle childhood.

A variety of factors lead some children to be unpopular and socially isolated from their peers.

sharing personal thoughts and feelings. They are also somewhat exclusive. By the end of middle childhood, children seek friends who will be loyal, and view friendship less in terms of shared activities than in terms of the psychological benefits it brings (Newcomb and Bagwell, 1995).

Children also develop clear ideas about which behaviours they like and dislike in friends, preferring others who invite them to share in activities and who are helpful, both physically and psychologically. They dislike behaviours such as physical or verbal aggression.

Individual Differences in Friendship: What Makes a Child Popular?

Why is it that some children are the schoolyard equivalent of the life of the party, while others are social isolates whose overtures toward peers are dismissed or disdained? Developmentalists have attempted to answer this question by examining individual differences in popularity.

Status Among School-Age Children: Establishing One's Position. Children's friendships exhibit clear status hierarchies. **Status** is the evaluation of a role or person by other relevant members of a group. Children who have high status have greater access to resources such as games, toys, books, and information. Lower-status children are more likely to follow their lead. Status can be measured in several ways. Often, children are asked directly how much they like or dislike particular classmates. They also might be asked whom they would most (and least) like to play or work with.

Status is an important determinant of friendships. High-status children tend to befriend those of a higher status, while lower-status children are likely to have friends of lower status. Status is also related to the number of friends a child has: Higher-status children tend to have more friends than those of lower status.

But it is not only the quantity of social interactions that separates high-status children from low-status children; the nature of their interactions also differs. Higher-status children are more likely to be viewed as friends by other children. They are more likely to form cliques—groups viewed as exclusive and desirable—and to interact with a greater number of children. Lower-status children tend to play with younger or less popular children (Ladd, 1983). Popularity is a reflection of children's status. Mid- to high-status children are more likely to initiate and coordinate social interaction, making their general level of social activity higher than the activity of children of low status (Erwin, 1993).

What Personal Characteristics Lead to Popularity? Popular children share several personality traits. They are usually helpful, co-operating with others on joint projects. They also tend to be funny and to appreciate others' attempts at humour. Compared to less popular children, they are better at reading non-verbal behaviour and understanding the emotional experiences of others. They also control their non-verbal behaviour more effectively, presenting themselves well. In short, popular children are high in **social competence**, the collection of social skills that permits individuals to perform successfully in social settings (Feldman et al., 1991; Feldman et al., 1999).

Although generally popular children are friendly, open, and co-operative, one subset of popular boys displays an array of negative behaviours, including being aggressive, disruptive, and causing trouble. Despite these behaviours, they are often remarkably popular, being viewed as cool and tough by their peers. This popularity may occur because they are seen as boldly breaking rules that others feel constrained to follow (Farmer et al., 2003; de Bruyn and Cillessen, 2006; Vaillancourt and Hymel, 2006).

Social Problem-Solving Abilities. Another factor in popularity is children's skill at social problem-solving. **Social problem-solving** is the use of strategies for solving social conflicts in mutually satisfactory ways. Because social conflicts are frequent—even among best friends—successful strategies for dealing with them are an important element of social success (Laursen et al., 1996; Rose and Asher, 1999; Murphy and Eisenberg, 2002).

According to developmental psychologist Kenneth Dodge, successful social problem-solving proceeds through a series of steps that correspond to children's information-processing

status the evaluation of a role or person by other relevant members of a group

social competence the collection of social skills that permit individuals to perform successfully in social settings

social problem-solving the use of strategies for solving social conflicts in ways that are satisfactory both to oneself and to others

strategies (see Figure 5-8). Dodge argues that the ways children solve social problems are a result of the decisions they make at each point in the sequence (Dodge and Crick, 1990; Dodge and Price, 1994; Dodge et al., 2003).

By carefully delineating each of the stages, Dodge provides a means to target interventions toward a specific child's deficits. For instance, some children routinely misinterpret the meaning of others' behaviour (Step 2), and then respond according to their misinterpretation.

Generally, popular children are better at interpreting others' behaviour. They also possess a wider inventory of techniques for dealing with social problems. In contrast, less popular children tend to show less understanding of others' behaviour, and thus their reactions may be inappropriate. Their strategies for dealing with social problems are more limited; they sometimes simply don't know how to apologize or help someone who is unhappy feel better (Vitaro and Pelletier, 1991; Rose and Asher, 1999; Rinaldi, 2002).

Teaching Social Competence. Happily, unpopular children can learn social competence. Several programs aim to teach children the skills that seem to underlie general social competence. In one experimental program, a group of unpopular grade 5 and grade 6 students were taught how to converse with friends. They were taught ways to disclose material about themselves, to learn about others by asking questions, and to offer help and suggestions in a nonthreatening way.

Compared with a group who did not receive training, the children in the experiment interacted more with their peers, held more conversations, developed higher self-esteem, and—most critically—were more accepted by their peers than before training (Bierman and Furman, 1984; Asher and Rose, 1997).

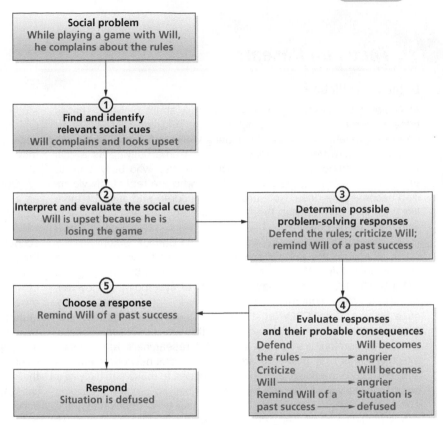

FIGURE 5-8 **Problem-Solving Steps**
Children's problem-solving proceeds through several steps involving different information-processing strategies.
Source: *Educational psychology* by K. A. Dodge. Copyright 1985 by Taylor & Francis Informa UK Ltd—Journals. Reproduced with permission of Taylor & Francis Informa UK Ltd—Journals in the format Textbook via Copyright Clearance Center.

Bullying: Schoolyard and Online Victimization

For some children, school represents a battleground where they live in constant fear of being bullied. One-third of children are involved in bullying in some way—as bullies, as victims, or as both, and teachers are often unaware of the extent of bullying that occurs in their school. Bullying is a worldwide problem: Cross-cultural studies find significant bullying in Asian and European countries as well (Charach et al., 1995; Eslea et al., 2004; Espelage and Swearer, 2004; Kanetsuna et al., 2006).

The newest form of bullying takes place on the Web. Cyberbullies use the Internet to make fun of others, start rumours, or post doctored photos. This type of bullying is often anonymous, leaving victims unable to identify the bully—and feeling particularly vulnerable and helpless. The public nature of cyberbullying humiliates victims in ways that can cause deep damage (Ybarra and Mitchell, 2004; Patchin and Hinduja, 2006; Thomas, 2006; Raskauskas and Stoltz, 2007).

About 10 to 15 percent of students bully others at some time. About half of all bullies come from abusive homes. They watch more violent television, and they misbehave more at home and at school than nonbullies. When their bullying brings them trouble, they may lie about events, and they show little remorse for their victims. Compared with their peers, bullies are more likely to break the law as adults (Kaltiala-Heino et al., 2000; Haynie et al., 2001; Ireland and Archer, 2004).

The victims of bullies typically share several characteristics. Often they are loners who are fairly passive. They may cry easily and lack the social skills to defuse a tense situation. For example, they tend not to think of humorous comebacks to bullies' taunts. But though such children are more likely to be bullied, even children without these characteristics occasionally are bullied: Some 90 percent of students report being bullied at some point in their school years, beginning as early as preschool (Egan and Perry, 1998; Crick et al., 1999; Ahmed and Braithwaite, 2004).

◉─Watch on **mydevelopmentlab**

Has your virtual child encountered issues with bullying? How have you handled it?
Check MyDevelopmentLab for an Observations Video on bullying.

Focus on Research

Bullies and Victims

At Queen's University, there is a lot of talk about bullying. That is because Professor Wendy Craig is also co-director of PREVNet: Promoting Relationships and Eliminating Violence Network. Craig and colleague Debra Pepler at York University frame bullying as a "destructive relationship problem" in which children who bully learn to use power to control others and children who are repeatedly victimized become powerless. Not surprisingly, children who bully are more likely to have parents who themselves were bullies as children, and who may still be power-assertive adults.

Is bullying a problem in Canada? Yes. Canada actually ranks rather poorly on the world stage when it comes to dealing with the problem of bullying. You might be surprised to learn that bullying has not increased, despite increased visibility of cyberbullying. However, relative to other countries, we've made very little progress to reduce bullying. Enter PREVNet. The mandate of PREVNet is to deliver research-based anti-bullying solutions through education, assessment, intervention, and policy. In all, 58 researchers representing 24 universities across Canada are involved in this network. Members aim to educate the public and change attitudes to make anti-bullying a priority, devise ways to assess the extent of bullying problems, develop effective intervention programs for individuals and communities, and shape public policy to deal with the problem.

The factors that underly bullying are very similar the world over: negative school perceptions, including academic achievement, student social relationships, teacher–student relationships, rules and regulations, and general school perceptions. No one aspect of negative school perceptions is more important than another; rather they operate under a cumulative stress model. The more negative the school atmosphere, the more bullying occurs.

Does this mean bullying can be prevented by treating the school as a whole? Yes. The following is just one example of a research-based intervention that can be implemented in a school.

Norway was the first country to implement research-based school-level anti-bullying programs. The Olweus Bullying Prevention Program operates at various levels, and researchers measure performance along the way. At the general level, adults need to be aware of what goes on in the school and be involved. At the school level, a school-wide anti-bullying conference or awareness day is held. Importantly, effective supervision of children during recess and noon hour is essential. At the classroom level, class rules are posted and meetings are held with students and with parents. At the individual level, serious discussion is held with bullies and victims, and with their parents, and individual intervention plans are developed to deal with the problems that arise. This model of treating bullying at the school-level is currently being tested in Canada, but while efforts are focused on children, we need to remain vigilant about bullying by adults as well (Olweus, 2004; Craig and Pepler, 2007; Harel-Fisch et al., 2011).

Gender and Friendships: The Sex Segregation of Middle Childhood

Girls rule; boys drool.

Boys are idiots. Girls have cooties.

Boys go to college to get more knowledge; girls go to Jupiter to get more stupider.

Those are some of the views of elementary school boys and girls regarding members of the other sex. Avoidance of the other sex becomes quite pronounced at this age, with social networks often consisting almost entirely of same-sex groupings (Adler et al., 1992; Lewis and Phillipsen, 1998; McHale et al., 2003).

Interestingly, this segregation of friendships occurs in almost all societies. In nonindustrialized societies, same-gender segregation can result from the types of activities children engage in. For instance, in many cultures, boys are assigned one type of chore and girls another (Whiting and Edwards, 1988). Participation in different activities may not wholly explain sex segregation, however: Children in more developed countries, who attend the same schools and participate in many of the same activities, still tend to avoid members of the other sex.

When boys and girls make occasional forays into the other gender's territory, the action often has romantic overtones. For instance, girls may threaten to kiss a boy, or boys might try to lure girls into chasing them. Such behaviour, termed "border work," emphasizes the clear boundaries between the two sexes. In addition, it might pave the way for adolescent interactions that do involve romantic or sexual interests, when cross-sex interactions become socially endorsed (Thorne, 1986; Beal, 1994).

The lack of cross-gender interaction in middle childhood means that boys' and girls' friendships are restricted to their own sex. The nature of friendships within these two groups is quite different (Lansford and Parker, 1999; Rose, 2002).

Boys typically have larger networks of friends, and they tend to play in groups, rather than pairing off. Differences in status within the group are usually pronounced, with an acknowledged leader and a hierarchy of members. Because of the fairly rigid rankings that represent the relative social power of those in the group, known as the **dominance hierarchy**, members of higher status can safely question and oppose those lower in the hierarchy (Beal, 1994).

Boys tend to be concerned with their place in the dominance hierarchy, and they attempt to maintain and improve their status. This makes for a style of play known as *restrictive*. In restrictive play, interactions are interrupted when a child feels his status is challenged. A boy who feels that he is unjustly challenged by a lower-status peer may attempt to end the interaction by scuffling over a toy or otherwise behaving assertively. Consequently, boys tend to play in bursts, rather than in more extended, tranquil episodes (Boulton and Smith, 1990; Benenson and Apostoleris, 1993).

The language of friendship used among boys reflects their concern over status and challenge. Consider this conversation between two boys who were good friends:

Child 1: Why don't you get out of my yard?

Child 2: Why don't you *make* me get out of the yard?

Child 1: I *know* you don't want that.

Child 2: You're not gonna make me get out of the yard cuz you can't.

Child 1: Don't force me.

Child 2: You can't. Don't force me to hurt you (*snickers*). (Goodwin, 1990, p. 37)

Friendship patterns among girls are quite different. Rather than a wide network of friends, girls focus on one or two "best friends." In contrast to boys, who seek out status differences, girls avoid differences, preferring to maintain equal-status friendships.

Conflicts among girls are usually solved through compromise, by ignoring the situation, or by giving in, rather than by seeking to make one's point of view prevail. The goal is to smooth over disagreements, making social interaction easy and nonconfrontational (Goodwin, 1990).

According to developmental psychologist Carole Beal, the motivation of girls to solve social conflict indirectly does not stem from a lack of self-confidence or from apprehension over the use of more direct approaches. In fact, when school-age girls interact with other girls who are not friends or with boys, they can be quite confrontational. However, among friends their goal is to maintain equal-status relationships, with no dominance hierarchy (Beal, 1994).

The language used by girls tends to reflect their view of relationships. Rather than blatant demands ("Give me the pencil"), girls are more apt to use less confrontational and directive language. Girls tend to use indirect forms of verbs, such as "Let's go to the movies" or "Would you want to trade books with me?" rather than "I want to go to the movies" or "Let me have these books" (Goodwin, 1980, 1990).

> **dominance hierarchy** rankings that represent the relative social power of those in a group

Cross-Race Friendships: Integration In and Out of the Classroom

For the most part, friendships are not colour-blind. Children's closest friendships tend to be with others of the same ethnic group. In fact, as children age there is a decline in the number and depth of friendships outside their own ethnic group. By age 11 or 12, children in minority groups appear to become particularly aware of and sensitive to the prejudice and discrimination directed toward members of their ethnic group. At that point, they are likely to make distinctions between members of ingroups (groups to which people feel they belong) and members of outgroups (groups to which they feel they do not belong) (Bigler et al., 1997; Aboud et al., 2003; Kao and Vaquera, 2006).

In a classic US study, when grade 3 students from one long-integrated school were asked to name a best friend, around one-quarter of white children and two-thirds of African American children chose a child of the other group. In contrast, by grade 10, fewer than 10 percent of whites and

As children age, the number of and depth of friendships outside their own ethnic group declines. What are some ways in which schools can foster mutual acceptance?

5 percent of African Americans named a different-race best friend (Singleton and Asher, 1979; Asher et al., 1982).

> **From a social worker's perspective:** How might it be possible to decrease the segregation of friendships along ethnic lines? What factors would have to change in individuals or in society?

We might ask, Has anything changed in more than 30 years? Yes and no. A more recent examination of cross-racial friendships in Toronto found that most adolescents still reported large numbers of outgroup friends, but there was still a tendency for best friends to be ingroup members. The diversity of children's classrooms and neighbourhoods has a significant impact. A good deal of research shows that contact between majority and minority group members can reduce prejudice and discrimination (Kerner and Aboud, 1998; Hewstone, 2003; Smith and Schneider, 2000).

Increasing Children's Social Competence

Becoming an Informed Consumer of Development

Clearly, building and maintaining friendships is critical in children's lives. Fortunately, parents and teachers can use several strategies to increase children's social competence.

- **Encourage social interaction.** Teachers can devise ways to get children to take part in group activities, and parents can encourage membership in such groups as Brownies and Cub Scouts or participation in team sports.

- **Teach listening skills to children.** Show them how to listen carefully and respond to the underlying meaning of a communication as well as its overt content.

- **Make children aware that people display emotions and moods non-verbally** and that, consequently, attention should be given

to others' non-verbal behaviour, not just to what others are saying.

- **Teach conversational skills, including self-disclosure and the importance of asking questions.** Encourage students to use "I" statements in which they clarify their own feelings or opinions, and avoid making generalizations about others.

- **Don't ask children to choose teams or groups publicly.** Instead, assign children randomly: It works just as well in ensuring a distribution of abilities across groups and avoids the public embarrassment of being chosen last.

REVIEW, CHECK, AND APPLY

REVIEW

- Children's understanding of friendship changes from the sharing of enjoyable activities, to the consideration of personal traits that can meet their needs, to a focus on intimacy and loyalty.

- Friendships in childhood display status hierarchies. Improvements in social problem-solving and social information-processing can lead to better interpersonal skills and greater popularity.

- Boys and girls engage increasingly in same-sex friendships, with boys' friendships involving group relationships and girls' friendships characterized by pairings of girls with equal status.

CHECK YOURSELF

1. Which of the following statements about friendship in middle childhood are true? Check all that apply.

   a. Friendships provide information about the world.
   b. Friends provide emotional support that is different from the support provided by parents.
   c. Children with friends are less likely to be the target of aggression.
   d. Friendships provide training in communication.
   e. Friendships protect children from interactions with others, which can enhance their intellectual growth.
   f. Children are only able to learn how to manage their emotions within the context of family.

2. _____ is the evaluation of the role or person by other relevant members of the group and is usually discussed in reference to children and their peer groups.

3. Which of the following descriptions best characterizes friendships in middle childhood?

   a. Boys and girls tend to remain in sex-segregated friendship networks.
   b. Boys and girls begin playing in larger groups including males and females.
   c. Boys are much more likely than girls to engage in activities considered more appropriate for the opposite sex.
   d. Girls typically have larger networks of friends than do boys.

APPLYING LIFESPAN DEVELOPMENT

- Do you think the stages of friendship are a childhood phenomenon, or do adults' friendships display similar stages?

Answers: 1) a, b, d; 2) Status; 3) a

Family Life in Middle Childhood

L013   **How do today's diverse family and care arrangements affect children?**

When Emily and Evan married, Evan's 8-year-old son, Peter, suddenly went from being an only child to having two older siblings, 10-year-old Patty and 16-year-old Tom. Peter was still coming to grips with his parents' divorce and living half-time with each. Emily had divorced when Patty was two years old, so her children were used to seeing their father only on odd weekends. But in some ways it was a bigger change for Patty and Tom. After living their entire lives in the same apartment, they moved into a house with a backyard.

We've seen in earlier chapters how the structure of the family has changed over the last few decades. With more parents who both work outside the home, a high divorce rate, and a rise in single-parent families, children passing through middle childhood in the twenty-first century face an environment different than the one faced by prior generations.

One of the biggest challenges of middle childhood is the increasing independence that characterizes children's behaviour. Children move from being controlled to increasingly controlling their own destinies—or at least conduct. Middle childhood, then, is a period of **coregulation** in which children and parents jointly control behaviour. Increasingly, parents provide broad guidelines for conduct, while children control their everyday behaviour. For instance, parents may urge their daughter to buy a nutritious school lunch, but their daughter's decision to buy pizza and two desserts is her own.

Family Life

During middle childhood, children spend less time with their parents. Still, parents remain a major influence, providing essential assistance, advice, and direction (Parke, 2004).

Siblings also have important influence, for good and for ill. Although brothers and sisters can provide support, companionship, and security, they can also be a source of strife. *Sibling rivalry* can occur, especially when the siblings are the same sex and similar in age. Parents may intensify sibling rivalry by seeming to favour one child over another—a perception that might or might not be accurate. Something as simple as granting older siblings more freedom can be interpreted as favouritism. In some cases, perceived favouritism can damage the self-esteem of the younger sibling. Sibling rivalry is not inevitable, however (Ciricelli, 1995; Branje et al., 2004; McHale et al., 2006).

What about children who have no siblings? Despite the stereotype suggesting that only-children are spoiled and self-centred, they are as well-adjusted as children with brothers and sisters. In fact, in some ways, only-children are better adjusted, with higher self-esteem and stronger motivation to achieve. In China, where a strict one-child policy is in effect, studies show that only-children often academically outperform children with siblings (Jiao et al., 1996; Miao and Wang, 2003).

Home and Alone: What Do Children Do?

When 10-year-old Johnetta Colvin comes home after a day at school, the first thing she does is grab a few cookies and turn on the computer. She takes a quick look at her email, and then typically spends an hour watching television. During commercials, she looks at her homework.
What she doesn't do is chat with her parents. She's home alone.

Johnetta is a **self-care child**. Self-care children let themselves into their homes after school and wait alone until their parents return from work. An estimated 12 to 14 percent of children between the ages of 5 and 12 spend some time alone after school, without adult supervision (Lamorey et al., 1998; Berger, 2000).

In the past, such children were called *latchkey children*, a term connoting sadness, loneliness, and neglect. Today a new view is emerging. According to sociologist Sandra Hofferth, given the hectic schedule of many children's lives, a few hours alone can provide a helpful

coregulation a period in which parents and children jointly control children's behaviour

self-care children children who let themselves into their homes after school and wait alone until their caretakers return from work; previously known as latchkey children

period of decompression and give children an opportunity to develop autonomy (Hofferth and Sandberg, 2001).

Research has identified few differences between self-care children and others. Although some children report negative experiences (such as loneliness), they do not seem emotionally damaged by the experience. In addition, if they stay by themselves rather than "hanging out" unsupervised with friends, they can avoid activities that lead to difficulties (Belle, 1999; Goyette-Ewing, 2000).

Time alone also gives children a chance to focus on homework and school or personal projects. In fact, children with employed parents can have higher self-esteem because they feel they are contributing to the household (Goyette-Ewing, 2000).

Divorce

Having divorced parents is not unusual: Approximately three-quarters of children spend their entire childhood in the same household with both parents. The rest will live in single-parent homes or with stepparents, grandparents, or other nonparental relatives; some end up in foster care (Harvey and Fine, 2004).

How do children react to divorce? The answer is complex. For six months to two years after the separation, children and parents can show signs of psychological maladjustment such as anxiety, depression, sleep disturbances, and phobias. Even though most children stay with their mothers, the quality of the mother–child relationship mostly declines, often because children feel caught in the middle between their mothers and fathers, and parenting often becomes more permissive (Holyrod and Sheppard, 1997; Wallerstein et al., 2000; Amato and Afifi, 2006).

During the early stage of middle childhood, children often blame themselves for the breakup. By age 10, they feel pressure to choose sides and they experience some degree of divided loyalty (Shaw et al., 1999).

The long-term consequences of divorce are less clear. Some studies have found that 18 months to 2 years later, most children begin to return to their predivorce state of adjustment. For many children, long-term consequences are minimal (Hetherington and Kelly, 2002; Guttmann and Rosenberg, 2003; Harvey and Fine, 2004).

Other evidence suggests that the fallout from divorce lingers. For example, compared with children from intact families, twice as many children of divorced parents enter psychological counselling (although sometimes counselling is mandated by a judge as part of the divorce). In addition, people who have experienced parental divorce are more at risk for experiencing divorce themselves later in life (Wallerstein et al., 2000; Amato and Booth, 2001; Wallerstein and Resnikoff, 2005; Huurre et al., 2006).

Another factor in children's reactions to divorce is the economic standing of the family. Divorce often brings a decline in both parents' standards of living. When this occurs, children may be thrown into poverty (Ozawa and Yoon, 2003).

On the other hand, if the household before the divorce was overwhelmed by parental strife—as is the case in around 30 percent of divorces—the greater calm of a postdivorce household may be beneficial to children. This is particularly true for children who maintain a close, positive relationship with the parent with whom they do not live (Davies et al., 2002). This means, of course, that in the 70 percent of divorces where the predivorce level of conflict is not high, children can have a more difficult time adjusting (Amato and Booth, 1997).

⊙ From the perspective of a health-care provider: How might the development of self-esteem in middle childhood be affected by a divorce? Can constant hostility and tension between parents lead to a child's health problems?

Single-Parent Families

Approximately 18 percent of children under age 14 live with only one parent; half the parents are divorced or separated, one-fifth are widowed, and 3 in 10 single parents were never married. By contrast, in 1951 most single parents were widowed. Eighty percent of single-parent households are headed by women (Statistics Canada, 2006).

What are the consequences for children in one-parent homes? Much depends on whether a second parent was present earlier and on the nature of the parents' relationship at that time.

Furthermore, the economic status of the single-parent family plays a role. Single-parent families are often less well-off financially than two-parent families, and living in relative poverty has a negative impact on children (Davis, 2003; Harvey and Fine, 2004).

Multigenerational Families

In some households, children, parents, and grandparents live together. Multigenerational families can make for a rich living experience for children, but the potential for conflict arises if "layers" of adults act as disciplinarians without coordinating what they do.

The incidence of three-generational families living together is increasing, according to 2006 census data. In addition to having traditional roots among Aboriginal families and immigrant families (for example, in India, where the practice is commonplace), multigenerational living arrangements have also been embraced by families seeking to economize or who are concerned about aging parents. The help of grandparents in everyday childcare is often a key component of life in these families (Baydar and Brooks-Gunn, 1998; Baird et al., 2000; Crowther and Rodriguez, 2003).

Blended families are created when couples with children marry or remarry.

Living in Blended Families

For some children, the aftermath of divorce includes a remarriage. Twice as often, the remarriage involves only the addition of a stepparent to the mix, but for many families, new siblings move in together as well, creating **blended families**.

Children in a blended family face challenges. They often have to deal with *role ambiguity*, in which roles and expectations are unclear. They can be uncertain about their responsibilities, how to behave toward stepparents and stepsiblings, and how to make a host of tough everyday decisions. For instance, they might have to choose which parent to spend holidays and vacations with, or decide between conflicting advice from a biological parent and a stepparent. Some find the disruption of routine and of established family relationships difficult. For instance, a child used to her mother's complete attention may find it hard to see her mother showing interest and affection to a stepchild (Cath and Shopper, 2001; Belcher, 2003).

Still, school-age children in blended families often adjust relatively smoothly—especially compared with adolescents—for several reasons. For one thing, the family's financial situation is often improved. In addition, there are usually more people to share the burden of household chores. Finally, the higher "population" of the family increases opportunities for social interaction (Hetherington and Clingempeel, 1992; Greene et al., 2003; Hetherington and Elmore, 2003).

Families blend most successfully when the parents create an environment that supports self-esteem and a climate of family togetherness. Generally, the younger the children, the easier the transition (Jeynes, 2007; Kirby, 2006).

Families with Gay and Lesbian Parents

An increasing number of children have two mothers or two fathers. Three percent of male same-sex couples have children, while 16 percent of female same-sex couples have children. Couples who are married are more likely to have children than those in a common-law union (Statistics Canada, 2007).

Relatively little research has been done on the effects of same-sex parenting on children, and the results are not definitive. However, most studies find that children in lesbian and gay households develop similarly to children in heterosexual families. Their sexual orientation is unrelated to that of their parents, their behaviour is no more or less gender-typed, and they seem equally well adjusted (Patterson, 2002, 2003, 2006; Parke, 2004).

Furthermore, children of lesbian and gay parents and children of heterosexual parents have similar relationships with their peers; relate to adults—both gay and straight—no differently; and when they reach adolescence, have similar romantic relationships and sexual behaviour (Patterson, 1995; Golombok et al., 2003; Wainright et al., 2004).

blended families comprising remarried couples who have at least one stepchild living with them

👁 Watch on mydevelopmentlab

Put yourself in the role of an educator, social worker, or health-care worker; how would you handle the issues presented in the video? Check MyDevelopmentLab for an Observations Video on neglected children.

Some research has even suggested that children of same-sex parents fared better than children in heterosexual homes. In interpreting this research, we have to consider the number one way in which families with same-sex parents differ from the average family: An estimated 50 percent of children of heterosexual parents are unplanned to some degree, but not in same-sex homes. Same-sex parents go through a lengthy and deliberate process to bring each and every child into their home, whether through artificial insemination or adoption. Landmark adoption rights for same-sex couples were not won by couples seeking to adopt a child from outside, but by a couple in which one was the biological mother (using donor sperm), and the other parent had no legal parental rights. When compared to families who are similar in terms of education and income, and who used non-traditional means to have a family, same-sex families are the same as opposite-sex families.

Poverty and Family Life

Children in economically disadvantaged families face hardships. Low-income families have fewer everyday resources, and more disruptions occur in children's lives. For example, parents might be forced to look for less expensive housing or a different job and, as a result, parents might be less responsive to their children's needs and provide less social support (Evans, 2004).

The stress of difficult family environments, along with other stress in the lives of children living in low-income households—such as living in unsafe neighbourhoods with high rates of violence and attending low-resource schools—ultimately takes its toll. Economically disadvantaged children are at risk for poorer academic performance, higher rates of aggression, and conduct problems. In addition, declines in economic well-being have been linked to mental health problems (Solantaus et al., 2004; Sapolsky, 2005; Morales and Guerra, 2006).

Orphanages in the Twenty-first Century

The term "orphanage" can evoke either stereotypical images of grim institutional life or the musical *Annie*. The reality of large institutional care for children was deemed to be so detrimental to children that all but one member of the United Nations agreed to eliminate these facilities. Children who would have once been placed in an orphanage are today placed in *foster care*, with a family who might have biological children of their own in the home. The intention is to provide a family atmosphere during what is certainly a period of intense upheaval.

An estimated 88 000 children are in foster care in Canada. Most children are removed from their homes after allegations of abuse or neglect, and some can be returned to their homes after social workers intervene with their families. In other situations, the family remains in turmoil, but parents are reluctant to relinquish rights that would permit adoption. Other children are so psychologically damaged that they are likely to remain in foster care throughout childhood. Adoption becomes a challenge for most of these children, who have developed severe emotional and behavioural problems, such as high levels of aggression or anger (Bass et al., 2004; Chamberlain et al., 2006).

Across Canada, a large number of children in foster care are eligible for adoption. Older children and children with special needs are particularly difficult to place permanently in new adoptive homes. Formerly restrictive policies on who could adopt have been changed in some provinces in an effort to place all children in loving, permanent homes.

Most countries in the United Nations pledged to eliminate orphanages. Most children are cared for in foster care.

REVIEW, CHECK, AND APPLY

REVIEW

- Self-care children may develop independence and enhanced self-esteem from their experience.

- How divorce affects children depends on such factors as financial circumstances and the comparative levels of tension in the family before and after the divorce.

- The effects of being raised in a single-parent household depend on financial circumstances, the amount of parent–child interaction, and the level of tension in the family.

CHECK YOURSELF

1. According to sociologist Sandra Hofferth, self-care children can benefit from their situation by having more time to decompress from a hectic schedule and the opportunity to develop greater _____ or independence.

2. Which of the following characteristics have been associated with a child's response to divorce? Check all that apply.

   a. phobias

   b. increased anxiety

   c. schizophrenia

   d. sleep disturbances

   e. depression

3. The impact of living in a single-parent family is less about the number of parents and more about the economic status, stress level, and time spent together in the family.

   - True

   - False

APPLYING LIFESPAN DEVELOPMENT

- Politicians often speak of "family values." How does this term relate to diverse family situations such as divorced parents, single parents, blended families, working parents, self-care children, and foster care?

Answers: 1) autonomy; 2) a, b, d, e; 3) True

Putting It All Together
Middle Childhood

RYAN (the student we met in the chapter prologue) entered grade 1 with boundless hope and a keen desire to read. Unfortunately, an undiagnosed vision problem interfered with his reading, and fine motor deficits made writing difficult. In most other ways, Ryan was at least the equal of his peers: physically active, imaginative, and highly intelligent. Socially, however, he was hampered by spending time in special education classes. Because he had been singled out and because he could not do some of the things his classmates could do, he was ignored, even bullied, by some of them. When he finally got the right treatment, though, most of his problems vanished. His physical and social skills advanced to match his cognitive abilities. He became more engaged in his schoolwork and more open to friend-ships. Ryan's story had a happy ending.

MODULE **5.1** Physical Development

- Steady growth and increased abilities characterized Ryan's physical development in these years **(p. 191)**.

- Ryan's gross and fine motor skills developed as muscle coordination improved and he practised new skills **(pp. 194–195)**.

- Ryan's sensory problems interfered with his schoolwork **(pp. 198–199)**.

MODULE **5.2** Cognitive Development

- Ryan's intellectual abilities, such as language and mem-ory, became more skilled in middle childhood **(p. 204)**.

- Fluent reading and appropriate comprehension were key academic tasks for Ryan **(p. 209)**.

- Ryan displayed many components and types of intel-ligence, and the development of his intellectual skills was aided by his social interactions **(p. 212)**.

- In this period, Ryan mastered many of the challenges presented by school and peers, both of which took on central importance in his life **(p. 222).**

- The development of Ryan's self-esteem was particularly crucial; when Ryan felt inadequate, his self-esteem suffered **(p. 223).**

- Ryan's friendships helped provide emotional support and fostered intellectual growth **(p. 229).**

What would a PARENT do?

- What strategies would you use to help Ryan overcome his difficulties and function effectively? How would you bolster his self-esteem?

  HINT Review pages 223–224.

  What's your response?

What would a HEALTH-CARE PROVIDER do?

- How might you respond to Ryan's vision and motor problems? What if Ryan's parents had refused to believe that there was anything physically wrong with Ryan? How would you persuade them to get treatment for Ryan?

  HINT Review pages 195, 198–199.

  What's your response?

What would an EDUCATOR do?

- How would you deal with Ryan's difficulties in reading and writing? What would you do to help integrate him into his class and help him make friends with his classmates? Who would you recommend in terms of educational specialists to deal with his problems?

  HINT Review pages 209–210, 223–224

  What's your response?

What would YOU do?

- How would you deal with a situation in which your child had physical disabilities that prevented him or her from progressing in school? How would you encourage your child? How would you deal with your child's frustration at falling behind in school?

  HINT Review pages 219–221, 223.

  What's your response?

CHAPTER 6

Adolescence

At 13, Mariah appeared to be navigating adolescence with ease. A petite, pretty girl from an affluent home, she earned good grades and was known among her friends for her razor-sharp wit.

But as she entered high school, Mariah began to withdraw. She gave up biking with her friends and spent long afternoons in her room "brooding," as her parents called it. She began a more serious exploration of the drugs her friends only flirted with, and she started cutting school.

Two days after she turned 15, Mariah swallowed a bottle of sleeping pills. She survived the suicide attempt, and she was diagnosed with depression. Over the next two years, Mariah—and her family—struggled. She received intensive individual therapy, and she also participated in family therapy with her parents.

Prior to this period, Mariah says, "Everyone thought I had it all together. I had had lots of friends, and I was in this crowd that was considered cool. But I didn't see myself that way. I didn't really know who I was or what I wanted."

Happily, with the help of mental health professionals, Mariah worked her way to a healthier self-concept. The path wasn't smooth. She broke several ribs in a car accident, the result of impulsively going for a ride with a boy she knew had been drinking.

MODULE 6.1 Physical Development in Adolescence

Teenage boys are affected by early maturation differently than girls. How? What about late maturation? see page 244.

MODULE 6.2 Cognitive Development in Adolescence

How does socioeconomic status affect school performance? What about race and ethnicity?

see page 258.

But by age 17, she was on the road to recovery. She developed an interest in photography and applied to colleges that offered courses in the subject.

Today, Mariah feels she has a much stronger sense of who she is and what she wants in life. She gets along well with her parents (formerly rejected as "clueless"). Her boyfriend of a year encourages her. "He treats me really nicely, and I guess I'm learning to treat myself that way, too," she says. "I'm excited about what's ahead. It's like I've come home to me, and it's good."

In this chapter we study adolescence, the transitional stage between childhood and adulthood. Adolescents face many challenges in all aspects of their lives. Physically, their bodies are maturing quickly—sometimes distressingly quickly. Adolescents become interested in sex, and many of them face worries about their bodies. We will look at some of the physical issues that sometimes plague adolescents, including those relating to obesity and nutrition, harmful substances, and sexually transmitted infections.

Beyond the physical aspects of development, adolescents grow cognitively as well. The most notable change we will discuss is adolescents' growing awareness of their own thought processes. We also consider how adolescents deal with the institution that occupies a great deal of their waking time—school—and discuss the growing impact of the Internet on adolescents' lives, learning, and relationships.

Finally, we turn to the changes that adolescents undergo in their relationships with others. We begin with a consideration of the ways in which they create their concepts of themselves and how they form and protect their self-esteem and identity. We discuss their relationships with parents as adolescents redefine their place within the family. Finally, we discuss dating and sex, which achieve central importance during this period and which encompass issues of intimacy.

MODULE 6.3 Social and Personality Development in Adolescence

What determines sexual orientation? see page 267.

MyVirtualLife

As your virtual child reaches adolescence, are you seeing any of the changes that Mariah went through? How would you deal with Mariah as her parent, educator, doctor, or friend?

Log onto MyVirtualLife to help your virtual child navigate the tumultuous adolescent stage.

MODULE 6.1 Physical Development in Adolescence

A Teenager's Day

5:45 a.m. The alarm goes off in Wendy Vacarro's bedroom.

5:55 a.m. The alarm rings again; this time Wendy gets up.

7:10 a.m. After washing and dressing, Wendy grabs a bagel and heads out the door to wait for the school bus.

8:05 a.m. The bus drops Wendy at Glenwood High School, where a full day of classes awaits her. Today, they consist of English, algebra, advanced biology, criminal justice, German, and phys. ed., with lunch and orchestra practice sandwiched in.

3:30 p.m. Field hockey practice begins. For two hours, Wendy runs laps and participates in scrimmages.

5:30 p.m. Wendy catches a ride home with a friend.

6:15 p.m. She eats dinner with her family.

7:00 p.m. Wendy watches a little TV, while looking over her homework.

8:00 p.m. She spends an hour working on a criminal justice paper, doing research on the Web while text messaging her friends. Then she tackles algebra and finishes a biology lab. Her major task is to study vocabulary and grammar for the next day's German test. She does this, interrupted only twice by friends calling to plan the weekend's activities.

11:30 p.m. Trying to unwind a bit, she watches a little TV.

12:00 midnight. Goes to bed. Sets her alarm for 5:15 a.m. to get in some extra study time for her German test.

This day was typical of Wendy Vacarro's life, in which academic and social demands fill virtually every waking moment. It's also typical of the lives of many adolescents, who struggle to meet society's—and their own—demands in the teenage years.

Adolescence is the developmental stage between childhood and adulthood. It is generally said to start just before the teenage years, and end just after them. Considered neither children nor adults, adolescents are in a transitional stage marked by considerable growth.

This module focuses on physical growth during adolescence. We first consider the extraordinary physical maturation that occurs during adolescence, triggered by the onset of puberty. We then discuss the consequences of early and late maturation and how they differ for males and females. We also consider nutrition. After examining the causes—and consequences—of obesity, we discuss eating disorders, which are surprisingly common at this stage.

The module concludes with a discussion of several major threats to adolescents' well-being: drugs, alcohol, tobacco, and sexually transmitted infections.

adolescence the developmental stage that lies between childhood and adulthood

Physical Maturation

LEARNING OBJECTIVES

LO1 What physical changes do adolescents experience?

LO2 What are the consequences of early and late maturation?

LO3 What are the nutritional needs and concerns of adolescents?

For young males of the Awa tribe, adolescence begins with an elaborate and—to Western eyes—gruesome ceremony to mark the passage from childhood to adulthood. The boys are whipped for two or three days with sticks and prickly branches. Throughout the whipping, the boys atone for their previous infractions and honour tribesmen who were killed in warfare. This ritual continues for days.

We are no doubt grateful to have been spared such physical trials when we entered adolescence. But members of Western cultures have their own rites of passage (admittedly less fearsome), such as bar mitzvahs at age 13 for Jewish boys, and bat mitzvahs at age 12 for Jewish girls, and confirmation ceremonies in many Christian denominations (Herdt, 1998; Eccles et al., 2003; Hoffman, 2003).

> ⟳ **From an educator's perspective:** Why do you think many cultures regard the passage to adolescence as a significant transition that calls for unique ceremonies?

> **puberty** the period during which the sexual organs mature

Regardless of their nature, the underlying purpose of these ceremonies tends to be the same across cultures: symbolically celebrating the physical changes that transform a child's body into an adult body capable of reproduction.

Growth During Adolescence: The Rapid Pace of Physical and Sexual Maturation

In only a few months, adolescents can grow several inches as they are transformed, at least physically, from children to young adults. During this growth spurt—a period of very rapid increases in height and weight—boys, on average, grow 10.4 cm a year and girls 8.9 cm. Some adolescents grow as much as 12 cm in a single year (Tanner, 1972; Caino et al., 2004).

Growth spurts begin at different ages for boys and girls. As you can see in Figure 6-1, a girl's growth spurt begins around age 10, while a boy's growth spurt starts at around age 12. During the two-year period from age 11, girls tend to be taller than boys, but by 13, boys, on average, are taller than girls—a state that persists for the remainder of the lifespan.

Puberty: The Start of Sexual Maturation

Puberty, the period when the sexual organs mature, begins when the pituitary gland in the brain signals other glands to begin producing at adult levels the sex hormones known as *androgens* (male hormones) or *estrogens* (female hormones). Males and females produce both

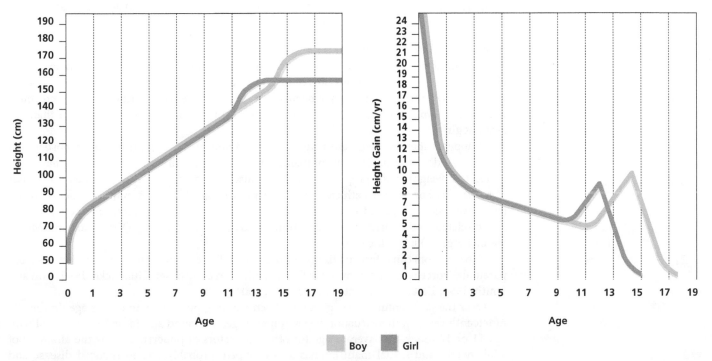

Boy   Girl

FIGURE 6-1 Growth Patterns
Patterns of growth are depicted in two ways. The first figure shows height at a given age, while the second shows the height *increase* that occurs from birth through the end of adolescence. Notice that girls begin their growth spurt around age 10, while boys begin the growth spurt at about age 12. However, by the age of 13, boys tend to be taller than girls. What are the social consequences of being taller or shorter than average for boys and girls?
Source: Adapted from Cratty, 1986.

Note the changes that have occurred in just a few years in these pre- and post-puberty photos of the same boy.

types of sex hormones, but males have higher levels of androgens and females have higher levels of estrogens. The pituitary gland also signals the body to produce more growth hormones. These interact with the sex hormones to cause the growth spurt and puberty. The hormone *leptin* also appears to play a role in the onset of puberty.

Like the growth spurt, puberty begins earlier for girls, starting at around age 11 or 12, whereas boys begin at about age 13 or 14. However, this varies widely. Some girls begin puberty as early as 7 or 8 or as late as age 16.

Puberty in Girls. Although it is not clear why puberty begins when it does, environmental and cultural factors play a role. For example **menarche**, the onset of menstruation and probably the most obvious sign of puberty in girls, varies greatly around the world. In poorer, developing countries, menstruation begins later than in more economically advantaged countries. Even within wealthier countries, more affluent girls begin to menstruate earlier than less affluent girls.

It appears that girls who are better nourished and healthier tend to start menstruation earlier than do those suffering from malnutrition or chronic disease. Some studies have suggested that weight or the proportion of fat to muscle in the body play a key role in the onset of menarche. For example, athletes with a low percentage of body fat may start menstruating later than less active girls. Conversely, obesity—which increases the secretion of leptin, a hormone related to the onset of menstruation—leads to earlier puberty (Vizmanos and Marti-Henneberg, 2000; Woelfle et al., 2007).

Other factors can affect the timing of menarche. For example, environmental stress from parental divorce or intense family conflict can affect an early onset (Hulanicka, 1999; Kim and Smith, 1999; Kaltiala-Heino et al., 2003; Ellis, 2004).

Over the past century or so, girls have been entering puberty at an earlier age. In the late nineteenth century, menstruation began, on average, at around age 14 or 15, compared with age 11 or 12 today. The average age for other indicators of puberty, such as the attaining of adult height and sexual maturity, has also dropped, probably due to reduced disease and improved nutrition, but potentially also from chemical exposures. For example, some chemicals, such as BPA in plastics, mimic estrogen when ingested (altering numerous hormonally mediated systems, especially if the exposure happens in early development—as if the body had really received more estrogen). These chemicals can leach into foods and drinks stored, and especially heated, in plastic containers (Richter et al., 2007).

menarche the onset of menstruation

The earlier start of puberty is an example of a significant **secular trend**. Secular trends occur when a physical characteristic changes over the course of several generations—for example, the earlier onset of menstruation or increased height resulting from better nutrition over the centuries.

Menstruation is one of several changes in puberty related to the development of primary and secondary sex characteristics. **Primary sex characteristics** are associated with the development of the organs and body structures related directly to reproduction. **Secondary sex characteristics** are the visible signs of sexual maturity that do not involve the sex organs directly.

In girls, developing primary sex characteristics involves changes in the vagina and uterus. Secondary sex characteristics include the development of breasts and pubic hair. Breasts begin to grow around age 10, and pubic hair appears at about age 11. Underarm hair appears about two years later.

For some girls, signs of puberty start unusually early—before age eight. The reasons for this earlier onset are unclear, and what defines normal and abnormal onset is a controversy among specialists (Lemonick, 2000; The Endocrine Society, 2001; Ritzen, 2003).

Puberty in Boys. The sexual maturation of boys follows a somewhat different course. Growth of the penis and scrotum accelerates around age 12, reaching adult size about three or four years later. As boys' penises enlarge, other primary sex characteristics develop. The prostate gland and seminal vesicles, which produce semen (the fluid that carries sperm), enlarge. A boy's first ejaculation, known as *spermarche,* usually occurs around age 13, more than a year after the body begins producing sperm. At first, the semen contains relatively few sperm, but the sperm count increases significantly with age. Secondary sex characteristics are also developing. Pubic hair begins to grow around age 12, followed by the growth of underarm and facial hair. Finally, boys' voices deepen as the vocal cords become longer and the larynx larger. (Figure 6-2 summarizes the changes that occur in sexual maturation during early adolescence.)

The surge in hormones that triggers puberty can also lead to rapid mood swings. Boys might have feelings of anger and annoyance associated with higher hormone levels. In girls, higher levels of hormones are associated with depression as well as anger (Buchanan et al., 1992).

Body Image: Reactions to Physical Changes in Adolescence. Unlike infants, who also undergo rapid growth, adolescents are aware of what is happening to their bodies, and they can react with horror or joy. Few, though, are neutral about the changes they are experiencing (Jansen et al., 2001).

Some of the changes of adolescence carry psychological weight. In the past, girls tended to view menarche with anxiety because Western society emphasized the negative aspects of menstruation—its cramps and messiness. Today, however, society views menstruation more positively, in part because more open discussion has demystified it; for example, television commercials for tampons are commonplace. As a result, menarche now typically increases

secular trend   a pattern of change occurring over several generations

primary sex characteristics   characteristics associated with the development of the organs and structures of the body that directly relate to reproduction

secondary sex characteristics   the visible signs of sexual maturity that do not directly involve the sex organs

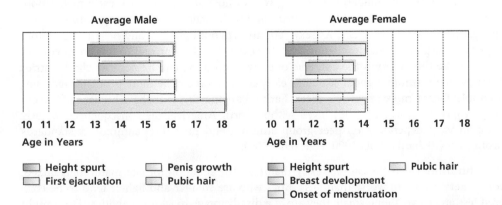

FIGURE 6-2 Sexual Maturation
The changes in sexual maturation that occur for males and females during early adolescence.
Source: Adapted from Tanner, 1978.

self-esteem, enhances status, and provides greater self-awareness, as girls see themselves as young adults (Johnson et al., 1999; Matlin, 2003).

A boy's first ejaculation is roughly equivalent to menarche. However, while girls generally tell their mothers about the onset of menstruation, boys rarely mention their first ejaculation to their parents or even their friends (Stein and Reiser, 1994). Why? One reason is that mothers provide the tampons or sanitary napkins girls need. For boys, the first ejaculation may be seen as a sign of their budding sexuality, an area they feel both uncertain about and reluctant to discuss with others.

Menstruation and ejaculations occur privately, but changes in body shape and size are quite public. Teenagers frequently are embarrassed by these changes. Girls, in particular, are often unhappy with their new bodies. Western ideals of beauty call for extreme thinness that is at odds with the actual shape of most women. Puberty considerably increases the amount of fatty tissue, and enlarges the hips and buttocks—a far cry from the pencil-thin bodies society seems to demand (Attie and Brooks-Gunn, 1989; Unger and Crawford, 2004).

How children react to the onset of puberty depends in part on when it happens. Girls and boys who mature either much earlier or later than most of their peers are especially affected.

The Timing of Puberty: The Consequences of Early and Late Maturation. There are social consequences for early or late maturation, and these social consequences are very important to adolescents.

Early Maturation. For boys, early maturation is largely a plus. Early-maturing boys tend to be more successful athletes, presumably because of their larger size. They also tend to be more popular and to have a more positive self-concept.

Early maturation in boys, though, does have a downside. Boys who mature early are more apt to have difficulties in school, and to become involved in delinquency and substance abuse. Being larger in size, they are more likely to seek the company of older boys and become involved in age-inappropriate activities. Early-maturers are also more conforming and lacking in humour, although they are more responsible and co-operative in adulthood. Overall, though, early maturation is positive for boys (Taga et al., 2006; Costello et al., 2007; Lynne et al., 2007).

The story differs for early-maturing girls. Early maturation tends to come at a very young age for girls, as they mature earlier than boys, in general. The obvious changes in their bodies (for example, the development of breasts) can make them feel uncomfortable and different from their peers. Less mature classmates might ridicule them (Williams and Currie, 2000; Franko and Striegel-Moore, 2002; Olivardia and Pope, 2002).

Early maturation, though, is not a completely negative experience for girls. Those who mature earlier are more often sought as dates, and their popularity might enhance their self-concept. This can be psychologically challenging, however. Early-maturers might not be socially ready for the kind of one-on-one dating situations that most girls deal with at a later age. Moreover, the obvious deviation from their later-maturing peers may produce anxiety, unhappiness, and depression (Kaltiala-Heino et al., 2003).

Cultural norms and standards play a big role in how girls experience early maturation. In North America, female sexuality is looked upon with some incongruity—promoted in the media, yet frowned upon socially. A "sexy" girl attracts both positive and negative attention. Conspicuous displays of her developing sexuality can bring disapproval. Unless an adolescent girl can handle this scrutiny, the outcome of early maturation can be negative. In countries with more liberal attitudes about sexuality, early maturation can be more positive. Germany, for example, takes a more open view of sex. Early-maturing girls there have higher self-esteem than such girls in North America. Even within North America, the consequences of early maturation vary, depending on peer group attitudes and prevailing community standards regarding sex (Richards et al., 1990; Petersen, 2000).

Late Maturation. As is the case for early-maturers, the situation for late-maturers is mixed, although here boys fare worse than girls. Boys who are smaller and lighter tend to be considered less attractive. Being small, they are at a disadvantage in sports activities. They might also suffer socially, as boys are expected to be taller than their dates. If these difficulties diminish a boy's self-concept, the disadvantages of late maturation could extend well into

👁 **Watch** on **mydevelopmentlab**

Log onto MyDevelopmentLab to watch 12-year-old Kianna, her mother, and her best friend talk about how important body image is in adolescence.

adulthood. Coping with the challenges of late maturation may actually help males, however. Late-maturing boys grow up to be assertive and insightful, and are more creatively playful than early maturers (Livson and Peskin, 1980; Kaltiala-Heino et al., 2003).

The picture for late-maturing girls is quite positive, even though they might be overlooked in dating and other mixed-sex activities during junior high and middle school, and can have relatively low social status (Apter et al., 1981; Clarke-Stewart and Friedman, 1987). In fact, late-maturing girls may suffer fewer emotional problems. Before they reach grade 10 and have begun to mature visibly, they are more apt to fit the slender, "leggy" body type society idealizes than their early-maturing peers, who tend to look heavier in comparison (Simmons and Blythe, 1987; Peterson, 1988).

The reactions to early and late maturation paint a complex picture. As we have seen, an individual's development is affected by a constellation of factors. Some developmentalists suggest that changes in peer groups, family dynamics, and particularly schools and other societal institutions, may determine an adolescent's behaviour more than age of maturation, and the effects of puberty in general (Dorn et al., 2003; Stice, 2003).

Nutrition, Food, and Eating Disorders: Fuelling the Growth of Adolescence

Heather's typical lunch throughout junior high was a Diet Coke. In the evening, she ate a few crackers with cheese. If she felt hungry, she had a glass of water. Heather was becoming increasingly afraid that she was fat. She stopped swimming because she didn't want anyone to see her in a bathing suit. She wore baggy sweaters to hide her "flab." Now 24, Heather eats a healthy, balanced diet, but still only sees "flab" when she looks in the mirror. "I'm a much healthier weight. I was under 40 kg at my worst. Ironic—40 kg was my goal, but even when I reached it, all I saw was flab."

Heather's problem: a severe eating disorder, anorexia nervosa. As we have seen, the cultural ideal of slim and fit favours late-developing girls. But when development does occur, how do girls, and increasingly, boys, cope with an image in the mirror that deviates from the popular media ideal?

A dramatic increase in food consumption fuels the rapid physical growth of adolescence. During the growth spurt, the average girl requires some 2200 calories a day, and the average boy requires 2800. Of course, not just any calories nourish this growth. Several nutrients are essential, particularly calcium and iron. Milk and certain vegetables provide calcium for bone growth, and calcium may prevent osteoporosis—the thinning of bones—which affects 25 percent of women in later life. Iron is also necessary, as iron-deficiency anemia is not uncommon among teenagers.

For most adolescents, the major eating issue involves getting a sufficient balance of nutritious foods. Two extremes of nutrition—obesity and eating disorders like the one afflicting Heather—concern a substantial minority of adolescents and can create real threats to health.

Obesity. The most common nutritional concern in adolescence is obesity. One in five adolescents is overweight, and one in eleven can be classified as obese. The proportion of females classified as obese increases over the course of adolescence (Brook and Tepper, 1997; Critser, 2003; Kimm et al., 2002).

Adolescents are obese for the same reasons that younger children are, but special concerns with body image may have severe psychological consequences in adolescence. The potential health consequences of obesity during adolescence are also problematic. Obesity taxes the circulatory system, increasing the risk of high blood pressure and diabetes. Obese adolescents also have an 80 percent chance of becoming obese adults (Blaine et al., 2007).

Lack of exercise is a major culprit. One survey found that by the end of the teenage years, few females get much exercise outside of school physical education classes. In fact, the older they get, the less they exercise (Burke et al., 2006; Deforche et al., 2006).

Obesity has become the most common nutritional concern during adolescence. In addition to issues of health, what are some psychological concerns about obesity in adolescence?

This young woman suffers from anorexia nervosa, a severe eating disorder in which people refuse to eat, while denying that their behaviour and appearance are out of the ordinary.

This lack of exercise might reflect a lack of organized sports or good athletic facilities for women. It could be the result of lingering cultural norms that suggest athletic participation is more the realm of boys than of girls. Whatever the reason, lack of exercise contributes to the increase in obesity.

A lack of healthy eating choices is a second culprit in obesity. Unlike younger children, adolescents make more decisions and exert more control over their diets. If children do not learn healthy eating habits early and are exposed to unhealthy models of eating and to advertising for junk foods, they are very likely to make poor dietary choices.

Anorexia Nervosa and Bulimia.   Fear of growing obese can create its own problems—for example, Heather suffered from **anorexia nervosa**, a severe eating disorder in which individuals refuse to eat. A troubled body image leads some adolescents to deny that their behaviour and appearance, which may become skeletal, are out of the ordinary.

Anorexia is a dangerous psychological disorder; some 15 to 20 percent of its victims starve themselves to death. It primarily afflicts women between the ages of 12 and 40; intelligent, successful, and attractive white adolescent girls from affluent homes are the most susceptible. Once thought of as a Western problem, eating disorders are on the rise in countries as diverse as Japan and Iran. Anorexia is also becoming a problem for boys; about 10 percent of the adolescents who suffer from it are male. This percentage is rising and is often associated with the use of steroids (Jacobi et al., 2004; Ricciardelli and McCabe, 2004; Crisp et al., 2006).

Though they eat little, individuals with anorexia tend to focus on food. They may shop often, collect cookbooks, talk about food, or cook huge meals for others. They may be incredibly thin but their body images are so distorted that they see themselves as disgustingly fat and try to lose more weight. Even when they grow skeletal, they cannot see what they have become.

Bulimia, another eating disorder, is characterized by *binge eating*: consuming large amounts of food, followed by *purging* through vomiting or the use of laxatives. Bulimics may eat an entire gallon of ice cream or a whole package of tortilla chips, but then feel such powerful guilt and depression that they intentionally rid themselves of the food. The disorder poses real risks. Though a sufferer's weight remains fairly normal, the constant vomiting and diarrhea of the binge-and-purge cycles can produce a chemical imbalance that triggers heart failure. Recently, binge eating disorder (without purging) has also been recognized as a psychiatric condition. As there is no compensatory purge, those with binge eating disorder tend to be overweight, if not obese, depending on the magnitude, frequency, and duration of the binging.

Why eating disorders occur is not clear, but several factors may be at work. Dieting often precedes the onset of eating disorders, as society exhorts even normal-weight individuals to be ever thinner. Losing weight may lead to feelings of control and success that encourage more dieting. Girls who mature early and have a higher level of body fat are more susceptible to eating disorders in later adolescence as they try to trim their mature bodies to fit the cultural ideal of a thin, boyish physique. Clinically depressed adolescents and girls who have been sexually abused are also at increased risk of developing eating disorders (Pratt et al., 2003; Walcott et al., 2003; Giordana, 2005).

A biological cause may underlie both anorexia nervosa and bulimia. In fact, twin studies suggest genetic components are involved. In addition, hormonal imbalances sometimes occur in sufferers (Irwin, 1993; Treasure and Tiller, 1993; Kaye et al., 2004). Other explanations emphasize psychological and social factors. Some experts suggest that perfectionist, over-demanding parents or other family difficulties can lead to the disorders.

Culture also plays a role. Anorexia nervosa was not seen in the seventeenth and eighteenth centuries, when the ideal female body was plump. The increasing number of anorexic boys might reflect a male ideal that emphasizes muscles and spurns body fat (Mangweth et al., 2004; Makino et al., 2006; Greenberg et al., 2007).

Because eating disorders involve both biological and environmental factors, treatment typically requires a mix of approaches (for example, both psychological therapy and dietary modifications). In more extreme cases, hospitalization might be necessary. Anti-depressant drug treatment is often not effective in anorexia until the patient reaches a healthy weight (Porzelius et al., 2001; Stice and Shaw, 2004; Robergeau et al., 2006).

anorexia nervosa   a severe eating disorder in which individuals refuse to eat, while denying that their behaviour and appearance, which may become skeletal, are out of the ordinary

bulimia   an eating disorder characterized by binges on large quantities of food, followed by purges of the food through vomiting or the use of laxatives

The prefrontal cortex, the area of the brain responsible for impulse control, is biologically immature during adolescence, leading to some of the risky and impulsive behaviour associated with the age group.

Brain Development and Thought: Paving the Way for Cognitive Growth

Teenagers tend to assert themselves more as they gain greater independence. This independence is, in part, the result of changes in the brain that bring significant advances in cognitive abilities. As the number of neurons (the cells of the nervous system) continues to grow, and their interconnections become richer and more complex, adolescent thinking becomes more sophisticated (Thompson and Nelson, 2001; Toga and Thompson, 2003).

The brain produces an oversupply of grey matter during adolescence, which is later pruned back by 1 to 2 percent each year (see Figure 6-3). Myelination—the process of insulating nerve cells with fat cells—increases, making the transmission of neural messages more efficient. Both pruning and increased myelination contribute to the growing cognitive abilities of adolescents (Sowell et al., 2001; Sowell et al., 2003).

The prefrontal cortex of the brain, which is not fully developed until the early 20s, undergoes considerable development during adolescence. The *prefrontal cortex* allows people to think, evaluate, and make complex judgments in a uniquely human way. It underlies the increasingly complex intellectual achievements that are possible during adolescence.

At this stage, the prefrontal cortex becomes increasingly efficient in communicating with other parts of the brain, creating a communication system that is more distributed and sophisticated, which permits the different areas of the brain to process information more effectively (Scherf et al., 2006).

The prefrontal cortex also provides impulse control. An individual with a fully developed prefrontal cortex is able to inhibit the desire to act on such emotions as anger or rage. In adolescence, however, the prefrontal cortex is biologically immature; the ability to inhibit impulses is not fully developed. This brain immaturity may lead to the risky and impulsive behaviours that characterize adolescence—and some behaviours that are even more extreme (Weinberger, 2001; Steinberg and Scott, 2003).

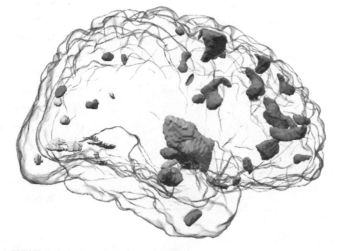

FIGURE 6-3 Pruning Grey Matter

This three-dimensional view of the brain shows areas of grey matter that are pruned from the brain between adolescence and adulthood.

Source: Reprinted by permission from Macmillan Publishers Ltd: Nature Neuroscience, 10. Sowell, E.R., Thompson, P.M., Holmes, C.J., Jernigan, T.L., & Toga, A.W. In vivo evidence for post-adolescent brain maturation in frontal and striatal regions. 859–861. Copyright 1999.

Some neuroscientists argue that adolescents are not capable of making sound decisions because their brains differ from those of adults. For example, neurons that make up unnecessary grey matter begin to disappear. The volume of white matter begins to increase. This change permits more sophisticated, thoughtful cognitive processing; however, this process continues throughout adolescence. When the brain's frontal lobes develop more white matter, we become better at restraining impulsivity. As neuroscientist Ruben Gur puts it, "If you've been insulted, your emotional brain says, 'Kill,' but your frontal lobe says you're in the middle of a cocktail party, 'so let's respond with a cutting remark'" (Beckman, 2004, p. 597). In adolescence, that censoring process is still developing. Teenagers may act impulsively, responding with emotion rather than reason. Their ability to foresee consequences can also be hindered by their less mature brains.

At the same time, adolescents can be capable of great creativity for precisely the same reason. Because of their relative lack of experience, adolescents can more easily "think outside the box," whereas adults, over time, might become increasingly boxed in by their cumulative experience and habits.

Brain development also produces changes in regions involving dopamine sensitivity and production. As a result, adolescents can become less affected by alcohol, requiring more drinks to experience its effects—leading to higher alcohol intake. Changes in dopamine sensitivity can also increase sensitivity to stress, leading to further alcohol use (Spear, 2002).

Sleep Deprivation. With increasing academic and social demands, adolescents go to bed later and get up earlier, leaving them sleep-deprived. This deprivation coincides with a shift in their internal clocks. Older adolescents have a need to go to bed later and to sleep later in the morning, requiring nine hours of sleep to feel rested. In the conflict between late nights and early morning classes, however, they get far less sleep than their bodies crave. Sleep-deprived teens have lower marks, are more depressed, and have greater difficulty controlling their moods. They are also at increased risk for auto accidents (Fredriksen et al., 2004; Dorofaeff and Denny, 2006; Fuligni and Hardway, 2006).

REVIEW, CHECK, AND APPLY

REVIEW

- Adolescence is a period of rapid physical growth, including the changes puberty brings.

- Adolescents' responses to puberty range widely—from confusion to increased self-esteem.

- Adequate nutrition is essential to fuel adolescents' physical growth. Changing physical needs and environmental pressures can cause obesity or eating disorders.

CHECK YOURSELF

1. The hormone _____ appears to play a role in the start of puberty for males and females.

   a. estrogen
   b. pituitary
   c. serotonin
   d. leptin

2. Which of the following is an example of a primary sex characteristic?

   a. growth of pubic hair
   b. development of breasts
   c. changes in the uterus
   d. sudden increase in height

3. The most common nutritional concern in adolescence is _____.

   a. anorexia
   b. bulimia
   c. sleep deprivation
   d. obesity

APPLYING LIFESPAN DEVELOPMENT

- How can societal and environmental influences contribute to eating disorders?

Answers: 1) d; 2) c; 3) d

Threats to Adolescents' Well-Being

LEARNING OBJECTIVES

LO4 What are some threats to the well-being of adolescents?

LO5 What dangers do adolescent sexual practices present, and how can these dangers be avoided?

AMY'S STORY...

My story begins the summer before 7th grade—I was 11 years old. My older brother, who was very popular in school and someone I looked up to, introduced me to opium. A week later, I began smoking marijuana. At first, I was only using drugs about three times a month. Then it became two times a week. By the middle of my sophomore year in high school, I was using daily and by my junior year, it was multiple times a day. After an injury that kept me from competitive gymnastics, I had to find something else to give my time to...something that could help me meet new friends. (www.theantidrug.com/advice/teens-today/teens-and-technology/real-teen-stories. aspx. Amy is not her real name.)

The use of marijuana among high school students has decreased in recent years but the drug remains heavily used among youth.

Drug use, along with other kinds of substance use and abuse, is one of several health threats in adolescence—usually one of the healthiest periods of life. While the extent of risky behaviour is unknown, drugs, alcohol, and tobacco pose serious threats to adolescents' health and well-being.

Illegal Drugs

Illegal drug use in adolescence is very common, but has declined slightly in recent years. A 2009 survey by Health Canada indicated that 26 percent of youth age 15 to 24 used cannabis in the past year, and 6 percent used a drug other than cannabis. Drug use is higher in this age range than in any other, but is on the decline (see Figure 6-4; Health Canada, 2012).

Adolescents use drugs for many reasons. Some seek the pleasure they provide. Others hope to escape the pressures of everyday life, however temporarily. Some adolescents try drugs simply for the thrill of doing the illegal. The alleged drug use of popular celebrities might also entice. And peer pressure plays a role: Adolescents are especially influenced by their peer groups (Urberg et al., 2003; Nation and Heflinger, 2006; Young et al., 2006).

The use of illegal drugs poses several dangers. Some drugs are addictive. **Addictive drugs** produce a biological or psychological dependence, leading users to increasingly crave the drugs.

With a biological addiction, the drug's presence becomes so common that the body cannot function in its absence. Addiction causes actual physical—and potentially lingering—changes in the nervous system. The drug may no longer provide a "high," but may be necessary to maintain the perception of normalcy (Cami and Farré, 2003; Munzar et al., 2003).

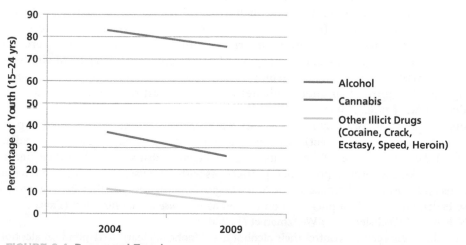

FIGURE 6-4 Downward Trend
Youth (15–24 years old) were asked about drug and alcohol use in the previous year. The percentage of youth who had used these substances has declined in recent years. What might account for the decline?
Source: Adapted from Health Canada, 2010 with the permission from the Minister of Health, 2012. Canadian alcohol and drug use monitoring survey (CADUMS). Adapted from "Table 4: Changes between CAS 2004 and CADUMS 2008 and 2009 by age: Drugs" and from "Table 9: Changes between CAS 2004 and CADUMS 2008 and 2009 by age: Alcohol." Retrieved September 28, 2012 from http://www.hc-sc. gc.ca/hc-ps/drugs-drogues/stat/_2009/tablestableaux-eng.pho

addictive drugs drugs that produce a biological or psychological dependence in users, leading to increasingly powerful cravings for them

Males

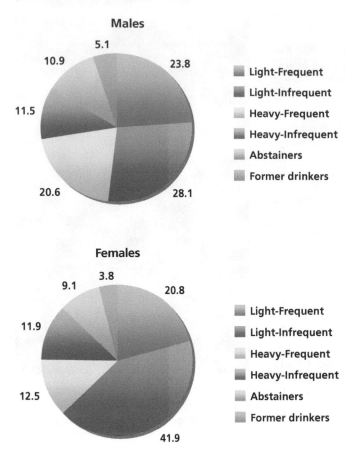

- Light-Frequent
- Light-Infrequent
- Heavy-Frequent
- Heavy-Infrequent
- Abstainers
- Former drinkers

Females

- Light-Frequent
- Light-Infrequent
- Heavy-Frequent
- Heavy-Infrequent
- Abstainers
- Former drinkers

FIGURE 6-5 Binge Drinking Among Post-Secondary Students
Eighty-five percent of students reported drinking in the past year. Binge drinking (heavy drinking) is defined as consuming five or more drinks in one sitting. Frequent drinking is defined as drinking on a weekly basis. Former drinkers are defined as not having consumed alcohol in the past 12 months. Abstainers are defined as having never consumed alcohol. Why is binge drinking popular?
Source: Based on raw data obtained from Adlaf et al. 2005.

alcoholics people who have learned to depend on alcohol and are unable to control their drinking

Drugs also can produce psychological addiction. People grow to depend on drugs to cope with everyday stress. If used as an escape, drugs can prevent adolescents from confronting—and solving—the problems that led to drug use in the first place. Even casual use of less hazardous drugs can escalate to dangerous forms of substance abuse (Segal and Stewart, 1996).

Alcohol: Use and Abuse

The prevalence of frequent, heavy drinking is three times higher among youth 15 to 24 than among adults 25 and older (12 percent versus 4 percent; Health Canada, 2009). Post-secondary students are the group most associated with frequent heavy drinking behaviour, although the legal drinking age may skew reporting. Most students have already started drinking when they enter university or college, but the culture condones and encourages them to drink more. In surveys of students at major Canadian universities, more than 75 percent of students report having consumed at least one alcoholic drink in the last 30 days. More than 40 percent say they've had five or more drinks in one sitting within the past two weeks, 17 percent had eight or more drinks in one sitting within the past two weeks, and 32 percent reported harmful or hazardous patterns of drinking (Adlaf et al., 2005).

Binge drinking is commonly perceived to be a problem on campuses across the country. Binge drinking is defined as having five or more drinks in one sitting; overall one in four post-secondary students report binge drinking, some at least once per week (16 percent) and others less frequently. Great regional variation exists in binge drinking as well, with more binge drinking in the Atlantic Provinces and Ontario and less in Quebec and BC. Male students are more likely to report binge drinking than females, especially at the heaviest consumption levels. Among students who reported drinking in the past month, the average student drank 1.3 times per week and consumed 6.4 drinks per occasion; nearly 6 in 10 had binged at least twice during the past month (Adlaf et al., 2005; see Figure 6-5).

Binge drinking affects even those who don't drink or who drink very little. One-third of students reported having their sleep or studies disturbed by drunken students. Nearly 10 percent had experienced sexual harassment and 10 percent had been assaulted by a drunken student. The drinkers reported hazardous behaviour including unplanned sex (14 percent), unsafe sex (6 percent), and drunk driving (11 percent). Drinkers also experienced harm from their drinking, including hangovers (53 percent) or missing class due to hangover (19 percent). One-quarter of drinkers reported experiencing memory loss and regrets as a consequence of their drinking. Nearly a third of all undergraduates reported at least one indicator of alcohol dependency (Adlaf et al., 2005).

Young people drink for many reasons. Most report that they drink to celebrate (29 percent) or to be sociable (25 percent), but 7 percent report intoxication as their goal (Adlaf et al., 2005). For some—especially male athletes, who tend to drink more than their peers, generally—drinking is a way to prove their prowess. As with drug use, others drink to release inhibitions and tension, and reduce stress. Many begin drinking because they believe everyone else is drinking heavily, a phenomenon known as the *false consensus effect* (Pavis et al., 1997; Nelson and Wechsler, 2003; Weitzman et al., 2003).

Some adolescents cannot control their alcohol use. **Alcoholics** learn to depend on alcohol and are unable to stop drinking. They develop an increasing tolerance for it, and need to drink ever-larger amounts to get the positive effects they crave. Some drink throughout the day, while others go on binges (NIAAA, 1990; Morse and Flavin, 1992).

Why some adolescents become alcoholics is not fully understood. Genetics plays a role: Alcoholism runs in families, though not all alcoholics have family members with alcohol problems. For adolescents with an alcoholic parent or family member, alcoholism can be triggered by efforts to deal with the stress (Bushman, 1993; Berenson, 2005).

Hooked on Drugs or Alcohol?

Becoming an Informed Consumer of Development

It is not always easy to know if an adolescent is abusing drugs or alcohol, but there are signals. Among them are the following:

Identification with the drug culture

- Drug-related magazines or slogans on clothing
- Conversation and jokes that involve drugs
- Hostility discussing drugs
- Collection of beer cans

Signs of physical deterioration

- Memory lapses, short attention span, difficulty concentrating
- Poor physical coordination, slurred or incoherent speech
- Unhealthy appearance, indifference to hygiene and grooming
- Bloodshot eyes, dilated pupils

Dramatic changes in school performance

- Marked downturn in grades—not just from Cs to Fs, but also from As to Bs and Cs; assignments not completed
- Increased absenteeism or tardiness

Changes in behaviour

- Chronic dishonesty (lying, stealing, cheating); trouble with the police
- Changes in friends; evasiveness in talking about new ones
- Possession of large amounts of money
- Increasing and inappropriate anger, hostility, irritability, secretiveness
- Reduced motivation, energy, self-discipline, self-esteem
- Diminished interest in extracurricular activities and hobbies (Adapted from Franck and Brownstone, 1991; National Institute on Drug Abuse, 2007)

If an adolescent—or anyone else—fits any of these descriptions, help is probably needed.

Of course, the origins of an adolescent's alcohol or drug problem matter less than getting help. Parents, teachers, and friends can help a teen—if the teen realizes there is a problem. Some of the telltale signs are described in the preceding box.

Tobacco: The Dangers of Smoking

Despite an awareness of the dangers of smoking, many adolescents indulge in it. According to recent data, 3 percent of students in grades 6 to 9 self-identify as smokers, as well as 13 percent of students in grades 10 to 12, with more boys than girls taking up the habit (Health Canada, 2010). Smoking is on the rise among girls, and in several countries, including Austria, Norway, and Sweden, the proportion of girls who smoke is higher than for boys (Harrell et al., 1998; Stolberg, 1998; Baker et al., 2004; Fergusson et al., 2007).

Smoking is becoming a difficult habit to maintain. Social sanctions against it are growing, and more places, including schools and places of business, have become smoke-free. Even so, a good number of adolescents still smoke, despite knowing the dangers of smoking and of second-hand smoke. Furthermore, youth who smoke are more likely to also drink alcohol and use drugs. Among smokers in grades 7 to 9, 88 percent had drunk alcohol and 83 percent had used cannabis in the past year. Among students in grades 7 to 9 who had never tried smoking, 20 percent had drunk alcohol and only 4 percent had used cannabis in the past year (Health Canada, 2010).

Nicotine is just one of the more than 3000 active chemical ingredients in cigarettes that can produce biological and psychological dependency very quickly, making cigarettes addicting. Many chemicals in cigarettes are psychoactive, acting directly upon the brain and contributing to the addiction (Barrett, 2010). Although one or two cigarettes do not usually create a lifetime habit, addiction comes easily. People who smoke as few as 10 cigarettes early in their lives stand an 80 percent chance of becoming habitual smokers (Stacy et al., 1992; Haberstick et al., 2007).

Smoking can produce a pleasant emotional state. Seeing parents and peers smoking increases the chances that an adolescent will adopt the habit. Some adolescents see smoking as a rite of passage, a sign of growing up, and might not think that it will become a lifelong habit or have a long-term impact on their health (Kodl and Mermelstein, 2004; Wills et al., 2007).

sexually transmitted infection (STI) an infection that is spread through sexual contact

Sexually Transmitted Infections

The New Start people came to my college to conduct free counselling and testing and i decided to go. Anyway it turns out that I was HIV positive.

They gave me that referral letter to take to the doctor and i kept it for about a month. I decided that i needed to know my CD4 count after reading the stories that are on here. Needless to say it was under 150 and a high viral load. My doc said that she was surprised i wasnt sick.

So now I am on ART and I am worried about telling my boyfriend cause i really like him and we just started dating. The thing is i really want him to know and yet a part of me is afraid that he will leave me. But I have decided that if he can't accept me the way that I am then maybe he is not the one. So will tell him this weekend.

Wish me luck.

AIDS. The personal story above was posted by an anonymous youth to a support website. This teen is not alone: *acquired immunodeficiency syndrome,* or *AIDS,* is a leading cause of death among young people around the world. AIDS has no cure, but treatments have improved greatly in recent years and AIDS is no longer the sure death sentence that it used to be.

Because AIDS is spread mostly through sexual contact, it is classified as a **sexually transmitted infection (STI)**. Already, 20 million people have died from AIDS, and almost 40 million people worldwide live with it. In Canada, nearly 2500 people are diagnosed each year; slightly more women than men test positive each year, and one in four are Aboriginal. The Public Health Agency of Canada estimates that more than 65 000 Canadians are living with HIV/AIDS and that one-quarter of those infected don't know it (Centers for Disease Control, 2006; UNAIDS and World Health Organization, 2006; Public Health Agency of Canada, 2010).

Other Sexually Transmitted Infections. Although AIDS is the deadliest of sexually transmitted infections, there are a number of other more common STIs (see Figure 6-6).

The most common STI, according to US data, is *human papilloma virus (HPV)*. Data on infection rates in Canada are not available as, historically, HPV has not been reported to the Public Health Agency of Canada. HPV can be transmitted through genital contact without intercourse. Often there are no symptoms, but HPV can produce genital warts and in some

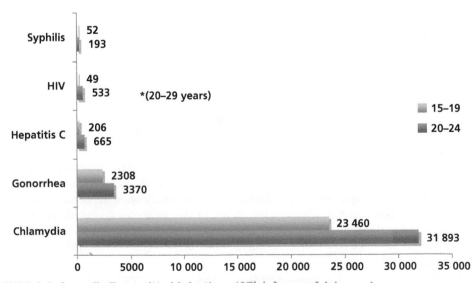

FIGURE 6-6 Sexually Transmitted Infections (STIs) Among Adolescents
Number of new cases of STIs reported to the Public Health Agency of Canada in 2009.
Why are adolescents in particular in danger of contracting an STI?
*Note: HIV was reported for 15- to 19-year-olds and 20- to 29-year-olds.
Sources: Public Health Agency of Canada, 2010.

cases lead to cervical cancer. A vaccine for certain strains of HPV is now available and recommended for all young women—a stance that has provoked much political reaction (Friedman et al., 2006; Kahn, 2007).

Another common STI is *chlamydia*, a bacterial infection that starts with few symptoms, but later causes burning urination and a discharge from the penis or vagina. It can lead to pelvic inflammation and even to sterility. Chlamydia can be treated with antibiotics. *Gonorrhea* and *syphilis* are the oldest known STIs, with cases recorded by ancient historians. Both infections were deadly before antibiotics, but can now be treated effectively.

Genital herpes is a virus not unlike the cold sores that appear around the mouth. Its first symptoms are often small blisters or sores around the genitals; these blisters can break open and become quite painful. Although the sores usually heal after a few weeks, the infection often recurs and the cycle repeats itself. When the sores reappear, this incurable infection is contagious. *Trichomoniasis* is an infection in the vagina or penis, which is caused by a parasite. Initially without symptoms, it can eventually cause a painful discharge. Neither herpes nor trichomoniasis are reported to the Public Health Agency of Canada; thus, rates are hard to estimate. US data suggests that infection rates are comparable to those of chlamydia.

Contracting an STI is a problem during not only adolescence; it can also become a problem later in life, as some infections increase the chances of infertility and cancer.

> **From a health-care provider's perspective:** Why do adolescents' increased cognitive abilities, including the ability to reason and to think experimentally, fail to deter them from drug and alcohol abuse, tobacco use, and sexually transmitted infections? How might you use these abilities to design a program to prevent these problems?

Avoiding STIs.   Short of abstinence, there is no certain way to avoid STIs. However, there are ways to make sex safer; these are listed in Table 6-1.

Even with substantial sex education, the use of safer sex practices is far from universal. Teenagers believe their chances of contracting STIs are minimal. This is particularly true when they view their partner as "safe"—someone they know well and with whom they have had a relatively long-term relationship (Lefkowitz et al., 2000; Tinsley et al., 2004).

Unfortunately, unless one knows a partner's complete sexual history and STI status, unprotected sex remains a risk. Personal information like this is difficult to get. Not only is it embarrassing to ask, partners might not be accurate reporters, whether out of ignorance regarding their own exposure, or embarrassment, forgetfulness, or a sense of privacy. As a result, STIs remain a significant problem.

TABLE 6-1 SAFER SEX PRACTICES

The only foolproof method of avoiding a sexually transmitted infection (STI) is abstinence. However, by following the "safer sex" practices listed here, one can significantly reduce the risk of contracting an STI:

- *Know your sexual partner—well.* Before having sex with someone, learn about his or her sexual history.

- *Use condoms.* For those in sexual relationships, condoms are the most reliable means of preventing transmission of STIs.

- *Avoid the exchange of bodily fluids, particularly semen.* In particular, avoid anal intercourse. The AIDS virus in particular can spread through small tears in the rectum, making anal intercourse without condoms particularly dangerous. Oral sex, once thought relatively safe, is now viewed as potentially dangerous for contracting the AIDS virus.

- *Stay sober.* Using alcohol and drugs impairs judgment and can lead to poor decisions—and it makes correctly using a condom more difficult.

- *Consider the benefits of monogamy.* People in long-term, monogamous relationships with partners who have been faithful are at a lower risk of contracting STIs.

REVIEW, CHECK, AND APPLY

REVIEW

- The use of illegal drugs and alcohol as a way to find pleasure, avoid pressure, or gain the approval of peers is prevalent among adolescents.

- Despite the well-known dangers of smoking, adolescents often smoke to enhance their images or emulate adults.

- AIDS is the most serious of the sexually transmitted infections. Safe sex practices or abstinence can prevent AIDS, but adolescents often ignore these strategies.

CHECK YOURSELF

1. Adolescents have a variety of reasons for using drugs. Circle all that apply.
   a. pleasurable feelings
   b. escape from everyday life
   c. thrill of doing something illegal
   d. parental pressure
   e. peer pressure

2. Youth who smoke are _____ likely to use alcohol and cannabis than youth who have never tried smoking.

   a. more
   b. less
   c. equally

3. _____ is the only sexually transmitted infection for which young women can be vaccinated.

APPLYING LIFESPAN DEVELOPMENT

- How might adolescents' concerns about self-image contribute to smoking and alcohol use?

Answers: 1) a, b, c, e; 2) a; 3) Human papilloma virus (HPV)

MODULE 6.2 Cognitive Development in Adolescence

Overcoming the Obstacles

A Nova Scotia student's invention to prevent cars from rolling over is getting some attention from GM Canada.

Brandon Fillmore, 14, came up with his design for a science fair. It places an air-pressured spring at each wheel of the vehicle. As the car leans, the outside springs pump up, levelling out the body of the car so it won't roll over.

***

Kevin Sibley was floored when he saw Brandon's design. The engineering professor at the Nova Scotia Agricultural College reviewed the teen's project.

"I've never seen anything like that. I've seen active suspension systems and so forth, but I've never seen anything that simple," Sibley said.

"A fellow like that, that's in Grade 9, that can think conceptually like that is very rare. I've been teaching engineering students for over 20 years and I would stack him against a first-year engineering student right now." (CBC, 2011)

In this module, we examine adolescents' cognitive development. The module begins with a look at several theories. We first consider the Piagetian approach, discussing how adolescents use formal operations to solve problems. We then look at a different viewpoint: the increasingly influential information-processing perspectives. We consider the growth of metacognitive abilities, through which adolescents gain awareness of their own thinking processes. We also look at the ways in which metacognition leads to egocentrism and the invention of personal fables.

The module then examines school performance. After discussing the profound impact that socioeconomic status has on school achievement, we consider school performance and ethnicity. We then look at the impact cyberspace has on education, the skills students must learn to use the Internet effectively, and the dangers the Internet poses. We close with a discussion of the role socioeconomic status plays in high school drop-out rates.

Cognitive Development

LEARNING OBJECTIVES

LO6 How does cognitive development proceed during adolescence?

LO7 What aspects of cognitive development cause difficulties for adolescents?

Mrs. Kirby smiled as she read a highly creative paper. She had asked her grade 8 social studies students to write about what their lives would be like if France had won the battle on the Plains of Abraham. She had tried a similar task with her grade 6 students, but many of them were unable to imagine anything other than what they knew. Her grade 8 students, however, were inventing some very interesting scenarios. One boy imagined himself as Lord Lucas; a girl imagined that she would serve a rich landowner; another that she would plot to overthrow the government.

The ability to think beyond the concrete, current situation to what *might* or *could be* distinguishes adolescent thinking from that of younger children. Adolescents are able to consider a variety of abstract possibilities; they can see issues in relative, as opposed to absolute, terms. When problems arise, they can perceive shadings beyond the black-and-white solutions of younger days (Keating, 1980, 1990).

There are several explanations for adolescents' cognitive development. We'll begin by revisiting Piaget's theory, which has greatly influenced how developmentalists perceive adolescent cognition.

Piagetian Approaches to Cognitive Development: Using Formal Operations

Leigh, age 14, is asked to solve the following problem: What determines the speed at which a pendulum moves back and forth? Leigh is given a weight hanging from a string and told that she can vary several things: the length of the string, the weight of the object, the amount of force used to push the string, and the height to which the weight is raised in an arc before it is released.

Leigh doesn't remember, but she was asked to solve the same problem at age eight as part of a longitudinal research study. She was then in the concrete operational period, and her efforts were not very successful. Her haphazard approach showed no systematic plan of action. For instance, she simultaneously tried to push the pendulum harder *and* shorten the length of the string *and* increase the weight on the string. Because she varied so many factors at once, when the pendulum's speed changed, she had no way of knowing what had made the difference.

Now, Leigh is more systematic. Rather than immediately pushing and pulling at the pendulum, she stops to think about which factors to consider. She ponders how she might test which factor is important, forming a hypothesis. Then, just as a scientist conducts an experiment, she varies only one factor at a time. By examining each variable separately and systematically, she comes to the correct solution: The length of the string determines the speed of the pendulum.

Using Formal Operations to Solve Problems. Leigh's approach to the pendulum question, a problem devised by Piaget, shows she has moved into the formal operational period of cognitive development (Piaget and Inhelder, 1958). In the **formal operational stage** people develop the ability to think abstractly. Piaget suggested that people reach it at the start of adolescence, around age 12.

Adolescents can consider problems in abstract rather than concrete terms by using formal principles of logic. They can test their understanding by systematically conducting rudimentary experiments and observing the results. Thus, as an adolescent, Leigh could think about the pendulum problem abstractly, and she understood how to test her hypotheses.

Adolescents are able to use formal reasoning, starting with a general theory about what causes a certain outcome, and then deducing explanations for the situations in which that outcome occurs. Like the scientists who form hypotheses, discussed in Chapter 1, they can test their theories. What distinguishes this kind of thinking from earlier stages is the ability to start with the abstract and move to the concrete; in previous stages, children are tied to the concrete present. At age eight, Leigh just moved things around to see what would happen in the pendulum problem—a concrete approach. At age 12, she began with the abstract idea that each variable should be tested separately.

formal operational stage the stage at which people develop the ability to think abstractly

Like scientists who form hypotheses, adolescents in the formal operational stage use systematic reasoning. They start with a general theory about what produces a particular outcome and then deduce explanations for specific situations in which they see that particular outcome.

Adolescents also can use propositional thought during this stage. *Propositional thought* is reasoning that uses abstract logic in the absence of concrete examples. Such thinking allows adolescents to understand that if certain premises are true, then a conclusion must also be true. For example:

All men are mortal.	*[premise]*
Socrates is a man.	*[premise]*
Therefore, Socrates is mortal.	*[conclusion]*

Adolescents understand that if both premises are true, then so is the conclusion. They are capable of using similar reasoning when premises and conclusions are stated more abstractly, as follows:

All As are B.	*[premise]*
C is an A.	*[premise]*
Therefore, C is a B.	*[conclusion]*

Although Piaget proposed that the formal operational stage begins at the onset of adolescence, he also hypothesized that—as with all the stages—full cognitive capabilities emerge gradually through a combination of physical maturation and environmental experiences. Not until around age 15, Piaget says, do adolescents fully settle into the formal operational stage.

In fact, evidence suggests that many people hone these skills at a later age, and some never fully employ them. Most studies show that only 40 to 60 percent of college students and adults achieve formal operational thinking completely, with some estimates as low as 25 percent. But many adults who do not use formal operational thought in every domain are fully competent in *some* aspects (Keating and Clark, 1980; Sugarman, 1988).

The culture in which they are raised affects how adolescents use formal operations. People with little formal education who live in isolated, technologically unsophisticated societies are less likely to use formal operations than formally educated people in more sophisticated societies (Jahoda, 1980; Segall et al., 1990).

It is not that adolescents (and adults) from cultures using few formal operations are incapable of attaining them. It is more likely that what characterizes formal operations—scientific reasoning—is not equally valued in all societies. If everyday life does not require or promote a certain type of reasoning, it is not likely that people will use such reasoning when confronting a problem (Greenfield, 1976; Shea, 1985; Gauvain, 1998). Our formal education system just happens to promote and encourage students to use formal operations and provides students with a lot of practice doing so.

The Consequences of Adolescents' Use of Formal Operations. The ability to reason abstractly—to use formal operations—changes adolescents' everyday behaviour. Whereas earlier they might have blindly accepted rules and explanations, their increased abstract reasoning abilities can lead to strenuous questioning of their parents and other authority figures.

In general, adolescents become more argumentative. They enjoy using abstract reasoning to poke holes in others' explanations, and their increased critical thinking abilities zero in on parents' and teachers' perceived shortcomings. For instance, they might see their parents' arguments against using drugs as inconsistent if their parents used drugs in adolescence without consequence. But adolescents can be indecisive, too, as they are able to see the merits of multiple sides of an issue (Elkind, 1996).

Coping with these new critical abilities can be challenging for parents, teachers, and other adults who deal with adolescents. But this makes adolescents more interesting as they actively seek to understand the values and justifications they encounter.

Evaluating Piaget's Approach. Each time we've considered Piaget's theory, several concerns have arisen. Let's summarize some of them here:

- Piaget suggests that cognitive development proceeds in universal, step-like stages. Yet significant differences exist in cognitive abilities from one person to the next, especially when we compare individuals from different cultures. We also find inconsistencies within the same individual. People indicate they have reached a certain level of thinking in some tasks but not others. If Piaget were correct, a person ought to perform uniformly well upon reaching a given stage (Siegler, 2007).

- The Piagetian notion of stages suggests that cognitive growth occurs in relatively rapid shifts from one stage to the next. Many developmentalists, however, argue that cognitive development is more continuous—increasing in quantitative accumulations rather than qualitative leaps forward. They also contend that Piaget's theory better *describes* behaviour at a given stage than *explains* why the shift to a new stage occurs (Case, 1999; Birney and Sternberg, 2006).

- Citing the nature of the tasks Piaget used to measure cognitive abilities, critics suggest that he underestimated the age at which certain abilities emerge. It is now widely accepted that infants and children are more sophisticated than Piaget asserted (Siegler, 2007).

- Some developmentalists argue that formal operations are not the epitome of thinking and that more sophisticated forms do not emerge until early adulthood. Developmental psychologist Giesela Labouvie-Vief (2006) argues that a complex society requires thought not necessarily based on pure logic. Instead, thinking must be flexible, allowing for interpretive processes, and reflecting the subtlety of cause and effect in real world events—something that Labouvie-Vief calls *postformal thinking* (Labouvie-Vief, 2006).

These criticisms regarding Piaget's approach to cognitive development have genuine merit. Yet Piaget's theory has inspired countless studies on the development of thinking capacities and processes, and it also has spurred much classroom reform. His bold statements about the nature of cognitive development sparked opposition that brought forth new approaches, such as the information-processing perspective we examine next (Zigler and Gilman, 1998; Taylor, 2005).

Information-Processing Perspectives: Gradual Transformations in Abilities

From an information-processing perspective, adolescents' cognitive abilities grow gradually and continuously. Unlike Piaget's view that increasing cognitive sophistication is a reflection of stage-like spurts, the **information-processing perspective** sees changes in adolescents' cognitive abilities as gradual transformations in the capacity to take in, use, and store information. Multiple progressive changes occur in the ways people organize their thinking, develop strategies to deal with new situations, sort facts, and advance in memory capacity and perceptual abilities (Wellman and Gelman, 1992; Pressley and Schneider, 1997; Wyer, 2004).

Adolescents' general intelligence—as measured by traditional IQ tests—remains stable, but dramatic improvements occur in the specific abilities that underlie intelligence. Verbal, mathematical, and spatial abilities increase. Memory capacity grows, and adolescents become adept at handling more than one stimulus at a time—as when they study for a biology test while listening to a CD.

As Piaget noted, adolescents grow increasingly sophisticated in understanding problems, grasping abstract concepts and hypothetical thinking, and comprehending the possibilities inherent in situations. This permits them, for instance, to endlessly dissect the course their relationships might hypothetically take.

Adolescents know more about the world, too. Their store of knowledge increases as the amount of material they are exposed to grows and their memory capacity enlarges. In sum, mental abilities markedly improve during adolescence (Kail, 2003, 2004).

According to information-processing theories of cognitive development, one of the main reasons for adolescents' advances in mental abilities is the growth of metacognition.

information-processing perspective   the model that seeks to identify the way that individuals take in, use, and store information

Adolescents' personal fables may lead them to feel invulnerable and to engage in risky behaviour, like these Brazilian boys (known as "surfistas") riding on the roof of a high-speed train.

Watch on **mydevelopmentlab**

Can you remember a time in your life when you developed an imaginary audience?
Watch the video on MyDevelopmentLab in which a teenager displays the concept of imaginary audience.

Watch on **mydevelopmentlab**

Imagine you were a parent, an educator, or a health-care worker: how would you deal with a teenager's personal fables?
In the "Invincibility Fable" video on MyDevelopmentLab, a popular and intelligent young woman is asked why she felt that she could engage in unprotected sex without getting pregnant.

metacognition the knowledge that people have about their own thinking processes, and their ability to monitor their cognition

adolescent egocentrism a state of self-absorption in which the world is viewed from one's own point of view

imaginary audience an adolescent's belief that his or her own behaviour is a primary focus of others' attention and concerns

Metacognition is the knowledge of one's own thinking processes, and the ability to monitor one's own cognition. Although younger children can use some metacognitive strategies, adolescents are much more adept at understanding their own mental processes.

For example, as their understanding of their memory capacity improves, adolescents can better gauge how long they need to memorize given material for a test. They also can judge when the material is fully memorized much more accurately than in younger days. Their improved metacognition permits adolescents to comprehend and master school material more effectively (Kuhn, 2000; Desoete et al., 2003).

These new abilities also can make adolescents deeply introspective and self-conscious—two characteristics which, as we see next, can produce a high degree of egocentrism.

Egocentrism in Thinking: Adolescents' Self-Absorption

Carlos thinks his parents are "control freaks"; he cannot figure out why they insist he call and let them know where he is when he borrows the car. Jeri views Molly's purchase of earrings just like hers as the ultimate compliment, even though Molly might have been unaware Jeri had a similar pair when she bought them. Lu is upset with his biology teacher for giving a long, difficult midterm exam on which he did poorly.

Adolescents' newly sophisticated metacognitive abilities make them readily imagine that others are focused on them, and they may create elaborate scenarios about others' thoughts. This is the source of the egocentrism that can dominate adolescents' thinking. **Adolescent egocentrism** is a state of self-absorption in which the world is seen as focused on oneself. This egocentrism makes adolescents highly critical of authority figures, hostile to criticism, and quick to find fault with others' behaviour (Elkind, 1985; Rycek et al., 1998; Greene et al., 2002).

Adolescents may develop an **imaginary audience**, fictitious observers who pay as much attention to their behaviour as they do themselves. Unfortunately, these scenarios suffer from the same kind of egocentrism as the rest of their thinking. For instance, a student sitting in a class may be sure a teacher is focusing on her, and a teenager at a basketball game may be convinced that everyone is staring at the pimple on his chin.

Egocentrism leads to a second distortion in thinking: that one's experiences are unique. Adolescents develop **personal fables**, the view that what happens to them is unique, exceptional, and shared by no other. Teenagers whose romantic relationships have ended may feel that no one has ever hurt the way they do, that no one was ever treated so badly, that no one can understand their pain.

> **personal fables** the view held by some adolescents that what happens to them is unique, exceptional, and shared by no one else

> ➡ **From a social worker's perspective:** In what ways does egocentrism complicate adolescents' social and family relationships? Do adults entirely outgrow egocentrism and personal fables?

Personal fables may make adolescents feel invulnerable to the risks that threaten others. They may see no need to use condoms during sex because, in the personal fables they construct, pregnancy and sexually transmitted infections only happen to other kinds of people, not to them. They may drink and drive because in their personal fables they are careful drivers, always in control (Greene et al., 2000; Vartanian, 2000; Reyna and Farley, 2006).

REVIEW, CHECK, AND APPLY

REVIEW

- Adolescence corresponds to Piaget's formal operations period, a stage characterized by abstract reasoning and an experimental approach to problems.

- According to the information-processing perspective, cognitive advances in adolescence are quantitative and gradual, as many aspects of thinking and memory improve. Growth in metacognition enables the monitoring of thought processes and mental capacities.

- Adolescents are susceptible to egocentrism and the perception that their behaviour is constantly observed by an imaginary audience. They also construct personal fables about their uniqueness and immunity to harm.

CHECK YOURSELF

1. Fifteen-year-old year old Wyatt is able to solve the physics problem from class in abstract rather than in concrete terms. According to Piaget, Wyatt is now capable of _____.

   a. preoperational thought

   b. formal operational thought

   c. egocentrism

   d. sensorimotor thought

2. _____ is the knowledge that people have about their own thinking processes and their ability to monitor their cognition.

3. Rorie refuses to go to the grade 8 dance because she is sure that the only thing everyone will see is the pimple on her face. Which of the following limitations in thinking associated with adolescence is at work here?

   a. imaginary audience

   b. personal fable

   c. invincibility fable

   d. hysteria

APPLYING LIFESPAN DEVELOPMENT

- When facing complex problems, do you think most adults spontaneously apply formal operations like those used to solve the pendulum problem? Why or why not?

Answers: 1) b; 2) Metacognition; 3) a

School Performance

LO8 What factors affect adolescent school performance?

LO9 Who attends university and how is the university experience different for men and women?

> **LEARNING OBJECTIVES**

Jeri Camber is annoyed. His iPod has stopped working and now he has to pull out his earbuds, put his calculus textbook down, and pause the game he's playing on his Playstation 3. He fiddles with the iPod and finally gets it working. As he puts his earbuds back in and returns to his calculus book and video game, he shouts to his father to find out the score of the basketball game he hears playing in the next room. To his surprise, his father answers that he doesn't know because he's been reading a book instead of paying attention. Jeri rolls his eyes and silently judges his dad a bit dim-witted for being unable to do both things at the same time.

Jeri's ability at age 17 to listen to music, do his homework, and play a video game all at the same time may or may not signal some kind of advance over his father's limit of doing only one thing at a time. In part, Jeri's talent for multitasking is surely due to the different eras in which he and his father were raised, but it might also be partly attributable to the cognitive changes that accompanied his advance into adolescence. Think of it this way: It is *possible* that Jeri actually can perform more mental tasks simultaneously than his father, but it is *certain* that he can do more tasks *well* than he could do just a few years earlier.

Do the advances in adolescents' metacognition, reasoning, and other cognitive abilities lead to improved school performance? If we use grades as the measure of performance, the answer is yes. High school students' grades have risen in the last decade. Several universities brag that average entrance grades exceed 85 percent.

At the same time, independent measures of achievement, such as standardized test scores, have not risen. A more likely explanation for the higher grades is the phenomenon of grade inflation: Students have not changed; instead, instructors are awarding higher grades for the same performance (Anglin and Meng, 2000; Cardman, 2004).

Socioeconomic Status and School Performance: Individual Differences in Achievement. All students are entitled to an equal education, but some groups enjoy more advantages than others, as the relationship between educational achievement and socioeconomic status (SES) clearly indicates.

Middle- and high-SES students, on average, earn higher grades, score higher on standardized achievement tests, and complete more years of school than students from lower-SES homes. This disparity does not start in adolescence; the same findings hold for children in lower grades. However, by high school, the effects of socioeconomic status are more pronounced.

Middle- and high-SES students enjoy greater academic success for several reasons. Children living in poverty lack many of the advantages of their more affluent peers. Their nutrition and health might be poorer. If they live in crowded conditions or attend inadequate schools, they might have few places to study. Their homes might lack the books and computers common in more affluent households (Adams and Singh, 1998; Bowen and Bowen, 1999; Prater, 2002).

For these reasons, impoverished students can be disadvantaged from their first day of school. As they grow up, their school performance can continue to lag and, in fact, the difference can snowball. High school success builds heavily on basic skills presumably learned earlier. Children who experience early problems can find themselves falling ever further behind (Huston, 1991; Phillips et al., 1994).

Cyberspace: Adolescents Online

The educational promise of the Internet is significant. Through the Internet, students can peruse library catalogues, gather government statistics, view the landscape of Mars transmitted by onsite cameras, and much more. As adolescents become increasingly familiar with computers, they use them in a variety of ways (see Figure 6-7).

The Internet is clearly changing education, but the nature of these changes—and how positive they will be—is less clear. Schools must teach students a key skill for effective Internet use: how to identify what is most useful among the vast body of available information. In order to create new knowledge, students must be able to search for, select, and integrate information (Trotter, 2004).

Despite its substantial benefits, the Internet has a drawback. Claims that cyberspace is overrun with child molesters might be exaggerated, but cyberspace does make material available that many parents and other adults find highly objectionable. Internet gambling is also a growing problem. High school and college students can use credit cards to bet on sports events and play games such as poker on the Web (Dowling et al., 2005; Winters et al., 2005; Fleming et al., 2006; Mitchell et al., 2007).

On the positive side, adolescents might also be using their time online to improve their relationships. In one survey, 57 percent of students reported using instant messaging. Students' use of instant messaging with their friends was related to the quality of their relationships—the more they chatted with their friends, the stronger and better their relationships. Virtual chatting can facilitate intimate disclosure between friends, as individuals are often less inhibited than when communicating in person or even speaking on the telephone (Blais et al., 2008).

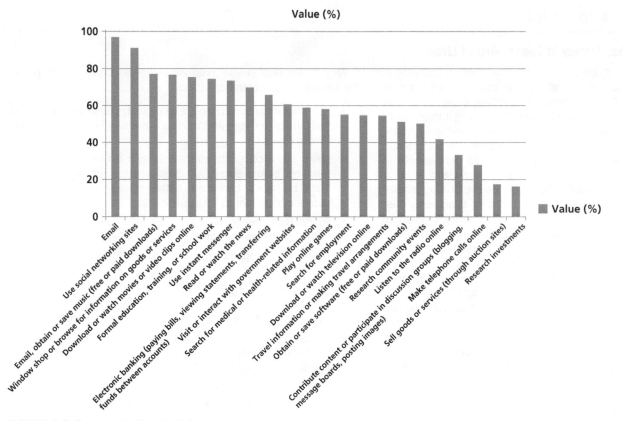

FIGURE 6-7 Teenage Online Activity
Today, a large majority of teenagers use the Internet for entertainment and communication, and many also use the new technology for education-related material and research. How will this trend affect the way educators teach in the future?
Source: Statistics Canada. (2010). Table 358-0153—Canadian Internet use survey, Internet use, by age group and Internet activity, occasional (percent). CANSIM (database).

Dropping Out of School. Most students complete high school, but 8 percent do not. This percentage is a considerable decline from 1990–1991 when 16 percent did not complete high school. The consequences of dropping out are severe. One-quarter of high school dropouts are unemployed, and those who are employed earn, on average, $70 less per week than graduates of high school.

Adolescents leave school for a variety of reasons. Some leave because of pregnancy or problems with the English language. Some must leave for economic reasons, needing to support themselves or their families.

Dropout rates differ according to gender and ethnicity. Males are more likely to drop out than females. Nearly one-quarter of Aboriginal youth drop out, and drop-out rates are highest in the North and in rural areas, and lower in urban centres. Immigrant youth have lower drop-out rates than Canadian-born youth, especially immigrants who arrived as younger children. The low drop-out rate among immigrants is attributed to the strong emphasis on and support for education among immigrant parents, and is also connected to the lower urban drop-out rate, as most immigrants settle in major urban centres (Gilmore, 2010).

Poverty is one important factor in whether a student completes high school. Students from lower-income households are three times more likely to drop out than those from middle- and upper-income households. Because economic success is so dependent on education, dropping out often perpetuates a cycle of poverty (National Center for Education Statistics, 2002). Engagement is another important factor. For example, teens' perceived irrelevance of the educational program is cited as a factor in the high drop-out rate in Aboriginal communities. Culturally meaningful curricula that celebrate Aboriginal heritage and preserve language might be used to improve academic outcomes (Castellano, 2008).

From Research to Practice

Living in Glass Houses: Privacy in Teens' Virtual Lives

In the 1986 film *Ferris Bueller's Day Off*, the lead character and friends con parents and school officials in order to skip school and have a day of fun. They narrowly avoid getting caught on a few occasions—but getting caught meant physically running into an adult: while the school principal had suspicions, he had no evidence of the students' truancy. If the film were made today, chances are the students' antics would have been tweeted or captured permanently in some form online and, voila! Evidence! In recent years a number of news stories have emerged about people's online lives having consequences for their real lives: teens suing or bringing charges against online bullies; professional careers ruined over "sexting"; potential employers researching applicants on Google or Facebook and finding long-forgotten inappropriate photos. It seems everything about our lives is online, and it's *more* permanent than that tattoo you thought was a good idea at the time. Bad judgment is everywhere. How does one keep indiscretions private in the social media age?

Social media is designed to elicit the sharing of information and blurs the line between public and private. Do teens disclose too much? Do teens understand how to manage their online privacy? At least one survey suggests that while teens do disclose more information than adults do on sites such as Facebook, teens also spend more time on the site and don't disclose more than adults per hour of use. Interestingly, whether and what teens and adults disclose is influenced by the same two basic factors: the need for popularity and the awareness of the potential future consequences of disclosure. Social media is changing our concept of privacy, but how much privacy is desirable is still different for different people (Christofides et al., 2012).

Amy Muise and Emily Christofides of the University of Guelph offer the following recommendations:

- Parents and children should sit down together to learn about the privacy settings and to read the privacy policy on social media sites.

- Never add a complete stranger to your list of friends—check them out before accepting. Even among your regular contacts, be sure to consider whether someone is really a friend before adding him to your friends list.

- Friendships change, so if you no longer consider someone a friend, delete her or limit her access to your information.

- Learn what happens when you share information online. Teachers and families should talk about how this information might be used now and in the future.

- Come up with a plan for dealing with situations that make you uncomfortable on Facebook—what to do and who to tell.

- Check to see how your page looks to others so you know what you are sharing. Are you sharing something with everyone that you would rather keep private?

- Remember that Facebook makes popularity seem more important. Think twice about what you are sharing and with whom you are sharing it.

Source (for recommendations): Pamphlet. **www.psychology.uoguelph.ca/faculty/desmarais/files/Facebook_Education_Pamplet.pdf**

REVIEW, CHECK, AND APPLY

REVIEW

- Academic performance is linked in complex ways to socioeconomic status and to race and ethnicity.

- Both gender and ethnicity affect the incidence of dropping out.

- The educational benefits of the Internet are many, but it also introduces adolescents to objectionable material and online gambling.

CHECK YOURSELF

1. The gradual shift upward of adolescents' grades in the last decade has been attributed to

    _____.

    a. increased immigration
    b. grade inflation
    c. increased achievement
    d. decreased motivation

2. Students who experience socioeconomic disadvantages and, consequently, academic disadvantages as young children usually overcome those disadvantages by adolescence.

    - True
    - False

3. Who is least likely to drop out of high school prior to graduation?

    a. males
    b. females

APPLYING LIFESPAN DEVELOPMENT

- What could schools do to improve high school completion rates?

Answers: 1) b; 2) False; 3) b

MODULE 6.3 Social and Personality Development in Adolescence

Adolescent Trio

Carly, a freshman at a school for gifted kids, says she has no interest in politics or social issues. "It's probably because of my mom—she's filled my brain with statistics and feminism and the environment," she says. "I'm like, 'Well, what do you want me to do?'" Since her parents split when she was three, Carly has lived mainly with her mother. So what is she passionate about? "My friends."

***

Trevor is the third of four sons of Richard Kelson, 56, a retired truck driver, and his wife, JoAnn, 46, a medical tape transcriber. The family lives in a four-bedroom home across from the school, where Trevor is in grade 9. He spent the summer volunteering in a leadership-training program at the Boys & Girls Club. "I guess it gives you a good feeling to help somebody else," he says. In off-hours, he plays videogames with pal Andy Muhlestein, 15. "When we don't have anything else to do, and we're tired of playing videos," he says, "we sit around and talk about girls." (Adapted from Fields-Meyer, 1995, p. 53)

* * *

Although Carly and Trevor lead very different lives, they are remarkably similar in their focus on friends, family, and school. They also typify adolescent life far more than the stereotype of wild and confused teenagers.

In truth, most teenagers pass through adolescence with little turmoil. They may "try on" different roles and flirt with activities their parents object to, but the majority find adolescence an exciting time during which friendships grow, intimate relationships develop, and their sense of themselves deepens.

This is not to say that the transitions adolescents pass through are unchallenging. As the discussion of personality and social development shows in this module, adolescence brings major changes in the ways teenagers deal with the world.

We begin by considering how adolescents form their views of themselves. We look at self-concept, self-esteem, and identity development. We also examine two major psychological difficulties: depression and suicide.

Next, we discuss relationships. We consider how adolescents reposition themselves within the family and how the influence of family members declines in some spheres as peers take on new importance. We also examine how adolescents interact with their friends, and how popularity is determined.

Finally, the module considers dating and sexual behaviour. We look at the role of dating and close relationships, and we consider sexual behaviour and the standards that govern adolescents' sex lives. We conclude by looking at teenage pregnancy and at programs that seek to prevent unwanted pregnancy.

Identity: Asking "Who Am I?"

LO10 **How do the development of self-concept, self-esteem, and identity proceed during adolescence?**

LO11 **What dangers do adolescents face as they deal with the stresses of adolescence?**

LEARNING OBJECTIVES

Fourteen was a hard year. I have my friends, but I'm not part of the popular crowd. I don't dress right. I don't say the right things. I'm not the smartest in my class; in fact, while I'm in the smart class, I am near the bottom of that pile. I stink at sports and music. I was diagnosed with depression last week, but I don't know how that is going to change anything. I want to be special. I want to do something meaningful with my life, but I don't really fit in. I don't know what the point of it all is. I don't know where I'm going in life. What's the point of it all? Who am I?

The thoughts of this teen demonstrate a clear awareness—and self-consciousness—regarding his new place in society. During adolescence, questions like "Who am I?" and "Where do I belong in the world?" begin to take a front seat.

One reason issues of identity become so important is that adolescents' intellectual capacities become more adult-like. They see how they stack up to others and realize they are individuals, separate from everyone else. The dramatic physical changes of puberty make adolescents acutely aware of their own bodies and aware that others are reacting to them in new ways. Whatever the cause, adolescence brings major changes in teenagers' self-concepts and self-esteem—in sum, in their views of their own identity.

Self-Concept: What Am I Like?

Valerie describes herself this way: "Others look at me as laid-back, relaxed, and not worrying too much. But really, I'm often nervous and emotional."

The fact that Valerie distinguishes others' views from her own represents a developmental advance. In childhood, she would have characterized herself by traits that would not differentiate her view from others'. However, when adolescents describe who they are, they take into account both their own and others' views (Harter, 1990a; Cole et al., 2001; Updegraff et al., 2004).

This broader view of themselves is one aspect of adolescents' increasing sense of identity. They can see various aspects of the self simultaneously, and this view becomes more organized and coherent. They look at the self from a psychological perspective, viewing traits not as concrete entities but as abstractions (Adams et al., 1996). For example, teenagers are more likely than younger children to define themselves by their ideology (for example, "I'm an environmentalist") than by physical characteristics (for example, "I'm the fastest runner in my class").

This broader, multifaceted self-concept, however, can be a mixed blessing, especially during early adolescence. At that time, adolescents can be troubled by the complexity of their personalities. Younger adolescents might want to view themselves in a certain way ("I'm a sociable person and love to be with people"), and might become concerned when their behaviour contradicts that view ("Even though I want to be sociable, sometimes I can't stand being around my friends and just want to be alone"). By the end of adolescence, however, teenagers find it easier to accept that behaviours and feelings change with the situation (Trzesniewski et al., 2003; Hitlin et al., 2006).

Self-Esteem: How Do I Like Myself?

Although adolescents increasingly perceive who they are (develop their self-concept), this does not mean they like themselves (have high self-esteem). Their increasingly accurate self-concept permits them to see themselves fully—warts and all. What they do with these perceptions determines their self-esteem.

The same cognitive sophistication that differentiates various aspects of the self also leads adolescents to evaluate those aspects in different ways (Chan, 1997; Cohen, 1999). An adolescent might have high self-esteem regarding academic performance, but lower self-esteem in relationships. Or the opposite might apply, as this adolescent notes:

How much do I like the kind of person I am? Well, I like some things about me, but I don't like others. I'm glad that I'm popular since it's really important to me to have friends. But in school I don't do as well as the really smart kids. That's OK, because if you're too smart you'll lose your friends. So being smart is just not that important. Except to my parents. I feel like I'm letting them down when I don't do as well as they want. (Harter, 1990b, p. 364)

Gender Differences in Self-Esteem. Several factors determine an adolescent's self-esteem, among them gender. Notably in early adolescence, girls' self-esteem tends to be lower and more vulnerable than boys' (Watkins et al., 1997; Byrne, 2000; Miyamoto et al., 2000; Ah-Kion, 2006).

Compared to boys, girls tend to worry more about physical appearance and social success—as well as academic achievement. Although boys care about these things, their attitudes are often more casual. Stereotypical societal messages suggesting brains and popularity do not mix pose a difficult bind for girls: If girls do well academically, they jeopardize their social success. No wonder their self-esteem is more fragile than boys' (Unger, 2001; Ricciardelli and McCabe, 2003).

Although boys tend to have higher self-esteem, they have their vulnerabilities too. Gender stereotypes can lead boys to believe they should always be confident, tough, and fearless. Boys facing difficulties (for example, not making a sports team or being rejected for a date) can feel incompetent as males as well as miserable about their defeat (Pollack, 1999; Pollack et al., 2001).

Socioeconomic Status and Ethnic Group Membership Differences in Self-Esteem. Socioeconomic status (SES) and ethnic group membership also influence self-esteem. Adolescents of higher SES tend to have higher self-esteem than those of lower SES, especially in middle and later adolescence. Social status factors that enhance one's standing and self-esteem, such as having more expensive clothes or a car, can become more conspicuous at this time (Savin-Williams and Demo, 1983; Van Tassel-Baska et al., 1994).

Minority group status also influences self-esteem, but less biased treatment of minorities has eased this impact. Early studies argued that minority status would lead to lower self-esteem, and this was initially supported by research. Minority groups, researchers explained, had lower self-esteem because society's prejudice made them feel disliked and rejected, and this was incorporated into their self-concepts. Most recent research, however, suggests that other factors, such as minority cultural identity and community are important. For example, Black adolescents differ little from whites in their levels of self-esteem (Harter, 1990b); this is thought to occur because social movements within the Black community to bolster racial pride have helped. Research finds that a stronger sense of racial identity is related to higher self-esteem in several minority groups (Phinney et al., 1990; Gray-Little and Hafdahl, 2000; Verkuyten, 2003).

Another reason for similarity in self-esteem between adolescents of different ethnic groups is that teenagers tend to focus their preferences and priorities on what they excel at. Consequently, minority youth might concentrate on what they most enjoy and gain self-esteem from their successes in that domain, regardless of what another group might value (Gray-Little and Hafdahl, 2000; Yang and Blodgett, 2000; Phinney, 2005).

Self-esteem can be influenced not just by ethnic group membership, but also by a complex combination of factors. Some developmentalists have considered ethnicity and gender simultaneously, coining the term *ethgender* to refer to the joint influence of these factors, as cultural differences in gender roles and expectations can create greater disparity between boys and girls in some groups than in others (King, 2003; Saunders et al., 2004; Biro et al., 2006).

Identity Formation: Change or Crisis?

According to Erik Erikson, whose theory we discussed earlier, the search for identity inevitably leads some adolescents to an identity crisis involving substantial psychological turmoil (Erikson, 1963). Erikson's theory of this stage, which is summarized with his other stages in Table 6-2, suggests teenagers try to figure out what is unique and distinctive about themselves—a task they manage with increasing sophistication due to the cognitive gains of adolescence.

Erikson argues that adolescents strive to discover their strengths and weaknesses and the roles that best suit their future lives. This often involves "trying on" different roles or choices to see if they fit their capabilities and views about themselves. In this process, adolescents seek to understand who they are by narrowing and making choices about their personal, occupational, sexual, and political commitments. Erikson calls this the **identity-versus-identity-confusion stage**.

In Erikson's view, adolescents who do not find a suitable identity may go off course in several ways. They may adopt socially unacceptable roles to express what they do *not* want to be.

> **identity-versus-identity-confusion stage** the period during which teenagers seek to determine what is unique and distinctive about themselves

TABLE 6-2 A SUMMARY OF ERIKSON'S STAGES

Stage	Approximate Age	Positive Outcomes	Negative Outcomes
1. Trust versus mistrust	Birth–1.5 years	Feelings of trust from others' support	Fear and concern regarding others
2. Autonomy versus shame and doubt	1.5–3 years	Self-sufficiency if exploration is encouraged	Doubts about self; lack of independence
3. Initiative versus guilt	3–6 years	Discovery of ways to initiate actions	Guilt from actions and thoughts
4. Industry versus inferiority	6–12 years	Development of sense of competence	Feelings of inferiority; little sense of mastery
5. Identity versus identity confusion	Adolescence	Awareness of uniqueness of self; knowledge of roles	Inability to identify appropriate roles in life
6. Intimacy versus isolation	Early adulthood	Development of loving, sexual relationships and close friendships	Fear of relationships with others
7. Generativity versus stagnation	Middle adulthood	Sense of contribution to continuity of life	Trivialization of one's activities
8. Ego-integrity versus despair	Late adulthood	Sense of unity in life's accomplishments	Regret over lost opportunities of life

Source: "Figure of Erikson's Stages of Personality Development," from CHILDHOOD AND SOCIETY by Erik H. Erikson. Copyright 1950, © 1963 by W. W. Norton & Company, Inc., renewed © 1978, 1991 by Erik H. Erikson. Used by permission of W. W. Norton & Company, Inc.

Forming and maintaining lasting close relationships might elude them. In general, their sense of self becomes "diffuse," failing to organize around a unified core identity.

In contrast, those who forge an appropriate identity set a foundation for future psychosocial development. They learn their unique capabilities and believe in them, and they develop an accurate sense of self. They are prepared to take full advantage of their unique strengths (Archer and Waterman, 1994; Allison and Schultz, 2001).

Societal Pressures and Reliance on Friends and Peers. Societal pressures are also high during the identity-versus-identity-confusion stage. Adolescents feel pressure from parents and friends to decide whether their post-high-school plans include work or further education and, if the former, which occupation to follow. Up to this point, their educational lives have followed a universal track, laid out by society. However, the track ends at high school, leaving adolescents with difficult choices about which path to follow (Kidwell et al., 1995).

During this period, friends and peers are increasingly sought out as sources of information. Dependence on adults declines. As we discuss later, this increasing dependence on peers enables adolescents to forge close relationships. Comparing themselves to others helps to clarify their own identities.

This reliance on peers to help define their own identities and learn to form relationships links this stage of psychosocial development to the next stage Erikson proposed, known as *intimacy versus isolation*. Reliance on peers also relates to gender differences in identity formation. Erikson suggested that males and females move through the identity-versus-identity-confusion period differently. He argued that males are more likely to experience the social development stages in the order shown in Table 6-2, developing a stable identity before committing to an intimate relationship. In contrast, he suggested that females reverse the order, seeking intimate relationships and then defining their identities through these relationships. These ideas largely reflect the social conditions at the time Erikson wrote them down—when women were less likely to go to college or establish their own careers and, instead, often married early. Today, the experiences of boys and girls seem relatively similar during the identity-versus-identity-confusion period.

Psychological Moratorium. Because of the pressures of the identity-versus-identity-confusion period, Erikson suggested that many adolescents pursue a *psychological moratorium*, a period during which they take time off from the upcoming responsibilities of adulthood to explore various roles and possibilities. For example, many post-secondary students take a semester or year off to travel, work, or find another way to examine their priorities.

Many adolescents, for practical reasons, cannot pursue a psychological moratorium to leisurely explore various identities. For economic reasons, some must work part-time after school and then take jobs immediately after high school, leaving them little time to experiment. By no means does this mean that such adolescents are psychologically damaged. Successfully holding a part-time job while attending school may offer a psychological reward that outweighs the lack of opportunity to try out various roles.

Limitations of Erikson's Theory. Erikson has been criticized for using male identity development as the standard against which to compare female identity. He saw males as developing intimacy only after achieving a stable identity, which is viewed as the norm. To critics, Erikson's view is based on male-oriented concepts of individuality and competitiveness. Alternatively, psychologist Carol Gilligan suggests that women develop identity while establishing relationships. In this view, the building of caring networks between herself and others is key to a woman's identity (Brown and Gilligan, 1990; Gilligan, 2004; Kroger, 2006).

Marcia's Approach to Identity Development: Updating Erikson

Using Erikson's theory as a springboard, psychologist James Marcia suggests that identity can be seen in terms of which of two characteristics—crisis or commitment—is present or absent. *Crisis* is a period in which an adolescent consciously chooses between various alternatives and makes decisions. *Commitment* is psychological investment in a course of action or an ideology. One adolescent might career from one activity to another, nothing lasting beyond a few weeks, while another becomes totally absorbed in volunteering at a homeless shelter (Marcia, 1980; Peterson et al., 2004).

After conducting lengthy interviews with adolescents, Marcia proposed four categories of identity.

1. **Identity achievement.** Teenagers in this category have successfully explored and thought through who they are and what they want to do. Following a period of crisis during which they considered various alternatives, these adolescents have committed to a particular identity. Teens who have reached this identity status tend to be psychologically healthier, and higher in achievement motivation and moral reasoning, than adolescents of any other status.

2. **Identity foreclosure.** These are adolescents who have committed to an identity without passing through a period of crisis in which they explored alternatives. Instead, they accepted others' decisions about what was best for them. Typical of this category is a son who enters the family business because it is expected, or a daughter who becomes a physician because her mother is one. Foreclosers are not necessarily unhappy but they tend to have something called "rigid strength": Happy and self-satisfied, they have a high need for social approval and tend to be authoritarian.

3. **Moratorium.** Adolescents in this category have explored some alternatives but made no commitments. As a result, Marcia suggests, they show relatively high anxiety and experience psychological conflict, though they are often lively and appealing, seeking intimacy with others. Such adolescents typically settle on an identity, but only after a struggle.

4. **Identity diffusion.** These adolescents neither explore nor commit to various alternatives. They tend to shift from one thing to the next. While appearing carefree, according to Marcia, their lack of commitment impairs their ability to form close relationships. They are often socially withdrawn.

Some adolescents shift among the four categories, for example, moving between moratorium and identity achievement in what is called a "MAMA" cycle (**m**oratorium—identity **a**chievement—**m**oratorium—identity **a**chievement). Similarly, a forecloser who selected a career path without much thought in early adolescence might reassess and make a more active choice later. For some individuals, identity formation takes place beyond adolescence. However, for most people, identity gels in the late teens and early twenties (Kroger, 2000; Meeus, 1996, 2003).

> ⮕ **From a social worker's perspective:** Do you believe that all four of Marcia's identity statuses can lead to reassessment and different choices later in life? Are there stages in Marcia's theory that might be difficult for adolescents who live in poverty to achieve? Why?

identity achievement the status of adolescents who commit to a particular identity following a period of crisis during which they consider various alternatives

identity foreclosure the status of adolescents who prematurely commit to an identity without adequately exploring alternatives

moratorium the status of adolescents who may have explored various identity alternatives to some degree, but have not yet committed themselves

identity diffusion the status of adolescents who consider various identity alternatives, but never commit to one or never even consider identity options in any conscious way

According to Marcia's approach, psychologically healthy identity development can be seen in adolescents who choose to commit to a course of action or ideology.

Identity and Ethnicity

Forming an identity is often difficult for adolescents, but it is especially challenging for members of ethnic groups that face discrimination. Society's contradictory values tell these adolescents that society should be colour-blind, that ethnic background should not affect opportunities and achievement, and that if they do achieve, society will accept them. Many people follow a *cultural assimilation model*, the view that individual cultural identities should be assimilated into a unified national culture—the melting-pot model.

In contrast, the *pluralistic society model* suggests that society is made up of diverse, coequal cultural groups that should preserve their individual features. This model grew from the belief that cultural assimilation denigrates the heritage of minority groups and lowers their self-esteem. According to the pluralistic view, ethnic factors form a central part of identity and are not submerged in an attempt to assimilate. While Canada officially follows a pluralistic model, there is a long history of attempted assimilation, especially of Aboriginal groups, and there continue to be many members of society, both majority and minority members, who are in favour of assimilation.

The middle ground says minority group members can form a *bicultural identity*, drawing from their own culture while integrating themselves into the dominant culture. This view suggests an individual can hold two cultural identities, without having to prefer one over the other (LaFromboise et al., 1993). Choosing a bicultural identity is increasingly common. Sometimes bicultural identity is a source of conflict; however, research shows that if individuals perceive the differences between the two cultures as small, then they are better able to see themselves as fitting in with both cultures simultaneously. This in turn improves self-esteem and satisfaction with life. Individuals who see their two cultures as very different, on the other hand, find they fit into neither (Stroink and Lalonde, 2009).

The process of identity formation is always complex and can be doubly so for minority group members. Ethnic identity takes time to form. For some, it requires a prolonged period, but the result can be a rich, multifaceted identity (Roberts et al., 1999; Grantham and Ford, 2003; Nadal, 2004; Umana-Taylor and Fine, 2004).

Depression and Suicide: Psychological Difficulties in Adolescence

Becky came from an ideal home—caring parents who were still affectionate with one another, good friends, good grades, and a comfortable life. Despite all that, an overwhelming despair invaded her life in grade 9. She lost interest in school, and found it easier to claim illness and sleep all day than get dressed.

When she did venture out with friends, Becky started drinking and experimenting with drugs. At home, she drank cough syrup to get "numb." She was experiencing chronic headaches and taking large quantities of Tylenol. Her grades were slipping and Becky was finding it hard to picture the future. One night, rather than just taking two Tylenol for her headache, Becky swallowed the whole bottle.

Although the vast majority of teenagers weather the search for identity—as well as other challenges of the age—without major psychological difficulties, some find adolescence very stressful and some develop severe psychological problems. Two of the most serious are depression and suicide.

Adolescent Depression. No one is immune to sadness and bad moods, including adolescents. The end of a relationship, failure at an important task, the death of a loved one—all can produce profound feelings of sadness, loss, and grief. In such situations, depression is a typical reaction.

Between 25 and 40 percent of girls, and 20 to 35 percent of boys, experience occasional episodes of depression during adolescence, although the incidence of major depression is far lower.

More than one-quarter of adolescents report feeling so sad or hopeless for two or more weeks in a row that they stop doing their normal activities. Almost two-thirds of teenagers say they have experienced such feelings at some point. In contrast, only a small minority of adolescents—some 3 percent—experience *major depression*, a full-blown psychological disorder that is severe and lingers for long periods (Grunbaum et al., 2001; Galambos et al., 2004).

Gender and ethnic differences also affect depression rates. As is true for adults, adolescent females experience depression more often than males. The crisis of suicide among Aboriginal youth is the subject of this chapter's Focus on Research (Jacques and Mash, 2004; Hightower, 2005; Li et al., 2006).

Biological factors are often involved in cases of severe, long-term depression. Some adolescents do seem genetically predisposed to experience depression, but environmental and social factors related to the extraordinary changes in their social lives also have impact. An adolescent who loses a loved one to death, for example, or who grows up with an alcoholic or depressed parent, is at a higher risk of depression. Being unpopular, having few close friends, and rejection are also associated with adolescent depression (Goldsmith et al., 2002; Eley et al., 2004; Zalsman et al., 2006).

Why the depression rate is higher for girls than for boys is puzzling. There is little evidence of a link to hormone differences or a particular gene. Some psychologists speculate that stress is greater for girls in adolescence due to the many, often conflicting, demands of the traditional female role. Recall the girl, quoted in our discussion of self-esteem, who feared academic achievement would endanger her popularity. Such conflict might make her feel helpless. Add to this the fact that traditional gender roles still give higher status to men than women (Nolen-Hoeksema, 2003; Gilbert, 2004).

Girls' higher levels of depression in adolescence might reflect gender differences in coping with stress, rather than differences in mood. Girls might be more likely to react to stress by turning inward, resulting in a sense of helplessness and hopelessness. Girls tend to *ruminate*, obsessing over the stress or conflict. In contrast, boys more often externalize the stress and act more impulsively or aggressively, or turn to drugs and alcohol (Hankin and Abramson, 2001; Winstead and Sanchez, 2005; Papadakis et al., 2006).

Adolescent Suicide. Approximately 300 adolescents commit suicide each year, and for each successful suicide, there are an estimated 10 to 100 attempted suicides. The reported rate might actually understate the true number; parents and medical personnel often prefer to report a death as accidental rather than as suicide. Even so, suicide is the second most common cause of death for 15- to 24-year-olds, after motor vehicle accidents. Despite this rise in suicide—more than for other age groups—the highest suicide rate is actually found in late adulthood (Grunbaum et al., 2002; Furi and Guimont, 2003; Joe and Marcus, 2003; Conner and Goldston, 2007).

The rate of adolescent suicide is four times higher for boys, although girls *attempt* suicide more frequently (twice as many girls are treated in hospital for failed attempts). Attempts among males are more likely to be fatal because boys tend to use more violent means, such as guns or strangulation, while girls tend to choose less violent means, such as drug overdose, which are slower acting and allow more time for medical intervention (Gelman, 1994; Joseph et al., 2003; Dervic et al., 2006).

In the second half of the twentieth century, suicide among youth increased 600 percent. The reasons for the increase in adolescent suicide are unclear. The most obvious explanation is that adolescent stress has increased (Elkind, 1994). But why should stress have increased only for teenagers? The suicide rate for other age groups has also increased by 78 percent over the same time period. Though we are not yet sure why adolescent suicide has increased so dramatically, certain factors, such as depression, raise the risk. Depressed teenagers who feel profound hopelessness are at greater risk for suicide (although most depressed individuals do not commit suicide). Social inhibition, perfectionism, and high levels of stress and anxiety are also related to an increased risk (Huff, 1999; Goldston, 2003).

Some suicide cases are associated with family conflicts and relationship or school difficulties. Some stem from a history of abuse and neglect. The rate of suicide among drug and alcohol abusers is also relatively high. Teens who called a hotline because they were considering suicide mentioned other factors as well (Lyon et al., 2000; Bergen et al., 2003; Wilcox et al., 2004).

In *cluster suicide*, one suicide leads others to attempt to kill themselves. Some high schools have experienced a series of suicides following a well-publicized case. As a result, many schools have established crisis intervention teams to counsel students when a suicide occurs (Haas, 2003; Arenson, 2004).

The warning signs of potential suicide include the following:

- direct or indirect talk about suicide, such as "I wish I were dead" or "You won't have me to worry about any longer"
- school difficulties, such as missed classes or a decline in grades
- making arrangements as if preparing for a long trip, such as giving away prized possessions or arranging for the care of a pet
- writing a will
- loss of appetite or excessive eating
- general depression, including a change in sleeping patterns, slowness and lethargy, and uncommunicativeness
- dramatic changes in behaviour, such as a shy person suddenly acting outgoing
- preoccupation with death in music, art, or literature

Focus on Research

The Crisis of Suicide among Aboriginal Youth

While not all Aboriginal communities are affected by high suicide rates, in some communities the rate of adolescent suicide was eight times higher than the national average. While troubling in its own right, this number is even more troubling given the youthful makeup of the Aboriginal population—50 percent of Aboriginals in Canada are under the age of 25. Aboriginal youth face numerous challenges: poverty, high rates of teen pregnancy, low educational attainment, overrepresentation in prisons, and substance abuse. But with a youthful population and high fertility rate, opportunities are also presented when considered next to the rapidly aging Canadian population. Some of the challenges faced by Aboriginal youth are not unique: Two-thirds of Aboriginals live off reserve and thus face challenges such as discrimination and acculturation common to many minority groups. Many live in remote, rural areas, which present another set of geographical challenges, especially for education and career prospects. However, these challenges are also faced by non-Aboriginals in remote areas. What Aboriginals across Canada share is a history of traumas:

> The shocks of epidemics, displacement from lands, depleted food supply, suppression of ceremonies and languages, and the loss of children to residential schools and child welfare agencies reverberate through tight knit communities, provoking adaptive and maladaptive responses. These responses become embedded in the collective memory and are passed on in oral narratives, shaping perceptions and behaviour in successive generations. When the shocks follow one another without intervals for recovery, pain and dysfunction are laid down layer upon layer and the original causes and effects become obscured (Brant Castellano, 2008, pp. 8–9).

What children growing up in Aboriginal communities face are something psychologists call *risk factors*, factors including living conditions that don't particularly help an individual get ahead in life. Most individuals can overcome a risk factor or two with the help of *protective factors*, which can include individual skills, or access to resources or opportunities that offset risk. But when the risk factors pile up, few individuals can prevail.

Researchers at the University of British Columbia and the University of Victoria have examined the issue of Aboriginal suicide from the perspective of risk and protective factors and have come to some very positive conclusions. In general, suicide risk among individuals is more or less the same, regardless of Aboriginal status. The stresses and identity crises that underlie adolescent suicide in general also underlie Aboriginal youth suicide, but the marginalization of Aboriginal culture puts youth at increased risk. Cultural continuity serves to protect youth in general, and research demonstrates that those communities in which cultural continuity is preserved, encouraged, and thriving are protected against the "epidemic" of suicide. In British Columbia, 90 percent of suicides occurred in fewer than 10 percent of communities, and 20 percent of communities experienced no suicides. Communities differ both in the degree to which they "weathered" non-Aboriginal contact over the years and the degree to which they have "rehabilitated" their culture.

Michael Chandler and colleagues devised a way to measure cultural continuity. Issues such as self-government, success in land claims, control over education, health services, and policing, and the establishment of community facilities for the preservation of culture were found to protect communities against suicide. In communities featuring all six factors, suicide was nonexistent. Other factors that protected communities were active participation of women in band council (50 percent representation) and control over child welfare services (Chandler and Lalonde, 2008). In other words, communities in crisis were communities stripped of all control.

The youthful Aboriginal culture might represent a new beginning: New generations with the support to embrace and preserve their culture means communities with a vision of growth and the future.

Unlike the aging majority population in Canada, the Aboriginal population is young and ready to embrace new opportunities for growth.

Preventing Adolescent Suicide

Becoming an Informed Consumer of Development

If you suspect an adolescent, or anyone else, is contemplating suicide, act! Here are several suggestions:

- Talk to the person. Listen with understanding and without judging.

- Talk specifically about suicidal thoughts; ask questions such as: Do you have a plan? Have you bought a gun? Where is it? Have you stockpiled pills? Where are they? Public health officials note that, "contrary to popular belief, such candour will not give a person dangerous ideas or encourage a suicidal act."

- Try to distinguish between general upset and more serious danger, as when suicide plans *have* been made. If the crisis is acute, *do not leave the person alone.*

- Be supportive, let the person know you care, and try to break down his or her feelings of isolation.

- Take charge of finding help. Do not fear invading the person's privacy. Do not try to handle the problem alone. Get professional help immediately.

- Make the environment safe, removing (not just hiding) weapons such as guns, razors, scissors, medication, and other potentially dangerous items.

- Do not keep suicide talk or threats secret; these are calls for help and call for immediate action.

- Do not challenge, dare, or use verbal shock treatment on the person to correct his or her thinking.

- Make a contract with the person, getting a promise or commitment, preferably in writing, not to attempt suicide until you have talked further.

- Don't be overly reassured by a sudden improvement of mood. Such quick "recoveries" may be merely the relief of deciding to commit suicide or the temporary release of talking to someone; most likely, the underlying problems have not been resolved.

Telephone helplines are available in all regions, including the Kids Help Phone 1-800-668-6868, which serves all of Canada.

REVIEW, CHECK, AND APPLY

REVIEW

- Self-concept during adolescence grows more differentiated as the view of the self becomes more organized, broader, and more abstract, and takes account of the views of others.

- Both Erikson's identity-versus-identity-confusion stage and Marcia's four identity statuses focus on the adolescent's struggle to determine an identity and a role in society.

- One of the dangers that adolescents face is depression, which affects girls more than boys.

CHECK YOURSELF

1. It is not uncommon for younger adolescents to be troubled by the multiple aspects of their personalities, especially when these aspects appear inconsistent with one another.

- True
- False

2. One of the reasons Erikson suggested that males and females moved through the identity-versus-identity-confusion period differently involved the

   a. inherent genetic differences between men and women related to goals and needs.

   b. lack of apparent interest men had in raising children.

   c. social conditions at the time he was writing.

   d. lack of effort expended by women in reaching goals as compared to men.

3. Which of the following hypotheses do Nolen-Hoeksema (2003) and Gilbert (2004) suggest might explain the higher incidence of depression in adolescent girls?

   a. Stress is more pronounced for girls due to the conflicting demands of the traditional female role.

   b. Females traditionally are less able to deal with stress than are males.

   c. Females are more likely to turn to drugs and alcohol than are males; therefore their problems are more apparent.

   d. Parents are more concerned and protective of their daughters than their sons; therefore they notice depression in girls earlier.

APPLYING LIFESPAN DEVELOPMENT

- What are some consequences of the shift from reliance on adults to reliance on peers? Are there advantages? Dangers?

Answers: 1) True; 2) c; 3) a

Relationships: Family and Friends

LO12 How does the quality of relationships with family and peers change during adolescence?

LO13 What are gender and ethnic relations like in adolescence?

LO14 What does it mean to be popular or unpopular in adolescence, and how do adolescents respond to peer pressure?

LEARNING OBJECTIVES

autonomy having independence and a sense of control over one's life

When Paco Lizzagara entered junior high school, his good relationship with his parents changed drastically. Paco felt his parents were always "on his case." Instead of giving him the freedom he felt he deserved at age 13, they seemed to be more restrictive. Paco's parents saw things differently. They felt that they were not the source of tension in the house—he was. In their eyes, Paco, with whom they'd always enjoyed a stable, loving relationship, suddenly seemed transformed. They saw him shutting them out, and when he did speak with them, he criticized their politics, their dress, their preferences in TV shows. To his parents, Paco's behaviour was upsetting and bewildering.

Family Ties: Changing Relations with Relations

The social world of adolescents is far wider than that of younger children. As relationships outside the home grow in significance, interactions with family evolve, taking on a new, and sometimes difficult, character (Collins and Andrew, 2004).

The Quest for Autonomy. Parents are sometimes angered, and more frequently puzzled, by adolescents' conduct. Children who previously accepted their parents' judgments, declarations, and guidelines begin to question—and sometimes rebel against—their parents' views.

One cause of these clashes is the shifting roles children and parents confront during adolescence. Adolescents seek **autonomy**, independence, and a sense of control over their lives. Most parents intellectually view this shift as a normal part of adolescence—a primary developmental task of the period—and in many ways they welcome it as a sign of growth. However, the day-to-day realities of adolescents' increasing autonomy may prove difficult for parents to deal with (Smetana, 1995). An intellectual appreciation of this growing independence and allowing a teen to attend an unsupervised party are two different things. To the adolescent, her parents' refusal indicates a lack of trust or confidence. To the parents, it's simply good sense: "I trust you," they might say. "It's the others who will be there that I worry about."

In most families, teenagers' autonomy grows gradually over the adolescent years. One study of adolescents' changing views of their parents found that as autonomy increases, parents are seen more realistically as people in their own right. Rather than viewing their parents as tyrants nagging them about homework, they might realize their parents' concern reflects regrets about their own academic experience and a hope that their children do better. At the same time, adolescents become more self-reliant and feel more autonomous.

The increase in adolescent autonomy changes the parent–child relationship, which tends to be asymmetrical in early adolescence, when parents hold most of the power and influence. By the end of adolescence, power and influence are more balanced; the relationship is more egalitarian, although parents typically retain the upper hand.

Culture and Autonomy. The degree of autonomy achieved varies from one family to the next. Cultural factors play a role. In Western societies, which value individualism, adolescents seek autonomy at a relatively early stage. In contrast, Asian societies are more collectivistic, believing the welfare of the group is more important than that of the individual. In such societies, adolescents' aspirations to autonomy are less pronounced (Kim et al., 1994; Raeff, 2004).

> **From a social worker's perspective:** In what ways do you think parents with different styles—authoritarian, authoritative, permissive, and uninvolved—react to attempts to establish autonomy during adolescence? Are the styles of parenting different for a single parent? Are there cultural differences?

A sense of obligation to family also varies among cultures. In collectivistic cultures, adolescents tend to feel a greater obligation to fulfill their family's expectations—to provide assistance, show respect, and offer financial support. In such societies, the push for autonomy is weaker and its development is slower (Fuligni et al., 1999; Chao, 2001; Fuligni and Zhang, 2004; Leung et al., 2006; Feldman and Rosenthal, 1991; Feldman and Wood, 1994).

The extended timetable for autonomy in collectivistic cultures appears to have no negative consequences for adolescents. What matters is the match between cultural expectations and developmental patterns, not the specific timetable (Rothbaum et al., 2000; Zimmer-Gembeck and Collins, 2005; Updegraff et al., 2006).

Compared with adolescents from more individualistic societies, adolescents from more collectivistic cultures tend to feel greater obligation to their families.

Gender also affects autonomy. Males are usually allowed more autonomy at an earlier age than females. This is consistent with traditional gender stereotypes, in which males are seen as more independent and females as more dependent on others. In fact, parents who hold traditional views on gender are less likely to encourage their daughters' autonomy (Bumpus et al., 2001).

The Myth of the Generation Gap. Teen movies often depict adolescents and their parents in total opposition, victims of a **generation gap**, a deep divide in attitudes, values, aspirations, and world views. For example, the parent of an environmentalist might turn out to own a factory that pollutes. These exaggerations are funny because they contain a truth: Parents and teenagers often see things differently.

The reality, however, is another matter. The generation gap, when it exists, is really quite narrow. Adolescents and their parents tend to agree on many things. Liberal parents generally have liberal children; members of the Christian Right have children with similar views; parents who advocate for abortion rights have children who are pro-choice. On social, political, and religious issues, parents and adolescents tend to be in sync, and children's worries mirror those of their parents. Adolescents' concerns about society's problems (see Figure 6-8) reflect those of many adults (Flor and Knap, 2001; Knafo and Schwartz, 2003; Smetana, 2005).

Most adolescents and their parents get along quite well. Despite their quest for autonomy and independence, most teenagers have deep love, affection, and respect for their parents—as their parents do for them. Although some parent–adolescent relationships are seriously troubled, the majority are positive and help adolescents avoid the kind of peer pressure discussed later in the module (Gavin and Furman, 1996; Resnick et al., 1997; Black, 2002).

Even though teenagers spend less time with their families in general, the amount of time they spend alone with each parent remains remarkably stable across adolescence (see Figure 6-9). There is no evidence that suggests family problems are worse in adolescence than at other stages of development (Steinberg, 1993; Larson et al., 1996; Granic et al., 2003).

Conflicts with Parents. Of course, if most adolescents get along with their parents most of the time, that means sometimes they don't. No relationship is always smooth. Parents and teens may agree about social and political issues, but they often differ on matters of personal taste, such as music and clothing. Also, parents and children may disagree when children act on their autonomy and independence sooner than parents feel is right. Consequently, parent–child conflicts are more likely to occur during adolescence, particularly in the early stages, although not every family is affected to the same degree (Arnett, 2000; Smetana et al., 2003).

According to developmental psychologist Judith Smetana, conflict is greater in early adolescence because of differing definitions of, and rationales for, appropriate and inappropriate conduct. Parents might frown on multiple ear piercings because society traditionally deems them inappropriate, while adolescents view the issue as one of personal choice (Smetana, 2005).

The newly sophisticated reasoning of adolescents (discussed in the previous module) leads them to regard parental rules in more complex ways. Arguments that might convince a school-age child ("Do it because I tell you to do it") are less compelling to an adolescent.

The argumentativeness and assertiveness of early adolescence might first increase conflict, but they play a key role in the evolution of parent–child relationships. While parents may initially react defensively to their children's challenges and grow inflexible and rigid, in

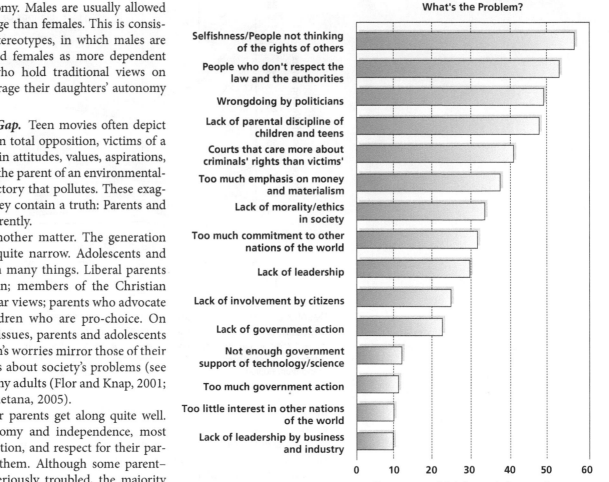

What's the Problem?

FIGURE 6-8 **What's the Problem?**
Adolescents' views of society's ills are ones with which their parents would likely agree.
Source: PRIMEDIA/Roper National Youth Survey, 1999.

generation gap a divide between parents and adolescents in attitudes, values, aspirations, and world views

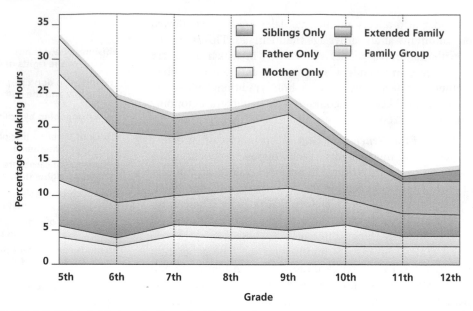

FIGURE 6-9 Time Adolescents Spend with Parents
Despite their quest for autonomy and independence, most adolescents have deep love, affection, and respect for their parents, and the amount of time they spend alone with each parent (the lower two segments) remains remarkably stable across adolescence.
Source: From Reed Larson et al., *Developmental Psychology*. Copyright © 1996 by the American Psychological Association. Reproduced with permission.

most cases they come to realize their children *are* growing up and they want to support their children in that process.

As parents realize that their children's arguments are often compelling and fairly reasonable, and that their children can be trusted with more freedom, they become more yielding, allowing and perhaps even encouraging independence. As this process occurs in mid-adolescence, the conflict of the early years of adolescence declines.

This does not hold true for all adolescents. The majority of teenagers maintain stable relations with their parents, but as many as 20 percent pass through a fairly rough time (Dryfoos, 1990; Dmitrieva et al., 2004).

Cultural Differences in Parent–Child Conflicts during Adolescence. Parent–child conflicts are found in every culture, but there does seem to be less conflict between parents and teenagers in "traditional," preindustrial cultures. Teens in such cultures experience fewer mood swings and instances of risky behaviour than teens in industrialized countries (Arnett, 2000; Nelson et al., 2004).

The reason may be the degree of independence that adolescents expect and adults permit. In more industrialized societies, with an emphasis on individualism, independence is expected of adolescents. Consequently, adolescents and their parents must negotiate the amount and timing of that independence—a process that often leads to strife. In more traditional societies, individualism is less valued; therefore, adolescents are less inclined to seek independence. The result is less parent–child conflict (Dasen, 2000, 2002).

Relationships with Peers: The Importance of Belonging

For many parents, the key symbols of adolescence are cellphones or computers. For their children, communicating with friends is an indispensable lifeline, a compulsive need that underscores their significance at this stage. Continuing the trend from middle childhood, adolescents spend increasing hours with their peers as these relationships grow in importance. In fact, there is probably no period of life in which peer relationships matter as much as in adolescence (Youniss and Haynie, 1992).

Social Comparison. Peers become more important for many reasons. They enable adolescents to compare and evaluate opinions, abilities, and even physical changes—a process called *social comparison.* Because the physical and cognitive changes of this age are unique and so pronounced, especially in early puberty, adolescents turn to others who share and can shed light on their own experiences. Parents, being well beyond these changes, cannot provide social comparison. Adolescents' questioning of adult authority and their desire for autonomy also render parents—and adults in general—inadequate sources of knowledge (Schutz et al., 2002; Rankin et al., 2004).

Reference Groups. As noted, adolescence is a time of trying out new identities, roles, and conduct. Peers provide information about what roles and behaviour are most acceptable by serving as a reference group. **Reference groups** are people with whom one compares oneself. Just as a professional ballplayer compares his performance to that of other pro players, so do teenagers compare themselves to peers similar to them.

Reference groups offer a set of *norms*, or standards, by which abilities and social success can be judged. A teenager need not belong to a group for it to serve as a reference. Unpopular adolescents, belittled and rejected by members of a popular group, might yet use it as a reference group (Berndt, 1999).

Cliques and Crowds: Belonging to a Group. Increased cognitive sophistication allows adolescents to group others in more discriminating ways. Even if they do not belong to their reference group, they typically are part of some identifiable group. Rather than defining people in concrete terms by what they do ("football players" or "musicians") as a younger child might, adolescents use more abstract terms ("jocks" or "skaters" or "stoners") (Brown, 1990; Montemayor et al., 1994).

Adolescents form two types of groups: cliques and crowds. **Cliques** are groups of from 2 to 12 people whose members have frequent social interactions with one another. **Crowds** are larger, comprising individuals who share certain characteristics but do not necessarily interact. "Jocks" and "nerds" represent crowds found in many high schools.

Membership in a clique or a crowd is determined by the degree of similarity with other members. One key similarity is substance use; adolescents tend to choose friends whose alcohol and drug use matches their own. Their friends often mirror their academic success and general behaviour patterns, although this is not always true. For instance, in early adolescence, peers who are aggressive may be more attractive than those who are well behaved (Bukowski et al., 2000; Farmer et al., 2003; Kupersmidt and Dodge, 2004).

The emergence of distinct cliques and crowds at this stage reflects adolescents' increased cognitive capabilities. Group labels are abstractions, requiring teens to judge people they might seldom interact with and have little direct knowledge about. Not until mid-adolescence do teenagers cognitively make the subtle judgments that distinguish between different cliques and crowds (Burgess and Rubin, 2000; Brown and Bradford, 2003).

Gender Relations. As children enter adolescence, their social groups are composed almost universally of same-sex friends. Boys hang out with boys; girls hang out with girls. This sex segregation is called the **sex cleavage.**

The situation changes with the onset of puberty. Boys and girls experience the hormonal surge that causes the sex organs to mature. At the same time, society suggests it is time for romantic involvement. These developments change the ways the opposite sex is viewed. Where a 10-year-old is likely to see every member of the other sex as "annoying" and "a pain," heterosexual teenage boys and girls regard each others' personalities and sexuality with greater interest. (For gay and lesbian youth, pairing off holds other complexities, as we will see when we discuss adolescent dating.)

In early puberty, boys' and girls' cliques, previously on parallel but separate tracks, begin to converge. Adolescents attend boy–girl dances or parties, although the boys still tend to socialize with boys, and the girls with girls (Richards et al., 1998). Soon, adolescents spend more time with the other sex. New cliques emerge, composed of both genders. Not everyone participates initially: Early on, the leaders of the same-sex cliques and those with the highest status lead the way. Eventually, however, most teenagers belong to mixed-gender cliques. At the end of adolescence, cliques and crowds become less influential. Many dissolve as pairing off occurs.

The sex segregation of childhood continues during the early stages of adolescence. However, by the time of middle adolescence, this segregation decreases, and boys' and girls' cliques begin to converge.

Watch on **mydevelopmentlab**

As your virtual child reaches adolescence, what changes have you seen between your child and his or her friends? What about between you and your child?
Log onto MyDevelopmentLab and watch the video on adolescence to see teenagers aged 16 to 20 talk about making decisions, the transition to university, first relationships, and their relationships with their parents.

reference groups groups of people with whom one compares oneself

cliques groups of from 2 to 12 people whose members have frequent social interactions with one another

crowds larger groups than cliques, composed of individuals who share particular characteristics but who might not interact with one another

sex cleavage sex segregation in which boys interact primarily with boys and girls primarily with girls

Cultural Dimensions

Ethnic Segregation: The Great Divide of Adolescence

A pattern of ethnic segregation is repeated in schools and colleges throughout the country: Even when they attend schools with significant diversity, people of different ethnicities interact very little. Even if they have a friend of a different ethnicity within the confines of a school, most adolescents don't interact with that friend outside of school (DuBois and Hirsch, 1990).

It doesn't start out this way. During elementary school and early adolescence, integration is common among students of differing ethnicities. However, by middle and late adolescence, students segregate (Spencer and Dornbusch, 1990; Ennett and Bauman, 1996).

Why is ethnic segregation the rule? One reason is that minority students may seek support from others who share their status (where "minority," used in its sociological sense, indicates a subordinate group lacking power compared to a dominant group). By associating with others of their own group, members of minority groups are able to affirm their own identity.

Members of different ethnic groups might be segregated in the classroom as well. As discussed earlier, members of groups that have experienced discrimination tend to be less successful in school. Thus, ethnic segregation in high school might be based on academic achievement as well.

Lower academic performance can place minority students in classes with fewer majority students, and vice versa. Such class assignment practices can maintain and promote ethnic segregation, especially in schools where rigid academic tracking assigns students to "low," "medium," and "high" tracks depending on their prior achievement (Lucas and Berends, 2002).

Segregation in school can also reflect prejudice, both perceived and real, toward members of other groups. Students of minority Group A might feel that majority Group B is discriminatory and hostile, and might thus prefer to stick to their own group. Group B students might assume that Group A students are antagonistic and unfriendly.

Such mutually destructive attitudes make meaningful interaction difficult (Phinney et al., 1997; Tropp, 2003).

Is this voluntary ethnic segregation inevitable? No. Adolescents who have interacted regularly and extensively with other ethnicities in childhood are more likely to have diverse friends. Schools that actively promote integration in classes create an environment that fosters diverse friendships (Hewstone, 2003).

Still, many societal pressures prevent social integration. Peer pressure, too, can discourage clique members from crossing ethnic lines to form new friendships.

Unpopular adolescents fall into several categories. Controversial adolescents are liked by some and disliked by others; rejected adolescents are uniformly disliked; and neglected adolescents are neither liked nor disliked.

Popularity and Rejection

Most adolescents are highly tuned in to who is popular and who is not. In fact, for some, popularity—or lack of it—is the central focus of their lives.

The social world of adolescents is more complex than just who is popular or unpopular. Some adolescents are controversial. In contrast to *popular* adolescents, who are mostly liked, **controversial adolescents** are liked by some and disliked by others. A controversial adolescent may be highly popular within a particular group, such as the string orchestra, but less so among other classmates. There are also **rejected adolescents**, who are uniformly disliked, and **neglected adolescents**, who are neither liked nor disliked (see Figure 6-10)—whose status is so low everyone overlooks them.

In most cases, both popular and controversial adolescents tend to enjoy a higher status, while rejected and neglected teenagers share a lower status. Popular and controversial adolescents have more close friends, engage in more activities with their peers, and disclose more about themselves than less popular students. They participate in more extracurricular school activities. Well aware of their own popularity, they are not as lonely than their less popular classmates (Englund et al., 2000; Farmer et al., 2003; Zettergren, 2004; Becker and Luthar, 2007).

controversial adolescents children who are liked by some peers and disliked by others

rejected adolescents children who are actively disliked, and whose peers may react to them in an obviously negative manner

neglected adolescents children who receive relatively little attention from their peers in the form of either positive or negative interactions

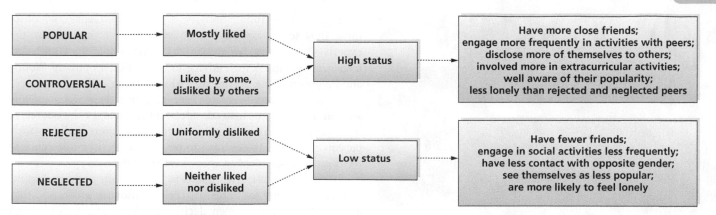

FIGURE 6-10 The Social World of Adolescence

An adolescent's popularity can fall into one of four categories, depending on the opinions of his or her peers. Popularity is related to differences in status, behaviour, and adjustment.

The social world of rejected and neglected adolescents is far less pleasant. They have fewer friends, engage in fewer social activities, and have less contact with the opposite sex. They see themselves—accurately—as less popular, and they are more likely to feel lonely.

As illustrated in Table 6-3, men and women differ in their ideas of what determines status in high school. College men suggest that appearance is what most determines a girl's status, while college women believe it is her grades and intelligence (Suitor et al., 2001).

Conformity: Peer Pressure in Adolescence

Whenever Aldos Henry said he wanted a particular brand of sneakers or a certain style of shirt, his parents blamed it on peer pressure and told him to think for himself.

In arguing with Aldos, his parents were taking a view prevalent in our society: that teenagers are highly susceptible to **peer pressure**, the pressure to conform to the behaviour and attitudes of one's peers. Were his parents correct?

Adolescents *are* highly susceptible to the influence of their peers when considering what to wear, whom to date, and what movies to see. Wearing the right clothes, down to the right brand, can be a ticket to popularity. It shows you know what's what. But when it comes to nonsocial matters, such as choosing a career path or trying to solve a problem, they are more likely to consult an adult (Phelan, Yu, and Davidson, 1994).

Watch on mydevelopmentlab

Log onto MyDevelopmentLab and watch a video of 18-year-old Tim and his mom talk about how peer pressure has affected Tim's life.

peer pressure the influence of one's peers to conform to their behaviour and attitudes.

TABLE 6-3 HIGH SCHOOL STATUS

What Makes High School Girls High in Status:		What Makes High School Boys High in Status:	
According to College Men:	**According to College Women:**	**According to College Men:**	**According to College Women:**
1. Physical attractiveness	1. Grades/intelligence	1. Participation in sports	1. Participation in sports
2. Grades/intelligence	2. Participation in sports	2. Grades/intelligence	2. Grades/intelligence
3. Participation in sports	3. General sociability	3. Popularity with girls	3. General sociability
4. General sociability	4. Physical attractiveness	4. General sociability	4. Physical attractiveness
5. Popularity with boys	5. Clothes	5. Car	5. School clubs/government

Source: From Suitor, J. J., Minyard, S. A., & Carter, R. S. (2001), "'Did you see what I saw?' Gender differences in perceptions of avenues to prestige among adolescents," *Sociological Inquiry*, 71, 437–454. Copyright © 2001 Blackwell Publishing. Reprinted with permission.

Undersocialized delinquents are raised with little discipline or by harsh, uncaring parents, and they begin anti-social activities at a relatively early age. In contrast, socialized delinquents know and usually follow the norms of society, and they are highly influenced by their peers.

Especially in middle and late adolescence, teenagers look to those they see as experts. For social concerns, they turn to the experts—their peers. For arenas where adults hold the knowledge, teenagers tend to ask their advice and accept their opinions (Young and Ferguson, 1979; Perrine and Aloise-Young, 2004).

Overall, susceptibility to peer pressure does not suddenly soar in adolescence. Instead, adolescence changes the source of influence. Whereas children conform fairly consistently to their parents, pressures to conform to peers increase in adolescence as teens establish an identity apart from their parents'.

Ultimately, adolescents conform less to both peers *and* adults as their autonomy increases. As their confidence grows and they are able to make their own decisions, adolescents are apt to act independently and to reject pressures from others. Before they learn to resist peer pressure, however, teenagers can get into trouble, often along with their friends (Steinberg, 1993; Crockett and Crouter, 1995).

Juvenile Delinquency: The Crimes of Adolescence

Adolescents, along with young adults, commit more crimes than any other age group. This is a somewhat misleading statistic: Because certain behaviours (such as drinking) are illegal for adolescents, it is easy for them to break the law. But even disregarding such crimes, adolescents disproportionately commit violent crimes and property crimes involving theft, robbery, and arson.

Youth violent crime has risen in recent decades, as much as 30 percent since 1991, whereas property crime has declined. As much as 40 percent of chargeable youth offenses involved violence, and homicides and assaults have risen dramatically. The largest increase, though, was in disturbing the peace, increasing 217 percent between 1997 and 2006. Dramatic increases were also seen for mischief, weapons, and illegal drugs (Statistics Canada, 2007).

What steers adolescents toward criminal activity? Some offenders, known as **undersocialized delinquents**, were raised with little discipline or by harsh, uncaring parents. Although they are influenced by peers, their parents did not teach them appropriate social behaviour or how to regulate their own conduct. Undersocialized delinquents typically begin criminal activities well before the onset of adolescence.

Undersocialized delinquents share several characteristics. They tend to be aggressive and violent early in life, leading to peer rejection and academic failure. They are more likely to have been diagnosed with attention deficit disorder as children, and they tend to be less intelligent than average (Silverthorn and Frick, 1999; Rutter, 2003).

Undersocialized delinquents often suffer from psychological problems, and as adults fit a pattern called antisocial personality disorder. They are unlikely to be successfully rehabilitated, and many undersocialized delinquents live on the margins of society their entire lives (Lynam, 1996; Frick et al., 2003).

A larger group of adolescent offenders are socialized delinquents. **Socialized delinquents** know and subscribe to the norms of society; they are fairly normal psychologically. For them, offenses committed in adolescence do not lead to a life of crime. Instead, most socialized delinquents engage in some petty crimes (such as shoplifting) during adolescence, but these crimes do not continue into adulthood.

Socialized delinquents are typically highly peer-influenced, their delinquency often occurring in groups. Some research also suggests that their parents supervise their behaviour less than other parents, but these minor delinquencies are often a result of giving in to group pressure or seeking to establish one's identity as an adult (Fletcher et al., 1995; Thornberry and Krohn, 1997).

undersocialized delinquents adolescent delinquents who are raised with little discipline or with harsh, uncaring parental supervision

socialized delinquents adolescent delinquents who know and subscribe to the norms of society and who are fairly normal psychologically

REVIEW

- The search for autonomy may change relations between teenagers and their parents, but the generation gap is narrower than is generally thought.

- Cliques and crowds serve as reference groups in adolescence, offering a means of social comparison. Sex cleavage gradually diminishes until boys and girls begin to pair off.

- Ethnic separation increases in adolescence, bolstered by socioeconomic status differences, different academic experiences, and mutually distrustful attitudes.

CHECK YOURSELF

1. Depending on their cultural framework, some adolescents can expect less autonomy from their parents than others.

   - True

   - False

2. _____ groups are groups of people with whom one compares oneself. For example, teens would compare themselves to other teens.

3. Cross-sex cliques begin forming

   a. once parents and teachers begin rewarding students for cross-sex interactions.

   b. once the leaders in the same-sex cliques begin dating.

   c. after grade 6.

   d. when same-sex peers become bored with one another.

APPLYING LIFESPAN DEVELOPMENT

- Thinking back to your own high school days, what was the dominant clique in your school, and what factors were related to group membership?

Answers: 1) True; 2) Reference; 3) b

Dating, Sexual Behaviour, and Teenage Pregnancy

LEARNING OBJECTIVES

L015 What are the functions and characteristics of dating during adolescence?

L016 How does sexuality develop in the adolescent years?

It took him almost a month, but Sylvester Chiu finally got up the courage to ask Jackie Durbin to the movies. It was hardly a surprise to Jackie, though. Sylvester had first told his friend Erik about his plans, and Erik had told Jackie's friend Cynthia, who had in turn told Jackie, who was primed to say "yes" when Sylvester finally called.

Welcome to the complex world of adolescent dating, an important ritual in the liturgy of adolescent relationships.

Dating: Close Relationships in the Twenty-First Century

Changing cultural factors largely determine when and how adolescents begin to date. Until recently, exclusive dating was a cultural ideal, viewed in the context of romance. Society encouraged dating as a way for adolescents to explore relationships that might lead to marriage. Today, some adolescents believe that dating is outmoded and limiting, and in some places "hooking up"—a vague term that covers everything from kissing to sexual intercourse—is regarded as more appropriate. Still, despite changing cultural norms, dating remains the dominant form of social interaction that leads to intimacy among adolescents (Denizet-Lewis, 2004; Manning et al., 2006).

The Functions of Dating. Dating serves functions other than courtship. It is a way to learn intimacy. It can provide entertainment and prestige. It can even help to develop an adolescent's identity (Skipper and Nass, 1966; Savin-Williams and Berndt, 1990; Sanderson and Cantor, 1995).

Unfortunately, dating, at least in early and middle adolescence, does not serve the function of developing intimacy very well. On the contrary, it is often a superficial activity in which the participants rarely let down their guard and never reveal themselves emotionally. Psychological intimacy can be lacking even when sex is part of the relationship (Savin-Williams and Berndt, 1990; Collins, 2003; Furman and Shaffer, 2003).

True intimacy becomes more common during later adolescence. At that point, both participants may take dating more seriously as a way to select a possible mate for marriage.

For homosexual adolescents, dating presents special challenges. In some cases, prejudice can cause gay and lesbian teens to try to fit in by dating members of the other sex. Even if they seek same-gender relationships, partners can be hard to find because many are not openly expressing their sexual orientation. Meanwhile, homosexual teens who openly date often face harassment (Savin-Williams, 2003).

Dating and Ethnicity. Culture influences dating patterns among adolescents of different ethnic groups, particularly those whose parents have emigrated from other countries. Foreign-born parents might try to control dating behaviour to preserve traditional values or confine dating to their own ethnic group.

Some parents might hold especially conservative attitudes because they themselves are living in an arranged marriage and might never have experienced dating. They might insist that there will be no dating without chaperones, a position that will inevitably lead to conflict with their children (Kibria, 2003; Hamon and Ingoldsby, 2003; Hoelter et al., 2004).

Sexual Relationships

The hormonal changes of puberty trigger not only the maturation of the sexual organs, but also a new range of feelings. Sexual behaviour and thoughts are among the central concerns of adolescents, occupying the minds of almost all adolescents a good deal of the time (Kelly, 2001; Ponton, 2001).

Masturbation. Often the first sex act in which adolescents engage is solitary sexual self-stimulation, or masturbation. By age 15, 80 percent of teenage boys and 20 percent of teenage girls report that they have masturbated. In males, frequency is high in the early teens and then begins to decline, while in females, frequency is lower initially and increases throughout adolescence (Schwartz, 1999; Hyde and DeLamater, 2003).

Although masturbation is widespread, it still may produce feelings of shame and guilt, a legacy from years of misguided views. In the nineteenth century, people were warned about the horrible effects of masturbation, which were thought to include "dyspepsia, spinal disease, headache, epilepsy, various kinds of fits, . . . impaired eyesight, palpitation of the heart, pain in the side and bleeding at the lungs, spasm of the heart, and sometimes sudden death" (Gregory, 1856). Suggested remedies included bandaging the genitals, covering them with a cage, tying the hands, male circumcision without anesthesia (so that it might better be remembered), and for girls, the administration of carbolic acid to the clitoris. One physician, J. W. Kellogg, believed that certain grains would be less likely to provoke sexual excitation—leading to his invention of corn flakes (Hunt, 1974; Michael et al., 1994).

Today, experts on sexual behaviour view masturbation as a normal, healthy, and harmless activity. In fact, some suggest that it provides a useful way to learn about one's own sexuality (Hyde and DeLamater, 2003).

Sexual Intercourse. Although it may be preceded by other types of sexual intimacy, sexual intercourse remains a major milestone for many adolescents. The perception is that teens are fornicating everywhere—an idea that must come from popular media because surveys suggest fewer teens are having sex than a decade earlier. Only 8 percent of teens report their first sexual intercourse before age 15, while 43 percent report first sexual intercourse between 15 and 19 years of age; notably there is no gender difference. Among sexually active teens, 75 percent reported using a condom the last time they had sex (see Figure 6-11) (Rotermann, 2008).

Strong societal norms govern sexual conduct. A few decades ago the prevailing norm was the *double standard*: Premarital sex was permissible for males but not females, but men should be sure to marry virgins. Today the double standard has begun to give way to *permissiveness with affection*. Under this standard, premarital intercourse is permissible for both men and women in the context of a long-term, committed, or loving relationship (Hyde and Delamater, 2004). A recent survey found a very open attitude towards sexuality among adolescent girls, coupled with declining frequency—adolescent girls in Canada are taking control of their sexuality, but the frequency of sexual intercourse for teens is less than that of their grandparents (Gulli, 2009).

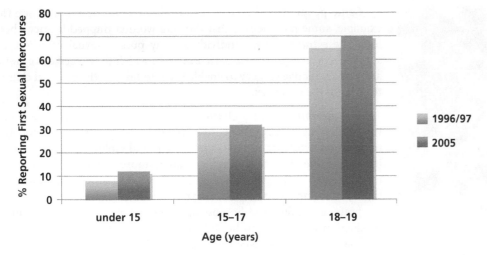

FIGURE 6-11 Adolescents and Sexual Activity

The age at which adolescents have sexual intercourse for the first time is rising, and many adolescents are not having sex.
Source: Rotermann, 2008.

> **From the perspective of a health-care provider:** A parent asks you how to prevent her 14-year-old son from engaging in sexual activity until he is older. What would you tell her?

While attitudes among Canadian youth are changing, the demise of the double standard is far from complete. Attitudes toward sexual conduct are still typically more lenient for males than for females, even in socially liberal cultures. And in some cultures, the standards for men and women are quite distinct. For example, in North Africa, the Middle East, and the majority of Asian countries, women are expected to abstain from sexual intercourse until they are married. In Mexico, males are considerably more likely than females to have premarital sex. In contrast, in Sub-Saharan Africa, women are more likely to have sexual intercourse before marriage, and intercourse is common among unmarried teenage women (Liskin, 1985; Spira et al., 1992; Johnson et al., 1992; Peltzer and Pengpid, 2006).

Sexual Orientation: Heterosexuality, Homosexuality, and Bisexuality

The most frequent pattern of adolescents' sexual development is *heterosexuality*, sexual attraction and behaviour directed to the other sex. Some teenagers are *homosexual*, with sexual attraction and behaviour oriented to members of their own sex. Others are *bisexual*, sexually attracted to people of both sexes.

Many teens experiment with homosexuality. Around 20 to 25 percent of adolescent boys and 10 percent of adolescent girls have at least one same-sex sexual encounter. In fact, homosexuality and heterosexuality are not completely distinct sexual orientations. Alfred Kinsey, a pioneer sex researcher, argued that sexual orientation should be viewed as a continuum in which "exclusively homosexual" is at one end and "exclusively heterosexual" at the other (Kinsey et al., 1948). In between are people who show both homosexual and heterosexual behaviour. Although accurate figures are difficult to obtain, most experts believe that between 4 and 10 percent of both men and women are exclusively homosexual during extended periods of their lives (Michael et al., 1994; Diamond, 2003a, 2003b; Russell and Consolacion, 2003).

Sexuality is further complicated by the distinction between sexual orientation (which refers to a person's sexual interests) and gender identity—the gender a person believes he or she is psychologically. Sexual orientation and gender identity are not necessarily related to one another: A man with a strong masculine gender identity might be attracted to other men, and traditional "masculine" or "feminine" behaviour is not necessarily related to a person's sexual orientation or gender identity (Hunter and Mallon, 2000).

This 16-year-old mother and her child are representative of a major social problem: teenage pregnancy. Why is teenage pregnancy a greater problem in the United States and Britain than in Canada?

Some people feel they have been born the wrong physical sex (for example, some men believe that they are women trapped in men's bodies). These *transgendered* individuals may pursue sexual reassignment surgery, a prolonged course of treatment in which they receive hormones and reconstructive surgery to enable them to take on the physical characteristics of the other sex.

What Determines Sexual Orientation? The factors that induce people to develop as heterosexual, homosexual, or bisexual are not well understood. Evidence suggests that genetic and biological factors play an important role. Among siblings who are homosexual, identical twins are more likely to both be homosexual than pairs of siblings who don't share their genetic makeup. Other research finds that various structures of the brain are different in homosexuals and heterosexuals, and hormone production also seems to be linked to sexual orientation (Lippa, 2003; Rahman and Wilson, 2003; Kraemer et al., 2006).

Other researchers have suggested that family or peer environmental factors play a role. For example, Freud argued that homosexuality was the result of inappropriate identification with the opposite-sex parent (Freud, 1922/1959). The difficulty with Freud's theoretical perspective and other, similar perspectives that followed is that there simply is no evidence to suggest that any particular family dynamic or childrearing practice is consistently related to sexual orientation. Similarly, explanations based on learning theory, which suggest that homosexuality arises because of rewarding, pleasant homosexual experiences and unsatisfying heterosexual ones, do not appear to be the complete answer (Bell and Weinberg, 1978; Isay, 1990; Golombok and Tasker, 1996).

In short, there is no accepted explanation of why some adolescents develop a heterosexual orientation and others a homosexual orientation. Most experts believe that sexual orientation develops out of a complex interplay of genetic, physiological, and environmental factors (LeVay and Valente, 2003).

Challenges Facing Gay and Lesbian Adolescents. Adolescents who are attracted to members of the same sex face a more difficult time than other teens. Gay and lesbian teens may be rejected by their family or peers and harassed or even assaulted by others. As a result, adolescents who are homosexual are at greater risk for depression, with suicide rates significantly higher than for heterosexual adolescents (Ryan and Rivers, 2003; Harris, 2004; Murdock and Bolch, 2005; Koh and Ross, 2006; Lester, 2006).

Ultimately, though, most people become comfortable with their sexual orientation. And while lesbian, gay, and bisexual adolescents may experience mental health difficulties, homosexuality is no longer considered a psychological disorder by any of the major psychological or medical associations (Stone, 2003; van Wormer and McKinney, 2003; Davison, 2005).

Teenage Pregnancies

Feedings at 3:00 a.m., diaper changes, and visits to the pediatrician are not part of most people's vision of adolescence. While the general trend in Canada is that, as a whole, women are becoming mothers later, approximately 2.5 percent of teenage girls become pregnant. The teen pregnancy rate in Canada is substantially lower than in the US or Britain, although the reasons remain unclear. One factor could be that fewer Canadian teens are having sex—in the previous section we saw that 8 percent of teens under 15 have had sex, whereas similar surveys suggest 20 percent of US teens under 15 have had sex. Canadian teenagers who become pregnant are also more likely to choose abortion than American or British teens (slightly more than 50 percent of adolescent pregnancies are electively terminated), reducing the rate of teenage motherhood even further. Still, nearly 1 in 20 sexually active teenage girls gets pregnant in Canada.

An adolescent mother faces a heightened risk of pregnancy complications both for herself and her child, in large part because young mothers fail to receive appropriate prenatal care. They also face heightened mortality rates and low-birth-weight babies. The Canadian

Paediatric Society (2006) identifies the following adolescents to be at risk of unprotected intercourse and subsequent pregnancy:

- those who are experiencing social and family difficulties
- those whose mothers were adolescent mothers
- those undergoing early puberty
- those who have been sexually abused
- those who have frequent social absenteeism or lack vocational goals
- those with siblings who were pregnant during adolescence
- those who use tobacco, alcohol, and other substances
- those who live in group homes or detention centres or who are street-involved

One thing that apparently hasn't led to a reduction in teenage pregnancies is asking adolescents to take a virginity pledge. These public pledges—a centrepiece of some forms of sex education—apparently are ineffective. In one study of 12 000 teenagers who had taken the pledge, 88 percent reported eventually having sexual intercourse. However, pledges did delay the start of sex an average of 18 months (Bearman and Bruckner, 2004).

An unintended pregnancy can be devastating to mother and child. Few put their children up for adoption, and many who consider adoption change their minds. Teenage mothers today are much less likely than in earlier years to be married. In many cases, mothers care for their children without the help of the father. Lacking financial and emotional support, the mother might have to abandon her own education and be relegated to unskilled, poorly paying jobs for the rest of her life. In some cases, she develops long-term dependency on welfare. Furthermore, her physical and mental health can suffer as she faces unrelenting stress from the continuous demands on her time (Manlove et al., 2004; Gillmore et al., 2006; Oxford et al., 2006).

REVIEW, CHECK, AND APPLY

REVIEW

- Dating in adolescence serves a number of functions, including intimacy, entertainment, and prestige.
- Sexual intercourse is a major milestone that most people reach during adolescence. The age of first intercourse reflects cultural differences and has been declining over the last 50 years.
- Sexual orientation, which is most accurately viewed as a continuum rather than categorically, develops as the result of a complex combination of factors.

CHECK YOURSELF

1. Dating has several functions in adolescence. Check all that apply.
   a. It usually leads to marriage.
   b. It provides entertainment.
   c. It can provide prestige depending on the status of the person one is dating.
   d. It assists in developing identity.
   e. It is a way to learn how to establish intimacy.

2. Overall, _____ of adolescents begin having intercourse between the ages of 15 and 18.
   a. 20%
   b. 10%
   c. 70%
   d. 50%

3. Teenage pregnancy presents a medical risk to both mother and child.
   a. True
   b. False

APPLYING LIFESPAN DEVELOPMENT

- What aspects of the social world of adolescents work against the achievement of true intimacy in dating?

Answers: 1) b, c, d, e; 2) d; 3) a

Putting It All Together
Adolescence

FROM AGE 13 TO 18, Mariah, the young woman we met in the chapter opener, changed from a seemingly "together" teenager to a troubled young adolescent to an increasingly confident and independent late adolescent. Early in her adolescence, she struggled to define herself and responded to the "Who am I?" question with some decidedly unwise answers. She dabbled with—and then nearly drowned in—drugs, and she attempted suicide. At last seeking help for her difficulties, she kicked her bad habits, began to work on her self-concept, returned to school and became interested in photography, repaired her family life, and entered a positive relationship with a boyfriend.

MODULE **6.1** Physical Development

- Adolescents have many physical issues to deal with **(pp. 244–249).**

- Mariah's resorting to drugs is a strategy used by some adolescents for coping with the stresses of the period **(p. 245).**

- Adolescent brain development permits Mariah to engage in complex thinking, which can sometimes lead to confusion **(p. 251).**

- Mariah displays a lack of impulse control, which is typical of a not yet fully developed prefrontal cortex **(p. 252).**

MODULE **6.2** Cognitive Development

- Adolescents' personal fables include a sense of invulnerability, which probably contributed to Mariah's impulsive decisions **(pp. 262–263).**

- Mariah's depression might have stemmed from the adolescent tendency toward introspection and self-consciousness **(pp. 259–261).**

- Mariah might have used drugs to escape the pressures of everyday life **(pp. 253–255).**

- It is not unusual for an adolescent like Mariah to have school difficulties **(p. 264).**

What would a PARENT do?

■ What warning signs should Mariah's parents have seen as their daughter descended into depression and attempted suicide? Is there anything they should have done?

HINT Review pages 272–274.

What's your response?

MODULE **6.3** Social and Personality Development

■ Mariah's struggles with identity represent the characteristic internal conflict of adolescence **(p. 268).**

■ In balancing friendships with the desire to be alone, Mariah is struggling to accommodate her increasingly complex personality **(p. 270).**

■ Her more accurate self-concept may in fact lower Mariah's self-esteem **(pp. 268–269).**

■ In relying on her "cool" crowd, Mariah is defining her identity in terms of a questionable reference group **(p. 279).**

■ Mariah's struggle with depression reflects the higher incidence of this ailment among adolescent girls **(p. 272).**

■ Mariah benefited from a moratorium that enabled her to re-establish connection with her "clueless" parents and begin to assume true independence **(p. 271).**

■ Her relationship with her boyfriend indicates a return to a normal social pattern **(pp. 280–281).**

What would a HEALTH-CARE PROVIDER do?

■ When an adolescent such as Mariah shows a definite decline in academic performance, are the symptoms likely to be interpreted differently depending on whether the adolescent comes from an affluent or impoverished background? How can a professional care provider prevent different interpretation and treatment?

HINT Review page 264.

What's your response?

What would an EDUCATOR do?

■ What signals might a teacher have observed in Mariah's classroom performance to suggest that she was having a drug problem? What steps might the teacher have taken?

HINT Review pages 253–255.

What's your response?

What would YOU do?

■ If you were Mariah's friend, what advice and support would you give her before she attempted suicide? What advice and support would you provide during her recovery?

HINT Review pages 273–275.

What's your response?

7 Early Adulthood

A t 27, Bella Arnoff was feeling pressure to marry. She and Theodore Choi had been living together for more than four years, but suddenly their personal atmosphere was filled with what they called "The Urge to Wed."

The funny thing was that the pressure was not coming from their parents. Admittedly, his Korean family occasionally extolled the blessings of grandchildren and sometimes even reminded her that Theodore was an only child (and therefore the sole hope for the continuation of the Choi bloodline), but the Korean front had been surprisingly restrained, and her free-spirited Jewish parents even more so.

Less restrained was peer pressure. It seemed that everyone they knew was marrying. Bella had just accepted her sixth bridesmaid invitation, and Theodore was slated to be best man twice in the next three months and usher twice more in the next year. There was, in their circle, a sense of ticking clocks and a determination to raise children while still young.

MODULE 7.1 Physical Development in Early Adulthood

How does stress affect the body? What are some strategies for coping with stress? see page 292

MODULE 7.2 Cognitive Development in Early Adulthood

What does gender bias in the classroom look like?

see page 301

As Bella and Theodore discussed the tidal wave of marriages, they meandered through topics such as their present and future health, the nature of love and commitment, the "right" age for childrearing, their desired number of children, the need for one of them to become a stay-at-home parent, the temporary sacrifice of one of their incomes, the postponement of his return to graduate school, and many other things. Slowly they realized that somewhere during their conversation they had decided to marry.

Early adulthood, the period from approximately age 20 to 40, is a time of continued development. In fact, young adults like Bella and Theodore face some of the most pressing questions they will ever face and experience considerable stress as they answer them.

At their physical peak in their twenties, they are on the threshold of the worrisome thirties, when the body begins to send messages of decline and to exact a price for excess and inattention. Cognitively, most have stopped their formal learning, but some want to take it up again either in college or in some other setting. Socially, young adults are often settling into a career, and sometimes they have to consider whether the path they are on is right for them after all. And they still have to answer the really big questions about marriage and children. Staring so many weighty decisions in the face can cause young adults a great deal of stress.

In this chapter, we look at the physical, cognitive, and social and personality changes that accompany young adulthood. This period of life, in which people are too often considered "developed" rather than "developing," in fact harbours many changes. Like Bella and Theodore, young adults continue to develop throughout the period.

MODULE 7.3 Social and Personality Development in Early Adulthood

Is love the only thing that matters in seeking a spouse?

see page 316

MyVirtualLife

Log onto MyDevelopmentLab and watch two young people, just like Bella and Theodore, talk about all the issues and emotions that they've experienced as young adults.

MODULE 7.1 Physical Development in Early Adulthood

The Chess Match

As Anton ate his lunch one sunny day in the park, he idly watched two young men playing a high-speed chess game at the next table. One of the players was sitting in a wheelchair. As the game proceeded, with first one player then the other announcing his moves and slamming his timer, Anton found himself hoping that the guy in the wheelchair would win the match.

No such luck. After only a few more moves, the opponent loudly and triumphantly called "Check," and the handicapped player, after surveying the board, tipped his king and conceded defeat. Anton was disappointed: He had hoped that the able-bodied player would go easy on his opponent.

But Anton almost choked on his sandwich when he saw the winner reach for his cane as he rose to shake the hand of the man in the wheelchair. The winner was blind. Both players had a disability, and the one who couldn't even see the board had won the match.

As Anton learned, many people have disabilities, and focusing on what they lack instead of what they have is itself a kind of blindness. It is also a mistake to offer sympathy for the handicap instead of understanding of the individual who has it.

Most people are at their physical peak in early adulthood. For them, the body acts as if it's on automatic pilot: Physical health and fitness are never better. Others have mild or severe disabilities, and they too are developing during this period. Often, aside from the area of their disability, they too are at their peak.

Physical development proceeds throughout early adulthood, which starts at the end of adolescence (around age 20) and continues until roughly the start of middle age (around age 40). As we see throughout this unit, significant changes occur as new opportunities arise and people choose to take on (or forgo) new roles in society.

This module focuses on physical development during this period. It begins with a look at the physical changes that extend into early adulthood. Though more subtle than the physical changes of adolescence, growth continues and various motor skills change as well. We look at diet and weight, examining the prevalence of obesity in this age group. We also consider physical disabilities and the ways that people deal with them. Finally, we discuss stress and coping during the early years of adulthood.

Physical Development

LEARNING OBJECTIVES

LO1 How does the body develop during early adulthood, and to what risks are young adults exposed?

Grady McKinnon grinned as his mountain bike briefly left the ground. The 27-year-old financial auditor was delighted to be out for a camping and biking weekend with four of his college buddies. Grady had been worried that an upcoming deadline at work would make him miss this trip. When they were still in school, Grady and his friends used to go biking nearly every weekend, but jobs, marriage—and even a child for one of the guys—started taking up a lot of their attention. This was their only trip this summer. He was sure glad he hadn't missed it.

Grady and his friends were probably in the best physical condition of their lives when they began mountain biking regularly in college. Even now, as Grady's life becomes more complicated and sports starts to take a back seat to work and other personal demands, he is still enjoying one of the healthiest periods of his life. Still, Grady has to cope with the stress produced by the challenges of adult life.

Physical Development and the Senses

In most respects, physical development and maturation are complete at early adulthood. Most people have attained their full height, with limbs proportional to their size, rendering the gangliness of adolescence a memory. People in their early twenties tend to be healthy, vigorous, and energetic. Although **senescence**, the natural physical decline brought about by increasing age, has begun, age-related changes are not usually obvious until later in life. At the same time, some growth continues; for example, some people, particularly late maturers, continue to gain height in their early twenties.

Other parts of the body also reach full maturity. The brain grows in both size and weight, reaching its maximum during early adulthood (and then subsequently contracting later in life). The grey matter continues to be pruned back, and myelination (the process in which nerve cells are insulated by a covering of fat cells) continues to increase. These brain changes help support the cognitive advances of early adulthood (Sowell et al., 2001; Toga et al., 2006).

The senses are as sharp as they will ever be. Although changes occur in the elasticity of the eye—a process that can begin as early as age 10—they are so minor that they produce no deterioration in vision. Hearing, too, is at its peak, although women can detect higher tones more readily than men (McGuinness, 1972). Under quiet conditions, the average young adult can hear the ticking of a watch 20 feet away. The other senses, including taste, smell, and sensitivity to touch and pain, are good and remain so throughout early adulthood.

People in their early twenties tend to be healthy, vigorous, and energetic, but they often experience quite a lot of stress.

Motor Functioning, Fitness, and Health: Staying Well

If you are a professional athlete, you are generally considered over the hill by the end of your twenties. Although there are notable exceptions, even athletes who train constantly tend to lose their physical edge once they reach their thirties. In some sports, the peak passes even sooner. Swimmers are at their best in their late teens, and gymnasts even younger (Schultz and Curnow, 1988).

Psychomotor abilities also peak during early adulthood. Reaction time is quicker, muscle strength greater, and eye–hand coordination better than at any other period (Sliwinski et al., 1994; Salthouse, 1993).

Physical Fitness. The fitness of early adulthood doesn't come naturally or to everyone. To reach their physical potential, people must exercise and maintain a proper diet.

A small commitment of time is enough to yield significant health benefits. According to the Canadian Society for Exercise Physiology, adults should accumulate at least 30 minutes of moderate physical activity at least 5 days a week. Exercise time can be continuous or in bouts of at least 10 minutes, as long as the daily total reaches 30 minutes. Moderate activity includes walking briskly at 3 to 6 kmh, biking at speeds up to 16 kmh, golfing while carrying or pulling clubs, fishing by casting from shore, playing ping-pong, or canoeing at 3 to 6 kmh. Even common household chores, such as weeding, vacuuming, and mowing with a power mower, provide moderate exercise (CSEP, 2011).

> ◯▶ **From an educator's perspective:** Can people be taught the lifelong advantages of regular exercise? Should school-based physical education programs be changed to foster a lifelong commitment to exercise?

The advantages of exercise are many. Exercise increases cardiovascular fitness, meaning that the heart and circulatory system operate more efficiently. Furthermore, lung capacity increases, raising endurance. Muscles become stronger, and the body is more flexible and manoeuvrable. The range of movement becomes greater, and the muscles, tendons, and ligaments become more elastic. Moreover, exercise during this period helps reduce *osteoporosis*, the thinning of the bones, in later life.

Exercise also can optimize the immune response of the body, helping it fight off disease. It can even decrease stress and anxiety and reduce depression. It can provide a sense of control over the body and a feeling of accomplishment (Mutrie, 1997; Faulkner and Biddle, 2004; Harris et al., 2006; Wise et al., 2006). The kicker is its ultimate reward: It is associated with increased longevity (see Figure 7-1; Stevens et al., 2002).

Health. Health risks in general are slight during early adulthood. People are less susceptible to colds and other minor illnesses than they were as children, and they recover quickly from those that they do come down with.

Adults in their twenties and thirties stand a higher risk of dying from accidents, primarily car accidents, than from most other causes. But there are other killers: Among the leading sources of death for people 25 to 34 are suicide, cancer, heart disease, and homicide. Amid the

senescence the natural physical decline brought about by aging

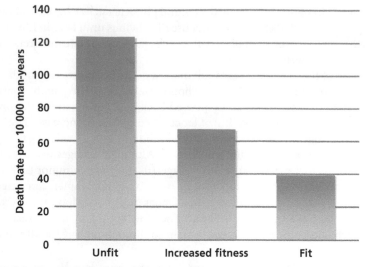

FIGURE 7-1 The Result of Fitness: Longevity

The greater the fitness level, the lower the death rate tends to be for both men and women.

Source: Adapted from Blair et al., Physical fitness and all-cause mortality: A prospective study of healthy men and women. *Journal of the American Medical Association,* 262 (1989), pp. 2395–2401. Copyright © 1989 American Medical Association.

grim statistics of mortality, the age 35 represents a significant milestone. It is at that point that illness and disease overtake accidents as the leading cause of death.

Not all people fare equally well during early adulthood. Lifestyle decisions, such as the use—or abuse—of alcohol, tobacco, or drugs or engaging in unprotected sex, can hasten *secondary aging,* physical declines brought about by environmental factors or behavioural choices. These substances can also increase the mortality risk from the causes just mentioned.

Cultural factors, including gender and race, are related to the risk of dying. For instance, men are more apt to die than women, primarily in automobile accidents. Furthermore, Aboriginal groups have significantly shorter life expectancies than non-Aboriginal groups (Tjepkema et al., 2009). While the causes of death are largely similar, Aboriginals' life expectancy at age 25 is nearly five years less than their non-Aboriginal peers.

Cultural factors also influence young adults' lifestyles and health-related behaviour, as examined in the Cultural Dimensions feature.

Cultural Dimensions

How Cultural Beliefs Influence Health and Health Care

Manolita recently suffered a heart attack. She was advised by her doctor to change her eating and activity habits or face the risk of another life-threatening heart attack. During the period that followed, Manolita dramatically changed her eating and activity habits. She also began going to church and praying extensively. After a recent check-up, Manolita is in the best shape of her life. What are some of the reasons for Manolita's amazing recovery? (Murguia et al., 1997, p. 16)

After reading the passage above, would you conclude that Manolita recovered her health because (a) she changed her eating and activity habits; (b) she became a better person; (c) God was testing her faith; or (d) her doctor prescribed the correct changes?

When asked this question in a survey, more than two-thirds of Latino immigrants from Central America, South America, or the Caribbean believed that "God was testing her faith" had a moderate or great effect on her recovery, although most also agreed

that a change in eating and activity habits was important (Murguia et al., 1997).

According to psychologists Alejandro Murguia, Rolf Peterson, and Maria Zea (1997), cultural health beliefs, along with demographic and psychological barriers, can affect the use of physicians and medical care. They suggest that, for example, Latinos are more likely than non-Hispanic whites to believe in supernatural causes of illness, which may explain why Latinos are the least likely of any Western ethnic group to seek the help of a physician when they are ill.

Health-care providers need to take cultural beliefs into account when treating members of different cultural groups. For example, if a patient believes that the source of his or her illness is a spell cast by a jealous romantic rival, the patient might not comply with medical regimens that ignore that perceived source. To provide effective health care, then, health-care providers must be sensitive to such cultural health beliefs.

REVIEW, CHECK, AND APPLY

REVIEW

- By young adulthood, the body and the senses are at their peak, but growth still proceeds, particularly in the brain.

- Young adults are generally as fit and healthy as they will ever be.

- Young adults are more likely to die of accidents than disease.

CHECK YOURSELF

1. _____ is the natural physical decline brought about by aging.

2. At the age of _____, illness and disease overtake accidents as the leading cause of death.

   a. 25

   b. 35

   c. 40

   c. 50

3. One of the greatest risks for death in young adult men is automobile accidents.

   - True

   - False

APPLYING LIFESPAN DEVELOPMENT

- What factors do you think contribute to the comparatively high risk of automobile accidents during young adulthood? How can this be changed?

Answers: 1) Senescence; 2) b; 3) True

Physical Limitations and Challenges

LO2: What are the physical changes that occur in young adulthood?

> LEARNING OBJECTIVES

Aidan Tindell, accustomed to the shaving mirror in his own apartment, got a shock when he glimpsed his image in a friend's full-length mirror. It was not a pretty sight. Aidan had somehow developed a belly—and a pretty good-sized one. As if in a vision, he conjured up the long evenings he spent in a local sports bar with his friends. He saw the beers he downed without a second thought, the bar snacks he ate incessantly, and the burgers and fries and pizzas that were his basic food groups. Aidan knew something had to give, and he was afraid it was going to be his lifestyle.

For many young adults, this period is the first time that they have to deal seriously with the negative consequences of developmental change. As they leave adolescence, they gradually learn that they can't simply extend their living habits indefinitely. One particularly painful area of change is diet.

Good Nutrition: No Such Thing as a Free Lunch?

Most young adults know which foods are nutritionally sound and how to maintain a balanced diet; they just don't bother to follow the rules—even though the rules are not that hard to follow. According to Health Canada, people can achieve good nutrition by eating foods that are low in fat and salt. Such foods—whole-grain foods and cereal products, vegetables (including dried beans and peas), and fruit—also help people maintain their intake of complex carbohydrates and fiber. Milk and other sources of calcium are also needed to prevent osteoporosis (Canada's Food Guide, Health Canada, 2011).

Adolescents don't suffer too much from a diet high in junk foods and fat because they are undergoing tremendous growth. The body is less forgiving to young adults, who must reduce their caloric intake to maintain their health (Insel and Roth, 1991).

Obesity: A Weighty Concern

The adult population is growing—in more ways than one. Body Mass Index is calculated using the following equation: weight in kilograms divided by the square of the height in metres. A body mass index of 18.5 to 24.9 is considered normal, 25 to 29.9 is considered overweight, and 30 or higher is considered obese. From 2003 to 2009, obesity increased

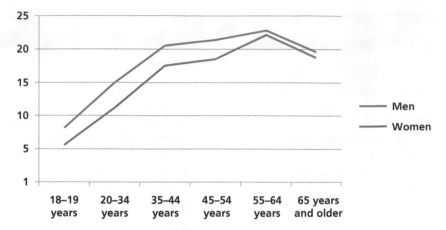

FIGURE 7-2 Obesity on the Rise
In spite of greater awareness of the importance of good nutrition, obesity among Canadian adults has risen dramatically over the past decade. Why do you think this rise has occurred?
Source: Statistics Canada, 2009.

2.5 percent, based on self-report measures from the general population. These data can be considered an underestimate as direct measurement of height and weight of adults suggests that women tend to underreport their weight and men overreport their height, resulting in an estimated 7 percent underreporting of obesity (see Figure 7-2; Statistics Canada, 2009).

Weight control is a difficult, and often losing, battle for many young adults. Most diets fail, producing nothing more than a seesaw cycle of gain and loss. Some obesity experts argue that the rate of dieting failure is so great that people should avoid dieting altogether and instead eat the foods they like, but in moderation (Polivy and Herman, 2002; Lowe and Timko, 2004; Putterman and Linden, 2004; Quatromoni et al., 2006; Annunziato and Lowe, 2007).

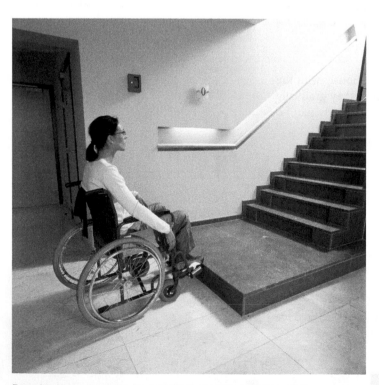

Despite laws guaranteeing access, people with physical disabilities still encounter numerous barriers, including access to many older buildings, poorly maintained sidewalks and crossings, and general inconsideration.

Physical Disabilities: Coping with Physical Challenge

Over 3 million people in Canada are physically or mentally challenged, according to the official definition of *disability*—a condition that substantially limits a major life activity such as walking or vision. In fact, we encountered people with both of these disabilities in the vignette about the chess players.

People with disabilities are, in large part, an undereducated and underemployed minority group. Thirty-seven percent of adults with major handicaps did not finish high school, fewer than 45 percent of men and 39 percent of women with disabilities are employed, and unemployment rates are high among those eligible to work (Statistics Canada 2001). Further, the jobs that people with disabilities find are often routine and low-paying positions (Schaefer and Lamm, 1992; Albrecht, 2005). The median income for adults with disabilites (for those with an income) is 60 percent of that of adults without disabilities.

Some barriers to a full life are physical. Individuals with mobility issues and those who use wheelchairs or motorized scooters face barriers such as older buildings with poor accessibility; inaccessible public transit; insufficient accessible parking; poorly maintained accessible entrances, sidewalks, and crossings; and thoughtlessly placed obstacles.

From a social worker's perspective: What sorts of interpersonal barriers do people with disabilities face? How can those barriers be removed?

Prejudice is another barrier. People with disabilities sometimes face pity or are avoided, as others focus so much on the disability that they overlook abilities. Others treat people with disabilities as if they were children. This can take its toll on the way people with disabilities think about themselves (French and Swain, 1997).

REVIEW, CHECK, AND APPLY

REVIEW

- Even in young adulthood, health must be maintained by proper diet and exercise. Obesity is increasingly a problem for young adults.

- People with physical disabilities face not only physical barriers but also psychological barriers caused by prejudice.

CHECK YOURSELF

1. As age increases, fewer individuals are classified as obese.

   - True

   - False

2. Over 3 million individuals in Canada are living with a _____, or a condition that substantially limits a major life activity such as walking or vision.

APPLYING LIFESPAN DEVELOPMENT

- What developmental factors make it hard for young adults to understand that they may have to change their eating habits and personal choices?

Answers: 1) False; 2) disability

Stress and Coping: Dealing with Life's Challenges

LO3 What are the effects of stress and what can be done about it?

LEARNING OBJECTIVES

It's 5:00 p.m. Rosa Convoy, a 25-year-old single mother, has just finished her work as a receptionist at a dentist's office and is on her way home. She has exactly two hours to pick up her daughter Zoe from childcare, get home, make and eat dinner, pick up and return with a babysitter from down the street, say goodbye to Zoe, and get to her seven o' clock programming class at a local community college. It's a marathon she runs every Tuesday and Thursday night, and she knows she doesn't have a second to spare if she wants to reach the class on time.

Rosa Convoy is experiencing **stress**, the physical and emotional response to events that threaten or challenge us. Our lives are crowded with events and circumstances known as stressors that threaten our equilibrium. Stressors need not be unpleasant events: Even the happiest events—starting a long-sought job or planning a wedding—can produce stress (Crowley et al., 2003; Shimizu and Pelham, 2004). How well people cope with stress depends on a complex interplay of physical and psychological factors (Hetherington and Blechman, 1996).

Researchers in the new field of **psychoneuroimmunology (PNI)**—the study of the relationship between the brain, the immune system, and psychological factors—have examined the outcomes of stress. The most immediate is a biological reaction, as hormones secreted by the adrenal glands cause a rise in heart rate, blood pressure, respiration rate, and sweating. In some situations, these immediate effects are beneficial because the "emergency reaction" they produce in the sympathetic nervous system enables people to defend themselves from a sudden, threatening situation (Parkes, 1997; Ray, 2004).

On the other hand, long-term, continuous exposure to stressors may reduce the body's ability to deal with stress. As stress-related hormones are constantly secreted, the heart, blood vessels, and other body tissues may deteriorate. As a consequence, people become more susceptible to diseases as their ability to fight off germs declines (Cohen et al., 1997; Lundberg, 2006).

⊙─Watch on **mydevelopmentlab**

Young adults experience many kinds of stress, and cope in different ways.
Log onto MyDevelopmentLab to hear two young adults, Amanda and Gary, talk about the stress in their lives.

stress   the physical and emotional response to events that threaten or challenge us

psychoneuroimmunology (PNI)   the study of the relationship between the brain, the immune system, and psychological factors

primary appraisal the assessment of an event to determine whether its implications are positive, negative, or neutral

secondary appraisal the assessment of whether one's coping abilities and resources are adequate to overcome the harm, threat, or challenge posed by the potential stressor

The Origins of Stress

Experienced interviewers, college counsellors, and owners of bridal shops all know that not everyone reacts the same way to a potentially stressful event. What makes the difference? According to psychologists Arnold Lazarus and Susan Folkman, people move through a series of stages that determine whether they will experience stress (Lazarus and Folkman, 1984; Lazarus, 1968, 1991).

Primary appraisal is the first stage—the individual's assessment of an event to determine whether its implications are positive, negative, or neutral. If a person sees the event as primarily negative, he or she appraises it in terms of the harm that it has caused in the past, how threatening it is likely to be, and how likely it is that the challenge can be resisted successfully. For example, you are likely to feel differently about an upcoming French test if you passed the last one with flying colours than if you did poorly.

Secondary appraisal follows. **Secondary appraisal** is the person's answer to the question, "Can I handle it?"—an assessment of whether the coping abilities and resources on hand are adequate. If resources are lacking and the threat is great, the person will feel stress. For example, a traffic ticket is always upsetting, but if you can't afford the fine, the stress is greater.

Stress varies with the person's appraisal, and that appraisal varies with the person's temperament and circumstances. Some general principles help predict when an event will be appraised as stressful. Psychologist Shelley Taylor (1991) suggests the following characteristics of events that have a high likelihood of producing stress:

- Events and circumstances that produce negative emotions—for example, dealing with the illness of a loved one produces more stress than planning for the adoption of a new baby.

- Situations that are uncontrollable or unpredictable—for example, professors who give surprise quizzes produce more stress than those who schedule them in advance.

- Events and circumstances that are ambiguous and confusing—for example, a new job that does not have a clear job description is likely to produce more stress than a well-defined position.

- Having to simultaneously accomplish many tasks that strain a person's capabilities—for example, a graduate student who is expecting her first child the same month she is scheduled to submit her dissertation is likely to be feeling more stress than a student with less on her agenda.

Although we commonly think of negative events, such as auto mishaps, as leading to stress, even welcome events, like getting married, can be stressful.

From the perspective of a health-care provider: Are there periods of life that are relatively stress-free, or do people of all ages experience stress? Do stressors differ from age to age?

The Consequences of Stress

Over the long run, the constant wear and tear of fighting off stress can have formidable costs. Headaches, backaches, skin rashes, indigestion, chronic fatigue, and even the common cold are stress-related illnesses (Cohen et al., 1993, 1997; Suinn, 2001).

In addition, the immune system—the organs, glands, and cells that defend the body against disease—can be damaged by stress. Stress can interfere with the immune system's ability to stop germs from reproducing or cancer cells from spreading. In addition, stress may overstimulate the immune system into attacking the body itself and damaging healthy tissue (Ader et al., 2001; Miller and Cohen, 2001; Cohen et al., 2002).

Stress can also lead to **psychosomatic disorders**—medical problems caused by the interaction of psychological, emotional, and physical difficulties. For instance, ulcers, asthma, arthritis, and high blood pressure can sometimes be produced by stress (Lepore et al., 1991).

To get a sense of how much stress you have in your own life, complete the questionnaire in Table 7-1.

> **psychosomatic disorders**   medical problems caused by the interaction of psychological, emotional, and physical difficulties

---

TABLE 7-1 HOW STRESSED ARE YOU?

Test your level of stress by answering these questions, and adding the score from each box. Questions apply to the last month only. A key below will help you determine the extent of your stress.

1. How often have you been upset because of something that happened unexpectedly?

   ☐ 0 = never, 1 = almost never, 2 = sometimes, 3 = fairly often, 4 = very often

2. How often have you felt that you were unable to control the important things in your life?

   ☐ 0 = never, 1 = almost never, 2 = sometimes, 3 = fairly often, 4 = very often

3. How often have you felt nervous and "stressed"?

   ☐ 0 = never, 1 = almost never, 2 = sometimes, 3 = fairly often, 4 = very often

4. How often have you felt confident about your ability to handle your personal problems?

   ☐ 4 = never, 3 = almost never, 2 = sometimes, 1 = fairly often, 0 = very often

5. How often have you felt that things were going your way?

   ☐ 4 = never, 3 = almost never, 2 = sometimes, 1 = fairly often, 0 = very often

6. How often have you been able to control irritations in your life?

   ☐ 4 = never, 3 = almost never, 2 = sometimes, 1 = fairly often, 0 = very often

7. How often have you found that you could not cope with all the things that you had to do?

   ☐ 0 = never, 1 = almost never, 2 = sometimes, 3 = fairly often, 4 = very often

8. How often have you felt that you were on top of things?

   4 = never, 3 = almost never, 2 = sometimes, 1 = fairly often, 0 = very often

9. How often have you been angered because of things that were outside your control?

   ☐ 0 = never, 1 = almost never, 2 = sometimes, 3 = fairly often, 4 = very often

10. How often have you felt difficulties were piling up so high that you could not overcome them?

    ☐ 0 = never, 1 = almost never, 2 = sometimes, 3 = fairly often, 4 = very often

How You Measure Up

Stress levels vary among individuals—compare your total score to the averages below:

Age		Gender		Marital Status	
18–29	14.2	Men	12.1	Widowed	12.6
30–44	13.0	Women	13.7	Married or living with	12.4
45–54	12.6			Single or never wed	14.1
55–64	11.9			Divorced	14.7
65 and over	12.0			Separated	16.6

Source: From Cohen, S., Kamarck, T., & Mermelstein, R. (1983). "A global measure of perceived stress." *Journal of Health and Social Behavior, 24*, 385–396.
Copyright © 1983 American Sociological Association. Reprinted with permission.

coping the effort to control, reduce, or learn to tolerate the threats that lead to stress

defensive coping coping that involves unconscious strategies that distort or deny the true nature of a situation

hardiness a personality characteristic associated with a lower rate of stress-related illness

Coping with Stress

Stress is a normal part of every life. But some young adults are better than others at **coping**, which is the effort to control, reduce, or learn to tolerate the threats that lead to stress. What's the secret to coping? It turns out that people use a variety of strategies.

Some people use *problem-focused coping*—managing a threatening situation by directly changing it to make it less stressful. For example, a man having difficulties on the job might ask his boss to change his responsibilities, or he might look for another job.

Other people employ *emotion-focused coping*—the conscious regulation of emotion. For instance, a mother having trouble finding appropriate care for her child while she is at work might tell herself that she should look at the bright side: At least she has a job in a difficult economy (Folkman and Lazarus, 1980, 1988).

Sometimes people acknowledge that they are in a stressful situation that cannot be changed, but they cope by managing their reactions. For example, they might take up meditation or exercise to reduce their physical reactions.

Coping is also aided by the presence of *social support*, assistance and comfort supplied by others. Turning to others can provide both emotional support (in the form of a shoulder to cry on) and practical, tangible support (such as a temporary loan) (Spiegel, 1993; Giacobbi et al., 2004; Jackson, 2006).

Finally, even if people do not consciously cope with stress, some psychologists suggest that they may unconsciously use defensive coping mechanisms. **Defensive coping** involves unconscious strategies that distort or deny the true nature of a situation. For instance, people may trivialize a life-threatening illness or tell themselves that failing a major test is unimportant.

Another type of defensive coping is *emotional insulation,* through which people unconsciously try to block emotions and thereby avoid pain. But if defensive coping becomes a habitual response to stress, its reliance on avoidance can stand in the way of dealing with the reality of the situation (Ormont, 2001).

In some cases, people use drugs or alcohol to escape from stressful situations. Like defensive coping, drinking and drug use do not help address the situation causing the stress, and they can increase a person's difficulties. For example, people may become addicted to the substances that initially provided them with a pleasurable sense of escape.

Hardiness, Resilience, and Coping. The success with which young adults deal with stress depends in part on their *coping style*, their general tendency to deal with stress in a particular way. For example, people with a "hardy" coping style are especially successful. **Hardiness** is a personality characteristic associated with a lower rate of stress-related illness.

Hardy individuals are take-charge people who revel in life's challenges. People who are high in hardiness are more resistant to stress-related illness than those with less hardiness. Hardy people react to stressors with optimism, convinced that they can respond effectively. By turning threats into challenges, they are less apt to experience high levels of stress (Horner, 1998; Maddi, 2006; Maddi et al., 2006).

For people who face the most profound difficulties—such as the unexpected death of a loved one—a key factor in their reactions is their level of resilience. As we discussed earlier, *resilience* is the ability to withstand, overcome, and even thrive after profound adversity (Bonanno, 2004; Werner, 2005; Norlander et al., 2005; Kim-Cohen, 2007).

Resilient young adults tend to be easy-going and good-natured, with good social and communication skills. They are independent, feeling that they can shape their own fate and are not dependent on others or luck. They work with what they have and make the best of any situation (Humphreys, 2003; Spencer et al., 2003; Deshields et al., 2005; Friborg et al., 2005).

Coping with Stress

Becoming an Informed Consumer of Development

Some general guidelines can help people cope with stress, including the following (Sacks, 1993; Kaplan et al., 1993; Bionna, 2006):

- Seek control over the situation. Taking charge of a situation that is producing stress can take you a long way toward coping with it. For example, if you are feeling stress about a test, do something about it—such as start to study.

- Redefine "threat" as "challenge." Changing the definition can make a situation seem less threatening. "Look for the silver lining" is not bad advice. For example, if you're fired, look at it as an opportunity to get a new and better job.

- Find social support. Almost any difficulty can be faced more easily with the help of others. Friends, family members, and even telephone hotlines staffed by trained counsellors can provide significant support.

- Use relaxation techniques. Reducing the physiological arousal brought about by stress can be effective in coping with stress. Techniques that produce relaxation, such as transcendental meditation, Zen and yoga, progressive muscle relaxation, and even hypnosis, have been shown to be effective.

- Maintain a healthy lifestyle that will reinforce your body's natural coping mechanisms. Exercise, eat nutritiously, get enough sleep, and avoid or reduce use of alcohol, tobacco, or other drugs.

- If all else fails, keep in mind that a life without stress would be dull. Stress is natural, and successfully coping with it can be gratifying.

REVIEW, CHECK, AND APPLY

REVIEW

- Stress, which is healthy in small doses, can be harmful to body and mind if it is frequent or long-lasting.

- Long-term exposure to stressors may cause deterioration in the heart, blood vessels, and other body tissues. Stress is linked to many common ailments.

- Strategies for coping with stress include problem-focused coping, emotion-focused coping, the use of social support, and defensive coping.

CHECK YOURSELF

1. Stressful events are limited to the negative events in our lives.

    - True
    - False

2. Researchers in the field of _____ study the relationship between the brain, the immune system, and psychoanalysis factors and have found that stress can produce several outcomes.

    a. psychoanalysis

    b. disease management

    c. pilates

    d. psychoneuroimmunology

3. Avoiding thinking about a stressful situation by drinking, doing drugs, or just denying the true nature of a situation are all examples of _____ coping.

    a. defensive

    b. emotion-focused

    c. social support

    d. hardiness

APPLYING LIFESPAN DEVELOPMENT

- In what circumstances can stress be an adaptive, helpful response? In what circumstances is it maladaptive?

Answers: 1) False; 2) d; 3) a

MODULE 7.2 Cognitive Development in Early Adulthood

A Tale of Two Students

Malik Saleh Al-Fulan never had any doubt: He was headed for university. Malik, the son of a wealthy Iraqi immigrant who had made a fortune in the medical supply business after fleeing Iraq five years before Malik's birth, had had the importance of education drummed into him by his family. In fact, the question was never whether he would go to university, but which university he would be able to get into. As a consequence, Malik found high school to be a pressure cooker: Every grade and extracurricular activity was seen as helping—or hindering—his chances of admission to a "good" school.

***

Matthew Williams' letter of acceptance to Holland College is framed on the wall of his mother's apartment. To her, the letter represents nothing short of a miracle, an answer to her prayers. Growing up in a neighbourhood saturated with drugs and gangs, Matthew had always been a hard worker and a "good boy," in his mother's view. But when he was growing up, she had never even entertained the possibility of his making it to college. To see him reach this stage in his education fills her with joy.

Although Malik and Matthew followed two very different paths, they share the goal of post-secondary education. They represent the increasing diversity in family background, socioeconomic status, race, and ethnicity that characterizes post-secondary populations today.

This module focuses on cognitive development during early adulthood. Although traditional approaches to cognitive development regarded adulthood as an inconsequential plateau, we will examine some new theories that suggest that significant cognitive growth occurs during the period. We also consider the nature of adult intelligence and the impact of life events on cognitive development.

The last part of the module considers post-secondary education, institutions that shape intellectual growth. We examine who attends, and how gender and ethnicity can influence achievement. We end by looking at some reasons why students drop out, and we examine some of the adjustment problems that post-secondary students face.

Cognitive Development

LEARNING OBJECTIVES

LO4 Does cognitive development continue in young adulthood?

Ben is known to be a heavy drinker, especially when he goes to parties. Tyra, Ben's wife, warns him that if he comes home drunk one more time, she will leave him and take the children. Tonight Ben is out late at an office party. He comes home drunk. Does Tyra leave Ben?

To the typical adolescent this case (drawn from research by Adams and Labouvie-Vief, 1986) is open-and-shut: Tyra leaves Ben. But in early adulthood, the answer is less clear. People become less concerned with sheer logic and instead take into account real-life concerns that can influence and temper behaviour.

Intellectual Growth in Early Adulthood

If we subscribed to the traditional view of cognitive development, we would expect to find little intellectual growth in early adulthood. Piaget argued that by the time people left adolescence, their thinking, at least qualitatively, had largely become what it would be for the rest of their lives. They might gather more information, but the ways in which they thought about it would not change.

Was Piaget's view correct? Increasing evidence suggests that he was mistaken.

Postformal Thought

Developmental psychologist Giesela Labouvie-Vief suggests that the nature of thinking changes during early adulthood. She asserts that thinking based solely on formal operations (Piaget's final stage, reached during adolescence) is insufficient to meet the demands placed on young adults. The complexity of society, which requires specialization, and the challenge of finding one's way through that complexity require thought that transcends logic to include practical experience, moral judgments, and values (Labouvie-Vief, 1990, 2006).

For example, imagine a young, single woman in her first job. Her boss, a married man whom she respects greatly and who is in a position to help her career, invites her to go with him to make an important presentation to a client. When the presentation (which has gone very well) is over, he suggests they go out to dinner and celebrate. Later that evening, after sharing a bottle of wine, he invites her to accompany him to a hotel room. What should she do?

Logic alone doesn't answer such questions. Labouvie-Vief suggests that young adults' thinking must develop to handle ambiguous situations like these. She suggests that young adults learn to use analogies

The nature of thought changes qualitatively during early adulthood.

and metaphors to make comparisons, confront society's paradoxes, and become comfortable with a more subjective understanding. This requires weighing all aspects of a situation according to one's values and beliefs. It allows for interpretive processes and reflects the fact that reasons behind events in the real world are painted in shades of grey rather than black and white (Labouvie-Vief, 1990; Sinnott, 1998; Thornton, 2004).

> **postformal thought**   thinking that acknowledges that adult predicaments must sometimes be solved in relativistic terms

To demonstrate how this sort of thinking develops, Labouvie-Vief presented experimental subjects, ranging in age from 10 to 40, with scenarios similar to the Ben and Tyra scenario presented earlier. Each story had a clear, logical conclusion, but it could be interpreted differently if real-world demands and pressures were taken into account.

In responding to the scenarios, adolescents relied heavily on the logic of formal operations. They tended to predict that Tyra would immediately pack up her bags and leave with the children when Ben came home drunk. After all, that's what she said she would do. In contrast, young adults were more apt to consider various real-life possibilities: Would Ben be apologetic and beg Tyra not to leave? Did Tyra really mean it when she said she would leave? Does Tyra have someplace to go?

Young adults exhibited what Labouvie-Vief calls postformal thinking. **Postformal thought** is thinking that goes beyond Piaget's formal operations. Rather than being based on purely logical processes, with absolutely right and wrong answers to problems, postformal thought acknowledges that adult predicaments must sometimes be solved in relativistic terms.

Postformal thought also encompasses *dialectical thinking*, an interest in and appreciation for argument, counterargument, and debate (Basseches, 1984). Dialectical thinking accepts that issues are not always clear-cut, and that answers to questions must sometimes be negotiated. According to psychologist Jan Sinnott (1998b), postformal thinkers shift back and forth between an abstract, ideal solution and real-world constraints that might prevent implementation of that solution. Postformal thinkers understand that just as there can be multiple causes of a situation, there can be multiple solutions.

Perry's Approach to Postformal Thinking

To psychologist William Perry (1970, 1981), the developmental growth of early adulthood involves mastering new ways of understanding the world. To examine intellectual and moral growth during post-secondary education, Perry interviewed students over the course of their studies. He found that students at the beginning of post-secondary education tended to use *dualistic thinking* in their views of the world: something was either right or wrong; people were either good or bad; others were either for them or against them.

However, as these students encountered new ideas and points of view from other students and their professors, their dualistic thinking declined. Consistent with postformal thinking, students began to accept that issues can have more than one plausible side. Furthermore, they understood that it is possible to hold multiple perspectives on an issue. Their attitude toward authorities also changed: Instead of assuming that experts had all the answers, they began to realize that their own thinking had validity if their position was well-thought-out and rational.

In fact, according to Perry, they had reached a stage in which knowledge and values were regarded as relativistic. Rather than seeing the world as having absolute standards and values, they argued that different societies, cultures, and individuals could have different standards and values, and all of them could be equally valid.

It's important to keep in mind that Perry's theory is based on a sample of interviews conducted with well-educated students attending an elite institution. His findings might not apply as well to people who have never learned how to examine multiple points of view.

 From an educator's perspective: Do you think it is possible for adolescent students to learn postformal thinking (for example, by direct instruction on breaking the habit of dualistic thinking)? Why or why not?

Schaie's Stages of Development

Developmental psychologist K. Warner Schaie offers another perspective on postformal thought. Taking up where Piaget left off, Schaie suggests that adults' thinking follows a set pattern of stages (illustrated in Figure 7-3). But Schaie focuses on the ways in which information is *used* during adulthood, rather than on changes in the acquisition and understanding of new information, as in Piaget's approach (Schaie and Willis, 1993; Schaie and Zanjani, 2006).

Schaie suggests that before adulthood, the main cognitive developmental task is acquisition of information. Consequently, he labels the first stage of cognitive development, which encompasses all of childhood and adolescence, the **acquisitive stage**. Information gathered before we grow up is largely squirreled away for future use. In fact, much of the rationale for education during childhood and adolescence is to prepare people for future activities.

The situation changes considerably in early adulthood when the focus shifts from the future to the here and now. According to Schaie, young adults are in the achieving stage, applying their intelligence to attain long-term goals regarding their careers, family, and contributions to society. During the **achieving stage**, young adults must confront and resolve several major issues, and the decisions they make—such as what job to take and whom to marry—have implications for the rest of their lives.

During the late stages of early adulthood and in middle adulthood, people move into the responsible and executive stages. In the **responsible stage**, middle-aged adults are mainly concerned with protecting and nourishing their spouses, families, and careers.

Sometime later, further into middle adulthood, many people (but not all) enter the **executive stage** in which they take a broader perspective, becoming more concerned about the larger world (Sinnott, 1997). People in the executive stage put energy into nourishing and sustaining societal institutions. They may become involved in town government, religious congregations, service clubs, charitable groups, factory unions—organizations that have a larger purpose in society.

Finally, the **reintegrative stage** is the period of late adulthood during which people focus on tasks that have personal meaning. They no longer focus on acquiring knowledge to solve potential problems that they may encounter. Instead, they acquire information about issues that specifically interest them. Furthermore, they have less interest in—and patience for—things that they do not see as having some immediate application to their lives.

acquisitive stage according to Schaie, the first stage of cognitive development, encompassing all of childhood and adolescence, in which the main developmental task is to acquire information

achieving stage the point reached by young adults in which intelligence is applied to specific situations involving the attainment of long-term goals regarding careers, family, and societal contributions

responsible stage the stage where the major concerns of middle-aged adults relate to their personal situations, including protecting and nourishing their spouses, families, and careers

executive stage the period in middle adulthood when people take a broader perspective than earlier, including concerns about the world

reintegrative stage the period of late adulthood during which the focus is on tasks that have personal meaning

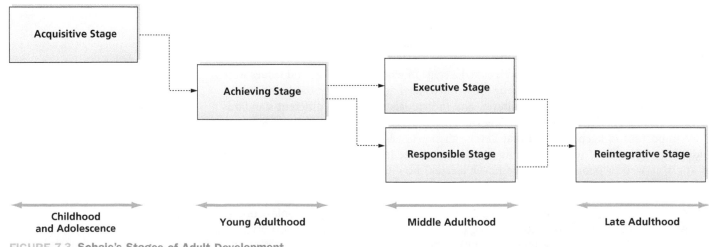

FIGURE 7-3 Schaie's Stages of Adult Development
Source: Schaie, 1977–1978.

REVIEW, CHECK, AND APPLY

REVIEW

- Cognitive development continues into young adulthood with the emergence of postformal thought, which goes beyond logic to encompass interpretive and subjective thinking.

- Perry suggests that people move from dualistic thinking to relativistic thought during early adulthood.

- According to Schaie, people pass through five stages in the way they use information: acquisitive, achieving, responsible, executive, and reintegrative.

CHECK YOURSELF

1. The idea that problem solving in adulthood has to consider previous experiences, logical thinking, and the relative benefits and costs of a decision is also known as _____.

   a. formal operational thought

   b. concrete operational thought

   c. postformal thought

   d. dualistic thinking

2. Postformal thought and dialectical thinking acknowledge that the world sometimes lacks clearly right or wrong solutions to problems.

   - True
   - False

APPLYING LIFE SPAN DEVELOPMENT

- Can you think of situations that you would deal with differently as an adult than as an adolescent? Do the differences reflect postformal thinking?

Answers: 1) c; 2) True

Intelligence: What Matters in Early Adulthood?

LO5 How is intelligence defined today, and what causes cognitive growth in young adults?

LEARNING OBJECTIVES

Your year on the job has been generally favourable. Performance ratings for your department are at least as good as they were before you took over, and perhaps even a little better. You have two assistants. One is quite capable. The other just seems to go through the motions and is of little real help. Even though you are well liked, you believe that there is little that would distinguish you in the eyes of your superiors from the nine other managers at a comparable level in the company. Your goal is rapid promotion to an executive position. (Based on Wagner and Sternberg, 1985, p. 447)

How do you achieve your goal?

The way adults answer this question may affect their future success. The question is one of a series designed to assess a particular type of intelligence that may have more of an impact on future success than the IQ measured by traditional tests.

Smart Thinking: Alternative Views of Intelligence

Many researchers argue that the kind of intelligence measured by IQ tests is not the only valid kind. Depending on what one wants to know about individuals, other theories of intelligence—and other measures of it—might be more appropriate.

In his *triarchic theory of intelligence* (also discussed in Chapter 5), psychologist Robert Sternberg, who is responsible for the executive question just posed, suggests that intelligence is made up of three major components: componential/analytic, experiential/creative, and contextual/practical. The *componential* aspect involves the mental components used to solve problems (for example, selecting and using formulas, choosing problem-solving strategies, and, in general, making use of what has been learned in the past). The *experiential* component refers to the relationship between intelligence, prior experience, and the ability to cope with new situations. This is the insightful aspect of intelligence, which allows people to relate what they already know to a new situation and facts never before encountered. Finally, the *contextual* component of intelligence takes account of the demands of everyday, real-world environments. For instance, the contextual component is involved in adapting to on-the-job professional demands (Sternberg, 2005).

Traditional IQ tests tend to focus on the componential aspect. Yet increasing evidence suggests that a more useful measure, particularly when comparing and predicting adult success, is the contextual component—the aspect of intelligence that has come to be called practical intelligence.

Practical and Emotional Intelligence. According to Sternberg, traditional IQ scores relate quite well to academic success but not to other types of achievement, such as career success. Although it is clear that success in business requires some level of the IQ sort of intelligence, the rate of career advancement and the ultimate success of business executives is only marginally related to IQ scores (Ree and Carretta, 2002; Cianciolo et al., 2006; Sternberg, 2006).

Sternberg contends that success in a career necessitates practical intelligence (Sternberg et al., 1997). While academic success is based on knowledge obtained largely from reading and listening, **practical intelligence** is learned primarily by observing others and modelling their behaviour. People with practical intelligence have good "social radar." They understand and handle even new situations effectively, reading people and circumstances insightfully based on their previous experiences. (See Figure 7-4 for sample items from a test of practical intelligence).

> **practical intelligence** according to Sternberg, intelligence that is learned primarily by observing others and modelling their behaviour

---

Management

You are responsible for selecting a contractor to renovate several large buildings. You have narrowed the choice to two contractors on the basis of their bids, and after further investigation, you are considering awarding the contract to the Wilson & Sons Company. Rate the importance of the following pieces of information in making your decision to award the contract to Wilson & Sons.

_____ The company has provided letters from satisfied former customers.

_____ The Better Business Bureau reports no major complaints about the company.

_____ Wilson & Sons has done good work for your company.

_____ Wilson & Sons' bid was $2000 less than the other contractor's (approximate total cost of the renovation is $325 000).

_____ Former customers whom you have contacted strongly recommended Wilson & Sons for the job.

Sales

You sell a line of photocopy machines. One of your machines has relatively few features and is inexpensive, at $700, although it is not the least expensive model you carry. The $700 photocopy machine is not selling well and it is overstocked. There is a shortage of the more elaborate photocopy machines in your line, so you have been asked to do what you can to improve sales of the $700 machine. Rate the following strategies for maximizing your sales of the slow-moving photocopy machine.

_____ Stress to potential customers that although this model lacks some desirable features, the low price more than makes up for it.

_____ Stress that there are relatively few models left at this price.

_____ Arrange as many demonstrations as possible of the machine.

_____ Stress simplicity of use, since the machine lacks confusing controls that other machines might have.

Academic Psychology

It is your second year as an assistant professor in a prestigious psychology department. This past year you published two unrelated empirical articles in established journals. You haven't yet, however, identified a research area as your own. You believe yourself to be about as productive as others. The feedback about your first year of teaching has been generally good. You have yet to serve on a university committee. There is one graduate student who has chosen to work with you. You have no external source of funding, nor have you applied for any.

Your goals are to become one of the top people in your field and to get tenure in your department. The following is a list of things you are considering doing in the next two months. You obviously cannot do them all. Rate the importance of each by its priority as a means of reaching your goals.

_____ Improve the quality of your teaching.

_____ Write a grant proposal.

_____ Begin a long-term research project that might lead to a major theoretical article.

_____ Concentrate on recruiting more students.

_____ Begin several related short-term research projects, each of which might lead to an empirical article.

_____ Participate in a series of panel discussions to be shown on the local public television station.

College Student Life

You are enrolled in a large introductory lecture course. Requirements consist of three exams and a final. Please indicate how characteristic it would be of your behaviour to spend time doing each of the following if your goal were to receive an A in the course.

_____ Attend class regularly.

_____ Attend optional weekly review sections with the teaching fellow.

_____ Read assigned text chapters thoroughly.

_____ Take comprehensive class notes.

_____ Speak with the professor after class and during office hours.

FIGURE 7-4 Sample Items from a Test That Taps Four Domains of Practical Intelligence
Source: Sternberg, 1993.

There is another, related type of intelligence. **Emotional intelligence** is the set of skills that underlies the accurate assessment, evaluation, expression, and regulation of emotions. Emotional intelligence is what enables people to get along well with others, to understand what they are feeling and experiencing, and to respond appropriately to their needs. Emotional intelligence is of obvious value to career and personal success as a young adult (Zeidner et al., 2004; Mayer et al., 2004; Carmeli and Josman, 2006; Sy et al., 2006).

> **From an educator's perspective:** Do you think educators can teach people to be more intelligent? Are there components or varieties of intelligence that might be more "teachable" than others? If so, which: componential, experiential, contextual, practical, or emotional?

> **emotional intelligence**   the set of skills that underlie the accurate assessment, evaluation, expression, and regulation of emotions

Focus on Research

Why Do People Act So Stupid?

We've all said it on occasion. How could he or she have been so stupid? Sometimes we say it about ourselves. Sometimes we feel like we're surrounded by stupidity. But what exactly is stupidity? As a folk psychology term, it is generally used to refer to that which is unintelligent, which is why we are always puzzled when someone whom we otherwise thought to be intelligent (such as ourselves) could do or say something so clearly unintelligent. One researcher tackling this problem is Keith Stanovich, Canada Research Chair in Cognitive Science at the Ontario Institute for Studies in Education. According to Stanovich, the source of our stupidity is what he calls *dysrationalia*, or a dysfunction in using rational thought. The crux of his research is that rational, logical thought has little to do with measured intelligence because it is missing from traditional IQ tests.

Two factors seem to predispose us to dysrational thought and behaviour, and they are unrelated to traditional measures of IQ. First, humans are cognitive misers—our default is to process problems in the most computationally efficient manner, even if it's less accurate. A feature of this lazy processing is the "me bias" wherein we tend to be very egocentric in our reasoning, stuck in our own perspective. This egocentrism is, of course, illogical and leads to errors in reasoning. For example, when students were given a problem of a hazardous foreign-made car and asked whether it should be banned, nearly 3/4 of students agreed. When presented with the same problem of an equally hazardous but domestic-made car, less than half of students thought it should be banned. The information about the hazard was the same in both problems. The irrational difference in responses is an example of *me bias*.

The second factor is referred to as the "mindware gap": We tend to be weak in calculating probabilities and in scientific hypothesis testing. Recall the concept of formal operations, which we discussed in the previous chapter. A classic test of formal operations is the following: Participants are shown four cards, one showing a vowel, one showing a consonant, one showing an even number, and one showing an odd number. Participants are told each card has a letter on one side and a number on the other. They are then given the rule "if a card has a vowel on one side, then it has an even number on the other side". Participants are asked which cards must be turned over in order to determine if the rule is true or false. While Piaget claimed that adolescents become capable of the reasoning required to solve the problem, most adults don't actually use that reasoning. In decades of research using this task, anywhere from 40% to 75% of adults fail the task—illustrating the mindware gap. Most adults correctly choose to check that the vowel card has an even number, but then choose the even number to check for a vowel. The rule stated that vowels must have even numbers on the other side, but not that even numbers must have vowels. The correct second choice is the odd number, which cannot have a vowel.

"My goal in proposing the term 'dysrationalia' is to separate intelligence from rationality, a trait that IQ tests do not measure. The concept of dysrationalia, and the empirical evidence indicating that the condition is not rare, should help create a conceptual space in which we value abilities at least as important as those currently measured on IQ tests—abilities to form rational beliefs and to take rational action" (Stanovich, 2009).

Creativity: Novel Thought

The hundreds of musical compositions of Wolfgang Amadeus Mozart, who died at the age of 35, were largely written during early adulthood. This pattern—major works produced during early adulthood—is true of many other creative individuals (Dennis, 1966a; see Figure 7-5).

One reason for the productivity of early adulthood might be that, after this period, creativity can be stifled by a phenomenon that psychologist Sarnoff Mednick (1963) called "familiarity breeds rigidity." By this he meant that the more people know about a subject, the less likely they are to be creative. Early adulthood might be the peak of creativity because many problems encountered professionally are novel.

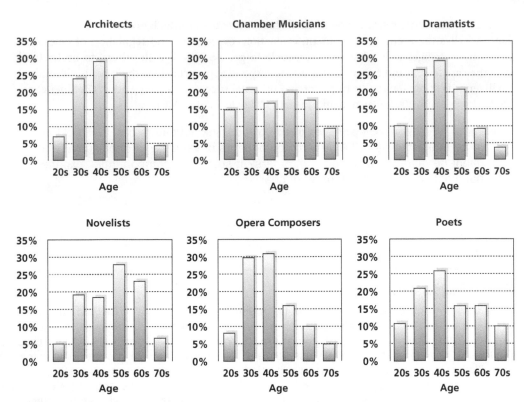

FIGURE 7-5 Creativity and Age
The period of maximum creativity differs depending on the particular field. The percentages refer to the total lifetime major works produced during the particular age period. Why do poets peak earlier than novelists?
Source: *Journal of Gerontology*, by W. Dennis. Copyright 1966 by The Gerontological Society of America. Reproduced with permission of The Gerontological Society of America in the format Textbook via Copyright Clearance Center.

On the other hand, many people do not reach their pinnacle of creativity until much later in life. For instance, Buckminster Fuller did not devise the geodesic dome until he was in his 50s. Frank Lloyd Wright designed the Guggenheim Museum in New York at age 70. Charles Darwin and Jean Piaget were still writing influential works well into their 70s, and Picasso was painting in his 90s. Furthermore, overall productivity, as opposed to the period of a person's most important output, remains fairly steady throughout adulthood, particularly in the humanities (Dennis, 1966b; Simonton, 1989).

Overall, the study of creativity reveals few consistent developmental patterns. One reason is the difficulty of determining just what constitutes **creativity**, which is defined as combining responses or ideas in novel ways. Because creativity is so loosely defined, and definitions of what is "novel" may vary from one person to the next, it is hard to identify a particular behaviour unambiguously as creative (Isaksen and Murdock, 1993; Sasser-Coen, 1993).

This hasn't stopped psychologists from trying. One suggested component of creativity is a person's willingness to take risks that might yield high payoffs. Creative people are like successful stock market investors who follow the "buy low, sell high" rule. Creative people develop and endorse ideas that are unfashionable or regarded as wrong ("buying low"), assuming that eventually others will see the value of these ideas and embrace them ("selling high"). According to this theory, creative adults take a fresh look at ideas that were initially discarded, particularly if the problem is a familiar one. These people are flexible enough to move away from tried-and-true ways of doing things and to consider new approaches (Sternberg and Lubart, 1992; Sternberg et al., 2002).

creativity combining responses or ideas in novel ways

Profound events such as the birth of a child or the death of a loved one can stimulate cognitive development by offering an opportunity to re-evaluate our place in the world. What are some other profound events that might stimulate cognitive development?

Life Events and Cognitive Development

Marriage. The death of a parent. Starting a first job. The birth of a child. Buying a house. Milestones such as these, whether welcome or unwanted, can cause stress. But do they also cause cognitive growth?

Some research evidence—spotty and largely based on case studies—suggests that the answer might be yes. For instance, the birth of a child can trigger fresh insights into the nature of relationships, one's place in the world, and one's role in perpetuating humanity. Similarly, the death of a loved one can cause a re-evaluation of what is important and a new look at the way life should be led (Aldwin, 1994; Woike and Matic, 2004).

Experiencing the ups and downs of life may lead young adults to think about the world in novel, more complex and sophisticated, less rigid ways. They are now capable of using postformal thought to see and grasp trends and patterns, personalities and choices. This allows them to deal effectively with the complex social worlds of which they are a part.

REVIEW, CHECK, AND APPLY

REVIEW

- New views of intelligence encompass the triarchic theory, practical intelligence, and emotional intelligence.

- Creativity seems to peak during early adulthood, with young adults viewing even long-standing problems as novel situations.

- Major life events contribute to cognitive growth by providing opportunities and incentives to rethink one's self and one's world.

CHECK YOURSELF

1. Sternberg's _____ theory of intelligence suggests that intelligence is made up of three major components.

2. According to psychologist Sarnoff Mednick (1963), creativity is at its highest in young adulthood because as we get older and more familiar with our areas of study (or occupations), creativity can be stunted.
   - True
   - False

3. Major life events can influence our cognitive development because positive and negative life circumstances lead us to think differently about our relationships with others, what's important to us, or our place in the world.
   - True
   - False

APPLYING LIFESPAN DEVELOPMENT

- What does "familiarity breeds rigidity" mean? Can you think of examples of this phenomenon from your own experience?

Answers: 1) triarchic; 2) True; 3) True

College: Pursuing Higher Education

LO6 Who attends post-secondary education today, and how is that population changing?

LO7 What difficulties do students face in post-secondary education?

LEARNING OBJECTIVES

The others don't always notice that Nicole Allen is actually the same age as the professor, not her classmates; the wardrobe of student life and a youthful appearance work to her advantage. But unlike her classmates, who might have just rolled out of bed, Nicole has been up since 5:00 a.m. She studies a little and gets lunch ready for her two kids and then sends them off to school. Then she takes the bus in to school herself—an hour and fifteen minutes and only one transfer. "I try to study on the bus, but some days it's too crowded and noisy." She made sure all her classes were finished by 2:30 so she could get home in time to meet her kids. After supper, she and her two kids sit around the dining table and everyone does homework together. Studying full-time now, Nicole will finally get her degree next spring.

Nicole Allen, like Matthew Williams (whom we met in the module prologue), faces challenges in her pursuit of post-secondary education. In some ways, Nicole and Matthew are "the new typical." One-third of university students are above age 24, just one example of the increasing diversity—in family background, socioeconomic status, and ethnicity—that characterizes university campuses today.

The Demographics of Higher Education

As a nation, Canadians clearly value education. More than 60 percent of Canadians aged 25 to 64 have completed at least some post-secondary education, and 48 percent hold a college or university degree—more than any other country. Higher education is becoming more accessible to all, and the group taking greatest advantage is women. Among older adults age 55 to 64, 16 percent of women and 21 percent of men have university degrees. Among their children's generation (25- to 34-year–olds), 33 percent of women and 25 percent of men have degrees (Statistics Canada, 2006).

Immigration is an important factor in Canada's claim to such a highly educated population: 20 percent of those born in Canada have a degree, compared to 51 percent of new immigrants (Statistics Canada, 2006). Within Canada, some groups continue to be underrepresented. Individuals from economically disadvantaged areas, especially rural areas, face the financial challenge of moving away for school, but also might be unable to leave family responsibilities or social supports. The increasing availability of distance education on the Internet might improve access in the future for those in more remote areas.

If you are reading this book, you too are likely pursuing higher education. Maybe you were told that post-secondary education was necessary to get a good job and earn a decent income. The downside to having such a well-educated population is that while the average income of university graduates is higher than the average income of those with only a high school diploma, Canada also has the largest proportion of highly educated low earners. That university degree is worth its weight in gold for the one-third in the highest income group, but nearly one-fifth of university graduates are in the lowest income group (Figure 7-6).

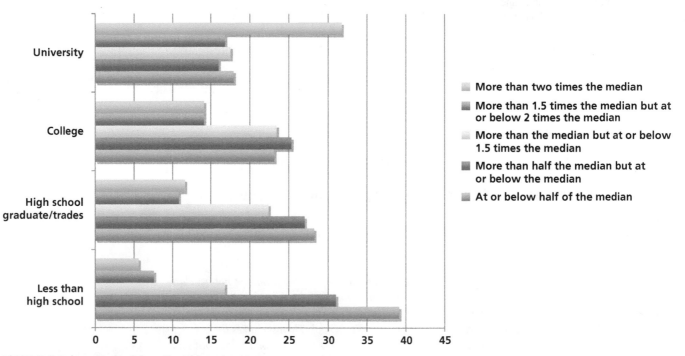

FIGURE 7-6 Income by Educational Level

For individuals with low education, high income is hard to achieve. But higher education doesn't always equal high income either. The median income is the middle, wherein half the population earns more and half earns less than this amount. If, for example, the median income was $32 000, the lowest income group earns less than $16 000 per year, the second group earns $16 000–$32 000, the third group earn $32 000–$40 000, the fourth group earn $40 000–$64 000, and the highest income group earns more than $64 000.

Source: Statistics Canada. Survey of Labour and Income Dynamics, 2006.

Who are these highly educated low-income individuals and why are there so many of them? Forty-two percent of them work only part-time, and working (the source of the income) is not their main activity—for example, artists, continuing students, and parents. Many are also self-employed. They are also twice as likely to be women (Zeman et al., 2010).

The Changing Post-Secondary Student: Never Too Late To Go back To School?

Approximately 50 percent of post-secondary students are between 18 and 23 years old, whereas the other half are older. And despite perceptions of increasing numbers of "mature" students on campuses (the term used for students over 25 who are not entering directly from high school), students are actually getting younger. Between 1992 and 2007, the percentage of university students aged 18 doubled, likely due to the elimination of grade 13 in Ontario, home to 38 percent of the Canadian population. The percentage of students in their thirties and forties, on the other hand, decreased, although mature students are still a substantial part of post-secondary life (Dale, 2011).

The number of older students starting or returning to college continues to grow. More than a third of post-secondary students are 25 years old or older. Why are so many older, non-traditional students taking post-secondary courses?

Why are so many older, non-traditional students going back to school? One reason is economics. An advanced degree might offer new opportunities—for a promotion or a career change. Many employers encourage or require workers to undergo post-secondary training to learn new skills or update old ones. For those who live in communities centred around a single industry, downsizing is sometimes a good opportunity to make a change.

In addition, as young adults age, they begin to feel the need to settle down with a family. This change in attitude can reduce their risk-taking behaviour and make them focus more on acquiring the ability to support their family—a phenomenon that has been labeled *maturation reform*.

According to developmental psychologist Sherry Willis (1985), several broad goals underlie adults' participation in learning. First, adults sometimes seek to understand their own aging, trying to figure out what is happening to them and what to expect in the future. Second, some adults seek to understand more fully the rapid technological and cultural changes of modern life.

Third, some adult learners might be seeking a practical edge in combating obsolescence on the job by acquiring new vocational skills. Finally, education might be seen as helpful in preparing for future retirement. Concerned about shifting from a work orientation to a leisure orientation, they may see education as a means of broadening their possibilities.

> **From an educator's perspective:** How is the presence of older students likely to affect the post-secondary classroom, given what you know about human development? Why?

Post-Secondary Adjustment: Reacting to the Demands of College Life

When you arrived on campus, did you feel depressed, lonely, anxious, withdrawn? If so, you weren't alone. Many students, particularly recent high school graduates living away from home for the first time, have problems adjusting during their first year in college. The **first-year adjustment reaction** is a cluster of psychological symptoms, including loneliness, anxiety, and depression, relating to the university experience. Although any first-year student can experience this reaction, it is particularly prevalent among students who were unusually successful, either academically or socially, in high school. In their new environment, their sudden change in status may cause distress.

Most often, first-year adjustment reaction passes as students make friends, experience academic success, and integrate themselves into campus life. In other cases, though, problems remain and can lead to more serious psychological difficulties.

first-year adjustment reaction a cluster of psychological symptoms, including loneliness, anxiety, withdrawal, and depression, suffered by first-year students.

Students who have been successful and popular in high school are particularly vulnerable to first-year adjustment reaction in college. Counselling, as well as increasing familiarity with campus life, can help a student adjust.

From Research to Practice

Depression 101

Recent Canadian surveys suggest that as many as 14 percent of female and 7 percent of male first-year university students suffer a major depressive episode, and 30 percent of graduate students experience clinically significant depressive symptoms (Peluso et al., 2011; Price et al., 2006). An estimated 40 percent of students visiting a campus counselling centre are experiencing depression.

Depression can have a serious negative impact on the student's academic performance. Concentration is poor, sleep is irregular, eating habits change, and classes, assignments, or tests might be missed. Depression has a way of spiralling out of control, changing the way the brain functions. The best course of treatment for most is a combination of drug treatment (to get brain chemistry back on track) and cognitive behavioural therapy (to stay on track).

The aim of cognitive behavioural therapy is to both identify the thought patterns/beliefs, and the resulting behaviour, that make problems worse instead of better. This therapy can help the individual who might be susceptible to depression change paths. Take the following two examples:

Olivia and Chantal were both A+ students in high school and received scholarships to attend Acadia University. They left their families and high school friends behind, including boyfriends. They both tried to maintain the long-distance relationship but it was difficult. When they went home for Thanksgiving, they fought with their boyfriends and broke up.

Olivia was devastated, but told herself "I'll find someone else." Her mood was a bit down, but she found ways to distract herself. If she missed her ex-boyfriend, she watched a movie or went out with her new friends. She joined a volleyball team, and made sure to eat well. By December, she was still single, but her marks were good, and she was looking forward to coming back after the holidays.

Chantal was devastated and locked herself in her room. She cried for days. She slept most of the time and rarely had an appetite for anything. Her floormates invited her to the movies and to parties, but she always said no and they stopped asking. She found it difficult to drag herself out of bed and as a result missed a lot of classes. She was falling farther and farther behind. She thought she was a failure that no one could love—in her mind she had failed at her relationship, she'd made no friends, and now she was failing at school. She went back to bed and cried. She wanted to drop out and go home. Eventually, she called the campus counselling centre for help.

While both students experienced a similar event, the paths they took resulted from the unique ways they viewed their situations and the behaviour they engaged in, whether it was productive in helping to get over the stressful situation, or whether it made the situation worse. Behaviours like exercise and eating well and keeping up with other routines are all productive. Disrupting routines, ruminating, catastrophizing, and focusing on negatives are all counterproductive.

When Do College Students Need Professional Help with Their Problems?

Becoming an Informed Consumer of Development

How can you tell if a student who is feeling depressed and unhappy needs professional help? Although there are no hard-and-fast rules, some signals indicate that professional help is warranted (Engler and Goleman, 1992). Among them are the following:

- psychological distress that lingers and interferes with a person's sense of well-being and ability to function
- feelings that one is unable to cope effectively with the stress
- hopeless or depressed feelings, with no apparent reason
- the inability to build close relationships
- physical symptoms—such as headaches, stomach cramps, or skin rashes—that have no apparent underlying cause

If some of these signals are present, talking with a help-provider, such as a counselling psychologist, clinical psychologist, or other mental health worker, would be helpful. The best place to start is the campus medical centre. A personal physician, neighbourhood clinic, or local board of health can also provide a referral.

How prevalent are psychological problems? Surveys find that almost half of university students report having at least one significant psychological issue. Other research finds that more than 40 percent of students who visited a campus counselling centre reported being depressed (see Figure 7-7). Remember, though, that these figures include only the students who sought help and, consequently, might not be representative of the entire post-secondary population (Benton et al., 2003).

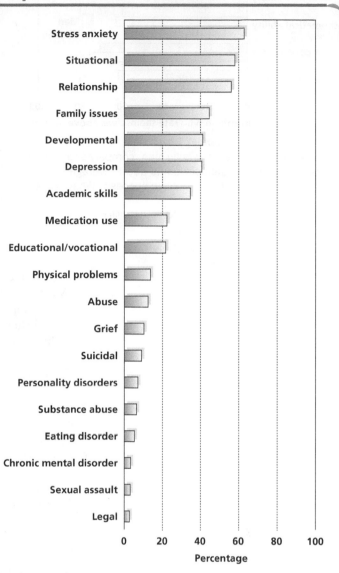

FIGURE 7-7 Post-Secondary Problems
The difficulties most frequently reported by post-secondary students visiting a campus counselling centre.
Source: Benton et al., 2003.

Gender and Post-Secondary Performance

I registered for a calculus course my first year at DePauw. Even twenty years ago I was not timid, so on the very first day I raised my hand and asked a question. I still have a vivid memory of the professor rolling his eyes, hitting his head with his hand in frustration, and announcing to everyone, "Why do they expect me to teach calculus to girls?" I never asked another question. Several weeks later I went to a football game, but I had forgotten to bring my ID. My calculus professor was at the gate checking IDs, so I went up to him and said, "I forgot my ID but you know me, I'm in your class." He looked right at me and said, "I don't remember you in my class." I couldn't believe that someone who changed my life and whom I remember to this day didn't even recognize me. (Sadker and Sadker, 1994, p. 162)

Although such blatant sexism is less likely today, gender bias is still a fact of post-secondary life. For instance, the next time you are in class, consider the gender of your classmates—and the subject matter of the class. Although men and women attend in roughly equal proportions, they tend to take different courses. Classes in education and the social sciences, for instance, typically have a larger proportion of women, and classes in engineering, the physical sciences, and mathematics tend to have more men.

Even women who start out in mathematics, engineering, and the physical sciences are more than twice as likely as men to drop out. And although the number of women seeking

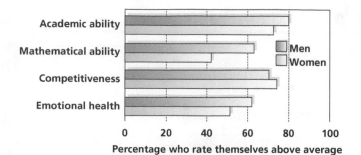

FIGURE 7-8 The Great Gender Divide
During their first year of university, men, compared to women, are more likely to view themselves as above average in several spheres relevant to academic success. What is the root of this difference?
Source: CIRE, 1990; Astin, Korn, & Berz, Higher Education Research Institute, UCLA.

graduate degrees in science and engineering quadrupled over one generation, women still lag behind men (National Science Foundation, 2002). Furthermore, as the number of women increases in a particular field, it often becomes labelled "girly" and devalued by male students. For example, female students in chemical engineering at a top Canadian university recounted that approximately 1 in 4 students was female and thus the male students referred to it as the "girly engineering." Approximately three out of five medical students today are female, yet they are less likely to pursue more financially lucrative specialties like dermatology.

These differences are no accident. They reflect the powerful influence of gender stereotypes and a lifetime of gender bias in classrooms. For instance, when women in their first year of college are asked to name a likely career choice, they are much less likely to choose careers that have traditionally been dominated by men, such as engineering or computer programming, and more likely to choose professions that have traditionally been populated by women, such as nursing and social work (Glick et al., 1988; CIRE, 1990).

Women also expect to earn less than men, both when they start their careers and when they are at their peaks (Jackson et al., 1992; Desmarais and Curtis, 1997; Pelham and Hetts, 2001). These expectations reflect reality: On average, women still earn 69 cents for every dollar that men earn (Statistics Canada, 2009).

Male and female post-secondary students also have different expectations regarding their areas of competence. For instance, one survey asked first-year students whether they were above or below average on a variety of traits and abilities. As shown in Figure 7-8, men were more likely than women to think of themselves as above average in overall academic and mathematical ability, competitiveness, and emotional health.

Both male and female professors treat men and women differently, even though the different treatment is largely unintentional and the professors are unaware of their actions. Professors call more frequently on men than on women and make more eye contact with men than with women. Furthermore, male students are more likely to receive extra help. Finally, the quality of the responses received by male and female students differs, with male students receiving more positive reinforcement for their comments than female students. These patterns began in early life—parents treat male and female infants differently; elementary school teachers pay more attention to boys (both competitive star students and trouble-makers) such that, by the time they grow up, once enthusiastic and confident girls become quiet women with lowered expectations, watching the men. Gender bias also negatively affects men, as male students are socialized even more rigidly than females, who are largely ignored (Epperson, 1988; AAUW, 1992; Sadker and Sadker, 1994; Sadker and Zittleman, 2009).

Benevolent Sexism: When Being Nice Is Not So Nice. Although some cases of unequal treatment represent *hostile sexism* in which people treat women in a way that is overtly harmful, in other cases women are the victims of benevolent sexism. In *benevolent sexism,* women are placed in stereotyped and restrictive roles that appear, on the surface, to be positive.

For instance, a male professor may compliment a female student on her good looks or offer to give her an easier research project so she won't have to work so hard. While the professor might feel that he is merely being thoughtful, in fact he might be making the woman feel that she is not taken seriously and undermining her view of her competence. Benevolent sexism can be just as harmful as hostile sexism (Glick et al., 2000; Greenwood and Isbell, 2002).

Stereotype Threat and Disidentification with School

Boys and girls perform virtually identically on standardized math tests in elementary and middle school, but that changes when they reach high school. At that level, and even more so in university, males tend to do better than females in math. In fact, when women take math, science, and engineering courses, they are more likely to do poorly than men who entered university with the same level of preparation and identical standardized test scores. Strangely, though, this phenomenon does not hold true for other areas of the curriculum, where men and women perform at similar levels (Hyde et al., 1990).

According to psychologist Claude Steele, the reason behind the declining levels of performance for women and some minority groups is the same: *academic disidentification,* a lack of personal identification with an academic domain. For women, disidentification is specific to math and science; for some minority groups, it is more generalized across academic domains. In both cases, negative societal stereotypes produce a state of **stereotype threat** in which members of the group fear that their behaviour will confirm the stereotype (Steele, 1997).

For instance, women seeking to achieve in fields that rely on math and science might worry about the failure that society predicts for them. They might decide, paradoxically, that failure in a male-dominated field (because it would confirm societal stereotypes) presents such great risks that the struggle to succeed is not worth the effort—they might not try very hard (Inzlicht and Ben-Zeev, 2000).

Similarly, members of minority groups might feel intense pressure to disconfirm the negative stereotype regarding their academic performance. The pressure can be anxiety-provoking and threatening and can reduce their performance below their true ability level. Ironically, stereotype threat might be most severe for better, more confident students, who have not internalized the negative stereotype and have never questioned their own abilities (Steele, 1997). In the end, students might perform less well and disidentify with schooling and academic pursuits relevant to the stereotype.

To examine this hypothesis, Steele and colleagues conducted an experiment in which Black and white students were given identical tests composed of difficult verbal skills questions from the Graduate Record Exam, a standardized test for graduate school admission. However, the stated purpose of the test was varied across participant groups. Some participants were told that the test measured "psychological factors involved in solving verbal problems"—information that presumably had little to do with underlying ability. It was stressed that the test would not evaluate their ability. In contrast, other participants were told that the test was concerned with various "personal factors involved in performance on problems requiring reading and verbal reasoning abilities," and that the test would be helpful in identifying their personal strengths and weaknesses.

The results provided clear evidence for the stereotype vulnerability hypothesis. The Black participants who thought the test measured psychological factors performed as well as white participants. But the Black participants who thought the test measured core abilities and limitations scored significantly lower than white participants. In contrast, white participants scored equally, regardless of the test description. Clearly, having to contend with the stereotype resulted in poorer performance (Steele and Aronson, 1995).

> **stereotype threat** obstacles to performance that come from awareness of the stereotypes held by society about academic abilities

Both male and female professors might unintentionally favour their male students over their female students, calling on male students more and making more eye contact with them than with the female students. Why do you think unconscious sexism like this persists?

In short, members of groups that are traditionally discriminated against are vulnerable to expectations regarding their future success. Happily, though, even relatively subtle changes in a situation—such as the way an assessment is described—can reduce vulnerability to stereotyping. Intervention programs designed to inform members of minority groups about the consequences of negative stereotypes can offer a means of reducing the impact of those stereotoypes (Lesko and Corpus, 2006; McGlone and Aronson, 2006; McGlone et al., 2006; Rosenthal and Crisp, 2006).

REVIEW, CHECK, AND APPLY

REVIEW

- While students with post-secondary degrees earn, on average, more than those without, some highly educated people earn low incomes.

- Approximately half of post-secondary students are "mature students."

- The phenomena of academic disidentification and stereotype threat help explain the lower performance of certain groups.

CHECK YOURSELF

1. The percentage of Canadian adults with a post-secondary degree is _____.

   a. 60%

   b. 48%

   c. 38%

   d. 21%

2. More women than men attend and graduate from university, and the proportion of women, relative to men, is increasing.

   - True

   - False

3. Jared is having difficulty in his first year of college. Psychological symptoms include loneliness, anxiety, withdrawal, and depression. It appears Jared is suffering from a cluster of symptoms called _____.

4. For women, failing to identify as successful in a certain academic domain such as math and science is known as _____.

   a. stereotype threat

   b. academic disidentification

   c. inadequate self-concept

   d. psychosomatic illness

APPLYING LIFESPAN DEVELOPMENT

- How would you educate professors who behave differently toward male and female students? What factors contribute to this phenomenon? Can this situation be changed?

Answers: 1) b; 2) True; 3) first-year adjustment reaction; 4) b

MODULE 7.3 Social and Personality Development in Early Adulthood

Love Without Borders

"Wedding ceremonies.... I grew up with certain expectations about my wedding, attended a lot of family weddings," says Gloria. "Then I met Raymond. We met at a work function, but we didn't work closely so it seemed OK to start dating. We had a lot in common. When we got engaged, suddenly I learned how different we were. His family had certain expectations too—and they were very different. The stress of balancing his family and my family was just too much. It's just a wedding. It's just a big party. We ditched them all, ran off to a sunny Caribbean island for our wedding and honeymoon, then came back and had a big family party. I'm happy to blend cultures over time, but we couldn't fit it all into one day."

Life hasn't gotten any less complicated for Gloria and Raymond. Their families accepted the elopement (after all, what could they do?) but will continue to try to steer the cultural influences now that there is a baby on the way.

In early adulthood, as Gloria and Raymond are discovering, we face many developmental tasks (see Table 7-2). We come to grips with the notion that we are no longer just other people's children, and we begin to perceive ourselves as adults, full members of society with significant responsibilities (Arnett, 2000).

This module examines those challenges, concentrating on relationships with others. First, we consider the question of love in its many varieties. We look at how people choose partners, influenced by societal and cultural factors.

TABLE 7-2 THE DEVELOPMENTAL TASKS OF ADULTHOOD

Early Adulthood (Ages 20–40)	Middle Adulthood (Ages 40–60)	Late Adulthood (Ages 60+)
1. Psychological separation from parents.	1. Dealing with body changes or illness and altered body image.	1. Maintaining physical health.
2. Accepting responsibility for one's own body.	2. Adjusting to middle-life changes in sexuality.	2. Adapting to physical infirmities or permanent impairment.
3. Becoming aware of one's personal history and time limitation.	3. Accepting the passage of time.	3. Using time in gratifying ways.
4. Integrating sexual experience (homosexual or heterosexual).	4. Adjusting to aging.	4. Adapting to losses of partner and friends.
5. Developing a capacity for intimacy with a partner.	5. Living through illness and death of parents and contemporaries.	5. Remaining oriented to present and future, not preoccupied with the past.
6. Deciding whether to have children.	6. Dealing with realities of death.	6. Forming new emotional ties.
7. Having and relating to children.	7. Redefining relationship to spouse or partner.	7. Reversing roles of children and grandchildren (as caretakers).
8. Establishing adult relationships with parents.	8. Deepening relations with grown children or grandchildren.	8. Seeking and maintaining social contacts: companionship vs. isolation and loneliness.
9. Acquiring marketable skills.	9. Maintaining longstanding friendships and creating new ones.	9. Attending to sexual needs and (changing) expressions.
10. Choosing a career.	10. Consolidating work identity.	10. Continuing meaningful work and play (satisfying use of time).
11. Using money to further development.	11. Transmitting skills and values to the young.	11. Using financial resources wisely, for self and others.
12. Assuming a social role.	12. Allocating financial resources effectively.	12. Integrating retirement into new lifestyle.
13. Adapting ethical and spiritual values.	13. Accepting social responsibility.	
	14. Accepting social change.	

Source: Colarusso and Nemiroff, 1981.

Then we examine marriage, including the choice of whether to marry and the factors that influence the success of marriage. We consider how children affect marital happiness and we look at the roles children play in a marriage. Also, we discuss the shapes and sizes of families today, which reflect the complexity of relationships in early adulthood.

Finally, we move to careers, another major preoccupation of young adults. We see how identity during early adulthood is often tied to one's job and how people decide on the kind of work they do. The chapter ends with a discussion of why people work and looks at ways to choose a career.

Forging Relationships: Intimacy, Liking, and Loving during Early Adulthood

LO8 **How do young adults form loving relationships, and how does love change over time?**

LO9 **How do people choose spouses, and what makes relationships work and cease working?**

LEARNING OBJECTIVES

Noelle and Philippe met at a party during grad school. A week later they ran into each other on the street, and headed in the same direction, starting to chat. They went for ice cream, then a drink, then supper, then karaoke. It was an impromptu date that neither wanted to end. "We stopped by her apartment to drop off her bag. I saw the movie titles on her shelf and knew any girl who likes the same silly movies as me—she's a keeper." Two years later they were married.

The road to love is not as smooth for everyone. For some it is tortuous, meandering through soured relationships and fallen dreams; for others, it is a road never taken. For some, love leads to marriage and the storybook picture of home, children, and long years together. For many, it leads to a less happy ending—to divorce and custody battles.

Intimacy and relationships are major considerations during early adulthood. Relationships are the core of young adults' happiness, and many worry whether they are developing serious relationships "on time." Even those who are not interested in forming long-term relationships typically are focused, to some extent, on connecting with others.

The Components of Happiness: Fulfilling Psychological Needs

Think back over the last seven days of your life. What made you happiest?

According to research on young adults, it probably wasn't money or material objects. It was more likely the product of feelings of independence, competence, self-esteem, or relating well to other people (Sheldon et al., 2001).

Asked to recall a time when they were happy, young adults are most likely to mention an experience or moment when their psychological needs rather than material needs were satisfied. Typical answers include being chosen for a new job, developing a deep relationship, or moving into an apartment or home of their own. Conversely, when they remember times when they were least satisfied, they mention incidents in which basic psychological needs were left unfulfilled.

Culture apparently influences which psychological needs are considered most important to happiness. For example, young adults in Korea more often associate satisfaction with experiences involving other people, whereas young adults in the United States associate satisfaction with experiences relating to the self and self-esteem (Diener et al., 2003; Sedikides et al., 2003; Jongudomkarn and Camfield, 2006).

The Social Clocks of Adulthood

Having children. Receiving a promotion. Getting divorced. Changing jobs. Becoming a grand-parent. Each of these events marks a moment on what has been called the social clock of life.

The term **social clock** is used to describe the psychological timepiece that records the major milestones in people's lives. A personal social clock tells each of us whether we have reached the major benchmarks of life early, late, or right on time in comparison to our peers. Our social clocks are culturally determined, reflecting the expectations of the society in which we live.

Until the mid-twentieth century, the social clocks of adulthood were fairly uniform—at least for upper-class and middle-class people in Western societies. The typical man completed his education by his early twenties, started a career, married in his mid-twenties, and was providing for a growing family by his thirties. Women also followed a set pattern, which focused on getting married and raising children—but not, in most cases, entering a profession and developing a career.

Today, there is considerably more heterogeneity in the social clocks of both men and women. The timing of major life events has changed, and women's social clocks have changed dramatically as a result of social and cultural changes.

Women's Social Clocks. Developmental psychologist Ravenna Helson and colleagues suggest that people choose from several social clocks, and the selection they make has implications for personality development during middle adulthood. Focusing on a sample of women who graduated from college during the early 1960s, Helson's longitudinal research has examined women whose social clocks were focused either on their families, on careers, or on a more individualistic target (Helson and Moane, 1987).

Helson found that, over the course of the study, which assessed participants at the ages of 21, 27, and 43, the women generally became more self-disciplined and committed to their duties. They also felt greater independence and confidence and could cope with stress and adversity more effectively.

Finding a spouse and embarking on motherhood meant that many women exhibited what Helson called traditional feminine behaviour from about age 21 to 27. But as children grew up and maternal duties diminished, women took on less traditional roles.

The study also found some intriguing similarities in women who chose to focus on family compared with those who focused on career. Both groups showed generally positive changes.

social clock the culturally determined psychological timepiece providing a sense of whether we have reached the major benchmarks of life at the appropriate time in comparison to our peers

In contrast, women who had no strong focus on either family or career tended to show either little change or more negative shifts in personality development, such as becoming less satisfied over time.

Helson's conclusion is that the critical factor in personality development is not which social clock a woman chooses, but the *process* of choosing a social clock, whether it involves motherhood or career. Whether the woman chooses a career first and then motherhood, or the opposite pattern, or an entirely different path, is less important than investing in and focusing on a particular trajectory.

It is important to keep in mind that social clocks are culturally determined. The timing of motherhood and the course of a woman's career are both influenced by the social, economic, and cultural worlds in which the woman lives (Helson et al., 1995; Stewart and Ostrove, 1998).

Seeking Intimacy: Erikson's View of Young Adulthood

Erik Erikson believed that the **intimacy-versus-isolation stage** originates in young adulthood, spanning postadolescence to the early thirties. During this period, the focus is on developing close, intimate relationships with others.

To Erikson, intimacy comprises several aspects. One is selflessness, the sacrifice of one's own needs to those of another. Another is sexuality, the experience of joint pleasure from focusing not just on one's own gratification but also on that of one's partner. Finally, there is deep devotion, marked by efforts to fuse one's identity with the identity of a partner.

According to Erikson, those who experience difficulties during this stage are often lonely, isolated, and fearful of relationships. Their difficulties may stem from an earlier failure to develop a strong identity. In contrast, young adults who are able to form intimate relationships on a physical, intellectual, and emotional level successfully resolve the crisis of this stage of development.

Erikson's approach has been influential, but it is troubling today because he limited healthy intimacy to heterosexuality. Same-sex partnerships, couples childless by choice, and other relationships different from Erikson's ideal were regarded as less than satisfactory. Furthermore, Erikson focused more on men than women, and did not consider ethnic identity, which greatly limits the applicability of his theory (Yip et al., 2006).

Always culturally determined, women's social clocks have changed over the years.

Friendship

Most of our relationships are friendships, and maintaining them is an important part of adult life. Why? One reason is that people have a basic *need for belongingness* that leads them, in early adulthood, to establish and maintain at least a minimum number of relationships that foster a sense of belonging with others (Manstead, 1997; Rice, 1999).

But how do particular people end up becoming our friends? One of the most important factors is proximity—people form friendships with others who live nearby and with whom they have frequent contact. People who are nearby can reap the rewards of friendship, such as companionship, social approval, and the occasional helping hand, at relatively little cost.

Also, birds of a feather *do* flock together: People are more attracted to others who hold attitudes and values similar to their own (McCaul et al., 1995; Simpkins et al., 2006; Morry, 2007).

We also choose friends for their personal qualities. What's most important? According to results of surveys, people are most attracted to others who keep confidences and are loyal, warm, and affectionate. In addition, people like those who are supportive, frank, and have a good sense of humor (Parlee, 1979; Hartup and Stevens, 1999).

Falling in Love: When Liking Turns to Loving

After a few chance encounters at the laundromat each week, Rebecca and Jerry begin talking. They find they have a lot in common, and they begin to look forward to what are now semi-planned meetings. After several weeks, they go out on their first official date and discover that they are well suited to each other.

If such a pattern seems predictable, it is: Most relationships develop by following a surprisingly regular progression (Burgess and Huston, 1979; Berscheid, 1985):

- Two people interact more often and for longer periods, and the range of settings increases.
- They increasingly seek each other's company.

intimacy-versus-isolation stage   according to Erikson, the period from postadolescence into the early thirties that focuses on developing close relationships with others

- They open up more and more, disclosing more intimate information. They begin to share physical intimacies.
- They are more willing to share both positive and negative feelings, and they may offer criticism in addition to praise.
- They begin to agree on their goals for the relationship.
- Their reactions to situations become more similar.
- They begin to feel that their own psychological well-being is tied to the success of the relationship, viewing it as unique, irreplaceable, and cherished.
- Finally, their definition of themselves and their behaviour changes: They begin to see themselves and act as a couple, rather than as two separate individuals.

Another view of the evolution of a relationship was put forward by psychologist Bernard Murstein (Murstein, 1976, 1986, 1987). According to **stimulus-value-role (SVR) theory**, relationships proceed in three stages.

In the first stage, the *stimulus stage*, relationships are built on surface, physical characteristics such as the way a person looks. Usually this represents just the initial encounter. The second stage, the *value stage*, usually occurs between the second and the seventh encounter. In the value stage, the relationship is characterized by increasing similarity of values and beliefs. Finally, in the third stage, the *role stage*, the relationship is built on specific roles played by the participants. For instance, the couple may define themselves as boyfriend–girlfriend or husband–wife.

SVR theory has come under criticism because not every relationship follows a similar pattern (Gupta and Singh, 1982; Sternberg, 1986). For instance, there is no logical reason why value factors, rather than stimulus factors, could not predominate early in a relationship. Two people who meet at a political meeting could be attracted to each other's views of current issues.

Passionate and Companionate Love: The Two Faces of Love

Is "love" just a lot of "liking"? Most developmental psychologists would say no; love not only differs quantitatively from liking, it represents a qualitatively different state. For example, love, at least in its early stages, involves relatively intense physiological arousal, all-encompassing interest, recurrent fantasies, and rapid swings of emotion (Lamm and Wiesmann, 1997). As distinct from liking, love includes closeness, passion, and exclusivity (Walster and Walster, 1978; Hendrick and Hendrick, 2003).

Not all love is the same. We don't love our mothers the same way we love girlfriends or boyfriends, brothers or sisters, or lifelong friends. What distinguishes these different types of love? Some psychologists suggest that our love relationships can fall into two different categories: passionate or companionate.

Passionate (or romantic) love is a state of powerful absorption in someone. It includes intense physiological interest and arousal, and caring for another's needs. In comparison, **companionate love** is the strong affection that we have for those with whom our lives are deeply involved (Hecht et al., 1994; Lamm and Wiesman, 1997; Hendrick and Hendrick, 2003).

What is it that fuels the fires of passionate love? According to one theory, strong emotions—even negative ones such as jealousy, anger, or fear of rejection—can be the source of deepening passionate love.

In psychologists Elaine Hatfield and Ellen Berscheid's **labelling theory of passionate love**, individuals experience romantic love when two events occur together: intense physiological arousal and situational cues that indicate that "love" is the appropriate label for the feelings being experienced (Berscheid and Walster, 1974). The physiological arousal can be produced by sexual arousal, excitement, or even negative emotions such as jealousy. If that arousal is subsequently labelled as "I must be falling in love" or "He really turns me on," the experience is attributed to passionate love.

The theory helps to explain why people may feel deepened love even in the face of rejection or hurt. If negative emotions produce strong physiological arousal and this arousal is interpreted as "love," then people may decide that they are even more in love than they were before they experienced the negative emotions.

But why should people label an emotional experience "love" when there are so many alternative explanations? One answer is that in Western cultures, romantic love is seen as possible,

stimulus-value-role (SVR) theory the theory that relationships proceed in a fixed order of three stages: stimulus, value, and role

passionate (or romantic) love a state of powerful absorption in someone

companionate love the strong affection for those with whom our lives are deeply involved

labelling theory of passionate love the theory that individuals experience romantic love when two events occur together: intense physiological arousal and situational cues suggesting that the arousal is due to love

acceptable, and desirable. The virtues of passion are extolled in songs, commercials, TV shows, and films. Young adults are primed and ready to experience love in their lives (Dion and Dion, 1988; Hatfield and Rapson, 1993; Florsheim, 2003).

This is not universal across cultures; in many cultures, passionate, romantic love is a foreign concept. Marriages are arranged on the basis of economic and status considerations. The concept of romantic love was "invented" during the Middle Ages, when social philosophers first suggested that love ought to be a requirement for marriage. Their goal was to provide an alternative to the raw sexual desire that had served as the primary basis for marriage before (Xiaohe and Whyte, 1990; Haslett, 2004).

Sternberg's Triangular Theory: The Three Faces of Love

Psychologist Robert Sternberg suggests that love is made up of three components: intimacy, passion, and decision/commitment. The **intimacy component** encompasses feelings of closeness, affection, and connectedness. The **passion component** comprises the motivational drives relating to sex, physical closeness, and romance. The **decision/commitment component** embodies both the initial cognition that one loves another person and the longer-term determination to maintain that love (Sternberg, 1997b).

These components can be combined to form eight different types of love, depending on which of the three components is either present or missing from a relationship (see Table 7-3). For instance, nonlove refers to people who have only the most casual of relationships; it consists of the absence of the three components of intimacy, passion, and decision/commitment. *Liking* develops when only intimacy is present; *infatuated love* exists when only passion is felt; and *empty love* exists when only decision/commitment is present.

Other types of love involve a mix of two or more components. For instance, romantic love occurs when intimacy and passion are present, and *companionate love* when intimacy and decision/commitment occur jointly. When two people experience romantic love, they are drawn together physically and emotionally, but they do not necessarily view the relationship as lasting. Companionate love, on the other hand, can occur in long-lasting relationships in which physical passion has taken a backseat.

Fatuous love exists when passion and decision/commitment, without intimacy, are present. Fatuous love is a kind of mindless loving in which there is no emotional bond between the partners.

Finally, the eighth kind of love is *consummate love*. In consummate love, all three components of love are present. But don't assume that consummate love is the "ideal" love.

intimacy component the component of love that encompasses feelings of closeness, affection, and connectedness

passion component the component of love that comprises the motivational drives relating to sex, physical closeness, and romance

decision/commitment component the third aspect of love that embodies both the initial cognition that one loves another person and the longer-term determination to maintain that love

TABLE 7-3 THE COMBINATIONS OF LOVE

Type of Love	Component			Example
	Intimacy	Passion	Decision/Commitment	
Nonlove	Absent	Absent	Absent	The way you might feel about the person who takes your ticket at the movies.
Liking	Present	Absent	Absent	Good friends who have lunch together at least once or twice a week.
Infatuated love	Absent	Present	Absent	A "fling" or short-term relationship based only on sexual attraction.
Empty love	Absent	Absent	Present	An arranged marriage or a couple who have decided to stay married "for the sake of the children."
Romantic love	Present	Present	Absent	A couple who have been happily dating a few months, but have not made any plans for a future together.
Companionate love	Present	Absent	Present	A couple who enjoy each other's company and their relationship, although they no longer feel much sexual interest in each other.
Fatuous love	Absent	Present	Present	A couple who decides to move in together after knowing each other for only two weeks.
Consummate love	Present	Present	Present	A loving, sexually vibrant, long-term relationship.

Many long-lasting and entirely satisfactory relationships are based on other types of love. Furthermore, the type of love that predominates in a relationship varies over time. In strong, loving relationships the level of decision/commitment peaks and remains fairly stable. By contrast, passion tends to peak early in a relationship, but then declines and levels off. Intimacy also increases fairly rapidly, but can continue to grow over time.

Sternberg's triangular theory of love emphasizes both the complexity of love and its dynamic, evolving quality. As people and relationships develop, so does their love.

◉ Watch on **mydevelopmentlab**

Log onto MyDevelopmentLab to watch videos of Stephanie and Ralf, two young adults searching for love, but who approach it in different ways.

Choosing a Partner: Recognizing Mr. or Ms. Right

For many young adults, the search for a partner is a major pursuit during early adulthood. Society offers a wealth of advice, as a glance at the magazines at supermarket check-out counters confirms. Still, the road to identifying a life partner is not always easy.

Seeking a Spouse: Is Love the Only Thing That Matters?   Most people have no hesitation in declaring that the major factor in choosing a spouse is love. Most people in the West, that is: If we ask people in other societies, love becomes a secondary consideration. For instance, college students were asked in a survey if they would marry someone they did not love. Hardly anyone in the United States, Japan, or Brazil would consider it. On the other hand, a high proportion of college students in Pakistan and India would find it acceptable to marry without love (Levine, 1993).

What else matters? The characteristics differ considerably from one culture to another (see Table 7-4). For instance, a survey of nearly 10 000 people from around the world found that in China men ranked good health most important and women rated emotional stability and maturity most critical. In South Africa men from a Zulu background rated emotional stability first, and Zulu women rated dependable character the greatest concern (Buss et al., 1990; Buss, 2003b).

TABLE 7-4 MOST DESIRED CHARACTERISTICS IN A MARRIAGE PARTNER

	China		South African (Zulu)		United States	
	Males	**Females**	**Males**	**Females**	**Males**	**Females**
Mutual Attraction—Love	4	8	10	5	1	1
Emotional Stability and Maturity	5	1	1	2	2	2
Dependable Character	6	7	3	1	3	3
Pleasing Disposition	13	16	4	3	4	4
Education and Intelligence	8	4	6	6	5	5
Good Health	1	3	5	4	6	9
Sociability	12	9	11	8	8	8
Desire for Home and Children	2	2	9	9	9	7
Refinement, Neatness	7	10	7	10	10	12
Ambition and Industriousness	10	5	8	7	11	6
Good Looks	11	15	14	16	7	13
Similar Education	15	12	12	12	12	10
Good Financial Prospects	16	14	18	13	16	11
Good Cook and Housekeeper	9	11	2	15	13	16
Favourable Social Status or Rating	14	13	17	14	14	14
Similar Religious Background	18	18	16	11	15	15
Chastity (no prior sexual intercourse)	3	6	13	18	17	18
Similar Political Background	17	17	15	17	18	17

Note: numbers indicate rank ordering of characteristics.
Source: Buss et al., 1990.

On the other hand, love and mutual attraction, even if not at the top of a culture's list, were relatively highly desired across all cultures. Furthermore, traits such as dependability, emotional stability, pleasing disposition, and intelligence were highly valued almost universally.

Certain gender differences were similar across cultures—as confirmed by other surveys (for example, Sprecher et al., 1994). More men than women prefer a potential marriage partner who is physically attractive. In contrast, more women than men prefer a potential spouse who is ambitious and industrious.

One explanation for cross-cultural similarities in gender differences rests on evolutionary theory. According to psychologist David Buss and colleagues (Buss, 2004), human beings, as a species, seek out certain characteristics in their mates that are likely to maximize the availability of beneficial genes. He argues that males in particular are genetically programmed to seek out mates with traits that indicate they have high reproductive capacity. Consequently, physically attractive, younger women might be more desirable since they are more capable of having children over a longer time period.

In contrast, women are genetically programmed to seek out men who have the potential to provide scarce resources in order to increase the likelihood that their offspring will survive. Consequently, they are attracted to mates who offer the highest potential of providing economic well-being (Li et al., 2002).

The evolutionary explanation for gender differences has come under heavy fire. Not only is the explanation untestable, but the similarities across cultures relating to different gender preferences may simply reflect similar patterns of gender stereotyping that have nothing to do with evolution. In addition, although some of the gender differences in what men and women prefer are consistent across cultures, numerous inconsistencies exist as well.

Finally, some critics of the evolutionary approach suggest that finding that women prefer a partner who has good earning potential may have nothing to do with evolution and everything to do with the fact that men generally hold more power, status, and other resources fairly consistently across different cultures. Consequently, it is a rational choice for women to prefer a high-earning-potential spouse. On the other hand, because men don't need to take economic considerations into account, they can use more inconsequential criteria—like physical attractiveness—in choosing a spouse. In short, the consistencies that are found across cultures might be due to the realities of economic life that are similar throughout different cultures (Eagly and Wood, 2003).

Filtering Models: Sifting Out a Spouse. While surveys help to identify valued characteristics, they are less helpful in illuminating how individual partners are chosen. According to the *filter explanation*, people seeking a mate screen potential candidates through successively finer-grained filters. The explanation assumes that people first filter for factors relating to broad determinants of attractiveness. Once these early screens have done their work, more sophisticated types of screening are used. The end result is a choice based on compatibility between the two individuals (Janda and Klenke-Hamel, 1980).

What determines compatibility? People often marry according to the principle of homogamy. **Homogamy** is the tendency to marry someone who is similar in age, ethnicity, education, religion, and other basic demographic characteristics. Homogamy, long the dominant standard, has been declining recently, at least in terms of visible characteristics like skin colour. For example, 4 percent of Canadians are in a mixed union, and the rate of mixed unions varies by ethnic group. Chinese Canadians are the single largest visible minority in Canada, and as a group have a relatively low rate of mixed unions (17 percent), whereas nearly three-quarters of Japanese Canadians are in mixed unions (Milan et al., 2010). In contrast, other aspects of homogamy, especially education and religion, continue to be important selection factors (Botwin et al., 1997)

Another important societal standard is the **marriage gradient**, the tendency for men to marry women who are slightly younger, smaller, and lower in status, and women to marry men who are slightly older, larger, and higher in status (Bernard, 1982).

homogamy the tendency to marry someone who is similar in age, race, education, religion, and other basic demographic characteristics

marriage gradient the tendency for men to marry women who are slightly younger, smaller, and lower in status, and women to marry men who are slightly older, larger, and higher in status

From a social worker's perspective: How do the principles of homogamy and the marriage gradient work to limit options for high-status women? How do they affect men's options? How might we expect the marriage picture to change given increasing rates of higher education among women relative to men?

Some psychologists believe that our attachment style as infants is repeated in the quality of our intimate relationships as adults.

The marriage gradient has important—and unfortunate—effects on partner choice. For one thing, it limits the number of potential mates for women, especially as they age, while allowing men a wider choice of partners throughout life. But it is unfortunate for low-status men, who do not marry because they cannot find women of low enough status or cannot find women of the same or higher status who are willing to accept them as mates. Consequently, these men are, in the words of sociologist Jessie Bernard (1982), "bottom of the barrel" men. On the other hand, some women will be unable to marry because they are higher in status or seek someone of higher status than anyone in the available pool of men. Bernard refers to these women as "cream of the crop" women.

Attachment Styles and Romantic Relationships: Do Adult Loving Styles Reflect Attachment in Infancy?

"I want a girl just like the girl that married dear old Dad." So go the lyrics of an old song, suggesting that the songwriter would like to find someone who loves him as much as his mother did. Is this just a corny tune, or is there a kernel of truth in this sentiment? Put more broadly, is the kind of attachment that people experience during infancy reflected in their adult romantic relationships?

Increasing evidence suggests that it very well might be. As we discussed earlier, attachment refers to the positive emotional bond that develops between a child and a particular individual. Most infants fall into one of three attachment categories: securely attached infants, who have healthy, positive, trusting relationships with their caregivers; avoidant infants, who are relatively indifferent to caregivers and avoid interactions with them; and ambivalent infants, who show great distress when separated from a caregiver but appear angry upon the caregiver's return.

According to psychologist Phillip Shaver and his colleagues, attachment styles continue into adulthood and affect the nature of romantic relationships (Tracy et al., 2003; Davis et al., 2006; Mikulincer and Shaver, 2007). For instance, consider the following statements:

Research finds that the quality of lesbian and gay relationships differs little from that of heterosexual relationships.

1. I find it relatively easy to get close to others and am comfortable depending on them and having them depend on me. I don't often worry about being abandoned or about someone getting too close to me.

2. I am somewhat uncomfortable being close to others; I find it difficult to trust them completely, difficult to allow myself to depend on them. I am nervous when anyone gets too close, and often love partners want me to be more intimate than I feel comfortable being.

3. I find that others are reluctant to get as close as I would like. I often worry that my partner doesn't really love me or won't want to stay with me. I want to merge completely with another person, and this desire sometimes scares people away. (Shaver et al., 1988)

According to Shaver, agreement with the first statement reflects a secure attachment style. Adults who agree with this statement readily enter into relationships and feel happy and confident about the future success of their relationships. Most young adults—just over half—display the secure style of attachment (Hazan and Shaver, 1987).

In contrast, adults who agree with the second statement typically display the avoidant attachment style. These individuals, who make up about a quarter of the population, tend to be less invested in relationships, have higher break-up rates, and often feel lonely.

Finally, agreement with the third category is reflective of an ambivalent style. Adults with an ambivalent style have a tendency to become overly invested in relationships, have repeated break-ups with the same partner, and have relatively low self-esteem. Around 20 percent of adults fall into this category (Simpson, 1990).

Attachment style is also related to the care that adults give their romantic partners when they need assistance. Secure adults tend to provide more sensitive and supportive care, responding to their partner's psychological needs. In contrast, anxious adults are more likely to provide compulsive, intrusive (and ultimately less helpful) assistance (Feeney and Collins, 2001; Gleason et al., 2003).

Cultural Dimensions

Gay and Lesbian Relationships: Men with Men and Women with Women

Most developmental research has examined heterosexual relationships, but an increasing number of studies have looked at gay and lesbian relationships. The findings suggest that gay relationships are similar to straight relationships.

For example, gay men describe successful relationships in much the same way heterosexual couples do. They believe that successful relationships involve greater appreciation for the partner and the couple as a whole, less conflict, and more positive feelings toward the partner. Similarly, lesbian women in a relationship show high levels of attachment, caring, intimacy, affection, and respect (Brehm, 1992; Beals et al., 2002; Kurdek, 2006).

Furthermore, the age preferences expressed in the marriage gradient for heterosexuals also extend to homosexual men, who also prefer partners who are the same age or younger. On the other hand, lesbians' age preferences fall somewhere between those of heterosexual women and heterosexual men (Kenrick et al., 1995).

Finally, most gay and lesbian adults seek loving, long-term, and meaningful relationships. They aspire to relationships that differ little from those desired by heterosexuals (Division 44, 2000; Diamond and Savin-Williams, 2003).

In Canada, 0.1 percent of married couples are same-sex couples. While same-sex couples are less likely to marry (more than 65 percent of heterosexual couples marry, compared to 16 percent of homosexual couples), of those who do, slightly more are male (53.7%). These numbers should be treated with caution, however, as they come from the 2006 Census, less than one year after same-sex marriage was legalized nationally. A more complete picture, including rates of divorce, will likely emerge as data is released from the 2011 Census. Will the marriage rate increase? Will the rate decline after an initial surge of enthusiasm? The number of common-law couples might hint at the answer: Where 83 percent of same-sex couples were living common-law, the national rate of common-law unions was 15.5 percent (Statistics Canada, 2006).

One thing is certain: same-sex marriage is here to stay. According to public opinion polling, 81 percent of Canadians under 30 support it (compared to 61 percent of Americans under 30), as do 43 percent of Canadians over 65 (compared to 18 percent of Americans over 65) (Angus Reid, 2010; Deakin, 2004).

REVIEW

- According to Erikson, young adults are in the intimacy-versus-isolation stage.

- Types of love include passionate and companionate love. Sternberg's triangular theory identifies three basic components (intimacy, passion, and decision/commitment).

- In general, the values applied to relationships by heterosexual, gay, and lesbian couples are more similar than different.

CHECK YOURSELF

1. According to Erikson, adults spend their early adult years _____.

a. consolidating careers

b. developing their identities

c. being industrious

d. focusing on developing relationships with others

2. _____ love is the strong affection we have for those individuals with whom our lives are deeply involved.

3. According to Sternberg, to determine the type of love that best describes a relationship, one must look at the presence or absence of intimacy, passion, and commitment.

- True

- False

APPLYING LIFESPAN DEVELOPMENT

- Consider a long-term marriage with which you are familiar. Do you think the relationship involves passionate love or companionate love (or both)? What changes when a relationship moves from passionate to companionate love? From companionate to passionate love? In which direction is it more difficult for a relationship to move? Why?

Answers: 1) d; 2) Companionate; 3) True

The Course of Relationships

LEARNING OBJECTIVES

LO10 How does the arrival of children affect a relationship?

Cohabitation is increasing in popularity, especially among young adults.

He wasn't being a chauvinist or anything, expecting me to do everything and him nothing. He just didn't volunteer to do things that obviously needed doing, so I had to put down some ground rules. Like if I'm in a bad mood, I may just yell: "I work eight hours just like you. This is half your house and half your child, too. You've got to do your share!" Jackson never changed the kitty litter box once in four years, but he changes it now, so we've made great progress. I just didn't expect it to take so much work. We planned this child together and we went through Lamaze together, and Jackson stayed home for the first two weeks. But then—wham—the partnership was over. (Cowan and Cowan, 1992, p. 63)

Relationships are especially challenging in early adulthood. One of the primary questions young adults face is whether and when to marry.

Marriage, Cohabitation, and Other Relationship Choices: Sorting Out the Options of Early Adulthood

For some people, the primary issue is not *whom* to marry, but *whether* to marry. Although surveys show that most heterosexuals (and a growing number of homosexuals) say they want to get married, a significant number choose some other route. For instance, the past three decades have seen both a decline in the number of married couples and a significant rise in couples living together without being married, a status known as **cohabitation** (see Figure 7-9). Also known as a common-law union, this choice is increasingly popular among younger adults, with one in five adults between 20 and 35 cohabiting. This is a significant increase over previous generations, although across the generations, young adulthood appears to be the time when couples are more likely to cohabitate. Census data across several generations suggests that cohabitation during young adulthood eventually is replaced by marriage for many adults in their late thirties and forties.

Other countries, such as Sweden, where cohabitation is the norm, have even higher cohabitation rates. In Latin America, cohabitation has a long history and is widespread (Tucker and Mitchell-Kernan, 1995). Quebec stands out from the rest of Canada as having a particularly

cohabitation couples living together without being married.

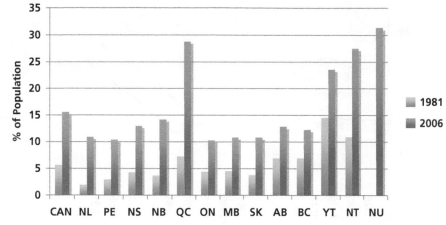

FIGURE 7-9 **Common-law Unions in Canada, 1981–2006**
The number of common-law unions has risen considerably in the last three decades.
Why do you think this is the case?
Note: Northwest Territories includes Nunavut in 1981. Same-sex couples were included beginning in 2001.
Source: Statistics Canada, 2006.

high rate of cohabitation, more than double the rate of the rest of the country. This trend is tied to the Quiet Revolution of the 1960s when marriage, seen as a religious institution, was rejected as part of a larger social rejection of the Catholic church. Formal legal marriage is also uncommon in the northern territories; the marriage rate in Nunavut is even lower than that of Quebec. Common-law unions in Canada carry many of the legal rights of marriage without the hassles of divorce should the relationship end. In some parts of the world however, cohabitation is illegal.

Why cohabit? Some couples feel they are not ready for a lifelong commitment. Others feel that cohabitation provides "practice" for marriage. Some reject marriage altogether, maintaining that marriage is outmoded and that it is unrealistic to expect a couple to spend a lifetime together (Hobart and Grigel, 1992; Cunningham and Antill, 1994; Martin et al., 2001).

Those who feel that cohabiting increases their chances of a happy marriage are incorrect. In fact, the chances of divorce are higher for those who have previously cohabited, according to data collected in both the United States and Western Europe (Brown, 2003; Doyle, 2004a; Hohmann-Marriott, 2006; Rhoades et al., 2006).

Despite the prevalence of cohabitation, marriage remains the preferred alternative for many people during early adulthood. Many see marriage as the appropriate culmination of a loving relationship, while others feel it is the "right" thing to do after reaching a particular age. Others seek marriage because spouses fill many roles, including economic, sexual, therapeutic, and recreational roles. Marriage is also the only *fully* accepted way to have children across much of our society. Finally, marriage offers some legal benefits and protections (Furstenberg, 1996).

Marriage is not a static institution. Fewer adults are now married than at any time on record. In part this is attributable to higher divorce rates, but the tendency of people to marry later in life is also a contributing factor. The median age of first marriage in Canada is now 30 for men and 28 for women—the oldest age for both men and women since national statistics were first collected in 1921 (see Figure 7-10; Statistics Canada, 2011).

Why are people getting married later in life? The delay reflects economic and career concerns. Choosing and starting a career present a series of increasingly difficult decisions, and some young adults decide to put marriage on hold until they get a foothold on a career path and an adequate salary (Dreman, 1997).

◉ **Watch** on **mydevelopmentlab**

There are different types of marriage.
Log onto MyDevelopmentLab to watch videos of Rati and Subas, who are in an arranged marriage, and Scherazade and Roderick, who are in a typical love marriage.

⟶ **From a social worker's perspective:** Why do you think society has established such a powerful norm in favour of marriage? What effects might such a norm have on a person who prefers to remain single?

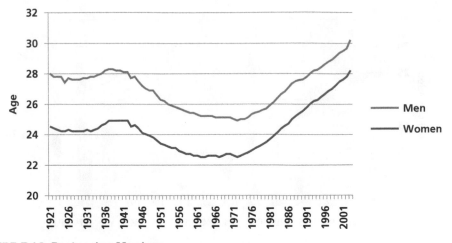

FIGURE 7-10 **Postponing Marriage**
The age at which women and men first marry is the highest since national statistics were first collected in 1921. What factors account for this?
Source: Statistics Canada, 2011

What Makes Marriage Work?

Successful marriages share several characteristics. The partners visibly show affection and communicate with relatively little negativity. They tend to perceive themselves as an interdependent couple rather than as two independent individuals. They experience social homogamy, having similar interests and agreeing on role distribution, such as who takes out the garbage and who takes care of the children (Gottman et al., 1996; Carrere et al., 2000; Huston et al., 2001; Stutzer and Frey, 2006).

Despite an increasing understanding of the components of successful marriages, many marriages still end in divorce. The divorce rate has increased over time, but these increases are tied to legislative changes that facilitated divorce. The rate first began to increase in Canada following the introduction of the Divorce Act in 1968, which introduced "no-fault" divorce. The rate spiked again following the 1986 amendment to the Divorce Act, which decreased the necessary period of separation in no-fault divorce from three or more years to just one. The divorce rate peaked in 1987 and appears to be on the decline. This decline could be related to a decreasing marriage rate. In fact, the rate of relationship failure among married couples is reported to be the same as among common-law couples. It's estimated that 35–40% of all new marriages in Canada will end in divorce within 30 years.

There is also evidence for a genetic risk for divorce. This is not to say there is a "divorce gene," but various genetically determined factors, such as temperament and IQ, might contribute to behaviours such as mate selection, tolerance for conflict, motivation to resolve conflict and effective problem solving, coping strategies, and realistic or unrealistic expectations for one's partner. Together, these factors may combine to lead identical twins to choose very similar lives, lifestyles, and partners with similar consequences.

Early Marital Conflict. Conflict in marriage is not unusual. According to some statistics, nearly half of newly married couples experience a significant degree of conflict. One of the major reasons is that partners may initially idealize one another, but as reality sets in they become more aware of flaws. In fact, spousal perceptions of marital quality over the first 10 years of marriage decline in the early years, followed by a period of stabilization, and then additional decline (Kurdek, 1999, 2002, 2003b; Huston et al., 2001; Karney and Bradbury, 2005).

Common sources of marital conflict include difficulty making the transition from childhood to adulthood; trouble developing a separate identity; and the challenge of allocating time across spouse, friends, and family members (Caughlin, 2002; Crawford et al., 2002; Murray et al., 2003).

Still, most married couples view the early years of marriage as deeply satisfying. In negotiating changes in their relationship and learning more about each other, many couples find themselves more deeply in love than before. In fact, the newlywed period is for many couples one of the happiest of their married lives (Bird and Melville, 1994; Orbuch et al., 1996; McNulty and Karney, 2004).

Parenthood: Choosing to Have Children

What makes a couple decide to have children? Certainly not economics: A middle-class family with two children spends around $233 000 per child to age 18. Add the cost of post-secondary education and the figure could rise to over $300 000 per child (Lino, 2001).

The most commonly cited reasons for having children are psychological. Parents expect to derive pleasure from helping their children grow, fulfillment from their children's accomplishments, satisfaction from seeing them become successful, and enjoyment from forging a close bond with them. For some there might also be a self-serving element in the decision that focuses on the hope that their children will provide for them in their old age, maintain a family business or farm, or offer companionship. Others have children because of a strong societal norm: More than 90 percent of married couples have at least one child.

In some cases children are unplanned, resulting from the failure or the absence of birth control. If the couple had planned to have children in the future, the pregnancy might be welcome. But in families that had actively not wanted children, or already had "enough" children, another pregnancy can be problematic (Clinton and Kelber, 1993; Leathers and Kelley, 2000; Pajulo et al., 2006).

The couples most likely to have unwanted pregnancies are often the most vulnerable—younger, poorer, and less educated couples. Fortunately, there has been a dramatic rise in the use and effectiveness of contraceptives, and the incidence of undesired pregnancies has declined in recent decades (Villarosa, 2003).

Family Size.   The availability of effective contraceptives has also dramatically decreased the number of children in the average family. According to a 1945 Gallup Poll, Canadians believed the ideal number of children was approximately four, a number that has declined ever since (Boyd, 1974). Today, most families seek to have no more than two children—although some say that three or more is ideal if money is no object (Kate, 1998; Gallup Poll, 2004).

These preferences have been translated into changes in the actual birth rate. Until 1965, the *fertility rate* hovered near three children per woman and then began to decline. Today, the rate is at 1.67 children per woman, which is less than the *replacement level* of 2.1—the number of children that one generation must produce to replenish its numbers. In contrast, in some underdeveloped countries, the fertility rate is as high as 6.9 (Fraser, 1983; Statistics Canada, 2008; World Bank, 2004).

What has produced this decline in the fertility rate? In addition to the availability of birth control, increasing numbers of women have joined the workforce. The pressures of simultaneously holding a job and raising a child have convinced many women to have fewer children.

Furthermore, many women who are developing their careers choose to have children later. In fact, women between 30 and 34 are the only ones whose rate of births has actually increased over earlier decades. Still, women who have their first child in their thirties do not have as many children as women who begin earlier. Also, research suggesting that there are health benefits for mothers who space their children apart might lead families to have fewer children (Marcus, 2004).

Financial considerations, particularly the increasing costs of childcare, extracurricular activities, and post-secondary education, can also act as a disincentive for bearing larger numbers of children. Finally, some couples doubt they will be good parents or simply don't want the work and responsibility involved in childrearing.

Dual-Earner Couples.   One of the major historical shifts affecting young adults began in the last half of the twentieth century, when a marked increase began in the number of families in which both parents work. Close to three-quarters

As increasing numbers of women have joined the workforce, more are choosing to have fewer children and to have them later.

of married women with children under 16 are employed outside the home, and nearly 65 percent of mothers with children under age 3 are working. In 1976, only 39 percent of mothers, and 28 percent of mothers with children under age 3, were engaged in paid work. In the majority of families, 69 percent, both husband and wife work. In the 21 percent of families with a stay-at-home parent, fathers accounted for only 11 percent of the parents at home (Marshall, 2006; Statistics Canada, 2010a).

The availability of two incomes brings economic benefits, but it also takes a toll, particularly on women. Even when both spouses work similar hours, the wife generally spends more time on housework, other household tasks such as groceries, and caring for the children—even though the time men spend with their children has risen by 25 percent in the last 20 years (Kitterod and Pettersen, 2006).

Furthermore, what husbands and wives contribute to the household often differs. "Men's chores" (for example, lawn mowing, home repairs) are more easily scheduled in advance, while "women's chores" tend to need immediate attention (for example, child care, meal preparation), which can cause anxiety and stress (Haddock and Rattenborg, 2003; Lee et al., 2003). For men and women, the length of the workday—for both paid and unpaid work—has increased over time (Figure 7-11).

The Transition to Parenthood: Two's a Couple, Three's a Crowd? Consider this quote from a spouse who just became a parent:

> *We had no idea what we were getting into when our first child was born. We certainly prepared for the event, reading magazine articles and books and even attending a class on child care. But when Sheanna was actually born, the sheer enormity of the task of taking care of her, her presence at every moment of the day, and the awesome responsibility of raising another human being weighed on us like nothing we'd ever faced. Not that it was a burden. But it did make us look at the world with an entirely different perspective.*

The arrival of a child alters virtually every aspect of family life. Spouses are suddenly placed in new roles—"mother" and "father"—which may overwhelm their older, continuing roles of "wife" and "husband." In addition, new parents face significant physical and psychological demands, including near-constant fatigue, new financial responsibilities, and an increase in household chores (Meijer and van den Wittenboer, 2007).

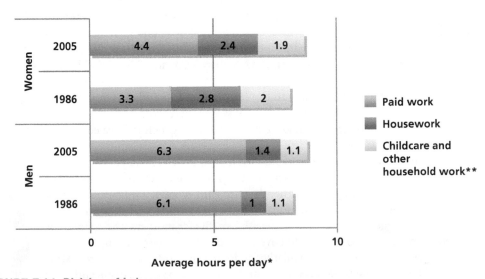

Average hours per day*

FIGURE 7-11 Division of Labour
Even when husbands and wives work at their paying jobs a similar number of hours on average each day, wives are apt to spend more time than their husbands doing home chores and in child-care activities. Why do you think this pattern exists?
* averaged across a seven-day week
** tasks such as household shopping
Source: Marshall, 2006.

Furthermore, in contrast with cultures in which childrearing is regarded as a communal task, Western culture's emphasis on individualism leaves parents to forge their own paths after the birth of a child, often without community support (Rubin and Chung, 2006; Lamm and Keller, 2007).

The consequence is that many couples experience the lowest level of marital satisfaction of any point in their marriage. This is particularly true for women, who tend to be more dissatisfied than men with their marriages after the arrival of children. The most likely reason is that women often bear the brunt of childrearing, even if both parents seek to share these responsibilities (Levy-Shiff, 1994; Laflamme et al., 2002; Lu, 2006).

Marital satisfaction does not decrease for all couples upon the birth of a child. According to work by John Gottman and colleagues (Shapiro et al., 2000), satisfaction can stay steady or even rise. Three factors permit couples to successfully weather the stress that follows the birth of a child:

- working to build fondness and affection toward each other
- remaining aware of events in each other's lives, and responding to those events
- considering problems as controllable and solvable

In addition, couples who are well satisfied with their marriages as newlyweds are more likely to be satisfied as they raise their children. Couples who harbour realistic expectations regarding the effort involved in childrearing also tend to be more satisfied after they become parents. Furthermore, parents who work together as a *coparenting team,* thoughtfully adopting common childrearing goals and strategies, are more apt to be satisfied with their parenting roles (Schoppe-Sullivan et al., 2006; McHale and Rotman, 2007).

In short, having children can lead to greater marital satisfaction for couples already satisfied with their marriage. For dissatisfied couples, having children may make a bad situation worse (Shapiro et al., 2000; Driver et al., 2003).

Gay and Lesbian Parents

In increasing numbers, children are being raised in families with two moms or two dads. Some 9 percent of gay and lesbian couples have children living in the home; the rate is higher for married than unmarried couples, and is five times higher for women than for men (Statistics Canada, 2009).

How do lesbian and gay households compare to heterosexual households? Studies of couples before children arrive show that, compared to heterosexual households, homosexual partners tend to divide labour more evenly and the ideal of an egalitarian allocation of household work is more strongly held (Patterson, 1994; Parks, 1998; Kurdek, 1993, 2003a).

However, the arrival of a child (usually through adoption or artificial insemination) changes the dynamics of household life considerably. As in heterosexual unions, role specialization develops. According to recent research on lesbian mothers, for instance, childrearing tends to fall more to one member of the couple, while the other spends more time in paid employment. Although both partners usually say they share household tasks and decision-making equally, the birth mother is more involved in child care (Patterson, 1995).

For children, being in a household with same-sex parents is similar to being in a household with opposite-sex parents. Most research suggests that children raised in both types of households show no differences in terms of eventual adjustment. Although they can face greater challenges from a society with deep roots of prejudice against homosexuality, children who have two moms or two dads ultimately seem to fare well (Tasker and Golombok, 1997; Wainwright et al., 2004; Bos et al., 2007; Short, 2007).

Staying Single: I Want to Be Alone

For some people, living alone is the right path, consciously chosen, through life. In fact, *singlehood,* living alone without an intimate partner, has increased significantly in the last several decades; singles now outnumber married adults. Almost 10 percent will probably spend their entire lives in singlehood, and expect to never marry (Crompton, 2005; Statistics Canada, 2006).

People who choose singlehood give several reasons for their decision. One is that they view marriage negatively. Rather than seeing marriage in idealized terms, they focus more on high divorce rates and marital strife. Ultimately, they conclude that the risks of forming a lifetime union are too high.

Others view marriage as too restrictive, valuing their personal change and growth, and reasoning that growth would be impeded by the stable, long-term commitment of marriage. Finally, some people simply do not meet anyone with whom they wish to spend their lives. Instead, they value their independence and autonomy (DePaulo and Morris, 2006).

Singlehood does have some drawbacks. Society often stigmatizes single individuals, particularly women. Furthermore, singles often lack companionship and sexual outlets, and they may feel that their futures are less secure financially (Byrne, 2000).

REVIEW, CHECK, AND APPLY

REVIEW

- Cohabitation is an increasingly popular option for young adults, but many still choose marriage.
- Divorce is prevalent, particularly within the first 10 years of marriage.
- Couples overwhelmingly desire to produce children, although the availability of contraception and changes in women's roles in the workplace have combined to decrease average family size.

CHECK YOURSELF

1. During the past three decades there has been both a decline in the number of married couples and the number of individuals living together without being married.

    - True
    - False

2. According to your text, divorce is most likely to occur at what point during marriage?

    a. during the first 6 months

    b. after 20 or more years

    c. during the first 10 years

    d. after one or both spouses retire

3. When asked why they want to have children, most young adults cite _____ reasons.

    a. personal

    b. physical

    c. psychological

    d. societal

APPLYING LIFESPAN DEVELOPMENT

- In what ways do you think cognitive changes in early adulthood (for example, the emergence of postformal thought and practical intelligence) affect how young adults deal with questions of marriage, divorce, and childrearing?

Answers: 1) False; 2) c; 3) c

Work: Choosing and Embarking on a Career

LEARNING OBJECTIVES

LO11 Why is choosing a career such an important issue for young adults, and what factors influence the choice of a career?

LO12 Why do people work, and what elements of a job bring satisfaction?

Why did I decide that I wanted to be a lawyer? The answer is embarrassing. When I started my fourth year of university, I began to worry about what I was going to do when I graduated. My parents kept asking what kind of work I was thinking about, and I felt the pressure rising with each call from home. At the time, a big celebrity murder trial was in the news, and it got me thinking about what it might be like to be an attorney. I had always been fascinated by legal dramas on television, and I could envision myself in one of those big corner offices with a view of the city. For these reasons, and just about none other, I decided to take the LSAT and apply to law school.

Early adulthood is a period of making decisions with lifelong implications. One of the most critical is the choice of a career path. This decision influences financial prosperity, of course, but also status, the sense of self-worth, and the contribution that a person will make in life. Decisions about work go to the core of a young adult's identity.

Identity During Young Adulthood: The Role of Work

According to psychiatrist George Vaillant, young adults reach the stage of development known as career consolidation. During **career consolidation**, which begins between 20 and 40, young adults become centred on their careers. Vaillant based his conclusion on a comprehensive longitudinal study of male graduates of Harvard, begun when they were freshmen in the 1930s (Vaillant, 1977; Vaillant and Vaillant, 1990).

In their early twenties, the men tended to be influenced by their parents' authority. But in their late twenties and early thirties, they started to act with greater autonomy. They married, had children, and began to focus on their careers—the period of career consolidation.

Vaillant draws a relatively uninspiring portrait of people in this stage. His participants worked very hard as they climbed the corporate ladder. They tended to be rule-followers conforming to the norms of their professions. Rather than showing the independence and questioning that they had displayed in college, they threw themselves unquestioningly into their work.

Vaillant argues that work plays such an important role that the career consolidation stage should be seen as an addition to Erikson's intimacy-versus-isolation stage of psychosocial identity. In Vaillant's view, career concerns supplant the focus on intimacy, and the career consolidation stage marks a bridge between intimacy-versus-isolation and generativity-versus-stagnation. (Generativity refers to an individual's contribution to society, as we discuss later.)

The reaction to Vaillant's viewpoint has been mixed. Critics point out that Vaillant's sample, although relatively large, comprised a highly restricted, unusually bright group of men. Furthermore, societal norms have changed considerably since the 1930s, and people's views of the importance of work might have shifted. Finally, the lack of women in the sample and the fact that there have been major changes in the role of work in *women's* lives make Vaillant's conclusions even less generalizable.

Still, it is hard to dispute the importance of work in most people's lives, and research suggests that it makes up a significant part of both men's and women's identity—if for no other reason than it occupies so much of their time (Deaux et al., 1995).

Picking an Occupation: Choosing Life's Work

Some people know from childhood what they want to do for a living; for others, career choice is a matter of chance. Many of us fall somewhere in the middle.

Ginzberg's Career Choice Theory. According to Eli Ginzberg (1972), people typically move through stages in choosing a career. The first stage is the **fantasy period**, which lasts until around age 11. During the fantasy period, people make and discard career choices without regard to skills, abilities, or available job opportunities. A child may decide she wants to be a rock star—despite being unable to carry a tune.

During the **tentative period**, which spans adolescence, people begin to think more practically about the requirements of various jobs and their own abilities and interests. They also consider how well a particular occupation might satisfy their personal values and goals.

Finally, in early adulthood, people enter the **realistic period**, in which young adults explore specific career options either through actual experience on the job or through training for a profession. After initially exploring what they might do, people begin to narrow their choices and eventually commit to a particular career.

Critics have charged that Ginzberg's theory oversimplifies the process of choosing a career. Because it was based on subjects from middle socioeconomic levels, his theory might overstate the choices available to people in lower socioeconomic levels. Furthermore, the ages associated with the various stages might be too rigid. For instance, a person who begins to work immediately after high school most likely makes serious career decisions earlier than a person who attends university. In addition, economic factors cause many people to change careers at different points in their adult lives.

Holland's Personality Type Theory. Other theories of career choice emphasize how personality affects career decisions. According to John Holland, certain personality types match particularly well with certain careers. If the correspondence between personality and career is

> **career consolidation** a stage that is entered between the ages of 20 and 40, when young adults become centred on their careers
>
> **fantasy period** according to Ginzberg, the period, lasting until about age 11, when career choices are made, and discarded, without regard to skills, abilities, or available job opportunities
>
> **tentative period** the second stage of Ginzberg's theory, which spans adolescence, when people begin to think in pragmatic terms about the requirements of various jobs and how their own abilities might fit with those jobs
>
> **realistic period** the third stage of Ginzberg's theory, which occurs in early adulthood, when people begin to explore specific career options, either through actual experience on the job or through training for a profession, and then narrow their choices and make a commitment

According to one theory, people move through a series of life stages in choosing a career. The first stage is the fantasy period, which lasts until a person is around 11 years old.

good, people will enjoy their careers more and be more likely to stay in them; but if the match is poor, they will be unhappy and more likely to shift to other careers (Holland, 1973, 1987; Gottfredson and Holland, 1990).

According to Holland, six personality types are important in career choice:

- Realistic. These are down-to-earth, practical problem-solvers, physically strong but with mediocre social skills. They make good farmers, labourers, and truck drivers.
- Intellectual. Intellectual types are oriented toward the theoretical and abstract. Although not particularly good with people, they are well suited to careers in math and science.
- Social. People with this personality type have strong verbal skills and are good with people. They make good salespeople, teachers, and counsellors.
- Conventional. Conventional types prefer highly structured tasks. They make good clerks, secretaries, and bank tellers.
- Enterprising. These are risk-takers and take-charge types. They are good leaders and can be particularly effective as managers or politicians.
- Artistic. These individuals use art to express themselves and often prefer the world of art to interactions with people. They are best suited to occupations involving the arts.

Holland's theory suffers from a central flaw: Not everyone fits neatly into personality types. Furthermore, clear exceptions exist, with people holding jobs that are "wrong" for their personality type. Still, the basics of the theory have been validated, and they form the foundation of several of the "job quizzes" that people take to see what occupations they might be right for (Randahl, 1991).

Gender and Career Choices: Women's Work

WANTED: Full-time employee for small family firm. DUTIES: Including but not limited to general cleaning, cooking, gardening, laundry, ironing and mending, purchasing, bookkeeping and money management. Child care may also be required. HOURS: Avg. 55/wk but standby duty required 24 hours/day, 7 days/wk. Extra workload on holidays. SALARY AND BENEFITS: No salary, but food, clothing, and shelter provided at employer's discretion; job security and benefits depend on continued goodwill of employer. No vacation. No retirement plan. No opportunities for advancement. REQUIREMENTS: No previous experience necessary, can learn on the job. Only women need apply. (Unger and Crawford, 1992, p. 446)

A generation or two ago, many women entering early adulthood assumed that this admittedly exaggerated job description matched the position that they would occupy: housewife. Even women who sought work outside the home were relegated to certain professions. For example, employment ads in a 1945 Canadian newspaper featured job ads that specified not only gender, but age and sometimes marital status. The men's ads included such professions as police officer, construction worker, and legal counsel; the women's ads were for cleaners, secretaries, teachers, cashiers, and librarians.

The breakdown of jobs reflected society's view of what the two genders were best suited for. Traditionally, women were considered most appropriate for **communal professions**, occupations associated with relationships, such as nursing. In contrast, men were perceived as best suited for agentic professions. **Agentic professions** are associated with getting things accomplished, such as carpentry. It is probably no coincidence that communal professions typically have lower status and pay than agentic professions (Eagly and Steffen, 1984, 1986; Hattery, 2000).

> ⊙ **From a social worker's perspective:** How does the division of jobs into communal and agentic relate to traditional views of male–female differences?

Although discrimination based on gender is far less blatant today than it was several decades ago—it is now illegal, for instance, to advertise a position specifically for one gender—remnants of gender prejudice persist. Women are less likely to be found in traditionally male-dominated professions such as engineering and computer programming, and men applying for jobs as teachers or child-care staff are sometimes blatantly excluded (and judged harshly).

communal professions occupations that are associated with relationships

agentic professions occupations that are associated with getting things accomplished

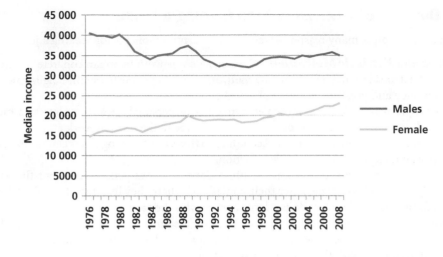

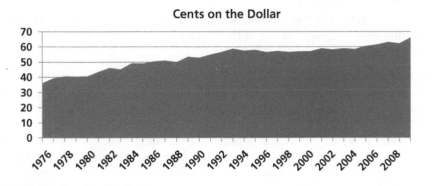

FIGURE 7-12 The Gender–Wage Gap
Women's median earnings relative to men's have improved since 1976, but still women earn 66¢ for every dollar earned by men overall (83¢ hourly).
Source: Adapted from Statistics Canada, CANSIM table 202-0409.

As shown in Figure 7-12, despite significant progress in the last 40 years, women's earnings still lag behind those of men. In fact, women in many professions earn significantly less than men in identical jobs; overall women earn 66 cents for every dollar earned by men, and even comparing hourly wages, women earn 83 cents (Frome et al., 2006; Statistics Canada, 2010b; CANSIM table 202-0409).

More women than ever are working outside the home, so why do they earn less? One factor is that women are far more likely to work part-time: Seven out of ten part-time workers are women. Another factor is that women continue to be overrepresented in lower-paying, traditionally female occupations. But increasing numbers of women are employed in business, medicine, and dentistry (Ferrao and Williams, 2011). Why might men and women in the same profession earn different incomes? There are several potential factors, including imbalances in the strain (or perceived strain) of childrearing that might lead to promotions for men over women, as well as experience with negotiation that might leave women short-changed from the very beginning of their careers. For example, female bus drivers are more apt to have part-time school bus routes, while men hold better-paying full-time routes in cities. Female pharmacists are more likely to work in hospitals, while men work in higher-paying jobs in retail stores (Crawford and Unger, 2004).

Women and minorities in high-status, visible, professional roles often hit what has come to be called the "glass ceiling." The glass ceiling is an invisible barrier in an organization that prevents individuals from being promoted beyond a certain level. It operates subtly, and often the people responsible for it are unaware of how their actions perpetuate discrimination (Goodman et al., 2003; Stockdale et al., 2004).

extrinsic motivation motivation that drives people to obtain tangible rewards, such as money and prestige

intrinsic motivation motivation that causes people to work for their own enjoyment, not for the rewards work might bring

status the evaluation of a role or person by other relevant members of a group or society

Why Do People Work? More than Earning a Living

Young adults express many reasons—well beyond earning money—for seeking a job.

Intrinsic and Extrinsic Motivation. Certainly, people work to obtain concrete rewards, or because of extrinsic motivation. **Extrinsic motivation** drives people to obtain tangible rewards, such as money and prestige (Singer et al., 1993).

But people also work for their own enjoyment—for personal rewards, or **intrinsic motivation**. People in many Western societies tend to subscribe to the Puritan work ethic, the notion that work is important in and of itself. According to this view, working is a meaningful act that brings psychological well-being and satisfaction.

Work also contributes to personal identity. Consider what people say about themselves when they first meet someone. After their names and where they live, they typically tell what they do for a living. What they do is a large part of who they are.

Work can also be central to people's social lives, a source of friends and activities. Work relationships can easily become personal friendships. In addition, work brings social obligations, such as dinner with the boss or the annual year-end party.

Finally, the kind of work people do helps to determine **status**, the evaluation by society of the role a person plays. Many jobs are associated with a particular status. For instance, physicians and professors are near the top of the status hierarchy, while ushers and shoe-shiners occupy the bottom.

Satisfaction on the Job. Status affects job satisfaction: The higher the status of the job, the more satisfied people tend to be. Furthermore, the status of the job of the major wage-earner can affect the status of the other members of the family (Green, 1995; Schieman et al., 2003).

Of course, status isn't everything: Worker satisfaction depends on a number of factors, not least the nature of the job itself. For example, consider the example of Patricia Alford, who worked at an insurance company. Her job consisted of entering data into a computer 9 hours each day except for two 15-minute breaks and an hour off for lunch. She never knew how much she was earning because her salary depended on how many insurance claims she entered each day. The pay standards were so complicated that her pay varied from $217 to $400 a week, giving her a weekly surprise at paycheck time (Booth, 1987; Ting, 1997).

Other people who work at computers are monitored on a minute-by-minute basis; supervisors can consistently see how many keystrokes they are entering. In some firms in which workers use the telephone for sales or to take customer orders, supervisors monitor their conversations. Many employers monitor or restrict workers' Internet use and email. Not surprisingly, such forms of job stress produce worker dissatisfaction (MacDonald, 2003).

Job satisfaction is higher when workers have input into the nature of their jobs and feel their ideas and opinions are valued. They also prefer jobs that offer variety over those that require only a few repeated skills. Finally, the more influence employees have over others, either directly as supervisors or more informally, the greater their job satisfaction (Peterson and Wilson, 2004; Thompson and Prottas, 2006).

Choosing a Career

Becoming an Informed Consumer of Development

One of the greatest challenges of early adulthood is making a decision that will have lifelong implications: the choice of a career. Although most people can be happy in a variety of jobs, choosing among the options can be daunting. Here are some guidelines for facing the career question.

- Systematically evaluate your choices. Libraries contain a wealth of career information and most colleges and universities have helpful career centres.

- Know yourself. Evaluate your strengths and weaknesses, perhaps by completing a questionnaire on your interests, skills, and values at a college career centre.

- Create a "balance sheet," listing the gains and losses from a particular profession. First list gains and losses for yourself and then for others, such as family members. Next, write down your

projected self-approval or self-disapproval from the potential career—and the projected social approval or disapproval you are likely to receive from others.

- "Try out" different careers through paid or unpaid internships. By seeing a job first-hand, interns get a sense of what an occupation is truly like.

- Remember that there are no permanent mistakes. People today increasingly change careers in early adulthood and even beyond. No one should feel locked into a decision made earlier in life. As we have seen throughout this book, people develop substantially over the course of their lives.

- It is reasonable to expect that shifting values, interests, abilities, and life circumstances might make a different career more appropriate later in life than the one chosen during early adulthood.

REVIEW, CHECK, AND APPLY

REVIEW

- Choosing a career is an important step in early adulthood.

- Gender stereotypes are changing, but women still experience subtle prejudice in career choices, roles, and wages.

- People work because of both extrinsic and intrinsic motivation factors.

CHECK YOURSELF

1. According to Vaillant, during young adulthood, individuals become centred on their careers. This stage is known as _____.

   a. career consolidation
   b. life comprehension
   c. personal attainment
   d. realism

2. Which of the following is *not* one of the six personality types Holland indicates is important when it comes to career choice?

   a. social
   b. realistic
   c. intellectual
   d. enterprising

3. Even though there are now more job opportunities for women in many fields, women are often not

afforded the same opportunities for advancement within those fields. Specifically, many women are not promoted because they have hit what is known as the _____—an invisible barrier to advancement.

APPLYING LIFESPAN DEVELOPMENT

- If Vaillant's study were performed today on women, in what ways do you think the results would be similar to or different from those of the original study?

Answers: 1) a; 2) b; 3) glass ceiling

Putting It All Together
Early Adulthood

BELLA ARNOFF AND THEODORE CHOI, the couple we encountered in the chapter opener, face many developmental issues typical of young adults. They have to consider the questions of health and aging, and the unspoken admission that they do not have all the time in the world. They have to look at their relationship and decide whether to take what society and nearly all their friends consider the next logical step: marriage. They have to face the question of children and career, and the possibility of giving up the luxury of being a two-earner family. They even have to reconsider Theodore's intention to continue his education. Fortunately they have each other to help deal with the stress of this weighty combination of questions and decisions—and a considerable developmental arsenal of useful skills and abilities.

MODULE **7.1** Physical Development

- Bella and Theodore's bodies and senses are at their peak, with their physical development nearly complete **(pp. 292–293).**

- During this period the couple will increasingly need to pay attention to diet and exercise **(pp. 293–294).**

- Because they face so many important decisions, Bella and Theodore are prime candidates for stress **(pp. 297–299).**

MODULE **7.2** Cognitive Development

- Bella and Theodore are in Schaie's achieving stage, confronting major life issues, including career and marriage **(p. 304).**

- They are able to apply postformal thought to the complex issues they face **(p. 304).**

- While dealing with major life events can cause stress, it can also foster cognitive growth in both of them **(p. 309).**

- Theodore's desire to return to university is not unusual today, when schools are serving a diversity of students, including many older students **(p. 311).**

- Bella and Theodore have reached a time when love and friendship relationships are of major importance **(p. 319).**

- The couple are likely to be experiencing a combination of intimacy, passion, and decision/commitment **(p. 321).**

- Bella and Theodore have been cohabiting and are now exploring marriage as a relationship option **(pp. 326–328).**

- Bella and Theodore are not unusual in thinking about marriage and children—decisions with major implications for the relationship. **(pp. 329–332)**

- The couple must also decide how to handle the shift from two careers to one, at least temporarily—a decision that has far more than just financial implications. **(p. 330)**

What would a HEALTH-CARE PROVIDER do?

- Given that Bella and Theodore are young, in good health, and physically fit, what strategies would you advise them to pursue to stay that way?

  HINT Review pages 292–294.

  What's your response?

What would a CAREER COUNSELLOR do?

- Assuming Bella and Theodore decide to have children, what advice would you give them about handling the major expenses they face and the impact of children on their careers? Would you advise one of them to put his or her career on hold and pursue childrearing full-time? If so, how would you counsel them to decide whose career should be put on hold?

  HINT Review pages 329–331.

  What's your response?

What would YOU do?

- If you were a friend of Bella and Theodore, what factors would you advise them to consider as they contemplate moving from cohabitation to marriage? Would your advice be the same if only Bella or only Theodore asked you?

  HINT Review pages 326–328.

  What's your response?

What would an EDUCATOR do?

- A friend of Theodore's has told him that he would be "a fish out of water" if he went back to graduate school such a long time after getting his undergraduate degree. Do you agree? Would you advise Theodore to pursue his graduate school studies right away, before he gets too old, or to wait until his life settles down?

  HINT Review pages 309–313.

  What's your response?

Middle Adulthood

A t 50, Leigh Ryan is considered "youthful" by her friends. Still as tall and as slim as she was in college, she keeps fit with regular dance workouts. Dance and gardening—both lifelong loves—reduce the stress of balancing two jobs, school, and family life.

Just as many of her friends are talking about retirement, Leigh has closed the knit design business she operated for 22 years. She has taken a full-time position as director of a small non-profit literacy project, and at the same time has begun taking classes toward a doctoral degree in sociology. Though she had to scramble to learn about the populace the literacy project serves, her expertise in management made her the top choice for the job.

Leigh also continues to teach two dance classes a week at the local university. "It makes life a bit crazy some days," she concedes. No matter how busy life gets, though, Leigh still makes time on weekends to entertain her friends, usually by hosting potlucks. "I've always been outgoing," she says. "People recharge my batteries. They give me energy."

Leigh's situation at midlife seems almost perfect. She's challenging her mind with a new course of study. She has a job that makes her feel she is giving

MODULE **8.1** Physical Development in Middle Adulthood

Do men experience the equivalent of menopause? see page 342

MODULE **8.2** Cognitive Development in Middle Adulthood

Does intelligence decline in adulthood? see page 354

something back to the community. Her health is good, thanks to regular exercise and good eating habits. But her life is hardly perfect.

"I just don't feel a connection to my husband anymore," she says. "We haven't been close in years, but I didn't realize how far we'd drifted apart until my older daughter left home." Leigh is not yet sure if she'll seek a divorce, but more and more of her future plans seem not to include her husband. Ultimately, she'd like to move back to Montreal where she has family, but it's a move her husband has no interest in. "If it comes to Montreal or marriage, I'm choosing Montreal," she says. "But I'll wait to see what happens when my youngest leaves home next year."

Middle adulthood is a time of significant transitions. Grown children leave home. People change the way they view their careers. Sometimes they change careers entirely, as Leigh did. Marriages undergo re-evaluation. Often, couples find this a period of strengthened ties as the "empty nest" leaves them free for uninterrupted intimacy. But sometimes they divorce. Middle age is also a period of deepening roots. Family and friends ascend in importance as career ambitions begin to take a backseat. And there is more time for leisure activities.

In this chapter, we first look at the physical changes of middle adulthood and how people cope with them. Then we consider sexuality and menopause and debate the use of hormone replacement drugs for women. We also look at health issues, especially heart disease and cancer, which become increasingly of concern in midlife.

Next we consider the changing intellectual abilities of middle-aged adults, and ask the question: Does intelligence decline over time? We investigate

MODULE **8.3** Social and Personality Development in Middle Adulthood

The midlife crisis: reality or myth? see page 361

MyVirtualLife

Many adults in this stage of life are going through the same changes that Leigh is.

Log onto MyDevelopmentLab to watch a video of several adults speaking about their experiences in middle adulthood.

various types of intelligence and look at how each is affected by the aging process. We also look at memory. Does it decline in middle age, and what are some strategies for strengthening recall?

Finally, we look at social development and examine what changes and what remains stable over time in an adult's personality. We consider the evidence for the so-called midlife crisis and discuss how family relationships change in the face of changed circumstances. We end by considering work and leisure in middle age, examining how people are spending their increased leisure time.

MODULE 8.1 Physical Development in Middle Adulthood

Fit for Life

Jennifer Zinck of Timmins became a fitness instructor at the age of 43. The gruelling training required for certification is nearly a full-time job in itself, but Jennifer managed it while working full-time in the nuclear medicine department of the local hospital and balancing home life with her husband and two children.

I had been active and athletic as a kid and even into most of my adult years. Then I finished school, got a job, moved provinces, got married, and started having kids. Phew. And that is when I started to become soft. Boo. Years passed and pounds crept on. I finally came to the proverbial "last straw" about three years ago. I ended up in a weight-loss clinic looking for help. What I found was a little "spitfire" named Lisa who was running a boot camp twice a week. She pushed me and inspired me to give 110 percent in every workout. I hated her twice a week for an hour, and loved her all the rest of the time! It was great, but I wanted more. A friend told me about a spin class she was taking. So I went and immediately fell in love with the pounding music, the encouraging instructor, and the absolute high I felt after crawling off the bike, drenched in sweat! What an absolute rush!

At that point I was just enjoying myself. I never saw myself as an instructor. I don't like being in front of crowds. I'm a team player, not a team leader, and why would anyone be inspired by me? But Lisa pushed me to take the instructor training. I thought she was crazy! So training weekend arrived. I have NEVER done anything so physically demanding in my entire life! It ran from 8:00 a.m. to 6:00 p.m. on Saturday and Sunday. Each day we rode the one-hour class about four times. It was intense, sometimes overwhelming, and yet I just kept telling myself, Get through it and see what happens.

Did I mention that I was the oldest in this group of 11 by about 9 years? Yeah. There were lots of much younger, much slimmer, people in there, and I held my own on the bike. We all worked so hard and knew that we would get a chance to teach if we passed, so there was no competition, only loads of support. It was truly amazing. We all passed the weekend, which meant we could go on to the three-month certification training. It was an intense three months. If I wasn't teaching the class, I was riding in the class of one of the other instructors in-training. I was on the bike at least every day, and sometimes I would ride twice on the weekends. There was no way I was going through all this and not getting certified. I can honestly say I have never, ever worked so hard for anything in my life, and to go through all the training, well, it was a dream come true.

The satisfaction of putting that much effort into one thing and staying with it—because along the way I was questioning why I was doing this—is beyond words! When I get on my bike in the front of those 25 or more people, I see the looks that some of the younger people give me—and that's OK, because I know by the end of the class they will be looking at me in a whole new light. I love teaching my spin class. I love being able to encourage people to go outside their comfort zone for an hour, to try something new, and to push my regulars harder each time so we can improve our health and fitness together.

Did I ever in my wildest dreams figure I could or would be a spin instructor at 44 years of age? Nope. But look at me now! Oh, and by the way, I am the team leader, and all my other instructors are at least 10 years my junior.

Jennifer Zinck's enthusiasm for her fitness classes illustrates the current revolution in midlife physical activity. People are joining health clubs in record numbers in midlife, seeking to remain healthy and agile as they age.

It is in middle adulthood, roughly the period from age 40 to 65, that people often first notice and feel the effects of aging. Their bodies and, to some extent, their cognitive abilities begin to change in unwelcome ways. Looking at the physical, cognitive, and social changes of midlife, however, we see this is also a time when many people reach the height of their capabilities, when they are engaged in shaping their lives as never before.

We begin the module by considering physical development. We consider changes in height, weight, and strength, and discuss the subtle declines in various senses.

We also look at sexuality in middle adulthood. We examine the effects of change in hormone production for both men and women—particularly, menopause—and the various therapies available to ease this transition. We consider, too, the role that attitude plays.

We then examine both health and illness in midlife, with special attention to two major health problems—heart disease and cancer.

Physical Development

LO1   What physical changes affect people in middle adulthood?

LEARNING OBJECTIVES

Soon after turning 40, Sharon Boker-Tov noticed that it took longer to bounce back from minor illnesses such as colds and the flu. Then she noticed changes in her eyesight: She needed more light to read fine print, and she had to adjust how far she held newspapers from her face in order to read them easily. Finally, she couldn't deny that the grey strands in her hair, which had first appeared in her late twenties, were becoming a virtual forest.

Physical Transitions: The Gradual Change in the Body's Capabilities

In middle adulthood, people become aware of the gradual changes that aging brings in their bodies. Some of these changes are the result of senescence, or naturally occurring declines. Other changes, however, are related to lifestyle choices such as diet, exercise, smoking, and alcohol or drug use. As we'll see, lifestyle choices can have a major impact on people's physical, and even cognitive, fitness in midlife.

Although physical changes occur throughout life, they take on new significance in midlife, particularly in Western cultures that highly value a youthful appearance. The psychological significance of aging may far exceed the relatively minor and gradual changes a person experiences. Sharon Boker-Tov had gray hairs in her twenties, but in her forties they multiplied to an extent she could not ignore. She was no longer young.

People's emotional reactions to midlife's physical changes depend in part on their self-concepts. When self-image is tied closely to one's physical attributes—as it is for very athletic men and women or those who are physically quite attractive—middle adulthood can be particularly difficult, as the changes the mirror reveals signal aging and mortality as well as a loss of physical attractiveness. On the other hand, because most people's self-concepts are not so closely tied to physical attributes, middle-aged adults generally report no less satisfaction with their body images than younger adults (Eitel, 2003).

Physical appearance often plays a significant role in how women see themselves. This is particularly true in Western cultures, where women face strong societal pressures to retain a youthful look. Society applies a double standard to men and women regarding appearance: Older women tend to be viewed in unflattering terms, while older men are frequently seen as attractively "mature" (Andreoni and Petrie, 2008).

👁 **Watch** on **mydevelopmentlab**

To learn more about physical changes during middle adulthood, go to MyDevelopmentLab.

Height, Weight, and Strength: The Benchmarks of Change

Most people reach their maximum height in their twenties and remain close to that height until around age 55. People then begin a "settling" process in which the bones attached to the spinal column become less dense. Although the loss of height is very slow, women average a 5 cm decline and men a 2.5 cm decline over the rest of the lifespan (Rossman, 1977).

Beginning at or around the age of 40, visual acuity—the ability to discern fine spatial detail—begins to decline. Most people begin to suffer from presbyopia, a decline in near vision.

Women are more prone to this decline because they are at greater risk of osteoporosis. **Osteoporosis**, a condition in which the bones become brittle, fragile, and thin, is often caused by a lack of calcium in the diet. Although it has a genetic component, osteoporosis is one aspect of aging that can be affected by lifestyle choices. Women—and men—can reduce the risk of osteoporosis by eating a calcium-rich diet (calcium is found in milk, yogourt, cheese, and other dairy products) and by exercising regularly (Prince et al., 1991; Alvarez-Leon et al., 2006; Schoenmaker et al., 2006).

Body fat tends to increase in middle adulthood. Even those who have always been slim might begin to gain weight. Because height is not increasing, and actually may be declining, these weight gains increase the incidence of obesity. This gain can often be avoided; lifestyle choices play a major role. People who exercise regularly tend to avoid obesity, as do those who live in cultures where life is more active than it is in many Western cultures.

Declines in strength accompany height and weight changes. Strength gradually decreases, particularly in the back and leg muscles. By age 60, people average a 10 percent loss of their maximum strength. Still, such a loss is relatively minor, and most people are easily able to compensate for it (Spence, 1989). Again, lifestyle choices matter. Regular exercise tends to make people feel stronger and more able to compensate for any losses.

The Senses: The Sights and Sounds of Middle Age

The vision changes Sharon Boker-Tov experienced are so common that reading glasses and bifocals have become a stereotypical emblem of middle age. Like Sharon, most people notice changes in the sensitivity not only of their eyes but also of other sense organs. All the organs seem to shift at about the same rate, but the changes are particularly marked in vision and hearing.

Vision. Starting at around age 40, *visual acuity*—the ability to discern fine spatial detail in both close and distant objects—begins to decline. The shape of the eye's lens changes and its elasticity deteriorates, which makes it harder to focus images sharply onto the retina. The lens becomes less transparent, so less light passes through the eye (Pitts, 1982; DiGiovanna, 1994).

A nearly universal change in midlife is the loss of near vision, called **presbyopia**. Even people who have never needed glasses or contact lenses find themselves holding print at an increasing distance in order to bring it into focus. Eventually, they need reading glasses. For those who were already near-sighted, presbyopia might require bifocals or two sets of glasses (Kalsi et al., 2001; Koopmans and Kooijman, 2006).

Midlife brings other vision changes. Depth perception, distance perception, and the ability to see in three dimensions all decline. The loss of elasticity in the lens also impairs people's ability to adapt to darkness, making it more difficult to navigate a dark room (Artal et al., 1993; Spear, 1993).

Although normal aging brings its own changes in vision, in some cases disease is the culprit. Glaucoma is one of the most frequent eye problems and, if left untreated, it can lead to blindness. **Glaucoma** occurs when pressure in the fluid of the eye increases, either because the fluid cannot drain properly or because too much is produced. Around 1 to 2 percent of people over age 40 are afflicted (Wilson, 1989).

Initially, the increased pressure may constrict the neurons involved in peripheral vision and lead to tunnel vision. Ultimately, the pressure can become so high that all nerve cells are constricted, which causes complete blindness. Fortunately, with early detection, glaucoma can be treated. Medication can reduce the pressure, as can surgery to restore normal drainage of eye fluid (Plosker and Keam, 2006).

Hearing. Hearing declines in acuity in midlife, though the changes tend to be less evident than changes affecting vision.

Environmental factors cause some hearing losses. People who work near loud noises—such as airplane mechanics and construction workers—are more apt to suffer debilitating and permanent hearing loss.

Many changes are simply related to aging. Age brings a loss of *cilia* or *hair cells* in the inner ear; these transmit neural messages to the brain when vibrations bend them. Like the lens of the eye, the eardrum becomes less elastic with age, reducing sensitivity to sound (Wiley et al., 2005).

The ability to hear high-pitched, high-frequency sounds usually degrades first, a problem called **presbycusis**. About 12% of people between 45 and 65 suffer from presbycusis. Men

osteoporosis a condition, often brought about by a lack of calcium in the diet, in which the bones become brittle, fragile, and thin

presbyopia a nearly universal change in eyesight during middle adulthood that results in some loss of near vision

glaucoma a condition in which pressure in the fluid of the eye increases, either because the fluid cannot drain properly or because too much fluid is produced

presbycusis loss of the ability to hear sounds of high frequency

are more prone to hearing loss than women, starting at around age 55. People with hearing problems can also have trouble identifying the direction and origin of a sound, a process called *sound localization* (Schneider, 1997; Veras and Mattos, 2007).

Declines in hearing do not markedly affect most people in middle age. Many people compensate for any losses relatively easily—by asking people to speak up, turning up the volume of a television set, or paying closer attention to what others are saying.

Reaction Time: Not-So-Slowing Down

One common concern is that people slow down once they reach middle adulthood. Such a worry is not valid in most cases. Reaction time does increase (that is, it takes longer to react to a stimulus), but usually the increase is mild and hardly noticeable. For instance, reaction time in responding to a loud noise increases by about 20 percent from age 20 to 60. Tasks requiring the coordination of various skills—such as driving a car—show less of an increase. Still, it takes more time to move the foot from the gas pedal to the brake when a driver faces an emergency situation. Changes in the speed at which the nervous system processes nerve impulses increases reaction time (Nobuyuki, 1997; Roggeveen et al., 2007).

Despite increased reaction time, middle-aged drivers have fewer accidents than younger ones, partly because they tend to be more careful and take fewer risks. Moreover, older drivers' greater experience benefits them. The minor slowing of reaction time is compensated for by their expertise (MacDonald et al., 2003; Marczinski et al., 2003).

Lifestyle choices can retard the process of slowing down. An active exercise program counteracts the effects of aging, improving health, muscle strength, and endurance (see Figure 8-1). Developmentalists would agree: "Use it or lose it" (Conn et al., 2003).

The advantages of exercise include

Muscle System

Slower decline in energy molecules, muscle cell thickness, number of muscle cells, muscle thickness, muscle mass, muscle strength, blood supply, speed of movement, stamina

Slower increase in fat and fibers, reaction time, recovery time, development of muscle soreness

Nervous System

Slower decline in processing impulses by the central nervous system

Slower increase in variations in speed of motor neuron impulses

Circulatory System

Maintenance of lower levels of LDLs and higher HDL/cholesterol and HDL/LDL ratios

Decreased risk of high blood pressure, atherosclerosis, heart attack, stroke

Skeletal System

Slower decline in bone minerals

Decreased risk of fractures and osteoporosis

Ψ **Psychological Benefits**

Enhanced mood

Feelings of well-being

Reduced stress

FIGURE 8-1 The Benefits of Exercise

Many benefits are derived from maintaining a high level of physical activity throughout life.

Source: From "The Benefits of Exercise," from A. G. DiGiovanna, *Human Aging: Biological Perspectives.*
Copyright © 1994 The McGraw-Hill Companies, Inc. Reprinted with permission.

REVIEW, CHECK, AND APPLY

REVIEW

- People in middle adulthood experience gradual changes in physical characteristics and appearance.
- The acuity of the senses, particularly vision and hearing, and speed of reaction declines slightly during middle age.
- Weight gain—commonly referred to as "middle-age spread"—can be controlled through regular exercise and a healthy diet.

CHECK YOURSELF

1. Starting at around age 40, visual acuity, the ability to discern fine spatial detail in both close and distant objects, begins to decline.
   - True
   - False

2. _____ occurs when pressure of the fluid in the eye increases, either because the fluid cannot drain properly or because too much is produced.

3. Although general reaction time increases in middle age, reaction time involving complex tasks such as driving a car shows less of an increase.
   - True
   - False

APPLYING LIFESPAN DEVELOPMENT

- Would you rather fly on an airplane with a middle-aged pilot or a young one? Why?

Answers: 1) True; 2) Glaucoma; 3) True

Sexuality in Middle Adulthood

LEARNING OBJECTIVES

LO2 What changes occur in sexuality for midlife men and women?

At age 51, Elaine was really looking forward to her postmenopausal life. Her youngest child had just left home to study art, and she had recently reduced her work schedule to a comfortable 30 hours a week. She envisioned the year to come as an opportunity for a "second honeymoon" with her husband, Greg, with no need for contraceptives or fears of becoming pregnant.

Her imagined honeymoon quickly evaporated in a heat wave of hot flashes and night sweats. Though Elaine recognized these as normal symptoms of menopause, she was having to change her clothing three or more times a day. And she was having more headaches. Her doctor prescribed hormone therapy to replace the estrogen she was losing through menopause. As she was not a likely candidate for any of the drug's negative side effects, she took her doctor's recommendation. The hormone therapy eased her symptoms and revitalized her spirits. Four months later, she and Greg booked a month's romantic getaway in Greece.

Although interest in sex remains fairly high for many people in middle adulthood, as Elaine's story illustrates, the physical changes associated with aging, such as menopause for women, can throw a curve ball at romance. We will look at some of the factors that affect men's and women's sexuality in midlife, and the roles that both attitude and prescription drugs can play in alleviating some of the problems commonly associated with this life stage.

Sexuality continues to be a vital part of most couples' lives in middle adulthood.

The Ongoing Sexuality of Middle Age

The frequency of sexual intercourse declines with age, but sexual pleasure remains a vital part of most middle-aged adults' lives. About half of men and women age 45 to 59 report having sexual intercourse once a week or more. Sex also remains an important activity for middle-aged gay and lesbian couples (Michael et al., 1994; Gabbay and Wahler, 2002; Cain et al., 2003; Kimmel and Sang, 2003; Duplassie and Daniluk, 2007).

For many, midlife brings a sexual enjoyment and freedom that was missing earlier. With their children grown and away from home, married couples have more time for uninterrupted sex. Women who have gone through menopause no longer fear pregnancy or need to use birth control (Sherwin, 1991; Lamont, 1997).

Both men and women can face challenges to their sexuality in midlife. A man often needs more time to achieve an erection, and it takes longer after an orgasm to have another. The volume of fluid that is ejaculated declines, as does the production of *testosterone*, the male sex hormone (Hyde and Delameter, 2003).

For women, the vaginal walls thin and grow less elastic. The vagina begins to shrink and its entrance becomes compressed, which can make intercourse painful. For most women, though, the changes do not reduce sexual pleasure. Those women who do find intercourse less enjoyable can seek help from an increasing array of drugs, such as topical creams and testosterone patches, designed to increase sexual pleasure (Laumann et al., 1999; Freedman and Ellison, 2004).

The Female Climacteric and Menopause. At around age 45, women enter a period known as the climacteric, which lasts for 15 to 20 years. The **female climacteric** marks the transition that ends the childbearing years.

The most notable sign of this transition is menopause. **Menopause** is the cessation of menstruation. Menstrual periods begin to occur irregularly and less frequently during a two-year period starting at around age 47 or 48, although this may begin as early as age 40 or as late as age 60. Menopause is completed when a woman passes a year without a menstrual period.

Menopause is important because it marks the end of a woman's natural fertility (although eggs implanted in a postmenopausal woman can produce a pregnancy). In addition, estrogen and progesterone levels—the female sex hormones—begin to drop (Schwenkhagen, 2007).

These changes in hormone production can produce a variety of symptoms, although they vary significantly for individuals. One of the most prevalent symptoms is "hot flashes," in which women experience a surge of heat above the waist. A woman might get red and begin to sweat when a hot flash occurs. Afterward, she may feel chilled. Some women have hot flashes several times a day; others, not at all.

During menopause, headaches, feelings of dizziness, heart palpitations, and aching joints are relatively common, though not universal. In one survey, only half of the women reported having hot flashes, and only about one-tenth of all women experience severe distress during menopause. Many women—perhaps as many as half—have no significant symptoms at all (Hyde and DeLamater, 2003; Grady, 2006).

female climacteric the period that marks the transition from being able to bear children to being unable to do so

menopause the cessation of menstruation

From Research to Practice

The Dilemma of Hormone Replacement Therapy: No Easy Answer

A few years ago, physicians would have prescribed regular doses of a hormone replacement drug for hot flashes and other uncomfortable symptoms caused by the onset of menopause.

For millions of women who experienced such difficulties, it was a solution that worked. In *hormone replacement therapy* (HRT), estrogen and progesterone are administered to alleviate the worst menopause symptoms. HRT reduces a variety of problems, such as hot flashes and loss of skin elasticity. HRT may also reduce coronary heart disease by changing the ratio of "good" cholesterol to "bad" cholesterol. And HRT decreases the thinning of the bones related to osteoporosis, which poses a problem for many people in late adulthood (Palan et al., 2005; McCauley, 2007; Birkhäuser et al., 2008).

Some studies also show that HRT reduces the risks of stroke and colon cancer. Estrogen might even slow the mental deterioration in Alzheimer's patients, and some research shows that it improves memory and cognitive performance in healthy women. Finally, increased estrogen might lead to a greater sex drive (Sarrel, 2000; O'Hara et al., 2005; Stephens et al., 2006; Schwenkhagen, 2007).

Although hormone replacement therapy might sound like a cure-all, in fact, since it became popular in the early 1990s, its risks have been well known. For instance, it seemed to increase the risk of breast cancer and blood clots. It was thought, though, that the benefits outweighed the risks. All that changed after 2002, when a large study conducted by the Women's Health Initiative determined that the long-term risks of HRT outweighed the benefits. Women taking a combination of estrogen and progestin were found to be at higher risk for breast cancer, stroke, pulmonary embolism, and heart disease. Increased risk of stroke and pulmonary embolism were later found to be associated with estrogen-alone therapy (Parker-Pope, 2003).

These results led to a profound rethinking of the benefits of HRT, calling into question the wisdom that HRT could protect against chronic disease. Many women stopped taking hormone replacement drugs, choosing instead to use alternative herbal and dietary therapies for menopausal symptoms; unfortunately, the most popular of such remedies have proven ineffective (Ness et al., 2006; Newton et al., 2006).

The sharp decline in HRT use is probably an overreaction, however. The most recent thinking among medical experts is that some women are simply better candidates for HRT than others. While HRT seems to be less appropriate for older, postmenopausal women (such as the participants in the Women's Health Initiative study) because of the increased risk of coronary heart disease and other health complications, younger women at the onset of menopause, who are experiencing severe symptoms, might still benefit from the therapy, at least on a short-term basis (Plonczynski and Plonczynski, 2007; Rossouw et al., 2007; Birkhäuser et al., 2008).

HRT remains a gamble. Women nearing menopause need to read literature on the topic, consult their physicians, and make an informed decision.

- How might the frequently changing opinions of medical experts regarding hormone replacement therapy affect women's decisions about what course of action to follow?

- What is most important for a woman to consider when deciding whether or not to try hormone replacement therapy?

male climacteric the period of physical and psychological change relating to the male reproductive system that occurs during late middle age

For many women, menopause symptoms may begin a decade before menopause actually occurs. *Perimenopause* describes this period prior to menopause when hormone production begins to change. It is marked by sometimes radical fluctuations in hormone levels, resulting in some of the same symptoms found in menopause (Winterich, 2003; Shea, 2006).

For some women, the symptoms of perimenopause and menopause are considerable. Treating these problems, though, can be challenging, as we consider in the *From Research to Practice* box.

The Psychological Consequences of Menopause. Traditionally, many people, including experts, believed that menopause was linked directly to depression, anxiety, crying spells, lack of concentration, and irritability. Some researchers estimated that as many as 10 percent of menopausal women suffered severe depression, the assumption being that the physiological changes of menopause caused such problems (Schmidt and Rubinow, 1991).

Today, most researchers take a different view, regarding menopause as a normal part of aging that does not, by itself, produce psychological symptoms. Some women do experience psychological difficulties, but they do so at other times in life as well (Dell and Stewart, 2000; Matthews et al., 2000; Freeman et al., 2004; Somerset et al., 2006).

Research shows that a woman's expectations can significantly affect her experience of menopause. Women who expect to have difficulties are more likely to attribute every physical symptom and emotional swing to menopause, while those with more positive attitudes are less apt to do so. A woman's attribution of physical symptoms, then, can affect her perception of menopause and thus her actual experience of the period (Dell and Stewart, 2000; Breheny and Stephens, 2003).

> ⟹ **From the perspective of a health-care professional:** What cultural factors might contribute to a woman's negative experience of menopause? How?

The Male Climacteric. Do men experience the equivalent of menopause? Not really. Lacking anything akin to menstruation, they cannot experience its discontinuation. But men do experience changes in midlife that are referred to as the male climacteric. The **male climacteric** is the period of physical and psychological change in the reproductive system that occurs late in midlife, typically in a man's fifties.

Because the changes are gradual, the exact period of the male climacteric is hard to pinpoint. For instance, despite declines in testosterone levels and sperm count, men are able to father children throughout middle age. And it is no easier in men than in women to attribute psychological symptoms to subtle physiological changes.

One physical change that occurs frequently is enlargement of the *prostate gland*. By age 40, about 10 percent of men have enlarged prostates, and the percentage increases to half of all men by the age of 80. Enlargement of the prostate produces problems with urination, including difficulty starting urination or a need to urinate frequently at night.

REVIEW, CHECK, AND APPLY

REVIEW

- Sexuality in middle adulthood changes slightly, but couples, freed from childbearing and parenting, can enjoy a new level of intimacy and pleasure.

- Physical changes affecting sexuality occur in both genders. Both the female climacteric, which includes menopause, and the male climacteric seem to have physical and perhaps psychological symptoms.

- Controversy attends the use of estrogen replacement therapy in postmenopausal women to induce pregnancy.

CHECK YOURSELF

1. The period of time that marks a woman's transition from being able to bear children to not being able to do so is also known as the _____.

2. In hormone replacement therapy, _____ and progesterone are administered to alleviate the worst of the symptoms experienced by menopausal women.

3. Roger is a middle-aged man who has started having difficulty urinating. Sometimes he has difficulty starting to urinate. Other times he needs to urinate frequently at night. One of the first things his doctor will check is the functioning of his _____.

a. liver

b. gallbladder

c. testicles

d. prostate

APPLYING LIFESPAN DEVELOPMENT

- How do you think society's view that women lose their sexual allure in middle age affects women's physical and psychological experience of menopause?

Answers: 1) female climacteric; 2) estrogen; 3) d

Sexual problems also increase as men age. In particular, *erectile dysfunction*, in which men are unable to achieve or maintain an erection, becomes more common. Drugs such as Viagra, Levitra, and Cialis, as well as patches that deliver doses of testosterone, often provide effective treatment (Noonan, 2003b; Kim and Park, 2006).

Men, like women, undergo psychological development in middle adulthood, but the extent to which psychological changes—discussed in the next module—are related to reproductive or other physical changes remains an open question.

Health

LO3   Is midlife a time of health or disease for men and women?

LO4   Who is likely to get coronary disease?

LO5   What causes cancer, and what tools are available to diagnose and treat it?

LEARNING OBJECTIVES

It was a normal exercise session for Jerome Yanger. Up at 5:30 a.m., he climbed onto his exercise bike and began vigorously pedalling, hoping to meet, and exceed, his average speed of 22 kms per hour. Stationed in front of the television, he used the remote control to tune to the morning business news. Occasionally glancing up at the television, he began reading a report he had begun the night before, silently cursing some of the poor sales figures he was seeing. By the time his half-hour of exercise was over, he had finished the report, signed a few letters his administrative assistant had typed for him, and left two voice-mail messages for some colleagues.

Most of us would be ready for a nap after such a packed half-hour. For Jerome Yanger, however, it was routine: He always tried to multitask, thinking it more efficient. Developmentalists might see it as symptomatic of a behaviour style that puts Jerome at risk for coronary heart disease.

Although most people are healthy in middle adulthood, they also grow increasingly susceptible to many health problems. We will look at some typical midlife health issues, focusing on coronary heart disease and cancer.

Health is of increasing concern during middle adulthood.

Wellness and Illness: The Ups and Downs of Middle Adulthood

Health concerns become increasingly important to people in middle age. Surveys asking adults what worries them most show that health—as well as national and global issues—is an issue of concern. (Skarborn and Nicki, 2000; see Figure 8-2).

For most people, however, midlife is a period of health. According to surveys, the vast majority of middle-aged adults report no chronic health difficulties and face no limitations on their activities.

In fact, in some ways, health is better in middle adulthood than in earlier periods of life. People ages 45 to 65 are less likely than younger adults to experience infections, allergies, respiratory diseases, and digestive problems. They may contract fewer of these diseases now because they have already experienced them and built up immunities (Sterns et al., 1985).

Certain chronic diseases do begin to appear in middle adulthood. Arthritis typically begins after age 40, and diabetes is most likely to occur between ages 50 and 60, particularly in those who are overweight. Hypertension (high blood pressure) is one of the most frequent chronic disorders. Often called the "silent killer" because it is symptomless, hypertension, if left untreated, greatly increases the risk of strokes and heart disease. For such reasons, many preventive and diagnostic medical tests are routinely recommended for midlife adults.

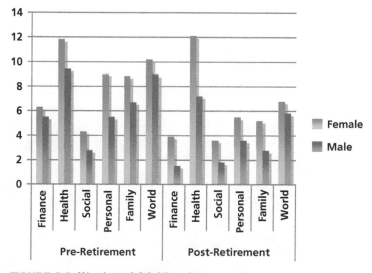

FIGURE 8-2 Worries of Adulthood
Pre- and post-retirement adults aged 50–78 were surveyed about their worries on 88 different issues in 6 categories. Worries are greater among pre-retirement adults and women.
Source: Adapted from Skarborn and Nicki, 2000, Table 4.

Cultural Dimensions

Individual Variation in Health: Ethnic and Gender Differences

Overall figures for the health of middle-aged adults mask vast individual differences. While most people are healthy, some are beset by a variety of ailments. Genetics play a role. For instance, hypertension often runs in families.

Members of lower-income families, however, are more likely to experience a disabling illness. There are many reasons for this. People in lower-SES households are more apt to work in dangerous occupations, such as mining or construction work. Lower-income individuals visit doctors more often, and are more likely to smoke. Crime rates and environmental pollutants are generally higher in lower-income neighbourhoods. A higher incidence of accidents and health hazards, and thus a higher death rate, are linked to lower levels of income (Fingerhut and MaKuc, 1992; Dahl and Birkelund, 1997; Scott, 2002).

Gender also makes a difference. Women's overall mortality rate is lower than men's—a trend that holds true from birth—but the incidence of illness among midlife women is higher than for men.

Women are more susceptible to minor, short-term illness and chronic, but non-life-threatening diseases such as migraine headaches, while men are more susceptible to serious illnesses such as heart disease. Fewer women smoke than men, which reduces their risk for cancer and heart disease; women drink less alcohol than men, which lowers their incidence of cirrhosis of the liver and auto accidents; and they work at less dangerous jobs (McDonald, 1999).

Another reason for the higher rate of illness in women might be that more medical research targets men and the disorders they suffer. The vast majority of medical research money goes to preventing life-threatening diseases faced mostly by men, rather than to chronic conditions such as heart disease that can cause disability and suffering, but not necessarily death. Typically, research on diseases that strike both men and women focused on men as subjects rather than women. This bias is now being addressed in research, but the historical pattern has been one of gender discrimination by a male-dominated research community (Vidaver et al., 2000).

The onset of chronic diseases in middle age boosts the death rate above that of earlier periods, and the rate increases steadily with age. Still, death remains rare in this period: Only 7 out of every 2000 40-year-olds are expected to die before age 50, and 16 out of every 2000 50-year-olds are expected to die before age 60. Cultural variations in health also exist, as we consider next (Smedley and Syme, 2000).

Stress in Middle Adulthood

Stress continues to have a significant impact on health, as it did in young adulthood, although the stressors might have changed. For example, parents might now worry about their adolescent child's potential drug use where before they worried about whether their toddler was ready to give up his soother.

No matter what events trigger stress, the results are similar. *Psychoneuroimmunologists*, who study the relationship between the brain, the immune system, and psychological factors,

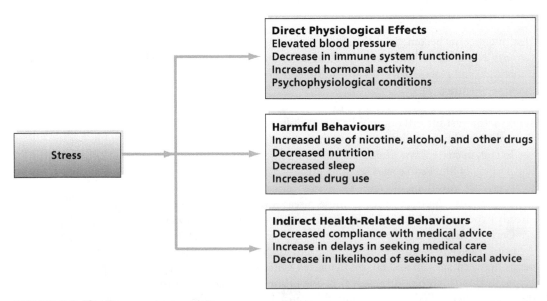

Direct Physiological Effects
Elevated blood pressure
Decrease in immune system functioning
Increased hormonal activity
Psychophysiological conditions

Harmful Behaviours
Increased use of nicotine, alcohol, and other drugs
Decreased nutrition
Decreased sleep
Increased drug use

Indirect Health-Related Behaviours
Decreased compliance with medical advice
Increase in delays in seeking medical care
Decrease in likelihood of seeking medical advice

FIGURE 8-3 The Consequences of Stress
Stress produces three major consequences: direct physiological effects, harmful behaviours, and indirect health-related behaviours.
Source: Adapted from Baum, 1994.

report that stress has three main consequences, summarized in Figure 8-3. First, stress has direct physiological effects, ranging from increased blood pressure and hormonal activity to decreased immune system response. Second, stress leads people to engage in unhealthy behaviours such as cutting back on sleep, smoking, drinking, or taking other drugs. Finally, stress has indirect effects on health-related behaviour. People under a lot of stress can be less likely to seek out good medical care, to exercise, or to comply with medical advice (Suinn, 2001; Suls and Wallston, 2003; Zellner et al., 2006). All of these can lead to or affect serious health conditions, including heart disease.

Coronary Heart Disease

Every seven minutes someone in Canada dies from heart disease or stroke, together accounting for 27 percent of deaths. These diseases are also responsible for substantial loss of work days and for disability days due to hospitalization.

Risk Factors for Heart Disease. Although heart and circulatory diseases are a major problem, some people have a much lower risk than others. The death rate in some countries, such as Japan and France, is nearly one-third the rate in Canada and the United States, whose rates are similar. A few other countries, such as Slovakia and Hungary have a considerably higher death rate. Why?

The answer is both genetics and environment. Some people seem genetically predisposed to heart disease. If a person's parents suffered from it, the likelihood is greater that she or he will too. Similarly, sex and age are risk factors: Men are more likely to suffer from heart disease, and the risk rises as people age.

Environment and lifestyle choices are also important. Cigarette smoking, a diet high in fats and cholesterol, and a lack of physical exercise all increase the risk of heart disease and might may explain country-to-country variations in the rate of heart disease. For example, the death rate from heart disease in Japan is relatively low and could be due to differences in diet: The typical Japanese diet is much lower in fat than the typical Canadian diet (Zhou et al., 2003; Wilcox et al., 2006; De Meersman and Stein, 2007).

Diet is not the only factor in heart disease. Psychological factors—particularly how stress is perceived and experienced—appear to be related as well. For instance, a set of personality characteristics, known as Type A behaviour, appears to be a factor in the development of coronary heart disease.

The **Type A behaviour pattern** is characterized by competitiveness, impatience, and a tendency toward frustration and hostility. Type A people are extremely ambitious and they engage in *polyphasic activities*—multiple activities carried out simultaneously. They are the true multitaskers whom you see talking on their phones while working on their laptop computers while riding the commuter train—and eating breakfast. Easily angered, they become both verbally and nonverbally hostile if prevented from reaching their goals.

In contrast, many people have virtually the opposite characteristics in what is known as the Type B behaviour pattern. The **Type B behaviour pattern** is characterized by noncompetitiveness, patience, and a lack of aggression. In contrast to Type As, Type Bs experience little sense of time urgency, and they are rarely hostile.

Few people are purely Type A or Type B. In fact, these types represent the ends of a continuum, and most people fall somewhere in between. Still, the majority come close to one or the other of the two categories. These categories become important in midlife because research suggests the distinction is related to the risk of coronary heart disease. Type A men have twice the rate of coronary heart disease, a greater number of fatal heart attacks, and five times as many heart problems as Type B men (Strube, 1990; Wielgosz and Nolan, 2000).

The Threat of Cancer

Few diseases are as frightening as cancer, and many middle-aged adults view a cancer diagnosis as a death sentence. Although the reality is different—many forms of cancer respond well to medical treatment, and 62 percent of those diagnosed are still alive five years later—the disease raises many fears. There is no denying that cancer is now the leading cause of death in Canada for both men and women (Statistics Canada, 2011; Canadian Cancer Society, 2011).

In addition to being characterized as competitive, people with Type A personalities also tend to engage in polyphasic activities—doing a number of things at once. Does a Type A personality deal with stress differently than a Type B personality?

Type A behaviour pattern behaviour characterized by competitiveness, impatience, and a tendency toward frustration and hostility

Type B behaviour pattern behaviour characterized by noncompetitiveness, patience, and a lack of aggression

"To other Canadians who are on journeys to defeat cancer and to live their lives, I say this: Please don't be discouraged that my own journey hasn't gone as well as I had hoped. You must not lose your own hope. Treatments and therapies have never been better in the face of this disease. You have every reason to be optimistic, determined, and focused on the future." — Jack Layton, 2011.

The precise trigger for cancer is still not known, but the process by which it spreads is clear. Certain cells in the body begin to multiply rapidly and uncontrollably. As they increase in number, these cells form tumours. Unimpeded, they draw nutrients from healthy cells and body tissue. Eventually, they destroy the body's ability to function.

Cancer is associated with a variety of genetic and environmental risk factors. Some cancers have clear genetic components. For example, a family history of breast cancer—the second most common cause of cancer death among women—raises the risk for a woman.

Several environmental and behavioural factors are also related to the risk of cancer. Poor nutrition, smoking, alcohol use, exposure to sunlight, exposure to radiation, and particular occupational hazards (such as exposure to certain chemicals or asbestos) are all known to increase the chances of developing cancer.

After a diagnosis, several forms of treatment are possible, depending on the type of cancer. One treatment is *radiation therapy*, in which radiation targets the tumour in an attempt to destroy it. Patients undergoing *chemotherapy* ingest controlled doses of toxic substances meant to poison the tumour. Finally, surgery can be used to remove the tumour (and often the surrounding tissue). Treatment is determined by how far the cancer has spread when it is first identified.

Because early detection improves a patient's chances of survival, diagnostic techniques that help identify the first signs of cancer are of great importance. This is especially true in middle adulthood, when the risk of certain cancers increases.

Physicians urge women to do routine breast exams and men to regularly check their testicles for signs of cancer. Cancer of the prostate gland, the most common type of cancer in men, can be detected by routine rectal exams and by a blood test that identifies prostate-specific antigen (PSA).

Mammograms provide internal scans of women's breasts to help identify early-stage cancer. However, at what age women should begin to routinely have the procedure has been controversial.

Figure 8-4 shows the incidence of and mortality rates for cancer in men and women.

Routine Mammograms: At What Age Should Women Start?

My mother was first diagnosed when I was thirteen years old and she died when I was twenty-four. My notion of womanhood has always been intertwined with breast cancer. So, when I was diagnosed with breast cancer two weeks ago, I was instantly transported back to 1989, back to the beginning of my relationship with my breasts, womanhood, and (in many ways) my mother. In that moment, I started to know.

However, I don't want to stay in 1989 nor do I want to be stuck in a state of knowing; I want to be doing. I will have a bilateral mastectomy at the end of April and then will begin the lengthy process of reconstruction. There is no doubt that this is the right course of action as I have the "breast cancer gene" (BRCA-1) and am considered "high risk." In fact, I have been mentally preparing for this surgery for the last 10 years as the threat of breast cancer was always salient. But, I am completely unprepared for how to negotiate my life as it interacts with my cancer. I have many unanswered questions: How will I tell my 6-year-old daughter about this? How will I occupy my time on my leave from work? Will I look remotely normal? Will I be able to have a casual fling without having to address my medical history before I take my top off? (Flanagan, http://cancerchic.blogspot.ca/2011/03/welcome-to-jungle.html 2011)

For Tara Flanagan, blogger and McGill University professor, feeling healthy, exercising, and eating a good diet was not enough: She still got cancer. But she was also lucky, and after aggressive treatment she stands a good chance of a full recovery.

Her good luck is partly a result of early identification of the cancer. Statistically, the earlier breast cancer is diagnosed, the better the chances for survival. But the question of how to go about identifying cancer early has caused some contention in the medical field. The controversy surrounds the age at which *mammograms*, a kind of weak X-ray used to examine breast tissue, should be routinely administered to women.

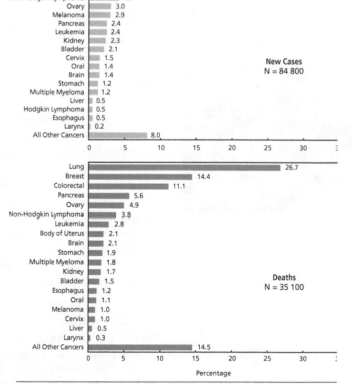

Percentage Distribution of Estimated New Cases and Deaths for Selected Cancers, Males, Canada, 2011

New Cases
N = 93 000

Cancer	Percentage
Prostate	27.5
Lung	14.1
Colorectal	13.4
Bladder	5.8
Non-Hodgkin Lymphoma	4.5
Kidney	3.4
Melanoma	3.3
Leukemia	3.2
Oral	2.5
Pancreas	2.2
Stomach	2.1
Brain	1.7
Liver	1.6
Esophagus	1.4
Multiple Myeloma	1.4
Thyroid	1.3
Testis	1.0
Larynx	1.0
Hodgkin Lymphoma	0.5
All Other Cancers	7.8

Deaths
N = 39 900

Cancer	Percentage
Lung	28.3
Colorectal	12.5
Prostate	10.2
Pancreas	4.7
Non-Hodgkin Lymphoma	4.2
Leukemia	3.7
Esophagus	3.6
Bladder	3.3
Stomach	2.8
Kidney	2.6
Brain	2.6
Oral	1.9
Multiple Myeloma	1.8
Liver	1.6
Melanoma	1.5
Larynx	1.0
Breast	0.1
All Other Cancers	13.4

Note: New cases exclude an estimated 40 700 new cases of non-melanoma skin cancer (basal and squamous). The number of deaths for "All Other Cancers" includes about 170 deaths with underlying cause "other malignant neoplasma" of skin.

Analysis by: Chronic Disease Surveillance and Monitoring Division, CCDPC, Public Health Agency of Canada
Data sources: Canadian Cancer Registry and Canadian Vital Statistics Death databases at Statistics Canada

Percentage Distribution of Estimated New Cases and Deaths for Selected Cancers, Females, Canada, 2011

New Cases
N = 84 800

Cancer	Percentage
Breast	27.6
Lung	14.4
Colorectal	11.4
Body of Uterus	5.6
Thyroid	5.3
Non-Hodgkin Lymphoma	4.1
Ovary	3.0
Melanoma	2.9
Pancreas	2.4
Leukemia	2.4
Kidney	2.3
Bladder	2.1
Cervix	1.5
Oral	1.4
Brain	1.4
Stomach	1.2
Multiple Myeloma	1.2
Liver	0.5
Hodgkin Lymphoma	0.5
Esophagus	0.5
Larynx	0.2
All Other Cancers	8.0

Deaths
N = 35 100

Cancer	Percentage
Lung	26.7
Breast	14.4
Colorectal	11.1
Pancreas	5.6
Ovary	4.9
Non-Hodgkin Lymphoma	3.8
Leukemia	2.8
Body of Uterus	2.1
Brain	2.1
Stomach	1.9
Multiple Myeloma	1.8
Kidney	1.7
Bladder	1.5
Esophagus	1.2
Oral	1.1
Melanoma	1.0
Cervix	1.0
Liver	0.5
Larynx	0.3
All Other Cancers	14.5

Note: New cases exclude an estimated 33 300 cases of non-melanoma skin cancer (basal and squamous). Deaths for "All Other Cancers" include about 100 deaths with underlying cause "other maligr neoplasms" of skin.

Analysis by: Chronic Disease Surveillance and Monitoring Division, CCDPC, Public Health Agency of Canada
Data sources: Canadian Cancer Registry and Canadian Vital Statistics Death databases at Statistics Canada

FIGURE 8-4 Incidence and Mortality of Different Cancers in Men and Women
Breast and prostate cancers are more prevalent, but lung cancer is far more deadly. Why do you think this would be the case?
Source: Canadian Cancer Society, 2011. Reprinted with permission.

Mammograms are among the best means for early detection of breast cancer. The procedure allows tumours to be identified while they are still very small. Patients can be treated before tumours grow and spread. Mammograms save many lives, and nearly all medical professionals suggest that women routinely obtain them at some point in midlife. The question is when. The risk of breast cancer begins to rise at around the age of 30 and then increases. Ninety-five percent of new cases occur in women aged 40 and above (SEER, 2005). The current recommendation is that women who are at high risk (for example, if your mother had breast cancer or you know that you carry the BRCA1 or BRAC2 genes) should have annual mammograms in their forties (if not earlier), and that low-risk women (aged 50 to 69) have mammograms every two years. Women 70 and older should discuss with their doctors whether and how often they should continue to have mammograms.

REVIEW, CHECK, AND APPLY

REVIEW

- In general, middle adulthood is a period of good health, although susceptibility to chronic diseases such as arthritis, diabetes, and hypertension increases.

- Heart disease is a risk for middle-aged adults. Both genetic and environmental factors, including the Type A behaviour pattern, contribute to heart disease.

- Therapies such as radiation, chemotherapy, and surgery can successfully treat cancer.

CHECK YOURSELF

1. Insecurity, anxiety, and having a negative outlook put people at risk for heart attacks. This behaviour is referred to as _____.
   a. Type D
   b. Type B
   c. Disassociative Identity Disorder
   d. Type A

2. Cancer is the _____ leading cause of death in middle adulthood.

APPLYING LIFESPAN DEVELOPMENT

- What social policies might be developed to lower the incidence of disabling illness among members of lower socioeconomic groups?

Answers: 1) d; 2) number one

MODULE 8.2 Cognitive Development in Middle Adulthood

Playing Her Trump Card

When Kate Dalton went back to school at the age of 46 to pursue a master's degree in education, she was the oldest student in her program by some 20 years—and the only one to carry the considerable responsibilities for a family, as well. Though Kate possessed a high level of energy and was in excellent health, she was long past the point in life where she could stay up all night writing lesson plans or researching a paper. And two decades had passed since she had sat in a lecture hall.

But Kate had three things in her favour. First, she had confidence. She knew exactly who she was and what she wanted from her advanced degree. Second, she knew her own strengths and weaknesses—how to play to the former and how to compensate for the latter. Third, and most significant, she had expertise in her field of study. Kate had been a parent for 15 years, and she had spent many hours in the classroom, helping teachers and taking on major school projects. She had also spent a year substitute-teaching in schools to gain experience both in teaching and in classroom management. Her insights into children, their development and needs, not only earned her the highest rank in her program, but she was also hired on the spot in her second interview.

Like many people in midlife, Kate took on the challenge of a new career. Not only did she have to learn and respond to a considerable amount of new material, but she had to compete against people half her age, both in the classroom and in the job search.

But Kate had something that younger people in her classes could not match: her experience and expertise. She also had the patience to allow herself extra time to learn new skills, many centred on the computer, which hadn't existed in student life the last time she was in college.

The second part of this module focuses on cognitive development in middle age. We look at the tricky question of whether intelligence declines during the period, and we consider the difficulty of answering the question fully. We also examine memory and how its capabilities change in middle adulthood.

Cognitive Development

LO6   What happens to a person's intelligence in middle adulthood?

It began innocently enough. Forty-five-year-old Bina Clingman couldn't remember whether she had mailed the letter that her husband had given her, and she wondered, briefly, whether this was a sign of aging. The next day, the question recurred when she spent 20 minutes looking for a phone number she knew she had written down on a piece of paper—somewhere. By the time she found it, she was surprised and even a little anxious. "Am I losing my memory?" she asked herself, feeling both annoyance and a degree of concern.

Many people in their forties feel more absentminded than they did 20 years earlier and are concerned about becoming less mentally able as they age. Common wisdom suggests that people lose some mental sharpness in midlife. But how accurate is this notion?

Does Intelligence Decline in Adulthood?

For years, experts provided an unwavering response when asked whether intelligence declined in adulthood: Intelligence peaks at age 18, stays fairly steady until the mid-twenties, and then gradually declines until the end of life.

Today, developmentalists view questions about changes in intelligence across the lifespan as more complicated—and they have come to different, and more complex, conclusions.

The Difficulties in Answering the Question. The conclusion that intelligence starts to diminish in our mid-twenties was based on extensive research. *Cross-sectional studies*—which test people of different ages at the same point in time—clearly showed that older subjects were less likely than younger subjects to score well on traditional intelligence tests of the sort discussed earlier.

But consider the drawbacks of cross-sectional research—in particular, the possibility that it might suffer from *cohort effects*. Recall that cohort effects are influences associated with growing up at a particular historical time; they affect people of a particular age. For instance, suppose that, compared to younger subjects, the older people in a cross-sectional study had had less adequate educations, less stimulating jobs, or were less healthy. In that case, the lower IQ scores of the older group could not be attributed solely, or perhaps even partially, to differences in intelligence based on age. Because they do not control for cohort effects, cross-sectional studies may well *underestimate* intelligence in older subjects.

To overcome the cohort problems of cross-sectional studies, developmentalists began to use *longitudinal studies* in which the same people are studied periodically over a span of time. These studies revealed a different developmental pattern for intelligence: Adults tended to show stable and even increasing intelligence test scores until their mid-thirties, and in some cases, into their fifties. Then the scores began to decline (Bayley and Oden, 1955).

But let's consider the drawbacks of longitudinal studies, too. People taking an intelligence test repeatedly may perform better because they become familiar—and comfortable—with the testing situation. Similarly, through repeated exposure to the same test, they might begin to remember some of the test items. Consequently, practice effects can account for the superior performance of people on longitudinal measures of intelligence as opposed to cross-sectional measures.

It is also difficult for researchers using longitudinal studies to keep their samples intact. Participants move away, decide they no longer want to participate, or become ill and die. Over time, the participants who remain might represent a healthier, more stable, and more psychologically positive group of people than those who are no longer part of the sample. If this is the case, longitudinal studies may *overestimate* intelligence in older subjects.

Crystallized and Fluid Intelligence. Drawing conclusions about age-related changes in intelligence is challenging. For instance, many IQ tests include sections based on physical performance, such as arranging a group of blocks. These sections are timed and scored on the basis of how quickly an item is completed. If older people take longer on physical tasks—recall that reaction time slows with age—then their poorer performance on IQ tests may result from physical rather than cognitive changes (Schaie, 1991; Nettelbeck and Rabbit, 1992).

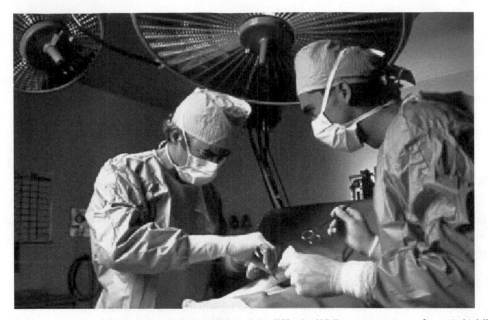

Evaluating cognitive abilities in middle adulthood is difficult. While some types of mental abilities might begin to decline, crystallized intelligence holds steady and actually can increase.

To complicate the issue further, many researchers believe there are two kinds of intelligence: fluid intelligence and crystallized intelligence. As noted earlier, **fluid intelligence** reflects information-processing capabilities, reasoning, and memory. To arrange a series of letters according to some rule or to memorize a set of numbers uses fluid intelligence. **Crystallized intelligence** is the information, skills, and strategies that people have accumulated through experience and that they can apply to solve problems. Someone who is solving a crossword puzzle or attempting to identify the murderer in a mystery story is using crystallized intelligence, relying on past experience as a resource.

Researchers once believed that fluid intelligence was largely determined by genetic factors, and crystallized intelligence by experiential, environmental factors. They later abandoned this distinction when they found that crystallized intelligence is determined in part by fluid intelligence. For instance, a person's ability to solve a crossword puzzle (which involves crystallized intelligence) relies on that person's proficiency with letters and patterns (a manifestation of fluid intelligence).

When developmentalists examined the two kinds of intelligence separately, they discovered there are two answers to the question of whether intelligence declines with age: Yes and No. Yes, because fluid intelligence does decline with age; No, because crystallized intelligence holds steady and can actually improve (Ryan et al., 2000; Salthouse et al., 2003; Bugg et al., 2006; see Figure 8-5).

If we look at more specific types of intelligence, true age-related differences and developments begin to show up. According to developmental psychologist K. Warner Schaie, who has conducted extensive longitudinal research on adult intellectual development, we should consider many types of ability, such as spatial orientation, numeric ability, verbal ability, and so on, rather than the broad divisions of crystallized and fluid intelligence (Schaie et al., 2005).

Examined this way, the question of how intelligence changes in adulthood yields yet another, more specific, answer. Schaie has found that certain abilities, such as inductive reasoning, spatial orientation, perceptual speed, and verbal memory, begin to decline very gradually at around age 25 and continue to do so through old age. Numeric and verbal abilities show a different pattern. Numeric ability tends to increase until the mid-forties, is lower at age 60, and then remains steady. Verbal ability rises until the start of middle adulthood, around age 40, then stays fairly steady (Schaie et al., 2005).

fluid intelligence information-processing capabilities, reasoning, and memory

crystallized intelligence the accumulation of information, skills, and strategies that people have learned through experience and that they can apply in problem-solving situations

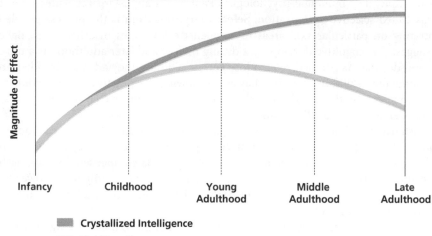

FIGURE 8-5 Changes in Crystallized and Fluid Intelligence
Although crystallized intelligence increases with age, fluid intelligence begins to decline in middle age. What are the implications for general competence in middle adulthood?
Source: From K. W. Schaie, "Longitudinal Studies of Adult Psychological Development," 1985. Copyright © Guilford Press. Reprinted with permission.

One reason these changes occur is that brain functioning begins to change in middle adulthood. Researchers have found that 20 genes that are vital to learning, memory, and mental flexibility begin to function less efficiently as early as age 40 (Lu et al., 2004).

Reframing the Issue: What Is the Source of Competence during Middle Adulthood? It is during midlife that people come to hold some of the most important and powerful positions in society, despite gradual declines in certain cognitive abilities. How do we explain such continuing, even growing, competence?

Psychologist Timothy Salthouse (1989, 1990, 1994a) suggests four reasons why this discrepancy exists. First, typical measures of cognitive skills might tap a different type of cognition than what is required to be successful in certain occupations. Recall the earlier discussion of practical intelligence, in which we found that traditional IQ tests fail to measure cognitive abilities that are related to occupational success. Perhaps we would find no discrepancy between intelligence and cognitive abilities in midlife if we used measures of practical intelligence rather than traditional IQ tests to assess intelligence.

A second factor also relates to the measurement of IQ and occupational success. It is possible that the most successful middle-aged adults are not representative of midlife adults in general. It might be that only a small proportion of people are highly successful, and the rest, who experience only moderate or little success, have changed occupations, retired, or become sick and died. Highly successful people, then, could be an unrepresentative sample.

Also, the degree of cognitive ability required for professional success might simply not be that high. According to this argument, people can succeed professionally and still be on the decline in certain cognitive abilities. In other words, they have brains to spare.

Finally, it could be that older people are successful because they have developed specific kinds of expertise and particular competencies. Whereas IQ tests measure reactions to novel situations, occupational success might be influenced by very specific, well-practised abilities. Consequently, middle-aged individuals might maintain and even expand the distinctive talents they need for professional accomplishment, despite a decline in overall intellectual skills. This explanation has generated research on expertise.

From the perspective of an educator: How do you think the apparent discrepancy between declining IQ scores and continuing cognitive competence in middle adulthood might affect the learning ability of middle adults who return to school?

selective optimization the process by which people concentrate on particular skill areas to compensate for losses in other areas

expertise the acquisition of skill or knowledge in a particular area

For example, developmental psychologists Paul Baltes and Margaret Baltes have studied a strategy called selective optimization. **Selective optimization** is the process people use in concentrating on particular skill areas to compensate for losses in other areas. Baltes and Baltes suggest that cognitive development during middle and later adulthood is a mixture of growth and decline. As people begin to lose certain abilities, they advance in other areas by strengthening their skills. In so doing, they avoid showing any practical deterioration. Overall cognitive competence, then, remains stable and may even improve (Bajor and Baltes, 2003; Baltes and Carstensen, 2003; Baltes and Freund, 2003a; Ebner et al., 2006).

For instance, recall that reaction time lengthens as people age. Because reaction time is a component of typing skill, we would expect that typists would slow as they age. This is not the case. Though their reaction time is increasing, older typists compensate by looking further ahead in the material as they type. Similarly, a business executive might be slower to recall names, but he could have a mental file of deals he has completed and be able to forge new agreements easily because of it.

Selective optimization is one of several strategies adults use to maintain high performance.

The Development of Expertise: Separating Experts from Novices

If you were ill and needed a diagnosis, would you rather visit a young physician fresh out of medical school, or a more experienced, middle-aged physician?

If you chose the older physician, you probably assumed that he or she would have more expertise. **Expertise** is the skill or knowledge acquired in a particular area. More focused than broad intelligence, expertise develops as people devote attention and practice to a subject or skill and, in so doing, gain experience. For example, physicians become better at diagnosing the symptoms of a medical problem as they gain experience. A person who does a lot of cooking comes to know how a recipe will taste if certain modifications are made.

What separates the experts from the less skilled? While beginners use formal procedures and rules, often following them very strictly, experts rely on experience and intuition, and they often bend the rules. Their experience allows them to process information automatically. Experts often have trouble articulating how they draw conclusions; their solutions just seem right to them—and *are* likely to be right. Brain imaging studies show that experts use different neural pathways than novices to solve problems (Grabner et al., 2006).

Finally, experts develop better problem-solving strategies than nonexperts and they're more flexible in their approach. Experience provides them with alternative solutions to the same problem, increasing the probability of success (Willis, 1996; Clark, 1998; Arts et al., 2006).

Not everyone develops an area of expertise in middle adulthood. Professional responsibilities, amount of leisure time, educational level, income, and marital status all affect the development of expertise.

Expertise develops as people become more experienced in a particular domain and are able to be flexible with procedures and rules.

REVIEW, CHECK, AND APPLY

REVIEW

- The question of whether intelligence declines in middle adulthood is complicated by limitations in cross-sectional studies and longitudinal studies.

- Intelligence appears to be divided into components, some of which decline while others hold steady or even improve.

- In general, cognitive competence in middle adulthood holds fairly steady despite declines in some areas of intellectual functioning.

CHECK YOURSELF

1. According to _____ studies that test people of different ages at the same time, older subjects scored lower than younger subjects on traditional intelligence tests.

2. Because cross-sectional studies do not control for cohort effects, these research designs may underestimate intelligence in older subjects.
   - True
   - False

3. Over the years, one of the types of intelligence that increases with age is _____ intelligence, or

the accumulation of information, skills, and strategies that people have learned through experience.

APPLYING LIFESPAN DEVELOPMENT

- How might crystallized and fluid intelligence work together to help middle-aged people deal with novel situations and problems?

Memory

LO7 How does aging affect memory, and how can memory be improved?

Mary Donovan races around the kitchen and makes one last frantic search through her purse. "I must be losing my memory," she mutters. "I always leave my keys on the counter next to the toaster." It's not until her son David comes downstairs ready for hockey practice that Mary remembers she lent him her car the day before. Sure enough, David produces the keys from the pocket of his varsity jacket. Relieved to have her keys in hand once more, Mary sighs. After all, she is 47. Such episodes are to be expected, she supposes.

Like Bina Clingman, who was worried about forgetting letters and phone numbers, Mary probably believes that memory loss is common in middle age. However, if she is a typical midlife adult, her assessment might not be accurate. Research shows that most people exhibit minimal or no memory loss. Because of societal stereotypes, however, people often attribute their absentmindedness to aging, even though they have been that way all their lives. It is the *meaning* they give to their forgetfulness that changes, rather than their actual ability to remember (Erber et al., 1991; Grossi et al., 2007).

Types of Memory

To understand the nature of memory changes, we must consider that memory is traditionally viewed as three sequential components: sensory memory, short-term memory (also called working memory), and long-term memory. *Sensory memory* is an initial, momentary storage of information. Information is recorded by the sensory system as a raw, meaningless stimulus. Next, information moves into *short-term memory*, where it is held for 15 to 25 seconds. If the information is rehearsed, it then moves into *long-term memory*, where it is stored on a relatively permanent basis.

Both sensory memory and short-term memory show virtually no weakening in middle age. Long-term memory, however, declines for some people. It appears this decline is not a fading or a complete loss of memory, but rather a less efficient registering and storing of information. Age also makes people less efficient at retrieving information. Even if the information was adequately stored in long-term memory, locating or isolating the memory might become more difficult (Salthouse, 2007).

Memory declines in middle age are relatively minor, and most can be compensated for by various cognitive strategies. Paying greater attention to material when it is first encountered can aid in its later recall. Your lost car keys might have more to do with your inattentiveness when you put them down than with a decline in memory.

Many middle adults find it hard to pay attention to certain things for some of the same reasons that expertise develops. They are used to using memory shortcuts, *schemas*, to ease the burden of remembering the many things they experience each day.

Memory Schemas. To recall information, people often use **schemas**, organized bodies of information stored in memory. Schemas represent the way the world is organized, allowing people to categorize and interpret new information. For example, if we have a schema for eating in a restaurant, we don't regard a meal in a new restaurant as a completely new experience. We know we will be seated at a table or counter and offered a menu from which to select food. Our schema for eating out tells us how to treat the server, what sorts of food to eat first, and that we should leave a tip.

People hold schemas for individuals (such as the particular behaviour patterns of one's mother, wife, or child) as well as for categories of people (mail carriers, lawyers, or professors) and behaviours or events (dining in a restaurant or visiting the dentist). People's schemas organize their behaviour and help them to interpret social events. A person who knows the schema for visiting the doctor will not be surprised when he is asked to undress.

Schemas also convey cultural information. Psychologists Susan Fiske and Shelley Taylor (1991) use the example of an old Aboriginal folktale in which the hero participates with

schemas organized bodies of information stored in memory

Effective Strategies for Remembering

Becoming an Informed Consumer of Development

We are all forgetful at times. However, there are techniques for more effective recall. **Mnemonics** (pronounced "nee-MON-iks") are formal strategies for organizing material in ways that make it easier to remember. Among the mnemonics that work are the following (Bloom and Lamkin, 2006; Morris and Fritz, 2006; Collins, 2007):

- **Get organized.** For people who have trouble recalling where they left their keys or remembering appointments, the simplest approach is to become more organized. Using a date book, hanging keys on a hook, or using Post-It notes can aid recall.

- **Pay attention.** You can improve your recall by paying close attention to new information, and purposefully thinking that you will need to recall it. For example, when you park your car at the mall, pay attention at the moment you park, and remind yourself that you really want to remember the location.

- **Use the encoding specificity phenomenon.** According to the encoding specificity phenomenon, people are most likely to recall information in environments that are similar to those in which they initially learned ("encoded") it (Tulving and Thompson, 1973). For instance, people are best able to recall information on a test if the test is held in the room in which they studied.

- **Visualize.** Making mental images of ideas can help you recall them later. For example, if you want to remember that global warming might lead to rising oceans, think of yourself on a beach on a hot day, with the waves coming closer and closer to where you're sitting.

- **Rehearse.** Practice makes memory perfect, or, if not perfect, at least better. By practising or rehearsing what you wish to recall, you can substantially improve your memory.

⊙ **Watch** on **mydevelopmentlab**

To learn more about mnemonics, try out the simulation on MyDevelopmentLab.

mnemonics formal strategies for organizing material in ways that make it easier to remember

several companions in a battle and is shot by an arrow. He feels no pain. When he returns home and tells the story, something black emerges from his mouth, and he dies the next morning.

This tale puzzles most people who are not familiar with the particular Aboriginal culture from which the story comes. However, to someone familiar with that culture, the story makes perfect sense: The hero feels no pain because his companions are ghosts, and the "black thing" coming from his mouth is his departing soul.

For an Aboriginal, it might be easy to recall the story because it makes sense in a way that it doesn't to members of other cultures. Material that fits into existing schemas is easier to recall than material that doesn't fit. For example, a person who usually puts her keys in her purse might well lose them because she doesn't recall putting them on the counter, which is not the "usual place" (Tse et al., 2007).

REVIEW, CHECK, AND APPLY

REVIEW

- Memory might appear to decline in middle age, but, in fact, long-term memory deficits are probably due to ineffective strategies of storage and retrieval.

- People categorize and interpret new information according to the schemas they have developed about how the world is organized and how it operates.

- Mnemonics help people organize material in ways that improve recall. These formal strategies include getting organized, visualizing, rehearsing, paying attention, and using the encoding specificity phenomenon.

CHECK YOURSELF

1. Both sensory memory and short-term memory show virtually no weakening during middle adulthood.
   - True
   - False

2. Middle-aged individuals find it hard to pay attention to everything that is going on around them and often rely on _____, or mental shortcuts, to reduce the stress of remembering so many things.

3. _____ are formal strategies for organizing material in ways that make it more likely to be remembered.

a. Mnemonics
b. Schemas
c. Perceptions
d. Heuristics

APPLYING LIFESPAN DEVELOPMENT

- In what ways do schemas give midlife adults an edge over younger adults?

Starting Over at 42

Ivan was a 42-year-old car salesman. He was in good shape financially, but mentally he was bored. "I just didn't like what I was doing, day in day out. I struggled to get out of bed in the morning. I was in a funk. I needed something to change." Ivan's oldest daughter was beginning high school and starting to think about what she wanted to do when she grew up. "She asked me for advice. I asked her what made her excited. That's when I realized I had to ask myself the same question. I had to find what excited me. I was too young to retire, but I didn't want to sell cars for another 20 years. Did I want to go back to school? Did I want to do something creative? With my hands? What will make me happy?"

The twists and turns in Ivan's life path are not unusual: Few lives follow a set, predictable pattern through middle adulthood. In fact, one of the remarkable characteristics of midlife is its variety.

In this module we focus on the personality and social development that occurs in midlife. We begin by examining the changes that typify this period. We also explore some of the controversies in developmental psychologists' understandings of midlife, including whether the midlife crisis, a phenomenon popularized in the media, is fact or fiction.

Next we consider the various familial ties that bind people together (or come unglued) in middle adulthood, including marriage, divorce, the empty nest, and grandparenting. We also look at a bleak, but common, side of family relations: family violence.

Finally, the module examines work and leisure in midlife. We consider the changing role of work in people's lives and look at work-related problems such as burnout and unemployment. The module concludes with a discussion of leisure time, which becomes more important during middle age.

Personality Development

LO8   In what ways does personality develop during middle adulthood?

LO9   Is there continuity in personality development during adulthood?

LEARNING OBJECTIVES

My fortieth birthday was not an easy one. I did not wake up feeling different—that's never been the case. But during my fortieth year, I did come to realize the finiteness of life. The die was cast. Time had become more of an adversary than an ally. But it was curious: My usual pattern of focusing on the future, planning each step, began to shift. I started appreciating what I had. I looked at my life and was pretty satisfied with some of my accomplishments. I began focusing on what was going right, not on what I was lacking. This didn't happen in a day; it took several years after turning 40 before I felt this way. Even now, it is hard to fully accept that I am middle-aged.

As this 47-year-old man suggests, realizing that one has reached midlife can be difficult. In many Western societies, age 40 undeniably marks one as middle-aged—at least in the public eye—and suggests that one is on the threshold of a "midlife crisis." How true this view is, as we'll see, depends on your perspective.

Two Perspectives on Adult Personality Development: Normative-Crisis versus Life Events

Traditional views of adult personality development have suggested that people move through a fixed series of stages, each tied closely to age. These stages are related to specific crises in which an individual undergoes an intense period of questioning and psychological turmoil. This perspective is a feature of the normative-crisis models of personality development.

Normative-crisis models see personality development as universal stages of sequential, age-related crises. For example, Erik Erikson's psychosocial theory predicts that people move through a series of stages and crises throughout their lifespan.

Some critics suggest that normative-crisis approaches might be outmoded. These approaches arose at a time when society had fairly rigid and uniform roles for people. Traditionally, men were expected to work and support a family; women were expected to stay at home and take care of the children. These roles played out at relatively uniform ages.

Today, there is considerable variety in both the roles and the timing. Some people marry and have children at 40. Others have children and marry later. Others never marry, and live with a partner and perhaps adopt a child or forego children altogether. In sum, social changes have called into question the normative-crisis models closely tied to age (Fugate and Mitchell, 1997; Barnett and Hyde, 2001; Fraenkel, 2003).

> ⭢ **From a social worker's perspective:** In what ways might normative-crisis models of personality development be specific to Western culture?

Because of this variation, some theorists, such as Ravenna Helson, focus on **life events models**, which suggest that particular events, rather than age per se, determine how personality develops. For instance, a woman who has her first child at age 21 might experience similar psychological forces as a woman who has her first child at age 39. These two women, despite their very different ages, share certain commonalities of personality development (Helson and Wink, 1992; Helson and Srivastava, 2001; Roberts et al., 2002).

It is not clear whether the normative-crisis view or the life events perspective more accurately depicts personality development and change in adulthood. What is clear is that developmental theorists all agree that midlife is a time of continuing, significant psychological growth.

Erikson's Stage of Generativity versus Stagnation

As we discussed earlier, psychoanalyst Erik Erikson characterized midlife as a period of **generativity versus stagnation**. One's middle adulthood, according to Erikson, is either spent in generativity—making a contribution to family, community, work, and society—or in stagnation. Generative people strive to guide and encourage future generations. Often, people find generativity through parenting, but other roles can fill this need, such as working directly with young people, acting as mentors. Or the need for generativity might be satisfied through creative and artistic output, seeking to leave a lasting contribution. The focus of generativity, then, is beyond the self, as one looks toward the continuation of one's own life through others (Pratt et al., 2001; McAdams and Logan, 2004; An and Cooney, 2006; Peterson, 2006).

A lack of psychological growth in this period results in stagnation. Focusing on their own trivial activities, people may feel they have contributed little to the world, that their presence has counted for little. Some people find themselves floundering, still seeking new, potentially more fulfilling careers. Others become frustrated and bored.

Erikson provides a broad overview, but some psychologists suggest that we need a more precise look at midlife changes in personality. We'll consider three alternative approaches.

Building on Erikson's Views: Vaillant, Gould, and Levinson. Developmentalist George Vaillant (1977) argues that an important period between ages 45 and 55 centres on "keeping the meaning" versus rigidity. Seeking to extract meaning from their lives, adults also seek to "keep the meaning" by accepting the strengths and weaknesses of others. Although they realize it is not perfect, they strive to safeguard their world, and they are relatively content. The man quoted at the beginning of this section, for example, appears content with the meaning he has found in his life. People who are unable to achieve this state risk becoming rigid and increasingly isolated from others.

Psychiatrist Roger Gould (1978) offered an alternative to Erikson's and Vaillant's views. He agrees that people move through a series of stages and potential crises, but he suggests that adults pass through seven stages associated with specific age periods (see Table 8-1). According to Gould, people in their late thirties and early forties begin to feel a sense of

normative-crisis models the approach to personality development that is based on fairly universal stages tied to a sequence of age-related crises

life events models the approach to personality development that is based on the timing of particular events in an adult's life rather than on age per se

generativity versus stagnation according to Erikson, the stage during middle adulthood in which people consider their contributions to family and society

TABLE 8-1   GOULD'S TRANSFORMATIONS IN ADULT DEVELOPMENT

Stage	Approximate Age	Development(s)
1	16 to 18	Desire to escape parental control
2	18 to 22	Leaving the family; peer-group orientation
3	22 to 28	Developing independence, commitment to a career and to children
4	29 to 34	Questioning self; role confusion; marriage and career vulnerable to dissatisfaction
5	35 to 43	Period of urgency to attain life's goals; awareness of time limitation, realignment of life's goals
6	43 to 53	Settling down; acceptance of one's life
7	53 to 60	More tolerance; acceptance of phase; less negativism, general mellowing

Source: From *Transformations*, by R. L. Gould and M. D. Gould, 1978, New York: Simon & Schuster.

urgency about attaining life's goals as they realize that their life is finite. Coming to grips with this reality can propel people toward maturity.

Gould based his model of development on a small sample and relied heavily on his own clinical judgments. Little research has supported his description of the various stages, which was heavily influenced by the psychoanalytic perspective.

Another alternative to Erikson's work is psychologist Daniel Levinson's *seasons of life* theory. According to Levinson (1986, 1992), who intensively interviewed men, the early forties are a period of transition and crisis. He suggests that adult men pass through a series of stages beginning with early adulthood, around age 20, and continuing into midlife. The beginning stages centre on leaving one's family and entering the adult world.

However, at around age 40 or 45, people move to what Levinson calls the midlife transition. The *midlife transition* is a time of questioning, a focus on the finite nature of life. People begin to question some of their fundamental assumptions. They experience the first signs of aging, and they confront the fact that they will not accomplish all their aims before they die.

In Levinson's view, this assessment can lead to a **midlife crisis**, a stage of uncertainty and indecision. Facing signs of physical aging, men might also discover that even the accomplishments of which they are proudest have brought them less satisfaction than they expected. They might try to define what went wrong and seek ways to correct past mistakes. The midlife crisis is a painful and tumultuous period of questioning.

Levinson's view is that most people are susceptible to a fairly profound midlife crisis. Before accepting his perspective, we need to consider some critical drawbacks in his research. First, his initial theory was based on 40 men, and his work with women was conducted years later and, again, on a small sample. Levinson also overstated the consistency and generality of the patterns he found. In fact, the notion of a universal midlife crisis has come under considerable criticism (McCrae and Costa, 1990; Stewart and Ostrove, 1998).

The Midlife Crisis: Reality or Myth? Central to Levinson's model is the concept of midlife crisis, a period in the early forties presumed to be marked by intense psychological turmoil. The notion has taken on a life of its own: There is a general expectation in our society that age 40 is an important psychological juncture.

Such a view is problematic: The evidence is simply lacking. In fact, most research suggests that most people pass into middle age with relative ease. The majority regard midlife as a particularly rewarding time. If they are parents, the physically demanding period of childrearing is usually over, and in some cases children have left the home, allowing parents the opportunity to rekindle their intimacy. Many people find that their careers have blossomed, and they feel quite content with their lives. Focusing on the present, they seek to maximize their involvement with family, friends, and other social groups. Those who regret

midlife crisis a stage of uncertainty and indecision brought about by the realization that life is finite

Despite there being no strong evidence that people universally experience a "midlife crisis," the belief that it is commonplace remains. Why is this belief so prevalent?

the course of their lives might be motivated to change directions, and those who do change end up better off psychologically (Stewart and Vandewater, 1999).

Furthermore, most people feel younger entering midlife than they actually are (Miller et al., 1997; Wethington et al., 1997).

Evidence for the inevitability of midlife crisis is no more compelling than the evidence for stormy adolescence, discussed earlier, yet the notion of a universal midlife crisis seems well entrenched in common wisdom. Why?

One reason might be that turmoil in middle age is both obvious and easily remembered by observers. A 40-year-old man who divorces his wife, trades his Ford Taurus station wagon for a red Saab convertible, and marries a much younger woman makes a greater impression than a happily married man who remains with his spouse (and Taurus) through middle adulthood. We are more likely to notice and recall marital difficulties than the lack of them. In this way, the myth of a blustery and universal midlife crisis is perpetuated. For most people, though, a midlife crisis is more the stuff of fiction than of reality. In fact, for some people, midlife brings few, if any, changes. As we consider in the Cultural Dimensions segment, middle age is not even considered a separate period of life in some cultures.

Stability versus Change in Personality

Harry Hennesey, age 53, is a vice-president of an investment banking firm. He says he still feels like a kid. Many middle-aged adults would agree. Although most people say they have changed a good deal since adolescence—and mostly for the better—many also perceive important similarities in basic personality traits between their present and younger selves.

The degree to which personality is stable across the lifespan or changes as we age is a major issue of personality development in middle adulthood. Theorists such as Erikson and Levinson clearly suggest that substantial change occurs over time. Erikson's stages and Levinson's seasons describe set patterns of change. The change might be predictable and age-related, but it is substantial.

An impressive body of research, however, suggests that for individual traits, personality is quite stable and continuous over the lifespan. Developmental psychologists Paul Costa and Robert McCrae find remarkable stability in particular traits. Even-tempered 20-year-olds are even-tempered at 75; affectionate 25-year-olds become affectionate 50-year-olds; and

Cultural Dimensions

Middle Age: In Some Cultures It Doesn't Exist

There's no such thing as middle age.

One could draw that conclusion by looking at the women living in the Oriya culture in Orissa, India. According to research by developmental anthropologist Richard Shweder, who studied how high-caste Hindu women view aging, a distinct period of middle age does not exist. These women view their life course not by chronological age, but by the nature of one's social responsibility, family management issues, and moral sense at a given time (Shweder, 1998, 2003).

The model of aging of the Oriyan women encompasses two phases of life: life in her father's house (*bapa gharo*), followed by life in her husband's mother's house (*sasu gharo*). These two segments fit the context of Oriyan family life, which consists of multigenerational households in which marriages are arranged. After they are married, husbands remain with their parents, and wives are expected to move in with their in-laws. Upon marriage, a wife changes social status from a child (someone's daughter) to a sexually active female (a daughter-in-law).

The shift from child to daughter-in-law typically occurs around the ages of 18 or 20. However, chronological age, per se, does not mark significant boundaries in life for Oriyan women, nor do physical changes, such as the onset of menstruation, nor its cessation at menopause. It is the change from daughter to daughter-in-law to mother-in-law that significantly alters social responsibility. Women must shift their focus from their own parents to the parents of their husband when they marry, and they must become sexually active in order to perpetuate the husband's family line. When a woman becomes mother-in-law, she enters the most prized period of life, described as a more leisurely time of supervision and management of the house rather than work. In this period, called *prauda*, women are in regular communication with God, acting as an intermediary between the family and God.

To a Western eye, the life course of these women might seem restricted, because they rarely have careers outside the home, but Oriyan women do not see themselves in this light. In fact, in the Oriya culture, domestic work is highly respected and valued. Oriyan women also view themselves as more cultured and civilized than men, who must work outside the home.

The notion of a separate middle age is clearly a cultural construction. The significance of a particular biological age range differs widely, depending on the culture in which one lives.

---

disorganized 26-year-olds are still disorganized at age 60. Similarly, self-concept at age 30 is a good indication of self-concept at age 80 (Costa and McCrae, 2002; McCrae and Costa, 2003; Srivastava et al., 2003; Terracciano et al., 2006; also see Figure 8-6).

There is also evidence that traits become more ingrained as people age. For instance, some research suggests that confident adolescents become more confident in their mid-fifties, while shy people become more diffident with age.

Stability and Change in the "Big Five" Personality Traits. Quite a bit of research has centred on the personality traits known as the "Big Five"—so known because they represent the five major clusters of personality characteristics. These include the following:

- neuroticism—the degree to which a person is moody, anxious, and self-critical
- extroversion—how outgoing or shy a person is
- openness—a person's level of curiosity and interest in new experiences

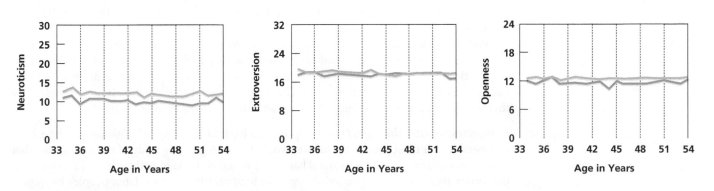

FIGURE 8-6 The Stability of Personality
According to Paul Costa and Robert McCrae, basic personality traits such as neuroticism, extroversion, and openness are stable and consistent throughout adulthood.
Source: Adapted from Costa et al., 1989, p. 148.

While Erikson and Levinson suggest there is substantial personality change over time, other research has shown that personality, in terms of individual traits, remains stable over the lifespan. How many of these high school swimmers do you think are still physically active after 40 years? Why?

- agreeableness—how easy-going and helpful a person tends to be
- conscientiousness—a person's tendencies to be organized and responsible

The majority of studies find that the big five traits are relatively stable past the age of 30, although variations exist for specific traits. In particular, neuroticism, extroversion, and openness to experience decline somewhat from early adulthood, while agreeableness and conscientiousness tend to increase—findings that are consistent across cultures. The basic pattern, however, is one of stability through adulthood (McCrae and Costa, 2003; Srivastava et al., 2003).

Does evidence for the stability of traits contradict the theories of personality change championed by Erikson, Gould, and Levinson? Not necessarily, for the contradictions may be more apparent than real.

People's basic traits do show continuity over the course of their adult lives. But people are also susceptible to changes, and adulthood is packed with major changes in family status, career, and even the economy. The physical changes of aging, illness, the death of a loved one, and an increased awareness of life's finite span also can spur changes in how people view themselves and the world at large (Krueger and Heckhausen, 1993; Roberts et al., 2006).

Happiness across the Lifespan. Suppose you hit it big on *Jeopardy*. Would you be a happier person? For most people, the answer would be no. A growing body of research shows that adults' *subjective well-being* or general happiness remains stable over their lives. Even winning the lottery increases subjective well-being only temporarily; one year later, people's happiness tends to return to pre-lottery levels (Diener, 2000).

The stability of subjective well-being suggests that most people have a "set point" for happiness—a level that is consistent despite the ups and downs of life. Specific events may temporarily elevate or depress a person's mood (for example, an outstanding job evaluation or being laid off from work), but people eventually return to their general level of happiness.

Most people's happiness set points seem to be fairly high. Some 30 percent of people rate themselves as "very happy," while only 10 percent rate themselves as "not too happy." Most people say they are "pretty happy." These findings are similar across different social groups. Men and women rate themselves as equally happy. Regardless of their economic situation, residents of countries across the world have similar levels of happiness (Schkade and Kahneman, 1998; Diener, 2000; Diener et al., 2003; Kahneman et al., 2006). The conclusion: Money doesn't buy happiness.

REVIEW, CHECK, AND APPLY

REVIEW

- In normative-crisis models, people pass through age-related stages of development; life events models focus on how people change in response to various life events.

- Levinson argues that the transition to middle age can lead to a midlife crisis, but there is little evidence that this is so for the majority of people.

- Broad, basic personality characteristics are relatively stable. Specific aspects of personality do seem to change in response to life events.

CHECK YOURSELF

1. According to _____ models, researchers understand personality development as the product of universal stages tied to age-related crises.

2. According to the _____ model, individuals at different ages can experience the same emotional and personality changes because they have shared common occurrences in their lives.

   a. normative-crisis

   b. psychosexual

   c. life events

   d. self-understanding

3. According to Roger Gould (1978, 1980) people in their late thirties and early forties feel a sense of urgency in terms of reaching their life goals because they realize their lives are limited.

   - True

   - False

APPLYING LIFESPAN DEVELOPMENT

- How do you think the midlife transition is different for a middle-aged person whose child has just entered adolescence versus a middle-aged person who has just become a parent for the first time?

Answers: 1) normative-crisis; 2) c; 3) True

Relationships: Family in Middle Age

LO10 What are typical patterns of marriage and divorce in middle adulthood?

LO11 What changing family situations do middle-aged adults face?

LO12 What are the causes and characteristics of family violence?

LEARNING OBJECTIVES

For Kathy and Bob, going to their son Jon's university orientation was a shockingly new experience in the life of their family. It hadn't really registered that he would be leaving home when he was accepted at a university on the other side of the country. It didn't hit them just how much this would change their family until they said goodbye and left him on his new campus. It was a wrenching experience. Kathy and Bob worried about their son in the ways that parents always do, but they also felt a profound loss—the job of raising their son, basically, was done. Now he was largely on his own. This thought filled them with pride and anticipation for his future, but with great sadness, too. They would miss him.

For members of many non-Western cultures who live in extended families in which multiple generations spend their lives in the same household or village, middle adulthood is nothing special. But in Western cultures, family dynamics change significantly in midlife. For most parents, there are major shifts in their relationships with their children and with other family members as well. It is a period of changing roles that, in twenty-first-century Western cultures, encompasses an increasing number of combinations and permutations. We'll start by looking at how marriage develops and changes over this period, and then consider some of the many alternative forms of family life today (Kaslow, 2001).

Marriage

Fifty years ago, midlife was similar for most people. Men and women, married since early adulthood, were still married to each other. One hundred years ago, when life expectancy was much shorter, people in their forties were usually married—but not necessarily to the persons they had first married. Spouses often died; people might be well into their second marriage by middle age.

Today, the story is different and more varied. More people are single at midlife, having never married. Single people might live alone or with a partner. Gay and lesbian adults might marry. Some couples have divorced, lived alone, and then remarried. Many people's marriages end in divorce, and many families "blend" together into new households comprising children and stepchildren from previous marriages. Some couples still spend 40 or 50 years together, the bulk of those years during middle adulthood. Many experience the peak of marital satisfaction during middle age.

The Ups and Downs of Marriage. Even happily married couples have their ups and downs, with satisfaction rising and falling over the course of the marriage. In the past, most research has suggested that marital satisfaction follows the U-shaped configuration shown in Figure 8-7. (Figley, 1973). Specifically, marital satisfaction begins to decline just after the marriage, falling until it reaches its lowest point following the births of the couple's children. At that point, satisfaction begins to grow, eventually returning to the same level as before the marriage (Karney and Bradbury, 1995; Noller, Feeney, and Ward, 1997; Harvey and Weber, 2002).

Middle-aged couples cite several sources of satisfaction. Both men and women typically say their spouse is "their best friend" and that they like them as people. They also view marriage as a long-term commitment and agree on their aims and goals. Finally, most also feel that their spouses have grown more interesting over the years (Levenson et al., 1993; Schmitt et al., 2007).

Sexual satisfaction is related to general marital satisfaction. What matters is not how often couples have sex. Instead, satisfaction is related to *agreeing* about their sex lives (Spence 1997; Litzinger and Gordon, 2005.)

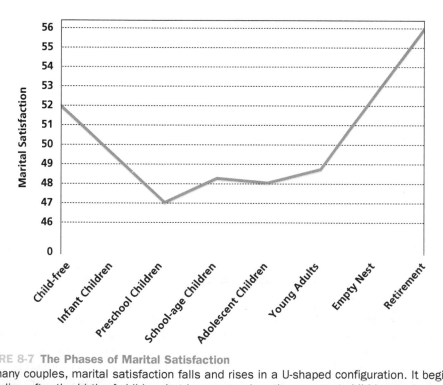

FIGURE 8-7 The Phases of Marital Satisfaction
For many couples, marital satisfaction falls and rises in a U-shaped configuration. It begins to decline after the birth of children but increases when the youngest child leaves home and eventually returns to a level of satisfaction similar to that at the start of marriage. Why do you think this pattern of satisfaction occurs?
Source: Adapted from Rollins and Cannon, 1974.

Divorce

Jane Burroughs knew 10 years into her marriage that it wasn't working. She and her husband argued constantly. He made all the decisions; she felt she had no say. But instead of divorcing, she stayed for 21 more years. It wasn't until she was 50, when her children were grown with kids of their own, that she finally got up the nerve to leave. Although she had wanted the divorce for years—and her husband eventually did, too—Burroughs, now 58, concedes it was the most difficult experience of her life and one that triggered conflicting emotions. "The hardest part was learning how to be alone," she says. "But I liked being independent." (Enright, 2004, p. 54)

Divorce among midlife couples is actually rising, despite a decline in divorces overall in recent decades (Uhlenberg et al., 1990; Stewart et al., 1997; Enright, 2004; Kelly, 2010). By examining trends in divorce across the country, researchers have noticed that divorce is more common among those who married young, and that divorce rates peak not at seven years, as the popular saying goes, but at four years (Clark and Crompton, 2006).

Marriages unravel for many reasons. One is that people spend less time together in middle adulthood than in earlier years. In individualistic Western cultures, people are concerned with their personal happiness. If their marriage is not satisfying, they feel that divorce might increase their happiness. Divorce is also more socially acceptable than in the past, and there are fewer legal impediments to it. In some cases—but certainly not all—the financial costs are not high. And as the opportunities for women grow, wives might feel less dependent on their husbands, both emotionally and economically (Wallerstein et al., 2000; Amato and Previti, 2003; Fincham, 2003).

Another reason for divorce is that romantic, passionate feelings may fade over time. Because Western culture emphasizes romance and passion, people might feel they have cause to divorce if the passion goes. Finally, a great deal of strain is put on marriages when both parents work. Energy once directed toward families and maintaining relationships is now spent on work and other obligations outside the home (Macionis, 2001).

Whatever the causes, divorce can be especially difficult in midlife. It can be particularly hard for women who have played the traditional role of mother and never performed substantial work outside the home. They may face age discrimination, finding that younger people are preferred even in jobs with minimal requirements. Without a good deal of training and support, these divorced women, lacking recognized job skills, can remain virtually unemployable (McDaniel and Coleman, 2003; Williams and Dunne-Bryant, 2006).

Many people who divorce in midlife, though, end up happy. Women, in particular, are apt to find that developing a new, independent self-identity is a positive outcome. Both men and women who divorce in midlife are also likely to form new relationships, and they typically remarry (Enright, 2004).

Remarriage. Nearly half of those who divorce marry again, and only 1 in 5 of those second marriages end in divorce. Divorcees are likely to marry people who are also divorced, partly because they tend to be available, but also because divorced people share a similar experience. Second marriages might be more successful because partners are more mature and realistic in their expectations of marriage. They often view marriage in less romantic terms than younger couples, and they are more cautious. They are also likely to be more flexible about roles and duties; they share household chores and decision making more equitably (Clark and Crompton, 2006; Hetherington, 1999).

Although the rate of remarriage is high, it is far higher in some groups than in others. For instance, it is harder for women to remarry than men, particularly older women. Whereas 90 percent of women under age 25 remarry after divorce, less than one-third of women over age 40 remarry (Bumpass et al., 1990; Besharov and West, 2002).

This age difference stems from the *marriage gradient* we discussed earlier: Societal norms push men to marry women who are younger, smaller, and lower in status than they are. The older a woman is, the fewer socially acceptable men she has available to her since men her age are likely to be looking for younger women. Women are also disadvantaged by double standards regarding physical attractiveness. Older women can be perceived as unattractive, while older men are seen as "distinguished" and "mature" (Bernard, 1982; Buss, 2003b; Doyle, 2004b).

For several reasons, marrying again might be more appealing than remaining single. A person who remarries avoids the social consequences of divorce. Even in the twenty-first century,

Most divorced adults do not remarry, but they are more likely to live in a common-law relationship.

when divorce is common, it carries with it a certain stigma. In addition, divorced people overall report less satisfaction with life than married people (Lucas, 2005).

The majority of divorced adults do not remarry, and attitude might have a very important role in whether or not one remarries. Less than one-quarter of divorced adults expect to remarry, and three out of five say they do not want to remarry. More women than men state that they do not intend to marry again. Those with children are also less likely to want to remarry, and the desire to remarry declines with age. This is not to say divorced adults are lonely, as they are more likely than never-married adults to live in a common-law relationship (Beaupré, 2008).

A minority of adults have experienced more than one divorce. Second (and third) marriages may include stresses not present in first marriages, such as the blending of different families. In some cases, having experienced and survived one divorce, partners can be less committed and more ready to walk away from an unhappy second marriage. Finally, some people might have personality and emotional characteristics that don't make them easy to live with (Cherlin, 1993; Warshak, 2000; Coleman et al., 2001).

Family Evolutions: From Full House to Empty Nest

For many parents, a major midlife transition is the departure of children who are going to university, getting married, joining the military, or taking a job far from home. Even people who become parents at a relatively late age are likely to face this transition, since the middle adulthood spans nearly a quarter century. As we saw in Kathy and Bob's story, a child's departure can be wrenching—so much so, in fact, that it has been labelled the "empty nest syndrome." The **empty nest syndrome** refers to the unhappiness, worry, loneliness, and depression some parents feel when their children leave home (Lauer and Lauer, 1999).

Many parents report that major adjustments are required. For women who were stay-at-home mothers, the loss can be very difficult. Traditional homemakers, who focus significant time and energy on their children, face a challenging time.

While the loss can be difficult, parents also find that some aspects of this transition are quite positive. Even mothers who have stayed at home find they have time for other interests, such as community or recreational activities, when the children leave. They may also enjoy the opportunity to get a job or return to school. Finally, many women find that motherhood is not easy; surveys show that most people regard motherhood as harder than it used to be. Such women might now feel liberated from a difficult set of responsibilities (Heubusch, 1997; Morfei et al., 2004).

empty nest syndrome the experience that relates to parents' feelings of unhappiness, worry, loneliness, and depression resulting from their children's departure from home

Though feelings of loss are common for most people, there is little, if any, evidence that the departure of children produces anything more than temporary feelings of sadness and distress. This is especially true for women who have worked outside the home (Antonucci, 2001; Crowley et al., 2003).

In fact, there are discernible benefits when children leave home. Spouses have more time for one another. Married or unmarried people can attend to their own work without having to worry about helping the kids with homework, carpools, and the like. The house stays neater, and the telephone rings less often.

Most research on the so-called empty nest syndrome has focused on women. Men, traditionally not as involved in childrearing, were assumed to weather the transition more smoothly. However, some research suggests that men also experience feelings of loss when their children depart, although these feelings may differ from those felt by women.

One survey found that although most fathers felt either happy or neutral about the departure of their children, almost a quarter felt unhappy (Lewis et al., 1979). Those fathers tended to mention lost opportunities, regretting things they had not done with their children. Some felt they had been too busy for their children or hadn't been sufficiently nurturing or caring.

The concept of the empty nest syndrome arose at a time when grown children tended to leave home for good. Today, as we discuss next, "boomerang children" frequently return to refill that empty nest.

> **boomerang children** young adults who return, after leaving home for some period, to live in the homes of their middle-aged parents
>
> **sandwich generation** adults who, in middle adulthood, must fulfill the needs of both children and aging parents

Boomerang Children: Refilling the Empty Nest

Carole Olis doesn't know what to make of her 23-year-old son, Rob. He has been living at home since his graduation from university more than two years ago. Her six older children returned to the nest for just a few months and then bolted.

"I ask him, 'Why don't you move out with your friends?'" says Mrs. Olis. Rob has a ready answer: "They all live at home, too."

Carole Olis is not alone in being surprised by the return of her son. A significant number of young adults are coming back to live with their middle-aged parents.

Known as **boomerang children**, they typically cite money as the main reason for returning. In the current economy, many graduates cannot find jobs, or the jobs they do find don't pay enough to make ends meet. Others return home after a divorce. Nearly 60 percent of all 20- to 24-year-olds in Canada live with their parents. In some European countries, the proportion is even higher. Further, children of European, South American, and Asian immigrants are more likely to live with their parents longer into adulthood, reflecting cultural differences (Bianchi and Casper, 2000; Lewin, 2003a; Buss, 2005; Statistics Canada, 2006).

Parents' reactions to the return of their children depend largely on the reasons for the children's return. If their children are unemployed, their return can be a major irritant. Fathers in particular might not grasp what a difficult job market graduates encounter, and may be decidedly unsympathetic. There may also be some subtle parent–child rivalry for the attention between the child and either spouse (Wilcox, 1992; Mitchell, 2006).

Mothers tend to sympathize more with children who are unemployed. Single mothers in particular may welcome the help and security returning children provide. Both mothers and fathers feel fairly positive about returning children who work and contribute to the household (Quinn, 1993; Veevers and Mitchell, 1998).

The Sandwich Generation: Between Children and Parents.
At the same time children are leaving the nest, or returning as boomerang children, many middle-aged adults face another challenge: the care of their own aging parents. The term **sandwich generation** refers to these midlife adults who are squeezed between the needs of children and parents (Riley and Bowen, 2005; Grundy and Henretta, 2006).

The sandwich generation is a relatively new phenomenon, produced by several converging trends. First, people are marrying later and having children at an older age. At the same time, people are living longer. Thus, midlife adults will often have both parents who are alive and require care, and children who need a significant amount of nurturing.

> **Watch** on **mydevelopmentlab**
>
> To better understand the sandwich generation, log onto MyDevelopmentLab to watch a video of Amy, a woman in her mid-forties who cares for her 6-year-old son and her 82-year-old mother while balancing work and other responsibilities.

The care of aging parents can be psychologically tricky. There is a degree of role reversal as children become more parental and parents become more dependent. As we'll discuss later, much older adults, who are used to being independent, may resent and resist their children's help. They do not want to be burdens. Almost all much older adults who live alone say they do not wish to live with their children (CFCEPLA, 1986; Merrill, 1997).

Middle-aged adults provide a range of care for their parents. They might provide financial support to supplement a parent's pension and also help manage a household, doing tasks such as removing storm windows in the spring or shovelling snow in the winter.

In some cases, aging parents are invited to live in their child's home. Multigenerational households—three or more generations—represent 4 percent of all households and are more prevalent among Aboriginal families and recent emigrants, although this is probably more for cultural reasons than to provide care for aging parents (Statistics Canada, 2004).

Multigenerational families present a delicate situation, as roles are renegotiated. Typically, the adult children—who are no longer children—are in charge of the household, but this can vary with culture and family circumstances. Both adult children and their parents must make adjustments and find some common ground in making decisions. Aging parents might find their new dependence difficult, and this can be wrenching for adult child as well. The youngest generation might resist including the oldest generation.

In many cases, the burden of care is not shared equally; the larger share is most often assumed by women. Even when both husband and wife are in the labour force, women tend to be more involved in day-to-day care, even when the parent is (or parents are) not their own (Soldo, 1996; Putney and Bengtson, 2001).

Culture also influences how caregivers view their roles. Members of Asian cultures, which are more collectivistic, are more likely to view caregiving as a traditional and ordinary duty. In contrast, members of more individualistic cultures might feel that familial ties are less central, and that caring for the older generation is a burden (Ho et al., 2003; Kim and Lee, 2003).

Despite the burden of being sandwiched in between two generations, which can stretch the caregiving child's resources, there are significant rewards. The psychological attachment between middle-aged children and their older parents can continue to grow. Both sides can see each other more realistically. They may grow closer, more accepting of each other's weaknesses and more appreciative of each other's strengths (Vincent et al., 2006).

Becoming a Grandparent: Who, Me?

When her eldest son and daughter-in-law had their first child, Leah couldn't believe it. At age 54, she was a grandmother! She kept telling herself she felt far too young to be anybody's grandparent.

Middle adulthood often brings one of the unmistakable symbols of aging: becoming a grandparent. For some people, the new role has been eagerly awaited. They might miss the energy and excitement and even the demands of young children, and see grandparenthood as the next stage in the natural progression of life. Others are less pleased with the prospect, seeing it as a clear signpost of aging.

Grandparenting tends to fall into different styles. *Involved* grandparents are actively engaged in and have influence over their grandchildren's lives. They hold clear expectations about the ways their grandchildren should behave. A retired grandparent who takes care of a grandchild while the child's parents work is an example of an involved grandparent (Cherlin and Furstenberg, 1986; Mueller et al., 2002).

In contrast, *companionate* grandparents are more relaxed. Rather than taking responsibility for their grandchildren, they act as supporters and buddies to them. Grandparents who visit and call frequently, and perhaps occasionally take their grandchildren on vacations or invite them to visit without their parents, are companionate grandparents.

Finally, the most aloof type of grandparents are *remote*. They are detached and distant, showing little interest in their grandchildren. Remote grandparents, for example, might rarely visit their grandchildren and might complain about childish behaviour when they did see their grandchildren.

There are marked gender differences in the extent to which people enjoy grandparenthood. Generally, grandmothers are more interested and experience greater satisfaction than grandfathers, particularly when they have a high level of interaction with younger grandchildren (Smith, 1995; Smith and Drew, 2002).

Grandparents are more apt to be involved when they are part of multigenerational households and when the family is headed by a single parent. In both circumstances, parents often rely substantially on the help of grandparents in everyday child care, and cultural norms tend to be highly supportive of grandparents taking an active role (Baydar and Brooks-Gunn, 1998; Baird et al., 2000; Crowther and Rodriguez, 2003; Stevenson et al., 2007).

Family Violence: The Hidden Epidemic

In November 2007, Karen Beck was strangled to death by her ex-husband, who then set fire to her house and hanged himself. Karen had a restraining order against her husband after he had threatened her with a gun (Vancouver Sun, 2008).

In June 2004, Sylvia Lyall-Ritchie was strangled to death by her partner. Family and friends had long tried to persuade her to end the relationship, but still felt guilty they had not done enough (CBC News, 2008).

It is not difficult to find media reports such as these about spousal violence ending in homicide. Despite these calls to action to end violence, to help victims leave abusive relationships, and to protect those who have, statistics on spousal violence have remained stable (Statistics Canada, 2011).

The Prevalence of Spousal Abuse. Domestic violence occurs in approximately 10 to 17 percent of all couples, and victims are more likely to be young, have a disability, be homosexual or bisexual, or Aboriginal. Spousal violence does not differ by income or education, or between minorities, immigrants, and the majority Canadian-born population. While men and women are equally likely to be abusive and report current abuse, the nature of the abuse is more violent when men are abusive towards women. Women are also more likely to report repeated incidents of violence and are more likely to report the violence to police, although only 22 percent do (Statistics Canada, 2009).

In addition, 17 percent of Canadians report psychological abuse, such as verbal or emotional abuse, and financial abuse, which includes limiting access to family finances, and prohibiting or forcing an individual to work. Domestic violence is a worldwide problem. Estimates suggest that one in three women around the globe experiences violent victimization during her life (Walker, 1999; Garcia-Moreno et al., 2005).

Certain factors increase the likelihood of abuse. Spousal abuse is more apt to occur in large families for whom both financial strain and verbal aggression are common. Those husbands and wives who grew up in families where violence was present are also more likely to be violent themselves (Straus and Yodanis, 1996; Ehrensaft et al., 2003; Lackey, 2003).

Marital aggression by a husband typically occurs in three stages (Walker, 1999). In the initial *tension-building* stage, a batterer becomes upset and shows dissatisfaction through verbal abuse. He might also use some physical aggression, such as shoving or grabbing. The wife may desperately try to avoid the impending violence, attempting to calm her spouse or withdraw from the situation. Such behaviour might only enrage the husband, who senses his wife's vulnerability. Her efforts to escape might escalate his anger.

In the next stage—an *acute battering incident*—the physical abuse actually occurs, lasting from several minutes to hours. Wives might be shoved against walls, choked, slapped, punched, kicked, and stepped on. Their arms might be twisted or broken, they might be shaken severely, thrown down a flight of stairs, or burned with cigarettes or scalding liquids. About a quarter of wives are forced to engage in sexual activity, which takes the form of aggressive sexual acts and rape.

Finally, in some—but not all—cases, the episode ends with the *loving contrition* stage. At this point, the husband feels remorse and apologizes for his actions. He may provide first aid and sympathy, assuring his wife that he will never act violently again. Because wives can feel they were somehow partly at fault, they might accept the apology and forgive their husbands. They want to believe that the aggression will never occur again.

The loving contrition stage helps explain why many wives remain with abusive husbands and continue to be victims. Wishing desperately to keep their marriages intact, and believing that they have no good alternatives, some wives remain out of a vague sense that they

Parents who abuse their own spouses and children were often victims of abuse themselves as children, reflecting a cycle of violence.

cycle of violence hypothesis the theory that abuse and neglect of children leads them to be predisposed to abusiveness as adults

are responsible for the abuse. In other cases, wives might be financially dependent on their partners or fear that their partners will come after them if they leave.

There is good reason for this fear. Many women report that their abusers threatened to harm the women, themselves, their children, or family pets if they leave. A much larger number of women report abuse from ex-partners (20%) than from current partners only (3%) or from both current and ex-partners (7%). One factor might be that women are more comfortable discussing abuse by an ex-partner, but the extent to which abuse continues after the relationship ends is very troubling. Spousal homicide accounts for 16 percent of all solved homicides in Canada. While men are more likely to be victims of homicide in general, women are far more likely to be victims of spousal homicide, which is more than twice as likely to occur after separation (Statistics Canada, 2009).

The Cycle of Violence. Still other wives stay with batterers because they learned in childhood, as their husbands did, that violence is an acceptable means of settling disputes.

Individuals who abuse their spouses and children were often the victims of abuse themselves. According to the **cycle of violence hypothesis**, abuse and neglect of children predisposes them to abusiveness as adults. In line with social learning theory, the cycle of violence hypothesis suggests that family aggression is perpetuated from one generation to another. It is a fact that individuals who abuse their wives often witnessed spousal abuse at home as children, just as parents who abuse their children frequently were the victims of abuse as children (McCloskey and Bailey, 2000; Serbin and Karp, 2004; Renner and Slack, 2006).

Growing up in an abusive home does not invariably lead to abusiveness as an adult. Only about one-third of people who were abused or neglected as children abuse their own children

> **From the perspective of a health-care provider:** What can be done to end the cycle of violence, in which people who were abused as children grow up to be abusers of others?

as adults, and two-thirds of abusers were not themselves abused as children. The cycle of violence, then, does not tell the full story of abuse (Jacobson and Gottman, 1998).

Whatever the causes of abuse, there are ways to deal with it, as we consider next.

The Cultural Roots of Violence. On December 10, 2007, at approximately 7:20 a.m., 16-year-old Aqsa Parvez was taken from a school bus stop in Mississauga by her brother. Half an hour

Dealing with Spousal Abuse

Becoming an Informed Consumer of Development

Spousal abuse occurs in up to 20 percent of all couples (sometimes not appearing until the relationship breaks down), but efforts to deal with victims of abuse are underfunded and inadequate to meet current needs. In fact, some psychologists argue that the same factors that led society to underestimate the magnitude of the problem for many years now hinder the development of effective interventions. Still, several measures can help the victims of spousal abuse (Browne, 1993; Koss et al., 1993):

- **Teach both wives and husbands a basic premise:** Violence is *never,* under *any* circumstances, an acceptable means of resolving disagreements.

- **Call the police.** Assault, including spousal assault, is against the law. It might be difficult to involve law enforcement officers, but this is a realistic way of handling the problem. Judges can also issue restraining orders requiring abusive husbands to stay away from their wives.

- **Understand that the remorse shown by a spouse, no matter how heartfelt, might have no bearing on possible future violence.** Even if a husband shows loving regret and vows that he will never be violent again, such a promise is no guarantee against future abuse.

- **If you are the victim of abuse, seek a safe haven.** Many communities have shelters for the victims of domestic violence that can house women and their children. Because addresses of shelters are kept confidential, an abusive spouse will not be able to find you. Telephone numbers are listed in the yellow or blue pages of phone books, and local police should also have the numbers.

- **If you feel in danger from an abusive partner, seek a restraining order** from a judge in court. A restraining order forbids a spouse to come near you, under penalty of law.

later, her father called 911 and confessed to killing his daughter. Aqsa was the youngest of eight children and was staying with a friend's family because of conflicts over cultural differences at home. Her father and brother pled guilty to her murder; their reason was that Aqsa's disobedience was an insult and embarrassment to the family. Aqsa's mother told police that disobedient daughters are sometimes killed in their native Pakistan. One of Aqsa's sisters told police that the killer should not go to jail and that Aqsa should have obeyed.

Although domestic violence and aggression are often seen as a particularly North American phenomenon, other cultures have traditions that regard violence as acceptable (Rao, 1997). Wife battering is especially prevalent in cultures that view women as inferior to men and treat them as property.

In Western societies, too, domestic violence varies in acceptability, both historically and regionally. Some commonly cited myths claim certain forms of spousal violence were once publicly endorsed and legal in our society (Sommers, 1994). Other forms of spousal violence sometimes slip through legal cracks, and spousal violence would often go unpunished by police, while the public turned a blind eye. Sadly, in some communities this attitude persists. For example, when a woman reported to a store security guard a domestic assault taking place in the store, the security guard told her to mind her own business. The woman acknowledged that, in this community, the level of open domestic violence was much higher than in the community she was raised.

Some experts on abuse suggest that its root cause is the traditional power structure in which women and men function. They argue that the more a society differentiates between men's and women's status, the more likely it is that abuse will occur.

They cite research examining the legal, political, educational, and economic roles of women and men. For example, some research has compared battering statistics across different regions in North America. Abuse is more likely to occur in regions where women are of particularly low or high status compared with women in other regions. Apparently, relatively low status makes women easy targets of violence, while unusually high status may make husbands feel threatened and thus more likely to behave abusively (Dutton, 1994; Vandello and Cohen, 2003).

REVIEW, CHECK, AND APPLY

REVIEW

- Family changes in middle adulthood include the departure of children. In recent years, the "boomerang children" phenomenon has emerged.

- Middle-aged adults often have increasing responsibilities for their aging parents.

- Marital violence tends to pass through three stages: tension building, an acute battering incident, and loving contrition.

CHECK YOURSELF

1. According to the U-shaped curve illustrating the changes in marital satisfaction, marriage satisfaction typically tends to decrease after marriage, reach its lowest point after the birth of children, and then

a. take a sharper dip that relates to more marriages ending in divorce.

b. slowly begin to increase again, eventually returning to the same level it was before marriage.

c. begin a drastic increase to levels surpassing premarriage levels of satisfaction.

d. steadily decrease until children leave the house.

2. Both men and women who divorce during midlife are likely to enter new relationships, but typically do not remarry.

- True

- False

3. Couples who, in middle adulthood, need to take care of their aging parents and their children are often referred to by psychologists as the _____.

4. Match each of the following descriptions of spousal violence to its appropriate stage.

a. Batterer expresses remorse and apologizes for actions.

b. Batterer becomes upset and shows dissatisfaction through verbal abuse.

c. Physical abuse actually occurs.

1. Tension-building stage

2. Acute battering incident

3. Loving contrition stage

APPLYING LIFESPAN DEVELOPMENT

- Are the phenomena of the empty nest, boomerang children, the sandwich generation, and grandparenting culturally dependent? Why might such phenomena be different in societies where multigenerational families are the norm?

Answers: 1) b; 2) True; 3) sandwich generation; 4) a-3, b-1, c-2

Work and Leisure

LO13 What are the characteristics of work and career in middle adulthood?

Enjoying a weekly game of golf . . . starting a neighbourhood watch program . . . coaching a Little League baseball team . . . joining an investment club . . . travelling . . . taking a cooking class . . . attending a theatre series . . . running for the local town council . . . going to the movies with friends . . . attending lectures on Buddhism . . . fixing up a porch in the back of the house . . . chaperoning a high school class on an out-of-town trip . . . lying on a beach, reading a book during an annual vacation . . . .

Adults in their middle years actually enjoy a rich variety of activities. Although middle adulthood often represents the peak of career success and earning power, it is also a time when people throw themselves into leisure and recreational activities. In fact, midlife may be the period when work and leisure activities are balanced most easily. No longer feeling a need to prove themselves on the job, and increasingly valuing their contributions to family, community, and—more broadly—society, middle-aged adults may find that work and leisure complement one another in ways that enhance overall happiness.

Work and Careers: Jobs at Midlife

For many, productivity, success, and earning power are greatest in middle age, but occupational success may become far less alluring than it once was. This is particularly true for those who have not achieved the career success they had hoped for. In such cases, family and other off-the-job interests become more important than work (Howard, 1992; Simonton, 1997).

The factors that make a job satisfying change during middle age. Younger adults focus on abstract and future-oriented concerns, such as the opportunity for advancement or the possibility of recognition and approval. Middle-aged employees care more about the here-and-now qualities of work. They are more concerned with pay, working conditions, and specific policies, such as how vacation time is calculated. As at earlier stages of life, changes in overall job quality are associated with changes in stress levels for both men and women (Hattery, 2000; Peterson and Wilson, 2004; Cohrs et al., 2006).

In general, though, the relationship between age and work is positive: The older workers are, the more overall job satisfaction they experience. This is not altogether surprising since younger adults who are dissatisfied with their jobs will quit them and find new positions that they like better. Also, because older workers have fewer opportunities to change jobs, they may learn to live with what they have and accept that it is the best they are likely to get. Such acceptance might ultimately translate into satisfaction (Tangri et al., 2003).

Challenges of Work: On-the-Job Dissatisfaction

Job satisfaction is not universal in middle adulthood. For some people, dissatisfaction with working conditions or with the nature of the job increases their stress. Conditions may become so bad that the result is burnout or a decision to change jobs.

Burnout. For 44-year-old Peggy Augarten, her early-morning shifts in the intensive care unit of a suburban hospital were becoming increasingly difficult. It had always been hard to lose a patient, but recently she found herself crying over patients at the strangest moments: while she was doing the laundry, washing the dishes, or watching TV. When she began to dread going to work, she knew that her feelings about her job were undergoing a fundamental change.

Augarten's response probably reflects the phenomenon of burnout. **Burnout** occurs when workers experience dissatisfaction, disillusionment, frustration, and weariness from their jobs. It occurs most often in jobs that involve helping others, and it often strikes those who once were the most idealistic and driven. In some ways, such workers can be overcommitted to their jobs. Realizing that they can make only minor dents in huge social problems such

burnout a situation that occurs when highly trained professionals experience dissatisfaction, disillusionment, frustration, and weariness from their jobs

as poverty and medical care can be disappointing and demoralizing (Demir et al., 2003; Taris et al., 2004; Bakker and Heuven, 2006).

A growing cynicism about one's work characterizes burnout. An employee might say to himself, "Why am I working so hard? No one is going to notice that I've come in on budget for the last two years." Workers also might feel indifferent about their job performance. The idealism a worker felt entering a profession can give way to pessimism and the attitude that no meaningful solution to a problem exists (Lock, 1992).

People can combat burnout, even in professions with high demands and seemingly insurmountable burdens. The nurse who despairs of not having enough time for every patient can adopt a more feasible, yet nurturing, goal—such as giving patients a quick backrub. Jobs can also be structured so that workers (and their supervisors) note the small, daily victories, such as a client's gratitude, even though disease, poverty, racism, and an inadequate educational system remain problems.

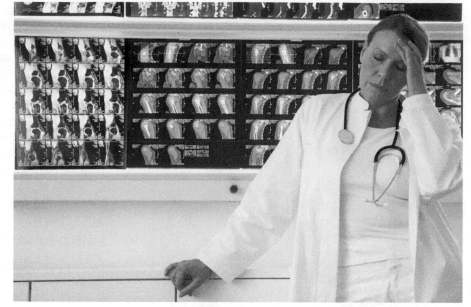

Burnout occurs when a worker experiences dissatisfaction, disillusionment, frustration, or weariness from his or her job. Those who experience it grow increasingly cynical or indifferent toward their work.

Unemployment: The Dashing of the Dream

For many workers, unemployment is a hard reality, affecting them psychologically and economically. For those who have been fired, laid-off by corporate downsizing, or forced out of jobs by technological advances, being out of work can be psychologically and even physically devastating (Sharf, 1992).

Unemployment can leave people feeling anxious, depressed, and irritable. Their self-confidence can plummet, and they might be unable to concentrate. According to one analysis, every time the unemployment rate goes up 1 percent, suicide rises 4 percent, and admissions to psychiatric facilities go up by some 4 percent for men and 2 percent for women (Kates et al., 1990; Connor, 1992; Inoue et al., 2006).

Even seemingly positive aspects of unemployment, such as having more time, can affect people negatively. Unemployed people can feel depressed and at loose ends, making them less apt than employed people to take part in community activities, use libraries, and read. They are more likely to be late for appointments and even for meals (Ball and Orford, 2002; Tyre and McGinn, 2003).

Focus on Research

The Curse of Perfectionism

At a job interview, a candidate is asked, "Tell me about your biggest weakness." "I'm a perfectionist, but I'm working on it. I still give 100 percent but I don't waste as much time triple-checking and second-guessing." You are the interviewer—did you roll your eyes? Is perfectionism a clichéd non-flaw, or a true obstacle? According to Dr. Simon Sherry, Dalhousie University, perfectionism actually sets individuals up for self-defeating behaviour.

Because perfection is unattainable, perfectionists have difficulty getting things done. They spend too much time preparing or reviewing and avoid other tasks that are challenging. Dr. Sherry and colleagues examined perfectionism and productivity in a large group of professors across Canada and the United States. While we have an image of perfectionists producing high-quality work, Sherry and colleagues found that the more perfectionist the individual, the less productive they were. There were also no indications that the smaller quantity of work was of higher quality; perfectionist professors produced fewer publications, published in less prestigious journals, and were cited by others less often. Because university faculty live by the motto "publish or perish," this lower productivity can seriously jeopardize careers—clear evidence that, for a group that collectively believes perfectionism is good, it does, in fact, cause harm.

Perfectionism is harmful in other ways as well. Dr. Sherry and his research team examine how perfectionism can lead to depression and eating disorders, including binge eating. And while perfectionism should be easy to treat with therapy, perfectionists are also very resistant to therapy, according to Dr. Sherry and colleagues (Graham et al., 2010; Sherry et al., 2010; Sherry and Hall, 2009). The widespread belief that perfectionism is a desirable trait only makes it harder for perfectionists to lower their standards, accept "good enough" and find better balance in their lives.

Becoming unemployed in midlife can be a shattering experience. It can taint your view of the world.

These problems can linger. Middle-aged adults tend to stay unemployed longer than younger workers and have fewer opportunities for gratifying work as they age. Employers might discriminate against older applicants, making finding a new job more difficult. Such discrimination is both illegal and based on misguided assumptions: Research finds that older workers miss fewer work days, hold their jobs longer, are more reliable, and are more willing to learn new skills (Connor, 1992).

Midlife unemployment is a shattering experience. For some people, especially those who never find meaningful work again, it taints their view of life. Such involuntary—and premature—retirement can lead to pessimism, cynicism, and despondency. Accepting the new situation takes time and a good deal of psychological adjustment. And there are challenges for those who *do* find a new career, too (Waters and Moore, 2002).

Switching—and Starting—Careers at Midlife

For some people, midlife brings a hunger for change. For those who are dissatisfied with their jobs, who switch careers after a period of unemployment, or who return to a job market they left years ago, development leads to new careers.

People change careers in middle adulthood for several reasons. Perhaps their jobs offer little challenge or they have achieved mastery, making the once difficult, routine. Other people switch because their jobs have changed in ways they do not like, or they have lost their jobs. They might be asked to accomplish more with fewer resources, or technology might have so drastically changed their daily activities that they no longer enjoy what they do.

Still others are unhappy with their status and wish to make a fresh start. Some are burned out or feel that they are on a treadmill. And some people simply want something new. They view middle age as the last chance to make a meaningful occupational change.

Finally, a significant number of people, most of them women, return to the job market after raising children. Some need to find paying work after a divorce. Since the mid-1980s, the number of women in the workforce who are in their fifties has grown significantly. Around half of women between the ages of 55 and 64—and an even larger percentage of those who graduated from university—are now in the workforce.

People can enter new professions with unrealistically high expectations and then be disappointed by the realities. Middle-aged people, starting new careers, might also be placed in entry-level positions; their peers on the job might be considerably younger than they are (Sharf, 1992; Barnett and Hyde, 2001). But in the long run, starting a new career in midlife can be invigorating. Those who switch or begin new careers can be especially valued employees (Connor, 1992; Adelmann et al., 1990; Bromberger and Matthews, 1994).

Some forecasters suggest that career changes will become the rule, not the exception. According to this view, technological advances will occur so rapidly that people will be forced periodically to change their profession, often dramatically. People will have not one, but several, careers during their lifetimes. As the Cultural Dimensions segment shows, this is especially true for those who make another major life and career change: immigrating to another country as adults.

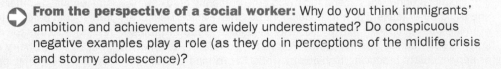

From the perspective of a social worker: Why do you think immigrants' ambition and achievements are widely underestimated? Do conspicuous negative examples play a role (as they do in perceptions of the midlife crisis and stormy adolescence)?

Cultural Dimensions

Immigrants on the Job

Remzi Cej was only a teenager when he was forced to flee war-torn Kosovo with his family. Over the next year and a half, he walked hundreds of kilometers to cross borders, lived in seven refugee camps, and waited. Finally, his family were told they were accepted to go to St. John's, Newfoundland, sponsored by three families in the community.

"What kind of country must this be where total strangers who don't even know us want us to come to their community?"

Ten years later, Remzi is a Rhodes Scholar and works as a policy advisor for the provincial government of Newfoundland and Labrador.

"I belong here. I decided I wanted to give something back to the community which has helped me become the person I am today" (Citizenship and Immigration Canada, 2011).

Public opinion often portrays immigrants as straining the educational, health-care, welfare, and prison systems while contributing little to society. But—as Remzi's story shows—these assumptions are quite wrong.

Approximately 150 000 foreign workers, 90 000 foreign students, and thousands of refugees enter Canada each year. According to 2006 Census data, foreign-born residents now represent nearly 20 percent of the population.

Today's immigrants differ from those who arrived a generation ago. Prior to 1991, more immigrants came to Canada from the UK than any other country. Today, the vast majority of immigrants arrive from China. Critics argue that many new immigrants lack the high-tech skills needed to contribute to today's economy,

But the critics are wrong in many respects. A higher proportion of recent immigrants entered Canada with a university degree than were obtained by Canadian-born citizens.

While qualified, a significant (and arguably exploitative) wage gap exists. Among men with less education, recent immigrants earn 61¢ for every dollar earned by Canadian-born men. Among men with university degrees, recent immigrants earn only 48¢ for every dollar earned by their Canadian-born peers (Statistics Canada, 2006).

Consider the following US. data as well (Topolnicki, 1995; Camarota, 2001):

- **Most legal *and* illegal immigrants ultimately succeed financially.** Although they initially experienced higher rates of poverty, immigrants who arrived prior to 1980 and established themselves have a higher family income than native-born Americans. Immigrants match non-immigrants in entrepreneurship, with one in nine owning their own business.

- **Only a few immigrants come to get on welfare.** Instead, most say they come for the opportunities to work and prosper. Non-refugee immigrants of working age are less likely to be on welfare than native-born US citizens.

- **Given time, immigrants contribute more to the economy than they take away.** Although initially costly to the government—often because they hold low-paying jobs and thus pay no income taxes—immigrants become more productive as they age. Immigrants pay $25 billion to $30 billion a year more in taxes than they use in government services.

One reason immigrants are often financially successful in the long run is that those who choose to leave their native countries are particularly motivated and driven, whereas those who choose *not* to emigrate might be less motivated.

In short, the majority of immigrants become contributing members of their adopted society. They may alleviate labour shortages, and the money they send to relatives back home may invigorate the world economy (World Bank, 2003).

Remzi Cej is one of many immigration success stories.

Leisure Time: Life beyond Work

Leisure time is important for our physical and mental well-being and has decreased in recent years. The availability of leisure time also changes throughout adulthood, with demands of career and family changing over time. Leisure time dips to its lowest level for adults 35 to 44 years old (averaging 4.3 hours per day) and then increases again as we get older. Leisure time is divided into active pursuits such as socializing, hobbies, and sports, and passive pursuits such as watching television or listening to music (which are considered relaxing but are largely sedentary).

Across all ages, Canadians spend more time in active leisure (mostly social activity) than in passive leisure activities such as watching television. For many people, midlife offers a renewed opportunity to take up activities outside the home. As children leave, parents have substantial time to participate in leisure activities such as sports or participating in town committees (Robinson and Godbey, 1997; Lindstrom et al., 2005).

A significant number of people find leisure so alluring that they take early retirement. For early retirees who have adequate financial resources to last the remainder of their years, life can be quite gratifying. Early retirees tend to be in good health, and they may take up a variety of new activities (Cliff, 1991).

Although midlife offers the opportunity for more leisure, most people report that the pace of their lives does not seem slower. Much of their free time is scattered throughout the week in 15- and 30-minute chunks as they pursue a variety of activities (Robinson and Godbey, 1997).

One reason extra leisure time seems to evaporate is that the pace of life in Canada is considerably faster than in many countries. By measuring the length of time average pedestrians cover 60 feet, the time it takes to purchase a stamp, and the accuracy of public clocks, research has compared the tempo of living in a variety of countries. According to a composite of these measures, Canada has a quicker tempo than many other countries, particularly Latin American, Asian, Middle Eastern, and African countries. But, many countries outpace Canada. Western European countries and Japan move more quickly than Canada, with Switzerland ranking first (Levine, 1999).

REVIEW, CHECK, AND APPLY

REVIEW

- People in middle age view their jobs differently than before, placing more emphasis on short-term factors and less on career striving and ambition.

- Midlife career changes are becoming more prevalent, motivated usually by dissatisfaction, the need for more challenge or status, or the desire to return to the workforce after childrearing.

- People in midlife usually have increased leisure time. Often they use it to become more involved outside the home in recreational and community activities.

CHECK YOURSELF

1. Burnout is more likely to strike individuals who are in helping professions.

   - True
   - False

2. Compared to younger adults, middle-aged adults who lose their jobs

   a. tend to stay unemployed longer and have fewer opportunities for gratifying work as they age.

   b. tend to find jobs quickly because of their skills but find it difficult to stay employed.

   c. find it difficult to get new jobs, but once employed have a stable work history.

   d. are less likely to become depressed, which makes it easier for them to obtain employment.

APPLYING LIFESPAN DEVELOPMENT

- Why might striving for occupational success be less appealing in middle age than before? What cognitive and personality changes might contribute to this phenomenon?

Answers: 1) True; 2) a

Putting It All Together
Middle Adulthood

LEIGH RYAN, who is active physically and mentally, and unsure about her marriage, is, at 50, chronologically and developmentally right in the middle of middle adulthood. She has continued to grow through the first half of middle adulthood, and she has firm plans to keep developing through the second half. She is active and engaged in her hobbies (dance and gardening), and she is pursuing further education while working full-time and teaching part-time. Socially, she enjoys entertaining her friends and giving back to her community, but she finds that her long marriage is unsatisfying, and she is quietly working to resolve that matter. In midlife she is feeling the pull of family connections in Montreal, and might, in fact, make a move in that direction. Undoubtedly, her development will continue wherever she chooses to live, with or without her husband.

MODULE 8.1 Physical Development in Middle Adulthood

- Leigh shows few signs of the physical declines of midlife, and she has maintained a high activity level **(p. 343)**.

- The fact that she is keeping physically fit may help her stave off osteoporosis and other ailments **(pp. 343–344)**.

- It is possible that Leigh's marital discontent may reflect changes in her or her husband's sexuality **(pp. 346–348)**.

- Leigh appears to be generally healthy and her many activities seem to be life-enhancing rather than stress-inducing **(pp. 349–350)**.

MODULE 8.2 Cognitive Development in Middle Adulthood

- Leigh is pursuing a doctoral degree, which demands intellectual alertness and activity **(p. 354)**.

- Leigh's love of teaching indicates an active mind and a commitment to using her intelligence **(p. 355)**.

- It is likely that Leigh has a great deal of practical intelligence in addition to the more traditional kind **(p. 357)**.

- Her memory shows little signs of decline, and allows for new skills to be learned **(p. 359)**.

- Leigh shares with many people in middle adulthood the experience of raising children and seeing them off to university **(pp. 370–371)**.

- Her contributions to her community and her family indicate that she is successfully managing Erikson's generativity-versus-stagnation stage **(p. 362)**.

- Leigh is working on her marital situation, which shows clear signs of a gradual decline rather than a reawakening **(p. 368)**.

- Leigh faces the prospect of an empty nest, which might have an effect on whether she decides to stay married **(p. 370)**.

What would YOU do?

- Would you advise Leigh to consider lightening her schedule, perhaps by giving up her teaching job or reducing her course load? Why or why not?

  HINT Review pages 349–350.

  What's your response?

What would a MARRIAGE COUNSELLOR do?

- What factors in her marriage would you advise Leigh to consider as she contemplates divorce, given her age and situation? How can she tell if her marital discontent is a genuine issue to resolve or just a "midlife crisis"?

  HINT Review pages 361, 366, 367.

  What's your response?

What would a HEALTH-CARE PROVIDER do?

- How would you check that Leigh's many activities are healthful for her and not potentially stress-inducing and harmful?

  HINT Review pages 343, 349–350.

  What's your response?

What would a CAREER COUNSELLOR do?

- Would you advise Leigh to consider studying something other than sociology—perhaps something more practical—given her age? Is she too old for a doctorate? Will she be able to keep up with younger students?

  HINT Review pages 376–378.

  What's your response?

Late Adulthood

Ben Tufty rolls over and checks his alarm clock, which has been silent for every one of the 27 years since he retired at age 63. It's 8:42.

Now 90, Tufty considers whether to have an active day: walking to town for a cup of decaf and a paper, then maybe stopping at the library—or a leisurely day: making his own decaf at home, listening to the news on the radio, and reading until it's time to plan his afternoon.

Asked if he misses working, the former aircraft engine technician laughs. "I retired as soon as I could. Not that I didn't like my job—I did. I just prefer doing my own thing with no particular schedule. I don't need constant companionship or the structure of the workday. I guess I'm a natural homebody. I don't even like to travel—maybe because I've seen jet engines up close," he says with a grin.

"My wife is long gone and there's been no one else I've been serious about," he adds. "I have grandkids and great-grandkids, but honestly, I'd rather hear from them long-distance. They know this and keep in touch by phone and the Internet."

Tufty's life might be quiet, but he manages to fill his days. "I'm not looking for things to do. My days are full enough. I exercise every day and keep up with the

MODULE 9.1 Physical Development in Late Adulthood

Life expectancy: How long have I got? see page 386

MODULE 9.2 Cognitive Development in Late Adulthood

How can you exercise your brain to stay sharp? see page 401

newest books and magazines. I occasionally call my friends, and we get together for a movie or a meal. Sometimes they come over and we play low-pressure *Scrabble* or checkers, and we always discuss politics and have a good laugh. All of us have seen just about everything, and we're always amazed when someone comes up with a 'new' idea that we know was tried a long, long time ago—to no effect.

"Am I happy? You bet I am. I wish I could have figured out how to do this 37 years ago instead of just 27. I was *made* for retirement."

The period of late adulthood, which starts around age 65, is characterized by great changes—and ongoing personal development. Older adults face profound physical, cognitive, and social changes, and by and large they figure out strategies for adjusting to them. No two strategies are exactly alike, but most older adults manage this stage successfully.

In late adulthood, people begin the decline that will be part of their lives until death. But we will see that all aspects of this period—physical, cognitive, and social—are largely misrepresented in popular stereotypes. Older people can maintain physical and mental strength virtually until the day they die, and their social worlds can also remain as vital and active as they want.

Physically, people over 65 certainly begin a gradual transition from full strength and health to an increasing concern about illness, pain, and disease. But this is not the only thing going on in their lives. They can stay healthy for quite a long time and can continue most, if not all, of the activities they enjoyed when younger. Cognitively, we find that older people adjust quite well to the changes that seem designed to impede

MODULE 9.3 Social and Personality Development in Late Adulthood

How does culture affect how we treat people in late adulthood? see page 406

MyVirtualLife

What are some of the many changes that occur in late adulthood?

Log onto MyDevelopmentLab and listen to several men and women in their sixties talk about changes in their health, their day-to-day lives, and losing loved ones.

them by adopting new strategies for solving problems and compensating for lost abilities. And socially, many of them become adept at coping with the changes in their lives, such as the death of a spouse and retirement from work.

Ben Tufty is typical only in being atypical. Through his unique approaches to aging, he makes the point that old age can be what people want it to be—not what society thinks it ought to be.

MODULE 9.1 Physical Development in Late Adulthood

Cycling through Late Adulthood

At the age of 60, Marlene Gervin dreamed of cycling across Canada. Five years later, at 65, she did it. Her husband Gordon purchased a motorhome to accompany her and they set off from Vancouver on their adventure. Ten provinces, 164 cycling days, and 7220 km later, she dipped her tire in the ocean at Mile 0 in Newfoundland, just as she'd always dreamt. (Winter, 2011)

Marlene Gervin is not alone in showing vitality in late adulthood. Consider runner Philip Rabinowitz, who, at 100, broke the centenarian 100-metre world record with a time of 30.86 seconds. For an increasing number of people in late adulthood, vigorous physical activity remains an important part of everyday life.

Old age used to be equated with loss: loss of brain cells, intellectual capabilities, energy, and sex drive. That view is being displaced as **gerontologists**, specialists who study aging, paint a very different picture. Rather than a period of decline, late adulthood is seen as a stage in which people continue to change—to grow in some areas and, yes, to decline in others.

Even the definition of "old" is changing. Many people in late adulthood, which begins around age 65 and continues to death, are as vigorous and involved with life as people several decades younger. We can no longer define old age by chronological years alone; we also must take into account people's physical and psychological well-being, their *functional ages*. Some researchers divide people into three groups according to functional ages: the *young old* are healthy and active; the *old old* have some health problems and difficulties with daily activities; and the *oldest old* are frail and need care. According to functional age, an active, healthy 100-year-old would be considered young old, while a 65-year-old in the late stages of emphysema would be among the oldest old.

We begin this module with a discussion of the myths and realities of aging, examining some stereotypes that colour our understanding of late adulthood. We look at the outward and inward signs of aging and the ways the nervous system and senses change with age.

Next, we consider health and well-being. After examining some of the major disorders that affect older adults, we look at what determines wellness and why older adults are susceptible to disease. We also focus on theories that seek to explain the aging process, as well as on gender and ethnic differences in life expectancy.

Physical Development in Late Adulthood

LEARNING OBJECTIVES

LO1 What sorts of physical changes occur in old age?

LO2 How are the senses affected by aging?

gerontologists specialists who study aging

The astronaut-turned-politician John Glenn was 77 years old when he returned to space on a 10-day mission to help NASA study how older adults adjust to space travel. Although sheer altitude sets Glenn apart from others, many people lead active, vigorous lives during late adulthood, fully engaged with life.

Aging: Myth and Reality

Late adulthood holds a unique distinction among life's stages: Because people are living longer, late adulthood is getting longer. Whether we start counting at 65 or 70, there is today a greater proportion of people alive in late adulthood than at any time in world history. In fact, demographers have divided the period using the same terms—but with different meanings— used by researchers of functional aging. For demographers, the terms are purely chronological. The *young old* are 65 to 74 years old. The *old old* are between 75 and 84, and the *oldest old* are 85 and older.

ageism prejudice and discrimination directed at older people

The Demographics of Late Adulthood. One in seven Canadians is 65 or older, and projections suggest that by 2050 nearly one-quarter of the population will be 65 and above. The number of people over 85 is projected to quadruple by 2050 (see Figure 9-1; Schneider, 1999; Statistics Canada, 2010).

The fastest growing segment of the population is the oldest old—people 85 or older. In the last two decades, the size of this group has nearly doubled. The population explosion among older people is not limited to Canada. As can be seen in Figure 9-2, the number of older adults is increasing substantially in countries around the globe. By 2050, the number of adults worldwide over 60 will exceed the number of people under 15 for the first time in history (Sandis, 2000; United Nations, 2002).

Ageism: Confronting the Stereotypes of Late Adulthood. Crotchety. Old codger. Old coot. Senile. Geezer. Old hag.

Such are the labels of late adulthood. They don't draw a pretty picture: These words are demeaning and biased, representing both overt and subtle ageism. **Ageism** is prejudice and discrimination directed at older people.

Ageism suggests that older adults are in less than full command of their mental faculties. Many attitude studies find that older adults are viewed more negatively than younger ones on a variety of traits, particularly those relating to general competence and attractiveness (Thornton, 2002; Cuddy and Fiske, 2004; Angus and Reeve, 2006).

Even when older and younger adults perform exactly the same behaviour, the behaviour is likely to be interpreted differently. Imagine you hear someone describing his search for his house keys. Would your perception of the person be different depending on whether he was 20 or 80? Research says yes. Older adults are more likely to be viewed as chronically forgetful and perhaps suffering from some mental disorder. Young adults are judged more charitably, perhaps as temporarily forgetful because they have too much on their minds (Erber et al., 1990; Nelson, 2004).

Many Western societies revere youth and admire a youthful appearance. It is the rare advertisement that includes an older adult, unless the ad is for a product

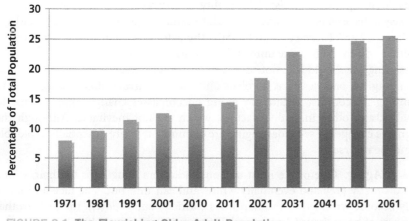

FIGURE 9-1 The Flourishing Older Adult Population
The percentage of people over the age of 65 is projected to rise to almost 25% of the population by the year 2050. Can you name two factors that contribute to this increase?
Source: Adapted from Statistics Canada, 2010.

FIGURE 9-2 The Older Adult Population Worldwide
Longer life is transforming population profiles worldwide, with the proportion of those over the age of 60 predicted to increase substantially by the year 2050.
Source: United Nations Population Division, 2002.

What do you see when you look at this woman? Ageism is found in widespread negative attitudes toward older people, and suggests that they are in less than full command of their faculties.

specifically designed for older adults. On TV, older adults are often presented as someone's parents or grandparents rather than as individuals in their own right (Vernon, 1990; McVittie et al., 2003).

Ageism is manifested not only in attitudes, but also in behaviour. For instance, older job seekers can face open prejudice, being told in job interviews that they lack the stamina for particular jobs. Sometimes they are relegated to jobs for which they are overqualified. Such job discrimination is illegal, but it persists (Hays-Thomas, 2004; Hedge et al., 2006; Rupp et al., 2006). An older person in a nursing home is often addressed in "baby talk." An 84-year-old woman might be addressed as "honey" or "baby," for example, and told that she has to go "night-night" (Whitbourne and Wills, 1993; Whitbourne and Sneed, 2004).

Today's ageism is, in some ways, a peculiarly modern and Western cultural phenomenon. In past centuries, a long life was an indication of a virtuous life, and older people were held in high esteem. Similarly, elders are venerated in most Asian societies because they have attained special wisdom by living so long, and many Aboriginal societies have traditionally viewed elders as storehouses of information about the past (Cowgill and Holmes, 1972; Ng, 2002).

Today, however, negative views of older people prevail in Western society—and these views are based on misinformation. Test your knowledge about aging by answering the questions in Table 9-1. Most people score no higher than chance, getting about 50 percent correct (Palmore, 1988, 1992). Given the prevalence of ageist stereotypes, it is reasonable to ask if there is a kernel of truth in them.

The answer is largely no. The effects of aging vary enough to defy stereotyping. Some older adults are frail, have cognitive difficulties, and require constant care; others are vigorous and independent—and sharp thinkers. Furthermore, some problems that older adults have are actually a result of illness or improper nutrition. As we will see, change and growth in late adulthood match those of life's earlier periods (Whitbourne, 1996).

> **From a social worker's perspective:** When older adults win praise and attention for being "vigorous," "active," and "youthful," is this a message that combats or supports ageism?

Physical Transitions in Older Adults

"Feel the burn." That's what the exercise tape says, and many of the 14 women in the group are doing just that. As the tape continues through its drills, some of the women stretch and reach vigorously, while others mostly just sway to the music. It's not much different from thousands of exercise classes across the country, and yet there is one surprise: The youngest woman in the group is 66 years old, and the oldest, dressed in sleek Spandex leotards, is 81.

The surprise registered by this observer reflects the stereotype that people over 65 are sedentary, incapable of vigorous exercise. The reality is different. Although their physical capabilities are likely to have changed, many older adults remain agile and fit long into old age (Fiatarone and Garnett, 1997; Riebe et al., 2002). Still, the outer and inner changes that began subtly during middle adulthood become unmistakable during old age.

As we discuss aging, we should take note of the distinction between primary and secondary aging. **Primary aging**, or *senescence*, involves universal and irreversible changes due to genetic programming. In contrast, **secondary aging** encompasses changes that are due to illness, health habits, and other individual factors, which are not inevitable. Although the physical and cognitive changes of secondary aging are common, they are potentially avoidable and can sometimes be reversed.

Outward Signs of Aging. One of the most obvious indicators of aging is the hair, which usually becomes distinctly grey and eventually white, and can thin out. The face and other parts of the body become wrinkled as the skin loses elasticity and *collagen*, the protein that forms the basic fibres of body tissue (Bowers and Thomas, 1995; Medina, 1996).

People can become shorter by as much as 10 cm (4 inches)—partially due to changes in posture, but mostly because the cartilage in the disks of the backbone becomes thinner. This is particularly true for women, who are more susceptible than men to **osteoporosis**, or thinning of the bones, largely a result of reduced estrogen production.

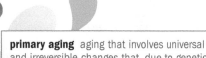

primary aging aging that involves universal and irreversible changes that, due to genetic programming, occur as people get older

secondary aging changes in physical and cognitive functioning that are due to illness, health habits, and other individual differences, but are not due to increased age itself and are not inevitable

osteoporosis a condition in which the bones become brittle, fragile, and thin, often brought about by a lack of calcium in the diet

TABLE 9-1   THE MYTHS OF AGING

1. The majority of old people (age 65 and older) have defective memory, are disoriented, or are demented. T or F?

2. The five senses (sight, hearing, taste, touch, and smell) all tend to weaken in old age. T or F?

3. The majority of old people have no interest in, nor capacity for, sexual relations. T or F?

4. Lung capacity tends to decline in old age. T or F?

5. The majority of old people are sick most of the time. T or F?

6. Physical strength tends to decline in old age. T or F?

7. At least one-tenth of the aged are living in long-stay institutions (such as nursing homes, mental hospitals, and homes for the aged). T or F?

8. Many older adults maintain large social networks of friends. T or F?

9. Older workers usually cannot work as effectively as younger workers. T or F?

10. Over three-quarters of the aged are healthy enough to carry out their normal activities. T or F?

11. The majority of old people are unable to adapt to change. T or F?

12. Old people usually take longer to learn something new. T or F?

13. It is almost impossible for the average old person to learn something new. T or F?

14. Older people tend to react slower than do younger people. T or F?

15. In general, old people tend to be pretty much alike. T or F?

16. The majority of old people say they are seldom bored. T or F?

17. The majority of old people are socially isolated. T or F?

18. Older workers have fewer accidents than do younger workers. T or F?

Scoring

All odd-numbered statements are false; all even-numbered statements are true. Most university students miss about six, and high school students miss about nine. Even university instructors miss an average of about three.

Source: From "The Myths of Aging" from Palmore, E. B. (1982). *The Facts on Aging Quiz*. New York: Springer. Reprinted with permission from the author.

Osteoporosis, which affects 25 percent of women over 60, is a primary cause of broken bones among older people. It is largely preventable if exercise is adequate and calcium and protein intake are sufficient earlier in life (Moyad, 2004; Picavet and Hoeymans, 2004).

Although negative stereotypes against appearing old affect both genders, they are particularly potent for women. In fact, in Western cultures there is a *double standard* for appearance, by which women are judged more harshly than men. For instance, grey hair in men is often viewed as "distinguished"; in women it is a sign of being "over the hill" (Sontag, 1979; Bell, 1989).

As a consequence, women feel considerably more pressure than men to hide the signs of aging by dyeing their hair, undergoing cosmetic surgery, and using age-concealing cosmetics (Unger and Crawford, 1992). This double standard is diminishing, however, as more men grow interested in looking younger and are falling prey to a new wave of male-oriented cosmetic products, such as wrinkle creams. Ironically, as the double standard eases, ageism is becoming more of a concern for both sexes.

Internal Aging. As the outward signs become more apparent, there are also changes in the internal functioning of the organ systems (Whitbourne, 2001; Aldwin and Gilmer, 2004).

The brain becomes smaller and lighter. As it shrinks, the brain pulls away from the skull, and the space between brain and skull doubles between ages 20 and 70. The brain uses less oxygen and glucose, and blood flow is reduced. The number of neurons, or brain cells, declines in some parts of the brain, although not as much as was once thought. Recent research suggests that the number of cells in the cortex might drop only minimally, or not at all. In fact,

Although grey hair is often characterized as "distinguished" in men, the same trait in women is viewed more often as a sign of being "over the hill"—a clear double standard.

some evidence suggests that certain types of neuronal growth might continue throughout the lifespan (Tisserand and Jolles, 2003; Lindsey and Tropepe, 2006; Raz et al., 2007).

The reduced flow of blood in the brain is due in part to the heart's reduced ability to pump blood through hardening and shrinking blood vessels. A 75-year-old man pumps less than three-quarters of the blood that he could pump during early adulthood (Kart, 1990; Yildiz, 2007).

Other bodily systems also work at lower capacity. The respiratory system is less efficient, and the digestive system produces less digestive juice and is less efficient in pushing food through the system—thereby increasing the incidence of constipation. Some hormones are produced at lower levels. Muscle fibres decrease both in size and in amount, and they become less efficient at using oxygen from the bloodstream and storing nutrients (Fiatarone and Garnett, 1997; Lamberts et al., 1997).

Although these changes are normal, they often occur earlier in people who have less healthy lifestyles. For example, smoking accelerates declines in cardiovascular capacity at any age.

Lifestyle factors can also slow the changes associated with aging. For instance, people whose exercise program includes weightlifting may lose muscle fibre at a slower rate than those who are sedentary. Similarly, physical fitness is related to better performance on mental tests, may prevent a loss of brain tissue, and may even aid in the development of new neurons. In fact, studies suggest that sedentary older adults who begin aerobic fitness training ultimately show cognitive benefits (Elder et al., 2006; Colcombe et al., 2006; Kramer et al., 2006; Pereira et al., 2007).

Slowing Reaction Time

Karl winced as the "game over" message came up on his grandsons' video game system. He enjoyed trying out their games, but he just couldn't shoot down those bad guys as quickly as his grandkids could.

As people get older, they take longer: longer to put on a tie, reach a ringing phone, press the buttons in a video game. One reason is a lengthening of reaction time, which begins to increase in middle age and can rise significantly by late adulthood (Fozard et al., 1994; Benjuya et al., 2004; Der and Deary, 2006).

It is not clear why people slow down. One explanation, known as the **peripheral slowing hypothesis**, suggests that the peripheral nervous system, which encompasses the nerves that branch from the spinal cord and brain to the extremities of the body, becomes less efficient with age. Because of this, it takes longer for information from the environment to reach the brain and for commands from the brain to be transmitted to the muscles (Salthouse, 1989, 2006).

peripheral slowing hypothesis the theory that suggests that overall processing speed declines in the peripheral nervous system with increasing age

According to the **generalized slowing hypothesis**, on the other hand, processing in all parts of the nervous system, including the brain, is less efficient. As a consequence, slowing occurs throughout the body, including the processing of both simple and complex stimuli and the transmission of commands to the muscles (Cerella, 1990).

Although we don't know which explanation is more accurate, some data suggest that the slowing of reaction time and general processing results in a higher incidence of accidents for older adults. Slowed reaction and processing time means they can't efficiently receive from the environment information that might indicate a dangerous situation. Slowed decision-making processes impair their ability to remove themselves from harm's way. Drivers over 70 have as many fatal accidents per kilometre driven as teenagers, although when taken as a proportion of licensed drivers, teenagers are three times as likely to be involved in an accident (Insurance Corporation of British Columbia, British Columbia Traffic Statistics, 2009; Whitbourne et al., 1996; see Figure 9-3).

Although response time slows, the *perception* of time actually seems to speed up with age. The days and weeks seem to go by more quickly and time seems to rush by faster for older adults, perhaps because of changes in the way the brain coordinates its internal time clock (Mangan, 1997).

> **generalized slowing hypothesis** the theory that processing in all parts of the nervous system, including the brain, is less efficient as we age

The Senses: Sight, Sound, Taste, and Smell

Old age brings declines in the sense organs. This decline has major psychological consequences—because the senses are our link with the world.

Vision. More than 80 percent of older adults report vision problems. Changes in the physical apparatus of the eye—the cornea, lens, retina, and optic nerve—diminish visual abilities. The lens becomes less transparent, allowing only a third as much light to reach the retina at 60 as at 20. The optic nerve also becomes less efficient in transmitting nerve impulses (Gawande, 2007). As a result, vision declines along several dimensions. We see distant objects less well, need more light to see clearly, and take longer to adjust from dark to light and vice versa.

These changes cause everyday problems. Driving, particularly at night, becomes more challenging. Reading requires more light, and eye strain comes more easily. Of course, eyeglasses and contact lenses can correct many of these problems, and the majority of older people see reasonably well (Horowitz, 1994; Ball and Rebok, 1994; Owsley et al., 2003).

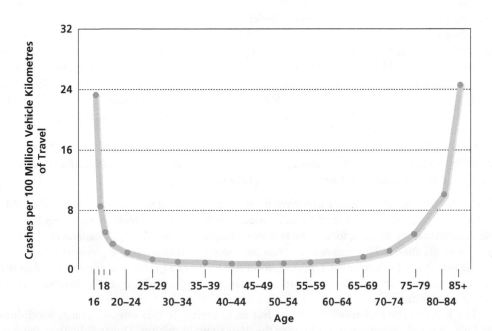

FIGURE 9-3 Vehicle Fatalities Across the Lifespan
Drivers over age 70 have a fatal accident record comparable to that of teenagers when crashes are calculated per kilometre of driving. Why is this the case?
Source: National Highway Traffic Safety Administration, 1994.

FIGURE 9-4 The World Through Macular Degeneration
Macular degeneration leads to a gradual deterioration of the centre of the retina, leaving only peripheral vision. This is an example of what a person with macular degeneration might see.
Source: AARP, 2005, p. 34.

Several eye diseases become more common during late adulthood. For instance, *cataracts*—cloudy or opaque areas on the lens of the eye that interfere with the passage of light—frequently develop. Cataracts bring blurred vision and glare in bright light. If cataracts are left untreated, the lens becomes milky white and blindness results. However, cataracts can be surgically removed, and eyesight can be restored with eyeglasses, contact lenses, or *intraocular lens implants*, in which a plastic lens is permanently placed in the eye (Walker et al., 2006).

Glaucoma is another serious problem among older adults. As we noted earlier, *glaucoma* occurs when pressure in the fluid of the eye increases, either because the fluid cannot drain properly or because too much fluid is produced. If it is detected early enough, glaucoma can be treated by drugs or surgery.

The most common cause of blindness in people over 60 is *age-related macular degeneration* (AMD), which affects the *macula*, a yellowish area near the retina at which visual perception is most acute. When a portion of the macula thins and degenerates, the eyesight gradually deteriorates (see Figure 9-4). If diagnosed early, macular degeneration can sometimes be treated with medication or lasers. There is also some evidence that a diet rich in antioxidant vitamins (C, E, and A) can reduce the risk of AMD (Mayo Clinic, 2000; Sun and Nathans, 2001; Rattner and Nathans, 2006; Wiggins and Uwaydat, 2006).

Hearing. Around 30 percent of adults between 65 and 74 have some hearing loss, and the figure rises to 50 percent among people over 75. Overall, more than 1 million older adults in Canada have hearing impairments of one kind or another (*HHL*, 1997; Chisolm et al., 2003).

Aging particularly affects the ability to hear higher frequencies. This makes it hard to hear conversations amid background noise or when several people are speaking simultaneously. Some older adults actually find loud noises painful.

Although hearing aids would probably be helpful around 75 percent of the time, only 20 percent of older adults wear them. One reason is that hearing aids are far from perfect. They amplify background noises as much as conversations, making it difficult for wearers to separate what they want to hear from other sounds. Furthermore, many people feel that hearing aids make them appear even older and encourage others to treat them as if they were disabled (Lesner, 2003; Meister and von Wedel, 2003).

A hearing loss can be deadly to one's social life. Unable to hear conversations fully, some older adults with hearing problems withdraw from others, unwilling to respond since they are unsure what was said to them. They can easily feel left out and lonely. Hearing loss can also lead to feelings of paranoia as conversational blanks are filled according to fear rather than reality. If someone hears "I hate going to Maude's" instead of "I hate going to the mall," a bland opinion about shopping can be interpreted as an expression of personal animosity (Knutson and Lansing, 1990; Myers, 2000).

Hearing loss may hasten cognitive decline. The struggle to understand what is being said can shunt mental resources away from processing information, causing difficulties in remembering and understanding information (Wingfield et al., 2005).

Taste and Smell. Older adults who have always enjoyed eating may experience a real decline in the quality of life because of changes in sensitivity to taste and smell. Both senses become less discriminating, causing food to be less appetizing than it was earlier (Kaneda et al., 2000; Nordin et al., 2003). The decrease in taste and smell sensitivity has a physical cause. The tongue loses taste buds over time, making food less tasty. The problem is compounded as the olfactory bulbs in the brain begin to shrivel. Because taste depends on smell, this makes food taste even blander.

The loss of taste and smell sensitivity has an unfortunate side effect: Because food does not taste as good, people eat less and open the door to malnutrition. They might also over-salt their food, thereby increasing their risk of *hypertension*, or high blood pressure, one of the most common health problems of old age (Smith et al., 2006).

REVIEW, CHECK, AND APPLY

REVIEW

- Older adults are often subject to ageism—prejudice and discrimination against people based on their age.

- Old age brings many physical transitions, internal changes, and changes in sensory perception.

- Many of the changes associated with aging can cause social and psychological difficulties for older adults.

CHECK YOURSELF

1. The fastest-growing segment of the older adult population is the oldest old, or people who are 85 and older.

- True
- False

2. _____ aging involves universal and irreversible changes that, due to genetic programming, occur as people get older.

3. According to the _____ slowing hypothesis, for older adults, processing in all parts of the nervous system, including the brain, is less efficient.

  a. automated

  b. global

  c. generalized

  d. peripheral

APPLYING LIFESPAN DEVELOPMENT

- Should older adults be subject to strict examinations to renew their drivers' licences? Should such tests cover more than eyesight (for example, response time, mental abilities)? What issues should be taken into consideration?

Answers: 1) True; 2) Primary; 3) c

Health and Wellness in Late Adulthood

LO3 What is the general state of health of older people, and to what disorders are they susceptible?

LO4 Can wellness and sexuality be maintained in old age?

LO5 How long can people expect to live, and why do they die?

LEARNING OBJECTIVES

I watched my mother's gradual and then rapid decline at the end. I know she went through the same with her mother 20 years earlier. I feel like I haven't just seen a preview of my future, but the full-length feature film. It is very depressing.

In reality, as we have seen, most older adults are in relatively good health for most of old age. Almost three-quarters of people 65 years old and above rate their health as good, very good, or excellent (USDHHS, 1990; Kahn and Rowe, 1999; Turcotte and Schellenberg, 2007).

On the other hand, to be old is in fact to be susceptible to diseases. We now consider some of the major physical and psychological disorders of older adults.

Health Problems in Older People: Physical and Psychological Disorders

Most of the illnesses and diseases of late adulthood are not peculiar to old age; people of all ages suffer from cancer and heart disease, for instance. However, the incidence of these diseases rises with age, raising the odds that a person will be ill during old age. Moreover, older adults bounce back more slowly from illnesses than younger people, and a full recovery might be impossible.

Common Physical Disorders. The leading causes of death in older adults are heart disease, cancer, and stroke, which claim close to three-quarters of people in late adulthood. Because aging weakens the immune system, older adults are also more susceptible to infectious diseases (Feinberg, 2000). In addition, most older adults have at least one chronic, long-term condition (AARP, 1990). For instance, *arthritis*, an inflammation of one or more joints, afflicts roughly half of older adults. Arthritis can cause painful swelling, and it can be disabling, preventing people from performing the simplest of everyday tasks, such as unscrewing a jar

Outspoken and popular retired Alberta Premier Ralph Klein was diagnosed with fronto-temporal dementia. According to the Alzheimer's Society of Canada, more than half a million Canadians are living with Alzheimer's or a related dementia.

dementia the most common mental disorder of older adults, it covers several diseases, each of which includes serious memory loss accompanied by declines in other mental functioning

Alzheimer's disease a progressive brain disorder that produces memory loss and confusion

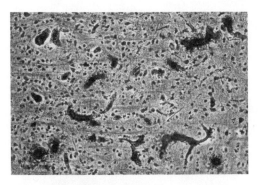

Brain scans of a patient with Alzheimer's disease show twisted clumps of nerve cells that are characteristic of the disease.

of food or turning a key in a lock. Although aspirin and other drugs can relieve some of the swelling and reduce the pain, arthritis cannot be cured (Burt and Harris, 1994).

Around one-third of older adults have *hypertension*, or high blood pressure. Many people who have high blood pressure are unaware of their condition because it has no symptoms, which makes it more dangerous. Left untreated, higher tension within the circulatory system can weaken the blood vessels and heart and raise the risk of cerebrovascular disease or stroke (Wiggins and Uwaydat, 2006).

Psychological and Mental Disorders.

Some 15 to 25 percent of people over 65 are thought to show some symptoms of psychological disorder, a lower percentage than in younger adults. The behavioural symptoms related to these disorders are sometimes different in older and younger adults (Whitbourne, 2001).

One of the more prevalent problems is major depression, which is characterized by feelings of intense sadness, pessimism, and hopelessness. Among the reasons cited for depression are the cumulative loss of spouses and friends, and their own declining health and physical capabilities (Penninx et al., 1998; Kahn et al., 2003).

Some older adults suffer from psychological disorders induced by the combinations of drugs they might be taking for various medical conditions. They might also be taking inappropriate doses of some medications because the metabolism of a 75-year-old and that of a 25-year-old differ, and the doses appropriate for them can differ too. Because of these possibilities, older adults who take medications must be careful to inform their physicians and pharmacists of every drug—with dosage information—that they take. They should also avoid medicating themselves with over-the-counter drugs, because a combination of non-prescription and prescription drugs can be dangerous.

The most common mental disorder among older adults is **dementia**, a broad category of diseases encompassing serious memory loss accompanied by declines in other mental functioning. Although dementia has many causes, the symptoms are similar: declining memory, lessened intellectual abilities, and impaired judgment. The chances of experiencing dementia increase with age. One in 11 Canadians over 65 has some form of dementia (Alzheimer Society of Canada, 2010).

Alzheimer's Disease.

The most common form of dementia is **Alzheimer's disease**, a progressive brain disorder that produces memory loss and confusion. The disease is one of the most serious mental health problems among the aging population. Nineteen percent of people 75 to 84, and nearly half of people over 90, have Alzheimer's. As the proportion of older adults grows, the number of adults living with Alzheimer's is expected to more than double.

The first sign of Alzheimer's is usually forgetfulness. A person might have trouble recalling words during a conversation or may return to the grocery store several times after having already done the shopping. At first, recent memories are affected, and then older ones. Eventually, people with the disease are totally confused, unable to speak intelligibly or to recognize even their closest family and friends. In the final stages, they lose voluntary control of their muscles and are bedridden. Because individuals with the disorder are initially aware of the future course of the disease, they may understandably suffer from anxiety, fear, and depression.

Biologically, Alzheimer's occurs when production of the protein *beta amyloid precursor protein*—which normally promotes the production and growth of neurons—goes awry, creating large clumps of cells that trigger inflammation and deterioration of nerve cells. The brain shrinks, and several areas of the hippocampus and frontal and temporal lobes show deterioration. Furthermore, certain neurons die, which leads to a shortage of various neurotransmitters, such as acetylcholine (Lanctot et al., 2001; Blennow and Vanmechelen, 2003; Wolfe, 2006; Medeiros et al., 2007). Figure 9.5 shows a comparison of a normal healthy brain and a brain with advanced Alzheimer's disease.

Although the physical changes that produce Alzheimer's are clear, what triggers the disease is not. Genetics clearly play a role, with some families showing a much higher incidence of Alzheimer's than others. In fact, in certain families half the children appear to inherit the disease from their parents. Furthermore, years before Alzheimer's symptoms emerge, people who are genetically at high risk for the disease show differences in brain functioning when they are trying to recall information (Bookheimer et al., 2000; Coon et al., 2007; Nelson et al., 2007; Thomas and Fenech, 2007).

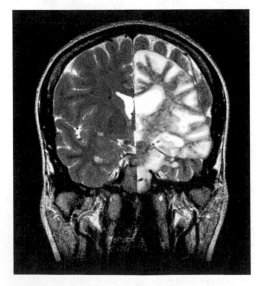

FIGURE 9-5
Composite MRI brain scans of a normal brain (in brown) and the brain of an adult with advanced Alzheimer's disease (in green). Note the atrophy, or shrinkage, of the brain with Alzheimer's disease.

Focus on Research

Bilingualism: A Life-Long Advantage?

York University's Professor Ellen Bialystok is best known for her research on the cognitive advantages of bilingualism for young children, but she and her colleagues have also demonstrated cognitive advantages in later life for life-long bilinguals. The research is based on the somewhat contentious idea of "cognitive reserve"—that individuals who engage in cognitively demanding activity seem to remain cognitively sharp. A few studies even suggested that this cognitive reserve could keep individuals with brain pathology from showing outward symptoms (Valenzuela and Sachdev, 2006). Given that the cognitive exercise that is bilingualism might give children an advantage, Bialystok and colleagues asked the question, Is bilingualism a form of cognitive reserve?

Bialystok and colleagues examined the medical records of 228 patients referred to the Memory Clinic at Baycrest Hospital in Toronto over a four-year period. As luck would have it, the numbers of bilingual and monolingual individuals was nearly even. All the patients in the study had Alzheimer's or a related form of dementia, but the bilingual patients' onset occurred on average four years later than the monolinguals. After that, the course of the disease appeared the same. The researchers considered various ways in which the two groups could differ—other variables such as education, occupational status, and cultural factors. Every way they examined the data, bilinguals showed substantially later onset of dementia. The conclusion? That life-long bilingualism is good exercise, keeping the brain in shape.

"In general, it is increasingly clear that biological factors interact with environmental experiences to determine cognitive outcomes; the present findings suggest that bilingualism is one experiential factor that can provide a positive benefit in this respect." (Bialystok et al., 2007, p. 464)

While evidence suggests that Alzheimer's has a substantially genetic origin, nongenetic lifestyle factors such as high blood pressure or diet also increase susceptibility. In one cross-cultural study, poor Black residents in a Nigerian town were less likely to develop Alzheimer's than a comparable sample of African Americans living in the United States. The researchers speculate that variations in diet between the two groups—the residents of Nigeria ate mainly vegetables—might account for the differences in the Alzheimer's rates (Hendrie et al., 2001; Friedland, 2003; Wu et al., 2003; Lahiri et al., 2007).

Scientists are also studying certain viruses, dysfunctions of the immune system, and hormone imbalances that might produce the disease. Other studies have found that lower levels of linguistic ability in the early twenties are associated with declines in cognitive capabilities due to Alzheimer's much later in life (Small et al., 1995; Snowdon et al., 1996; Alisky, 2007).

As individuals with Alzheimer's lose the ability to feed and clothe themselves, or even to control bladder and bowel functions, they must be cared for 24 hours a day. Because of this, most people with Alzheimer's live out their lives in nursing homes, accounting for some two-thirds of the residents of nursing homes (Prigerson, 2003; Sparks, 2008).

Caregivers often become secondary victims of the disease. It is easy to become frustrated, angry, and exhausted by the demands of Alzheimer's patients, whose needs may be overpowering. In addition to the physical chore of providing total care, caregivers face the loss of a loved one who not only is visibly deteriorating but who can act emotionally unstable and even fly into rages (Ferrario et al., 2003; Danhauer et al., 2004; Kosmala and Kloszewska, 2004; Thomas et al., 2006).

Caring for People with Alzheimer's Disease

Becoming an Informed Consumer of Development

Alzheimer's disease is one of the most difficult illnesses to deal with, but several steps can be taken to help both patient and caregiver deal with Alzheimer's.

- Make patients feel secure in their home environments by keeping them occupied in everyday tasks of living as long as possible.

- Label everyday objects, furnish calendars and detailed but simple lists, and give oral reminders of time and place.

- Keep clothing simple: Provide clothes with few zippers and buttons, and lay them out in the order in which they should be put on.

- Put bathing on a schedule. People with Alzheimer's may be afraid of falling and of hot water, and might therefore avoid needed bathing.

- Prevent driving. Although patients often want to continue driving, their accident rate is high—some 20 times higher than average.

- Monitor telephone use. Alzheimer patients who answer the phone may agree to offers from telephone salespeople and investment counsellors.

- Provide opportunities for exercise, such as a daily walk. This prevents muscle deterioration and stiffness.

- Caregivers should remember to take time off and lead their own lives. Seek out support from community service organizations.

Wellness in Late Adulthood: The Relationship between Aging and Illness

Sickness is not inevitable in old age. Whether an older person is ill or well depends less on age than on a variety of factors, including genetic predisposition, past and present environmental factors, and psychological factors.

Certain diseases, such as cancer and heart disease, have a clear genetic component, but a genetic predisposition does not automatically mean that a person will get a particular illness. People's lifestyles—smoking, diet, exposure to cancer-causing agents such as sunlight or asbestos—can raise or lower the chances of coming down with such a disease.

Education also plays a role. Among older adults with a university degree, 58 percent rated themselves as being in very good or excellent health, higher than younger adults (48%) and older adults (30%) with less than a high school education. Economics plays less of a role in accessing health care, although income is related to overall life expectancy. Older adults are more likely than younger adults to have a family doctor, and while older adults make more use of health care, they actually report fewer problems accessing health care than younger adults. As well, unlike with younger adults, income does not play a role (Turcotte and Schellenberg, 2007).

Finally, psychological factors play an important role in determining susceptibility to illness. For example, a sense of control over one's environment, such as making choices involving everyday matters, leads to a better psychological state and superior health outcomes (Taylor et al., 1991; Levy et al., 2002).

Promoting Good Health.   People can enhance their physical well-being—and longevity—simply by doing what people of all ages should do: Eat wisely, exercise, and avoid obvious threats to health, such as smoking. The goal of medical and social service professionals is now to extend people's *active lifespans*, the amount of time they remain healthy and able to enjoy their lives (Burns, 2000; Resnick, 2000; Sawatzky and Naimark, 2002; Gavin and Myers, 2003; Katz and Marshall, 2003).

Older Canadian adults are in relatively good shape financially and physically. Fewer than 6 percent of older adults live in poverty, one of the lowest rates internationally. Older adults report better eating habits, less smoking, and less alcohol use than younger adults. We would expect older adults to be less active and engage in less exercise than younger adults due to increasing limitations, but the difference is surprisingly small. It's likely that these older adults are less active than they used to be, but also that today's younger adults are shockingly inactive themselves. It's also very likely that the relatively healthy state of older adults reflects the fact that the unhealthiest younger adults don't make it to old age (Turcotte and Schellenberg, 2007).

The number of Canadian older adults living in poverty is among the lowest in the world. Most older adults own their own home, mortgage-free.

Sexuality in Old Age: Use It or Lose It

Do your grandparents have sex?

Quite possibly, yes. Increasing evidence suggests that people are sexually active well into their eighties and nineties, despite societal stereotypes suggesting that it is somehow improper for two 75-year-olds to have sexual intercourse, and even worse for a 75-year-old to masturbate. In many other cultures, older adults are expected to remain sexually active, and in some societies, people are expected to become less inhibited as they age (Hyde, 1994; Hillman, 2000).

Two major factors determine whether an older adult will engage in sexual activity (Masters et al., 1982). One is good physical and mental health. The other is previous regular sexual activity. "Use it or lose it" seems an accurate description of sexual functioning in older adults. Sexual activity can and often does continue throughout the lifespan. Furthermore, there's some intriguing evidence that having sex may have some unexpected side benefits: One study found that having sex regularly is associated with a *lower risk of death* (Gelfand, 2000; Kellett, 2000; Henry and McNab, 2003)!

One survey found that 43 percent of men and 33 percent of women over the age of 70 masturbate. The average frequency for those who masturbated was once a week. Around two-thirds of married men and women had sex with their spouses—again averaging around once a week. In addition, the percentage of people who view their sexual partners as physically attractive actually increases with age (Brecher et al., 1984; Budd, 1999; Araujo et al., 2004).

Of course, some changes occur in sexual functioning. Testosterone declines during adulthood by approximately 30 to 40 percent from the late forties to the early seventies. It takes a longer time, and more stimulation, for men to get a full erection. The refractory period—the time following an orgasm before a man can become aroused again—may last one or more days. Women's vaginas become thin and inelastic, and they produce less natural lubrication, making intercourse more difficult. It is important to realize that older adults—like younger ones—are susceptible to sexually transmitted diseases. In fact, 10 percent of people diagnosed with AIDS are over 50 (Sidman, 2003; National Institute of Aging, 2004).

Approaches to Aging: Why Is Death Inevitable?

Hovering over late adulthood is the spectre of death. At some point, no matter how healthy we have been throughout life, we know that we will experience physical declines and that life will end. But why?

There are two major approaches to explaining why we undergo physical deterioration and death: genetic programming theories and wear-and-tear theories.

Genetic programming theories of aging suggest that our body's DNA contains a built-in time limit for the reproduction of human cells. After a genetically determined period, the cells can no longer divide and the individual begins to deteriorate (Finch and Tanzi, 1997; Rattan et al., 2006).

The theory comes in several variants. One is that the genetic material contains a "death gene" programmed to tell the body to deteriorate and die. Researchers who take an evolutionary viewpoint suggest that a long lifespan after the reproductive years is unnecessary for the survival of the species. According to this view, genetic diseases that strike later in life continue to exist because they allow people time to have children, thus passing along genes that are "programmed" to cause diseases and death.

Another variant is that the cells can duplicate only a certain number of times. Throughout our lives, new cells are produced through cell duplication to repair and replenish our various tissues and organs. According to this view, the genetic instructions for running the body can be read only a certain number of times before they become illegible and cells stop reproducing. Because the body is not being renewed at the same rate, bodily deterioration and death ensue (Hayflick, 1974; Thoms et al., 2007).

Evidence for the genetic programming theory comes from research showing that human cells permitted to divide in the laboratory can do so successfully only around 50 times. Each time they divide, *telomeres*, which are tiny, protective areas of DNA at the tip of chromosomes, grow shorter. When a cell's telomere has just about disappeared, the cell stops replicating, making it susceptible to damage and producing signs of aging (Chung et al., 2007).

On the other hand, **wear-and-tear theories of aging** argue that the mechanical functions of the body simply wear out—the way cars and washing machines do. In addition, some wear-and-tear theorists suggest that the body's constant manufacture of energy to fuel its activities

Watch on **mydevelopmentlab**

What effect does lifestyle have on health? Log onto MyDevelopmentLab and watch a video of Joan and Bill, a couple in their seventies; they both are avid hikers and rowers, and play tennis, ski, and compete athletically.

genetic programming theories of aging theories that suggest that our body's DNA genetic code contains a built-in time limit for the reproduction of human cells

wear-and-tear theories of aging the theory that the mechanical functions of the body simply wear out with age

According to genetic preprogramming theories of aging, our DNA genetic code contains a built-in limit on the length of life.

creates by-products. These by-products, combined with the toxins and threats of everyday life (such as radiation, chemical exposure, accidents, and disease), eventually reach such high levels that they impair the body's normal functioning. The ultimate result is deterioration and death.

One specific category of by-products that has been related to aging includes free radicals, electrically charged molecules or atoms that are produced by the cells of the body. Because of their electrical charge, free radicals may cause negative effects on other cells of the body. A great deal of research suggests that oxygen free radicals may be implicated in a number of age-related problems, including cancer, heart disease, and diabetes (Vajragupta et al., 2000; Birlouez-Aragon and Tessier, 2003; Poon et al., 2004; Sierra, 2006).

Reconciling the Theories of Aging.

Genetic programming theories and wear-and-tear theories make different suggestions about the inevitability of death. Genetic programming theories suggest that there is a built-in time limit to life. Wear-and-tear theories, particularly those that focus on toxin build-up, suggest that if a means can be found to eliminate toxins and environmental threats, aging might be slowed.

We don't know which class of theories provides the more accurate account. Each is supported by some research, and each seems to explain certain aspects of aging. Ultimately, though, the mystery remains (Horiuchi et al., 2003).

Life Expectancy: How Long Have I Got?

Although why we die is not fully understood, we do know how to calculate our average life expectancy: Most of us can expect to live into old age. The **life expectancy**—the average age of death for members of a population—of a person born in 1980, for instance, is 74. And a lifespan of 100 years is by no means as uncommon as it once was.

Average life expectancy is on the rise. A woman born in 1901 expected to live on average to age 50 and a man to age 47. By 2003, the life expectancy for Canadians was 80, and life expectancy continues to increase by one year every four years (see Figure 9-6).

There are several reasons for this. Health and sanitation are generally better, and many diseases, such as smallpox, have been wiped out entirely. Vaccines and preventive measures are available for many diseases, such as measles and mumps, that used to kill young people. Working conditions are better and products are safer. Many people are making healthy lifestyle choices such as keeping their weight down, eating fresh fruits and vegetables, and exercising, all of which can extend the active lifespan—the years spent in health and enjoyment of life.

Just how much can the lifespan be increased? The most common answer is around 120 years, the age reached by Jeanne Calment, the oldest person in the world until she died in 1997 at 122. Living longer would probably require major genetic alterations that are both technically and ethically improbable. Still, recent scientific and technological advances suggest that significantly extending the lifespan is not impossible.

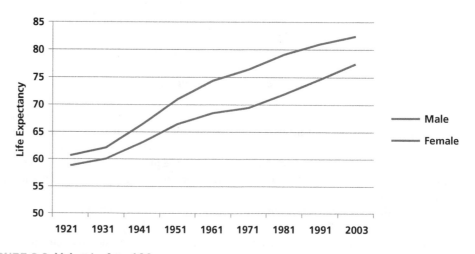

FIGURE 9-6 Living to Age 100

If increases in life expectancy continue, it might become common for people to live to 100 by the end of this century. What implications does this have for society?
Source: Statistics Canada, 2009.

life expectancy the average age of death for members of a population.

Postponing Aging: Can Scientists Find the Fountain of Youth?

Are researchers close to finding the scientific equivalent of the fountain of youth?

Not yet, but they're getting closer, at least in nonhuman species. For instance, researchers have extended the lives of nematodes (microscopic, transparent worms that typically live for just 9 days) to 50 days—the equivalent of extending human life to 420 years. Researchers have also doubled fruit flies' lives (Whitbourne, 2001; Libert et al., 2007; Ocorr et al., 2007).

The following are the most promising avenues for increasing the length of life:

- **Telomere therapy.** Telomeres are the tiny areas at the tip of chromosomes that grow shorter each time a cell divides and eventually disappear, ending cell replication. Some scientists believe that if telomeres could be lengthened, aging could be slowed. Researchers are now looking for genes that control the production of telomerase, an enzyme that seems to regulate the length of telomeres (Steinert et al., 2000; Urquidi et al., 2000; Chung et al., 2007).

Cultural Dimensions

Gender and Ethnic Differences in Average Life Expectancy: Separate Lives, Separate Deaths

- A male born in Canada today is expected to live to age 78; a female will probably live 5 years longer.

- A child born in Japan has a life expectancy of 79; for a child born in Gambia, life expectancy is less than 45.

Let's consider the gender gap, which is particularly pronounced. Across the industrialized world, women live longer than men by 4 to 10 years (Holden, 1987). The female advantage begins just after conception: Although slightly more males are conceived, males are more likely to die during the prenatal period, infancy, and childhood. Consequently, by age 30 there are roughly equal numbers of men and women. The numbers remain nearly equal through age 69. But by age 80, nearly twice as many females than males are still alive. For those over 90, the gender gap grows wider: For every male, 3 women are still alive (Turcotte and Schellenberg, 2007).

One suggested explanation for this is that the naturally higher levels of hormones such as estrogen and progesterone in women provide some protection from diseases such as heart attacks. It is also possible that women engage in healthier behaviour during their lives, such as eating well. However, there is no conclusive evidence for either explanation (DiGiovanna, 1994; Baerlocher, 2007).

Life Expectancy at Birth, by Sex, 1991 and 2001, Canada

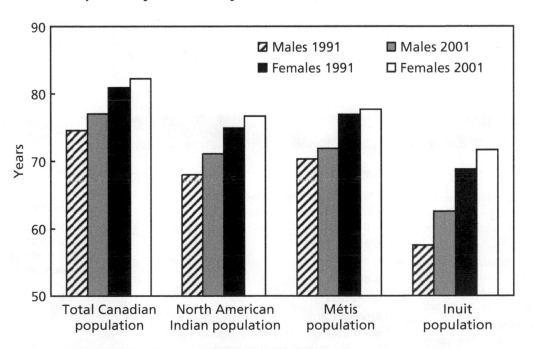

Source: Statistics Canada, Demography Division.

FIGURE 9-7 Life Expectancy of Aboriginal and Non-Aboriginal Canadians
Both male and female Aboriginals have a shorter life expectancy than male and female non-Aboriginals. Are the reasons for this genetic, cultural, or both?
Source: Turcotte and Schellenberg, 2007. Reprinted with permission.

- **Unlocking longevity genes.** Certain genes control the body's ability to cope with environmental challenges and physical adversity. If harnessed, those genes may provide a way to increase the lifespan. One particularly promising family of genes is *sirtuins*, which might regulate and promote longer life (Guarente, 2006; Sinclair and Guarente, 2006).

- **Reducing free radicals through antioxidant drugs.** Free radicals—unstable molecules that drift through the body—damage other cells and lead to aging. Antioxidant drugs that can reduce the number of free radicals might eventually be perfected. Furthermore, it might be possible to insert into human cells genes that produce enzymes that act as anti-oxidants. In the meantime, nutritionists urge a diet rich in antioxidant vitamins, which are found in fruits and vegetables (Vajragupta et al., 2000; Birlouez-Aragon and Tessier, 2003; Kedziora-Kornatowska et al., 2007).

- **Restricting calories.** For at least the last decade, researchers have known that laboratory rats who are fed an extremely low-calorie diet, providing 30 to 50 percent of their normal intake, often live 30 percent longer than better-fed rats, providing they get all the vitamins and minerals they need. The reason appears to be that they produce fewer free radicals. Researchers hope to develop drugs that mimic the effects of calorie restriction without forcing people to feel hungry all the time (Mattson, 2003; Ingram et al., 2007).

- **The bionic solution: replacing worn-out organs.** Heart transplants, liver transplants, lung transplants—we live in an age when replacing damaged or diseased organs seems nearly routine.

One major problem remains: Transplants often fail because the body rejects the foreign tissue. To overcome this problem, some researchers advocate growing replacement organs from the person's own cloned cells, which will not be rejected. Even more radically, genetically engineered cells from nonhumans that do not provoke rejection could be cloned, harvested, and transplanted into humans. Finally, it may be possible to create artificial organs that can completely replace diseased or damaged ones (Cascalho et al., 2006; Kwant et al., 2007; Li and Zhu, 2007).

Sci-fi ideas for extending human life are exciting, but society must work to solve a more immediate problem: the significant disparity in life expectancies between members of different groups. We discuss this important issue in the preceding Cultural Dimensions segment.

> ⊙ **From the perspective of a health-care professional:** Given what you've learned about explanations of life expectancy, how might you try to extend your own life? Should you? Would you want to?

REVIEW, CHECK, AND APPLY

REVIEW

- Proper diet, exercise, and avoidance of health risks can lead to prolonged wellness during old age, and sexuality can continue throughout the lifespan in healthy adults.

- Whether death is caused by genetic programming or by general physical wear and tear is an unresolved question. Life expectancy, which has risen for centuries, varies with gender, race, and ethnicity.

- New approaches to increasing life expectancy include telomere therapy, reducing free radicals through antioxidant drugs, restricting caloric intake, and replacing worn-out organs.

CHECK YOURSELF

1. Although we might expect older adults to be in poor health or sickly, approximately _____ of people 65 and older rate their health as good, very good, or excellent.

    a. one-half

    b. three-quarters

    c. two-thirds

    d. one-quarter

2. Which of the following is *not* a physical change in the brain associated with Alzheimer's?

    a. The hippocampus shows deterioration.

    b. The frontal and temporal lobes show deterioration.

    c. Specific neurons die, leading to a shortage of transmitters such as acetylcholine.

    d. The brain enlarges.

3. A strong relationship exists between economic well-being and illness in that those individuals who can afford to maintain good health care in their later years remain in better health.

    - True

    - False

APPLYING LIFESPAN DEVELOPMENT

- In what ways is socioeconomic status related to wellness in old age and to life expectancy?

Answers: 1) b; 2) d; 3) False

MODULE 9.2 Cognitive Development in Late Adulthood

Don't Knock Old Age

Three women were talking about the inconveniences of growing old.

"Sometimes," one of them confessed, "when I go to my refrigerator, I can't remember if I'm putting something in or taking something out."

"Oh, that's nothing," said the second woman. "There are times when I find myself at the foot of the stairs wondering if I'm going up or if I've just come down."

"Well, my goodness!" exclaimed the third woman. "I'm certainly glad I don't have any problems like that"—and she knocked on wood. "Oh," she said, starting up out of her chair, "there's someone at the door." (Dent, 1984, p. 38)

The old joke at the start of this module sums up the stereotypic view of older people as befuddled and forgetful. Today the view is different. Researchers have come to discount the view that the cognitive abilities of older people inevitably decline. Overall intellectual ability and specific cognitive skills, such as memory and problem solving, are more likely to remain strong. In fact, with appropriate practice and environmental stimuli, cognitive skills can actually improve.

This module discusses intellectual development during late adulthood. We look at the nature of intelligence in older people and the various ways cognitive abilities change. We also assess how different types of memory fare during late adulthood, and we consider ways to reverse intellectual declines in older people.

Intelligence

LO6 How well do older people function intellectually?

LO7 Must intellectual abilities inevitably decline during old age or can the decline be slowed?

Some have credited Dr. Brenda Milner with creating the field of cognitive neuroscience. Recipient of the Order of Canada, 20 honourary degrees, and countless prizes and awards, Dr. Milner has been a mainstay at the Montreal Neurological Institute for more than 60 years. Now in her 90s, she shows no signs of retiring.

"I'm doing it out of sheer curiosity and interest in how the brain works, and fascination in behaviour. If it has a spin-off, so much the better." Her research has long focused on memory, a topic all the more relevant today for an aging population.

"Memory was not a fashionable topic when I started working on it. I only started working on it because the patients complained of poor memory. And if a patient complains of memory, you don't say, 'No, no, I'm interested in perception,' and then forget about memory. You study memory or you take a different job." (Rockel, 2010)

Brenda Milner's story of durable intellectual activity is unusual but not unique. A growing number of people who depend on their wits for a livelihood, or just to keep going, have reached ages that would have been considered unthinkable when they started out—and have remained intellectually active.

Intelligence in Older People

The notion that older people become less cognitively adept initially arose from misinterpretations of research evidence comparing younger and older people's performance on the same IQ test, using traditional cross-sectional experimental methods. For example, a group of 30-year-olds and 70-year-olds might have taken the same test and had their performances compared.

However, cross-sectional methods do not take into account *cohort effects*—influences attributable to growing up in a particular era. If the younger group—because of when they grew up—has more education, on average, they will probably do better on the test for that reason alone. Furthermore, older people might do worse on any intelligence test with a timed portion simply because of their slower reaction time.

Longitudinal studies, which follow the same individuals for many years, are not much better. As we discussed earlier, repeated exposure to the same test might cause over-familiarity; as well, participants might become unavailable over time, leaving a smaller and possibly more cognitively skilled group of subjects.

Recent Conclusions

More recent research attempts to address these drawbacks. In an ambitious—and ongoing—study of intelligence in older people, developmental psychologist K. Warner Schaie uses sequential methods, which combine cross-sectional and longitudinal methods by examining several different age groups at a number of points in time.

In Schaie's massive study, 500 randomly chosen individuals took a battery of tests of cognitive ability. The people belonged to different age groups, starting at age 20 and extending at five-year intervals to age 70. The participants were tested, and continue to be tested, every seven years, and more people are recruited every year. At this point, more than 5000 participants have been tested (Schaie et al., 2005).

The study, along with other research, supports several generalizations (Craik and Salthouse, 1999, 2008):

- Some abilities gradually decline starting at around age 25, while others stay relatively steady (see Figure 9-8). There is no uniform pattern of age-related intellectual changes. For example, fluid intelligence (the ability to deal with new problems and situations) declines with age, while crystallized intelligence (the store of information, skills, and strategies that people have acquired) remains steady and in some cases improves (Schaie, 1993).

- On average, some cognitive declines are found in all abilities by age 67, but they are minimal until the eighties. Even at age 81, fewer than half of those tested showed consistent declines over the previous seven years.

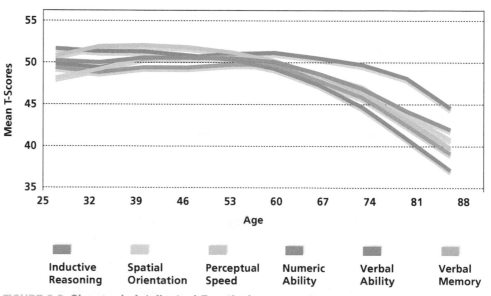

FIGURE 9-8 **Changes in Intellectual Functioning**
Although some intellectual abilities decline across adulthood, others stay relatively steady.
Source: Changes in Intellectual Functioning from Schaie, K. W. (1994). "The course of adult intellectual development." p. 307 *American Psychologist*, 49, 304–313. Copyright © 1994 by the American Psychological Association. Reproduced with permission.

- There are also significant individual differences. Some people begin to show declines in their thirties, while others show no declines until their seventies. In fact, around a third of people in their seventies score higher than the average young adult.

- Environmental and cultural factors play a role. People with no chronic disease and with higher socioeconomic status (SES), involvement in an intellectually stimulating environment, a flexible personality style, a bright spouse, good perceptual processing speed, and satisfaction with their accomplishments in midlife or early old age showed less decline.

> **plasticity** the degree to which a developing structure or behaviour is susceptible to experience

The relationship between environmental factors and intellectual skills suggests that with stimulation, practice, and motivation, older adults can maintain their mental abilities. Such **plasticity** illustrates that the changes that occur in intellectual abilities during late adulthood are not fixed. In mental life, as in so many other areas of human development, the motto "Use it or lose it" fits.

This suggests that there may be interventions to help older adults maintain their information-processing skills, as we discuss in the *From Research to Practice* box.

However, not all developmentalists accept the "use it or lose it" hypothesis. Developmental psychologist Timothy Salthouse suggests that the rate of true, underlying cognitive decline in late adulthood is unaffected by mental exercise. Instead, he argues that some people—the kind who have consistently engaged in high levels of mental activity such as completing crossword puzzles—enter late adulthood with a "cognitive reserve." This allows them to continue to perform at relatively high mental levels, despite underlying declines. Still, most developmentalists accept the hypothesis that mental exercise is beneficial (Salthouse, 2006).

From Research to Practice

Exercising the Aging Brain

My friend Joyce walks six miles a day, unless the weather is rotten: then she does just three or four. She's a voracious reader and contributes to various philosophical e-discussion groups. Joyce is in her 70s and is one of those people whose life, far from becoming empty in retirement, has filled almost to overflowing. Keen to speak to her, I found I had to leave several phone messages and send a number of e-mails: she is always busy. (McCartney, 2006, p. 1)

Research shows that continued intellectual stimulation keeps cognitive abilities sharp, although as people pass retirement age, their opportunities and motivation for cognitive challenges can decline. Recent studies suggest that a relatively small investment of time and effort in mental workouts can pay big dividends.

Sherry L. Willis and her colleagues examined the benefits of cognitive training in older adults. Participants—healthy adults over 65 with good cognitive and functional abilities—received 10 one-hour cognitive training sessions, with each successive session becoming more challenging. Three groups of participants received memory training (such as mnemonic strategies for memorizing word lists), reasoning training (such as finding the pattern in a series of numbers), or processing speed training (such as identifying objects that flashed briefly on a computer screen). Some participants also received four sessions of "booster" training one year and three years later (Willis et al., 2006).

Remarkably, cognitive benefits were evident five years after the original training sessions. Compared to a no-training control group, participants who received reasoning training performed 40 percent better on reasoning tasks at the five-year mark, those who received memory training performed 75 percent better on memory tasks, and those who received speed training performed a staggering 300 percent better on speed tasks. This is a bit like spending just two weeks at the gym for an hour a day and then giving up entirely—but still seeing noticeable improvement five years later (Vedantam, 2006; Willis et al., 2006)!

In terms of benefits to real-world functioning (such as interpreting labels on medicine bottles or looking up a telephone number), only the participants who received the processing speed training followed by booster sessions showed improvement at the five-year mark. However, participants in all three cognitive training groups reported having more confidence in their ability to complete cognitively complex daily tasks such as housework, meal preparation, finances, and shopping. Such confidence is important by itself, because it is associated with greater independence, less reliance on health services, and longer life (Willis et al., 2006).

Willis interprets these findings as evidence that mental exercise, as long as it is done regularly, seems to slow down cognitive declines. Engaging in some form of mental workout consistently—and continually increasing the level of difficulty to keep yourself challenged—are the keys to success (Vedantam, 2006; Willis et al., 2006).

- Why might the benefits of cognitive training in healthy, well-functioning older adults become evident five years afterward?

- If you were the director of a community centre for older adults, how might you apply this research in creating new programs to improve cognitive functioning in the centre's patrons?

REVIEW, CHECK, AND APPLY

REVIEW

- Although some intellectual abilities gradually decline throughout adulthood, starting at around age 25, others stay relatively steady.

- The intellect retains considerable plasticity and can be maintained with stimulation, practice, and motivation.

CHECK YOURSELF

1. One problem with conducting cross-sectional research on aging and cognition is that this method does not take into consideration _____, the influences attributable to growing up in a particular area.

2. Based on the sequential study of aging and cognition conducted by Schaie (1994), there is no uniform pattern in adulthood of age-related change across all intellectual abilities.

- True

- False

3. Not all developmentalists believe in the "use it or lose it" hypothesis. For example, Salthouse suggests that the rate of true, underlying cognitive decline in late adulthood is unaffected by mental exercise and the lack of decline is a function of a larger cognitive reserve.

- True

- False

APPLYING LIFESPAN DEVELOPMENT

- Do you think steady or increasing crystallized intelligence can partially or fully compensate for declines in fluid intelligence? Why or why not?

Answers: 1) cohort effects; 2) True; 3) True

Memory

LEARNING OBJECTIVES

LO8 What factors contribute to memory changes in old age?

Is memory loss inevitable? Not necessarily. Cross-cultural research reveals that in societies that hold older adults in relatively high esteem, such as China, older people are less likely to show memory loss. In these cultures, positive expectations can lead people to think more positively about their own capabilities (Levy and Langer, 1994; Hess et al., 2003).

Those memory declines that do occur are limited primarily to *episodic memories*, which relate to specific life experiences, such as when you first visited Vancouver. Other types of memory, such as *semantic memories* (general knowledge and facts, such as the capital of New Brunswick) and *implicit memories* (memories about which people are not consciously aware, such as how to ride a bike), are largely unaffected by age (Nilsson et al., 1997; Dixon, 2003; Nilsson, 2003).

Memory capacity changes during old age. For instance, *short-term memory* slips gradually until age 70, when the decline becomes more pronounced. The largest drop is for information that is presented quickly and orally, such as when someone at a computer helpline rattles off a series of complicated steps for fixing a computer problem. In addition, older adults find it harder to recall information about unfamiliar things, such as prose passages, names and faces of people, and the directions on a medicine label, possibly because new information is not registered and processed effectively when initially encountered. Still, these changes are minor, and most older adults automatically learn to compensate for them (Cherry and Park, 1993; Carroll, 2000; Light, 2000).

Autobiographical Memory: Recalling the Days of Our Lives. When it comes to **autobiographical memory** (memories about one's own life), older adults are as subject to lapses as younger individuals. For instance, recall frequently follows the *Pollyanna principle*, in which pleasant memories are more likely to be recalled than unpleasant memories. Similarly, people tend to forget information that is not congruent with the way they currently see themselves. Thus a strict parent who forgets that she got drunk at her high school prom is making her memories "fit" her current conception of herself (Rubin, 1996; Eacott, 1999; Rubin and Greenberg, 2003; Skowronski et al., 2003; Loftus, 2003).

Everyone tends to recall particular periods of life better than others. As can be seen in Figure 9-9, 70-year-olds tend to recall autobiographical details from their twenties and thirties

autobiographical memory memories of information about one's own life

Memory loss is not as common among older Chinese as it is in the West. What are some factors that contribute to cultural differences in memory loss of older adults?

best, while 50-year-olds are likely to have more memories of their teenage years and their twenties. In both cases, recall is better for earlier years than for more recent decades, but not as complete as for very recent events (Fromholt and Larsen, 1991; Rubin, 2000).

Explaining Memory Changes in Old Age. Explanations for memory changes in older people focus on three main categories: environmental factors, information-processing deficits, and biological factors.

- **Environmental factors.** Certain environmental factors common to many older adults can cause declines in memory. For example, older adults often take prescription drugs that hinder memory, and this, rather than age *per se*, might account for their lower performance on memory tasks.

    In addition, retirees, no longer facing job challenges, might use their memory less. Further, their motivation to recall information might be lower than before, and they might be less motivated than younger people to do their best in experimental testing situations.

- **Information-processing deficits.** Memory declines might also be linked to changes in information-processing capabilities. The ability to inhibit irrelevant information and thoughts that interfere with problem solving may decrease, and the speed of information-processing can decline (Bashore et al., 1998; Palfai et al., 2003; Salthouse et al., 2003).

    Another information-processing view suggests that older adults lose the ability to concentrate on new material and have difficulty paying attention to appropriate stimuli and organizing material in memory. According to this information-processing-deficit approach, which has substantial research support, older adults use less efficient processes to retrieve information from memory. This leads to declines in recall abilities (Craik, 1994; Castel and Craik, 2003).

- **Biological factors.** The last of the major approaches concentrates on biological factors. According to this view, memory changes are a result of brain and body deterioration. For instance, declines in episodic memory may be related to the deterioration of the frontal lobes of the brain or a reduction in estrogen. Some studies also show a loss of cells in the hippocampus, which is critical to memory. However, some memory deficits occur without any evidence of underlying biological deterioration (Eberling et al., 2004; Lye et al., 2004; Bird and Burgess, 2008).

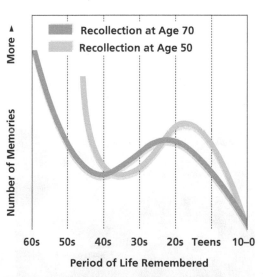

FIGURE 9-9 Remembrances of Things Past
Recall of autobiographical memories varies with age, with 70-year-olds recalling details from their twenties and thirties best, and 50-year-olds recalling memories from their teenage years and twenties. People of both ages also recall more recent memories best of all.
Source: Rubin, 1986.

Learning in Later Life: Never Too Late to Learn

Many universities encourage older adults to enrol in classes by offering them free tuition. In addition, some retirement communities are located at or near campuses—an added bonus being that universities with medical schools are located near major hospitals, popular locations for some older adults. Such central locations, in addition to facilitating medical treatment, also tend to be well served by public transit (Powell, 2004).

Although some older adults are doubtful about their intellectual capabilities and consequently hesitate to compete with younger students in regular classes, their concern is largely misplaced. Older adults often have no trouble maintaining their standing in rigorous university classes. Furthermore, professors and other students generally find the presence of older people, with their varied and substantial life experiences, a real educational benefit (Simson et al., 2006).

REVIEW, CHECK, AND APPLY

REVIEW

- Declines in memory affect mainly episodic memories and short-term memory.

- Explanations for memory changes in old age have focused on environmental factors, information-processing declines, and biological factors.

CHECK YOURSELF

1. When it comes to autobiographical memories, older individuals, like younger individuals, follow the _____, in that they are more likely to remember pleasant memories.

   a. saliency effect

   b. environmental effect

   c. Pollyanna principle

   d. positive effect

2. Explanations for changes in memory tend to focus on three main categories: environmental factors, biological factors, and _____.

   a. social support

   b. life changes

   c. information-processing deficits

   d. personal influences

3. Despite concerns about memory and intellectual capabilities, older adults have no trouble maintaining their standing in rigorous university classes.

   - True

   - False

APPLYING LIFESPAN DEVELOPMENT

- How might cultural factors, such as the esteem in which a society holds its older members, work to affect an older person's memory performance?

Answers: 1) c; 2) c; 3) True

MODULE 9.3 Social and Personality Development in Late Adulthood

Late Love

Gerry, 76, and Dot, 73, met at the Botanical Gardens. "I went to the Gardens frequently because I missed having my own garden," Gerry said, "and there was this lovely lady there every time I went . . . ."

Both Gerry and Dot enjoyed gardening, but they enjoyed seeing each other every Wednesday afternoon even more. Dot always wore the same bright hat, "so he'd notice me," she blushes. They struck up a conversation and began sharing tea. Then they began to see each other outside the Gardens.

"My children were surprised when I told them I had a boyfriend. They were even more surprised at the idea we might be intimate. They didn't know what to think," said Dot, "but I just told them, I'm in my seventies, I've been through menopause . . . ."

We turn in this module to the social and emotional aspects of late adulthood, which remain as central as in earlier stages of the lifespan. We begin by considering how personality continues to develop, and then we examine various ways people can age successfully.

Next, we consider how various societal factors affect older adults. We discuss living arrangements and economic and financial issues. We also look at how culture governs the way we treat older adults, and we examine the influence of work and retirement on older adults.

Finally, we consider relationships in late adulthood among married couples, relatives, and friends. We will see how social networks play an important—and sustaining—role in people's lives. We examine how events such as the divorce of a parent, decades earlier, can still affect people's lives. We end with a discussion of elder abuse.

Personality Development and Successful Aging

LO9 In what ways does personality develop during late adulthood?

LO10 How do people deal with aging?

LEARNING OBJECTIVES

The mayor of Spring Garden Road—that's what they called Leroy. If you went out for coffee with him, no matter where you were, everyone knew him. Mr. Popularity. He didn't let his physical limitations slow him down. He was a shameless flirt, and a resourceful businessman . . . but most of all, he was loved.

For older adults, time and circumstances can bring changes in their outlook on life, their views of themselves, and perhaps even their basic personalities. In fact, one of the fundamental questions asked by lifespan developmentalists concerns the degree to which personality remains stable or changes in later adulthood.

Continuity and Change in Personality during Late Adulthood

Is personality relatively stable throughout adulthood, or does it vary significantly? The answer depends on which facets of personality we consider. According to developmental psychologists Paul Costa and Robert McCrae, whose work we discussed earlier, the "Big Five" basic personality traits (neuroticism, extroversion, openness, agreeableness, and conscientiousness) are remarkably stable across adulthood. For instance, even-tempered people at 20 are still even-tempered at 75, and people who hold positive self-concepts early in adulthood still view themselves positively in late adulthood. There seems to be a fundamental continuity to personality (Costa and McCrae, 1988, 1989, 1997; McCrae and Costa, 1990, 2003; Field and Millsap, 1991).

Despite this continuity, change is still possible. Profound changes in people's social environments can produce personality changes. What is important to a person at 80 is not necessarily the same as what was important at 40.

To account for these changes, some theorists have focused on the discontinuities of development. As we'll see next, Erik Erikson, Robert Peck, Daniel Levinson, and Bernice Neugarten have examined personality changes that accompany new challenges in later adulthood.

Ego Integrity versus Despair: Erikson's Final Stage. Psychoanalyst Erik Erikson characterizes late adulthood as the time when people move into the last of life's eight stages of psychosocial development. Labelled the **ego-integrity-versus-despair stage**, this period is characterized by a process of looking back over one's life, evaluating it, and coming to terms with it.

People who are successful in this stage of development experience satisfaction and accomplishment, which Erikson terms "integrity." When people achieve integrity, they feel they have fulfilled the possibilities that have come their way in life, and they have few regrets. Other people look back on their lives with dissatisfaction. They might feel that they have missed important opportunities and have not accomplished what they wished. Such individuals might be unhappy, depressed, angry, or despondent over what they have done, or failed to do, with their lives—in short, they despair.

Peck's Developmental Tasks. Although Erikson's approach provides a picture of the broad possibilities of later adulthood, other theorists offer a more differentiated view of the final

ego-integrity-versus-despair stage Erikson's final stage of life, characterized by a process of looking back over one's life, evaluating it, and coming to terms with it

redefinition of self versus preoccupation with work role the theory that those in old age must redefine themselves in ways that do not relate to their work roles or occupations

body transcendence versus body preoccupation a period in which people must learn to cope with and move beyond changes in physical capabilities as a result of aging

ego transcendence versus ego preoccupation the period in which older adults must come to grips with their coming death

stage of life. The psychologist Robert Peck (1968) suggests that personality development in older adults is occupied by three major developmental tasks.

In Peck's view—part of a comprehensive description of change across adulthood—the first task in old age is to redefine oneself in ways that do not relate to work roles or occupations. He labels this stage the **redefinition of self versus preoccupation with work role**. As we will see, the changes that occur when people stop working can trigger a difficult adjustment in the way they view themselves. Peck suggests that people must adjust their values to place less emphasis on themselves as workers or professionals and more on attributes that don't involve work, such as being a grandparent or a gardener.

The second major developmental task in late adulthood, according to Peck, is **body transcendence versus body preoccupation**. Older individuals can undergo significant changes in their physical abilities as a result of aging. In the body-transcendence-versus-body-preoccupation stage, people must learn to cope with and move beyond those physical changes (transcendence). If they don't, they become preoccupied with their physical deterioration, to the detriment of their personality development.

The third developmental task in old age is **ego transcendence versus ego preoccupation**, in which older adults must come to grips with their coming death. They need to understand that although death is inevitable, and probably not too far off, they have made contributions to society. If they see these contributions, which can take the form of children or work and civic activities, as lasting beyond their own lives, they will experience ego transcendence. If not, they may become preoccupied with asking whether their lives had value and worth to society.

Levinson's Final Season: The Winter of Life. Daniel Levinson's theory of adult development does not focus as much on the challenges that aging adults must overcome. Instead, he looks at the processes that can lead to personality change as we grow old. According to Levinson, people enter late adulthood by passing through a transition stage that typically occurs around ages 60 to 65 (Levinson, 1986, 1992). During this stage, people come to view themselves as entering late adulthood—or, ultimately, as being "old." Knowing full well society's negative stereotypes about older adults, they struggle with the notion that they are now in this category.

According to Levinson, people come to realize that they are no longer on the centre stage, but rather are playing bit parts. This loss of power, respect, and authority can be difficult for individuals accustomed to having control in their lives.

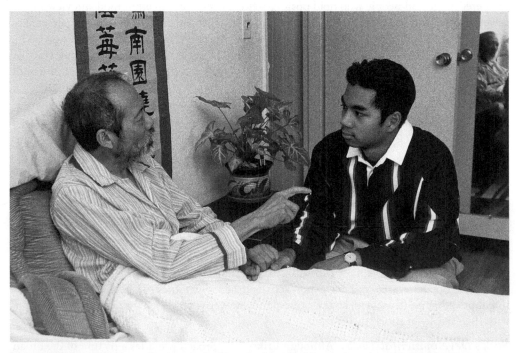

Older adults may become "venerated elders," whose advice is sought and relied upon.

On the other hand, people in late adulthood can serve as resources to younger individuals, and they might find that they are viewed as "venerated elders" whose advice is sought and relied upon. Furthermore, old age can bring a new freedom to do things simply for enjoyment and pleasure, rather than as obligations.

Coping with Aging: Neugarten's Study.   In what became a classic study, Bernice Neugarten (1972, 1977) examined the different ways that people cope with aging. Neugarten found four different personality types in her research on people in their seventies:

- **Disintegrated and disorganized personalities.** Some people are unable to accept aging and experience despair as they get older. They are often found in long-term care facilities.

- **Passive-dependent personalities.** Others become fearful—of falling ill, of the future, of their own inability to cope. They are so fearful that they might seek help from family and care providers, even when they don't need it.

- **Defended personalities.** Others respond to the fear of aging quite differently—by trying to stop it in its tracks. They might attempt to act young, exercising vigorously and engaging in youthful activities. Unfortunately, they might set unrealistic expectations and run the risk of disappointment.

- **Integrated personalities.** The most successful individuals cope comfortably with aging. They accept it with a sense of self-dignity.

Neugarten found that the majority of the people she studied fell into the final category. They acknowledged aging and could look back at their lives and gaze into the future with acceptance.

Life Review and Reminiscence: The Common Theme of Personality Development.
Life review, in which people examine and evaluate their lives, is a major thread running through the work of Erikson, Peck, Neugarten, and Levinson, and a common theme among personality theorists who focus on late adulthood.

According to gerontologist Robert Butler (2002), life review is triggered by the increasingly obvious prospect of death. People look back on their lives, remembering and reconsidering what has happened to them. Far from being a harmful process of reliving the past, wallowing in past problems, and reopening old wounds, life review usually leads to a better understanding of the past. People might resolve lingering problems and conflicts with others, such as an estrangement from a child, and they might feel they can face their current lives with greater serenity (Bohlmeijer et al., 2003; Arkoff et al., 2004; McKee et al., 2005).

Life review offers other benefits, including a sense of mutuality—a feeling of interconnectedness with others. Moreover, it can be a source of social interaction, as older adults share their experiences with others (Sherman, 1991; Parks et al., 2003).

Reminiscence can even have cognitive benefits, improving memory. By reflecting on the past, people activate a variety of memories, which can trigger other memories and bring back sights, sounds, and even smells of the past (Thorsheim and Roberts, 1990; Kartman, 1991).

On the other hand, life review can sometimes produce declines in psychological functioning. If people become obsessive about the past, reliving old insults and mistakes that cannot be rectified, they can end up feeling guilt, depression, and anger against acquaintances who might not even be alive (DeGenova, 1993).

Overall, though, the process of life review and reminiscence can play an important role by providing continuity between past and present and increasing awareness of the contemporary world. It also can provide new insights into the past and into others, allowing people to continue personality growth and to function more effectively in the present (Stevens-Ratchford, 1993; Turner and Helms, 1994; Webster and Haight, 2002; Coleman, 2005; Haber, 2006).

Age Stratification Approaches to Late Adulthood

Age, like race and gender, provides a way of ranking people within a society. **Age stratification theories** suggest that economic resources, power, and privilege are distributed unequally among people at different stages of life. Such inequality is particularly pronounced during late adulthood.

Even as medical advances have lengthened the lifespan, power and prestige for older adults have eroded—at least in highly industrialized societies. The peak earning years are

life review the point in life in which people examine and evaluate their lives

age stratification theories the view that an unequal distribution of economic resources, power, and privilege exists among people at different stages of the life course

the fifties; later, earnings tend to decline. Furthermore, younger people are often physically removed from their elders, and their increased independence can make older adults feel less important. In addition, rapidly changing technology makes older adults seem out of date and lacking in important skills. Ultimately, they are seen as not particularly productive members of society and, in some cases, simply irrelevant (Cohn, 1982; Macionis, 2001). According to Levinson's theory, older people are keenly aware of their decline in status, and adjusting to it is the major transition of late adulthood.

Age stratification theories help explain why aging is viewed more positively in less industrialized societies. In predominantly agricultural societies, older people accumulate control over important resources such as animals and land. In such societies, the concept of retirement is unknown. Older individuals (especially males) are highly respected because they continue to be involved in daily activities central to the society. Furthermore, because the pace of change in agricultural societies is slower than in more technological societies, people in late adulthood have considerable relevant wisdom. Nor is respect for elders limited to agricultural countries; it is a characteristic of a variety of cultures.

Cultural Dimensions

How Culture Shapes the Way We Treat People in Late Adulthood

Views of late adulthood are coloured by culture. For example, compared to Western cultures, Asian societies generally hold older adults, particularly family members, in higher esteem. Although this is changing in rapidly industrializing areas of Asia, such as Japan, the view of aging and the treatment of people in late adulthood still tend to be more positive than in Western cultures (Fry, 1985; Ikels, 1989; Cobbe, 2003; Degnen, 2007).

What is it about Asian cultures that leads to esteem for old age? In general, cultures that value older adults are relatively homogeneous in socioeconomic terms. In addition, the roles that people play in those societies entail greater responsibility with increasing age, and older adults control resources to a relatively large extent.

Moreover, the roles of people in Asian societies display more continuity throughout the lifespan than in Western cultures, and older adults continue to engage in activities that are valued by society. Finally, Asian cultures are more organized around extended families in which the older generations are well integrated into the family structure (Fry, 1985; Sangree, 1989). In such an arrangement, younger family members tend to rely on older members to share their considerable accumulated wisdom.

On the other hand, even societies that articulate strong ideals regarding older adults do not always live up to those standards. For instance, the attitudes of Chinese people, typified by admiration, respect, and even worship for individuals in late adulthood, are more positive than their actual behaviour in all but the most elite segment of the society. Furthermore, sons and their wives—but not daughters—are typically expected to care for older parents; parents with only daughters may find

themselves with no one to care for them. In short, broad, global statements about how older adults are treated in a given society almost always mask exceptions (Comunian and Gielen, 2000).

Asian cultures are not alone in esteeming their elders. In Aboriginal cultures, elders play a prominent, vital, and respected role, and are considered "teachers of heritage and survival and strength." In many Latin American cultures, the elders are thought to have a special inner strength, and in many African cultures, reaching an old age is seen as a sign of divine intervention (Diop, 1989; Holmes and Holmes, 1995; Lehr et al., 2000; Métis National Council of Women, 2006).

What aspects of Asian cultures lead them to hold their elders at higher levels of esteem?

Does Age Bring Wisdom?

One of the benefits of age is supposed to be wisdom. But do people gain wisdom as they become older?

In fact we don't know for sure, because the concept of **wisdom**—expert knowledge in the practical aspects of life—is only recently receiving attention from gerontologists and other researchers. This is partly due to the difficulty of defining and measuring the concept (Helmuth, 2003; Brugman, 2006). Wisdom can be seen as reflecting an accumulation of knowledge, experience, and contemplation, and by this definition, aging contributes to wisdom (Baltes and Staudinger, 2000; Dixon and Cohen, 2003; Wink and Dillon, 2003; Kunzmann and Baltes, 2005).

Distinguishing wisdom from intelligence is tricky. Some researchers have made suggestions: While knowledge derived from intelligence is related to the here-and-now, wisdom is more timeless. While intelligence permits a person to think logically and systematically, wisdom provides an understanding of human behaviour. According to psychologist Robert Sternberg, intelligence permits humans to invent the atom bomb, while wisdom prevents them from using it (Seppa, 1997).

Measuring wisdom is difficult. Ursula Staudinger and Paul Baltes (2000) designed a study showing that it is possible to assess people reliably on the concept. Pairs of people ranging in age from 20 to 70 discussed difficulties relating to life events. One problem involved someone who gets a phone call from a friend who is planning to commit suicide. Another involved a 14-year-old girl who wanted to move out of her family home immediately. Participants were asked what they should do and consider.

Although there were no absolute right or wrong answers, the responses were evaluated against several criteria, including how much factual knowledge they brought to bear; their knowledge of decision-making strategies; how well the participants considered the context of the central character's lifespan and values; and their recognition that there might not be a single, absolute solution. Using these criteria, the older participants' responses were wiser than those of younger participants.

The study also found that the older participants benefited more from an experimental condition designed to promote wise thinking, and other research suggests that the very wisest individuals may be older adults.

Other research has looked at wisdom in terms of the development of a theory of mind: the ability to make inferences about others' thoughts, feelings, and intentions—their mental states. Older adults, drawing on their years of experience, appear to have a more sophisticated theory of mind (Happe et al., 1998).

Successful Aging: What Is the Secret?

At age 77, Elinor Reynolds spends most of her time at home, leading a quiet, routine existence. Never married, Elinor receives visits from her two sisters every few weeks, and some of her nieces and nephews stop by on occasion. But for the most part, she keeps to herself. When asked, she says she is quite happy.

In contrast, Carrie Masterson, also 77, is involved in something different almost every day. If she is not visiting the senior centre and participating in some activity, she is out shopping. Her daughter complains that Carrie is "never home" when she tries to reach Carrie by phone, and Carrie replies that she has never been busier—or happier.

Clearly, there is no single way to age successfully. How people age depends on personality factors and people's circumstances. Some people become progressively less involved with the day-to-day, while others maintain active ties to people and their personal interests. Three major approaches provide explanations: disengagement theory, activity theory, and continuity theory.

Disengagement Theory: Gradual Retreat. According to **disengagement theory**, late adulthood often involves a gradual withdrawal from the world on physical, psychological, and social levels (Cummings and Henry, 1961). On a physical level, older adults have lower energy levels and slow down progressively. Psychologically, they begin to withdraw, showing less interest in the world around them and spending more time looking inward. Finally, on a social level, they engage in fewer interactions—both day-to-day, face-to-face encounters and participation in society as a whole. Older adults also become less involved and invested in the lives of others (Quinnan, 1997).

wisdom expert knowledge in the practical aspects of life

disengagement theory the period in late adulthood that marks a gradual withdrawal from the world on physical, psychological, and social levels

Disengagement theory suggests that withdrawal is a mutual process. Because of norms and expectations about aging, society begins to disengage from those in late adulthood. For example, mandatory retirement ages compel older adults to withdraw from work, which accelerates disengagement.

Such withdrawal is not necessarily negative. In fact, most theorists who subscribe to the theory maintain that the outcomes of disengagement are largely positive. As people withdraw they become more reflective about their lives and less constrained by social roles. Furthermore, they can become more discerning in their social relationships, focusing on those who best meet their needs. Thus, disengagement can be liberating (Settersten, 2002; Wrosch et al., 2005).

Similarly, decreased emotional investment in others can be beneficial. By investing less emotional energy in others, people in late adulthood are better able to adjust to serious illness and death among their peers.

Evidence for disengagement comes from a study examining close to 300 people aged 50 to 90 which found that specific events, such as retirement or the death of a spouse, were accompanied by a gradual disengagement in which the level of social interaction with others plummeted (Cummings and Henry, 1961). Consistent with the theory, disengagement was related to successful aging.

Activity Theory: Continued Involvement. Although early findings were consistent with disengagement theory, later research was not so supportive. For example, a follow-up study found that although some of the subjects were happily disengaged, others, who had remained involved and active, were as happy as—and sometimes happier than—those who disengaged. Furthermore, people in many non-Western cultures remain engaged, active, and busy throughout old age, and are expected to do so. Clearly, disengagement is not a universal process (Havighurst, 1973; Bergstrom and Holmes, 2000; Crosnoe and Elder, 2002).

The lack of support for disengagement theory led to an alternative. **Activity theory** suggests that successful aging occurs when people maintain the interests and activities of middle age and the amount and type of their social interactions. According to this perspective, happiness and satisfaction with life spring from involvement with the world (Charles et al., 2001; Consedine et al., 2004; Hutchinson and Wexler, 2007).

Activity theory suggests that continuation of activities is important. Even when continuation is no longer possible—such as continuing work after retirement—activity theory argues that successful aging occurs when replacement activities are found.

But activity theory, like disengagement theory, is not the full story. For one thing, activity theory makes little distinction among activities. Not every activity will have an equal impact on a person's satisfaction with life; in fact, the nature and quality of the activities are likely to be more critical than mere quantity or frequency (Burrus-Bammel and Bammel, 1985; Adams, 2004).

A more significant concern is that for some people in late adulthood, the principle of "less is more" clearly holds: less activity brings greater enjoyment because they can slow down and do only the things that bring them the greatest satisfaction. In fact, some people view the ability to moderate their pace as one of the bounties of late adulthood. For them, a relatively inactive, and perhaps even solitary, existence is welcome (Ward, 1984; Hansson and Carpenter, 1994).

From a social worker's perspective: How might cultural factors affect an older adult's likelihood of pursuing either the disengagement strategy or the activity strategy?

Continuity Theory: A Compromise Position. Neither disengagement theory nor activity theory provides a complete picture of successful aging (Johnson and Barer, 1992; Rapkin and Fischer, 1992; Ouwehand et al., 2007). A compromise view is needed. **Continuity theory** suggests that people simply need to maintain their desired level of involvement in society in order to maximize their sense of well-being and self-esteem (Whitbourne, 2001; Atchley, 2003).

According to continuity theory, those who were highly active and social will be happiest if they largely remain so. Those who enjoy solitude and solitary interests, such as reading or walks in the woods, will be happiest pursuing that level of sociability (Holahan and Chapman, 2002).

It is also clear that most older adults experience positive emotions as frequently as younger individuals. Furthermore, they become more skilled at regulating their emotions.

activity theory the theory suggesting that successful aging occurs when people maintain the interests, activities, and social interactions with which they were involved during middle age

continuity theory the theory suggesting that people need to maintain their desired level of involvement in society in order to maximize their sense of well-being and self-esteem

Other factors enhance happiness during late adulthood. The importance of physical and mental health cannot be overestimated, and having enough financial security to provide for basic needs is critical. In addition, a sense of autonomy, independence, and personal control over one's life is a significant advantage (Carstensen et al., 2000; Lawton, 2001; Morris, 2001; Charles et al., 2003).

Finally, as we discussed earlier, people's perceptions can influence their happiness and satisfaction. Those who view late adulthood favourably are apt to perceive themselves more positively than those who view old age in a more pessimistic way (Levy et al., 2002; Levy, 2003).

Selective Optimization with Compensation: A General Model of Successful Aging.

In considering the factors that lead to successful aging, developmental psychologists Paul Baltes and Margret Baltes focus on the "selective optimization with compensation" model. As we noted earlier, the assumption underlying the model is that late adulthood brings with it changes and losses in underlying capabilities, which vary from one person to another. However, it is possible to overcome such shifts in capabilities through selective optimization.

Selective optimization is the process by which people concentrate on particular skill areas to compensate for losses in other areas. They do this to fortify their general motivational, cognitive, and physical resources. A person who has run marathons all her life might have to cut back or give up entirely other activities in order to increase her training. By giving up other activities, she might be able to maintain her running skills through concentration on them (Bajor and Baltes, 2003; Baltes and Carstensen, 2003; Baltes and Freund, 2003a, 2003b; Rapp et al., 2006).

Similarly, older adults engage in compensation for age-related losses. For instance, a person may compensate for a hearing loss by using a hearing aid. Piano virtuoso Arthur Rubinstein provides another example of selective optimization with compensation. In his later years, he maintained his concert career by reducing the number of pieces he played at concerts (an example of being selective) and by practising those pieces more often (optimization). Finally, in an example of compensation, he slowed down the tempo of musical passages immediately preceding faster passages, thereby fostering the illusion that he was playing as fast as ever (Baltes and Baltes, 1990).

In short, the model of selective optimization with compensation illustrates the fundamentals of successful aging. Although late adulthood can bring changes in capabilities, people who focus on making the most of particular areas might be able to compensate for limitations and losses. The outcome is a life that is reduced in some ways, but transformed and modified and, ultimately, successful.

> **selective optimization** the process by which people concentrate on selected skills areas to compensate for losses in other areas

---

REVIEW, CHECK, AND APPLY

REVIEW

- Erikson calls older adulthood the ego-integrity-versus-despair stage; Peck focuses on three tasks that define the period; Levinson suggests that older people can experience liberation and self-regard; and Neugarten focuses on the ways people cope with aging.

- Societies in which older adults are respected are generally characterized by social homogeneity, extended families, responsible roles for older adults, and control of significant resources by older adults.

- Disengagement theory suggests that older adults gradually withdraw from the world, while activity theory suggests that the happiest people continue to be engaged with the world. A compromise theory—continuity theory—might be the most useful approach to defining successful aging, and the most successful model for aging might be selective optimization with compensation.

CHECK YOURSELF

1. According to Erikson, individuals in late adulthood engage in looking back over their lives, evaluating their experiences, and coming to terms with decisions. This is also known as _____.
   a. ego transcendence versus ego preoccupation
   b. acceptance of growing old
   c. generativity versus stagnation
   d. ego integrity versus despair

2. According to Peck, the first major developmental task is to decide on your identity even though you are no longer employed. This is also known as _____.

   a. redefinition of self versus preoccupation with work role
   b. ego integrity versus despair
   c. body transcendence versus body preoccupation
   d. ego transcendence versus ego preoccupation

3. According to Levinson, as individuals enter late adulthood one of the hardest struggles they experience is the acceptance that they are "old."
   - True
   - False

APPLYING LIFESPAN DEVELOPMENT

- How might personality traits account for success or failure in achieving satisfaction through the life review process?

Answers: 1) d; 2) a; 3) True

The Daily Life of Late Adulthood

L011 What is it like to retire?

Living in a multigenerational setting with children and their families can be rewarding and helpful for those in late adulthood. Are there any disadvantages to this type of situation? What are some solutions?

When Susan was first offered a seniors' discount, she was offended. She had always had compliments about how young she looked. Not this day. She was shopping in The Bay, her hair covered by a scarf because it was raining, and a 20-something sales lady just offered her a seniors' discount. Susan didn't consider herself a senior. When she told her husband the story later, his only comment was, "How much did you save?"

Although not all retirees are so fortunate, many, if not most, find their post-work lives happy and involving. We will consider some of the ways in which people lead their lives in late adulthood, beginning with where they live.

Living Arrangements: The Places and Spaces of Their Lives

Think "old age" and your thoughts are likely to turn to long-term care facilities. But the reality is different. Only 7 percent of older adults live in long-term care facilities; most live out their entire lives in home environments, typically with at least one family member.

Living at Home. More than one quarter of older adults live alone, and nearly half live with their spouse. Some older adults live with their siblings, and others live in multigenerational settings with their children, grandchildren, and even great-grandchildren. The number of older adults living alone or in long-term care facilities increases with age as fewer older adults continue to live with a spouse. Among those over the age of 85, nearly one-third live alone and an equal number live in long-term care facilities (Turcotte and Schellenberg, 2007).

The setting in which an older adult lives has varied effects. For married couples, living with a spouse represents continuity. On the other hand, moving in with children represents an adjustment to a multigenerational setting that can be jarring. Not only is there a potential loss of independence and privacy, but older adults might feel uncomfortable with the way their children are raising their grandchildren. Unless there are household ground rules about people's roles, conflicts can arise (Sussman and Sussman, 1991; Navarro, 2006).

Specialized Living Environments. For approximately 1 in 30 older adults, home is a long-term care facility, although there are many types of specialized environments in which older adults live. More than two-thirds of Canada's long-term care facilities are privately owned, and the cost of accommodation ranges from $50 to $100 per day.

One of the more recent innovations is the **continuing-care community**, typically an environment in which all the residents are of retirement age or older. The community provides various levels of care, and residents sign contracts for the level they need. In many such communities, people start out in separate houses or apartments, living either independently or with occasional home care. As they age, they may move into *assisted living*, which involves independent housing supported by medical providers to the extent required. Continuing care ultimately extends all the way to full-time nursing care, which is often provided at an onsite hospital-like facility.

Continuing-care communities tend to be fairly homogeneous in terms of religious, racial, and ethnic backgrounds, and they are often organized by private or religious organizations. Because joining can involve a substantial initial payment, members tend to be relatively well-off. Increasingly, though, continuing-care communities are making efforts to increase diversity and also to enhance intergenerational interaction by establishing daycare centres on the premises and developing programs that involve younger populations (Barton, 1997; Chaker, 2003; Berkman, 2006).

Several types of facilities exist, ranging from those that provide part-time daycare to homes that offer 24-hour-a-day, live-in care. In **adult daycare facilities**, older adults receive care only during the day, but spend nights and weekends in their own homes. When

continuing-care community a community that offers an environment in which all the residents are of retirement age or older and need various levels of care

adult daycare facilities facilities in which older adults receive care only during the day; they spend nights and weekends in their own homes

they are at the facility, they receive nursing care, take their meals, and participate in scheduled activities. Sometimes adult facilities are combined with infant and child daycare programs, an arrangement that allows for interaction between the old and the young, although the obvious analogy might be offensive to some (Quade, 1994; Ritchie, 2003; Tse and Howie, 2005; Gitlin et al., 2006).

Other institutional settings offer more extensive care. The most intensive are **skilled-nursing facilities**, which provide full-time nursing care for people who have chronic illnesses and require 24-hour care. While a minority of those 65 and older live in nursing homes, the number increases dramatically with age. The percentages are 1.1 percent for people 65 to 74 years old; 4.7 percent for those 75 to 84; and 18.2 percent for people 85 and older. Many adults requiring this level of care have dementia or have had strokes (Administration on Aging, 2006).

The more intensive the care, the greater the adjustment required of residents. Although some newcomers adjust relatively rapidly, the loss of independence can lead to difficulties. In addition, older adults are as susceptible as other people to society's stereotypes about "nursing homes," and their expectations can be negative. They might see themselves as just marking time until they die, forgotten and discarded by a society that venerates youth (Biedenharn and Normoyle, 1991; Baltes, 1996).

Institutionalism and Learned Helplessness. Although the fears of those in long-term care facilities might be exaggerated, those fears can lead to **institutionalism**, a psychological state in which people develop apathy, indifference, and a lack of caring about themselves. Institutionalism is brought about, in part, by *learned helplessness*, a belief that one has no control over one's environment (Butler and Lewis, 1981; Peterson and Park, 2007).

The sense of helplessness brought about by institutionalism can be literally deadly. When people enter long-term care facilities in late adulthood, they lose control over their most basic activities. They might be told when and what to eat, when to sleep, and even when to go to the bathroom (Kane et al., 1997; Wolinsky et al., 2003).

A classic experiment showed the consequences of such a loss of control. Psychologists Ellen Langer and Irving Janis (1979) divided residents of a long-term care facility into two groups. One group was encouraged to make choices about their day-to-day activities. The other group was given no choices and was encouraged to let the staff care for them. The results

skilled-nursing facilities facilities that provide full-time nursing care for people who have chronic illnesses or who are recovering from a temporary medical condition

institutionalism a psychological state in which people in nursing homes develop apathy, indifference, and a lack of caring about themselves

During late adulthood, the range of socioeconomic well-being mirrors that of earlier years.

were clear. The participants who had choices were not only happier, they were also healthier. In fact, 18 months after the experiment began, only 15 percent of the choice group had died—compared to 30 percent of the comparison group.

In short, loss of control can have a profound effect on well-being. The best long-term care facilities go out of their way to permit residents to make basic life decisions and maintain a sense of control over their lives.

> **From the perspective of a health-care professional:** What policies might a long-term care facility institute to minimize the chances that its residents will develop "institutionalism"? Why are such policies relatively uncommon?

Financial Issues: The Economics of Late Adulthood

Like everyone, people in late adulthood range from one end of the socioeconomic spectrum to the other. Those who were relatively affluent during their working years tend to remain relatively affluent, while those who were poor tend to remain poor when they reach late adulthood.

However, social inequities affecting various groups earlier in life are magnified with increasing age. Even so, everyone who reaches late adulthood today might experience growing economic pressure because the increasing human lifespan means it is more likely they will run through their savings.

Overall, 6 percent of people age 65 and older live in poverty, a proportion about half that for people under 65. However, there are significant gender differences. Women are almost twice as likely as men to be living in poverty. Married couples are the least likely to live in poverty, but living alone is more detrimental to women. About 19 percent of older adult women without a spouse live on incomes below the poverty line. A married woman might also slip into poverty if she becomes widowed, for she might well have used up savings to pay for costs associated with her husband's final illness, and the husband's pension might cease with his death. Divorced women are even more likely to live in poverty than widows. Substantial regional differences also exist (Turcotte and Schellenberg, 2007; Spraggins, 2003; see Figure 9-10).

One source of financial vulnerability is the reliance on a fixed income. The income of an older adult, which typically comes from a combination of Canada Pension Plan, employee pensions, and savings/investments, rarely keeps up with inflation. What might have been a

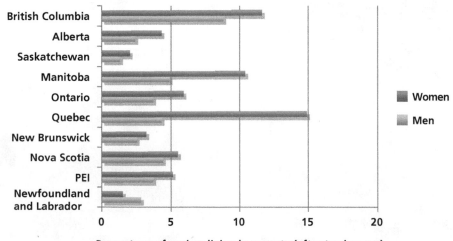

Percentage of seniors living in poverty (after tax income)

FIGURE 9-10 **Poverty and Older Adults**
While 6 percent of those 65 years of age and older live in poverty, significant gender and regional differences exist.
Source: Turcotte and Schellenberg, 2007.

reasonable income at age 65 is worth much less 20 years later, as the older adult gradually slips into poverty. Today, many retirees are also concerned about outliving their savings. As a young adult, they might have anticipated living 10 or 15 years after retirement, only to witness their own parents live 20 or more years past retirement.

While accommodation, transportation, and food costs comprise the bulk of older adults' expenses, rising medical costs add to financial vulnerability. On average, older adults spend 6 to 8 percent of their income on health related expenses, including equipment and medication, and dental and vision care, costs that are often not covered by provincial medicare. For those who require care in long-term care facilities, a private room can cost thousands of dollars per month (Turcotte and Schellenberg, 2007).

The Canada Pension Plan has made a positive difference in the lives of today's older adults, but concerns are frequently expressed that, as baby boomers begin to retire, they will bankrupt the system. This dilemma could lead to increasing friction among and segregation between younger and older generations, and is a key factor for many people when deciding how long to work.

Work and Retirement in Late Adulthood

Deciding when to retire is a major decision faced by the majority of individuals in late adulthood. Some wish to work as long as they can. Others retire the moment their financial circumstances permit it. A decreasing number of adults are subject to mandatory retirement—a controversial topic.

When they do retire, many people have some difficulty with the identity shift from "worker" to "retiree." They lack a professional title, they may no longer have people asking them for advice, and they can't say "I work for the Diamond Company."

For others, though, retirement offers the chance to lead, perhaps for the first time in adulthood, a life of leisure. Because a significant number of people retire as early as age 55 or 60, and because lifespans are expanding, many people spend far more time in retirement than in previous generations. Moreover, because the number of people in late adulthood continues to increase, retirees are an increasingly significant and influential segment of the population.

Older Workers: Combatting Age Discrimination.   Many people continue to work, either full- or part-time, for some part of late adulthood. Some employers continue to have a mandatory retirement policy, while other companies have raised the age of mandatory retirement or eliminated it altogether.

Whether older adults continue to work for intellectual and social reasons, or for financial reasons, many encounter age discrimination—a reality, despite laws against it. Some employers encourage older workers to leave their jobs so they can be replaced with younger employees who will earn lower salaries. In tough economic times, encouraging retirement without replacing the worker can be a way to avoid or reduce layoffs. And some employers believe that older workers are not up to the demands of the job or are less willing to adapt to a changing workplace—enduring stereotypes that laws can't change (Moss, 1997).

There is little evidence to support the idea that older workers lose their ability to perform their jobs. In many fields, such as art, literature, science, politics, and entertainment, examples abound of people who have made some of their greatest contributions during late adulthood. Even in those few professions that were specifically exempted from laws that prohibit mandatory retirement—those involving public safety—the evidence does not support the notion that workers should be retired early.

For instance, one large-scale, careful study of older police officers, firefighters, and prison guards concluded that age was not a good predictor of whether a worker was likely to be incapacitated on the job, or of the level of his or her general work performance. Accurate prediction required a case-by-case analysis of individual workers' performance (Landy and Conte, 2004).

◉ Watch on mydevelopmentlab

Mary and George, a couple in their seventies, have recently retired and have gone through many of the same issues you've just read about.
Log onto MyDevelopment to hear them talk about how they dealt with the changes that come with retirement.

Retirement is a different journey for each individual. Some are content with a more sedate lifestyle, while others remain active and, in some cases, pursue new activities. Can you explain why many non-Western cultures do not follow the disengagement theory of retirement?

Although age discrimination remains a problem, market forces might help reduce its severity. As baby boomers retire and the workforce drastically shrinks, companies might begin to offer incentives to older adults to either remain in or return to the workforce. Still, for most older adults, retirement is the norm.

Retirement: Filling a Life of Leisure. Why do people retire? Although the basic reason seems apparent—to stop working—there are actually many factors. For instance, sometimes workers burn out after a lifetime of work and seek to ease the tension and frustration of their jobs and the sense that they have not accomplished as much as they wished. Others retire because their health has declined, and still others because they receive incentives from their employers. Finally, some people have planned for years to retire and intend to use their increased leisure to travel, study, or spend more time with their children and grandchildren (Beehr et al., 2000; Nimrod and Adoni, 2006; Sener et al., 2007).

Whatever the reason they retire, people often pass through a series of retirement stages. Retirement might begin with a *honeymoon* period, in which people engage in a variety of activities, such as travel, that were previously hindered by work. The next phase might be *disenchantment*, in which they conclude that retirement is not all they thought it would be because they miss the stimulation and companionship of work or find it hard to keep busy (Atchley and Barusch, 2003).

The next phase is *reorientation*, in which retirees reconsider their options and become engaged in new, more fulfilling activities. If successful, this leads to the *retirement routine* stage, in which they come to grips with the realities of retirement and feel fulfilled. Not all people reach this stage; some can feel disenchanted for years.

The last phase is *termination*. Although for some people this occurs when they go back to work, for most it follows major physical deterioration. In this case, health becomes so bad that the person can no longer function independently.

Obviously, not everyone passes through all stages, and the sequence is not universal. In large measure, a person's reactions to retirement stem from the reasons he or she retired in the first place. For example, a person forced to retire for health reasons will have a different experience from a person who eagerly chose to retire at a particular age. Similarly, the retirement of people who loved their jobs can differ from that of people who despised their work.

In short, the psychological consequences of retirement vary from one individual to the next. For many people, retirement is a continuation of a life well-lived. Moreover, as we see next, there are ways to plan a good retirement.

Planning for—and Living—a Good Retirement

Becoming an Informed Consumer of Development

What makes for a good retirement? Gerontologists suggest several factors (Kreitlow and Kreitlow, 1997; Rowe and Kahn, 1998; Borchard, 2008):

- **Plan ahead financially.** Because Canada Pension Plan pensions are likely to be inadequate in the future, personal savings are critical.

- **Consider tapering off from work gradually.** Sometimes it is helpful to prepare for retirement by shifting from full-time to part-time work.

- **Explore your interests before you retire.** Assess what you like about your current job and think about how to translate those things into leisure activities.

- **If you are married or in a long-term partnership, spend some time discussing your views of the ideal retirement with your partner.** You might find that you need to negotiate a vision that will suit you both.

- **Consider where you want to live.** Try out, temporarily, a community to which you are thinking of moving.

- **Determine the advantages and disadvantages of downsizing your current home.**

- **Plan to volunteer your time.** People who retire have a wealth of skills that are often needed by non-profit organizations.

REVIEW, CHECK, AND APPLY

REVIEW

- Older adults live in a variety of settings, although most live at home with a family member.

- Financial issues can trouble older adults, largely because their incomes are fixed, costs of living are increasing, and the lifespan is lengthening.

- After retirement, many people pass through stages that include a honeymoon period, disenchantment, reorientation, retirement routine, and termination.

CHECK YOURSELF

1. Older adults living in communities that offer an environment in which all the residents are of retirement age or older and need various levels of care reside in a _____ home.

   a. retirement

   b. single-family

   c. continuing-care

   d. multifamily

2. After age 65, women are twice as likely as men to be living in poverty.

   - True

   - False

3. Which of the following is *not* cited in your text as a reason older adults decide to retire?

   a. declining health

   b. job burnout

   c. incentives from their employers

   d. spouses have retired

APPLYING LIFESPAN DEVELOPMENT

- Based on the research on successful aging, what advice would you give someone who is nearing retirement?

Answers: 1) c; 2) True; 3) d

Relationships: Old and New

L012 How do marriages fare in late adulthood?

L013 What sorts of relationships are important in late adulthood?

LEARNING OBJECTIVES

Rita and Theo met in high school. He joined the RCAF and they were married straight after graduation. Theo travelled the world but he always came back to "his girl." Even at 82 years young, they were still as affectionate as two 18-year-olds. Now, they often sit quietly, reading or listening to the radio, or enjoying old photographs of their 5 children, 12 grandchildren, and 8 great-grandchildren. Rita loves to cook and Theo does the dishes. They can complete each other's sentences, but often they just sit in a comfortable, contented, silence, watching birds or sometimes deer out their big picture window.

The warmth and affection between Rita and Theo are unmistakable. Their relationship, spanning eight decades, continues to bring them quiet joy, and their life is the sort to which many couples aspire. Yet it is also rare for the last stage of life. For every older adult who is part of a couple, many more are alone.

What is the social world of late adulthood like? To answer the question, we will first consider marriage.

Marriage in the Later Years: Together, then Alone

It's a man's world—at least when it comes to marriage after 65. The proportion of men who are married is far greater than that of women (see Figure 9-11). One reason is that 70 percent of women outlive their husbands by at least a few years. Because fewer men are available (many have died), these widowed women are unlikely to remarry (Barer, 1994).

Furthermore, the marriage gradient that we discussed earlier is still a powerful influence. Reflecting societal norms that women should marry older men, the marriage gradient keeps women single even in the later years of life. At the same time, it makes remarriage for men much easier, since the pool of eligible partners is much larger (Treas and Bengtson, 1987; AARP, 1990).

The vast majority of people who are still married in later life report that they are satisfied with their marriages. Their partners provide substantial companionship and emotional support. Because at this period in life they have typically been together for a long time, they have great insight into their partners (Brubaker, 1991; Levenson et al., 1993; Jose and Alfons, 2007).

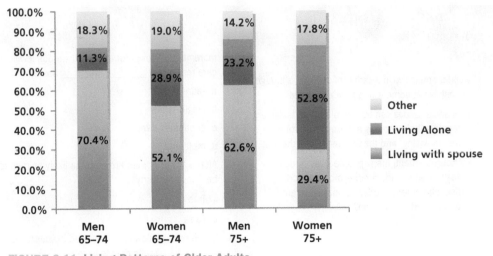

FIGURE 9-11 Living Patterns of Older Adults
What, if anything, do these patterns suggest about the relative health and adjustment of men and women?
Source: Statistics Canada, 2004, CANSIM table 12-0003.

Still, not every aspect of marriage is satisfying, and marriages may undergo stress as spouses experience changes in their lives. For instance, the retirement of one or both spouses can shift the nature of a couple's relationship (Askham, 1994; Henry et al., 2005).

For some couples, the stress is so great that one spouse or the other seeks a divorce—although the divorce rate for older adults is the lowest of all age groups, with fewer than 1 in 500 married adults over 65 seeking a divorce (Statistics Canada, 2005).

The reasons for divorce so late in life are varied. Often, women divorce because their husbands are abusive or alcoholic. But more frequently a husband divorces his wife because he has found a younger woman. Often the divorce occurs soon after retirement, when men who have been highly involved in their careers are in psychological turmoil (Cain, 1982; Solomon et al., 1998).

Divorce so late in life is particularly difficult for women. Between the marriage gradient and the limited pool of eligible men, an older divorced woman is unlikely to remarry. For many women in this age cohort, marriage has been their primary role and the centre of their identities, and they might view divorce as a major failure. As a consequence, happiness and the quality of life for divorced women often plummet (Goldscheider, 1994; Davies and Denton, 2002).

Seeking a new relationship becomes a priority for many men and women who are divorced or whose spouses have died. People seeking to develop relationships use the same strategies to meet potential partners as younger people, such as joining singles organizations or even using the Internet to seek out companionship (Durbin, 2003).

Of course, some people enter late adulthood having never married. For this group—about 5 percent of the population—late adulthood may bring fewer transitions, since living status does not change. In fact, never-married individuals report feeling less lonely than do most people their age, and they have a greater sense of independence (Essex and Nam, 1987; Newston and Keith, 1997).

Dealing with Retirement: Too Much Togetherness? When Morris Abercrombie finally stopped working full-time, his wife, Roxanne, found some aspects of his increased presence at home troubling. Although their marriage was strong, his intrusion into her daily routine and his constant questioning about whom she was on the phone with and where she was going were irksome. Finally, she began to wish he would spend less time around the house. This was ironic: She had passed much of Morris's preretirement years wishing that he would spend more time at home.

The situation in which Morris and Roxanne found themselves is not unique. For many couples, relationships need to be renegotiated since the couple will probably spend more time together than at any other point in their marriage. For others, retirement alters the longstanding distribution of household chores, with men taking on more responsibility than before for the everyday functioning of the household.

One of the most difficult responsibilities of later adulthood can be caring for one's ill spouse.

In fact, research suggests that an interesting role-reversal often takes place. In contrast to the early years of marriage, in late adulthood husbands' companionship needs tend to be greater than their wives'. The power structure of marriage also changes: Men become more affiliative and less competitive following retirement. At the same time, women become more assertive and autonomous (Blumstein and Schwartz, 1989; Bird and Melville, 1994).

Caring for an Aging Spouse. The shifts in health that accompany late adulthood sometimes require women and men to care for their spouses in ways that they never envisioned. Consider, for example, one woman's comments of frustration:

> *I cry a lot because I never thought it would be this way. I didn't expect to be mopping up the bathroom, changing him, doing laundry all the time. I was taking care of babies at twenty; now I'm taking care of my husband. (Doress et al., 1987, pp. 199–200)*

At the same time, some people view caring for an ailing and dying spouse as a final opportunity to demonstrate love and devotion. In fact, some caregivers report feeling satisfied at fulfilling what they see as their responsibility to their spouse. And some of those who initially experience emotional distress find that the distress declines as they successfully adapt (Zarit and Reid, 1994).

Yet there is no getting around the fact that giving care is arduous, made more difficult by the fact that the spouses providing the care are probably not in the peak of health themselves. In fact, caregiving may be detrimental to the provider's own physical and psychological health. For instance, caregivers report lower levels of satisfaction with life than do non-caregivers (Vitaliano et al., 1994; Grant et al., 2004; Choi and Marks, 2006).

It should be noted that in almost three-quarters of the cases, the spouse who provides the care is the wife. Part of the reason is demographic: Men tend to die earlier than women and, consequently, to contract the diseases leading to death earlier than women. A second reason, though, relates to society's traditional gender roles, which view women as "natural" caregivers. As a consequence, health-care providers might be more likely to suggest that a wife care for her husband than that a husband care for his wife (Polansky, 1976; Unger and Crawford, 1992).

The Death of a Spouse: Becoming Widowed. Few events are more painful and stressful than the death of a spouse. Especially for those who married young, the death leads to profound feelings of loss and often brings drastic changes in economic and social circumstances. If the marriage was a good one, the death means the loss of a companion, a lover, a confidante, a helper.

Upon a partner's death, spouses suddenly assume a new and unfamiliar societal role: widowhood. At the same time, they lose the role with which they were most familiar: spouse. Suddenly, they are no longer part of a couple; instead they are viewed by society, and themselves, as individuals. All this occurs as they are dealing with profound and sometimes overwhelming grief (which we discuss more in the next chapter).

Widowhood brings new demands and concerns. There is no longer a companion to share the day's events. If the deceased spouse primarily did the household chores, the surviving spouse must learn how to do these tasks every day. Although initially family and friends provide a great deal of support, this assistance quickly fades and newly widowed people are left to make the adjustment on their own (Wortman and Silver, 1990; Hanson and Hayslip, 2000).

People's social lives often change drastically. Married couples tend to socialize with other married couples; widowed people can feel like "fifth wheels" as they seek to maintain the friendships they enjoyed as part of a couple. Eventually, such friendships might cease, although they may be replaced by friendships with other single people (van den Hoonaard, 1994).

Economic issues are a major concern to many widowed people. Although many have insurance, savings, and pensions to provide economic security, some people (most often women) experience a decline in their economic well-being as the result of a spouse's death. This can force wrenching decisions, such as whether to sell the house in which the couple spent their married lives (Meyer et al., 2006).

The process of adjusting to widowhood encompasses three stages. In the first stage, known as *preparation*, spouses prepare (in some cases, for years or even decades) for the eventual death of the partner. Consider, for instance, the purchase of life insurance, the preparation of a will, and the decision to have children who might eventually provide care in one's old age. Each of these actions helps prepare for the eventuality that one will be widowed and will require some degree of assistance (Heinemann and Evans, 1990; Roecke and Cherry, 2002).

The second stage of adjustment to widowhood, *grief and mourning*, is an immediate reaction to the death of a spouse. It starts with the shock and pain of loss and continues as the survivor works through the emotions the loss brings up. The time a person spends in this period depends on the support received from others, as well as on personality factors. In some cases, grief and mourning may last for years, while in others it lasts a few months.

The last stage of adjustment to the death of a spouse is *adaptation*. In adaptation, the widowed individual starts a new life. The period begins with the acceptance of loss and continues with the reorganization of roles and the formation of new friendships. The adaptation stage also encompasses a period of reintegration in which a new identity—as an unmarried person—is developed.

Of course, neither the details nor the timing of the three-stage model of loss and change applies to everyone. Still, for most people, life returns to normal and becomes enjoyable again.

Without exception, the death of a spouse is a profound event in any period of life. During late adulthood, its implications are particularly powerful, since it can be seen as a forewarning of one's own mortality. Friends can help the surviving spouse move forward.

◉─[**Watch** on **mydevelopmentlab**

Log onto MyDevelopmentLab to watch a video of Bob, a man who recently lost his wife of 48 years. He talks about how her loss has affected him and how he still manages to keep a positive outlook on life.

➡ **From a social worker's perspective:** What are some factors that can combine to make late adulthood a more difficult time for women than for men?

The Social Networks of Late Adulthood

Older adults enjoy friends as much as younger people do, and friendships play an important role in their lives. In fact, time spent with friends is often valued more highly during late adulthood than time spent with family, with friends often seen as more important providers of support. Furthermore, around a third of older adults report that they made a new friend within the past year, and many older adults engage in significant interaction (see Figure 9-12; Hartshorne, 1994; Hansson and Carpenter, 1994; Ansberry, 1997).

Friendship: Why Friends Matter in Late Adulthood. Friendships are characterized by a sense of control: In friendship, unlike in family relationships, we choose whom we like and whom we dislike. Because late adulthood often causes a gradual loss of control in other areas, such as in health, the ability to maintain friendships can take on more importance than in other stages of life (Pruchno and Rosenbaum, 2003; Stevens et al., 2006).

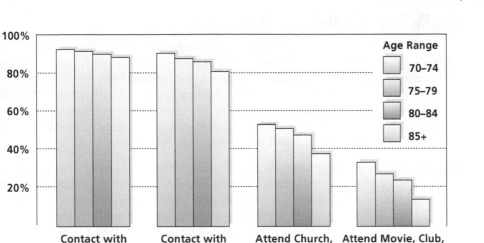

FIGURE 9-12 Social Activity in Late Adulthood
Friends and family play an important role in the social activity of older adults.
Source: Federal Interagency Forum on Age Related Statistics, 2000.

In addition, friendships—especially recent ones—can be more flexible than family relationships since they lack the long history of obligations and conflicts that often typify family ties and that can reduce the emotional sustenance they provide (Hartshorne, 1994; Magai and McFadden, 1996).

Friendships in late adulthood are also important because of the increasing likelihood, over time, that one will be without a marital partner. When a spouse dies, people typically seek out friends to help deal with their loss and for some of the companionship that was provided by the deceased spouse.

Of course, spouses are not the only ones who die during old age; friends die too. The way adults view friendship in late adulthood determines how vulnerable they are to the death of a friend. If they have defined the friendship as irreplaceable, the loss of the friend can be quite difficult. On the other hand, if the friendship is defined as one of many, the death of a friend might be less traumatic (Hartshorne, 1994).

Social Support: The Significance of Others. Friendships also provide one of the basic social needs: social support. **Social support** is assistance and comfort supplied by a network of caring, interested people. Such support plays a critical role in successful aging (Antonucci, 1990; Antonucci and Akiyama, 1991; Avlund et al., 2004).

Social support brings considerable benefits. A social support network can offer emotional support by lending a sympathetic ear and providing a sounding board for concerns. Furthermore, people who are experiencing similar problems—such as the loss of a spouse—can provide an unmatched degree of understanding and a pool of helpful suggestions for coping strategies that would be less credible coming from others.

Finally, people can furnish material support, such as helping with rides or picking up groceries. They can provide help in solving problems, such as dealing with a difficult landlord or fixing a broken appliance.

The benefits of social support extend to the provider as well as the recipient. People who offer support experience feelings of usefulness and heightened self-esteem, knowing that they are making a contribution to someone else's welfare.

What kinds of social support are most effective and appropriate? Certainly preparing food, accompanying someone to a movie, or inviting someone to dinner are helpful. But the opportunity for reciprocity is important, too. Reciprocity is the expectation that if someone provides something positive to another person, eventually, the favour will be returned. In Western societies, older adults—like younger people—value relationships in which reciprocity is possible (Clark and Mills, 1993; Becker et al., 2003).

With increasing age, it can be progressively more difficult to reciprocate the social support that one receives. As a consequence, relationships can become more asymmetrical, placing the recipient in a difficult psychological position (Selig et al., 1991).

social support assistance and comfort supplied by another person or a network of caring, interested people

Family Relationships: The Ties That Bind

Even after the death of a spouse, most older adults are part of a larger family unit. Connections with siblings, children, grandchildren, and even great-grandchildren continue and may be an important source of comfort to adults in the last years of their lives.

Siblings can provide unusually strong emotional support because they often share old, pleasant memories of childhood, and because they usually represent a person's oldest existing relationships. While not every memory of childhood may be pleasant, continuing interaction with brothers and sisters can enhance late adulthood (Moyer, 1992).

Children. Even more important than siblings are children and grandchildren. Even in an age in which geographic mobility is high, most parents and children remain fairly close, both geographically and psychologically. Some 75 percent of children live within a 30-minute drive of their parents, and parents and children visit and talk with one another frequently. Daughters tend to be in more frequent contact with their parents than sons, and mothers tend to be the recipients of communication more often than fathers (Field and Minkler, 1988; Krout, 1988; Ji-liang et al., 2003).

Because the great majority of older adults have at least one child who lives fairly close, family members still provide significant aid to one another. Moreover, parents and children tend to share similar views of how adult children should behave toward their parents. In particular, they expect that children should help their parents understand their resources, provide emotional support, and talk over such important matters as medical issues. Furthermore, it is most often children who end up caring for their aging parents when they require assistance (Wolfson et al., 1993; Dellmann-Jenkins and Brittain, 2003; Ron, 2006).

The bonds between parents and children are sometimes asymmetrical, with parents seeking a closer relationship and children a more distant one. Parents have a greater *developmental stake* in close ties, since they see their children as perpetuating their beliefs, values, and standards. On the other hand, children are motivated to maintain their autonomy and live independently from their parents. These divergent perspectives make parents more likely to minimize conflicts they experience with their children, and children more likely to maximize them (Bengtson et al., 1985; O'Connor, 1994).

For parents, their children remain a source of great interest and concern. Some surveys show, for instance, that even in late adulthood parents talk about their children nearly every day, particularly if the children are having some sort of problem. At the same time, adult children might turn to their parents for advice, information, and sometimes tangible help, such as money (Greenberg and Becker, 1988).

Grandchildren and Great-Grandchildren. As we discussed earlier, not all grandparents are equally involved with their grandchildren. Even those who take great pride in their grandchildren may be relatively detached, avoiding any direct care role (Cherlin and Furstenberg, 1986).

As we saw, grandmothers tend to be more involved than grandfathers, and most young adult grandchildren feel closer to their grandmothers. In addition, most express a preference for their maternal grandmothers over their paternal grandmothers (Kalliopuska, 1994; Chan and Elder, 2000; Hayslip et al., 2000; Lavers-Preston and Sonuga-Barke, 2003).

Great-grandchildren play less of a role in the lives of great-grandparents. Most great-grandparents do not have close relationships with their great-grandchildren. Close relationships tend to occur only when the great-grandparents and great-grandchildren live relatively near one another (Doka and Mertz, 1988).

There are several explanations for this relative lack of involvement. One is that by the time people reach great-grandparenthood, they are so old that they do not have much physical or psychological energy to expend on relationships with their great-grandchildren. Another is that there might be so many great-grandchildren that great-grandparents do not feel strong emotional ties to them and might not even be able to keep track of them. As parents delay having children until later in life, however, grandparents will become older, as will great-grandparents.

Still, great-grandparents profit emotionally from the mere fact that they have great-grandchildren. They may see their great-grandchildren as representing both their own and

⊙⊣ Watch on **mydevelopmentlab**

How involved were your grandparents in your life? What effects do you think that had on your grandparents' life?

To see one grandmother's perspective, log onto MyDevelopmentLab and watch a video of Maria, a 68-year-old woman who lives with her daughter and watches her grandchildren while their parents are at work.

their family's continuation, as well as providing a concrete sign of their longevity (Doka and Mertz, 1988).

Elder Abuse: Relationships Gone Wrong

With good health and a sizable pension, 76-year-old Mary T. should have been enjoying a comfortable retirement. But in fact, her life was made miserable by a seemingly endless barrage of threats, insults, and indignities from her live-in adult son.

A habitual gambler and drug user, the son was merciless: he spat at Mary, brandished a knife in her face, stole her money, and sold her possessions. After several emergency room trips and two hospitalizations, social workers convinced Mary to move out and join a support group of other elderly people abused by their loved ones. With a new apartment and understanding friends, Mary finally had some peace. But her son found her, and feeling a mother's guilt and shame, Mary took him back—and opened another round of heartache. (Minaker and Frishman, 1995, p. 9)

Media reports of telemarketing scams targeting older adults, and public service announcements aimed at educating the public about elder abuse give the impression that older adults are the highest risk group for victimization, but in fact, older adults are the group least likely to be victims of crime. According to some estimates, **elder abuse**, the physical or psychological mistreatment or neglect of older adults, might affect between 1 and 2 per 1000 older adults each year, and nearly 10 percent of older adults report being victims of crime (in contrast to 27 percent of the adult population as a whole). These estimates could be low, since people who are abused are often too embarrassed to report their plight, and older adults with the most severe health problems may be unaware of a crime or unable to report it, especially when victimized by family or caregivers. As the number of older adults increases, experts believe that elder abuse will also rise (Brubaker, 1991; Turcotte and Schellenberg, 2007).

Elder abuse is most frequently directed at family members and particularly at parents. Those most at risk are likely to be less healthy and more isolated than average, and they are more likely to be living in a caregiver's home. Although there is no single cause for elder abuse, it often stems from economic, psychological, and social pressures on caregivers who must provide high levels of care 24 hours a day. Thus, people with Alzheimer's disease or other sorts of dementia are particularly likely to be targets of abuse (Dyer et al., 2000; Arai, 2006; Jayawardena and Liao, 2006; Nahmiash, 2006; Tauriac and Scruggs, 2006; Baker, 2007).

The best way to deal with elder abuse is to prevent it. Family members caring for an older adult should take breaks and should contact social support agencies for advice and concrete support. Anyone suspecting that an older adult is being abused should contact local authorities.

> **elder abuse** the physical or psychological mistreatment or neglect of older adults

REVIEW, CHECK, AND APPLY

REVIEW

- While marriages in older adulthood are generally happy, the many changes of the period cause stresses that can bring divorce.

- The death of a spouse has major psychological, social, and material effects on the survivor and makes the formation and continuation of friendships highly important.

- Family relationships are a continuing part of most older people's lives, especially relationships with siblings and children.

CHECK YOURSELF

1. Individuals still married in later life report being significantly less satisfied with their marriages than they were in earlier years.

   - True
   - False

2. Older adults often rely on _____, or the assistance and comfort supplied by another person or network of people, for successful aging.

3. Which of the following characteristics is associated with elder abuse?

   a. being healthy

   b. being a victim of Alzheimer's

   c. being less isolated

   d. having a caregiver who lives outside of the home

APPLYING LIFESPAN DEVELOPMENT

- What are some ways the retirement of a spouse can bring stress to a marriage? Is retirement likely to be less stressful in households where both spouses work, or twice as stressful?

Answers: 1) False; 2) social support; 3) b

Putting It All Together
Late Adulthood

BEN TUFTY couldn't wait to retire and now enjoys his leisure to the fullest. He is committed to maintaining his physical health, intellectual activity, and key relationships—important even if older adults choose radically different ways to do these things. By paying attention to his needs in all three spheres, Ben remains optimistic and cheerful. Clearly, he looks forward to every day he spends in the world.

MODULE **9.1** Physical Development

- Though Ben is chronologically among the "oldest old," he is "young old" in his functional ages **(p. 386)**.

- Ben defies ageist stereotypes in his health and attitudes **(p. 387)**.

- Ben appears to have avoided Alzheimer's and most of the other physical and psychological disorders associated with old age **(p. 394)**.

- Ben has made healthy lifestyle choices—exercising, eating right, and avoiding bad habits **(p. 396)**.

MODULE **9.2** Cognitive Development

- Ben is apparently rich in crystallized intelligence—his store of information, skills, and strategies **(p. 401)**.

- He demonstrates plasticity by using stimulation, practice, and motivation to maintain his mental abilities **(p. 403)**.

- Ben might have slight memory problems, such as a decline in episodic or autobiographical memory **(pp. 404–405)**.

- Ben is navigating Erikson's ego-integrity-versus-despair stage, and has successfully navigated Peck's developmental task of redefinition-of-self-versus-preoccupation-with-work role **(p. 407–408)**.

- He appears to have an "integrated personality," according to Neugarten's personality categories **(p. 409)**.

- He seems to have acquired wisdom with age, knowing who he is and how to deal with others **(p. 411)**.

- In playing "low-pressure" games, Ben might be engaging in compensation for slowed reaction time or less-than-perfect recall **(p. 413)**.

- He has chosen to continue living at home **(p. 414)**.

- Ben doesn't seem to have gone through the classic retirement stages **(p. 418)**.

What would a RETIREMENT COUNSELLOR do?

- What advice would you give someone like Ben, who wants to retire early? What advice would you give a person who instead wants to stay on the job forever? What characteristics would you look for in these individuals that would help you give the right advice?

  HINT Review pages 417–418.

  What's your response?

What would a HEALTH-CARE PROVIDER do?

- Why do you think Ben is in such good mental health? What strategies has Ben used? What strategies has he overlooked?

  HINT Review pages 401–405, 411.

  What's your response?

What would YOU do?

- If you were asked to do an oral history project involving Ben, how complete and accurate would you expect his recollections to be? Would he be more reliable about the 1950s or the 1990s?

  HINT Review pages 404–405.

  What's your response?

What would an EDUCATOR do?

- Would you recommend cognitive training for Ben? What about university courses? Why or why not?

  HINT Review pages 405, 408.

  What's your response?

10 Death and Dying

You see most everything around here, but I tell you, the little ones—babies and kids—they really get to me," says James Tiburon.

"I've done six-month rotations on the maternity ward, oncology, organ transplant, the geriatric ward, intensive care—you name it. You get to help hundreds of people of all different ages and backgrounds every year. But fairly often you have to attend a death. Old people, middle agers, adolescents, even infants—death strikes at any age. And to tell you the truth, I hate it. Every one is a defeat if you're a health professional. You may pretend you get used to death, but unless you're inhuman, you don't really. You suppress it—that's the way you cope with it. But you still grieve every time one of your patients dies. Every time.

"I've worked with the families too. Sometimes, with a DNR—you know, Do Not Resuscitate—you have to work closely with them. And if there's an unexpected death, sometimes a doctor really doesn't want to be the first to tell the family, so they call me in.

MODULE 10.1 Dying and Death across the Lifespan

What are the moral and ethical issues that surround defining death? see page 430

MODULE 10.2 Confronting Death

DNR, assisted suicide, euthanasia.... Where do you stand? see page 436

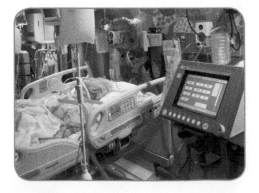

"You know that stage thing, the stages of death? Well, I've seen every one of those stages in the patients and in their families. You know, anger, denial, the whole range? You get used to the symptoms and you deal with the situation that you're presented with. If they're angry, you know what to do. Same if they're denying or depressed. You meet them where they are.

"In the end, you do your best for the patients and the families, the dead and the living. You help the family members keep moving—mourning but moving. You try to nudge them to the next step. You can't give them back their loved one, but you give them what you can."

Appropriately enough, in this last chapter we discuss the final period of life. We begin by considering how the moment of death is defined, and we examine how people view and react to death at different points in the lifespan. Then we look at how people confront their own deaths, examining the theory that people pass through stages as they come to grips with their approaching death. We also look at how people endeavour to exert control over the circumstances of their death by using living wills and assisted suicide. Finally, we consider bereavement and grief. We distinguish normal from unhealthy grief, and we discuss the consequences of a loss. Finally, we look at mourning and funerals, and discuss how people acknowledge the passing of a loved one.

MODULE **10.3** Grief and Bereavement

What is the difference between bereavement and grief? see page 443

MyVirtualLife

You've just read about death and dying from a health-care worker's point of view.

Now, log onto MyDevelopmentLab and watch a video in which Bob talks about the loss of both his daughter and his wife and the effects it had on him and his family.

MODULE 10.1 Dying and Death across the Lifespan

Choosing Death

Mrs. Morrison's family were all gathered, knowing the end was near. At age 82, her lengthy battle with cancer was nearly over. The priest came after Sunday service to perform the last rites.

"There was a moment there when the priest told her it was OK to let go and to go be with God," said her daughter Beatrice, "I thought that would be it. If it were a movie, that would be when she took her last breath."

But it wasn't a movie. Her last breath came at 5:45 the following morning.

Death is an experience that will happen to all of us, as universal to the human condition as birth. As such, understanding it is central to understanding the lifespan.

Only recently have lifespan developmentalists given serious study to the developmental implications of dying. In this module we will discuss death and dying from several perspectives. We begin by considering how we define death—a determination that is more complex than it seems. We then examine how people view and react to death at different points in the lifespan. And we consider the very different views of death held by various societies.

Defining Death: Determining the Point at Which Life Ends

LEARNING OBJECTIVES

LO1 What defines the moment of death?

Sue Rodriguez brought to the Supreme Court of Canada her challenge for the right to commit suicide with the assistance of a doctor. Should doctors be allowed to help a patient commit suicide?

"If I cannot give consent to my own death, whose body is this? Who owns my life?" In 1992, Sue Rodriguez' famous statement to the Supreme Court of Canada challenging prohibition of assisted suicide launched the topics of euthanasia and assisted suicide to the forefront of public debate. The 42-year-old British Columbia woman suffered from ALS, a devastating neurodegenerative disease. She lost her case 5–4, but ultimately succeeded in committing suicide with the assistance of an anonymous doctor. (CBC News, 2009)

Such difficult questions illustrate the complexity of what are, literally, matters of life and death. Death is not only a biological event; it involves psychological aspects as well. We need to consider not only what defines death, but also how our conception of death changes across the lifespan.

What is death? The question seems clear, but defining the point at which life ceases is surprisingly complex. Medicine has advanced to the point where some people who would have been considered dead a few years ago would now be considered alive.

Functional death is defined by an absence of heartbeat and breathing. This definition, however, is more ambiguous than it seems. For example, a person whose heartbeat and breathing have ceased for as long as five minutes might be resuscitated and suffer little damage from the experience. Was the person who is now alive once dead, as the functional definition would have it?

Because of this imprecision, brain functioning is now used to determine the moment of death rather than heartbeat or respiration. In **brain death**, all signs of brain activity, as measured by electrical brain waves, have ceased. When brain death occurs, it is impossible to restore functioning.

Some medical experts suggest that defining death only as a lack of brain waves is too restrictive. They argue that losing the ability to think, reason, feel, and experience the world might define death, as well. In this view, which considers the psychological ramifications, a person who suffers irreversible brain damage, who is in a coma, and who will never experience anything approaching a human life can be considered dead, even if some sort of primitive brain activity continues (Ressner, 2001).

This argument, which moves us from strictly medical criteria to moral and philosophical considerations, is controversial. As a result, death is legally defined often as the absence of brain functioning, although some laws still include the absence of respiration and heartbeat in their definition. In reality, no matter where a death occurs, brain waves are seldom measured. Usually, they are closely monitored only in special circumstances—when the time of death is significant, when organs may be transplanted, or when criminal or legal issues are involved.

The difficulty in establishing legal and medical definitions of death reflect changes in understanding and attitudes that occur over the course of people's lives.

Death across the Lifespan: Causes and Reactions

L02   How is death perceived at different stages of the lifespan?

Cheryl played flute in the school band. She had shoulder-length brown hair, brown eyes, and a smile that often gave way to a lopsided grin when her friends or older brother said something funny.

Cheryl's family owned a small farm, and it was her job to feed the chickens and gather any eggs every morning before the school bus arrived. After she completed her chores, she gathered up whatever sewing project she was working on in Family and Consumer Sciences—Cheryl loved designing and creating her own clothing—and waved goodbye to her parents. "Don't take any wooden nickels," her dad always called after her. Cheryl thought it was a really dumb joke, but she loved that her dad never forgot to say it.

One Friday night, Cheryl's dad suggested they hop in the truck and go get pizza. There were only two seat belts in the narrow cab, but Cheryl felt safe wedged in between her dad and her brother. They were riding down a two-lane highway, singing along with some silly song on the radio, when a car in the lane opposite lost control and crossed the centre line, slamming into the truck. Without a seat belt, Cheryl flew through the windshield. Her father and brother survived, but at 13, Cheryl's life was over.

We associate death with old age, but for many individuals, death comes earlier. Because it seems "unnatural" for a young person like Cheryl to die, reactions to such a death are particularly extreme. In fact, some people believe that children should be sheltered from the reality of death. Yet people of every age can experience the death of friends and family members, as well as their own death. How do our reactions to death evolve as we age? We will consider several age groups.

Death in Infancy and Childhood. While most infants are born healthy and without complications, approximately 5 of every 1000 newborns do not live to see their first birthday. As there are, on average, more than 1000 babies born each day in Canada, the number of parents who lose an infant is significant. The death of a child arouses all the typical reactions one would have to a more timely death, but family members can suffer severe effects as they struggle to deal with death at such an early age. One common reaction is extreme depression (Murphy et al., 2003).

Prenatal death, or *miscarriage*, is an exceptionally difficult death to confront. Parents often form a psychological bond with their unborn child, and may feel profound grief if the child dies before birth. Moreover, friends and relatives often fail to understand the emotional impact of miscarriage, making parents feel their loss all the more keenly (Wheeler and Austin, 2001).

Sudden infant death syndrome produces extreme stress, in part because it is so unanticipated. In cases of **sudden infant death syndrome**, or **SIDS** (which usually occurs between the ages of two and four months), a seemingly healthy baby stops breathing and dies inexplicably.

In cases of SIDS, parents often feel intense guilt, and acquaintances might have suspicions about the "true" cause of death. However, the cause of SIDS is still unknown; it seems to strike randomly, and parents' guilt is unwarranted (Dyregrov et al., 2003; Hunt and Hauck, 2006; Krueger, 2006; Paterson et al., 2006).

functional death   the absence of a heartbeat and breathing

brain death   a diagnosis of death based on the cessation of all signs of brain activity, as measured by electrical brain waves

sudden infant death syndrome (SIDS)   the unexplained death of a seemingly healthy baby

For children, accidents are the most frequent cause of death—motor vehicle crashes, fires, and drowning. Cancer and congenital conditions are the second and third leading causes of death in children under 14 (Statistics Canada, 2011).

For parents, the death of a child produces a profound sense of loss and grief. There is no worse death for most parents, including the loss of a spouse or of one's own parents. They might feel their trust in the natural order of the world—where children should outlive their parents—has been violated. Believing that their primary responsibility is to protect their children from harm, they can feel they have failed when a child dies (Strength, 1999).

Parents are almost never prepared to deal with the death of a child, and they may obsessively ask themselves why the death occurred. Because the bond between children and parents is so strong, parents sometimes feel that a part of themselves has died as well. The stress is so profound that it significantly increases the risk of hospitalization for a mental disorder (Wayment and Vierthaler, 2002; Li et al., 2005; Mahgoub and Lantz, 2006).

Childhood Conceptions of Death. Children do not really begin to develop a concept of death until around age five. Although they are already well aware of death, they tend to view it as a temporary, reduced state of living, rather than a cessation. A preschool-age child might say, "Dead people don't get hungry—well, maybe a little" (Kastenbaum, 1985, p. 629).

Some preschool children think of death as a sleep people can wake from, just as Sleeping Beauty awoke in the fairy tale. For these children, death is not particularly fearsome; rather, it is a curiosity. If people merely tried hard enough—by administering medicine, providing food, or using magic—dead people might "return" (Lonetto, 1980).

Children's misunderstanding of death can have devastating emotional consequences. Children might believe they are somehow responsible for a person's death. They might assume their bad behaviour caused the death. They might also think that if the dead person really wanted to, she or he could return.

> ⮕ **From an educator's perspective:** Given their developmental level and understanding of death, how do you think preschool children react to the death of a parent?

Around age five, children can better grasp the finality and irreversibility of death. They may personify death as a ghostlike or devilish figure. They do not regard death as universal, however, but as something that happens only to certain people. It is not until about age nine that they accept the universality and finality of death (Nagy, 1948). By middle childhood, there is an awareness of the customs around death, such as funerals, cremation, and cemeteries.

Death in Adolescence. We might expect the significant cognitive development that occurs in adolescence to bring about a sophisticated, thoughtful, and reasoned view of death. However, in many ways, adolescents' views of death are as unrealistic as those of younger children, although along different lines.

Adolescents understand the finality and irreversibility of death, yet they tend to think it can't happen to them—a belief that can lead to risky behaviour. As we discussed earlier, adolescents develop a *personal fable*, a set of beliefs that makes them feel unique and special. Thus, they might believe they are invulnerable and that the bad things that happen to other people won't happen to them (Elkind, 1985). This risky behaviour causes many deaths in adolescence. For instance, accidents, often involving motor vehicles, are the most frequent cause of death at this age.

Other frequent causes include suicide, homicide, and cancer (Statistics Canada, 2011). When adolescent feelings of invulnerability confront a fatal illness, the results can be shattering. Adolescents who learn they are terminally ill often feel angry and cheated—that life has been unjust to them. Because they feel—and act—so negatively, it can be difficult for medical personnel to treat them effectively.

In contrast, some adolescents who are terminally ill react with total denial. Feeling indestructible, they might not accept the seriousness of their illness. Some degree of denial might be useful—if it does not cause the adolescent to reject medical treatment—as it allows an adolescent to continue living a normal life as long as possible (Blumberg et al., 1984).

Death in Young Adulthood. Young adults feel primed to begin their lives. Past the preparatory time of childhood and adolescence, they are ready to make their mark on the

Adolescents' views of death can be highly romanticized and dramatic.

world. Because death at such a point seems close to unthinkable, its occurrence is particularly difficult. In active pursuit of life goals, they are angry and impatient with any illness that threatens their future.

For young adults, the leading cause of death continues to be accidents, followed by suicide, and cancer. By the end of early adulthood, however, death from cancer becomes most prevalent.

For young adults facing death, several concerns are acutely important. One is the desire to develop intimate relationships and express sexuality, each of which is inhibited, or completely prevented, by a terminal illness. For instance, people who test positive for the AIDS virus can find it quite difficult to start new relationships. In evolving relationships, sexual activities present even more challenging issues (Rabkin et al., 1994).

Planning for the future is another concern of young adults. At a time when most people are mapping out careers and deciding when to start a family, young adults who are terminally ill face additional burdens. Should they marry, even though they might soon leave a partner widowed? Should a couple seek to conceive if the child is likely to be raised by only one parent? How soon should one's employer be told about a terminal illness, when the revelation might cost the young adult his or her job? None of these questions is easily answered.

Death in Middle Adulthood. For middle-aged people, the shock of a life-threatening disease—the most common cause of death in this period—is not so great. By this point, people are well aware that they will die someday, and they might be able to accept this possibility in a realistic manner.

Their sense of realism, though, doesn't make the possibility of dying any easier. Fears about death are often greater in midlife than at any time previously—or even in later life. These fears may lead people to switch their focus to the number of years they have remaining rather than the number of years they have already lived (Levinson, 1992).

The most frequent causes of death in midlife are cancer and heart disease. Dying unexpectedly from a heart attack does not allow for preparation, but it might be easier than a slow and painful battle with cancer. It is the kind of death most people prefer: When asked, they say they would like an instant and painless death that does not involve loss of any body part (Taylor, 1991).

Death in Late Adulthood. By late adulthood, people know that the end is approaching. They face an increasing number of deaths in their environment: Spouses, siblings, and friends might have already died, providing a constant reminder of their own mortality.

At this age, the most likely causes of death are cancer, heart disease, and stroke. What would happen if these were eliminated? According to demographers' estimates, the average 70-year-old's life expectancy would increase around 7 years (Hayward et al., 1997).

The prevalence of death in the lives of older adults makes them less anxious about dying. This does not mean that people in late adulthood welcome death. Rather, they are more realistic and reflective about it. They think about death, and they might begin to prepare for it. Some begin to pull away from the world as physical and psychological energy diminishes (Turner and Helms, 1994).

Impending death is sometimes accompanied by rapid declines in cognitive functioning. In what is known as the *terminal decline*, a significant drop in memory and reading ability can foreshadow death within the next few years (Wilson et al., 2003; Sliwinski et al., 2006; Wilson et al., 2007).

Some older adults actively seek out death, turning to suicide. In fact, the suicide rate for men climbs steadily during late adulthood, and no age group has a higher suicide rate than men age 85 to 89. (Adolescents and young adults commit suicide in greater numbers, but their *rate* of suicide—the number of suicides as a proportion of the general adolescent population—is actually lower.) Suicide is often a consequence of severe depression or some form of dementia, or it might arise from the loss of a spouse (Chapple et al., 2006).

A critical issue for older adults who are terminally ill is whether their lives still have value. More than younger adults, older adults who are dying worry that they are burdens to their family or to society. They might even be given the message, sometimes inadvertently, that society no longer values them and that they are viewed as "dying" rather than being "very sick" (Kastenbaum, 2000).

Cultural Dimensions

Differing Conceptions of Death

In the midst of a tribal celebration, an older man waits for his oldest son to place a cord around his neck. The older man has been sick, and he is ready to relinquish his ties to this earthly world. He asks that his son lift him to his death, and the son complies.

***

To Hindus in India, death is not an ending, but rather part of a continual cycle. Because they believe in reincarnation, death is thought to be followed by rebirth into a new life. Death, then, is seen as a companion to life.

Differing conceptions of death lead to different rituals, as this ceremony in India illustrates.

People's responses to death take many forms, particularly in different cultures. But even in Western societies, reactions to death and dying are quite diverse. For instance, is it better for a man to die after a full life in which he has raised a family and been successful in his job, or for a courageous and valiant young soldier to die defending his country in wartime? Has one person died a better death than the other?

The answer depends on one's values, which reflect cultural and subcultural teachings, often shared through religious beliefs. Some societies view death as a punishment or as a judgment about one's contributions to the world. Others see death as redemption from an earthly life of travail. Some view death as the start of an eternal life, while others believe that an earthly life is all there is (Bryant, 2003).

Aboriginal peoples see death as a continuation of life, a "transition from Mother Earth." Various traditional ceremonies and practices exist; for example, in both Haudenosaunee and Anishnabe cultures, the deceased is not mentioned by name (Hampton et al., 2010; Longboat, 2002).

The age at which people learn about death varies among cultures. In countries with high levels of violence and death, an awareness of death can come earlier in life. Research shows that children in Northern Ireland and Israel understood the finality, irreversibility, and inevitability of death at an earlier age than children in the United States and Britain (Atchley, 2000; Braun et al., 2000).

👁 **Watch** on **mydevelopmentlab**

To discover how various cultures remember and honour their ancestors, watch the video on MyDevelopmentLab.

In most cases, older adults want to know if death is impending. Like younger patients, who usually prefer to know the truth about an illness, older adults want the details. Ironically, caregivers usually wish to avoid telling patients that they are dying (Goold et al., 2000; Hagerty et al., 2004).

Not all people, however, wish to know about their condition or that they are dying. Individuals react to death in substantially different ways, in part due to personality factors. For example, people who are generally anxious worry more about death. Significant cultural differences exist in how people view and react to death, as we consider in the Cultural Dimensions box.

Death Education: Preparing for the Inevitable?

LEARNING OBJECTIVES

LO3 Why is it helpful to educate people about death and dying?

"When will Mom come back from being dead?"
"Why did Barry have to die?"
"Did Grandpa die because I was bad?"

Children's questions such as these illustrate why many developmentalists, as well as **thanatologists**—people who study death and dying—have suggested that death education should be a component of everyone's schooling. Recently, such instruction has emerged. *Death education* encompasses programs designed to help people of all ages deal better with death, dying, and grief—both others' deaths and their own.

> **thanatologists**   people who study death and dying

Death education arose as a response to the way we hide death, at least in most Western societies. We typically let hospitals deal with the dying, and we do not talk to children about death or allow them to go to funerals for fear that the children will be disturbed. Even emergency workers and medical specialists are uncomfortable talking about it. Because it is seldom discussed and is so removed from everyday life, people often have little opportunity to confront their feelings about death or to gain a realistic sense of it (McGovern and Barry, 2000; Lowton and Higginson, 2003; Wass, 2004).

Several types of death education programs exist. Among them are the following:

- **Crisis intervention education.** When school shootings occur, such as the 2006 Dawson College shooting in Montreal or the 1999 shooting in Taber, Alberta, several kinds of crisis intervention are mobilized to deal with the anxieties of students. When crises affect younger children, whose conceptions of death are shaky, explanations for the loss of life need to be geared to their cognitive development.

- **Routine death education.** Although relatively little curricular material on death exists for elementary students, coursework in high schools is increasingly common. Colleges and universities increasingly include courses about death in such departments as psychology, human development, sociology, and education.

- **Death education for members of the helping professions.** Professionals who will deal with death, dying, and grief in their careers have a special need for death education. Almost all medical and nursing schools now offer some form of death education. The most successful programs not only offer providers ways to help people deal with their own impending death or those of family members, but also allow students to explore their feelings about the topic.

Although death education will not completely demystify death, the programs just described can help people come to grips with what is, along with birth, the most universal—and certain—of all human experiences.

REVIEW, CHECK, AND APPLY

REVIEW

- Functional death is defined as the cessation of heartbeat and respiration; brain death is defined by the absence of electrical brain waves.

- What defines death has changed as medical advances now allow us to resuscitate people who would once have been considered dead. Some medical experts believe that a person is in fact dead when they can no longer think, reason, or feel, and can never again live anything resembling a human life.

- The death of an infant or young child can be particularly difficult for parents, and for adolescents, death appears to be unthinkable.

- Cultural differences in attitudes and beliefs about death strongly influence people's reactions to it.

- Thanatologists recommend that death education become a normal part of learning.

CHECK YOURSELF

1. Once an individual is no longer breathing or has a heartbeat, he or she is said to have experienced a _____ death.

2. Parents' extreme reaction to their child's death is partly based on the sense that the natural order of the world, in which children should outlive their parents, has now been violated.
   - True
   - False

3. While adolescents understand death, they tend to think it won't happen to them.
   - True
   - False

4. _____ are people who study death and dying.

APPLYING LIFESPAN DEVELOPMENT

- Do you think people who are going to die should be told? Does your response depend on the person's age?

MODULE 10.2 Confronting Death

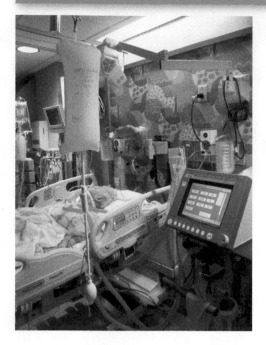

Deciding to Say Goodbye

Susan was a 52-year-old woman who had end-stage breast cancer with metastases to the brain and bone. She had completed two years of college before dropping out, aspired to be a writer but never pursued it, and regarded herself as a lesbian but repressed her sexuality.

I have to find a way of forgiving myself and maybe that is a part of what is going on, you know, what I am supposed to be doing, forgiving myself for not giving myself a chance, not helping myself to a better education when I could have, maybe, and done some of the things that I wanted to do. You know, wanting to do that, having that in me and yet, never leaving the ground. It is sort of like someone went and clipped my wings and the person who did that was me. (Yedidia and MacGregor, 2001)

How do people come to terms with death, and how do they react and adapt to it? Lifespan developmentalists and other specialists in death and dying have struggled to find answers.

In this module, we look at how people confront their own deaths. We discuss the theory that people move through stages as they come to grips with their approaching death. We also look at how people use living wills and assisted suicide.

The Process of Dying: Taking Steps toward Death

LEARNING OBJECTIVES

LO4 In what ways do people face the prospect of their own death?

No individual has influenced our understanding of the way people confront death more than Elisabeth Kübler-Ross. A psychiatrist, Kübler-Ross developed a theory of death and dying based on interviews with dying people and those caring for them (Kübler-Ross, 1969, 1982).

Kübler-Ross initially suggested that people pass through five basic steps as they move toward death (summarized in Figure 10-1).

Denial. "No, I can't be dying. There must be some mistake." It is typical for people to protest when they learn that they have a terminal disease. *Denial* is the first stage of dying. In denial, people resist the idea that they are going to die. They might argue that their test results have

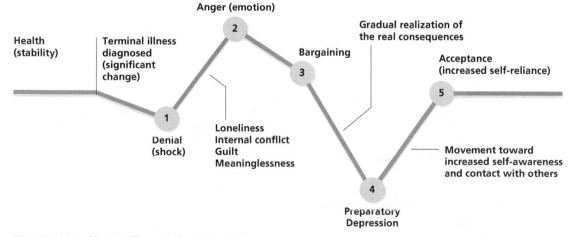

FIGURE 10-1 **Moving Toward the End of Life**
The steps toward death, according to Kübler-Ross (1975). Do you think there are cultural differences in the steps?

been mixed up, an X-ray has been misread, or their physician is just wrong. They might flatly reject the diagnosis, simply refusing to believe the news. In extreme cases, memories of weeks in the hospital are forgotten. In other forms of denial, patients fluctuate between refusing to accept the news and confiding that they know they are going to die (Teutsch, 2003).

Far from being a sign of a lost sense of reality and deteriorating mental health, denial is a defense mechanism that helps people absorb the news on their own terms and at their own pace, after which they can move on and come to grips with the reality of their death.

Anger. After denial, people may express *anger*. They might be angry at everyone: people in good health, spouses and family members, caregivers, children. They might lash out and wonder—sometimes aloud—why *they* are dying and not someone else. They might be furious at God, reasoning that they have led good lives and far worse people in the world should be dying.

It is not easy to be around people in the anger stage. They might say and do things that are painful and sometimes unfathomable. Eventually, though, most people move beyond anger to another development—bargaining.

Bargaining. "If you're good, you'll be rewarded." Many people try to apply this pearl of childhood wisdom to their impending death, promising to be better people if they are rewarded with their life.

In *bargaining*, dying people try to negotiate their way out of death. They might swear to dedicate their lives to the poor if God saves them. They might promise that if they can just live long enough to see a son married, they will willingly accept death later.

However, these promises are rarely kept. If one request appears to be granted, people typically seek another, and yet another. Furthermore, they might be unable to fulfill their promises because their illness keeps progressing and prevents them from achieving what they said they would do.

In some ways, bargaining can have positive consequences. Although death cannot be postponed indefinitely, having a goal of attending a particular event or living until a certain time can in fact delay death until then. For instance, death rates of Jewish people fall just before the Passover and rise just after. Similarly, the death rate among older Chinese women falls before and during important holidays and rises after (Phillips, 1992).

In the end, of course, no one can bargain away death. When people eventually realize this, they often move into the depression stage.

Depression. Many dying people experience *depression*. Realizing that the issue is settled and can't be bargained away, they are overwhelmed with a deep sense of loss. They know that they are leaving their loved ones and reaching the end of their lives.

Their depression may be reactive or preparatory or both. In *reactive depression*, the sadness is based on events that have already occurred: the loss of dignity with many medical procedures, the end of a job, goals unachieved, or the knowledge that they will never return home. In *preparatory depression*, people feel sadness over future losses. They know that death will end their relationships and that they will never see future generations. Just as their loved ones will miss them when they are gone, the individual who is dying grieves these losses to come. The reality of death is inescapable in this stage, and it brings profound sadness.

Acceptance. Kübler-Ross suggested that the final step of dying is *acceptance*. Acceptance is not "giving up" or feeling defeated by the illness. People who have developed acceptance are fully aware that death is impending. They may have an increased self-awareness. Unemotional and uncommunicative, they have virtually no feelings—positive or negative—about the present or future. They have made peace with themselves, and they might wish to be left alone, withdrawing contact even from their closest loved ones. This may be particularly difficult for the family members.

➡ **From an educator's perspective:** Do you think Kübler-Ross's five steps of dying might be subject to cultural influences? Age differences? Why or why not?

Evaluating Kübler-Ross's Theory. Kübler-Ross has had an enormous impact on the way we look at death. She is recognized as a pioneer in observing systematically how people approach their own deaths. She was almost single-handedly responsible for bringing the phenomenon of death into public awareness. Her contributions have been particularly influential among those who provide direct care to the dying.

On the other hand, there are some obvious limitations to her conception of dying. It is largely limited to those who are aware that they are dying and who die relatively slowly. It does not apply as well to people who suffer from diseases where the outcome and timing are uncertain.

The most important criticisms concern the "stages" in Kübler-Ross's theory. Not every person passes through every step, and some move through them in a different sequence. Some people even go through the same steps several times. Depressed patients can show bursts of anger, and an angry patient may bargain for more time (Kastenbaum, 1992). Furthermore, because Kübler-Ross's stages have become so familiar, well-meaning caregivers sometimes encourage patients to work through the steps in a prescribed order, without consideration of individual needs. The stages are descriptive, not prescriptive.

Finally, people's reactions to impending death differ. The cause of death; the duration of the dying process; the person's age, sex, and personality; and the social support available from family and friends all influence the course of dying and one's responses to it (Stroebe et al., 1993; Carver and Scheier, 2002).

Other theorists have developed alternative ideas in response to concerns about Kübler-Ross's account. Psychologist Edwin Shneidman, for example, suggests that "themes" in people's reactions to dying can occur—and recur—in any order. These include incredulity, a sense of unfairness, fear of pain or even general terror, and fantasies of being rescued (Leenaars and Shneidman, 1999).

Choosing the Nature of Death: Is DNR the Way to Go?

LEARNING OBJECTIVES

LO6 **How do people exercise some control over the place and the manner in which they die?**

When Colin's mother was diagnosed with lung cancer, she chose to enjoy the time she had left. "I don't want to waste my last few months sick from chemo and radiation," she said. So she had her doctor write a No Cardiopulmonary Resuscitation order and she went home to her family. One evening while they were watching television, Colin's mother stopped breathing. Colin panicked and called 911. When the paramedics arrived, he apologized and showed them the no CPR order.

The letters "DNR" on a patient's medical chart have a simple and clear meaning: "Do Not Resuscitate." DNR means that no extraordinary means are to be taken to keep a patient alive. For terminally ill patients, DNR can mean the difference between dying immediately or living additional days, months, or even years, kept alive only by the most extreme, invasive, and even painful medical procedures. No Cardiopulmonary Resuscitation (no CPR) is also becoming common; patients choosing to die at home may have a doctor's note or medical alert bracelet expressing this wish.

The DNR decision entails several issues. One is differentiating "extreme" and "extraordinary" measures from routine ones. There are no hard-and-fast rules; people making the decision must consider the needs of the patient, his or her prior medical history, and factors such as age and even religion. For instance, different standards might apply to a 12-year-old and an 85-year-old with the same medical condition. Other questions concern quality of life. How can we determine an individual's current quality of life and whether it will be improved or diminished by a medical intervention? Who makes these decisions—the patient, a family member, or medical personnel?

Although one-third of patients ask not to be resuscitated, less than half of their physicians say they know their patients' preferences. In addition, only 49 percent of patients have their wishes entered on their medical charts. Physicians and other providers might be reluctant to act on DNR requests, in part because they are trained to save patients, not permit them to die, and in part to avoid legal liability (Knaus et al., 1995; Goold et al., 2000; McArdle, 2002).

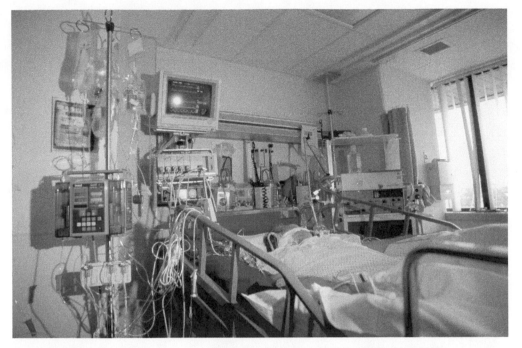

Many terminally ill patients choose "DNR" (Do Not Resuscitate) or "No Cardiopulmonary Resuscitation" as a way to avoid extraordinary medical interventions, so that they can die peacefully when the time comes.

Living Wills. To gain more control over decisions regarding their own death, many people sign living wills. A **living will** is a legal document that designates the medical treatments a person does or does not want if unable to express his or her wishes (see Figure 10-2).

Some people designate a specific person, called a *health-care proxy*, to act as their representative for health-care decisions. Health-care proxies are authorized either in living wills or in a legal document known as a *durable power of attorney*. Health-care proxies may be authorized to deal with all medical care problems (such as how to proceed in the event of a coma) or only terminal illnesses.

As with DNR orders, living wills are ineffective unless people make sure their health-care proxies and doctors know their wishes. Although people might be reluctant to do this, they should have frank conversations with their health-care proxies.

Euthanasia and Assisted Suicide. Dr. Jack Kevorkian became well known in the 1990s for his invention and promotion of a "suicide machine," which allowed patients to push a button and release anesthesia and a drug that stops the heart. By supplying the machine and the drugs, which patients administered themselves, Kevorkian was participating in *assisted suicide*, providing the means for a terminally ill person to commit suicide. Kevorkian spent eight years in prison for second-degree murder for his participation in an assisted suicide shown on the television show *60 Minutes*.

Assisted suicide is bitterly controversial and illegal in much of the world. The exception in North America is Oregon, which passed a "right to die law" in 1998. Far from releasing a flood of assisted suicides, in its first decade fewer than 300 people took medication to end their lives (Ganzini et al., 2006; Davey, 2007).

In some countries, assisted suicide is accepted. For instance, in The Netherlands medical personnel may help end their patients' lives if several conditions are met: At least two physicians must determine that the patient is terminally ill; there must be unbearable physical or mental suffering; the patient must give informed consent in writing; and relatives must be informed beforehand (Galbraith and Dobson, 2000; Rosenfeld et al., 2000; Naik, 2002; Kleespies, 2004).

Assisted suicide generally assumes that the individual who wishes to commit suicide is physically incapable of committing suicide alone, like Sue Rodriguez. In contrast, **euthanasia** is the practice of helping terminally ill people die more quickly, and does not assume the individual is capable of expressing his or her wishes (such as individuals in

living wills legal documents designating what medical treatments people want or do not want if they cannot express their wishes

euthanasia the practice of assisting people who are terminally ill to die more quickly

I,_____,
being of sound mind, make this statement as a directive to be followed if I
become permanently unable to participate in decisions regarding my
medical care. These instructions reflect my firm and settled commitment to
decline medical treatment under the circumstances indicated below:

I direct my attending physician to withhold or withdraw treatment that
merely prolongs my dying, if I should be in **an incurable or irreversible
mental or physical condition** with no reasonable expectation of recovery,
including but not limited to: (a) a **terminal condition**; (b) a **permanently
unconscious condition**; or (c) a **minimally conscious condition in which I am
permanently unable to make decisions or express my wishes.**

I direct that treatment be limited to measures to keep me comfortable and
to relieve pain, including any pain that might occur by withholding or
withdrawing treatment.

While I understand that I am not legally required to be specific about future
treatments, **if I am in the condition(s) described above I feel especially
strongly about the following treatments:**

I do not want cardiac resuscitation.
I do not want mechanical respiration.
I do not want tube feeding.
I do not want antibiotics.

However, I **do want** maximum pain relief, even if it may hasten my death.

Other directions (insert personal instructions):

These directions express my legal right to refuse treatment under federal
and state law. I intend my instructions to be carried out, unless I have
revoked them in a new writing or by clearly indicating that I have changed
my mind.

Signed:_____ Date:_____

Address:_____

– –

Statement by Witnesses
I declare that the person who signed this document appears to be at least
eighteen (18) years of age, of sound mind, and under no constraint or
undue influence. The person who signed this document appeared to do so
willingly and free from duress. He or she signed (or asked another to sign
for him or her) this document in my presence.

Witness:_____

Address:_____

– –

Witness:_____

Address:_____

– –

FIGURE 10-2 **An Example of a Living Will**
What steps can people take to make sure the wishes they write into their living wills are
carried out?

comas). Popularly known as "mercy killing," euthanasia has several forms. *Passive eutha-nasia* involves removing respirators or other medical equipment that might be sustaining a patient's life, to allow them to die naturally—such as when medical staff follow a DNR order. In *voluntary active euthanasia* caregivers or medical staff act to end a person's life before death would normally occur, perhaps by administering a lethal dose of pain medication. When a parent euthanizes a severely disabled child, the issue becomes headline news. But for all the controversy surrounding the practice, euthanasia is surprisingly widespread. One survey of nurses in intensive care units found that 20 percent had deliberately hastened a patient's death at least once, and other experts assert that euthanasia is far from rare (Asch, 1996).

The controversy arises from the question of who should control life. Does the right to one's life belong to the individual, the person's physicians, his or her dependants, the government, or some deity? Because we claim to have the absolute right to create lives in the form of babies, some people argue that we should also have the absolute right to end our lives (Solomon, 1995; Lester, 1996; Allen et al., 2006).

Many opponents argue that the practice of euthanasia is morally wrong. In their view, prematurely ending the life of a person, no matter how willing the person is, is murder. Others point out that physicians are often inaccurate in predicting how long a person will live. For example, a large-scale study known as SUPPORT—the Study to Understand Prognoses and Preferences for Outcomes and Risks of Treatment—found that patients often outlive physicians' predictions of when they will die—in some cases living years after being given no more than a 50 percent chance of living six more months (Bishop, 2006).

Another argument against euthanasia focuses on the emotional state of the patient. Even if patients beg health-care providers to help them die, they might be suffering from a form of depression that could be treated with antidepressant drugs. Once the depression lifts, patients can change their minds about wanting to die (Becvar, 2000; Gostin, 2006).

Caring for the Terminally Ill: The Place of Death

Dina Bianga loves her work. Dina is a registered nurse whose job is to meet the physical and psychologi-cal needs of the terminally ill.

"You need compassion and a good clinical background," she says. "You also have to be flex-ible. You go into the home, hospital, nursing home, adult foster care—wherever the patient is."

Dina likes the interdisciplinary approach that hospice work requires. "You form a team with others who provide social work, spiritual care, home health aid, grief support, and administra-tive support."

Surprisingly, the patients are not the most challenging part of the job. Families and friends are.

"Families are frightened, and everything seems out of control. They're not always ready to accept that death is coming soon, so you have to be careful and sensitive how you word things. If they are well informed on what to expect, the transition is smoother and a more comfortable atmosphere is created for the patient."

More than half the people in Canada who die do so in hospitals. Yet hospitals are among the least desirable places in which to face death. They are typically impersonal, with staff rotating through the day. But for those requiring palliative care, also known as end-of-life and hospice care, the hospital is often where they end up.

Palliative care is care for the dying and their families. It is designed to provide a warm, supportive environment for the dying. It does not focus on extending people's lives, but on making their final days pleasant and meaningful. The emphasis is on managing symptoms, maximizing quality of life for the patient, as well as supporting caregivers.

In **home care**, dying people stay in their homes and receive treatment from their families and visiting medical staff. Many dying patients prefer home care, because they can spend their final days in a familiar environment, with people they love and a lifetime accumulation of treasures around them.

Watch on **mydevelopmentlab**

You've just read about home care, now log onto MyDevelopmentLab to watch an interview of a nurse manager discuss the goals and structure of hospice care.

palliative care   care provided for the comfort and support of the dying

home care   an alternative to hospitalization in which dying people stay in their homes and receive treatment from their families and visiting medical staff

But home care can be quite difficult for family members. True, giving something precious to people they love offers family members substantial emotional solace, but being on call 24 hours a day is extraordinarily draining, both physically and emotionally. Furthermore, because most relatives are not trained in nursing, they might provide less than optimal medical care (Perreault et al., 2004).

Focus on Research

End-of-Life Care in Canada

With an aging population, the health care system faces a new challenge—end-of-life care. Most older adults report that they would prefer to die at home rather than in a long-term care facility or hospital, but very few will. Between 1950 and 1994 an increasing number of Canadians died in hospital rather than at home or in a long-term care facility. One factor was economics: for individuals needing palliative care, that care was provided free in a hospital but was not necessarily available in a long-term care facility or community based home-care. Where available, such care often involved private fees. Beginning in 1994, however, University of Alberta Nursing faculty Donna Wilson and colleagues noted a change: More people were dying in long-term care facilities or the comfort of their own home and fewer were dying in hospitals. This trend was seen for almost all causes of death, and was occurring independently of any formal health-care policy changes. In 1994, 80 percent of deaths occurred in a hospital. By 2004, it was down to 60 percent—male, female, urban, rural, regardless of age or place of birth. Across the board, palliative care was leaving the hospital. Wilson and colleagues noted a few factors that might underlie the shift in location of death:

1. Fewer hospital beds. With budgets squeezed tighter and tighter, terminally ill patients who could be cared for elsewhere might not be admitted to hospital. For example, older patients with dementia are now more likely to die in long-term care facilities, and the shortage of hospital beds might have forced long-term care facilities to improve their palliative care. Some circumstances still require palliative care be delivered in a hospital, the most prominent being management of severe pain.

2. Family support. While home care can be a tremendous burden for family members, when the family together sets the goal of dying at home, benefits can also result. Slowly, public policy is shifting to facilitate home-based palliative care. For example, Compassionate Care Benefits allow individuals to take time off work to care for terminally ill family members. (Wilson et al., 2009)

REVIEW, CHECK, AND APPLY

REVIEW

- Elisabeth Kübler-Ross identified five steps toward dying: denial, anger, bargaining, depression, and acceptance.

- Issues surrounding dying are highly controversial, including the measures that physicians should apply to keep dying patients alive, and who should make the decisions about those measures.

- Assisted suicide and euthanasia are highly controversial and are illegal across Canada, although many people believe they should be legalized if they are regulated.

- Although most people in Canada die in hospitals, increasing numbers are choosing home care for their final days.

CHECK YOURSELF

1. Kübler-Ross initially suggested that individuals pass through basic steps or stages as they approach death. Match each of the following examples with its appropriate stage.

   a. "You can't mean me. I have never been sick a day in my life."

   b. "If I could just live a little longer so I can see my daughter get married, I will do anything."

   c. "I know I only have a little time left; can you help me accomplish a few things before that time comes?"

   d. "I don't know what to do. I can't eat, I can't sleep. I don't want to do anything or talk to anyone."

   e. "I hate you; I hate this disease. Leave me alone."

2. In the medical community, DNR stands for
   _____.

   a. Do Not Renew

   b. Daily Notice of Revision

   c. Do Not Revive

   d. Do Not Resuscitate

3. _____ is the practice of assisting people who are terminally ill to die more quickly.

APPLYING LIFESPAN DEVELOPMENT

- Do you think assisted suicide should be permissible? Euthanasia? Why or why not?

Answers: 1) a-denial, b-bargaining, c-acceptance, d-depression, e-anger; 2) d; 3) euthanasia

Facing the Void

No one ever told me that grief felt so like fear. I am not afraid, but the sensation is like being afraid. The same fluttering in the stomach, the same restlessness, the yawning. I keep on swallowing.

At other times it feels like being mildly drunk, or concussed. There is a sort of invisible blanket between the world and me. I find it hard to take in what anyone says. Or perhaps, hard to want to take it in. It is so uninteresting. (Lewis, 1985, p. 394)

It is a universal experience, but most of us are surprisingly ill-prepared for the grief that follows the death of a loved one. Particularly in Western societies, where life expectancy is long and mortality rates are low, people view death as atypical rather than expected. This attitude makes grief all the more difficult to bear.

In this module, we consider bereavement and grief. We examine the difficulties in distinguishing normal from unhealthy grief and the consequences of loss. The module also looks at mourning and funerals, discussing how people can prepare themselves for the inevitability of death.

Mourning and Funerals: Final Rites

L06 What are the basic components of a Western funeral rite, and how are other cultures' rites similar and different?

In our culture, only babies are buried; just about everyone else is cremated. When my father died, my elder brother took the lead and, with the other men observing, approached the pyre and lit it.

My father's body burned well. After the fire died down, my brother oversaw the gathering of the ashes and bone fragments, and we all took a bath to purify us. Despite this and subsequent baths, we in the close family were considered polluted for 13 days.

Finally, after the 13 days, we gathered for a big meal. The centrepiece was the preparation of rice balls (pinda), which we offered to the spirit of my father. At the end of the meal we dedicated gifts for distribution to the poor.

In Hindu culture, the idea behind these ceremonies is to honour the dead person's memory. More traditional people believe that it helps the soul pass to the realm of Yama, the god of death, rather than hanging on in this world as a ghost.

This ritual is specifically Hindu, and yet, in its carefully prescribed roles for survivors and its focus on honouring the dead, it shares key elements with Western rituals. The first step in grieving, for most survivors in Western countries, is some sort of funeral. Death is a big business. The average funeral and burial costs $7000 to $10 000, including an ornate, polished coffin, limousine transportation, and preservation and viewing of the body (Bryant, 2003; AARP, 2004).

Funerals are grandiose in part because of the vulnerability of the survivors who typically make the arrangements. Wishing to demonstrate love and affection, the survivors are susceptible to suggestions that they should "provide the best" for the deceased (Culver, 2003).

But in large measure, social norms and customs determine the nature of funerals just as they do for weddings. In a sense, a funeral is not only a public acknowledgment that an individual has died, but recognition of everyone's mortality and an acceptance of the cycle of life.

In Western societies, funeral rituals follow a typical pattern. The body is prepared in some way and dressed in special clothing. There is usually a religious rite, a eulogy, a procession of some sort, and some formal period, such as the wake for Irish Catholics and shivah for Jews,

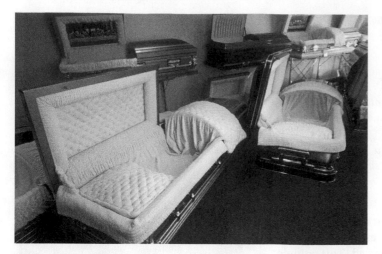

Because an individual's death represents an important transition, not only for loved ones but for an entire community, the rites associated with death take on an added importance. The emotional significance of death, combined with the pressure of enterprising salespersons, leads many to overspend on funerals.

in which relatives and friends visit the family and pay their respects. Military funerals typically include the firing of weapons and a flag draped over the coffin.

Cultural Differences in Grieving. As we saw in the prologue, non-Western funerals are different. In some societies mourners shave their heads as a sign of grief, while in others they allow the hair to grow and stop shaving for a time. In other cultures, mourners may be hired to wail and grieve. Sometimes noisy celebrations take place, while in other cultures silence is the norm. Culture determines even the nature of emotional displays, such as the amount and timing of crying (Rosenblatt, 1988, 2001).

Mourners in Balinese funerals in Indonesia show little emotion because they believe the gods will hear their prayers only if they are calm. In contrast, mourners at African American funerals show their grief, and funeral rituals allow attendees to display their feelings (Rosenblatt and Wallace, 2005; Collins and Doolittle, 2006).

Historically, some cultures developed rather extreme funeral rites. For example, in *suttee*, a traditional Hindu practice in India that is now illegal, a widow was expected to throw herself into the fire that consumed her husband's body. In ancient China, servants were sometimes buried (alive) with their masters' bodies.

Ultimately, no matter the ritual, all funerals basically serve the same function: They mark the endpoint of the life of the person who has died—and provide a formal forum for the feelings of the survivors, a place where they can come together, share their grief, and comfort one another.

Bereavement and Grief: Adjusting to the Death of a Loved One

LEARNING OBJECTIVES

LO7 How do survivors react to and cope with death?

When Princess Diana of Britain was killed in a car crash in 1997, it seemed that everyone in the world was instantly aware of the tragedy and eager to share in the mourning process. It is estimated that 2.5 billion people watched her funeral, a number undoubtedly swelled by the youth, beauty, and popularity of the princess, and by the sudden and tragic circumstances of her death.

The funeral route in London was lined with thousands of people, dozens deep. People had camped overnight just to catch a glimpse of the funeral cortège as it passed. Many held hand-drawn posters with sentiments such as "Diana, Princess of Hearts" and "The People's Princess."

To some, this unique display signalled the public's insistence on participating in the private grief of the princess's family. In truth it signified more than this—that, to billions of people around the world, Diana was family and their grief was entirely natural.

After the death of a loved one, a painful period of adjustment follows, involving bereavement and grief. **Bereavement** is acknowledgment of the objective fact that one has experienced a death, while **grief** is the emotional response to one's loss.

The first stage of grief typically entails shock, numbness, disbelief, or outright denial. People try to avoid the reality of the situation and pursue their usual routines, although the pain may break through, causing anguish, fear, and deep sorrow and distress. In some ways, numbness may be beneficial, since it permits the survivor to make funeral arrangements and carry out other psychologically difficult tasks. Typically, people pass through this stage in a few days or weeks.

In the next phase, people begin to confront the death and realize the extent of their loss. They fully experience their grief and begin to acknowledge that the separation from the dead person will be permanent. They may suffer deep unhappiness or even depression, a normal feeling in this situation. They may yearn for the dead individual. Emotions can range from impatient to lethargic. However, they also begin to view their past relationship with

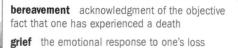

bereavement acknowledgment of the objective fact that one has experienced a death

grief the emotional response to one's loss

the deceased realistically, good and bad. In so doing, they begin to free themselves from some of the bonds that tied them to the loved one (de Vries et al., 1997).

Finally, they reach the accommodation stage. They begin to pick up the pieces of their lives and to construct new identities. For instance, rather than seeing herself as a widowed spouse, a woman whose husband has died may come to regard herself as a single person. Still, there are moments when intense feelings of grief occur.

Ultimately, most people emerge from grieving and live new, independent lives. They form new relationships, and some even find that coping with the death has helped them to grow as individuals. They become more self-reliant and more appreciative of life.

Of course, people display vast individual differences because of their personalities, the nature of the relationship with the deceased, and the opportunities that are available to them for continuing their lives after the loss. The stages of grieving do not unfold in the same way for all people.

After a death, people move through a painful period of bereavement and grief, even for those they might not have known well, as this tribute to Michael Jackson suggests.

Differentiating Unhealthy Grief from Normal Grief. Although ideas abound about what separates normal grief from unhealthy grief, careful research has shown that many assumptions are simply wrong. There is no correct timetable for grieving, particularly not the year that common knowledge prescribes for grieving after a spouse has died. Increasing evidence suggests that grieving may sometimes take considerably longer than a year. Research also contradicts the assumption that depression inevitably follows a death; only 15 to 30 percent of people show relatively deep depression following the loss of a loved one (Prigerson et al., 1995; Bonanno et al., 2002; Hensley, 2006).

Similarly, it is often assumed that people who show little initial distress are not facing up to reality, and that they are likely to have problems later. In fact, those who show the most intense distress immediately after a death are the most apt to have adjustment difficulties and health problems later (Gluhoski et al., 1994; Boerner et al., 2005).

The Consequences of Grief and Bereavement. In a sense, death is catching. Evidence suggests that widowed people are particularly at risk of death. Some studies find that the risk of death can be seven times higher than normal in the first year after the death of a spouse, particularly for men and younger women. Remarriage seems to lower the risk of death, especially for widowed men, although the reasons are not clear (Gluhoski et al., 1994; Martikainen and Valkonen, 1996; Aiken, 2000).

Bereavement is more likely to produce depression or other negative consequences if the person is already insecure, anxious, or fearful and therefore less able to cope effectively. Relationships marked by ambivalence before death are more apt to cause poor post-death outcomes than secure relationships. Highly dependent people are apt to suffer more after the death, as are those who spend a lot of time reflecting on the death and their own grief. Bereaved people who lack social support from family, friends, or some other group, religious or otherwise, are more likely to feel lonely, and therefore are more at risk. Finally, people who are unable to make sense of the death or find meaning in it (such as a new appreciation of life) show less successful adjustment (Nolen-Hoeksema, 2001; Nolen-Hoeksema and Davis, 2002).

The suddenness of the death also affects the course of grieving. People who unexpectedly lose their loved ones are less able to cope than those who could anticipate the death. In one study, people who experienced a sudden death had not fully recovered four years later. In part, this could be because sudden deaths are often the result of violence, which occurs more frequently among younger individuals (Rando, 1993; Burton et al., 2006).

> **From a social worker's perspective:** Why do you think the risk of death is so high for people who have recently lost a spouse? Why might remarriage lower the risk?

As we noted earlier, children need special help understanding and mourning the death of someone they love.

Helping a Child Cope with Grief

Becoming an Informed Consumer of Development

Because of their limited understanding of death, younger children need special help in coping with grief. Among the strategies that can help are the following:

- **Be honest.** Don't say that the person is "sleeping" or "on a long trip." Use age-appropriate language to tell the truth. Gently but clearly point out that death is final and universal.

- **Encourage expressions of grief.** Don't tell children not to cry or show their feelings. Instead, tell them that it is understandable to feel terrible, and that they may always miss the deceased. Encourage them to draw a picture, write a letter, or express their feelings some other way.

- **Reassure children that they are not to blame.** Children sometimes attribute a loved one's death to their own behaviour—if they had not misbehaved, they mistakenly reason, the person would not have died.

- **Understand that children's grief can surface in unanticipated ways.** Children can show little initial grief but later might become upset for no apparent reason, or revert to behaviours like thumbsucking or wanting to sleep with their parents.

REVIEW, CHECK, AND APPLY

REVIEW

- After a death, most cultures prescribe some sort of funeral ritual to honour the passing of a community member.

- Funeral rites play a significant role in helping people acknowledge the death of a loved one, recognize their own mortality, and proceed with their lives.

- Bereavement refers to the loss of a loved one; grief refers to the emotional response to that loss.

- For many people, grief passes through denial, sorrow, and accommodation stages.

CHECK YOURSELF

1. According to Rosenblatt (1998, 2001) the nature of emotional displays, such as the amount and timing of crying in response to someone's death, are determined culturally.

   - True
   - False

2. Bereaved people who lack _____ are more likely to experience feelings of loneliness and are therefore at greater risk for more negative post-death outcomes.

   a. ambivalence
   b. rituals
   c. independence
   d. social support

3. In the final stage of grief, people tend to

   a. reach the accommodation stage, where they pick up the pieces of their lives and construct new identities.
   b. cycle back to numbness if the pain is too severe.
   c. avoid the reality of the situation through denial.
   d. suffer deep unhappiness and even depression.

APPLYING LIFESPAN DEVELOPMENT

- Why do so many people feel reluctant to think and talk about death? Why do people in other cultures feel less reluctant?

Answers: 1) True; 2) d; 3) a

Putting It All Together
Death and Dying

JAMES TIBURON, the nurse we met in the chapter opener, admitted to never quite getting accustomed to death, despite his many encounters with it. As part of his job, James saw deaths at every stage of the lifespan, from infancy to old age, and from every cause imaginable. He dealt with grieving families, working with them to determine when it might be necessary to follow a DNR order and to walk them through the painful process of claiming their loved one's body from the hospital morgue. He witnessed firsthand the stages of death and dying and at least the initial stages of grief. For all his close-ups with death, James remains decisively positive and life-affirming, serving as a model for a plainspoken acceptance of death and moving on with life.

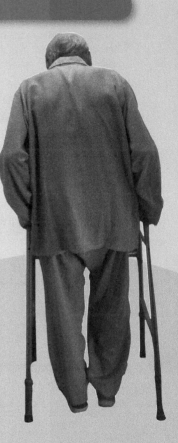

MODULE **10.1** Death across the Lifespan

- James is familiar with facing the question of when life ends **(p. 430).**

- James has seen death at every age, including during infancy **(p. 431).**

- He has dealt with family members who have lost loved ones at every point in the lifespan **(pp. 432–433).**

- As part of his job, James has studied death education and informally educated survivors about death **(p. 435).**

MODULE **10.2** Confronting Death

- James has dealt with patients who are passing through the steps of dying **(pp. 436–437).**

- He has worked with doctors and families in making life-or-death (for example, DNR) decisions **(p. 438).**

- He has probably been asked by patients to help them die **(p. 439).**

- James has experience with the hospital as a place to die **(p. 441).**

What would YOU do?

■ Given what you know about possible places to die, which would you recommend for your closest loved one, in the event it was needed: hospitalization, home care, or hospice care? Why? Would other choices be more appropriate for other loved ones you know?

HINT Review pages 441–442.

What's your response?

MODULE **10.3** Grief and Bereavement

■ As a worker in a metropolitan hospital, James has undoubtedly encountered many culturally different expressions of grief and many forms of bereavement **(p. 443)**.

■ He has seen mostly the first stage of grief—shock, numbness, denial—in dealing with the survivors of deceased patients **(pp. 444–445)**.

■ James is likely to have had to talk to children about death, a particularly difficult task **(p. 432)**.

What would a POLICYMAKER do?

■ Should the government be involved in determining if individuals should be permitted to decide whether to continue their own lives in times of critical illness or extreme pain? Should this be a matter of law or of personal conscience?

HINT Review pages 439–441.

What's your response?

What would a HEALTH-CARE PROVIDER do?

■ Which criteria are most important in deciding whether to discontinue life-support systems? Do you think the criteria differ in different cultures?

HINT Review pages 438–439.

What's your response?

What would an EDUCATOR do?

■ What sorts of topics should be covered in depth in death education courses for health providers? For laypeople?

HINT Review page 435.

What's your response?

References

AAMR (American Association on Mental Retardation). (2002). *Mental retardation: Definition, classification, and systems of support.* Washington, DC: Author.

AARP (American Association of Retired Persons). (1990). *A profile of older Americans.* Washington, DC: Author.

AARP. (2004, May 25). Funeral arrangements and memorial service. Available online at http://www.aarp.org/griefandloss/articles/73_a.html.

AARP. (2005, October). I can see clearly now. *AARP Bulletin*, p. 34.

AAUW (American Association of University Women). (1992). *How schools shortchange women: The A.A.U.W. report.* Washington, DC: American Association of University Women Educational Foundation.

Aber, J. L., Bishop-Josef, S. J., Jones, S. M., McLearn, K. T., & Phillips, D. A. (Eds.). (2007). *Child development and social policy: Knowledge for action.* Washington, DC: American Psychological Association.

Aboud, F., Mendelson, M., & Purdy, K. (2003). Cross-race peer relations and friendship quality. *International Journal of Behavioral Development, 27*, 165–173.

Achenbach, T. A. (1992). Developmental psychopathology. In M. H. Bornstein and M. E. Lamb (Eds.), *Developmental psychology: An advanced textbook.* Hillsdale, NJ: Erlbaum.

Ackerman, B. P., & Izard, C. E. (2004). Emotion cognition in children and adolescents: Introduction to the special issue. *Journal of Experimental Child Psychology, 89* [Special issue: Emotional cognition in children], 271–275.

Acocella, J. (August 18 and 25, 2003). Little people. *The New Yorker*, 138–143.

ACOG. (2002). *Guidelines for perinatal care.* Elk Grove, IN: Author.

Adams, C., & Labouvie-Vief, G. (1986, November 20). Modes of knowing and language processing. Symposium on developmental dimensions of adult adaptations. Perspectives in mind, self, and emotion. Paper presented at the meeting of the Gerontological Association of America, Chicago, IL.

Adams, C. R., & Singh, K. (1998). Direct and indirect effects of school learning variables on the academic achievement of African American 10th graders. *Journal of Negro Education, 67*, 48–66.

Adams, G. R., Montemayor, R., & Gullotta, T. P. (Eds.). (1996). *Psychosocial development during adolescence.* Thousand Oaks, CA: Sage Publications.

Adams, K. B. (2004). Changing investment in activities and interests in elders' lives: Theory and measurement. *International Journal of Aging and Human Development, 58*, 87–108.

Adams, R. J., Mauer, D., & Davis, M. (1986). Newborns' discrimination of chromatic from achromatic stimuli. *Journal of Experimental Child Psychology, 41*, 267–281.

Adams Hillard, P. J. (2001). Gynecologic disorders and surgery. In N. L. Stotland & D. E. Stewart. (Eds.), *Psychological aspects of women's health care: The interface between psychiatry and obstetrics and gynecology* (2nd ed.). Washington, DC: American Psychiatric Publishing.

Adamson, L., and Frick, J. (2003). The still face: A history of a shared experimental paradigm. *Infancy, 4*, 451–473.

Adelmann, P. K., Antonucci, T. C., & Crohan, S. E. (1990). A causal analysis of employment and health in midlife women. *Women and Health, 16*, 5–20.

Ader, R., Felten, D., & Cohen, N. (2001). *Psychoneuroimmunology* (3rd ed.). San Diego: Academic Press.

Adesman, A. (2011). Restricted elimination diet for ADHD. *Lancet, 377(9777)*, 1567.

Adlaf, E. M., Demers, A., & Gliksman, L. (Eds.). (2005). Canadian campus survey 2004. Toronto: Centre for Addiction and Mental Health.

Adler, P. A., Kless, S. J., & Adler, P. (1992). Socialization to gender roles: Popularity among elementary school boys and girls. *Sociology of Education, 65*, 169–187.

Administration on Aging. (2006). *Profiles of older Americans 2005: Research report.* Washington, DC: U.S. Department of Health and Human Resources.

Adolph, K. E. (1997). Learning in the development of infant locomotion. With commentary by B. I. Bertenthal, S. M. Boker, E. C. Goldfield, & E. J. Gibson. *Monographs of the Society for Research in Child Development, 62*, 238–251.

Afifi, T., Brownridge, D., Cox, B., & Sareen, J. (2006, October). Physical punishment, childhood abuse and psychiatric disorders. *Child Abuse and Neglect, 30*, 1093–1103.

Aguiar, A., & Baillargeon, R. (2002). Developments in young infants' reasoning about occluded objects. *Cognitive Psychology, 45*, 267–336.

Ah-Kion, J. (2006, June). Body image and self-esteem: A study of gender differences among mid-adolescents. *Gender and Behaviour, 4*, 534–549.

Ahmed, E., & Braithwaite, V. (2004). Bullying and victimization: Cause for concern for both families and schools. *Social Psychology of Education, 7*, 35–54.

Ahn, W., Gelman, S., & Amsterlaw, J. (2000). Causal status effect in children's categorization. *Cognition, 76*, B35–B43.

Aiken, L. R. (2000). *Dying, death, and bereavement* (4th ed.). Mahwah, NJ: Erlbaum.

Ainsworth, M. D. S. (1973). The development of infant–mother attachment. In B. M. Caldwell & H. N. Ricciuti (Eds.), *Review of child development research* (Vol. 3). Chicago: University of Chicago Press.

Ainsworth, M. D. S. (1993). Attachment as related to mother–infant interaction. *Advances in Infancy Research, 8*, 1–50.

Ainsworth, M. D. S., Blehar, M. C., Waters, E., & Wall, S. (1978). *Patterns of attachment: A psychological study of the strange situation.* Hillsdale, NJ: Erlbaum.

Aitken, R. J. (1995, July 7). The complexities of conception. *Science, 269*, 39–40.

Akshoomoff, N. (2006). Autism spectrum disorders: Introduction. *Child Neuropsychology, 12*, 245–246.

Albers, L. L., Migliaccio, L., Bedrick, E. J., Teaf, D., & Peralta, P. (2007). Does epidural analgesia affect the rate of spontaneous obstetric lacerations in normal births? *Journal of Midwifery and Women's Health, 52*, 31–36.

Albrecht, G. L. (2005). *Encyclopedia of disability* (General ed.). Thousand Oaks, CA: Sage Publications.

Aldwin, C., & Gilmer, D. (2004). *Health, illness, and optimal aging: Biological and psychosocial perspectives.* Thousand Oaks, CA: Sage Publications, Inc.

Aldwin, C. M. (1994). *Stress, coping, and development: An integrative perspective.* New York: Guilford Press, 1994.

Ales, K. L., Druzin, M. L., & Santini, D. L. (1990). Impact of advanced maternal age on the outcome of pregnancy. *Surgery, Gynecology and Obstetrics, 171*, 209–216.

Alexander, G. M., & Hines, M. (2002). Sex differences in response to children's toys in nonhuman primates. *Evolution and Human Behavior, 23*, 467–479.

Alfonso, V. C., Flanagan, D. P., & Radwan, S. (2005). The impact of the Cattell-Horn-Carroll theory on test development and interpretation of cognitive and academic abilities. In D. P. Flanagan & P. L. Harrison (Eds.), *Contemporary intellectual assessment: Theories, tests, and issues.* New York: Guilford Press.

Alisky, J. M. (2007). The coming problem of HIV-associated Alzheimer's disease. *Medical Hypotheses, 12*, 47–55.

Allen, J., Chavez, S., DeSimone, S., Howard, D., Johnson, K., LaPierre, L., et al. (2006, June). Americans' attitudes toward euthanasia and physician-assisted suicide, 1936–2002. *Journal of Sociology and Social Welfare, 33*, 5–23.

Allison, B., & Schultz, J. (2001). Interpersonal identity formation during early adolescence. *Adolescence, 36*, 509–523.

Altholz, S., & Golensky, M. (2004). Counseling, support, and advocacy for clients who stutter. *Health and Social Work, 29*, 197–205.

Alvarez-Leon, E. E., Roman-Vinas, B., & Serra-Majem, L. (2006). Dairy products and health: A review of the epidemiological evidence. *British Journal of Nutrition, 96*, Supplement, S94–S99.

Amato, P., & Afifi, T. (2006, February). Feeling caught between parents: Adult children's relations with parents and subjective well-being. *Journal of Marriage and Family, 68*, 222–235.

Amato, P., & Booth, A. (1997). *A generation at risk.* Cambridge, MA: Harvard University Press.

Amato, P., & Previti, D. (2003). People's reasons for divorcing: Gender, social class, the life course, and adjustment. *Journal of Family Issues, 24*, 602–626.

Amato, P. R., & Booth, A. (2001). The legacy of parents' marital discord: Consequences for children's marital quality. *Journal of Personality and Social Psychology, 81*, 627–638.

American Academy of Family Physicians. (2002). *Position paper on neonatal circumcision.* Leawood, KS: American Academy of Family Physicians.

American Academy of Pediatrics. (1999, August). Media education. *Pediatrics, 104*, 341–343.

American Academy of Pediatrics. (2004, June 3). *Sports programs.* Available online at http://www.medem.com/medlb/article_detaillb_for_printer.cfm?article_ID=ZZZD2QD5M7Candsub_cat=405.

American Academy of Pediatrics (Committee on Psychosocial Aspects of Child and Family Health). (1998, April). Guidance for effective discipline. *Pediatrics, 101*, 723–728.

American Academy of Pediatrics (Committee on Sports Medicine and Committee on School Health). (1989). Organized athletics for preadolescent children. *Pediatrics, 84(3)*, 583–584.

Amsterlaw, J., & Wellman, H. (2006). Theories of mind in transition: A microgenetic study of the development of false belief understanding. *Journal of Cognition and Development, 7*, 139–172.

An, J., & Cooney, T. (2006, September). Psychological well-being in mid to late life: The role of generativity development and parent–child relationships across the lifespan. *International Journal of Behavioral Development, 30*, 410–421.

Anand, K. J. S., & Hickey, P. R. (1992). Halothane-morphine compared with high-dose sufentanil for anesthesia and post-operative analgesia in neonatal cardiac surgery. *New England Journal of Medicine, 326(1)*, 1–9.

Anders, T. F., & Taylor, T. (1994). Babies and their sleep environment. *Children's Environments, 11*, 123–134.

Andersen, A. M. N., Wohlfahrt, J., Christens, P., Olsen, J., & Melbye, M. (2000). Maternal age and fetal loss: Population based register linkage study. *BMJ, 320*, 1708–1712.

Anderson, C., Berkowitz, L., Donnerstein, E., Huesmann, L., Johnson, J., Linz, D., Malamuth, N., & Wartella, E. (2003). The influence of media violence on youth. *Psychological Science in the Public Interest, 4*, 81–110.

Anderson, C. A., Funk, J. B., & Griffiths, M. D. (2004). Contemporary issues in adolescent video game playing: Brief overview and introduction to the special issue. *Journal of Adolescence, 27*, 1–3.

Anderson, D., & Pempek, T. (2005). Television and very young children. *American Behavioral Scientist, 48*, 505–522.

Anderson, P., & Butcher, K. (2006, March). Childhood obesity: Trends and potential causes. *The Future of Children, 16*, 19–45.

Andrews, G., Halford, G., & Bunch, K. (2003). Theory of mind and relational complexity. *Child Development, 74*, 1476–1499.

Anglin, P. M., & Meng, R. (2000). *Canadian public policy— analyse de politiques, 26(3)*, 361–368.

Angus, J., & Reeve, P. (2006, April). Ageism: A threat to "aging well" in the 21st century. *Journal of Applied Gerontology, 25*, 137–152.

Angus-Reid (2010, July 26). Canadians and Britons are more open on same-sex relations than Americans. Retrieved from http://www.angus-reid.com/polls/43149/canadians-and-britons-are-more-open-on-same-sex-relations-than-americans/.

Anisfeld, M. (1996). Only tongue protrusion modeling is matched by neonates. *Developmental Review, 16*, 149–161.

Annunziato, R., & Lowe, M. (2007, April). Taking action to lose weight: Toward an understanding of individual differences. *Eating Behaviors, 8*, 185–194.

Antonucci, T. C. (1990). Social supports and social relationships. In R. H. Binstock & L. K. George (Eds.), *Handbook of aging and the social sciences*. San Diego: Academic Press.

Antonucci, T. C. (2001). Social relations: An examination of social networks, social support, and sense of control. In J. E. Birren & K. W. Schaie (Eds.), *Handbook of the psychology of aging* (5th ed.). San Diego: Academic Press.

Antonucci, T. C., & Akiyama, H. (1991). Social relationships and aging well. *Generations, 15*, 39–44.

Apgar, V. (1953). A proposal for a new method of evaluation in the newborn infant. *Current research in anesthesia and analgesia, 32*, p. 260. Lippincott Williams & Wilkins.

Apperly, I., & Robinson, E. (2002). Five-year-olds' handling of reference and description in the domains of language and mental representation. *Journal of Experimental Child Psychology, 83*, 53–75.

Apter, A., Galatzer, A., Beth-Halachmi, N., & Laron, Z. (1981). Self-image in adolescents with delayed puberty and growth retardation. *Journal of Youth and Adolescence, 10*, 501–505.

Arai, M. (2006, January). Elder abuse in Japan. *Educational Gerontology, 32*, 13–23.

Archer, S. L., & Waterman, A. S. (1994). Adolescent identity development: Contextual perspectives. In C. B. Fisher & R. M. Lerner (Eds.), *Applied developmental psychology*. New York: McGraw-Hill.

Arenson, K. W. (2004, December 3). Worried colleges step up efforts over suicide. *The New York Times*, p. A1.

Aries, P. (1962). *Centuries of childhood*. New York: Knopf.

Arkoff, A., Meredith, G., & Dubanoski, J. (2004). Gains in well-being achieved through retrospective-proactive life review by independent older women. *Journal of Humanistic Psychology, 44*, 204–214.

Arnett, J. J. (2000). Emerging adulthood: A theory of development from the late teens through the twenties. *American Psychologist, 55*, 469–480.

Arnold, R., & Colburn, N. (2007) Brain food. *School Library Journal, 53*, 29.

Arredondo, E., Elder, J., Ayala, G., Campbell, N., Baquero, B., & Duerksen, S. (2006, December). Is parenting style related to children's healthy eating and physical activity in Latino families? *Health Education Research, 21*, 862–871.

Arseneault, L., Moffitt, T. E., & Caspi, A. (2003). Strong genetic effects on cross-situational antisocial behavior among 5-year-old children according to mothers, teachers, examiner-observers, and twins' self-reports. *Journal of Child Psychology and Psychiatry and Allied Disciplines, 44*, 832–848.

Artal, P., Ferro, M., Miranda, I., & Navarro, R. (1993). Effects of aging in retinal image quality. *Journal of the Optical Society of America, 10*, 1656–1662.

Asch, D. A. (1996, May 23). The role of critical care nurses in euthanasia and assisted suicide. *The New England Journal of Medicine, 334*, 1374–1379.

Asendorpf, J. B., Warkentin, V., & Baudonniere, P. (1996). Self-awareness and other-awareness II: Mirror self-recognition, social contingency awareness, and synchronic imitation. *Developmental Psychology, 32*, 313–321.

Asher, S. & Rose, A. (1997). Promoting children's social-emotional adjustment with peers. *Emotional development and emotional intelligence: Educational implications* (pp. 196–230). New York, NY: Basic Books.

Asher, S. R., Singleton, L. C., & Taylor, A. R. (1982). Acceptance vs. friendship. Paper presented at the meeting of the American Research Association, New York.

Askham, J. (1994). Marriage relationships of older people. *Reviews in Clinical Gerontology, 4*, 261–268.

Aslin, R. N. (1987). Visual and auditory development in infancy. In J. D. Osofsky (Ed.), *Handbook of infant development* (2nd ed.). New York: Wiley.

Atchley, R. (2003). Why most people cope well with retirement. In J. Ronch & J. Goldfield (Eds.), *Mental wellness in aging: Strengths-based approaches*. Baltimore, MD: Health Professions Press.

Atchley, R. C. (2000). *Social forces and aging* (9th ed.). Belmont, CA: Wadsworth Thomson Learning.

Atchley, R. C., & Barusch, A. (2005). *Social forces and aging* (10th ed.). Belmont, CA: Wadsworth.

Attie, I., & Brooks-Gunn, J. (1989). The development of eating problems in adolescent girls: A longitudinal study. *Developmental Psychology, 25*, 70–79.

Auestad, N., Scott, D. T., Janowsky, J. S., Jacobsen, C., Carroll, R. E., Montalto, M. B., & Halter, R…Hall, R. T. (2003). Visual cognitive and language assessments at 39 months: A follow-up study of children fed formulas containing long-chain polyunsaturated fatty acids to 1 year of age. *Pediatarics, 112*, e177–e183.

Aviezer, O., Sagi, A., & Resnick, G. (2002). School competence in young adolescence: Links to early attachment relationships beyond concurrent self-perceived competence and representations of relationships. *International Journal of Behavioral Development, 26*, 397–409.

Avlund, K., Lund, R., & Holstein, B. (2004). Social relations as determinant of onset of disability in aging. *Archives of Gerontology and Geriatrics, 38*, 85–99.

Axia, G., Bonichini, S., & Benini, F. (1995). Pain in infancy: Individual differences. *Perceptual and Motor Skills, 81*, 142.

Aylward, G. P., & Verhulst, S. J. (2000). Predictive utility of the Bayley Infant Neurodevelopmental Screener (BINS) risk status classifications: Clinical interpretation and application. *Developmental Medicine and Child Neurology, 42*, 25–31.

Ayoub, N. C. (2005, February 25). A pleasing birth: Midwives and maternity care in the Netherlands. *Chronicle of Higher Education*, p. 9.

Bacchus, L., Mezey, G., & Bewley, S. (2006). A qualitative exploration of the nature of domestic violence in pregnancy. *Violence Against Women, 12*, 588–604.

Bader, A. P. (1995). Engrossment revisited: Fathers are still falling in love with their newborn babies. In J. L. Shaptro, M. J. Diamond, & M. Grenberg (Eds.), *Becoming a father*. New York: Springer.

Baer, J. S., Sampson, P. D., & Barr, H. M. (2003). A 21-year longitudinal analysis of the effects of prenatal alcohol exposure on young adult drinking. *Archives of General Psychiatry, 60*, 377–385.

Baillargeon, R. (2004). Infants' physical world. *Current Directions in Psychological Science, 13*, 89–94.

Baird, A., John, R., & Hayslip, Jr., B. (2000). Custodial grandparenting among African Americans: A focus group perspective. In B. Hayslip, Jr. and R. Goldberg-Glen (Eds.), *Grandparents raising grandchildren: Theoretical, empirical, and clinical perspectives*. New York: Springer.

Bajor, J., & Baltes, B. (2003). The relationship between selection optimization with compensation, conscientiousness, motivation, and performance. *Journal of Vocational Behavior, 63*, 347–367.

Baker, M. (2007, December). Elder mistreatment: Risk, vulnerability, and early mortality. *Journal of the American Psychiatric Nurses Association, 12*, 313–321.

Baker, T., Brandon, T., & Chassin, L. (2004). Motivational influences on cigarette smoking. *Annual Review of Psychology, 55*, 463–491.

Bakker, A., & Heuven, E. (2006, November). Emotional dissonance, burnout, and in-role performance among nurses and police officers. *International Journal of Stress Management, 13*, 423–440.

Ball, K., & Rebok, G. W. (1994). Evaluating the driving ability of older adults. [Special Issue: Research translation in gerontology: A behavioral and social perspective], *Journal of Applied Gerontology, 13*, 20–38.

Ball, M., & Orford, J. (2002). Meaningful patterns of activity amongst the long-term inner city unemployed: A qualitative study. *Journal of Community and Applied Social Psychology, 12*, 377–396.

Ballen, L., and Fulcher, A. (2006). Nurses and doulas: Complementary roles to provide optimal maternity care. *Journal of Obstetric, Gynecologic, and Neonatal Nursing: Clinical Scholarship for the Care of Women, Childbearing Families, and Newborns, 35*, 304–311.

Baltes, M., & Carstensen, L. (2003). The process of successful aging: Selection, optimization and compensation. In U. Staudinger & U. Lindenberger (Eds.), *Understanding human development: Dialogues with lifespan psychology*. Netherlands: Kluwer Academic Publishers.

Baltes, M. M. (1996). *The many faces of dependency in old age*. New York: Cambridge University Press.

Baltes, P., & Freund, A. (2003a). Human strengths as the orchestration of wisdom and selective optimization with compensation. In L. Aspinwall & U. Staudinger (Eds.), *A psychology of human strengths: Fundamental questions and future directions for a positive psychology*. Washington, DC: American Psychological Association.

Baltes, P., and Freund, A. (2003b). The intermarriage of wisdom and selective optimization with compensation: Two meta-heuristics guiding the conduct of life. In C. Keyes & J. Haidt (Eds.), *Flourishing: Positive psychology and the life well-lived*. Washington, DC: American Psychological Association.

Baltes, P. B. (2003). On the incomplete architecture of human ontogeny: Selection, optimization and compensation as foundation of developmental theory. In U. M. Staudinger & U. Lindenberger (Eds.), *Understanding human development: Dialogues with lifespan psychology*. Dordrecht, Netherlands: Kluwer Academic Publishers.

Baltes, P. B., and Baltes, M. M. (1990). Psychological perspectives on successful aging: The model of selective optimization with compensation. In P. B. Baltes & M. M. Baltes (Eds.), *Successful aging: Perspectives from the behavioral sciences*. Cambridge, England: Cambridge University Press.

Baltes, P. B., & Staudinger, U. M. (2000). Wisdom: A meta-heuristic (pragmatic) to orchestrate mind and virtue toward excellence. *American Psychologist, 55*, 122–136.

Baltes, P. B., Staudinger, U. M., & Lindenberger, U. (1999). Lifespan psychology: Theory and application to intellectual functioning. *Annual Review of Psychology, 50*, 471–507.

Bamshad, M. J., & Olson, S. E. (2003, December). Does race exist? *Scientific American*, 78–85.

Bamshad, M. J., et al. (2003). Human population genetic structure and inference of group membership. *American Journal of Human Genetics, 72*, 578–589.

Bandura, A. (1977). *Social learning theory*. Englewood Cliffs, NJ: Prentice-Hall.

Bandura, A. (1994). Social cognitive theory of mass communication. In J. Bryant & D. Zillmann (Eds.), *Media effects: Advances in theory and research. LEA's communication series*. Hillsdale, NJ: Erlbaum.

Bandura, A. (2002). Social cognitive theory in cultural context. *Applied Psychology: An International Review, 51* [Special Issue], 269–290.

Bandura, A., Grusec, J. E., & Menlove, F. L. (1967). Vicarious extinction of avoidance behavior. *Journal of Personality and Social Psychology, 5*, 16–23.

Bandura, A., Ross, D., & Ross, S. (1963). Vicarious extinction of avoidance behavior. *Journal of Personality and Social Psychology, 67,* 601–607.

Barberá, E. (2003). Gender schemas: Configuration and activation processes. *Canadian Journal of Behavioural Science, 35,* 176–180.

Barer, B. M. (1994). Men and women aging differently. *International Journal of Aging and Human Development, 38,* 29–40.

Barinaga, M. (2000, June 23). A critical issue for the brain. *Science, 288,* 2116–2119.

Barker, V., Giles, H., & Noels, K. (2001). The English-only movement: A communication analysis of changing perceptions of language vitality. *Journal of Communication, 51,* 3–37.

Barnett, R. C., & Hyde, J. S. (2001). Women, men, work, and family. *American Psychologist, 56,* 781–796.

Barrett, D. E., & Frank, D. A. (1987). *The effects of undernutrition on children's behavior.* New York: Gordon and Breach.

Barrett, S. P. (2010). The effects of nicotine, denicotinized tobacco, and nicotine-containing tobacco on cigarette craving, withdrawal, and self-administration in male and female smokers. *Behavioural Pharmacology 21,* 144–152.

Barton, L. J. (1997, July). A shoulder to lean on: Assisted living in the U.S. *American Demographics,* 45–51.

Bashore, T. R., Ridderinkhof, K. R., & van der Molen, M. W. (1998). The decline of cognitive processing speed in old age. *Current Directions in Psychological Science, 6,* 163–169.

Bass, S., Shields, M. K., & Behrman, R. E. (2004). Children, families, and foster care: Analysis and recommendations. *The Future of Children, 14,* 5–30.

Basseches, M. (1984). *Dialectical thinking and adult development.* Norwood, NJ: Ablex.

Bates, J. E., Marvinney, D., Kelly, T., Dodge, K. A., Bennett, D. S., & Pettit, G. S. (1994). Child-care history and kindergarten adjustment. *Developmental Psychology, 30,* 690–700.

Bauer, P. J. (2004). Getting explicit memory off the ground: Steps toward construction of a neuro-developmental account of changes in the first two years of life. *Developmental Review, 24* [Special Issue: Memory development in the new millennium], 347–373.

Bauer, P. J., Wiebe, S. A., Carver, L. J., Waters, J. M., & Nelson, C. A. (2003). Developments in long-term explicit memory late in the first year of life: Behavioral and electrophysiological indices. *Psychological Science, 14,* 629–635.

Baum, A. (1994). Behavioral, biological, and environmental interactions in disease processes. In S. Blumenthal, K. Matthews, & S. Weiss (Eds.), *New research frontiers in behavioral medicine: Proceedings of the National Conference.* Washington, DC: NIH Publications.

Baumrind, D. (1971). Current patterns of parental authority. *Developmental Psychology Monographs, 4* (1, pt. 2).

Baumrind, D. (1980). New directions in socialization research. *Psychological Bulletin, 35,* 639–652.

Baydar, N., & Brooks-Gunn, J. (1998). Profiles of grandmothers who help care for their grandchildren in the United States. *Family Relations, 47,* 385–393.

Bayley, N. (1969). *Manual for the Bayley scales of infant development.* New York: The Psychological Corporation.

Bayley, N., & Oden, M. (1955). The maintenance of intellectual ability in gifted adults. *Journal of Gerontology, 10,* 91–107.

Beach, B. A. (2003). Rural children's play in the natural environment. In D. E. Lytle (Ed.), *Play and educational theory and practice.* Westport, CT: Praeger Publishers/Greenwood Publishing Group.

Beal, C. R. (1994). *Boys and girls: The development of gender roles.* New York: McGraw-Hill.

Beal, C. R., & Belgrad, S. L. (1990). The development of message evaluation skills in young children. *Child Development, 61,* 705–712.

Beals, K., Impett, E., & Peplau, L. (2002). Lesbians in love: Why some relationships endure and others end. *Journal of Lesbian Studies, 6,* 53–63.

Bearce, K., & Rovee-Collier, C. (2006). Repeated priming increases memory accessibility in infants. *Journal of Experimental Child Psychology, 93,* 357–376.

Beardslee, W. R., & Goldman, S. (2003, September 22.) Living beyond sadness. *Newsweek,* p. 70.

Bearman, P., & Bruckner, H. (2004). Study on teenage virginity pledge. Paper presented at meeting of the National STD Prevention Conference, Philadelphia, PA.

Beauchaine, T. P. (2003). Taxometrics and developmental psychopathology. *Development and Psychopathology: Special Issue, 15,* 501–527.

Beaupre, P. (2008, July). I do…take two? Changes in intentions to remarry among divorced Canadians during the past 20 years. Statistics Canada Catalogue no. 89-630-x. Retrieved from http://www.statcan.gc.ca/pub/89-630-x/2008001/article/10659-eng.pdf.

Becker, B., & Luthar, S. (2007, March). Peer-perceived admiration and social preference: Contextual correlates of positive peer regard among suburban and urban adolescents. *Journal of Research on Adolescence, 17,* 117–144.

Becker, G., Beyene, Y., & Newsom, E. (2003). Creating continuity through mutual assistance: Intergenerational reciprocity in four ethnic groups. *Journals of Gerontology: Series B: Psychological Sciences and Social Sciences, 58B,* S151–S159.

Beckman, M. (2004, July 30). Neuroscience: Crime, culpability, and the adolescent brain. *Science,* pp. 305, 596–599.

Becvar, D. S. (2000). Euthanasia decisions. In F. W. Kaslow et al. (Eds.), *Handbook of couple and family forensics: A sourcebook for mental health and legal professionals.* New York: Wiley.

Beehr, T. A., Glazer, S., Nielson, N. L., & Farmer, S. J. (2000). Work and nonwork predictors of employees' retirement ages. *Journal of Vocational Behavior, 57,* 206–225.

Beilin, H. (1996). Mind and meaning: Piaget and Vygotsky on causal explanation. *Human Development, 39,* 277–286.

Beilin, H., & Pufall, P. (Eds.). (1992). *Piaget's theory: Prospects and possibilities.* Hillsdale, NJ: Erlbaum.

Belcher, J. R. (2003). Stepparenting: Creating and recreating families in America today. *Journal of Nervous and Mental Disease, 191,* 837–838.

Bell, A., & Weinberg, M. S. (1978). *Homosexuality: A study of diversities among men and women.* New York: Simon and Schuster.

Bell, I. P. (1989). The double standard: Age. In J. Freeman (Ed.), *Women: A feminist perspective* (4th ed.). Mountain View, CA: Mayfield.

Belle, D. (1999). *The after-school lives of children: Alone and with others while parents work.* Mahwah, NJ: Erlbaum.

Belsky, J., Rovine, M., & Taylor, D. G. (1984). The Pennsylvania infant and family development project, III: The origins of individual differences in infant–mother attachment: Maternal and infant contributions. *Child Development, 55,* 718–728.

Belsky, J., Vandell, D. L., Burchinal, M., Clarke-Stewart, A. K., McCartney, K., & Owen, M. T. (2007). Are there long-term effects of early child care? *Child Development, 78,* 188–193.

Bender, H., Allen, J., McElhaney, K., Antonishak, J., Moore, C., Kelly, H., et al. (2007, December). Use of harsh physical discipline and developmental outcomes in adolescence. *Development and Psychopathology, 19,* 227–242.

Benedict, H. (1979). Early lexical development: Comprehension and production. *Journal of Child Language, 6,* 183–200.

Benelli, B., Belacchi, C., Gini, G., & Lucangeli, D. (2006, February). "To define means to say what you know about things": The development of definitional skills as metalinguistic acquisition. *Journal of Child Language, 33,* 71–97.

Benenson, J. F., & Apostoleris, N. H. (1993, March). Gender differences in group interaction in early childhood. Paper presented at the biennial meeting of the Society for Research in Child Development, New Orleans, LA.

Bengtson, V. L., Cutler, N. E., Mangen, D. J., & Marshall, V. W. (1985). Generations, cohorts, and relations between age groups. In R. H. Binstock & E. Shanas (Eds.), *Handbook of aging and the social sciences* (2nd ed.). New York: Van Nostrand Reinhold.

Benjamin, J., Ebstein, R. P., & Belmaker, R. H. (2002). Personality genetics, 2002. *Israel Journal of Psychiatry and Related Sciences* [Special Issue], *39,* 271–279.

Benjuya, N., Melzer, I., & Kaplanski, J. (2004). Aging-induced shifts from a reliance on sensory input to muscle cocontraction during balanced standing. *Journal of Gerontology, Series A: Biological Sciences and Medical Sciences, 59,* 166–171.

Benson, E. (2003, March). "Goo, gaa, grr?" *Monitor on Psychology,* 50–51.

Benson, H. (1993). The relaxation response. In D. Goleman & J. Guerin (Eds.), *Mind–body medicine: How to use your mind for better health.* Yonkers, NY: Consumer Reports Publications.

Benton, S. A., Robertson, J. M., Tseng, W-C., Newton, F. B., & Benton, S. L. (2003). Changes in counseling center client problems across 13 years. *Professional Psychology: Research and Practice, 34,* 66–72.

Berenbaum, S. A., & Bailey, J. M. (2003). Effects on gender identity of prenatal androgens and genital appearance: Evidence from girls with congenital adrenal hyperplasia. *Journal of Clinical Endocrinology and Metabolism, 88,* 1102–1106.

Berenbaum, S. A., & Hines, M. (1992). Early androgens are related to sex-typed toy preferences. *Psychological Science, 3,* 202–206.

Berenson, P. (2005). *Understand and treat alcoholism.* New York: Basic Books.

Bergen, H., Martin, G., & Richardson, A. (2003). Sexual abuse and suicidal behavior: A model constructed from a large community sample of adolescents. *Journal of the American Academy of Child and Adolescent Psychiatry, 42,* 1301–1309.

Berger, L. (2000, April 11). What children do when home and alone. *New York Times,* p. F8.

Bergstrom, M. J., & Holmes, M. E. (2000). Lay theories of successful aging after the death of a spouse: A network text analysis of bereavement advice. *Health Communication, 12,* 377–406.

Berkman, R. (Ed.) (2006). *Handbook of social work in health and aging.* New York: Oxford University Press.

Berko, J. (1958). The child's learning of English morphology. *Word, 14,* 150–177.

Bernard, J. (1982). *The future of marriage.* New Haven, CT: Yale University Press.

Berndt, T. J. (1999). Friends' influence on students' adjustment to school. *Educational Psychologist, 34,* 15–28.

Berndt, T. J. (2002). Friendship quality and social development. *Current Directions in Psychological Science, 11,* 7–10.

Berry, G. L. (2003). Developing children and multicultural attitudes: The systemic psychosocial influences of television portrayals in a multimedia society. *Cultural Diversity and Ethnic Minority Psychology, 9,* 360–366.

Berry, J. W., Poortinga, Y. H., Segall, M. H., & Dasen, P. (1992). *Cross-cultural psychology: Research and application.* New York: Cambridge University Press.

Berscheid, E. (1985). Interpersonal attraction. In G. Lindzey & E. Aronson (Eds.), *Handbook of social psychology* (3rd ed.). New York: Random House.

Berscheid, E., & Walster, E. (1974). Physical attractiveness. In G. Lindzey & E. Aronson (Eds.), *Handbook of social psychology* (3rd ed.). New York: Random House.

Bertin, E., & Striano, T. (2006, April). The still-face response in newborn, 1.5-, and 3-month-old infants. *Infant Behavior and Development, 29,* 294–297.

Besharov, D. J., & West, A. (2002). African American marriage patterns. In A. Thernstrom & S. Thernstrom (Eds.), *Beyond the color line: New perspectives on race and ethnicity in America.* Stanford, CA: Hoover Institution Press.

Bialystok, E., Craik, F. I. M., & Freedman, M. (2007). Bilingualism as a protection against the onset of symptoms of dementia. *Neuropsychologia, 45,* 459–464.

Bianchi, S. M., & Casper, L. M. (2000). American Families. *Population Bulletin, 55(4).*

Biedenharn, B. J., & Normoyle, J. B. (1991). Elderly community residents' reactions to the nursing home: An analysis of nursing home-related beliefs. *Gerontologist, 31,* 107–115.

Bierman, K. L., & Furman, W. (1984). The effects of social skills training and peer involvement on the social adjustment of preadolescents. *Child Development, 55,* 151–162.

Bigelow, A., & Rochat, P. (2006). Two-month-old infants' sensitivity to social contingency in mother–infant and stranger–infant interaction. *Infancy, 9,* 313–325.

Bigelow, A. E., & Power, M. (2012). The effect of mother–infant skin-to-skin contact on infants' response to the still face task from newborn to three months of age. *Infant Behavior and Development, 35,* 240–251.

Bigler, R. S., Jones, L. C., & Lobliner, D. B. (1997). Social categorization and the formation of intergroup attitudes in children. *Child Development, 68,* 530–543.

Bijeljac-Babic, R., Bertoncini, J., & Mehler, J. (1993). How do 4-day-old infants categorize multisyllabic utterances? *Developmental Psychology, 29,* 711–721.

Bionna, R. (2006). *Coping with stress in a changing world.* New York: McGraw-Hill.

Birch, E. E., Garfield, S., Hoffman, D. R., Uauy, R., & Birch, D. G. (2000). A randomized controlled trail of early dietary supply of long-chain polyunsaturated fatty acids and mental development in term infants. *Developmental Medicine and Child Neurology, 42,* 174–181.

Bird, G., & Melville, K. (1994). *Families and intimate relationships.* New York: McGraw-Hill.

Birkhauser, M. H., Panay, N., Archer, D. F., Barlow, D., Burger, H., Gambacciani, M., et al. (2008). Updated practical recommendations for hormone replacement therapy in the peri- and postmenopause. *Climacteric, 11(2),* 108–123.

Birlouez-Aragon, I., & Tessier, F. (2003). Antioxidant vitamins and degenerative pathologies: A review of vitamin C. *Journal of Nutrition, Health and Aging, 7,* 103–109.

Birney, D. P., & Sternberg, R. J. (2006). Intelligence and cognitive abilities as competencies in development. In E. Bialystok and F. I. M. Craik (Eds.), *Lifespan cognition: Mechanisms of change.* New York: Oxford University Press.

Biro, F., Striegel-Moore, R., Franko, D., Padgett, J., & Bean, J. (2006, October). Self-esteem in adolescent females. *Journal of Adolescent Health, 39,* 501–507.

Bishop, D. V. M., & Leonard, L. B. (Eds.). (2001). *Speech and language impairments in children: Causes, characteristics, intervention and outcome.* Philadelphia, PA: Psychology Press.

Bishop, J. (2006, April). Euthanasia, efficiency, and the historical distinction between killing a patient and allowing a patient to die. *Journal of Medical Ethics, 32,* 220–224.

Bjorklund, D. F. (1997). In search of a metatheory of cognitive development (or Piaget is dead and I don't feel so good myself). *Child Development, 68,* 144–148.

Bjorklund, D. F., & Hernandez Blasi, C. (2005). Evolutionary developmental psychology. In D. Buss (Ed.), *Evolutionary psychology handbook* (pp. 828–850). New York: Wiley.

Bjorklund, D. F., Schneider, W., Cassel, W. S., & Ashley, E. (1994). Training and extension of a memory strategy: Evidence of utilization deficiencies in the acquisition of an organizational strategy in high- and low-IQ children. *Child Development, 65,* 951–965.

Black, M. M., and Matula, K. (1999). *Essentials of Bayley Scales of Infant Development II assessment.* New York: Wiley.

Blaine, B. E., Rodman, J., and Newman, J. M. (2007). Weight loss treatment and psychological well-being: A review and meta-analysis. *Journal of Health Psychology, 12,* 66–82.

Blair, S. N., Kohl, H. W., Paffenberger, R. S., Clark, D. G., Cooper, K. H., and Gibbons, L. W. (1989). Physical fitness and all-cause mortality: A prospective study of healthy men and women. *Journal of the American Medical Association, 262,* 2395–2401.

Blais, J. J., Craig, W. M., Pepler, D., & Connolly, J. (2008). Adolescents online: The importance of internet activity choices to salient relationships. *Journal of Youth and Adolescence, 37,* 522–536. doi: 10.1007/s10964-007-9262-7.

Blake, J., & de Boysson-Bardies, B. (1992). Patterns in babbling: A cross-linguistic study. *Journal of Child Language, 19,* 51–74.

Blakemore, J. (2003). Children's beliefs about violating gender norms: Boys shouldn't look like girls, and girls shouldn't act like boys. *Sex Roles, 48,* 411–419.

Blank, M., & White, S. J. (1999). Activating the zone of proximal development in school: Obstacles and solutions. In P. Lloyd & C. Fernyhough (Eds.), *Lev Vygotsky: Critical assessments: The zone of proximal development, Vol. III.* New York: Routledge.

Blasi, H., & Bjorklund, D. F. (2003). Evolutionary developmental psychology: A new tool for better understanding human ontogeny. *Human Development, 46,* 259–281.

Blass, E. M., Ganchrow, J. R., & Steiner, J. E. (1984). Classical conditioning in newborn humans 2–48 hours of age. *Infant Behavior and Development, 7,* 223–235.

Blennow, K., & Vanmechelen, E. (2003). CSF markers for pathogenic processes in Alzheimer's disease: Diagnostic implications and use in clinical neurochemistry. *Brain Research Bulletin, 61,* 235–242.

Bloom, C., & Lamkin, D. (2006). The Olympian struggle to remember the cranial nerves: Mnemonics and student success. *Teaching of Psychology, 33,* 128–129.

Bloom, L. (1993). *The transition from infancy to language: Acquiring the power of expression.* New York: Cambridge University Press.

Blount, B. G. (1982). Culture and the language of socialization: Parental speech. In D. A. Wagner & H. W. Stevenson (Eds.), *Cultural perspectives on child development.* San Francisco: Freeman.

Blumberg, B. D., Lewis, M. J., & Susman, E. J. (1984). Adolescence: A time of transition. In M. G. Eisenberg, L. C. Sutkin, & M. A. Jansen (Eds.), *Chronic illness and disability through the life span: Effects on self and family.* New York: Springer.

Blumenthal, S. (2000). Developmental aspects of violence and the institutional response. *Criminal Behaviour and Mental Health, 10,* 185–198.

Blumstein, P., & Schwartz, P. (1989). *American couples: Money, work, sex.* New York: Morrow.

Blundon, J., & Schaefer, C. (2006). The role of parent–child play in children's development. *Psychology and Education: An Interdisciplinary Journal, 43,* 1–10.

Bober, S., Humphry, R., & Carswell, H. (2001). Toddlers' persistence in the emerging occupations of functional play and self-feeding. *American Journal of Occupational Therapy, 55,* 369–376.

Bochner, S. (1996). The learning strategies of bilingual versus monolingual students. *British Journal of Educational Psychology, 66,* 83–93.

Boehm, K. E., & Campbell, N. B. (1995). Suicide: A review of calls to an adolescent peer listening phone service. *Child Psychiatry and Human Development, 26(1),* pp. 61–66.

Boerner, K., Wortman, C. B., & Bonanno, G. A. (2005). Resilient or at risk? A 4-year study of older adults who initially showed high or low distress following conjugal loss. *Journal of Gerontology, B, Psychological Sciences and Social Sciences, 60,* P67–P73.

Bohlmeijer, E., Smit, F., & Cuijpers, P. (2003). Effects of reminiscence and life review on late-life depression: A meta-analysis. *International Journal of Geriatric Psychiatry, 18,* 1088–1094.

Bonanno, G., Galea, S., Bucciarelli, A., & Vlahov, D. (2006). Psychological resilience after disaster: New York City in the aftermath of the September 11th terrorist attack. *Psychological Science, 17,* 181–186.

Bonanno, G. A. (2004). Loss, trauma, and human resilience: Have we underestimated the human capacity to thrive after extremely aversive events? *American Psychologist, 59,* 20–28.

Bonanno, G. A., Wortman, C. B., Lehman, D. R., Tweed, R. G., Haring, M., Sonnega, J., et al. (2002). Resilience to loss and chronic grief: A prospective study from preloss to 18-months postloss. *Journal of Personality and Social Psychology, 83,* 1150–1164.

Bonke, B., Tibben, A., Lindhout, D., Clarke, A. J., & Stijnen, T. (2005). Genetic risk estimation by healthcare professionals. *Medical Journal of Autism, 182,* 116–118.

Bookheimer, S. Y., Strojwas, M. H., Cophen, M. S., Saunders, A. M., Pericak-Vance, M. A., Mazziotta, J. C., & Small, G. W. (2000, August 17). Patterns of brain activation in people at risk for Alzheimer's disease. *New England Journal of Medicine, 343,* 450–456.

Bookstein, F. L., Sampson, P. D., Streissguth, A. P., & Barr, H. M. (1996). Exploiting redundant measurement of dose and developmental outcome: New methods from the behavioral teratology of alcohol. *Developmental Psychology, 32,* 404–415.

Booth, W. (1987, October 2). Big Brother is counting your keystrokes. *Science, 238,* 17.

Bornstein, M., & Arterberry, M. (2003). Recognition, discrimination and categorization of smiling by 5-month-old infants. *Developmental Science, 6,* 585–599.

Bornstein, M. H., Cote, L., & Maital, S. (2004). Cross-linguistic analysis of vocabulary in young children: Spanish, Dutch, French, Hebrew, Italian, Korean, and American English. *Child Development, 75,* 1115–1139.

Bornstein, M. H., Putnick, D. L., Suwalsky, T. D., & Gini, M. (2006). Maternal chronological age, prenatal and perinatal history, social support, and parenting of infants. *Child Development, 77,* 875–892.

Boruch, R. F. (1998). Randomized controlled experiments for evaluation and planning. In L. Bickman & D. J. Rog (Eds.), *Handbook of applied social research methods* (pp. 161–191). Thousand Oaks, CA: Sage.

Bos, C. S., & Vaughn, S. S. (2005). *Strategies for teaching students with learning and behavior problems* (6th Ed.). Boston: Allyn and Bacon.

Bos, H., van Balen, F., & van den Boom, D. (2007, January). Child adjustment and parenting in planned lesbian-parent families. *American Journal of Orthopsychiatry, 77,* 38–48.

Botwin, M. D., Buss, D. M., & Shackelford, T. K. (1997). Personality and mate preferences: Five factors in mate selection and marital satisfaction. *Journal of Personality, 65,* 107–136.

Bouchard, T. J., Jr. (1997, September/October). Whenever the twain shall meet. *The Sciences,* 52–57.

Bouchard, T. J., Jr. (2004). Genetic influence on human psychological traits: A survey. *Current Directions in Psychological Science, 13,* 148–153.

Bouchard, T. J., Jr., Lykken, D. T., McGue, M., Segal, N. L., & Tellegen, A. (1990, October 12). Sources of human psychological differences: The Minnesota study of twins reared apart. *Science, 250,* 223–228.

Bouchard, T. J., & McGue, M. (1981). Familial studies of intelligence: A review. *Science, 212,* 1055–1059.

Bouchard, T. J., Jr., & Pedersen, N. (1999). Twins reared apart: Nature's double experiment. In M. C. LaBuda, E. L. Grigorenko, et al. (Eds.), *On the way to individuality: Current methodological issues in behavioral genetics.* Commack, NY: Nova.

Boulton, M. J., and Smith, P. K. (1990). Affective bias in children's perceptions of dominance relationships. *Child Development, 61,* 221–229.

Bourne, V., & Todd, B. (2004). When left means right: An explanation of the left cradling bias in terms of right hemisphere specializations. *Developmental Science, 7,* 19–24.

Bowen, N. K., & Bowen, G. L. (1999). Effects of crime and violence in neighborhoods and schools on the school behavior and performance of adolescents. *Journal of Adolescent Research, 14,* 319–342.

Bower, T. G. R. (1977). *A primer of infant development*. San Francisco: Freeman.

Bowers, K. E., & Thomas, P. (1995, August). Handle with care. *Harvard Health Letter*, pp. 6–7.

Boyd, M. (1974). Family size ideals of Canadians. A methodological note. *Canadian Review of Sociology & Anthropology, 11, 4*, 360–371.

Bracey, J., Bamaca, M., & Umana-Taylor, A. (2004). Examining ethnic identity and self-esteem among biracial and monoracial adolescents. *Journal of Youth and Adolescence, 33*, 123–132.

Bracken, B., & Brown, E. (2006, June). Behavioral identification and assessment of gifted and talented students. *Journal of Psychoeducational Assessment, 24*, 112–122.

Bracken, B., & Lamprecht, M. (2003). Positive self-concept: An equal opportunity construct. *School Psychology Quarterly, 18*, 103–121.

Brainerd, C. (2003). Jean Piaget, learning research, and American education. In B. Zimmerman (Ed.), *Educational psychology: A century of contributions*. Mahwah, NJ: Lawrence Erlbaum Associates.

Branje, S. J. T., van Lieshout, C. F. M., van Aken, M. A. G., & Haselager, G. J. T. (2004). Perceived support in sibling relationships and adolescent adjustment. *Journal of Child Psychology and Psychiatry, 45*, 1385–1396.

Brant, M. (2003, September 8). Log on and learn. *Newsweek*, E14.

Brant Castellano, M. (2008). Reflections on identity and empowerment: Recurring themes in the discourse on and with Aboriginal youth. *Horizons, 10*(1), 7–12.

Branum, A. (2006). Teen maternal age and very preterm birth of twins. *Maternal and Child Health Journal, 10*, 229–233.

Braun, K. L., Pietsch, J. H., & Blanchette, P. L. (Eds.). (2000). *Cultural issues in end-of-life decision making*. Thousand Oaks, CA: Sage Publications.

Brazelton, T. B. (1973). *The neonatal behavioral assessment scale*. Philadelphia: Lippincott.

Brazelton, T. B. (1983). *Infants and mothers: Differences in development* (Rev. ed.). New York: Dell.

Brazelton, T. B. (1990). Saving the bathwater. *Child Development, 61*, 1661–1671.

Brazelton, T. B. (1997). *Toilet training your child*. New York: Consumer Visions.

Brazelton, T. B., Christophersen, E. R., Frauman, A. C., Gorski, P. A., Poole, J. M., Stadtler, A. C., & Wright, C. L. (1999). Instruction, timeliness, and medical influences affecting toilet training. *Pediatrics, 103*, 1353–1358.

Brazelton, T. B., & Sparrow, J. D. (2003). *Discipline: The Brazelton way*. New York: Perseus.

Brecher, E. M., & the Editors of Consumer Reports Books. (1984). *Love, sex, and aging*. Mount Vernon, New York: Consumers Union.

Breedlove, G. (2005). Perceptions of social support from pregnant and parenting teens using community-based doulas. *Journal of Perinatal Education, 14*, 15–22.

Breheny, M., & Stephens, C. (2003). Healthy living and keeping busy: A discourse analysis of mid-aged women's attributions for menopausal experience. *Journal of Language and Social Psychology, 22*, 169–189.

Brehm, K. (2003). Lessons to be learned at the end of the day. *School Psychology Quarterly, 18*, 88–95.

Brehm, S. S. (1992). *Intimate relationships* (2nd ed.). New York: McGraw-Hill.

Bremmer, J. D. (2003). Long-term effects of childhood abuse on brain and neurobiology. *Child Adolescent Psychiatric Clinics of North America, 12*, 271–292.

Bridges, J. S. (1993). Pink or blue: Gender-stereotypic perceptions of infants as conveyed by birth congratulations cards. *Psychology of Women Quarterly, 17*, 193–205.

Brody, N. (1993). Intelligence and the behavioral genetics of personality. In R. Plomin & G. E. McClearn (Eds.), *Nature, nurture, and psychology*. Washington, DC: American Psychological Association.

Bromberger, J. T., & Matthews, K. A. (1994). Employment status and depressive symptoms in middle-aged women: A longitudinal investigation. *American Journal of Public Health, 84*, 202–206.

Brook, U., & Tepper, I. (1997). High school students' attitudes and knowledge of food consumption and body image: Implications for school-based education. *Patient Education and Counseling, 30*, 282–288.

Brooks-Gunn, J. (2003). Do you believe in magic? What we can expect from early childhood intervention programs. *Social Policy Report, 17*, 1–16.

Brown, A. L., & Ferrara, R. A. (1999). Diagnosing zones of proximal development. In P. Llyod & C. Fernyhough (Eds.), *Lev Vygotsky: Critical assessments: The zone of proximal development, Vol. III*. New York: Routledge.

Brown, B. (1990). Peer groups. In S. Feldman & G. Elliott (Eds.), *At the threshold: The developing adolescent*. Cambridge, MA: Harvard University Press.

Brown, J. D. (1998). *The self*. New York: McGraw-Hill.

Brown, J. L., & Pollitt, E. (1996, February). Malnutrition, poverty and intellectual development. *Scientific American*, 38–43.

Brown, J. V., Bakeman, R., Coles, C. D., Platzman, K. A., & Lynch, M. E. (2004). Prenatal cocaine exposure: A comparison of 2-year-old children in prenatal and non-parental care. *Child Development, 75*, 1282–1295.

Brown, S. (2003). Relationship quality dynamics of cohabitating unions. *Journal of Family Issues, 24*, 583–601.

Brown, W. M., Hines, M., & Fane, B. A. (2002). Masculinized finger length patterns in human males and females with congenital adrenal hyperplasia. *Hormones and Behavior, 42*, 380–386.

Browne, A. (1993). Violence against women by male partners: Prevalence, outcomes, and policy implications. *American Psychologist, 48*, 1077–1087.

Browne, B. A. (1998). Gender stereotypes in advertising on children's television in the 1990s: A cross-national analysis. *Journal of Advertising, 27*, 83–96.

Browne, K. (2006, March). Evolved sex differences and occupational segregation. *Journal of Organizational Behavior, 27*, 143–162.

Brubaker, T. (1991). Families in later life: A burgeoning research area. In A. Booth (Ed.), *Contemporary families*. Minneapolis, MN: National Council on Family Relations.

Bruck, M., & Ceci, S. (2004). Forensic developmental psychology: Unveiling four common misconceptions. *Current Directions in Psychological Science, 13*, 229–232.

Brugman, G. (2006). *Wisdom and aging*. Amsterdam, Netherlands: Elsevier.

Bryant, C. D. (Ed.). (2003). *Handbook of death and dying*. Thousand Oaks, CA: Sage Publications.

Bryant, J., & Bryant, J. (2003). Effects of entertainment televisual media on children. In E. Palmer & B. Young (Eds.), *The faces of televisual media: Teaching, violence, selling to children*. Mahwah, NJ: Lawrence Erlbaum Associates.

Bryant, J., & Bryant, J. A. (Eds.). (2001). *Television and the American family* (2nd ed.). Mahwah, NJ: Lawrence Erlbaum.

Bryson, S. E., Zwaigenbaum, L., Brian, J., Roberts, W., Szatmari, P., Rombough, V., et al. (2007). A prospective case series of high-risk infants who developed autism. *Journal of Autism and Developmental Disorders, 37*, 12–24.

Buchanan, C. M., Eccles, J. S., & Becker, J. B. (1992). Are adolescents the victims of raging hormones? Evidence for activational effects of hormones on moods and behavior at adolescence. *Psychological Bulletin, 111*, 62–107.

Bugg, J., Zook, N., DeLosh, E., Davalos, D., & Davis, H. (2006, October). Age differences in fluid intelligence: Contributions of general slowing and frontal decline. *Brain and Cognition, 62*, 9–16.

Bukowski, W. M., Sippola, L. K., & Newcomb, A. F. (2000). Variations in patterns of attraction to same- and other-sex peers during early adolescence. *Developmental Psychology, 36*, 147–154.

Bullinger, A. (1997). Sensorimotor function and its evolution. In J. Guimon (Ed.), *The body in psychotherapy* (pp. 25–29). Basil, Switzerland: Karger.

Bumpass, L., Sweet, J., & Martin, T. (1990). Changing patterns of remarriage. *Journal of Marriage and the Family, 52*, 747–756.

Bumpus, M. F., Crouter, A. C., & McHale, S. M. (2001). Parental autonomy granting during adolescence: Exploring gender differences in context. *Developmental Psychology, 37*, 163–173.

Burd, L., Cotsonas-Hassler, T. M., Martsolf, J. T., & Kerbeshian, J. (2003). Recognition and management of fetal alcohol syndrome. *Neurotoxicological Teratology, 25*, 681–688.

Burgess, K. B., & Rubin, K. H. (2000). Middle childhood: Social and emotional development. In A. E. Kazdin (Ed.), *Encyclopedia of psychology, Vol. 5*. Washington, DC: American Psychological Association.

Burgess, R. L., & Huston, T. L. (Eds.). (1979). *Social exchanges in developing relationships*. New York: Academic Press.

Burke, V., Beilin, L., Durkin, K., Stritzke, W., Houghton, S., & Cameron, C. (2006, November). Television, computer use, physical activity, diet and fatness in Australian adolescents. *International Journal of Pediatric Obesity, 1*, 248–255.

Burnett, P., & Proctor, R. (2002). Elementary school students' learner self-concept, academic self-concepts and approaches to learning. *Educational Psychology in Practice, 18*, 325–333.

Burnham, M., Goodlin-Jones, B., & Gaylor, E. (2002). Nighttime sleep–wake patterns and self-soothing from birth to one year of age: A longitudinal intervention study. *Journal of Child Psychology and Psychiatry and Allied Disciplines, 43*, 713–725.

Burns, D. M. (2000). Cigarette smoking among the elderly: Disease consequences and the benefits of cessation. *American Journal of Health Promotion, 14*, 357–361.

Burrus-Bammel, L. L., & Bammel, G. (1985). Leisure and recreation. In J. E. Birren & K. W. Schaie (Eds.), *Handbook of the psychology of aging*. New York: Van Nostrand Reinhold.

Burt, V. L., & Harris, T. (1994). The third National Health and Nutrition Examination Survey: Contributing data on aging and health. *Gerontologist, 34*, 486–490.

Burton, A., Haley, W., & Small, B. (2006, May). Bereavement after caregiving or unexpected death: Effects on elderly spouses. *Aging and Mental Health, 10*, 319–326.

Bushman, B. J. (1993). Human aggression while under the influence of alcohol and other drugs: An integrative research review. *Current Directions in Psychological Science, 2*, 148–152.

Bushman, B. J., & Anderson, C. A. (2001). Media violence and the American public: Scientific facts versus media misinformation. *American Psychologist, 56*, 477–489.

Bushman, B. J., & Anderson, C. A. (2002). Violent video games and hostile expectations: A test of the general aggression model. *Personality and Social Psychology Bulletin, 28*, 1679–1689.

Bushnik, T. (2006). Child Care in Canada. Statistics Canada Catalogue No. 89-599-MIE. Ottawa. 99 p. Children and Youth Research Paper Series, No. 3. Retrieved from www.statcan.gc.ca/pub/89-599-m/89-599-m2006003-eng.pdf. Accessed March 11, 2011.

Buss, D. (2005, January 23). Sure, come back to the nest. Here are the rules. *The New York Times*, p. 8.

Buss, D. M. (2003b). *The evolution of desire: Strategies of human mating* (Revised ed.). New York: Basic Books.

Buss, D. M. (2004). *Evolutionary psychology: The new science of the mind* (2nd ed.). Boston: Allyn and Bacon.

Buss, D. M., et al. (1990). International preferences in selecting mates: A study of 37 cultures. *Journal of Cross-Cultural Psychology, 21*, 5–47.

Buss, K. A., & Kiel, E. J. (2004). Comparison of sadness, anger, and fear facial expressions when toddlers look at their mothers. *Child Development, 75*, 1761–1773.

Butler, K. G., & Silliman, E. R. (2002). *Speaking, reading, and writing in children with language learning disabilities: New paradigms in research and practice*. Mahwah, NJ: Lawrence Erlbaum Associates, Publishers, 2002.

Butler, R. N. (2002). The life review. *Journal of Geriatric Psychiatry, 35*, 7–10.

Butler, R. N., & Lewis, M. I. (1981). *Aging and mental health*. St. Louis: Mosby.

Butterworth, G. (1994). Infant intelligence. In J. Khalfa (Ed.), *What is intelligence? The Darwin College lecture series* (pp. 49–71). Cambridge, England: Cambridge University Press.

Byrne, A. (2000). Singular identities: Managing stigma, resisting voices. *Women's Studies Review, 7*, 13–24.

Cadinu, M. R., & Kiesner, J. (2000). Children's development of a theory of mind. *European Journal of Psychology of Education, 15*, 93–111.

Cain, B. S. (1982, December 19). Plight of the gray divorcee. *The New York Times Magazine*, 89–93.

Cain, V., Johannes, C., & Avis, N. (2003). Sexual functioning and practices in a multi-ethnic study of midlife women: Baseline results from SWAN. *Journal of Sex Research, 40*, 266–276.

Caino, S., Kelmansky, D., Lejarraga, H., & Adamo, P. (2004). Short-term growth at adolescence in healthy girls. *Annals of Human Biology, 31*, 182–195.

Calhoun, F., & Warren, K. (2007). Fetal alcohol syndrome: Historical perspectives. *Neuroscience and Biobehavioral Reviews, 31*, 168–171.

Callister, L. C., Khalaf, I., Semenic, S., Kartchner, R., & Vehvilainen-Julkunen, K. (2003). The pain of childbirth: Perceptions of culturally diverse women. *Pain Management Nursing, 4*, 145–154.

Calvert, S. L., Kotler, J. A., Zehnder, S., & Shockey, E. (2003). Gender stereotyping in children's reports about educational and informational television programs. *Media Psychology, 5*, 139–162.

Camarota, S. A. (2001). *Immigrants in the United States—2000: A snapshot of America's foreign-born population*. Washington, DC: Center for Immigration Studies.

Cami, J., & Farré, M. (2003). Drug addiction. *New England Journal of Medicine, 349*, 975–986.

Campbell, A., Shirley, L., & Candy, J. (2004). A longitudinal study of gender-related cognition and behaviour. *Developmental Science, 7*, 1–9.

Campbell, F., Ramey, C., & Pungello, E. (2002). Early childhood education: Young adult outcomes from the Abecedarian Project. *Applied Developmental Science, 6*, 42–57.

Campos, J. J., Langer, A., & Krowitz, A. (1970). Cardiac responses on the visual cliff in prelocomotor human infants. *Science, 170*, 196–197.

Camras, L., Meng, Z., Ujiie, T., Dharamsi, S., Miyake, K., Oster, H...Campos, J. (2002). Observing emotion in infants: Facial expression, body behavior, and rater judgments of responses to an expectancy-violating event. *Emotion, 2*, 179–193.

Canadian Cancer Society. (2011). Retrieved from http://www.cancer.ca/Canada-wide.aspx?sc_lang=en.

Canadian Cancer Society. (2011). Canadian Cancer Society's Steering Committee on Cancer Statistics. *Canadian Cancer Statistics 2011*. Toronto, ON: Canadian Cancer Society.

Canadian Institute for Health Information. (2009). *Children's mental health in Canada: Preventing disorders and promoting population health*. Ottawa, ON: CIHI.

Canadian Institute for Health Information. (2009). *Too early, too small: A profile of small babies across Canada*. Ottawa, ON: CIHI 2009.

Canadian Institutes of Health Research, Natural Sciences and Engineering Research Council of Canada, and Social Sciences and Humanities Research Council of Canada. (2010, December). Tri-council policy statement: Ethical conduct for research involving humans. Retrieved from http://www.pre.ethics.gc.ca/eng/policy-politique/initiatives/tcps2-eptc2/Default/.

Canadian Language and Literacy Research Network. (2009). National strategy for early literacy: Report and recommendations.

Canadian Paediatric Society. (2000). Toilet learning: Anticipatory guidance with a child-oriented approach. *Paediatrics & Child Health, 5*, 333–335. Retrieved from http://www.cps.ca/english/statements/CP/cp00-02.htm. Accessed March 17, 2011.

Canadian Paediatric Society. (2002). Healthy active living: Physical activity guidelines for children and adolescents. Position Statement HAL02-01.

Canadian Paediatric Society. (2003). Impact of media use on children and youth. Position Statement (PP 2003-01). Retrieved from www.cps.ca/english/statements/CP/pp03-01.htm. Accessed March 17, 2011.

Canadian Paediatric Society. (2004). Recommendations for safe sleeping environments for infants and children. *Paediatrics & Child Health, 9*, 659–663. http://www.cps.ca/english/statements/cp/cp04-02.htm. Accessed June 3, 2012.

Canadian Paediatric Society. (2004). Effective discipline for children. Position Statement (PP 2004-01). Retrieved from www.cps.ca/english/statements/CP/pp04-01.htm. Accessed May 3, 2011.

Canadian Paediatric Society. (2004b). Weaning from the breast. *Paediatrics & Child Health 9(4)*, 249–253. http://www.cps.ca/english/statements/CP/cp04-01.htm. Accessed June 3, 2012.

Canadian Paediatric Society. (2005). Exclusive breastfeeding should continue to six months. *Paediatr Child Health, 10(3)*, 148. Retrieved from http://www.cps.ca/english/statements/n/breastfeedingmar05.htm. Accessed June 3, 2012.

Canadian Paediatric Society. (2006). Read, speak, sing: Promoting literacy in the physician's office. *Paediatr Child Health 11(9)*, 601–606. Retrieved from http://www.cps.ca/english/statements/CP/pp06-01.htm. Accessed June 3, 2012.

Canadian Paediatric Society. (2006). Adolescent pregnancy. Position Statement AH06-02. *Paediatric Child Health, 11(4)*, 243–246.

Canals, J., Fernandez-Ballart, J., & Esparo, G. (2003). Evolution of Neonatal Behavior Assessment Scale scores in the first month of life. *Infant Behavior and Development, 26*, 227–237.

CancerChic, (2011, Mar 26). Welcome to 1989... [web log post] Retrieved from http://cancerchic.blogspot.ca/2011_03_01_archive.html.

Cardman, M. (2004). Rising GPAs, course loads a mystery to researchers. *Education Daily, 37*, 1–3.

Carlson, E., & Hoem, J. M. (1999). Low-weight neonatal survival paradox in the Czech Republic: Original contributions. *American Journal of Epidemiology, 149*, 447–453.

Carmeli, A., & Josman, Z. (2006). The relationship among emotional intelligence, task performance, and organizational citizenship behaviors. *Human Performance, 19*, 403–419.

Carmichael, M. (2004, May 10). Have it your way: Redesigning birth. *Newsweek*, 70–72.

Carrere, S., Buehlman, K. T., Gottman, J. M., Coan, J. A., & Ruckstuhl, L. (2000). Predicting marital stability and divorce in newlywed couples. *Journal of Family Psychology, 14*, 42–58.

Carroll, L. (2000, February 1). Is memory loss inevitable? Maybe not. *The New York Times*, pp. D1, D7.

Carson, T. (2009). *The Parenting Coach*. Retrieved from http://www.theparentingcoach.ca/index.php/id/172. Accessed May 23, 2012.

Carstensen, L. L., Pasupathi, M., Mayr, U., & Nesselroade, J. R. (2000). Emotional experience in everyday life across the adult life span. *Journal of Personality and Social Psychology, 79*, 644–655.

Carver, L., & Vaccaro, B. (2007, January). 12-month-old infants allocate increased neural resources to stimuli associated with negative adult emotion. *Developmental Psychology, 43*, 54–69.

Cascalho, M., Ogle, B. M., & Platt, J. L. (2006). The future of organ transplantation. *Annals of Transplantation, 11*, 44–47.

Case, R. (1991). Stages in the development of the young child's first sense of self. *Developmental Review, 11*, 210–230.

Case, R. (1999). Conceptual development in the child and in the field: A personal view of the Piagetian legacy. In E. K. Scholnick, K. Nelson, S. A. Gelman, & P. H. Miller (Eds.), *Conceptual development: Piaget's legacy*. Mahwah, NJ: Lawrence Erlbaum Associates Publishers.

Case, R. (1999). Conceptual development. In M. Bennett, *Developmental psychology: Achievements and prospects*. Philadelphia, PA: Psychology Press.

Case, R., Demetriou, A., & Platsidou, M. (2001). Integrating concepts and tests of intelligence from the differential and developmental traditions. *Intelligence, 29*, 307–336.

Case, R., & Okamoto, Y. (1996). The role of central conceptual structures in the development of children's thought. *Monographs of the Society for Research in Child Development, 61*, v–265.

Caspi, A. (2000). The child is father of the man: Personality continuities from childhood to adulthood. *Journal of Personality and Social Psychology, 78*, 158–172.

Caspi, A., & Moffitt, T. E. (1993). *Continuity amidst change: A paradoxical theory of personality coherence*. Manuscript submitted for publication.

Cassidy, J., & Berlin, L. J. (1994). The insecure/ambivalent pattern of attachment: Theory and research. *Child Development, 65*, 971–991.

Castel, A., & Craik, F. (2003). The effects of aging and divided attention on memory for item and associative information. *Psychology and Aging, 18*, 873–885.

Catell, R. B. (1967). *The scientific analysis of personality*. Chicago: Aldine.

Catell, R. B. (1987). *Intelligence: Its structure, growth, and action*. Amsterdam: North-Holland.

Cath, S., & Shopper, M. (2001). *Stepparenting: Creating and recreating families in America today*. Hillsdale, NJ: Analytic Press, Inc.

Caughlin, J. (2002). The demand/withdraw pattern of communication as a predictor of marital satisfaction over time. *Human Communication Research, 28*, 49–85.

Cavallini, A., Fazzi, E., & Viviani, V. (2002).Visual acuity in the first two years of life in healthy term newborns: An experience with the Teller Acuity Cards. *Functional Neurology: New Trends in Adaptive and Behavioral Disorders, 17*, 87–92.

CBC News. (2008). Family of woman killed in Iqaluit speaks out against violence. Retrieved from http://www.cbc.ca/news/canada/north/story/2008/02/18/nu-death.html.

CBC News. (2009). The fight for the right to die. Retrieved from http://www.cbc.ca/news/canada/story/2009/02/09/f-assisted-suicide.html. Last updated June 15, 2012.

Ceci, S.J., & Bruck, M. (1993). The suggestibility of the child witness: A historical review and synthesis. *Psychological Bulletin, 113*, 403–439.

Centers for Disease Control and Prevention. (2006). *HIV/AIDS surveillance report*. Atlanta: Author.

Cerella, J. (1990). Aging and information-processing rate. In J. E. Birren & K. W. Schaie (Eds.), *Handbook of the psychology of aging* (3rd ed.). San Diego, CA: Academic Press.

CFCEPLA (Commonwealth Fund Commission on Elderly People Living Alone). (1986). *Problems facing elderly Americans living alone*. New York: Louis Harris and Associates.

Chaffin, M. (2006). The changing focus of child maltreatment research and practice within psychology. *Journal of Social Issues, 62*, 663–684.

Chaiklin, S. (2003). The zone of proximal development in Vygotsky's analysis of learning and instruction. In A. Kozulin & B. Gindis (Eds.), *Vygotsky's educational theory in cultural context*. New York: Cambridge University Press.

Chaker, A. M. (2003, September 23). Putting toddlers in a nursing home. *The Wall Street Journal*, D1.

Chall, J. (1992). The new reading debates: Evidence from science, art, and ideology. *Teachers College Record, 94*, 315–328.

Chall, J. S. (1979). The great debate: Ten years later, with a modest proposal for reading stages. In L. B. Resnick & P. A. Weaver (Eds.), *Theory and practice of early reading*. Hillsdale, NJ: Erlbaum.

Chamberlain, P., Price, J., Reid, J., Landsverk, J., Fisher, P., & Stoolmiller, M. (2006, April). Who disrupts from placement in foster and kinship care? *Child Abuse and Neglect, 30*, 409–424.

Chan, C. G., & Elder, G. H., Jr. (2000). Matrilineal advantage in grandchild–grandparent relations. *Gerontologist, 40*, 179–190.

Chan, D. W. (1997). Self-concept and global self-worth among Chinese adolescents in Hong Kong. *Personality and Individual Differences, 22*, 511–520.

Chao, R. K. (1994). Beyond parental control and authoritarian parenting style: Understanding Chinese parenting through the cultural notion of training. *Child Development, 65*, 1111–1119.

Chao, R. K. (2001). Extending research on the consequences of parenting style for Chinese Americans and European Americans. *Child Development, 72*, 1832–1843.

Chapple, A., Ziebland, S., McPherson, A., & Herxheimer, A. (2006, December). What people close to death say about euthanasia and assisted suicide: A qualitative study. *Journal of Medical Ethics, 32*, 706–710.

Charles, S. T., Mather, M., & Carstensen, L. L. (2003). Aging and emotional memory: The forgettable nature of negative images for older adults. *Journal of Experimental Psychology: General, 132*, 237–244.

Charles, S. T., Reynolds, C. A., & Gatz, M. (2001). Age-related differences and change in positive and negative affect over 23 years. *Journal of Personality and Social Psychology, 80*, 136–151.

Chen, J., & Gardner, H. (2005). Assessment based on multiple-intelligences theory. In D. P. Flanagan & P. L. Harrison (Eds.), *Contemporary intellectual assessment: Theories, tests, and issues*. New York, Guilford Press.

Chen, X., Hastings, P. D., Rubin, K. H., Chen, H., Cen, G., & Stewart, S. L. (1998). Child-rearing attitudes and behavioral inhibition in Chinese and Canadian toddlers: A cross-cultural study. *Developmental Psychology, 34*, 677–686.

Cherlin, A. (1993). *Marriage, divorce, remarriage*. Cambridge, MA: Harvard University Press.

Cherlin, A., & Furstenberg, F. (1986). *The new American grandparent*. New York: Basic Books.

Cherney, I. (2003). Young children's spontaneous utterances of mental terms and the accuracy of their memory behaviors: A different methodological approach. *Infant and Child Development, 12*, 89–105.

Cherney, I., Kelly-Vance, L., & Glover, K. (2003). The effects of stereotyped toys and gender on play assessment in children aged 18–47 months. *Educational Psychology, 23*, 95–105.

Cherry, K. E., & Park, D. C. (1993). Individual difference and contextual variables influence spatial memory in younger and older adults. *Psychology and Aging, 8*, 517–526.

Chien, S., Bronson-Castain, K., Palmer, J., & Teller, D. (2006). Lightness constancy in 4-month-old infants. *Vision Research, 46*, 2139–2148.

Chisolm, T., Willott, J., & Lister, J. (2003). The aging auditory system: Anatomic and physiologic changes and implications for rehabilitation. *International Journal of Audiology, 42*, 2S3–2S10.

Choi, H. (2002). Understanding adolescent depression in ethnocultural context. *Advances in Nursing Science, 25*, 71–85.

Choi, H., & Marks, N. (2006, December). Transition to caregiving, marital disagreement, and psychological well-being: A prospective U.S. National Study. *Journal of Family Issues, 27*, 1701–1722.

Chomsky, N. (1968). *Language and mind*. New York: Harcourt Brace Jovanovich.

Chomsky, N. (1978). On the biological basis of language capacities. In G. A. Miller & E. Lennenberg (Eds.), *Psychology and biology of language and thought* (pp. 199–220). New York: Academic Press.

Chomsky, N. (1991). Linguistics and cognitive science: Problems and mysteries. In A. Kasher (Ed.), *The Chomskyan turn*. Cambridge, MA: Blackwell.

Chomsky, N. (1999). On the nature, use, and acquisition of language. In W. C. Ritchie & T. J. Bhatia (Eds.), *Handbook of child language acquisition*. San Diego: Academic Press.

Chomsky, N. (2005). Editorial: Universals of human nature. *Psychotherapy and Psychosomatics [serial online], 74*, 263–268.

Choy, C. M., Yeung, Q. S., Briton-Jones, C. M., Cheung, C. K., Lam, C. W., & Haines, C. J. (2002). Relationship between semen parameters and mercury concentrations in blood and in seminal fluid from subfertile males in Hong Kong. *Fertility and Sterility, 78*, 426–428.

Christakis, D. A., Zimmerman, F. J., DiGiuseppe, D. L., & McCarthy, C. A. (2004). Early television exposure and subsequent attentional problems in children. *Pediatrics, 113*, 708–713.

Christofides, E., Muise, A., & Desmarais, S. (2012). Hey mom, what's on your Facebook? Comparing Facebook disclosure and privacy in adolescents and adults. *Social Psychological and Personality Science, 3(1)*, 48–54.

Christophersen, E. R., & Mortweet, S. L. (2003). Disciplining your child effectively. In E. R. Christophersen & S. L. Mortweet (Eds.), *Parenting that works: Building skills that last a lifetime*. Washington, DC: American Psychological Association.

Chronis, A., Jones, H., & Raggi, V. (2006, June). Evidence-based psychosocial treatments for children and adolescents with attention-deficit/hyperactivity disorder. *Clinical Psychology Review, 26*, 486–502.

Chung, S. A., Wei, A. Q., Connor, D. E., Webb, G. C., Molloy, T., Pajic, M., & Diwan, A. D. (2007). Nucleus pulposus cellular longevity by telomerase gene therapy. *Spine, 15*, 1188–1196.

Chyi, L. J., Lee, H. C., Hintz, S. R., Gould, J. B., & Sutcliffe, T. L. (2008). School outcomes for late preterm infants: Special needs and challenges for infants born at 32 to 36 weeks gestation. *The Journal of Pediatrics,153*, 25–31.

Cianciolo, A. T., Matthew, C., & Sternberg, R. J. (2006). Tacit knowledge, practical intelligence, and expertise. In K. A. Ericsson, N. Charness, P. J. Feltovich, & R. R. Hoffman (Eds.), *The Cambridge handbook of expertise and expert performance*. New York: Cambridge University Press.

Cicchetti, D. (1996). Child maltreatment: Implications for developmental theory and research. *Human Development, 39*, 18–39.

Cicchetti, D. (2003). Neuroendocrine functioning in maltreated children. In D. Cicchetti & E. Walker (Eds.), *Neurodevelopmental mechanisms in psychopathology*. New York: Cambridge University Press.

Cicchetti, D., & Cohen, D. J. (2006). *Developmental Psychopathology, Vol. 1: Theory and method* (2nd ed.). Hoboken, NJ: John Wiley and Sons.

CIRE (Cooperative Institutional Research Program of the American Council on Education). (1990). *The American freshman: National norms for fall 1990*. Los Angeles: American Council on Education.

Ciricelli, V. G. (1995). *Sibling relationships across the life span*. New York: Plenum.

Cirulli, F., Berry, A., & Alleva, E. (2003). Early disruption of the mother–infant relationship: Effects on brain plasticity and implications for psychopathology. *Neuroscience and Biobehavioral Reviews, 27*, 73–82.

Citizenship and Immigration Canada. (2011, June). Success stories. Remzi: from refugee to Rhodes scholar. [cached copy] Retrieved from http://www.cic.gc.ca/english/department/media/stories/remzi.asp.

Claes, M., Lacourse, E., & Bouchard, C. (2003). Parental practices in late adolescence, a comparison of three countries: Canada, France and Italy. *Journal of Adolescence, 26*, 387–399.

Clark, E. (1983). Meanings and concepts. In J. Flavell & E. Markham (Eds.), *Handbook of child psychology: Cognitive development (Vol. 3)*. New York: Wiley.

Clark, K. B., & Clark, M. P. (1947). Racial identification and preference in Negro children. In T. M. Newcomb & E. L. Hartley (Eds.), *Readings in social psychology*. New York: Holt, Rinehart and Winston.

Clark, R. (1998). *Expertise*. Silver Spring, MD: International Society for Performance Improvement.

Clark, W., & Crompton, S. (2006). Till death do us part? The risk of first and second marriage dissolution. Statistics Canada [archived content]. Retrieved from http://www.statcan.gc.ca/pub/11-008-x/2006001/9198-eng.htm.

Clarke-Stewart, A., & Friedman, S. (1987). *Child development: Infancy through adolescence*. New York: Wiley.

Clarke-Stewart, K., & Allhusen, V. (2002). Nonparental caregiving. (2002). In M. Bornstein (Ed.), *Handbook of parenting: Vol. 3: Being and becoming a parent* (2nd ed.). Mahwah, NJ: Lawrence Erlbaum Associates.

Claxton, L. J., Keen R., & McCarty, M. E. (2003). Evidence of motor planning in infant reaching behavior. *Psychological Science, 14*, 354–356.

Clearfield, M., & Nelson, N. (2006, January). Sex differences in mothers' speech and play behavior with 6-, 9-, and 14-month-old infants. *Sex Roles, 54*, 127–137.

Cliff, D. (1991). Negotiating a livable retirement: Further paid work and the quality of life in early retirement. *Aging and Society, 11*, 319–340.

Clinton, J. F., & Kelber, S. T. (1993). Stress and coping in fathers of newborns: Comparisons of planned versus unplanned pregnancy. *International Journal of Nursing Studies, 30*, 437–443.

Cnattingius, S., Berendes, H., & Forman, M. (1993). Do delayed childbearers face increased risks of adverse pregnancy outcomes after the first birth? *Obstetrics and Gynecology, 81*, 512–516.

Cobbe, E. (2003, September 25). France ups heat toll. *CBS Evening News*.

Cohen, J. (1999, March 19). Nurture helps mold able minds. *Science, 283*, 1832–1833.

Cohen, L. B., & Cashon, C. H. (2003). Infant perception and cognition. In R. M. Lerner & M. A. Easterbrooks (Eds.), *Handbook of psychology: Developmental psychology (Vol. 6)*. New York: John Wiley and Sons.

Cohen, S., Hamrick, N., Rodriguez, M. S., Feldman, P. J., Rabin B. S., & Manuck, S. B. (2002). Reactivity and vulnerability to stress-associated risk for upper respiratory illness. *Psychosomatic Medicine, 64*, 302–310.

Cohen, S., Tyrell, D. A., & Smith, A. P. (1993). Negative life events, perceived stress, negative affect, and susceptibility of the common cold. *Journal of Personality and Social Psychology, 64*, 131–140.

Cohen, S., Tyrell, D. A., & Smith, A. P. (1997). Psychological stress in humans and susceptibility to the common cold. In T. W. Miller (Ed.), *International Universities Press stress and health series, Monograph 7. Clinical disorders and stressful life events* (pp. 217–235). Madison, CT: International Universities Press.

Cohn, R. M. (1982). Economic development and status change of the aged. *American Journal of Sociology, 87*, 1150–1161.

Cohrs, J., Abele, A., & Dette, D. (2006, July). Integrating situational and dispositional determinants of job satisfaction: Findings from three samples of professionals. *Journal of Psychology: Interdisciplinary and Applied, 140*, 363–395.

Colby, A., & Damon, W. (1987). Listening to a different voice: A review of Gilligan's in a different voice. In M. R. Walsh (Ed.),

The psychology of women. New Haven, CT: Yale University Press.

Colby, A., & Kohlberg, L. (1987). *The measurement of moral adjudgment (Vols. 1–2).* New York: Cambridge University Press.

Colcombe, S. J., Erickson, K. I., Scalf, P. E., Kim, J. S., Prakash, R., McAuley, E., Elavsky, S...Kramer, A. F. (2006). Aerobic exercise training increases brain volume in aging humans. *Journal of Gerontology, A. Biological Sciences and Medical Sciences, 61,* 1166–1170.

Cole, D. A., Maxwell, S. E., Martin, J. M., Peeke, L. G., Seroczynski, A. D., Tram, J. M., Joffman, K. B...Maschman, T. (2001). The development of multiple domains of child and adolescent self-concept: A cohort sequential longitudinal design. *Child Development, 72,* 1723–1746.

Cole, M. (1992). Culture in development. In M. H. Bornstein & M. E. Lamb (Eds.), *Developmental psychology: An advanced textbook* (3rd ed.). Hillsdale, NJ: Erlbaum.

Cole, S. A. (2005). Infants in foster care: Relational and environmental factors affecting attachment. *Journal of Reproductive and Infant Psychology, 23,* 43–61.

Coleman, M., Ganong, L., & Weaver, S. (2001). Relationship maintenance and enhancement in remarried families. In J. Harvey & A. Wenzel (Eds.), *Close romantic relationships: Maintenance and enhancement.* Mahwah, NJ: Lawrence Erlbaum Associates.

Coleman, P. (2005, July). Editorial: Uses of reminiscence: Functions and benefits. *Aging and Mental Health, 9,* 291–294.

Collett, B. R., Gimpel, G. A., Greenson, J. N., & Gunderson, T. L. (2001). Assessment of discipline styles among parents of preschool through school-age children. *Journal of Psychopathology and Behavioral Assessment, 23,* 163–170.

Collins, W. (2003). More than myth: The developmental significance of romantic relationships during adolescence. *Journal of Research on Adolescence, 13,* 1–24.

Collins, W., & Andrew, L. (2004). Changing relationships, changing youth: Interpersonal contexts of adolescent development. *Journal of Early Adolescence, 24,* 55–62.

Collins, W., & Doolittle, A. (2006, December). Personal reflections of funeral rituals and spirituality in a Kentucky African American family. *Death Studies, 30,* 957–969.

Colom, R., Lluis-Font, J. M., & Andrés-Pueyo, A. (2005). The generational intelligence gains are caused by decreasing variance in the lower half of the distribution: Supporting evidence for the nutrition hypothesis. *Intelligence, 33,* 83–91.

Coltrane, S., & Adams, M. (1997). Children and gender. In T. Arendell (Ed.), *Contemporary parenting: Challenges and issues. Understanding families* (Vol. 9, pp. 219–253). Thousand Oaks, CA: Sage.

Compton, R., & Weissman, D. (2002). Hemispheric asymmetries in global-local perception: Effects of individual differences in neuroticism. *Laterality, 7,* 333–350.

Comunian, A. L., & Gielen, U. P. (2000). Sociomoral reflection and prosocial and antisocial behavior: Two Italian studies. *Psychological Reports, 87,* 161–175.

Condly, S. (2006, May). Resilience in children: A review of literature with implications for education. *Urban Education, 41,* 211–236.

Condry, J., & Condry, S. (1976). Sex differences: A study of the eye of the beholder. *Child Development, 47,* 812–819.

Conel, J. L. (1939/1976). *Postnatal development of the human cortex (Vols. 1–8).* Cambridge, MA: Harvard University Press.

Conklin, H. M., & Iacono, W. G. (2002). Schizophrenia: A neurodevelopmental perspective. *Current Directions in Psychological Science, 11,* 33–37.

Conn, V. S. (2003). Integrative review of physical activity intervention research with aging adults. *Journal of the American Geriatrics Society, 51,* 1159–1168.

Conner, K., & Goldston, D. (2007, March). Rates of suicide among males increase steadily from age 11 to 21: Developmental

framework and outline for prevention. *Aggression and Violent Behavior, 12(2),* 193–207.

Connor, R. (1992). *Cracking the over-50 job market.* New York: Penguin Books.

Consedine, N., Magai, C., & King, A. (2004). Deconstructing positive affect in later life: A differential functionalist analysis of joy and interest. *International Journal of Aging and Human Development, 58,* 49–68.

Coon, K. D., Myers, A. J., Craig, D. W., Webster, J. A., Pearson, J. V., Lince, D. H., Zismann, V. L...Stephan, D. A. (2007). A high-density whole-genome association study reveals that APOE is the major susceptibility gene for sporadic late-onset Alzheimer's disease. *Journal of Clinical Psychiatry, 68,* 613–618.

Cooperstock, M. S., Bakewell, J., Herman, A., & Schramm W. F. (1998). Effects of fetal sex and race on risk of very preterm birth in twins. *American Journal of Obstetrics and Gynecology, 179,* 762–765.

Corballis, P. (2003). Visuospatial processing and the right-hemisphere interpreter. *Brain and Cognition, 53,* 171–176.

Corenblum, B. (1996). Development of identity in Native Indian children: Review and possible futures. *The Canadian Journal of Native Studies, 16,* 81–103.

Costa, P. T., & McCrae, R. (2002). Looking backward: Changes in the mean levels of personality traits from 80 to 12. In D. Cervone & W. Mischel (Eds.), *Advances in personality science.* New York: Guilford Press.

Costa, P. T., Jr., & McCrae, R. R. (1988). Personality in adulthood: A six-year longitudinal study of self-report and spouse ratings on the NEO Personality Inventory. *Journal of Personality and Social Psychology, 54,* 853–863.

Costa, P. T., & McCrae, R. R. (1997). Longitudinal stability of adult personality. In R. Hogan, J. A. Johnson, & S. R. Briggs (Eds.), *Handbook of personality psychology* (pp. 269–290). San Diego, CA: Academic Press.

Costa, P. T., Jr., & McCrae, R. R. (1989). Personality continuity and the changes of adult life. In M. Storandt & G. R. VandenBos (Eds.), *The adult years: Continuity and change.* Washington, DC: American Psychological Association.

Costello, E., Compton, S., & Keeler, G. (2003). Relationships between poverty and psychopathology: A natural experiment. *Journal of the American Medical Association, 290,* 2023–2029.

Costello, E., Sung, M., Worthman, C., & Angold, A. (2007, April). Pubertal maturation and the development of alcohol use and abuse. *Drug and Alcohol Dependence, 88,* S50–S59.

Couperus, J., & Nelson, C. (2006). Early brain development and plasticity. *Blackwell handbook of early childhood development.* New York: Blackwell Publishing.

Courchesne, E., Carper, R., &S Akshoomoff, N. (2003). Evidence of brain overgrowth in the first year of life in autism. *Journal of the American Medical Association, 290,* 337–344.

Couzin, J. (2002, June 21). Quirks of fetal environment felt decades later. *Science, 296,* 2167–2169.

Cowan, C., and Cowan, D. *When partners become parents: The big life change* (1992). Permission conveyed through Copyright Clearance Center, Inc.

Cowan, N., Saults, J., & Elliot, E. (2002). The search for what is fundamental in the development of working memory. In R. Kail & H. Reese (Eds.), *Advances in child development and behavior* (Vol. 29). San Diego: Academic Press.

Cowgill, D. O., & Holmes, L. D. (1972). *Aging and modernization.* New York: Appleton-Century-Crofts.

Craig, W. M., & Pepler, D. J. (2007). Understanding bullying: From research to practice. *Canadian Psychology, 48,* 86–93.

Craik, F., & Salthouse, T. A. (Eds.). (1999). *The handbook of aging and cognition* (2nd ed.). Mahwah, NJ: Erlbaum.

Craik, F. I. M. (1994). Memory changes in normal aging. *Current Directions in Psychological Science, 3,* 155–158.

Crane, E., & Morris, J. (2006). Changes in maternal age in England and Wales—Implications for Down syndrome. *Down Syndrome: Research and Practice, 10,* 41–43.

Cratty, B. (1979). *Perceptual and motor development in infants and children* (2nd ed.). Englewood Cliffs, NJ: Prentice-Hall.

Cratty, B. (1986). *Perceptual and motor development in infants and children* (3rd ed.). Englewood Cliffs, NJ: Prentice-Hall.

Crawford, M., & Unger, R. (2004). *Women and gender: A feminist psychology* (4th ed). New York: McGraw-Hill.

Crawley, A., Anderson, D., & Santomero, A. (2002). Do children learn how to watch television? The impact of extensive experience with *Blue's Clues* on preschool children's television viewing behavior. *Journal of Communication, 52,* 264–280.

Crews, D. (1993). The organizational concept and vertebrates without sex chromosomes. *Brain, Behavior, and Evolution, 42,* 202–214.

Crick, N. R., Casas, J. G., & Ku, H. (1999). Relational and physical forms of peer victimization in preschool. *Developmental Psychology, 35,* 376–385.

Crisp, A., Gowers, S., Joughin, N., McClelland, L., Rooney, B., Nielsen, S., et al. (2006, May). Anorexia nervosa in males: Similarities and differences to anorexia nervosa in females. *European Eating Disorders Review, 14,* 163–167.

CSEP. (2011). Canadian Physical Activity Guidelines. Retrieved from http://www.csep.ca/english/View .asp?x=587. Accessed May 3, 2012.

Critser, G. (2003). *Fat land: How Americans became the fattest people in the world.* Boston: Houghton Mifflin.

Crockett, L. J., & Crouter, A. C. (Eds.). (1995). *Pathways through adolescence: Individual development in relation to social contexts.* Hillsdale, NJ: Erlbaum.

Crompton, S. (2005, Summer). Always the bridesmaid: People who don't expect to marry. Canadian Social Trends. Statistics Canada Catalogue No. 11-008-XPE.

Crosnoe, R., & Elder, G. H., Jr. (2002). Successful adaptation in the later years: A life course approach to aging. *Social Psychology Quarterly, 65,* 309–328.

Crowley, B., Hayslip, B., & Hobdy, J. (2003). Psychological hardiness and adjustment to life events in adulthood. *Journal of Adult Development, 10,* 237–248.

Crowther, M., & Rodriguez, R. (2003). A stress and coping model of custodial grandparenting among African Americans. In B. Hayslip & J. Patrick (Eds.), *Working with custodial grandparents.* New York: Springer Publishing.

Crutchley, A. (2003). Bilingualism in development: Language, literacy and cognition. *Child Language Teaching and Therapy, 19,* 365–367.

Cruz, N., & Bahna, S. (2006, October). Do foods or additives cause behavior disorders? *Psychiatric Annals, 36,* 724–732.

Cuddy, A. J. C., & Fiske, S. T. (2004). Doddering but dear: Process, content, and function in stereotyping of older persons. In T. Nelson (Ed.), *Ageism: Stereotyping and prejudice against older persons.* Cambridge, MA: MIT Press.

Culbertson, J. L., & Gyurke, J. (1990). Assessment of cognitive and motor development in infancy and childhood. In J. H. Johnson & J. Goldman (Eds.), *Developmental assessment in clinical child psychology: A handbook* (pp. 100–131). New York: Pergamon Press.

Culver, V. (2003, August 26). Funeral expenses overwhelm survivors: $10,000-plus tab often requires aid. *The Denver Post,* p. B2.

Cummings, E., & Henry, W. E. (1961). *Growing old.* New York: Basic Books.

Cummings, E. M., Iannotti, R. J., & Zahn-Waxler, C. (1989). Aggression between peers in early childhood: Individual continuity and developmental change. *Child Development, 60,* 887–895.

Cunningham, J. D., & Antill, J. K. (1994). Cohabitation and marriage: Retrospective and predictive comparisons. *Journal of Social and Personal Relationships, 11,* 77–93.

Curtis, W. J., & Cicchetti, D. (2003). Moving research on resilience into the 21st century: Theoretical and methodological considerations in examining the biological contributors to resilience. *Development and Psychopathology, 15*, 126–131.

Dahl, E., & Birkelund, E. (1997). Health inequalities in later life in a social democratic welfare state. *Social Science and Medicine, 44*, 871–881.

Dale, M. (2011). Trends in the age composition of college and university students and graduates. *Education matters: Insights on education, learning and training in Canada.* Statistics Canada Catalogue no. 81-004-X, Vol. 7, no. 5. Retrieved from http://www.statcan.gc.ca/pub/81-004-x/2010005/article/11386-eng.htm.

Daley, K. C. (2004). Update on sudden infant death syndrome. *Current Opinion in Pediatrics, 16*, 227–232.

Damon, W. (1983). *Social and personality development.* New York: Norton.

Damon, W., & Hart, D. (1988). *Self-understanding in childhood and adolescence.* New York: Cambridge University Press.

Danhauer, S., McCann, J., & Gilley, D. (2004). Do behavioral disturbances in persons with Alzheimer's disease predict caregiver depression over time? *Psychology and Aging, 19*, 198–202.

Daniels, H. (Ed.). (1996). *An introduction to Vygotsky.* New York: Routledge.

Dare, W. N., Noronha, C. C., Kusemiju, O. T., & Okanlawon, O. A. (2002). The effect of ethanol on spermatogenesis and fertility in male Sprague-Dawley rats pretreated with acetylsalicylic acid. *Nigeria Postgraduate Medical Journal, 9*, 194–198.

Dasen, P., Inhelder, B., Lavallee, M., & Retschitzki, J. (1978). *Naissance de l'intelligence chez l'enfant Baoule de Cote d'Ivorie.* Berne: Hans Huber.

Dasen, P., Ngini, L., & Lavallee, M. (1979). Cross-cultural training studies of concrete operations. In L. H. Eckenberger, W. J. Lonner, & Y. H. Poortinga (Eds.), *Cross-cultural contributions to psychology.* Amsterdam: Swets and Zeilinger.

Dasen, P. R. (2000). Rapid social change and the turmoil of adolescence: A cross-cultural perspective. *International Journal of Group Tensions, 29*, 17–49.

Davey, M. (2007, June 2). Kevorkian freed after years in prison for aiding suicide. *The New York Times*, p. A1.

Davey, M., Eaker, D. G., & Walters, L. H. (2003). Resilience processes in adolescents: Personality profiles, self-worth, and coping. *Journal of Adolescent Research, 18*, 347–362.

Davies, P. T., Harold, G. T., Goeke-Morey, M. C., & Cummings, E. M. (2002). Child emotional security and interparental conflict. *Monographs of the Society for Research in Child Development, 67.*

Davies, S., & Denton, M. (2002). The economic well-being of older women who become divorced or separated in mid- or later life. *Canadian Journal on Aging, 21*, 477–493.

Davis, A. (2003). *Your divorce, your dollars: Financial planning before, during, and after divorce.* Bellingham, WA: Self-Counsel Press.

Davis, D., Shaver, P., Widaman, K., Vernon, M., Follette, W., & Beitz, K. (2006, December). "I can't get no satisfaction": Insecure attachment, inhibited sexual communication, and sexual dissatisfaction. *Personal Relationships, 13*, 465–483.

Davis, M., & Emory, E. (1995). Sex differences in neonatal stress reactivity. *Child Development, 66*, 14–27.

Davis-Kean, P. E., & Sandler, H. M. (2001). A meta-analysis of measures of self-esteem for young children: A framework for future measures. *Child Development, 72*, 887–906.

Davison, G. C. (2005). Issues and nonissues in the gay-affirmative treatment of patients who are gay, lesbian, or bisexual. *Clinical Psychology: Science and Practice, 12*, 25–28.

de Bruyn, E., & Cillessen, A. (2006, November). Popularity in early adolescence: Prosocial and antisocial subtypes. *Journal of Adolescent Research, 21*, 607–627.

De Meersman, R., & Stein, P. (2007, February). Vagal modulation and aging. *Biological Psychology, 74*, 165–173.

de Rosnay, M., Cooper, P., Tsigaras, N., & Murray, L. (2006, August). Transmission of social anxiety from mother to infant: An experimental study using a social referencing paradigm. *Behaviour Research and Therapy, 44*, 1165–1175.

De Roten, Y., Favez, N., & Drapeau, M. (2003). Two studies on autobiographical narratives about an emotional event by preschoolers: Influence of the emotions experienced and the affective closeness with the interlocutor. *Early Child Development and Care, 173*, 237–248.

de Vries, B., Davis, C. G., Wortman, C. B., & Lehman, D. R. (1997). Long-term psychological and somatic consequences of later life parental bereavement. *Omega—Journal of Death and Dying, 35*, 97–117.

Deakin, M. B. (2004, May 9). The (new) parent trap. *Boston Globe Magazine*, pp. 18–21, 28–33.

Deater-Deckard, K., & Cahill, K. (2006). Nature and nurture in early childhood. *Blackwell handbook of early childhood development* (pp. 3–21). New York: Blackwell Publishing.

Deaux, K., Reind, A., Mizrahi, K., & Ethier, K. A. (1995). Parameters of social identity. *Journal of Personality and Social Psychology, 68*, 280–291.

Deb, S., & Adak, M. (2006, July). Corporal punishment of children: Attitude, practice and perception of parents. *Social Science International, 22*, 3–13.

Decarrie, T. G. (1969). A study of the mental and emotional development of the thalidomide child. In B. M. Foss (Ed.), *Determinants of infant behavior (Vol. 4).* London: Methuen.

DeCasper, A. J., & Fifer, W. P. (1980). Of human bonding: Newborns prefer their mothers' voices. *Science, 208*, 1174–1176.

DeCasper, A. J., & Spence, M. J. (1986). Prenatal material speech influences newborns' perception of speech sounds. *Infant Behavior and Development, 9*, 133–150.

Decety, J., & Jackson, P. L. (2006). A social-neuroscience perspective on empathy. *Current Directions in Psychological Science, 15*, 54–61.

deChateau, P. (1980). Parent–neonate interaction and its long-term effects. In E. G. Simmel (Ed.), *Early experiences and early behavior.* New York: Academic Press.

Deforche, B., De Bourdeaudhuij, I., & Tanghe, A. (2006, May). Attitude toward physical activity in normal-weight, overweight and obese adolescents. *Journal of Adolescent Health, 38*, 560–568.

DeGenova, M. K. (1993). Reflections of the past: New variables affecting life satisfaction in later life. *Educational Gerontology, 19*, 191–201.

Degnen, C. (2007). Minding the gap: The construction of old age and oldness amongst peers. *Journal of Aging Studies, 21*, 69–80.

Dehaene-Lambertz, G., Hertz-Pannier, L., & Dubois, J. (2006). Nature and nurture in language acquisition: Anatomical and functional brain-imaging studies in infants. *Neurosciences, 29* [Special issue: Nature and nurture in brain development and neurological disorders], 367–373.

DeHart, T., Pelham, B., & Tennen, H. (2006, January). What lies beneath: Parenting style and implicit self-esteem. *Journal of Experimental Social Psychology, 42*, 1–17.

Dejin-Karlsson, E., Hanson, B. S., Oestergren, P. O., Sjoeberg, N. O., & Marsal, K. (1998). Does passive smoking in early pregnancy increase the risk of small-for-gestational age infants? *American Journal of Public Health, 88*, 1523–1527.

DeLisi, L., & Fleischhaker, W. (2007). Schizophrenia research in the era of the genome, 2007. *Current Opinion in Psychiatry, 20*, 109–110.

Dell, D. L., & Stewart, D. E. (2000). Menopause and mood. Is depression linked with hormone changes? *Postgraduate Medicine, 108*, 34–36, 39–43.

Dellmann-Jenkins, M., & Brittain, L. (2003). Young adults' attitudes toward filial responsibility and actual assistance to elderly family members. *Journal of Applied Gerontology, 22*, 214–229.

Demir, A., Ulusoy, M., & Ulusoy, M. (2003). Investigation of factors influencing burnout levels in the professional and private lives of nurses. *International Journal of Nursing Studies, 40*, 807–827.

Denizet-Lewis, B. (2004, May 30). Friends, friends with benefits and the benefits of the local mall. *New York Times Magazine*, pp. 30–35, 54–58.

Dennis, T. A., Cole, P. M., Zahn-Wexler, C., & Mizuta, I. (2002). Self in context: Autonomy and relatedness in Japanese and U.S. mother–preschooler dyads. *Child Development, 73*, 1803–1817.

Dennis, W. (1966a). Age and creative productivity. *Journal of Gerontology, 21*, 1–8.

Dennis, W. (1966b). Creative productivity between the ages of 20 and 80 years. *Journal of Gerontology, 11*, 331–337.

Dennison, B., Edmunds, L., Stratton, H., & Pruzek, R. (2006). Rapid infant weight gain predicts childhood overweight. *Obesity, 14*, 491–499.

Dent, C. (1984). Development of discourse rules: Children's use of indexical reference and cohesion. *Developmental Psychology, 20*, 229–234.

DePaulo, B. M., & Morris W. L. (2006). The unrecognized stereotyping and discrimination against singles. *Current Directions in Psychological Science, 15*, 251–254.

Der, G., Batty, G., & Deary, I. (2006). Effect of breast feeding on intelligence in children: Prospective study, sibling pairs analysis, and meta-analysis. *BMJ: British Medical Journal, 333*, 723–732.

Der, G., and Deary, I. (2006, March). Age sex differences in reaction time in adulthood: Results from the United Kingdom health and lifestyle survey. *Psychology and Aging, 21(1)*, 62–73.

Dervic, K., Friedrich, E., Oquendo, M., Voracek, M., Friedrich, M., & Sonneck, G. (2006, October). Suicide in Austrian children and young adolescents aged 14 and younger. *European Child and Adolescent Psychiatry, 15*, 427–434.

Deshields, T., Tibbs, T., Fan, M. Y., & Taylor, M. (2005, August 12). Differences in patterns of depression after treatment for breast cancer. *Psycho-Oncology*, published online, John Wiley and Sons.

Desmarias, S., & Curtis, J. (1997). Gender and perceived pay entitlement: Testing for effects of experience with income. *Journal of Personality and Social Psychology, 72*, 141–150.

Desoete, A., Roeyers, H., & De Clercq, A. (2003). Can offline metacognition enhance mathematical problem solving? *Journal of Educational Psychology, 95*, 188–200.

Deurenberg, P., Deurenberg-Yap, M., & Guricci, S. (2002). Asians are different from Caucasians and from each other in their body mass index/body fat percent relationship. *Obesity Review, 3(3)*, 141–146.

Deurenberg, P., Deurenberg-Yap, M., Foo, L. F., Schmidt, G., & Wang, J. (2003). Differences in body composition between Singapore Chinese, Beijing Chinese and Dutch children. *European Journal of Clinical Nutrition, 57(3)*, pp. 405–409.

Deveny, K. (1994, December 5). Chart of kindergarten awards. *The Wall Street Journal*, p. B1.

deVilliers, P. A., & deVilliers, J. G. (1992). Language development. In M. H. Bornstein & M. E. Lamb (Eds.), *Developmental psychology: An advanced textbook.* Hillsdale, NJ: Erlbaum.

Devlin, B., Daniels, M., & Roeder, K. (1997). The heritability of IQ. *Nature, 388*, 468–471.

deVries, R. (1969). Constancy of generic identity in the years 3 to 6. *Monographs of the Society for Research in Child Development, 34* (3, Serial No. 127).

Dey, A. N., & Bloom, B. (2005). Summary health statistics for U.S. children: National Health Interview Survey, 2003. *Vital Health Statistics, 10, 223*, 1–78.

Diambra, L. & Menna-Barretio, L. (2004). Infradian rhythmicity in sleep/wake ratio in developing infants. *Chronobiology International, 21*, 217–227.

Diamond, L. (2003a). Love matters: Romantic relationships among sexual-minority adolescents. In P. Florsheim (Ed.), *Adolescent romantic relations and sexual behavior: Theory, research, and practical implications.* Mahwah, NJ: Lawrence Erlbaum Associates.

Diamond, L. (2003b). Was it a phase? Young women's relinquishment of lesbian/bisexual identities over a 5-year period. *Journal of Personality and Social Psychology, 84,* 352–364.

Diamond, L., & Savin-Williams, R. (2003). The intimate relationships of sexual-minority youths. In G. Adams & M. Berzonsky (Eds.), *Blackwell handbook of adolescence.* Malden, MA: Blackwell Publishers.

DiCicco-Bloom, E., Lord, C., Zwaigenbaum, L., Courchesne, E., Dager, S. R., et al. (2006). Developmental neurobiology of autism spectrum disorder. *The Journal of Neuroscience, 26,* 6897–6906.

Dick, D., Rose, R., & Kaprio, J. (2006). The next challenge for psychiatric genetics: Characterizing the risk associated with identified genes. *Annals of Clinical Psychiatry, 18,* 223–231.

Diener, E. (2000). Subjective well-being: The science of happiness and a proposal for a national index. *American Psychologist, 55,* 34–43.

Diener, E., Oishi, S., & Lucas, R. (2003). Personality, culture, and subjective well-being: Emotional and cognitive evaluations of life. *Annual Review of Psychology, 54,* 403–425.

Dietz, W. H., & Stern, L. (Eds.). (1999). American Academy of Pediatrics guide to your child's nutrition: Making peace at the table and building healthy eating habits for life. New York: Villard.

DiGiovanna, A. G. (1994). *Human aging: Biological perspectives.* New York: McGraw-Hill.

DiLalla, L. F., Thompson, L. A., Plomin, R., Phillips, K., Fagan, J. F., Haith, M. M., Cyphers, L. H., & Fulker, D. W. (1990). Infant predictors of preschool and adult IQ: A study of infant twins and their parents. *Developmental Psychology, 26,* 433–440.

Dildy, G. A., et al. (1996). Very advanced maternal age: Pregnancy after 45. *American Journal of Obstetrics and Gynecology, 175,* 668–674.

Dion, K. L., & Dion, K. K. (1988). Romantic love: Individual and cultural perspectives. In R. J. Sternberg & M. L. Barnes (Eds.), *The psychology of love.* New Haven, CT: Yale University Press.

Diop, A. M. (1989). The place of the elderly in African society. *Impact of Science on Society, 153,* 93–98.

DiPietro, J. A. (2004). The role of prenatal maternal stress in child development. *Current Directions in Psychological Science, 13,* 71–74.

DiPietro, J. A., Bornstein, M. H., & Costigan, K. A. (2002). What does fetal movement predict about behavior during the first two years of life? *Developmental Psychobiology, 40,* 358–371.

Dittman, M. (2005). Generational differences at work. *Monitor on Psychology, 36,* 54–55.

Division 44/Committee on Lesbian, Gay, and Bisexual Concerns Joint Task Force on Guidelines for Psychotherapy with Lesbian, Gay, and Bisexual Clients. (2000). Guidelines for psychotherapy with lesbian, gay, and bisexual clients. *American Psychologist, 55,* 1440–1451.

Dixon, R. (2003). Themes in the aging of intelligence: Robust decline with intriguing possibilities. In R. Sternberg & J. Lautrey (Eds.), *Models of intelligence: International perspectives.* Washington, DC: American Psychological Association.

Dixon, R., & Cohen, A. (2003). Cognitive development in adulthood. In R. Lerner & M. Easterbrooks (Eds.), *Handbook of psychology: Developmental psychology, Vol. 6.* New York: John Wiley and Sons, Inc.

Dmitrieva, J., Chen, C., & Greenberger, E. (2004). Family relationships and adolescent psychosocial outcomes: Converging findings from Eastern and Western cultures. *Journal of Research on Adolescence. 14(4),* pp. 425–447.

Dodge, K. A. (1985). A social information processing model of social competence in children. In M. Perlmutter (Ed.), *Minnesota Symposia on Child Psychology, 18,* 77–126.

Dodge, K. A., & Coie, J. D. (1987). Social information-processing factors in reactive and proactive aggression in children's peer groups. *Journal of Personality and Social Psychology, 53,* 1146–1158.

Dodge, K. A., & Crick, N. R. (1990). Social information-processing bases of aggressive behavior in children. *Personality and Social Psychology Bulletin, 16,* 8–22.

Dodge, K. A., Lansford, J. E., & Burks, V. S. (2003). Peer rejection and social information-processing factors in the development of aggressive behavior problems in children. *Child Development, 74,* 374–393.

Dodge, K. A., & Price, J. M. (1994). On the relation between social information processing and socially competent behavior in early school-aged children. *Child Development, 65,* 1385–1397.

Doka, K. J., & Mertz, M. E. (1988). The meaning and significance of great-grandparenthood. *Gerontologist, 28,* 192–197.

Doman, G., & Doman, J. (2002). *How to teach your baby to read.* Gentle Revolution Press.

Dominguez, H. D., Lopez, M. F., & Molina, J. C. (1999). Interactions between perinatal and neonatal associative learning defined by contiguous olfactory and tactile stimulation. *Neurobiology of Learning and Memory, 71,* 272–288.

Donat, D. (2006, October). Reading their way: A balanced approach that increases achievement. *Reading and Writing Quarterly: Overcoming Learning Difficulties, 22,* 305–323.

Dondi, M., Simion, F., & Caltran, G. (1999). Can newborns discriminate between their own cry and the cry of another newborn infant? *Developmental Psychology, 35,* 418–426.

Doress, P. B., Siegal, D. L., & The Midlife and Old Women Book Project. (1987). *Ourselves, growing older.* New York: Simon and Schuster.

Dorofaeff, T., & Denny, S. (2006, September). Sleep and adolescence. Do New Zealand teenagers get enough? *Journal of Paediatrics and Child Health, 42,* 515–520.

Dowling, N., Smith, D., & Thomas, T. (2005). Electronic gaming machines: Are they the 'crack-cocaine' of gambling? *Addiction, 100,* 33–45.

Doyle, R. (2004a, January). Living together. *Scientific American,* p. 28.

Doyle, R. (2004b, April). By the numbers: A surplus of women. *Scientific American, 290,* 33.

Dreman, S. (Ed.). (1997). *The family on the threshold of the 21st century.* Mahwah, NJ: Erlbaum.

Driver, J., Tabares, A., & Shapiro, A. (2003). Interactional patterns in marital success and failure: Gottman laboratory studies. In F. Walsh (Ed.), *Normal family processes: Growing diversity and complexity* (3rd ed.). New York: Guilford Press.

Dromi, E. (1987). *Early lexical development.* Cambridge, England: Cambridge University Press.

Dryfoos, J. G. (1990). *Adolescents at risk: Prevalence and prevention.* New York: Oxford University Press.

DuBois, D. L., & Hirsch, B. J. (1990). School and neighborhood friendship patterns of blacks and whites in early adolescence. *Child Development, 61,* 524–536.

Duenwald, M. (2003, July 15). After 25 years, new ideas in the prenatal test tube. *The New York Times,* p. D5.

Duenwald, M. (2004, May 11). For couples, stress without a promise of success. *The New York Times,* p. D3.

Dukes, R., & Martinez, R. (1994). The impact of gender on self-esteem among adolescents. *Adolescence, 29,* 105–115.

Dulitzki, M., Soriano, D., Schiff, E., Chetrit, A., Mashiach, S., & Seidman, D. S. (1998). Effect of very advanced maternal age on pregnancy outcome and rate of cesarean delivery. *Obstetrics and Gynecology, 92,* 935–939.

DuPaul, G., & Weyandt, L. (2006, June). School-based intervention for children with attention deficit hyperactivity disorder: Effects on academic, social, and behavioural functioning. *International Journal of Disability, Development and Education, 53,* 161–176.

Duplassie, D., & Daniluk, J. C. 2007). Sexuality: Young and middle adulthood. In A. Owens & M. Tupper (Eds.), *Sexual health: Volume 1, psychological foundations.* Westport, CT: Praeger.

Durbin, J. (2003, October 6). Internet sex unzipped. *Macleans,* p. 18.

Durik, A. M., Hyde, J. S., & Clark, R. (2000). Sequelae of cesarean and vaginal deliveries: Psychosocial outcomes for mothers and infants. *Developmental Psychology, 36,* 251–260.

Durkin, K., & Nugent, B. (1998). Kindergarten children's gender-role expectations for television actors. *Sex Roles, 38,* 387–402.

Durrant, Joan E., (1993–1994). Sparing the rod: Manitobans' attitudes toward the abolition of physical discipline and implications for policy change. *Canada's Mental Health, 41(4),* 2–6.

Dutton, D. G. (1994). *The domestic assault of women: Psychological and criminal justice perspectives* (2nd ed.). Vancouver, BC, Canada: University of British Columbia Press.

Dwairy, M., Achoui, M., Abouserie, R., & Farah, A. (2006, May). Parenting styles, individuation, and mental health of Arab adolescents: A third cross-regional research study. *Journal of Cross-Cultural Psychology, 37,* 262–272.

Dweck, C. (2002). The development of ability conceptions. In A. Wigfield & J. Eccles (Eds.), *Development of achievement motivation.* San Diego: Academic Press.

Dyer, C. B., Pavlik, V. N., Murphy, K. P., & Hyman, D. J. (2000). The high prevalence of depression and dementia in elder abuse or neglect. *Journal of the American Geriatrics Society, 48,* 205–208.

Dyregrov, K., Nordanger, D., & Dyregrov, A. (2003). Predictors of psychosocial distress after suicide, SIDS and accidents. *Death Studies, 27,* 143–165.

Dyson, A. H. (2003). "Welcome to the jam": Popular culture, school literacy and making of childhoods. *Harvard Educational Review, 73,* 328–361.

Eacott, M. J. (1999). Memory of the events of early childhood. *Current Directions in Psychological Science, 8,* 46–49.

Eagly, A. H., & Steffen, V. J. (1984). Gender stereotypes stem from the distribution of women and men into social roles. *Journal of Personality and Social Psychology, 46,* 735–754.

Eagly, A. H., & Steffen, V. J. (1986). Gender and aggressive behavior: A meta-analytic review of the social psychological literature. *Psychological Bulletin, 100,* 309–330.

Eagly, A. H., & Wood, W. (2003). In C. B. Travis, *Evolution, gender, and rape.* Cambridge, MA: MIT Press.

Eastman, Q. (2003, June 20). Crib death exoneration in new gene tests. *Science, 300,* 1858.

Eaton, W. O., & Enns, L. R. (1986). Sex differences in human motor activity level. *Psychological Bulletin, 100,* 19–28.

Eaton, W. O., & Yu, A. P. (1989). Are sex differences in child motor activity level a function of sex differences in maturational status? *Child Development, 60,* 1005–1011.

Eberling, J. L., Wu, C., Tong-Turnbeaugh, R., & Jagust, W. J. (2004). Estrogen- and tamoxifen-associated effects on brain structure and function. *Neuroimage, 21,* 364–371.

Ebner, N., Freund, A., & Baltes, P. (2006, December). Developmental changes in personal goal orientation from young to late adulthood: From striving for gains to maintenance and prevention of losses. *Psychology and Aging, 21,* 664–678.

Ebstein, R. P., Novick, O., Umansky, R., Priel, B., Osher, Y., Blaine, D., Bennett, E. R...Belmaker, R. H. (1996). Dopamine D4 receptor (1996) exon III polymorphism associated with the human personality trait of novelty seeking. *Nature and Genetics, 12,* 78–80.

Eccles, J., Templeton, J., & Barber, B. (2003). Adolescence and emerging adulthood: The critical passage ways to adulthood. In M. Bornstein & L. Davidson (Eds.), *Well-being: Positive development across the life course*. Mahwah, NJ: Lawrence Erlbaum Associates.

Eckerman, C. & and Peterman, K. (2001). Peers and infant social/communicative development. In G. Bremner & A. Fogel (Eds.), *Blackwell handbook of infant development* (pp. 326–350). Malden, MA: Blackwell Publishers.

Eckerman, C. O. & Oehler, J. M. (1992). Very-low-birthweight newborns and parents as early social partners. In S. L. Friedman and M. D. Sigman (Eds.), *The psychological development of low-birthweight children*. Norwood, NJ: Ablex.

Edwards, C. P. (2000). Children's play in cross-cultural perspective: A new look at the Six Cultures study. *Cross-Cultural Research: The Journal of Comparative Social Science, 34*, 318–338.

Edwards, S. (2005). Constructivism does not only happen in the individual: Sociocultural theory and early childhood education. *Early Child Development and Care, 175*, 37–47.

Effer, S. B., Moutquin, J.-M., Farine, D., Saigal, S., Nimrod, C., Kelly, E. & Niyonsenga, T. (2002). Neonatal survival rates in 860 singleton live births at 24 and 25 weeks gestational age. A Canadian multicentre study. *BJOG: An International Journal of Obstetrics & Gynaecology, 109*, 740–745. doi: 10.1111/j.1471-0528.2002.01067.x.

Egan, S. K., & Perry, D. G. (1998). Does low self-regard invite victimization? *Developmental Psychology, 34*, 299–309.

Ehrensaft, M., Cohen, P., & Brown, J. (2003). Intergenerational transmission of partner violence: A 20-year prospective study. *Journal of Consulting and Clinical Psychology, 71*, 741–753.

Eichstedt, J., Serbin, L., & Poulin-Dubois, D. (2002). Of bears and men: Infants' knowledge of conventional and metaphorical gender stereotypes. *Infant Behavior and Development, 25*, 296–310.

Eiden, R., Foote, A., & Schuetze, P. (2007). Maternal cocaine use and caregiving status: Group differences in caregiver and infant risk variables. *Addictive Behaviors, 32*, 465–476.

Eigsti, I., & Cicchetti, D. (2004). The impact of child maltreatment on expressive syntax at 60 months. *Developmental Science, 7*, 88–102.

Eisbach, A. O. (2004). Children's developing awareness of diversity in people's trains of thought. *Child Development, 75*, 1694–1707.

Eisenberg, N. (2004). Another slant on moral judgment. *psycCRITQUES, 12*–15.

Eisenberg, N., Guthrie, I. K., Murphy, B. C., Shepard, S. A., Cumberland, A., & Carlo, G. (1999). Consistency and development of prosocial dispositions: A longitudinal study. *Child Development, 70*, 1360–1372.

Eisenberg, N., & Valiente, C. (2002). Parenting and children's prosocial and moral development. In M. Bornstein (Ed.), *Handbook of parenting: Vol. 5: Practical issues in parenting*. Mahwah, NJ: Lawrence Erlbaum Associates.

Eisenberg, N., & Zhou, Q. (2000). Regulation from a developmental perspective. *Psychological Inquiry, 11*, 166–172.

Eitel, B. J. (2003). Body image satisfaction, appearance importance, and self-esteem: A comparison of Caucasian and African-American women across the adult lifespan. *Dissertation Abstracts International: Section B. The Sciences and Engineering, 63*, pp. 5511.

Elder, G. A., De Gasperi, R., & Gama Sosa, M. A. (2006). Research update: Neurogenesis in adult brain and neuropsychiatric disorders. *Mt. Sinai Journal of Medicine, 73*, 931–940.

Eley, T., Liang, H., & Plomin, R. (2004). Parental familial vulnerability, family environment, and their interactions as predictors of depressive symptoms in adolescents. *Child and Adolescent Social Work Journal, 21*, 298–306.

Eley, T. C., Bolton, D., & O'Connor, T. G. (2003). A twin study of anxiety-related behaviours in pre-school children. *Journal of Child Psychology and Psychiatry and Allied Disciplines, 44*, 103–121.

Eley, T. C., Lichtenstein, P., & Moffitt, T. E. (2003). A longitudinal behavioral genetic analysis of the etiology of aggressive and nonaggressive antisocial behavior. *Development and Psychopathology, 15*, 383–402.

Elkind, D. (1985). Egocentrism redux. *Developmental Review, 5*, 218–226.

Elkind, D. (1994). *Ties that stress: The new family imbalance*. Cambridge, MA: Harvard University Press.

Elkind, D. (1996). Inhelder and Piaget on adolescence and adulthood: A postmodern appraisal. *Psychological Science, 7*, 216–220.

Elliott, K., & Urquiza, A. (2006). Ethnicity, culture, and child maltreatment. *Journal of Social Issues, 62*, 787–809.

Ellis, B. J. (2004). Timing of pubertal maturation in girls: An integrated life history approach. *Psychological Bulletin, 130*, 920–958.

Ellis, L. (2006, July). Gender differences in smiling: An evolutionary neuroandrogenic theory. *Physiology and Behavior, 88*, 303–308.

Else-Quest, N. M., Hyde, J. S., & Clark, R. (2003). Breastfeeding, bonding, and the mother–infant relationship. *Merrill-Palmer Quarterly, 49*, 495–517.

Emslie, G. J., Rush, A. J., Weinberg, W. A., Kowatch, R. A., Hughes, C. W., Carmody, T., & Rintelmann, J. A. (1997). Double-blind, randomized, placebo-controlled trial of fluoxetine in children and adolescents with depression. *Archives of General Psychiatry, 54*, 1031–1037.

Endo, S. (1992). Infant–infant play from 7 to 12 months of age: An analysis of games in infant–peer triads. *Japanese Journal of Child and Adolescent Psychiatry, 33*, 145–162.

Engler, J., & Goleman, D. (1992). *The consumer's guide to psychotherapy*. New York: Simon and Schuster.

Englund, K., & Behne, D. (2006). Changes in infant directed speech in the first six months. *Infant and Child Development, 15(2)*, 139–160.

Englund, M. M., Levy, A. K., Hyson, D. M., & Sroufe, L. A. (2000). Adolescent social competence: Effectiveness in a group setting. *Child Development, 71*, 1049–1060.

Ennett, S. T., & Bauman, K. E. (1996). Adolescent social networks: School, demographic, and longitudinal considerations. *Journal of Adolescent Research, 11*, 194–215.

Enright, E. (2004, July and August). A house divided. *AARP Magazine*, pp. 54, 57.

Ensenauer, R. E., Michels, V. V., & Reinke, S. S. (2005). Genetic testing: Practical, ethical, and counseling considerations. *Mayo Clinic Proceedings, 80*, 63–73.

Epperson, S. E. (1988, September 16). Studies link subtle sex bias in schools with women's behavior in the workplace. *The Wall Street Journal*, p. 19.

Erber, J. T., Rothberg, S. T., & Szuchman, L. T. (1991). Appraisal of everyday memory failures by middle-aged adults. *Educational Gerontology, 17*, 63–72.

Erber, J. T., Szuchman, L. T., & Rothberg, S. T. (1990). Everyday memory failure: Age differences in appraisal and attribution. *Psychology and Aging, 5*, 236–241.

Erikson, E. H. (1963). *Childhood and society*. New York: Norton.

Eron, L. (1982). Parent-child interaction, television violence, and aggression of children. *American Psychologist, 37*, 197–211. doi: 10.1037/0003-066X.37.2.197.

Erwin, P. (1993). *Friendship and peer relations in children*. Chichester, England: Wiley.

Eslea, M., Menesini, E., Morita, Y., O'Moore, M., Mora-Nerchan, J. A., Pereira, B., & Smith, P. K. (2004). Friendship and loneliness among bullies and victims: Data from seven countries. *Aggressive Behavior, 30*, 71–83.

Espelage, D. L., & Swearer, S. M. (2004). *Bullying in American schools*. Mahwah, NJ: Lawrence Erlbaum.

Espenschade, A. (1960). Motor development. In W. R. Johnson (Ed.), *Science and medicine of exercise and sports*. New York: Harper and Row.

Essex, M. J., & Nam, S. (1987). Marital status and loneliness among older women: The differential importance of close family and friends. *Journal of Marriage and the Family, 49*, 92–106.

Ethier, L., Couture, G., & Lacharite, C. (2004). Risk factors associated with the chronicity of high potential for child abuse and neglect. *Journal of Family Violence, 19*, 13–24.

Evans, G. W. (2004). The environment of childhood poverty. *American Psychologist, 59*, 77–92.

Eyer, D. (1992). The bonding hype. In M. E. Lamb & J. B. Lancaster (Eds.), *Birth management: Biosocial perspectives*. Hawthorne, New York: Aldine de Gruyter.

Faith, M. S., Johnson, S. L., & Allison, D. B. (1997). Putting the behavior into the behavior genetics of obesity. *Behavior Genetics, 27*, 423–439.

Fantz, R. (1963). Pattern vision in newborn infants. *Science, 140*, 296–297.

Fantz, R. L. (1961). The origin of form perception. *Scientific American*, p. 72.

Farine, D., Shenhav, M., Barnea, O., Jaffa, A., & Fox, H. E. (2006). The need for a new outlook on labor monitoring. *Journal of Maternal and Fetal and Neonatal Medicine, 19*, 161–164.

Farmer, T. W., Estell, D. B., Bishop, J. L., O'Neal, K. K., & Cairns, B. D. (2003). Rejected bullies or popular leaders? The social relations of aggressive subtypes of rural African American early adolescents. *Developmental Psychology, 39*, 992–1004.

Faulkner, G., & Biddle, S. (2004). Exercise and depression: Considering variability and contextuality. *Journal of Sport and Exercise Psychology, 26*, 3–18.

Federal Interagency Forum on Age-Related Statistics. (2000). *Older Americans 2000: Key indicators of well-being*. Hyattsville, MD: Federal Interagency Forum on Age-Related Statistics.

Feeney, B., & Collins, N. (2001). Predictors of caregiving in adult intimate relationships: An attachment theoretical perspective. *Journal of Personality and Social Psychology, 80*, 972–994.

Feinberg, J. L. (2000). Ensuring appropriate, effective, and safe medication use for older people. *Medication and Aging*.

Feldman, R., & Eidelman, A. (2003). Direct and indirect effects of breast milk on neurobehavioral and cognitive development of premature infants. *Developmental Psychobiology, 43*, 109–119.

Feldman, R., & Masalha, S. (2007). The role of culture in moderating the links between early ecological risk and young children's adaptation. *Development and Psychopathology, 19*, 1–21.

Feldman, R. S. (Ed.). (1992). *Applications of nonverbal behavioral theories and research*. Hillsdale, NJ: Erlbaum.

Feldman, R. S., Philippot, P., & Custrini, R. J. (1991). Social competence and nonverbal behavior. In R. S. Feldman & B. Rime (Eds.), *Fundamentals of nonverbal behavior*. Cambridge, England: Cambridge University Press.

Feldman, R. S., Tomasian, J., & Coats, E. J. (1999). Adolescents' social competence and nonverbal deception abilities: Adolescents with higher social skills are better liars. *Journal of Nonverbal Behavior, 23*, 237–249.

Feldman, S. S., & Rosenthal, D. A. (1990). The acculturation of autonomy expectations in Chinese high schoolers residing in two Western nations. *International Journal of Psychology, 25*, 259–281.

Feldman, S. S., & Wood, D. N. (1994). Parents' expectations for preadolescent sons' behavioral autonomy: A longitudinal study of correlates and outcomes. *Journal of Research on Adolescence, 4*, 45–70.

Fenson, L., Dale, P. S., Reznick, J. S., Bates, E., Thal, D. J., & Pethick, S. J. (1994). Variability in early communicative development. *Monographs of the Society for Research in Child Development, 59* (5, Serial No. 242).

Fenwick, K., & Morrongiello, B. (1991). Development of frequency perception in infants and children. *Journal of Speech, Language Pathology, and Audiology, 15,* 7–22.

Fergusson, D. M., Horwood, L. J., & Ridder, E. M. (2006). Abortion in young women and subsequent mental health. *Journal of Child Psychology and Psychiatry, 47,* 16–24.

Fernald, A. (2001). Hearing, listening, and understanding: Auditory development in infancy. In G. Bremner & A. Fogel (Eds.), *Blackwell handbook of infant development.* Malden, MA: Blackwell Publishers.

Fernald, A., & Marchman, V. A. (2006). Language learning in infancy. In Traxler, M. J. & Gernsbacher, M. A. (Eds.) *Handbook of psycholinguistics* (2nd ed).

Fernyhough, C. (1997). Vygotsky's sociocultural approach: Theoretical issues and implications for current research. In S. Hala (Ed.), *The development of social cognition* (pp. 65–92). Hove, England: Psychology Press/Erlbaum, Taylor and Francis.

Ferrao, V. (2011). Women in Canada: A gender-based statistical report: Paid work. Statistics Canada Catalogue no. 89-503-XWE. Retrieved from http://www.statcan.gc.ca/pub/89-503-x/2010001/article/11388/c-g/c-g001-eng.htm.

Ferrao, V., & Williams, C. (2010). Women in Canada: A Gender-based statistical report. Statistics Canada Catalogue no. 89-503-XWE. Ottawa. Retrieved from http://www.statcan.gc.ca/pub/89-503-x/89-503-x2010001-eng.htm. Accessed March 28, 2011.

Ferrario, S., Vitaliano, P., & Zotti, A. (2003). Alzheimer's disease: Usefulness of the Family Strain Questionnaire and the Screen for Caregiver Burden in the study of caregiving-related problems. *International Journal of Geriatric Psychiatry, 18,* 1110–1114.

Fetterman, D. M. (1998). Ethnography. In L. Bickman & D. J. Rog (Eds.), *Handbook of applied social research methods* (pp. 473–504). Thousand Oaks, CA: Sage.

Fiatarone, M. S. A., & Garnett, L. R. (1997, March). Keep on keeping on. *Harvard Health Letter,* pp. 4–5.

Field, D., & Minkler, M. (1988). Continuity and change in social support between young-old and old-old or very-old age. *Journal of Gerontology, 43(4),* 100–106.

Field, T. (2001). Massage therapy facilitates weight gain in preterm infants. *Current Directions in Psychological Science, 10,* 51–54.

Field, T., Diego, M., & Hernandez-Rief, M. (2008). Prematurity and potential predictors. *International Journal of Neuroscience, 118,* 277–289.

Field, T., Greenberg, R., Woodson, R., Cohen, D., & Garcia, R. (1984). Facial expression during Brazelton neonatal assessments. *Infant Mental Health Journal, 5,* 61–71.

Field, T., & Walden, T. (1982). Perception and production of facial expression in infancy and early childhood. In H. Reese & L. Lipsitt (Eds.), *Advances in child development and behavior* (Vol. 16). New York: Academic Press.

Field, T. M. (1982). Individual differences in the expressivity of neonates and young infants. In R. S. Feldman (Ed.), *Development of nonverbal behavior in children.* New York: Springer-Verlag.

Field, T. M. (1990). Alleviating stress in newborn infants in the intensive care unit. In B. M. Lester & E. Z. Tronick (Eds.), *Stimulation and the preterm infant: The limits of plasticity.* Philadelphia: Saunders.

Field, T. M., & Millsap, R. E. (1991). Personality in advanced old age: Continuity or change? *Journal of Gerontology: Psychological Sciences, 46,* P299–P308.

Fields-Meyer, T. (1995, September 25). Having their say. *People,* 50–60.

Fifer, W.P., & Moon, C. (2003). Prenatal development. In A. Slater & G. Bremner (Eds.), *An Introduction to Developmental Psychology* (pp. 95–114). Blackwell.

Figley, C. R. (1973). Child density and the marital relationship. *Journal of Marriage and the Family, 35,* 272–282.

Finch, C. E., & Tanzi, R. E. (1997, October 17). Genetics of aging. *Science, 278,* 407–410.

Fincham, F. D. (2003). Marital conflict: Correlates, structure, and context. *Current Directions in Psychological Science, 12,* 23–27.

Fingerhut, L. A., & MaKuc, D. M. (1992). Mortality among minority populations in the United States. *American Journal of Public Health, 82,* 1168–1170.

Finkbeiner, A. K. (1996). *After the death of a child: Living with loss through the years.* New York: The Free Press.

First, J. M., & Cardenas, J. (1986). A minority view on testing. *Educational Measurement Issues and Practice, 5,* 6–11.

Fisch, S. M. (2004). *Children's learning from educational television: Sesame Street and beyond.* Mahwah, NJ: Routledge.

Fischer, K. W., & Rose, S. P. (1995). Concurrent cycles in the dynamic development of brain and behavior. *Newsletter of the Society for Research in Child Development,* p. 16.

Fish, J. M. (Ed.). (2001). *Race and intelligence: Separating science from myth.* Mahwah, NJ: Erlbaum.

Fiske, S. T., & Taylor, S. E. (1991). *Social cognition* (2nd ed.). New York: McGraw-Hill.

Fivush, R., Kuebli, J., & Clubb, P. A. (1992). The structure of events and event representations: A developmental analysis. *Child Development, 63,* 188–201.

Flavell, J. H. (1994). Cognitive development: Past, present, and future. In R. D. Parke, P. A. Ornstein, J. J. Rieser, & C. Zahn-Waxler (Eds.), *A century of developmental psychology.* Washington, DC: American Psychological Association.

Flavell, J. H. (1996). Piaget's legacy. *Psychological Science, 7,* 200–203.

Fletcher, A. C., Darling, N. E., Steinberg, L., & Dornbusch, S. M. (1995). The company they keep: Relation of adolescents' adjustment and behavior to their friends' perceptions of authoritative parenting in the social network. *Developmental Psychology, 31,* 300–310.

Flom, R., & Bahrick, L. (2007). The development of infant discrimination of affect in multimodal and unimodal stimulation: The role of intersensory redundancy. *Developmental Psychology, 43,* 238–252.

Flor, D. L., & Knap, N. F. (2001). Transmission and transaction: Predicting adolescents' internalization of parental religious values. *Journal of Family Psychology, 15,* 627–645.

Florsheim, P. (2003). Adolescent romantic and sexual behavior: What we know and where we go from here. In P. Florsheim (Ed.), *Adolescent romantic relations and sexual behavior: Theory, research, and practical implications.* Mahwah, NJ: Lawrence Erlbaum Associates.

Flouri, E. (2005). *Fathering and child outcomes.* New York: Wiley and Sons.

Flynn, E., O'Malley, C., & Wood, D. (2004). A longitudinal, microgenetic study of the emergence of false belief understanding and inhibition skills. *Developmental Science, 7,* 103–115.

Fogel, A., Hsu, H., Shapiro, A., Nelson-Goens, G., & Secrist, C. (2006, May). Effects of normal and perturbed social play on the duration and amplitude of different types of infant smiles. *Developmental Psychology, 42,* 459–473.

Fowers, B. J., & Davidov, B. J. (2006). The virtue of multiculturalism: Personal transformation, character, and openness to the other. *American Psychologist, 61,* 581–594.

Fozard, J. L., Vercruyssen, M., Reynolds, S. L., Hancock, P. A., et al. (1994). Age differences and changes in reaction time: The Baltimore Longitudinal Study of Aging. *Journal of Gerontology, 49,* 179–189.

Fraenkel, P. (2003). Contemporary two-parent families: Navigating work and family challenges. In F. Walsh (Ed.), *Normal family processes: Growing diversity and complexity* (3rd ed., pp. 61–95). New York: Guilford Press.

Franko, D. L., & Striegel-Moore, R. H. (2002). The role of body dissatisfaction as a risk factor for depression in adolescent girls: Are the differences Black and White? *Journal of Psychosomatic Research, 53(5),* pp. 975–983.

Franck, I., & Brownstone, D. (1991). *The parent's desk reference.* New York: Prentice-Hall.

Frankenburg, W. K., Dodds, J., Archer, P., Shapiro, H., & Bresnick, B. (1992). The Denver II: A major revision and restandardization of the Denver Developmental Screening Test. *Pediatrics, 89,* 91–97.

Fransen, M., Meertens, R., & Schrander-Stumpel, C. (2006). Communication and risk presentation in genetic counseling: Development of a checklist. *Patient Education and Counseling, 61,* 126–133.

Fraser, R. D. (1983), Historical statistics of Canada, section B: Vital statistics and health. Catalogue no. 11-516-XWE. Retrieved May 3, 2012.

Frazier, L. M., Grainger, D. A., Schieve, L. A., & Toner, J. P. (2004). Follicle-stimulating hormone and estradiol levels independently predict the success of assisted reproductive technology treatment. *Fertility and Sterility, 82,* 834–840.

Fredriksen, K., Rhodes, J., Reddy, R., & Way, N. (2004). Sleepless in Chicago: Tracking the effects of adolescent sleep loss during the middle school years. *Child Development, 75,* 84–95.

Freedman, A. M., & Ellison, S. (2004, May 6). Testosterone patch for women shows promise. *The Wall Street Journal,* pp. A1, B2.

Freedman, D. G., & DeBoer, M. M. (1979). Biological and cultural differences in early child development. *Annual Review of Anthropology, 8,* 579–600.

Freedman, D. S., Khan, L. K., Serdula, M. K., Dietz, W. H., Sriniasan, S. R., & Berenson, G. S. (2004). Inter-relationships among childhood BMI, childhood height, and adult obesity: The Bogalusa Heart Study. *International Journal of Obesity and Related Metabolic Disorders, 28,* 10–16.

Freeman, E., Sammel, M., & Liu, L. (2004). Hormones and menopausal status as predictors of depression in women in transition to menopause. *Archives of General Psychiatry, 61,* 62–70.

French, S., & Swain, J. (1997). Young disabled people. In J. Roche & S. Tucker (Eds.), *Youth in society: Contemporary theory, policy and practice* (pp. 199–206). London Sage.

Freud, S. (1920). *A general introduction to psychoanalysis.* New York: Boni and Liveright.

Freud, S. (1922/1959). *Group psychology and the analysis of the ego.* London: Hogarth.

Friborg, O., Barlaug, D., Martinussen, M., Rosenvinge, J. H., & Hjemdal, O. (2005). Resilience in relation to personality and intelligence. *International Journal of Methods in Psychiatric Research, 14,* 29–42.

Frick, P. J., Cornell, A. H., Bodin, S. D., Dane, H. A., Barry, C. T., & Loney, B. R. (2003). Callous-unemotional traits and developmental pathways to severe conduct problems. *Developmental Psychology, 39,* 246–260.

Friedland, R. (2003). Fish consumption and the risk of Alzheimer disease: Is it time to make dietary recommendations? *Archives of Neurology, 60,* 923–924.

Friedman, L., Kahn, J., Middleman, A., Rosenthal, S., & Zimet, G. (2006, October). Human papillomavirus (HPV) vaccine: A position statement of the society for adolescent medicine. *Journal of Adolescent Health, 39,* 620.

Friendly, M., Ferns, C., & Prabhu, N. (2009). Ratios for four and five year olds: What does the research say? What else is important? Retrieved from www.childcarecanada.org/pubs/pdf/BN_ratios.pdf. Accessed May 3, 2011.

Frisch, M., Friis, S., Kjear, S. K., & Melbye, M. (1995). Falling incidence of penis cancer in an uncircumcised population (Denmark 1943–90). *British Medical Journal, 311,* 1471.

Fritz, G., & Rockney, R. (2004). Summary of the practice parameter for the assessment and treatment of children and adolescents with enuresis. *Work Group on Quality Issues; Journal of the American Academy of Child and Adolescent Psychiatry, 43,* 123–125.

Frome, P., Alfeld, C., Eccles, J., & Barber, B. (2006, August). Why don't they want a male-dominated job? An investigation of young women who changed their occupational aspirations. *Educational Research and Evaluation, 12,* 359–372.

Fromholt, P., & Larsen, S. F. (1991). Autobiographical memory in normal, aging and primary degenerative dementia (dementia of the Alzheimer type). *Journal of Gerontology, 46,* 85–91.

Fry, C. L. (1985). Culture, behavior, and aging in the comparative perspective. In J. E. Birren & K. W. Schaie (Eds.), *Handbook of the psychology of aging.* New York: Van Nostrand Reinhold.

Fu, G., Xu, F., Cameron, C., Heyman, G., & Lee, K. (2007, March). Cross-cultural differences in children's choices, categorizations, and evaluations of truths and lies. *Developmental Psychology, 43(2),* 278–293.

Fugate, W. N., & Mitchell, E. S. (1997). Women's images of midlife: Observations from the Seattle Midlife Women's Health Study. *Health Care for Women International, 18,* 439–453.

Fuligni, A., & Hardway, C. (2006, September). Daily variation in adolescents' sleep, activities, and psychological well-being. *Journal of Research on Adolescence, 16,* 353–378.

Fuligni, A., & Yoshikawa, H. (2003). Socioeconomic resources, parenting, and child development among immigrant families. In M. Bornstein & R. Bradley (Eds.), *Socioeconomic status, parenting, and child development.* Mahwah, NJ: Lawrence Erlbaum Associates.

Fuligni, A., & Zhang, W. (2004). Attitudes toward family obligation among adolescents in contemporary urban and rural China. *Child Development, 75,* 180–192.

Fulgini, A. J. (1998). The adjustment of children from immigrant families. *Current Directions in Psychological Science, 7,* 99–103.

Fuligni, A. J., Tseng, V., & Lam, M. (1999). Attitudes toward family obligations among American adolescents with Asian, Latin American, and European backgrounds. *Child Development, 70,* 1030–1044.

Funk, J., Buchman, D., & Jenks, J. (2003). Playing violent video games, desensitization, and moral evaluation in children. *Journal of Applied Developmental Psychology, 24,* 413–436.

Furi, M., & Guimont, A. (2003). Teen suicide in Canada. Library of Parliament Catalogue PRB 03-42E.

Furman, W., & Shaffer, L. (2003). The role of romantic relationships in adolescent development. In P. Florsheim (Ed.), *Adolescent romantic relations and sexual behavior: Theory, research, and practical implications.* Mahwah, NJ: Lawrence Erlbaum Associates.

Furstenberg, Jr., F. F. (1996, June). The future of marriage. *American Demographics,* 34–40.

Gabbay, S., & Wahler, J. (2002). Lesbian aging: Review of a growing literature. *Journal of Gay and Lesbian Social Services: Issues in Practice, Policy and Research, 14,* 1–21.

Gagné, M.-H., Tourigny, M., Joly, J., & Pouliot-Lapointe, J. (2007). Predictors of adult attitudes toward corporal punishment of children. *Journal of Interpersonal Violence.* Retrieved from http://jiv.sagepub.com/content/22/10/1285.short.

Gagnon, S. G., & Nagle, R. J. (2000). Comparison of the revised and original versions of the Bayley Scales of Infant Development. *School Psychology International, 21,* 293–305.

Galambos, N., Leadbeater, B., & Barker, E. (2004). Gender differences in and risk factors for depression in adolescence: A 4-year longitudinal study. *International Journal of Behavioral Development, 28,* 16–25.

Galbraith, K. M., & Dobson, K. S. (2000). The role of the psychologist in determining competence for assisted suicide/euthanasia in the terminally ill. *Canadian Psychology, 41,* 174–183.

Gallagher, L., Becker, K., & Kearney, G. (2003). A case of autism associated with del(2)(q32.1q32.2) or (q32.2q32.3). *Journal of Autism and Developmental Disorders, 33,* 105–108.

Gallup, G. G., Jr. (1977). Self-recognition in primates: A comparative approach to the bidirectional properties of consciousness. *American Psychologist, 32,* 329–337.

Gallup Poll. (2004). How many children? *The Gallup Poll Monthly.*

Gamliel, I., Yirmiya, N., Jaffe, D. H., Manor, O., & Sigman, M. (2009). Developmental trajectories in siblings of children with autism: Cognition and language from 4 months to 7 years. *Journal of Autism and Developmental Disorders, 39,* 1131–1144.

Ganger, J., & Brent, M. R. (2004). Reexamining the vocabulary spurt. *Developmental Psychology, 40,* 621–632.

Ganzini, L., Beer, T., & Brouns, M. (2006, September). Views on physician-assisted suicide among family members of Oregon cancer patients. *Journal of Pain and Symptom Management, 32,* 230–236.

Garcia-Moreno, C., Heise, L., Jansen, H. A. F. M., Ellsberg, M., & Watts, C. (2005, November 25). Violence against women. *Science, 310,* 1282–1283.

Gardner, H. (2000). *Intelligence reframed: Multiple intelligences for the 21st century.* New York: Basic Books.

Gardner, H. (2003). Three distinct meanings of intelligence. In R. Sternberg & J. Lautrey (Eds.), *Models of intelligence: International perspectives.* Washington, DC: American Psychological Association.

Gardner, H., & Moran, S. (2006). The science of multiple intelligences theory: A response to Lynn Waterhouse. *Educational Psychologist, 41,* 227–232.

Garland, J. E. (2004). Facing the evidence: Antidepressant treatment in children and adolescents. *Canadian Medical Association Journal, 17,* 489–491.

Garlick, D. (2003). Integrating brain science research with intelligence research. *Current Directions in Psychological Science, 12,* 185–189.

Garrison, M., & Christakis, D. (2005). *A teacher in the living room? Educational media for babies, toddlers and preschoolers.* Menlo Park, CA: Kaiser Family Foundation.

Gartstein, M., Slobodskaya, H., & Kinsht, I. (2003). Cross-cultural differences in temperament in the first year of life: United States of America (US) and Russia. *International Journal of Behavioral Development, 27,* 316–328.

Gaulden, M. E. (1992). Maternal age effect: The enigma of Down syndrome and other trisomic conditions. *Mutation Research, 296,* 69–88.

Gauthier, Y. (2003). Infant mental health as we enter the third millennium: Can we prevent aggression? *Infant Mental Health Journal, 24,* 101–109.

Gauvain, M. (1998). Cognitive development in social and cultural context. *Current Directions in Psychological Science, 7,* 188–194.

Gavin, T., & Myers, A. (2003). Characteristics, enrollment, attendance, and dropout patterns of older adults in beginner Tai-Chi and line-dancing programs. *Journal of Aging and Physical Activity, 11,* 123–141.

Gawande, A. (2007, April 30). The way we age now. *The New Yorker,* 49–59.

Gazmararian, J. A., Petersen, R., Spitz, A. M., Goodwin, M. M., Saltzman, L. E., & Marks, J. S. (2000). Violence and reproductive health: Current knowledge and future research directions. *Mat Child Health, 4,* 79–84.

Gazzaniga, M. S. (1983). Right-hemisphere language following brain bisection: A twenty-year perspective. *American Psychologist, 38,* 525–537.

Geangu, E., Benga, O., Stahl, D., & Striano, T. (2010). Contagious crying beyond the first days of life. *Infant Behavior and Development.* doi:10.1016/j.infbeh.2010.03.004.

Gee, H. (2004). *Jacob's ladder: The history of the human genome.* New York: Norton.

Gelfand, M. M. (2000). Sexuality among older women. *Journal of Womens Health and Gender-Based Medicine, 9*(Suppl 1), S-15–S-20.

Gelman, D. (1994, April 18). The mystery of suicide. *Newsweek,* 44–49.

Gelman, R. (2006, August). Young natural-number arithmeticians. *Current Directions in Psychological Science, 15,* 193–197.

Gelman, R. (1982). Accessing one-to-one correspondence: Still another paper about conservation. *British Journal of Psychology, 73,* 209–220. doi: 10.1111/j.2044-8295.1982.tb01803.x.

Gelman, R., & Baillargeon, R. (1983). A review of some Piagetian concepts. In P. H. Mussen (Ed.), *Handbook of child psychology: Vol 3. Cognitive development* (4th ed., pp. 167–230). New York: Wiley.

Gelman, R., and Gallistel, C. R. (2004, October 15). Language and the origin of numerical concepts. *Science, 306,* 441–443.

Gelman, S. A., Taylor, M. G., & Nguyen, S. (2004). Mother-child conversations about gender. *Monographs of the Society for Research in Child Development, 69.*

Genovese, J. (2003). Piaget, pedagogy, and evolutionary psychology. *Evolutionary Psychology, 4,* 127–137.

Gerard, C. M., Harris, K. A., & Thach, B. T. (2002). Spontaneous arousals in supine infants while swaddled and unswaddled during rapid eye movement and quiet sleep. *Pediatrics, 110,* 70.

Gerber, P., & Coffman, K. (2007). Nonaccidental head trauma in infants. *Child's Nervous System, 23,* 499–507.

Gershoff, E. T. (2002). Parental corporal punishment and associated child behaviors and experiences: A meta-analytic and theoretical review. *Pychological Bulletin, 128,* 539–579.

Gersten, R., & Dimino, J. (2006, January). RTI (response to intervention): Rethinking special education for students with reading difficulties (yet again). *Reading Research Quarterly, 41,* 99–108.

Gervais, J., & Tremblay, R. E. (Producers). (2005). *The origins of human aggression: The other story.* National Film Board.

Gesell, A. L. (1946). The ontogenesis of infant behavior. In L. Carmichael (Ed.), *Manual of child psychology.* New York: Harper.

Giacobbi, P., Lynn, T., & Wetherington, J. (2004). Stress and coping during the transition to university for first-year female athletes. *Sport Psychologist, 18,* 1–20.

Gibbs, N. (2002, April 15). Making time for a baby. *Time,* 48–54.

Gibson, E.J., & Walk, R.D. (1960). The "visual cliff". *Scientific American, 202,* 64–71.

Gilbert, S. (2004, March 16). New clues to women veiled in black. *The New York Times,* pp. D1.

Gilbert, W. M., Nesbitt, T. S., & Danielsen, B. (1999). Childbearing beyond age 40: Pregnancy outcome in 24,032 cases. *Obstetrics and Gynecology, 93,* 9–14.

Giles-Sims, J., & Lockhart, C. (2005). Culturally shaped patterns of disciplining children. *Journal of Family Issues, 26,* 196–218.

Gilligan, C. (2004). Recovering psyche: Reflections on life-history and history. *Annual of Psychoanalysis, 32,* 131–147.

Gillespie, N. A., Cloninger, C., R., & Heath, A. C. (2003). The genetic and environmental relationship between Cloninger's dimensions of temperament and character. *Personality and Individual Differences, 35,* 1931–1946.

Gillies, R., & Boyle, M. (2006, May). Ten Australian elementary teachers' discourse and reported pedagogical practices during cooperative learning. *The Elementary School Journal, 106,* 429–451.

Gilligan, C., Brown, L. M. & Rogers, A. G. (1990). Psyche embedded: A place for body, relationships, and culture in personality theory. In A. I. Rabin, R. A. Zucker, R. A. Emmons & S. Frank (Eds.), *Studying persons and lives.* New York, NY: Springer Publishing Co.

Gilligan, C., Ward, J. V., & Taylor, J. M. (Eds.). (1988). *Mapping the moral domain: A contribution of women's thinking to psychological theory and education*. Cambridge, MA: Harvard University Press.

Gilliland, A. L., & Verny, T. R. (1999). The effects of domestic abuse on the unborn child. *Journal of Prenatal and Perinatal Psychology and Health, 13* [Special Issue], 235–246.

Gilmore, J. (2010). Trends in dropout rates and the labour market outcomes of young dropouts. *Education matters: Insights on education, learning and training in Canada*. Statistics Canada Catalogue no. 81-004-XIE, Vol. 7, no. 4. Retrieved from http://www.statcan.gc.ca/pub/81-004-x/2010004/article/11339-eng.htm.

Ginzberg, E. (1972). Toward a theory of occupational choice: A restatement. *Vocational Guidance Quarterly, 12*, 10–14.

Giordana, S. (2005). *Understanding eating disorders: Conceptual and ethical issues in the treatment of anorexia (Issues in biomedical ethics)*. New York: Oxford University Press.

Gitlin, L., Reever, K., Dennis, M., Mathieu, E., & Hauck, W. (2006, October). Enhancing quality of life of families who use adult day services: Short- and long-term effects of the Adult Day Services Plus Program. *The Gerontologist, 46*, 630–639.

Gleason, M., Iida, M., & Bolger, N. (2003). Daily supportive equity in close relationships. *Personality and Social Psychology Bulletin, 29*, 1036–1045.

Gleitman, L., & Landau, B. (1994). *The acquisition of the lexicon*. Cambridge, MA: Bradford.

Glick, P., Fiske, S. T., Mladinic, A., Saiz, J. L., et al. (2000). Beyond prejudice as simple antipathy: Hostile and benevolent sexism across cultures. *Journal of Personality and Social Psychology, 79*, 763–775.

Glick, P., Zion, C., & Nelson, C. (1988). What mediates sex discrimination in hiring decisions? *Journal of Personality and Social Psychology, 55*, 178–186.

Gluhoski, V., Leader, J., & Wortman, C. B. (1994). Grief and bereavement. In V. S. Ramachandran (Ed.), *Encyclopedia of human behavior*. San Diego: Academic Press.

Goetz, A., & Shackelford, T. (2006). Modern application of evolutionary theory to psychology: Key concepts and clarifications. *American Journal of Psychology, 119*, 567–584.

Goldberg, A. E. (2004). But do we need universal grammar? Comment on Lidz et al. *Cognition, 94*, 77–84.

Goldberg, J., Pereira, L., & Berghella, V. (2002). Pregnancy after uterine artery emoblization. *Obstetrics and Gynecology, 100*, 869–872.

Goldman, R. (2004, November). [0]Circumcision policy: A psychosocial perspective. *Paediatr Child Health. 9(9)*, 630–633.

Goldman, R. D. (2010). ADHD: Stimulants and their effect on height in children. *Canadian Family Physician, 56(2)*, 145–146.

Goldscheider, F. K. (1994). Divorce and remarriage: Effects on the elderly population. *Reviews in Clinical Gerontology, 4*, 253–259.

Goldsmith, L. T. (2000). Tracking trajectories of talent: Child prodigies growing up. In R. C. Friedman & B. M. Shore et al. (Eds.), *Talents unfolding: Cognition and development*. Washington, DC: American Psychological Association.

Goldsmith, S. K., Pellmar, T. C., Kleinman, A. M., & Bunney, W. E. (2002). *Reducing suicide: A national imperative*. Washington, DC: The National Academies Press.

Goldston, D. B. (2003). *Measuring suicidal behavior and risk in children and adolescents*. Washington, DC: American Psychological Association.

Golinkoff, R. M. (1993). When is communication a "meeting of minds"? *Journal of Child Language, 20*, 199–207.

Golombok, S., Golding, J., Perry, B., Burston, A., Murray, C., Mooney-Somers, J., & Stevens, M. (2003). Children with lesbian parents: A community study. *Developmental Psychology, 39*, 20–33.

Golombok, S., & Tasker, F. (1996). Do parents influence the sexual orientation of their children? Findings from a longitudinal study of lesbian families. *Developmental Psychology, 32*, 3–11.

Goode, E. (1999, January 12). Clash over when, and how, to toilet-train. *The New York Times*, pp. A1, A17.

Goode, E. (2004, February 3). Stronger warning is urged on antidepressants for teenagers. *The New York Times*, p. A12.

Goodman, G. S. (2006). Children's eyewitness memory: A modern history and contemporary commentary. *Journal of Social Issues, 62*, 811–832.

Goodman, J. S., Fields, D. L., & Blum, T. C. (2003). Cracks in the glass ceiling: In what kinds of organizations do women make it to the top? *Group and Organization Management, 28*, 475–501.

Goodstein, R., & Ponterotto, J. G. (1997). Racial and ethnic identity: Their relationship and their contribution to self-esteem. *Journal of Black Psychology, 23*, 275–292.

Goodwin, M. H. (1980). Directive-response speech sequences in girls' and boys' task activities. In S. McConnell-Ginet, R. Borker, & N. Furman (Eds.), *Women and language in literature and society* (pp. 157–173). New York: Praeger.

Goodwin, M. H. (1990). Tactical uses of stories: Participation frameworks within girls' and boys' disputes. *Discourse Processes, 13*, 33–71.

Goold, S. D., Williams, B., & Arnold, R. M. (2000). Conflicts regarding decisions to limit treatment: A differential diagnosis. *Journal of the American Medical Association, 283*, 909–914.

Gordon, N. (2007). The cerebellum and cognition. *European Journal of Paediatric Neurology, 30*, 214–220.

Gostin, L. (2006, April). Physician-assisted suicide A legitimate medical practice? *JAMA: Journal of the American Medical Association, 295*, 1941–1943.

Gottesman, I. I. (1991). *Schizophrenia genesis: The origins of madness*. New York: Freeman.

Gottfredson, G. D., & Holland, J. L. (1990). A longitudinal test of the influence of congruence: Job satisfaction, competency utilization, and counterproductive behavior. *Journal of Counseling Psychology, 37*, 389–398.

Gottlieb, G. (2003). On making behavioral genetics truly developmental. *Human Development, 46*, 337–355.

Gottlieb, G., &S Blair, C. (2004). How early experience matters in intellectual development in the case of poverty. *Preventive Science, 5*, 245–252.

Gottman, J. M., Fainsilber-Katz, L., & Hooven, C. (1996). *Meta-emotion: How families communicate emotionally*. Mahwah, NJ: Erlbaum.

Gould, R. L. (1978). *Transformations: Growth and change in adult life*. New York: Simon Schuster.

Gould, S. J. (1977). *Ontogeny and phylogeny*. Cambridge, MA: Harvard University Press.

Goyette-Ewing, M. (2000). Children's after school arrangements: A study of self-care and developmental outcomes. *Journal of Prevention and Intervention in the Community, 20*, 55–67.

Grabner, R. H., Neubauer, A., C., & Stern, E. (2006). Superior performance and neural efficiency: The impact of intelligence and expertise. *Brain Research Bulletin, 69*, 422–439.

Grady, D. (2006, November). Management of menopausal symptoms. *New England Journal of Medicine, 355*, 2338–2347.

Graham, A. R., Sherry, S. B., Stewart, S. H., Sherry, D. L., McGrath, D., Fossum, K., & Allen, S. L. (2010). The existential model of perfectionism and depressive symptoms: A short-term, four-wave longitudinal study. *Journal of Counseling Psychology, 57*, 423–438.

Graham, I., Carroli, G., Davies, C., & Medves, J. (2005). Episiotomy rates around the world: An update. *Birth: Issues in Perinatal Care, 32*, 219–223.

Granic, I., Hollenstein, T., & Dishion, T. (2003). Longitudinal analysis of flexibility and reorganization in early adolescence: A dynamic systems study of family interactions. *Developmental Psychology, 39*, 606–617.

Grant, J., Weaver, M., & Elliott, T. (2004). Family caregivers of stroke survivors: Characteristics of caregivers at risk for depression. *Rehabilitation Psychology, 49*, 172–179.

Grantham, T., & Ford, D. (2003). Beyond self-concept and self-esteem: Racial identity and gifted African American students. *High School Journal, 87*, 18–29.

Grantham-McGregor, S., Ani, C., & Fernald, L. (2001). The role of nutrition in intellectual development. In R. J. Sternberg & E. L. Grigorenko (Eds.), *Environmental effects on cognitive abilities*. Mahwah, NJ: Erlbaum.

Grantham-McGregor, S., Powell, C., Walker, S., Chang, S., & Fletcher, P. (1994). The long-term follow-up of severely malnourished children who participated in an intervention program. *Child Development, 65*, 428–439.

Gratch, G., & Schatz, J. A. (1987). Cognitive development: The relevance of Piaget's infancy books. In J. D. Osofsky (Ed.), *Handbook of infant development* (2nd ed.). New York: Wiley.

Grattan, M. P., DeVos, E. S., Levy, J., & McClintock, M. K. (1992). Asymmetric action in the human newborn: Sex differences in patterns of organization. *Child Development, 63*, 273–289.

Gray, C., Ferguson, J., Behan, S., Dunbar, C., Dunn, J., & Mitchell, D. (2007, March). Developing young readers through the linguistic phonics approach. *International Journal of Early Years Education, 15*, 15–33.

Gray-Little, B., & Hafdahl, A. R. (2000). Factors influencing racial comparisons of self-esteem: A quantitative review. *Psychological Bulletin, 126*, 26–54.

Green, M. H. (1995). Influences of job type, job status, and gender on achievement motivation. *Current Psychology: Developmental, Learning, Personality, Social, 14*, 159–165.

Greenberg, J., & Becker, M. (1988). Aging parents as family resources. *Gerontologist, 28*, 786–790.

Greenberg, L., Cwikel, J., & Mirsky, J. (2007, January). Cultural correlates of eating attitudes: A comparison between native-born and immigrant university students in Israel. *International Journal of Eating Disorders, 40*, 51–58.

Greene, K., Krcmar, M., & Rubin, D. (2002). Elaboration in processing adolescent health messages: The impact of egocentrism and sensation seeking on message processing. *Journal of Communication, 52*, 812–831.

Greene, K., Krcmar, M., Walters, L. H., Rubin, D L., & Hale, J. L. (2000). Targeting adolescent risk-taking behaviors: The contribution of egocentrism and sensation-seeking. *Journal of Adolescence, 23*, 439–461.

Greene, S., Anderson, E., & Hetherington, E. (2003). Risk and resilience after divorce. In F. Walsh (Ed.), *Normal family processes: Growing diversity and complexity*. New York: Guilford Press.

Greenfield, P. M. (1976). Cross-cultural research and Piagetian theory: Paradox and progress. In K. F. Riegel & J. A. Meacham (Eds.), *The developing individual in a changing world; Vol, 1*, The Hague, The Netherlands: Mouton.

Greenfield, P. M. (1997). You can't take it with you. Why ability assessments don't cross cultures. *American Psychologist, 52*, 1115–1124.

Greenway, C. (2002). The process, pitfalls and benefits of implementing a reciprocal teaching intervention to improve the reading comprehension of a group of year 6 pupils. *Educational Psychology in Practice, 18*, 113–137.

Greenwood, D., & Isbell, L. (2002). Ambivalent sexism and the dumb blonde: Men's and women's reactions to sexist jokes. *Psychology of Women Quarterly, 26*, 341–350.

Greenwood, D. N., & Pietromonaco, P. R. (2004). The interplay among attachment orientation, idealized media images of women, and body dissatisfaction: A social psychological analysis. In L. J. Shrum (Ed.), *Psychology of entertainment media: Blurring the lines between entertainment and persuasion*. Mahwah, NJ: Lawrence Erlbaum Associates.

Gregory, K. (2005). Update on nutrition for preterm and full-term infants. *Journal of Obstetrics and Gynecological Neonatal Nursing, 34*, 98–108.

Griffith, D. R., Azuma, S. D., & Chasnoff, I. J. (1994). Three-year outcome of children exposed prenatally to drugs. *Journal of the American Academy of Child and Adolescent Psychiatry, 33,* 20–27.

Grigorenko, E. (2003). Intraindividual fluctuations in intellectual functioning: Selected links between nutrition and the mind. In R. Sternberg & J. Lautrey (Eds.), *Models of intelligence: International perspectives.* Washington, DC: American Psychological Association.

Groome, L. J., Swiber, M. J., Bentz, L. S., Holland, S. B., & Atterbury, J. L. (1995). Maternal anxiety during pregnancy: Effect on fetal behavior at 38 to 40 weeks of gestation. *Developmental and Behavioral Pediatrics, 16,* 391–396.

Groopman, J. (1998, February). Decoding destiny. *The New Yorker.*

Gross, R. T., Spiker, D., & Haynes, C. W. (Eds.). (1997). *Helping low-birthweight, premature babies: The Infant Health and Development Program.* Stanford, CA: Stanford University Press.

Grossmann, K. E., Grossman, K., Huber, F., & Wartner, U. (1982). German children's behavior towards their mothers at 12 months and their fathers at 18 months in Ainsworth's Strange Situation. *International Journal of Behavioral Development, 4,* 157–181.

Grossman, K. E., Grossmann, K., & Waters, E. (Eds.). (2005). *Attachment from infancy to adulthood: The major longitudinal studies.* New York: Guilford Press.

Grunbaum, J. A., Kann, L., Kinchen, S. A., Williams, B., Ross, J. G., Lowry, R., & Kolbe, L. (2002). *Youth risk behavior surveillance—United States, 2001.* Atlanta, GA: Centers for Disease Control.

Grunbaum, J. A., Lowry, R., & Kann, L. (2001). Prevalence of health-related behaviors among alternative high school students as compared with students attending regular high schools. *Journal of Adolescent Health, 29,* 337–343.

Grundy, E., & Henretta, J. (2006, September). Between elderly parents and adult children: A new look at the intergenerational care provided by the "sandwich generation." *Ageing and Society, 26,* 707–722.

Grusec, J. E. (1982). Socialization processes and the development of altruism. In J. P. Rushton & R. M. Sorrentino (Eds.), *Altruism and helping behavior.* Hillsdale, NJ: Erlbaum.

Grusec, J. E. (1991). The socialization of altruism. In M. S. Clark (Ed.), *Prosocial behavior.* Newbury Park, CA: Sage.

Grusec, J. E., & Kuczynski, L. E. (Eds.). (1997). *Parenting and children's internalization of values: A handbook of contemporary theory.* New York: Wiley.

Guarente, L. (2006, December 14). Sirtuins as potential targets for metabolic syndrome. *Nature, 14,* 868–874.

Guasti, M. T. (2002). *Language acquisition: The growth of grammar.* Cambridge, MA: MIT Press.

Guerrini, I., Thomson, A., & Gurling, H. (2007). The importance of alcohol misuse, malnutrition and genetic susceptibility on brain growth and plasticity. *Neuroscience and Biobehavioral Reviews, 31,* 212–220.

Gulli, C. (2009, Apr 10). Youth survey: Teen girls in charge. *Macleans.* Retrieved from http://www2.macleans .ca/2009/04/10/teen-girls-in-charge/.

Gump, L. S., Baker, R. C., & Roll, S. (2000). Cultural and gender differences in moral judgment: A study of Mexican Americans and Anglo-Americans. *Hispanic Journal of Behavioral Sciences, 22,* 78–93.

Gunnarsdottir, I., & Thorsdottir, I. (2003). Relationship between growth and feeding in infancy and body mass index at the age of 6 years. *International Journal of Obesity and Metabolic Disorders, 27,* 1523–1527.

Gupta, A., & State, M. (2007). Recent advances in the genetics of autism. *Biological Psychiatry, 61,* 429–437.

Gupta, U., & Singh, P. (1982). An exploratory study of love and liking and type of marriages. *Indian Journal of Applied Psychology, 19,* 92–97.

Gur, R. C., Gur, R. E., Obrist, W. D., Hungerbuhler, J. P., Younkin, D., Rosen, A. D., Skilnick, B. E., & Reivich, M. (1982). Sex and handedness differences in cerebral blood flow during rest and cognitive activity. *Science, 217,* 659–661.

Guterl, F. (2002, November 11). What Freud got right. *Newsweek,* 50–51.

Guttmann, J., & Rosenberg, M. (2003). Emotional intimacy and children's adjustment: A comparison between single-parent divorced and intact families. *Educational Psychology, 23,* 457–472.

Haber, D. (2006). Life review: Implementation, theory, research, and therapy. *International Journal of Aging and Human Development, 63,* 153–171.

Haberstick, B. C., Timberlake, D., Ehringer, M. A., Lessem, J. M., Hopfer, C. J., Smolen, A., & Hewitt, J. K. (2007). Can cigarette warnings counterbalance effects of smoking scenes in movies? *Addiction, 102,* 655–665.

Hack, M. (2009, October). [0]Adult outcomes of preterm children. *J Dev Behav Pediatr. 30(5),* 460–470.

Haddock, S., & Rattenborg, K. (2003). Benefits and challenges of dual-earning: Perspectives of successful couples. *American Journal of Family Therapy, 31,* 325–344.

Hagerty, R. G., Butow, P. N., Ellis, P. A., Lobb, E. A., Pendlebury, S., Leighl, N., Goldstein, D….Tattersall, M. H. (2004). Cancer patient preferences for communication of prognosis in the metastatic setting. *Journal of Clinical Oncology, 22,* 1721–1730.

Haight, W. (2002). *African-American children at church: A sociocultural perspective.* Cambridge: Cambridge University Press. Retrieved from http://www.questia.com/library/105180581/african-american-children-at-church-a-sociocultural.

Haith, M. H. (1986). Sensory and perceptual processes in early infancy. *Journal of Pediatrics, 109*(1), 158–171.

Haith, M. H. (1991, April). Setting a path for the 90s: Some goals and challenges in infant sensory and perceptual development. Paper presented at the biennial meeting of the Society for Research in Child Development, Seattle, WA.

Hales, K. A., Morgan, M. A., & Thurnau, G. R. (1993). Influence of labor and route of delivery on the frequency of respiratory morbidity in term neonates. *International Journal of Gynecology and Obstetrics, 43,* 35–40.

Halford, G. S., Maybery, M. T., O'Hare, A. W., & Grant, P. (1994). The development of memory and processing capacity. *Child Development, 65,* 1338–1356.

Hall, E. G., & Lee, A. M. (1984). Sex differences in motor performance of young children: Fact or fiction? *Sex Roles, 10,* 217–230.

Hall, R. E., & Rowan, G. T. (2003). Identity development across the lifespan: Alternative model for biracial Americans. *Psychology and Education: An Interdisciplinary Journal, 40,* 3–12.

Hallahan, D. P., Kauffman, J. M., & Lloyd, J. W. (2000). *Introduction to learning disabilities* (4th ed.). Boston: Allyn and Bacon.

Halliday, M. A. K. (1975). *Learning how to mean—Explorations in the development of language.* London: Edward Arnold.

Hamilton, R. J., Bowers, B. J., & Williams, J. K. (2005, February). Disclosing genetic test results to family members. *Journal of Nursing Scholarship, 37(1),* 18–24. doi: 10.1111/j.1547-5069.2005.00007.x.

Hamon, R. R., & Ingoldsby, B. B. (Eds.) (2003). *Mate selection across cultures.* Thousand Oaks, CA: Sage Publications.

Hampton, M., Baydala, A., Bourassa, C., McKay-McNabb, K., Placsko, C., Goodwill, K., McKenna, B., McNabb, P., & Boekelder, R. (2010). Completing the circle. Elders speak about end-of-life care with Aboriginal families in Canada. *Journal of Palliative Care, 26,* 6–15.

Hane, A., Feldstein, S., & Dernetz, V. (2003). The relation between coordinated interpersonal timing and maternal sensitivity in four-month-old infants. *Journal of Psycholinguistic Research, 32,* 525–539.

Hankin, B. L., & Abramson, L. Y. (2001). Development of gender differences in depression: An elaborated cognitive vulnerability-transactional stress theory. *Psychological Bulletin, 127,* 773–796.

Hanley, W. B. (2005). Newborn screening in Canada—are we out of step? *Paediatr Child Health, 10,* 203–207. Retrieved from http://www.ncbi.nlm.nih.gov/pmc/articles/PMC2722527/.

Hanson, D. R., & Gottesman, I. I. (2005). Theories of schizophrenia: A genetic-inflammatory-vascular synthesis. *BMC Medical Genetics, 6,* 7.

Hanson, R., & Hayslip, B. (2000). Widowhood in later life. In J. Harvey & E. Miller (Eds.), *Loss and trauma: General and close relationship perspectives.* New York: Brunner-Routledge.

Hansson, R. O., & Carpenter, B. N. (1994). *Relationship in old age: Coping with the challenge of transition.* New York: Guilford Press.

Happe, F. G. E., Winner, E., & Brownell, H. (1998). The getting of wisdom: Theory of mind in old age. *Developmental Psychology, 34,* 358–362.

Harel-Fisch, Y., Walsh, S. D., Fogel-Grinvald, H., Amitai, G., Pickett, W., Molcho, M., et al. (2011). Negative school perceptions and involvement in school bullying: A universal relationship across 40 countries. *Journal of Adolescence, 34,* 639–652.

Harrell, J. S., Bangdiwala, S. I., Deng, S., Webb, J. P., & Bradley, C. (1998). Smoking initiation in youth: The roles of gender, race, socioeconomics, and developmental status. *Journal of Adolescent Health, 23,* 271–279.

Harris, A., Cronkite, R., & Moos, R. (2006, July). Physical activity, exercise coping, and depression in a 10-year cohort study of depressed patients. *Journal of Affective Disorders, 93,* 79–85.

Harris, C. M. (2004). Personality and sexual orientation. *College Student Journal, 38,* 207–211.

Harris, J., Vernon, P., & Jang, K. (2007). Rated personality and measured intelligence in young twin children. *Personality and Individual Differences, 42,* 75–86.

Harris, J. R. (1998). *The nurture assumption: Why children turn out the way they do.* New York: Free Press.

Harris, K. (1999). The health status and risk behaviors of adolescents in immigrant families. In D. J. Hernandez (Ed.), *Children of immigrants: Health, adjustment, and public assistance.* Washington, D.C.: The National Academy Press.

Hart, B. (2004). What toddlers talk about. *First Language, 24,* 91–106.

Hart, C. H., Yang, C., Nelson, D. A., Jin, S., Bazarskaya, N., & Nelson, L. (1998). Peer contact patterns, parenting practices, and preschoolers' social competence in China, Russia, and the United States. In P. Slee & K. Rigby (Eds.), *Peer relations amongst children: Current issues and future directions.* London: Routledge.

Hart, D., Burock, D., & London, B. (2003). Prosocial tendencies, antisocial behavior, and moral development. In A. Slater & G. Bremner (Eds.), *An introduction to developmental psychology.* Malden, MA: Blackwell Publishers.

Harter, S. (1990a). Identity and self-development. In S. Feldman & G. Elliott (Eds.), *At the threshold: The developing adolescent.* Cambridge, MA: Harvard University Press.

Harter, S. (1990b). Issues in the assessment of self-concept of children and adolescents. In A. LaGreca (Ed.), *Through the eyes of a child.* Boston: Allyn and Bacon.

Hartshorne, T. S. (1994). Friendship. In V. S. Ramachandran (Ed.), *Encyclopedia of human behavior.* San Diego: Academic Press.

Hartup, W. W., & Stevens, N. (1999). Friendships and adaptation across the life span. *Current Directions in Psychological Science, 8,* 76–79.

Harvey, J. H., & Fine, M. A. (2004). *Children of divorce: Stories of loss and growth.* Mahwah, NJ: Lawrence Erlbaum Associates.

Harwood, R. L., Schoelmerich, A., Ventura-Cook, E., Schulze, P. A., & Wilson, S. P. (1996). Culture and class influences on Anglo and Puerto Rican mothers' beliefs regarding long-term socialization goals and child behavior. *Child Development, 67,* 2446–2461.

Hasher, L., & Zacks, R. T. (1984). Automatic processing of fundamental information: The case of frequency of occurrence. *American Psychologist, 39,* 1372–1388.

Haskett, M., Nears, K., Ward, C., & McPherson, A. (2006, October). Diversity in adjustment of maltreated children: Factors associated with resilient functioning. *Clinical Psychology Review, 26,* 796–812.

Haslett, A. (2004, May 31). Love supreme. *The New Yorker,* 76–80.

Hatfield, E., & Rapson, R. L. (1993). Historical and cross-cultural perspectives on passionate love and sexual desire. *Annual Review of Sex Research, 4,* 67–97.

Hattery, A. (2000). *Women, work, and family: Balancing and weaving.* Thousand Oaks, CA: Sage.

Hauser, M., Chomsky, N., & Fitch, W. (2002). The faculty of language: What is it, who has it, and how did it evolve? *Science, 298,* 1569–1579.

Havighurst, R. J. (1973). Social roles, work, leisure, and education. In C. Eisdorfer & M. P. Lawton (Eds.), *The psychology of adult development and aging.* Washington, DC: American Psychological Association.

Hay, D. F., Pawlby, S., & Angold, A. (2003). Pathways to violence in the children of mothers who were depressed postpartum. *Developmental Psychology, 39,* 1083–1094.

Hayflick, L. (1974). The strategy of senescence. *The Journal of Gerontology, 14,* 37–45.

Haynie, D. L., Nansel, T., Eitel, P., Crump, A. D., Saylor, K., Yu, K., and Simons-Morton, B. (2001). Bullies, victims, and bully/victims: Distinct groups of at-risk youth. *Journal of Early Adolescence, 21,* 29–49.

Hayslip, B., Jr., Shore, R. J., & Henderson, C. E. (2000). Perceptions of grandparents' influence in the lives of their grandchildren. In B. Hayslip, Jr., Goldberg, & G. Robin (Eds.), *Grandparents raising grandchildren: Theoretical, empirical, and clinical perspectives.* New York: Springer.

Hayward, M., Crimmins, E., & Saito, Y. (1997). Cause of death and active life expectancy in the older population of the United States. *Journal of Aging and Health,* 122–131.

Hazan, C., & Shaver, P. (1987). Romantic love conceptualized as an attachment process. *Journal of Personality and Social Psychology, 52,* 511–524.

Health Canada. (1998). Health Canada, Laboratory Centre for Disease Control, Canadian Hospitals Injury Reporting and Prevention Program (CHIRPP) Database, 1998. Reported in *Statistical Report on the Health of Canadians.* Statistics Canada Catalogue no.: 82-570-XWE1997001. Retrieved from http://www.statcan.gc.ca/pub/82-570-x/4198590-eng.pdf. Accessed March 11, 2011.

Health Canada. (2000). The Canadian tobacco use monitoring survey 2000. Retrieved from http://www.hc-sc.gc.ca/hc-ps/tobac-tabac/research-recherche/stat/_ctums-esutc_fs-if/2000-youth-eng.php

Health Canada. (2001). The Canadian incidence study of reported child abuse and neglect, final report. Prepared by Trocmé, N., et al. Retrieved from http://www.phac-aspc.gc.ca/publicat/cisfr-ecirf/index-eng.php.

Health Canada. (2004). Correction: Health Canada advises Canadians under the age of 18 to consult physicians if they are being treated with newer anti-depressants. *Health Canada Advisory 2004-02-03.* Retrieved from http://www.hc-sc.gc.ca/ahc-asc/media/advisories-avis/_2004/2004_02-eng.php.

Health Canada (2009). The Canadian alcohol and drug use monitoring survey. Retrieved from http://www.hc-sc.gc.ca/hc-ps/drugs-drogues/stat/index-eng.php.

Health Canada. (2010). Summary of results of the 2008–09 youth smoking survey. Retrieved from http://www.hc-sc.gc.ca/hc-ps/tobac-tabac/research-recherche/stat/_survey-sondage_2008-2009/result-eng.php.

Health Canada. (2011). Canada's food guide. Retrieved from http://www.hc-sc.gc.ca/fn-an/food-guide-aliment/index-eng.php.

Hecht, M. L., Marston, P. J., & Larkey, L. K. (1994). Love ways and relationship quality in heterosexual relationships. *Journal of Social and Personal Relationships, 11,* 25–43.

Heck, A., Lieb, R., Ellgas, A., Pfister, H., Lucae, S., Roeske, D., Pütz, B…Ising, M. (2009). Investigation of 17 candidate genes for personality traits confirms effects of the *HTR2A* gene on novelty seeking. *Genes, Brain and Behavior, (8)* 464–472. Retrieved from doi: 10.1111/j.1601-183X.2009.00494.x.

Hedge, J., Borman, W., & Lammlein, S. (2006). *Age stereotyping and age discrimination.* Washington, DC: American Psychological Association.

Heffner, L. J. (2004). Advanced maternal age—how old is too old? *New England Journal of Medicine, 351*(19), 1927–1929.

Heimann, M. (2001). Neonatal imitation—a "fuzzy" phenomenon? In F. Lacerda & C. von Hofsten (Eds.), *Emerging cognitive abilities in early infancy.* Mahwah, NJ: Lawrence Erlbaum Associates.

Heimann, M. (Ed.). (2003). *Regression periods in human infancy.* Mahwah, NJ: Lawrence Erlbaum Associates.

Heinemann, G. D., & Evans, P. L. (1990). Widowhood: Loss, change, and adaptation. In T. H. Brubaker (Ed.), *Family relationships in later life.* Newbury Park, CA: Sage.

Helms, J. E., Jernigan, M., & Mascher, J. (2005). The meaning of race in psychology and how to change it: A methodological perspective. *American Psychologist, 60,* 27–36.

Helmuth, L. (2003, February 28). The wisdom of the wizened. *Science, 299,* 1300–1302.

Helson R., & Moane, G. (1987). Personality change in women from college to midlife. *Journal of Personality and Social Psychology, 53,* 176–186.

Helson, R., & Srivastava, S. (2001). Three paths of adult development: Conservers, seekers, and achievers. *Journal of Personality and Social Psychology, 80,* 995–1010.

Helson, R., Stewart, A. J., & Ostrove, J. (1995). Identity in three cohorts of midlife women. *Journal of Personality and Social Psychology, 69,* 544–557.

Helson, R., & Wink, P. (1992). Personality change in women from the early 40s to the early 50s. *Psychology and Aging, 7,* 46–55.

Hendrick, C., & Hendrick, S. (2003). Romantic love: Measuring cupid's arrow. In S. Lopez & C. Snyder (Eds.), *Positive psychological assessment: A handbook of models and measures.* Washington, DC: American Psychological Association.

Hendrie, H. C., Ogunniyi, A., Hall, K. S., Baiyewu, O., Unverzagt, F. W., Gureje, O., Gao, S…Hui, S. L. (2001). Incidence of dementia and Alzheimer disease in 2 communities: Yoruba residing in Ibadan, Nigeria, and African Americans residing in Indianapolis, Indiana. *Journal of the American Medical Association, 285,* 739–747.

Henry, J., & McNab, W. (2003). Forever young: A health promotion focus on sexuality and aging. *Gerontology and Geriatrics Education, 23,* 57–74.

Henry, R., Miller, R., & Giarrusso, R. (2005). Difficulties, disagreements, and disappointments in late-life marriages. *International Journal of Aging and Human Development, 61,* 243–264.

Hensley, P. (2006, July). Treatment of bereavement-related depression and traumatic grief. *Journal of Affective Disorders, 92,* 117–124.

Hepper, P. G., Wells, D. L. & Lynch, C. (2005). Prenatal thumb sucking is related to postnatal handedness. *Neuropsychologia, 43,* 313–315. doi:10.1016/j.neuropsychologia.2004.08.009.

Herbert, M. R., Ziegler, D. A., Deutsch, C. K., O'Brien, L. M., Kennedy, D. N., Filipek, P. A., Bakardjiev, A. I… Caviness, Jr., V. S. (2005). Brain asymmetries in autism and developmental language disorder: A nested whole-brain analysis. *Brain, 128,* 213–226.

Herdt, G. H. (Ed.). (1998). *Rituals of manhood: Male initiation in Papua New Guinea.* Somerset, NJ: Transaction Books.

Hernandez-Reif, M., Field, T., Diego, M., Vera, Y., & Pickens, J. (2006, January). Brief report: Happy faces are habituated more slowly by infants of depressed mothers. *Infant Behavior and Development, 29,* 131–135.

Herrnstein, R. J., & Murray, C. (1994). *The bell curve: Intelligence and class structure in American life.* New York: Free Press.

Hertelendy, F., & Zakar, T. (2004). Prostaglandins and the myometrium and cervix. *Prostaglandins Leukot Essent Fatty Acids, 70,* 207–222.

Hetherington, E., & Elmore, A. (2003). Risk and resilience in children coping with their parents' divorce and remarriage. In S. Luthar (Ed.), *Resilience and vulnerability: Adaptation in the context of childhood adversities.* New York: Cambridge University Press.

Hetherington, E. M. (Ed.). (1999). *Coping with divorce, single parenting, and remarriage: A risk and resiliency perspective.* Mahwah, NJ: Erlbaum.

Hetherington, E. M., & Blechman, E. A. (Eds.). (1996). *Stress, coping, and resiliency in children and families.* Hillsdale, NJ: Erlbaum.

Hetherington, E. M., & Clingempeel, W. (1992). Coping with marital transitions: A family systems perspective. *Monographs of the Society for Research in Child Development, 57(2–3, Serial No. 227).*

Hetherington, E. M., & Kelly, J. (2002). For better or worse: Divorce reconsidered. New York: Norton.

Heubusch, K. (1997, September). A tough job gets tougher. *American Demographics,* p. 39.

Hewstone, M. (2003). Intergroup contact: Panacea for prejudice? *Psychologist, 16,* 352–355.

Heyman, R., & Slep, A. M. (2002). Do child abuse and interparental violence lead to adulthood family violence? *Journal of Marriage and Family, 64,* 864–870.

Hietala, J., Cannon, T. D., & van Erp, T. G. M. (2003). Regional brain morphology and duration of illness in never-medicated first-episode patients with schizophrenia. *Schizophrenia, 64,* 79–81.

Higgins, D., & McCabe, M. (2003). Maltreatment and family dysfunction in childhood and the subsequent adjustment of children and adults. *Journal of Family Violence, 18,* 107–120.

Hildreth, K., Sweeney, B., & Rovee-Collier, C. (2003). Differential memory-preserving effects of reminders at 6 months. *Journal of Experimental Child Psychology, 84,* 41–62.

Hillman, J. (2000). *Clinical perspectives on elderly sexuality.* Dordrecht, Netherlands: Kluwer Academic Publishers.

Hines, M., & Kaufman, F. R. (1994). Androgen and the development of human sex-typical behavior: Rough-and-tumble play and sex of preferred playmates in children with congenital adrenal hyperplasia (CAH). *Child Development, 65,* 1042–1053.

Hirsh-Pasek, K., & Michnick-Golinkoff, R. (1995). *The origins of grammar: Evidence from early language comprehension.* Cambridge, MA: MIT Press.

Hitlin, S., Brown, J. S., & Elder, G. H., Jr. (2006). Racial self-categorization in adolescence: Multiracial development and social pathways. *Child Development, 77,* 1298–1308.

HMHL (Harvard Mental Health Letter). (2005). The treatment of attention deficit disorder: New evidence. *Harvard Mental Health Letter, 21,* 6.

Ho, B., Friedland, J., Rappolt, S., Noh, S. (2003). Caregiving for relatives with Alzheimer's disease: Feelings of Chinese-Canadian women. *Journal of Aging Studies, 17,* 301–321.

Hobart, C., & Grigel, F. (1992). Cohabitation among Canadian students at the end of the eighties. *Journal of Comparative Family Studies, 23,* 311–337.

Hoek, J., & Gendall, P. (2006). Advertising and obesity: A behavioral perspective. *Journal of Health Communication, 11,* 409–423.

Hoekstra, R. E., Ferrara, T. B., Couser, R. J., Payne, N. R., & Connett, J. E. (2004). Survival and long-term neurodevelopmental outcome of extremely premature infants born at 23–26 weeks' gestational age at a tertiary centre. *Pediatrics, 113,* e1–e6. Retrieved from http://www.pediatricsdigest .mobi/content/113/1/e1.full.

Hoelter L. F., Axinn, W. G., & Ghimire, D. J. (2004). Social change, premarital nonfamily experiences, and marital dynamics. *Journal of Marriage and Family, 66(5),* 1131–1151.

Hofer, M. A. (2006). Psychobiological roots of early attachment. *Current Directions in Psychological Science, 15,* 84–88.

Hofferth, S., & Sandberg, J. F. (2001). How American children spend their time. *Journal of Marriage and the Family, 63,* 295–308.

Hoffman, L. (2003). Why high schools don't change: What students and their yearbooks tell us. *High School Journal, 86,* 22–37.

Hoffman, M. L. (1987) Empathy: Justice and moral judgment. In N. Eisenberg & J. Strayer (Eds.), *Empathy and its development.* (pp. 47–80). Cambridge: Cambridge University Press.

Hohmann-Marriott, B. (2006, November). Shared beliefs and the union stability of married and cohabiting couples. *Journal of Marriage and Family, 68,* 1015–1028.

Holahan, C., & Chapman, J. (2002). Longitudinal predictors of proactive goals and activity participation at age 80. *Journals of Gerontology: Series B: Psychological Sciences and Social Sciences, 57B,* P418–P425.

Holden, C. (1987, October 9). Why do women live longer than men? *Science, 233,* 158–160.

Holden, G. W., & Miller, P. C. (1999). Enduring and different: A meta-analysis of the similarity in parents' child rearing. *Psychological Bulletin, 125,* 223–254.

Holland, J. L. (1973). *Making vocational choices: A theory of careers.* Englewood Cliffs, NJ: Prentice-Hall.

Holland, J. L. (1987). Current status of Holland's theory of careers: Another perspective. *Career Development Quarterly, 36,* 24–30.

Holland, N. (1994, August). Race dissonance—Implications for African American children. Paper presented at the annual meeting of the American Psychological Association, Los Angeles, CA.

Holmes, E. R., & Holmes, L. D. (1995). *Other cultures, elder years.* Thousand Oaks, CA: Sage Publications.

Holtzman, N. A., Murphy, P. D., Watson, M. S., & Barr, P. A. (1997, October 24). Predictive genetic testing: From basic research to clinical practice. *Science, 278(5338),* pp. 602–605. doi: 10.1126/science.278.5338.602.

Holyrod, R., & Sheppard, A. (1997). Parental separation: Effects on children; implications for services. *Child: Care, Health and Development, 23,* 369–378.

Holzman, L. (1997). *Schools for growth: Radical alternatives to current educational models.* Mahwah, NJ: Erlbaum.

Honey, J. L., Bennett, P., & Morgan, M. (2003). Predicting postnatal depression. *Journal of Affective Disorders, 76,* 201–210.

Hook, E. B., Cross, P. K., & Schreinemachers, D. M. (1983). Chromosomal abnormality rates at amniocentesis and in liveborn infants. *Journal of the American Medical Association, 249(15),* 2034–2038.

Hopkins, B., & Westra, T. (1989). Maternal expectations of their infants' development: Some cultural differences. *Developmental Medicine and Child Neurology, 31,* 384–390.

Horiuchi, S., Finch, C., & Mesle, F. (2003). Differential patterns of age-related mortality increase in middle age and old age. *Journals of Gerontology: Series A: Biological Sciences and Medical Sciences, 58A,* 495–507.

Horner, K. L. (1998). Individuality in vulnerability: Influences on physical health. *Journal of Health Psychology, 3,* 71–85.

Horowitz, A. (1994). Vision impairment and functional disability among nursing home residents. *Gerontologist, 34,* 316–323.

Howard, A. (1992). Work and family crossroads spanning the career. In S. Zedeck (Ed.), *Work, families and organizations.* San Francisco: Jossey-Bass.

Howe, M. J. (1997). *IQ in question: The truth about intelligence.* London, England: Sage.

Howe, M. J. (2004). Some insights of geniuses into the causes of exceptional achievement. In L. V. Shavinina & M. Ferrari (Eds.), *Beyond knowledge: Extracognitive aspects of developing high ability.* Mahwah, NJ: Lawrence Erlbaum Associates.

Howe, M. L. (2003). Memories from the cradle. *Current Directions in Psychological Science, 12,* 62–65.

Howe, M. L., Courage, M. L., & Edison, S. C. (2004). When autobiographical memory begins. In S. Algarabel, A. Pitarque, T. Bajo, S. E. Gathercole, & M. A. Conway (Eds.), *Theories of memory: Vol. 3.* New York: Psychology Press.

Howes, C., Galinsky, E., & Kontos, S. (1998). Child care caregiver sensitivity and attachment. *Social Development, 7,* 25–36.

Howes, C., Unger, O., & Seidner, L. B. (1989). Social pretend play in toddlers: Parallels with social play and with solitary pretend. *Child Development, 60,* 77–84.

Hubel, D. H., & Wiesel, T. N. (1979). Brain mechanisms of vision. *Scientific American, 241,* 150–162.

Hubel, D. H., & Wiesel, T. N. (2004). *Brain and visual perception: The story of a 25-year collaboration.* New York: Oxford University Press.

Hudson, J. A., Sosa, B. B., & Shapiro, L. R. (1997). Scripts and plans: The development of preschool children's event knowledge and event planning. In S. L. Friedman & E. K. Scholnick (Eds.), *The developmental psychology of planning: Why, how and when do we plan?* (pp. 77–102). Mahwah, NJ: Erlbaum.

Huesmann, L. R., Moise-Titus, J., & Podolski, C. L. (2003). Longitudinal relations between children's exposure to TV violence and their aggressive and violent behavior in young adulthood: 1977–1992. *Developmental Psychology, 39,* 201–221.

Huff, C. O. (1999). Source, recency, and degree of stress in adolescence and suicide ideation. *Adolescence, 34,* 81–89.

Hughes, F. P. (1995). *Children, play, and development* (2nd ed.). Boston: Allyn and Bacon.

Huizink, A., & Mulder, E. (2006). Maternal smoking, drinking or cannabis use during pregnancy and neurobehavioral and cognitive functioning in human offspring. *Neuroscience and Biobehavioral Reviews, 30,* 24–41.

Huizink, A., Mulder, E., & Buitelaar, J. (2004). Prenatal stress and risk for psychopathology: Specific effects or induction of general susceptibility? *Psychological Bulletin, 130,* 115–142.

Hulanicka, B. (1999). Acceleration of menarcheal age of girls from dysfunctional families. *Journal of Reproductive and Infant Psychology,17,* 119–132.

Hulei, E., Zevenbergen, A., & Jacobs, S. (2006, September). Discipline behaviors of Chinese American and European American mothers. *Journal of Psychology: Interdisciplinary and Applied, 140,* 459–475.

Human Genome Program. (2003). *Genomics and its impact on science and society: A 2003 primer.* Washington, DC: U.S. Department of Energy.

Human Genome Project. (2006). Available online at http://www.ornl.gov/sci/techresources/Human_Genome/ medicine/genetest.shtml.

Humphreys, J. (2003). Resilience in sheltered battered women. *Issues in Mental Health Nursing, 24,* 137–152.

Hunt, C., & Hauck, F. (2006). Sudden infant death syndrome. *Canadian Medical Association Journal, 174,* 1861–1869.

Hunt, M. (1974). *Sexual behaviors in the 1970s.* New York: Dell.

Hunt, M. (1993). *The story of psychology.* New York: Doubleday.

Hunter, J., & Mallon, G. P. (2000). Lesbian, gay, and bisexual adolescent development: Dancing with your feet tied together. In B. Greene & G. L. Croom (Eds.), *Education, research, and practice in lesbian, gay, bisexual, and transgendered psychology: A resource manual, Vol. 5.* Thousand Oaks, CA: Sage.

Huston, A. (Ed.). (1991). *Children in poverty: Child development and public policy.* Cambridge, England: Cambridge University Press.

Huston, T. L., Caughlin, J. P., Houts, R. M., & Smith, S. E. (2001). The connubial crucible: Newlywed years as predictors of marital delight, distress, and divorce. *Journal of Personality and Social Psychology, 80,* 237–252.

Hutchinson, A., Whitman, R., & Abeare, C. (2003). The unification of mind: Integration of hemispheric semantic processing. *Brain and Language, 87,* 361–368.

Hutchinson, S., & Wexler, B. (2007, January). Is "raging" good for health? Older women's participation in the Raging Grannies. *Health Care for Women International, 28,* 88–118.

Hutton, P. H. (2004). *Philippe Aries and the politics of French cultural history.* Amherst: University of Massachusetts Press.

Huurre, T., Junkkari, H., & Aro, H. (2006, June). Long-term psychosocial effects of parental divorce: A follow-up study from adolescence to adulthood. *European Archives of Psychiatry and Clinical Neuroscience, 256,* 256–263.

Hyde, J. S. (1994). *Understanding human sexuality* (5th ed.). New York: McGraw-Hill.

Hyde, J. S., & DeLamater, J. D. (2003). *Understanding human sexuality* (8th ed.). New York: McGraw-Hill.

Hyde, J. S., Fennema, E., & Lamon, S. J. (1990). Gender differences in mathematics performance: A meta-analysis. *Psychological Bulletin, 107,* 139–155.

Hyssaelae L., Rautava, P., & Helenius, H. (1995). Fathers' smoking and use of alcohol: The viewpoint of maternity health care clinics and well-baby clinics. *Family Practice, 12,* 22–27.

Iglesias, J., Eriksson, J., Grize, F., Tomassini, M., & Villa, A. E. (2005). Dynamics of pruning in simulated large-scale spiking neural networks. *Biosystems, 79,* 11–20.

Ikels, C. (1989). Becoming a human being in theory and practice: Chinese views of human development. In D. I. Kertzer & K. W. Schaie (Eds.), *Age structuring in comparative perspective.* Hillsdale, NJ: Erlbaum.

Insurance Corporation of British Columbia. (2009). British Columbia traffic statistics. Rising tide—the impact of dementia on Canadian society. Alzheimer Society of Canada.

Ingersoll, E. W., & Thoman, E. B. (1999). Sleep/wake states of preterm infants: Stability, developmental change, diurnal variation, and relation with caregiving activity. *Child Development, 70,* 1–10.

Ingram, D. K., Young, J., & Mattison, J. A. (2007). Calorie restriction in nonhuman primates: Assessing effects on brain and behavioral aging. *Neuroscience, 14,* 1359–1364.

Inoue, K., Tanii, H., Abe, S., Kaiya, H., Nata, M., & Fukunaga, T. (2006, December). The correlation between rates of unemployment and suicide rates in Japan between 1985 and 2002. *International Medical Journal, 13,* 261–263.

Insel, P. M., & Roth, W. T. (1991). *Core concepts in health* (6th ed.). Mountain View, CA: Mayfield.

International Cesarean Awareness Network. (2004). Available online at http://www.ican-online.org/.

International Human Genome Sequencing Consortium. (2001). Initial sequencing and analysis of the human genome. *Nature, 409,* 860–921.

Inzlicht, M., & Ben-Zeev, T. (2000). A threatening intellectual environment: Why females are susceptible to experiencing problem-solving deficits in the presence of males. *Psychological Science, 11,* 365–371.

Ireland, J. L., & Archer, J. (2004). Association between measures of aggression and bullying among juvenile young offenders. *Aggressive Behavior, 30,* 29–42.

Irwin, E. G. (1993). A focused overview of anorexia nervosa and bulimia: I. Etiological issues. *Archives of Psychiatric Nursing, 7,* 342–346.

Isaksen, S. G., & Murdock, M. C. (1993). The emergence of a discipline: Issues and approaches to the study of creativity. In S. G. Isaksen, M. C. Murdock, R. L. Firestein, & D. J. Treffinger

(Eds.), *The emergence of a discipline* (Vol. 1). Norwood, NJ: Ablex.

Isay, R. A. (1990). *Being homosexual: Gay men and their development*. New York: Avon.

Jackson, H. (2006, November 27). Boosting brain power: Computer program gives retirees a workout to keep memory sharp, thinking clear. *St. Louis Post-Dispatch*, p. H4.

Jackson, L. A., Gardner, P. D., & Sullivan, L. A. (1992). Explaining gender differences in self-pay expectations: Social comparison standards and perceptions of fair pay. *Journal of Applied Psychology, 77*, 651–663.

Jacobson, N., & Gottman, J. (1998). *When men batter women*. New York: Simon and Schuster.

Jacques, H., & Mash, E. (2004). A test of the tripartite model of anxiety and depression in elementary and high school boys and girls. *Journal of Abnormal Child Psychology, 32*, 13–25.

Jahoda, G. (1980). Theoretical and systematic approaches in mass-cultural psychology. In H. C. Triandis & W. W. Lambert (Eds.), *Handbook of cross-cultural psychology* (Vol. 1). Boston: Allyn and Bacon.

Jahoda, G. (1983). European "lag" in the development of an economic concept: A study in Zimbabwe. *British Journal of Developmental Psychology, 1*, 113–120.

Janda, L. H., & Klenke-Hamel, K. E. (1980). *Human sexuality*. New York: Van Nostrand.

Jansen, B. R. J., Van der Maas, W. L., & Black J. E. (2001). Evidence for the phase transition from rule I to rule II on the balance scale task. *Developmental Review, 21*, 450–494.

Janssens, J. M. A. M., and Dekovic, M. (1997). Child rearing, prosocial moral reasoning, and prosocial behaviour. *International Journal of Behavioral Development, 20*, 509–527.

Javawant, S., & Parr, J. (2007). Outcome following subdural hemorrhages in infancy. *Archives of the Disabled Child, 92*, 343–347.

Jayawardena, K., & Liao, S. (2006, January). Elder abuse at end of life. *Journal of Palliative Medicine, 9*, 127–136.

Jazwinski, S. M. (1996, July 5). Longevity, genes, and aging. *Science, 273*, 54–59.

Jeng, S., Yau, K. T., & Teng, R. (1998). Neurobehavioral development at term in very low-birthweight infants and normal term infants in Taiwan. *Early Human Development, 51*, 235–245.

Jensen, A. (2003). Do age-group differences on mental tests imitate racial differences? *Intelligence, 31*, 107–121.

Jeynes, W. (2007). The impact of parental remarriage on children: A meta-analysis. *Marriage and Family Review, 40*, 75–102.

Ji-liang, S., Li-qing, Z., & Yan, T. (2003). The impact of intergenerational social support and filial expectation on the loneliness of elder parents. *Chinese Journal of Clinical Psychology, 11*, 167–169.

Jiao, S., Ji, G., & Jing, Q. (1996). Cognitive development of Chinese urban only children and children with siblings. *Child Development, 67*, 387–395.

Jimenez, J., & Guzman, R. (2003). The influence of code-oriented versus meaning-oriented approaches to reading instruction on word recognition in the Spanish language. *International Journal of Psychology, 38*, 65–78.

Joe, S., & Marcus, S. (2003). Datapoints: Trends by race and gender in suicide attempts among U.S. adolescents, 1991–2001. *Psychiatric Services, 54*, 454.

Johannes, L. (2003, October 9). A better test for Down syndrome. *The Wall Street Journal*, pp. D1, D3.

Johnson, A. M., Wadsworth, J., Wellings, K., & Bradshaw, S. (1992). Sexual lifestyles and HIV risk. *Nature, 360*, 410–412.

Johnson, C. H., Vicary, J. R., Heist, C. L., & Corneal, D. A. (2001). Moderate alcohol and tobacco use during pregnancy and child behavior outcomes. *Journal of Primary Prevention, 21*, 367–379.

Johnson, C. L., & Barer, B. M. (1992). Patterns of engagement and disengagement among the oldest old. *Journal of Aging Studies, 6*, 351–364.

Johnson, D., Jin, Y., & Truman, C. (2002). Early discharge of Alberta mothers post-delivery and the relationship to potentially preventable newborn readmissions. *Canadian Journal of Public Health, 93*, 276–280.

Johnson, K., & Eilers, A. (1998). Effects of knowledge and development on subordinate level categorization. *Cognitive Development, 13*, 515–545.

Johnson, M. H. (1998). The neural basis of cognitive development. In D. Kuhn & R. S. Siegler (Eds.), *Handbook of child psychology: Vol. 2: Cognition, perception, and language* (5th ed.), pp. 1–49. New York: Wiley.

Johnson, N. G., Roberts, M. C., & Worell, J. (Eds.). (1999). *Beyond appearance: A new look at adolescent girls*. Washington, DC: American Psychological Association.

Johnson, S. L., & Birch, L. L. (1994). Parents' and children's adiposity and eating style. *Pediatrics, 94*, 653–661.

Jones, H. (2006). Drug addiction during pregnancy: Advances in maternal treatment and understanding child outcomes. *Current Directions in Psychological Science, 15*, 126–130.

Jones, S. (2006). Exploration or imitation? The effect of music on 4-week-old infants' tongue protrusions. *Infant Behavior and Development, 29*, 126–130.

Jongudomkarn, D., & Camfield, L. (2006, September). Exploring the quality of life of people in northeastern and southern Thailand. *Social Indicators Research, 78*, 489–529.

Jorgensen, G. (2006, June). Kohlberg and Gilligan: Duet or duel? *Journal of Moral Education, 35*, 179–196.

Jose, O., & Alfons, V. (2007). Do demographics affect marital satisfaction? *Journal of Sex and Marital Therapy, 33*, 73–85.

Joseph, H., Reznik, I., & Mester, R. (2003). Suicidal behavior of adolescent girls: Profile and meaning. *Israel Journal of Psychiatry and Related Sciences, 40*, 209–219.

Joseph, R. (1999). Environmental influences on neural plasticity, the limbic system, emotional development and attachment: A review. *Child Psychiatry and Human Development, 29*, 189–208.

Jost, H., & Songtag, L. (1944). The genetic factor in autonomic nervous system function. *Psychosomatic Medicine, 6*, 308–310.

Jurimae, T., & Saar, M. (2003). Self-perceived and actual indicators of motor abilities in children and adolescents. *Perception and Motor Skills, 97*, 862–866.

Jusko, T. A., Henderson, C. R., Lanphear, B. P., Cory-Slechta, D. A., Parsons, P. J., et al. (2008). Blood lead concentrations < 10 μg/dL and child intelligence at 6 years of age. *Environ Health Perspect, 116*, 243–248.

Kagan, J. (2003). An unwilling rebel. In R. J. Sternberg (Ed.), *Psychologists defying the crowd: Stories of those who battled the establishment and won*. Washington, DC: American Psychological Association.

Kagan, J. (2010). *The temperamental thread: How genes, culture, time, and luck make us who we are*. New York, NY: Dana Press.

Kagan, J., Arcus, D., & Snidman, N. (1993). The idea of temperament: Where do we go from here? In R. Plomin & G. E. McClearn (Eds.), *Nature, nurture, and psychology*. Washington, DC: American Psychological Association.

Kagan, J., Arcus, D., Snidman, N., Feng, W. Y., Hendler, J., & Greene, S. (1994). Reactivity in infants: A cross-national comparison. *Developmental Psychology, 30*, 342–345.

Kagan, J., Kearsley, R., & Zelazo, P. R. (1978). *Infancy: Its place in human development*. Cambridge, MA: Harvard University Press.

Kagan, J., & Snidman, N. (1991). Infant predictors of inhibited and uninhibited profiles. *Psychological Science, 2*, 40–44.

Kahn, J. (2007, February). Maximizing the potential public health impact of HPV vaccines: A focus on parents. *Journal of Adolescent Health, 40*, 101–103.

Kahn, J., Hessling, R., & Russell, D. (2003). Social support, health, and well-being among the elderly: What is the role of negative affectivity? *Personality and Individual Differences, 35*, 5–17.

Kahn, R. L., & Rowe, J. W. (1999). *Successful aging*. New York: Dell.

Kahneman, D., Krueger, A., Schkade, D., Schwarz, N., & Stone, A. (2006, June). Would you be happier if you were richer? A focusing illusion. *Science, 312*, 1908–1910.

Kail, R. (2003). Information processing and memory. In M. Bornstein & L. Davidson (Eds.), *Well-being: Positive development across the life course*. Mahwah, NJ: Lawrence Erlbaum Associates.

Kail, R. V. (2004). Cognitive development includes global and domain-specific processes. *Merrill-Palmer Quarterly, 50* [Special issue: 50th anniversary issue: Part II, the maturing of the human development sciences: Appraising past, present, and prospective agendas], 445–455.

Kaiser, L. L., Allen, L., & American Dietetic Association. (2002). Position of the American Dietetic Association: Nutrition and lifestyle for a healthy pregnancy outcome. *Journal of the American Dietetic Association, 102*, 1479–1490.

Kalb, C. (1997, Spring/Summer). The top 10 health worries. *Newsweek Special Issue*, 42–43.

Kalb, C. (2003, March 10). Preemies grow up. *Newsweek*, 50–51.

Kalb, C. (2004, January 26). Brave new babies. *Newsweek*, 45–53.

Kalb, C. (2006, December 11). Peering into the future. *Newsweek*, 52.

Kalliopuska, M. (1994). Relations of retired people and their grandchildren. *Psychological Reports, 75*, 1083–1088.

Kalsi, M., Heron, G., & Charman, W. (2001). Changes in the static accommodation response with age. *Ophthalmic and Physiological Optics, 21*, 77–84.

Kaltiala-Heino, R., Kosunen, E., & Rimpela, M. (2003). Pubertal timing, sexual behaviour and self-reported depression in middle adolescence. *Journal of Adolescence, 26*, 531–545.

Kaltiala-Heino, R., Rimpelae, M., Rantanen, P., & Rimpelae, A. (2000). Bullying at school—an indicator of adolescents at risk for mental disorders. *Journal of Adolescence, 23*, 661–674.

Kane, R. A., Caplan, A. L., Urv-Wong, E. K., & Freeman, I. C. (1997). Everyday matters in the lives of nursing home residents: Wish for and perception of choice and control. *Journal of the American Geriatrics Society, 45*, 1086–1093.

Kaneda, H., Maeshima, K., Goto, N., Kobayakawa, T., Ayabe-Kanamura, S., & Saito, S. (2000). Decline in taste and odor discrimination abilities with age, and relationship between gustation and olfaction. *Chemical Senses, 25*, 331–337.

Kanetsuna, T., Smith, P., & Morita, Y. (2006, November). Coping with bullying at school: Children's recommended strategies and attitudes to school-based interventions in England and Japan. *Aggressive Behavior, 32*, 570–580.

Kao, G. (2000). Psychological well-being and educational achievement among immigrant youth. In D. J. Hernandez (Ed.), *Children of immigrants: Health, adjustment, and public assistance*. Washington, DC: National Academy Press.

Kao, G., & Tienda, M. (1995). Optimism and achievement: The educational performance of immigrant youth. *Social Science Quarterly, 76*, 1–19.

Kao, G., & Vaquera, E. (2006, February). The salience of racial and ethnic identification in friendship choices among Hispanic adolescents. *Hispanic Journal of Behavioral Sciences, 28*, 23–47.

Kaplan, H., & Dove, H. (1987). Infant development among the Ache of Eastern Paraguay. *Developmental Psychology, 23*, 190–198.

Kaplan, R. M., Sallis, J. F., Jr., & Patterson, T. L. (1993). *Health and human behavior*. Age specific breast cancer annual incidence. New York: McGraw-Hill.

Kaplan, S., Heiligenstein, J., West, S., Busner, J., Harder, D., Dittmann, R., Casat, C., & Wernicke, J. F. (2004). Efficacy and safety of atomoxetine in childhood attention-deficit/hyperactivity disorder with comorbid oppositional defiant disorder. *Journal of Attention Disorders, 8*, 45–52.

Karney, B. R., & Bradbury, T. N. (2005). Contextual influences on marriage. *Current Directions in Psychological Science, 14*, 171–174.

Karpov, Y. V., & Haywood, H. C. (1998). Two ways to elaborate Vygotsky's concept of mediation: Implications for instruction. *American Psychologist, 53*, 27–36.

Kart, C. S. (1990). *The realities of aging* (3rd ed.). Boston: Allyn and Bacon.

Kartman, L. L. (1991). Life review: One aspect of making meaningful music for the elderly. *Activities, Adaptations, and Aging, 15*, 42–45.

Kaslow, F. W. (2001). Families and family psychology at the millennium: Intersecting crossroads. *American Psychologist, 56*, 37–44.

Kastenbaum, R. (1999). Dying and bereavement. In J. C. Cavanaugh & S. K. Whitbourne (Eds.), *Gerontology: An interdisciplinary perspective*. New York: Oxford University Press.

Kate, N. T. (1998, March). How many children? *American Demographics*, p. 35.

Kates, N., Grieff, B., & Hagen, D. (1990). *The psychosocial impact of job loss*. Washington, DC: American Psychiatric Press.

Kantrowitz, B., & Springen, K. (2005, May 16.) A peaceful adolescence. *Newsweek International Edition*, pp. 50–52.

Katz, D. L. (2001). Behavior modification in primary care: The Pressure System Model. *Preventive Medicine: An International Devoted to Practice and Theory, 32*, 66–72.

Katz, L. G. (1989, December). Beginners' ethics. *Parents*, p. 213.

Katz, L. Y., Kozyrskyj, A. L., Prior, H. J., Enns, M. W., Cox, B. J., & Sareen, J. (2008). Impact of regulatory warnings on anti-depressant prescription rates, use of health services and outcomes among children, adolescents and young adults. *Canadian Medical Association Journal, 178*, 1005–1011. doi: 10.1503/cmaj.071265.

Katz, S., & Marshall, B. (2003). New sex for old: Lifestyle, consumerism, and the ethics of aging well. *Journal of Aging Studies, 17*, 3–16.

Kavale, K. (2002). Mainstreaming to full inclusion: From orthogenesis to pathogenesis of an idea. *International Journal of Disability, Development and Education, 49*, 201–214.

Kavale, K. A., & Forness, S. R. (2000, Sep.–Oct.). History, rhetoric, and reality: Analysis of the inclusion debate. *RASE: Remedial and Special Education, 21*, 279–296.

Kaye, W. H., Devlin, B., Barbarich, N., Bulik, C. M., Thornton, L., Bacanu, S. A., Fichter, M. M...Berrettini, W. H. (2004). Genetic analysis of bulimia nervosa: Methods and sample description. *Journal of Eating Disorders, 35*, 556–570.

Kazdin, A. E., & Benjet, C. (2003). Spanking children: Evidence and issues. *Current Directions in Psychological Science, 12*, 99–103.

Keating, D. (1980). Thinking processes in adolescence. In J. Adelson (Ed.), *Handbook of adolescent psychology*. New York: Wiley.

Keating, D. (1990). Adolescent thinking. In S. S. Feldman & G. R. Elliott (Eds.), *At the threshold*. Cambridge, MA: Harvard University Press.

Keating, D. P., & Clark, L. V. (1980). Development of physical and social reasoning in adolescence. *Developmental Psychology, 16*, 23–30.

Kecskes, I., & Papp, T. (2000). *Foreign language and mother tongue*. Mahwah, NJ: Erlbaum.

Kedziora-Kornatowska, K., Szewczyk-Golec, K. Czuczejko, J., van Marke de Lumen, K., Pawluk, H., Motyl, J., Karasek, M., & Kedziora, J. (2007). Effect of melatonin on the oxidative stress in erythrocytes of healthy young and elderly subjects. *Journal of Pineal Research, 42*, 153–158.

Keefer, B. L., Kraus, R. F., Parker, B. L., Elliott, R., et al. (1991). A state university collaboration program: Residents' perspectives. Annual Meeting of the American Psychiatric Association (1990, New York, New York). *Hospital and Community Psychiatry, 42*, 62–66.

Kellett, J. M. (2000). Older adult sexuality. In L. T. Szuchman & F. Muscarella et al. (Eds.), *Psychological perspectives on human sexuality*. New York: Wiley.

Kellman, P., & Arterberry, M. (2006). Infant visual perception. In W. Damon & R. M. Lerner (Eds.), *Handbook of child psychology: Vol. 2, Cognition, perception, and language* (6th ed.). New York: John Wiley and Sons Inc.

Kelly, G. (2001). *Sexuality today: A human perspective*. (7th ed.) New York: McGraw-Hill.

Kelly, M. B. (2010). The processing of divorce cases through civil court in seven provinces and territories. Statistics Canada, 2001 Source. For 1988: Statistics Canada. Divorces, 1991, Shelf Tables. Cat. no. 84-213; For 1989 to 1992: Statistics Canada. Divorces, 1992, Shelf Tables. Cat. no. 84-213; For 1993 to 1995: Statistics Canada. Divorces, 1996 and 1997, Shelf Tables. Cat. no. 84F0213XPB; For 1996 and 1997: Statistics Canada. Divorces, 1999 and 2000, Shelf Tables. Cat. no. 84F0213XPB; For 1998 to 2002: Statistics Canada. Divorces 2001 and 2002, Shelf Tables. Cat. no. 84F0213XPB; and for 2003: Statistics Canada. Divorces 2003, Shelf Tables. Cat. no. 84F0213XPB.

Kemper, R. L., & Vernooy, A. R. (1994). Metalinguistic awareness in first graders: A qualitative perspective. *Journal of Psycholinguistic Research, 22*, 41–57.

Kennell, J. H. (2002). On becoming a family: Bonding and the changing patterns in baby and family behavior. In J. Gomes-Pedro & J. K. Nugent (Eds.), *The infant and family in the twenty-first century*. New York: Brunner-Routledge.

Kenrick, D. T., Keefe, R. C., Bryna, A., Barr, A., & Brown, S. (1995). Age preferences and mate choice among homosexuals and heterosexuals: A case for modular psychological mechanisms. *Journal of Personality and Social Psychology, 69*, 1166–1172.

Kerner, M., & Aboud, F. E. (1998). The importance of friendship qualities and reciprocity in a multi-racial school. *The Canadian Journal of Research in Early Childhood Education, 7*, 117–125.

Kibria, N. (2003). *Becoming Asian American: Second-generation Chinese and Korean American identities*. Baltimore, MD: Johns Hopkins University Press.

Kidwell, J. S., Dunyam, R. M., Bacho, R. A., Pastorino, E., & Portes, P. R. (1995). Adolescent identity exploration: A test of Erikson's theory of transitional crisis. *Adolescence, 30*, 785–793.

Killen, M., & Hart, D. (Eds.). (1995). *Morality in everyday life: Developmental perspectives*. New York: Cambridge University Press.

Kim, J., & Cicchetti, D. (2003). Social self-efficacy and behavior problems in maltreated children. *Journal of Clinical Child and Adolescent Psychology, 32*, 106–117.

Kim, J.-S., & Lee, E.-H. (2003). Cultural and noncultural predictors of health outcomes in Korean daughter and daughter-in-law caregivers. *Public Health Nursing, 20*, 111–119.

Kim, K., & Smith, P. K. (1999). Family relations in early childhood and reproductive development. *Journal of Reproductive and Infant Psychology, 17*, 133–148.

Kim, S., & Park, H. (2006, January). Five years after the launch of Viagra in Korea: Changes in perceptions of erectile dysfunction treatment by physicians, patients, and the patients' spouses. *Journal of Sexual Medicine, 3*, 132–137.

Kim, U., Triandis, H. C., Kagitçibasi, Ç., Choi, S., & Yoon, G. (Eds.). (1994). *Individualism and collectivism: Theory, method, and applications*. Thousand Oaks, CA: Sage.

Kim-Cohen, J. (2007). Resilience and developmental psychopathology. *Child and Adolescent Psychiatric Clinics of North America, 16*, 271–283.

Kimm, S. Y., Glynn, N. W., Kriska, A. M., Barton, B. A., Kronsberg, S. S., Daniels, S. R., Crawford, P. B., Sabry, Z. I., & Liu, K. (2002). Decline in physical activity in black girls and white girls during adolescence. *New England Journal of Medicine, 347*, 709–715.

Kimmel, D., & Sang, B. (2003). Lesbians and gay men in midlife. In L. Garnets & D. Kimmel (Eds.), *Psychological perspectives on lesbian, gay, and bisexual experiences*. New York: Columbia University Press.

Kimura, M., & Kato, Y. (2006). Young children's understanding of video images. *Japanese Journal of Developmental Psychology, 17*, 126–137.

King, K. (2003). Racism or sexism? Attributional ambiguity and simultaneous memberships in multiple oppressed groups. *Journal of Applied Social Psychology, 33*, 223–247.

King, S., & Laplante, D. P. (2005). The effects of prenatal maternal stress on children's cognitive development: Project ice storm. *Stress, 8 (1)*, 35–45.

Kinney, H. C., Randall, L. L., Sleeper, L. A., Willinger, M., Beliveau, R. A., Zec, N., Rava, L. A...Welty, T. K. (2003). Serotonergic brainstem abnormalities in Northern Plains Indians with the sudden infant death syndrome. *Journal of Neuropathology and Experimental Neurology, 62*, 1178–1191.

Kinsey, A. C., Pomeroy, W. B., & Martin, C. E. (1948). *Sexual behavior in the human male*. Philadelphia: Saunders.

Kirby, J. (2006, May). From single-parent families to stepfamilies: Is the transition associated with adolescent alcohol initiation? *Journal of Family Issues, 27*, 685–711.

Kirchengast, S., & Hartmann, B. (2003). Impact of maternal age and maternal-somatic characteristics on newborn size. *American Journal of Human Biology, 15*, 220–228.

Kisilevsky, B. S., Hains, S. M., Lee, K., Xie, X., Huang, H., Ye, H. H., Zhang, K., & Wang, Z. (2003). Effects of experience on fetal voice recognition. *Psychological Science, 14*, 220–224.

Kitchener, R. F. (1996). The nature of the social for Piaget and Vygotsky. *Human Development, 39*, 243–249.

Kitterod, R., & Pettersen, S. (2006, September). Making up for mothers' employed working hours? Housework and childcare among Norwegian fathers. *Work, Employment and Society, 20*, 473–492.

Kleespies, P. (2004). The wish to die: Assisted suicide and voluntary euthanasia. In P. Kleespies (Ed.), *Life and death decisions: Psychological and ethical considerations in end-of-life care*. Washington, DC: American Psychological Association.

Klier, C. M., Muzik, M., Dervic, K., Mossaheb, N., Benesch, T., Ulm, B., & Zeller, M. (2007). The role of estrogen and progesterone in depression after birth. *Journal of Psychiatric Research, 41*, 273–279.

Knafo, A., & Schwartz, S. H. (2003). Parenting and accuracy of perception of parental values by adolescents. *Child Development, 73*, 595–611.

Knaus, W. A., Conners, A. F., Dawson, N. V., Desbiens, N. A., Fulkerson, W. J., Jr., Goldman, L., Lynn, J., & Oye, R. K. (1995, November 22). A controlled trial to improve care for seriously ill hospitalized patients. The study to understand prognoses and preferences for outcomes and risks of treatments (SUPPORT). *Journal of the American Medical Association, 273*, 1591–1598.

Knickmeyer, R., & Baron-Cohen, S. (2006, December). Fetal testosterone and sex differences. *Early Human Development, 82*, 755–760.

Knight, K. (1994, March). Back to basics. *Essence*, 122–138.

Knutson, J. F., & Lansing, C. R. (1990). The relationship between communication problems and psychological difficulties in persons with profound acquired hearing loss. *Journal of Speech and Hearing Disorders, 55*, 656–664.

Kochanska, G. (1998). Mother–child relationship, child fearfulness, and emerging attachment: A short-term longitudinal study. *Developmental Psychology, 34*, 480–490.

Kodl, M., & Mermelstein, R. (2004). Beyond modeling: Parenting practices, parental smoking history, and adolescent cigarette smoking. *Addictive Behaviors, 29*, 17–32.

Koenig, A., Cicchetti, D., & Rogosch, F. (2004). Moral development: The association between maltreatment and young children's prosocial behaviors and moral transgressions. *Social Development, 13*, 97–106.

Koenig, L. B., McGue, M., Krueger, R. F., & Bouchard, Jr., T. J. (2005). Genetic and environmental influences on religiousness: Findings for retrospective and current religiousness ratings. *Journal of Personality, 73*, 471–488.

Koh, A., & Ross, L. (2006). Mental health issues: A comparison of lesbian, bisexual and heterosexual women. *Journal of Homosexuality, 51*, 33–57.

Kohlberg, L. (1984). *The psychology of moral development: Essays on moral development (Vol. 2)*. San Francisco: Harper and Row.

Koivisto, M., & Revonsuo, A. (2003). Object recognition in the cerebral hemispheres as revealed by visual field experiments. *Laterality: Asymmetries of Body, Brain and Cognition, 8*, 135–153.

Kolata, G. (2004, May 11). The heart's desire. *The New York Times*, p. D1.

Koopmans, S., & Kooijman, A. (2006, November). Presbyopia correction and accommodative intraocular lenses. *Gerontechnology, 5*, 222–230.

Koska, J., Ksinantova, L., Sebokova, E., Kvetnansky, R., Klimes, I., Chrousos, G., & Pacak, K. (2002). Endocrine regulation of subcutaneous fat metabolism during cold exposure in humans. *Annals of the New York Academy of Science, 967*, 500–505.

Kosmala, K., & Kloszewska, I. (2004). The burden of providing care for Alzheimer's disease patients in Poland. *International Journal of Geriatric Psychiatry, 19*, 191–193.

Koss, M. P., Goodman, L. A., Browne, A., Fitzgerald, L. F., Keita, G. P., & Russo, N. F. (1993). *No safe haven: Violence against women, at home, at work, and in the community*. Final report of the American Psychological Association Women's Programs Office Task Force on Violence Against Women. Washington, DC: American Psychological Association.

Kotre, J., & Hall, E. (1990). *Seasons of life*. Boston: Little, Brown.

Kozulin, A. (2004). Vygotsky's theory in the classroom: Introduction. *European Journal of Psychology of Education, 19*, 3–7.

Kraemer, B., Noll, T., Delsignore, A., Milos, G., Schnyder, U., & Hepp, U. (2006). Finger length ratio (2D:4D) and dimensions of sexual orientation. *Neuropsychobiology, 53*, 210–214.

Kramer, A. F., Erickson, K. I., & Colcombe, S. J. (2006). Exercise, cognition, and the aging brain. *Journal of Applied Physiology, 101*, 1237–1242.

Kreitlow, B., & Kreitlow, D. (1997). *Creative planning for the second half of life*. Duluth, MN: Whole Person Associates.

Krishnamoorthy, J. S., Hart, C., & Jelalian, E. (2006). The epidemic of childhood obesity: Review of research and implications for public policy. *Social Policy Report, 19*, 3–19.

Kroger, J. (2000). *Identity development: Adolescence through adulthood*. Thousand Oaks, CA: Sage.

Kroger, J. (2006). *Identity development: Adolescence through adulthood*. Thousand Oaks, CA: Sage Publications.

Krojgaard, P. (2005). Infants' search for hidden persons. *International Journal of Behavioral Development, 29*, 70–79.

Kronenfeld, J. J. (2002). *Health care policy: Issues and trends*. New York: Praeger.

Krout, J. A. (1988). Rural versus urban differences in elderly parents' contact with their children. *Gerontologist, 28*, 198–203.

Krueger, G. (2006, September). Meaning-making in the aftermath of sudden infant death syndrome. *Nursing Inquiry, 13*, 163–171.

Kübler-Ross, E. (1969). *On death and dying*. New York: Macmillan.

Kübler-Ross, E. (Ed.). (1975). *Death: The final stage of growth*. Englewood Cliffs, NJ: Prentice-Hall.

Kübler-Ross, E. (1982). *Working it through*. New York: Macmillan.

Kuczynski, L., & Kochanska, G. (1990). Development of children's noncompliance strategies from toddlerhood to age 5. *Developmental Psychology, 26*, 398–408.

Kuhl, P. K. (2007). Is speech learning 'gated' by the social brain? *Developmental Science, 10*, 110–120.

Kuhl, P., Tsao, F.-M., & Liu, H.-M. (2003). Foreign-language experience in infancy: Effects of short-term exposure and social interaction on phonetic learning. *Proceedings of the National Academy of Sciences, 100*, 9096–9101.

Kuhl, P. K., Andruski, J. E., Chistovich, I. A., Chistovich, L. A., Kozhevnikova, E. V., Ryskina, V. L., Stolyarova, E. I...Lacerda, F. (1997, August 1). Cross-language analysis of phonetic units in language addressed to infants. *Science, 277*, 684–686.

Kuhn, D. (2000). Metacognitive development. *Current Directions in Psychological Science, 9*, 178–181.

Kuhn, D., Garcia-Mila, M., Zohar, A., & Andersen, C. (1995). Strategies of knowledge acquisition. With commentary by S. H. White, D. Klahr, & S. M. Carver, and a reply by D. Kuhn. *Monographs of the Society for Research in Child Development, 60*, 122–137.

Kunkel, D., Wilcox, B. L., Cantor, J., Palmer, E., Linn, S., & Dowrick, P. (2004, February 20). *Report of the APA task force on advertising and children*. Washington, DC: American Psychological Association.

Kunzmann, U., & Baltes, P. (2005). *The psychology of wisdom: Theoretical and empirical challenges*. New York: Cambridge University Press.

Kupersmidt, J. B., & Dodge, K. A. (Eds.). (2004). *Children's peer relations: From development to intervention*. Washington, DC: American Psychological Association.

Kurdek, L. (2002). Predicting the timing of separation and marital satisfaction: An eight-year prospective longitudinal study. *Journal of Marriage and Family, 64*, 163–179.

Kurdek, L. (2003a). Differences between gay and lesbian cohabiting couples. *Journal of Social and Personal Relationships, 20*, 411–436.

Kurdek, L. (2003b). Negative representations of the self/spouse and marital distress. *Personal Relationships, 10*, 511–534.

Kurdek, L. (2006, May). Differences between partners from heterosexual, gay, and lesbian cohabiting couples. *Journal of Marriage and Family, 68*, 509–528.

Kurdek, L. A. (1993). The allocation of household labor in gay, lesbian, and heterosexual married children. *Journal of Social Issues, 49*, 127–139.

Kurdek, L. A. (1999). The nature and predictors of the trajectory of change in marital quality for husbands and wives over the first 10 years of marriage. *Developmental Psychology, 35*, 1283–1296.

Kurtines, W. M., & Gewirtz, J. L. (1987). *Moral development through social interaction*. New York: Wiley.

Kwant, P. B., Finocchiaro, T., Forster, F., Reul, H., Rau, G., Morshuis, M., El Banayosi, A...Steinseifer, U. (2007). The MiniACcor: Constructive redesign of an implantable total artificial heart, initial laboratory testing and further steps. *International Journal of Artificial Organs, 30*, 345–351.

Labouvie-Vief, G. (1990). Modes of knowledge and the organization of development. In M. L. Commons, C. Armon, L. Kohlberg, F. A. Richards, T. A. Grotzer, & J. Sinnott (Eds.), *Adult development (Vol. 2). Models and methods in the study of adolescent thought*. New York: Praeger.

Labouvie-Vief, G. (2006). Emerging structures of adult thought. In J. J. Arnett & J. L. Tanner (Eds.), *Emerging adults in America: Coming of age in the 21st century*. Washington, DC: American Psychological Association.

Lacerda, F., von Hofsten, C., & Heimann, M. (2001). *Emerging cognitive abilities in early infancy*. Mahwah, NJ: Lawrence Erlbaum Associates.

Lachmann, T., Berti, S., Kujala, T., & Schroger, E. (2005). Diagnostic subgroups of developmental dyslexia have different deficits in neural processing of tones and phonemes. *International Journal of Psychophysiology, 56*, 105–120.

Lackey, C. (2003). Violent family heritage, the transition to adulthood, and later partner violence. *Journal of Family Issues, 24*, 74–98.

Laflamme, D., Pomerleau, A., & Malcuit, G. (2002). A comparison of fathers' and mothers' involvement in childcare and stimulation behaviors during free-play with their infants at 9 and 15 months. *Sex Roles, 47*, 507–518.

LaFromboise, T., Coleman, H. L., & Gerton, J. (1993). Psychological impact of biculturalism: Evidence and theory. *Psychological Bulletin, 114*, 395–412.

Lafuente, M. J., Grifol, R., Segarra, J., & Soriano, J. (1997). Effects of the Firstart method of prenatal stimulation on psychomotor development: The first six months. *Pre- and PeriNatal Psychology, 11*, 151–162.

Lahiri, D. K., Maloney, B., Basha, M. R., Ge, Y. W., & Zawia, N. H. (2007). How and when environmental agents and dietary factors affect the course of Alzheimer's disease: The "LEARn" model (latent early-life associated regulation) may explain the triggering of AD. *Current Alzheimer Research, 4*, 219–228.

Lam, V., & Leman, P. (2003). The influence of gender and ethnicity on children's inferences about toy choice. *Social Development, 12*, 269–287.

Lambert, W. E., & Peal, E. (1972). The relation of bilingualism to intelligence. In A. S. Dil (Ed.), *Language, psychology, and culture* (3rd ed.). New York: Wiley.

Lamberts, S. W. J., van den Beld, A. W., & van der Lely, A.-J. (1997, October 17). The endocrinology of aging. *Science, 278*, 419–424.

Lamm, B., & Keller, H. (2007). Understanding cultural models of parenting: The role of intracultural variation and response style. *Journal of Cross-Cultural Psychology, 38*, 50–57.

Lamm, H., & Wiesmann, U. (1997). Subjective attributes of attraction: How people characterize their liking, their love, and their being in love. *Personal Relationships, 4*, 271–284.

Lamont, J. A. (1997). Sexuality. In D. E. Stewart & G. E. Robinson (Eds.), *A clinician's guide to menopause. Clinical practice* (pp. 63–75). Washington, DC: Health Press International.

Lamorey, S., Robinson, B. E., & Rowland, B. H. (1998). *Latchkey kids: Unlocking doors for children and their families*. Newbury Park, CA: Sage.

Lanctot, K. L., Herrmann, N., & Mazzotta, P. (2001). Role of serotonin in the behavioral and psychological symptoms of dementia. *Journal of Neuropsychiatry and Clinical Neurosciences, 13*, 5–21.

Landy, F., & Conte, J. M. (2004). *Work in the 21st century*. New York: McGraw-Hill.

Lane, W. K. (1976, November). The relationship between personality and differential academic achievement within a group of highly gifted and high achieving children. *Dissertation Abstracts International, 37(5-A)*, 2746.

Langford, P. E. (1995). *Approaches to the development of moral reasoning*. Hillsdale, NJ: Erlbaum.

Lansford, J. E., Chang, L., Dodge, K. A., Malone, P. S., Oburu, P., Palmérus, K., Bacchini, D...Quinn, N. (2005). Physical discipline and children's adjustment: Cultural normativeness as a moderator. *Child Development, 76*, 1234–1246.

Lansford, J. E., & Parker, J. G. (1999). Children's interactions in triads: Behavioral profiles and effects of gender and patterns of friendships among members. *Developmental Psychology, 35*, 80–93.

Laplante, D. P., Barr, R. G., Brunet, A., Galbaud du Fort, G., Meaney, M., Saucier, J.-F., et al. (2004). Stress during pregnancy affects intellectual and linguistic functioning in human toddlers. *Pediatric Research, 56*, 400–410.

Larson, R. W., Richards, M. H., Moneta, G., Holmbeck, G., & Duckett, E. (1996). Changes in adolescents' daily interactions with their families from ages 10 to 18: Disengagement and transformation. *Developmental Psychology, 32*, 744–754.

Lau, I., Lee, S., & Chiu, C. (2004). Language, cognition, and reality: Constructing shared meanings through communication. In

M. Schaller & C. Crandall (Eds.), *The psychological foundations of culture*. Mahwah, NJ: Lawrence Erlbaum Associates.

Lauer, J. C., & Lauer, R. H. (1999). *How to survive and thrive in an empty nest*. Oakland, CA: New Harbinger Publications.

Laugharne, J., Janca, A., & Widiger, T. (2007). Posttraumatic stress disorder and terrorism: 5 years after 9/11. *Current Opinion in Psychiatry, 20*, 36–41.

Laumann, E. O., Paik, A., & Rosen, R. C. (1999). Sexual dysfunction in the United States: Prevalence and predictors. *Journal of the American Medical Association, 281*, 537–544.

Laursen, B., Hartup, W. W., & Koplas, A. L. (1996). Towards understanding peer conflict. *Merrill-Palmer Quarterly, 42*, 76–102.

Lauter, J. L. (1998). Neuroimaging and the trimodal brain: Applications for developmental communication neuroscience. *Phoniatrica et Logopaedica, 50*, 118–145.

Lavelli, M., & Fogel, A. (2005). Developmental changes in the relationship between the infant's attention and emotion during early face-to-face communication: The 2-month transition. *Developmental Psychology [serial online], 41*, 265–280.

Lavers-Preston, C., & Sonuga-Barke, E. (2003). An intergenerational perspective on parent–child relationships: The reciprocal effects of tri-generational grandparent–parent–child relationships. In R. Gupta & D. Parry-Gupta (Eds.), *Children and parents: Clinical issues for psychologists and psychiatrists*. London: Whurr Publishers, Ltd.

Lavzer, J. I., & Goodson, B. D. (2006). The "quality" of early care and education settings: Definitional and measurement issues. *Evaluation Review, 30*, 556–576.

Lawton, M. P. (2001). Emotion in later life. *Current Directions in Psychological Science, 10*, 120–123.

Layton, J. (2011). Letter to Canadians. Retrieved from http://www.cbc.ca/news/politics/story/2011/08/22/pol-layton-last-letter.html.

Lazarus, R. S. (1968). Emotions and adaptations: Conceptual and empirical relations. In W. Arnold (Ed.), *Nebraska symposium on motivation*. Lincoln: University of Nebraska.

Lazarus, R. S. (1991). *Emotion and adaptation*. New York: Oxford University Press.

Lazarus, R. S., & Folkman, S. (1984). *Stress, appraisal, and coping*. New York: Springer.

Leaper, C. (2002). Parenting girls and boys. In M. Bornstein (Ed.), *Handbook of parenting: Vol. 1: Children and parenting*. Mahwah, NJ: Lawrence Erlbaum Associates.

Leathers, H. D., & Foster, P. (2004). *The world food problem: Tackling causes of undernutrition in the third world*. Boulder, CO: Lynne Rienner Publishers.

Leathers, S., & Kelley, M. (2000). Unintended pregnancy and depressive symptoms among first-time mothers and fathers. *American Journal of Orthopsychiatry, 70*, 523–531.

Lecours, A. R. (1982). Correlates of developmental behavior in brain maturation. In T. Bever (Ed.), *Regressions in mental development*. Hillsdale, NJ: Erlbaum.

Lee, B. H., Schofer, J. L., & Koppelman, F. S. (2005). Bicycle safety helmet legislation and bicycle-related non-fatal injuries in California. *Accident Analysis and Prevention, 37*, 93–102.

Lee, M., Vernon-Feagans, L., & Vazquez, A. (2003). The influence of family environment and child temperament on work/family role strain for mothers and fathers. *Infant and Child Development, 12*, 421–439.

Lee, R. M. (2005). Resilience against discrimination: Ethnic identity and other-group orientation as protective factors for Korean Americans. *Journal of Counseling Psychology, 52*, 36–44.

Lee, S., Perlman, M., Ballantyne, M., Elliott, I., & To, T. (1995). Association between duration of neonatal hospital stay and readmission rate. *The Journal of Pediatrics, 127*, 758–766.

Leenaars, A. A., & Shneidman, E. S. (Eds.). (1999). *Lives and deaths: Selections from the works of Edwin S. Shneidman*. New York: Bruuner-Routledge.

Lefkowitz, E. S., Sigman, M., & Kit-fong Au, T. (2000). Helping mothers discuss sexuality and AIDS with adolescents. *Child Development, 71*, 1383–1394.

Legerstee, M., Anderson, D., & Schaffer, A. (1998). Five- and eight-month-old infants recognize their faces and voices as familiar and social stimuli. *Child Development, 69*, 37–50.

Lehman, D., Chiu, C., & Schaller, M. (2004). Psychology and culture. *Annual Review of Psychology, 55*, 689–714.

Lehr, U., Seiler, E., & Thomae, H. (2000). Aging in a cross-cultural perspective. In A. L. Comunian, & U. P. Gielen (Eds.), *International perspectives on human development*. Lengerich, Germany: Pabst Science Publishers.

Lemonick, M. D. (2000, October 30). Teens before their time. *Time, 67*, 68–74.

Leonard, C. M., Lombardino, L. J., Mercado, L. R., Browd, S. R., Breier, J. I., & Agee, O. F. (1996). Cerebral asymmetry and cognitive development in children: A magnetic resonance imaging study. *Psychological Science, 7*, 89–95.

Leonard, T. (2005, March 22). Need parenting help? Call your coach. *The Daily Telegraph (London)*, p. 15.

Lerner, J. W. (2002). *Learning disabilities: Theories, diagnosis, and teaching strategies*. Boston: Houghton Mifflin.

Lerner, R. M., Theokas, C., & Jelicic, H. (2005). Youth as active agents in their own positive development: A developmental systems perspective. In W. Greve, K. Rothermund, & D. Wentura (Eds.), *Adaptive self: Personal continuity and intentional self-development*. Ashland, OH: Hogrefe and Huber Publishers.

Lesko, A., & Corpus, J. (2006, January). Discounting the difficult: How high math-identified women respond to stereotype threat. *Sex Roles, 54*, 113–125.

Leslie, C. (1991, February 11). Classrooms of Babel. *Newsweek*, 56–57.

Lesner, S. (2003). Candidacy and management of assistive listening devices: Special needs of the elderly. *International Journal of Audiology, 42*, 2S68–2S76.

Lester, D. (1996). Psychological issues in euthanasia, suicide, and assisted suicide. *Journal of Social Issues, 52*, 51–62.

Lester, D. (2006, December). Sexual orientation and suicidal behavior. *Psychological Reports, 99*, 923–924.

Leung, C., Pe-Pua, R., & Karnilowicz, W. (2006, January). Psychological adaptation and autonomy among adolescents in Australia: A comparison of Anglo-Celtic and three Asian groups. *International Journal of Intercultural Relations, 30*, 99–118.

Leung, K. (2005). Special issue: Cross-cultural variations in distributive justice perception. *Journal of Cross-Cultural Psychology, 36*, 6–8.

LeVay, S., & Valente, S. M. (2003). *Human sexuality*. Sunderland, MA: Sinauer Associates.

Levenson, R. W., Carstensen, L. L., & Gottman, J. M. (1993). Long-term marriage: Age, gender, and satisfaction. *Psychology and Aging, 8*, 301–313.

Levine, R. V. (1993, February). Is love a luxury? *American Demographics*, 29–37.

Levine, S. C., Huttenlocher, J., Taylor, A., & Langrock, A. (1999). Early sex differences in spatial skill. *Developmental Psychology, 35*, 940–949.

Levinson, D. (1992). *The seasons of a woman's life*. New York: Knopf.

Levinson, D. J. (1986). A conception of adult development. *American Psychologist, 41*, 3–13.

Levy, B. L., & Langer, E. (1994). Aging free from negative stereotypes: Successful memory in China and among the American deaf. *Journal of Personality and Social Psychology, 66*, 989–997.

Levy, B. R. (2003). Mind matters: Cognitive and physical effects of aging self-stereotypes. *Journal of Gerontology: Series B: Psychological Sciences and Social Sciences, 58B*, P203–P211.

Levy, B. R., Slade, M. D., & Kasl, S. V. (2002). Longitudinal benefit of positive self-perceptions of aging on functioning health. *Journal of Gerontology: Psychological Sciences, 57*, 166–195.

Levy-Shiff, R. (1994). Individual and contextual correlates of marital change across the transition to parenthood. *Developmental Psychology, 30*, 591–601.

Lewin, T. (2003a, December 22). For more people in their 20s and 30s, going home is easier because they never left. *The New York Times*, p. A27.

Lewis, B., Legato, M., & Fisch, H. (2006). Medical implications of the male biological clock. *JAMA: Journal of the American Medical Association, 296*, 2369–2371.

Lewis, C., & Mitchell, P. (Eds.). (1994). *Children's early understanding of mind: Origins and development*. Hillsdale, NJ: Erlbaum.

Lewis, C. S. (1985). A grief observed. In E. S. Shneidman (Ed.), *Death: Current perspectives* (3rd ed.). Palo Alto, CA: Mayfield.

Lewis, R., Freneau, P., & Roberts, C. (1979). Fathers and the postparental transition. *Family Coordinator, 28*, 514–520.

Lewis, T. E., & Phillipsen, L. C. (1998). Interactions on an elementary school playground: Variations by age, gender, race, group size, and playground area. *Child Study Journal, 28*, 309–320.

Lewkowicz, D. (2002). Heterogeneity and heterochrony in the development of intersensory perception. *Cognitive Brain Research, 14*, 41–63.

Leyens J.-P., Camino, L., Parke, R., & Berkowitz L. (1975, August). Effects of movie violence on aggression in a field setting as a function of group dominance and cohesion. *J Pers Soc Psychol. 32(2)*, 346–360.

Li, C., DiGiuseppe, R., & Froh, J. (2006, September). The roles of sex, gender, and coping in adolescent depression. *Adolescence, 41*, 409–415.

Li, G. R., & Zhu, X. D. (2007). Development of the functionally total artificial heart using an artery pump. *ASAIO Journal, 53*, 288–291.

Li, J., Laursen, T. M., Precht, D. H., Olsen, J., & Mortensen, P. B. (2005). Hospitalization for mental illness among parents after the death of a child. *New England Journal of Medicine, 352*, 1190–1196.

Li, N. P., Bailey, J. M., Kenrick, D. T., & Linsenmeier, J. A. W. (2002). The necessities and luxuries of mate preferences: Testing the tradeoffs. *Journal of Personality and Social Psychology, 82*, 947–955.

Li, S. (2003). Biocultural orchestration of developmental plasticity across levels: The interplay of biology and culture in shaping the mind and behavior across the life span. *Psychological Bulletin, 129*, 171–194.

Libert, S., Zwiener, J., Chu, X., Vanvoorhies, W., Roman, G., & Pletcher, S. D. (2007, February 23). Regulation of Drosophila life span by olfaction and food-derived odors. *Science, 315*, 1133–1137.

Lickliter, R., and Bahrick, L. E. (2000). The development of infant intersensory perception: Advantages of a comparative convergent-operations approach. *Psychological Bulletin, 126*, 260–280.

Lidz, J., & Gleitman, L. R. (2004). Yes, we still need Universal Grammar: Reply. *Cognition, 94*, 85–93.

Liem, D. G., & Mennella, J. A. (2002). Sweet and sour preferences during childhood: Role of early experiences. *Developmental Psychology, 41*, 388–395.

Light, L. L. (2000). Memory changes in adulthood. In S. H. Qualls & N. Abeles et al. (Eds.), *Psychology and the aging revolution: How we adapt to longer life* (pp. 73–97). Washington, DC: American Psychological Association.

Lindsey, B. W., & Tropepe, V. (2006). A comparative framework for understanding the biological principles of adult neurogenesis. *Progressive Neurobiology, 80*, 281–307.

Lindsey, E., & Colwell, M. (2003). Preschoolers' emotional competence: Links to pretend and physical play. *Child Study Journal, 33*, 39–52.

Lindstrom, H., Fritsch, T., Petot, G., Smyth, K., Chen, C., Debanne, S., et al. (2005, July). The relationships between television viewing in midlife and the development of Alzheimer's disease in a case-control study. *Brain and Cognition, 58,* 157–165.

Lino, Mark. 2001. *Expenditures on children by families, 2000 annual report.* Washington, DC: U.S. Department of Agriculture, Center for Nutrition Policy and Promotion. Miscellaneous Publication No. 1528-2000.

Lippa, R. A. (2003). Are 2D:4D finger-length rations related to sexual orientation? Yes for men, no for women. *Journal of Personality and Social Psychology, 85,* 179–188.

Lipsett, L. (2003). Crib death: A biobehavioral phenomenon? *Current Directions in Psychological Science, 12,* 164–170.

Liskin, L. (1985, Nov.–Dec.). Youth in the 1980s: Social and health concerns: 4. *Population Reports,* 85.

Litzinger, S., & Gordon, K. (2005, October). Exploring relationships among communication, sexual satisfaction, and marital satisfaction. *Journal of Sex and Marital Therapy, 31,* 409–424.

Liu, H., Kuhl, P., & Tsao, F. (2003). An association between mothers' speech clarity and infants' speech discrimination skills. *Developmental Science, 6,* F1–F10.

Livson, N., & Peskin, H. (1980). Perspectives on adolescence from longitudinal research. In J. Adelson (Ed.), *Handbook of adolescent psychology.* New York: Wiley.

Lock, R. D. (1992). *Taking charge of your career direction* (2nd ed.). Pacific Grove, CA: Brooks/Cole.

Loehlin, J. C., Neiderhiser, J. M., & Reiss, D. (2005). Genetic and environmental components of adolescent adjustment and parental behavior: A multivariate analysis. *Child Development, 76,* 1104–1115.

Loftus, E. F. (2003, November). Make-believe memories. *American Psychologist,* 867–873.

Loftus, E. F., & Bernstein, D. M. (2005). Rich false memories: The royal road to success. In A. F. Healy (Ed.), *Experimental cognitive psychology and its applications.* Washington, DC: American Psychological Association.

Lonetto, R. (1980). *Children's conception of death.* New York: Springer.

Longboat, D. 2002. Indigenous perspectives on death and dying. Retrieved from http://www.cme.utoronto.ca/endoflife/Modules/Indigenous%20Perspectives%20on%20Death%20and%20Dying.pdf. Accessed May 6, 2012.

Lorenz, K. (1957). Companionship in bird life. In C. Scholler (Ed.), *Instinctive behavior.* New York: International Universities Press.

Lorenz, K. (1966). *On aggression.* New York: Harcourt Brace Jovanovich.

Lorenz, K. (1974). *Civilized man's eight deadly sins.* New York: Harcourt Brace Jovanovich.

Lourenco, O., & Machado, A. (1996). In defense of Piaget's theory: A reply to 10 common criticisms. *Psychological Review, 103,* 143–164.

Love, J. M., Harrison, L., Sagi-Schwartz, A., van Ijzendoorn, M. H., Ross, C., Ungerer, J. A., Raikes, H…Chazan-Cohen, R. (2003). Child care quality matters: How conclusions may vary with context. *Child Development, 74,* 1021–1033.

Lowe, M. R., & Timko, C. A. (2004). What a difference a diet makes: Towards an understanding of differences between restrained dieters and restrained nondieters. *Eating Behaviors, 5,* 199–208.

Lowrey, G. H. (1986). *Growth and development of children* (8th ed.). Chicago: Year Book Medical Publishers.

Lowton, K., & Higginson, I. (2003). Managing bereavement in the classroom: A conspiracy of silence? *Death Studies, 27,* 717–741.

Lu, L. (2006). The transition to parenthood: Stress, resources, and gender differences in a Chinese society. *Journal of Community Psychology, 34,* 471–488.

Lu, X. (2001). Bicultural identity development and Chinese community formation: An ethnographic study of Chinese schools in Chicago. *Howard Journal of Communications, 12,* 203–220.

Lubinski, D. (2004). Introduction to the special section on cognitive abilities: 100 years after Spearman's (1904) "'General Intelligence,' objectively determined and measured." *Journal of Personality and Social Psychology, 86,* 96–111.

Lucas, S. R., & Berends, M. (2002). Sociodemographic diversity, correlated achievement, and de facto tracking. *Sociology of Education, 75,* 328–349.

Lui, S., Wen, S., McMillan, D., & Fowler, D. (2000). Increased neonatal readmission rate associated with decreased length of hospital stay at birth in Canada. *Canadian Journal of Public Health, 91,* 46–50.

Lundberg, U. (2006, July). Stress, subjective and objective health. *International Journal of Social Welfare, 15,* S41–S48.

Luthar, S. S., Cicchetti, D., & Becker, B. (2000). The construct of resilience: A critical evaluation and guidelines for future work. *Child Development, 71,* 543–562.

Lye, T. C., Piguet, O., Grayson, D. A., Creasey, H., Ridley, L. J., Bennett, H. P., & Broe, G. A. (2004). Hippocampal size and memory function in the ninth and tenth decades of life: The Sydney Older Persons Study. *Journal of Neurology, Neurosurgery, and Psychiatry, 75,* 548–554.

Lynam, D. R. (1996). Early identification of chronic offenders: Who is the fledgling psychopath? *Psychological Bulletin, 120,* 209–234.

Lynch, M. E., Coles, C. D., & Corely, T. (2003). Examining delinquency in adolescents: Risk factors. *Journal of Studies on Alcohol, 64,* 678–686.

Lynne, S., Graber, J., Nichols, T., Brooks-Gunn, J., & Botvin, G. (2007, February). Links between pubertal timing, peer influences, and externalizing behaviors among urban students followed through middle school. *Journal of Adolescent Health, 40,* 35–44.

Lyon, M. E., Benoit, M., O'Donnell, R. M., Getson, P. R., Silber, T., & Walsh, T. (2000). Assessing African American adolescents' risk for suicide attempts: Attachment theory. *Adolescence, 35,* 121–134.

Lyons, M. J., Bar, J. L., & Kremen, W. S. (2002). Nicotine and familial vulnerability to schizophrenia: A discordant twin study. *Journal of Abnormal Psychology, 111,* 687–693.

Mabbott, D. J., Noseworthy, M., Bouffet, E., Laughlin, S., & Rockel, C. (2006). White matter growth as a mechanism of cognitive development in children. *Neuroimaging, 15,* 936–946.

Maccoby, E. B. (1999). *The two sexes: Growing up apart, coming together.* New York: Belknap.

Maccoby, E. E., & Lewis, C. C. (2003). Less day care or different day care? *Child Development, 74,* 1069–1075.

MacDonald, S., Hultsch, D., & Dixon, R. (2003). Performance variability is related to change in cognition: Evidence from the Victoria Longitudinal Study. *Psychology and Aging, 18,* 510–523.

MacDonald, W. (2003). The impact of job demands and workload stress and fatigue. *Australian Psychologist, 38,* 102–117.

MacDorman, M. F., Martin, J. A., Mathews, T. J., Hoyert, D. L., & Ventura, S. J. (2005). Explaining the 2001–02 infant mortality increase: Data from the linked birth/infant death data set. *National Vital Statistics Report, 53,* 1–22.

Macionis, J. J. (2001). *Sociology.* Upper Saddle River, NJ: Prentice Hall.

Mackey, M. C. (1990). Women's preparation for the childbirth experience. *Maternal-Child Nursing Journal, 19,* 143–173.

Maddi, S. R., (2006). Hardiness: The courage to grow from stresses. *Journal of Positive Psychology, 1,* 160–168.

Maddi, S. R., Harvey, R. H., Khoshaba, D. M., Lu, J. L., Persico, M., & Brow, M. (2006). The personality construct of hardiness, III: Relationships with repression, innovativeness, authoritarianism, and performance. *Journal of Personality, 74,* 575–598.

Magai, C., & McFadden, S. H. (Eds.). (1996). *Handbook of emotion, adult development, and aging.* New York: Academic Press.

Mahgoub, N., & Lantz, M. (2006, December). When older adults suffer the loss of a child. *Psychiatric Annals, 36,* 877–880.

Major, B., Appelbaum, M., Beckman, L., Dutton, M. A., Russo, N. F., & West, C. (2009). Abortion and mental health: Evaluating the evidence. *American Psychologist, 64,* 863–890. doi: 10.1037/a0017497.

Makino, M., Hashizume, M., Tsuboi, K., Yasushi, M., & Dennerstein, L. (2006, September). Comparative study of attitudes to eating between male and female students in the People's Republic of China. *Eating and Weight Disorders, 11,* 111–117.

Maller, S. (2003). Best practices in detecting bias in nonverbal tests. In R. McCallum (Ed.), *Handbook of nonverbal assessment.* New York: Kluwer Academic/Plenum Publishers.

Mangan, P. A. (1997, November). *Time perception.* Paper presented at the annual meeting of the Society for Neuroscience, New Orleans.

Mangweth, B., Hausmann, A., & Walch, T. (2004). Body fat perception in eating-disordered men. *International Journal of Eating Disorders, 35,* 102–108.

Manlove, J., Franzetta, K., McKinney, K., Romano-Papillo, A., & Terry-Humen, E.(2004). *No time to waste: Programs to reduce teen pregnancy among middle school-aged youth.* Washington, DC: National Campaign to Prevent Teen Pregnancy.

Manning, M., & Hoyme, H. (2007). Fetal alcohol spectrum disorders: A practical clinical approach to diagnosis. *Neuroscience and Biobehavioral Reviews, 31,* 230–238.

Manning, W., Giordano, P., & Longmore, M. (2006, September). Hooking up: The relationship contexts of "nonrelationship" sex. *Journal of Adolescent Research, 21,* 459–483.

Manstead, A. S. R. (1997). Situations, belongingness, attitudes, and culture: Four lessons learned from social psychology. In C. McGarty & S. A. Haslam et al. (Eds.), *The message of social psychology: Perspectives on mind in society.* Oxford, England: Blackwell Publishers, Inc.

Mao, A., Burnham, M. M., Goodlin-Jones, B. L., Gaylor, E. E., & Anders, T. F. (2004). A comparison of the sleep-wake patterns of cosleeping and solitary-sleeping infants. *Child Psychiatry and Human Development, 35,* 95–105.

Marchant, M., Young, K. R., & West, R. P. (2004). The effects of parental teaching on compliance behavior of children. *Psychology in the Schools, 41,* 337–350.

Marcia, J. E. (1980). Identity in adolescence. In J. Adelson (Ed.), *Handbook of adolescent psychology.* New York: Wiley.

Marcus, A. D. (2004, February 3). The new math on when to have kids. *The Wall Street Journal,* pp. D1, D4.

Marczinski, C., Milliken, B., & Nelson, S. (2003). Aging and repetition effects: Separate specific and non specific influences. *Psychology and Aging, 18,* 780–790.

Markus, H. R., & Kitayama, S. (1991). Culture and the self: Implications for cognition, emotion, and motivation. *Psychological Review, 98,* 224–253.

Marlier, L., Schaal, B., & Soussignan, R. (1998). Neonatal responsiveness to the odor of amniotic and lacteal fluids: A test of perinatal chemosensory continuity. *Child Development, 69,* 611–623.

Marmar, C. R., Neylan, T. C., & Schoenfeld, F. B. (2002). New directions in the pharmacotherapy of posttraumatic stress disorder. *Psychiatric Quarterly, 73,* 259–270.

Marschark, M., & Spencer, P. E. (Eds.). (2003). *Oxford handbook of deaf studies, language and education.* New York, NY: Oxford University Press.

Marsh, H., & Hau, K. (2004). Explaining paradoxical relations between academic self-concepts and achievements: Cross-cultural generalizability of the internal/external frame of reference predictions across 26 countries. *Journal of Educational Psychology, 96,* 56–67.

Marsh, H., Ellis, L., & Craven, R. (2002). How do preschool children feel about themselves? Unraveling measurement and multidimensional self-concept structure. *Developmental Psychology, 38*, 376–393.

Marsh, H. W., & Ayotte, V. (2003). Do multiple dimensions of self-concept become more differentiated with age? The differential distinctiveness hypothesis. *International Review of Education, 49*, 463.

Marshall, E. (2000, November 17). Planned Ritalin trial for tots heads into uncharted waters. *Science, 290*, 1280–1282.

Marshall, K. (2006, July). Converging gender roles. *Perspectives on labour and income*. Statistics Canada Catalogue no. 75-001-XIE.

Martikainen, P., & Valkonen, T. (1996). Mortality after the death of a spouse: Rates and causes of death in a large Finnish cohort. *American Journal of Public Health, 86*, 1087–1093.

Martin, C., & Fabes, R. (2001). The stability and consequences of young children's same-sex peer interactions. *Developmental Psychology, 37*, 431–446.

Martin, C. L. (2000). Cognitive theories of gender development. In T. Eckes & H. M. Trautner et al. (Eds.), *The developmental social psychology of gender*. Mahwah, NJ: Erlbaum.

Martin, C. L., & Ruble, D. (2004). Children's search for gender cues: Cognitive perspectives on gender development. *Current Directions in Psychological Science, 13*, 67–70.

Martin, C. L., Ruble, D. N., & Szkrybalo, J. (2002). Cognitive theories of early gender development. *Psychological Bulletin, 128*, 903–933.

Martin, P., Martin, D., & Martin, M. (2001). Adolescent premarital sexual activity, cohabitation, and attitudes toward marriage. *Adolescence, 36*, 601–609.

Martin, S., Li, Y., Casanueva, C., Harris-Britt, A., Kupper, L., & Cloutier, S. (2006). Intimate partner violence and women's depression before and during pregnancy. *Violence Against Women, 12*, 221–239.

Masataka, N. (1996). Perception of motherese in a signed language by 6-month-old deaf infants. *Developmental Psychology, 32*, 874–879.

Masataka, N. (1998). Perception of motherese in Japanese sign language by 6-month-old hearing infants. *Developmental Psychology, 34*, 241–246.

Masataka, N. (2000). The role of modality and input in the earliest stage of language acquisition: Studies of Japanese sign language. In C. Chamerlain & J. P. Morford (Eds.), *Language acquisition by eye*. Mahwah, NJ: Lawrence Erlbaum Associates.

Mash, E. J., & Barkley, R. A., (Eds.). (2003). *Child psychopathology* (2nd ed.). New York: Guilford Press.

Masling, J. M., & Bornstein, R. F. (Eds.). (1996). *Psychoanalytic perspectives on developmental psychology*. Washington, DC: American Psychological Association.

Matlin, M. (2003). From menarche to menopause: Misconceptions about women's reproductive lives. *Psychology Science, 45*, 106–122.

Maton, K. I., Schellenbach, C. J., Leadbeater, B. J., & Solarz, A. L. (Eds.). (2004). *Investing in children, youth, families and communities*. Washington, DC: American Psychological Association.

Matsumoto, D., & Yoo, S. H. (2006). Toward a new generation of cross-cultural research. *Perspectives on Psychological Science, 1*, 234–250.

Matthews, K. A., Wing, R. R., Kuller, L. H., Meilahn, E. N., & Owens, J. F. (2000). Menopause as a turning point in midlife. In S. B. Manuck & R. Jennings et al. (Eds.), *Behavior, health, and aging*. Mahwah, NJ: Erlbaum.

Mattson, S., Calarco, K., & Lang, A. (2006). Focused and shifting attention in children with heavy prenatal alcohol exposure. *Neuropsychology, 20*, 361–369.

Matusov, E., & Hayes, R. (2000). Sociocultural critique of Piaget and Vygotsky. *New Ideas in Psychology, 18*, 215–239.

Mauritzson, U., & Saeljoe, R. (2001). Adult questions and children's responses: Coordination of perspectives in studies of children's theories of other minds. *Scandinavian Journal of Educational Research, 45*, 213–231.

Mayer, J. D., Salovey, P., & Caruso, D. R. (2004). Emotional intelligence: Theory, findings, and implications. *Psychological Inquiry, 15*, 197–215.

Mayo Clinic. (2000, March). Age-related macular degeneration: Who gets it and what you can do about it. *Women's Healthsource, 4*, 1–2.

Mayseless, O. (1996). Attachment patterns and their outcomes. *Human Development, 39*, 206–223.

McAdams, D., & Logan, R. (2004). What is generativity? In E. de St. Aubin & D. McAdams (Eds.), *Generative society: Caring for future generations* (pp. 15–31). Washington, DC: American Psychological Association.

McArdle, E. F. (2002). New York's Do-Not-Resuscitate law: Groundbreaking protection of patient autonomy or a physician's right to make medical futility determinations? *DePaul Journal of Health Care Law, 8*, 55–82.

McAuliffe, S. P., & Knowlton, B. J. (2001). Hemispheric differences in object identification. *Brain and Cognition, 45*, 119–128.

McCall, R. B. (1979). *Infants*. Cambridge, MA: Harvard University Press.

McCartney, M. (2006, March 11). Mind gains: We are living longer but will we be able to keep our minds active enough to enjoy it? *Financial Times* (London, England), p. 1. Retrieved March 4, 2007, from LexisNexis Academic.

McCarty, M., & Ashmead, D. H. (1999). Visual control of reaching and grasping in infants. *Developmental Psychology, 35*, 620–631.

McCaul, K. D., Ployhart, R. E., Hinsz, V. B., & McCaul, H. S. (1995). Appraisals of a consistent versus a similar politician: Voter preferences and intuitive judgments. *Journal of Personality and Social Psychology, 68*, 292–299.

McCauley, K. M. (2007). Modifying women's risk for cardiovascular disease. *Journal of Obstetric and Gynecological Neonatal Nursing, 36*, 116–124.

McClelland, D. C. (1993). Intelligence is not the best predictor of job performance. *Current Directions in Psychological Science, 2(1)*, pp. 5–6.

McCloskey, L. A., & Bailey, J. A. (2000). The intergenerational transmission of risk for child sexual abuse. *Journal of Interpersonal Violence, 15*, 1019–1035.

McCrae, R., & Costa, P. (2003). *Personality in adulthood: A five-factor theory perspective* (2nd ed.). New York: Guilford Press.

McCrae, R. R., & Costa, P. T., Jr. (1990). *Personality in adulthood*. New York: Guilford.

McCrae, R. R., Costa, P. T., Jr., Ostendorf, F., Angleitner, A., Hebíková, M., Avia, M. D., Sanz, J...Smith, P. B. (2000). Nature over nurture: Temperament, personality, and life span development. *Journal of Personality and Social Psychology, 78*, 173–186.

McCrink, K., & Wynn, K. (2004). Large-number addition and subtraction by 9-month-old infants. *Psychological Science, 15*, 776–782.

McDaniel, A., & Coleman, M. (2003). Women's experiences of midlife divorce following long-term marriage. *Journal of Divorce and Remarriage, 38*, 103–128.

McDonald, K. A. (1999, June 25). Studies of women's health produce a wealth of knowledge on the biology of gender differences. *Chronicle of Higher Education, 45*, pp. A19, A22.

McDonald, L., & Stuart-Hamilton, I. (2003). Egocentrism in older adults: Piaget's three mountains task revisited. *Educational Gerontology, 29*, 417–425.

McDonald, M. A., Sigman, M., Espinosa, M. P., & Neumann, C. G. (1994). Impact of a temporary food shortage on children and their mothers. *Child Development, 65*, 404–415.

McDonough, L. (2002). Basic-level nouns: First learned but misunderstood. *Journal of Child Language, 29*, 357–377.

McElwain, N., & Booth-LaForce, C. (2006, June). Maternal sensitivity to infant distress and nondistress as predictors of infant–mother attachment security. *Journal of Family Psychology, 20*, 247–255.

McGlone, M., & Aronson, J. (2006, September). Stereotype threat, identity salience, and spatial reasoning. *Journal of Applied Developmental Psychology, 27*, 486–493.

McGlone, M., Aronson, J., & Kobrynowicz, D. (2006, December). Stereotype threat and the gender gap in political knowledge. *Psychology of Women Quarterly, 30*, 392–398.

McGough, R. (2003, May 20). MRIs take a look at reading minds. *The Wall Street Journal*, p. D8.

McGovern, M., & Barry, M. M. (2000). Death education: Knowledge, attitudes, and perspectives of Irish parents and teachers. *Death Studies, 24*, 325–333.

McGreal, D., Evans, B. J., & Burrows, G. D. (1997). Gender differences in coping following loss of a child through miscarriage or stillbirth: A pilot study. *Stress Medicine, 13*, 159–165.

McGrew, K. S. (2005). The Cattell-Horn-Carroll theory of cognitive abilities: Past, present, and future. In D. P. Flanagan & P. L. Harrison (Eds.), *Contemporary intellectual assessment: Theories, tests, and issues*. New York, Guilford Press.

McGue, M., Bouchard, J., Thomas, J., Iacono, W. G., & Lykken, D. T. (1993). Behavioral genetics of cognitive ability: A life-span perspective. In Plomin, R., & McClearn, G. E. (Eds.), *Nature, nurture & psychology*, (pp. 59–76). Washington, DC, US: American Psychological Association. doi: 10.1037/10131-003.

McGuffin, P., Riley, B., & Plomin, R. (2001, February 16.) Toward behavioral genomics. *Science, 291*, 1232–1233.

McGuinness, D. (1972). Hearing: Individual differences in perceiving. *Perception, 1*, 465–473.

McHale, J. P., & Rotman, T. (2007). Is seeing believing? Expectant parents' outlooks on coparenting and later coparenting solidarity. *Infant Behavior and Development, 30*, 63–81.

McHale, S., Dariotis, J., & Kauh, T. (2003). Social development and social relationships in middle childhood. In R. Lerner & M. Easterbrooks (Eds.), *Handbook of psychology: Developmental psychology, Vol. 6*. New York: John Wiley and Sons, Inc.

McHale, S. M., Kim, J-Y., & Whiteman, S. D. (2006). Sibling relationships in childhood and adolescence. In P. Noller & J. A. Feeney (Eds.), *Close relationships: Functions, forms and processes*. Hove, England: Psychology Press/Taylor and Francis.

McKee, K., Wilson, F., Chung, M., Hinchliff, S., Goudie, F., Elford, H., et al. (2005, November). Reminiscence, regrets and activity in older people in residential care: Associations with psychological health. *British Journal of Clinical Psychology, 44*, 543–561.

McNulty, J. K., & Karney, B. R. (2004). Positive expectations in the early years of marriage: Should couples expect the best or brace for the worst? *Journal of Personality and Social Psychology, 86*, 729–743.

McVittie, C., McKinlay, A., & Widdicombe, S. (2003). Committed to (un)equal opportunities? "New ageism" and the older worker. *British Journal of Social Psychology, 42*, 595–612.

Mead, M. (1942). Environment and education, a symposium held in connection with the fiftieth anniversary celebration of the Univeristy of Chicago. Chicago: University of Chicago.

Mealey, L. (2000). *Sex differences: Developmental and evolutionary strategies*. Orlando, FL: Academic Press.

Medeiros, R., Prediger, R. D., Passos, G. F., Pandolfo, P., Duarte, F. S., Franco, J. L., Dafre, A. L...Calixto, J. B. (2007). Connecting TNF-alpha signaling pathways to iNOS expression in a mouse model of Alzheimer's disease: Relevance for the behavioral and synaptic deficits induced by amyloid beta protein. *Journal of Neuroscience, 16*, 5394–5404.

Medina, J. J. (1996). *The clock of ages: Why we age—How we age—Winding back the clock*. New York: Cambridge University Press.

Mednick, S. A. (1963). Research creativity in psychology graduate students. *Journal of Consulting Psychology, 27*, 265–266.

Meeus, W. (1996). Studies on identity development in adolescence: An overview of research and some new data. *Journal of Youth and Adolescence, 25*, 569–598.

Meeus, W. (2003). Parental and peer support, identity development and psychological well-being in adolescence. *Psychology: The Journal of the Hellenic Psychological Society, 10*, 192–201.

Meier, A., Bukusi, E., & Cohen, C. (2006). Independent association of hygiene, socioeconomic status, and circumcision with reduced risk of HIV infection among Kenyan men. *Journal of Acquired Immune Deficiency Syndromes, 43*, 117–118.

Meijer, A. M., & van den Wittenboer, G. L. H. (2007). Contribution of infants' sleep and crying to marital relationship of first-time parent couples in the first year after childbirth. *Journal of Family Psychology, 21*, 49–57.

Meisels, S. J., & Plunkett, J. W. (1988). Developmental consequences of preterm birth: Are there long-term deficits? In P. B. Baltes, D. L. Featherman, & R. M. Lerner (Eds.), *Lifespan development and behavior (Vol. 9)*. Hillsdale, NJ: Erlbaum.

Meister, H., & von Wedel, H. (2003). Demands on hearing aid features—special signal processing for elderly users? *International Journal of Audiology, 42*, 2S58–2S62.

Meltzoff, A. N. (1981). Imitation, intermodal coordination and representation in early infancy. In G. Butterworth (Ed.), *Infancy and epistemology*. Brighton: Harvester Press.

Meltzoff, A. N., & Moore, M. K. (1977). Imitation of facial and manual gestures by human neonates. *Science, 198*, 75–78.

Meltzoff, A. N., & Moore, M. (2002). Imitation, memory, and the representation of persons. *Infant Behavior and Development, 25*, 39–61.

Mendoza, C. (2006, September). Inside today's classrooms: Teacher voices on No Child Left Behind and the education of gifted children. *Roeper Review, 29*, 28–31.

Menken, J., Trussell, J., & Larsen, U. (1986). Age and infertility. *Science, 233*, 1389–1394.

Merill, D. M. (1997). *Caring for elderly parents: Juggling work, family, and caregiving in middle and working class families.* Westport, CT: Auburn House/Greenwood Publishing Group.

Mervis, J. (2004, June 11). Meager evaluations make it hard to find out what works. *Science, 304*, 1583.

Messer, S. B., & McWilliams, N. (2003). The impact of Sigmund Freud and *The Interpretation of Dreams*. In R. J. Sternberg (Ed.), *The anatomy of impact: What makes the great works of psychology great* (pp. 71–88). Washington, DC: American Psychological Association.

Metis National Council of Women. (2006). Retrieved from http://www.metiswomen.ca/culture/tradition/elders.htm. Accessed May 6, 2012.

Meyer, M., Wolf, D., and Himes, C. (2006, March). Declining eligibility for Social Security spouse and widow benefits in the United States? *Research on Aging, 28*, 240–260.

Miao, X., & Wang, W. (2003). A century of Chinese developmental psychology. *International Journal of Psychology, 38*, 258–273.

Michael, R. T., Gagnon, J. H., Laumann, E. O., & Kolata, G. (1994). *Sex in America: A definitive survey.* Boston: Little, Brown.

Mikulincer, M., & Shaver, P. R. (2005). Attachment security, compassion, and altruism. *Current Directions in Psychological Science, 14*, 34–38.

Mikulincer, M., & Shaver, P. R. (2007). *Attachment in adulthood: Structure, dynamics, and change.* New York: Guilford Press.

Milan, A., Maheux, H., & Chui, T. (2010). A portrait of couples in mixed unions. *Canadian Social Trends.* Statistics Canada Catalogue no. 11-008-X No. 89 2010001. Retrieved from http://www.statcan.gc.ca/pub/11-008-x/2010001/article/11143-eng.htm.

Milan, A., & Martel, L. (2009). Report on the demographic situation in Canada: 2005 and 2006. Part 1: Nuptuality and divorce. Statistics Canada Catalogue No. 91-209-X.

Milan, A., Vézina, M. & Wells, C. (2006). Family portrait. Statistics Canada Census of the Population. Retrieved from http://www12.statcan.gc.ca/census-recensement/2006/as-sa/97-553/figures/c3-eng.cfm.

Milan, A., Vézina, M., & Wells, C. (2006). 2006 Census: Family portrait: Continuity and change in Canadian families and households in 2006: Findings. Statistics Canada Catalogue no. 97-553-XWE2006001.

Miles, R., Cowan, F., Glover, V., Stevenson, J., & Modi, N. (2006). A controlled trial of skin-to-skin contact in extremely preterm infants. *Early Human Development, 2(7)*, 447–455.

Miller, E. M. (1998). Evidence from opposite-sex twins for the effects of prenatal sex hormones. In L. Ellis & L. Ebertz (Eds.), *Males, females, and behavior: Toward biological understanding.* Westport, CT: Praeger Publishers/Greenwood Publishing Group.

Miller G. (2010). Epigenetics: The seductive allure of behavioral epigenetics. *Science. 329(5987)* 24–7.

Miller, G., & Cohen, S. (2001). Psychological interventions and the immune system: A meta-analytic review and critique. *Health Psychology, 20*, 47–63.

Miller, P. A., & Jansen op de Haar, M. A. (1997). Emotional, cognitive, behavioral, and temperament characteristics of high-empathy children. *Motivation and Emotion, 21*, 109–125.

Miller, P. H., & Seier, W. L. (1994). *Strategy utilization deficiencies in children: When, where, and why.* San Diego, CA: Academic Press.

Miller-Perrin, C. L., & Perrin, R. D. (1999). *Child maltreatment: An introduction.* Thousand Oaks, CA: Sage.

Mills, E., & Siegfried, N. (2006). Cautious optimism for new HIV/AIDS prevention strategies. *Lancet, 368*, 1236–1236.

Mimura, K., Kimoto, T., & Okada, M. (2003). Synapse efficiency diverges due to synaptic pruning following overgrowth. *Phys Rev E Stat Nonlinear Soft Matter Physics, 68*, 124–131.

Mirmiran, M., Maas, Y. G. H., & Ariagno, R. L. (2003). Development of fetal and neonatal sleep and circadian rhythms. *Sleep Medicine Review, 4(4)*, 321–334. doi:10.1053/smrv.2002.0243.

Mishra, R. C. (1997). Cognition and cognitive development. In J. W. Berry, P. R. Dasen, & T. S. Saraswathi (Eds.), *Handbook of cross-cultural psychology, Vol. 2: Basic processes and human development* (2nd ed.), pp. 143–175. Boston, MA: Allyn and Bacon.

Mistry, J., & Saraswathi, T. (2003). The cultural context of child development. In R. Lerner & M. Easterbrooks (Eds.), *Handbook of psychology: Developmental psychology (Vol. 6)*, pp. 267–291. New York: John Wiley and Sons, Inc.

Mitchell, B. A. (2006). *The boomerang age: Transitions to adulthood in families.* New Brunswick, NJ: AldineTransaction.

Mitchell, K., Wolak, J., & Finkelhor, D. (2007, February). Trends in youth reports of sexual solicitations, harassment and unwanted exposure to pornography on the Internet. *Journal of Adolescent Health, 40*, 116–126.

Mitchell, S. (2002). *American generations: Who they are, how they live, what they think.* Ithaca, NY: New Strategists Publications.

Mittendorf, R., Williams, M. A., Berkey, C. S., & Cotter, R. F. (1990). The length of uncomplicated human gestation. *Obstetrics and Gynecology, 75*, 73–78.

Miyamoto, R. H., Hishinuma, E. S., Nishimura, S. T., Nahulu, L. B., Andrade, N. N., & Goebert, D. A. (2000). Variation in self-esteem among adolescents in an Asian/Pacific-Islander sample. *Personality and Individual Differences, 29*, 13–25.

Mizuno, K., & Ueda, A. (2004). Antenatal olfactory learning influences infant feeding. *Early Human Development, 76*, 83–90.

Molfese, V. J., & Acheson, S. (1997). Infant and preschool mental and verbal abilities: How are infant scores related to preschool scores? *International Journal of Behavioral Development, 20*, 595–607.

Money, J., & Ehrhardt, A. A. (1972). *Man and woman, boy and girl: The differentiation and dimorphism of gender identity from conception to maturity.* Baltimore: Johns Hopkins University Press.

Montemayor, R., Adams, G. R., & Gulotta, T. P. (Eds.). (1994). *Personal relationships during adolescence.* Newbury Park, CA: Sage.

Montgomery-Downs, H., & Thomas, E. B. (1998). Biological and behavioral correlates of quiet sleep respiration rates in infants. *Physiology and Behavior, 64*, 637–643.

Moon, C. (2002). Learning in early infancy. *Advances in Neonatal Care, 2*, 81–83.

Moore, L., Gao, D., & Bradlee, M. (2003). Does early physical activity predict body fat change throughout childhood? *Preventive Medicine: An International Journal Devoted to Practice and Theory, 37*, 10–17.

Morales, J. R., & Guerra, N. F. (2006). Effects of multiple context and cumulative stress on urban children's adjustment in elementary school. *Child Development, 77*, 907–923.

Morelli, G. A., Rogoff, B., Oppenheim, D., & Goldsmith, D. (1992). Cultural variation in infants' sleeping arrangements: Questions of independence [Special section: Cross-cultural studies of development]. *Developmental Psychology, 28*, 604–613.

Moreton, C. (2007). World's first test tube baby Louise Brown has a child of her own. *The Independent.* Retrieved from http://www.independent.co.uk/life-style/health-and-families/health-news/worlds-first-testtube-baby-louise-brown-has-a-child-of-her-own-432080.html.

Morfei, M. Z., Hooker, K., Carpenter, J., Blakeley, E. & Mix, C. (2004). Agentic and communal generative behavior in four areas of adult life: Implications for psychological well-being. *Journal of Adult Development, 11*, 55–58.

Morris, L. B. (2001, March 21). For elderly, relief for emotional ills can be elusive. *The New York Times*, p. A6.

Morris, P., & Fritz, C. (2006, October). How to improve your memory. *The Psychologist, 19*, 608–611.

Morrongiello, B., & Hogg, K. (2004). Mothers' reactions to children misbehaving in ways that can lead to injury: Implications for gender differences in children's risk taking and injuries. *Sex Roles, 50*, 103–118.

Morrongiello, B., Midgett, C., & Stanton, K. (2000). Gender biases in children's appraisals of injury risk and other children's risk-taking behaviors. *Journal of Experimental Child Psychology, 77*, 317–336.

Morry, M. (2007, February). The attraction-similarity hypothesis among cross-sex friends: Relationship satisfaction, perceived similarities, and self-serving perceptions. *Journal of Social and Personal Relationships, 24*, 117–138.

Morse, R. M., & Flavin, D. K. (1992). The definition of alcoholism. *Journal of the American Medical Association, 268*, 1012–1014.

Moshman, D., Glover, J. A., & Bruning, R. H. (1987). *Developmental psychology.* Boston: Little, Brown.

Moss, M. (1997, March 31). Golden years? For one 73-year-old, punching time clock isn't a labor of love. *The Wall Street Journal*, pp. A1, A8.

Moyad, M. A. (2004). Preventing male osteoporosis: Prevalence, risks, diagnosis and imaging tests. *Urological Clinics of North America, 31*, 321–330.

Mueller, M., Wilhelm, B., & Elder, G. (2002). Variations in grandparenting. *Research on Aging, 24*, 360–388.

Muir, D., Lee, K., Hains, C., & Hains, S. (2005). Infant perception and production of emotions during face-to-face interactions with live and "virtual" adults. In Nadel, J., & Muir, D. (Eds.) *Emotional Development: Current and future research directions.* (pp. 207–234). Oxford University Press.

Mumme, D., & Fernald, A. (2003). The infant as onlooker: Learning from emotional reactions observed in a television scenario. *Child Development, 74*, 221–237.

Munzar, P., Cami, J., & Farré, M. (2003). Mechanisms of drug addiction. *New England Journal of Medicine, 349*, 2365.

Murdock, T. B., & Bolch, M. B. (2005). Risk and protective factors for poor school adjustment in lesbian, gay, and bisexual (LGB) high school youth: Variable and person-centered analyses. *Psychology in the Schools, 42*, 159–172.

Murguia, A., Peterson, R. A., & Zea, M. C. (1997, August). Cultural health beliefs. Paper presented at the annual meeting of the American Psychological Association, Toronto, Canada.

Murphy, B., & Eisenberg, N. (2002). An integrative examination of peer conflict: Children's reported goals, emotions, and behaviors. *Social Development, 11*, 534–557.

Murphy, S., Johnson, L., & Wu, L. (2003). Bereaved parents' outcomes 4 to 60 months after their children's death by accident, suicide, or homicide: A comparative study demonstrating differences. *Death Studies, 27*, 39–61.

Murray, R. B., & Zentner, J. P., (2009). *Health promotion strategies through the life span* (8th ed.). (p. 233). Upper Saddle River, NJ: Prentice Hall.

Murray, J. A., Terry, D. J., Vance, J. C., Battistutta, D., & Connolly, Y. (2000). Effects of a program of intervention on parental distress following infant death. *Death Studies, 4*, 275–305.

Murray, S., Bellavia, G., & Rose, P. (2003). Once hurt, twice hurtful: How perceived regard regulates daily marital interactions. *Journal of Personality and Social Psychology, 84*, 126–147.

Murstein, B. I. (1976). *Who will marry whom? Theories and research in marital choice*. New York: Springer.

Murstein, B. I. (1986). *Paths to marriage*. Beverly Hills, CA: Sage.

Murstein, B. I. (1987). A clarification and extension of the SVR theory of dyadic pairing. *Journal of Marriage and the Family, 49*, 929–933.

Mutrie, N. (1997). The therapeutic effects of exercise on the self. In K. R. Fox (Ed.), *The physical self: From motivation to well being* (pp. 287–314). Champaign, IL: Human Kinetics.

Myers, D. (2000). *A quiet world: Living with hearing loss*. New Haven: Yale University Press.

Myers, R. H. (2004). Huntington's disease genetics. *NeuroRx, 1*, 255–262.

Myklebust, B. M., & Gottlieb, G. L. (1993). Development of the stretch reflex in the newborn: Reciprocal excitation and reflex irradation. *Child Development, 64*, 1036–1045.

Nadal, K. (2004). Filipino American identity development model. *Journal of Multicultural Counseling and Development, 32*, 45–62.

Nadeau, L., Boivin, M., Tessier, R., Lefebvre, F. & Robaey, P. (2001). Mediators of behavioral problems in 7-year-old children born after 24 to 28 weeks of gestation. *Journal of Developmental and Behavioral Pediatrics, 22*, 1–10.

Nagy, E., Compagne, H., Orvos, H., Pal, A., Molnar, P., Janszky, I., Loveland, K. A., & Bardos, G. (2005, October). Index finger movement imitation by human neonates: motivation, learning, and left-hand preference. *Pediatr Res. 58(4)*, 749–753.

Nagy, M. (1948). The child's theories concerning death. *Journal of Genetic Psychology, 73*, 3–27.

Nahmiash, D. (2006). *Abuse and neglect of older adults: What do we know about it and how can we identify it*? Westport, CT: Praeger Publishers/Greenwood Publishing Group.

Naik, G. (2002, November 22). The grim mission of a Swiss group: Visitor's suicides. *The Wall Street Journal*, pp. A1, A6.

Nakagawa, M., Lamb, M. E., & Miyaki, K. (1992). Antecedents and correlates of the Strange Situation behavior of Japanese infants. *Journal of Cross-Cultural Psychology, 23*, 300–310.

Nathanson, A., Wilson, B., & McGee, J. (2002). Counteracting the effects of female stereotypes on television via active mediation. *Journal of Communication, 52*, 922–937.

Nation, M., & Heflinger, C. (2006). Risk factors for serious alcohol and drug use: The role of psychosocial variables in predicting the frequency of substance use among adolescents. *American Journal of Drug and Alcohol Abuse, 32*, 415–433.

National Center for Educational Statistics. (2002). *Dropout rates in the United States: 2000*. Washington, DC: NCES.

National Highway Traffic Safety Administration. (1994). *Age-related incidence of traffic accidents*. Washington, DC: National Highway Traffic Safety Administration.

National Institute of Aging. (2004, May 31). Sexuality in later life. Available online at http://www.niapublications .org/engagepages/sexuality.asp.

National Institute of Child Health and Human Development (NICHD). (1999). Child care and mother–child interaction in the first 3 years of life. *Developmental Psychology, 35*, 1399–1413.

National Institute on Drug Abuse. (2007). *Marijuana: Facts parents need to know (revised)*. Washington, DC: National Institute on Drug Abuse.

National Institutes of Health. (2006, December 13). Adult male circumcision significantly reduces risk of acquiring HIV. NIH news release. Retrieved January 7, 2006, from http://www.nih. gov/news/pr/dec2006/niaid-13.htm.

National Science Foundation (NSF), Division of Science Resources Statistics. (2002). *Women, minorities, and persons with disabilities in science and engineering: 2002*. Arlington, VA: National Science Foundation.

Navarro, M. (2006, May 25). Families add 3rd generation to households. *The New York Times*, pp. A1, A22.

Nazzi, T., & Bertoncini, J. (2003). Before and after the vocabulary spurt: Two modes of word acquisition? *Developmental Science, 6*, 136–142.

Needleman, H. L., & Bellinger, D. (Eds.). (1994). *Prenatal exposure to toxicants: Developmental consequences*. Baltimore: Johns Hopkins University Press.

Negy, C., Shreve, T., & Jensen, B. (2003). Ethnic identity, self-esteem, and ethnocentrism: A study of social identity versus multicultural theory of development. *Cultural Diversity and Ethnic Minority Psychology, 9*, 333–344.

Neisser, U. (2004). Memory development: New questions and old. *Developmental Review, 24*, 154–158.

Nelson, C. A. (1987). The recognition of facial expressions in the first two years of life: Mechanisms of development. *Child Development, 58*, 889–909.

Nelson, C. A., & Bosquet, M. (2000). Neurobiology of fetal and infant development: Implications for infant mental health. In C. H. Zeanah, Jr. (Ed.), *Handbook of infant mental health* (2nd ed.). New York: Guilford Press.

Nelson, K. (1996). *Language in cognitive development: Emergence of the mediated mind*. New York: Cambridge University Press.

Nelson, K., & Fivush, R. (2004). The emergence of autobiographical memory: A social cultural developmental theory. *Psychological Review, 111*, 486–511.

Nelson, L., Badger, S., & Wu, B. (2004). The influence of culture in emerging adulthood: Perspectives of Chinese college students. *International Journal of Behavioral Development, 28*, 26–36.

Nelson, L. D., Scheibel, K. E., & Ringman, J. M. (2007). An experimental approach to detecting dementia in Down syndrome: A paradigm for Alzheimer's disease. *Brain and Cognition, 64*, 92–103.

Nelson, T., & Wechsler, H. (2003). School spirits: Alcohol and collegiate sports fans. *Addictive Behaviors, 28*, 1–11.

Nesheim, S., Henderson, S., Lindsay, M., Zuberi, J., Grimes, V., Buehler, J., Lindegren, M. L., & Bulterys, M. (2004). *Prenatal HIV testing and antiretroviral prophylaxis at an urban hospital—Atlanta, Georgia, 1997-2000*. Atlanta, GA: Centers for Disease Control.

Ness, J., Aronow, W., & Beck, G. (2006). Menopausal symptoms after cessation of hormone replacement therapy. *Maturitas, 53*, 356–361.

Nettelbeck, T., & Rabbitt, P. M. (1992). Aging, cognitive performance, and mental speed. *Intelligence, 16*, 189–205.

Neugarten, B. L. (1972). Personality and the aging process. *The Gerontologist, 12*, 9–15.

Neugarten, B. L. (1977). Personality and aging. In J. E. Birren & K. W. Schaie (Eds.), *Handbook for the psychology of aging*. New York: Van Nostrand Reinhold.

Newcomb, A. F., & Bagwell, C. L. (1995). Children's friendship relations: A meta-analytic review. *Psychological Bulletin, 117*, 306–347.

Newman, R., & Hussain, I. (2006). Changes in preference for infant-directed speech in low and moderate noise by 4.5- to 13-month-olds. *Infancy, 10*, 61–76.

Newston, R. L., & Keith, P. M. (1997). Single women later in life. In J. M. Coyle (Ed.), *Handbook on women and aging* (pp. 385–399). Westport, CT: Greenwood Press.

Newton, K., Reed, S., LaCroix, A., Grothaus, L., Ehrlich, K., & Guiltinan, J. (2006). Treatment of vasomotor symptoms of menopause with black cohosh, multi-botanicals, soy, hormone therapy, or placebo. *Annals of Internal Medicine, 145*, 869–879.

Ng, S. (2002). Will families support their elders? Answers from across cultures. In T. Nelson (Ed.), *Ageism: Stereotyping and prejudice against older persons*. Cambridge, MA: The MIT Press.

Nguyen, L., & Frye, D. (1999). Children's theory of mind: Understanding of desire, belief and emotion with social referents. *Social Development, 8*, 70–92.

NIAAA (National Institute on Alcohol Abuse and Alcoholism). (1990). *Alcohol and health*. Washington, DC: U.S. Government Printing Office.

Niederhofer, H. (2004). A longitudinal study: Some preliminary results of association of prenatal maternal stress and fetal movements, temperament factors in early childhood and behavior at age 2 years. *Psychological Reports, 95*, 767–770.

Nieto, S. (2005). Public education in the twentieth century and beyond: High hopes, broken promises, and an uncertain future. *Harvard Educational Review, 75*, 43–65.

Nigg, J. T. (2001). Is ADHD a disinhibitory disorder? *Psychological Bulletin, 127*, 571–598.

Nihart, M. A. (1993). Growth and development of the brain. *Journal of Child and Adolescent Psychiatric and Mental Health Nursing, 6*, 39–40.

Nilsson, L. (2003). Memory function in normal aging. *Acta Neurologica Scandinavica, 107*, 7–13.

Nilsson, L. G., Bäckman, L., Erngrund, K., Nyberg, L., et al. (1997). The Betula prospective cohort study: Memory, health, and aging. *Aging Neuropsychology and Cognition, 4*, 1–32.

Nimrod, G., and Adoni, H. (2006, July). Leisure-styles and life satisfaction among recent retirees in Israel. *Ageing and Society, 26*, 607–630.

Nobuyuki, I. (1997). Simple reaction times and timing of serial reactions of middle-aged and old men. *Perceptual and Motor Skills, 84*, 219–225.

Nolen-Hoeksema, S. (2001). Ruminative coping and adjustment to bereavement. In M. Stroebe & R. Hansson (Eds.), *Handbook of bereavement research: Consequences, coping, and care*. Washington, DC: American Psychological Association.

Nolen-Hoeksema, S. (2003). *Women who think too much: How to break free of overthinking and reclaim your life*. New York: Henry Holt.

Nolen-Hoeksema, S., & Davis, C. (2002). Positive responses to loss: Perceiving benefits and growth. In C. Snyder & S. Lopez (Eds.), *Handbook of positive psychology*. London: Oxford University Press.

Noonan, D. (2003a, September 22). When safety is the name of the game. *Newsweek*, 64–66.

Noonan, D. (2003b, September 29). High on testosterone. *Newsweek*, 50–52.

Nordin, S., Razani, L., & Markison, S. (2003). Age-associated increases in intensity discrimination for taste. *Experimental Aging Research, 29*, 371–381.

Norlander, T., Von Schedvin, H., & Archer, T. (2005). Thriving as a function of affective personality: Relation to personality factors, coping strategies and stress. *Anxiety, Stress and Coping: An International Journal, 18*, 105–116.

Norman, R. M. G., & Malla, A. K. (2001). Family history of schizophrenia and the relationship of stress to symptoms: Preliminary findings. *Australian and New Zealand Journal of Psychiatry, 35*, 217–223.

Nowak, M. A., Komarova, N. L., & Niyogi, P. (2001, January 5). Evolution of universal grammar. *Science, 291*, 114–116.

Nyiti, R. M. (1982). The validity of "culture differences explanations" for cross-cultural variation in the rate of Piagetian cognitive development. In D. Wagner & H. Stevenson (Eds.), *Cultural perspectives on child development*. New York: Freeman.

Nylen, K., Moran, T., Franklin, C., & O'Hara, M. (2006). Maternal depression: A review of relevant treatment approaches for mothers and infants. *Infant Mental Health Journal, 27*, 327–343.

O'Connor, P. (1994). Very close parent/child relationships: The perspective of the elderly person. *Journal of Cross-Cultural Gerontology, 9*, 53–76.

O'Grady, W., & Aitchison, J. (2005). *How children learn language*. New York: Cambridge University Press.

O'Hara, R., Schroder, C., Bloss, C., Bailey, A., Alyeshmerni, A., Mumenthaler, M., Friedman, L., & Yesavage, J. (2005). Hormone replacement therapy and longitudinal cognitive performance in postmenopausal women. *American Journal of Geriatric Psychiatry, 13*, 1107–1110.

O'Leary, S. G. (1995). Parental discipline mistakes. *Current Directions in Psychological Science, 4*, 11–13.

Ocorr, K., Reeves, N. L., Wessells, R. J., Fink, M., Chen, H. S., Akasaka, T., Yasuda, S...Bodmer, R. (2007). KCNQ potassium channel mutations cause cardiac arrhythmias in Drosophila that mimic the effects of aging. *Proceedings of the National Academy of Sciences, 104*, 3943–3948.

Office of the Privacy Commissioner of Canada. (n.d.) [pamphlet]. Christofedes, E., & Muise, A: Authors. Retrieved from http://www.psychology.uoguelph.ca/faculty/desmarais/files/Facebook_Education_Pamplet.pdf.

Ogden, C. L., Kuczmarski, R. J., Flegal, K. M., Mei, Z., Guo, S., Wei, R., Grummer-Strawn, L. M...Johnson, C. L. (2002). Centers for Disease Control and Prevention 2000 growth charts for the United States: Improvements to the 1977 National Center for Health Statistics Version. *Pediatrics, 109*, 45–60.

Okie, S. (2005). *Winning the war against childhood obesity*. Washington, DC: Joseph Henry Publications.

Olivardia, R., & Pope, H. (2002). Body image disturbance in childhood and adolescence. In D. Castle & K. Phillips (Eds.), *Disorders of body image*. Petersfield, England: Wrightson Biomedical Publishing.

Oller, D. K., Eilers, R. E., Urbano, R., & Cobo-Lewis, A. B. (1997). Development of precursors to speech in infants exposed to two languages. *Journal of Child Language, 24*, 407–425.

Olness, K. (2003). Effects on brain development leading to cognitive impairment: A worldwide epidemic. *Journal of Developmental and Behavioural Pediatrics, 24*, 120–130.

Olshansky, S. J., Passaro, D. J., Hershow, R. C., Layden, J., Carnes, B. A., Brody, J., Hayflick, L...Ludwig, D. S. (2005, March 17). Special report: A potential decline in life expectancy in the United States in the 21st century. *The New England Journal of Medicine, 352*, 1138–1145.

Olweus, D. (2004). The Olweus Bullying Prevention Programme: Design and implementation issues and a new national initiative in Norway. In P. K. Smith, D. Pepler, & K. Rigby (Eds.), *Bullying in schools: How successful can interventions be?* (pp. 13–36). Cambridge, UK: Cambridge University Press.

Oostindjer, M., Bolhuis, J. E., van den Brand, H., & Kemp, B. (2009, November). Prenatal flavor exposure affects flavor recognition and stress-related behavior of piglets. Adaptation Physiology Group, Wageningen Institute of Animal Sciences, Wageningen University, *34(9)*, pp. 775–787.

Orbuch, T. L., House, J. S., Mero, R. P., & Webster, P. S. (1996). Marital quality over the life course. *Social Psychology Quarterly, 59*, 162–171.

Ormont, L. R. (2001). Developing emotional insulation (1994). In L. B. Fugeri (Ed.), *The technique of group treatment: The collected papers of Louis R. Ormont*. Madison, CT: Psychosocial Press.

Ortiz, S. O., & Dynda, A. M. (2005). Use of intelligence tests with culturally and linguistically diverse populations. In D. P. Flanagan & P. L. Harrison (Eds.), *Contemporary intellectual assessment: Theories, tests, and issues*. New York, Guilford Press.

Ostrov, J., Gentile, D., & Crick, N. (2006, November). Media exposure, aggression and prosocial behavior during early childhood: A longitudinal study. *Social Development, 15*, 612–627.

Ouwehand, C., de Ridder, D. T., & Bensing, J. M. (2007). A review of successful aging models: Proposing proactive coping as an important additional strategy. *Clinical Psychology Review, 43*, 101–116.

Owsley, C., Stalvey, B., & Phillips, J. (2003). The efficacy of an educational intervention in promoting self-regulation among high-risk older drivers. *Accident Analysis and Prevention, 35*, 393–400.

Oxford, M., Gilchrist, L., Gillmore, M., & Lohr, M. (2006, July). Predicting variation in the life course of adolescent mothers as they enter adulthood. *Journal of Adolescent Health, 39*, 20–26.

Oyserman, D., Kemmelmeier, M., Fryberg, S., Brosh, H., & Hart-Johnson, T. (2003). Racial ethnic self-schemas. *Social Psychology Quarterly, 66*, 333–347.

Ozawa, M., & Yoon, H. (2003). Economic impact of marital disruption on children. *Children and Youth Services Review, 25*, 611–632.

Pajulo, M., Helenius, H., & Mayes, L. (2006, May). Prenatal views of baby and parenthood: Association with sociodemographic and pregnancy factors. *Infant Mental Health Journal, 27*, 229–250.

Palan, P. R., Connell, K., Ramirez, E. Inegbenijie, C., Gavara, R. Y., Ouseph, J. A., & Mikhail, M. S. (2005). Effects of menopause and hormone replacement therapy on serum levels of coenzyme Q10 and other lipid-soluble antioxidants. *Biofactors, 25*, 61–66.

Palfai, T., Halperin, S., & Hoyer, W. (2003). Age inequalities in recognition memory: Effects of stimulus presentation time and list repetitions. *Aging, Neuropsychology, and Cognition, 10*, 134–140.

Palincsar, A. S., Brown, A. L., & Campione J. C. (1993). First-grade dialogues for knowledge acquisition and use. In E. Forman, N. Minick, & C. A. Stone (Eds.), *Contexts for learning: Sociocultural dynamics in children's development*. New York: Oxford University Press.

Palmore, E. B. (1988). *The facts on aging quiz*. New York: Springer.

Palmore, E. B. (1992). Knowledge about aging: What we know and need to know. *Gerontologist, 32*, 149–150.

Paneth, N. S. (1995). The problem of low birth weight. *The Future of Children, 5*, 19–34.

Papadakis, A., Prince, R. P., Jones, N. P., & Strauman, T. J. (2006). Self-regulation, rumination, and vulnerability to depression in adolescent girls. *Development and Psychopathology, 18*, 815–829.

Papousek, H., & Papousek, M. (1991). Innate and cultural guidance of infants' integrative competencies: China, the United States, and Germany. In M. H. Borstein (Ed.), *Cultural approaches to parenting*. Hillsdale, NJ: Erlbaum.

Parents: The Anti-Drug. (n.d.). Amy's story. *Real teen stories*. Retrieved from http://www.theantidrug.com/advice/teens-today/teens-and-technology/real-teen-stories.aspx.

Paris, J. (1999). *Nature and nurture in psychiatry: A predisposition–stress model of mental disorders*. Washington, DC: American Psychiatric Press.

Park, K. A., Lay, K., & Ramsay, L. (1993). Individual differences and developmental changes in preschoolers' friendships. *Developmental Psychology, 29*, 264–270.

Parke, R., Simpkins, S., & McDowell, D. (2002). Relative contributions of families and peers to children's social development. In P. Smith & C. Hart (Eds.), *Blackwell handbook of childhood social development*. Malden, MA: Blackwell Publishers.

Parke, R. D. (1996). *New fatherhood*. Cambridge, MA: Harvard University Press.

Parke, R. D. (2004). Development in the family. *Annual Review of Psychology, 55*, 365–399.

Parker-Pope, T. (2003, October 21). The case for hormone therapy. *The Wall Street Journal*, pp. R1, R3.

Parkes, C. M. (1997). Normal and abnormal responses to stress—a developmental approach. In D. Black, M. Newman, J. Harris-Hendricks, & G. Mezey (Eds.), *Psychological trauma: A developmental approach* (pp. 10–18). London, England: Gaskell/Royal College of Psychiatrists.

Parks, C., Sanna, L., & Posey, D. (2003). Retrospection in social dilemmas: How thinking about the past affects future cooperation. *Journal of Personality and Social Psychology, 84*, 988–996.

Parks, C. A. (1998). Lesbian parenthood: A review of the literature. *American Journal of Orthopsychiatry, 68*, 376–389.

Parlee, M. B. (1979, October). The friendship bond. *Psychology Today, 13*, 43–45.

Parmalee, A. H., Jr., & Sigman, M. D. (1983). Prenatal brain development and behavior. In P. H. Mussen (Ed.), *Handbook of child psychology (Vol. 2)*, (4th ed.). New York: Wiley.

Parten, M. B. (1932). Social participation among preschool children. *Journal of Abnormal and Social Psychology, 27*, 243–269.

Pascalis, O., de Haan, M., & Nelson, C. A. (2002). Is face processing species-specific during the first year of life? *Science, 296*, 1321–1323.

Pasqualotto, F. F., Lucon, A. M., Sobreiro, B. P., Pasqualotto, E. B., & Arap, S. (2005). Effects of medical therapy, alcohol, smoking, and endocrine disruptors on male infertility. *Revista do Hospital das Clinicas, 59*, 375–382.

Patchin, J., & Hinduja, S. (2006, April). Bullies move beyond the schoolyard: A preliminary look at cyberbullying. *Youth Violence and Juvenile Justice, 4*, 148–169.

Patenaude, A. F., Guttmacher, A. E., & Collins, F. S. (2002). Genetic testing and psychology: New roles, new responsibilities. *American Psychologist, 57*, 271–282.

Paterson, D. S., Trachtenberg, F. L., Thompson, E. G., Belliveau, R. A., Beggs, A. H., Darnall, R., Chadwick, A. E... Kinney, H. C. (2006). Multiple serotonergic brainstem abnormalities in sudden infant death syndrome. *JAMA: Journal of the American Medical Association, 296*, 2124–2132.

Patterson, C. (2003). Children of lesbian and gay parents. In L. Garnets & D. Kimmel (Eds.), *Psychological perspectives on lesbian, gay, and bisexual experiences* (2nd ed.). New York: Columbia University Press.

Patterson, C. (2006, October). Children of lesbian and gay parents. *Current Directions in Psychological Science, 15*, 241–244.

Patterson, C. J. (1994). Lesbian and gay families. *Current Directions in Psychological Science, 3*, 62–64.

Patterson, C. J. (1995). Families of the baby boom: Parents' division of labor and children's adjustment [Special issue: Sexual orientation and human development]. *Developmental Psychology, 31*, 115–123.

Patterson, C. J. (2002). Lesbian and gay parenthood. In M. Bornstein (Ed.), *Handbook of parenting*. Mahwah, NJ: Erlbaum.

Paulesu, E., Démonet, J. F., Fazio, F., McCrory, E., Chanoine, V., Brunswick, N., Cappa, S. F...Frith, U. (2001, March 16). Dyslexia: Cultural diversity and biological unity. *Science, 291*, 2165–2167.

Pauli-Pott, U., Mertesacker, B., & Bade, U. (2003). Parental perceptions and infant temperament development. *Infant Behavior and Development, 26*, 27–48.

Pavis, S., Cunningham-Burley, S., & Amos, A. (1997). Alcohol consumption and young people: Exploring meaning and social context. *Health Education Research, 12,* 311–322.

Pavlov, I. P. (1927). *Conditioned reflexes.* London: Oxford University Press.

Peck, R. C. (1968). Psychological developments in the second half of life. In B. L. Neugarten (Ed.), *Middle age and aging.* Chicago: University of Chicago Press.

Peirano, P., Algarin, C., & Uauy, R. (2003). Sleep-wake states and their regulatory mechanisms throughout early human development. *Journal of Pediatrics, 143,* Supplement, S70–S79.

Pelham, B., & Hetts, J. (2001). Underworked and overpaid: Elevated entitlement in men's self-pay. *Journal of Experimental Social Psychology, 37,* 93–103.

Pelsser, L. M., Buitelaar, J. K., & Savelkoul, H. F. (2009). ADHD as a (non) allergic hypersensitivity disorder: A hypothesis. *Pediatric Allergy Immunology, 20(2),* 107–112.

Peltonen, L., & McKusick, V. A. (2001, February 16). Dissecting the human disease in the postgenomic era. *Science, 291,* 1224–1229.

Peltzer, K., & Pengpid, S. (2006). Sexuality of 16- to 17-year-old South Africans in the context of HIV/AIDS. *Social Behavior and Personality, 34,* 239–256.

Penninx, B., Guralnik, J. M., Ferrucci, L., Simonsick, E. M., Deeg, D., & Wallace, R. B. (1998). Depressive symptoms and physical decline in community-dwelling older persons. *Journal of the American Medical Association, 279,* 1720–1726.

Pennisi, E. (2000, May 19). And the gene number is . . . ? *Science, 288,* 1146–1147.

Pereira, A. C., Huddleston, D. E., Brickman, A. M., Sosunov, A. A., Hen, R., McKhann, G. M., Sloan, R...Small, S. A. (2007). An in vivo correlate of exercise-induced neurogenesis in the adult dentate gyrus. *Proceedings of the National Academy of Sciences, 104,* 5638–5643.

Perozzi, J. A., & Sanchez, M. C. (1992). The effect of instruction in L1 on receptive acquisition of L2 for bilingual children with language delay. *Language, Speech, and Hearing Services in Schools, 23,* 348–352.

Perreault, A., Fothergill-Bourbonnais, F., & Fiset, V. (2004). The experience of family members caring for a dying loved one. *International Journal of Palliative Nursing, 10,* 133–143.

Perry, W. G. (1970). *Forms of intellectual and ethical development in the college years.* New York: Holt.

Persson, G. E. B. (2005). Developmental perspectives on prosocial and aggressive motives in preschoolers' peer interactions. *International Journal of Behavioral Development, 29,* 80–91.

Petersen, A. (2000). A longitudinal investigation of adolescents' changing perceptions of pubertal timing. *Developmental Psychology 36,* 37–43.

Peterson, A. C. (1988, September). Those gangly years. *Psychology Today,* 28–34.

Peterson, C., & Park, N. (2007). Explanatory style and emotion regulation. In J. J. Gross (Ed.), *Handbook of emotion regulation.* New York: Guilford Press.

Peterson, D. M., Marcia, J. E., & Carpendale, J. I. (2004). Identity: Does thinking make it so? In C. Lightfoot, C. Lalonde, & M. Chandler (Eds.), *Changing conceptions of psychological life.* Mahwah, NJ: Lawrence Erlbaum Associates.

Peterson, M., & Wilson, J. F. (2004). Work stress in America. *International Journal of Stress Management, 11,* 91–113.

Peterson, R. A., & Brown, S. P. (2005). On the use of beta coefficients in meta-analysis. *Journal of Applied Psychology, 90,* 175–181.

Petersson, K. M., Silva, C., Castro-Caldas, A., Ingvar, M., & Reis, A. (2007). Literacy: A cultural influence on functional left–right differences in the inferior parietal cortex. *European Journal of Neuroscience, 26,* 791–799.

Petit, G., & Dodge, K. A. (2003). Violent children: Bridging development, intervention, and public policy. *Developmental Psychology, Special Issues: Violent Children, 39,* 187–188.

Petrou, S. (2006). Preterm birth—What are the relevant economic issues? *Early Human Development, 82(2),* 75–76.

Phillips, D. (1992, September). Death postponement and birthday celebrations. *Psychosomatic Medicine, 26,* 12–18.

Phillips, D. A., Voran, M., Kisker, E., Howes, C., & Whitebook, M. (1994). Child care for children in poverty: Opportunity or inequity? *Child Development, 65,* 472–492.

Phinney, J., Lochner, B., & Murphy, R. (1990). Ethnic identity development and psychological adjustment in adolescence. In A. Stiffman & L. Davis (Eds.), *Advances in adolescent mental health. Vol. 5. Ethnic issues.* Greenwich, CT: JAI Press.

Phinney, J. S. (2005). Ethnic identity in late modern times: A response to Rattansi and Phoenix. *Identity, 5,* 187–194.

Phinney, J. S., Ferguson, D. L., & Tate, J. D. (1997). Intergroup attitudes among ethnic minority adolescents: A causal model. *Child Development, 68,* 955–969.

Piaget, J. (1932). *The moral judgment of the child.* New York: Harcourt, Brace and World.

Piaget, J. (1952). *The origins of intelligence in children.* New York: International Universities Press.

Piaget, J. (1962). *Play, dreams and imitation in childhood.* New York: Norton.

Piaget, J. (1983). Piaget's theory. In W. Kessen (Ed.), P. H. Mussen (Series Ed.), *Handbook of child psychology: Vol 1. History, theory, and methods* (pp. 103–128). New York: Wiley.

Piaget, J., & Inhelder, B. (1958). *The growth of logical thinking from childhood to adolescence* (A. Parsons and S. Seagrin, Trans.). New York: Basic Books.

Picavet, H. S., & Hoeymans, N. (2004). Health related quality of life in multiple musculoskeletal diseases: SF-36 and EQ-5D in the DMC3 study. *Annals of the Rheumatic Diseases, 63,* 723–729.

Pinker, S. (1994). *The language instinct.* New York: William Morrow.

Pinker, S. (2005). So how does the mind work? *Mind and Language, 20,* 1–24.

Pitts, D. G. (1982). The effects of aging upon selected visual functions. In R. Sekuler, D. Kline, & K. Dismukes (Eds.), *Aging and human visual function.* New York: Alan R. Liss.

Plomin, R. (1994a). *Genetics and experience: The interplay between nature and nurture.* Newbury Park, CA: Sage.

Plomin, R. (1994b). Nature, nurture, and social development. *Social Development, 3,* 37–53.

Plomin, R., & Caspi, A. (1998). DNA and personality. *European Journal of Personality, 12,* 387–407.

Plomin, R., & McClearn, G. E. (Eds.). (1993). *Nature, nurture, and psychology.* Washington, DC: American Psychological Association.

Plonczynski, D. J., & Plonczynski, K. J. (2007). Hormone therapy in perimenopausal and postmenopausal women: Examining the evidence on cardiovascular disease risks. *Journal of Gerontological Nursing, 33,* 48–55.

Plosker, G., & Keam, S. (2006). Bimatoprost: A pharmacoeconomic review of its use in open-angle glaucoma and ocular hypertension. *PharmacoEconomics, 24,* 297–314.

Poest, C. A., Williams, J. R., Witt, D. D., & Atwood, M. E. (1990). Challenge me to move: Large muscle development in young children. *Young Children, 45,* 4–10.

Polansky, E. (1976). Take him home, Mrs. Smith. *Healthright, 2(2).*

Polivy, J., & Herman, C. (2002). If at first you don't succeed: False hopes of self-change. *American Psychologist, 57,* 677–689.

Pollack, W. (1999). *Real boys: Rescuing our sons from the myths of boyhood.* Owl Books.

Pollack, W., Shuster, T., & Trelease, J. (2001). *Real boys' voices.* Penguin.

Pollak, S., Holt, L., & Wismer Fries, A. (2004). Hemispheric asymmetries in children's perception of nonlinguistic human affective sounds. *Developmental Science, 7,* 10–18.

Ponton, L. E. (2001). *The sex lives of teenagers: Revealing the secret world of adolescent boys and girls.* New York: Penguin Putnam.

Poon, H. F., Calabrese, V., Scapagnini, G., & Butterfield, D. A. (2004). Free radicals and brain aging. *Clinical Geriatric Medicine, 20,* 329–359.

Population Council Report. (1995, May 30). The decay of families is global, studies says. *The New York Times,* p. A5.

Porath, A. J., & Fried, P. A. (2005). Effects of prenatal cigarette and marijuana exposure on drug use among offspring. *Neurotoxicological Teratology, 27,* 267–277.

Porges, S. W., Lipsitt, & Lewis P. (1993). Neonatal responsivity to gustatory stimulation: The gustatory-vagal hypothesis. *Infant Behavior and Development, 16,* 487–494.

Porter, R. H., Bologh, R. D., & Malkin, J. W. (1988). Olfactory influences on mother–infant interactions. In C. Rovee-Collier & L. Lipsitt (Eds.), *Advances in infancy research* (Vol. 5). Norwood, NJ: Ablex.

Portes, A., & Rumbaut, R. (2001). *Legacies: The story of the immigrant second generation.* Los Angeles: University of California Press.

Porzelius, L. K., Dinsmore, B. D., & Staffelbach, D. (2001). Eating disorders. In M. Hersen & V. B. Van Hasselt (Eds.), *Advanced abnormal psychology* (2nd ed.). New York: Kluwer Academic/Plenum Publishers.

Posthuma, D., & de Geus, E. (2006, August). Progress in the molecular-genetic study of intelligence. *Current Directions in Psychological Science, 15,* 151–155.

Poulin-Dubois, D. (1999). Infants' distinction between animate and inanimate objects: the origins of naive psychology. In P. Rochat (Ed.), *Early social cognition.* Hillsdale, NJ: Lawrence Erlbaum Associates.

Poulin-Dubois, D., Serbin, L., & Eichstedt, J. (2002). Men don't put on make-up: Toddlers' knowledge of the gender stereotyping of household activities. *Social Development, 11,* 166–181.

Poulin-Dubois, D., Serbin, L. A., Kenyon, B., & Derbyshire, A. (1994). Infants' intermodal knowledge about gender. *Developmental Psychology, 30,* 436–442.

Poulton, R., & Caspi, A. (2005). Commentary: How does socioeconomic disadvantage during childhood damage health in adulthood? Testing psychosocial pathways. *International Journal of Epidemiology, 23,* 51–55.

Powell, G. F., Brasel, J. A., & Blizzard, R. M. (1967). Emotional deprivation and growth retardation simulating idiopathic hypopituitarism: I. Clinical evaluation of the syndrome. *New England Journal of Medicine, 276,* 1272–1278.

Powell, M. B., Thomson, D. M., & Ceci, S. J. (2003). Children's memory of recurring events: Is the first event always the best remembered? *Applied Cognitive Psychology, 17,* 127–146.

Powell, R. (2004, June 19). Colleges construct housing for elderly: Retiree students move to campus. *The Washington Post,* p. F13.

Power, T. G. (1999). *Play and exploration in children and animals.* Mahwah, NJ: Erlbaum.

Prater, L. (2002). African American families: Equal partners in general and special education. In F. Obiakor & A. Ford (Eds.), *Creating successful learning environments for African American learners with exceptionalities.* Thousand Oaks, CA: Corwin Press, Inc.

Pratt, H., Phillips, E., & Greydanus, D. (2003). Eating disorders in the adolescent population: Future directions. *Journal of Adolescent Research, 18,* 297–317.

Pratt, M. W., Danso, H. A., Arnold, M. L., Norris, J. E., & Filyer, R. (2001). Adult generativity and the socialization of adolescents: Relations to mothers' and fathers' parenting beliefs, styles, and practices. *Journal of Personality, 69,* 89–120.

Prechtl, H. F. R. (1982). Regressions and transformations during neurological development. In T. G. Bever (Ed.), *Regressions in mental development.* Hillsdale, NJ: Erlbaum.

Prescott, C., & Gottesman, I. (1993). Genetically mediated vulnerability to schizophrenia. *Psychiatric Clinics of North America, 16,* 245–267.

Prescott, C. A., Caldwell, C. B., Carey, G., Vogler, G. P., Trumbetta, S. L., & Gottesman, I. I. (2005). The Washington University Twin Study of Alcoholism. *American Journal of Medical Genetics, B, Neuropsychiatric Genetics, 31.*

Pressley, M. (1987). Are keyword method effects limited to slow presentation rates? An empirically based reply to Hall and Fuson (1986). *Journal of Educational Psychology, 79,* 333–335.

Pressley, M., & Levin, J. R. (1983). *Cognitive strategy research: Psychological foundations.* New York: Springer-Verlag.

Pressley, M., & Schneider, W. (1997). *Introduction to memory development during childhood and adolescence.* Mahwah, NJ: Lawrence Erlbaum.

Pressley, M., & VanMeter, P. (1993). Memory strategies: Natural development and use following instruction. In R. Pasnak & M. L. Howe (Eds.), *Emerging themes in cognitive development (Vol. II).* New York: Springer-Verlag.

Prezbindowski, A. K., & Lederberg, A. R. (2003). Vocabulary assessment of deaf and hard-of-hearing children from infancy through the preschool years. *Journal of Deaf Studies and Deaf Education, 8,* 383–400.

Price, R., & Gottesman, I. (1991). Body fat in identical twins reared apart: Roles for genes and environment. *Behavior Genetics, 21,* 1–7.

Prigerson, H. (2003). Costs to society of family caregiving for patients with end-stage Alzheimer's disease. *New England Journal of Medicine, 349,* 1891–1892.

Prigerson, H. G., Frank, E., Kasl, S. V., et al. (1995). Complicated grief and bereavement-related depression as distinct disorders: Preliminary empirical validation in elderly bereaved spouses. *American Journal of Psychiatry, 152,* 22–30.

PRIMEDIA/Roper National Youth Survey. (1999). *Adolescents' view of society's ills.* Storrs, CT: Roper Center for Public Opinion Research.

Prince, M. (2000, November 13). How technology has changed the way we have babies. *The Wall Street Journal,* pp. R4, R13.

Prince, R. L., Smith, M., Dick, I. M., Price, R. I., Webb, P. G., Henderson, N. K., & Harris, M. M. (1991). Prevention of postmenopausal osteoporosis. A comparative study of exercise, calcium supplementation, and hormone replacement therapy. *New England Journal of Medicine, 325,* 1189–1195.

Propper, C., & Moore, G. (2006, December). The influence of parenting on infant emotionality: A multi-level psychobiological perspective. *Developmental Review, 26,* 427–460.

Public Health Agency of Canada. (2009). Child and youth injury in review (2009 ed). *Spotlight on consumer product safety.* Ottawa.

Public Health Agency of Canada. (2009). What mothers say: The Canadian maternity experiences survey. Retrieved from Public Health Agency of Canada website http://www.phac-aspc.gc.ca/rhs-ssg/pdf/survey-eng.pdf.

Public Health Agency of Canada (2010). *HIV and AIDS in Canada. Surveillance report to December 31, 2009.* Surveillance and Risk Assessment Division, Centre for Communicable Diseases and Infection Control. Retrieved from http://www.nwac.ca/programs/sexually-transmitted-infections

Public Health Agency of Canada (n.d.). STIs and hepatitis C statistics. Last updated June 22, 2011. Retrieved from http://www.phac-aspc.gc.ca/sti-its-surv-epi/surveillance-eng.php.

Puchalski, M., & Hummel, P. (2002). The reality of neonatal pain. *Advances in Neonatal Care, 2,* 245–247.

Puntambekar, S., & Hübscher, R. (2005). Tools for scaffolding students in a complex learning environment: What have we gained and what have we missed? *Educational Psychologist, 40,* 1–12.

Putney, N. M., & Bengtson, V. L. (2001). Families, intergenerational relationships and kinkeeping in midlife. In M. E. Lachman, (Ed.), *Handbook of midlife development.* Hoboken, NJ: John Wiley and Sons.

Putterman, E., & Linden, W. (2004). Appearance versus health: Does the reason for dieting affect dieting behavior? *Journal of Behavioral Medicine, 27,* 185–204.

Quade, R. (1994, July 10). Day care brightens young and old. *The New York Times,* p. B8.

Quatromoni, P., Pencina, M., Cobain, M., Jacques, P., & D'Agostino, R. (2006, August). Dietary quality predicts adult weight gain: Findings from the Framingham Offspring Study. *Obesity, 14,* 1383–1391.

Quinn, J. B. (1993, April 5). What's for dinner, Mom? *Newsweek,* 68.

Quinnan, E. J. (1997). Connection and autonomy in the lives of elderly male celibates: Degrees of disengagement. *Journal of Aging Studies, 11,* 115–130.

Raag, T. (2003). Racism, gender identities and young children: Social relations in a multi-ethnic, inner-city primary school. *Archives of Sexual Behavior, 32,* 392–393.

Rabain-Jamin, J., & Sabeau-Jouannet, E. (1997). Maternal speech to 4-month-old infants in two cultures: Wolof and French. *International Journal of Behavioral Development, 20,* 425–451.

Rabin, R. (2006, June 13). Breast-feed or else. *The New York Times,* p. D1.

Rabkin, J., Remien, R., & Wilson, C. (1994). *Good doctors, good patients: Partners in HIV treatment.* New York: NCM Publishers.

Raeff, C. (2004). Within-culture complexities: Multifaceted and interrelated autonomy and connectedness characteristics in late adolescent selves. In M. E. Mascolo & J. Li (Eds.), *Culture and developing selves: Beyond dichotomization.* San Francisco, CA: Jossey-Bass.

Rahman, Q., & Wilson, G. (2003). Born gay? The psychobiology of human sexual orientation. *Personality and Individual Differences, 34,* 1337–1382.

Rakison, D., & Oakes, L. (2003). *Early category and concept development: Making sense of the blooming, buzzing confusion.* London: Oxford University Press.

Ramsey-Rennels, J. L., & Langlois, J. H. (2006). Infants' differential processing of female and male faces. *Current Directions in Psychological Science, 15,* 59–62.

Ranade, V. (1993). Nutritional recommendations for children and adolescents. *International Journal of Clinical Pharmacology, Therapy, and Toxicology, 31,* 285–290.

Randahl, G. J. (1991). A typological analysis of the relations between measured vocational interests and abilities. *Journal of Vocational Behavior, 38,* 333–350.

Rando, T. A. (1993). *Treatment of complicated mourning.* Champaign, IL: Research Press.

Rankin, J., Lane, D., & Gibbons, F. (2004). Adolescent self-consciousness: Longitudinal age changes and gender differences in two cohorts. *Journal of Research on Adolescence, 14,* 1–21.

Rao, V. (1997). Wife-beating in rural South India: A qualitative and econometric analysis. *Social Science and Medicine, 44,* 1169–1180.

Rapkin, B. D., & Fischer, K. (1992). Personal goals of older adults: Issues in assessment and prediction. *Psychology and Aging, 7,* 127–137.

Rapp, M., Krampe, R., & Balles, P. (2006, January). Adaptive task prioritization in aging: Selective resource allocation to postural control is preserved in Alzheimer disease. *American Journal of Geriatric Psychiatry, 14,* 52–61.

Raskauskas, J., & Stoltz, A. D. (2007). Involvement in traditional and electronic bullying among adolescents. *Developmental Psychology, 43,* 564–575.

Ratanachu-Ek, S. (2003). Effects of multivitamin and folic acid supplementation in malnourished children. *Journal of the Medical Association of Thailand, 4,* 86–91.

Rattan, S. I. S., Kristensen, P., & Clark, B. F. C. (Eds.). (2006). *Understanding and modulating aging.* Malden, MA: Blackwell Publishing on behalf of the New York Academy of Sciences.

Rattner, A., & Nathans, J. (2006, November). Macular degeneration: Recent advances and therapeutic opportunities. *Nature Reviews Neuroscience, 7,* 860–872.

Raudsepp, L., & Liblik, R. (2002). Relationship of perceived and actual motor competence in children. *Perception and Motor Skills, 94,* 1059–1070.

Ray, O. (2004). How the mind hurts and heals the body. *American Psychologist, 59,* 29–40.

Rayner, K., Foorman, B. R., Perfetti, C. A., Pesetsky, D., & Seidenberg, M. S. (2002, March). How should reading be taught? *Scientific American,* 85–91.

Raz, N., Rodrigue, K., Kennedy, K., & Acker, J. (2007, March). Vascular health and longitudinal changes in brain and cognition in middle-aged and older adults. *Neuropsychology, 21,* 149–157.

Reddy, V. (1999). Prelinguistic communication. In M. Barrett (Ed.), *The development of language* (pp. 25–50). Philadelphia: Psychology Press.

Redshaw, M. E. (1997). Mothers of babies requiring special care: Attitudes and experiences. *Journal of Reproductive and Infant Psychology, 15,* 109–120.

Ree, M., & Carretta, T. (2002). g2K. *Human Performance, 15,* 3–24.

Reifman, A. (2000). Revisiting *The Bell Curve. Psychology,* 11.

Reiner, W. G., & Gearhart, J. P. (2004). Discordant sexual identity in some genetic males with cloacal exstrophy assigned to female sex at birth. *The New England Journal of Medicine, 350,* 333–341.

Reis, H. T., Collins, W. A., & Berscheid, E. (2000). The relationship context of human behavior and development. *Psychological Bulletin, 126,* 844–872.

Reis, S., & Renzulli, J. (2004). Current research on the social and emotional development of gifted and talented students: Good news and future possibilities. *Psychology in the Schools, 41,* 119–130.

Renner, L., & Slack, K. (2006, June). Intimate partner violence and child maltreatment: Understanding intra- and intergenerational connections. *Child Abuse and Neglect, 30,* 599–617.

Rescorla, L., Alley, A., & Christine, J. (2001). Word frequencies in toddlers' lexicons. *Journal of Speech, Language, and Hearing Research, 44,* 598–609.

Resnick, B. (2000). A seven step approach to starting an exercise program for older adults. *Patient Education and Counseling, 39,* 243–252.

Resta, R., Biesecker, B. B., Bennett, R. L., Blum, S., Estabrooks. H. S., Strecker, M. N., & Williams J. L. (2006). A new definition of genetic counseling: National Society of Genetic Counselors' Task Force Report. *Journal of Genetic Counseling, 15,* 77–83.

Reuters Health eLine. (2002, June 26). Baby's injuring points to danger of kids imitating television. *Reuters Health eLine.*

Reutzel, D., Fawson, P., & Smith J. (2006). Words to Go!: Evaluating a first-grade parent involvement program for "making" words at home. *Reading Research and Instruction* [serial online], *45,* 119–159.

Reyna, V. F. (1997). Conceptions of memory development with implications for reasoning and decision making. In R. Vasta (Ed.), *Annals of child development: A research annual (Vol. 12),* pp. 87–118. London, England: Jessica Kingsley Publishers.

Reyna, V. F., & Farley, F. (2006). Risk and rationality in adolescent decision making. *Psychological Science in the Public Interest, 7,* 1–44.

Rhoades, G., Stanley, S., & Markman, H. (2006, December). Pre-engagement cohabitation and gender asymmetry in marital commitment. *Journal of Family Psychology, 20,* 553–560.

Rhule, D. (2005). Take care to do no harm: Harmful interventions for youth problem behavior. *Professional Psychology: Research and Practice, 36*, 618–625.

Ricciardelli, L., & McCabe, M. (2003). Sociocultural and individual influences on muscle gain and weight loss strategies among adolescent boys and girls. *Psychology in the Schools, 40*, 209–224.

Ricciardelli, L. A., & McCabe, M. P. (2004). A biopsychosocial model of disordered eating and the pursuit of muscularity in adolescent boys. *Psychological Bulletin, 130*, 179–205.

Rice, F. P. (1999). *Intimate relationships, marriages, and families* (4th ed.). Mountain View, CA: Mayfield.

Richards, M. H., Crowe, P. A., Larson, R., & Swarr, A. (1998). Developmental patterns and gender differences in the experience of peer companionship during adolescence. *Child Development, 69*, 154–163.

Richards, R., Kinney, D. K., Benet, M., & Merzel, A. P. C. (1990). Assessing everyday creativity: Characteristics of the lifetime creativity scales and validation with three large samples. *Journal of Personality and Social Psychology, 54*, 476–485.

Richardson, K., & Norgate, S. (2007). A critical analysis of IQ studies of adopted children. *Human Development, 49*, 319–335.

Richter, C. A. (2007). In vivo effects of bisphenol A in laboratory rodent studies. *Reprod Toxic, 24*, 199–224.

Rideout V., Vandewater, E., & Wartella, E. (2003). *Zero to six: Electronic media in the lives of infants, toddlers, and preschoolers*. Menlo Park, CA: Kaiser Family Foundation.

Riebe, D., Burbank, P., & Garber, C. (2002). Setting the stage for active older adults. In P. Burbank & D. Riebe (Eds.), *Promoting exercise and behavior change in older adults: Interventions with the transtheoretical mode*. New York: Springer Publishing Co.

Riley, L., & Bowen, C. (2005, January). The sandwich generation: Challenges and coping strategies of multigenerational families. *The Family Journal, 13*, 52–58.

Rinaldi, C. (2002). Social conflict abilities of children identified as sociable, aggressive, and isolated: Developmental implications for children at-risk for impaired peer relations. *Developmental Disabilities Bulletin, 30*, 77–94.

Ritchie, L. (2003). Adult day care: Northern perspectives. *Public Health Nursing, 20*, 120–131.

Ritzen, E. M. (2003). Early puberty: What is normal and when is treatment indicated? *Hormone Research, 60*, Supplement, 31–34.

Roberto, K. A. (1987). Exchange and equity in friendships. In R. G. Admas & R. Blieszner (Eds.), *Older adult friendships: Structure and process*. Newbury Park, CA: Sage.

Roberts, B., Helson, R., & Klohnen, E. (2002). Personality development and growth in women across 30 years: Three perspectives. *Journal of Personality, 70*, 79–102.

Roberts, R. E., Phinney, J. S., Masse, L. C., Chen, Y. R., Roberts, C. R., & Romero, A. (1999). The structure of ethnic identity of young adolescents from diverse ethnocultural groups. *Journal of Early Adolescence, 19*, 301–322.

Robertson, A. (2012, Jan 10). Goal of SFU graduation kept cancer patient going. Retrieved from http://www.sfu.ca/continuing-studies/news/features/2012/goal-of-sfu-graduation-kept-cancer-patient-going.html.

Robins, R. W., & Trzesniewski, K. H. (2005). Self-esteem development across the lifespan. *Current Directions in Psychological Science, 14*, 158–162.

Robinson, G. E. (2004, April 16). Beyond nature and nurture. *Science, 304*, 397–399.

Robinson, J. P., & Bianchi, S. (1997, December). The children's hours. *American Demographics*, 20–23.

Robinson, J. P., & Godbey, G. (1997). *Time for life: The surprising ways Americans use their time*. College Park: Pennsylvania State University Press.

Robinson, N. M., Zigler, E., & Gallagher, J. J. (2000). Two tails of the normal curve: Similarities and differences in the study of mental retardation and giftedness. *American Psychologist, 55*, 1413–1421.

Rochat, P. (2004). Emerging co-awareness. In G. Bremner & A. Slater (Eds.), *Theories of infant development*. Malden, MA: Blackwell Publishers.

Rockel, N. (2010, November 30). Brenda Milner unlocks the mysteries of memory. *The Globe and Mail*. Retrieved from: http://www.theglobeandmail.com/report-on-business/25/brenda-milner-unlocks-the-mysteries-of-memory/article1817681/.

Roecke, C., & Cherry, K. (2002). Death at the end of the 20th century: Individual processes and developmental tasks in old age. *International Journal of Aging and Human Development, 54*, 315–333.

Roelofs, J., Meesters, C., Ter Huurne, M., Bamelis, L., & Muris, P. (2006, June). On the links between attachment style, parental rearing behaviors, and internalizing and externalizing problems in non-clinical children. *Journal of Child and Family Studies, 15*, 331–344.

Roffwarg, H. P., Muzio, J. N., & Dement, W. C. (1966). Ontogenic development of the human sleep–dream cycle. *Science, 152*, 604–619.

Rogers, S. (2009). What are infant siblings teaching us about autism in infancy? *Autism Research, 2*, 125–137.

Rogers, S., & Willams, J. (2006). *Imitation and the social mind: Autism and typical development*. Guilford Press.

Roggeveen, A. B., Prime, D. J., & Ward, L. M. (2007). Lateralized readiness potentials reveal motor slowing in the aging brain. *Journal of Gerontology, B, Psychological Science and Social Science, 62*, P78–P84.

Rogoff, B. (1995). Observing sociocultural activity on three planes: Participatory appropriation, guided participation, and apprenticeship. New York: Cambridge University Press.

Rogoff, B., & Chavajay, P. (1995). What's become of research on the cultural basis of cognitive development? *American Psychologist, 50*, 859–877.

Rolls, E. (2000). Memory systems in the brain. *Annual Review of Psychology, 51*, 599–630.

Romaine, S. (1994). *Bilingualism* (2nd ed.). London: Blackwell.

Ron, P. (2006). Care giving offspring to aging parents: How it affects their marital relations, parenthood, and mental health. *Illness, Crisis, and Loss, 14*, 1–21.

Roopnarine, J. (2002). *Conceptual, social-cognitive, and contextual issues in the fields of play*. Westport, CT: Ablex Publishing.

Rose, A. J. (2002). Co-rumination in the friendships of girls and boys. *Child Development, 73*, 1830–1843.

Rose, A. J., & Asher, S. R. (1999). Children's goals and strategies in response to conflicts within a friendship. *Developmental Psychology, 35*, 69–79.

Rose, R. J., Viken, R. J., Dick, D. M., Bates, J. E., Pulkkinen, L., & Kaprio, J. (2003). It *does* take a village: Nonfamilial environments and children's behavior. *Psychological Science, 14*, 273–278.

Rose, S., Jankowski, J., & Feldman, J. (2002). Speed of processing and face recognition at 7 and 12 months. *Infancy, 3*, 435–455.

Rose, S. A., Feldman, J. F., & Jankowski, J. J. (2004). Infant visual recognition memory. *Developmental Review, 24*, 74–100.

Rosenblatt, P. C. (1988). Grief: The social context of private feelings. *Journal of Social Issues, 44*, 67–78.

Rosenblatt, P. C. (2001). A social constructionist perspective on cultural differences in grief. In M. S. Stroebe, R. O. Hansson, W. Stroebe, & H. Schut (Eds.), *Handbook of bereavement research: Consequences, coping, and care*. Washington, DC: American Psychological Association Press.

Rosenblatt, P. C., & Wallace, B. R. (2005). *African American grief*. New York: Brunner-Routledge.

Rosenfeld, B., Krivo, S., Breitbart, W., & Chochinov, H. M. (2000). Suicide, assisted suicide, and euthanasia in the terminally ill. In H. M. Chochinov and W. Breitbart (Eds.), *Handbook of psychiatry in palliative medicine*. New York: Oxford University Press.

Rosenthal, H., & Crisp, R. (2006, April). Reducing stereotype threat by blurring intergroup boundaries. *Personality and Social Psychology Bulletin, 32*, 501–511.

Ross, G., Kagan, J., Zelazo, P., & Kotelchuk, M. (1975). Separation protest in infants in home and laboratory. *Developmental Psychology, 11*, 256–257.

Ross, M., & Wilson, A. E. (2003). Autobiographical memory and conceptions of self: Getting better all the time. *Current Directions in Psychological Science, 12*, 66–69.

Rossman, I. (1977). Anatomic and body composition changes with aging. In C. E. Finch & L. Hayflick (Eds.), *Handbook of the biology of aging*. New York: Van Nostrand Reinhold.

Rossouw, J. E., Prentice, R. L., Manson, J. E., Wu, L., Barad, D., Barnabei, V. M., Ko, M…Stefanick, M. L. (2007). Postmenopausal hormone therapy and risk of cardiovascular disease by age and years since menopause. *Journal of the American Medical Association, 297*, 1465–1477.

Rotermann, M. (2008, September). Trends in teen sexual behaviour and condom use. Health Matters. Statistics Canada Catalogue no. 82-003-XPE. *Health Reports, Vol. 19, no. 3*. Retrieved from http://www.statcan.gc.ca/pub/82-003-x/2008003/article/10664-eng.pdf. Accessed May 2, 2012.

Roth, D., Slone, M., & Dar, R. (2000). Which way cognitive development? An evaluation of the Piagetian and the domain-specific research programs. *Theory and Psychology, 10*, 353–373.

Rothbart, M., & Derryberry, D. (2002). Temperament in children. In C. von Hofsten & L. Backman (Eds.), *Psychology at the turn of the millennium, Vol. 2: Social, developmental, and clinical perspectives*. Florence, KY: Taylor and Frances/Routledge.

Rothbaum, F., Weisz, J., Pott, M., Miyake, K., & Morelli, G. (2000). Attachment and culture: Security in the United States and Japan. *American Psychologist, 55*, 1093–1104.

Rowe, D. C. (1994). *The effects of nurture on individual natures*. New York: Guilford Press.

Rowe, J. W., & Kahn, R. L. (1998). *Successful aging*. New York: Pantheon.

Rubenstein, A. J., Kalakanis, L., & Langlois, J. H. (1999). Infant preferences for attractive faces: A cognitive explanation. *Developmental Psychology, 35*, 848–855.

Rubin, D., & Greenberg, D. (2003). The role of narrative in recollection: A view from cognitive psychology and neuropsychology. In G. Fireman & T. McVay (Eds.), *Narrative and consciousness: Literature, psychology, and the brain*. London: Oxford University Press.

Rubin, D. C. (1986). *Autobiographical memory*. Cambridge, England: Cambridge University Press.

Rubin, D. C. (2000). Autobiographical memory and aging. In C. D. Park & N. Schwarz et al. (Eds.), *Cognitive aging: A primer*. Philadelphia: Psychology Press/Taylor and Francis.

Rubin, K. H., & Chung, O. B. (Eds.) (2006). *Parenting beliefs, behaviors, and parent-child relations: A cross-cultural perspective*. New York: Psychology Press.

Rubin, K. H., Fein, G., & Vandenberg, B. (1983). In E. M. Hetherington (Ed.), *Handbook of child psychology. Vol. 4. Socialization, personality and social development* (pp. 693–774). New York: Wiley.

Rudy, D., & Grusec, J. (2006, March). Authoritative parenting in individualist and collectivist groups: Associations with maternal emotion and cognition and children's self-esteem. *Journal of Family Psychology, 20*, 68–78.

Ruff, H. A. (1989). The infant's use of visual and haptic information in the perception and recognition of objects. *Canadian Journal of Psychology, 43*, 302–319.

Rupp, D., Vodanovich, S., & Credé, M. (2006, June). Age bias in the workplace: The impact of ageism and causal attributions. *Journal of Applied Social Psychology, 36*, 1337–1364.

Rusen, I. D., Liu, S., Sauve, R., Joseph, K. S., & Kramer, M. S. (2004). Sudden infant death syndrome in Canada: Trends in rates and risk factors, 1985–1998. *Chronic Diseases in Canada, 25*. Public Health Agency of Canada. Retrieved from http://www.phac-aspc.gc.ca/publicat/cdic-mcc/25-1/a-eng.php. Accessed June 3, 2012.

Russell, S., & Consolacion, T. (2003). Adolescent romance and emotional health in the United States: Beyond binaries. *Journal of Clinical Child and Adolescent Psychology, 32*, 499–508.

Rust, J., Golombok, S., Hines, M., Johnston, K., & Golding, J. ALSPAC Study Team. (2000). The role of brothers and sisters in the gender development of preschool children. *Journal of Experimental Child Psychology, 77*, 292–303.

Rutter, M. (2003). Commentary: Causal processes leading to antisocial behavior. *Developmental Psychology, 39*, 372–378.

Rutter, M. (2006). *Genes and behavior: Nature-nurture interplay explained.* New York: Blackwell Publishing.

Ryan, B. P. (2001). *Programmed therapy for stuttering in children and adults* (2nd ed.). Springfield, IL: Charles C. Thomas.

Ryan, C., & Rivers, I. (2003). Lesbian, gay, bisexual and transgender youth: Victimization and its correlates in the USA and UK. *Culture, Health and Sexuality, 5*, 103–119.

Ryan, J. J., Sattler, J. M., & Lopez, S. J. (2000). Age effects on Wechsler Adult Intelligence Scale-III subtests. *Archives of Clinical Neuropsychology, 15*, 311–317.

Rycek, R. F., Stuhr, S. L., McDermott, J., Benker, J., & Swartz, M. D. (1998). Adolescent egocentrism and cognitive functioning during late adolescence. *Adolescence, 33*, 745–749.

Sacks, M. H. (1993). Exercise for stress control. In D. Goleman & J. Gurin (Eds.), *Mind–body medicine.* Yonkers, NY: Consumer Reports Books.

Sadker, M., & Sadker, D. (1994). *Failing at fairness: How America's schools cheat girls.* New York: Scribner's.

Saffran, J. R. (2003). Statistical language learning: Mechanisms and constraints. *Current Directions in Psychological Science, 12*, 110–114.

Sallis, J., & Glanz, K. (2006, March). The role of built environments in physical activity, eating, and obesity in childhood. *The Future of Children, 16*, 89–108.

Salthouse, T. A. (1989). Age-related changes in basic cognitive processes. In APA Master Lectures, *The adult years: Continuity and change.* Washington, DC: American Psychological Association.

Salthouse, T. A. (1990). Cognitive competence and expertise in aging. In J. E. Birren & W. K. Schaie, et al. (Eds.), *Handbook of the psychology of aging* (3rd ed.). San Diego, CA: Academic Press.

Salthouse, T. A. (1993). Speed mediation of adult age differences in cognition. *Developmental Psychology, 29*, 722–738.

Salthouse, T. A. (1994a). Aging associations: Influence of speed on adult age differences in associative learning. *Journal of Experimental Psychology: Learning, Memory, and Cognition, 20*, 1486–1503.

Salthouse, T. A. (2006). Mental exercise and mental aging: Evaluating the validity of the "Use it or lose it" hypothesis. *Perspectives on Psychological Science, 1*, 68–87.

Salthouse, T. A., Atkinson, T. M., & Berish, D. E. (2003). Executive functioning as a potential mediator of age-related cognitive decline in normal adults. *Journal of Experimental Psychology, General, 132*, 566–594.

Samuelsson, I., & Johansson, E. (2006, January). Play and learning—inseparable dimensions in preschool practice. *Early Child Development and Care, 176*, 47–65.

Sanderson, C. A., & Cantor, N. (1995). Social dating goals in late adolescence: Implications for safer sexual activity. *Journal of Personality and Social Psychology, 68*, 1121–1134.

Sandis, E. (2000). The aging and their families: A cross-national review. In A. L. Comunian & U. P. Gielen (Eds.), *International perspectives on human development.* Lengerich, Germany: Pabst Science Publishers.

Sang, B., Miao, X., & Deng, C. (2002). The development of gifted and nongifted young children in metamemory knowledge. *Psychological Science (China), 25*, 406–409, 424.

Sangree, W. H. (1989). Age and power: Life-course trajectories and age structuring of power relations in East and West Africa. In D. I. Kertzer & K. W. Schaie (Eds.), *Age structuring in comparative perspective.* Hillsdale, NJ: Erlbaum.

Sapolsky, R. (2005, December). Sick of poverty. *Scientific American*, 93–99.

Sarrel, P. M. (2000). Effects of hormone replacement therapy on sexual psychophysiology and behavior in postmenopause. *Journal of Womens Health and Gender-Based Medicine, 9 (Suppl. 1)*, S-25–S-32.

Sasser-Coen, J. R. (1993). Qualitative changes in creativity in the second half of life: A life-span developmental perspective. *Journal of Creative Behavior, 27*, 18–27.

Satel, S. (2004, May 25). Antidepressants: Two countries, two views. *The New York Times*, p. H2.

Saunders, J., Davis, L., & Williams, T. (2004). Gender differences in self-perceptions and academic outcomes: A study of African American high school students. *Journal of Youth and Adolescence, 33*, 81–90.

Savin-Williams, R., & Demo, D. (1983). Situational and transituational determinants of adolescent self-feelings. *Journal of Personality and Social Psychology, 44*, 824–833.

Savin-Williams, R. C. (2003). Are adolescent same-sex romantic relationships on our radar screen? In P. Florsheim (Eds.), *Adolescent romantic relations and sexual behavior: Theory, research, and practical implications.* Mahwah, NJ: Lawrence Erlbaum.

Savin-Williams, R. C., & Berndt, T. J. (1990). Friendship and peer relations. In S. Feldman & G. Elliott (Eds.), *At the threshold: The developing adolescent.* Cambridge, MA: Harvard University Press.

Sawatzky, J., & Naimark, B. (2002). Physical activity and cardiovascular health in aging women: A health-promotion perspective. *Journal of Aging and Physical Activity, 10*, 396–412.

Sax, L., & Kautz, K. J. (2003). Who first suggests the diagnosis of attention-deficit/hyperactivity disorder? *Annals of Family Medicine, 1*, 171–174.

Scarr, S. (1993). Biological and cultural diversity: The legacy of Darwin for development. *Child Development, 64*, 1333–1353.

Scarr, S. (1998). American child care today. *American Psychologist, 53*, 95–108.

Scarr, S., & Carter-Saltzman, L. (1982). Genetics and intelligence. In R. J. Sternberg (Ed.), *Handbook of human intelligence* (pp. 792–896). Cambridge, England: Cambridge University Press.

Schaefer, R. T., & Lamm, R. P. (1992). *Sociology* (4th ed.). New York: McGraw-Hill.

Schaie, K. W. (1977–1978). Toward a stage of adult theory of adult cognitive development. *Journal of Aging and Human Development, 8*, 129–138.

Schaie, K. W. (1991). Developmental designs revisited. In S. H. Cohen & H. W. Reese (Eds.), *Life-span developmental psychology: Methodological innovations.* Hillsdale, NJ: Erlbaum.

Schaie, K. W. (1993). The Seattle longitudinal studies of adult intelligence. *Current Directions in Psychological Science, 2*, 171–175.

Schaie, K. W. (1994). The course of adult intellectual development. *American Psychologist, 49*, 304–313.

Schaie, K. W., & Willis, S. L. (1993). Age difference patterns of psychometric intelligence in adulthood: Generalizability within and across ability domains. *Psychology and Aging, 8*, 44–55.

Schaie, K. W., & Zanjani, F. A. K. (2006). Intellectual development across adulthood. In C. Hoare, *Handbook of adult development and learning.* New York: Oxford University Press.

Schaller, M., & Crandall, C. S. (Eds.). (2004). *The psychological foundations of culture.* Mahwah, NJ: Lawrence Erlbaum Associates.

Scharfe, E. (2000). Development of emotional expression, understanding, and regulation in infants and young children. In R. Bar-On & J. Parker (Eds.), *The handbook of emotional intelligence: Theory, development, assessment, and application at home, school, and in the workplace.* San Francisco: Jossey-Bass/Pfeiffer.

Scharrer, E., Kim, D., Lin, K., & Liu, Z. (2006). Working hard or hardly working? Gender, humor, and the performance of domestic chores in television commercials. *Mass Communication and Society, 9*, 215–238.

Schatz, M. (1994). *A toddler's life.* New York: Oxford University Press.

Schechter, T., Finkelstein, Y., & Koren, G. (2005). Pregnant "DES daughters" and their offspring. *Canadian Family Physician, 51*, 493–494.

Schellenberg, E. G., & Trehub, S. E. (1996). Natural musical intervals: Evidence from infant listeners. Psychological *Science, 7*, 272–277.

Schemo, D. J. (2004, March 2). Schools, facing tight budgets, leave gifted programs behind. *The New York Times*, pp. A1, A18.

Scherf, K. S., Sweeney, J. A., & Luna, B. (2006). Brain basis of developmental change in visuospatial working memory. *Journal of Cognitive Neuroscience, 18*, 1045–1058.

Schieman, S., McBrier, D. B., & van Gundy, K. (2003). Home-to-work conflict, work qualities, and emotional distress. *Sociological Forum, 18*, 137–164.

Schkade, D. A., & Kahneman, D. (1998). Does living in California make people happy? A focusing illusion on judgments of life satisfaction. *Psychological Science, 9*, 340–346.

Schmidt, P. J., & Rubinow, D. R. (1991). Menopause-related affective disorders: A justification for further study. *American Journal of Psychiatry, 148*, 844–852.

Schneider, B. (1997). Psychoacoustics and aging: Implications for everyday listening. *Journal of Speech-Language Pathology and Audiology, 21*, 111– 124.

Schneider, W., & Pressley, M. (1989). *Memory between two and twenty.* New York: Springer-Verlag.

Schoppe-Sullivan, S., Diener, M., Mangelsdorf, S., Brown, G., McHale, J., & Frosch, C. (2006, July). Attachment and sensitivity in family context: The roles of parent and infant gender. *Infant and Child Development, 15*, 367–385.

Schoppe-Sullivan, S., Mangelsdorf, S., Brown, G., & Sokolowski, M. (2007, February). Goodness-of-fit in family context: Infant temperament, marital quality, and early coparenting behavior. *Infant Behavior and Development, 30*, 82–96.

Schreiber, G. B., Robins, M., Striegel-Moore, R., Obarzanek, M., Morrison, J. A., & Wright, D. J. (1996). Weight modification efforts reported by black and white preadolescent girls: National Heart, Lung, and Blood Institute Growth and Health Study. *Pediatrics, 98*, 63–70.

Schultz, A. H. (1969). *The life of primates.* New York: Universe.

Schuster, C. S., & Ashburn, S. S. (1986). *The process of human development* (2nd. ed.). Boston: Little, Brown.

Schutt, R. K. (2001). *Investigating the social world: The process and practice of research.* Thousand Oaks, CA: Sage.

Schutz, H., Paxton, S., & Wertheim, E. (2002). Investigation of body comparison among adolescent girls. *Journal of Applied Social Psychology, 32*, 1906–1937.

Schwartz, I. M. (1999). Sexual activity prior to coital interaction: A comparison between males and females. *Archives of Sexual Behavior, 28*, 63–69.

Schwenkhagen, A. (2007). Hormonal changes in menopause and implications on sexual health. *The Journal of Sexual Medicine, 4* [Supplement], 220–226.

Scopesi, A., Zanobini, M., & Carossino, P. (1997). Childbirth in different cultures: Psychophysical reactions of women delivering in U.S., German, French, and Italian hospitals. *Journal of Reproductive and Infant Psychology, 15*, 9–30.

Scott, K. (2002). *A lost decade: Income equality and the health of Canadians.* Paper presented at The Social Determinants of Health Across the Life-Span Conference, Toronto, Canada, November 2002.

Scrimsher, S., and Tudge, J. (2003). The teaching/learning relationship in the first years of school: Some revolutionary implications of Vygotsky's theory. *Early Education and Development, 14* [Special issue], 293–312.

Sears, R. R. (1977). Sources of life satisfaction of the Terman gifted men. *American Psychologist, 32,* 119–129.

Seavey, C., Katz, P., & Zalk, S. (1975). Baby X: The effect of gender labels on adult responses to infants. *Sex Roles, 1,* 103–109.

Sedikides, C., Gaertner, L., & Toguchi, Y. (2003). Pancultural self-enhancement. *Journal of Personality and Social Psychology, 84,* 60–79.

SEER. (2005). Surveillance, Epidemiology, and End Results (SEER) Program. (www.seer.cancer.gov) SEER*Stat Database: Incidence—SEER 9 Regs Public-Use, Nov 2004 Sub (1973–2002), National Cancer Institute, DCCPS, Surveillance Research Program, Cancer Statistics Branch, released April 2005, based on the November 2004 submission.

Segal, B. M., & Stewart, J. C. (1996). Substance use and abuse in adolescence: An overview. *Child Psychiatry and Human Development, 26,* 193–210.

Segal, J., & Segal, Z. (1992, September). No more couch potatoes. *Parents,* p. 235.

Segal, N. L. (1993). Twin, sibling, and adoption methods: Tests of evolutionary hypotheses. *American Psychologist, 48,* 943–956.

Segal, N. L. (2000). Virtual twins: New findings on within-family environmental influences on intelligence. *Journal of Educational Psychology, 92,* 188–194.

Segall, M. H., Dasen, P. R., Berry, J. W., & Poortinga, Y. H. (1990). *Human behavior in global perspective.* Boston: Allyn and Bacon.

Selig, S., Tomlinson, T., & Hickey, T. (1991). Ethical dimensions of intergenerational reciprocity: Implications for practice. *Gerontologist, 31,* 624–630.

Semerci, Ç. (2006). The opinions of medicine faculty students regarding cheating in relation to Kohlberg's moral development concept. *Social Behavior and Personality, 34,* 41–50.

Sener, A., Terzioglu, R., & Karabulut, E. (2007, January). Life satisfaction and leisure activities during men's retirement: A Turkish sample. *Aging and Mental Health, 11,* 30–36.

Seppa, N. (1997, February). Wisdom: A quality that may defy age. *APA Monitor,* pp. 1, 9.

Serbin, L., & Karp, J. (2004). The intergenerational transfer of psychosocial risk: Mediators of vulnerability and resilience. *Annual Review of Psychology, 55,* 333–363.

Serbin, L. A., Poulin-Dubois, D., Colburne, K. A., Sen, M. G., & Eichstedt, J. A. (2001). Gender stereotyping in infancy: Visual preferences for and knowledge of gender-stereotyped toys in the second year. *International Journal of Behavioral Development, 25,* 7–15.

Serbin, L., Poulin-Dubois, D., & Eichstedt, J. (2002). Infants' response to gender-inconsistent events. *Infancy, 3,* 531–542.

Serpell, R., & Hatano, G. (1997). Education, schooling, and literacy. In J. Berry, P. Dasen, & T. Saraswathi (Eds.), *Handbook of cross-cultural psychology. Vol. 2: Basic processes and human development.* Boston: Allyn & Bacon.

Servin, A., Nordenström, A., Larsson, A., & Bohlin, G. (2003). Prenatal androgens and gender-typed behavior: A study of girls with mild and severe forms of congenital adrenal hyperplasia. *Developmental Psychology, 39,* 440–450.

Settersten, R. (2002). Social sources of meaning in later life. In R. Weiss & S. Bass (Eds.), *Challenges of the third age: Meaning and purpose in later life.* London: Oxford University Press.

Seven, R. (2006, November 26). The road taken. *The Seattle Times Pacific Northwest Sunday Magazine,* p. 6.

Shapiro, A. F., Gottman, J. M., & Carrère, S. (2000). The baby and the marriage: Identifying factors that buffer against decline in marital satisfaction after the first baby arrives. *Journal of Family Psychology, 14,* 124–130.

Shapiro, L. (1997, Spring/Summer). Beyond an apple a day. *Newsweek Special Issue,* 52–56.

Sharf, R. S. (1992). *Applying career development theory to counseling.* Pacific Grove, CA: Brooks/Cole.

Shaunessy, E., Suldo, S., Hardesty, R., & Shaffer, E. (2006, December). School functioning and psychological well-being of international baccalaureate and general education students: A preliminary examination. *Journal of Secondary Gifted Education, 17,* 76–89.

Shaver, P. R., Hazan, C., & Bradshaw, D. (1988). Love as attachment: The integration of three behavioral systems. In R. J. Sternberg & M. L. Barnes (Eds.), *The psychology of love* (pp. 68–99). New Haven, CT: Yale University Press.

Shaw, D. S., Winslow, E. B., & Flanagan, C. (1999). A prospective study of the effects of marital status and family relations on young children's adjustment among African American and European American families. *Child Development, 70,* 742–755.

Shaw, M. L. (2003). Creativity and whole language. In J. Houtz (Ed.), *The educational psychology of creativity.* Cresskill, NJ: Hampton Press.

Shaywitz, S. (2004). *Overcoming dyslexia: A new and complete science-based program for reading problems at any level.* New York: Vintage.

Shea, J. (2006, September). Cross-cultural comparison of women's midlife symptom-reporting: A China study. *Culture, Medicine and Psychiatry, 30,* 331–362.

Shea, J. D. (1985). Studies of cognitive development in Papua, New Guinea. *International Journal of Psychology, 20,* 33–61.

Shea, K. M., Wilcox, A. J., & Little, R. E. (1998). Postterm delivery: A challenge for epidemiologic research. *Epidemiology, 9,* 199–204.

Sheets, R. H., & Hollins, E. R. (1999). *Racial and ethnic identity in school practices.* Mahwah, NJ: Lawrence Erlbaum.

Sheilds, M. (2004). Measured obesity: Overweight Canadian children and adolescents. *Nutrition: Findings from the Canadian Community Health Survey. Issue 1.* Component of Statistics Canada Catalogue no. 82-620-MWE2005001.

Sheldon, K. M., Elliot, A. J., Kim, Y., & Kasser, T. (2001). What is satisfying about satisfying events? Testing 10 candidate psychological needs. *Journal of Personality and Social Psychology, 80,* 325–339.

Sherman, E. (1991). *Reminiscence and the self in old age.* New York: Springer.

Sherwin, B. B. (1991). The psychoendocrinology of aging and female sexuality. *Annual Review of Sex Research, 2,* 181–198.

Sherry, S. B., & Hall, P. A. (2009). The perfectionism model of binge eating: Tests of an integrative model. *Journal of Personality and Social Psychology, 96,* 690–709.

Sherry, S. B., Hewitt, P. L., Sherry, D. L., Flett, G. L. & Graham, A. R. (2010). Perfectionism dimensions and research productivity in psychology professors: Implications for understanding the (mal)adaptiveness of perfectionism. *Canadian Journal of Behavioural Science, 42,* 273–283.

Shi, L. (2003). Facilitating constructive parent–child play: Family therapy with young children. *Journal of Family Psychotherapy, 14,* 19–31.

Shimizu, M., & Pelham, B. (2004). The unconscious cost of good fortune: Implicit and explicit self-esteem, positive life events, and health. *Health Psychology, 23,* 101–105.

Shiner, R., Masten, A., & Roberts, J. (2003). Childhood personality foreshadows adult personality and life outcomes two decades later. *Journal of Personality, 71,* 1145–1170.

Shiono, P. H., & Behrman, R. E. (1995). Low birth weight: Analysis and recommendations. *The Future of Children, 5,* 4–18.

Shonk, S. M., & Cicchetti, D. (2001). Maltreatment, competency deficits, and risk for academic and behavioral maladjustment. *Developmental Psychology, 37,* 3–17.

Shor, R. (2006, May). Physical punishment as perceived by parents in Russia: Implications for professionals involved in the care of children. *Early Child Development and Care, 176,* 429–439.

Short, L. (2007, February). Lesbian mothers living well in the context of heterosexism and discrimination: Resources, strategies and legislative change. *Feminism and Psychology, 17,* 57–74.

Shurkin, J. N. (1992). *Terman's kids: The groundbreaking study of how the gifted grow up.* Boston: Little, Brown.

Shute, N. (1997, Nov 10). No more hard labor. High-tech and high-touch remedies for easing the pain of childbirth. *US News World Rep, 123(18),* 92–95.

Shweder, R. A. (1998). *Welcome to middle age! (And other cultural fictions).* New York: Oxford University Press.

Shweder, R. A. (2003). *Why do men barbecue? Recipes for cultural psychology.* Cambridge, MA: Harvard University Press.

Sidorowicz, L., & Lunney, G. (1980). Baby X Revisited. *Sex Roles, 6,* 67–73.

Siegal, M. (1997). *Knowing children: Experiments in conversation and cognition* (2nd ed.). Hove, England: Psychology Press/Erlbaum, Taylor and Francis.

Siegler, R. (2003). Thinking and intelligence. In M. Bornstein & L. Davidson (Eds.), *Well-being: Positive development across the life course* (pp. 311–320). Mahwah, NJ: Lawrence Erlbaum Associates.

Siegler, R. S. (1994). Cognitive variability: A key to understanding cognitive development. *Current Directions in Psychological Science, 3,* 1–5.

Siegler, R. S. (1995). How does change occur? A microgenetic study of number conservation. *Cognitive Psychology, 28,* 225–273.

Siegler, R. S. (1998). *Children's thinking* (3rd ed.). Upper Saddle River, NJ: Prentice Hall.

Siegler, R. S. (2007). Cognitive variability. *Developmental Science, 10(1),* pp. 104–109.

Siegler, R. S., & Ellis, S. (1996). Piaget on childhood. *Psychological Science, 7,* 211–215.

Siegler, R. S., & Richards, D. (1982). The development of intelligence. In R. Sternberg (Ed.), *Handbook of human intelligence.* London: Cambridge University Press.

Sierra, F. (2006, June). Is (your cellular response to) stress killing you? *Journals of Gerontology: Series A: Biological Sciences and Medical Sciences, 61,* 557–561.

Silveira, P. P., Portella, A. K., Crema, L., Correa, M., Nieto, F. B., Diehl, L., Lucion, A. B., & Dalmaz, C. (2007). Both infantile stimulation and exposure to sweet food lead to an increased sweet food ingestion in adult life. *Physiological Behavior, 15,* 88–97.

Silverthorn, P., & Frick, P. J. (1999). Developmental pathways to antisocial behavior: The delayed-onset pathway in girls. *Developmental and Psychopathology, 11,* 101–126.

Simmons, R., & Blyth, D. (1987). *Moving into adolescence.* New York: Aldine de Gruyter.

Simons, L., & Conger, R. (2007, February). Linking mother–father differences in parenting to a typology of family parenting styles and adolescent outcomes. *Journal of Family Issues, 28,* 212–241.

Simons, S. H., van Dijk, M., Anand, K. S., Roofthooft, D., van Lingen, R. A., & Tibboel. D. (2003). Do we still hurt newborn babies? A prospective study of procedural pain and analgesia in neonates. *Archives of Pediatrics and Adolescence, 157,* 1058–1064.

Simonton, D. K. (1989). The swan-song phenomenon: Last-works effects for 172 classical composers. *Psychology and Aging, 4,* 42–47.

Simonton, D. K. (1997). Creative productivity: A predictive and explanatory model of career trajectories and landmarks. *Psychological Review, 104,* 66–89.

Simpkins, S., Parke, R., Flyr, M., & Wild, M. (2006, November). Similarities in children's and early adolescents' perceptions of friendship qualities across development, gender, and friendship qualities. *Journal of Early Adolescence, 26,* 491–508.

Simpson, J., Collins, W., Tran, S., & Haydon, K. (2007, February). Attachment and the experience and expression of emotions in romantic relationships: A developmental perspective. *Journal of Personality and Social Psychology, 92,* 355–367.

Simpson, J. A. (1990). Influence of attachment styles on romantic relationships. *Journal of Personality and Social Psychology, 59,* 971–980.

Simson, S. P., Wilson, L. B., & Harlow-Rosentraub, K. (2006). Civic engagement and lifelong learning institutes: Current status and future directions. In L. Wilson & S. P. Simson (Eds.), *Civic engagement and the baby boomer generation: Research, policy, and practice perspectives.* New York: Haworth Press.

Sinclair, D. A., & Guarente, L. (2006). Unlocking the secrets of longevity genes. *Scientific American, 294,* 48–51, 54–57.

Singer, D. G., & Singer, J. L. (Eds.). (2000). *Handbook of children and the media.* Thousand Oaks, CA: Sage.

Singer, L. T., Arendt, R., Minnes, S., Farkas, K., & Salvator, A. (2000). Neurobehavioral outcomes of cocaine-exposed infants. *Neurotoxicology and Teratology, 22,* 653–666.

Singer, L. T., Minnes, S., Short, E., Arendt, R., Farkas, K., Lewis, B., et al. (2004). Cognitive outcomes of preschool children with prenatal cocaine exposure. *Journal of the American Medical Association, 291,* 2448–2456. doi: 10.1001/jama.291.20.2448.

Singer, M. S., Stacey, B. G., & Lange, C. (1993). The relative utility of expectancy-value theory and social cognitive theory in predicting psychology student course goals and career aspirations. *Journal of Social Behavior and Personality, 8,* 703–714.

Singleton, L. C., & Asher, S. R. (1979). Racial integration and children's peer preferences. *Child Development, 50,* 936–941.

Sinnott, J. D. (1997). Developmental models of midlife and aging in women: Metaphors for transcendence and for individuality in community. In J. Coyle (Ed.), *Handbook on women and aging* (pp. 149–163). Westport, CT: Greenwood.

Skarborn, M., & Nicki, R. (2000). Worry in pre- and post-retirement persons. *International Journal of Aging and Human Development, 50(1)* 61–71.

Skinner, B. F. (1957). *Verbal behavior.* New York: Appleton-Century-Crofts.

Skinner, B. F. (1975). The steep and thorny road to a science of behavior. *American Psychologist, 30,* 42–49.

Skinner, J. D., Ziegler, P., Pac, S., & Devaney, B. (2004). Meal and snack patterns of infants and toddlers. *Journal of the American Dietary Association, 104,* S65–S70.

Skipper, J. K., & Nass, G. (1966). Dating behavior: A framework of analysis and an illustration. *Journal of Marriage and the Family, 28,* 412–420.

Skowronski, J., Walker, W., & Betz, A. (2003). Ordering our world: An examination of time in autobiographical memory. *Memory, 11,* 247–260.

Slater, A., Field, T., & Hernandez-Reif, M. (2007). The development of the senses. In Slater & Lewis (Eds.) (2nd ed.) *Introduction to infant development.* New York: Oxford University Press.

Slater, A., & Johnson, S. P. (1998). Visual sensory and perceptual abilities of the newborn: Beyond the blooming, buzzing confusion. In F. Simion, G. Butterworth et al. (Eds.), *The development of sensory, motor and cognitive capacities in early infancy: From perception to cognition.* Hove, England: Psychology Press/Erlbaum (UK) Taylor and Francis.

Slater, A., Mattock, A., & Brown, E. (1990). Size constancy at birth: Newborn infants' responses to retinal and real size. *Journal of Experimental Child Psychology, 49,* 314–322.

Slater, M., Henry, K., & Swaim, R. (2003). Violent media content and aggressiveness in adolescents: A downward spiral model. *Communication Research, 30,* 713–736.

Slavin, R. E. (1995). Enhancing intergroup relations in schools: Cooperative learning and other strategies. In W. D. Hawley & A. W. Jackson (Eds.), *Toward a common destiny: Improving race and ethnic relations in America.* San Francisco: Jossey-Bass.

Sliwinski, M., Buschke, H., Kuslansky, G., & Senior, G. (1994). Proportional slowing and addition speed in old and young adults. *Psychology and Aging, 9,* 72–80.

Sliwinski, M., Stawski, R., Hall, C., Katz, M., Verghese, J., & Lipton, R. (2006). Distinguishing preterminal and terminal cognitive decline. *European Psychologist, 11,* 172–181.

Smedley, A., & Smedley, B. D. (2005). Race as biology is fiction, racism as a social problem is real: Anthropological and historical perspectives on the social construction of race. *American Psychologist, 60,* 16–26.

Smedley, B. D., & Syme, S. L. (Eds.). (2000). *Promoting health: Intervention strategies from social and behavioral research.* Washington, DC: National Academy of Sciences.

Smetana, J., Daddis, C., & Chuang, S. (2003). "Clean your room!" A longitudinal investigation of adolescent–parent conflict and conflict resolution in middle-class African American families. *Journal of Adolescent Research, 18,* 631–650.

Smetana, J. G. (1995). Parenting styles and conceptions of parental authority during adolescence. *Child Development 66,* 299–316.

Smetana, J. G. (2005). Adolescent–parent conflict: Resistance and subversion as developmental process. In L. Nucci (Ed.), *Conflict, contradiction, and contrarian elements in moral development and education.* Mahwah, NJ: Lawrence Erlbaum Associates.

Smith, A., & Schneider, B. H. (2000). The inter-ethnic friendships of adolescent students: a Canadian study. *International Journal of Intercultural Relations, 24,* 247–258.

Smith, G. C., et al. (2003). Interpregnancy interval and risk of preterm birth and neonatal death. *British Medical Journal, 327,* 313–316.

Smith, I. M., Koegel, R. L., Koegel, L. K., Openden, D. A., Fossum, K. L., & Bryson, S. E. (2010). Effectiveness of a novel community based early intervention model for children with autistic spectrum disorder. *American Journal on Intellectual and Developmental Disabilities, 115(6),* 504–523. doi: 10.1352/1944-7558-115.6.504.

Smith, J. (2005, April 7). Coaches help mom, dad see "big picture" in parenting. *The Oregonian,* 8.

Smith, P. K. (1995). Grandparenthood. In M. H. Bornstein (Ed.), *Handbook of parenting.* Hillsdale, NJ: Erlbaum.

Smith, P. K., & Drew, L. M. (2002). Grandparenthood. In M. Bornstein (Ed.), *Handbook of parenting.* Mahwah, NJ: Erlbaum.

Smith, R. (1999, March). The timing of birth. *Scientific American,* 68–75.

Smith, R. J., Bale, J. F., Jr., & White, K. R. (2005, March 2). Sensorineural hearing loss in children. *Lancet, 365,* 879–890.

Smith, S., Quandt, S., Arcury, T., Wetmore, L., Bell, R., & Vitolins, M. (2006, January). Aging and eating in the rural, southern United States: Beliefs about salt and its effect on health. *Social Science and Medicine, 62,* 189–198.

Snarey, J. R. (1995). In a communitarian voice: The sociological expansion of Kohlbergian theory, research, and practice. In W. M. Kurtines & J. L. Gerwirtz (Eds.), *Moral development: An introduction.* Boston: Allyn and Bacon.

Snowdon, D. A., Kemper, S. J., Mortimer, J. A., Greiner, L. H., Wekstein, D. R., & Markesbery, W. R. (1996, February 21). Linguistic ability in early life and cognitive function and Alzheimer's disease in late life: Findings from the nun study. *Journal of the American Medical Association, 275,* 528–532.

Snyder, J., Cramer, A., & Afrank, J. (2005). The contributions of ineffective discipline and parental hostile attributions of child misbehavior to the development of conduct problems at home and school. *Developmental Psychology, 41,* 30–41.

Society of Obstetricians and Gynaecologists of Canada. (2007). Non-medical use of fetal ultrasound. *J Obstet Gynaecol Can 2007.29(4),* 364–365.

Society of Obstetricians and Gynaecologists (2008). Joint policy statement on normal childbirth. *J Obstet Gynaecol Can, 30,* 1163–1165.

Solantaus, T., Leinonen, J., & Punamäki, R-L. (2004). Children's mental health in times of economic recession: Replication and extension of the family economic stress model in Finland. *Developmental Psychology, 40,* 412–429.

Soldo, B. J. (1996). Cross-pressures on middle-aged adults: A broader view. *Journal of Gerontology: Psychological Sciences and Social Sciences, 51B,* 271–273.

Solomon, A. (1995, May 22). A death of one's own. *New Yorker,* 54–69.

Solomon, W., Richards, M., Huppert, F. A., Brayne, C., & Morgan, K. (1998). Divorce, current marital status and well-being in an elderly population. *International Journal of Law, Policy and the Family, 12,* 323–344.

Somerset, W., Newport, D., Ragan, K., & Stowe, Z. (2006). Depressive disorders in women: From menarche to beyond the menopause. In L. M. Keyes & S. H. Goodman (Eds.), *Women and depression: A handbook for the social, behavioral, and biomedical sciences.* New York: Cambridge University Press.

Sommers, C. H. (1994). *Who stole feminism? How women have betrayed women.* New York, NY: Touchstone.

Sontag, S. (1979). The double standard of aging. In J. H. Williams (Ed.), *Psychology of women: Selected readings.* New York: Norton.

Sophian, C., Garyantes, D., & Chang, C. (1997). When three is less than two: Early developments in children's understanding of fractional quantities. *Developmental Psychology, 33,* 731–744.

Sorensen, T., Nielsen, G., Andersen, P., & Teasdale, T. (1988). Genetic and environmental influences on premature death in adult adoptees. *New England Journal of Medicine, 318,* 727–732.

Sotiriou, A., & Zafiropoulou, M. (2003). Changes of children's self-concept during transition from kindergarten to primary school. *Psychology: The Journal of the Hellenic Psychological Society, 10,* 96–118.

Sousa, D. L. (2005). *How the brain learns to read.* Thousand Oaks, CA: Corwin Press.

Sowell, E. R., Peterson, B. S., Thompson, P. M., Welcome, S. E., Henkenius, A. L., & Toga, A. W. (2003). Mapping cortical change across the human life span. *Nature Neuroscience, 6,* 309–315.

Sowell, E. R., Thompson, P. M., Holmes, C. J., Jerrigan, T. L., & Toga, A. W. (1999). In vivo evidence for post-adolescent brain maturation in frontal and striatal regions. *Nature Neuroscience, 10,* 859–861.

Sowell, E. R., Thompson, P. M., Tessner, K. D., & Toga, A. W. (2001). Mapping continued brain growth and gray matter density reduction in dorsal frontal cortex: Inverse relationships during postadolescent brain maturation. *Journal of Neuroscience, 21,* 8819–8829.

Spear, L. P. (2002). The adolescent brain and the college drinker: Biological basis of propensity to use and misuse alcohol. *Journal of Studies on Alcohol [Special issue: College drinking, what it is, and what to do about it: Review of the state of the science], Suppl. 14,* 71–81.

Spear, P. D. (1993). Neural bases of visual deficits during aging. *Vision Research, 33,* 2589–2609.

Spearman, C. (1927). *The abilities of man.* London: Macmillan.

Spence, S. H. (1997). Sex and relationships. In W. K. Halford & H. J. Markman (Eds.), *Clinical handbook of marriage and couples interventions* (pp. 73–105). Chichester, England: Wiley.

Spencer, M. B. & Dornbusch, S. M. (1990). Challenges in studying minority youth. In S. S. Feldman & G. R. Elliott (Eds.), *At the threshold: The developing adolescent.* Cambridge, MA: Harvard University Press.

Spencer, S. J., Fein, S., Zanna, M. P., & Olson, J. M. (Eds.). (2003). *Motivated social perception: The Ontario Symposium* (Vol. 9). Mahwah, NJ: Erlbaum.

Spiegel, D. (1993). Social support: How friends, family, and groups can help. In D. Goleman & J. Gurin (Eds.), *Mind-body medicine.* Yonkers, NY: Consumer Reports Books.

Spira, A., Bajos, N., Bejin, A., & Beltzer, N. (1992). AIDS and sexual behavior in France. *Nature, 360*, 407–409.

Spraggins, R. E. (2003). *Women and men in the United States: March 2002*. Washington, DC: U.S. Department of Commerce.

Sprecher, S., Sullivan, Q., & Hatfield, E. (1994). Mate selection preferences: Gender differences examined in a national sample. *Journal of Personality and Social Psychology, 66*, 1074–1080.

Springer, S. P., & Deutsch, G. (1989). *Left brain, right brain* (3rd ed.). New York: Freeman.

Srivastava, S., John, O., & Gosling, S. (2003). Development of personality in early and middle adulthood: Set like plaster or persistent change? *Journal of Personality and Social Psychology, 84*, 1041–1053.

Sroufe, L. A. (1994). Pathways to adaptation and maladaptation: Psychopathology as developmental deviation. In D. Cicchetti (Ed.), *Developmental psychopathology: Past, present, and future*. Hillsdale, NJ: Erlbaum.

Sroufe, L. A. (1996). *Emotional development: The organization of emotional life in the early years*. New York: Oxford University Press.

Stacy, A. W., Sussman, S., Dent, C. W., Burton, D., et al. (1992). Moderators of peer social influence in adolescent smoking. *Personality and Social Psychology Bulletin, 18*, 163–172.

Stanjek, K. (1978). Das Uberreichen von Gaben: Funktion und Entwicklung in den ersten Lebensjahren. *Zeitschrift fur Entwicklungpsychologie und Pedagogische Psychologie, 10*, 103–113.

Stanovich, K. E. (2009, Nov/Dec). Rational and irrational thought: The thinking that IQ tests miss. *Scientific American Mind*, 34–39.

Statistics Canada (n. d.) Income of individuals, by sex, age group and income source, 2009 constant dollars, annual (67200 series). Table 202-0407, CANSIM (database). Last updated June 13, 2011. Retrieved from http://www5.statcan.gc.ca/cansim/a16?lang=eng&smonth=1&syear=1976&emonth=1&eyear=2009&requestID=2011081510533820461&csid=. Accessed August 15, 2011.

Statistics Canada. (2001). Participation and activity limitation survey. Catalogue no. 89-587-XIE.

Statistics Canada. (2004, February 17). *StatsCan, Infomat, a Weekly Review*. Catalogue no. 11-002-XWE

Statistics Canada. (2005). Vital statistics divorce database 3235.

Statistics Canada. (2006). Population by mother tongue, by province and territory. 2006 Census of the Population (summary table). Retrieved from: http://www.statcan.gc.ca/tables-tableaux/sum-som/l01/cst01/demo11a-eng.htm.

Statistics Canada. (2006). Educational portrait of Canada, 2006 census. Catalogue no. 97-560-XIE2006001.

Statistics Canada. (2006). Statistics Canada, Canadian Social Trends, 2006. Catalogue no. 11-008.

Statistics Canada. (2006). Census of the population, Fig 8-11.

Statistics Canada. (2007, September 12). *The Daily*. Retrieved from: http://www.statcan.gc.ca/daily-quotidien/070912/dq070912a-eng.htm.

Statistics Canada. (2008, May 16). Youth crime. *The Daily*. Retrieved from http://www.statcan.gc.ca/daily-quotidien/080516/dq080516a-eng.htm.

Statistics Canada. (2008, December 4). Leading causes of death. *The Daily*. Retrieved from http://www.statcan.gc.ca/daily-quotidien/081204/dq081204c-eng.htm.

Statistics Canada. (2009). Ethnic diversity and immigration. *Canada Year Book*, Catalogue no. 11-402-X. Retrieved from http://www41.statcan.gc.ca/2009/30000/cybac30000 000-eng.htm.

Statistics Canada. (2009, Jun 25). Canadian community health survey. *The Daily*.

Statistics Canada. (2009). Average earnings by sex and work pattern. Table 202-0102, CANSIM (database). Last updated

June 15, 2011. Retrieved from http://www40.statcan.gc.ca/l01/cst01/labor01a-eng.htm.

Statistics Canada. (2009). Family violence in Canada. *The Daily*. Retrieved from http://www.statcan.gc.ca/daily-quotidien/110127/dq110127a-eng.htm.

Statistics Canada. (2009). Life Tables, Canada, Provinces and Territories, Catalogue no. 84-537-XPB; and Canadian Vital Statistics, Birth and Death Databases; and Demography Division (population estimates).

Statistics Canada. (2009). Table 5.7. Leading causes of death of children and youth, by age group, 2003 to 2005. [cached copy]. Retrieved from http://www41.statcan.gc.ca/2009/20000/tbl/cybac20000_2009_000_t07-eng.htm.

Statistics Canada. (2010) Infant mortality. Catalogue no. 84F0211X. Retrieved from http://www40.statcan.gc.ca/l01/cst01/health21a-eng.htm.

Statistics Canada. (2010). Canadian Internet use survey: Internet use, by age group and Internet activity, occasional (percent). Table 358-0153. CANSIM (database).

Statistics Canada, (2010a). Women in Canada: Paid work. *The Daily*. Retrieved from http://www.statcan.gc.ca/daily-quotidien/101209/dq101209a-eng.htm.

Statistics Canada. (2010b). Study: Why has the gender wage gap narrowed? *The Daily*. Retrieved from http://www.statcan.gc.ca/daily-quotidien/101220/dq101220b-eng.htm.

Statistics Canada. (2011). *Births 2008*. Catalogue no. 84F0210XWE. Accessed May 16, 2011.

Statistics Canada. (2011). Fig 6-13. Source: For 1921-1975: Statistics Canada. Marriage and Conjugal Life in Canada, Current Demographic Analysis. Cat. number 91-543E, Table I; for 1976-2002: Statistics Canada. Demography Division; and for 2003: Statistics Canada. Mean age and median age of males and females, by type of marriage and marital status, Canada, provinces and territories, annual. CANSIM no. 101-1002.

Statistics Canada. (2011). Family violence in Canada. Catalogue no. 85-224-X. Retrieved from [0]http://www.statcan.gc.ca/pub/85-224-x/85-224-x2010000-eng.pdf.

Statistics Canada. (2012). Live births and fetal deaths (stillbirths), by type (single or multiple), Canada, provinces and territories. Table 102-4515. Retrieved from http://www5.statcan.gc.ca/cansim/a05?lang=eng&id=1024515.

Statistics Canada. (2012, Jul 25). Leading causes of death, total population, by sex (2009 data). CANSIM table 102-0561. Accessed August, 22, 2012.

Staunton, H. (2005). Mammalian sleep. *Naturwissenschaften, 35*, 15.

Stearns, E., & Glennie, E. (2006, September). When and why dropouts leave high school. *Youth and Society, 38*, 29–57.

Steele, C. M. (1997). A threat in the air: How stereotypes shape intellectual identity and performance. *American Psychologist, 52*, 613–629.

Steele, C. M., & Aronson, J. (1995). Stereotype threat and the intellectual test performance of African Americans. *Journal of Personality and Social Psychology, 69*, 797–811.

Stein, J. A., Lu, M. C., & Gelberg, L. (2000). Severity of homelessness and adverse birth outcomes. *Health Psychology, 19*, 524–534.

Stein, J. H., & Reiser, L. W. (1994). A study of white middle-class adolescent boys' responses to "semenarche" (the first ejaculation). *Journal of Youth and Adolescence, 23*, 373–384.

Stein, M. T., Kennell, J. H., & Fulcher, A. (2003). Benefits of a doula present at the birth of a child. *Journal of Developmental and Behavioral Pediatrics, 24*, 195–198.

Stein, Z., Susser, M., Saenger, G., & Marolla, F. (1975). *Famine and human development: The Dutch hunger winter of 1944-1945*. New York: Oxford University Press.

Steinberg, L. (1993). *Adolescence*. New York: McGraw-Hill.

Steinberg, L. D., & Scott, S. S. (2003). Less guilty by reason of adolescence: Developmental immaturity, diminished responsibility, and the juvenile death penalty. *American Psychologist, 58*, 1009–1018.

Steinert, S., Shay, J. W., & Wright, W. E. (2000). Transient expression of human telomerase extends the life span of normal human fibroblasts. *Biochemical and Biophysical Research Communications, 273*, 1095–1098.

Steinhausen, H. C., & Spohr, H. L. (1998). Long-term outcome of children with fetal alcohol syndrome: Psychopathology, behavior, and intelligence. *Alcoholism, Clinical and Experimental Research, 22*, 334–338.

Stephens, C., Pachana, N., & Bristow, V. (2006). The effect of hormone replacement therapy on mood and everyday memory in younger and mid-life women. *Psychology, Health and Medicine, 11*, 461–469.

Steri, A. O., & Spelke, E. S. (1988). Haptic perception of objects in infancy. *Cognitive Psychology, 20*, 1–23.

Sternberg, R. (2003a). A broad view of intelligence: The theory of successful intelligence. *Consulting Psychology Journal: Practice and Research, 55*, 139–154.

Sternberg, R. (2003b). Our research program validating the triarchic theory of successful intelligence: Reply to Gottfredson. *Intelligence, 31*, 399–413.

Sternberg, R. J. (1982). Reasoning, problem solving, and intelligence. In R. J. Sternberg (Ed.), *Handbook of human intelligence* (pp. 225–307). Cambridge, England: Cambridge University Press.

Sternberg, R. J. (1986). Triangular theory of love. *Psychological Review, 93*, 119–135.

Sternberg, R. J. (1987). Liking versus loving: A comparative evaluation of theories. *Psychological Bulletin, 102*, 331–345.

Sternberg, R. J. (1990). *Metaphors of mind: Conceptions of the nature of intelligence*. Cambridge, England: Cambridge University Press.

Sternberg, R. J. (1991). Theory-based testing of intellectual abilities: Rationale for the Sternberg triarchic abilities test. In H. A. H. Rowe (Ed.), *Intelligence: Reconceptualization and measurement*. Hillsdale, NJ: Erlbaum.

Sternberg, R. J. (2005). The triarchic theory of successful intelligence. In D. P. Flanagan & P. L. Harrison (Eds.), *Contemporary intellectual assessment: Theories, tests, and issues*. New York, Guilford Press.

Sternberg, R. J. (2006). Intelligence. In K. Pawlik, and G. d'Ydewalle, *Psychological concepts: An international historical perspective*. Hove, England: Psychology Press/Taylor and Francis.

Sternberg, R. J., Conway, B. E., Ketron, J. L., & Bernstein, M. (1981). People's conceptions of intelligence. *Journal of Personality and Social Psychology, 41*, 37–55.

Sternberg, R. J., & Grigorenko, E. L. (Eds.). (2002). *The general factor of intelligence: How general is it?* Mahwah, NJ: Lawrence Erlbaum.

Sternberg, R. J., Kaufman, J. C., & Pretz, J. E. (2002). *The creativity conundrum: A propulsion model of creative contributions*. Philadelphia, PA: Psychology Press.

Sternberg, R. J., & Lubart, T. I. (1992). Buy low and sell high: An investment approach to creativity. *Current Directions in Psychological Science, 1*, 1–5.

Sternberg, R. J., Wagner, R. K., Williams, W. M., & Horvath, J. A. (1997). Testing common sense. In D. Russ-Eft, H. Preskill, & C. Sleezer (Eds.), *Human resource development review: Research and implications* (pp. 102–132). Thousand Oaks, CA: Sage.

Sterns, H. L., Barrett, G. V., & Alexander, R. A. (1985). Accidents and the aging individual. In J. E. Birren & K. W. Schaie (Eds.), *Handbook of the psychology of aging* (2nd ed.). New York: Van Nostrand Reinhold.

Stevens, L. J., Kuczek, T., Burgess, J. R., Hurt, E., & Arnold, L. E. (2011, April). Dietary sensitivities and ADHD symptoms: Thirty-five years of research. *Clin Pediatr (Phila)50(4)* 279–293.

Stevens-Ratchford, R. G. (1993). The effect of life review reminiscence activities on depression and self-esteem in older adults. *American Journal of Occupational Therapy, 47*, 413–420.

Stevenson, J. (2003). Editorial, *Journal of Child Psychology and Psychiatry, 44(8),* pp. 1077–1078.

Stevenson, M., Henderson, T., & Baugh, E. (2007, February). Vital defenses: Social support appraisals of black grandmothers parenting grandchildren. *Journal of Family Issues, 28,* 182–211.

Stewart, A. J., Copeland, A. P., Chester, N. L., Mallery, J. E., & Barenbaum, N. B. (1997). *Separating together: How divorce transforms families.* New York: Guilford Press.

Stewart, A. J., & Ostrove, J. M. (1998). Women's personality in middle age: Gender, history, and midcourse corrections. *American Psychologist, 53,* 1185–1194.

Stewart, A. J., & Vandewater, E. A. (1999). "If I had it to do over again . . .": Midlife review, midcourse corrections, and women's well-being in midlife. *Journal of Personality and Social Psychology, 76,* 270–283.

Stice, E. (2003). Puberty and body image. In C. Hayward (Ed.), *Gender differences at puberty.* New York: Cambridge University Press.

Stice, E., & Shaw, H. (2004). Eating disorder prevention programs: A meta-analytic review. *Psychological Bulletin, 130,* 206–227.

Stigler, J. W., & Stevenson, H. W. (1991, Spring). How Asian teachers polish each lesson to perfection. *American Educator, 12–20,* 43–47.

Stockdale, M. S., & Crosby, F. J. (2004). *Psychology and management of workplace diversity.* Malden, MA: Blackwell Publishers.

Stolberg, S. G. (1998, April 3). Rise in smoking by young blacks erodes a success story in health. *The New York Times,* p. A1.

Stone, C. (2003). Counselors as advocates for gay, lesbian, and bisexual youth: A call for equity and action. *Journal of Multicultural Counseling and Development, 31,* 143–155.

Storfer, M. (1990). *Intelligence and giftedness: The contributions of heredity and early environment.* San Francisco: Jossey-Bass.

Strauch, B. (1997, August 10). Use of antidepression medicine for young patients has soared. *The New York Times,* pp. A1, A24.

Straus, M. A., Gelles, R. J., & Steinmetz, S. K. (2003). The marriage license as a hitting license. In M. Silberman (Eds.), *Violence and society: A reader.* Upper Saddle River, NJ: Prentice Hall.

Straus, M. A., & McCord, J. (1998). Do physically punished children become violent adults? In S. Nolen-Hoeksema (Ed.), *Clashing views on abnormal psychology: A Taking Sides custom reader* (pp. 130–155). Guilford, CT: Dushkin/McGraw-Hill.

Straus, M. A., Sugarman, D. B., & Giles-Sims, J. (1997). Spanking by parents and subsequent antisocial behavior of children. *Archives of Pediatrics and Adolescent Medicine, 151,* 761–767.

Straus, M. A., & Yodanis, C. L. (1996). Corporal punishment in adolescence and physical assaults on spouses in later life: What accounts for the link? *Journal of Marriage and the Family, 58,* 825–841.

Streissguth, A. (1997). *Fetal alcohol syndrome: A guide for families and communities.* Baltimore, MD: Paul H. Brookes.

Strelau, J. (1998). *Temperament: A psychological perspective.* New York: Plenum Publishers.

Strength, J. (1999). Grieving the loss of a child. *Journal of Psychology and Christianity, 18,* 338–353.

Striano, T., & Vaish, A. (2006, November). Seven- to 9-month-old infants use facial expressions to interpret others' actions. *British Journal of Developmental Psychology, 24,* 753–760.

Stroebe, M. S., Stroebe, W., & Hansson, R. O. (Eds.). (1993). *Handbook of bereavement: Theory, research, and intervention.* Cambridge, England: Cambridge University Press.

Stroink, M. L., & Lalonde, R. N. (2009). Bicultural identity conflict in second generation Asian-Canadians. *Journal of Social Psychology, 149,* 44–65.

Strube, M. (Ed.). (1990). Type A behavior. *Journal of Social Behavior and Personality, 5* [Special issue].

Stutzer, A., & Frey, B. (2006, April). Does marriage make people happy, or do happy people get married? *The Journal of Socio-Economics, 35,* 326–347.

Sugarman, S. (1988). *Piaget's construction of the child's reality.* Cambridge, England: Cambridge University Press.

Suinn, R. M. (2001). The terrible twos—Anger and anxiety: Hazardous to your health. *American Psychologist, 56,* 27–36.

Suitor, J. J., Minyard, S. A., & Carter, R. S. (2001). "Did you see what I saw?" Gender differences in perceptions of avenues to prestige among adolescents. *Sociological Inquiry, 71,* 437–454.

Sullivan, M., & Lewis, M. (2003). Contextual determinants of anger and other negative expressions in young infants. *Developmental Psychology, 39,* 693–705.

Suls, J., & Wallston, K. (2003). *Social psychological foundations of health and illness.* Malden, MA: Blackwell Publishers.

Sun, J., & Nathans, J. (2001, October). The challenge of macular degeneration. *Scientific American,* 69–75.

Super, C. M. (1976). Environmental effects on motor development: A case of African infant precocity. *Developmental Medicine and Child Neurology, 18,* 561–576.

Super, C. M., & Harkness, S. (1982). The infant's niche in rural Kenya and metropolitan America. In L. Adler (Ed.), *Issues in cross-cultural research.* New York: Academic Press.

Sussman, S. K., & Sussman, M. B. (Eds.). (1991). *Families: Intergenerational and generational connections.* Binghamton, NY: Haworth.

Sutherland, R., Pipe, M., & Schick, K. (2003). Knowing in advance: The impact of prior event information on memory and event knowledge. *Journal of Experimental Child Psychology, 84,* 244–263.

Sutton, J. (2002). Cognitive conceptions of language and the development of autobiographical memory. *Language and Communication, 22,* 375–390.

Swanson, H., Saez, L., & Gerber, M. (2004). Literacy and cognitive functioning in bilingual and nonbilingual children at or not at risk for reading disabilities. *Journal of Educational Psychology, 96,* 3–18.

Swanson, L. A., Leonard, L. B., & Gandour, J. (1992). Vowel duration in mothers' speech to young children. *Journal of Speech and Hearing Research, 35,* 617–625.

Swiatek, M. (2002). Social coping among gifted elementary school students. *Journal for the Education of the Gifted, 26,* 65–86.

Sy, T., Tram, S., & O'Hara, L. (2006, June). Relation of employee and manager emotional intelligence to job satisfaction and performance. *Journal of Vocational Behavior, 68,* 461–473.

Taga, K., Markey, C., & Friedman, H. (2006, June). A longitudinal investigation of associations between boys' pubertal timing and adult behavioral health and well-being. *Journal of Youth and Adolescence, 35,* 401–411.

Tajfel, H. (1982). *Social identity and intergroup relations.* London: Cambridge University Press.

Takahashi, K. (1986). Examining the Strange Situation procedure with Japanese mothers and 12-month-old infants. *Developmental Psychology, 22,* 265–270.

Takala, M. (2006, November). The effects of reciprocal teaching on reading comprehension in mainstream and special (SLI) education. *Scandinavian Journal of Educational Research, 50,* 559–576.

Tallandini, M., & Scalembra, C. (2006). Kangaroo mother care and mother–premature infant dyadic interaction. *Infant Mental Health Journal, 27,* 251–275.

Tan, H., Wen, S. W., Mark, W., Fung, K. F., Demissie, K., & Rhoads, G. G. (2004). The association between fetal sex and preterm birth in twin pregnancies. *Obstetrics and Gynecology, 103,* 327–332.

Tang, C., Wu, M., Liu, J., Lin, H., & Hsu, C. (2006). Delayed parenthood and the risk of Cesarean delivery—Is paternal age an independent risk factor? *Birth: Issues in Perinatal Care, 33,* 18–26.

Tangney, J., & Dearing, R. (2002). Gender differences in morality. In R. Bornstein & J. Masling (Eds.), *The psychodynamics of gender and gender role.* Washington, DC: American Psychological Association.

Tangri, S., Thomas, V., & Mednick, M. (2003). Predictors of satisfaction among college-educated African American women in midlife. *Journal of Adult Development, 10,* 113–125.

Tanner, E., & Finn-Stevenson, M. (2002). Nutrition and brain development: Social policy implications. *American Journal of Orthopsychiatry, 72,* 182–193.

Tanner, J. (1972). Sequence, tempo, and individual variation in growth and development of boys and girls aged twelve to sixteen. In J. Kagan & R. Coles (Eds.), *Twelve to sixteen: Early adolescence.* New York: Norton.

Tanner, J. M. (1978). *Education and physical growth* (2nd ed.). New York: International Universities Press.

Tappan, M. (2006, March). Moral functioning as mediated action. *Journal of Moral Education, 35,* 1–18.

Tappan, M. B. (1997). Language, culture and moral development: A Vygotskian perspective. *Developmental Review, 17,* 199–212.

Tardif, T. (1996). Nouns are not always learned before verbs: Evidence from Mandarin speakers' early vocabularies. *Developmental Psychology, 32,* 492–504.

Taris, T., van Horn, J., & Schaufeli, W. (2004). Inequity, burnout and psychological withdrawal among teachers: A dynamic exchange model. *Anxiety, Stress and Coping: An International Journal, 17,* 103–122.

Tartamella, L., Herscher, E., & Woolston, C. (2005). *Generation extra large: Rescuing our children from the epidemic of obesity.* New York: Basic.

Tasker, F. L., & Golombok, S. (1997). *Growing up in a lesbian family: Effects on child development.* New York: Guilford Press.

Tatum, B. (2007). *Can we talk about race? And other conversations in an era of school resegregation.* Boston: Beacon Press.

Tauriac, J., & Scruggs, N. (2006, January). Elder abuse among African Americans. *Educational Gerontology, 32,* 37–48.

Taveras, E., Sandora, T., Shih, M., Ross-Degnan, D., Goldmann, D., & Gillman, M. (2006, November). The association of television and video viewing with fast food intake by preschool-age children. *Obesity, 14,* 2034–2041.

Taylor, L. (2005). *Introducing cognitive development.* New York, NY: Psychology Press.

Taylor, R. J., Chatters, L. M., Tucker, M. B., & Lewis, E. (1991). Developments in research on black families. In A. Booth (Ed.), *Contemporary families.* Minneapolis, MN: National Council on Family Relations.

Taylor, S. E. (1991). *Health psychology* (2nd ed.). New York: McGraw-Hill.

Taylor-Butts, A., & Bressan, A. (2007). Youth crime in Canada, 2006. *Juristat, Vol. 28(3),* Statistics Canada Cat. 85-002-X. Retrieved from http://www.statcan.gc.ca/pub/85-002-x/2008003/article/10566-eng.htm.

Teerikangas, O. M., Aronen, E. T., Martin, R. P., & Huttunen, M. O. (1998). Effects of infant temperament and early intervention on the psychiatric symptoms of adolescents. *Journal of the American Academy of Child and Adolescent Psychiatry, 37,* 1070–1076.

Teicher, M. H., Anderson, S. L., Polcari, A., Anderson, C. M., & Navalta, C. P. (2002). Developmental neurobiology of childhood stress and trauma. *Psychiatric Clinics of North America, 25,* 397–426.

Teicher, M. H., Anderson, S. L., Polcari, A., Anderson, C. M., Navalta, C. P., & Kim, D. M. (2003). The neurobiological consequences of early stress and childhood maltreatment. *Neuroscience and Biobehavioral Review, 27,* 33–44.

Tellegen, A., Lykken, D. T., Bouchard, T. J., Jr., Wilcox, K. J., Segal, N. L., & Rich, S. (1988). Personality similarity in twins reared apart and together. *Journal of Personality and Social Psychology, 54,* 1031–1039.

Terman, L. M., & Oden, M. H. (1959). *The gifted group at mid-life: Thirty-five years follow-up of the superior child.* Stanford, CA: Stanford University Press.

Terracciano, A., Costa, P., & McCrae, R. (2006, August). Personality plasticity after age 30. *Personality and Social Psychology Bulletin, 32,* 999–1009.

Tessor, A., Felson, R. B., & Suls, J. M. (Eds.). (2000). *Psychological perspectives on self and identity.* Washington, DC: American Psychological Association.

Teutsch, C. (2003). Patient–doctor communication. *Medical Clinics of North America, 87,* 1115–1147.

Tharp, R.G. (1989). Psychocultural variables and constants: Effects on teaching and learning in schools. *American Psychologist, 44* [Special issue: Children and their development: Knowledge base, research agenda, and social policy application], 349–359.

The Endocrine Society. (2001, March 1). *The Endocrine Society and Lawson Wilkins Pediatric Endocrine Society call for further research to define precocious puberty.* Bethesda, MD: The Endocrine Society.

The World Factbook. (2007, April 17). Estimates of infant mortality. Retrieved from https://www.cia.gov/cia/publications/factbook/rankorder/2091rank.html. Accessed April 20, 2007.

Thelen, E., & Bates, E. (2003). Connectionism and dynamic systems: Are they really different? *Developmental Science, 6,* 378–391.

Thiessen, E. D., Hill, E. A., & Saffran, J. R. (2005). Infant-directed speech facilitates word segmentation. *Infancy, 7,* 53–71.

Thoman, E. B., & Whitney, M. P. (1990). Behavioral states in infants: Individual differences and individual analyses. In J. Colombo & J. Fagen (Eds.), *Individual differences in infancy: Reliability, stability, prediction* (pp. 113–136). Hillsdale, NJ: Erlbaum.

Thomas, A., & Chess, S. (1977). *Temperament and development.* New York: Brunner-Mazel.

Thomas, A., & Chess, S. (1980). *The dynamics of psychological development.* New York: Brunner-Mazel.

Thomas, A., Chess, S., & Birch, H. G. (1968). *Temperament and behavior disorders in children.* New York: New York University Press.

Thomas, P., & Fenech, M. (2007). A review of genome mutation and Alzheimer's disease. *Mutagenesis, 22,* 15–33.

Thomas, P., Lalloué, F., Preux, P., Hazif-Thomas, C., Pariel, S., Inscale, R., et al. (2006, January). Dementia patients' caregivers quality of life: The PIXEL study. *International Journal of Geriatric Psychiatry, 21,* 50–56.

Thomas, S. (2006, December). From the editor—the phenomenon of cyberbullying. *Issues in Mental Health Nursing, 27,* 1015–1016.

Thompson, C., & Prottas, D. (2006, January). Relationships among organizational family support, job autonomy, perceived control, and employee well-being. *Journal of Occupational Health Psychology, 11,* 100–118.

Thompson, R., Easterbrooks, M., & Padilla-Walker, L. (2003). Social and emotional development in infancy. In R. Lerner & M. Easterbrooks (Eds.), *Handbook of psychology: Developmental psychology, Vol. 6* (pp. 91–112). New York: John Wiley and Sons, Inc.

Thompson, R. A., & Nelson, C. A. (2001). Developmental science and the media. *American Psychologist, 56,* 5–15.

Thoms, K. M., Kuschal, C., & Emmert, S. (2007). Lessons learned from DNA repair defective syndromes. *Experimental Dermatology, 16,* 532–544.

Thomson, J. A., Ampofo-Boateng, K., Lee, D. N., Grieve, R., Pitcairn, T. K., & Demetre, J. D. (1998). The effectiveness of parents in promoting the development of road crossing skills in young children. *British Journal of Educational Psychology, 68,* 475–491.

Thornberry, T. P., & Krohn, M. D. (1997). Peers, drug use, and delinquency. In D. M. Stoff, J. Breiling, & J. D. Maser (Eds.), *Handbook of antisocial behavior* (pp. 218–233). New York: Wiley.

Thorne, B. (1986). Girls and boys together, but mostly apart. In W. W. Hartup & Z. Rubin (Eds.), *Relationships and development* (pp. 167–184). Hillsdale, NJ: Erlbaum.

Thornton, J. (2002). Myths of aging or ageist stereotypes. *Educational Gerontology, 28,* 301–312.

Thornton, J. (2004). Life-span learning: A developmental perspective. *International Journal of Aging and Human Development, 57,* 55–76.

Tincoff, R., & Jusczyk, P. W. (1999). Some beginnings of word comprehension in 6-month-olds. *Psychological Science, 10,* 172–175.

Ting, Y. (1997). Determinants of job satisfaction of federal government employees. *Public Personnel Management, 26,* 313–334.

Tinsley, B., Lees, N., & Sumartojo, E. (2004). Child and adolescent HIV risk: Familial and cultural perspectives. *Journal of Family Psychology, 18,* 208–224.

Tisserand, D., & Jolles, J. (2003). On the involvement of prefrontal networks in cognitive ageing. *Cortex, 39,* 1107–1128.

Tjepkema, M., Senécal, S., Guimond, E., & Penney, C. (2009). Mortality of Métis and registered Indian adults in Canada: An 11-year follow-up study. Component of Statistics Canada Catalogue no. 82-003-X Health Reports.

Toga, A. W., & Thompson, P. M. (2003). Temporal dynamics of brain anatomy. *Annual Review of Biomedical Engineering, 5,* 119–145.

Toga, A. W., Thompson, P. M., & Sowell, E. R. (2006). Mapping brain maturation. *Trends in Neuroscience, 29,* 148–159.

Tolan, P. H., & Dodge, K. A. (2005). Children's mental health as a primary care and concern: A system for comprehensive support and service. *American Psychologist, 60,* 601–614.

Tolchinsky, L. (2003). *The cradle of culture and what children know about writing and numbers before being taught.* Mahwah, NJ: Lawrence Erlbaum Associates.

Tomblin, J. B., Hammer, C. S., & Zhang, X. (1998). The association of prenatal tobacco use and SLI. *International Journal of Language and Communication Disorders, 33,* 357–368.

Tongsong, T., Iamthongin, A., Wanapirak, C., Piyamongkol, W., Sirichotiyakul, S., Boonyanurak, P., Tatiyapornkul, T., & Neelasri, C. (2005). Accuracy of fetal heart-rate variability interpretation by obstetricians using the criteria of the National Institute of Child Health and Human Development compared with computer-aided interpretation. *Journal of Obstetric and Gynaecological Research, 31,* 68–71.

Topolnicki, D. M. (1995, January). The real immigrant story: Making it big in America. *Money,* 129–138.

Torvaldsen, S., Roberts, C. L., Simpson, J. M., Thompson, J. F., & Ellwood, D. A. (2006). Intrapartum epidural analgesia and breastfeeding: A prospective cohort study. *International Breastfeeding Journal, 24,* 1–24.

Toschke, A. M., Grote, V., Koletzko, B., & von Kries, R. (2004). Identifying children at high risk for overweight at school entry by weight gain during the first 2 years. *Archives of Pediatric Adolescence, 158,* 449–452.

Tracy, J., Shaver, P., & Albino, A. (2003). Attachment styles and adolescent sexuality. In P. Florsheim (Ed.), *Adolescent romantic relations and sexual behavior: Theory, research, and practical implications.* Mahwah, NJ: Lawrence Erlbaum Associates.

Trainor, C., & Mihorean, K. (Eds.). (2001). Family violence in Canada: A statistical profile. Statistics Canada Catalogue no. 85-224-XIE. Ottawa. Retrieved from www.phac-aspc.gc.ca/ncfv-cnivf/pdfs/fv-85-224-x2000010-eng.pdf. Accessed March 11, 2011.

Trainor, L. J., Austin, C. M., & Desjardins, R. N. (2000). Is infant-directed speech prosody a result of the vocal expression of emotion? *Psychological Science, 11,* 188–195.

Treasure, J., & Tiller, J. (1993). The aetiology of eating disorders: Its biological basis. *International Review of Psychiatry, 5,* 23–31.

Trehub, S. E. (2003). The developmental origins of musicality. *Nature Neuroscience, 6,* 669–673.

Trickett, P. K., Kurtz, D. A., & Pizzigati, K. (2004). Resilient outcomes in abused and neglected children: Bases for strengths-based intervention and prevention policies. In K. I. Maton & C. J. Schellenbach (Eds.), *Investing in children, youth, families and communities: Strength-based research and policy.* Washington, DC: American Psychological Association.

Tronick, E. Z. (1995). Touch in mother–infant interactions. In T. M. Field (Ed.), *Touch in early development.* Hillsdale, NJ: Erlbaum.

Tropp, L. (2003). The psychological impact of prejudice: Implications for intergroup contact. *Group Processes and Intergroup Relations, 6,* 131–149.

Troseth, G. L., & DeLoache, J. S. (1998). The medium can obscure the message: Young children's understanding of video. *Child Development, 69,* 950–965.

Trotter, A. (2004, December 1). Web searches often overwhelm young researchers. *Education Week, 24,* 8.

Trzesniewski, K. H., Donnellan, M. B., & Robins, R. W. (2003). Stability of self-esteem across the life span. *Journal of Personality and Social Psychology, 84,* 205–220.

Tsao, F.-M., Liu, H-M., & Kuhl, P. K. (2004). Speech perception in infancy predicts language development in the second year of life: A longitudinal study. *Child Development, 75,* 1067–1084.

Tse, T., & Howie, L. (2005, September). Adult day groups: Addressing older people's needs for activity and companionship. *Australasian Journal on Ageing, 24,* 134–140.

Tucker, M. B., & Mitchell-Kernan, C. (Eds.). (1995). *The decline in marriage among African Americans: Causes, consequences, and policy implications.* New York: Russell Sage.

Tudge, J., & Scrimsher, S. (2003). Lev S. Vygotsky on education: A cultural-historical, interpersonal, and individual approach to development. In B. Zimmerman, (Ed.), *Educational psychology: A century of contributions.* Mahwah, NJ: Lawrence Erlbaum Associates.

Tulving, E., & Thompson, D. M. (1973). Encoding specificity and retrieval processes in episodic memory. *Psychological Review, 80,* 352–373.

Turati, C., Cassia, V. M., Simion, F., & Leo, I. (2006). Newborns' face recognition: Role of inner and outer facial features. *Child Development, 77,* 297–311.

Turcotte, M., & Schellenberg, G. (2007). A portrait of seniors in Canada. Statistics Canada Catalogue no. 89-519-XIE.

Turkheimer, E., Haley, A., Waldreon, M., D'Onofrio, B., & Gottesman, I. I. (2003). Socioeconomic status modifies heritability of IQ in young children. *Psychological Science, 14,* 623–628.

Turner, J. C., & Onorato, R. S. (1999). Social identity, personality, and the self-concept: A self-categorizing perspective. In T. R. Tyler & R. M. Kramer et al. *The psychology of the social self. Applied social research.* Mahwah, NJ: Lawrence Erlbaum Associates.

Turner, J. S., & Helms, D. B. (1994). *Contemporary adulthood* (5th ed.). Forth Worth, TX: Harcourt Brace.

Turner-Bowker, D. M. (1996). Gender stereotyped descriptors in children's picture books: Does "Curious Jane" exist in the literature? *Sex Roles, 35,* 461–488.

Twenge, J. M., & Campbell, W. K. (2001). Age and birth cohort differences in self-esteem: A cross-temporal meta-analysis. *Personality and Social Psychology Review, 5,* 321–344.

Twomey, J. (2006). Issues in genetic testing of children. *MCN: The American Journal of Maternal/Child Nursing, 31,* 156–163.

Tyre, P., & McGinn, D. (2003, May 12). She works, he doesn't. *Newsweek,* 45–52.

Tyre, P., & Scelfo, J. (2003, September 22). Helping kids get fit. *Newsweek,* 60–62.

Uhlenberg, P., Cooney, T., & Boyd, R. (1990). Divorce for women after midlife. *Journal of Gerontology, 45(1)*, S3–S11.

Umana-Taylor, A., & Fine, M. (2004). Examining ethnic identity among Mexican-origin adolescents living in the United States. *Hispanic Journal of Behavioral Sciences, 26*, 36–59.

Unger, R., & Crawford, M. (1992). *Women and gender: A feminist psychology* (2nd ed.). New York: McGraw-Hill.

Unger, R., & Crawford, M. (2004). *Women and gender: A feminist psychology* (4th ed.). New York, NY: McGraw-Hill.

Unger, R. K. (Ed.). (2001). *Handbook of the psychology of women and gender.* New York: John Wiley and Sons.

UNAIDS and World Health Organization. (2006). *AIDS epidemic update.* Paris: World Health Organization.

United Nations. (1990). *Declaration of the world summit for children.* New York: Author.

United Nations. (2002). *Building a society for all ages.* New York: United Nations.

United Nations. (2004). *Hunger and the world's children.* New York: Author.

University of Akron. (2006). *A longitudinal evaluation of the new curricula for the D.A.R.E. middle (7th grade) and high school (9th grade) programs: Take charge of your life.* Akron, OH: University of Akron.

Updegraff, K. A., Helms, H. M., McHale, S. M., Crouter, A. C., Thayer, S. M., & Sales, L. H. (2004). Who's the boss? Patterns of perceived control in adolescents' friendship. *Journal of Youth and Adolescence, 33*, 403–420.

Updegraff, K. A., McHale, S. M., Whiteman, S. D., Thayer, S. M., & Crouter, A. C. (2006). The nature and correlates of Mexican-American adolescents' time with parents and peers. *Child Development, 77*, 1470–1486.

Urberg, K., Luo, Q., & Pilgrim, C. (2003). A two-stage model of peer influence in adolescent substance use: Individual and relationship-specific differences in susceptibility to influence. *Addictive Behaviors, 28*, 1243–1256.

Urquidi, V., Tarin, D., & Goodison, S. (2000). Role of telomerase in cell senescence and oncogenesis. *Annual Review of Medicine, 51*, 65–79.

U.S. Food and Drug Administration. (2008). Avoid fetal "keepsake" images, heartbeat monitors. Consumer Updates. Retrieved from: http://www.fda.gov/forconsumers/consumerupdates/ucm095508.ht. Accessed June 3, 2012.

USDHHS (U.S. Department of Health and Human Services). (1990). *Health United States 1989* (DHHS Publication No. PHS 90–1232). Washington, DC: U.S. Government Printing Office.

Uylings, H. (2006). Development of the human cortex and the concept of "critical" or "sensitive" periods. *Language Learning, 56*, 59–90.

Vaillancourt, T., & Hymel, S. (2006, July). Aggression and social status. The moderating roles of sex and peer-valued characteristics. *Aggressive Behavior, 32*, 396–408.

Vaillant, G. E. (1977). *Adaptation to life.* Boston: Little, Brown.

Vaillant, G. E., & Vaillant, C. O. (1981). Natural history of male psychological health, X: Work as a predictor of positive mental health. *The American Journal of Psychiatry, 138*, 1433–1440.

Vaillant, G. E., & Vaillant, C. O. (1990). Natural history of male psychological health, XII: A 45-year study of predictors of successful aging. *American Journal of Psychiatry, 147(1)*, 31–37.

Vajragupta, O., Monthakantirat, O., Wongkrajang, Y., Watanabe, H., & Peungvicha, P. (2000). Chroman amide 12P inhibition of lipid peroxidation and protection against learning and memory impairment. *Life Sciences, 67*, 1725–1734.

Valenzuela, M. J., & Sachdev, P. (2006). Brain reserve and cognitive decline: A non-parametric systematic review. *Psychological Medicine, 36*, 1065–1073. doi:10.1017/S0033291706007744.

Valiente, C., Eisenberg, N., & Fabes, R. A. (2004). Prediction of children's empathy-related responding from their effortful control and parents' expressivity. *Developmental Psychology, 40*, 911–926.

van den Hoonaard, D. K. (1994). Paradise lost: Widowhood in a Florida retirement community. *Journal of Aging Studies, 8*, 121–132.

Van Tassel-Baska, J., Olszewski-Kubilius, P., & Kulieke, M. (1994). A study of self-concept and social support in advantaged and disadvantaged seventh and eighth grade gifted students. *Roeper Review, 16*, 186–191.

van Wormer, K., & McKinney, R. (2003). What schools can do to help gay/lesbian/bisexual youth: A harm reduction approach. *Adolescence, 38*, 409–420.

van't Spijker, A., & ten Kroode, H. F. (1997). Psychological aspects of genetic counseling: A review of the experience with Huntington's disease. *Patient Education and Counseling, 32*, 33–40.

Vancouver Sun (2008, May 23). Woman killed by ex-husband despite restraining order. Retrieved from http://www.canada.com/vancouversun/story.html?id=49cbba27-9cc0-4a50-b6e2-78978a754174.

Vandell, D. L. (2000). Parents, peer groups, and other socializing influences. *Developmental Psychology, 36*, 699–710.

Vandell, D. L. (2004). Early child care: The known and the unknown. *Merrill-Palmer Quarterly, 50 [Special issue: The maturing of human developmental sciences: Appraising past, present, and prospective agendas]*, 387–414.

Vandell, D. L., Burchinal, M. R., Belsky, J., Owen, M. T., Friedman, S. L., Clarke-Stewart, A., McCartney, K., & Weinraub, M. (2005). Early child care and children's development in the primary grades: Follow-up results from the NICHD Study of Early Child Care. Paper presented at the biennial meeting of the Society for Research in Child Development, Atlanta, GA.

Vandello, J., & Cohen, D. (2003). Male honor and female fidelity: Implicit cultural scripts that perpetuate domestic violence. *Journal of Personality and Social Psychology, 84*, 997–1010.

Vartanian, L. R. (2000). Revisiting the imaginary audience and personal fable constructs of adolescent egocentrism: A conceptual review. *Adolescence, 35*, 639–646.

Vedantam, S. (2004, April 23). Antidepressants called unsafe for children: Four medications singled out in analysis of many studies. *The Washington Post*, p. A03.

Vedantam, S. (2006, December 20). Short mental workouts may slow decline of aging minds, study finds. *The Washington Post*, p. A1.

Veevers, J. E., & Mitchell, B. A. (1998). Intergenerational exchanges and perceptions of support within "boomerang kid" family environments. *International Journal of Aging and Human Development, 46*, 91–108.

Vellutino, F. R. (1991). Introduction to three studies on reading acquisition: Convergent findings on theoretical foundations of code-oriented versus whole-language approaches to reading instruction. *Journal of Educational Psychology, 83*, 437–443.

Veneziano, R. (2003). The importance of paternal warmth. *Cross-Cultural Research: The Journal of Comparative Social Science, 37*, 265–281.

Veras, R. P., & Mattos, L. C. (2007). Audiology and aging: Literature review and current horizons. *Revista Brasileira de Otorrinolaringologia, 73*, 88–128.

Vereijken, C. M., Riksen-Walraven, J. M., & Kondo-Ikemura, K. (1997). Maternal sensitivity and infant attachment security in Japan: A longitudinal study. *International Journal of Behavioral Development, 21*, 35–49.

Verkerk, G., Pop, V., & Van Son, M. (2003). Prediction of depression in the postpartum period: A longitudinal follow-up study in high-risk and low-risk women. *Journal of Affective Disorders, 77*, 159–166.

Vernon, J. A. (1990). Media stereotyping: A comparison of the way elderly women and men are portrayed on prime-time television. *Journal of Women and Aging, 2*, 55–68.

Vidaver, R. M., et al. (2000). Women subjects in NIH-funded clinical research literature: Lack of progress in both representation and analysis by sex. *Journal of Women's Health, Gender-Based Medicine, 9*, 495–504.

Vilette, B. (2002). Do young children grasp the inverse relationship between addition and subtraction? Evidence against early arithmetic. *Cognitive Development, 17*, 1365–1383.

Vilhjalmsson, R., & Kristjansdottir, G. (2003). Gender differences in physical activity in older children and adolescents: The central role of organized sport. *Social Science Medicine, 56*, 363–374.

Villarosa, L. (2003, December 23). More teenagers say no to sex, and experts aren't sure why. *The New York Times*, p. D6.

Vincent, J. A., Phillipson, C. R., & Downs, M. (2006). *The futures of old age.* Thousand Oaks, CA: Sage Publications.

Vitaliano, P. P., Dougherty, C. M., & Siegler, I. C. (1994). Biopsychosocial risks for cardiovascular disease in spouse caregivers of persons with Alzheimer's disease. In R. P. Abeles, H. C. Gift, & M. G. Ory (Eds.), *Aging and quality of life.* New York: Springer.

Vitaro, F., & Pelletier, D. (1991). Assessment of children's social problem-solving skills in hypothetical and actual conflict situations. *Journal of Abnormal Child Psychology, 19*, 505–518.

Vizmanos, B., & Marti-Henneberg, C. (2000). Puberty begins with a characteristic subcutaneous body fat mass in each sex. *European Journal of Clinical Nutrition, 54*, 203–206.

Volkow, N. D., Wang, G. J., Fowler, J. S., Logan, J., Gerasimov, M., Maynard, L., Ding, Y. S., Gatley, S. J., Gifford, A., & Granceschi, D. (2001). Therapeutic doses of oral methylphenidate significantly increase extracellular dopamine in the human brain. *Journal of Neuroscience, 21*, 1–5.

Votruba-Drzal, E., Coley, R. L., & Chase-Lansdale, L. (2004). Child care and low-income children's development: Direct and moderated effects. *Child Development, 75*, 396–312.

Vyas, S. (2004). Exploring bicultural identities of Asian high school students through the analytic window of a literature club. *Journal of Adolescent and Adult Literacy, 48*, 12–18.

Vygotsky, L. S. (1926/1997). *Educational psychology.* Delray Beach, FL: St. Lucie Press.

Vygotsky, L. S. (1979). *Mind in society: The development of higher mental processes.* Cambridge, MA: Harvard University Press. (Original works published 1930, 1933, and 1935.)

Wachs, T. (2002). Nutritional deficiencies as a biological context for development. In W. Hartup, W. Silbereisen, & K. Rainer (Eds.), *Growing points in developmental science: An introduction.* Philadelphia, PA: Psychology Press.

Wachs, T. D. (1992). *The nature of nurture.* Newbury Park, CA: Sage.

Wachs, T. D. (1993). The nature–nurture gap: What we have here is a failure to collaborate. In R. Plomin & G. E. McClearn (Eds.), *Nature, nurture, and psychology.* Washington, DC: American Psychological Association.

Wachs, T. D. (1996). Known and potential processes underlying developmental trajectories in childhood and adolescence. *Developmental Psychology, 32*, 796–801.

Wade, N. (2001, October 4). Researchers say gene is linked to language. *The New York Times*, p. A1.

Wagner, R. K., & Sternberg, R. J. (1985). Alternate conceptions of intelligence and their implications for education. *Review of Educational Research, 54*, 179–223.

Wahlin, T. (2007). To know or not to know: A review of behaviour and suicidal ideation in preclinical Huntington's disease. *Patient Education and Counseling, 65*, 279–287.

Wainwright, J. L., Russell, S. T., & Patterson, C. J. (2004). Psychosocial adjustment, school outcomes, and romantic relationships of adolescents with same-sex parents. *Child Development, 75*, 1886–1898.

Wakefield, M., Reid, Y., & Roberts, L. (1998). Smoking and smoking cessation among men whose partners are pregnant: A qualitative study. *Social Science and Medicine, 47*, 657–664.

Wakschlag, L. S., Leventhal, B. L., Pine, D. S., Pickett, K. E., & Carter, A. S. (2006). Elucidating early mechanisms of developmental psychopathology: The case of prenatal smoking and disruptive behavior. *Child Development, 77*, 893–906.

Walcott, D., Pratt, H., & Patel, D. (2003). Adolescents and eating disorders: Gender, racial, ethnic, sociocultural and socioeconomic issues. *Journal of Adolescent Research, 18*, 223–243.

Walker, J., Anstey, K., & Lord, S. (2006, May). Psychological distress and visual functioning in relation to vision-related disability in older individuals with cataracts. *British Journal of Health Psychology, 11*, 303–317.

Walker, L. J., de Vries, B., & Trevethan, S. D. (1987). Moral stages and moral orientations in real-life and hypothetical dilemmas. *Child Development, 58*, 842–858.

Walker, L. E. (1999). Psychology and domestic violence around the world. *American Psychologist, 54*, 21–29.

Wallerstein, J., & Resnikoff, D. (2005). Parental divorce and developmental progression: An inquiry into their relationship. In L. Gunsberg & P. Hymowitz, *A handbook of divorce and custody: Forensic, developmental, and clinical perspectives.* Hillsdale, NJ: Analytic Press, Inc.

Wallerstein, J. S., Lewis, J. M., & Blakeslee, S. (2000). *The unexpected legacy of divorce.* New York: Hyperion.

Wallis, C. (1994, July 18). Life in overdrive. *Time*, 42–50.

Wals, M., & Verhulst, F. (2005). Child and adolescent antecedents of adult mood disorders. *Current Opinion in Psychiatry, 18*, 15–19.

Walster, H. E., & Walster, G. W. (1978). *Love.* Reading, MA: Addison-Wesley.

Walters, E., & Gardner, H. (1986). The theory of multiple intelligences: Some issues and answers. In R. J. Sternberg & R. K. Wagner (Eds.), *Practical intelligence.* New York: Cambridge University Press.

Wang, Q. (2004). The emergence of cultural self-constructs: Autobiographical memory and self-description in European American and Chinese children. *Developmental Psychology, 40*, 3–15.

Wang, Q. (2006). Culture and the development of self-knowledge. *Current Directions in Psychological Science, 15*, 182–187.

Wang, S., & Tamis-LeMonda, C. (2003). Do child-rearing values in Taiwan and the United States reflect cultural values of collectivism and individualism? *Journal of Cross-Cultural Psychology, 34*, 629–642.

Wang, S-H., Baillargeon, R., & Paterson, S. (2005). Detecting continuity violations in infancy: A new account and new evidence from covering and tube events. *Cognition, 95*, 129–173.

Ward, R. A. (1984). *The aging experience: An introduction to social gerontology* (2nd ed.). New York: Harper and Row.

Wardle, J., Guthrie, C., & Sanderson, S. (2001). Food and activity preferences in children of lean and obese parents. *International Journal of Obesity and Related Metabolic Disorders, 25*, 971–977.

Warneken, F., & Tomasello, M. (2006). Altruistic helping in human infants and young chimpanzees. *Science, 311*, 1301–1303.

Warnock, F., & Sandrin, D. (2004). Comprehensive description of newborn distress behavior in response to acute pain (newborn male circumcision). *Pain, 107*, 242–255.

Warshak, R. A. (2000). Remarriage as a trigger of parental alienation syndrome. *American Journal of Family Therapy, 28*, 229–241.

Wartella, E., Caplovitz, A., & Lee, J. (2004). From Baby Einstein to LeapFrog, from Dooms to the Sims, from instant messaging to Internet chat rooms: Public interest in the role of interactive media in children's lives. *Social Policy Report, 18(4)*, 7–8.

Warwick, P., & Maloch, B. (2003). Scaffolding speech and writing in the primary classroom: A consideration of work with literature and science pupil groups in the USA and UK. *Reading: Literacy and Language, 37*, 54–63.

Wass, H. (2004). A perspective on the current state of death education. *Death Studies, 28*, 289–308.

Wasserman, G., Factor-Litvak, P., & Liu, X. (2003). The relationship between blood lead, bone lead and child intelligence. *Child Neuropsychology, 9*, 22–34.

Waterhouse, J. M., & DeCoursey, P. J. (2004). Human circadian organization. In J. C. Dunlap & J. J. Loros, (Eds.), *Chronobiology: Biological timekeeping.* Sunderland, MA: Sinauer Associates.

Waterland, R. A., & Jirtle, R. L. (2004). Early nutrition, epigenetic changes at transposons and imprinted genes, and enhanced susceptibility to adult chronic diseases. *Nutrition*, 63–68.

Waters, L., & Moore, K. (2002). Predicting self-esteem during unemployment: The effect of gender financial deprivation, alternate roles and social support. *Journal of Employment Counseling, 39*, 171–189.

Watkins, D., Dong, Q., & Xia, Y. (1997). Age and gender differences in the self-esteem of Chinese children. *Journal of Social Psychology, 137*, 374–379.

Watson, J. B. (1925). *Behaviorism.* New York: Norton.

Watson, J. B., & Rayner, R. (1920). Conditioned, emotional reactions. *Journal of Experimental Psychology, 3*, 1–14.

Watts-English, T., Fortson, B. L., Gibler, N., Hooper, S. R., & De Bellis, M. D. (2006). The psychobiologic of maltreatment in childhood. *Journal of Social Issues, 62*, 717–736.

Wayment, H., & Vierthaler, J. (2002). Attachment style and bereavement reactions. *Journal of Loss and Trauma, 7*, 129–149.

Webster, J., & Haight, B. (2002). *Critical advances in reminiscence work: From theory to application.* New York: Springer Publishing Co.

Wechsler, D. (1975). Intelligence defined and undefined. *American Psychologist, 30*, 135–139.

Weed, K., Ryan, E. B., & Day, J. (1990). Metamemory and attributions as mediators of strategy use and recall. *Journal of Educational Psychology, 82*, 849–855.

Weigel, D., Martin, S., & Bennett, K. (2006). Contributions of the home literacy environment to preschool-aged children's emerging literacy and language skills. *Early Child Development and Care [serial online], 176*, 357–378.

Weinberg, R. A. (2004). The infant and the family in the twenty-first century. *Journal of the American Academy of Child and Adolescent Psychiatry, 43*, 115–116.

Weinberger, D. R. (2001, March 10). A brain too young for good judgment. *The New York Times*, p. D1.

Weiss, R. (2003, September 2). Genes' sway over IQ may vary with class. *The Washington Post*, p. A1.

Weiss, R., & Raz, I. (2006, July). Focus on childhood fitness, not just fatness. *Lancet, 368*, 261–262.

Weisz, A., & Black, B. (2002). Gender and moral reasoning: African American youth respond to dating dilemmas. *Journal of Human Behavior in the Social Environment, 5*, 35–52.

Weitzman, E., Nelson, T., & Wechsler, H. (2003). Taking up binge drinking in college: The influences of person, social group, and environment. *Journal of Adolescent Health, 32*, 26–35.

Wellman, H. M., & Gelman, S. A. (1992). Cognitive development: Foundational theories of core domains. *Annual Review of Psychology, 43*, 337–375.

Wen, S.W, Liu S., Marcoux, S., & Fowler, D. (1998). Trends and variations in length of hospital stay for childbirth in Canada. *Canadian Medical Association Journal, 158*, 875–880.

Werker, J. F., & Yeung, H. H. (2005). Infant speech perception bootstraps word learning. *Trends in Cognitive Science. 9*, 519–527.

Werker, J. F., Pons, F., Dietrich, C., Kajikawa, S., Fais, L., & Amano, S. (2007). Infant-directed speech supports phonetic category learning in English and Japanese. *Cognition, 103*, 147–162.

Werner, E. E. (1972). Infants around the world: Cross-cultural studies of psychomotor development from birth to two years. *Journal of Cross-Cultural Psychology, 3*, 111–134.

Werner, E. E. (1995). Resilience in development. *Current Directions in Psychological Science, 4*, 81–85.

Werner, E. E. (2005). What can we learn about resilience from large-scale longitudinal studies? In S. Goldstein & R. B. Brooks, *Handbook of resilience in children.* New York: Kluwer Academic/Plenum Publishers.

Werner, L. A., & Marean, G. C. (1996). *Human auditory development.* Boulder, CO: Westview Press.

Werner, N. E., & Crick, N. R. (2004). Maladaptive peer relationships and the development of relational and physical aggression during middle childhood. *Social Development, 13*, 495–514.

West, J. R., & Blake, C. A. (2005). Fetal alcohol syndrome: An assessment of the field. *Experimental Biology and Medicine, 230*, 354–356.

Wethington, E., Cooper, H., & Holmes, C. S. (1997). Turning points in midlife. In I. H. Gotlib & B. Wheaton (Eds.), *Stress and adversity over the life course: Trajectories and turning points* (pp. 215–231). New York: Cambridge University Press.

Wexler, B. (2006). *Brain and culture: Neurobiology, ideology, and social change.* Cambridge, MA: MIT Press.

Whalen, C. K., Jamner, L. D., Henker, B., Delfino, R. J., & Lozano, J. M. (2002). The ADHD spectrum and everyday life: Experience sampling of adolescent moods, activities, smoking, and drinking. *Child Development, 73*, 209–227.

Whaley, B. B., & Parker, R. G. (2000). Expressing the experience of communicative disability: Metaphors of persons who stutter. *Communication Reports, 13*, 115–125.

Wheeldon, L. R. (1999). *Aspects of language production.* Philadelphia: Psychology Press.

Wheeler, S., & Austin, J. (2001). The impact of early pregnancy loss. *American Journal of Maternal/Child Nursing, 26*, 154–159.

Whitaker, R. C., Wright, J. A., Pepe, M. S., Seidel, K. D., & Dietz, W. H. (1997, September 25). Predicting obesity in young adulthood from childhood and parental obesity. *The New England Journal of Medicine, 337*, 869–873.

Whitbourne, S., Jacobo, M., & Munoz-Ruiz, M. (1996). Adversity in the elderly. In R. S. Feldman (Ed.), *The psychology of adversity.* Amherst: University of Massachusetts Press.

Whitbourne, S. K. (1996). *The aging individual: Physical and psychological perspectives.* New York: Springer.

Whitbourne, S. K. (2001). *Adult development and aging: Biopsychosocial perspectives.* New York: Wiley.

Whitbourne, S. K., & Sneed, J. R. (2004). The paradox of well-being, identity processes, and stereotype threat: Ageism and its potential relationships to the self in later life. In T. Nelson (Ed.), *Ageism: Stereotyping and prejudice against older persons.* Cambridge, MA: MIT Press.

Whitbourne, S. K., & Wills, K. (1993). Psychological issues in institutional care of the aged. In S. B. Goldsmith (Ed.), *Long-term care.* Gaithersburg, MD: Aspen.

Whitbourne, S. K., Zuschlag, M. K., Elliot, L. B., & Waterman, A. S. (1992). Psychosocial development in adulthood: A 22-year sequential study. *Journal of Personality and Social Psychology, 63*, 260–271.

Whiting, B. B., & Edwards, C. P. (1988). *Children of different worlds: The formation of social behavior.* Cambridge, MA: Harvard University Press.

Whyte, H. E., Fitzhardinge, P. M., Shennan, A. T., Lennox, K., Smith, L., & Lacy, J. (1993). Extreme immaturity: Outcome of 568 pregnancies of 23–26 weeks' gestation. *Obstetrics and Gynecology, 82*, 1–7.

Wickelgren, W. A. (1999). Webs, cell assemblies, and chunking in neural nets: Introduction. *Canadian Journal of Experimental Psychology, 53*, 118–131.

Widom, C. S. (2000). Motivation and mechanisms in the "cycle of violence" In D. J. Hansen (Ed.), *Nebraska Symposium on Motivation Vol. 46, 1998: Motivation and child maltreatment* (Current theory and research in motivation series). Lincoln, NE: University of Nebraska Press.

Wielgosz, A. T., & Nolan, R. P. (2000). Biobehavioral factors in the context of ischemic cardiovascular disease. *Journal of Psychosomatic Research, 48*, 339–345.

Wiggins, M., & Uwaydat, S. (2006, January). Age-related macular degeneration: Options for earlier detection and improved treatment. *The Journal of Family Practice, 55*, 22–27.

Wilcox, H. C., Conner, K. R., & Caine, E. D. (2004). Association of alcohol and drug use disorders and completed suicide: An empirical review of cohort studies. *Drug and Alcohol Dependence, 76 [Special issue: Drug abuse and suicidal behavior]*, S11–S19.

Wilcox, M. D. (1992). Boomerang kids. *Kiplinger's Personal Finance Magazine, 46*, 83–86.

Wilcox, S., Castro, C. M., & King, A. C. (2006). Outcome expectations and physical activity participation in two samples of older women. *Journal of Health Psychology, 11*, 65–77.

Wilcox, T., Woods, R., Chapa, C., & McCurry, S. (2007). Multisensory exploration and object individuation in infancy. *Developmental Psychology, 43*, 479–495.

Wildberger, S. (2003, August). So you're having a baby. *Washingtonian, 85–86*, 88–90.

Wiley, T. L., Nondahl, D. M., Cruickshanks, K. J., & Tweed, T. S. (2005). Five-year changes in middle ear function for older adults. *Journal of the American Academy of Audiology, 16*, 129–139.

Williams, C. (2011). Women in Canada: A gender-based statistical report: Economic well-being. Statistics Canada Catalogue no. 89-503-XWE. Retrieved from http://www.statcan.gc.ca/pub/89-503-x/2010001/article/11388/c-g/c-g001-eng.htm.

Williams, J. M., & Currie, C. (2000). Self-esteem and physical development in early adolescence: Pubertal timing and body image. *Journal of Early Adolescence, 20*, 129–149.

Williams, K., & Dunne-Bryant, A. (2006, December). Divorce and adult psychological well-being: Clarifying the role of gender and child age. *Journal of Marriage and Family, 68*, 1178–1196.

Willis, S. (1996). Everyday problem solving. In J. E. Birren, K. W. Schaie, R. P. Abeles, M. Gatz, & T. A. Salthouse (Eds.), *Handbook of the psychology of aging* (4th ed.). San Diego: Academic Press.

Willis, S., Tennstedt, S., Marsiske, M., Ball, K., Elias, J., Koepke, K., Morris, J...Wright, E. (2006). Long-term effects of cognitive training on everyday functional outcomes in older adults. *Journal of the American Medical Association, 296*, 2805–2814.

Willis, S. L. (1985). Educational psychology of the older adult learner. In J. E. Birren & K. W. Schaie (Eds.), *Handbook of the psychology of aging* (2nd ed.). New York: Van Nostrand Reinhold.

Wills, T. A., Sargent, J. D., Stoolmiller, M., Gibbons, F. X., Worth, K. A., & Cin, S. D. (2007). Movie exposure to smoking cues and adolescent smoking onset: A test for mediation through peer affiliations. *Health Psychology, 26*, 769–776.

Wilson, D., Truman, C. D., Thomas, R., Fainsinger, R., Kovacs-Burns, K., Froggatt, K., & Justice, C. (2009). The rapidly changing location of death in Canada, 1994–2004. *Social Science and Medicine 68*, 1752–1758.

Wilson, M. N. (1989). Child development in the context of the black extended family. *American Psychologist, 44*, 380–385.

Wilson, R., Beck, T., Bienias, J., & Bennett, D. (2007, February). Terminal cognitive decline: Accelerated loss of cognition in the last years of life. *Psychosomatic Medicine, 69*, 131–137.

Wilson, R., Beckett, L., & Bienias, J. (2003). Terminal decline in cognitive function. *Neurology, 60*, 1782–1787.

Wines, M. (2006, August 24). Africa adds to miserable ranks for child workers. *New York Times*, p. D1.

Wingfield, A., Tun, P. A., & McCoy, S. L. (2005). Hearing loss in older adulthood: What it is and how it interacts with cognitive performance. *Current Directions in Psychological Science, 14*, 144–147.

Wink, P., & Dillon, M. (2003). Religiousness, spirituality, and psychosocial functioning in late adulthood: Findings from a longitudinal study. *Psychology and Aging, 18*, 916–924.

Winsler, A. (2003). Introduction to special issue: Vygotskian perspectives in early childhood education. *Early Education and Development, 14* [Special Issue], 253–269.

Winsler, A., De Leon, J. R., & Wallace, B. A. (2003). Private speech in preschool children: Developmental stability and change, across-task consistency, and relations with classroom behavior. *Journal of Child Language, 30*, 583–608.

Winstead, B. A., & Sanchez, J. (2005). Gender and psychopathology. In J. Maddux (Ed.), *Psychopathology: Foundations for a contemporary understanding*. Mahwah, NJ: Lawrence Erlbaum Associates.

Winter, J. W. (2011). Easy rider. *Senior Living Magazine*. Victoria, B.C.: Stratus Publishing. Retrieved from http://www.seniorlivingmag.com/articles/easy-rider.

Winterich, J. (2003). Sex, menopause, and culture: Sexual orientation and the meaning of menopause for women's sex lives. *Gender and Society, 17*, 627–642.

Winters, K. C., Stinchfield, R. D., & Botzet, A. (2005). Pathways fo youth gambling problem severity. *Psychology of Addictive Behaviors, 19*, 104–107.

Wise, L., Adams-Campbell, L., Palmer, J., & Rosenberg, L. (2006, August). Leisure time physical activity in relation to depressive symptoms in the Black Women's Health Study. *Annals of Behavioral Medicine, 32*, 68–76.

Witt, S. D. (1997). Parental influence on children's socialization to gender roles. *Adolescence, 32*, 253–259.

Woelfle, J. F., Harz, K., & Roth, C. (2007). Modulation of circulating IGF-I and IGFBP-3 levels by hormonal regulators of energy homeostasis in obese children. *Experimental and Clinical Endocrinology Diabetes, 115*, 17–23.

Woike, B., & Matic, D. (2004). Cognitive complexity in response to traumatic experiences. *Journal of Personality, 72*, 633–657.

Wolfe, M. S. (2006, May). Shutting down Alzheimer's. *Scientific American*, 73–79.

Wolfson, C., Handfield-Jones, R., Glass, K. C., McClaran, J., et al. (1993). Adult children's perceptions of their responsibility to provide care for dependent elderly parents. *Gerontologist, 33*, 315–323.

Wolinsky, F., Wyrwich, K., & Babu, A. (2003). Age, aging, and the sense of control among older adults: A longitudinal reconsideration. *Journals of Gerontology: Series B: Psychological Sciences and Social Sciences, 58B*, S212–S220.

Wood, N. S., Marlow, N., Costeloe, K., Gibson, A. T., & Wilkinson, A. R. (2000). Neurologic and developmental disability after extremely preterm birth. *New England Journal of Medicine, 343*, 378–384.

Woolfolk, A. E. (1993). *Educational psychology* (5th ed.). Boston: Allyn and Bacon.

World Bank. (2003). *Global development finance 2003—Striving for stability in development finance*. Washington, DC: Author.

World Bank. (2004). *World development indicators 2004 (WDI)*. Washington, DC: Author.

World Health Organization (2006). [Growth Charts] Based on the World Health Organization (WHO) Child Growth Standards (2006) and WHO Reference (2007). Adapted for Canada by Dietitians of Canada, Canadian Paediatric Society, the College of Family Physicians of Canada, and Community Health Nurses of Canada. Retrieved from http://www.dietitians.ca/Secondary-Pages/Public/Who-Growth-Charts. Accessed March 17, 2011.

Worrell, F., Szarko, J., & Gabelko, N. (2001). Multi-year persistence of nontraditional students in an academic talent development program. *Journal of Secondary Gifted Education, 12*, 80–89.

Wortman, C. B., & Silver, R. C. (1990). Successful mastery of bereavement and widowhood: A life-course perspective. In P. B. Baltes & M. M. Baltes (Eds.), *Successful aging: Perspectives from the behavioral sciences*. Cambridge, England: Cambridge University Press.

Wright, J. C., Huston, A. C., Reitz, A. L., & Piemyat, S. (1994). Young children's perceptions of television reality: Determinants and developmental differences. *Developmental Psychology, 30*, 229–239.

Wright, J. C., Huston, A. C., Truglio, R., Fitch, M., Smith, E., & Piemyat, S. (1995). Occupational portrayals on television: Children's role schemata, career aspirations, and perceptions of reality. *Child Development, 66*, 1706–1718.

Wright, S. C., & Taylor, D. M. (1995). Identity and the language of the classroom: Investigation of the impact of heritage versus second language instruction on personal and collective self-esteem. *Journal of Educational Psychology, 87*, 241–252.

Wrosch, C., Bauer, I., & Scheier, M. (2005, December). Regret and quality of life across the adult life span: The influence of disengagement and available future goals. *Psychology and Aging, 20*, 657–670.

Wu, C., Zhou, D., & Chen, W. (2003). A nested case-control study of Alzheimer's disease in Linxian, northern China. *Chinese Mental Health Journal, 17*, 84–88.

Wu, P., Robinson, C., & Yang, C. (2002). Similarities and differences in mothers' parenting of preschoolers in China and the United States. *International Journal of Behavioral Development, 26*, 481–491.

Wyer, R. (2004). The cognitive organization and use of general knowledge. In J. Jost & M. Banaji (Eds.), *Perspectivism in social psychology: The yin and yang of scientific progress*. Washington, DC: American Psychological Association.

Wynn, K. (1992, August 27). Addition and subtraction by human infants. *Nature, 358*, 749–750.

Xiaohe, X., & Whyte, M. K. (1990). Love matches and arranged marriages: A Chinese replication. *Journal of Marriage and the Family, 52*, 709–722.

Yan, Z., & Fischer, K. (2002). Always under construction: Dynamic variations in adult cognitive microdevelopment. *Human Development, 45*, 141–160.

Yang, R., & Blodgett, B. (2000). Effects of race and adolescent decision-making on status attainment and self-esteem. *Journal of Ethnic and Cultural Diversity in Social Work, 9*, 135–153.

Ybarra, M. L., & Mitchell, K. J. (2004). Online aggressor/targets, aggressors, and targets: A comparison of associated youth characteristics. *Journal of Child Psychology and Psychiatry, 45*, 1308–1316.

Yedidia, M. J., & MacGregor, B. (2001). Confronting the prospect of dying: Reports of terminally ill patients. *Journal of Pain and Symptom Management, 22*, 807–819.

Yelland, G. W., Pollard, J., & Mercuri, A. (1993). The metalinguistic benefits of limited contact with a second language. *Applied Psycholinguistics, 14*, 423–444.

Yildiz, O. (2007). Vascular smooth muscle and endothelial functions in aging. *Annals of the New York Academy of Sciences, 1100*, 353–360.

Yip, T., Sellers, R. M., & Seaton, E. K. (2006). African American racial identity across the lifespan: Identity status, identity content, and depressive symptoms. *Child Development, 77*, 1504–1517.

Yoshinaga-Itano, C. (2003). From screening to early identification and intervention: Discovering predictors to successful outcomes for children with significant hearing loss. *Journal of Deaf Studies and Deaf Education, 8*, 11–30.

Young, S., Rhee, S., Stallings, M., Corley, R., & Hewitt, J. (2006, July). Genetic and environmental vulnerabilities underlying adolescent substance use and problem use: General or specific? *Behavior Genetics, 36*, 603–615.

Youniss, J., & Haynie, D. L. (1992). Friendship in adolescence. *Journal of Developmental and Behavioral Pediatrics, 13*, 59–66.

Zafeiriou, D. I. (2004). Primitive reflexes and postural reactions in the neurodevelopmental examination. *Pediatric Neurology, 31*, 1–8.

Zalsman, G., Oquendo, M., Greenhill, L., Goldberg, P., Kamali, M., Martin, A., et al. (2006, October). Neurobiology of depression in children and adolescents. *Child and Adolescent Psychiatric Clinics of North America, 15*, 843–868.

Zampi, C., Fagioli, I., & Salzarulo, P. (2002). Time course of EEG background activity level before spontaneous awakening in infants. *Journal of Sleep Research, 11*, 283–287.

Zarit, S. H., & Reid, J. D. (1994). Family caregiving and the older family. In C. B. Fisher & R. M. Lerner (Eds.), *Applied developmental psychology.* New York: McGraw-Hill.

Zauszniewski, J. A., & Martin, M. H. (1999). Developmental task achievement and learned resourcefulness in healthy older adults. *Archives of Psychiatric Nursing, 13*, 41–47.

Zeedyk, M., & Heimann, M. (2006). Imitation and socio-emotional processes: Implications for communicative development and interventions. *Infant and Child Development, 15*, 219–222.

Zeidner, M., Matthews, G., & Roberts, R. D. (2004). Emotional intelligence in the workplace: A critical review. *Applied Psychology: An International Review, 53*, 371–399.

Zelazo, P. D., Muller, U., Frye, D., & Marcovitch, S. (2003). The development of executive function in early childhood. *Monographs of the Society for Research in Child Development, 68*, 103–122.

Zelazo, P. R. (1998). McGraw and the development of unaided walking. *Developmental Review, 18*, 449–471.

Zellner, D., Loaiza, S., Gonzalez, Z., Pita, J., Morales, J., Pecora, D., et al. (2006, April). Food selection changes under stress. *Physiology and Behavior, 87*, 789–793.

Zeman, J., Cassano, M., Perry-Parrish, C., & Stegall, S. (2006, April). Emotion regulation in children and adolescents. *Journal of Developmental and Behavioral Pediatrics, 27*, 155–168.

Zeman, K., McMullen, K., & de Broucker, P. (2010). The high education/low income paradox: College and university graduates with low earnings Ontario, 2006. *Culture, tourism and the centre for education statistics.* Statistics Canada Catalogue no. 81-595-M, No. 81. Retrieved from http://www.statcan.gc.ca/pub/81-595-m/81-595-m2010081-eng.htm.

Zernike, K., & Petersen, M. (2001, August 19). Schools' backing of behavior drugs comes under fire. *The New York Times,* pp. 1, 28.

Zhang, Y., Proenca, R., Maffel, M., Barone, M., Leopold, L., & Friedman, J. M. (1994). Positional cloning of the mouse obese gene and its human homologue. *Nature, 372*, 425–432.

Zhe, C., & Siegler, R. S. (2000). Across the great divide: Bridging the gap between understanding of toddlers' and older children's thinking. *Monographs of the Society for Research in Child Development, 65 (2, Serial No. 261).*

Zhou, B. F., Stamler, J., Dennis, B., Moag-Stahlberg, A., Okuda, N., Robertson, C., Zhao, L...INTERMAP Research Group. (2003). Nutrient intakes of middle-aged men and women in China, Japan, United Kingdom, and United States in the late 1990s: The INTERMAP study. *Journal of Human Hypertension, 17*, 623–630.

Zhu, J., & Weiss, L. (2005). The Wechsler Scales. In D. P. Flanagan & P. L. Harrison (Eds.), *Contemporary intellectual assessment: Theories, tests, and issues.* New York, Guilford Press.

Zigler, E., & Gilman, E. (1998). The legacy of Jean Piaget. In G. A. Kimble, M. Wertheimer et al. (Eds.), *Portraits of pioneers in psychology (Vol. 3).* Mahwah, NJ: American Psychological Association.

Ziv, M., & Frye, D. (2003). The relation between desire and false belief in children's theory of mind: No satisfaction? *Developmental Psychology, 39*, 859–876.

Zuckerman, M. (2003). Biological bases of personality. In T. Millon & M. J. Lerner, (Eds.), *Handbook of psychology: Personality and social psychology (Vol. 5).* New York: John Wiley and Sons.

Zwaigenbaum, L., Bryson, S., Rogers, T., Roberts, W., Brian, J., & Szatmari, P. (2005). Behavioral manifestation of autism in the first year of life. *International Journal of Developmental Neuroscience, 23*, 143–152.

Glossary

abstract modelling the process in which modelling paves the way for the development of more general rules and principles (p. 180)

acceleration special programs that allow gifted students to move ahead at their own pace, even if this means skipping to higher grade levels (p. 220)

accommodation changes in existing ways of thinking that occur in response to encounters with new stimuli or events (p. 104)

achieving stage the point reached by young adults in which intelligence is applied to specific situations involving the attainment of long-term goals regarding careers, family, and societal contributions (p. 304)

acquisitive stage according to Schaie, the first stage of cognitive development, encompassing all of childhood and adolescence, in which the main developmental task is to acquire information (p. 304)

activity theory the theory suggesting that successful aging occurs when people maintain the interests, activities, and social interactions with which they were involved during middle age (p. 412)

addictive drugs drugs that produce a biological or psychological dependence in users, leading to increasingly powerful cravings for those drugs (p. 253)

adolescence the developmental stage that lies between childhood and adulthood (p. 244)

adolescent egocentrism a state of self-absorption in which the world is viewed from one's own point of view (p. 262)

adult daycare facilities a facility in which elderly individuals receive care only during the day, but spend nights and weekends in their own homes (p. 414)

affordances the action possibilities that a given situation or stimulus provides (p. 102)

age stratification theories the view that an unequal distribution of economic resources, power, and privilege exists among people at different stages of the life course (p. 409)

ageism prejudice and discrimination directed at older people (p. 387)

agentic professions occupations that are associated with getting things accomplished (p. 335)

aggression intentional injury or harm to another person (p. 180)

Ainsworth Strange Situation a sequence of staged episodes that illustrate the strength of attachment between a child and (typically) his or her mother (p. 129)

alcoholics people with alcohol problems who have learned to depend on alcohol and are unable to control their drinking (p. 254)

Alzheimer's disease a progressive brain disorder that produces loss of memory and confusion (p. 394)

ambivalent attachment pattern a style of attachment in which children display a combination of positive and negative reactions to their mothers; they show great distress when the mother leaves, but upon her return they might simultaneously seek close contact but also hit and kick her (p. 130)

amniocentesis the process of identifying genetic defects by examining a small sample of fetal cells drawn by a needle inserted into the amniotic fluid surrounding the unborn fetus (p. 43)

androgynous a state in which gender roles encompass characteristics thought typical of both sexes (p. 168)

anorexia nervosa a severe eating disorder in which individuals refuse to eat, while denying that their behaviour and appearance, which can become skeletal, are out of the ordinary (p. 250)

anoxia a restriction of oxygen to the baby, lasting a few minutes during the birth process, that can produce brain damage (p. 65)

Apgar scale a standard measurement system that looks for a variety of indications of good health in newborns (p. 64)

applied research research meant to provide practical solutions to immediate problems (p. 27)

artificial insemination a process of fertilization in which a man's sperm is placed directly into a woman's vagina by a physician (p. 56)

assimilation the process in which people understand an experience in terms of their current stage of cognitive development and way of thinking (p. 104)

associative play play in which two or more children actually interact with one another by sharing or borrowing toys or materials, although they do not do the same thing (p. 170)

attachment the positive emotional bond that develops between a child and a particular individual (p. 129)

attention deficit hyperactivity disorder (ADHD) a learning disability marked by inattention, impulsiveness, a low tolerance for frustration, and generally a great deal of inappropriate activity (p. 200)

auditory impairment a special need that involves the loss of hearing or some aspect of hearing (p. 198)

authoritarian parents parents who are controlling, punitive, rigid, and cold, and whose word is law; they value strict, unquestioning obedience from their children and do not tolerate expressions of disagreement (p. 172)

authoritarian parents parents who are firm, setting clear and consistent limits, but who try to reason with their children, giving explanations for why they should behave in a particular way (p. 172)

autobiographical memory memories of information about one's own life (p. 155)

autonomy having independence and a sense of control over one's life (p. 276)

autonomy-versus-shame-and-doubt stage the period during which, according to Erikson, toddlers (aged 18 months to 3 years) develop independence and autonomy if they are allowed the freedom to explore, or shame and self-doubt if they are restricted and overprotected (p. 134)

avoidant attachment pattern a style of attachment in which children do not seek proximity to the mother; after the mother has left, they seem to avoid her when she returns as if they are angered by her behaviour (p. 130)

babbling making speech-like but meaningless sounds (p. 117)

Bayley Scales of Infant Development a measure that evaluates an infant's development from 2 to 42 months (p. 113)

behaviour modification a formal technique for promoting the frequency of desirable behaviours and decreasing the incidence of unwanted ones (p. 15)

behavioural genetics the study of the effects of heredity on behaviour (p. 41)

behavioural perspective the approach that suggests that the keys to understanding development are observable behaviour and outside stimuli in the environment (p. 14)

bereavement acknowledgment of the objective fact that one has experienced a death (p. 444)

bicultural identity Maintaining one's original cultural identity while integrating oneself into the dominant culture (p. 210)

bilingualism the use of more than one language (p. 207)

bioecological approach the perspective suggesting that different levels of the environment simultaneously influence individuals (p. 18)

blended families a family consisting of a remarried couple who have at least one stepchild living with them (p. 237)

body transcendence versus body preoccupation a period in which people must learn to cope with and move beyond changes in physical capabilities as a result of aging (p. 408)

bonding close physical and emotional contact between parent and child during the period immediately following birth, argued by some to affect later relationship strength (p. 65)

boomerang children young adults who return, after leaving home for some period, to live in the homes of their middle-aged parents (p. 371)

brain death a diagnosis of death based on the cessation of all signs of brain activity, as measured by electrical brain waves (p. 430)

Brazelton Neonatal Behavioral Assessment Scale (NBAS) a measure designed to determine infants' neurological and behavioural responses to their environment (p. 95)

bulimia an eating disorder characterized by binges on large quantities of food, followed by purges of the food through vomiting or the use of laxatives (p. 250)

burnout a situation that occurs when highly trained professionals experience dissatisfaction, disillusionment, frustration, and weariness from their jobs (p. 376)

Caesarean delivery a birth in which the baby is surgically removed from the uterus, rather than travelling through the birth canal (p. 70)

career consolidation a stage that is entered between the ages of 20 and 40, when young adults become centred on their careers (p. 333)

case studies studies that involve extensive, in-depth interviews with a particular individual or small group of individuals (p. 25)

centration the process of concentrating on one limited aspect of a stimulus and ignoring other aspects (p. 151)

cephalocaudal principle the principle that growth follows a pattern that begins with the head and upper body parts and then proceeds down to the rest of the body (p. 85)

cerebral cortex   the upper layer of the brain (p. 88)

chorionic villus sampling (CVS)   used to find genetic defects, a test that involves taking samples of hair-like material that surrounds the embryo (p. 43)

chromosomes   rod-shaped portions of DNA that are organized in XX pairs (p. 37)

chronological (or physical) age   the actual age of the child taking the intelligence test (p. 212)

classical conditioning   a type of learning in which an organism responds in a particular way to a neutral stimulus that normally does not bring about that type of response (p. 15)

cliques   groups of from 2 to 12 people whose members have frequent social interactions with one another (p. 279)

cognitive development   development involving the ways that growth and change in intellectual capabilities influence a person's behaviour (p. 5)

cognitive neuroscience approach   the approach that examines cognitive development through the lens of brain processes (p. 17)

cognitive perspective   the approach that focuses on the processes that allow people to know, understand, and think about the world (p. 16)

cohabitation   when couples live together without being married (p. 326)

cohort   a group of people born at around the same time in the same place (p. 8)

collectivistic orientation   a philosophy that promotes the notion of interdependence (p. 166)

communal professions   occupations that are associated with relationships (p. 335)

companionate love   the strong affection for those with whom our lives are deeply involved (p. 320)

concrete operational stage   the period of cognitive development between 7 and 12 years of age, which is characterized by the active and appropriate use of logic (p. 202)

conservation   the knowledge that quantity is unrelated to the arrangement and physical appearance of objects (p. 151)

constructive play   play in which children manipulate objects to produce or build something (p. 170)

contextual perspective   the theory that considers the relationship between individuals and their physical, cognitive, personality, and social worlds (p. 18)

continuing-care community   a community that offers an environment in which all the residents are of retirement age or older and need various levels of care (p. 414)

continuity theory   the theory suggesting that people need to maintain their desired level of involvement in society in order to maximize their sense of well-being and self-esteem (p. 412)

continuous change   gradual development in which achievements at one level build on those of previous levels (p. 9)

controversial adolescents   children who are liked by some peers and disliked by others (p. 280)

co-operative play   play in which children genuinely interact with one another, taking turns, playing games, or devising contests (p. 170)

coping   the effort to control, reduce, or learn to tolerate the threats that lead to stress (p. 300)

coregulation   a period in which parents and children jointly control children's behaviour (p. 235)

correlational research   research that seeks to identify whether an association or relationship between two factors exists (p. 23)

creativity   the combination of responses or ideas in novel ways (p. 308)

critical period   a specific time during development when a particular event has its greatest consequences and the presence of certain kinds of environmental stimuli are necessary for development to proceed normally (p. 9)

cross-sectional research   research in which people of different ages are compared at the same point in time (p. 28)

crowds   larger groups than cliques, composed of individuals who share particular characteristics but who may not interact with one another (p. 279)

crystallized intelligence   the accumulation of information, skills, and strategies that people have learned through experience and that they can apply in problem-solving situations (p. 356)

cultural assimilation model   the model that fostered the view of American society as the proverbial melting pot (p. 210)

cycle of violence hypothesis   the theory that the abuse and neglect that children suffer predisposes them as adults to abuse and neglect their own children (p. 374)

decentring   the ability to take multiple aspects of a situation into account (p. 202)

decision/commitment component   the third aspect of love that embodies both the initial cognition that one loves another person and the longer-term determination to maintain that love (p. 321)

defensive coping   coping that involves unconscious strategies that distort or deny the true nature of a situation (p. 300)

dementia   the most common mental disorder of the elderly, it covers several diseases, each of which includes serious memory loss accompanied by declines in other mental functioning (p. 394)

dependent variable   the variable that researchers measure in an experiment and expect to change as a result of the experimental manipulation (p. 26)

developmental quotient   an overall developmental score that relates to performance in four domains: motor skills, language use, adaptive behaviour, and personal-social (p. 113)

difficult babies   babies who have negative moods and are slow to adapt to new situations; when confronted with a new situation, they tend to withdraw (p. 135)

discontinuous change   development that occurs in distinct steps or stages, with each stage bringing about behaviour that is assumed to be qualitatively different from behaviour at earlier stages (p. 9)

disengagement theory   the period in late adulthood that marks a gradual withdrawal from the world on physical, psychological, and social levels (p. 411)

disorganized-disoriented attachment pattern   a style of attachment in which children show inconsistent, often contradictory behaviour, such as approaching the mother when she returns but not looking at her; they can be the least securely attached children of all (p. 130)

dizygotic twins   twins who are produced when two separate ova are fertilized by two separate sperm at roughly the same time (p. 38)

DNA (deoxyribonucleic acid) molecules   the substance that genes are composed of that determines the nature of every cell in the body and how each will function (p. 37)

dominance hierarchy   rankings that represent the relative social power of those in a group (p. 233)

dominant trait   the one trait that is expressed when two competing traits are present (p. 39)

Down's syndrome   a disorder produced by the presence of an extra chromosome on the twenty-first pair; once referred to as mongolism (p. 41)

easy babies   babies who have a positive disposition; their body functions operate regularly, and they are adaptable (p. 135)

ego transcendence versus ego preoccupation   the period in which elderly people must come to grips with their coming death (p. 408)

ego-integrity-versus-despair stage   Erikson's final stage of life, characterized by a process of looking back over one's life, evaluating it, and coming to terms with it (p. 407)

egocentric thought   thinking that does not take into account the viewpoints of others (p. 151)

elder abuse   the physical or psychological mistreatment or neglect of elderly individuals (p. 425)

embryonic stage   the period from two to eight weeks following fertilization during which significant growth occurs in the major organs and body systems (p. 54)

emotional intelligence   the set of skills that underlie the accurate assessment, evaluation, expression, and regulation of emotions (p. 307)

emotional self-regulation   the ability to adjust emotions to a desired state and level of intensity (p. 180)

empathy   an emotional response that corresponds to the feelings of another person (p. 180)

empty nest syndrome   the experience that relates to parents' feelings of unhappiness, worry, loneliness, and depression resulting from their children's departure from home (p. 370)

enrichment   an approach through which students are kept at grade level but are enrolled in special programs and given individual activities to allow greater depth of study on a given topic (p. 221)

episiotomy   an incision sometimes made to increase the size of the opening of the vagina to allow the baby to pass (p. 63)

Erikson's theory of psychosocial development   the theory that considers how individuals come to understand themselves and the meaning of others'—and their own—behaviour (p. 134)

euthanasia   the practice of assisting people who are terminally ill to die more quickly (p. 439)

evolutionary perspective   the theory that seeks to identify behaviour that is a result of our genetic inheritance from our ancestors (p. 20)

executive stage   the period in middle adulthood when people take a broader perspective than earlier, including concerns about the world (p. 304)

experiment   a process in which an investigator, called an experimenter, devises two different experiences for participants (p. 26)

experimental research research designed to discover causal relationships between various factors (p. 23)

expertise the acquisition of skill or knowledge in a particular area (p. 358)

expressive style a style of language use in which language is used primarily to express feelings and needs about oneself and others (p. 119)

extrinsic motivation motivation that drives people to obtain tangible rewards, such as money and prestige (p. 336)

fantasy period according to Ginzberg, the period, lasting until about age 11, when career choices are made, and discarded, without regard to skills, abilities, or available job opportunities (p. 333)

fast mapping instances in which new words are associated with their meaning after only a brief encounter (p. 159)

female climacteric the period that marks the transition from being able to bear children to being unable to do so (p. 347)

fertilization the process by which a sperm and an ovum—the male and female gametes, respectively—join to form a single new cell (p. 53)

fetal alcohol effects (FAE) a condition in which children display some, although not all, of the problems of fetal alcohol syndrome due to the mother's consumption of alcohol during pregnancy (p. 60)

fetal alcohol syndrome (FAS) a disorder caused by the pregnant mother consuming substantial quantities of alcohol during pregnancy, potentially resulting in mental retardation and delayed growth in the child (p. 60)

fetal monitor a device that measures the baby's heartbeat during labour (p. 72)

fetal stage the stage that begins at about eight weeks after conception and continues until birth (p. 54)

fetus a developing child, from eight weeks after conception until birth (p. 54)

field study a research investigation carried out in a naturally occurring setting (p. 27)

first-year adjustment reaction a cluster of psychological symptoms, including loneliness, anxiety, withdrawal, and depression, relating to the college experience suffered by first-year college students (p. 312)

fluid intelligence intelligence that reflects information-processing capabilities, reasoning, and memory (p. 215)

formal operational period the stage at which people develop the ability to think abstractly (p. 259)

fragile X syndrome a disorder produced by injury to a gene on the X chromosome, producing mild to moderate mental retardation (p. 41)

functional death the absence of a heartbeat and breathing (p. 430)

functional play play that involves simple, repetitive activities typical of three-year-olds (p. 170)

gender the sense of being male or female (p. 136)

gender constancy the belief that people are permanently males or females, depending on fixed, unchangeable biological factors (p. 168)

gender identity the perception of oneself as male or female (p. 168)

gender schema a cognitive framework that organizes information relevant to gender (p. 168)

generalized slowing hypothesis the theory that processing in all parts of the nervous system, including the brain, is less efficient as we age (p. 391)

generation gap a divide between parents and adolescents in attitudes, values, aspirations, and world views (p. 277)

generativity-versus-stagnation state according to Erikson, the stage during middle adulthood in which people consider their contributions to family and society (p. 362)

genes the basic unit of genetic information (p. 36)

genetic counselling the discipline that focuses on helping people deal with issues relating to inherited disorders (p. 42)

genetic programming theories of aging theories that suggest that our body's DNA genetic code contains a built-in time limit for the reproduction of human cells (p. 397)

genotype the underlying combination of genetic material present (but not outwardly visible) in an organism (p. 39)

germinal stage the first—and shortest—stage of the prenatal period, which takes place during the first two weeks following conception (p. 54)

gerontologists specialists who study aging (p. 386)

gifted a term for children who show evidence of high performance-capability in areas such as intellect, creativity, artistic ability, leadership capacity, or specific academic fields (p. 220)

glaucoma a condition in which pressure in the fluid of the eye increases, either because the fluid cannot drain properly or because too much fluid is produced (p. 344)

goodness-of-fit the notion that development is dependent on the degree of match between children's temperament and the nature and demands of the environment in which they are being raised (p. 135)

grammar the system of rules that determine how our thoughts can be expressed (p. 159)

grief the emotional response to one's loss (p. 444)

habituation the decrease in the response to a stimulus that occurs after repeated presentations of the same stimulus (p. 76)

handedness the preference of using one hand over another (p. 149)

hardiness a personality characteristic associated with a lower rate of stress-related illness (p. 300)

heterozygous inheriting from parents different forms of a gene for a given trait (p. 39)

holophrases one-word utterances that stand for a whole phrase, the meaning of which depends on the particular context in which they are used (p. 118)

home care an alternative to hospitalization in which dying people stay in their homes and receive treatment from their families and visiting medical staff (p. 441)

homogamy the tendency to marry someone who is similar in age, race, education, religion, and other basic demographic characteristics (p. 323)

homozygous inheriting from parents similar genes for a given trait (p. 39)

hostile aggression intentional injury or harm to another person (p.180)

hypothesis a prediction stated in a way that permits it to be tested (p. 23)

identity achievement the status of adolescents who commit to a particular identity following a period of crisis during which they consider various alternatives (p. 271)

identity diffusion the status of adolescents who consider various identity alternatives, but never commit to one or never even consider identity options in any conscious way (p. 271)

identity foreclosure the status of adolescents who prematurely commit to an identity without adequately exploring alternatives (p. 271)

identity-versus-identity-confusion stage the period during which teenagers seek to determine what is unique and distinctive about themselves (p. 269)

imaginary audience an adolescent's belief that his or her own behaviour is a primary focus of others' attention and concerns (p. 262)

in vitro fertilization (IVF) a procedure in which a woman's ova are removed from her ovaries, and a man's sperm are used to fertilize the ova in a laboratory (p. 56)

inclusive education an educational approach in which children with special needs are integrated into the traditional classroom and are provided with a broad range of in-class supports (p. 219)

independent variable the variable that researchers manipulate in an experiment (p. 26)

individualistic orientation a philosophy that emphasizes personal identity and the uniqueness of the individual (p. 166)

industry-versus-inferiority stage the period from age 6 to 12 characterized by a focus on efforts to attain competence in meeting the challenges presented by parents, peers, school, and the other complexities of the modern world (p. 222)

infant mortality death within the first year of life (p. 72)

infant-directed speech a type of speech directed toward infants, characterized by short, simple sentences (p. 121)

infantile amnesia the lack of memory for experiences that occurred prior to three years of age (p. 111)

infertility the inability to conceive after 12 to 18 months of trying to become pregnant (p. 56)

information-processing the model that seeks to identify the way that individuals take in, use, and store information (p. 17)

initiative-versus-guilt stage according to Erikson, the period during which children aged three to six years experience conflict between independence of action and the sometimes negative results of that action (p. 165)

institutionalism a psychological state in which people in nursing homes develop apathy, indifference, and a lack of caring about themselves (p. 415)

instrumental aggression aggression motivated by the desire to obtain a concrete goal (p. 181)

intellectual disability (mental retardation) a significantly below-average level of intellectual functioning that occurs with related limitations in two or more skill areas (p. 219)

intelligence the capacity to understand the world, think with rationality, and use resources effectively when faced with challenges (p. 212)

intelligence quotient (or IQ score) a measure of intelligence that takes into account a student's mental and chronological age (p. 212)

intimacy component the component of love that encompasses feelings of closeness, affection, and connectedness (p. 321)

intimacy-versus-isolation stage   according to Erikson, the period of postadolescence into the early thirties that focuses on developing close relationships with others (p. 319)

intrinsic motivation   motivation that causes people to work for their own enjoyment, not for the rewards work might bring (p. 336)

intuitive thought   thinking that reflects preschoolers' use of primitive reasoning and their avid acquisition of knowledge about the world (p. 153)

Kaufman Assessment Battery for Children, Second Edition (KABC-II)   an intelligence test that measures children's ability to integrate different stimuli simultaneously and step-by-step thinking (p. 214)

Klinefelter's syndrome   a disorder resulting from the presence of an extra X chromosome that produces underdeveloped genitals, extreme height, and enlarged breasts (p. 42)

labelling theory of passionate love   the theory that individuals experience romantic love when two events occur together: intense physiological arousal and situational cues suggesting that the arousal is due to love (p. 320)

laboratory study   a research investigation conducted in a controlled setting explicitly designed to hold events constant (p. 27)

language   the systematic, meaningful arrangement of symbols, which provides the basis for communication (p. 116)

language-acquisition device (LAD)   a neural system of the brain hypothesized to permit understanding of language (p. 120)

lateralization   the process in which certain cognitive functions are located more in one hemisphere of the brain than in the other (p. 146)

learning disabilities   difficulties in the acquisition and use of listening, speaking, reading, writing, reasoning, or mathematical abilities (p. 199)

learning theory approach   the theory that language acquisition follows the basic laws of reinforcement and conditioning (p. 120)

life events models   the approach to personality development that is based on the timing of particular events in an adult's life rather than on age per se (p. 362)

life expectancy   the average age of death for members of a population (p. 398)

life review   the point in life at which people examine and evaluate their lives (p. 409)

lifespan development   the field of study that examines patterns of growth, change, and stability in behaviour that occur throughout the entire lifespan (p. 5)

living wills   legal documents designating what medical treatments people want or do not want if they cannot express their wishes (p. 439)

longitudinal research   research in which the behaviour of one or more participants in a study is measured as they age (p. 27)

low-birth-weight infants   infants who weigh less than 2500 grams (around 5½ pounds) at birth (p. 68)

mainstreamed   an approach in which children with special needs attend the same school as children without special needs, sharing social activities but learning in a separate class (p. 219)

male climacteric   the period of physical and psychological change relating to the male reproductive system that occurs during late middle age (p. 348)

marriage gradient   the tendency for men to marry women who are slightly younger, smaller, and lower in status, and for women to marry men who are slightly older, larger, and higher in status (p. 323)

maturation   the predetermined unfolding of genetic information (p. 10)

memory   the process by which information is initially recorded, stored, and retrieved (p. 111)

menarche   the onset of menstruation (p. 246)

menopause   the cessation of menstruation (p. 347)

mental age   the typical intelligence level found for people at a given chronological age (p. 212)

metacognition   the knowledge that people have about their own thinking processes, and their ability to monitor their cognition (p. 262)

metalinguistic awareness   an understanding of one's own use of language (p. 206)

metamemory   an understanding about the processes that underlie memory, which emerges and improves during middle childhood (p. 204)

midlife crisis   a stage of uncertainty and indecision brought about by the realization that life is finite (p. 363)

mnemonics   formal strategies for organizing material in ways that make it more likely to be remembered (p. 360)

monozygotic twins   twins who are genetically identical (p. 38)

moral development   the changes in people's sense of justice and of what is right and wrong, and in their behaviour related to moral issues (p. 179)

moratorium   the status of adolescents who might have explored various identity alternatives to some degree, but have not yet committed themselves (p. 271)

multicultural education   a form of education in which the goal is to help minority students develop confidence in the culture of the majority group while maintaining positive group identities that build on their original cultures (p. 210)

multifactorial transmission   the determination of traits by a combination of both genetic and environmental factors in which a genotype provides a range within which a phenotype can be expressed (p. 45)

multimodal approach to perception   the approach that considers how information that is collected by various individual sensory systems is integrated and coordinated (p. 102)

myelin   protective insulation that surrounds parts of neurons—which speeds the transmission of electrical impulses along brain cells but also adds to brain weight (p. 88)

nativist approach   the theory that a genetically determined, innate mechanism directs language development (p. 120)

naturalistic observation   a type of correlational study in which some naturally occurring behaviour is observed without intervention in the situation (p. 25)

neglected adolescents   children who receive relatively little attention from their peers in the form of either positive or negative interactions (p. 280)

neonates   the term used for newborns (p. 63)

neuron   the basic nerve cell of the nervous system (p. 86)

nonorganic failure to thrive   a disorder in which infants stop growing due to a lack of stimulation and attention as the result of inadequate parenting (p. 97)

normative-crisis models   the approach to personality development that is based on fairly universal stages tied to a sequence of age-related crises (p. 362)

norms   the average performance of a large sample of children of a given age (p. 95)

obesity   body weight more than 20 percent higher than the average weight for a person of the same given age and height (p. 143)

object permanence   the realization that people and objects exist even when they cannot be seen (p. 106)

onlooker play   action in which children simply watch others at play, but do not actually participate themselves (p. 170)

operant conditioning   a form of learning in which a voluntary response is strengthened or weakened by its association with positive or negative consequences (p. 15)

operations   organized, formal, logical mental processes (p. 150)

osteoporosis   a condition in which the bones become brittle, fragile, and thin, often brought about by a lack of calcium in the diet (p. 344)

overextension   the overly broad use of words, overgeneralizing their meaning (p. 119)

palliative care   care provided for the comfort and support of the dying (p. 441)

parallel play   action in which children play with similar toys, in a similar manner, but do not interact with each other (p. 170)

passion component   the component of love that comprises the motivational drives relating to sex, physical closeness, and romance (p. 321)

passionate (or romantic) love   a state of powerful absorption in someone (p. 320)

peer pressure   the influence of one's peers to conform to their behaviour and attitudes (p. 281)

perception   the sorting out, interpretation, analysis, and integration of stimuli involving the sense organs and brain (p. 99)

peripheral slowing hypothesis   the theory that suggests that overall processing speed declines in the peripheral nervous system with increasing age (p. 390)

permissive parents   parents who provide lax and inconsistent feedback and require little of their children (p. 172)

personal fables   the view held by some adolescents that what happens to them is unique, exceptional, and shared by no one else (p. 263)

personality   the sum total of the enduring characteristics that differentiate one individual from another (p. 134)

personality development   development involving the ways that the enduring characteristics that differentiate one person from another change over the lifespan (p. 6)

phenotype   an observable trait; the trait that actually is seen (p. 39)

physical development   development involving the body's physical makeup, including the brain, nervous system, muscles, and senses, and the need for food, drink, and sleep (p. 5)

placenta   a conduit between the mother and fetus, providing nourishment and oxygen via the umbilical cord (p. 54)

plasticity   the degree to which a developing structure or behaviour is modifiable due to experience (p. 403)

pluralistic society model the concept that Canadian society is made up of diverse, coequal cultural groups that should preserve their individual cultural features (p. 210)

polygenic inheritance inheritance in which a combination of multiple gene pairs is responsible for the production of a particular trait (p. 40)

postformal thought thinking that acknowledges that adult predicaments must sometimes be solved in relativistic terms (p. 303)

postmature infants infants still unborn two weeks after the mother's due date (p. 70)

practical intelligence according to Sternberg, intelligence that is learned primarily by observing others and modelling their behaviour (p. 306)

pragmatics the aspect of language that relates to communicating effectively and appropriately with others (p. 160)

preoperational stage according to Piaget, the stage from approximately age two to age seven in which children's use of symbolic thinking grows, mental reasoning emerges, and the use of concepts increases (p. 150)

presbycusis loss of the ability to hear sounds of high frequency (p. 344)

presbyopia a nearly universal change in eyesight during middle adulthood that results in some loss of near vision (p. 344)

preterm infants infants who are born prior to 38 weeks after conception (also known as premature infants) (p. 68)

primary aging aging that involves universal and irreversible changes that, due to genetic programming, occur as people get older (p. 388)

primary appraisal the assessment of an event to determine whether its implications are positive, negative, or neutral (p. 298)

primary sex characteristics characteristics associated with the development of the organs and structures of the body that directly relate to reproduction (p. 247)

principle of hierarchical integration the principle that simple skills typically develop separately and independently but are later integrated into more complex skills (p. 85)

principle of the independence of systems the principle that different body systems grow at different rates (p. 85)

private speech speech by children that is spoken and directed to themselves (p. 160)

prosocial behaviour helping behaviour that benefits others (p. 179)

proximodistal principle the principle that development proceeds outward from the centre of the body (p. 85)

psychoanalytic theory the theory proposed by Freud that suggests that unconscious forces act to determine personality and behaviour (p. 12)

psychodynamic perspective the approach stating that behaviour is motivated by inner forces, memories, and conflicts that are generally beyond people's awareness and control (p. 12)

psychological maltreatment abuse that occurs when parents or other caregivers harm children's behavioural, cognitive, emotional, or physical functioning (p. 176)

psychoneuroimmunology (PNI) the study of the relationship between the brain, the immune system, and psychological factors (p. 297)

psychophysiological methods research that focuses on the relationship between physiological processes and behaviour (p. 25)

psychosexual development according to Freud, a series of stages that children pass through in which pleasure, or gratification, is focused on a particular biological function and body part (p. 12)

psychosocial development according to Erikson, development that encompasses changes both in the understandings individuals have of themselves as members of society and in their comprehension of the meaning of others' behaviour (p. 13)

psychosomatic disorders medical problems caused by the interaction of psychological, emotional, and physical difficulties (p. 299)

puberty the period during which the sexual organs mature (p. 245)

race dissonance the phenomenon in which minority children indicate preferences for majority values or people (p. 166)

rapid eye movement (REM) sleep the period of sleep that is found in older children and adults and is associated with dreaming (p. 90)

realistic period the third stage of Ginzberg's theory, which occurs in early adulthood, when people begin to explore specific career options either through actual experience on the job or through training for a profession, and then narrow their choices and make a commitment (p. 334)

recessive trait a trait within an organism that is present, but is not expressed (p. 39)

redefinition of self versus preoccupation with work role the theory that those in old age must redefine themselves in ways that do not relate to their work roles or occupations (p. 408)

reference groups groups of people with whom one compares oneself (p. 279)

referential style a style of language use in which language is used primarily to label objects (p. 119)

reflexes unlearned, organized involuntary responses that occur automatically in the presence of certain stimuli (p. 74)

reintegrative stage the period of late adulthood during which the focus is on tasks that have personal meaning (p. 304)

rejected adolescents children who are actively disliked, and whose peers might react to them in an obviously negative manner (p. 280)

relational aggression nonphysical aggression that is intended to hurt another person's psychological well-being (p. 181)

resilience the ability to overcome circumstances that place a child at high risk for psychological or physical damage (p. 177)

responsible stage the stage where the major concerns of middle-aged adults relate to their personal situations, including protecting and nourishing their spouses, families, and careers (p. 304)

rhythms repetitive, cyclical patterns of behaviour (p. 89)

sample a group of participants chosen for an experiment (p. 27)

sandwich generation people who in middle adulthood must fulfill the needs of both their children and their aging parents (p. 371)

scaffolding the support for learning and problem solving that encourages independence and growth (p. 157)

schemas organized bodies of information stored in memory (p. 359)

scheme an organized pattern of sensorimotor functioning (p. 104)

scientific method the process of posing and answering questions using careful, controlled techniques that include systematic, orderly observation and the collection of data (p. 23)

scripts broad representations in memory of events and the order in which they occur (p. 155)

secondary aging changes in physical and cognitive functioning that are due to illness, health habits, and other individual differences, but are not due to increased age itself and are not inevitable (p. 388)

secondary appraisal the assessment of whether one's coping abilities and resources are adequate to overcome the harm, threat, or challenge posed by the potential stressor (p. 298)

secondary sex characteristics the visible signs of sexual maturity that do not directly involve the sex organs (p. 247)

secular trend a pattern of change occurring over several generations (p. 247)

secure attachment pattern a style of attachment in which children use the mother as a kind of home base and are at ease when she is present; when she leaves, they become upset and go to her as soon as she returns (p. 129)

selective optimization the process by which people concentrate on particular skill areas to compensate for losses in other areas (p. 413)

self-awareness knowledge of oneself (p. 127)

self-care children children who let themselves into their homes after school and wait alone until their caretakers return from work; previously known as latchkey children (p. 235)

self-concept one's identity or set of beliefs about what one is like as an individual (p. 165)

self-esteem an individual's overall and specific positive and negative self-evaluation (p. 223)

senescence the natural physical decline brought about by aging (p. 293)

sensation the physical stimulation of the sense organs (p. 99)

sensitive period a point in development when organisms are particularly susceptible to certain kinds of stimuli in their environments, but the absence of those stimuli does not always produce irreversible consequences (p. 9)

sensorimotor stage (of cognitive development) Piaget's initial major stage of cognitive development, which can be broken down into six substages (p. 105)

separation anxiety the distress displayed by infants when a customary care provider departs (p. 125)

sequential studies research in which researchers examine a number of different age groups over several points in time (p. 29)

sex cleavage sex segregation in which boys interact primarily with boys, and girls primarily with girls (p. 279)

sexually transmitted infection (STI) an infection that is spread through sexual contact (p. 256)

sickle-cell anemia a blood disorder that gets its name from the shape of the red blood cells in those who have it (p. 41)

skilled-nursing facilities facilities that provide full-time nursing care for people who have chronic illnesses or are recovering from a temporary medical condition (p. 415)

slow-to-warm babies babies who are inactive, showing relatively calm reactions to their environment; their moods are generally negative, and they withdraw from new situations, adapting slowly (p. 135)

small-for-gestational-age infants infants who, because of delayed fetal growth, weigh 90 percent (or less) of the average weight of infants of the same gestational age (p. 68)

social clock the culturally determined psychological timepiece providing a sense of whether we have reached the major benchmarks of life at the appropriate time in comparison to our peers (p. 319)

social competence the collection of social skills that permit individuals to perform successfully in social settings (p. 230)

social development the way in which individuals' interactions with others and their social relationships grow, change, and remain stable over the course of life (p. 6)

social problem-solving the use of strategies for solving social conflicts in ways that are satisfactory both to oneself and to others (p. 230)

social referencing the intentional search for information about others' feelings to help explain the meaning of uncertain circumstances and events (p. 127)

social speech speech directed toward another person and meant to be understood by that person (p. 161)

social support assistance and comfort supplied by another person or a network of caring, interested people (p. 423)

social-cognitive learning theory learning by observing the behaviour of another person, called a model (p. 15)

socialized delinquents adolescent delinquents who know and subscribe to the norms of society and who are fairly normal psychologically (p. 282)

sociocultural theory the approach that emphasizes how cognitive development proceeds as a result of social interactions between members of a culture (p. 19)

speech impairment speech that deviates so much from the speech of others that it calls attention to itself, interferes with communication, or produces maladjustment in the speaker (p. 199)

Stanford-Binet Intelligence Scales, Fifth Edition (SB5) a test that consists of a series of items that vary according to the age of the person being tested (p. 213)

state the degree of awareness an infant displays to both internal and external stimulation (p. 89)

states of arousal different degrees of sleep and wakefulness through which newborns cycle, ranging from deep sleep to great agitation (p. 78)

status the evaluation of a role or person by other relevant members of a group or society (p. 336)

stereotype threat obstacles to performance that come from awareness of the stereotypes held by society about academic abilities (p. 315)

stillbirth the delivery of a child who is not alive, occurring in less than 1 delivery in 100 (p. 72)

stimulus-value-role (SVR) theory the theory that relationships proceed in a fixed order of three stages: stimulus, value, and role (p. 320)

stranger anxiety the caution and wariness displayed by infants when encountering an unfamiliar person (p. 125)

stress the physical and emotional response to events that threaten or challenge us (p. 297)

stuttering substantial disruption in the rhythm and fluency of speech; the most common speech impairment (p. 199)

sudden infant death syndrome (SIDS) the unexplained death of a seemingly healthy baby (p. 431)

survey research a type of study where a group of people chosen to represent some larger population are asked questions about their attitudes, behaviour, or thinking on a given topic (p. 25)

synapse the gap at the connection between neurons, through which neurons chemically communicate with one another (p. 86)

synaptic pruning the elimination of neurons as the result of non-use or lack of stimulation (p. 88)

syntax the way in which an individual combines words and phrases to form sentences (p. 159)

Tay-Sachs disease a disorder that produces blindness and muscle degeneration prior to death; there is no treatment (p. 42)

telegraphic speech speech in which words not critical to the message are left out (p. 119)

temperament patterns of arousal and emotionality that are consistent and enduring characteristics of an individual (p. 134)

tentative period the second stage of Ginzberg's theory, which spans adolescence, when people begin to think in pragmatic terms about the requirements of various jobs and how their own abilities might fit with them (p. 334)

teratogen a factor that produces a birth defect (p. 57)

thanatologists people who study death and dying (p. 435)

theoretical research research designed specifically to test some developmental explanation and expand scientific knowledge (p. 27)

theories broad explanations and predictions about phenomena of interest (p. 12)

theory of mind knowledge and beliefs about how the mind works and how it affects behaviour (p. 127)

transformation the process in which one state is changed into another (p. 151)

triarchic theory of intelligence Sternberg's theory that intelligence is made up of three major components: componential, experiential, and contextual (p. 215)

trust-versus-mistrust stage according to Erikson, the period during which infants develop a sense of trust or mistrust, largely depending on how well their needs are met by their caregivers (p. 134)

Type A behaviour pattern behaviour characterized by competitiveness, impatience, and a tendency toward frustration and hostility (p. 351)

Type B behaviour pattern behaviour characterized by noncompetitiveness, patience, and a lack of aggression (p. 351)

ultrasound sonography a process in which high-frequency sound waves scan the mother's womb to produce an image of the unborn baby, whose size and shape can then be assessed (p. 42)

underextension the overly restrictive use of words, common among children just mastering spoken language (p. 119)

undersocialized delinquents adolescent delinquents who are raised with little discipline or with harsh, uncaring parental supervision (p. 282)

uninvolved parents parents who show almost no interest in their children and indifferent, rejecting behaviour (p. 172)

universal grammar Noam Chomsky's theory that all the world's languages share a similar underlying structure (p. 120)

very-low-birth-weight infants infants who weigh less than 1250 grams (around 2.25 pounds) or, regardless of weight, have been in the womb less than 30 weeks (p. 68)

visual impairment a difficulty in seeing that can include blindness or partial sightedness (p. 199)

wear-and-tear theories of aging the theory that the mechanical functions of the body simply wear out with age (p. 397)

Wechsler Intelligence Scale for Children, Fourth Edition (WISC-IV) a test for children that provides separate measures of verbal and performance (or nonverbal) skills, as well as a total score (p. 213)

wisdom expert knowledge in the practical aspects of life (p. 411)

X-linked genes genes that are considered recessive and located only on the X chromosome (p. 40)

zone of proximal development (ZPD) according to Vygotsky, the level at which a child can almost, but not fully, perform a task independently, but can do so with the assistance of someone more competent (p. 157)

zygote the new cell formed by the process of fertilization (p. 36)

Photo Credits

Photographs

Front matter Page v Dorling Kindersley; p.vii Exactostock/SuperStock; p. viii iStockphoto/Thinkstock; p. ix Jupiterimages/Goodshoot/Getty Images/Thinkstock; p.x Kablonk/SuperStock; p.xv Jstudio/Dreamstime.com; p. xxi (bottom) Oriane Landry/Nick Pearce; p. xxi (top)Robert Feldman.

Chapter 1 Page 2 (left) AP Images/Alastair Grant; (bottom, right) Eddie Lawrence/DK Images; p. 3 (bottom, left) Jeff Greenberg/Alamy; (top) Exactostock/SuperStock; p. 4 67photo/Alamy; p. 7 Ben Edwards/Imagestate Media Partners Limited - Impact Photos/Alamy; p. 11 Bettmann/Corbis; p. 12 Photo Researchers/Alamy; p. 14 Library of Congress Photographs and Prints Division; p. 15 Hulton Archive/Archive Photos/Getty Images; p. 16 Photofest; p. 19 Eddie Lawrence/DK Images; p. 20 Nina Leen/Time & Life Pictures/Getty Images; p. 25 Peter Arnold/Stegerphoto/Getty Images; p. 27 Jeff Greenberg/Alamy; p. 32 Exactostock/SuperStock; p. 33 (top) Jim Esposito Photography L.L.C./Photodisc/Getty Images; (top, centre) Photodisc/Getty Images; (bottom) Asia Images Group/Getty Images; (bottom, centre) Mel Yates/Cultura/Getty Images.

Chapter 2 Page 34 (left) Chad Ehlers/Alamy; (right) Photo Researchers; p. 35 (bottom) AP Images/Al Goldis; (top) Andersen Ross/Blend Images/Getty Images; p. 37 (right) MedicalRF.com/Alamy; (bottom) MartinShields/Alamy; (centre) Custom Medical Stock Photo Custom Medical Stock Photo/Newscom; (left) Don W. Fawcett/Photo Researchers; p. 42 Eye of Science/Photo Researchers; p. 43 Sally and Richard Greenhill/Alamy; p. 48 Comstock/Thinkstock; p. 50 Mark Cator/Imagestate Media Partners Limited - Impact Photos/Alamy; p. 52 (top, right) Arco Images GmbH/Alamy; (centre, left) TheSupe87/Fotolia; (centre, right) baloss74/Fotolia; (top, right) Al Fenn//Time Life Pictures/Getty Images; p. 55 (left) Photo Researchers; (centre) Science Pictures Ltd./Photo Researchers; (right) Photo Researchers; p. 60 Chris Harvey/Stone/Getty Images; p. 62 AP Images/Al Goldis; p. 65 (top) Jennie Woodcock/Encyclopedia/Corbis; (bottom) George Lamson/Shutterstock; p. 66 Purestock/Alamy; p. 67 Molly Schlachter/Pearson Education/PH College; p. 69 John Cole/Photo Researchers; p. 71 Brian Gordon Green/National Geographic Image Collection/Alamy; p. 74 Geri Engberg; p. 77 LesliRicharJacobs/Corbis Premium RF/Alamy; p. 80 Andersen Ross/Blend Images/Getty Images; p. 81 (top) Photodisc/Getty Images; (top, centre) Mark Andersen/Rubberball/Getty Images; (bottom, centre) Jose Luis Pelaez Inc/Blend Images/Getty Images; (bottom) Image Source/Getty Images.

Chapter 3 Page 82 (right) Bob Ebbesen/Alamy; (left) Simon Ritter/Alamy; p. 83 (bottom, left) Dbtravel/Dbimages/Alamy; (top, right) DK Images; p. 84 Purestock/Getty Images; p. 90 Justin Guariglia/National Geographic Stock; p. 93 (bottom, left) DK Images; (top, left) Oriane Landry; (top, right) Oriane Landry; (bottom, right) Victoria MacDougall; p. 96 Nativestock/PhotoEdit; p. 99 Tim Ridley/DK Images; p. 100 Mark Richards/PhotoEdit, Inc; p. 101 (bottom) Creative Eye/MIRA.com; (top) Creatas/Jupiterimages/Thinkstock; p. 102 Dmitrijs Dmitrijevs/Fotolia; p. 103 Alain Schroeder/Getty Images; p. 104 Bettmann/Corbis; p. 108 (top) Brocreative/Shutterstock; (bottom) Thoron/Shutterstock; p. 111 Carolyn Rovee-Collier; p. 116 Geri Engberg; p. 117 Christina Kennedy/PhotoEdit; p. 118 Jennie Hart/Alamy; p. 120 Thierry Berrod/Mona LIsa Production/Science Photo Library/Photo Researchers; p. 121 (left) Angela Hampton Picture Library/Alamy; (right) Earl & Nazima Kowall/Documentary Value/Corbis; (centre) Giacomo Pirozzi/Panos Pictures; p. 123 Steve Nagy/Design Pics Inc/Alamy; p. 124 (top, left) Courtesy Dr. Carroll Izard; (bottom, left) Courtesy Dr. Carroll Izard; (top, right) Courtesy Dr. Carroll Izard; (bottom, right) Courtesy Dr. Carroll Izard; p. 125 Michael Newman/PhotoEdit, Inc; p. 127 Vanessa Davies/DK Images; p. 131 (bottom) Larry Williams/Flirt/Corbis; (top) Ruth Jenkinson/DK Images; p. 138 DK Images; p. 139 (top) Photodisc/Getty Images; (top, centre) Mark Andersen/Rubberball/Getty Images; (bottom) Asia Images Group/Getty Images; (bottom, centre) Jose Luis Pelaez Inc/Blend Images/Getty Images.

Chapter 4 Page 140 (right) Vladimir Godnik/Beyond Fotomedia GmbH/Alamy; (left)Geostock/Photodisc/Getty Images; p. 141 (top) Jstudio/Dreamstime.com; (bottom) Don Smetzer/PhotoEdit; p. 142 Ghislain & Marie David de Lossy/Cultura/Alamy; p. 143 Pedro Luz Cunha/Alamy; p. 144 David McGlynn/Taxi/Getty Images; p. 146 Science Photo Library/CMSP; p. 148 (bottom) Gondwana Photo Art/Alamy; (top) Poznyakov /Shutterstock; p. 150 Vladimir Godnik/Beyond Fotomedia GmbH/Alamy; p. 155 Alex Melnick/Shutterstock; p. 156 RIA Novosti/Alamy; p. 165 David R. Frazier Photolibrary, Inc/Alamy; p. 167 (top) Cedric Lim/Glow Images, Inc.; (bottom) Photo Researchers; p. 169 PhotoEdit; p. 170 Tony Freeman/PhotoEdit; p. 172 SW Productions/Design Pics Inc/Alamy; p. 174 AP Images/Cindy Loo/Department of Social Services; p. 176 AP Images/Come Alive New Testament Church, ho; p. 179 Stanley Fellerman/Spirit/Corbis; p. 180 Richard Hutchings/PhotoEdit, Inc; p. 182 (top, left) Albert Bandura, Stanford University; (top, centre) Albert Bandura, Stanford University; (top, centre) Albert Bandura, Stanford University; (top, right) Albert Bandura, Stanford University; (top, left) Albert Bandura, Stanford University; (top, centre) Albert Bandura, Stanford University; (top, centre) Albert Bandura, Stanford University; (top, right) Albert Bandura, Stanford University; (centre, left) Albert Bandura, Stanford University; (centre) Albert Bandura, Stanford University; (centre) Albert Bandura, Stanford University; (centre, right) Albert Bandura, Stanford University; p. 184 Bill Aron/PhotoEdit, Inc; p. 186 Jstudio/Dreamstime.com; p. 187 (top) Jim Esposito Photography L.L.C./Photodisc/Getty Images; (top, centre) Photodisc/Getty Images; (bottom, centre) Mel Yates/Cultura/Getty Images; (bottom) Asia Images Group/Getty Images.

Chapter 5 Page 188 (bottom) Con Tanasiuk/Design Pics Inc/Alamy; (top) George Doyle/Stockbyte/Getty Images; p. 189 (bottom) Myrleen Pearson/Alamy; (bottom, left) Anne Ackermann/Taxi/Getty Images; (top) Mike Kemp/Rubberball/Getty Images; p. 190 George Doyle/Stockbyte/Getty Images; p. 191 Jeff Greenberg/The Image Works; p. 192 zuma wire service/Alamy; p. 194 Myrleen Pearson/Alamy; p. 196 Leila Cutler/Alamy; p. 198 Michael Newman/PhotoEdit, Inc; p. 201 Con Tanasiuk/Design Pics Inc/Alamy; p. 202 Ryan McVay/Digital Vision/Thinkstock; p. 204 Stock Connection Distribution/Alamy; p. 209 Michele Burgess/Alamy; p. 211 Sally and Richard Greenhill/Alamy; p. 212 Bob Daemmrich/The Image Works; p. 217 purepix/alamy; Gladskikh Tatiana/DK Images; p. 218 Richard Hutchings/Photo Researchers; p. 221 Anne Ackermann/Taxi/Getty Images; p. 222 Steve Satushek/The Image Bank/Getty Images; p. 224 Merritt Vincent/PhotoEdit; p. 225 Richard Lord/The Image Works; p. 229 Jupiterimages/Thinkstock; p. 230 Angela Hampton/Bubbles Photolibrary/Alamy; p. 233 Photosindiacom, LLC / Shutterstock; p. 237 Michelle D. Bridwell/PhotoEdit; p. 238 Bubbles Photolibrary/Alamy; p. 240 Mike Kemp/Rubberball/Getty Images; p. 241 (top) Jim Esposito Photography L.L.C./Photodisc/Getty Images; (top, centre) Photodisc/Getty Images; (bottom, centre) Mel Yates/Cultura/Getty Images; (bottom) Asia Images Group/Getty Images.

Chapter 6 Page 242 (left) moodboard/Alamy; (right) Wesley Hitt/Alamy; p. 243 (bottom) Tony Freeman/PhotoEdit; (top) iStockphoto/Thinkstock; p. 244 Sally and Richard Greenhill/Alamy; p. 246 (left) Mark Edward Atkinson/Tetra Images/Alamy; (right) Radius Images/Alamy; p. 249 DK Images; p. 250 Angela Hampton/Bubbles Photolibrary/Alamy; p. 251 Syracuse Newspapers/John Berry/The Image Works; p. 253 ACE Stock Limited/Alamy; p. 258 Wesley Hitt/Alamy; p. 260 Denise Hager/Catchlight Visual Services/Alamy; p. 262 John Maier/Jr. Collection/Age Fotostock; p. 267 Tony Freeman/PhotoEdit; p. 272 (bottom) Richard Hutchings/PhotoEdit; (top) Marilyn Humphries/The Image Works; p. 274 Michelle Gilders Canada West/Alamy; p. 276 Peter Turnley/Corbis; p. 279 Adrian Sherratt/Alamy; p. 280 Richard T. Nowitz/Photo Researchers; p. 282 Bobby Deal/RealDealPhoto/Shutterstock; p. 286 Jacky Chapman/Janine Wiedel Photolibrary/Alamy; p. 288 iStockphoto/Thinkstock; p. 289 (top, centre) Photodisc/Getty Images; (top) Photodisc/Getty Images; (bottom, centre) Jose Luis Pelaez Inc/Blend Images/Getty Images; (bottom) Image Source/Getty Images.

Chapter 7 Page 290 (top) Nelson Hancock/Rough Guides/DK Images; (bottom) Bob Daemmrich/The Image Works; p. 291 (top) blue jean images/Getty Images; (bottom, left) PhotoEdit; p. 292 Nelson Hancock/Rough Guides/DK Images; p. 293 Christopher Bissell/The Image Bank/Getty Images; p. 296 David De Lossy/Photodisc/Thinkstock; p. 298 (left) Mikael Karlsson/Alamy; (right) Spencer Grant/Alamy; p. 301 Bob Daemmrich/The Image Works; p. 302 Manfred Vollmer/Das Fotoarchiv/Peter Arnold, Inc./Photolibrary; p. 308 Belinsky Yuri/ITAR-TASS /Landov; p. 311 (top) Mike Booth/Alamy; p. 312 Lisa F. Young/Alamy; p. 315 David Butow/Corbis; p. 316 PhotoEdit; p. 319 Altrendo images/Getty Images; p. 324 (bottom) Punchstock/Getty Images Inc.; (top) David Hughes/Robert Harding; p. 326 DAJ/amana images inc./Alamy; p. 329 Ariel Skelley/Blend Images/Alamy; p. 333 Annie Griffiths Belt/Encyclopedia/Corbis; p. 338 blue jean images/Getty Images; p. 339 (top, centre) Sheer Photo, Inc/Stockbyte/Getty Images; (bottom) Jose Luis Pelacz Inc/Blend Images/Getty Images; (top) Photodisc/Getty Images; (bottom, centre) PhotoAlto/Laurence Mouton/Jupiter Images.

Chapter 8 Page 340 (bottom) Ableimages/Digital Vision/Getty Images; (top) Jennifer Zinck/Kate Durst; p. 341 (bottom) John Foraste/Creative Eye/MIRA.com; (top) Jupiterimages/Goodshoot/Getty Images/Thinkstock; p. 342 Jennifer Zinck/Kate Durst; p. 343 Gretje Ferguson/Queerstock, Inc./Alamy; p. 344 Paul Bradbury/Alamy; p. 346 Ariel Skelley/Blend Images/Alamy; p. 349 Antonia Reeve/Photo Researchers; p. 351 Adrian Weinbrecht/Photolibrary/Getty Images; p. 352 ZUMA Wire Service/Alamy; p. 354 Ableimages/Digital Vision/Getty Images; p. 356 Stock Connection Blue/Alamy; p. 358 Tom Grill/Corbis Premium RF/Alamy; p. 361 John Foraste/Creative Eye/MIRA.com; p. 364 Corbis Flirt/Alamy; p. 366 Michael J. Doolittle/The Image Works; p. 370 auremar/Shutterstock; p. 373 Angela Hampton/Bubbles Photolibrary/Alamy; p. 377 FancyVeerSet15/Alamy; p. 378 Exactostock/SuperStock; p. 379 Source: Success Stories - Remzi: From a refugee to a Rhodes Scholar, http://www.cic.gc.ca/english/department/media/stories/remzi.asp, Citizenship and Immigration Canada, June 2011. Reproduced with the permission of the Minister of Public Works and Government Services Canada, 2012; p. 382 Jupiterimages/Goodshoot/Getty Images/Thinkstock; p. 383 (top) Asia Images Group/Getty Images; (bottom, centre) Mark Andersen/Rubberball/Getty Images; Jose Luis Pelaez Inc/Blend Images/Getty Images; (top, centre) Sheer Photo, Inc/Stockbyte/Getty Images.

Chapter 9 Page 384 (bottom) Yellow Dog Productions/Digital Vision/Getty Images; (top) PhotoEdit Inc.; p. 385 (top) Roy McMahon/Digital Vision/Getty Images; (bottom) Steve Mason/Photodisc/Thinkstock; p. 386 PhotoEdit; p. 388 Jack Sparticus/Alamy; p. 390 (right) Caroline Wood/Stone/Getty Images; (left) Kevin Dodge/Masterfile; p. 392 Pearson Education/PH College; p. 393 AP Images/Adrian Wyld; p. 394 (bottom) Medical Body Scans/Jessica Wilson/Science Source/Photo Researchers; (top) CNRI/Photo Researchers; p. 396 nyul/Fotolia; p. 398 Deco Images II/Alamy; p. 401 Yellow Dog Productions/Digital Vision/Jupiter Images; p. 405 jeremy sutton-hibbert/Alamy; p. 406 Cultura Creative/Alamy; p. 408 Rhoda Sidney/The Image Works; p. 410 Richard Hutchings/PhotoEdit; p. 414 Andresr/Shutterstock; p. 415 (left) Jupiter Images; (right) Comstock/Thinkstock; p. 417 Horizon International Images Limited/Alamy; p. 421 Bill Aron/PhotoEdit; p. 426 Roy McMahon/Digital Vision/Getty Images; p. 427 (top) IMAGEMORE Co., Ltd./Getty Images; Photodisc/Getty Images; (bottom) Jose Luis Pelaez Inc/Blend Images/Getty Images; (bottom, centre) Image Source/Getty Images.

Chapter 10 Page 428 (bottom) Mediscan/Medical-on-Line/Alamy; (top) Tim Brown/Stone/Getty Images; p. 429 (bottom) Stockbyte/Getty Images; (top) Kablonk/SuperStock; p. 430 (bottom) Chuck Stoody/CP Photo; (top) Tim Brown/Stone/Getty Images; p. 432 Tracy Whiteside/Shutterstock; p. 434 Fredrik Renander/Alamy; p. 436 Mediscan/Medical-on-Line/Alamy; p. 439 Mark Richards/PhotoEdit; p. 443 Stockbyte/Getty Images; p. 444 Randy Duchaine/Alamy; p. 445 David Pearson/Alamy; p. 448 Kablonk/SuperStock; p. 449 (bottom, centre) Mark Andersen/Rubberball/Getty Images; (bottom) Jose Luis Pelaez Inc/Blend Images/Getty Images; (top) PhotoAlto/Laurence Mouton/Jupiter Images; (top, centre) Fuse/Jupiter Images.

Name Index

Note: *f* indicates figure or illustration; *t* indicates table

Subject Index

Note: *f* indicates figure or illustration; *t* indicates table